WileyPLUS with ORION

Quickly identify areas of strength and weakness before the first exam, and use the information to build a learning path to success.

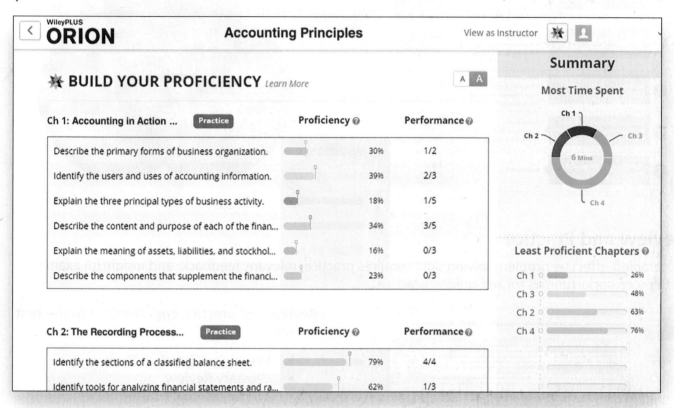

A little time with ORION goes a long way.

Based on usage data, students who engage in ORION adaptive practice—just a few minutes per week—get better outcomes. In fact, students who used ORION five or more times over the course of a semester reported the following results:

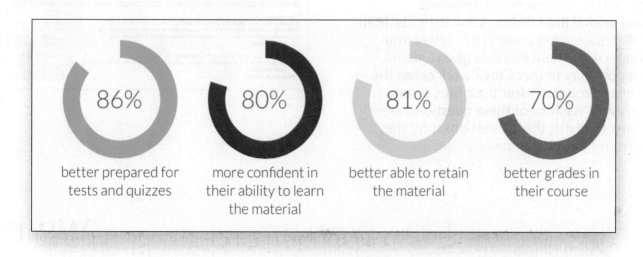

86% better prepared for tests and quizzes

80% more confident in their ability to learn the material

81% better able to retain the material

70% better grades in their course

Streamlined Learning Objectives

Newly streamlined learning objectives help students make the best use of their time outside of class. Each learning objective is addressed by reading content, watching educational videos, and answering a variety of practice and assessment questions, so that no matter where students begin their work, the relevant resources and practice are readily accessible.

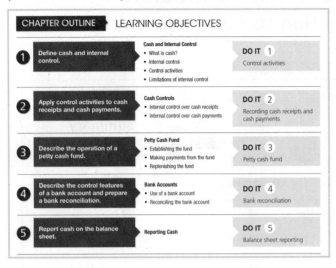

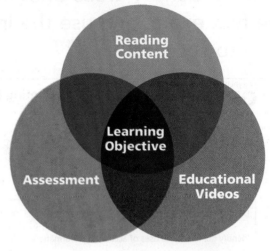

Review and Practice

Developing effective problem-solving skills requires practice, relevant feedback, and insightful examples with more opportunities for self-guided practice.

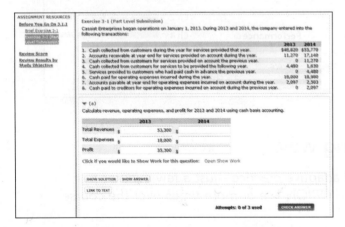

Review and practice opportunities in the text include:

- Learning Objectives Review
- Glossary Review
- Multiple-Choice Questions with Answers
- Do It Problems with Action Plans
- Demonstration Problems

In **WileyPLUS**, the practice assignments include several Brief Exercises and Exercises from the related exercises listed in the Before You Go On section. These exercises give students the opportunity to check their work or see the answer and solution after their final attempt. Algorithmic versions of these questions allow students to revisit these questions until they understand a topic completely.

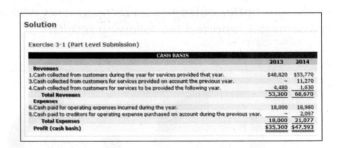

ACCOUNTING PRINCIPLES

SEVENTH CANADIAN EDITION

→ Jerry J. Weygandt *Ph.D., CPA*
University of Wisconsin—Madison

→ Donald E. Kieso *Ph.D., CPA*
Northern Illinois University

→ Paul D. Kimmel *Ph.D., CPA*
University of Wisconsin—Milwaukee

→ Barbara Trenholm *M.B.A., FCA*
University of New Brunswick—Fredericton

→ Valerie R. Warren *M.B.A., CPA, CA*
Kwantlen Polytechnic University

→ Lori Novak *H.B.Comm., CPA, CGA*
Red River College

WILEY

To our students—past, present, and future

Library and Archives Canada Cataloguing in Publication

Weygandt, Jerry J., author
Accounting principles / Jerry J. Weygandt, Ph.D., CPA (University of Wisconsin—Madison), Donald E. Kieso, Ph.D., CPA (Northern Illinois University), Paul D. Kimmel, Ph.D., CPA (University of Wisconsin—Milwaukee), Barbara Trenholm, MBA, FCA (University of New Brunswick—Fredericton), Valerie Warren, B.Comm., M.B.A., CPA, CA (Kwantlen Polytechnic University), Lori Novak, H.B.Comm., CPA, CGA (Red River College).—Seventh Canadian edition.

Includes indexes.
Revision of: Accounting principles / Jerry J. Weygandt, Donald E. Kieso, Barbara Trenholm; in collaboration with Donald C. Cherry.—1st Canadian ed.—Toronto: J. Wiley Canada, ©1999.
ISBN 978-1-119-04850-3 (volume 1: bound).—ISBN 978-1-119-04847-3 (volume 2: bound)

1. Accounting—Textbooks.   I. Kieso, Donald E., author   II. Kimmel, Paul D., author   III. Trenholm, Barbara, author   IV. Warren, Valerie, 1968-, author   V. Novak, Lori, author   VI. Title.

HF5635.W39 2015   657'.044   C2015-906305-1

Production Credits
Executive Editor: Zoë Craig
Vice President and Director, Market Solutions: Veronica Visentin
Marketing Manager: Anita Osborne
Editorial Manager: Karen Staudinger
Developmental Editor: Daleara Jamasji Hirjikaka
Media Editor: Luisa Begani
Production and Media Specialist: Meaghan MacDonald
Assistant Editor: Ashley Patterson
Cover and Interior Design: Joanna Vieira
Production Editing: Denise Showers, Senior Project Manager, Aptara Inc.
Typesetting: Aptara Inc.
Cover Photo: Background: ©raspu/Getty Images. Leaves in iPad: © View Stock/Getty Images. Ipad: © Mattjeacock/Getty Images. Falling leaves: ©bgfoto/Getty Images.

The inside back cover will contain printing identification and country of origin if omitted from this page. In addition, if the ISBN on the back cover differs from the ISBN on this page, the one on the back cover is correct.

Manufactured in the United States by LSC Communications

2 3 4 5 LSC 19 18 17

John Wiley & Sons Canada, Ltd.
Suite 300, 90 Eglinton Ave East
Toronto, Ontario, Canada, M4P 2Y3

Seventh Canadian Edition

Barbara Trenholm, B.Comm., M.B.A., FCPA, FCA, ICD.D, is a professor emerita at the University of New Brunswick, for which she continues to teach part-time locally and internationally. She is a recipient of the Leaders in Management Education Award, the Global Teaching Excellence Award, and the University of New Brunswick's Merit Award and Dr. Allan P. Stuart Award for Excellence in Teaching. She also served a three-year term as a Teaching Scholar of the University of New Brunswick.

Professor Trenholm is a member of the boards of several public, private, and Crown corporations, including Plaza Retail REIT and NB Power. She is a past board member of Atomic Energy of Canada Limited, the Canadian Institute of Chartered Accountants (now known as CPA Canada), and the Atlantic School of Chartered Accountancy, and past president of the New Brunswick Institute of Chartered Accountants (now known as CPA New Brunswick). She has also served as a chair of the Canadian Institute of Chartered Accountants Academic Research Committee, Interprovincial Education Committee, and Canadian Institute of Chartered Accountants/Canadian Academic Accounting Association Liaison Committee. She has served as a member of the Canadian Institute of Chartered Accountants Qualification Committee, International Qualifications Appraisal Board, and Education Reengineering Task Force and the American Accounting Association's Globalization Initiatives Task Force, in addition to numerous other professional committees at the international, national, and provincial levels.

Professor Trenholm also has an extensive record of service in leadership roles in the university and the community. She has served as acting dean of the Faculty of Administration, as a member of the University Senate, and as Co-Chair of the New Brunswick Pension Board of Trustees, in addition to chairing and/or serving on many university committees.

She has presented at many conferences and published widely in the field of accounting education and standard setting in journals including *Accounting Horizons, Journal of the Academy of Business Education, CAmagazine, CGA Magazine,* and *CMA Magazine.* She is also part of the Canadian author team of Kimmel, Weygandt, Kieso, Trenholm, and Irvine, *Financial Accounting: Tools for Business Decision-Making,* published by John Wiley & Sons Canada, Ltd.

Valerie Warren, M.B.A., CPA, CA, is an instructor at Kwantlen Polytechnic University in the Fraser Valley, British Columbia. She has a wide range of teaching experience in financial accounting and auditing. She is also currently the academic chair of the accounting program at Kwantlen. Ms. Warren has also been active in the accounting profession. She participated in the Institute of Chartered Accountants of British Columbia student education program in a variety of roles, including facilitator and marker. She also serves as a practice review officer for CPABC (Chartered Professional Accounts British Columbia), where she conducts practice reviews of national, regional, and local firms for compliance with current accounting and assurance standards. She is also the Canadian author of Moroney, Campbell, Hamilton, and Warren's *Auditing: A Practical Approach,* published by John Wiley & Sons Canada, Ltd.

Lori Novak, H.B.Comm., CPA, CGA, is an instructor at Red River College in Winnipeg, Manitoba. Her teaching experience includes course development and delivery in financial accounting, management accounting, and general business courses. Ms. Novak has a Bachelor of Commerce degree from Laurentian University and is in the process of completing a Masters of Business Administration. She has professional accounting experience with Palmer, Badger & Co, Chartered Professional Accountants, as well as industry experience working in management. She has served on various volunteer boards as treasurer and fundraising manager in her community.

U.S. Edition

Jerry J. Weygandt, Ph.D., CPA, is Arthur Andersen Alumni Emeritus Professor of Accounting at the University of Wisconsin—Madison. He holds a Ph.D. in accounting from the University of Illinois. Articles by Professor Weygandt have appeared in the *Accounting Review, Journal of Accounting Research, Accounting Horizons, Journal of Accountancy,* and other academic and professional journals. These articles have examined such financial reporting issues as accounting for price-level adjustments, pensions, convertible securities, stock option contracts, and interim reports. Professor Weygandt is author of other accounting and financial reporting books and is a member of the American Accounting Association, the American Institute of Certified Public Accountants, and the Wisconsin Society of Certified Public Accountants. He has served on numerous committees of the American Accounting Association and as a member of the editorial board of *The Accounting Review;* he also has served as President and Secretary-Treasurer of the American Accounting Association. In addition, he has been actively involved with the American Institute of Certified Public Accountants and has been a member of the Accounting Standards Executive Committee of that organization. He has served on the FASB task force that examined the reporting issues related to accounting for income taxes and served as a trustee of the Financial Accounting Foundation. Professor Weygandt has received the Chancellor's Award for Excellence in Teaching and the Beta Gamma Sigma Dean's Teaching Award. He is on the board of directors of M & I Bank of Southern Wisconsin. He is the recipient of the Wisconsin Institute of CPAs' Outstanding Educator's Award and the Lifetime Achievement Award. In 2001, he received the American Accounting Association's Outstanding Educator Award.

Donald E. Kieso, Ph.D., CPA, received his bachelor's degree from Aurora University and his doctorate in accounting from the University of Illinois. He has served as chairman of the Department of Accountancy and is currently the KPMG Emeritus Professor of Accounting at Northern Illinois University. He has public accounting experience with PricewaterhouseCoopers (San Francisco and Chicago) and Arthur Andersen & Co. (Chicago) and research experience with the Research Division of the American Institute of Certified Public Accountants (New York). He has done post-doctoral work as a Visiting Scholar at the University of California at Berkeley and is a recipient of NIU's Teaching Excellence Award and four Golden Apple Teaching Awards. Professor Kieso is the author of other accounting and business books and is a member of the American Accounting Association, the American Institute of Certified Public Accountants, and the Illinois CPA Society. He has served as a member of the board of directors of the Illinois CPA Society, the AACSB's Accounting Accreditation Committees, and the State of Illinois Comptroller's Commission; as secretary-treasurer of the Federation of Schools of Accountancy; and as secretary-treasurer of the American Accounting Association. He is the recipient of the Outstanding Accounting Educator Award from the Illinois CPA Society, the FSA's Joseph A. Silvoso Award of Merit, the NIU Foundation's Humanitarian Award for Service to Higher Education, the Distinguished Service Award from the Illinois CPA Society, and in 2003 an honorary doctorate from Aurora University.

Paul D. Kimmel, Ph.D., CPA, received his bachelor's degree from the University of Minnesota and his doctorate in accounting from the University of Wisconsin. He is an Associate Professor at the University of Wisconsin—Milwaukee, and has public accounting experience with Deloitte & Touche (Minneapolis). He was the recipient of the UWM School of Business Advisory Council Teaching Award, the Reggie Taite Excellence in Teaching Award, and is a three-time winner of the Outstanding Teaching Assistant Award at the University of Wisconsin. He is also a recipient of the Elijah Watts Sells Award for Honorary Distinction for his results on the CPA exam. He is a member of the American Accounting Association and the Institute of Management Accountants and has published articles in *Accounting Review, Accounting Horizons, Advances in Management Accounting, Managerial Finance, Issues in Accounting Education,* and *Journal of Accounting Education,* as well as other journals. His research interests include accounting for financial instruments and innovation in accounting education. He has published papers and given numerous talks on incorporating critical thinking into accounting education, and helped prepare a catalogue of critical thinking resources for the Federated Schools of Accountancy.

How to Use the Study Aids in This Book

3 ADJUSTING THE ACCOUNTS

CHAPTER PREVIEW

In Chapter 2, we learned the accounting cycle up to and including the preparation of the trial balance. In this chapter, we will learn that additional steps are usually needed before preparing the financial statements. These steps adjust accounts for timing mismatches, like what Maple Leaf Sports and Entertainment, in our feature story, does to account for advance ticket sales to games. In this chapter, we introduce the accrual accounting concepts that guide the adjustment process. The remainder of the accounting cycle is discussed in Chapter 4 and is illustrated here.

CHAPTER 2
1. Analyzing and recording Transactions
2. Posting Transactions
3. Trial Balance

CHAPTER 3
4. Journalize Adjusting Entries
5. Post Adjusting Entries
6. Adjusted Trial Balance
7. Financial Statements

CHAPTER 4
8. Closing Entries
9. Post-Closing Trial Balance

The **Preview** sums up the essence of the chapter in a few brief sentences.

The **Feature Story** helps you picture how the chapter topic relates to the real world of accounting and business. Throughout the chapter, references to the Feature Story will help you put new ideas in context, organize them, and remember them.

FEATURE STORY — ADVANCE SPORTS REVENUE IS JUST THE TICKET

TORONTO, Ont.—Professional sports teams sell millions of dollars worth of tickets before the players ever step onto the ice, court, or field. Some teams, such as the National Hockey League's Toronto Maple Leafs, have thousands of loyal season-ticket holders and a waiting list of season-ticket hopefuls.

Not only that, but the average price of a single ticket to a Leafs' game in the 2014–15 season was $373.50 on the resale market—the highest among all NHL teams.

Such strong ticket sales are good news to the Leafs' owner, Maple Leaf Sports and Entertainment Ltd. (MLSE), which also owns the Toronto Raptors National Basketball Association team, the Toronto FC professional soccer club, and the Toronto Marlies of the American Hockey League. MLSE also saw a revenue boost when the Raptors sold 3,000 season tickets for 2014–15.

How do these teams ac[...] which are considered unearn[...] company (jointly owned by [...] BCE Inc., and Kilmer Sports [...] ments are not made public. Bu[...] ticket sales as an increase in [...] Revenue, because they are ob[...] the game—that customers hav[...]

However, sports ticket rev[...] ferent accounting period than [...] most common method of recog[...] the accrual basis—transaction[...] which they occur, not when [...] means that when preparing fi[...] need to make journal entrie[...] timing. These adjusting entrie[...]

Abelimages/Getty Images

Based on the price of Leafs' tickets, an adjusting entry that MLSE might make for just one game held in a different accounting period could be for several million dollars.

Sources: Morgan Campbell, "Maple Leafs Won't Raise Prices on Season Tickets," *Toronto Star*, March 3, 2015; Brian Costello, "Toronto Maple Leafs Most Expensive Ticket in NHL; All Teams Listed 1 to 30," *The Hockey News*, October 7, 2014; Josh Rubin, "Toronto Raptors Ticket Sales Jump," *Toronto Star*, October 2, 2014; Grant Robertson and Tara Perkins, *The Globe and Mail*, "Rogers, Bell Agree to Deal for MLSE," BNN, December 10, 2011.

The **Chapter Outline** is a visual preview of the major topics and subtopics that will be discussed and gives you a mental framework upon which to arrange the new information you are about to learn. The Do It exercises are mini demonstration problems keyed to the various learning objectives.

Learning Objectives at the beginning of each chapter provide you with a framework for learning the specific concepts and procedures covered in the chapter. Each learning objective reappears at the point within the chapter where the concept is discussed. You can review all the learning objectives in the **Summary of Learning Objectives** at the end of the chapter. End-of-chapter material is keyed to learning objectives.

CHAPTER OUTLINE — LEARNING OBJECTIVES

1 Explain accrual basis accounting, and when to recognize revenues and expenses.

Timing Issues
- Accrual versus cash basis accounting
- Revenue and expense recognition

DO IT 1 Accrual accounting

2 Prepare adjusting entries for prepayments.

The Basics of Adjusting Entries
- Adjusting entries for prepayments

DO IT 2 Adjusting entries for prepayments

3 Prepare adjusting entries for accruals.

- Adjusting entries for accruals

DO IT 3 Adjusting entries for accruals

4 Describe the nature and purpose of an adjusted trial balance, and prepare one.

The Adjusted Trial Balance and Financial Statements
- Preparing the adjusted trial balance
- Preparing financial statements

DO IT 4 Trial balance

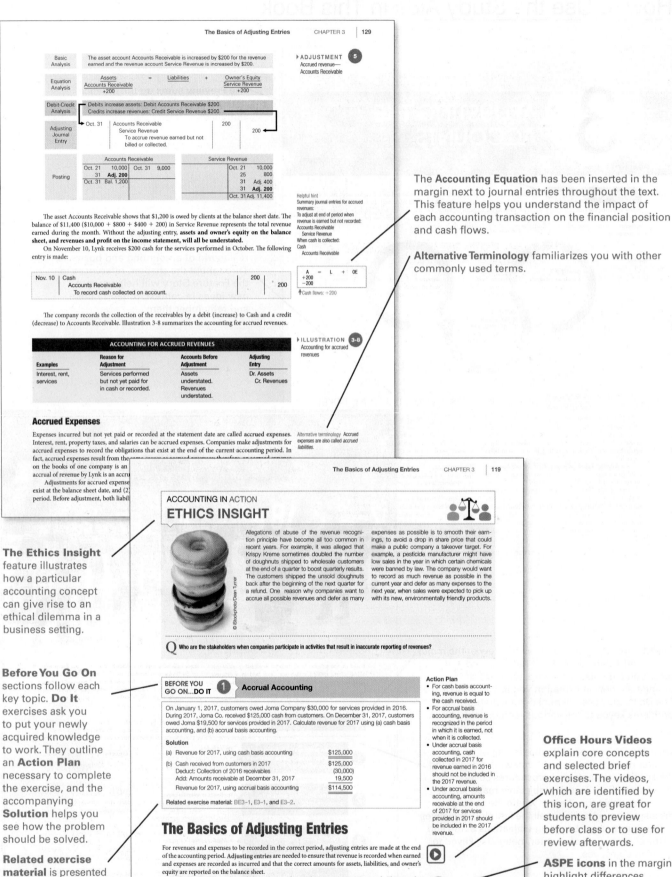

The Accounting Equation has been inserted in the margin next to journal entries throughout the text. This feature helps you understand the impact of each accounting transaction on the financial position and cash flows.

Alternative Terminology familiarizes you with other commonly used terms.

The Ethics Insight feature illustrates how a particular accounting concept can give rise to an ethical dilemma in a business setting.

Before You Go On sections follow each key topic. **Do It** exercises ask you to put your newly acquired knowledge to work. They outline an **Action Plan** necessary to complete the exercise, and the accompanying **Solution** helps you see how the problem should be solved.

Related exercise material is presented at the end of the Before You Go On section.

Office Hours Videos explain core concepts and selected brief exercises. The videos, which are identified by this icon, are great for students to preview before class or to use for review afterwards.

ASPE icons in the margin highlight differences between International Financial Reporting Standards (IFRS) and Accounting Standards for Private Enterprises.

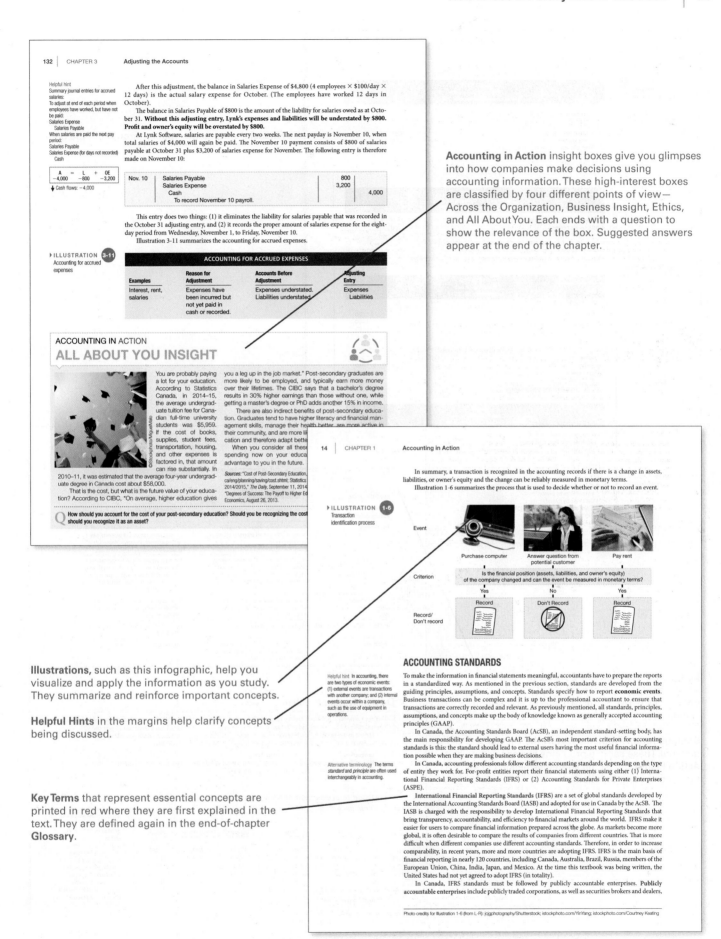

Accounting in Action insight boxes give you glimpses into how companies make decisions using accounting information. These high-interest boxes are classified by four different points of view—Across the Organization, Business Insight, Ethics, and All About You. Each ends with a question to show the relevance of the box. Suggested answers appear at the end of the chapter.

Illustrations, such as this infographic, help you visualize and apply the information as you study. They summarize and reinforce important concepts.

Helpful Hints in the margins help clarify concepts being discussed.

Key Terms that represent essential concepts are printed in red where they are first explained in the text. They are defined again in the end-of-chapter **Glossary**.

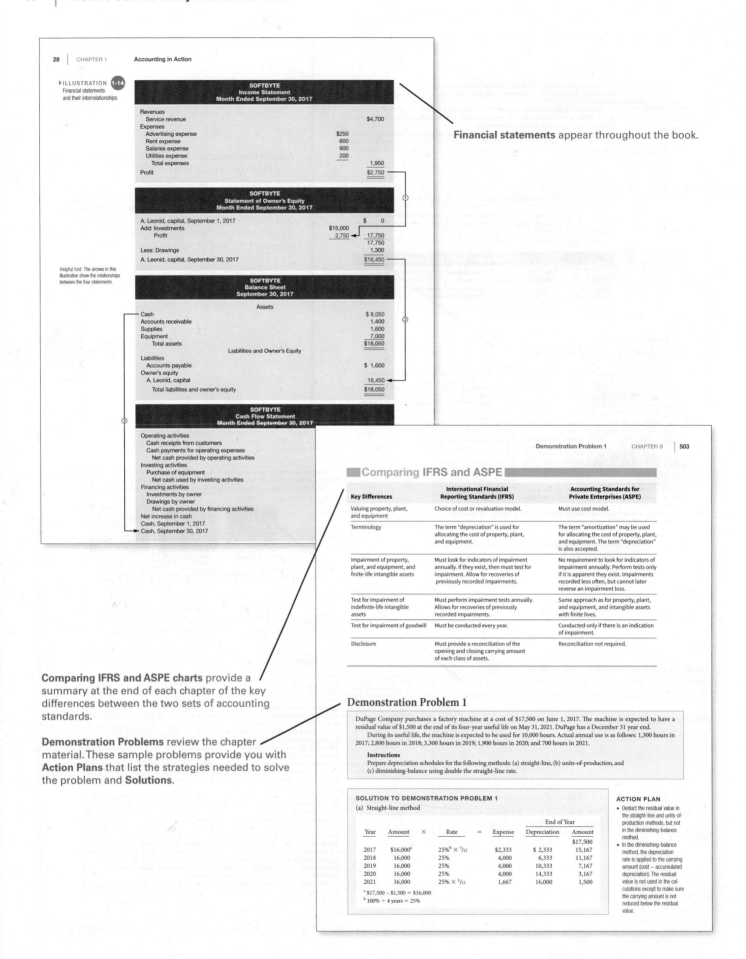

▶ILLUSTRATION 1-14
Financial statements
and their interrelationships

SOFTBYTE
Income Statement
Month Ended September 30, 2017

Revenues		
Service revenue		$4,700
Expenses		
Advertising expense	$250	
Rent expense	600	
Salaries expense	900	
Utilities expense	200	
Total expenses		1,950
Profit		$2,750

SOFTBYTE
Statement of Owner's Equity
Month Ended September 30, 2017

A. Leonid, capital, September 1, 2017		$ 0
Add: Investments	$15,000	
Profit	2,750	17,750
		17,750
Less: Drawings		1,300
A. Leonid, capital, September 30, 2017		$16,450

Helpful hint The arrows in this
illustration show the relationships
between the four statements.

SOFTBYTE
Balance Sheet
September 30, 2017

Assets	
Cash	$ 8,050
Accounts receivable	1,400
Supplies	1,600
Equipment	7,000
Total assets	$18,050
Liabilities and Owner's Equity	
Liabilities	
Accounts payable	$ 1,600
Owner's equity	
A. Leonid, capital	16,450
Total liabilities and owner's equity	$18,050

SOFTBYTE
Cash Flow Statement
Month Ended September 30, 2017

Operating activities	
Cash receipts from customers	
Cash payments for operating expenses	
Net cash provided by operating activities	
Investing activities	
Purchase of equipment	
Net cash used by investing activities	
Financing activities	
Investments by owner	
Drawings by owner	
Net cash provided by financing activities	
Net increase in cash	
Cash, September 1, 2017	
Cash, September 30, 2017	

Financial statements appear throughout the book.

▮Comparing IFRS and ASPE▮

Key Differences	International Financial Reporting Standards (IFRS)	Accounting Standards for Private Enterprises (ASPE)
Valuing property, plant, and equipment	Choice of cost or revaluation model.	Must use cost model.
Terminology	The term "depreciation" is used for allocating the cost of property, plant, and equipment.	The term "amortization" may be used for allocating the cost of property, plant, and equipment. The term "depreciation" is also accepted.
Impairment of property, plant, and equipment, and finite-life intangible assets	Must look for indicators of impairment annually. If they exist, then must test for impairment. Allow for recoveries of previously recorded impairments.	No requirement to look for indicators of impairment annually. Perform tests only if it is apparent they exist. Impairments recorded less often, but cannot later reverse an impairment loss.
Test for impairment of indefinite-life intangible assets	Must perform impairment tests annually. Allows for recoveries of previously recorded impairments.	Same approach as for property, plant, and equipment, and intangible assets with finite lives.
Test for impairment of goodwill	Must be conducted every year.	Conducted only if there is an indication of impairment.
Disclosure	Must provide a reconciliation of the opening and closing carrying amount of each class of assets.	Reconciliation not required.

Comparing IFRS and ASPE charts provide a
summary at the end of each chapter of the key
differences between the two sets of accounting
standards.

Demonstration Problems review the chapter
material. These sample problems provide you with
Action Plans that list the strategies needed to solve
the problem and **Solutions**.

Demonstration Problem 1

DuPage Company purchases a factory machine at a cost of $17,500 on June 1, 2017. The machine is expected to have a residual value of $1,500 at the end of its four-year useful life on May 31, 2021. DuPage has a December 31 year end.

During its useful life, the machine is expected to be used for 10,000 hours. Actual annual use is as follows: 1,300 hours in 2017; 2,800 hours in 2018; 3,300 hours in 2019; 1,900 hours in 2020; and 700 hours in 2021.

Instructions
Prepare depreciation schedules for the following methods: (a) straight-line, (b) units-of-production, and (c) diminishing-balance using double the straight-line rate.

SOLUTION TO DEMONSTRATION PROBLEM 1
(a) Straight-line method

						End of Year	
Year	Amount	×	Rate	=	Expense	Depreciation	Amount
							$17,500
2017	$16,000ᵃ		25%ᵇ × ⁷/₁₂		$2,333	$ 2,333	15,167
2018	16,000		25%		4,000	6,333	11,167
2019	16,000		25%		4,000	10,333	7,167
2020	16,000		25%		4,000	14,333	3,167
2021	16,000		25% × ⁵/₁₂		1,667	16,000	1,500

ᵃ $17,500 − $1,500 = $16,000
ᵇ 100% ÷ 4 years = 25%

ACTION PLAN
• Deduct the residual value in the straight-line and units-of-production methods, but not in the diminishing-balance method.
• In the diminishing-balance method, the depreciation rate is applied to the carrying amount (cost − accumulated depreciation). The residual value is not used in the calculations except to make sure the carrying amount is not reduced below the residual value.

▶ Summary of Learning Objectives

1. *Explain accrual basis accounting, and when to recognize revenues and expenses.* In order to provide timely information, accountants divide the life of a business into specific time periods. Therefore, it is important to record transactions in the correct time period. Under accrual basis accounting, events that change a company's financial statements are recorded in the periods in which the events occur, rather than in the periods in which the company receives or pays cash. The revenue recognition principle provides guidance about when to recognize revenues. Under ASPE, revenue is recognized when the service has been performed or the goods have been sold and delivered, the revenue can be reliably measured, and collection is reasonably certain. For IFRS, a contractual relationship to provide a performance obligation (goods or services) with the customer must exist. The transaction price must be determined and allocated if there are multiple goods and services to be provided. When the goods and services have been provided, the performance obligation is satisfied and revenue may be recognized. Expenses are recorded in the same period as revenue is recognized, if there is a direct association between the revenues and expenses. If there is no association between revenues and expenses, expenses are recorded in the period they are incurred.

2. *Prepare adjusting entries for prepayments.* Prepayments are either prepaid expenses or unearned revenues. Adjusting entries for prepayments record the portion of the prepayment

that applies to the expense or revenue of the current accounting period. The adjusting entry for prepaid expenses debits (increases) an expense account and credits (decreases) an asset account. For a long-lived asset, the contra asset account Accumulated Depreciation is used instead of crediting the asset account directly. The adjusting entry for unearned revenues debits (decreases) a liability account and credits (increases) a revenue account.

3. *Prepare adjusting entries for accruals.* Accruals are either accrued revenues or accrued expenses. Adjusting entries for accruals record revenues and expenses that apply to the current accounting period and that have not yet been recognized through daily journal entries. The adjusting entry for accrued revenue debits (increases) a receivable account and credits (increases) a revenue account. The adjusting entry for an accrued expense debits (increases) an expense account and credits (increases) a liability account.

4. *Describe the nature and purpose of an adjusted trial balance, and prepare one.* An adjusted trial balance shows the balances of all accounts, including those that have been adjusted, at the end of an accounting period. It proves that the total of the accounts with debit balances is still equal to the total of the accounts with credit balances after the adjustments have been posted. Financial statements are prepared from an adjusted trial balance in the following order: (1) income statement, (2) statement of owner's equity, and (3) balance sheet.

*The **Summary of Learning Objectives** relates the learning objectives to the key points in the chapter. It gives you another opportunity to review, as well as to see how all the key topics within the chapter are related.*

▶ Glossary

Accrual basis accounting A basis for accounting in which revenues are recorded when earned and expenses are recorded when incurred. (p. 117)

Accrued expenses Expenses incurred but not yet paid in cash or recorded. (p. 129)

Accrued revenues Revenues earned but not yet received in cash or recorded. (p. 128)

Accumulated depreciation The cumulative sum of the depreciation expense since the asset was purchased. (p. 124)

Adjusted trial balance A list of accounts and their balances after all adjustments have been posted. (p. 135)

Adjusting entries Entries made at the end of an accounting period to ensure that the revenue and expense recognition criteria are followed. (p. 119)

Carrying amount The difference between the cost of a depreciable asset and its accumulated depreciation; in other words, it is the unallocated or unexpired portion of the depreciable asset's cost. (p. 125)

Cash basis accounting A basis for accounting in which revenue is recorded when cash is received and an expense is recorded when cash is paid. (p. 117)

Contra asset account An account with the opposite balance (credit) compared with its related asset account, which has a debit

balance. A contra asset is deducted from the related asset on the balance sheet. (p. 124)

Depreciation The allocation of the cost of a long-lived asset to expense over its useful life in a rational and systematic manner. (p. 123)

Fiscal year An accounting period that is one year long. It does not need to start and end on the same days as the calendar year. (p. 116)

Interim periods Accounting time periods that are less than one year long, such as a month or a quarter of a year. (p. 116)

Matching concept Dictates that ⬛⬛⬛⬛⬛⬛⬛⬛⬛⬛⬛⬛⬛⬛ results (revenues). (p. 118)

Principal The amount borrowed ⬛⬛⬛⬛⬛⬛⬛⬛⬛⬛⬛⬛ loan, separate from interest. (p. 130)

Revenue recognition principle P⬛⬛⬛⬛⬛⬛⬛⬛⬛⬛ record revenue. In general, it is recor⬛⬛⬛⬛⬛⬛⬛⬛⬛⬛ gation has been satisfied, that is, the ⬛⬛⬛⬛⬛⬛⬛⬛⬛⬛ the goods sold and delivered. (p. 11⬛)

Straight-line depreciation metho⬛ ⬛⬛⬛⬛⬛⬛⬛⬛⬛⬛ which depreciation expense is calcu⬛⬛⬛⬛⬛⬛⬛⬛⬛⬛ useful life. (p. 123)

Useful life The length of service o⬛⬛⬛⬛⬛⬛⬛⬛⬛⬛

*The **Glossary** defines all the terms and concepts introduced in the chapter. Page references help you find any terms you need to study further.*

▶ Self-Study Questions
Answers are at the end of the chapter.

(LO 1) K 1. Which of the following statements about an account is true?
(a) The left side of an account is the credit or decrease side.
(b) An account is an individual accounting record of increases and decreases in specific asset, liability, and owner's equity items.
(c) There are separate accounts for specific assets and liabilities but only one account for owner's equity items.
(d) The right side of an account is the debit or increase side.

(LO 1) K 2. Credits:
(a) increase both assets and liabilities.
(b) decrease both assets and liabilities.
(c) increase assets and decrease liabilities.
(d) decrease assets and increase liabilities.

(LO 1) K 3. Accounts that normally have debit balances are:
(a) assets, expenses, and revenues.
(b) assets, expenses, and owner's capital.
(c) assets, liabilities, and drawings.
(d) assets, expenses, and drawings.

(LO 2) K 4. What is the correct sequence of steps in the recording process?
(a) Analyzing transactions; preparing a trial balance
(b) Analyzing transactions; entering transactions in a journal; posting transactions
(c) Entering transactions in a journal; posting transactions; preparing a trial balance
(d) Entering transactions in a journal; posting transactions; analyzing transactions

(LO 2) AP 5. Performing services for a customer on account should result in:
(a) a decrease in the liability account Accounts Payable and an increase in the revenue account Service Revenue.
(b) an increase in the asset account Cash and a decrease in the asset account Accounts Receivable.
(c) an increase to the asset account Accounts Receivable and an increase to the liability account Unearned Revenue.

(d) an increase to the asset account Accounts Receivable and an increase to the revenue account Service Revenue.

(LO 2) AP 6. The purchase of equipment on account should result in:
(a) a debit to Equipment and a credit to Accounts Payable.
(b) a debit to Equipment Expense and a credit to Accounts Payable.
(c) a debit to Equipment and a credit to Cash.
(d) a debit to Accounts Receivable and a credit to Equipment.

(LO 3) K 7. A ledger:
(a) contains only asset and liability accounts.
(b) should show accounts in alphabetical order.
(c) is a collection of the entire group of accounts maintained by a company.
(d) is a book of original entry.

(LO 3) K 8. Posting:
(a) is normally done before journalizing.
(b) transfers ledger transaction data to the journal.
(c) is an optional step in the recording process.
(d) transfers journal entries to ledger accounts.

(LO 4) K 9. A trial balance:
(a) is a list of accounts with their balances at a specific time.
(b) proves that journalized transactions are accurate.
(c) will not balance if a correct journal entry is posted twice.
(d) proves that all transactions have been recorded.

(LO 4) AP 10. A trial balance will not balance if:
(a) the collection of an account receivable is posted twice.
(b) the purchase of supplies on account is debited to Supplies and credited to Cash.
(c) a $100 cash drawing by the owner is debited to Drawings for $1,000 and credited to Cash for $100.
(d) a $450 payment on account is debited to Accounts Payable for $45 and credited to Cash for $45.

Self-Study Questions form a practice test that gives you an opportunity to check your knowledge of important topics. Answers appear on the last page of the chapter.

Self-study questions are keyed to learning objectives. In addition, the level of cognitive skill required to solve the question has been classified with a letter code following Bloom's Taxonomy. You will find more information about Bloom's Taxonomy and this coding system on page XIV of this Preface.

Questions allow you to explain your understanding of concepts and relationships covered in the chapter. (These are keyed to learning objectives and Bloom's Taxonomy.)

▶ Questions

(LO 1) C 1. What is an account? Will a company need more than one account? Explain.

(LO 1) K 2. What is debiting an account? What is crediting an account?

(LO 1) K 3. Explain the relationship between the normal balance in each type of account and the accounting equation.

(LO 1) C 4. Dmitri Karpov doesn't understand how a debit increases Equipment and a credit increases Accounts

Payable. He believes that debits and credits cannot both increase account balances. Explain to Dmitri why he is wrong.

(LO 1) C 5. Why are increases to drawings and expenses recorded as debits?

(LO 1) C 6. Gustave Orsen, an introductory accounting student, thinks that a double-entry accounting system means that each transaction is recorded twice. Is Gustave correct? Explain.

▶ Brief Exercises

Brief Exercises generally focus on one learning objective at a time. They help you build confidence in your basic skills and knowledge. (These are keyed to learning objectives and Bloom's Taxonomy.)

Determine profit using cash and accrual bases. (LO 1) AP

BE3–1 AA Lawn Care had the following transactions in May, its first month of business:
1. Collected $550 cash from customers for services provided in May.
2. Billed customers $725 for services provided in May.
3. Received $350 from customers for services to be provided in June.
4. Purchased $250 of supplies on account. All of the supplies were used in May but were paid for in June.
   (a) Calculate profit for May using cash basis accounting.
   (b) Calculate profit for May using accrual basis accounting.

Calculate missing data for supplies. (LO 2) AP

BE3–2 Calculate the missing information in each of the following independent situations:

	Red Co.	Blue Co.	Green Co.
Supplies on hand, May 31, 2016	$ 795	$ 985	$1,325
Supplies purchased during the year	3,830	3,070	2,395
Supplies on hand, May 31, 2017	665	?	1,700
Supplies used during the year	?	2,750	?

Identify the major types of adjusting entries. (LO 1, 2) C

BE3–3 Kee Company accumulates the following adjustment data at December 31. Indicate (a) the type of balance sheet account that requires adjustment (prepaid expense, accrued revenue, etc.); and (b) whether the identified balance sheet account is over- or understated before any adjustments are recorded.
1. Supplies of $100 are on hand. Kee Company started the year with $1,100 of supplies on hand.
2. Services were performed but not recorded.
3. Interest of $200 has accumulated on a note payable.
4. Rent collected in advance totalling $650 has been earned.

Prepare and post transaction and adjusting entries for supplies. (LO 2) AP

BE3–4 Hahn Consulting Company's general ledger showed $785 in the Supplies account on January 1, 2017. On May 31, 2017, the company paid $3,255 for additional supplies. A count on December 31, 2017, showed $1,035 of supplies on hand.
(a) Prepare the journal entry to record the purchase of supplies on May 31, 2017.
(b) Calculate the amount of supplies used in 2017.
(c) Prepare the adjusting entry required at December 31, 2017.

Prepare and post transaction and adjusting entries for insurance. (LO 2) AP

BE3–5 On March 1, 2017, Eire Co. paid $4,800 to Big North Insurance for a one-year insurance policy. Eire Co. has a December 31 fiscal year end and adjusts accounts annually. Complete the following for Eire Co.
(a) Prepare the March 1, 2017, journal entry for the purchase of the insurance.
(b) Calculate the amount of insurance that expired during 2017 and the unexpired cost at December 31, 2017.
(c) Prepare the adjusting entry required at December 31, 2017.

Prepare and post transaction and adjusting entries for insurance. (LO 2) AP

BE3–6 On July 1, 2017, Majors Co. buys a three-year insurance policy for $12,750. Majors Co. has a December 31 year end.
(a) Journalize the purchase of the insurance policy.
(b) Prepare the year-end adjusting entry for the amount of insurance expired.

Prepare transaction and adjusting entries for depreciation. (LO 2) AP

BE3–7 On July 1, 2017, Masood Company purchases equipment for $30,000. The company uses straight-line depreciation. It estimates the equipment will have a 10-year life. Masood Company has a December 31 year end.
(a) Record the purchase of the equipment.
(b) Calculate the amount of depreciation Masood Company should record for the year of the equipment purchase.
(c) Prepare the adjusting journal entry for the equipment at December 31, 20

Prepare transaction and adjusting entries for depreciation; show statement presentation. (LO 2) AP

BE3–8 Zhang Company paid $27,000 to purchase equipment on January 1, 20__ ber 31 fiscal year end and uses straight-line depreciation. The company estimat__ year useful life.
(a) Prepare the journal entry to record the purchase of the equipment on Janu__
(b) Prepare the adjusting entries required on December 31, 2017 and 2018.
(c) Show the balance sheet and income statement presentation of the equipme__

Prepare and post transaction and adjusting entries for unearned revenue. (LO 2) AP

BE3–9 On March 1, 2017, Big North Insurance received $4,800 cash from __ policy. Big North Insurance has an October 31 fiscal year end and adjusts accou__ ing for Big North Insurance.
(a) Prepare the March 1, 2017, journal entry.
(b) Calculate the amount of revenue earned during 2017 and the amount unea__

Exercises that gradually increase in difficulty help you to build your confidence in your ability to use the material learned in the chapter. (These are keyed to learning objectives and Bloom's Taxonomy.)

Each Problem helps you pull together and apply several concepts of the chapter. Two sets of problems—Set A and Set B—are usually keyed to the same learning objectives and cognitive level. These provide additional opportunities to apply concepts learned in the chapter.

Taking It Further is an extra question at the end of each problem designed to challenge you to think beyond the basic concepts covered in the problem, and to provide written explanations. Your instructor may assign problems with or without this extra element.

(c) If the amount in Insurance Expense is the January 31 adjusting entry, and the original insurance premium was for one year, what was the total premium, and when was the policy purchased? (*Hint*: Assume the policy was purchased on the first day of the month.)
(d) If the amount in Supplies Expense is the January 31 adjusting entry, and the balance in Supplies on January 1 was $800, what was the amount of supplies purchased in January?
(e) If the balance in Salaries Payable on January 1, 2017, was $1,200, what was the amount of salaries paid in cash during January?

Prepare adjusting entries from analysis of trial balances. (LO 2, 3, 4) AP

E3–15 The trial balances before and after adjustment for Lane Company at October 31, 2017, which is the end of its fiscal year, are as follows:

	Before Adjustment		After Adjustment	
	Debit	Credit	Debit	Credit
Cash	$ 9,100		$ 9,100	
Accounts receivable	8,700		9,230	
Supplies	2,450		710	
Prepaid insurance	3,775		2,525	
Equipment	34,100		34,100	
Accumulated depreciation—equipment		$ 3,525		$ 5,800
Accounts payable		5,900		5,900
Notes payable		40,000		40,000
Salaries payable		0		1,125
Interest payable		0		500
Unearned service revenue		1,600		900
E. Lane, capital		5,600		5,600
E. Lane, drawings	10,000		10,000	
Service revenue		45,000		46,230
Depreciation expense	0		2,275	
Insurance expense	0		1,250	
Interest expense	1,500		2,000	
Rent expense	15,000		15,000	
Salaries expense	17,000		18,125	
Supplies expense	0		1,740	
Totals	$101,625	$101,625	$106,055	$106,055

Instructions

Prepare the adjusting entries that were made.

Prepare financial statements from adjusted trial balance. (LO 4) AP

E3–16 The adjusted trial balance for Lane Company is given in E3–15.

Instructions

Prepare Lane Company's income statement, statement of owner's equity, and balance sheet.

▶ Problems: Set A

Determine profit on cash and accrual bases; recommend method. (LO 1) AP

P3–1A Your examination of the records of Southlake Co. shows the company collected $85,500 cash from customers and paid $48,400 cash for operating costs during 2017. If Southlake followed the accrual basis of accounting, it would report the following year-end balances:

	2017	2016
Accounts payable	$ 1,310	$ 2,250
Accounts receivable	4,230	2,650
Accumulated depreciation	11,040	10,400
Prepaid insurance	1,580	1,250
Supplies	910	490
Unearned revenue	1,260	1,480

Instructions

(a) Determine Southlake's profit on a cash basis for 2017.
(b) Determine Southlake's profit on an accrual basis for 2017.

TAKING IT FURTHER Which method do you recommend that Southlake use? Why?

Financial Reporting and Analysis   CHAPTER 9 | 525

Cumulative Coverage—Chapters 2 to 4

Alou Equipment Repair has a September 30 year end. The company adjusts and closes its accounts on an annual basis. On August 31, 2017, the account balances of Alou Equipment Repair were as follows:

In selected chapters, a **Cumulative Coverage Problem** follows the Set A and Set B Problems.

CHAPTER 9: BROADENING YOUR PERSPECTIVE

The **Broadening Your Perspective** section helps you pull together various concepts covered in the chapter and apply them to real-life business decisions.

Financial Reporting and Analysis

Financial Reporting Problem

BYP9-1   Refer to the financial statements and the Notes to Consolidated Statements for **Corus Entertainment Inc.**, which are reproduced in Appendix A.

Instructions

(a) For each type of property and equipment that Corus reports in note 6 to its consolidated statement of financial position, identify the following amounts at August 31, 2014: (1) cost, (2) accumulated depreciation, and (3) net carrying amount.

(b) For the broadcast licences (intangible asset) and goodwill that Corus reports in note 9 and in its consolidated statement of financial position, identify the following amounts at August 31, 2014: (1) cost, (2) accumulated amortization, and (3) net carrying amount.

(c) Refer to note 9 again and identify the amount of disposals and retirements for the fiscal year ended August 31, 2014.

(d) What total amount did Corus report for depreciation and amortization expense?

(e) Note 3 includes additional details regarding property, plant, and equipment accounting policies. Read the note and answer the following questions:
1. Does Corus use the cost model or revaluation model for property, plant, and equipment?
2. What depreciation method does Corus use for these assets?
3. For each property, plant, and equipment asset, identify the estimated useful life ranges used by Corus for depreciation.
4. When does Corus derecognize assets and how does it calculate gains and losses?

Interpreting Financial Statements

BYP9-2   **WestJet Airlines Ltd.** is one of Canada's leading airlines, offering service to destinations in Canada, the United States, Mexico, and the Caribbean. The following is a partial extract from its December 31, 2014, notes to the financial statements:

Financial Reporting Problems familiarize you with the format, content, and uses of financial statements prepared by Corus Entertainment, which are presented in Appendix A at the end of the text.

Interpreting Financial Statements asks you to apply the concepts you have learned to specific situations faced by actual companies.

All About You Activities ask you questions about the All About You feature in the chapter, helping you apply accounting principles to your personal finances.

Note. 1 (j) Statement of Significant Accounting Policies—Property and Equipment

Property and equipment is stated at cost and depreciated to its estimated residual value. Expected useful lives and depreciation methods are reviewed annually.

Asset class	Basis	Rate
Aircraft, net of estimated residual value	Straight-line	15–20 years
Engine, airframe and landing gear overhaul	Straight-line	5–15 years
Ground property and equipment	Straight-line	3–25 years
Spare engines and rotables, net of estimated residual value	Straight-line	15–20 years
Buildings	Straight-line	40 years
Leasehold improvements	Straight-line	5 years/Term of

Estimated residual values of the Corporation's aircraft range between $2,500 and $6,0[...] thousands of dollars) per aircraft. Spare engines have an estimated residual value equ[...] of the original purchase price. Residual values, where applicable, are reviewed annual[...] prevailing market rates at the consolidated statement of financial position date.

Major overhaul expenditures are capitalized and depreciated over the expected li[...] overhauls. All other costs relating to the maintenance of fleet assets are charged to th[...] statement of earnings on consumption or as incurred.

---

526 | CHAPTER 9   Long-Lived Assets

Instructions

(a) WestJet uses straight-line depreciation for all of its depreciable property and equipment. For which of the assets shown above might WestJet consider using units-of-production instead of straight-line depreciation? Should WestJet use units-of-production for those assets?

(b) According to this note, major overhaul expenditures are treated differently than other fleet maintenance costs. Explain how WestJet records these items. Is this appropriate? Why or why not?

(c) WestJet depreciates the cost of leasehold improvements over the terms of the leases. Is this appropriate? Are these terms the same as the physical lives of these assets?

(d) Does WestJet use component depreciation for any of its property and equipment assets? Explain.

Critical Thinking

Collaborative Learning Activity

Note to instructor: Additional instructions and material for this group activity can be found on the Instructor Resource Site and in *WileyPLUS*.

BYP9-3   In this learning activity, you will improve your understanding of depreciation by working in small groups to analyze and categorize, on a grid, information about the three methods of depreciation.

Communication Activity

BYP9-4   **Long Trucking Corporation** is a medium-sized trucking company with trucks that are driven across North America. The company owns large garages and equipment to repair and maintain the trucks. Ken Bond, the controller, knows that assets can be exchanged with or without money being paid or received. The company is considering exchanging a semi-truck with a carrying amount of $100,000 (original cost $165,000) for a garage in a rural area where the company can operate a branch of the repair operation. The garage has a fair value of $90,000 and the semi-truck has a fair value of $75,000. Long Trucking Corporation will also pay the seller an additional $15,000.

Santé Smoothie Saga

(**Note:** This is a continuation of the Santé Smoothie Saga from Chapters 1 through 8.)

BYP9-6   Natalie is thinking of buying a van that will be used only for business. She estimates that she can buy the van for $28,400. Natalie would spend an additional $3,000 to have the van painted. As well, she wants the back seat of the van removed so that she will have lots of room to transport her juicer inventory and smoothies and supplies. The cost of taking out the back seat and installing shelving units is estimated at $1,600. She expects the van to last about five years and to

Instructions

Write an e-mail to Jason Long (the owner) that explains (1) the financial impact of the exchange on assets and profit and (2) how the transaction should be recorded in the accounting records. (3) Suggest appropriate depreciation methods to use for the garage for future recording.

"All About You" Activity

BYP9-5   In the "All About You" feature, you learned about actions that were taken to strengthen Canada's copyright law and the radical changes in technology that drove the need to update the law. You have recently graduated from a music program and have composed two songs that you believe a recording artist may produce. You are wondering how you can best get copyright protection for your songs.

Instructions

Go to the Canadian Intellectual Property Office website at http://www.cipo.ic.gc.ca and search for its publication "A Guide to Copyright." The guide can be found by clicking on "Learn" in the "Copyright" box midway down the page. (Note that the links may change so a basic search of the site may be required.)

Answer the following questions:

(a) What is a copyright and to what does copyright apply?
(b) How can you obtain a copyright for your songs and what do you have to do to be protected?
(c) What are the benefits to you of getting copyright registration for your songs?
(d) How and where do you register a copyright?
(e) When you register a copyright, you are required to pay a fee for the registration. Should the registration fee for the copyright be recorded as an asset or an expense?
(f) Go to the glossary in "A Guide to Copyright." What is infringement of copyright? Provide a specific example of infringement.
(g) Go to frequently asked questions in "A Guide to Copyright." How long does a copyright last?

(b) Prepare depreciation schedules for the life of the van under the following depreciation methods:
1. straight-line.
2. diminishing-balance at double the straight-line rate.
3. units-of-production. It is estimated that the van will be driven as follows: January 2018–June 2018, 30,000 km; July 2018–June 2019, 37,500 km; July 2019–June 2020, 40,000 km; July 2020–June 2021, 47,500 km; July 2021–June 2022, 35,000 km; July 2022–July 2023, 10,000 km.

Collaborative Learning Activities prepare you for the business world, where you will be working with many people, by giving you practice in solving problems with colleagues. They also allow you to learn from fellow students.

Communication Activities ask you to engage in real-life business situations using your writing, speaking, or presentation skills.

The Santé Smoothie Saga is a serial problem found in each chapter. It follows the operations of a hypothetical small company, Santé Smoothies, throughout the text. The company is owned by a student and the purpose of the serial problem is to reinforce the application of accounting to the type of business a student could operate.

Answers to Chapter Questions offer suggested answers for questions that appear in the chapter's **Accounting in Action** insight boxes.

ANSWERS TO CHAPTER QUESTIONS

ANSWERS TO ACCOUNTING IN ACTION INSIGHT QUESTIONS

All About You, p. 367

Q: Who is responsible for losses due to unauthorized credit card use?

A: Most major credit card companies offer zero liability for credit card fraud, which protects the cardholder from losses due to fraud. You should find out if your cardholder agreement for any credit cards that you have offers protection from credit

card fraud so that you can avoid taking on the identity thief's debts.

Across the Organization Insight, p. 371

Q: How might an organization's marketing department assist in, and benefit from, the implementation of a mobile payments system?

The Use of Bloom's Taxonomy

Bloom's Taxonomy is a classification framework that you can use to develop your skills from the most basic to the most advanced competence levels: knowledge, comprehension, application, analysis, synthesis, and evaluation. These levels are in a hierarchy. In order to perform at each level, you must have mastered all prior levels.

Questions, exercises, and problems at the end of each chapter of this text have been classified by the knowledge level required in answering each one. Below you will learn what your role is in each of the six skill levels and how you can demonstrate mastery at each level. Key word clues will help you recognize the skill level required for a particular question.

(K) Knowledge (Remembering)

Student's role: "I read, listen, watch, or observe; I take notes and am able to recall information; ask and respond to questions."

Student demonstrates knowledge by stating who, what, when, why, and how in the same form in which they learned it.

Key word clues: define, identify, label, name, etc.

(C) Comprehension (Understanding)

Student's role: "I understand the information or skill. I can recognize it in other forms and I can explain it to others and make use of it."

Student demonstrates comprehension by giving an example of how the information would be used.

Key word clues: describe, distinguish, give example, compare, differentiate, explain, etc.

(AP) Application (Solving the Problem)

Student's role: "I can apply my prior knowledge and understanding to new situations."

Student demonstrates knowledge by solving problems independently, recognizing when the information or skill is needed and using it to solve new problems or complete tasks.

Key word clues: calculate, illustrate, prepare, complete, use, produce, etc.

(AN) Analysis (Detecting)

Student's role: "I can break down the information into simpler parts and understand how these parts are related."

Student demonstrates knowledge by recognizing patterns and hidden meanings, filling in missing information, correcting errors, and identifying components and effects.

Key word clues: analyze, break down, compare, contrast, deduce, differentiate, etc.

(S) Synthesis (Creating)

Student's role: "I use all knowledge, understanding, and skills to create alternatives. I can convey this information to others effectively."

Student demonstrates knowledge by acting as a guide to others, designing, and creating.

Key word clues: relate, tell, write, categorize, devise, formulate, generalize, create, design, etc.

(E) Evaluation (Appraisal)

Student's role: "I am open to and appreciative of the value of ideas, procedures, and methods and can make well-supported judgements, backed up by knowledge, understanding, and skills."

Student demonstrates knowledge by formulating and presenting well-supported judgement, displaying consideration of others, examining personal options, and making wise choices.

Key word clues: appraise, assess, criticize, critique, decide, evaluate, judge, justify, recommend, etc.

What TYPE of learner are you?

Understanding each of these basic learning styles enables the authors to engage students' minds and motivate them to do their best work, ultimately improving the experience for both students and faculty.

	Intake: To take in the information	To make a study package	Text features that may help you the most	Output: To do well on exams
VISUAL	• Pay close attention to charts, drawings, and handouts your instructors use. • Underline. • Use different colours. • Use symbols, flow charts, graphs, different arrangements on the page, white spaces.	Convert your lecture notes into "page pictures." To do this: • Use the "Intake" strategies. • Reconstruct images in different ways. • Redraw pages from memory. • Replace words with symbols and initials. • Look at your pages.	The Feature Story/Preview Infographics/Illustrations/Photos Accounting in Action Insight Boxes Accounting equation analyses Highlighted words Key Terms in red Demonstration Problem/ Action Plan Questions/Exercises/Problems Financial Reporting and Analysis	• Recall your "page pictures." • Draw diagrams where appropriate. • Practise turning your visuals back into words.
AURAL	• Attend lectures and tutorials. • Discuss topics with students and instructors. • Explain new ideas to other people. • Record your lectures. • Leave spaces in your lecture notes for later recall. • Describe pictures and visuals to somebody who was not in class.	You may take poor notes because you prefer to listen. Therefore: • Expand your notes by talking with others and with information from your textbook. • Record summarized notes and listen. • Read summarized notes out loud. • Explain your notes to another "aural" person.	Preview Accounting Matters! Insight Boxes Do It! Action Plan Summary of Learning Objectives Glossary Demonstration Problem/ Action Plan Self-Study Questions Questions/Exercises/Problems Financial Reporting and Analysis Critical Thinking, particularly the Collaborative Learning Activities Ethics Case	• Talk with the instructor. • Spend time in quiet places recalling the ideas. • Do extra assignments and attempt practice quizzes. • Say your answers out loud.
READING/ WRITING	• Use lists and headings. • Use dictionaries, glossaries, and definitions. • Read handouts, textbooks, and supplementary readings. • Use lecture notes.	• Write out words again and again. • Reread notes silently. • Rewrite ideas and principles in other words. • Turn charts, diagrams, and other illustrations into statements.	The Feature Story/Learning Objectives Preview Accounting equation analyses Do It! Action Plan Summary of Learning Objectives Glossary/Self-Study Questions Questions/Exercises/Problems Taking it Further Financial Reporting problem and Analysis Critical Thinking, particularly the Communication and Collaborative Learning Activities	• Do extra assignments. • Practise with multiple-choice questions. • Write paragraphs, beginnings, and endings. • Write your lists in outline form. • Arrange your words into hierarchies and points.
KINESTHETIC	• Use all your senses. • Go to labs, take field trips. • Listen to real-life examples. • Pay attention to applications. • Use hands-on approaches. • Use trial-and-error methods.	You may take poor notes because topics do not seem concrete or relevant. Therefore: • Put examples in your summaries. • Use case studies and applications to help with principles and abstract concepts. • Talk about your notes with another "kinesthetic" person. • Use pictures and photographs that illustrate an idea.	The Feature Story/Preview Infographics/Illustrations Do It! Action Plan Summary of Learning Objectives Demonstration Problem/Action Plan Self-Study Questions Questions/Exercises/Problems Financial Reporting and Analysis Critical Thinking, particularly the Communication and Collaborative Learning Activities	• Do extra assignments. • Role-play the exam situation.

Visit www.vark-learn.com and complete the Questionnaire to determine what type of learning style you have.

To the Instructor

Student-Focused and Instructor-Friendly—
The Solution for Your Accounting Principles Class!

In the previous editions of *Accounting Principles*, we sought to create a book about accounting that makes the subject clear and fascinating to students. And that is still our passion: to empower students to succeed by giving them the tools and the motivation they need to excel in their accounting courses and their future careers. We are confident that this new edition, with its strong pedagogical foundations, continuing currency and accuracy, and exciting new features, is the best edition yet.

Preparing the Seventh Canadian Edition

This revision of *Accounting Principles* provided us with an opportunity to improve a textbook that had already set high standards for quality. In the sixth edition, the new world of multiple GAAP standards was fully integrated. In this edition, we continue our incorporation of International Financial Reporting Standards (IFRS) and Accounting Standards for Private Enterprises (ASPE) into the text material. Differences between IFRS and ASPE are highlighted throughout each chapter with an ASPE logo (ASPE).

While we now live in a multiple GAAP world, the basic accounting cycle has not changed. Thus, our focus for introductory students continues to be the fundamental principles. We have undertaken to reduce unnecessary complexities where possible to ensure students stay focused on the concepts that really matter.

WileyPLUS is an innovative, research-based on-line environment for effective teaching and learning. It includes ORION, the powerful personalized adaptive learning tool to analyze students' proficiency and help improve their learning outcomes. Over 6,200 questions are available for practice and review allowing students to build proficiency in course topics.

WileyPLUS builds students' confidence because it takes the guesswork out of studying by providing students with a clear roadmap: **what to do, how to do it, if they did it right**. This interactive approach focuses on:

CONFIDENCE: Research shows that students experience a great deal of anxiety over studying. That's why we provide a structured learning environment that helps students focus on **what to do**, along with the support of immediate resources.

MOTIVATION: To increase and sustain motivation throughout the semester, *WileyPLUS* helps students learn **how to do it** at a pace that's right for them. Our integrated resources—available 24/7—function like a personal tutor, directly addressing each student's demonstrated needs with specific problem-solving techniques.

SUCCESS: *WileyPLUS* helps to assure that each study session has a positive outcome by putting students in control. Through instant feedback and learning objective reports, students know if they did it right, and where to focus next, so they achieve the strongest results.

With *WileyPLUS*, our efficacy research shows that students improve their outcomes by as much as one letter grade. *WileyPLUS* helps students take more initiative, so you'll have a greater impact on their achievement in the classroom and beyond.

What do students receive with *WileyPLUS*?

- The complete digital textbook, saving students up to 60% off the cost of a printed text.
- Question assistance, including links to relevant sections in the on-line digital textbook.
- Immediate feedback and proof of progress, 24/7.
- Integrated multimedia resources—Office Hours Videos, visual exhibits, animated tutorials, demonstration problems, and much more—that provide multiple study paths and encourage more active learning.

What do instructors receive with *WileyPLUS*?

- Reliable resources that reinforce course goals inside and outside of the classroom.
- Media-rich course materials and assessment content, including Instructor's Manual, Test Bank, PowerPoint® Slides, Solutions Manual, Computerized Test Bank, all text problems programmed and ready to assign to students, Additional Problems, and much more.
- The ability to easily identify those students who are falling behind.
- All end of chapter material is keyed to CPA technical and enabling competencies allowing the instructor to filter by competencies.

Relevance for Users

It has always been our goal to motivate both accounting and non-accounting majors to learn accounting. In order to illustrate the importance of financial accounting to non-accounting majors, we started Chapter 1 with a section about why accounting is important to everyone, not just accountants. We consistently emphasize this point throughout the text in our All About You Accounting in Action insight boxes. These boxes demonstrate how learning accounting is useful for students in managing their own financial affairs. We also have many Across the Organization Accounting in Action insight boxes. These clearly demonstrate how accounting is used to address issues in marketing, finance, management, and other functions. It is our sincere hope that non-accounting majors have the opportunity to appreciate accounting both personally and professionally.

This edition continues, and expands, the inclusion of user-oriented material to demonstrate the relevance of accounting to all students, no matter what their area of study is. We have a new focus company this edition—Corus Entertainment, an entertainment company with a specialty television and radio focus. Corus was chosen because of its appeal to post-secondary students. References to Corus have been made throughout each chapter, including in ratio analysis illustrations, end-of-chapter assignments, and examples cited from Corus's financial statements reproduced in Appendix A at the end of the textbook.

This edition was also subject to a comprehensive updating to ensure that it continues to be relevant and fresh. The textbook has a bold and colourful appearance. This new look is accompanied with appealing chapter opening stories. Over 85% of the chapter opening feature stories are new. The stories were carefully selected to ensure a balanced representation of private and public entities in a variety of industries to reflect the current economic reality in Canada. With the new colourful design comes an increased emphasis on the learning objectives at the beginning of each chapter, to ensure students can easily identify the key concepts to be mastered. Furthermore, many of the real-world examples were updated or replaced in the text as appropriate. Our textbook includes references to over 200 real companies. In addition, many of the Accounting in Action insight boxes are new.

Realizing that ethics is the basis for a strong business education, an Ethics Insight box has been added to each chapter. Each Ethics Insight box describes a real-world ethical dilemma. Students are encouraged to think of the impact and consequences of these situations. This exposure is so students begin to analyze ethical issues and to promote the development of their ethical reasoning skills.

Responding to instructor requests, we have also added a video feature called Office Hours Videos. These are short videos included in each chapter on core accounting concepts and problem walkthroughs for selected end-of-chapter material to supplement student learning. We continue to feature problem material that allows students to tie the concepts they are learning together and place them in context. Central to this is the Santé Smoothie Saga, a serial problem that allows students to apply chapter topics to an ongoing scenario where a young entrepreneur builds her small business.

Topical and Organization Changes

Where there is additional topical coverage, it was written to help students better prepare for the complexities of today's world. As always, each topic had to pass a strict test to warrant inclusion: an item was added only if it represented a major concept, issue, or procedure that a beginning student should understand. Changes to the text's organization were made to simplify chapters or to provide instructors with greater flexibility of coverage.

Some of the more significant additions in each chapter include the following:

- Chapter 1: Accounting in Action includes realigned learning objectives to clearly define GAAP. It contains expanded material on the building blocks of accounting, including a new visual representation of the conceptual framework hierarchy, which is introduced in the chapter and expanded in Chapter 11. The chapter includes references to expected future changes in the conceptual framework to ensure students are aware of differences that may be encountered between this course and future courses or the workplace. The revenue recognition discussion has been updated to incorporate the key concept of IFRS 15 *Revenue from Contracts with Customers*.

- Chapter 2: The Recording Process includes new visuals of the accounting cycle throughout the chapter to remind students of the cyclical nature of the accounting process and to provide a roadmap for Chapters 2 to 4. Journalizing and posting transactions to the general ledger are now separate learning objectives to represent the fact that these are distinct steps in the cycle.

- Chapter 3: Adjusting the Accounts includes an enhanced explanation of adjusting journal entries. The potential impact of failing to record adjusting entries has been added to emphasize the impact these entries have on the financial statements. Also, the terminology throughout the chapter has been updated to comply with the conceptual framework and the new revenue recognition standard, IFRS 15.

- Chapter 4: Completion of the Accounting Cycle now has greater emphasis on temporary and permanent accounts to help students understand which accounts are closed at the end of the accounting period. New visuals were added for further emphasis. The chapter now includes only the common Canadian balance sheet presentation to reflect current Canadian practice.

- Chapter 5: Accounting for Merchandising Operations includes an updated illustration of earnings measurements, and infographics were added for operating cycles. The introduction to perpetual and periodic inventory systems includes new infographics to identify the flow of costs through each system. The sales tax discussion has been reduced and students are referred to Appendix B for more detailed instruction so the focus remains on basic purchase and sales transactions.

- Chapter 6: Inventory Costing includes a refined discussion on inventory cost determination methods to focus on the mechanics of inventory costing. New illustrations have been added for FIFO and weighted average cost formulas in a perpetual inventory system. The illustrations are now on one page and show the entire process with instructional notes to explain critical steps. Journal entries have been added throughout the instructional notes to assist students in integrating knowledge from previous chapters. End-of-chapter material has been revised and updated to match the new illustrations in the chapter. The inventory errors discussion has been updated with additional illustrations to clarify the discussion.

- Chapter 7: Internal Control and Cash now begins with a definition of cash. It continues with consideration of the risks associated with cash and an introduction to internal controls. Internal controls focus primarily on control activities. A fraud example has been included in each control category to highlight the importance of good internal controls over cash. The discussion of cash receipts and payments has been combined into one learning objective and petty cash is now presented separately.

- Chapter 8: Accounting for Receivables now includes a discussion and illustration of credit card receivables, and discussion of nonbank credit card sales has been removed. The percentage of sales method for estimating uncollectible accounts has been added as part of the discussion on valuing accounts receivable. The end-of-chapter material has been updated with questions on the percentage of sales method.

- Chapter 9: Long-Lived Assets now includes a separate discussion and illustrations for partial period depreciation. Natural resources and depletion are now presented before intangible assets and goodwill.
- Chapter 10: Current Liabilities and Payroll now has an expanded discussion of unearned revenues. It also includes an updated discussion on customer loyalty programs to comply with IFRS 15.
- Chapter 11: Financial Reporting Concepts has been restructured to expand on the conceptual framework introduced in Chapter 1; the infographic used in Chapter 1 is repeated and expanded. The learning objectives are organized to follow the hierarchy of the conceptual framework. Each new learning objective includes the same infographic that highlights the concepts to be covered. Throughout the chapter, references are made to future changes in the conceptual framework to reflect the ongoing work of the IASB, and new ideas from the revised framework are incorporated when appropriate. The revenue recognition discussion now includes the impact of IFRS 15 *Revenue from Contracts with Customers*. A side-by-side comparison of the accounting under the contract-based approach and earnings approach for recognizing revenue is included at the end of the revenue recognition discussion. The illustrations and discussions on the percentage of completion method have been removed and replaced with illustrations of sales of goods and services, multiple performance obligations, warranties, and right of return revenue recognition situations. The discussion on measurement of elements has been refined to match the conceptual framework and incorporates some of the new ideas from the upcoming framework change. A section has been added to summarize the upcoming changes in the conceptual framework and IFRS 15. All "Do It" exercises and the end-of-chapter demonstration problem have been updated. End-of-chapter materials have been revised to match the changes in the chapter.
- Chapter 12: Accounting for Partnerships now has revised illustrations to show how profits are allocated and a simplified presentation of profit and loss ratios.
- Chapter 13: Introduction to Corporations has been refreshed. The discussion on preferred share dividends is now part of the cash dividends discussion and has been expanded with additional illustrations.
- Chapter 14: Corporations: Additional Topics and IFRS includes several new illustrations. An illustration was added to summarize the accounting for the reacquisition of share capital. T account illustrations have been added to demonstrate the use of the retained earnings and accumulated other comprehensive income accounts. Expanded discussions with additional guidance are included for intraperiod tax allocation related to discontinued operations and the calculation of comprehensive income. The example used to demonstrate accounting changes has been changed from inventory error corrections to property, plant, and equipment error corrections. The discussion, presentations, and illustrations related

to the statement of changes in shareholders' equity have been updated to incorporate current presentation practice. Step-by-step instructions have been added for earnings per share calculations. The earnings per share demonstration has been expanded and includes notes explaining each calculation.

- Chapter 15: Non-current Liabilities begins with a comprehensive introduction to long-term debt and bonds; however, a discussion of the types of bonds has been added. More emphasis has been placed on bond terminology and a new related Before You Go On has been added. Accounting for bonds has now been expanded into three separate learning objectives: bond pricing, accounting for bonds (with a new section added on issuing bonds between periods), and bond retirements. Each section now includes a related Before You Go On.
- Chapter 16: Investments has been substantially revised to reflect IFRS 9 *Financial Instruments*. Terminology and accounting techniques are updated throughout the chapter. Financial calculator demonstrations have been added for present value calculations related to bond acquisitions. The straight-line method of amortizing a discount has been added to demonstrate the alternative available under ASPE. The discussion on selling bonds before maturity has been simplified to focus on the journal entries. The illustration at the end of the chapter summarizing investment categories and valuation requirements has been revised.
- Chapter 17: The Cash Flow Statement has been reorganized. The preparation of the cash flow statement using the indirect method is now a separate learning objective. A new learning objective for preparing the operating section of the cash flow section using the direct method has been added. Also, additional T accounts have been included to help students better understand account analysis and the related impact on cash flows.
- Chapter 18: Financial Statement Analysis continues to separate the material on ratio analysis into the three types of ratios: liquidity, solvency, and profitability. The summary of each type of ratio remains in that section but a new summary of ratios was added to the end-of-chapter material.

Unparalleled End-of-Chapter Material

The seventh Canadian edition continues to have a complete range of end-of-chapter material to satisfy all courses. This material guides students through the basic levels of cognitive understanding—knowledge, comprehension, application, analysis, synthesis, and evaluation—in a step-by-step process, starting first with questions, followed by brief exercises, exercises, problems, and finally, integrative cases to broaden a student's perspective.

Using Bloom's Taxonomy of Learning, all of the end-of-chapter material was carefully reviewed. Topical gaps were identified and material added as required to facilitate progressive learning. A Taking It Further question is included at the end of every problem. These questions are designed to help you determine how far your students have taken their understanding of the material. To ensure maximum flexibility, problems can also be assigned with or without the Taking It Further question. They also make excellent classroom discussion questions.

The Santé Smoothie Saga, a serial problem in each chapter, follows the life of a simulated student-owned company. This edition has been revised to include moving the business into a family-owned corporation. The conceptual material in each problem attempts to integrate real-life experience and examples with the changing demands of financial accounting and reporting requirements.

The Collaborative Learning Activities address several major concerns related to improving student learning. They provide an effective method of actively engaging students that cannot be accomplished through traditional lecture and large group discussion. Students benefit from hearing multiple perspectives from their group members and enhance their learning through explaining ideas to other students. Instructor resource material includes information on how to use these activities in class as well as suggestions for modifying them depending on the amount of time available for the activity.

The All About You boxes mentioned earlier are mirrored in the Broadening Your Perspective section. The All About You activities have been designed to help students appreciate that learning accounting is helpful for everyone, regardless of their current and future career plans.

In total, we have over 1,877 end-of-chapter items for students to test their understanding of accounting. We have added more than 370 new questions, brief exercises, exercises, problems, and cases to the end-of-chapter material. That means that over one third of the end-of-chapter material is new! The remaining material was substantially updated and revised, as required.

Special Student Supplements

Accounting Principles is accompanied by special student supplements to help students master the material and achieve success in their studies.

Canadian Financial Accounting Cases by Camillo Lento and Jo-Anne Ryan provides additional cases at the introductory level that may be used either for assignment purposes or for in-class discussion.

Acknowledgements

During the course of developing *Accounting Principles,* Seventh Canadian Edition, the authors benefited from the feedback from instructors and students of accounting principles courses throughout the country, including many users of the previous editions of this text. The constructive suggestions and innovative ideas helped focus this revision on motivating students to want to learn accounting. In addition, the input and advice of the ancillary authors, contributors, and proofreaders provided valuable feedback throughout the development of this edition.

Reviewers

Peter Alpaugh, *George Brown College*
Alym Amlani, *Kwantlen Polytechnic University*
Mark Binder, *Red River College*
Joan Baines, *Red River College*
Maggie May Fitzpatrick, *Red River College*
Dave Fleming, *George Brown College*
Suzanne Iskander, *Humber College*
Leanne Vig, *Red Deer College*

Supplement Contributors

Maria Belanger, *Algonquin College*
Ted Cotton, *Red River College*
Angela Davis, *Booth University College*
Ilene Gilborn
Rosalie Harms, *University of Winnipeg*
Rhonda Heninger, *SAIT Polytechnic*

Cécile Laurin, *Algonquin College*
Chris Leduc, *Cambrian College*
Ross Meacher
Debbie Musil, *Kwantlen Polytechnic University*
Marie Sinnott, *College of New Caledonia*
Ruth Ann Strickland, *Western University*
Brian Trenholm
Leanne Vig, *Red Deer College*

Through their editorial contributions, Laurel Hyatt and Zofia Laubitz added to the real-world flavour of the text and its clarity.

Accuracy

We have made every effort to ensure that this text is error-free. *Accounting Principles* has been extensively reviewed and proofed at more than five different production stages prior to publication. Moreover, the end-of-chapter material has been independently solved and then checked by at least three individuals, in addition to the authors, prior to publication of the text. We would like to express our sincere gratitude to everyone who spent countless hours ensuring the accuracy of this text and the solutions to the end-of-chapter material.

Publications

We would like to thank Corus Entertainment Inc. for allowing us to reproduce its 2014 financial statements in Appendix A.

A Final Note of Thanks

We appreciate the exemplary support and professional commitment given us by the talented team in the Wiley Canada Learning Solutions division, including Luisa Begani, Media Editor; Zoë Craig, Executive Editor; Deanna Durnford, Supplements Coordinator; Daleara Hirjikaka, Developmental Editor; Meaghan MacDonald, Production Specialist; Anita Osborne, Marketing Manager; Ashley Patterson, Assistant Editor; Karen Staudinger, Editorial Manager; Kaitlyn Sykes, Editorial Intern; Maureen Talty, General Manager; Veronica Visentin, Vice-President and Director, Market Solutions; and Joanna Vieira, Multimedia Designer. We wish to also thank Wiley's dedicated sales representatives, who work tirelessly to serve your needs.

It would not have been possible to write this text without the understanding of our employer, colleagues, students, family, and friends. Together, they provided a creative and supportive environment for our work. We would particularly like to thank Oliver, Matthew, and Nicholas and Gary, James, and Matthew for their support through this lengthy writing process.

We have tried our best to produce a text and supplement package that is error-free and meets your specific needs. Suggestions and comments from all users—instructors and students alike—are encouraged and appreciated.

Valerie Warren
valerie.warren@kpu.caq
Surrey, BC
September 2015

Lori Novak
lenovak@rrc.ca
Winnipeg, Manitoba

BRIEF CONTENTS

Volume One

Volume Two

Volume Three

CONTENTS – VOLUME ONE

1

ACCOUNTING IN ACTION

The Chapter Preview outlines the major topics and subtopics you will see in the chapter.

CHAPTER PREVIEW

The feature story about Corus Entertainment highlights the importance of having good financial information to make good business decisions. This applies not just to companies but also to individuals. You cannot earn a living, spend money, buy on credit, make an investment, or pay taxes without receiving, using, or giving financial information. Good decision-making for companies and individuals depends on good information.

This chapter shows you that accounting is the system that produces useful financial information for decision-making.

The Feature Story helps you see how the chapter topic fits with the real world of accounting and business. The story will be mentioned throughout the chapter.

FEATURE STORY ▶ ACCOUNTING KEEPS CORUS ON AIR

TORONTO, Ont.—If you ever operated a babysitting or lawn-mowing service, you probably tried to make more money by finding as many customers as possible and keeping expenses down. Maybe you put up flyers in your neighbourhood, or borrowed your parents' lawn mower instead of buying your own. You were using the same principles that businesses use to maximize profit.

Enterprises need a successful business model—a way of generating regular sales that over the long run exceed expenses, which results in profit. Companies use accounting to record financial information, which they report in financial statements that internal users (such as management) and external users (such as shareholders and banks) use to make decisions. For example, internal users need to know how much to charge for products or services to maximize profits without losing sales to competitors. External users need to decide if the company is worth investing in or lending money to.

Take as an example Corus Entertainment, one of Canada's leading integrated media and content companies. It creates and broadcasts television and radio programming, including the specialty cable television channels YTV, HBO Canada, Treehouse, TELETOON, and W Network; 39 radio stations across the country including rock and alternative music stations CFOX and Q107; Nelvana, an international creator, producer, and distributor of animated children's programs such as the successful Franklin the Turtle series; and children's publisher Kids Can Press. Corus was founded by Canadian broadcast icon JR Shaw, created from the assets originally owned by Shaw Communications Inc., a major telecommunications company. Corus became its own publicly traded company in 1999.

What kinds of things does Corus need to keep track of in its accounts? Like any company, Corus records revenues (sales), which totalled $833.0 million in 2014, and expenses, which were $676.8 million, resulting in a profit of $156.2 million. It also records assets (the value of what it owns at a certain point in time) and liabilities (the value of what it owes to others).

Corus doesn't sell directly to consumers. Instead, its business model is to sell services to other businesses, such as Kids Can Press books to bookstores, commercials on its radio stations to advertisers, television channels to cable and satellite providers, and the rights to air TV programs to broadcasters in other countries. Companies such as Corus need to boost revenues and reduce expenses. To increase revenues, Corus can use several strategies, including charging more for its services, finding additional customers for its services, launching new services such as TV channels, investing in similar businesses, or acquiring competitors. To reduce expenses, Corus has used "disciplined cost controls" at its radio stations. All of these efforts are recorded by accounting—a crucial business tool that keeps Corus on the air.

Sources: Corus Entertainment 2014 annual report; Corus Entertainment website, www.corusent.com.

Courtesy of Corus Entertainment

Learning Objectives show what you should be able to do after learning the specific concepts presented in the chapter.

CHAPTER OUTLINE ▶ LEARNING OBJECTIVES

1 Identify the use and users of accounting and the objective of financial reporting.

Why Is Accounting Important?
- Using accounting information
- Objective of financial reporting

DO IT 1
Users of accounting information

---

2 Compare the different forms of business organization.

Forms of Business Organization
- Proprietorship
- Partnership
- Corporation

DO IT 2
Types of business organization

---

3 Explain the building blocks of accounting: ethics and the concepts included in the conceptual framework.

Generally Accepted Accounting Principles
- Ethics in financial reporting
- Conceptual framework
- Accounting standards

DO IT 3
Building blocks of accounting

---

4 Describe the components of the financial statements and explain the accounting equation.

The Accounting Model
- Financial statements
- The expanded accounting equation

DO IT 4
The accounting equation

---

5 Analyze the effects of business transactions on the accounting equation.

Transaction Analysis

DO IT 5
Tabular analysis

---

6 Prepare financial statements.

Preparing Financial Statements
- Income statement
- Statement of owner's equity
- Balance sheet
- Cash flow statement
- Understanding the information in the financial statements

DO IT 6
Financial statements

LEARNING OBJECTIVE **1** | Identify the use and users of accounting and the objective of financial reporting.

Why Is Accounting Important?

Essential (key) terms are printed in red when they first appear, and are defined in the end-of-chapter glossary.

Accounting is the information system that identifies, records, and communicates the economic events of an organization to a wide variety of interested users. The world's economic systems depend on highly transparent and relevant financial reporting that provides a true representation of the economic events. When that does not happen, it can have disastrous results. Lehman Brothers, a major United States bank, used misleading accounting practices to reduce its debt and make its financial position healthier than it was. Not only were Lehman Brothers' investors and lenders unaware of the bank's financial difficulties when the company went into bankruptcy, but economists believe the bankruptcy was a major contributor to the worldwide economic crises that began in 2008.

As a starting point to the accounting process, a company identifies the economic events relevant to its business. Examples of economic events are the delivery of radio shows and television programs by Corus Entertainment, the sale of coffee and donuts by Tim Hortons, and the payment of wages by BlackBerry. Once a company like Corus identifies economic events, it records those events in order to provide a history of its financial activities. Recording consists of keeping a systematic, chronological diary of events, measured in dollars and cents. The systematic collection of these data allows Corus to prepare financial statements that are used to then communicate financial information to interested users. Financial statements report the recorded data in a standardized way to make the reported information meaningful. For example, Corus accumulates all sales transactions over a certain period of time and reports the data as one amount in the company's financial statements. Such data are said to be reported in the aggregate. By presenting the recorded data in the aggregate, the accounting process simplifies the multitude of transactions and makes a series of activities understandable and meaningful.

A vital element in communicating economic events is the accountant's ability to analyze and interpret the reported information. Analysis involves using ratios, percentages, graphs, and charts to highlight significant financial trends and relationships. Interpretation involves explaining the uses, meaning, and limitations of reported data. Appendix A at the end of this text shows the financial statements of Corus Entertainment. We refer to these statements at various places throughout the textbook. At this point, these financial statements probably strike you as complex and confusing. By the end of this course, you'll be surprised at your ability to understand, analyze, and interpret them.

You should understand that the accounting process includes the bookkeeping function. Bookkeeping usually involves only the recording of economic events. It is therefore just one part of the accounting process. In total, accounting involves the entire process of identifying, recording, and communicating economic events.

You might think this is all well and good for students who want to become accountants, but what about someone who has plans to be anything *but* an accountant?

Understanding the basics of accounting is helpful for almost every endeavour you can think of. Whether you plan to own your own business in the future, work for someone else in their business, or invest in a business, learning how to read and interpret financial information is a valuable set of skills.

When you study accounting, you will also learn a lot about management, finance, and marketing, which will give you a solid foundation for your future studies. For example, you will learn how making a sale is meaningless unless it is a profitable sale and the money can eventually be collected from the customer. Marketing managers must also be able to decide pricing strategies based on costs. Accounting is what quantifies these costs and explains why a product or service costs what it does. So think of this textbook as your introduction to accounting across the organization.

It doesn't matter if you plan to become a doctor, lawyer, social worker, teacher, engineer, architect, or entrepreneur—whatever you choose, a working knowledge of accounting will be relevant and useful. Make the most of this course—it will serve you for a lifetime in ways you cannot now imagine.

ACCOUNTING IN ACTION
ALL ABOUT YOU INSIGHT

Getty Images/Fotografías de Rodolfo Velasco

We all know the importance of literacy. But what about financial literacy—the ability to understand and manage your finances? It seems Canadians don't place the same importance on financial literacy— but with rising household debt levels, falling savings levels, increasing personal bankruptcies, and continuing economic uncertainty, they should. According to Statistics Canada research, in 2014 only 7.1% of adult Canadians considered themselves "very knowledgeable" about their finances. In addition, survey respondents were asked a series of 14 questions concerning their knowledge of topics such as inflation, debt repayment, banking fees, and credit reports. Almost one third of respondents got half or more of the questions wrong.

There is movement on several fronts to improve financial literacy. For example, the federal government in 2014 appointed its first-ever financial literacy leader, who is among other things touring the country to promote financial literacy among targeted groups such as seniors and students. Some financial gurus are also spreading the word about the need to get a grip on personal finance. Gail Vaz-Oxlade, for instance, is urging Canadians to be "debt-free forever" through several best-selling books and popular TV shows. Financial literacy experts point out that making the right financial decisions can have a major impact on an individual's financial well-being, health, and happiness.

Learning the basics of accounting will help you make the right financial decisions. Accounting will help you make investment decisions, determine how much interest you are paying on your student loan or credit cards, and prepare your personal budget. To demonstrate the value of accounting to you, included in each chapter is an "All About You" feature and a related activity (BYP–5) that links accounting to your life as a student or to a situation you are likely to face.

Sources: Bruce Johnstone, "Financial Literacy Falling Short," *Regina Leader-Post*, March 27, 2015; "Canadian Financial Capability Survey, 2014," Statistics Canada, *The Daily*, November 6, 2014; Gail Vaz-Oxlade's personal website, www.gailvazoxlade.com.

Q How might learning accounting help you make sure that your employer or bank hasn't made an error with your paycheque or bank account?

USING ACCOUNTING INFORMATION

There are two broad groups of users of accounting information: internal users and external users.

Internal Users

Internal users of accounting information plan, organize, and run companies. They work for the company. This includes finance directors, marketing managers, human resources personnel, production supervisors, and company officers. In running a business, internal users must answer many important questions, as shown in Illustration 1-1.

Accounting in Action insights give examples of accounting situations from different perspectives: all about you, across the organization, and in terms of business and ethics. At the end of the chapter, you will find answers to the questions that are asked after each insight.

▶ ILLUSTRATION 1-1
Questions asked by internal users

Finance
Is there enough cash to pay the bills?

Marketing
What price should we sell smart phones for to maximize profits?

Human Resources
How many employees can we afford to hire this year?

Production
Which product line is the most profitable?

Photo credits for Illustration 1-1: Finance: Getty Images/John Kuczala; Marketing: Getty Images/Jonathan Kitchen; Production: Getty Images/Echo.

To answer these and other questions, users need detailed information on a timely basis; that is, it must be available when needed. Some examples of information that internal users need include:

- forecasts of cash flows for the next year,
- projections of profit from new sales campaigns,
- analyses of salary costs, and
- budgeted financial statements.

Internal users generally have direct access to the business's accounting information and are able to request a wide variety of custom reports designed for their specific needs.

External Users

There are several types of external users of accounting information.

1. **Investors,** who are owners—or potential owners—of the business, use accounting information to make decisions to buy, hold, or sell their ownership interest.
2. **Creditors**—persons or other businesses that are owed money by the business, such as suppliers and bankers—use accounting information to evaluate the risks of granting credit or lending money.

Investors and creditors are the main external users of accounting information, but there are also many other external users with a large variety of information needs and questions. Some examples of other external users and their information needs are the following.

- Labour unions want to know whether the owners can afford to pay increased salaries and benefits to their members.
- Customers are interested in whether a company will continue to honour its product warranties and support its product lines.
- Taxing authorities, such as the Canada Revenue Agency, want to know whether the company respects the tax laws.
- Regulatory agencies, such as provincial securities commissions that regulate companies that sell shares to the public, want to know whether the company is respecting established rules.
- Economic planners use accounting information to forecast economic activity.

Some questions that external users may ask about a company are shown in Illustration 1-2.

▶ **ILLUSTRATION 1-2**
Questions asked
by external users

Investors
Is the company earning enough to give
me a return on my investment?

Creditors
Does the company generate enough cash flow
to pay me the amounts I am owed?

Labour Unions
Can the company afford to increase
our members' benefits?

Customers
Will the company stay in business long enough
to service the products I buy from it?

Unlike internal users, external users have access to only the accounting information available publicly and/or provided to them by the business. Determining what information should be provided to external users, and how, is the focus of financial accounting.

OBJECTIVE OF FINANCIAL REPORTING

As stated, accounting information is communicated in financial reports, and the most common reports are financial statements. **The main objective of financial reporting is to provide useful information to investors and creditors (external users) to make decisions about providing resources to a business.** This information is most commonly supplied in general purpose financial statements, which we will discuss later in the chapter. Recall that internal users have access to a broader range of accounting information and do not necessarily need general purpose financial statements to make informed decisions, although they can be used by internal users as well.

To make the decision to invest in a business or to lend to a business, users need information about the business's ability to earn a profit and generate cash. Consequently, financial statements must give information about the following:

1. The business's economic resources. What resources does the business have that it can use to carry out its business activities?
2. The claims to the business's economic resources. What are the amounts owed by the business and the owner's rights to the business's resources?
3. Economic performance. Is the business generating a profit and enough cash to pay its debts, and provide a return to its owners?

We will learn more about financial statements in the following sections.

BEFORE YOU GO ON...DO IT — **Users of Accounting Information**

The following is a list of some users of accounting information. For each user indicate:

(a) whether they are an internal or external user and
(b) an example of a question that might be asked by that user.
1. Creditor
2. Canada Revenue Agency
3. Investor
4. General manager of the production department
5. Manager of the human resources department

Solution

User	(a) Internal or External	(b) Question
1. Creditor	External	Will the business be able to pay back the loan?
2. Canada Revenue Agency	External	Is the company following the tax laws?
3. Investor	External	Should I invest money in the company?
4. General manager of the production department	Internal	How much will it cost to produce the product?
5. Manager of the human resources department	Internal	Can the company afford to give the employees raises?

Related exercise material: BE1–1 and E1–1.

Before You Go On ... Do It exercises like the one here ask you to put your new knowledge to work. They also outline an Action Plan you need to follow to do the exercise. Related exercise material tells you which Brief Exercises (BE) and Exercises (E) at the end of the chapter have similar study objectives.

Action Plan
- Understand that internal users work for the company and have direct access to the business's accounting information.
- Understand that external users are users who do not work for the company and have access to only the accounting information available publicly and/or provided to them by the company.
- Understand that users require information to make decisions.

LEARNING OBJECTIVE 2 — **Compare the different forms of business organization.**

Forms of Business Organization

Now that we understand that accounting information is prepared to convey financial information to various users, it is important to note that how the financial statements are prepared depends on the form and nature of the business organization. Therefore, let's now discuss the different organizational forms a business can take. The most common forms of business organization are the proprietorship, partnership, and corporation.

PROPRIETORSHIP

A business owned by one person is a **proprietorship**. The owner is usually the operator of the business. Small service businesses (hair stylists, plumbers, and mechanics), farms, and small retail stores (antique shops, corner grocery stores, and independent bookstores) are often proprietorships.

Often only a relatively small amount of money (capital) is needed to start in business as a proprietorship. The owner (the proprietor) receives any profits, suffers any losses, and is personally liable (responsible) for all debts of the business. This is known as **unlimited liability**.

There is no legal distinction between the business as an economic unit and the owner. Thus the life of a proprietorship is limited to the life of the owner. This also means that the profits of the business are reported and taxed on the owner's personal income tax return. However, for accounting purposes, the records of the proprietorship's business activities are kept separate from the personal records and activities of the owner.

Many businesses in Canada are proprietorships, but they earn only a small percentage of the revenue earned by Canadian businesses as a whole. In this textbook, we start with proprietorships because many students organize their first business this way.

PARTNERSHIP

A business owned by two or more persons who are associated as partners is a **partnership**. In most aspects, a partnership is similar to a proprietorship, except that there is more than one owner. Partnerships are often used to organize service-type businesses, including professional practices (lawyers, doctors, architects, and accountants).

Typically, a partnership agreement (written or oral) defines the initial investments of each partner, the duties of each partner, how profit (or loss) will be divided, and what the settlement will be if a partner dies or withdraws. As in a proprietorship, for accounting purposes a partnership's business activities must be kept separate from the personal activities of each partner. The partners' share of the profit must be reported and taxed on the partners' personal income tax returns.

Each partner generally has unlimited liability for all debts of the partnership, even if one of the other partners created the debt. This means that any of the partners can be forced to give up his or her personal assets in order to repay the partnership debt, just as can happen to an owner in a proprietorship. We will learn more about partnerships in Chapter 12.

CORPORATION

A business that is organized (incorporated) as a separate legal entity under federal or provincial corporate law is a **corporation**. A corporation can have one owner or many owners. A corporation is responsible for its debts and paying taxes on its profit. A corporation's ownership is divided into transferable shares. The corporation's separate legal status provides the owners of the shares (shareholders) with **limited liability** because they risk losing only the amount that they have invested in the company's shares. They are not personally liable for the debts of the corporate entity. Shareholders, also known as investors, may sell all or part of their shares to other investors at any time. Easy changes of ownership are part of what makes it attractive to invest in a corporation. Because ownership can be transferred through the sale of shares and without dissolving the corporation, the corporation enjoys an unlimited life.

Although there are many more proprietorships and partnerships than corporations in Canada, the revenue produced by corporations is far greater. Most of the largest companies in Canada—for example, Suncor Energy, Bombardier Inc., Toronto-Dominion Bank, Barrick Gold, and Shaw Communications— are corporations.

Corporations such as these are publicly traded. That is, their shares are listed on Canadian stock exchanges and the public can buy the shares. Public corporations commonly distribute their financial statements to shareholders, creditors, other interested parties, and the general public upon request. Corus Entertainment Inc. is a public corporation, whose shares are traded on the Toronto Stock Exchange (TSX). You can access Corus's financial statements on its website and selected statements are also presented in Appendix A at the back of this textbook.

Helpful hints help clarify concepts or items that are being discussed.

Helpful hint You can usually tell if a company is a corporation by looking at its name. The words *Limited (Ltd.)*, *Incorporated (Inc.)*, or *Corporation (Corp.)* usually follow its name.

Other companies are private corporations, because they do not issue publicly traded shares. Some of the largest private companies in Canada include Hootsuite, Moosehead Breweries Limited, McCain Foods Limited, and EllisDon Inc. Like proprietorships and partnerships, these companies almost never distribute their financial statements publicly. We will discuss the corporate form of organization in Chapters 13 and 14.

Illustration 1-3 provides a summary of the important characteristics of each organizational form a business can take.

Characteristic	Proprietorship	Partnership	Corporation
Owners	Proprietor: one	Partners: two or more	Shareholders: one or more
Owner's liability	Unlimited	Unlimited	Limited
Private or public	Private	Usually private	Private or public
Taxation of profits	Paid by the owner	Paid by the partners	Paid by the corporation
Life of organization	Limited	Limited	Unlimited

▶ ILLUSTRATION 1-3
Characteristics of business organizations

BEFORE YOU GO ON...DO IT ② **Types of Business Organization**

For each type of organization (proprietorship, partnership, and corporation) indicate:

1. Number and type of owners.
2. If it has limited or unlimited liability.
3. If it is a separate legal entity from its owners.

Solution

	Proprietorship	Partnership	Corporation
1.	Proprietor: one	Partners: two or more	Shareholders: one or more
2.	Unlimited	Unlimited	Limited
3.	Not a separate legal entity from its owners	Not a separate legal entity from its owners	Separate legal entity from the shareholders

Related exercise material: BE1–3, BE1–4, and E1–2.

Action Plan
- Understand the characteristics of the most common forms of business organization.

LEARNING OBJECTIVE ③ **Explain the building blocks of accounting: ethics and the concepts included in the conceptual framework.**

Generally Accepted Accounting Principles

In order to prepare useful financial information, the accounting profession has developed standards that are generally accepted and universally practised. This common set of standards is called **generally accepted accounting principles (GAAP)**. Generally accepted accounting principles represent broad principles, procedures, concepts, and standards that act as guidelines for accountants. Taken together, GAAP guide the reporting of economic events. However, for these standards to be meaningful, a fundamental business concept must be present—ethical behaviour.

ETHICS IN FINANCIAL REPORTING

For financial information to have value to its users, whether internal or external, it must be prepared by individuals with high standards of ethical behaviour. The standards of conduct by which actions are judged as right or wrong, honest or dishonest, fair or not fair are **ethics**. Ethics in accounting is of the utmost importance to accountants and decision makers who rely on the financial information they produce. Effective financial reporting depends on sound ethical behaviour.

Fortunately, most individuals in business are ethical. Their actions are both legal and responsible. They consider the organization's interests when they make decisions. Accountants and other professionals have extensive rules of conduct to guide their behaviour with each other and the public. In addition, many companies today have codes of conduct, or statements of corporate values, that outline their commitment to ethical behaviour in their internal and external relationships. The behaviour of management is critical for creating the appropriate tone from the top of the organization.

Throughout this textbook, ethical considerations will be presented to highlight the importance of ethics in financial reporting. Every chapter includes an Accounting in Action Ethics Insight case that simulates a business situation that asks you to put yourself in the position of a key decision maker. When you analyze these ethical situations, you should follow the steps outlined in Illustration 1-4.

▸ ILLUSTRATION **1-4**
Steps used to analyze
ethics cases and situations

1. Identify the ethical issues involved.
- Use your personal ethics or an organization's code of ethics to identify ethical situations and issues.
- Some business and professional organizations provide written codes of ethics for guidance in common business situations.

2. Identify the stakeholders— the persons or groups that may benefit or face harm.
- Ask the questions: Who are the impacted parties? What are their responsibilities and obligations?

3. Consider the alternative courses of action and the consequences of each for the various stakeholders.
- There may not always be one right answer. Some situations require an evaluation of the alternatives and the impact of each alternative on the identified stakeholders.
- Select the most ethical alternative, considering all the consequences.

ACCOUNTING IN ACTION
ETHICS INSIGHT

Getty Images/Jennifer Trenchard

What would you do if you suspected a co-worker was stealing? Would you confront them or tell your employer or the authorities? Would you keep quiet if you feared losing your job? What to do about suspected fraud is an ethical question facing not just those working in the accounting field, but employees in any role. Workplace fraud can take many forms. It could be an employee forging a cheque or stealing inventory. But it could also be an executive who falsifies financial information to make their department's sales figure look better, to meet company targets and collect a bonus, or to keep their job.

Organizations need to send a strong message that they won't tolerate fraud. One way of doing that is to protect and encourage employees who suspect fraud and report it to their employers. The federal government and most provinces in Canada have enacted their own public employee protection legislation. Another way to discourage fraud is to set up an internal crime hotline for employees to report suspected wrongdoing. When fraud is not reported, everyone is potentially harmed, not just the employer. Colleagues may lose jobs, customers may be misled, and shareholders and the public will lose trust in the accuracy of financial information.

Consider the following scenario: Jennifer is an accountant who works for Currie Financial Services Company. Currie has recently been given the opportunity to provide financial services to a large transportation company but Currie must compete against other financial service companies. Jennifer's boss has instructed her to prepare a presentation for the transportation company and include some performance statistics that he created. The potential client wants reassurance that whichever financial services provider it chooses will be in business a long time to serve its needs. Consequently, it wants to see financial figures from bidders that show they have been profitable over several years. Jennifer knows that the financial figures her boss wants her to show the potential client do not reflect Currie's actual performance but her boss told her they must "get that contract at all costs." He also said that those statistics are "likely to reflect actual performance in the future."

Sources: Michael McKiernan, "Regulator at a Crossroads," *Canadian Lawyer*, April 2012; Association of Certified Fraud Examiners, "Report to the Nations on Occupational Fraud and Abuse," 2012; David Malamed, "Whistle Where You Work?" *CA Magazine*, January/February 2012; Marjo Johne, "Don't Fall Victim to an Inside Job," *Globe and Mail*, December 14, 2011.

Q Who are the stakeholders in this situation? How would they be impacted by this situation?

CONCEPTUAL FRAMEWORK

Some GAAP are so fundamental that we begin the study of them in introductory courses because they help us understand why we prepare and report accounting information in the manner we do.

As previously discussed in this chapter, the objective of financial reporting is to provide information to assist users in making decisions. Illustration 1-5 is a representation of the **conceptual framework of accounting**, which is a coherent system that guides the development and application of accounting principles and standards and leads to the objective of financial reporting. In this chapter, we introduce some of the central concepts contained in the conceptual framework. The entire framework will be covered in more detail in Chapter 11.

As this text is being written, the conceptual framework is in the process of being revised. The revision is expected to be released sometime in 2016. The revised framework is still in draft form and therefore not yet finalized. For our purposes, this textbook will cover the current existing framework contained in the 2015 edition of the *CPA Canada Handbook*. Whenever appropriate, we have incorporated ideas from the revised framework and highlighted items that will likely change.

▶ **ILLUSTRATION** **1-5**
The conceptual
framework of accounting

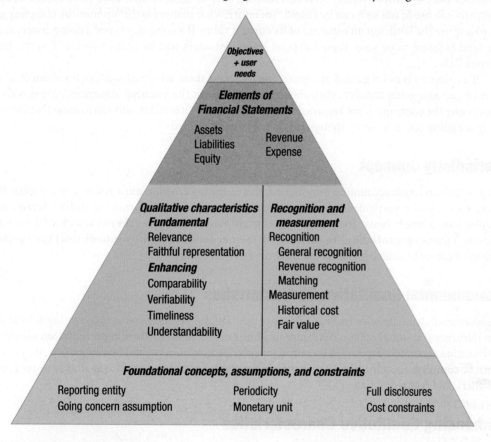

Reporting Entity Concept

Financial statements are prepared for a business or reporting entity. This is referred to as the **reporting entity concept. This concept requires that the accounting for a reporting entity's economic activities be kept separate and distinct from the accounting for the activities of its owner and all other reporting entities.** A reporting entity can be any organization or unit in society. Recall that proprietorships' and partnerships' records of their business activities are kept separate from the personal records of their owners. That is because proprietorships and partnerships are considered reporting entities for financial reporting purposes. Similarly, a corporation (such as Corus) is considered a reporting entity for financial reporting purposes. Other examples of reporting entities are a governmental unit (such as the Province of Manitoba), a municipality (such as the Ville de Montréal), a native band council (such as the Kingsclear Indian Band), a school board (such as the Burnaby School Board), and a club (such as the Melfort Rotary Club).

It is important to understand that a reporting entity may not necessarily be a separate legal entity. For example, proprietorships and partnerships are not separate *legal* entities from their owners, but the reporting entity concept requires that they are treated as separate entities for accounting purposes.

Going Concern Assumption

The **going concern assumption** is the assumption that the reporting entity will continue to operate in the foreseeable future. Although some businesses fail, most companies continue operating for a long time. **The going concern assumption presumes that the company will operate long enough to use its resources for their intended purpose and to complete the company's commitments.**

This assumption is one of the most important assumptions in GAAP because it has implications regarding what information is useful for decision makers and affects many of the accounting standards you will learn. If a company is a going concern, then financial statement users will find it useful for the company to report certain resources, such as land, at their cost. Land is acquired so a company can use it, not so it can be resold. Therefore, what matters is the amount the company gave up to acquire the land, not an estimate of its current value. If a company is not a going concern, and the land is going to be sold, then financial statement users will be more interested in the land's current value.

If a company is not regarded as a going concern, or if there are significant doubts about its ability to continue as a going concern, then this must be stated in the financial statements, along with the reason why the company is not regarded as a going concern. Otherwise, you can assume that the company is a going concern—even though this is not explicitly stated.

Periodicity Concept

Users require relevant accounting information; that is, the information must enhance or complete their understanding of a particular enterprise. In order for accounting information to be relevant, users require it on a timely basis. The **periodicity concept** (also sometimes referred to as the "time period concept") **guides organizations in dividing up their economic activities into distinct time periods**. The most common time periods are months, quarters, and years.

Fundamental Qualitative Characteristics

Fundamental characteristics include **relevance** and faithful representation. Accounting information has relevance if it would make a difference in a business decision. **Faithful representation** means that information accurately depicts what really happened. To provide a faithful representation, information must be **complete** (nothing important has been omitted), **neutral** (is not biased toward one position or another), and **free from error**.

Enhancing Qualitative Characteristics

In addition to the fundamental qualities, there are a number of enhancing qualities of useful information. These include **comparability**, **verifiability**, **timeliness**, and **understandability**. In accounting, **comparability** results when different companies use the same accounting principles. Comparability also implies that the accounting information should be consistent. **Consistency** means that a company uses the same accounting principles and methods from year to year. Information has the quality of **verifiability** if independent observers, using the same methods, obtain similar results. For accounting information to have relevance, it must be timely. This is referred to as **timeliness** and it means information must be available to decision makers before it loses its capacity to influence decisions. For example, public companies like Corus Entertainment, Apple, or Best Buy provide their annual financial statements to investors within 60 days of their year end. Information has the quality of **understandability** if it is presented in a clear and concise fashion, so that reasonably informed users of that information can interpret it and comprehend its meaning.

Recognition

Not all events are recorded and reported in the financial statements. For example, suppose a new employee is hired. Should this event be recorded in the company's accounting records? The answer is no. Why? Not all events are recorded and reported in the financial statements. Only events that cause changes in the business's economic resources or changes to the claims on those resources are recorded and reported. These transactions are called **accounting transactions**. While the hiring of an employee will lead to future accounting transactions (e.g., the payment of a salary after the work has been completed), an accounting transaction has not occurred at the time of hiring.

Recognition is the process of recording items in the accounting records. Once a transaction has been recognized or recorded, it will be included in the financial statements. One of the key recognition principles is the **revenue recognition principle**. When a company agrees to perform a service or sell a product to a customer, it has a **performance obligation**. When the company meets this performance obligation, it recognizes revenue. The **revenue recognition principle** therefore requires that companies recognize revenue in the accounting period in which the performance obligation is satisfied, not when cash is exchanged. To illustrate, assume that Landon's Laundry cleans clothing on June 30 but customers do not claim and pay for their clothes until the first week of July. When should Landon's recognize the revenue? Landon's should recognize the revenue and record the transaction in June when it performed the service (satisfied the performance obligation) rather than in July when it received the cash.

This then gives rise to the **matching concept**, which often drives when we recognize certain costs incurred to operate the business (known as expenses and discussed later in the chapter). Generally when there is a direct association between the costs incurred and the earning of revenue, accounting attempts to match these costs and revenues. In our Landon's Laundry example, this means that Landon's should recognize wage costs incurred in performing the June 30 cleaning service in the same period in which it recognizes the service revenue.

Measurement

Measurement is the process of determining the amount that should be recognized. At the time something is acquired, the transaction is first measured at the amount of cash that was paid or at the value exchanged. For example, if Echo Company purchased land for $100,000, the land is recorded in Echo's records at its cost of $100,000. The land is an economic resource of the business and $100,000 is referred to as the land's historical cost.

But what should Echo Company do if, by the end of the next year, the land's value has increased to $120,000? Historical cost is the primary basis of measurement used in financial statements, which means that Echo Company would continue to report the land at its historical cost of $100,000. This is often called the **historical cost** measurement method.

Alternative terminology The historical cost measurement method is also known as the *cost measurement method.*

Historical cost has an important advantage over other valuations. It is definite and verifiable. The values exchanged at the time something is acquired can be objectively measured. Users can therefore rely on the information that is supplied, because they know it is based on fact. Historical cost is relevant if a business is a going concern and the resource is going to continue to be used in the business. We can ask the question, "what did the business give up to acquire the resource to use in the business?"

However, historical cost may not always be the most relevant measure of certain types of resources. Fair value may provide more useful information. For example, with an investment purchased for the purpose of trading to make a gain, the current cost or market value of the investment provides more relevant information to the user. **Fair value** generally would be the amount the resource could be sold for in the market.

Fundamental to this discussion is that only transactions that can be reliably expressed as an amount of money can be included in the accounting records. This is known as the **monetary unit concept**. This concept makes it possible for accounting to quantify (measure) economic events. In Canada, we mainly use the Canadian dollar to record these transactions. However, some companies report their results in U.S. dollars. In Europe, the euro (€) is used; in China, the yuan (CNY) is used; and so on.

The monetary unit concept does prevent some relevant information from being included in the accounting records. For example, the health of the owner, the quality of service, and the morale of employees would not be included, because they cannot be reliably quantified in monetary amounts.

In summary, a transaction is recognized in the accounting records if there is a change in the business's economic resources or a change to the claims on those resources and the change can be reliably measured in monetary terms.

Illustration 1-6 summarizes the process that is used to decide whether or not to record an event.

▶ **ILLUSTRATION 1-6**
Transaction
identification process

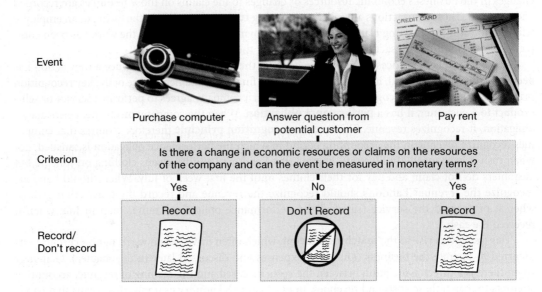

Event | Purchase computer | Answer question from potential customer | Pay rent

Criterion | Is there a change in economic resources or claims on the resources of the company and can the event be measured in monetary terms?

Yes | No | Yes

Record/Don't record | Record | Don't Record | Record

ACCOUNTING STANDARDS

Helpful hint In accounting, there are two types of economic events: (1) external events are transactions with another company; and (2) internal events occur within a company, such as the use of equipment in operations.

To make the information in financial statements meaningful, accountants have to prepare the reports in a standardized way. As mentioned in the previous section, standards are developed from the guiding principles, assumptions, and concepts. Standards specify how to report **economic events**. Business transactions can be complex and it is up to the professional accountant to ensure that transactions are correctly recorded and relevant. As previously mentioned, all standards, principles, assumptions, and concepts make up the body of knowledge known as generally accepted accounting principles (GAAP).

In Canada, the Accounting Standards Board (AcSB), an independent standard-setting body, has the main responsibility for developing GAAP. The AcSB's most important criterion for accounting standards is this: the standard should lead to external users having the most useful financial information possible when they are making business decisions.

Alternative terminology The terms *standard* and *principle* are often used interchangeably in accounting.

In Canada, accounting professionals follow different accounting standards depending on the type of entity they work for. For-profit entities report their financial statements using either (1) International Financial Reporting Standards (IFRS) or (2) Accounting Standards for Private Enterprises (ASPE).

International Financial Reporting Standards (IFRS) are a set of global standards developed by the International Accounting Standards Board (IASB) and adopted for use in Canada by the AcSB. The IASB is charged with the responsibility to develop International Financial Reporting Standards that bring transparency, accountability, and efficiency to financial markets around the world. IFRS make it easier for users to compare financial information prepared across the globe. As markets become more global, it is often desirable to compare the results of companies from different countries. That is more difficult when different companies use different accounting standards. Therefore, in order to increase comparability, in recent years, more and more countries are adopting IFRS. IFRS is the main basis of financial reporting in nearly 120 countries, including Canada, Australia, Brazil, Russia, members of the European Union, China, India, Japan, and Mexico. At the time this textbook was being written, the United States had not yet agreed to adopt IFRS (in totality).

In Canada, IFRS standards must be followed by publicly accountable enterprises. **Publicly accountable enterprises** include publicly traded corporations, as well as securities brokers and dealers, banks, and credit unions whose role is to hold assets for the public as part of their primary businesses. In this textbook, we will discuss publicly traded corporations. Discussion of the other types of businesses will be covered in more advanced courses. Corus is a publicly traded company and therefore it is required to follow IFRS.

The AcSB recognized that, for most private companies in Canada, users can generally obtain additional information from the company if required. Therefore, these users typically require less information in the financial statements. As a result, the AcSB developed **Accounting Standards for Private Enterprises (ASPE)**. Non-publicly traded companies can choose to use ASPE instead of IFRS. ASPE requires considerably less information in financial statements than is required by IFRS. Canadian private companies, such as McCain Foods and EllisDon Inc., have the choice to report under ASPE or IFRS. Because proprietorships and partnerships are private companies, these companies will generally follow ASPE for financial reporting.

While both IFRS and ASPE are "principle based" (designed to encourage the use of professional judgement in applying basic accounting principles), there are reporting differences. Therefore, financial statement users will need to know which standards the company is following. Companies are required to report this in their financial statements. In this textbook, as we proceed through the material, we will point out where there are differences in the two sets of standards. However, the two sets of standards have a great deal in common regarding the type of material covered in an introductory accounting textbook. The authoritative source of all accounting standards is the handbook produced by Chartered Professional Accountants Canada (CPA Canada), the main accounting professional body in Canada, called the *CPA Canada Handbook*.

Regardless of the financial reporting framework, it is important to understand that GAAP is not static and that it changes over time. Standard setters continue to develop new GAAP and modify existing GAAP. Changes to GAAP may take a long time before being finalized. Therefore, the length of time involved in changing existing accounting standards or adding new ones can make it difficult to determine what information we should include in this textbook. Should we cover the currently approved standard or the proposed new standard? Normally the textbook will cover only the currently approved standards, which includes standards that are approved and not yet effective. But where we believe it is important to do so, we will discuss new standards that were proposed at the time the textbook was written, as demonstrated in our previous discussion on the conceptual framework.

> **Helpful hint** Accounting standards use the word "enterprise" because it is a broader term than "company" or "business." The word "enterprise" means that the accounting standard applies to the different forms of business organization, as well as specific projects. Throughout this text, instead of using the word "enterprise," we will frequently use the words "company" or "business," because they are more common terms.

The ASPE Icon indicates where differences between IFRS and ASPE are explained. These differences are also summarized at the end of each chapter.

BEFORE YOU GO ON...DO IT ③	**Building Blocks of Accounting**

Indicate whether each of the five statements presented below is true or false.

1. The historical cost principle dictates that companies record economic resources at their cost. In later periods, however, the fair value of the resource must be used if fair value is higher than its cost.
2. Relevance means that financial information matches what really happened; the information is factual.
3. A business owner's personal expenses must be separated from expenses of the business to comply with accounting's reporting entity concept.
4. All events are recorded in the financial statements.
5. All companies in Canada must report their financial statements using IFRS.

Solution

1. False. The historical cost principle dictates that companies record economic resources at their cost. Under the historical cost principle, the company must also use cost in later periods.
2. False. Faithful representation, not relevance, means that financial information matches what really happened; the information is factual.
3. True.
4. False. Not all events are recorded and reported in the financial statements; only accounting transactions are recorded as business transactions. Accounting transactions are events that change the business's economic resources or claims on those resources.
5. False. In Canada, publicly accountable entities must use IFRS, while private entities may report using ASPE.

Related exercise material: BE1–3, BE1–4, and E1–2.

Action Plan
- Review the discussion of financial reporting standards.
- Develop an understanding of the key terms used.

The Accounting Model

We can think of the accounting model as what it takes to prepare financial statements, which are the end result of accounting. To prepare the financial statements, we need to use the accounting equation, which is the basis for recording and summarizing all transactions. The accounting model underpins everything we will do with transactions in the rest of the textbook.

FINANCIAL STATEMENTS

You will recall that the main objective of the financial statements is to provide information to allow investors and creditors (external users) to make decisions about a business. Here we will introduce four basic financial statements—the balance sheet, income statement, statement of owner's equity, and cash flow statement—and show how this information is included in these statements. Later in the chapter, we will illustrate how to prepare these statements.

The specific financial statements prepared differ depending on the nature of the business organization; however, all businesses prepare a balance sheet and income statement. As you go through this section, we recommend you refer to Corus's financial statements for the year ended August 31, 2014, in Appendix A of this textbook. We will refer to these statements often throughout the textbook.

Balance Sheet

Alternative terminology The balance sheet is sometimes called the *statement of financial position.*

Users need information on the economic resources that the business can use to carry out its business activities to earn a profit and the claims to these economic resources. In accounting, economic resources that are owned or controlled by a business are called "assets." Claims on the economic resources are the amounts owed by the business and the owner's rights to the resources. In accounting, amounts owed by the business are called "liabilities" and the owner's right to these resources is called "owner's equity." **Assets, liabilities, and owner's equity are referred to as elements of the financial statements and are reported in the balance sheet.**

The balance sheet is like a snapshot of the company's financial condition at a specific point in time (usually the end of a month, quarter, or year). The heading of a balance sheet must identify the company, statement, and date. To indicate that the balance sheet is at a specific point in time, the date only mentions the point in time (e.g., as at December 31, 2017). Let's look at the components of the balance sheet in more detail.

Assets. **Assets** are resources controlled by a business as a result of past events and from which future economic benefits are expected to flow to the business. In a business, economic benefits generally refer to cash inflows (receipts) but can include other assets.

Assets are used to carry out activities, such as the production and distribution of merchandise. For example, imagine that a local pizza restaurant, called Campus Pizza, owns a delivery truck. The truck provides economic benefits because it is used to deliver pizzas. Campus Pizza also owns other assets, such as tables, chairs, a sound system, a cash register, an oven, dishes, supplies, and, of course, cash.

Other common assets include merchandise held for resale (commonly referred to as merchandise inventory), investments, land, buildings, patents, and copyrights. **Accounts receivable** is the asset created when a company sells goods or services to customers who promise to pay cash in the future. **Prepaid expense**, another common asset, is the asset created when a business pays cash in advance and the goods or services will be used over time. Common types of prepaid expenses are insurance, rent, and supplies.

Liabilities. **Liabilities** are present obligations, arising from past events, the settlement of which will include an outflow of economic benefits. An economic benefit here generally refers to cash outflows (payments) but can also include other assets or services. For example, businesses of all sizes usually borrow money and purchase merchandise inventory on credit. If a business borrows money to do such things as purchase equipment, it usually has a note payable for the amount borrowed. A **note payable** is supported by a written promise to pay a specific amount, at a specific time, in the future. Obligations to pay cash to suppliers in the future are called **accounts payable**.

Sometimes customers might pay a business in advance of being provided a service or product. This advance by the customer is a liability called **unearned revenue**, because the business has an obligation to provide the service or product in the future. Businesses may also have salaries payable to employees, Goods and Services Tax (GST/HST) payable and Provincial Sales Tax (PST) payable to the federal and provincial governments (respectively), and property taxes payable to the municipality.

Recall that persons or other businesses that are owed money by the business, such as suppliers and bankers, are called "creditors." The law requires that creditor claims be paid before ownership claims are paid.

Owner's Equity. The owner's claim on the assets of the company is known as **owner's equity**. It is equal to total assets minus total liabilities. Since the claims of creditors must be paid before ownership claims, the owner's equity is often called "residual equity." If the equity is negative—that is, if total liabilities are more than total assets—the term "owner's deficiency" (or deficit) describes the shortage. Owner's equity is a general accounting term that could be used for any type of organization. It is used most frequently for proprietorships. Partnerships use the term "partners' equity"; corporations, such as Corus, use "shareholders' equity."

The revised conceptual framework will include updated definitions of assets and liabilities. The updated definitions will expand on the definition of a resource as well as refine and update the term "economic benefit."

A summary of the balance sheet accounts, assets, liabilities, and owner's equity is presented in Illustration 1-7.

ASSETS
- Resources controlled by the business that can produce economic benefits
  - Examples: accounts receivable, merchandise inventory, vehicles

LIABILITIES
- Present obligations to transfer an economic resource
  - Examples: accounts payable, salaries payable

OWNER'S EQUITY
- The owner's claim on the assets
  - Residual equity of assets minus liabilities

▶ ILLUSTRATION **1-7**
The balance sheet:
A snapshot in time

The Accounting Equation. The relationship between assets, liabilities, and owner's equity (which are shown on the balance sheet) is expressed as an equation, called the **accounting equation**. Assets must equal the sum of liabilities and owner's equity. Liabilities are shown before owner's equity in the accounting equation because creditors have the right to receive payment before owners. Illustration 1-8 shows the accounting equation for Corus as at August 31, 2014 (balances presented are in thousands).

Alternative terminology The accounting equation is sometimes referred to as the *balance sheet equation*.

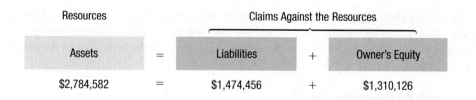

Resources		Claims Against the Resources		
Assets	=	Liabilities	+	Owner's Equity
$2,784,582	=	$1,474,456	+	$1,310,126

▶ ILLUSTRATION **1-8**
Accounting equation

The accounting equation is the same for all businesses regardless of their size, nature of business, or form of business organization. It applies to a small proprietorship such as a corner grocery store as much as it does to a large corporation such as Corus (where owner's equity is called shareholders' equity). Not only is the balance sheet based on the equation, but as we will see, the equation is the basis for recording and summarizing the economic events of a company.

Because the balance sheet is based on the accounting equation, you should never see a balance sheet where assets are not equal to liabilities plus owner's equity. If you do, it contains one or more errors. In that situation, we would say that the balance sheet is not balanced.

Income Statement

Users of the financial statements want to know if the business is generating a profit from its business activities. The main purpose of the **income statement** is to report the profitability of the business's operations over a specified period of time (a month, quarter, or year). **Profit is measured by the difference between revenues and expenses. Revenue and expense are referred to as elements of the financial statements and are reported in the income statement along with profit or loss. Profit results when revenues are greater than expenses and conversely a loss results when expenses are greater than revenues.**

Revenues. **Revenues** result from business activities that are undertaken to earn profit, such as performing services, selling merchandise inventory, renting property, and lending money. Revenues result in an increase in an asset or a decrease in a liability *and* an increase in owner's equity. They come from different sources and are given different names, depending on the type of business. Campus Pizza, for instance, has two categories of revenue: food sales and beverage sales. Common sources of revenue include sales, fees, services, commissions, interest, and rent.

Expenses. **Expenses** are the costs of assets that are consumed and services that are used in a company's business activities. Expenses are decreases in assets or increases in liabilities, *and* result in a decrease in owner's equity. Withdrawals of assets by an owner are not considered expenses. Like revenues, there are many kinds of expenses and they are identified by various names, depending on the type of asset consumed or service used. For example, Campus Pizza reports the following expenses: cost of ingredients (such as meat, flour, cheese, tomato paste, and mushrooms); cost of beverages; salaries expense; utilities expense (electric, gas, and water expense); telephone expense; repairs expense; fuel expense; supplies expense (such as napkins, detergents, and aprons); rent expense; insurance expense; and interest expense.

Illustration 1-9 shows the items reported on the income statement for a particular period of time.

▶ILLUSTRATION **1-9**
The income statement for a period of time

REVENUES
- Result from business activities undertaken to earn profit, such as performing services, selling merchandise inventory, renting property, and lending money
  - Examples: sales revenue, service revenue

EXPENSES
- The costs of assets consumed and services used in a company's business activities
  - Examples: cost of goods sold, salaries expense, rent expense, utility expense

PROFIT
- Measured by the difference between revenues and expenses

The balance sheet and income statement report balances for all of the elements of the financial statements; assets, liabilities, equity, revenue, and expense. The next financial statement that is prepared—the statement of owner's equity—reports the change in equity from the beginning of the period to the end of the period.

Statement of Owner's Equity

The **statement of owner's equity** shows the changes in owner's equity for the same period of time as the income statement. In a proprietorship, owner's equity is increased by investments made by the owner and decreased by withdrawals made by the owner. Owner's equity is also increased when a business generates a profit from business activities or decreased if the business has a loss. Let's look at each of these equity components in more detail.

Investments. **Investments by the owner** are contributions of cash or other assets (e.g., a vehicle or computer) made by the owners to the business. In a proprietorship, investments are recorded as increases to what is known as the owner's capital account. (Accounting records are made up of several accounts that group similar transactions, each one given a title such as Owner's Capital or Utilities Expense. An **account** records increases or decreases in assets, liabilities, or owner's equity items. We'll learn more about recording transactions in accounts in Chapter 2.) Accordingly, investments by owners result in an increase in an asset and an increase in owner's equity.

Drawings. An owner may withdraw cash (or other assets) for personal use. In a proprietorship, these withdrawals could be recorded as a direct decrease to the owner's capital account. However, it is generally considered better to use a separate account called **drawings** so that the total withdrawals for the accounting period can be determined. Drawings result in a decrease in an asset and a decrease in owner's equity.

Profit. As previously explained, revenues increase owner's equity and expenses decrease owner's equity. We also learned that profit results from revenues being greater than expenses and a loss results if expenses are greater than revenues. Therefore, profit increases owner's equity and losses decrease owner's equity.

Illustration 1-10 summarizes the transactions that change owner's equity.

Increases in owner's equity	Decreases in owner's equity
Investments by the owner	Drawings by the owner
Revenues	Expenses

▶ **ILLUSTRATION 1-10**
Transactions that increase and decrease owner's equity

We will see later in the chapter how this information is shown in the statement of owner's equity.

Cash Flow Statement

Investors and creditors need information on the business's ability to generate cash from its business activities and how the business uses cash. The **cash flow statement** gives information about the cash receipts and cash payments for a specific period of time. The cash flow statement gives answers to the following simple but important questions:

1. Where did the cash come from during the period?
2. What was the cash used for during the period?
3. What was the change in the cash balance during the period?

Alternative terminology The cash flow statement is sometimes called the *statement of cash flows.*

To help investors, creditors, and others analyze a company's cash, the cash flow statement reports the following:

1. the cash effects of the company's operating activities during a period;
2. the cash inflows and outflows from investing transactions (e.g., the purchase and sale of land, buildings, and equipment);
3. the cash inflows and outflows from financing transactions (e.g., borrowing and repayments of debt, and investments and withdrawals by the owner);
4. the net increase or decrease in cash during the period; and
5. the cash amount at the end of the period.

Accounting Differences by Type of Business Organization

Previously, you were introduced to different forms of business organization: the proprietorship, partnership, and corporation. Basically, accounting for assets, liabilities, revenues, expenses, and cash flows is the same, regardless of the form of business organization. The main distinction between the forms of organizations is found in (1) the terminology that is used to name the equity section, (2) the accounting for the owner's investments and withdrawals, and (3) the name of the statement showing the changes in owner's equity. In Illustration 1-11, we summarize these differences.

▶ ILLUSTRATION **1-11**
Accounting
differences by type
of business organization

	Proprietorship	**Partnership**	**Corporation (reporting under IFRS)**
Equity section called:	Owner's equity	Partners' equity	Shareholders' equity
Investments by owners added to:	Owner's capital	Partners' capital	Share capital
Profits added to:	Owner's capital	Partners' capital	Retained earnings
Withdrawals by owners called:	Drawings	Drawings	Dividends
Withdrawals deducted from:	Owner's capital	Partners' capital	Retained earnings
Name of statement:	Statement of owner's equity	Statement of partners' equity	Statement of changes in equity

In a proprietorship, equity is summarized and reported as one line item on the balance sheet called "capital" and prefaced by the owner's name. In a partnership, equity is summarized and reported as one line item for each partner and each account is referred to as "capital" prefaced by the individual partner's name. In the next sections of this chapter, transaction analysis will be demonstrated and the presentation of the balance sheet for a proprietorship will be illustrated. Chapter 12 will illustrate the balance sheet for a partnership. In a corporation, investments by all of the shareholders are grouped together and reported on the balance sheet as "share capital." In a corporation, regardless of the number of shareholders, one account called Retained Earnings is used to record the accumulated profit (or earnings) that has been retained (i.e., not paid out to shareholders) in the company and is also reported on the balance sheet. We will cover corporation accounting in more depth in Chapters 13 and 14. For now, note that account and statement names in a corporation are different from proprietorships and partnerships.

THE EXPANDED ACCOUNTING EQUATION

The basic accounting equation in Illustration 1-8 shows that assets are equal to liabilities plus owner's equity. Recall that the basic equation is a summary of the information shown on the balance sheet. But we also know that it is necessary to report on revenues, expenses, and other changes in owner's equity. In Illustration 1-12, we have expanded the basic accounting equation to show the different parts of owner's equity and the relationship between revenues, expenses, profit (or loss), and owner's equity.

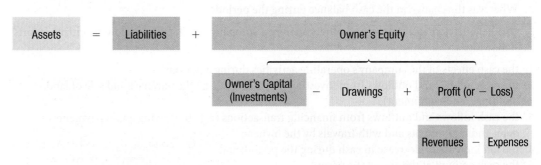

By expanding the equation, we have created a framework that can be used to report the information required in the income statement and the statement of owner's equity, as well as the balance sheet. The components in the expanded accounting equation are known as the **elements of the financial statements**.

Remember that the equation must always balance. Assets must equal liabilities plus owner's equity. From the expanded equation, we can see that if revenue increases, owner's equity increases and therefore either assets increase or liabilities decrease to keep the equation balanced. Conversely, if expenses increase, owner's equity decreases and therefore either assets decrease or liabilities increase to keep the equation balanced.

BEFORE YOU GO ON...DO IT	4	**The Accounting Equation**

The following are a few of the items that are reported in financial statements: (1) cash, (2) service revenue, (3) drawings, (4) accounts receivable, (5) accounts payable, and (6) salaries expense.

(a) Classify the items as assets, liabilities, or owner's equity. For the owner's equity items, indicate whether these items increase or decrease equity.
(b) Indicate which financial statement the item is reported in.

Solution

	(a) Type of Item	(b) Financial Statement
1. Cash	Asset	Balance sheet
2. Service revenue	Owner's equity—increase	Income statement
3. Drawings	Owner's equity—decrease	Statement of owner's equity
4. Accounts receivable	Asset	Balance sheet
5. Accounts payable	Liability	Balance sheet
6. Salaries expense	Owner's equity—decrease	Income statement

Related exercise material: BE1–5, BE1–6, BE1–7, BE1–8, BE1–9, E1–4, E1–5, and E1–6.

Action Plan
- Understand that assets are resources that are capable of providing future service or benefit that are owned or controlled by a business.
- Understand that liabilities are amounts owed by a business.
- Review which transactions affect owner's equity.
- Recall what information is included in each of the financial statements.

LEARNING OBJECTIVE	5	**Analyze the effects of business transactions on the accounting equation.**

Transaction Analysis

Once it has been determined that an event or transaction should be recognized, it must be analyzed for its effect on the components of the accounting equation before it can be recorded. This analysis must identify the specific items that are affected and the amount of change in each item.

Each transaction must have a dual effect on the equation for the two sides of the accounting equation to remain equal. For example, if an asset is increased, there must be a corresponding

1. decrease in another asset, or
2. increase in a liability, or
3. increase in owner's equity.

Two or more items could be affected by a transaction. For example, an asset (equipment) could increase by $10,000, a different asset (cash) could decrease by $6,000, and a liability (notes payable) could increase by $4,000.

As a general example, we will now look at transactions conducted by Softbyte, a fictitious computer programming business, during its first month of operations. You should study these transactions until you are sure you understand them. They are not difficult, but they are important to your success in this course. Being able to analyze how transactions affect the accounting equation is essential for understanding accounting.

To keep it simple, we will not include cents in the dollar amounts we record in the following analysis of Softbyte's transactions. In reality, it is important to understand that cents should be, and are, used when transactions are recorded in a company's internal accounting records.

Transaction (1): Investment by Owner. Andrew Leonid decides to open a computer programming business, which he names Softbyte. On September 1, 2017, he invests $15,000 cash in the business, which he deposits in a bank account opened under the name of Softbyte. This transaction results in an equal increase in both assets and owner's equity for Softbyte.

Office Hours Videos are short videos included in each chapter on core accounting concepts. The videos are indicated by the "play" icon in the margin beside the relevant topic.

Basic Analysis	The asset Cash is increased by $15,000 and the owner's equity account, A. Leonid, Capital, is increased by $15,000.

Equation Analysis		Assets	=	Liabilities	+	Owner's Equity
						A. Leonid, Capital
		Cash	=			
	(1)	+$15,000	=			+$15,000

Notice that the two sides of the basic equation remain equal. Note also that investments by an owner are **not** revenues and are not included in calculating profit. The increase therefore has to be recorded as an investment in the owner's capital account rather than as revenue from operations.

Transaction (2): Purchase of Equipment for Cash. Softbyte purchases computer equipment for $7,000 cash. This transaction results in an equal increase and decrease in total assets, though the composition of the assets changes. The specific effect of this transaction and the cumulative effect of the first two transactions are:

Basic Analysis	The asset Cash is decreased by $7,000 and the asset Equipment is increased by $7,000.

Equation Analysis		Assets		=	Liabilities	+	Owner's Equity
		Cash	+ Equipment	=			A. Leonid, Capital
	Old Balances	$15,000		=			$15,000
	(2)	−7,000	+$7,000				
	New Balances	$ 8,000 +	$7,000	=			$15,000
		$15,000					$15,000

Notice that total assets are still $15,000, and that Leonid's equity also remains at $15,000, the amount of his original investment.

Transaction (3): Purchase of Supplies on Credit. Softbyte purchases $1,600 of computer paper and other supplies that are expected to last several months from the Alpha Supply Company. Alpha Supply will allow Softbyte to pay this bill next month (in October). This transaction is referred to as a purchase on account, or a credit purchase. Assets are increased because the use of the paper and supplies is capable of producing economic benefits. Liabilities are increased by the amount that is due to Alpha Supply Company.

Basic Analysis	The asset Supplies is increased by $1,600 and the liability Accounts Payable is increased by the same amount.

Equation Analysis		Assets			=	Liabilities	+	Owner's Equity
						Accounts		A. Leonid,
		Cash +	Supplies +	Equipment	=	Payable	+	Capital
	Old Balances	$8,000 +		+ $7,000	=			$15,000
	(3)		+$1,600			+$1,600		
	New Balances	$8,000 +	$1,600 +	$7,000	=	$1,600	+	$15,000
			$16,600				$16,600	

Total assets are now $16,600. This total is matched by a $1,600 creditor's claim and a $15,000 ownership claim.

Transaction (4): Services Provided for Cash. Softbyte receives $1,200 cash from customers for programming services it has provided. This transaction is Softbyte's main revenue-producing activity. Remember that revenue increases profit, which then increases owner's equity.

Basic Analysis	The asset Cash is increased by $1,200 and the owner's equity account Service Revenue is increased by $1,200.

		Assets					=	Liabilities	+	Owner's Equity		
								Accounts		A. Leonid,		
		Cash	+	Supplies	+	Equipment	=	Payable	+	Capital	+	Revenues
Equation Analysis	Old Balances	$8,000	+	$1,600	+	$7,000	=	$1,600	+	$15,000		
	(4)	+1,200										+$1,200
	New Balances	$9,200	+	$1,600	+	$7,000	=	$1,600	+	$15,000	+	$1,200
				$17,800						$17,800		

The two sides of the equation still balance at $17,800.

We don't have room to give details for each revenue and expense account in this illustration, so revenues (and expenses when we get to them) will be summarized under one column heading for Revenues and one for Expenses. However, it is important to keep track of the account titles that are affected (e.g., Service Revenue), because they will be needed when the income statement is prepared in the next section.

Transaction (5): Purchase of Advertising on Credit. Softbyte receives a bill for $250 from the local newspaper for advertising the opening of its business. It postpones payment of the bill until a later date. The cost of advertising is an expense, and not an asset, because the benefits have already been used. Owner's equity decreases because an expense is incurred. Expenses reduce profit and owner's equity.

Basic Analysis	The liability Accounts Payable is increased by $250 and the owner's equity account Advertising Expense is increased by $250.

		Assets					=	Liabilities	+	Owner's Equity				
								Accounts		A. Leonid,				
		Cash	+	Supplies	+	Equipment	=	Payable	+	Capital	+	Revenues	−	Expenses
Equation Analysis	Old Balances	$9,200	+	$1,600	+	$7,000	=	$1,600	+	$15,000	+	$1,200		
	(5)							+250						−$250
	New Balances	$9,200	+	$1,600	+	$7,000	=	$1,850	+	$15,000	+	$1,200	−	$250
				$17,800						$17,800				

The two sides of the equation still balance at $17,800. Note that, although the expense increases, this is shown as a negative number because expenses reduce owner's equity.

Expenses do not have to be paid in cash at the time they are incurred. When payment is made on the later date, the liability Accounts Payable will be decreased and the asset Cash will also be decreased [see transaction (8)].

Transaction (6): Services Provided for Cash and Credit. Softbyte provides $3,500 of programming services for customers. Cash of $1,500 is received from customers, and the balance of $2,000 is billed to customers on account. This transaction results in an equal increase in assets and owner's equity.

Basic Analysis

Three specific items are affected: the asset Cash is increased by $1,500; the asset Accounts Receivable is increased by $2,000; and the owner's equity account Service Revenue is increased by $3,500.

Equation Analysis

		Assets				=	Liabilities	+		Owner's Equity		
			Accounts				Accounts		A. Leonid,			
		Cash +	Receivable +	Supplies +	Equipment =		Payable +		Capital +	Revenues −	Expenses
Old Balances		$ 9,200		+ $1,600 +	$7,000 =		$1,850 +		$15,000 +	$1,200 −	$250
(6)		+1,500	+$2,000							+3,500	
New Balances		$10,700 +	$2,000 +	$1,600 +	$7,000 =		$1,850 +		$15,000 +	$4,700 −	$250

$21,300 = $21,300

You might wonder why owner's equity is increased by $3,500 when only $1,500 has been collected. The reason is that the assets from earning revenues do not have to be in cash. Owner's equity is increased when revenues are recognized. In Softbyte's case, revenues are recognized when the service (performance obligation) is provided and complete. When collections on account are received at a later date, Cash will be increased and Accounts Receivable will be decreased [see transaction (9)].

Transaction (7): Payment of Expenses. The expenses paid in cash for September are store rent, $600; salaries of employees, $900; and utilities, $200. These payments result in an equal decrease in assets and owner's equity.

Basic Analysis

The asset Cash is decreased by $1,700 in total ($600 + $900 + $200) and owner's equity expense accounts are increased by the same amount, which then decreases owner's equity.

Equation Analysis

		Assets				=	Liabilities	+		Owner's Equity		
			Accounts				Accounts		A. Leonid,			
		Cash +	Receivable +	Supplies +	Equipment =		Payable +		Capital +	Revenues −	Expenses
Old Balances		$10,700 +	$2,000 +	$1,600 +	$7,000 =		$1,850 +		$15,000 +	$4,700 −	$ 250
(7)		−600									−600
		−900									−900
		−200									−200
New Balances		$ 9,000 +	$2,000 +	$1,600 +	$7,000 =		$1,850 +		$15,000 +	$4,700 −	$1,950

$19,600 = $19,600

The two sides of the equation now balance at $19,600. Three lines are needed in the analysis in order to show the different types of expenses that have been paid. Note that total expenses increase but, as explained in transaction (5), it is shown as a negative number because expenses decrease owner's equity.

Transaction (8): Payment of Accounts Payable. Softbyte pays its $250 advertising bill in cash. Remember that the bill was previously recorded in transaction (5) as an increase in Accounts Payable and a decrease in owner's equity.

Basic Analysis

The asset Cash is decreased by $250 and the liability Accounts Payable is decreased by $250.

Equation Analysis

		Assets				=	Liabilities	+		Owner's Equity		
			Accounts				Accounts		A. Leonid,			
		Cash +	Receivable +	Supplies +	Equipment =		Payable +		Capital +	Revenues −	Expenses
Old Balances		$9,000 +	$2,000 +	$1,600 +	$7,000 =		$1,850 +		$15,000 +	$4,700 −	$1,950
(8)		−250						−250				
New Balances		$8,750 +	$2,000 +	$1,600 +	$7,000 =		$1,600 +		$15,000 +	$4,700 −	$1,950

$19,350 = $19,350

Notice that the payment of a liability for an expense that has previously been recorded does not affect owner's equity. The expense was recorded in transaction (5) and should not be recorded again.

Transaction (9): Receipt of Cash on Account. The sum of $600 in cash is received from some customers who were billed for services in transaction (6). This transaction does not change total assets, but it does change the composition of those assets.

Basic Analysis	The asset Cash is increased by $600 and the asset Accounts Receivable is decreased by $600.

Equation Analysis		Assets					=	Liabilities	+		Owner's Equity		
		Cash +	Accounts Receivable +	Supplies +	Equipment	=	Accounts Payable +		A. Leonid, Capital +		Revenues −	Expenses
	Old Balances	$8,750 +	$2,000 +	$1,600 +	$7,000	=	$1,600 +		$15,000 +		$4,700 −	$1,950
	(9)	+600	−600									
	New Balances	$9,350 +	$1,400 +	$1,600 +	$7,000	=	$1,600 +		$15,000 +		$4,700 −	$1,950
			$19,350							$19,350		

Note that a collection of an account receivable for services that were billed and recorded earlier does not affect owner's equity. Revenue was already recorded in transaction (6) and should not be recorded again.

Transaction (10): Signed Contract to Rent Equipment in October. Andrew Leonid and an equipment supplier sign a contract for Softbyte to rent equipment for the months of October and November at the rate of $250 per month. Softbyte is to pay each month's rent at the start of the month. There is no effect on the accounting equation because the assets, liabilities, and owner's equity have not been changed by the signing of the contract. An accounting transaction has not occurred. At this point, Softbyte has not paid for anything, nor has it used the equipment, and therefore it has not incurred any expenses.

	Assets				=	Liabilities	+		Owner's Equity		
	Cash +	Accounts Receivable +	Supplies +	Equipment	=	Accounts Payable +		A. Leonid, Capital +		Revenues −	Expenses
Old Balances	$9,350 +	$1,400 +	$1,600 +	$7,000	=	$1,600 +		$15,000 +		$4,700 −	$1,950
(10) No entry											
New Balances	$9,350 +	$1,400 +	$1,600 +	$7,000	=	$1,600 +		$15,000 +		$4,700 −	$1,950
		$19,350							$19,350		

Note that the new balances are all identical to the old balances because nothing has changed.

Transaction (11): Withdrawal of Cash by Owner. Andrew Leonid withdraws $1,300 in cash from the business for his personal use. This transaction results in an equal decrease in assets and owner's equity.

Basic Analysis	The asset Cash is decreased by $1,300, and the owner's equity account Drawings is increased by $1,300, which then decreases owner's equity, as follows:

Equation Analysis		Assets				=	Liabilities	+		Owner's Equity			
		Cash +	Accounts Receivable +	Supplies +	Equipment	=	Accounts Payable +		A. Leonid, Capital −	A. Leonid, Drawings +	Revenues −	Expenses
	Old Balances	$9,350 +	$1,400 +	$1,600 +	$7,000	=	$1,600 +		$15,000		+ $4,700 −	$1,950
	(11)	−1,300								−$1,300		
	New Balances	$8,050 +	$1,400 +	$1,600 +	$7,000	=	$1,600 +		$15,000 −	$1,300 +	$4,700 −	$1,950
			$18,050							$18,050		

Note that both drawings and expenses reduce owner's equity, as shown in the accounting equation above. However, **owner's drawings are not expenses**. Expenses are incurred for the purpose of earning revenue and are reported in the income statement. Drawings do not generate revenue. They are a *disinvestment*; that is, the effect of an owner's cash withdrawal is the opposite of the effect of an owner's investment. Like owner's investments, drawings are not included in the determination of profit.

Summary of Transactions

▶ILLUSTRATION **1-13**
Tabular summary of
Softbyte transactions

Softbyte's transactions are summarized in Illustration 1-13 to show their cumulative effect on the accounting equation. The transaction number and the specific effects of each transaction are indicated.

		Assets			=	Liabilities	+		Owner's Equity			
	Cash +	Accounts Receivable +	Supplies +	Equipment	=	Accounts Payable +		A. Leonid, Capital −	A. Leonid, Drawings +	Revenues −	Expenses
(1)	+$15,000							+$15,000			
(2)	−7,000			+$7,000							
(3)			+$1,600			+$1,600					
(4)	+1,200									+$1,200	
(5)						+250					−$ 250
(6)	+1,500	+$2,000								+3,500	
(7)	−600										−600
	−900										−900
	−200										−200
(8)	−250					−250					
(9)	+600	−600									
(10)	No entry										
(11)	−1,300								−$1,300		
	$ 8,050 +	$1,400 +	$1,600 +	$7,000	=	$1,600 +		$15,000 −	$1,300 +	$4,700 −	$1,950
		$18,050							$18,050		

The illustration demonstrates some significant facts.

1. Each transaction must be analyzed for its effects on:
   (a) the three components (assets, liabilities, and owner's equity) of the accounting equation, and
   (b) specific items within each component.
2. The two sides of the equation must always be equal.

This section on transaction analysis does not show the formal method of recording transactions. We will start illustrating that in Chapter 2. But understanding how transactions change assets, liabilities, and owner's equity is fundamental to understanding accounting and also business in general.

BEFORE YOU GO ON...DO IT **5** ▶ **Tabular Analysis**

Transactions for the month of August by Dawd & Co., a public accounting firm, are shown below. Make a table that shows the effects of these transactions on the accounting equation, like the tabular analysis shown in Illustration 1-13.

1. The owner, John Dawd, invested $25,000 of cash in the business.
2. Equipment was purchased on credit, $7,000.
3. Services were performed for customers for $8,000. Of this amount, $2,000 was received in cash and $6,000 is due on account.
4. Rent of $850 was paid for the month.
5. Customers on account paid $4,000 (see transaction 3).
6. The owner withdrew $1,000 of cash for personal use.

(continued)

BEFORE YOU GO ON...DO IT **Tabular Analysis** *(continued)*

Solution

	Assets			=	Liabilities	+			Owner's Equity		
		Accounts	Office		Accounts		J. Dawd,	J. Dawd,			
Cash	+	Receivable	+	Equipment	=	Payable	+	Capital	–	Drawings	+	Revenues	–	Expenses
1. +$25,000								+$25,000						
2.			+$7,000		+$7,000						
3. +2,000	+$6,000										+$8,000	
4. –850												–$850
5. +4,000	–4,000										
6. –1,000								–$1,000			
$29,150 +	$2,000 +	$7,000	=	$7,000 +	$25,000 –	$1,000 +	$8,000 –	$850

$38,150 $38,150

Related exercise material: BE1–11, BE1–12, BE1–13, E1–7, E1–9, E1–10, E1–11, and E1–12.

LEARNING OBJECTIVE 6 **Prepare financial statements.**

Preparing Financial Statements

Once all transactions for the month have been recognized, financial statements can be prepared. You will recall that these include the balance sheet, income statement, statement of owner's equity, and cash flow statement.

Illustration 1-14 shows Softbyte's statements prepared from the transaction analysis in Illustration 1-13 and how the statements are interrelated. It is important to note that, because of the interrelationships of the financial statements, they are always prepared in the following order:

1. income statement,
2. statement of owner's equity,
3. balance sheet, and
4. cash flow statement.

The essential features of Softbyte's four financial statements, and their interrelationships, are briefly described in the following sections.

Helpful hint The income statement, statement of owner's equity, and cash flow statement all report information for a period of time. The balance sheet reports information at a point in time.

INCOME STATEMENT

The income statement is prepared from the data in the owner's equity columns (specifically the Revenues and Expenses columns) of Illustration 1-13. The statement's heading names the company and type of statement, and to indicate that it applies to a period of time, the income statement date names the time period. For Softbyte, this appears as Month Ended September 30, 2017, which means the statement is for a one-month period—September 1 to 30, 2017 (Illustration 1-14).

On the income statement, revenues of $4,700 appear first, followed by a list of the expenses totalling $1,950. Finally, profit of $2,750 is determined. The income statement is always prepared first in order to determine the amount of profit or loss to be used in the statement of owner's equity.

STATEMENT OF OWNER'S EQUITY

Data for preparing the statement of owner's equity are taken from the owner's equity columns (specifically the Capital and Drawings columns) of the tabular summary (Illustration 1-13) and from the income statement. The heading of this statement names the company and type of statement, and shows the time period covered by the statement. Because the time period is the same as it is for the income statement, it is also dated Month Ended September 30, 2017.

▶ ILLUSTRATION **1-14**
Financial statements
and their interrelationships

SOFTBYTE
Income Statement
Month Ended September 30, 2017

Revenues		
Service revenue		$4,700
Expenses		
Advertising expense	$250	
Rent expense	600	
Salaries expense	900	
Utilities expense	200	
Total expenses		1,950
Profit		$2,750

SOFTBYTE
Statement of Owner's Equity
Month Ended September 30, 2017

A. Leonid, capital, September 1, 2017		$ 0
Add: Investments	$15,000	
Profit	2,750	17,750
		17,750
Less: Drawings		1,300
A. Leonid, capital, September 30, 2017		$16,450

Helpful hint The arrows in this illustration show the relationships between the four statements.

SOFTBYTE
Balance Sheet
September 30, 2017

Assets	
Cash	$ 8,050
Accounts receivable	1,400
Supplies	1,600
Equipment	7,000
Total assets	$18,050
Liabilities and Owner's Equity	
Liabilities	
Accounts payable	$ 1,600
Owner's equity	
A. Leonid, capital	16,450
Total liabilities and owner's equity	$18,050

SOFTBYTE
Cash Flow Statement
Month Ended September 30, 2017

Operating activities		
Cash receipts from customers	$ 3,300	
Cash payments for operating expenses	(1,950)	
Net cash provided by operating activities		$ 1,350
Investing activities		
Purchase of equipment	$ (7,000)	
Net cash used by investing activities		(7,000)
Financing activities		
Investments by owner	$15,000	
Drawings by owner	(1,300)	
Net cash provided by financing activities		13,700
Net increase in cash		8,050
Cash, September 1, 2017		0
Cash, September 30, 2017		$ 8,050

The beginning owner's equity amount is shown on the first line of the statement. In this example, it is a zero balance because it is Softbyte's first period of operations. When financial statements are again prepared for Softbyte on October 31, 2017, the beginning owner's equity amount will be $16,450, which is the ending balance on September 30, 2017. For a company that is continuing its operations, the beginning balance is equal to the ending balance from the previous period. What if Softbyte reported a loss in its first month? The loss would reduce owner's capital. Instead of adding profit, the loss would be deducted in the same section as owner's drawings.

BALANCE SHEET

The balance sheet is prepared from the Assets and Liabilities column headings and the month-end data shown in the last line of the tabular summary (Illustration 1-13), and from the statement of owner's equity. Owner's capital of $16,450 at the end of the reporting period in the statement of owner's equity is reported on the balance sheet.

The heading of a balance sheet must identify the company, statement, and date. To indicate that the balance sheet is at a specific point in time, the date only mentions the point in time (there is no indication of a time period). For Softbyte, the date is September 30, 2017. Sometimes, the words "as at" precede the balance sheet date. Notice that the assets are listed at the top, followed by liabilities and owner's equity. This presentation is a common convention used in Canada but other orders of presentation are possible. Total assets must equal total liabilities and owner's equity. In other words, the balance sheet must balance.

CASH FLOW STATEMENT

Softbyte's cash flow statement, shown in Illustration 1-14, is for the same period of time as the income statement and the statement of owner's equity. Note that the positive numbers indicate cash inflows or increases. Numbers in parentheses indicate cash outflows or decreases. At this time, you do not need to know how these amounts are determined. In Chapter 17, we will look at the cash flow statement in detail. But you should note that Cash of $8,050 on the September 30, 2017, balance sheet is also reported at the bottom of the cash flow statement.

UNDERSTANDING THE INFORMATION IN THE FINANCIAL STATEMENTS

Illustration 1-14 showed the financial statements for Softbyte. Every set of financial statements also has explanatory notes and supporting schedules that are an essential part of the statements. For example, as previously mentioned, at the very least a company will have to indicate if it is following IFRS or ASPE.

Public corporations issue their financial statements and supplementary materials in an annual report. The **annual report** is a document that includes useful non-financial information about the company, as well as financial information.

Non-financial information may include a management discussion of the company's mission, goals, and objectives; market position; and the people involved in the company. Financial information may include a review of current operations and a historical summary of key financial figures and ratios, in addition to comparative financial statements. Public company financial statements are audited and include the auditors' report. There is also a statement of management responsibility for the statements.

Now is a good time to look again at Corus's financial statements in Appendix A. Carefully examine the format and content of each financial statement and compare them with Softbyte's financial statements in Illustration 1-14. What similarities can you find between Softbyte's financial statements and the more complicated financial statements for Corus?

You will see that Corus's transactions have been accumulated for the year ended August 31, 2014, and grouped together in categories. When similar transactions are grouped together, they are being reported in aggregate. By presenting recorded data in aggregate, the accounting information system simplifies a large number of transactions. As a result, the company's activities are easier to understand and are more meaningful. This simplification does mean less detail, however. Most companies report condensed information for two reasons: it's simpler, and it also avoids revealing significant details to competitors.

You should note that financial statement amounts are normally rounded to the nearest dollar, thousand dollars, or million dollars, depending on the size of the company. Corus rounds its numbers to the nearest thousand dollars. This is done to remove unimportant detail and make the information easier for the reader to understand.

Listed below, in alphabetical order, are the financial statement items for Park Accounting Services. Prepare an income statement, statement of owner's equity, and balance sheet for the month ended January 31, 2017.

Accounts payable	$ 5,000	M. Park, capital, January 1, 2017	$10,350
Accounts receivable	2,500	M. Park, drawings	3,000
Advertising expense	500	Prepaid rent	1,300
Cash	8,200	Rent expense	850
Equipment	10,000	Service revenue	11,000

Solution

PARK ACCOUNTING SERVICES
Income Statement
Month Ended January 31, 2017

Revenues		
Service revenue		$11,000
Expenses		
Advertising expense	$500	
Rent expense	850	
Total expenses		1,350
Profit		$ 9,650

PARK ACCOUNTING SERVICES
Statement of Owner's Equity
Month Ended January 31, 2017

M. Park, capital, January 1, 2017	$10,350
Add: Profit	9,650
	20,000
Less: Drawings	3,000
M. Park, capital, January 31, 2017	$17,000

①

PARK ACCOUNTING SERVICES
Balance Sheet
January 31, 2017

Assets	
Cash	$ 8,200
Accounts receivable	2,500
Prepaid rent	1,300
Equipment	10,000
Total assets	$22,000

②

Liabilities and Owner's Equity	
Liabilities	
Accounts payable	$ 5,000
Total liabilities	5,000
Owner's equity	
M. Park, capital	17,000
Total liabilities and owner's equity	$22,000

Related exercise material: BE1–14, BE1–15, BE1–16, BE1–17, BE1–18, E1–13, E1–14, E1–15, and E1–16.

▌Comparing **IFRS** and **ASPE** ▌

Key Differences	International Financial Reporting Standards (IFRS)	Accounting Standards for Private Enterprises (ASPE)
Accounting standards	Required for publicly accountable enterprises and optional for private enterprises	Private enterprises only
Level of accounting information required	Users require extensive detailed information	Users require less information
Equity reporting	Statement of changes in equity	• Proprietorships: Statement of owner's equity • Partnerships: Statement of partners' equity • Corporation: Statement of retained earnings

The Demonstration Problem is a final review before you work on the assignment material. The problem-solving strategies in the margins give you tips about how to approach the problem. The solution shows both the form and the content of complete answers.

Demonstration Problem

Adina Falk opened her own law office on July 1, 2017. During the first month of operations, the following transactions occurred:

1. Invested $15,000 in cash in the law practice.
2. Hired a legal assistant to work part-time for $1,500 per month.
3. Paid $1,800 for July rent on office space.
4. Purchased equipment on account, $3,000.
5. Provided legal services to clients for cash, $2,500.
6. Borrowed $7,000 cash from a bank on a note payable.
7. Provided legal services to a client on account, $4,000.
8. Collected $1,200 of the amount owed by a client on account (see transaction 7).
9. Paid monthly expenses: salaries, $1,500; telephone, $200; and utilities, $300.
10. Withdrew $2,000 cash for personal use.

Instructions
(a) Prepare a tabular analysis of the transactions.
(b) Prepare the income statement, statement of owner's equity, and balance sheet for Adina Falk, Barrister & Solicitor.

SOLUTION TO DEMONSTRATION PROBLEM
(a)

Transaction	Cash	+ Accounts Receivable	+ Equipment	= Notes Payable	+ Accounts Payable	+ A. Falk, Capital	− A. Falk, Drawings	+ Revenues	− Expenses
(1)	+$15,000					+$15,000			
(2) No Entry									
(3)	−1,800								−$1,800
(4)			+$3,000		+$3,000				
(5)	+2,500							+$2,500	
(6)	+7,000			+$7,000					
(7)		+$4,000						+4,000	
(8)	+1,200	−1,200							
(9)	−1,500								−1,500
	−200								−200
	−300								−300
(10)	−2,000						−$2,000		
	$19,900	+ $2,800	+ $3,000	= $7,000	+ $3,000	+ $15,000	− $2,000	+ $6,500	− $3,800

Assets: $25,700

Liabilities + Owner's Equity: $25,700

ACTION PLAN

- Make sure that assets equal liabilities plus owner's equity in each transaction.
- Investments and revenues increase owner's equity. Withdrawals and expenses decrease owner's equity.
- Prepare the financial statements in the order listed.
- The income statement shows revenues and expenses for a period of time.
- Profit (or loss) is calculated on the income statement and carried forward to the statement of owner's equity.
- The statement of owner's equity shows the changes in owner's equity for the same period of time as the income statement.
- The owner's capital at the end of the period is carried forward from the statement of owner's equity to the balance sheet.
- The balance sheet reports assets, liabilities, and owner's equity at a specific date.

(b)

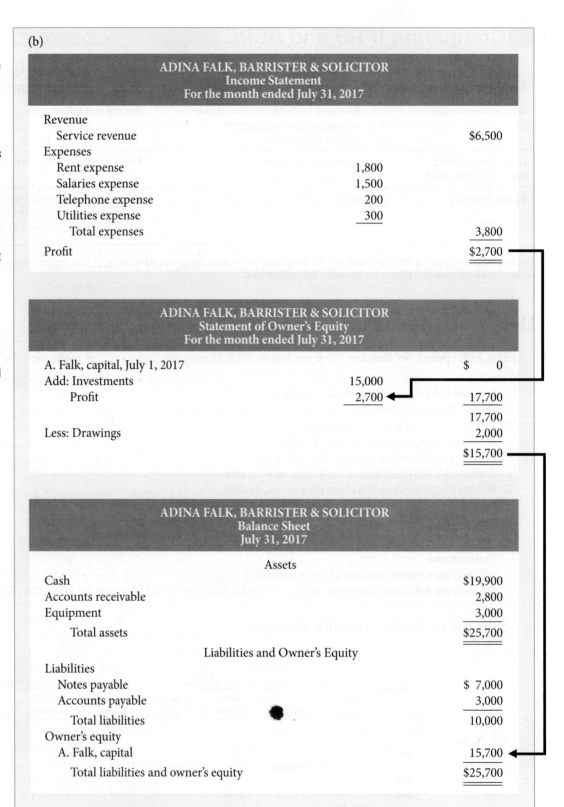

ADINA FALK, BARRISTER & SOLICITOR
Income Statement
For the month ended July 31, 2017

Revenue		
Service revenue		$6,500
Expenses		
Rent expense	1,800	
Salaries expense	1,500	
Telephone expense	200	
Utilities expense	300	
Total expenses		3,800
Profit		$2,700

ADINA FALK, BARRISTER & SOLICITOR
Statement of Owner's Equity
For the month ended July 31, 2017

A. Falk, capital, July 1, 2017		$ 0
Add: Investments	15,000	
Profit	2,700	17,700
		17,700
Less: Drawings		2,000
		$15,700

ADINA FALK, BARRISTER & SOLICITOR
Balance Sheet
July 31, 2017

Assets	
Cash	$19,900
Accounts receivable	2,800
Equipment	3,000
Total assets	$25,700

Liabilities and Owner's Equity	
Liabilities	
Notes payable	$ 7,000
Accounts payable	3,000
Total liabilities	10,000
Owner's equity	
A. Falk, capital	15,700
Total liabilities and owner's equity	$25,700

⏵ Summary of Learning Objectives

1. *Identify the use and users of accounting and the objective of financial reporting.* Accounting is the information system that identifies, records, and communicates the economic events of an organization to a wide variety of interested users. Good accounting is important to people both inside and outside the organization. Internal users, such as management, use accounting information to plan, control, and evaluate business operations. External users include investors and creditors, among others. Accounting data are used by investors (owners or potential owners) to decide whether to buy, hold, or sell their financial interests. Creditors (suppliers and bankers) evaluate the risks of granting credit or lending money based on the accounting information. The objective of financial reporting is to provide useful information to investors and creditors to make these decisions. Users need information about the business's ability to earn a profit and generate cash. For our economic system to function smoothly, reliable and ethical accounting and financial reporting are critical.

2. *Compare the different forms of business organization.* The most common examples of business organization are proprietorships, partnerships, and corporations. Proprietorships and partnerships are not separate legal entities but are separate entities for accounting purposes; income taxes are paid by the owners and owners have unlimited liability. Corporations are separate legal entities as well as separate entities for accounting purposes; income taxes are paid by the corporation and owners of the corporation have limited liability.

3. *Explain the building blocks of accounting: ethics and the concepts included in the conceptual framework.* Generally accepted accounting principles are a common set of guidelines that are used to prepare and report accounting information. The conceptual framework outlines some of the body of theory used by accountants to fulfill their goal of providing useful accounting information to users. Ethical behaviour is fundamental to fulfilling the objective of financial accounting. The reporting entity concept requires the business activities of each reporting entity to be kept separate from the activities of its owner and other economic entities. The going concern assumption presumes that a business will continue operations for enough time to use its assets for their intended purpose and to fulfill its commitments. The periodicity concept requires businesses to divide up economic activities into distinct periods of time. Qualitative characteristics include fundamental and enhancing characteristics that help to ensure accounting information is useful.

Only events that cause changes in the business's economic resources or changes to the claims on those resources are recorded. Recognition is the process of recording items and measurement is the process of determining the amount that should be recognized. The historical cost concept states that economic resources should be recorded at their historical (original) cost. Fair value may be a more appropriate measure for certain types of resources. Generally fair value is the amount the resource could be sold for in the market. The monetary unit concept requires that only transactions that can be expressed as an amount of money be included in the accounting records, and it assumes that the monetary unit is stable.

The revenue recognition principle requires companies to recognize revenue when a performance obligation(s) is satisfied. The matching concept requires that costs be recognized as expenses in the same period as revenue is recognized when there is a direct association between the cost incurred and revenue recognized.

In Canada, there are two sets of standards for profit-oriented businesses. Publicly accountable enterprises must follow International Financial Reporting Standards (IFRS) and private enterprises have the choice of following IFRS or Accounting Standards for Private Enterprises (ASPE).

4. *Describe the components of the financial statements and explain the accounting equation.* Assets, liabilities, and owner's equity are reported in the balance sheet. Assets are present economic resources controlled by the business as a result of past events that are capable of producing economic benefits. Liabilities are present obligations of a business to transfer an economic resource as a result of past events. Owner's equity is the owner's claim on the company's assets and is equal to total assets minus total liabilities. The balance sheet is based on the accounting equation: Assets = Liabilities + Owner's equity.

The income statement reports the profit or loss for a specified period of time. Profit is equal to revenues minus expenses. Revenues are the increases in assets, or decreases in liabilities, that result from business activities that are undertaken to earn profit. Expenses are the cost of assets consumed or services used in a company's business activities. They are decreases in assets or increases in liabilities, excluding withdrawals made by the owners, and result in a decrease to owner's equity.

The statement of owner's equity summarizes the changes in owner's equity during the period. Owner's equity is increased by investments by the owner and profits. It is decreased by drawings and losses. Investments are contributions of cash or other assets by owners. Drawings are withdrawals of cash or other assets from the business for the owner's personal use. Owner's equity in a partnership is referred to as partners' equity and in a corporation as shareholders' equity.

A cash flow statement summarizes information about the cash inflows (receipts) and outflows (payments) for a specific period of time.

5. *Analyze the effects of business transactions on the accounting equation.* Each business transaction must have a dual effect on the accounting equation. For example, if an individual asset is increased, there must be a corresponding (1) decrease in another asset, (2) increase in a liability, and/or (3) increase in owner's equity.

6. *Prepare financial statements.* The income statement is prepared first. Expenses are deducted from revenues to calculate the profit or loss for a specific period of time. Then

the statement of owner's equity is prepared using the profit or loss reported in the income statement. The profit is added to (losses are deducted from) the owner's equity at the beginning of the period. Drawings are then deducted to calculate owner's equity at the end of the period. A balance sheet reports the assets, liabilities, and owner's equity of a business as at the end of the accounting period. The owner's equity at the end of period, as calculated in the statement of owner's equity, is reported in the balance sheet in the owner's equity section.

▶ Glossary

Account A record of increases and decreases in a specific asset, liability, or owner's equity item. (p. 19)

Accounting The information system that identifies, records, and communicates the economic events of an organization to a wide variety of interested users. (p. 4)

Accounting equation Assets = Liabilities + Owner's equity. (p. 17)

Accounting Standards for Private Enterprises (ASPE) A set of standards developed by the Accounting Standards Board (AcSB) that may be used for financial reporting by private enterprises in Canada. (p. 15)

Accounting transaction An economic event that is recorded in the accounting records because it changes the assets, liabilities, or owner's equity items of the organization. (p. 13)

Accounts payable A liability created by buying services or products on credit. It is an obligation to pay cash to a supplier in the future. (p. 17)

Accounts receivable An asset created when selling services or products to customers who promise to pay cash in the future. (p. 16)

Annual report Information that a company gives each year to its shareholders and other interested parties about its operations and financial position. It includes the financial statements and auditors' report, in addition to information and reports by management. (p. 29)

Assets Resources controlled by a business as a result of past events and from which future economic benefits are expected to flow to the business. (p. 16)

Balance sheet A financial statement that reports the assets, liabilities, and owner's equity at a specific date. (p. 16)

Cash flow statement A financial statement that provides information about the cash receipts and cash payments for a specific period of time. (p. 19)

Comparability An enhancing qualitative characteristic that accounting information has if it can be compared with the accounting information of other companies because the companies all use the same accounting principles. (p. 12)

Conceptual framework of accounting A coherent system that guides the development and application of accounting principles. (p. 11)

Consistency The use of the same accounting policies from year to year. Consistency is part of the comparability enhancing qualitative characteristic of accounting information. (p. 12)

Corporation A business organized as a separate legal entity under corporation law, with ownership divided into transferable shares. (p. 8)

Creditors All of the persons or entities that a company owes money to. (p. 6)

Drawings Withdrawals of cash or other assets from an unincorporated business for the owner's personal use. Drawings result in a decrease in an asset and a decrease in owner's equity. (p. 19)

Elements of the financial statements The components in the financial statements: assets, liabilities, owner's equity, revenues, and expenses. (p. 20)

Ethics The standards of conduct by which actions are judged as right or wrong, honest or dishonest, fair or not fair. (p. 9)

Expenses The cost of assets consumed or services used in a company's ordinary business activities. Expenses are decreases in assets or increases in liabilities, excluding withdrawals made by the owners, and result in a decrease to owner's equity. (p. 18)

Fair value Generally the amount the asset could be sold for in the market assuming the company is a going concern, not the amount that a company would receive in an involuntary liquidation or distress sale. (p. 13)

Faithful representation A fundamental qualitative characteristic of accounting information meaning information accurately depicts what really happened. (p. 12)

Generally accepted accounting principles (GAAP) An accepted set of accounting standards that includes broad principles, procedures, concepts, and standards. GAAP guide the reporting of economic events. (p. 9)

Going concern assumption An assumption that a company will continue to operate in the foreseeable future. (p. 12)

Historical cost An accounting concept that states that assets should be recorded at their historical (original) cost. (p. 13)

Income statement A financial statement that presents the revenues and expenses and resulting profit (or loss) for a specific period of time. (p. 18)

International Financial Reporting Standards (IFRS) A set of global standards developed by the International Accounting Standards Board (IASB) used for financial reporting mostly by publicly accountable enterprises but also by certain private entities. (p. 14)

Investments by the owner The increase in owner's equity that results from assets put into the business by the owner. (p. 19)

Investors Owners or potential owners of a business. (p. 6)

Liabilities Present obligations, arising from past events, the settlement of which will include an outflow of economic benefits. (p. 16)

Limited liability The legal principle that the owners' liability for the debts of the business is limited to the amount they invested in the business. (p. 8)

Loss The amount by which expenses are greater than revenues. A loss decreases owner's equity. (p. 18)

Matching concept The accounting concept that prescribes when a cost incurred by a business should be recognized as an expense. The general concept states that, if a direct association exists between a cost incurred and a revenue recognized, the cost should be recognized as an expense in the same period as the revenue is recognized. (p. 13)

Measurement The process of determining the amount that should be recognized. (p. 13)

Monetary unit concept A concept that states that only transaction data that can be expressed as an amount of money may be included in the accounting records. It is also assumed that the monetary unit is stable. (p. 13)

Neutral The characteristic of accounting information when it is not biased toward one position or another. Neutrality is part of the faithful representation fundamental qualitative characteristic of accounting information. (p. 12)

Note payable A liability supported by a written promise to pay a specific amount, at a specific time, in the future. (p. 17)

Objective of financial reporting The goal of providing useful information to investors and creditors (external users) to make decisions about providing resources to a business. (p. 7)

Owner's equity The owner's claim on the assets of the company, which is equal to total assets minus total liabilities. (p. 17)

Partnership An association of two or more persons to carry on as co-owners of a business for profit. (p. 8)

Performance obligation The obligation of a company to perform a service or deliver goods to a customer. (p. 13)

Periodicity concept The accounting concept that guides organizations in dividing up their economic activities into distinct time periods. The most common time periods are months, quarters, and years. (p. 12)

Prepaid expense The asset created when a business pays cash for costs incurred in advance of being used or consumed. (p. 16)

Profit The amount by which revenues are greater than expenses. Profit increases owner's equity. (p. 18)

Proprietorship A small business owned by one person. (p. 8)

Publicly accountable enterprises Publicly traded companies, as well as securities brokers and dealers, banks, and credit unions, whose role is to hold assets for the public as part of their primary business. (p. 14)

Recognition The process of recording a transaction in the accounting records. (p. 13)

Relevance A fundamental qualitative characteristic that accounting information has if it makes a difference in a decision. (p. 12)

Reporting entity concept The concept that the accounting for a reporting entity's activities should be kept separate and distinct from the accounting for the activities of its owner and all other reporting entities. (p. 11)

Revenue recognition principle The principle that guides the recognition of revenue when a performance obligation is satisfied, not when cash is exchanged. (p. 13)

Revenues The result of business activities that are undertaken to earn profit, such as performing services, selling merchandise inventory, renting property, and lending money. Revenues result in an increase in assets, or decrease in liabilities, and an increase in owner's equity. (p. 18)

Statement of owner's equity A financial statement that summarizes the changes in owner's equity for a specific period of time. (p. 18)

Timeliness An enhancing qualitative characteristic that accounting information has if information is made available to decision makers before it loses its capacity to influence decisions. (p. 12)

Understandability An enhancing qualitative characteristic that requires information to be presented in a clear and concise fashion, so that reasonably informed users of that information can interpret it and comprehend its meaning. (p. 12)

Unearned revenue The liability created when a customer pays in advance of being provided with a service or product. (p. 17)

Unlimited liability The principle that the owners of a business are personally liable (responsible) for all debts of the business. (p. 8)

Verifiability Information is verifiable if independent observers, using the same methods, obtain similar results. Verifiability is an enhancing qualitative characteristic. (p. 12)

▶ Self-Study Questions
Answers are at the end of the chapter.

(LO 1) K 1. The main objective of the financial statements is to provide useful information to
    (a) government in deciding if the company is respecting tax laws
    (b) increase the value of the company

    (c) investors and creditors that is useful when they are making decisions about the business
    (d) management that is useful when they are making decisions about the business

(LO 1) K 2. Which of the following statements about users of accounting information is **incorrect?**
(a) Management is an internal user.
(b) Taxing authorities are external users.
(c) Present creditors are external users.
(d) Regulatory authorities are internal users.

(LO 2) K 3. The three types of business organization forms are:
(a) proprietorships, small businesses, and partnerships.
(b) proprietorships, partnerships, and corporations.
(c) proprietorships, partnerships, and large businesses.
(d) financial, manufacturing, and service companies.

(LO 3) K 4. Which of the following statements about International Financial Reporting Standards (IFRS) is correct?
(a) All Canadian enterprises must follow IFRS.
(b) Under IFRS, companies that operate in more than one country must produce separate financial statements for each of those countries.
(c) All Canadian publicly accountable enterprises must use IFRS.
(d) Canadian private enterprises are not allowed to use IFRS. They must use ASPE.

(LO 3) C 5. Which of the following statements about the going concern assumption is correct?
(a) The going concern assumption is the assumption that the reporting entity will continue to operate in the future.
(b) Under the going concern assumption, all of the business's assets must be reported at their fair value.
(c) The financial statements must report whether or not a company is a going concern.
(d) The going concern assumption is not followed under ASPE.

(LO 3) K 6. Which of the following best describes when an event should be recognized in the accounting records?
(a) An event should be recognized in the accounting records if there is a change in assets, liabilities, or owner's equity and the change can be measured in monetary terms.
(b) An event should be recognized in the accounting records if it involves an interaction between the company and another external entity.
(c) Where there is uncertainty about a future event occurring or not, it should not be recognized.

(d) Accountants use tradition to determine which events to recognize.

(LO 4) AP 7. As at December 31, after its first year of operations, Bruske Company has assets of $12,500; revenues of $10,000; expenses of $5,500; beginning owner's capital of $8,000; and drawings of $1,500. What are the liabilities for Bruske Company as at December 31?
(a) $1,500
(b) $2,500
(c) $500
(d) $3,500

(LO 5) AP 8. Performing services on account will have the following effects on the components of the basic accounting equation:
(a) increase assets and decrease owner's equity.
(b) increase assets and increase owner's equity.
(c) increase assets and increase liabilities.
(d) increase liabilities and increase owner's equity.

(LO 5) AP 9. Bing Company pays $700 for store rent for the month. The basic analysis of this transaction on the accounting records is:
(a) the asset Cash is increased by $700 and the expense Rent Expense is increased by $700.
(b) the asset Cash is decreased by $700 and the expense Rent Expense is increased by $700.
(c) the asset Cash is decreased by $700 and the liability Rent Payable is increased by $700.
(d) the asset Cash is increased by $700 and the liability Rent Payable is decreased by $700.

(LO 6) C 10. Which of the following statements is true?
(a) An income statement presents the revenues, expenses, and changes in owner's equity for a specific period of time.
(b) The income statement shows information as at a specific point in time; the balance sheet shows information for a specified time period.
(c) The statement of cash flows summarizes cash inflows (receipts) and outflows (payments) as at a specific point in time.
(d) The income statement shows information for a specified time period; the balance sheet shows information as at a specific point in time.

▶ Questions

(LO 1) C 1. "Accounting is ingrained in our society and it is vital to our economic system." Do you agree? Explain.

(LO 1) C 2. Distinguish between internal and external users of accounting information. Include in your answer what kinds of questions both internal and external users might want answered.

(LO 1) K 3. What is the main objective of financial reporting?

(LO 2) C 4. Explain the differences between the following forms of business organization: (a) proprietorship, (b) partnership, (c) corporation.

(LO 3) C 5. Why is ethics important to the accounting profession? To statement users?

(LO 3) K 6. Why are there two sets of standards for profit-oriented enterprises in Canada?

(LO 3) K 7. What is the reporting entity concept?

(LO 3) C 8. Describe the fundamental qualitative characteristics of relevance and faithful representation.

(LO 3) C 9. What is the difference between historical cost and fair value measurements?

(LO 3) C   10. What criteria must be fulfilled for an event to be recognized in the accounting records? Give two examples of events that would not be recognized.

(LO 3) C   11. Explain the monetary unit concept.

(LO 4) K   12. What is the accounting equation and what is its purpose?

(LO 4) K   13. (a) Define assets, liabilities, and owner's equity. (b) What items increase and decrease owner's equity?

(LO 4) K   14. What is the difference between Accounts Payable and Accounts Receivable?

(LO 4) C   15. How is profit or loss determined?

(LO 4) K   16. List the types of accounts that are reported on (a) the balance sheet and (b) the income statement.

(LO 5) C   17. Can a business have a transaction in which only the left (assets) side of the accounting equation is affected? If yes, give an example.

(LO 5) AP   18. Alessandro Bega withdrew $8,000 from his business, Bega Pharmacy, which is organized as a proprietorship. Bega's accountant recorded this withdrawal as an increase in an expense and a decrease in cash. Is this treatment correct? Why or why not?

(LO 6) K   19. In what order should the financial statements be prepared? Why?

(LO 6) C   20. James is puzzled as he reads **Corus Entertainment's** financial statements. He notices that the numbers have all been rounded to the nearest thousand. He thought financial statements were supposed to be accurate and he is now wondering what happened to the rest of the money. Respond to James's concern.

When the financial results of **real companies** are used in the end-of-chapter material, the company's name is shown in red.

▶ Brief Exercises

BE1–1   A list of decisions made by different users of accounting information follows:

1. Decide whether the company pays fair salaries.
2. Decide whether the company can pay its obligations.
3. Decide whether a marketing proposal will be cost-effective.
4. Decide whether the company's profit will permit an increase in drawings.
5. Decide how the company should finance its operations.

The different users are identified in the table that follows. (a) Insert the number (1–5) of the kind of decision described above that each user would likely make. (b) Indicate whether the user is internal or external.

Identify users of accounting information. (LO 1) K

User	(a) Kind of Decision	(b) Internal or External User
Owner		
Marketing manager		
Creditor		
Chief financial officer		
Labour union		

BE1–2   Match each of the following forms of business organization with the correct set of characteristics: proprietorship (PP), partnership (P), and corporation (C).

(a) _____ Shared control; combined skills and resources
(b) _____ Easier to transfer ownership and raise funds; no personal liability; entity pays income tax
(c) _____ Simple to set up; owner pays income tax

Identify forms of business organization. (LO 2) C

BE1–3   Describe an ethical dilemma that each of the following individuals might encounter:

(a) A student in an introductory accounting course
(b) A production supervisor
(c) A banker

Discuss ethical issues. (LO 3) AN

BE1–4   Indicate whether each of the following statements is true or false by placing a T or an F in the blank at the start of each statement.

(a) _____ Relevance is an enhancing qualitative characteristic.
(b) _____ Timeliness is enhanced when a business uses the same accounting methods from year to year.
(c) _____ Understandability is an enhancing qualitative characteristic that requires accounting information to be clear and concise.
(d) _____ Information is verifiable if two independent people, using similar methods, achieve similar results.
(e) _____ Information is neutral when it is unbiased.

Identify application of concepts. (LO 3) C

Identify application of IFRS and ASPE. (LO 3) C

BE1–5   Indicate whether each of the following statements is true or false by placing a T or an F in the blank at the start of each statement.

(a) _____ Canadian publicly accountable enterprises have the choice to report under IFRS or ASPE.
(b) _____ All private enterprises must follow ASPE.
(c) _____ Companies are required to include a note in their financial statements stating if they are using IFRS or ASPE.
(d) _____ Using IFRS may help Canadian public companies attract investors from around the globe.

Identify GAAP concepts. (LO 3) C

BE1–6   Match each of the following terms with the best description below:

1. Historical cost
2. Revenue recognition
3. Going concern assumption
4. Reporting entity concept
5. Monetary unit concept

(a) _____ Transactions are recorded in terms of units of money.
(b) _____ Transactions are recorded based on the actual amount received or paid.
(c) _____ Indicates that personal and business record keeping should be kept separate.
(d) _____ Performance obligation has been satisfied.
(e) _____ Businesses are expected to continue operating indefinitely.

Identify the components of the financial statements. (LO 4) (C)

BE1–7   Match the following components with the best description below and indicate if the component is reported on the balance sheet (BS) or income statement (IS).

1. Assets
2. Liabilities
3. Owner's equity
4. Revenues
5. Expenses
6. Profit

Description	Component	Balance Sheet or Income Statement
(a) The increase in assets, or decrease in liabilities, resulting from business activities carried out to earn profit.		
(b) Resources controlled by a business that are expected to provide future economic benefits.		
(c) The owner's claim on the residual assets of the company.		
(d) Present obligations which are expected to result in an outflow of economic resources as a result of a past transaction.		
(e) The cost of resources consumed or services used in the company's business activities.		

Solve accounting equation. (LO 4) AP

BE1–8   Presented below is the accounting equation. Determine the missing amounts:

Assets	=	Liabilities	+	Owner's Equity
$75,000		$24,000		(a)
(b)		$150,000		$91,000
$89,000		(c)		$52,000

Solve accounting equation. (LO 4) AP

BE1–9   Use the accounting equation to answer each of the following questions:

(a) The liabilities of Weber Company are $120,000 and the owner's equity is $232,000. What is the amount of Weber Company's total assets?
(b) The total assets of King Company are $190,000 and its owner's equity is $91,000. What is the amount of its total liabilities?
(c) The total assets of Smith Company are $800,000 and its liabilities are equal to one half of its total assets. What is the amount of Smith Company's owner's equity?

Solve accounting equation. (LO 4) AP

Office Hours Videos also walk students through the approach and solution to selected questions from the text.

BE1–10   Butler Company is owned by Rachel Butler. The company had total assets of $850,000 and total liabilities of $550,000 at the beginning of the year. Answer each of the following independent questions:

(a) During the year, total assets increased by $130,000 and total liabilities decreased by $80,000. What is the amount of owner's equity at the end of the year?

(b) Total liabilities decreased by $95,000 during the year. The company incurred a loss of $40,000. R. Butler made an additional investment of $100,000 and made no withdrawals. What is the amount of total assets at the end of the year?

(c) Total assets increased by $45,000, and total liabilities decreased by $50,000. There were no additional owner's investments, and R. Butler withdrew $40,000. What is the amount of profit or loss for the year?

BE1–11 Indicate whether each of the following items is an asset (A), liability (L), or part of owner's equity (OE).

_____ 1. Accounts receivable	_____ 4. Supplies
_____ 2. Salaries payable	_____ 5. Owner's capital
_____ 3. Equipment	_____ 6. Notes payable

Identify assets, liabilities, and owner's equity. (LO 4) K

BE1–12 Presented below are eight business transactions. Indicate whether the transactions increased (+), decreased (−), or had no effect (NE) on each element of the accounting equation.

(a) Purchased $250 of supplies on account.
(b) Performed $500 of services on account.
(c) Paid $300 of operating expenses.
(d) Paid $250 cash on account for the supplies purchased in item (a) above.
(e) Invested $1,000 cash in the business.
(f) Owner withdrew $400 cash.
(g) Hired an employee to start working the following month.
(h) Received $500 from a customer who had been billed previously in item (b) above.
(i) Purchased $450 of equipment in exchange for a note payable.

Determine effects of transactions on accounting equation. (LO 5) AP

Use the following format, in which the first one has been done for you as an example:

			Owner's Equity			
Transaction	Assets	Liabilities	Capital	Drawings	Revenues	Expenses
a	+$250	+$250	NE	NE	NE	NE

BE1–13 Match the following basic transaction analysis with the best description of the economic event.

1. Cash increased by $9,000 and the owner's equity account, M. Vijayakumar, Capital, is increased by $9,000.
2. Cash is decreased by $6,000 and the asset account Prepaid Rent is increased.
3. Supplies is increased by $1,000 and the liability account Accounts Payable is increased by $1,000.
4. Accounts receivable is increased by $900 and the revenue account Service Revenue is increased by $900.

Match basic transaction analysis with transaction description. (LO 5) AP

Description	Transaction Analysis
(a) Cash paid in advance for rent.	_____
(b) Owner invests cash in the business.	_____
(c) Supplies are purchased on account.	_____
(d) Company provides service on account.	_____

BE1–14 Classify each of the following items as owner's investments (I), drawings (D), revenue (R), expenses (E), or as having no effect on owner's equity (NE):

(a) _____ Advertising expense
(b) _____ Commission fees earned
(c) _____ Cash received from the company's owner
(d) _____ Amounts paid to employees
(e) _____ Services performed on account
(f) _____ Utilities incurred
(g) _____ Cash distributed to company owner

Determine effects of transactions on owner's equity. (LO 4, 5) AP

BE1–15 Presented below is information from the statements of owner's equity for Kerkan Consulting for the first three years of operation. Determine the missing amounts:

Determine missing items in owner's equity. (LO 4, 6) AP

	2015	2016	2017
J. Kerkan, capital, January 1	$ 0	$68,000	$ (c)
Investment in the year	50,000	0	20,000
Profit (loss) for the year	25,000	(b)	17,000
Drawings in the year	(a)	33,000	12,000
J. Kerkan, capital, December 31	68,000	65,000	(d)

BE1–16 Prairie Company is owned and operated by Natasha Woods. In alphabetical order below are the financial statement items for Prairie Company. Using the appropriate items, prepare an income statement for the month ended October 31, 2017.

Prepare an income statement. (LO 6) AP

Accounts payable	$90,000	N. Woods, capital, October 1, 2017	$36,000
Accounts receivable	77,500	N. Woods, drawings	6,000
Advertising expense	3,600	Rent expense	2,600
Cash	59,300	Service revenue	23,000

Prepare a statement of owner's equity. (LO 6) AP

BE1–17 Refer to the data in BE1–16. Using these data and the information from Prairie's income statement, prepare a statement of owner's equity.

Prepare a balance sheet. (LO 6) AP

BE1–18 Refer to the data in BE1–16. Using these data and the information from Prairie's statement of owner's equity prepared in BE1–17, prepare a balance sheet for Prairie Company.

▶ Exercises

Identify users of accounting information. (LO 1) C

E1–1   1. The following are users of financial information:

_____ Customers	_____ Store manager
_____ Canada Revenue Agency	_____ Supplier
_____ Labour unions	_____ Chief Financial Officer
_____ Marketing manager	_____ Loan officer

2. The following questions could be asked by an internal user or an external user.

_____ Can the company afford to give our members a pay raise?
_____ How does the company's profitability compare with other companies in the industry?
_____ Do we need to borrow money in the near future?
_____ What does it cost to manufacture each unit produced?
_____ Has the company paid all income tax amounts owing?
_____ Which product should we emphasize?

Instructions

(a) In part 1, identify the users as being either external users (E) or internal users (I).
(b) In part 2, identify each of the questions as being more likely asked by an internal user (I) or an external user (E).

Identify users and uses of accounting information. (LO 1) C

E1–2   **lululemon Athletica Inc.,** a public company, is known around the world for its clothing and accessories. It has more than 250 stores in Canada, the United States, Australia, and New Zealand.

Instructions

(a) Identify two internal users of lululemon's accounting information. Write a question that each user might try to answer by using accounting information.
(b) Identify two external users of lululemon's accounting information. Write a question that each user might try to answer by using accounting information.

Relate concepts to forms of business organization. (LO 2) C

E1–3   Listed below are several statements regarding different forms of business organization.

Instructions

For each statement, indicate if that statement is true or false for each of the forms of business organization by placing a T or an F in each column.

	Proprietorship	Partnership	Publicly Traded Corporation
(a) Owners have limited liability.	_____	_____	_____
(b) Records of the business are combined with the personal records of the owner or owners.	_____	_____	_____
(c) Required to follow IFRS.	_____	_____	_____
(d) Pays income taxes on its profits.	_____	_____	_____
(e) Owners are called "shareholders."	_____	_____	_____
(f) Will have more than one owner.	_____	_____	_____
(g) Has a limited life.	_____	_____	_____
(h) Has a separate legal existence from its owners.	_____	_____	_____

Match accounting concepts with descriptions. (LO 3) C

E1–4   Below is a list of accounting concepts:

1. Relevance
2. Faithful representation
3. Comparability
4. Verifiability

5. Neutrality
6. Understandability

Instructions

Match each concept with the best description that follows:

(a) _____ An economic event is reported so it represents what actually happened.
(b) _____ Users find the information in the financial statements helps them to make decisions.
(c) _____ The accounting information shows the profit of a business without consideration of what the owner may want to report.
(d) _____ Financial statements make sense to business people.
(e) _____ Henry is able to confirm the information presented in the financial statements.
(f) _____ Très Chic Boutique uses the same accounting methods as other similar boutiques.

E1-5   Here are some terms from the chapter:

Match words with descriptions. (LO 1, 3, 5) K

1. Accounts payable	7. Assets
2. Expenses	8. Corporation
3. Creditor	9. Unearned revenue
4. International Financial Reporting Standards (IFRS)	10. Generally accepted accounting principles (GAAP)
5. Prepaid expense	11. Accounts receivable
6. Profit	12. Owner's equity

Instructions

Match each term with the best description that follows:

(a) _____ A company that raises money by issuing shares
(b) _____ An accepted set of accounting standards that includes broad principles, procedures, and concepts.
(c) _____ Obligations to suppliers of goods
(d) _____ Amounts due from customers
(e) _____ Owner's claims against the residual company's resources
(f) _____ Payment of cash for costs incurred in advance of being used
(g) _____ A party that a company owes money to
(h) _____ Resources owned by a business that are expected to provide future economic benefit
(i) _____ The set of accounting standards that all publicly traded enterprises in Canada have to follow
(j) _____ Results when revenues exceed expenses
(k) _____ The cost of assets consumed or services used in a company's ordinary business activities
(l) _____ A liability arising when a customer pays in advance of receiving service

E1-6   Below is a partially completed income statement and statement of owner's equity for Gary Dickson Engineering Company.

Determine missing items. *(LO 4) AP

Consulting revenue		$18,000
Expenses		
Advertising expense	$ 400	
Rent expense	(a)	
Utilities expense	900	
Salaries expense	3,500	
		6,800
Profit (loss)		$ (b)
G. Dickson, capital, August 1		$ 5,000
Add: Investment	(e)	
Profit	(c)	21,200
		26,200
Less: Drawings		(d)
G. Dickson, capital, July 31		$21,700

Instructions

Fill in the missing amounts.

E1-7   Shane Cooke began a business, Cooke Company, on January 1, 2017, with an investment of $100,000. The company had the following assets and liabilities on the dates indicated:

Calculate profit (or loss). (LO 4) AP

December 31	Total Assets	Total Liabilities
2017	$370,000	$210,000
2018	440,000	290,000
2019	525,000	355,000

Instructions

Use the accounting equation and the change in owner's equity during the year to calculate the profit (or loss) for:

(a) 2017, assuming Shane Cooke's drawings were $50,000 for the year.

(b) 2018, assuming Shane Cooke made an additional investment of $40,000 and had no drawings in 2018.

(c) 2019, assuming Shane Cooke made an additional investment of $10,000 and his drawings were $60,000 for the year.

Classify accounts. (LO 5) C

E1–8   Below are some items found in the financial statements of Petra Zizler, Orthodontist.

	(a)	(b)
1. Accounts payable	L	BS
2. Accounts receivable		
3. Cash		
4. Equipment		
5. Interest payable		
6. Interest revenue		
7. Interest expense		
8. Investment by the owner		
9. Service revenue		
10. Prepaid rent		
11. P. Zizler, capital (opening balance)		
12. P. Zizler, drawings		
13. Salaries expense		
14. Supplies		
15. Supplies expense		
16. Unearned revenue		

Instructions

Indicate:

(a) whether each of the above items is an asset (A), liability (L), or part of owner's equity (Eq); and

(b) which financial statement—income statement (IS), statement of owner's equity (OE), or balance sheet (BS)—it would be reported on. The first one has been done for you as an example.

Identify GAAP. (LO 3, 5, 6) C

E1–9   James Company, a proprietorship, had the following selected business transactions during the year:

1. Land with a cost of $415,000 was recorded at its fair value of $465,000.

2. A lease agreement to rent equipment from an equipment supplier starting next year was signed. The rent is $500 per month and the lease is for two years. Payments are due at the start of each month. Nothing was recorded in James Company's accounting records when the lease was signed.

3. James paid the rent for an apartment for the owner's personal use and charged it to Rent Expense.

4. James prepaid for a one-year insurance policy for $1,200. The amount was charged to Insurance Expense.

5. James included a note in its financial statements stating the company is a going concern and is following ASPE.

Instructions

(a) In each situation, identify whether the accounting treatment is correct or not, and why.

(b) If it is incorrect, state what should have been done.

Determine events to be recognized. (LO 3, 5) C

E1–10   The following is a list of independent events:

1. A company pays $10,000 cash to purchase equipment at a bankruptcy sale. The equipment's fair value is $15,000.

2. A Canadian company purchases equipment from a company in the United States and pays US$5,000 cash. It cost the company $5,200 Canadian to purchase the U.S. dollars from its bank.

3. A company provides $4,000 of services to a customer on account.

4. A company hires a new chief executive officer, who will bring significant economic benefit to the company. The company agrees to pay the new executive officer $500,000 per year.

5. A company signs a contract to provide $10,000 of services to a customer. The customer pays the company $4,000 cash at the time the contract is signed. The performance obligation required by the company has not been completed.

Instructions

(a) Should the transaction be recorded in the accounting records? Explain why or why not.

(b) If the transaction should be recorded, indicate the amount. Explain.

Give examples of transactions. (LO 5) C

E1–11   A list of effects on the accounting equation follows.

1. Increases an asset and increases a liability.

2. Increases an asset and increases owner's equity.

3. Decreases an asset and decreases a liability.

4. Decreases owner's equity and decreases an asset.
5. Increases a liability and decreases owner's equity.
6. Increases one asset and decreases another asset.

Instructions

For each effect, give an example of a transaction that would cause it.

E1–12 At the beginning of March, Brister Software Company had Cash of $12,000, Accounts Receivable of $18,000, Accounts Payable of $4,000, and G. Brister, Capital of $26,000. During the month of March, the following transactions occurred:

Analyze effects of transactions for existing company. (LO 5) AP

1. Purchased equipment for $23,000 from Digital Equipment. Paid $3,000 cash and signed a note payable for the balance.
2. Received $12,000 from customers for contracts billed in February.
3. Paid $3,000 for March rent of office space.
4. Paid $2,500 of the amounts owing to suppliers at the beginning of March.
5. Provided software services to Kwon Construction Company for $7,000 cash.
6. Paid BC Hydro $1,000 for energy used in March.
7. G. Brister withdrew $5,000 cash from the business.
8. Paid Digital Equipment $2,100 on account of the note payable issued for the equipment purchased in transaction 1. Of this, $100 was for interest expense.
9. Hired an employee to start working in April.
10. Incurred advertising expense on account for March, $1,500.

Instructions

Prepare a tabular analysis of the above transactions, as shown in Illustration 1-13 in the text. The first row contains the amounts the company had at the beginning of March.

Analyze transactions. Calculate profit and increase in owner's equity. (LO 4, 5) AP

E1–13 A tabular summary of the transactions for Star & Co., an accounting firm, for its first month of operations, July 2017, follows:

	Cash	+	Accounts Receivable	+	Prepaid Insurance	+	Equipment	=	Accounts Payable	+	B. Star, Capital	−	B. Star, Drawings	+	Revenues	−	Expenses
1	$18,000						$6,000				$24,000						
2	−4,000						8,000		$4,000								
3	−750				$750												
4	3,500		$4,800												$8,300		
5	−2,000								−2,000								
6	−3,300												−3,300				
7	−800																−$800 Rent
8	1,350		−1,350														
9	−2,700																−2,700 Salaries
10									420								−420 Utilities

Instructions

(a) Describe each transaction that occurred in the month.
(b) Calculate the amount of profit for the month.
(c) Calculate the increase in owner's equity for the month.

E1–14 An analysis of transactions for Star & Co. for July 2017 was presented in E1–13.

Prepare financial statements. (LO 6) AP

Instructions

Prepare an income statement and statement of owner's equity for July and a balance sheet at July 31.

E1–15 Atlantic Cruise Co. is owned by Irina Temelkova. The following information is an alphabetical listing of financial statement items for the company for the year ended May 31, 2017:

Prepare income statement and statement of owner's equity. (LO 6) AP

Accounts payable	$ 47,750	Interest expense	$ 20,960
Accounts receivable	42,950	Investments by owner	5,847
Advertising expense	3,640	Maintenance expense	82,870
Building	122,570	Notes payable	379,000
Cash	20,080	Other expenses	66,500
Equipment	553,300	Prepaid insurance	1,283
I. Temelkova, capital, June 1, 2016	311,182	Salaries expense	126,950
I. Temelkova, drawings	33,950	Supplies	16,800
Insurance expense	2,566	Ticket revenue	350,640

Instructions

Prepare an income statement and a statement of owner's equity for the year.

Prepare balance sheet.
(LO 6) AP

E1–16 Refer to the financial information in E1–15 for Atlantic Cruise Co. at May 31, 2017.

Instructions

Prepare the balance sheet.

Calculate profit and owner's equity and prepare balance sheet. (LO 6) AP

E1–17 Judy Cumby is the sole owner of Deer Park, a public camping ground near Gros Morne National Park. Judy has gathered the following financial information for the year ended March 31, 2017:

Revenues—camping fees	$150,000	Revenues—general store	$ 40,000
Operating expenses	150,000	Cash on hand	9,400
Supplies on hand	2,500	Original cost of equipment	110,000
Fair value of equipment	125,000	Notes payable	70,000
Accounts payable	11,500	J. Cumby, capital, April 1, 2016	17,000
Accounts receivable	21,000	J. Cumby, drawings	5,000
Camping fees collected for April	10,000	Insurance paid for in advance for April to June 2017	600

Instructions

(a) Calculate Deer Park's profit for the year.
(b) Calculate Judy's owner's equity for the period ended March 31, 2017.
(c) Prepare a balance sheet at March 31, 2017.

▶ Problems: Set A

Identify users and uses of accounting information.
(LO 1) S

P1–1A Specific financial decisions often depend more on one type of accounting information than another. Consider the following independent, hypothetical situations:

1. Pierson Industries is thinking about extending credit to a new customer. The terms of credit would require the customer to pay within 45 days of receipt of the goods.
2. Dean Gunnerson owns Toys and Sports Co., a manufacturer of quality toys and sports equipment. The company manufactures a line of mountain bikes and a line of treadmills. Dean wants to know which line is more profitable.
3. The president of Hi-tech Adventure is trying to determine whether the company has enough cash to buy additional equipment.
4. Standen Bank is thinking about extending a loan to a small company. The company would be required to make interest payments at the end of each year for five years, and to repay the loan at the end of the fifth year.

Instructions

(a) Identify types of user(s) of accounting information in each situation and indicate if they are external or internal.
(b) For each situation, state whether the user making the decision would depend mostly on information about (1) the business's economic resources and claims to the resources, or (2) the economic performance of the business. Justify your choice.

Taking It Further is an extra question at the end of each problem designed to challenge you to think beyond the basic concepts covered in the problem and to provide written explanations. Your instructor may assign problems with or without this extra element.

TAKING IT FURTHER Why is it important to users of financial statements to know that the statements have been prepared by individuals who have high standards of ethical behaviour?

Determine forms of business organization and type of accounting standards.
(LO 2, 3) AP

P1–2A Four independent situations follow:

1. Tom Courtney, a student looking for summer employment, started a dog-walking service. He picks up the dog while its owner is at work and returns it after a walk.
2. Joseph Counsell and Sabra Surkis each own a bike shop. They have decided to combine their businesses and try to expand their operations to include snowboards. They expect that in the coming year they will need funds to expand their operations.
3. Three chemistry professors have formed a business that uses bacteria to clean up toxic waste sites. Each has contributed an equal amount of cash and knowledge to the venture. The use of bacteria in this situation is experimental, and legal obligations could result.
4. Abdur Rahim has run a successful but small organic food store for over five years. The increased sales at his store have made him believe the time is right to open a chain of organic food stores across the country. Of course, this will require a substantial investment for inventory and equipment, as well as for employees and other resources. Abdur has minimal personal savings.

Instructions

(a) In each case, explain what form of organization the business is likely to take: proprietorship, partnership, or corporation. Give reasons for your choice.

(b) In each case, indicate what accounting standards, IFRS or ASPE, the business is likely to use in its financial statements. Give reasons for your choice.

TAKING IT FURTHER   Frequently, individuals start a business as a proprietorship and later incorporate the business. What are some of the advantages of doing this?

P1-3A   The following selected data are for Carducci Importers for its first three years of operations:

Determine missing items.
(LO 4) AP

January 1:	2015	2016	2017
Total assets	$ 40,000	$ (f)	$ (j)
Total liabilities	0	50,000	(k)
Total owner's equity	(a)	75,000	(l)
December 31:			
Total assets	(b)	140,000	172,000
Total liabilities	50,000	(g)	65,000
Total owner's equity	(c)	97,000	(m)
Changes during year in owner's equity:			
Investments by owner during the year	7,000	0	(n)
Drawings by owner during the year	15,000	(h)	36,000
Profit or loss for the year	(d)	40,000	(o)
Total revenues for the year	132,000	(i)	157,000
Total expenses for the year	(e)	95,000	126,000

Instructions

Determine the missing amounts.

TAKING IT FURTHER   What information does the owner of a company need in order to decide whether he or she is able to withdraw cash from the business?

P1-4A   Listed in alphabetical order, the following selected items (in thousands) were taken from Parker Information Technology Company's December 31, 2017, financial statements:

Classify accounts and prepare accounting equation.
(LO 4) AP

1.	L	BS	Accounts payable	$ 810	7.	___ ___	Rent expense	$4,800
2.	___	___	Accounts receivable	900	8.	___ ___	S. Parker, capital, Jan. 1	6,600
3.	___	___	Cash	3,500	9.	___ ___	S. Parker, drawings	3,900
4.	___	___	Consulting revenue	15,730	10.	___ ___	Salaries expense	3,200
5.	___	___	Equipment	5,700	11.	___ ___	Utilities expense	350
6.	___	___	Interest expense	790				

Instructions

(a) In each case, identify on the blank line in the first column whether the item is an asset (A), liability (L), capital (C), drawings (D), revenue (R), or expense (E) item. The first one has been done for you as an example.

(b) Indicate on the blank line in the second column which financial statement—income statement (IS), statement of owner's equity (OE), or balance sheet (BS)—each item would be reported on. The first one has been done for you as an example.

(c) Calculate the company's profit or loss for the year ended December 31, 2017.

TAKING IT FURTHER   Is it important for Parker Information Technology Company to keep track of its different types of expenses as separate items? Explain.

P1-5A   Four independent situations follow:

Assess accounting treatment.
(LO 3, 5) C

1. Human Solutions Incorporated believes its people are its most significant asset. It estimates and records their value on its balance sheet.

2. Sharon Barton, president and owner of Barton Industries, has instructed the accountant to report the company's land and buildings at its current value of $500,000 instead of its cost of $350,000. "Reporting the land and buildings at $500,000 will make it easier to get a loan from the bank next month," Sharon states.

3. Will Viceira, owner of the Music To You Company, bought an electric guitar for his personal use. He paid for the guitar with company funds and debited the Equipment account.

4. West Spirit Oil Corp. is a very small oil and gas company that is listed on the Toronto Stock Exchange. The president asked each of the shareholders to approve using ASPE instead of IFRS to reduce expenses for accounting services. He received unanimous approval and has advised the company accountant to prepare the 2017 financial statements accordingly.

Instructions

(a) For each of the above situations, determine if the accounting treatment of the situation is correct or incorrect. Explain why.

(b) If the accounting treatment is incorrect, explain what should be done.

TAKING IT FURTHER   Why is it important for companies to follow generally accepted accounting principles when preparing their financial statements?

Analyze transactions and calculate owner's equity.
(LO 4, 6) AP

P1-6A   Frank Petronick decided to start an accounting practice after graduation from university. The following is a list of events that occurred concerning Frank's practice during June 2017, the first month of operations.

June 1	After shopping around, Frank found an office to lease and signed a lease agreement. The lease calls for a payment of $1,050 rent per month.
4	Borrowed $3,846 from his grandmother so that he could buy some office furniture for his new office.
4	Deposited the $3,846 plus $530 of his own cash in a new bank account at BMO under the name Petronick Accounting Services.
6	Paid the landlord the first month's rent.
8	Purchased furniture for $3,160 on account.
11	Moved into the office and obtained the first assignment from a client to prepare year-end financial statements for $1,865.
15	Performed the work on the assignment and sent an invoice to the customer for $1,865.
15	Paid half of the amount of the purchase of furniture.
18	Purchased supplies on account for $344.
26	Paid for Internet services, $49 cash.
28	Collected $900 of the June 15 billing to the customer.
30	Withdrew cash from the business of $128 for personal expenses.

Instructions

(a) Prepare a tabular analysis of the effects of the above transactions on the accounting equation.

(b) From an analysis of the owner's equity, calculate the account balance in F. Petronick, Capital, at June 30.

TAKING IT FURTHER   Assume on June 30 there is $144 of supplies on hand and that $200 of supplies had been used during June. What amount should be reported as an asset, Supplies, on the June 30 balance sheet? What amount should be reported as Supplies Expense?

Analyze transactions and prepare balance sheet.
(LO 3, 4, 5, 6) AP

P1-7A   The following events concern Anita LeTourneau, a Manitoba law school graduate, for March 2017:

1. On March 4, she spent $20 on a lottery ticket.
2. On March 7, she won $250,000 in the lottery and immediately quit her job as a junior lawyer.
3. On March 10, she decided to open her own law practice, and deposited $50,000 of her winnings in a business chequing account, LeTourneau Legal Services.
4. On March 14, she purchased a new luxury condominium with a down payment of $150,000 from her personal funds plus a home mortgage of $200,000.
5. On March 15, Anita signed a rental agreement for her law office space for $2,500 a month, starting March 15. She paid the first month's rent, as it is due on the 15th of each month.
6. On March 19, she hired a receptionist. He will be paid $500 a week and will begin working on March 24.
7. On March 20, she purchased equipment for her law practice from a company that had just declared bankruptcy. The equipment was worth at least $15,000 but Anita was able to buy it for only $10,000.
8. On March 21, she purchased $400 of supplies on account.
9. On March 24, she purchased an additional $6,500 of equipment for her law practice for $3,000 plus a $3,500 note payable due in six months.
10. On March 31, she performed $3,500 of legal services on account.
11. On March 31, she received $2,500 cash for legal services to be provided in April.
12. On March 31, she paid her receptionist $500 for the week.
13. On March 31, she paid $400 for the supplies purchased on account on March 21.

Instructions

(a) Prepare a tabular analysis of the effects of the above transactions on the accounting equation.

(b) Calculate profit and owner's equity for the month ended March 31.

(c) Prepare a balance sheet at March 31.

TAKING IT FURTHER   How should Anita determine which transactions should be recorded and which ones should not be recorded?

P1-8A   Izabela Jach opened a medical office under the name Izabela Jach, MD, on August 1, 2017. On August 31, the balance sheet showed Cash $3,000; Accounts Receivable $1,500; Supplies $600; Equipment $7,500; Accounts Payable $5,500; Note Payable $3,000; and I. Jach, Capital, $4,100. During September, the following transactions occurred:

Analyze transactions and prepare financial statements. (LO 4, 5, 6) AP

Sept. 4   Collected $800 of accounts receivable.
    5   Provided services of $10,500, of which $7,700 was collected from patients and the remainder was on account.
    7   Paid $2,900 on accounts payable.
    12   Purchased additional equipment for $2,300, paying $800 cash and leaving the balance on account.
    15   Paid salaries, $2,800; rent for August, $1,900; and advertising expenses, $275.
    18   Collected the balance of the accounts receivable from August 31.
    20   Withdrew $1,000 for personal use.
    26   Borrowed $3,000 from the Bank of Montreal on a note payable.
    28   Signed a contract to provide medical services, not covered under the government health plan, to employees of CRS Corp. in October for $5,700. CRS Corp. will pay the amount owing after the medical services have been provided.
    29   Received the telephone bill for September, $325.
    30   Billed the government $10,000 for services provided to patients in September.

Instructions

(a) Beginning with the August 31 balances, prepare a tabular analysis of the effects of the September transactions on the accounting equation.
(b) Prepare an income statement and statement of owner's equity for September, and a balance sheet at September 30.

TAKING IT FURTHER   What are the differences between purchasing an item on account and signing a note payable for the amount owing?

P1-9A   Pavlov's Home Renovations was started in 2008 by Jim Pavlov. Jim operates the business from an office in his home. Listed below, in alphabetical order, are the company's assets and liabilities as at December 31, 2017, and the revenues, expenses, and drawings for the year ended December 31, 2017:

Prepare financial statements. (LO 6) AP

Accounts payable	$ 7,850	Operating expenses	$ 3,545
Accounts receivable	10,080	Prepaid insurance	1,685
Cash	8,250	Salaries expense	88,230
Equipment	29,400	Service revenue	153,750
Insurance expense	3,375	Supplies	595
Interest expense	1,195	Supplies expense	20,095
J. Pavlov, drawings	44,800	Unearned revenue	15,000
Notes payable	30,800	Vehicles	42,000

Jim's capital at the beginning of 2017 was $45,850. He made no investments during the year.

Instructions

Prepare an income statement, statement of owner's equity, and balance sheet.

TAKING IT FURTHER   Why is it necessary to prepare the income statement first, then the statement of owner's equity, and the balance sheet last?

P1-10A   Here are incomplete financial statements for Lee Company:

Determine missing amounts, and comment. (LO 6) AN

LEE COMPANY
Balance Sheet
February 28, 2017

Assets		Liabilities and Owner's Equity	
Cash	$ 9,500	Liabilities	
Accounts receivable	5,300	Notes payable	$26,000
Land	(i)	Accounts payable	(iii)
Building and equipment	41,500	Total liabilities	43,800
Total assets	$ (ii)	M. Lee, Capital	(iv)
		Total liabilities and owner's equity	$91,300

LEE COMPANY
Income Statement
Year Ended February 28, 2017

Revenues		
Service revenues		$95,000
Expenses		
Salaries expense	$32,000	
Other expenses	(v)	
Supplies expense	1,500	
Total expenses		59,500
Profit		(vi)

LEE COMPANY
Statement of Owner's Equity
Year Ended February 28, 2017

M. Lee, capital, March 1, 2016	$22,000
Add: Investments	(vii)
Profit	(viii)
	62,500
Less: M. Lee, drawings	(ix)
M. Lee, capital, February 28, 2017	(x)

Instructions

(a) Calculate the missing amounts (i) to (x).
(b) Write a memo explaining (1) the sequence for preparing the financial statements, and (2) the interrelationships between the income statement, statement of owner's equity, and balance sheet.

TAKING IT FURTHER   Why isn't the balance sheet dated the same way as the income statement and statement of owner's equity: "Year Ended February 28, 2017"?

Discuss errors and prepare corrected balance sheet.
(LO 3, 4, 5, 6) AP

P1-11A   The balance sheet of Reflections Book Shop at April 30, 2017, is as follows:

REFLECTIONS BOOK SHOP
Balance Sheet
April 30, 2017

Assets		Liabilities and Owner's Equity	
Building	$110,000	Accounts payable	$ 15,000
Accounts receivable	37,000	Equipment	58,000
C. Dryfuss, capital	85,000	Supplies	1,000
Cash	10,000	"Plug"	338,000
Land	50,000		
Notes payable	120,000		
	$412,000		$412,000

Charles Dryfuss, the owner of the book shop, admits that he is not an accountant. In fact, he couldn't get the balance sheet to balance without "plugging" the numbers (making up numbers to give the desired result). He gives you the following additional information:

1. A professional real estate appraiser estimated the value of the land at $50,000. The actual cost of the land was $36,000.

2. Accounts receivable include amounts due from customers in China for 35,000 yuan, which is about $5,000 Canadian. Dryfuss didn't know how to convert the currency for reporting purposes so he added the 35,000 yuan to the $2,000 due from Canadian customers. He thought it more important to know how much he was owed by each customer in the currency they would likely pay him with anyway.

3. Dryfuss reasons that equipment is a liability because it will cost him money in the future to maintain these items.

4. Dryfuss reasons that the note payable must be an asset because getting the loan was good for the business. If he had not obtained the loan, he would not have been able to purchase the land and buildings.

5. Dryfuss believes that his capital account is also an asset. He has invested in the business, and investments are assets; therefore his capital account is an asset.

Instructions

(a) Identify any corrections that should be made to the balance sheet, and explain why by referring to the appropriate accounting principle, assumption, or concept.

(b) Prepare a corrected balance sheet for Reflections Book Shop at April 30. (*Hint:* The capital account may need to be adjusted in order to balance.)

TAKING IT FURTHER Explain to Dryfuss why all transactions affect at least two financial statement items.

⏵ Problems: Set B

P1–1B Specific financial decisions often depend more on one type of accounting information than another. Consider the following independent, hypothetical situations:

Identify users and uses of accounting information.
(LO 1) S

1. Samuel Colt owns a company called Organics To You, which operates a chain of 20 organic food stores across Canada. Samuel wants to determine which brand of pasta is the most profitable for the store.

2. The Backroads Company is considering extending credit to a new customer—Europe Tours Company. The terms of credit would require the customer to pay within 45 days of receipt of the goods.

3. The senior partner of Accountants R Us is trying to determine if the partnership is generating enough cash to increase the partners' drawings and still ensure the partnership has enough cash to expand its operations.

Instructions

(a) Identify types of user(s) of accounting information in each situation and indicate if they are external or internal.

(b) For each situation, state whether the user making the decision would depend mostly on information about (1) the business's economic resources and claims to the resources, or (2) the economic performance of the business. Justify your choice.

TAKING IT FURTHER Why is it important to users of financial statements to know that the statements have been prepared by individuals who have high standards of ethical behaviour?

P1–2B Four independent situations follow:

Determine forms of business organization and types of accounting standards.
(LO 2, 3) AP

1. Three computer science students have formed a business to develop a new social media application (app) for the Internet. Each has contributed an equal amount of cash and knowledge to the venture. While their app looks promising, they are concerned about the legal liabilities that their business might confront.

2. Shamira Hatami, a student looking for summer employment, opened a small cupcake shop out of her summer vacation home.

3. Robert Steven and Tom Cheng each own a snowboard manufacturing business and have now decided to combine their businesses. They expect that in the next year they will need funds to expand their operations.

4. Darcy Becker, Ellen Leboeuf, and Meg Dwyer recently graduated with marketing degrees. Friends since childhood, they have decided to start a consulting business that focuses on branding strategies for small and medium-sized businesses.

Instructions

(a) In each case, explain what form of organization the business is likely to take: proprietorship, partnership, or corporation. Give reasons for your choice.

(b) In each case indicate what accounting standards, IFRS or ASPE, the business is likely to use in its financial statements. Give reasons for your choice.

TAKING IT FURTHER   What are the advantages of two individuals first forming a partnership to run a business, and later incorporating?

Determine missing items.
(LO 4) AP

P1-3B   The following selected data are for Alexei Imports for its first three years of operations.

January 1:	2015	2016	2017
Total assets	(a)	$75,000	$127,000
Total liabilities	0	(e)	(k)
Total owner's equity	60,000	(f)	(l)
December 31:			
Total assets	75,000	(g)	170,000
Total liabilities	(b)	45,000	(m)
Total owner's equity	45,000	(h)	100,000
Changes during year in owner's equity:			
Investments by owner during the year	5,000	(i)	0
Drawings by owner during the year	0	10,000	(n)
Profit or loss for the year	(c)	35,000	30,000
Total revenues for the year	(d)	(j)	160,000
Total expenses for the year	120,000	95,000	(o)

Instructions

Determine the missing amounts.

TAKING IT FURTHER   What information does the owner of a company need in order to decide whether he or she needs to invest additional cash in the business?

Classify accounts and prepare accounting equation.
(LO 4) AP

P1-4B   Listed in alphabetical order, the following selected items (in thousands) were taken from Paradise Mountain Family Resort's December 31 financial statements:

1.	L	BS	Accounts payable	$ 195	10.			Operating expenses	$ 871
2.			Accounts receivable	160	11.			Other assets	615
3.			Cash	120	12.			Other liabilities	396
4.			Equipment	600	13.			Other revenue	52
5.			Insurance expense	15	14.			Rent revenues	1,295
6.			Interest expense	45	15.			Salaries payable	125
7.			Land and buildings	1,495	16.			T. Yuen, capital, January 1	934
8.			Notes payable	950	17.			T. Yuen, drawings	20
9.			Prepaid insurance	30	18.			Unearned rent revenue	24

Instructions

(a) In each case, identify on the blank line, in the first column, whether the item is an asset (A), liability (L), capital (C), drawings (D), revenue (R), or expense (E) item. The first one has been done for you as an example.

(b) Indicate on the blank line, in the second column, which financial statement—income statement (IS), statement of owner's equity (OE), or balance sheet (BS)—each item would be reported on. The first one has been done for you as an example.

(c) Calculate the company's profit or loss for December 31, 2017.

TAKING IT FURTHER   Is it important for Paradise Mountain Family Resort to keep track of its different types of expenses as separate items? Explain.

Assess accounting treatment.
(LO 3, 4) C

P1-5B   Three independent situations follow:

1. In preparing its financial statements, Karim Company estimated and recorded the impact of the recent death of its president.

2. Because of a "flood sale," equipment worth $300,000 was purchased by Montigny Company for only $200,000. The equipment was recorded at $300,000 on Montigny's books.

3. Vertical Lines Company was on the verge of filing for bankruptcy, but a turnaround in the economy has resulted in the company being very healthy financially. The company president insists that the accountant put a note in the financial statements that states the company is a real going concern now.

Instructions

(a) For each of the above situations, determine if the accounting treatment of the situation is correct or incorrect. Explain why.

(b) If the accounting treatment is incorrect, explain what should be done.

TAKING IT FURTHER   Why is it important for companies to follow generally accepted accounting principles when preparing their financial statements?

P1–6B   Kensington Bike Repair Shop was started on April 1 by L. Depres. A summary of the April transactions follows:

Analyze transactions and calculate owner's equity. (LO 4, 5, 6) AP

April	1	Invested $21,000 to start the repair shop.
	2	Purchased equipment for $9,000, paying $3,000 cash and signing a note payable for the balance.
	5	Paid rent for the month, $1,050.
	7	Purchased $975 of supplies on account.
	9	Received $3,200 in cash from customers for repair services.
	16	Provided repair services on account to customers, $2,900.
	26	Collected $1,200 on account for services billed on April 16.
	27	Paid for supplies purchased on April 7.
	28	Paid $290 for advertising.
	29	Withdrew $1,300 for personal use.
	30	Received April utility bill, $200.
	30	Paid part-time employee salaries, $1,400.
	30	Billed a customer $750 for repair services.
	30	Received an advance from a customer for repairs to be performed in May, $2,100.

Instructions

(a) Prepare a tabular analysis of the effects of the above transactions on the accounting equation.

(b) From an analysis of the owner's equity, calculate the account balance in L. Depres, Capital at April 30.

TAKING IT FURTHER   Assume on April 30 there is $500 of supplies on hand and that $475 of supplies had been used during April. What amount should be reported as an asset, Supplies, on the April 30 balance sheet? What amount should be reported as Supplies Expense?

P1–7B   Lynn Barry started her own consulting firm, Barry Consulting, on June 1, 2017. The following transactions occurred during the month of June:

Analyze transactions and prepare balance sheet. (LO 3, 4, 5, 6) AP

June	1	Sold her shares in Big Country Airlines for $7,000, which she deposited in her personal bank account.
	1	Transferred $6,000 from her personal account to a business account in the name of Barry Consulting.
	2	Paid $900 for office rent for the month.
	3	Purchased $545 of supplies on account.
	5	Paid $95 to advertise in the *County News*.
	9	Received $3,275 for services provided.
	12	Withdrew $600 for personal use.
	15	Performed $5,000 of services on account.
	17	Paid $1,800 for employee salaries.
	21	Received $3,000 for services provided on account on June 15.
	22	Paid for the supplies purchased on account on June 3.
	25	Signed a contract to provide consulting services to a client for $5,500. Services will be performed and paid for in July.
	26	Borrowed $5,500 from the bank and signed a note payable.
	29	Used part of the cash borrowed from the bank on June 26 to purchase equipment for $2,150.
	30	Paid $150 for telephone service for the month.
	30	Received $2,500 from client for consulting to be provided in July.

Instructions

(a) Prepare a tabular analysis of the effects of the above transactions on the accounting equation.

(b) Calculate profit and owner's equity for the month ended June 30.

(c) Prepare a balance sheet at June 30.

TAKING IT FURTHER How should Lynn determine which transactions should be recorded and which ones should not be recorded?

Analyze transactions and prepare financial statements.
(LO 4, 5, 6) AP

P1–8B Fraser Baker opened Baker's Accounting Service in Winnipeg on September 1, 2017. On September 30, the balance sheet showed Cash $5,700; Accounts Receivable $2,100; Supplies $350; Equipment $7,600; Accounts Payable $4,300; and F. Baker, Capital $11,450. During October, the following transactions occurred:

Oct.	1	Paid $3,800 of the accounts payable.
	1	Paid $900 rent for October.
	4	Collected $1,550 of the accounts receivable.
	5	Hired a part-time office assistant at $80 per day to start work the following week.
	8	Purchased additional equipment for $4,000, paying $500 cash and signing a note payable for the balance.
	14	Performed $900 of accounting services on account.
	15	Paid $300 for advertising.
	18	Collected $400 from customers who received services on October 14.
	20	Paid $500 for family dinner celebrating Fraser's son's university graduation.
	25	Borrowed $8,000 from the Manitoba Bank on a note payable.
	26	Sent a statement reminding a customer that he still owed the company money from September.
	28	Earned revenue of $5,400, of which $3,100 was paid in cash and the balance was due in November.
	29	Paid the part-time office assistant $720 for working nine days in October.
	29	Received $2,800 cash for accounting services to be performed in November.
	30	Received the telephone bill for the month, $205.
	30	Withdrew $1,200 cash for personal expenses.

Instructions

(a) Beginning with the September 30 balances, prepare a tabular analysis of the effects of the October transactions on the accounting equation.

(b) Prepare an income statement and statement of owner's equity for October, and a balance sheet at October 31.

TAKING IT FURTHER Fraser is confused about the accounting treatment of the October 20 transaction. Explain the reason for this treatment.

Prepare financial statements.
(LO 6) AP

P1–9B Judy Johansen operates an interior design business, Johansen Designs. Listed below, in alphabetical order, are the company's assets and liabilities as at December 31, 2017, and the revenues, expenses, and drawings for the year ended December 31, 2017:

Accounts payable	$ 6,590		Prepaid insurance	$ 600
Accounts receivable	6,745		Rent expense	18,000
Cash	11,895		Salaries expense	70,500
Equipment	9,850		Service revenue	132,900
Furniture	15,750		Supplies	675
Insurance expense	1,800		Supplies expense	3,225
Interest expense	350		Telephone expense	3,000
J. Johansen, drawings	40,000		Unearned revenue	2,500
Notes payable	7,000		Utilities expense	2,400

Judy's capital at the beginning of 2017 was $35,800. She made no investments during the year.

Instructions

Prepare an income statement, statement of owner's equity, and balance sheet.

TAKING IT FURTHER Why is the balance sheet prepared after the statement of owner's equity?

P1–10B   Here are incomplete financial statements for Deol Company:

Determine missing amounts, and comment. (LO 6) AN

DEOL COMPANY
Balance Sheet
October 31, 2017

Assets		Liabilities and Owner's Equity	
Cash	$ 5,000	Liabilities	
Accounts receivable	10,000	Notes payable	$59,600
Land	(i)	Accounts payable	(ii)
Building and equipment	45,000	Total liabilities	66,500
Total assets	$110,000	Owner's equity	
		B. Deol, capital	(iii)
		Total liabilities and owner's equity	$ (iv)

DEOL COMPANY
Income Statement
Year Ended October 31, 2017

Revenues		
Service revenue		$80,000
Expenses		
Salaries expense	$37,500	
Other expenses	(v)	
Supplies expense	6,000	
Total expenses		62,500
Profit		$ (vi)

DEOL COMPANY
Statement of Owner's Equity
Year Ended October 31, 2017

B. Deol, capital, November 1, 2016	$35,000
Add: Investments	(vii)
Profit	(viii)
	57,500
Less: B. Deol, drawings	(ix)
B. Deol, capital, October 31, 2017	$ (x)

Instructions

(a) Calculate the missing amounts (i) to (x).

(b) Write a memo explaining (1) the sequence for preparing the financial statements, and (2) the interrelationships between the income statement, statement of owner's equity, and balance sheet.

TAKING IT FURTHER   Why aren't the income statement and the statement of owner's equity dated the same way as the balance sheet: "October 31, 2017"?

P1–11B   GG Company was formed on January 1, 2017. On December 31, Gil Goodman, the owner, prepared a balance sheet:

Discuss errors and prepare corrected balance sheet. (LO 3, 4, 5, 6) AP

```
                              GG COMPANY
                              Balance Sheet
                            December 31, 2017

         Assets                          Liabilities and Owner's Equity

Cash                    $ 15,000      Accounts payable           $ 45,000
Accounts receivable       55,000      Boat loan payable            13,000
Supplies                  20,000      G. Goodman, capital          25,000
Boat                      18,000      Profit for 2017              25,000
                        $108,000                                 $108,000
```

Gil willingly admits that he is not an accountant. He is concerned that his balance sheet might not be correct. He gives you the following additional information:

1. The boat actually belongs to Gil Goodman, not to GG Company. However, because he thinks he might take customers out on the boat occasionally, he decided to list it as an asset of the company. To be consistent, he also listed as a liability of the company the personal bank loan that he took out to buy the boat.
2. Gil spent $15,000 to purchase more supplies than he usually does, because he heard that the price of the supplies was expected to increase. It did, and the supplies are now worth $20,000. He thought it best to record the supplies at $20,000, as that is what it would have cost him to buy them today.
3. Gil has signed a contract to purchase equipment in January 2018. The company will have to pay $5,000 cash for the equipment when it arrives and the balance will be payable in 30 days. Guy has already reduced Cash by $5,000 because he is committed to paying this amount.
4. The balance in G. Goodman, Capital is equal to the amount Gil originally invested in the company when he started it on January 1, 2017.
5. Gil paid $1,200 for a one-year insurance policy on December 31. He did not include it in the balance sheet because the insurance is for 2018 and not 2017.
6. Gil knows that a balance sheet needs to balance but on his first attempt he had $108,000 of assets and $83,000 of liabilities and owner's equity. He reasoned that the difference was the amount of profit the company earned this year and added that to the balance sheet as part of owner's equity.

Instructions

(a) Identify any corrections that should be made to the balance sheet, and explain why by referring to the appropriate accounting concept, assumption, or principle.
(b) Prepare a corrected balance sheet for GG Company. (*Hint:* To get the balance sheet to balance, adjust owner's equity.)

TAKING IT FURTHER　Assume that Gil did not make any withdrawals from the company in 2017, nor any investments other than his initial investment of $25,000. What was the actual profit for the year?

CHAPTER 1: BROADENING YOUR PERSPECTIVE

▶ Financial Reporting and Analysis

Financial Reporting Problem

BYP1–1　Corus Entertainment's financial statements have been reproduced in Appendix A at the back of the textbook.

Instructions

(a) Many companies use a calendar year for their financial statements. What does Corus use?

(b) Where in the financial statements does it indicate that Corus statements have been prepared using IFRS?
(c) What four financial statements has Corus presented in its financial statements?
(d) Where in the financial statements does it indicate that Corus reports the financial amounts in thousands of Canadian dollars?
(e) What were Corus's total assets as at August 31, 2014? As at August 31, 2013?
(f) What were Corus's total liabilities as at August 31, 2014? As at August 31, 2013?
(g) What is the amount of change in Corus's profit (Corus calls this "net income") from 2013 to 2014?

Interpreting Financial Statements

BYP1-2   Apple Inc. is an international corporation that designs, manufactures, and markets a range of mobile communication and media devices, personal computing products, and portable digital music players, as well as a variety of related software, networking solutions, and hardware products. In the assets section of its 2014 balance sheet, the following data were presented:

APPLE INC. Balance Sheets (partial) (in U.S. millions)		
Assets	September 27, 2014	September 28, 2013
Cash and cash equivalents	$ 13,844	$ 14,259
Short-term marketable securities	11,233	26,287
Accounts receivable, less allowance	17,460	13,102
Inventories	2,111	1,764
Deferred tax assets	4,318	3,453
Vendor non-trade receivables	9,759	7,539
Other current assets	9,806	6,882
Long-term marketable securities	130,162	106,215
Property, plant and equipment, net	20,624	16,597
Goodwill	4,616	1,577
Acquired intangible assets, net	4,142	4,179
Other assets	3,764	5,146
Total assets	$231,839	$207,000

Instructions

(a) For a company such as Apple, what do you think its most important economic resource is? Where is this recorded on the balance sheet? At what value (if any) should it be shown?

(b) Do the assets reported on the balance sheet above tell you what Apple is worth? What information does the balance sheet give you about the company's value?

▶ Critical Thinking

Collaborative Learning Activity

Note to instructor: Additional instructions and material for this group activity can be found on the Instructor Resource Site and in *WileyPLUS.*

BYP1-3   In this group activity, students will be asked to identify (or determine) the information they would require if they were making a decision whether or not to lend money or to invest in a company.

Communication Activity

BYP1-4   Robert Joote is the owner of Peak Company. Robert has prepared the following balance sheet:

PEAK COMPANY Balance Sheet Month Ended December 31, 2017	
Assets	
Equipment	$ 20,500
Cash	10,500
Supplies	2,000
Accounts payable	(5,000)
Total assets	$ 28,000
Liabilities and Owner's Equity	
R. Joote, capital	$ 23,500
Accounts receivable	(3,000)
R. Joote, drawings	(2,000)
Prepaid insurance	(2,500)
Notes payable	12,000
Total liabilities and owner's equity	$ 28,000

Robert didn't know how to determine the balance for his capital account so he just "plugged" the number. (He made up a number that would give him the result that he wanted.) He had heard somewhere that assets had to equal the total of liabilities and owner's equity so he made up a number for capital so that these would be equal.

Instructions

In a memo, explain to Robert (a) how to determine the balance for his capital account, (b) why his balance sheet is incorrect, and (c) what he should do to correct it. Include in your explanation how the financial statements are interrelated, and why the order of preparation is important.

"All About You" Activity

BYP1–5 In the "All About You" feature, we introduced the idea that being financially literate has a major impact on our ability to meet our financial goals and even on our health and happiness. We all face financial decisions each day. Some of these decisions are small and others are critical. Making the right financial decisions is important to your well-being. Following are three financial decisions that you as a student will likely have to make.

1. You have to pay for your tuition, books, and spending money during college. You are trying to decide what kind of summer job you should apply for and whether or not you need to work part-time during the school year.

2. You need to have transportation to get back and forth to college each day. You are trying to decide if you can afford to buy a second-hand car and pay for parking or whether you should use public transit. You will have to borrow money to purchase the car.

3. You will be graduating this year and have received job offers from two different companies. You are deciding which company you should work for, and you want to accept a position in a company that is financially stable and has growth potential.

Instructions

(a) For each decision, indicate what financial information you would want to have in order to make an optimal decision.
(b) Based on what you have learned in Chapter 1, how will learning about accounting help you with the above decisions?

The Santé Smoothie Saga starts in this chapter and continues in every chapter throughout the book. This feature chronicles the growth of a hypothetical small business to show how the concepts you learn in each chapter can be applied in the real world.

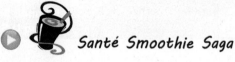
Santé Smoothie Saga

BYP1–6 Natalie Koebel spent much of her youth playing sports. She passed many hours on the soccer field and in the dance studio. As Natalie grew older, her passion for healthy living continued as she started practising yoga. Now, at the start of her second year in college, Natalie is investigating various possibilities for starting her own business as part of the requirements of the Entrepreneurship program she is taking. A long-time friend insists that Natalie has to somehow include healthy living in her business plan and, after a series of brainstorming sessions, Natalie settles on the idea of operating a smoothie business. She will start on a part-time basis. She will make the product at home, bottle it, and take it to the yoga studio where she exercises because they have agreed to purchase it on a regular basis. Now that she has started thinking about it, the possibilities seem endless. During the summer, she will concentrate on fresh fruit and vegetable smoothies. The first difficult decision is coming up with the perfect name for her business. In the end, she settles on "Santé Smoothies" and then moves on to more important issues.

Instructions

(a) What form of business organization—proprietorship, partnership, or corporation—do you recommend that Natalie use for her business? Discuss the benefits and weaknesses of each form and give the reasons for your choice.
(b) Will Natalie need accounting information? If yes, what information will she need and why? How often will she need this information?
(c) In addition to Natalie, who do you anticipate to be the users of Natalie's accounting information? What information will these identified users need and why?
(d) Identify specific asset, liability, and equity accounts that Santé Smoothies will likely use to record its business transactions.
(e) Should Natalie open a separate bank account for the business? Why or why not?

ANSWERS TO CHAPTER QUESTIONS

ANSWERS TO ACCOUNTING IN ACTION INSIGHT QUESTIONS

All About You Insight, p. 5

Q: How might learning accounting help you make sure that your employer or bank hasn't made an error with your paycheque or bank account?

A: Learning accounting will provide you with tools that will help you track your transactions and ensure that the bank balance is correct. You will learn how to calculate how much your

paycheque should be. You will learn how to calculate interest on loans and the total cost of borrowing. Examining your potential employer's financial statements will help you predict if the company will have enough cash to pay you now and if the company has growth potential. Stay tuned to the "All About You" features and related activities for more!

Ethics Insight, p. 10

Q: Who are the stakeholders in this situation? How would they be impacted by this situation?

A: The stakeholders include Jennifer, who risks violating her profession's ethical code of conduct if she goes along with the falsified performance statistics; Currie's employees, who may lose their jobs if the company doesn't get more contracts; Currie's competitors, who are at an unfair advantage if they lose the contract to Currie based on its falsified information; and the transportation company, which risks Currie not being able to fulfill its contract in the long term if it goes out of business because its performance is not as good as it presented.

ANSWERS TO SELF-STUDY QUESTIONS

1. c   2. d   3. b   4. c   5. a   6. a   7. a   8. b   9. b   10. d

2 THE RECORDING PROCESS

CHAPTER PREVIEW

In Chapter 1, we used the accounting equation to analyze transactions. The combined effects of these transactions were presented in a tabular form. This method could work for small companies like Softbyte (the fictitious company discussed in Chapter 1) because they have relatively few transactions. But imagine Tonica Kombucha, in the feature story that processes many more transactions, using the same tabular format as Softbyte. With the volume of kombucha sales during a year, the company has too many transactions to record each one this way. This would be impractical, expensive, and unnecessary. Instead, companies use a set of procedures and records to keep track of transaction data more easily.

The entire set of procedures used to prepare an entity's financial statements is called the accounting cycle. The accounting cycle begins with the analyzing, recording, and posting of transactions, which is the focus of this chapter. The remainder of the accounting cycle is discussed in Chapters 3 and 4 and is illustrated here.

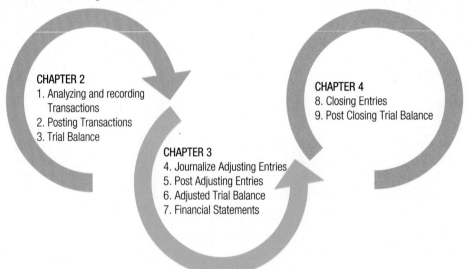

CHAPTER 2
1. Analyzing and recording Transactions
2. Posting Transactions
3. Trial Balance

CHAPTER 3
4. Journalize Adjusting Entries
5. Post Adjusting Entries
6. Adjusted Trial Balance
7. Financial Statements

CHAPTER 4
8. Closing Entries
9. Post Closing Trial Balance

FEATURE STORY　　SLAYING THE DRAGONS TO BREW UP SALES

TORONTO, Ont.—Tonica Kombucha went face to face with the dragons and prevailed. The idea for this beverage start-up was sparked when yoga instructor Zoey Shamai visited New Mexico. While there, she was introduced to a centuries-old fermented tea beverage called kombucha. It's said to have many health benefits, including helping digestion and metabolism and detoxing the liver. "Everyone was making it down there," said Ms. Shamai "But when I returned to Toronto, it wasn't really available, so I started making it myself."

Ms. Shamai originally brewed about 15 litres of kombucha a week in her kitchen and sold it to her yoga students. Then she started selling it in Toronto health food stores. Word spread, and she decided to turn her sideline into a full-fledged business.

To raise enough money to produce kombucha commercially, she faced the dragons on the CBC TV show *Dragons' Den*. Getting ready to pitch her idea to the potential investors meant she had to pore over her financial figures. "Just sitting down and combing through your numbers to put together a pitch is an eye-opening process, and one that I might not have done as carefully if I wasn't going on the show," said Ms. Shamai.

Doing her accounting homework paid off. The show's "dragons" pledged $125,000 in capital in return for a one-quarter interest in Tonica. Thanks to accounting, when the "dragons" asked Ms. Shamai what her projected sales were, she could answer—she told them that she expected to bring in $303,000 in the coming year and that she had about a 71% markup—the amount she charges customers above her costs.

The successful start-up is now making 500 cases of the beverage a week at a new 1,000-square-foot facility in Toronto. The product, in flavours such as peach, ginger, and blueberry, is sold in some 300 grocery stores across Canada, including Whole Foods and Pusateri's.

Ms. Shamai is certain to keep a close eye on her business transactions to determine how much to charge retailers and how much to expect in sales, to ensure her *Dragons' Den* investors receive a return on their investment.

Sources: Jump Branding and Design Inc., "Tonica Kombucha Slays the Dragons," www.howhigh.ca, November 22, 2012; Derek Flack, "Toronto Beverage Startup Set to Enter the Dragon's Den," blogTO.com, November 21, 2012; "Pitches: Tonica Kombucha," *Dragons' Den,* November 21, 2012, www.cbc.ca/dragonsden/pitches/tonica-kombucha; Wency Leung, "Bottoms Up to the Latest Health Beverage Craze: Kombucha," *Globe and Mail*, May 29, 2012; Tonica Kombucha website, www.tonicakombucha.com.

CHAPTER OUTLINE ▸ LEARNING OBJECTIVES

1 Describe how accounts, debits, and credits are used to record business transactions.

The Account
- Debits and credits
- Double-entry accounting

DO IT 1
Normal account balances

2 State how a journal is used in the recording process and journalize transactions.

Analyzing and Recording Transactions
- The accounting cycle and steps in the recording process
- The journal

DO IT 2
Recording business activities

3 Explain how a ledger helps in the recording process and post transactions.

The Ledger
- Posting
- The recording process illustrated
- Summary illustration of journalizing and posting

DO IT 3
Posting

4 Prepare a trial balance.

The Trial Balance
- Limitations of a trial balance
- Locating errors
- Some process explanations

DO IT 4
Trial balance

LEARNING OBJECTIVE 1   Describe how accounts, debits, and credits are used to record business transactions.

The Account

An **account** is an individual accounting record of increases and decreases in a specific asset, liability, or owner's equity item. For example, Softbyte has separate accounts called Cash, Accounts Receivable, Accounts Payable, Service Revenue, Salaries Expense, and so on.

In its simplest form, an account has three parts: (1) the title of the account, (2) a left or a debit side, and (3) a right or a credit side. Because these parts of an account are positioned like the letter T, it is called a **T account**. The basic form of an account is shown in Illustration 2-1.

▶ **ILLUSTRATION 2-1**
Basic form of T account

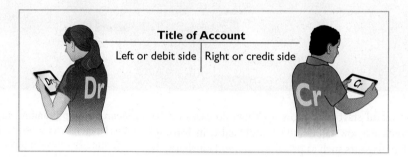

The actual format that is used in real life is more complex than the above T, and will be explained later in the chapter. The T account format is a learning tool that will be used throughout the book to explain basic accounting relationships. It is also a format used by professional accountants for analytical purposes.

DEBITS AND CREDITS

The term **debit** means left. The term **credit** means right. These terms are often abbreviated as "Dr." for debit and "Cr." for credit. Debit and credit are simply directional signals that describe where entries are made in the accounts. Entering an amount on the left side of an account is called debiting the account. Entering an amount on the right side is called crediting the account.

When the totals of the two sides are compared, an account will have a debit balance if the total of the debit amounts exceeds the credits. On the other hand, an account will have a credit balance if the credit amounts are more than the debits.

The recording of debits and credits in an account is shown in Illustration 2-2 for Softbyte's cash transactions. The data are taken from the Cash column of the tabular summary in Illustration 1-10.

▶ **ILLUSTRATION 2-2**
Tabular summary and account form comparison

Tabular Summary	
Cash	
+$15,000	
−7,000	
+1,200	
+1,500	
−600	
−900	
−200	
−250	
+600	
−1,300	
$ 8,050	

Account Form			
Cash			
(Debits)		(Credits)	
	15,000		7,000
	1,200		600
	1,500		900
	600		200
			250
			1,300
Balance	8,050		

In the tabular summary, every positive item is the receipt of cash. Every negative item is the payment of cash. Notice that in the account format, the increases in cash are recorded as debits, and the decreases in cash are recorded as credits. The account balance, a debit of $8,050, indicates that Softbyte had $8,050 more increases than decreases in cash. We will learn in the next section why debits and credits are used in this way.

Debit and Credit Procedure

It is very important to understand that debit does not mean increase nor does it mean decrease. Sometimes we use a debit to increase an account and sometimes we use a debit to decrease an account. Credits are the same—sometimes a credit is used to increase an account and sometimes a credit is used to decrease an account. The system of using debits and credits is based on the accounting equation, introduced in Chapter 1, and the definitions of debit and credit, as shown in the following diagram:

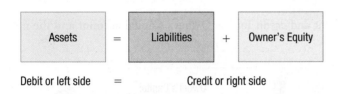

We will use this diagram to apply debit and credit procedures to each part of the accounting equation—assets, liabilities, and owner's equity—in the following sections.

Assets and Liabilities. All accounts have a normal balance, which is the side that *increases* the account balance. Because assets are on the left or debit side of the accounting equation, the normal balance of an asset is also on the left or debit side of the account. Logically, then, increases to asset accounts need to be recorded on the debit side and decreases in assets must be entered on the right or credit side. This is why in Illustration 2-2, the Softbyte illustration, increases in Cash—an asset account—were entered on the debit (left) side, and decreases in Cash were entered on the credit (right) side.

Similarly, because liabilities are on the right or credit side of the accounting equation, the normal balance of a liability account is on the right or credit side. This means increases in liabilities are entered on the right or credit side, and decreases in liabilities are entered on the left or debit side.

Debits	Credits
Increase assets	Decrease assets
Decrease liabilities	Increase liabilities

To summarize, because assets are on the left side of the accounting equation and this is the opposite of liabilities, increases and decreases in assets are recorded opposite from increases and decreases in liabilities. The effects that debits and credits have on assets and liabilities and the normal balances are as follows:

Helpful hint Increases in accounts are always on the same side as the normal balance for that account. For assets, increases are to the left, and for liabilities, increases are to the right.

Knowing the normal balance in an account may help you find errors. For example, a credit balance in an asset account such as Land or a debit balance in a liability account such as Wages Payable probably means there was a recording error. Occasionally, an abnormal balance may be correct. The Cash account, for example, will have a credit balance when a company has overdrawn its bank balance.

Owner's Equity. As liabilities and owner's equity are on the same side of the accounting equation, the rules of debit and credit are the same for these two types of accounts. Credits increase owner's equity and debits decrease owner's equity. And as explained in Chapter 1, owner's equity is increased by owner's investments and revenues. It is decreased by owner's drawings and expenses. Separate accounts are kept for each of these types of transactions.

Owner's Capital. The normal balance of the Owner's Capital account is a credit balance. Therefore, investments by owners are credited to the owner's capital account and this increases owner's equity. For example, when cash is invested in the business, the Cash account is debited and Owner's Capital is credited.

Debits	**Credits**
Decrease Owner's Equity	Increase Owner's Equity

The rules of debit and credit for the Owner's Capital account and the normal balance are as follows:

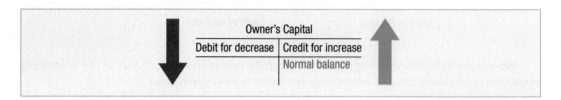

Owner's Capital
Debit for decrease	Credit for increase
	Normal balance

Owner's Drawings. An owner may withdraw cash or other assets for personal use. Withdrawals are recorded as debits because withdrawals decrease owner's equity. Withdrawals could be debited directly to Owner's Capital. However, it is better to have a separate account, called Drawings, as we did in Chapter 1. The separate account makes it easier to add up the total withdrawals for the accounting period and to prepare the statement of owner's equity.

Because withdrawals decrease owner's equity, the drawings account has a normal debit balance. Credits to an owner's drawings account are unusual, but might be used, for example, to correct a withdrawal recorded in error.

Debits	**Credits**
Increase Owner's Drawings	Decrease Owner's Drawings

The rules of debit and credit for the Drawings account and the normal balance are as follows:

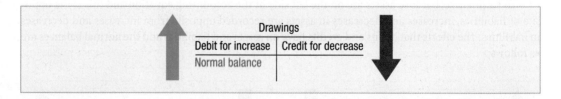

Drawings
Debit for increase	Credit for decrease
Normal balance	

Note that increases and decreases to the drawings account are recorded opposite to increases and decreases in Owner's Capital. That is because investments, which increase owner's equity, are recorded in Owner's Capital, and withdrawals, which decrease owner's equity, are recorded in Drawings.

Revenues and Expenses. Revenues normally have a credit balance; therefore, increases to revenues are credits. This is because when revenues are earned, this benefits the owners of the business, and so owner's equity increases. Therefore, like the Owner's Capital account, revenue accounts are increased by credits and decreased by debits. Credits to revenue accounts should exceed the debits.

Expenses normally have a debit balance; therefore, increases to expenses are debits. This is because as expenses are incurred, owner's equity decreases. Therefore, like the Owner's Drawings account, expense accounts are increased by debits and decreased by credits. Debits to expense accounts should exceed the credits.

Debits	Credits
Decrease revenues	Increase revenues
Increase expenses	Decrease expenses

Since revenues are the positive factor in calculating profit, and expenses are the negative factor, it is logical that the increase and decrease sides of revenue accounts should be the reverse of expense accounts.

The effect of debits and credits on revenues and expenses and the normal balances are as follows:

Summary of Debit and Credit Effects

Illustration 2-3 shows the expanded accounting equation and a summary of the debit/credit rules on each type of account.

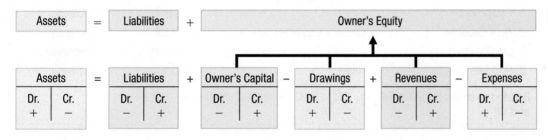

▶ **ILLUSTRATION** 2-3
Summary of debit/credit rules and effects for the expanded accounting equation

Remember, the normal balance of each account is on its increase side. So assets, drawings, and expense accounts have a normal debit balance, while liabilities, owner's capital, and revenue accounts have a normal credit balance.

DOUBLE-ENTRY ACCOUNTING

In Chapter 1, you learned that each transaction must affect two or more accounts to keep the basic accounting equation in balance. This means that, when we record transactions, **debits must equal credits**. This is known as the **double-entry accounting system** in which the dual (two-sided) effect of each transaction is recorded in the appropriate accounts.

Helpful hint Debits must equal credits for each transaction.

If every transaction is recorded with equal debits and credits, then the sum of all the debits to the accounts must equal the sum of all the credits. And, if the debit and credit procedures are correctly applied, the total amount of debits will always equal the total amount of credits and the accounting equation stays in balance. This provides a logical method for recording transactions and ensuring the amounts are recorded accurately.

The debit and credit conventions are the building blocks for understanding the double-entry accounting system and the accounting cycle.

BEFORE YOU GO ON...DO IT — Normal Account Balances

Brooke Schwenke has just rented space in a shopping mall where she will open a salon and spa called the Oasis Spa. Brooke has determined that the company will need the following accounts:

1. Accounts Payable
2. Cash
3. B. Schwenke, Capital
4. B. Schwenke, Drawings
5. Equipment
6. Rent Expense
7. Service Revenue
8. Supplies

   (a) Indicate whether each of these accounts is an asset, liability, or owner's equity account. If it is an owner's equity account, indicate what type it is (e.g., owner's capital, drawings, revenue, or expense).
   (b) What is the normal balance of these accounts?
   (c) Will a debit increase or decrease these accounts?

Action Plan

- Use the expanded accounting equation to determine the type of account.
- Remember that the normal balance of an account is on its increase side.
- Remember that assets are increased by debits, and that liabilities and owner's equity are increased by credits.

Helpful hint **Normal Balances**

DR	CR
Assets	Liabilities
Expenses	Revenues
Drawings	Owner's Capital

Solution

	(a)	(b)	(c)
Account	Type of Account	Normal Balance	Debit Effect
1. Accounts Payable	Liability	Credit	Decrease
2. Cash	Asset	Debit	Increase
3. B. Schwenke, Capital	Owner's Equity (capital)	Credit	Decrease
4. B. Schwenke, Drawings	Owner's Equity (drawings)	Debit	Increase
5. Equipment	Asset	Debit	Increase
6. Rent Expense	Owner's Equity (expense)	Debit	Increase
7. Service Revenue	Owner's Equity (revenue)	Credit	Decrease
8. Supplies	Asset	Debit	Increase

Related exercise material: BE2–1, BE2–2, BE2–3, BE2–4, BE2–5, E2–1, E2–2, E2–3, E2–4, and E2–5.

LEARNING OBJECTIVE 2 — State how a journal is used in the recording process and journalize transactions.

Analyzing and Recording Transactions

THE ACCOUNTING CYCLE AND STEPS IN THE RECORDING PROCESS

As stated in the chapter preview, the **accounting cycle** is a series of steps followed by accountants in preparing financial statements. There are nine steps in this cycle, as shown in Illustration 2-4.

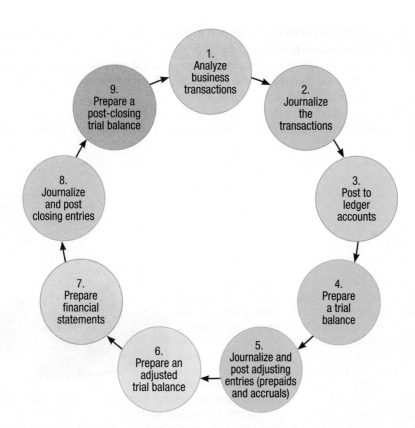

The procedures used in analyzing and recording transaction information are the first three steps, shown in Illustration 2-5. These three steps are also known as the **recording process**. This is the focus of the remainder of this chapter. We will consider the remaining six steps in Chapters 3 and 4.

Analyzing Business Transactions

As shown in Illustration 2-5, the recording process begins with analyzing the transaction. Recall that a transaction is recorded only if it causes the financial position of the entity, that is the assets, liabilities and/or owners' equity to change. Evidence of a transaction comes from a source document, such as a sales slip, cheque, bill, cash register tape, or bank statement. A company analyzes this evidence to determine the transaction's effects on specific accounts.

Recall also from Chapter 1 that we started to learn how to analyze transactions. Once we determined that a transaction should be recorded, we analyzed it to determine how the transaction affected the accounting equation. We saw in the transaction analysis process that we needed to identify the accounts that were changed, whether the account increased or decreased, and if so, by how much. This analysis is often referred to as the basic analysis of the transaction.

After the basic analysis is complete, then the debit and credit procedures you learned in the previous section of this chapter are applied to determine which account or accounts should be debited and which account or accounts should be credited. This is often referred to as the debit/credit analysis of the transaction.

Analyzing transactions is the most difficult part of the accounting cycle because there are so many different types of transactions. Throughout this textbook, and in later accounting courses, you will continue to be introduced to different transactions. As you learn about new transactions, remember to first do your basic analysis and then the debit/credit analysis. If you follow this system, you will improve your ability to correctly analyze and record transactions.

After the transaction has been analyzed, then it can be entered in the accounting records—steps 2 and 3 of the accounting cycle. We will explain how this is done in the following sections on the journal and the ledger.

ACCOUNTING IN ACTION
BUSINESS INSIGHT

Does hiring a great employee add value for a company? In the case of sports teams, owners, players, and fans all agree that having the most talented players makes a huge difference. But how does a team attract and keep those players? Is simply offering the player a contract enough to attract talent? Not these days. And accountants would agree that simply having a player sign a contract doesn't change the team's assets, liabilities, or owner's equity. This isn't a transaction that would get recorded in the team's accounting records even if it does bring value to the team.

Signing bonuses are different because they affect cash. In the National Hockey League, they are used partly to deal with the league's salary caps, which restrict how much can be included in individual players' and the whole team's salaries in each year. A signing bonus can be paid in one year but be included in the team's salary cap in a year that's financially advantageous to the team. For example, in July 2014, the Chicago Blackhawks signed star players Jonathan Toews and Patrick Kane to identical eight-year contract extensions reportedly worth $84 million each. It was reported that $44 million of that amount is signing bonuses, which drop from $7 million in the first year down to $4 million in the last year. The accounting question as to whether these bonuses should be considered assets or expenses is complicated.

Sources: Mike Brehm, "How Jonathan Toews-Patrick Kane Contracts Break Down," *USA TODAY*, July 12, 2014; Rory Boylen, "Jonathan Toews and Patrick Kane Sign Eight-Year Extensions with $10.5 Million Cap Hits—A Fair Market Price," *The Hockey News*, July 9, 2014; James Mirtle, "Big Signing Bonuses Becoming NHL's New Norm," *Globe and Mail* blog, July 20, 2011, http://www.theglobeandmail.com/sports/hockey/globe-onhockey/big-signing-bonuses-becoming-nhls-new-norm/article2103658/, accessed on January 18, 2012.

 What are the issues involved in determining if a signing bonus is an asset or an expense?

THE JOURNAL

We are all familiar with the term "journal." It usually refers to a book where personal events are recorded in chronological order. Similarly, accounting transactions are also recorded in a **journal** in chronological (date) order. For this reason, the journal is referred to as the book of original entry. As transactions are sequentially recorded, the debit and credit effects can be seen on specific accounts.

Companies can use various kinds of journals, but every company has a **general journal. Whenever we use the term "journal" in this textbook, we mean the general journal unless we specify otherwise.**

The journal makes some important contributions to the recording process:

- It discloses the complete effect of a transaction in one place.
- It provides a chronological record of transactions.
- It helps to prevent and locate errors, because the debit and credit amounts for each entry can be easily compared.

Journalizing Transactions

Entering transaction data in the journal is known as **journalizing**. A separate journal entry is made for each transaction. A complete entry consists of the following: (1) the date of the transaction, (2) the accounts and amounts to be debited and credited, and (3) a brief explanation of the transaction.

To illustrate the technique of journalizing, let's look at the first two transactions of Softbyte from Chapter 1. These transactions were (1) September 1, Andrew Leonid invested $15,000 cash in the business, and (2) computer equipment was purchased for $7,000 cash (we will assume that this transaction also occurred on September 1). In tabular form, as shown in Chapter 1, these transactions appeared as follows:

	Assets		=	Liabilities	+	Owner's Equity
	Cash	+ Equipment				A. Leonid, Capital
(1)	+$15,000					+$15,000
(2)	−7,000	+$7,000				

In standard journal entry form, these transactions would appear as follows (the boxed numbers correspond to explanations that follow):

	GENERAL JOURNAL				**J1**
Date	**Account Titles and Explanation**	**Ref**	**Debit**	**Credit**	
2017		5			
Sept. 1	Cash 2		15,000		
1	A. Leonid, Capital 3			15,000	
	4 Invested cash in business.				
1	Equipment		7,000		
	Cash			7,000	
	Purchased equipment for cash.				

A   =   L   +   OE
+15,000   +15,000

↑Cash flows: +15,000

A   =   L   +   OE
+7,000
−7,000

↓Cash flows: −7,000

In the margins next to journal entries are equation analyses that show the effect of the transaction on the accounting equation (A = L + OE) and on cash flows. You should think of these as part of Step 1 of the accounting cycle.

Since this is the first page of Softbyte's general journal, it is numbered J1. You should note the following features of journal entries:

1 The date of the transaction is entered in the Date column.

2 The debit account title (that is, the account to be debited) is entered first at the extreme left margin of the column headed "Account Titles and Explanation," and the amount of the debit is recorded in the Debit column.

3 The credit account title (that is, the account to be credited) is indented and entered on the next line in the column headed "Account Titles and Explanation," and the amount of the credit is recorded in the Credit column.

4 A brief explanation of the transaction appears on the line below the credit account title. A space is left between journal entries. The blank space separates individual journal entries and makes the entire journal easier to read.

5 The column titled Ref (which stands for Reference) is left blank when the journal entry is made. This column is used later when the journal entries are transferred to the ledger accounts.

It is important to use correct and specific account titles in journal entries. While there is some flexibility in creating account titles, **each title has to accurately describe the account's content**. For example, the account title used for the computer equipment purchased by Softbyte may be Equipment, Computer Equipment, Computers, or Office Equipment. However, once a company chooses the specific title to use, all transactions for the account should be recorded with the same title.

When you complete the assignments in this text, if specific account titles are given, you should use those. If account titles are not given, you should create account titles that identify the nature and content of each account. **Account titles used in journalizing should not contain explanations (such as Cash Paid or Cash Received).**

If an entry affects only two accounts, it will have one debit and one credit. This is considered a simple journal entry. Some transactions, however, involve more than two accounts. When three or more accounts are required in one journal entry, the entry is called a **compound entry**. To illustrate, recall from Chapter 1 that Softbyte provided $3,500 of programming services to customers (assume this was on September 9).

It received $1,500 cash from the customers for these services. The balance, $2,000, was owed on account. The compound entry to record this transaction is as follows:

GENERAL JOURNAL					J1
Date	**Account Titles and Explanation**		**Ref**	**Debit**	**Credit**
2017 Sept. 9	Cash			1,500	
	Accounts Receivable			2,000	
	Service Revenue				3,500
	Performed services for cash and credit.				

```
A    =   L   +   OE
+1,500          +3,500
+2,000
```

↑ Cash flows: +1,500

BEFORE YOU GO ON...DO IT 2   Recording Business Activities

Brooke Schwenke did the following activities in setting up her salon and spa, the Oasis Spa:

1. Opened a bank account in the name of the Oasis Spa and deposited $20,000 of her own money in this account as her initial investment.
2. Purchased equipment on account (to be paid in 30 days) for a total cost of $4,800.
3. Interviewed three people for the position of esthetician.
4. During the first two weeks, performed $1,280 of massage services, all collected in cash. (Note: Date this May 14.)
5. On May 15, paid the employee, hired on May 7, her $500 weekly salary.

For each of the transactions, prepare a basic analysis, a debit/credit analysis, and a journal entry.

Solution

Transaction 1:

Basic Analysis	The asset account Cash is increased by $20,000. The owner's equity account B. Schwenke, Capital is increased by $20,000.
Debit/Credit Analysis	Debits increase assets: debit Cash $20,000. Credits increase owner's equity: credit B. Schwenke, Capital $20,000.

Journal Entry	May 1 Cash 20,000
	             B. Schwenke, Capital 20,000
	                Invested cash in business.

Transaction 2:

Basic Analysis	The asset account Equipment is increased by $4,800. The liability account Accounts Payable is increased by $4,800.
Debit/Credit Analysis	Debits increase assets: debit Equipment $4,800. Credits increase liabilities: credit Accounts Payable $4,800.

Journal Entry	May 3 Equipment 4,800
	             Accounts Payable 4,800
	                Purchased equipment on account.

Transaction 3:

Basic Analysis	An accounting transaction has not occurred.

Transaction 4:

Basic Analysis	The asset account Cash is increased by $1,280. The revenue account Service Revenue is increased by $1,280.
Debit/Credit Analysis	Debits increase assets: debit Cash $1,280. Credits increase revenues: credit Service Revenue $1,280.

Journal Entry	May 14 Cash 1,280
	              Service Revenue 1,280
	               Performed services for cash.

(continued)

Action Plan

- Understand which activities need to be recorded and which do not.
- Analyze the transactions. Determine the accounts affected and whether the transaction increases or decreases the account.
- Apply the debit and credit rules.
- Record the transactions in the general journal following the formatting rules. Remember that the name of the account to be credited is indented and the amount is recorded in the right-hand column.

BEFORE YOU GO ON...DO IT › **Recording Business Activities** *(continued)*

Transaction 5:

Basic Analysis	The expense account Salaries Expense is increased by $500. The asset account Cash is decreased by $500.
Debit/Credit Analysis	Debits increase expenses: debit Salaries Expense $500. Credits decrease assets: credit Cash $500.
Journal Entry	May 14 Salaries Expense 500
	Cash 500
	Paid salary for a week.

Related exercise material: BE2–6, BE2–7, BE2–8, BE2–9, BE2–10, BE2–11, BE2–12, E2–5, E2–6, E2–7, E2–8, and E2–9.

LEARNING OBJECTIVE 3 › **Explain how a ledger helps in the recording process and post transactions.**

The Ledger

The entire group of accounts maintained by a company is called the **ledger**. The ledger provides the balance in each of the accounts and keeps track of changes in these balances.

Companies can use different kinds of ledgers, but every company has a general ledger. A **general ledger** contains accounts for all the asset, liability, equity, revenue, and expense accounts. Whenever we use the term "ledger" in this textbook, we are referring to the general ledger, unless we specify otherwise.

Companies arrange the ledger in the sequence in which they present the accounts, beginning with the balance sheet accounts. First in order are the asset accounts, followed by liability accounts, owner's capital, drawings, revenues, and expenses. Each account is numbered for easier identification.

The ledger provides the balance in each of the accounts. For example, the Cash account shows the amount of cash available to meet current obligations. The Accounts Receivable account shows amounts due from customers. Accounts Payable shows amounts owed to creditors.

There are different standard forms of accounts. One of them, the simple T account form, is used in accounting textbooks and is often very useful for analyzing illustrations, and for learning accounting. However, in practice, T accounts are not generally used in the accounting cycle. Generally, the account forms that are used in ledgers as presented below are the norm. A very popular form in both manual and computerized systems using the data (and assumed dates) from Softbyte's Cash account in Illustration 2-2 follows.

GENERAL LEDGER					
CASH					
Date	Explanation	Ref	Debit	Credit	Balance
2017					
Sept. 1			15,000		15,000
1				7,000	8,000
3			1,200		9,200
9			1,500		10,700
17				600	10,100
17				900	9,200
20				200	9,000
25				250	8,750
30			600		9,350
30				1,300	8,050

This form is often called the **three-column form of account** because it has three money columns: debit, credit, and balance. The balance in the account is determined after each transaction. The explanation and reference columns make it possible to give more information about the transaction. In manual accounting systems, the explanation column is usually left blank because it is too time-consuming to copy explanations from the general journal. Computerized accounting systems will automatically copy the explanation that was originally recorded in the journal entry into the ledger.

POSTING

Transferring journal entries to the ledger accounts is called **posting**. It is the third step in the accounting cycle (see Illustration 2-4). This phase of the recording process accumulates the effects of journalized transactions into the individual accounts.

Steps in the Posting Process

Posting has the following steps:

1 In the general ledger, to post to the debit account, enter the date, the journal page number, and the amount.

2 In the journal, enter the debit account number in the journal reference column.

3 In the general ledger, to post to the credit account, enter the date, the journal page number, and the amount.

4 In the journal, enter the credit account number in the journal reference column.

These steps are shown in Illustration 2-6 using Softbyte's first journal entry.

▶ILLUSTRATION 2-6
Posting a journal entry

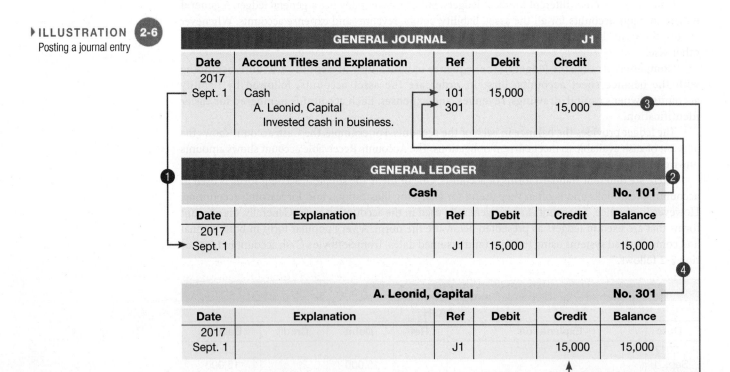

The reference column in the journal shows the entries that have been posted. The references also show the account numbers to which the amounts have been posted. The reference column of a ledger account indicates the journal page where the transaction was posted from.

Posting should be done in chronological order. That is, all the debits and credits of one journal entry should be posted before going to the next journal entry. Postings should be made on a timely basis to keep the ledger up to date. In a computerized accounting system, posting is done automatically, usually right after each journal entry is prepared.

Chart of Accounts

When creating an accounting system, the first step is to develop a framework for the accounting information. Whether using a computerized or manual system, this is done by creating a chart of accounts. The **chart of accounts** is a list of the accounts and account numbers that identify where the accounts are in the ledger. The numbering system used to identify the accounts usually starts with the balance sheet accounts and follows with the income statement accounts. Because each company is different, the types and number of accounts they have vary. The number of accounts depends on the amount of detail that management requires. For example, the management of one company may want to use one account for all utility expenses, while another company may keep separate expense accounts for each type of utility expense, such as gas, electricity, and water. Many companies, such as Tonica Kombucha, in our feature story, use different revenue accounts for difference sources of revenue.

We now introduce the chart of accounts for Lynk Software Services, a new technology company started by Tyler Jacobs, is presented in Illustration 2-7. Accounts 100–199 indicate asset accounts; 200–299 indicate liabilities; 300–399 indicate owner's equity accounts; 400–499, revenues; and 500–999, expenses. There are gaps in the numbering system to permit the insertion of new accounts as needed during the life of the business.

ILLUSTRATION 2-7
Chart of accounts

LYNK SOFTWARE SERVICES
CHART OF ACCOUNTS

Assets		Owner's Equity	
101	Cash	301	T. Jacobs, Capital
112	Accounts Receivable	306	T. Jacobs, Drawings
129	Supplies	350	Income Summary
130	Prepaid Insurance	**Revenues**	
151	Equipment		
152	Accumulated Depreciation— Equipment	400	Service Revenue
Liabilities		**Expenses**	
		711	Depreciation Expense
200	Notes Payable	722	Insurance Expense
201	Accounts Payable	726	Rent Expense
209	Unearned Revenue	729	Salaries Expense
212	Salaries Payable	740	Supplies Expense
230	Interest Payable	905	Interest Expense

In this and subsequent chapters, we will show the accounting cycle for Lynk Software Services. This proprietorship was started by Tyler Jacobs to provide consulting services to businesses looking to make e-commerce sales. Accounts shown in green are used in this chapter; accounts shown in black are explained in later chapters.

THE RECORDING PROCESS ILLUSTRATED

We will now show the three steps in the recording process—analyze, journalize, and post—using the October 2017 transactions of Lynk Software Services. The company's accounting period is one month. Because Lynk Software Services was started on October 1, 2017, there are no balances in its accounts from prior transactions. Had the business previously existed, each account would have an opening balance.

Study these transactions carefully. Remember that in Step 1 of the recording process, the transaction is analyzed to identify (1) the types of accounts involved, (2) whether the accounts are increased or decreased, and (3) whether the accounts need to be debited or credited. This is shown in the basic analysis and the debit/credit analysis for each transaction in the illustrations before journalizing and posting. For simplicity, the illustrations use the T account form to show posting instead of the standard account form.

▶ TRANSACTION 1
Investment of cash by owner

Transaction	October 1, Tyler Jacobs invests $10,000 cash in a technology venture to be known as Lynk Software Services
Basic Analysis	The asset Cash is increased by $10,000, and the owner's equity account T. Jacobs, Capital, is increased by $10,000.
Debit/Credit Analysis	Debits increase assets: debit Cash $10,000. Credits increase owner's equity: credit T. Jacobs, Capital, $10,000.

Journal Entry

Oct. 1	Cash	101	10,000	
	T. Jacobs, Capital	301		10,000
	Invested cash in business.			

Posting

Cash		101
Oct. 1	10,000	

T. Jacobs, Capital		301
	Oct. 1	10,000

▶ TRANSACTION 2
Purchase of office equipment

Transaction	October 2, office equipment costing $5,000 is purchased by signing a $5,000, 6% note payable, due in three months on January 2, 2018.
Basic Analysis	The asset account Equipment is increased by $5,000, and the liability account Notes Payable is increased by $5,000.
Debit/Credit Analysis	Debits increase assets: debit Equipment $5,000. Credits increase liabilities: credit Notes Payable $5,000.

Journal Entry

Oct. 2	Equipment	151	5,000	
	Notes Payable	200		5,000
	Issued a three-month, 6% note			
	for equipment.			

Posting

Equipment		151
Oct. 2	5,000	

Notes Payable		200
	Oct. 2	5,000

▶ TRANSACTION 3
Receipt of cash in advance from customer

Transaction	October 3, a $1,200 cash advance is received from R. Knox, a client, for consulting services that are expected to be completed by December 31.
Basic Analysis	The asset account Cash is increased by $1,200; the liability account Unearned Revenue is increased by $1,200 because the service has not been provided yet. That is, when an advance payment is received, unearned revenue (a liability) should be recorded in order to recognize the obligation that exists. Note also that unearned revenue is not a revenue account and does not increase owner's equity even though the word "revenue" is used.
Debit/Credit Analysis	Debits increase assets: debit Cash $1,200. Credits increase liabilities: credit Unearned Revenue $1,200.

Journal Entry

Oct. 3	Cash	101	1,200	
	Unearned Revenue	209		1,200
	Received advance from R. Knox for			
	future services.			

Posting

Cash		101
Oct. 1	10,000	
3	1,200	

Unearned Revenue		209
	Oct. 3	1,200

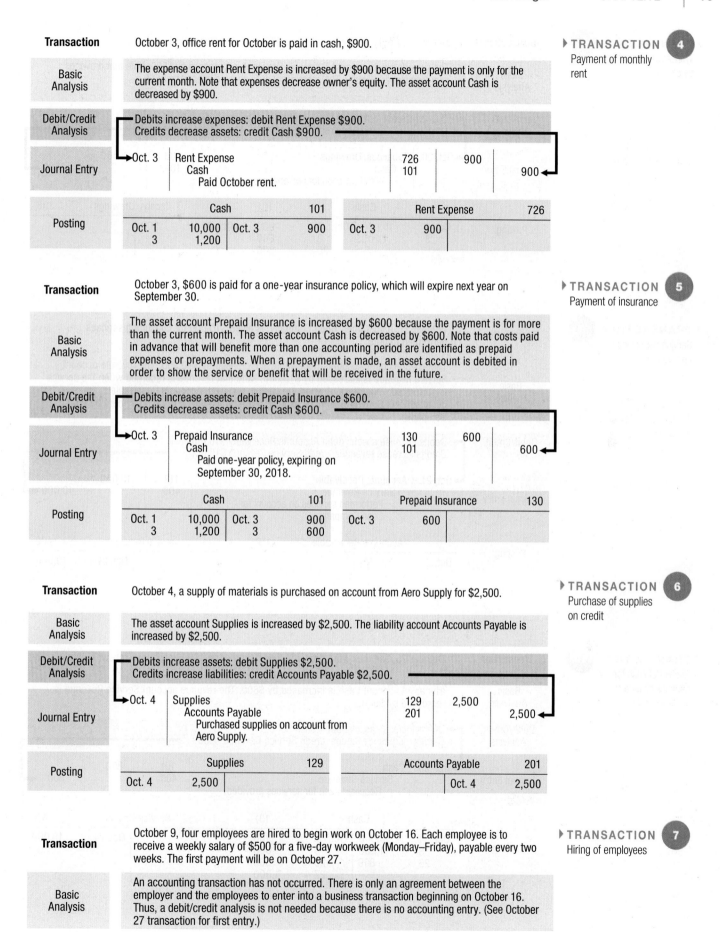

Transaction — October 3, office rent for October is paid in cash, $900.

▸ **TRANSACTION 4**
Payment of monthly rent

Basic Analysis — The expense account Rent Expense is increased by $900 because the payment is only for the current month. Note that expenses decrease owner's equity. The asset account Cash is decreased by $900.

Debit/Credit Analysis — Debits increase expenses: debit Rent Expense $900.
Credits decrease assets: credit Cash $900.

Journal Entry

Oct. 3	Rent Expense	726	900	
	Cash	101		900
	Paid October rent.			

Posting

Cash			101		Rent Expense		726
Oct. 1	10,000	Oct. 3	900	Oct. 3	900		
3	1,200						

Transaction — October 3, $600 is paid for a one-year insurance policy, which will expire next year on September 30.

▸ **TRANSACTION 5**
Payment of insurance

Basic Analysis — The asset account Prepaid Insurance is increased by $600 because the payment is for more than the current month. The asset account Cash is decreased by $600. Note that costs paid in advance that will benefit more than one accounting period are identified as prepaid expenses or prepayments. When a prepayment is made, an asset account is debited in order to show the service or benefit that will be received in the future.

Debit/Credit Analysis — Debits increase assets: debit Prepaid Insurance $600.
Credits decrease assets: credit Cash $600.

Journal Entry

Oct. 3	Prepaid Insurance	130	600	
	Cash	101		600
	Paid one-year policy, expiring on			
	September 30, 2018.			

Posting

Cash			101		Prepaid Insurance		130
Oct. 1	10,000	Oct. 3	900	Oct. 3	600		
3	1,200	3	600				

Transaction — October 4, a supply of materials is purchased on account from Aero Supply for $2,500.

▸ **TRANSACTION 6**
Purchase of supplies on credit

Basic Analysis — The asset account Supplies is increased by $2,500. The liability account Accounts Payable is increased by $2,500.

Debit/Credit Analysis — Debits increase assets: debit Supplies $2,500.
Credits increase liabilities: credit Accounts Payable $2,500.

Journal Entry

Oct. 4	Supplies	129	2,500	
	Accounts Payable	201		2,500
	Purchased supplies on account from			
	Aero Supply.			

Posting

Supplies		129		Accounts Payable		201
Oct. 4	2,500				Oct. 4	2,500

Transaction — October 9, four employees are hired to begin work on October 16. Each employee is to receive a weekly salary of $500 for a five-day workweek (Monday–Friday), payable every two weeks. The first payment will be on October 27.

▸ **TRANSACTION 7**
Hiring of employees

Basic Analysis — An accounting transaction has not occurred. There is only an agreement between the employer and the employees to enter into a business transaction beginning on October 16. Thus, a debit/credit analysis is not needed because there is no accounting entry. (See October 27 transaction for first entry.)

▶ TRANSACTION **8**
Withdrawal of cash
by owner

Transaction	October 20, Tyler Jacobs withdraws $500 cash for personal use.
Basic Analysis	The owner's equity account T. Jacobs, Drawings is increased by $500. Note that drawings decrease owner's equity. The asset account Cash is decreased by $500.
Debit/Credit Analysis	Debits increase drawings: debit T. Jacobs, Drawings, $500. Credits decrease assets: credit Cash $500.

Journal Entry	Oct. 20 T. Jacobs, Drawings 306 500
	                Cash 101 500
	                    Withdrew cash for personal use.

Posting

Cash			101
Oct. 1	10,000	Oct. 3	900
3	1,200	3	600
		20	500

T. Jacobs, Drawings		306
Oct. 20	500	

▶ TRANSACTION **9**
Service performed
on account

Transaction	October 21, a customer, Copa Company, is billed $10,000 for consulting services performed to date.
Basic Analysis	The asset account Accounts Receivable is increased by $10,000. The revenue account Service Revenue is increased by $10,000. Note that revenue is recorded when the service is performed, regardless of when the cash is received. Accounts Receivable is an asset because Lynk Software Services expects a future benefit—the cash payment by Copa Company.
Debit/Credit Analysis	Debits increase assets: debit Accounts Receivable $10,000. Credits increase revenues: credit Service Revenue $10,000.

Journal Entry	Oct. 21 Accounts Receivable 112 10,000
	                Service Revenue 400 10,000
	                    Performed services on account for
	                    Copa Company.

Posting

Accounts Receivable		112
Oct. 21	10,000	

Service Revenue		400
	Oct. 21	10,000

▶ TRANSACTION **10**
Receipt of cash for
services provided

Transaction	October 25, services were provided to a customer and $800 cash was received immediately.
Basic Analysis	The asset account Cash is increased by $800. The revenue account Service Revenue is increased by $800.
Debit/Credit Analysis	Debits increase assets: debit Cash $800. Credits increase revenues: credit Service Revenue $800

Journal Entry	Oct. 25 Cash 101 800
	                Service Revenue 400 800
	                    Received cash for services provided.

Posting

Cash			101
Oct. 1	10,000	Oct. 3	900
3	1,200	3	600
25	800	20	500
		27	4,000

Service Revenue		400
	Oct. 21	10,000
	25	800

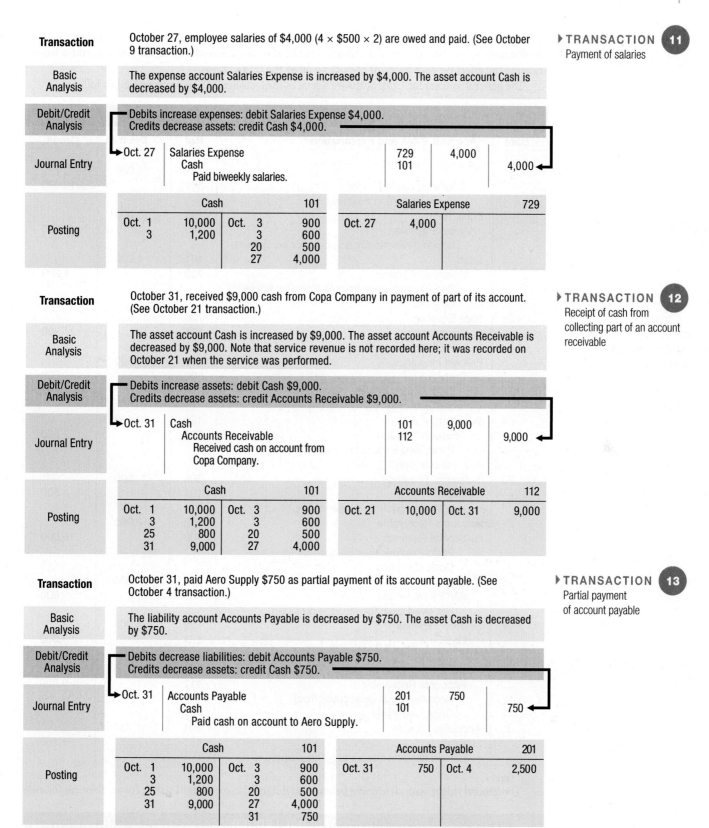

| | Transaction | | October 27, employee salaries of $4,000 (4 × $500 × 2) are owed and paid. (See October 9 transaction.) | | ▸TRANSACTION **11** Payment of salaries |

Transaction

October 27, employee salaries of $4,000 (4 × $500 × 2) are owed and paid. (See October 9 transaction.)

▸TRANSACTION **11**
Payment of salaries

Basic Analysis

The expense account Salaries Expense is increased by $4,000. The asset account Cash is decreased by $4,000.

Debit/Credit Analysis

Debits increase expenses: debit Salaries Expense $4,000.
Credits decrease assets: credit Cash $4,000.

Journal Entry

Oct. 27	Salaries Expense	729	4,000	
	Cash	101		4,000
	Paid biweekly salaries.			

Posting

	Cash		101			Salaries Expense		729
Oct. 1	10,000	Oct. 3	900		Oct. 27	4,000		
3	1,200	3	600					
		20	500					
		27	4,000					

Transaction

October 31, received $9,000 cash from Copa Company in payment of part of its account. (See October 21 transaction.)

▸TRANSACTION **12**
Receipt of cash from collecting part of an account receivable

Basic Analysis

The asset account Cash is increased by $9,000. The asset account Accounts Receivable is decreased by $9,000. Note that service revenue is not recorded here; it was recorded on October 21 when the service was performed.

Debit/Credit Analysis

Debits increase assets: debit Cash $9,000.
Credits decrease assets: credit Accounts Receivable $9,000.

Journal Entry

Oct. 31	Cash	101	9,000	
	Accounts Receivable	112		9,000
	Received cash on account from			
	Copa Company.			

Posting

	Cash		101			Accounts Receivable		112
Oct. 1	10,000	Oct. 3	900		Oct. 21	10,000	Oct. 31	9,000
3	1,200	3	600					
25	800	20	500					
31	9,000	27	4,000					

Transaction

October 31, paid Aero Supply $750 as partial payment of its account payable. (See October 4 transaction.)

▸TRANSACTION **13**
Partial payment of account payable

Basic Analysis

The liability account Accounts Payable is decreased by $750. The asset Cash is decreased by $750.

Debit/Credit Analysis

Debits decrease liabilities: debit Accounts Payable $750.
Credits decrease assets: credit Cash $750.

Journal Entry

Oct. 31	Accounts Payable	201	750	
	Cash	101		750
	Paid cash on account to Aero Supply.			

Posting

	Cash		101			Accounts Payable		201
Oct. 1	10,000	Oct. 3	900		Oct. 31	750	Oct. 4	2,500
3	1,200	3	600					
25	800	20	500					
31	9,000	27	4,000					
		31	750					

SUMMARY ILLUSTRATION OF JOURNALIZING AND POSTING

You should always think through the basic analysis and debit/credit analysis before journalizing a transaction. The analysis will help you understand the journal entries discussed in this chapter, as well as more complex journal entries in later chapters.

However, the actual accounting records will not show this analysis for each transaction. Instead, the accounting records will show a chronological list of the transactions in the journal, and a ledger showing the effect on each account of posting all of the transactions.

The general journal for Lynk Software Services for October 2017 is summarized as follows:

GENERAL JOURNAL				J1
Date	Account Titles and Explanation	Ref	Debit	Credit
2017 Oct. 1	Cash	101	10,000	
	T. Jacobs, Capital	301		10,000
	Invested cash in business.			
2	Equipment	151	5,000	
	Notes Payable	200		5,000
	Issued three-month, 6% note for equipment.			
3	Cash	101	1,200	
	Unearned Revenue	209		1,200
	Received advance from R. Knox for future services.			
3	Rent Expense	726	900	
	Cash	101		900
	Paid October rent.			
3	Prepaid Insurance	130	600	
	Cash	101		600
	Paid one-year policy, expiring on September 30, 2018.			
4	Supplies	129	2,500	
	Accounts Payable	201		2,500
	Purchased supplies on account from Aero Supply.			
20	T. Jacobs, Drawings	306	500	
	Cash	101		500
	Withdrew cash for personal use.			
21	Accounts Receivable	112	10,000	
	Service Revenue	400		10,000
	Performed services on account for Copa Company.			
25	Cash	101	800	
	Service Revenue	400		800
	Received cash for services provided.			
27	Salaries Expense	729	4,000	
	Cash	101		4,000
	Paid biweekly salaries.			
31	Cash	101	9,000	
	Accounts Receivable	112		9,000
	Received cash on account from Copa Company.			
31	Accounts Payable	201	750	
	Cash	101		750
	Paid cash on account to Aero Supply.			

The general ledger, with all account balances highlighted in green, for Lynk Software Services follows:

GENERAL LEDGER							
	Cash		101		Accounts Payable		201
Oct. 1	10,000	Oct. 3	900	Oct. 31	750	Oct. 4	2,500
3	1,200	3	600			Bal.	1,750
25	800	20	500				
31	9,000	27	4,000		Unearned Revenue		209
		31	750			Oct. 3	1,200
Bal.	14,250					Bal.	1,200

Accounts Receivable		112
Oct. 21	10,000	Oct. 31	9,000
Bal.	1,000		

T. Jacobs, Capital		301
		Oct. 1	10,000
		Bal.	10,000

Supplies		129
Oct. 4	2,500	
Bal.	2,500	

T. Jacobs, Drawings		306
Oct. 20	500	
Bal.	500	

Prepaid Insurance		130
Oct. 3	600	
Bal.	600	

Service Revenue		400
		Oct. 21	10,000
		25	800
		Bal.	10,800

Equipment		151
Oct. 2	5,000	
Bal.	5,000	

Rent Expense		726
Oct. 23	900	
Bal.	900	

Notes Payable		200
		Oct. 2	5,000
		Bal.	5,000

Salaries Expense		729
Oct. 27	4,000	
Bal.	4,000	

BEFORE YOU GO ON...DO IT **Posting**

Brooke Schwenke recorded the following transactions in the general ledger during the month of June:

June 4	Cash	2,280	
	Service Revenue		2,280
15	Salaries and Wages Expense	400	
	Cash		400
19	Utilities Expense	92	
	Cash		92

Post these entries to the Cash account of the general ledger to determine its ending balance. The beginning cash of June 1 was $600.

Solution

Cash					
June 1	Bal.	600	June 15		400
4		2,280	19		92
	Bal.	2,388			

Related exercise material: BE2–12, BE2–13, BE2–14, E2–10, E2–11, and E2–12.

Action Plan
- Posting involves transferring the journalized debits and credits to specific accounts in the ledger.
- Determine the ending balances by netting (calculating the difference between) the total debits and credits.

LEARNING OBJECTIVE **Prepare a trial balance.**

The Trial Balance

As discussed in the section Analyzing and Recording Transactions, the steps in the recording process are the first three steps in the accounting cycle. The fourth step in the accounting cycle, as shown in Illustration 2-8, is to prepare a trial balance.

▶ **ILLUSTRATION** 2-8
The accounting cycle—
Steps 1 to 4

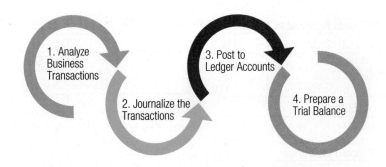

1. Analyze Business Transactions

2. Journalize the Transactions

3. Post to Ledger Accounts

4. Prepare a Trial Balance

A **trial balance** is a list of the accounts and their balances at a specific time. If any accounts have a zero balance, they can be omitted from the trial balance. It is prepared at the end of an accounting period. In the trial balance, the accounts are listed in the same order as they are in the ledger, with debit balances in the left column and credit balances in the right column.

The main purpose of a trial balance is to prove (check) that the debits equal the credits after posting. That is, the sum of the debit account balances must equal the sum of the credit account balances. If the totals are not the same, this means an error was made in journalizing or posting the transactions, or in preparing the trial balance. For example, the trial balance will not balance if an incorrect amount is posted in the ledger. If the trial balance does not balance, then the error must be located and corrected before proceeding.

A trial balance is also useful in preparing financial statements, as we will explain in the next two chapters. The procedure for preparing a trial balance is as follows:

Helpful hint When the totals of the two columns are equal, the trial balance is considered "balanced."

1. List the account titles and their balances in the same order as in the chart of accounts. Debit balances are entered in the debit column and credit balances are entered in the credit column.
2. Total the debit and credit columns.
3. Ensure that the totals of the two columns are equal.

To illustrate how a trial balance is prepared, we will continue with the Lynk Software Services illustration in the previous section of this chapter. We use the information in Lynk Software Services's general ledger to prepare its trial balance shown in Illustration 2-9.

▶ **ILLUSTRATION** 2-9
Lynk Software
Services's trial balance

LYNK SOFTWARE SERVICES
Trial Balance
October 31, 2017

	Debit	Credit
Cash	$14,250	
Accounts receivable	1,000	
Supplies	2,500	
Prepaid insurance	600	
Equipment	5,000	
Notes payable		$ 5,000
Accounts payable		1,750
Unearned revenue		1,200
T. Jacobs, capital		10,000
T. Jacobs, drawings	500	
Service revenue		10,800
Rent expense	900	
Salaries expense	4,000	
Totals	$28,750	$28,750

You should note the following:

1. The accounts are listed in the same order they were in the general ledger (and chart of accounts in Illustration 2-7).

2. The balance at October 31, 2017, of each account in the general ledger is included in the correct debit or credit column.
3. The total of the debit accounts, $28,750, is equal to the total of the credit accounts, $28,750.

LIMITATIONS OF A TRIAL BALANCE

Although a trial balance can reveal many types of bookkeeping errors, it does not prove that all transactions have been recorded or that the ledger is correct. There can be many errors even when the trial balance columns agree. For example, the trial balance may balance even when:

ETHICS NOTE
An error is the result of an unintentional mistake; it is neither ethical nor unethical. An irregularity is an intentional misstatement, which is viewed as unethical.

1. a transaction is not journalized,
2. a correct journal entry is not posted,
3. a journal entry is posted twice,
4. incorrect accounts are used in journalizing or posting, or
5. offsetting errors (errors that hide each other) are made in recording the amount of a transaction.

As long as equal debits and credits are posted, even to the wrong account or in the wrong amount, the total debits will equal the total credits when the trial balance is prepared.

ACCOUNTING IN ACTION
ETHICS INSIGHT

Vu Hung is the assistant chief accountant at Lim Company, a manufacturer of computer chips and cellular phones with annual sales of $20 million. At the end of the first quarter, Vu hurriedly tries to prepare a general ledger trial balance so that quarterly financial statements can be prepared and released to management and regulatory agencies. The credits on the trial balance add up to $1,000 more than the debits. In order to meet the 4:00 p.m. deadline, Vu decides to force the debits and credits into balance by adding the amount of the difference to the Equipment account. She chose Equipment because it is one of the larger account balances. Proportionally, it will be the least misstated. She believes that the difference will not affect anyone's decisions. She wishes that she had more time to find the error, but realizes that the financial statements are already late.

 Who are the stakeholders in this situation and what impact will Vu's action have on them?

LOCATING ERRORS

Errors generally result from mathematical mistakes, incorrect postings, or simply recopying data incorrectly. In a computerized system, the trial balance is usually balanced because most computerized systems will not let you enter an unbalanced journal entry, and because there are rarely software errors in posting or in the preparation of the trial balance.

What do you do if you have a manual trial balance that does not balance? First, determine the amount of the difference between the two columns of the trial balance. After you know this amount, try the following steps:

1. If the error is an amount such as $1, $100, or $1,000, re-add the trial balance columns and recalculate the account balances.
2. If the error can be evenly divided by two, scan the trial balance to see if a balance equal to half the error has been entered in the wrong column.

3. If the error can be evenly divided by nine, retrace the account balances on the trial balance to see whether they are incorrectly copied from the ledger. For example, if a balance was $12 but was listed as $21, a $9 error has been made. Reversing the order of numbers is called a transposition error.

4. If the error cannot be evenly divided by two or nine, scan the ledger to see whether an account balance in the amount of the error has been omitted from the trial balance. Scan the journal to see whether a posting in the amount of the error has been omitted.

ACCOUNTING IN ACTION
ALL ABOUT YOU INSIGHT

As a student, you need to do more than just eat macaroni and cheese and sleep on a second-hand futon to survive: you need to watch money coming in and going out so your bank account doesn't go in the red. The same is true for small businesses, which must track revenues and expenses to ensure that the employee payroll and cheques to suppliers don't bounce. Small business owners also need to know how much profit they're earning to see whether their hard work is paying off. Accounting experts recommend that business owners set aside time every week to organize receipts and track finances to determine whether to raise prices, add services, or cut back on certain spending. They also advise business owners to shop around for the best bank account fee package. Having good financial records through the year also helps when it's time to prepare an income tax return. You, too, can adopt these good bookkeeping habits to ensure your bank account is in the black and you won't have to borrow from the Bank of Mom and Dad at the end of the school year.

Sources: Kendra Murphy, "Small Business Accounting 101: Ten Steps to Get Your Startup on Track," Shopify.ca, September 9, 2014; Kirk Simpson, "5 Simple Tips to Keep Your Small-Business Finances in Order," Forbes.com, October 24, 2012; Osmond Vitez, "Why Is Accounting Important for the Start Up of a Business?," *Houston Chronicle,* n.d., http://smallbusiness.chron.com/accounting-important-start-up-business-52.html, accessed on April 20, 2015.

 Q What categories of expenses do you have that a small business would also have?

SOME PROCESS EXPLANATIONS

Use of Dollars and Cents

In this textbook, in order to simplify the process, we have not included cents in the amounts we record in journal entries, general ledger accounts, and trial balances. In reality, cents are used in the formal accounting records. When a transaction is recorded in the journal and then posted to the ledger, cents are always used. But when the financial statements are prepared, the account balances are normally rounded to the nearest dollar, and in larger companies, they may be rounded to the nearest thousand or even million. Even though the Canadian government has eliminated the penny for cash transactions, cheques will still be written to the nearest cent.

Use of Dollar Signs and Underlining

Both in practice and in accounting textbooks, dollar signs are not used in the journals or ledgers. Dollar signs are used only in the trial balance and the financial statements. Generally, a dollar sign is shown only for the first item in the column, and for the total of that column.

A single line is placed under a column of figures to be added or subtracted. Total amounts are double-underlined to indicate they are the final sum. In other words, a double underline under a number means that no further amounts will be added to, or subtracted from, that amount.

Account Numbers

As previously mentioned, in practice companies use both account names and account numbers. In this textbook, we have included account numbers in some of our examples and in some of the end-of-chapter exercises and problems. But in most of the examples throughout the textbook, we will use only account names, not account numbers, to simplify the process.

BEFORE YOU GO ON...DO IT ④ **Trial Balance**

Koizumi Kollections has the following alphabetical list of accounts and balances at July 31, 2017:

Account	Amount	Account	Amount
Accounts payable	$33,700	Land	$ 51,000
Accounts receivable	71,200	Notes payable	49,000
Building	86,500	Operating expenses	102,000
Cash	3,200	Prepaid insurance	3,100
Equipment	35,700	Service revenue	172,000
J. Koizumi, capital	99,000	Unearned revenue	3,000
J. Koizumi, drawings	4,000		

Each of the above accounts has a normal balance. Prepare a trial balance with the accounts in the same order as they would be in the ledger (in other words, in financial statement order).

Solution

KOIZUMI KOLLECTIONS
Trial Balance
July 31, 2017

	Debit	Credit
Cash	$ 3,200	
Accounts receivable	71,200	
Prepaid insurance	3,100	
Land	51,000	
Building	86,500	
Equipment	35,700	
Accounts payable		$ 33,700
Unearned revenue		3,000
Notes payable		49,000
J. Koizumi, capital		99,000
J. Koizumi, drawings	4,000	
Service revenue		172,000
Operating expenses	102,000	
Totals	$356,700	$356,700

Related exercise material: BE2–16, BE2–17, BE2–18, E2–17, E2–18, and E2–19.

Action Plan

- Reorder the accounts as they would normally be in the general ledger: balance sheet accounts are listed first (assets, liabilities, and equity) followed by income statement accounts (revenues and expenses).
- Determine whether each account has a normal debit or credit balance.
- List the amounts in the appropriate debit or credit column.
- Total the trial balance columns. Total debits must equal total credits or a mistake has been made.

Comparing IFRS and ASPE

Key Differences	International Financial Reporting Standards (IFRS)	Accounting Standards for Private Enterprises (ASPE)
No significant differences		

Demonstration Problem

Katrina Aung opened Katrina's Catering on September 1, 2017. During the first month of operations, the following transactions occurred:

Sept. 1   Invested $15,000 cash and cooking equipment worth $5,000 in the business.
2   Paid $1,000 cash for rent for the month of September.
3   Borrowed $15,000 cash from the bank and signed a $15,000, 6-month, 5% note payable.
3   Purchased an industrial oven for $20,000 cash.
6   Paid $1,200 for a one-year insurance policy.
10   Received a bill for $300 from *The Daily News* for advertising the opening of the catering company.
15   Billed a nearby law firm $500 for catering services performed on account.
20   Withdrew $700 cash for personal use.
25   Received $300 cash from the law firm billed on September 15. The balance of the account will be collected in October.
29   Received a $400 cash advance from a customer for services to be performed in October.
30   Cash receipts for catering services performed for the month were $6,200.
30   Paid employee salaries of $1,600.
30   Paid *The Daily News* $200 of the amount owed from the bill received September 10.

The chart of accounts for the company is the same as the one for Lynk Software Services in Illustration 2-7 except for the following: No. 610 Advertising Expense and the names of the capital and drawing accounts.

Instructions
(a) Journalize the September transactions.
(b) Open ledger accounts and post the September transactions.
(c) Prepare a trial balance at September 30, 2017.
(d) Prepare an income statement, statement of owner's equity, and balance sheet for Katrina's Catering.

ACTION PLAN

- Determine if the transaction should be recorded or not.
- Do a basic analysis of the transaction. Identify the accounts that were changed and determine if these accounts increased or decreased and by how much.
- Do a debit/credit analysis of the transaction. Determine which account or accounts should be debited and which account or accounts should be credited and make sure debits equal credits.
- In the journal entry, use specific account titles taken from the chart of accounts.
- Include an appropriate description of each journal entry.
- Arrange the ledger in statement order, beginning with the balance sheet accounts.
- Post in chronological order.
- Put account numbers in the reference column of the journal to indicate the amount has been posted.

SOLUTION TO DEMONSTRATION PROBLEM

(a)

GENERAL JOURNAL				J1
Date	Account Titles and Explanation	Ref	Debit	Credit
2017				
Sept. 1	Cash	101	15,000	
	Equipment	151	5,000	
	K. Aung, Capital	301		20,000
	Invested cash and equipment in business.			
2	Rent Expense	726	1,000	
	Cash	101		1,000
	Paid September rent.			
3	Cash	101	15,000	
	Notes Payable	200		15,000
	Borrowed from bank and signed a 6-month, 5% note payable.			
3	Equipment	151	20,000	
	Cash	101		20,000
	Purchased kitchen equipment for cash.			
6	Prepaid Insurance	130	1,200	
	Cash	101		1,200
	Paid for a one-year insurance policy.			
10	Advertising Expense	610	300	
	Accounts Payable	201		300
	Received bill from *The Daily News* for advertising.			

15	Accounts Receivable		112	500	
	Service Revenue		400		500
	Performed catering services on account.				
20	K. Aung, Drawings		306	700	
	Cash		101		700
	Withdrew cash for personal use.				
25	Cash		101	300	
	Accounts Receivable		112		300
	Received cash on account.				
29	Cash		101	400	
	Unearned Revenue		209		400
	Received cash in advance from customer.				
30	Cash		101	6,200	
	Service Revenue		400		6,200
	Received cash for catering services.				
30	Salaries Expense		729	1,600	
	Cash		101		1,600
	Paid employee salaries.				
30	Accounts Payable		201	200	
	Cash		101		200
	Made a partial payment to *The Daily News*.				

(b)

GENERAL LEDGER

Cash   101

Sept. 1	15,000	Sept. 2	1,000		
3	15,000	3	20,000		
25	300	6	1,200		
29	400	20	700		
30	6,200	30	1,600		
		30	200		
Bal.	12,200				

Accounts Receivable   112

Sept. 15	500	Sept. 25	300
Bal.	200		

Prepaid Insurance   130

Sept. 6	1,200	
Bal.	1,200	

Equipment   151

Sept. 1	5,000	
3	20,000	
Bal.	25,000	

Notes Payable   200

	Sept. 3	15,000
	Bal.	15,000

Accounts Payable   201

Sept. 30	200	Sept. 10	300
		Bal.	100

Unearned Revenue   209

	Sept. 29	400
	Bal.	400

K. Aung, Capital   301

	Sept. 1	20,000
	Bal.	20,000

K. Aung, Drawings   306

Sept. 20	700	
Bal.	700	

Service Revenue   400

	Sept. 15	500
	30	6,200
	Bal.	6,700

Advertising Expense   610

Sept. 10	300	
Bal.	300	

Rent Expense   726

Sept. 2	1,000	
Bal.	1,000	

Salaries Expense   729

Sept. 30	1,600	
Bal.	1,600	

- In the trial balance, list the accounts in the same order as in the ledger (financial statement order).
- List debit balances in the left column of the trial balance and credit balances in the right column.
- Prepare the income statement first, then the statement of owner's equity, then the balance sheet.
- Use the profit from the income statement when preparing the statement of owner's equity.
- Use the owner's capital balance at September 30, 2017, in the statement of owner's capital when preparing the balance sheet.
- Remember that an income statement and a statement of owner's equity are for a period of time. A balance sheet is at a point in time.

(c)

KATRINA'S CATERING
Trial Balance
September 30, 2017

	Debit	Credit
Cash	$12,200	
Accounts receivable	200	
Prepaid insurance	1,200	
Equipment	25,000	
Notes payable		$15,000
Accounts payable		100
Unearned revenue		400
K. Aung, capital		20,000
K. Aung, drawings	700	
Service revenue		6,700
Advertising expense	300	
Rent expense	1,000	
Salaries expense	1,600	
Totals	$42,200	$42,200

(d)

KATRINA'S CATERING
Income Statement
Month Ended September 30, 2017

Revenues		
Service revenue		$6,700
Expenses		
Advertising expense	$ 300	
Rent expense	1,000	
Salaries expense	1,600	2,900
Profit		$3,800

KATRINA'S CATERING
Statement of Owner's Equity
Month Ended September 30, 2017

K. Aung, capital, September 1		$ 0
Add: Investments	$20,000	
Profit	3,800	23,800
Less: Drawings		700
K. Aung, capital, September 30		$23,100

KATRINA'S CATERING
Balance Sheet
September 30, 2017

Assets	
Cash	$12,200
Accounts receivable	200
Prepaid insurance	1,200
Equipment	25,000
Total assets	$38,600

Liabilities and Owner's Equity	
Liabilities	
Notes payable	$15,000
Accounts payable	100
Unearned revenue	400
Total liabilities	15,500
Owner's equity	
K. Aung, capital	23,100
Total liabilities and owner's equity	$38,600

84

▶ Summary of Learning Objectives

1. ***Describe how accounts, debits, and credits are used to record business transactions.*** Debit means left and credit means right. The normal balance of an asset is a debit because assets are on the left side of the accounting equation. Assets are increased by debits and decreased by credits. The normal balance of liabilities and owner's capital is a credit because they are on the right side of the accounting equation. Liabilities and owner's capital are increased by credits and decreased by debits. Revenues increase owner's equity and therefore are recorded as credits because credits increase owner's equity. Credits increase revenues and debits decrease revenues. Expenses and drawings decrease owner's equity and therefore are recorded as debits because debits decrease owner's equity. Expenses and drawings are increased by debits and decreased by credits.

2. ***State how a journal is used in the recording process and journalize transactions.*** The steps in the recording process are the first three steps in the accounting cycle. These steps are: (a) analyze each transaction for its effect on the accounts, (b) record the transaction in a journal, and (c) transfer the journal information to the correct accounts in the ledger.

A journal (a) discloses the complete effect of a transaction in one place, (b) provides a chronological record of transactions, and (c) helps to prevent and locate errors because the debit and credit amounts for each entry can be easily compared.

3. ***Explain how a ledger helps in the recording process and post transactions.*** The ledger is the entire group of accounts maintained by a company. The ledger provides the balance in each of the accounts and keeps track of changes in these balances. Posting is the procedure of transferring journal entries to the ledger accounts. After the journal entries have been posted, the ledger will show all of the increases and decreases that have been made to each account.

4. ***Prepare a trial balance.*** A trial balance is a list of the accounts in the ledger and the account balances at a specific time. Its main purpose is to prove that debits and credits are equal after posting. A trial balance uncovers certain types of errors in journalizing and posting, and is useful in preparing financial statements. Preparing a trial balance is the fourth step in the accounting cycle.

▶ Glossary

Account A record of increases and decreases in a specific asset, liability, or owner's equity item. (p. 60)

Accounting cycle A series of steps followed by accountants in preparing financial statements. (p. 64)

Chart of accounts A list of accounts and the account numbers that identify where the accounts are in the ledger. (p. 71)

Compound entry A journal entry that affects three or more accounts. (p. 67)

Credit The right side of an account. (p. 60)

Debit The left side of an account. (p. 60)

Double-entry accounting system A system that records the dual (two-sided) effect of each transaction in appropriate accounts. (p. 63)

General journal The most basic form of journal in which transactions are recorded when they are not recorded in other specialized journals. (p. 66)

General ledger A ledger that contains accounts for all assets, liabilities, equities, revenues, and expenses. (p. 69)

Journal An accounting record where transactions are recorded in chronological (date) order. It shows the debit and credit effect of each transaction on specific accounts. (p. 66)

Journalizing The entering of transaction data in the journal. (p. 66)

Ledger A record that contains all of a company's accounts. It keeps all the information about changes in each account in one place. (p. 69)

Posting The procedure of transferring journal entries to the ledger accounts. (p. 70)

Recording process The first three steps of the accounting cycle. (p. 65)

T account A form of account that looks like the letter T. It has the title above the horizontal line. Debits are shown to the left of the vertical line, credits to the right. (p. 60)

Three-column form of account An account form with columns for debit, credit, and balance amounts in an account. (p. 70)

Trial balance A list of the accounts in the ledger and the account balances at a specific time, usually at the end of the accounting period. (p. 78)

Self-Study Questions

Answers are at the end of the chapter.

(LO 1) K 1. Which of the following statements about an account is true?
    (a) The left side of an account is the credit or decrease side.
    (b) An account is an individual accounting record of increases and decreases in specific asset, liability, and owner's equity items.
    (c) There are separate accounts for specific assets and liabilities but only one account for owner's equity items.
    (d) The right side of an account is the debit or increase side.

(LO 1) K 2. Credits:
    (a) increase both assets and liabilities.
    (b) decrease both assets and liabilities.
    (c) increase assets and decrease liabilities.
    (d) decrease assets and increase liabilities.

(LO 1) K 3. Accounts that normally have debit balances are:
    (a) assets, expenses, and revenues.
    (b) assets, expenses, and owner's capital.
    (c) assets, liabilities, and drawings.
    (d) assets, expenses, and drawings.

(LO 2) K 4. What is the correct sequence of steps in the recording process?
    (a) Analyzing transactions; preparing a trial balance
    (b) Analyzing transactions; entering transactions in a journal; posting transactions
    (c) Entering transactions in a journal; posting transactions; preparing a trial balance
    (d) Entering transactions in a journal; posting transactions; analyzing transactions

(LO 2) AP 5. Performing services for a customer on account should result in:
    (a) a decrease in the liability account Accounts Payable and an increase in the revenue account Service Revenue.
    (b) an increase in the asset account Cash and a decrease in the asset account Accounts Receivable.
    (c) an increase to the asset account Accounts Receivable and an increase to the liability account Unearned Revenue.
    (d) an increase to the asset account Accounts Receivable and an increase to the revenue account Service Revenue.

(LO 2) AP 6. The purchase of equipment on account should result in:
    (a) a debit to Equipment and a credit to Accounts Payable.
    (b) a debit to Equipment Expense and a credit to Accounts Payable.
    (c) a debit to Equipment and a credit to Cash.
    (d) a debit to Accounts Receivable and a credit to Equipment.

(LO 3) K 7. A ledger:
    (a) contains only asset and liability accounts.
    (b) should show accounts in alphabetical order.
    (c) is a collection of the entire group of accounts maintained by a company.
    (d) is a book of original entry.

(LO 3) K 8. Posting:
    (a) is normally done before journalizing.
    (b) transfers ledger transaction data to the journal.
    (c) is an optional step in the recording process.
    (d) transfers journal entries to ledger accounts.

(LO 4) K 9. A trial balance:
    (a) is a list of accounts with their balances at a specific time.
    (b) proves that journalized transactions are accurate.
    (c) will not balance if a correct journal entry is posted twice.
    (d) proves that all transactions have been recorded.

(LO 4) AP 10. A trial balance will not balance if:
    (a) the collection of an account receivable is posted twice.
    (b) the purchase of supplies on account is debited to Supplies and credited to Cash.
    (c) a $100 cash drawing by the owner is debited to Drawings for $1,000 and credited to Cash for $100.
    (d) a $450 payment on account is debited to Accounts Payable for $45 and credited to Cash for $45.

Questions

(LO 1) C 1. What is an account? Will a company need more than one account? Explain.

(LO 1) K 2. What is debiting an account? What is crediting an account?

(LO 1) K 3. Explain the relationship between the normal balance in each type of account and the accounting equation.

(LO 1) C 4. Dmitri Karpov doesn't understand how a debit increases Equipment and a credit increases Accounts Payable. He believes that debits and credits cannot both increase account balances. Explain to Dmitri why he is wrong.

(LO 1) C 5. Why are increases to drawings and expenses recorded as debits?

(LO 1) C 6. Gustave Orsen, an introductory accounting student, thinks that a double-entry accounting system means that each transaction is recorded twice. Is Gustave correct? Explain.

(LO 2) C   7. MacKenzie Harper doesn't understand why some events are recorded as accounting transactions but others are not. Explain.

(LO 2) K   8. What are the basic steps in the recording process?

(LO 2) C   9. What is involved in analyzing a business transaction?

(LO 2) K   10. What is the difference between a simple and a compound journal entry? What rule must be followed when recording a compound entry so the accounting equation remains balanced?

(LO 2) C   11. A company receives cash from a customer. List three different accounts that could be credited and the circumstances under which each of these accounts would be credited.

(LO 3) K   12. What are the advantages of first recording transactions in the journal?

(LO 3) C   13. Explain the differences between the format of a T account and the standard form of accounts. In your explanation, include the benefits of each format, and when each format is typically used.

(LO 3) C   14. What are the differences between a ledger and a chart of accounts?

(LO 4) K   15. What is a trial balance? What are its purposes?

(LO 4) C   16. Does it matter in what order the accounts are listed on a trial balance? Explain.

(LO 4) C   17. Yue Shin thinks it doesn't matter in what order the first four steps in the accounting cycle are completed, as long as they are all done before moving on to the remaining steps. Do you agree or disagree with Yue? Explain.

(LO 4) C   18. Jamal Nazari is doing the accounting for a company that has a December 31 year end. He is wondering if the heading on its trial balance should read "Year Ended December 31" or just "December 31." Which one is correct? Explain why.

(LO 4) AN   19. Two students are discussing the use of a trial balance. They wonder if the following errors in different companies would prevent a trial balance from balancing. For each error, tell the students whether the trial balance will balance or not.
(a) The bookkeeper debited Supplies for $750 and debited Accounts Payable for $750 for the purchase of supplies on account.
(b) Cash collected on account was debited to Cash for $1,000 and credited to Service Revenue for $1,000.
(c) A journal entry recording the payment of rent expense was posted to the general ledger as a $650 debit to Rent Expense and a $560 credit to Cash.

(LO 4) AP   20. Madison Melnyk has just prepared a trial balance for a company and found that the total debits were $450 higher than the total credits. Assuming that the account balances in the ledger are correct, give Madison three examples of things that she might have done incorrectly when preparing the trial balance.

Brief Exercises

BE2–1   For the three accounts that follow, fill in the missing amounts (a) through (f):

Accounts Receivable		Supplies		Notes Payable	
7,500		6,400			100,000
16,700		(c)		24,000	
	15,400		6,800		45,000
Bal. (a)		Bal. 3,800			Bal. (e)
13,100		7,700			(f)
	(b)		5,900	27,000	
Bal. 4,700		Bal. (d)			Bal. 149,000

Calculate missing amounts and account balances. (LO 1) AP

BE2–2   Identify the normal balance for the following accounts:

1. Prepaid Insurance
2. Accounts Payable
3. Land
4. Service Revenue
5. Utilities Expense
6. Owner's Capital
7. Equipment
8. Salaries Expense
9. Supplies
10. Unearned Revenue

Indicate the normal balance. (LO 1) K

BE2–3   For each the following accounts, indicate (a) if the account is an asset, liability, or owner's equity account; and (b) whether the account would have a normal debit or credit balance.

1. Accounts Receivable
2. Rent Expense
3. B. Damji, Drawings
4. Supplies
5. Unearned Revenue
6. Service Revenue
7. Prepaid Insurance
8. Notes Payable

Indicate type of account and normal balance. (LO 1) K

Determine the account balance. (LO 1) K

BE2–4 Calculate the account balance for the following accounts:

Cash		Service Revenue		Accounts Payable		Salary Expense	
Dr.	Cr.	Dr.	Cr.	Dr.	Cr.	Dr.	Cr.
500	8,720		9,500	1,720	6,740	4,550	
800	495		3,200	495	2,500	550	
8,920	6,750		4,500	6,750		3,750	
5,355			1,050			425	
10,435							

Indicate normal balance and debit and credit effects. (LO 1) K

BE2–5 For each of the following accounts, indicate (a) the normal balance, (b) the effect of a debit on the account, and (c) the effect of a credit on the account:

1. Accounts Payable
2. Supplies
3. J. Takamoto, Capital
4. J. Takamoto, Drawings
5. Prepaid Rent
6. Utilitites Expense
7. Service Revenue
8. Unearned Revenue

Indicate type of account and when to use debits and credits. (LO 2) K

BE2–6 For each of the following, indicate (a) if the account is an asset, liability, or owner's equity account; and (b) whether you would use a debit or credit to record the change:

1. Increase in D. Parmelee, Capital
2. Decrease in Cash
3. Decrease in Notes Payable
4. Increase in Rent Expense
5. Increase in D. Parmelee, Drawings
6. Increase in Equipment
7. Increase in Accounts Payable
8. Increase in Service Revenue

Prepare basic analysis and debit/credit analysis for transactions. (LO 2) C

BE2–7 Levine Legal Services had the following transactions:

1. Cash is paid for the purchase of $439 of office supplies.
2. Customer is billed $1,020 for services provided that day.
3. Equipment with a cost of $2,230 is purchased on account.
4. The current month's utility bill of $293 is paid in cash.
5. Cash of $750 is received for services provided that day.
6. Cash of $7,100 is received for services to be provided in the next month.

For each transaction, prepare a basic analysis and a debit/credit analysis. Use the following format, in which the first one has been done for you as an example:

Transaction 1:

Basic analysis	The asset Cash is decreased by $439. The asset Supplies is increased by $439.
Debit/credit analysis	Debits increase assets: debit Supplies $439. Credits decrease assets: credit Cash $439.

Identify accounts and debit/credit analysis. (LO 2) C

BE2–8 Fleming's Logistics Consulting has the following transactions during August.

Aug.	1	Received $17,970 cash from the company's owner, Barbara Fleming.
	4	Paid rent in advance for three months, $4,720.
	5	Purchased $625 of office supplies on account.
	6	Received $560 from clients for services provided.
	17	Billed clients $1,210 for services provided.
	27	Paid secretary $980 salary.
	29	Paid the company's owner, Barbara Fleming, $720 cash for personal use.

For each transaction, indicate (a) the basic type of account to be debited and credited (asset, liability, owner's equity); (b) the specific accounts to debit and credit (for example, Cash, Service Revenue, Accounts Payable); and (c) whether each account is increased (+) or decreased (−), and by what amount. Use the following format, in which the first one has been done for you as an example:

	Account Debited			Account Credited		
Transaction	(a) Basic Type	(b) Specific Account	(c) Effect	(a) Basic Type	(b) Specific Account	(c) Effect
Aug. 1	Asset	Cash	+$17,970	Owner's Equity	B. Fleming, Capital	+$17,970

BE2–9   Pridham Welding Company had the following transactions for June.

June	1	Tyler Pridham invested $8,430 cash in a small welding business.
	2	Bought used welding equipment on account for $2,620.
	5	Hired an employee to start work on July 15. Agreed on a salary of $3,760 per month.
	17	Billed R. Windl $2,500 for welding work done.
	27	Received $1,190 cash from R. Windl for work billed on June 17.

For each transaction, prepare a basic analysis and a debit/credit analysis, and journalize the transaction. Use the following format, in which the first one has been done for you as an example:

June 1 transaction:

Basic analysis	The asset account Cash is increased by $8,430. The owner's equity account T. Pridham, Capital is increased by $8,430.
Debit/credit analysis	Debits increase assets: debit Cash $8,430. Credits increase owner's equity: credit T. Pridham, Capital $8,430.

Journal entry	June 1 Cash 8,430
	                    T. Pridham, Capital 8,430
	                        Invested cash in business.

BE2–10   Presented below is information related to Berge Real Estate Agency:

Oct.	1	Lia Berge begins business as a real estate agent with a cash investment of $30,000.
	2	Paid rent, $700, on office space.
	3	Purchases office equipment for $2,800, on account.
	6	Sells a house and lot for Hal Smith; bills Hal Smith $4,400 for realty services performed.
	27	Pays $1,100 on the balance related to the transaction of October 3.
	30	Receives bill for October utilities, $130 (not paid at this time).

Journalize the transactions. (You may omit explanations.)

BE2–11   Using the data in BE2–7 for Levine Legal Services, journalize the transactions. Assume all of the transactions occurred on August 31.

BE2–12   Using the data in BE2–8 for Fleming's Logistics Consulting, journalize the transactions.

BE2–13   Using T accounts, post the journal entries from BE2–12 to the general ledger. Note that since this is the first year of operations, there are no opening balances to consider.

BE2–14   Tom Rast recorded the following transactions during the month of April:

April	3	Cash	3,400	
		Service Revenue		3,400
	16	Rent Expense	700	
		Cash		700
	20	Salaries Expense	250	
		Cash		250

Post these entries to the Cash T account of the general ledger to determine the ending balance in cash. The beginning balance in cash on April 1 was $1,600.

BE2–15   Using T accounts, post the following journal entries to the general ledger.

GENERAL JOURNAL			
Date	Account titles	Debit	Credit
Sept. 2	Accounts Receivable	4,400	
	Service Revenue		4,400
4	Cash	2,400	
	Accounts Receivable		2,400
10	Cash	3,000	
	Service Revenue		3,000
28	Cash	1,325	
	Accounts Receivable		1,325

Prepare trial balance.
(LO 4) AP

BE2–16 From the ledger balances given below, prepare a trial balance for Amaro Company at June 30, 2017. All account balances are normal.

Accounts Payable $8,100, Cash $5,800, Owner's Capital $15,000, Owner's Drawings $1,200, Equipment $17,000, Service Revenue $10,000, Accounts Receivable $3,000, Salaries Expense $5,100, and Rent Expense $1,000.

Prepare trial balance.
(LO 4) AP

BE2–17 Use the ledger balances that follow to prepare a trial balance for Pettipas Company at April 30, 2017. All account balances are normal.

Accounts payable	$ 3,300	Prepaid rent	$ 800
Accounts receivable	5,000	Rent expense	4,500
C. Pettipas, capital	22,500	Salaries expense	1,000
C. Pettipas, drawings	1,100	Service revenue	8,000
Cash	6,400	Supplies	650
Equipment	14,600	Unearned revenue	250

Explain errors in trial balance. (LO 4) AP

BE2–18 There are two errors in the following trial balance: (1) one account has been placed in the wrong column, and (2) there is a transposition error in the balance of the L. Bourque, Capital account. Explain the two errors.

BOURQUE COMPANY
Trial Balance
December 31, 2017

	Debit	Credit
Cash	$15,000	
Accounts receivable	1,800	
Prepaid insurance		$ 3,500
Accounts payable		2,000
Unearned revenue		2,200
L. Bourque, capital		15,400
L. Bourque, drawings	4,900	
Service revenue		27,500
Rent expense	2,400	
Salaries expense	18,600	
Totals	$42,700	$50,600

▶ Exercises

Analyze statements about accounting and the recording process. (LO 1) K

E2–1 Kim Yi has prepared the following list of statements about accounts.

1. An account is an accounting record of either a specific asset or a specific liability.
2. An account shows only increases, not decreases, in the item it relates to.
3. Some items, such as Cash and Accounts Receivable, are combined into one account.
4. An account has a left, or credit side, and a right, or debit side.
5. A simple form of an account consisting of just the account title, the left side, and the right side, is called a T account.

Instructions

Identify each statement as true or false. If false, indicate how to correct the statement.

Match concepts with descriptions. (LO 1, 2, 3, 4) K

E2–2 Here are some of the concepts discussed in the chapter:

1. Account	5. Debit	9. Posting
2. Analyzing transactions	6. Journal	10. Trial balance
3. Chart of accounts	7. Journalizing	
4. Credit	8. Ledger	

Instructions

Match each concept with the best description below. Each concept may be used more than once, or may not be used at all.

(a) _____ The normal balance for liabilities
(b) _____ The first step in the recording process
(c) _____ The procedure of transferring journal entries to the ledger accounts
(d) _____ A record of increases and decreases in a specific asset, liability, or owner's equity item
(e) _____ The left side of an account
(f) _____ The entering of transaction data in the journal

(g) _____ A list of accounts and their balances at a specific time
(h) _____ Used to decrease the balance in an asset account
(i) _____ A list of all of a company's accounts
(j) _____ An accounting record where transactions are recorded in chronological (date) order

E2–3　Kobayashi Company has the following accounts:

Identify type of account, financial statement, and normal balance. Explain normal balances. (LO 1) C

Account	(1) Type of Account	(2) Financial Statement	(3) Normal Balance
Cash	Asset	Balance Sheet	Debit
M. Kobayashi, Capital			
Accounts Payable			
Building			
Fees Earned			
Insurance Expense			
Interest Revenue			
M. Kobayashi, Drawings			
Notes Receivable			
Prepaid Insurance			
Rent Expense			
Supplies			

Instructions

(a) Complete the table. Identify (1) the type of account as asset, liability, or owner's equity (for owner's equity accounts, also identify if it is a capital, drawings, revenue, or expense account); (2) what financial statement it is presented on; and (3) the normal balance of the account. The first one has been done for you as an example.
(b) Explain why the normal balance for each of the different types of accounts is either a debit or credit. Refer to the accounting equation in your explanation.

E2–4　In the first month of business, Jakmak Interior Design Company had the following transactions:

Identify accounts and determine debits and credits. (LO 1) C

Mar. 5　The owner, Jackie MacKenzie, invested $10,220 cash in the business.
　　7　Paid $350 cash for advertising the launch of the business.
　　9　Purchased supplies on account for $1,050.
　　11　Purchased a used car for $8,770 cash, for use in the business.
　　13　Billed customers $1,520 for services performed.
　　25　Borrowed $10,880 from the bank and signed a note payable.
　　26　Received $1,140 cash from customers billed on March 13.
　　29　Paid for the supplies purchased on March 9.
　　30　Received $800 cash from a customer for services to be performed in April.
　　31　Paid Jackie MacKenzie $1,720 cash for her personal use.

Instructions

For each transaction, indicate:

(a) the basic type of account debited and credited (asset, liability, or owner's equity);
(b) the specific account debited and credited (Cash, Rent Expense, Service Revenue, etc.); and
(c) whether each account is increased (+) or decreased (−), and by what amount.

Use the following format to complete the exercise; the first one has been done for you as an example:

	Account Debited				Account Credited		
	(a) Basic	(b) Specific	(c)		(a) Basic	(b) Specific	(c)
Date	Type	Account	Effect		Type	Account	Effect
Mar. 5	Asset	Cash	+10,220		Owner's Equity	J. MacKenzie, Capital	+10,220

E2–5　Using the data in E2–4 for Jakmak Interior Design Company, journalize the transactions.

Record transactions. (LO 2) AP

E2–6　Bratt Plumbing Company had the following transactions for June.

Prepare basic analysis, debit/credit analysis. (LO 2) AP

June 1　Paid $550 for rent for the month of June.
　　2　Paid $175 for one month of insurance.
　　5　Collected an account of $1,255 for plumbing services provided in May. This account was billed and correctly recorded in May.

9 Provided Jeff Dupuis, a potential customer, with an estimate of $5,000 for plumbing work that will be performed in July if the customer hires Bratt Plumbing.
14 Paid $675 for supplies purchased on account in May. The purchase in May had been correctly recorded.
17 Billed Rudy Holland $1,420 for plumbing work done.
19 Jeff Dupuis agreed to hire Bratt Plumbing (see the June 9 transaction) and gave Bratt Plumbing a down payment of $1,000.
29 Purchased $1,575 of equipment on account.
30 Paid an employee $850.
30 Paid D. Bratt, the company owner, $1,250.

Instructions

For each transaction, prepare a basic analysis and a debit/credit analysis. Use the format shown in BE2–7.

Record transactions.
(LO 2) AP

E2–7 Data for Bratt Plumbing Company are presented in E2–6.

Instructions

Journalize the transactions.

Record transactions.
(LO 2) AP

E2–8 At the end of September 2017, total owner's equity for Beaulieu Group Company was $8,050. During October, the following transactions occurred:

1. Provided services to a client and received $1,820 cash.
2. Paid $1,095 for October's rent.
3. Purchased $450 of supplies on account.
4. Provided services to a client and billed the client $2,105.
5. Collected $1,225 from the client billed in transaction 4.
6. Received $7,960 cash from a client for services to be provided in November.
7. Paid $8,120 cash for radio advertising that will be aired in November.
8. Paid for the supplies purchased on account in transaction 3.
9. Shehla Beaulieu, the owner, withdrew $2,800 cash for personal use.

Instructions

Journalize the transactions.

Record transactions.
(LO 2) AP

E2–9 Selected transactions for Polland Real Estate Agency during its first month of business follow:

June 1 Samantha Polland opened Polland Real Estate Agency with an investment of $13,430 cash and $3,490 of equipment.
2 Paid $1,420 for a one-year insurance policy.
3 Purchased additional equipment for $4,580, paying $930 cash and signing a note payable for the balance.
10 Received $220 cash as a fee for renting an apartment.
16 Sold a house and lot to B. Rollins. The commission due from Rollins is $8,000. (It is not paid by Rollins at this time.)
27 Paid $650 for advertising during June.
29 Received an $80 bill for telephone service during the month of June. (The bill is paid in July.)
30 Paid an administrative assistant $1,830 in salary for June.
30 Received $8,000 cash from B. Rollins for the June 16 transaction.

Instructions

Journalize the transactions.

Post journal entries and prepare trial balance.
(LO 3, 4) AP

E2–10 Journal entries for Polland Real Estate Agency's transactions were prepared in E2–9.

Instructions

(a) Post the journal entries to the general ledger, using T accounts. Note, as this is the first year of operations, there are no opening balances to consider.
(b) Post transactions to T accounts and prepare a trial balance at June 30, 2017.

Analyze statements about the ledger. (LO 3) K

E2–11 McKenna Para has prepared the following list of statements about the general ledger.

1. The general ledger contains all the asset and liability but no owner's equity accounts.
2. The general ledger is sometimes referred to as simply the ledger.
3. The accounts in the general ledger are arranged in alphabetical order.
4. Each account in the general ledger is numbered for easier identification.
5. The general ledger is a book of original entry.

Instructions

Identify each statement as true or false. If false, indicate how to correct the statement.

E2–12 On June 1, Depot Company began operations. On September 1, Depot Company has the following accounts and account balances:

Post journal entries and prepare a trial balance. (LO 3, 4) AP

Cash $17,400, Accounts Receivable $2,000, Supplies $1,900, Accounts Payable $1,000, Unearned Service Revenue $1,600, Owner's Capital $16,000, Service Revenue $4,100, and Salaries Expense $1,400

During the month of September, the bookkeeper for Depot Corporation created the following journal entries:

1. Cash	1,200	
Service Revenue		1,200
To record cash received from services performed.		
2. Salaries Expense	700	
Cash		700
Paid salaries to date.		
3. Accounts Payable	200	
Cash		200
Paid creditors on account.		
4. Cash	1,000	
Accounts Receivable		1,000
Received cash in payment of account.		
5. Unearned Service Revenue	1,200	
Service Revenue		1,200
Provided services.		
6. Supplies	1,000	
Accounts Payable		1,000
To record supplies purchased on account.		

(a) Create T accounts and post the opening balances.
(b) Post the September transactions and determine the ending balance in each account.
(c) Using the balances determined in part (b), create a trial balance at September 30, 2017.

E2–13 Selected transactions from the journal of June Feldman, investment broker, are presented below:

Post journal entries and prepare a trial balance. (SO 3, 4) AP

Date	Account Titles and Explanation	Ref	Debit	Credit
Aug. 1	Cash		5,000	
	J. Feldman, Capital			5,000
	Owner's investment of cash in business.			
10	Cash		2,600	
	Service Revenue			2,600
	Received cash for services performed.			
12	Equipment		5,000	
	Cash			2,300
	Notes Payable			2,700
	Purchased equipment for cash and notes payable.			
25	Accounts Receivable		1,700	
	Service Revenue			1,700
	Billed clients for services performed.			
31	Cash		900	
	Accounts Receivable			900
	Received cash on account.			

Instructions

(a) Post the transactions to T accounts.
(b) Prepare the trial balance at August 31, 2017.

E2–14 Fortin Co.'s ledger is as follows:

Record transactions and prepare trial balance. (LO 2, 4) AP

		Cash			
Oct.	1	1,200	Oct. 3	400	
	10	650	12	500	
	15	3,000	30	600	
	21	800	31	250	
	25	2,000	31	500	

A. Fortin, Capital		
Oct. 1	1,200	
25	2,000	

A. Fortin, Drawings	
Oct. 30	600

Accounts Receivable				
Oct.	6	1,000	Oct. 21	800
	20	940		

Supplies		
Oct.	4	800

Equipment		
Oct.	3	5,400

Notes Payable			
		Oct. 3	5,000

Accounts Payable				
Oct. 12	500	Oct.	4	800
			28	400

Service Revenue			
		Oct. 6	1,000
		10	650
		15	3,000
		20	940

Advertising Expense		
Oct. 28	400	

Rent Expense		
Oct. 31	250	

Salaries Expense		
Oct. 31	500	

Instructions

(a) Journalize the October transactions.

(b) Determine the October 31, 2017, balance for each account. Prepare a trial balance at October 31, 2017.

Post journal entries and prepare trial balance.
(LO 3, 4) AP

E2-15 On July 31, 2017, Lee Meche, MD, had the following balances in the ledger for his medical practice: Cash $8,800, Accounts Receivable $2,750, Supplies $585, Equipment $15,550, Notes Payable $10,000, Accounts Payable $850, L. Meche, Capital $15,000, L. Meche, Drawings $5,125, Fees Earned $10,410, Rent Expense $1,200, and Salaries Expense $2,250. Selected transactions during August 2017 follow:

GENERAL JOURNAL				
Date	Account titles	Ref	Debit	Credit
2017				
Aug. 1	Rent Expense		1,200	
	Cash			1,200
10	Accounts Payable		420	
	Cash			420
12	Cash		2,400	
	Accounts Receivable			2,400
25	Salaries Expense		2,250	
	Cash			2,250
30	Notes Payable		500	
	Interest Expense		40	
	Cash			540
31	Cash		5,910	
	Accounts Receivable		2,550	
	Fees Earned			8,460
31	L. Meche, Drawings		4,770	
	Cash			4,770

Instructions

(a) Create T accounts and enter the July 31 balances.

(b) Post the transactions to the T accounts. Create new T accounts if needed.

(c) Prepare a trial balance at August 31.

Prepare and post journal entries. Prepare trial balance.
(LO 2, 3, 4) AP

E2-16 Ahuja Dental Services' general ledger at June 30, 2017, included the following: Cash $5,820, Supplies $1,180, Equipment $64,990, Notes Payable $50,020, Accounts Payable $680, and S. Ahuja, Capital, $21,290. During July 2017, the following transactions occurred:

July 2   Paid July's rent of $1,060.

    4   Purchased $790 supplies on account.

   15   Paid the accounts payable owing from June 30, 2017.

   31   Paid the dental assistant's salary of $2,420.

   31   Earned revenue of $10,340 for dental services during July. Collected $9,940 of this in cash.

Instructions

(a) Journalize July transactions.
(b) Using T accounts, enter the balances as at June 30, 2017.
(c) Post the July journal entries.
(d) Prepare a trial balance.

E2–17   A list of accounts and their balances of O'Neill's Psychological Services, at its year end July 31, 2017, is presented below.

Prepare trial balance and financial statements.
(LO 4) AP

Supplies	$ 790	Notes Payable	$22,960
Unearned Revenue	1,350	Salaries Expense	45,540
Supplies Expense	5,960	T. O'Neill, Drawings	57,980
Cash	6,470	Equipment	58,900
Accounts Receivable	7,340	T. O'Neill, Capital	64,340
Accounts Payable	9,030	Service Revenue	96,180
Rent Expense	10,880		

Instructions

(a) Prepare a trial balance in financial statement order.
(b) Prepare an income statement, statement of owner's equity, and balance sheet.

E2–18   The accountant for Smistad Guitar Repair Company made a number of errors in journalizing and posting, as described below:

Analyze errors and their effect on the trial balance.
(LO 4) AN

1. A credit posting of $400 to Accounts Payable was omitted.
2. A debit posting of $750 for Rent Expense was debited to Prepaid Rent.
3. A collection on account of $100 was journalized and posted as a $100 debit to Cash and a $100 credit to Service Revenue.
4. A credit posting of $500 to Accounts Payable was made twice.
5. A cash purchase of supplies for $250 was journalized and posted as a $25 debit to Supplies and a $25 credit to Cash.
6. A debit of $475 to Advertising Expense was posted as $457.
7. A journal entry for the payment of $1,200 of salaries expense was posted twice.

Instructions

Considering each error separately, indicate the following using the format below, where error number 1 is given as an example.

(a) Will the trial balance be in balance?
(b) What is the amount of the error if the trial balance will not balance?
(c) Which trial balance column will have the larger total?
(d) Which account or accounts have an incorrect balance? If the balance in all of the accounts is correct, write "all correct."

Error	(a) In Balance	(b) Difference	(c) Larger Column	(d) Incorrect Accounts
1	No	$400	Debit	Accounts Payable

E2–19   Terry Zelinski, the owner of Royal Mountain Tours, prepared the following trial balance at March 31, 2017.

Prepare corrected trial balance. (LO 4) AP

Cash	$12,800	
Accounts receivable	4,090	
Supplies	840	
Equipment	7,350	
Accounts payable		$ 2,500
T. Zelinski, capital		24,000
T. Zelinski, drawings		3,650
Service revenue	6,750	
Advertising expense	3,700	
Salaries expense	400	
Total	$35,930	$30,150

A review shows that Terry made the following errors in the accounting records:

1. A purchase of $400 of supplies on account was recorded as a credit to Cash. The debit entry was correct.
2. A $100 credit to Accounts Receivable was posted as $1,000.

3. A journal entry to record service revenue of $770 earned on account was not prepared or posted.

4. A journal entry to record the payment of $240 for an advertising expense was correctly prepared but the credit to Cash was posted as a debit. The debit to Advertising Expense was properly posted.

Instructions

Prepare the correct trial balance at March 31, 2017, using the format shown in the chapter. (*Hint*: You should also make sure that the account balances are recorded in the correct columns on the trial balance.)

▶ Problems: Set A

Perform transaction analysis and journalize transactions.
(LO 1, 2) AP

P2–1A ND Paint Designs began operations on April 1, 2017. The company completed the following transactions in its first month:

Apr. 1 The owner, Nazim Dhaliwal, invested $12,800 cash in the company.

2 Purchased equipment for $5,000 on account.

2 Purchased a one-year insurance policy effective April 1, and paid the first month's premium of $134.

2 Paid for $590 of supplies.

7 Paid cash for $600 of advertising expenses.

8 Finished a painting project for Maya Angelina and collected $630 cash.

10 Received a $1,270 contract from a customer, SUB Terrain Inc., to paint its new office space. SUB Terrain will pay when the project is complete.

25 The owner, Nazim Dhaliwal, withdrew $960 cash for his use.

28 Completed the contract with SUB Terrain Inc. from April 10 and collected the amount owing.

29 Received $1,800 cash from Memphis Shek for a painting project that ND Paint Designs will start on May 5.

30 Paid for the equipment purchased on account on April 2.

Instructions

(a) For each transaction, indicate: (1) the basic type of account debited and credited (asset, liability, or owner's equity); (2) the specific account debited and credited (Cash, Rent Expense, Service Revenue, etc.); and (3) whether each account is increased (+) or decreased (−), and by what amount. Use the following format, in which the first transaction is given as an example:

	Account Debited			Account Credited		
	(1)	(2)	(3)	(1)	(2)	(3)
	Basic	Specific		Basic	Specific	
Transaction	Type	Account	Effect	Type	Account	Effect
Apr. 1	Asset	Cash	+$12,800	Owner's Equity	N. Dhaliwal, Capital	+$12,800

(b) Prepare a journal entry for each transaction.

TAKING IT FURTHER Nazim doesn't understand why a debit increases the cash account and yet a credit to N. Dhaliwal, Capital increases that account. He reasons that debits and credits cannot both increase account balances. Explain to Nazim why he is wrong.

Journalize transactions.
(LO 2) AP

P2–2A Bucket Club Miniature Golf and Driving Range was opened on May 1. The following events and transactions are for May:

May 1 Amin Mawani, the owner, invested $73,800 cash in the business.

2 Purchased Lee's Golf Land for $251,900. The price consists of land $108,500, building $84,300, and equipment $59,100. Paid $60,300 cash and signed a note payable for the balance.

4 Purchased golf clubs and other equipment for $17,000 from Woods Company on account.

5 Hired a golf pro to teach lessons at the golf range at a rate of $40 per hour.

6 Paid $2,580 cash for a one-year insurance policy.

15 Collected $1,830 of golf fees earned in cash from customers.

19 Paid Woods Company $5,480 for the items purchased on May 4.

20 Billed a customer, Deer Fern Inc., $1,410 for golf fees earned. Deer Fern Inc. paid $350 and agreed to pay the remaining amount owing in 10 days.

30 Received $1,060 from Deer Fern Inc. for the May 20 transaction.

31 Collected $3,100 cash from customers for golf fees earned.
31 Paid salaries of $2,220.
31 Paid $710 of interest on the note payable.
31 Paid Amin Mawani $1,540 for his personal use.

The company's chart of accounts includes the following accounts: Cash; Accounts Receivable; Prepaid Insurance; Land; Buildings; Equipment; Accounts Payable; Notes Payable; A. Mawani, Capital; A. Mawani, Drawings; Fees Earned; Salaries Expense; and Interest Expense.

Instructions
Journalize the May transactions.

TAKING IT FURTHER After Amin has reviewed the journal entries, he complains that they don't seem to be very useful. Explain to Amin the purpose of the journal entries.

P2–3A You are presented with the following transactions for J. Green, a sole proprietorship established in the month of August:

Journalize transactions. (LO 2) AP

Aug. 2 The owner, Jason Green, invested $35,000 in the business.
2 Purchased supplies on account for $550.
5 Purchased equipment for $10,000 by signing a note payable due in three months.
9 Earned service revenue of $15,000. Of this amount, $7,500 was received in cash. The balance was on account.
14 Paid salaries of $1,200.
15 Paid Jason Green $4,300 for his use.
19 A customer paid $2,450 in advance for services to be provided next month.
22 Paid the balance owing for the supplies purchased on August 2.
25 Collected the $7,500 of the amount owing from the August 9 transaction.
26 Paid office expense of $3,200.
30 Paid interest of $50 on the note payable signed on August 5.

Instructions
Journalize the August transactions.

TAKING IT FURTHER Jason Green does not understand why service revenue and salaries expense are considered equity accounts. Explain why they are considered equity accounts. Include in your explanation the debit and credit conventions.

P2–4A Emily Valley is a licensed dentist. During the first month of operation of her business, the following events and transactions occurred.

Journalize transactions, post, and prepare a trial balance. (LO 1, 2, 3, 4) AP

Apr. 1 Invested $20,000 cash in her business.
1 Hired a secretary-receptionist at a salary of $700 per week, payable monthly.
2 Paid office rent for the month of $1,100.
3 Purchased dental supplies on account from Dazzle Company of $4,000.
10 Performed dental services and billed insurance companies $5,100.
11 Received $1,000 cash advance from Leah Mataruka for an implant.
20 Received $2,100 cash for services performed from Michael Santos.
30 Paid secretary-receptionist $2,800 for the month.
30 Paid $2,400 to Dazzle for accounts payable due.

Emily uses the following chart of accounts: No. 101 Cash, No. 112 Accounts Receivable, No. 126 Supplies, No. 201 Accounts Payable, No. 209 Unearned Revenue, No. 301 E. Valley, Capital, No. 400 Service Revenue, No. 726 Salaries Expense, and No. 729 Rent Expense.

Instructions
(a) Journalize the transactions.
(b) Post the journal entries directly to the ledger accounts. (Note: See Illustration 2.6).
(c) Prepare a trial balance at April 30, 2017.

TAKING IT FURTHER Emily Valley believes that now that she has posted the transactions for the month of April, she no longer needs to do any further accounting for that month. Explain to Emily the next step of the accounting cycle and the benefits of performing it.

Journalize transactions, post, and prepare trial balance. (LO 2, 3, 4) AP

P2–5A Grete Rodewald formed a dog grooming and training business called Grete Kanines on September 1, 2017. After consulting with a friend who had taken introductory accounting, Grete created a chart of accounts for the business as follows: No. 101 Cash; No. 112 Accounts Receivable; No. 130 Prepaid Insurance; No. 151 Equipment; No. 201 Accounts Payable; No. 209 Unearned Revenue; No. 301 G. Rodewald, Capital; No. 306 G. Rodewald, Drawings; No. 400 Service Revenue; No. 610 Advertising Expense; No. 726 Rent Expense; and No. 737 Utilities Expense. During September, the following events and transactions occurred:

Sept. 1	Grete transferred $9,630 from her personal bank account to a bank account under the company name Grete Kanines.
2	Signed a one-year rental agreement for $690 per month. Paid the first month's rent.
2	Paid $750 for a one-year insurance policy effective September 1, 2017.
5	Purchased $2,640 of equipment on credit.
7	Paid $420 for advertising in several community newsletters in September.
13	Collected $500 cash for providing dog grooming services.
21	Attended a dog show and provided $800 of dog grooming services for one of the major kennel owners. The kennel owner will pay the amount owing within two weeks.
24	Collected $540 from the kennel owner for the services provided on September 21. The kennel owner promised to pay the rest on October 2.
28	Paid $210 for utilities for the month of September.
29	Paid $1,470 of the amount owed from the September 5 equipment purchase.
30	Received $860 cash for dog training lessons that will start on October 10.
30	Collected $1,045 cash for providing dog grooming services.
30	Paid the owner, Grete Rodewald, $1,490 for her personal use.

Instructions

(a) Journalize the transactions.

(b) Post the journal entries directly to the ledger accounts. (Note: See Illustration 2.6.)

(c) Prepare a trial balance as at September 30, 2017.

TAKING IT FURTHER   Grete thinks she needs only one account for investments, drawings, revenues, and expenses because these are all owner's equity accounts. Explain to her why she needs separate accounts.

Journalize transactions, post, and prepare trial balance. (LO 2, 3, 4) AP

P2–6A Abramson Financial Services was formed on May 1, 2017. The following events and transactions are from its first month:

May 1	Jacob Abramson invested $44,810 cash and equipment worth $10,690 in the company.
1	Hired one employee to work in the office for a salary of $2,340 per month.
2	Paid $3,255 cash for a one-year insurance policy.
5	Signed a two-year rental agreement on an office and paid $4,550 cash. Half was for the May 2017 rent and the other half was for the final month's rent. (*Hint:* The portion for the final month is considered prepaid rent.)
8	Purchased additional equipment costing $15,870. A cash payment of $7,150 was made immediately. Signed a note payable for the balance.
9	Purchased supplies for $570 cash.
15	Purchased more supplies for $730 on account.
17	Completed a contract for a client for $3,200 on account.
22	Paid $320 for May's telephone bill.
25	Completed services for a client and immediately collected $1,120.
26	Paid Jacob Abramson $1,980 cash for his personal use.
28	Collected $2,720 from the client billed on May 17.
30	Paid for the supplies purchased on account on May 15.
30	Paid $67 interest expense on the note payable.
31	Received a cash advance of $500 for services to be completed in June.
31	Paid the employee's monthly salary, $2,340.

Instructions

(a) Prepare journal entries to record the transactions.

(b) Post the journal entries to ledger accounts. Use T accounts.

(c) Prepare a trial balance as at May 31, 2017.

TAKING IT FURTHER   Jacob asks if the change in his cash account balance, from the beginning to the end of the month, is equal to his profit or loss for the month. Explain to Jacob whether or not this is true and why.

P2-7A Sequel Theatre, owned by Nadia Wood, is unique as it shows only movies that are part of a theme with sequels. As at April 30, 2017, the ledger of Sequel Theatre showed the following: Cash $18,900, Land $75,000, Buildings $69,800, Equipment $17,000, Accounts Payable $4,990, Mortgage Payable $106,300, and N. Wood, Capital, $69,410. In May, the following events and transactions occurred:

Journalize transactions, post, and prepare trial balance.
(LO 2, 3, 4) AP

May 1	Rented the first four *Harry Potter* movies, to be shown in the first two weeks of May. The film rental was $25,000. Of that amount, $10,784 was paid in cash and the balance will be paid on May 10.
2	Hired M. Brewer to operate the concession stand. Brewer agreed to pay Sequel Theatre 15% of gross concession receipts, on the last day of each month, for the right to operate the concession stand.
7	Paid advertising expenses, $1,090.
10	Received $35,940 cash from customers for admissions.
10	Paid the balance due from the May 1 movie rental transaction.
15	Received the final four *Harry Potter* movies to be shown in the last two weeks of May. The film rental cost was $28,600. Paid $14,300 cash and the balance will be paid on June 1.
25	Paid the accounts payable owing at the end of April.
30	Paid salaries of $6,230.
31	Received statement from Brewer showing gross receipts from concessions of $27,700 and the balance due to Sequel Theatre of $4,155 ($27,700 × 15%) for May. Brewer paid $2,370 of the balance due and will pay the rest on June 5.
31	Received $41,800 cash from admissions.
31	Made a $1,790 mortgage payment. Of this amount, $1,185 is a principal payment, and $605 is interest on the mortgage.

In addition to the accounts identified above, Sequel Theatre's ledger includes the following: Accounts Receivable; Admission Revenue; Concession Revenue; Advertising Expense; Film Rental Expense; Interest Expense; and Salaries Expense.

Instructions

(a) Journalize the May transactions.
(b) Enter the beginning balances in the ledger as at May 1. Use the ledger format provided in Illustration 2.6.
(c) Post the May journal entries to the ledger.
(d) Prepare a trial balance at the end of May.

TAKING IT FURTHER A friend of yours is considering buying Sequel Theatre from the current owner. Using the information in the trial balance, comment on whether or not this may be a sound company for your friend to purchase.

P2-8A Aduke Zhawaki is a talented musician who runs a business teaching music and playing in gigs with a variety of other musicians. Her business is operated as a proprietorship, under the name A to Z Music, which has a December 31 year end. On November 30, 2017, the company's general ledger included the following accounts (all accounts have normal balances):

Journalize transactions, post, and prepare trial balance.
(LO 2, 3, 4) AP

A. Zhawaki, capital	$19,500	Insurance expense	$3,410
A. Zhawaki, drawings	31,350	Rent expense	5,225
Accounts payable	4,235	Supplies	1,450
Accounts receivable	2,200	Telephone expense	1,485
Cash	2,965	Travel expense	6,050
Equipment	17,500	Unearned revenue	825
Fees earned	47,075		

December transactions were as follows:

Dec. 1	Paid December rent on her studio space, $475.
1	Purchased additional sound equipment for $3,500 from a friend who was going back to school to study accounting. The equipment was probably worth $5,000, but the friend needed the cash for tuition and was anxious to sell it. Paid $1,500 cash and promised to pay the remaining amount by December 5.
3	Borrowed $2,500 cash from her parents and signed a note payable.
4	Paid her friend the remaining amount owing on the December 1 transaction.
4	Collected $1,800 from customers in payment of their accounts.
7	Paid the $310 monthly insurance premium.
8	Paid for $150 of supplies.
10	Paid $2,130 of the accounts payable from November.
15	Gave musical performances at two recitals and earned $825. The customers had paid her in November. (*Hint:* In November, Aduke had recorded the $825 received in advance as a liability, Unearned Revenue. By performing at the recitals, she has "paid" this obligation.)

20   Received $3,300 cash from students for music lessons provided in December.
21   Paid her monthly telephone bill of $135.
22   Billed customers $2,250 for providing music at several holiday parties.
24   Withdrew $3,000 for personal use.
29   Received $525 cash advance from a customer for a performance in January.
30   Paid travel expenses of $695 for December in cash.
31   Paid her parents $210. Of this amount, $10 is interest and the remainder is a principal payment on the note payable.

Instructions

(a) Enter the November 30 balances in ledger accounts. Use T accounts.
(b) Journalize the December transactions.
(c) Post the December journal entries to the T accounts. Add new accounts if needed.
(d) Prepare a trial balance at December 31, 2017.

TAKING IT FURTHER   Comment on A to Z Music's cash balance at December 31, 2017. What concerns or suggestions do you have for Aduke to consider in January?

Prepare trial balance.
(LO 4) AP

P2–9A   The following is an alphabetical list of accounts and balances for J. Saggit, proprietorship, at June 30, 2017:

Accounts Payable	$12,500	Notes Payable	$30,000
Accounts Receivable	10,250	Prepaid Expenses	3,000
Cash	8,000	Rent Expense	4,500
Equipment	18,250	Service Revenue	63,050
Interest Expense	500	Supplies	5,000
J. Saggit, Capital	28,000	Utilities Expense	550
J. Saggit, Drawings	12,000	Salaries Expense	7,500
Land	64,000		

Instructions

Prepare a trial balance at June 30, sorting each account into the debit or the credit column.

TAKING IT FURTHER   J. Saggit believes that once the trial balance is prepared, if the debits equal the credits, then his financial statements will be error free. Advise J. Saggit if he is correct in his belief.

Prepare financial statements.
(LO 4) AP

P2–10A   Refer to the trial balance for Abramson Financial Services prepared in P2–6A, part (c).

Instructions

(a) Prepare an income statement for May.
(b) Prepare a statement of owner's equity for May.
(c) Prepare a balance sheet at the end of May 2017.

TAKING IT FURTHER   Discuss how well the company performed in its first month of operations.

Journalize transactions, post, and prepare trial balance.
(LO 2, 3, 4) AP

P2–11A   Derek Scoffin owns and operates YH Curling School on evenings and weekends. The company had the following balances in its general ledger at January 31, 2017: Cash $2,100, Accounts Receivable $720, Equipment $12,400, Accounts Payable $1,470, and D. Scoffin, Capital $13,750. The following events and transactions occurred during February 2017.

Feb. 1   Received and paid a $430 advertising bill.
      2   Paid the YH Curling Club $1,050 rent for use of the ice for lessons during the first two weeks of February.
      3   Collected $4,240 cash for February's curling lessons.
      4   Collected all of the accounts receivable at January 31 in cash.
      6   Paid $970 of the accounts payable at January 31.
     14   Paid his part-time assistant $400.
     15   Paid the YH Curling Club $1,050 rent for use of the ice for lessons during the last two weeks of February.
     23   Provided $1,475 of coaching services to curlers preparing for a tournament. The curlers will pay him on March 2.
     26   Paid $185 cash for his Internet bill for February. This is a business, not a personal, expense.
     27   Received $2,830 cash for curling lessons in March.

27   Withdrew $575 cash. Used the cash to pay his Visa bill.
28   Paid his part-time assistant $400.
28   Paid the YH Curling Club $1,050 rent for use of the ice for lessons during the first two weeks of March.

Instructions

(a) Prepare journal entries to record each of YH Curling School's February transactions. (*Hint*: Use the revenue account Fees Earned for all revenue earned in February.)
(b) Open the required ledger accounts for the transactions that were journalized, and enter the January 31, 2017, balances. Use T accounts.
(c) Post the journal entries to the accounts in the ledger.
(d) Prepare a trial balance as at February 28, 2017.

TAKING IT FURTHER   Are the February payments to YH Curling Club for ice rental an asset, a reduction of a liability, or an expense? Explain.

P2–12A   Refer to the trial balance prepared in part (d) of P2–11A for YH Curling School.

Prepare financial statements. (LO 4) AP

Instructions

Use the trial balance to do the following:

(a) Prepare an income statement for YH Curling School.
(b) Prepare a statement of owner's equity.
(c) Prepare a balance sheet.

TAKING IT FURTHER   Derek has reviewed the financial statements. He does not understand why the company's revenue is not equal to the cash he collected from customers. Explain.

P2–13A   The ledger of Super Delivery Service has the following account balances at the company's year end, August 31, 2017:

Prepare trial balance and financial statements. (LO 4) AP

Accounts Payable	$ 3,250	Repairs Expense	$ 1,549
Accounts Receivable	4,226	Salaries Expense	5,698
Cash	?	Salaries Payable	883
Equipment	49,660	Service Revenue	37,800
Gas Expense	12,177	Supplies	299
Insurance Expense	2,016	Supplies Expense	2,606
Interest Expense	1,006	T. Rowe, Capital	48,840
Notes Payable	19,480	T. Rowe, Drawings	25,000
Prepaid Insurance	358	Unearned Revenue	643

Instructions

(a) Prepare a trial balance, with the accounts arranged in ledger (financial statement) order, as illustrated in the chapter, and determine the missing amount for Cash.
(b) Prepare an income statement, statement of owner's equity, and balance sheet.

TAKING IT FURTHER   The owner, Tom Rowe, is not sure how much cash he can withdraw from the company each year. After reviewing the financial statements, comment on the amount he withdrew this year.

P2–14A   A co-op student, working for Insidz Co., recorded the company's transactions for the month. At the end of the month, the owner of Insidz Co. reviewed the student's work and had some questions about the following transactions:

Analyze errors and effects on trial balance. (LO 4) AN

1. Insidz Co. received $425 cash from a customer on account, which was recorded as a debit to Cash of $425 and a credit to Accounts Receivable of $425.
2. A service provided for cash was posted as a debit to Cash of $2,000 and a credit to Service Revenue of $2,000.
3. A credit of $750 for interest earned was neither recorded nor posted. The debit was recorded and posted correctly.
4. The debit to record $1,000 of drawings was posted to the Salary Expense account. The credit was posted correctly.
5. Services of $325 were provided to a customer on account. The co-op student debited Accounts Receivable $325 and credited Unearned Revenue $325.
6. A purchase of supplies for $770 on account was recorded as a credit to Supplies and a credit to Accounts Payable.

7. Insidz Co. received a cash advance of $500 from a customer for work to be done next month. Cash was debited $500 but there was no credit because the co-op student was not sure what to credit.
8. A cash payment of $495 for salaries was recorded as a debit to Salaries Expense and a credit to Salaries Payable.
9. Insidz Co. purchased $2,600 of equipment on account and made a $6,200 debit to Equipment and a $2,600 credit to Accounts Payable.
10. A $650 utility bill for the month was received at the end of the month. It was not recorded because it had not been paid.

Instructions

(a) Indicate which transactions are correct and which are incorrect.
(b) For each error identified in part (a), answer the following:
     1. Will the trial balance be in balance?
     2. Which account(s) will be incorrectly stated because of the error?
     3. For each account you identified in (2) as being incorrect, is the account overstated or understated? By how much?
     4. Is the debit column total of the trial balance stated correctly? If not, does correcting the errors increase or decrease the total and by how much?
     5. Is the credit column total of the trial balance stated correctly? If not, does correcting the errors increase or decrease the total and by how much?

TAKING IT FURTHER   Your best friend thinks it is a waste of time to correct all of the above errors. Your friend reasons that, as long as the trial balance is balanced, then there is no need to correct an error. Do you agree or disagree with your friend? Explain, using at least two of the above errors to make your points.

Prepare correct trial balance. (LO 4) AN

P2–15A   The trial balance of Winter Co. does not balance:

WINTER CO. Trial Balance June 30, 2017		
	Debit	Credit
Cash	$ 2,835	
Accounts receivable	1,861	
Supplies	500	
Equipment		$ 7,900
Accounts payable		2,695
Unearned revenue	1,855	
F. Winter, capital		11,231
F. Winter, drawings	800	
Service revenue		3,460
Office expense	1,010	
Salaries expense	3,000	
	$11,861	$25,286

Your review of the ledger reveals that each account has a normal balance. You also discover the following errors:

1. Cash received from a customer on account was debited to Cash for $750 and Accounts Receivable was credited for the same amount. The actual collection was $570.
2. The purchase of supplies on account for $360 was recorded as a debit to Equipment for $360 and a credit to Accounts Payable for $360.
3. Services of $980 were performed on account for a client. Accounts Receivable was debited for $98 and Service Revenue was credited for $980.
4. A debit posting to Office Expense of $500 was not done.
5. A payment on account for $806 was credited to Cash for $806 and debited to Accounts Payable for $608.

6. The withdrawal of $400 cash for Winter's personal use was debited to Salaries Expense for $400 and credited to Cash for $400.
7. A transposition error (reversal of digits) was made when copying the balance in Service Revenue to the trial balance. The correct balance recorded in the account was $4,360.
8. The general ledger contained a Prepaid Insurance account with a debit balance of $655.

Instructions

Prepare a correct trial balance.

TAKING IT FURTHER   After the trial balance is corrected for the above errors, could there still be errors in any of the account balances? Explain why or why not.

▶ Problems: Set B

P2–1B   Battistella Couture & Design Co. began operations in 2017. During January 2017, the company had the following transactions:

Perform transaction analysis and journalize transactions.
(LO 1, 2) AP

Jan. 2   Paid January rent, $525.
    4   Finished sewing a suit, delivered it to the customer, and collected $1,055 cash.
    5   Purchased supplies for $420 on account.
    7   Received an order from another customer to design and sew a leather jacket for $1,085.
    10   Agreed to sew a wedding dress for a customer for $3,000. Received $1,500 cash from the customer as a down payment.
    12   The owner, Karen Battistella, withdrew $500 cash for personal use.
    18   Finished sewing the leather jacket (see January 7 transaction), and delivered it to the customer. The customer, a friend of Karen's, asked if she could pay at the end of the month. Karen agreed.
    25   Paid for the supplies purchased on January 5.
    27   The customer billed on January 18 paid the amount owing.
    28   Borrowed $5,000 cash from the bank and signed a one-year, 5% note payable.
    29   Used $1,950 of the note payable to purchase a new pressing machine.

Instructions

(a) For each transaction, indicate: (1) the basic type of account debited and credited (asset, liability, or owner's equity); (2) the specific account debited and credited (Cash, Rent Expense, Service Revenue, etc.); and (3) whether each account is increased (+) or decreased (−), and by what amount. Use the following format, in which the first transaction is given as an example:

	Account Debited				Account Credited		
Transaction	Basic Type	Specific Account	Effect	Basic Type	Specific Account	Effect
Jan. 2	Owner's Equity	Rent Expense	+$525	Asset	Cash	−$525

(b) Prepare a journal entry for each transaction.

TAKING IT FURTHER   Karen is confused about why credits are used to decrease cash. Explain.

P2–2B   Mountain Adventure Biking Park was started on May 1 by Dustin Tanner. The following events and transactions are for May:

Journalize transactions.
(LO 2) AP

May 1   Tanner invested $70,000 cash in the business.
    3   Purchased an out-of-use ski hill for $355,000, paying $35,000 cash and signing a five-year, 4.5% note payable for the balance. The $355,000 purchase price consisted of land $225,000, building $75,000, and equipment $55,000.
    3   Purchased a one-year insurance policy effective May 1 for $9,360. Paid the first month's premium of $780.

  8   Paid $1,950 for advertising expenses.

 15   Received $5,400 cash from customers for admission fees.

 16   Paid salaries to employees, $2,600.

 20   Billed a customer, Celtic Fern Ltd., $2,750 for admission fees for exclusive use of the park that day. Celtic Fern Ltd. paid $500 cash and agreed to pay the amount owing within 10 days.

 22   Hired a park manager to start June 1 at a salary of $4,000 per month.

 29   Received the balance owing cash from Celtic Fern Ltd. for the May 20 transaction.

 30   Received $5,750 cash for admission fees.

 31   Paid $6,533 on the note payable, of which $1,200 is interest expense.

 31   Dustin Tanner, the owner, withdrew $1,800 cash for his personal use.

 31   Paid salaries to employees, $3,800.

The company's chart of accounts includes the following accounts: Cash; Accounts Receivable; Prepaid Insurance; Land; Building; Equipment; Accounts Payable; Notes Payable; D. Tanner, Capital; D. Tanner, Drawings; Admissions Revenue; Advertising Expense; Salaries Expense; and Interest Expense.

Instructions

Journalize the May transactions.

TAKING IT FURTHER   After Dustin has reviewed the journal entries, he complains that they don't seem to be very useful. Explain to Dustin the purpose of the journal entries and the next step in the accounting cycle. Include in your answer whether or not Dustin will find any useful information after the next step is completed.

Journalize transactions.
(LO 2) AP

P2–3B   You are presented with the following transactions for A. Rai, a sole proprietorship established in the month of April:

Apr. 1   The owner, A. Rai, invested $27,750 in the business.

    2   Purchased equipment for $5,000 by signing a note payable due in three months.

    3   Purchased supplies on account for $250.

    5   Earned service revenue of $12,250. Of this amount, $6,300 was received in cash. The balance was on account.

  10   Paid A. Rai $4,300 for his personal use.

  13   Paid the balance owing for supplies purchased on April 3.

  15   A customer paid $2,450 in advance for services to be provided next month.

  25   Collected the balance from the April 5 transaction.

  26   Paid office expense of $1,200.

  30   Paid interest of $45 on the note payable signed on April 2.

Instructions

Journalize the August transactions.

TAKING IT FURTHER   Explain the relationship between the normal balance in each type of account and the basic accounting equation.

Journalize transactions, post, and prepare a trial balance.
(LO 1, 2, 3, 4), AP

P2–4B   Barbara Fair is a licensed architect. During the first month of operation of her business, the following events and transactions occurred.

Apr. 1   Invested $45,000 cash.

    1   Hired a secretary-receptionist at a salary of $500 per week payable monthly.

    2   Paid office rent for the month $800.

    3   Purchased architectural supplies on account from Dakin Company for $1,500.

  10   Completed blueprints on a carport and billed client $1,800 for services performed.

  11   Received $500 cash advance from D. Ellington for the design of a new home.

  20   Received $1,500 cash for services completed and delivered to L. Leno.

  30   Paid secretary-receptionist $2,000 for the month.

  30   Paid $600 to Dakin Company for accounts payable due.

Barbara uses the following chart of accounts:

No. 101 Cash, No. 112 Accounts Receivable, No. 126 Supplies, No. 201 Accounts Payable, No. 209 Unearned Service Revenue, No. 301 B. Fair, Capital, No. 400 Service Revenue, No. 726 Salaries Expense, and No. 729 Rent Expense.

Instructions

(a) Journalize the transactions.
(b) Post the journal entries directly to the ledger accounts. (Note: See Illustration 2.6).
(c) Prepare a trial balance on April 30, 2017.

TAKING IT FURTHER   Barbara believes credit balances are favourable and debit balances are unfavourable. Is Barbara correct? Discuss.

P2–5B   Thanh Nguyen started a business, Nguyen Import Services, on August 1, 2017. After consulting with a friend who had taken introductory accounting, Thanh created a chart of accounts for the business as follows: No. 101 Cash; No. 112 Accounts Receivable; No. 126 Supplies; No. 151 Equipment; No. 201 Accounts Payable; No. 209 Unearned Revenue; No. 301 T. Nguyen, Capital; No. 306 T. Nguyen, Drawings; No. 400 Service Revenue; No. 610 Advertising Expense; No. 726 Rent Expense; and No. 737 Utilities Expense. During August, the following events and transactions occurred:

Journalize transactions, post, and prepare trial balance. (LO 2, 3, 4) AP

Aug. 1	Thanh transferred $25,000 cash from his personal bank account to a bank account under the company name, Nguyen Import Services.
1	Signed a one-year rental agreement for $750 per month. Paid the first month's rent.
2	Paid $250 for utilities for August.
3	Purchased equipment for $5,250 cash.
5	Purchased $675 of supplies on account.
8	Provided services to a client and billed them $1,270.
12	Paid $945 for advertising the opening of the company.
20	Provided services to a client and collected $1,320 cash.
24	Received a $2,500 cash advance for a consulting engagement to be started in September.
25	Paid the balance due for the purchase of supplies on August 5.
28	Received $970 cash from the client billed in the August 8 transaction.
29	Paid Thanh, the owner, $1,225 cash for his personal use.
31	Received a $225 utility bill for August. It will be paid on September 1.

Instructions

(a) Journalize the transactions.
(b) Post the journal entries directly to the ledger accounts. (Note: See Illustration 2.6).
(c) Prepare a trial balance at August 31, 2017.

TAKING IT FURTHER   Thanh asks why separate drawings, revenue, and expense accounts are necessary since all of these accounts are owner's equity accounts. Thanh thinks he should be able to use one account. Explain if he is correct or not.

P2–6B   Kiersted Financial Services was formed on November 1, 2017. During the month of November, the following events and transactions occurred:

Journalize transactions, post, and prepare trial balance. (LO 2, 3, 4) AP

Nov. 1	Haakon Kiersted, the owner, invested $35,000 cash in the company. He also invested equipment that had originally cost Haakon $25,000 but was currently worth $12,000.
2	Hired one employee to work in the office for a monthly salary of $2,825.
3	Signed a three-year contract to lease office space for $2,140 per month. Paid the first and last month's rent in cash. (*Hint:* The payment for the final month's rent should be considered an asset and be recorded in Prepaid Rent.)
4	Purchased a one-year insurance policy for $4,740 to be paid in monthly instalments on the fourth day of each month. Paid the first month's premium.
5	Purchased additional equipment for $18,000. Paid $6,000 cash and signed a note payable for the balance.
6	Purchased supplies for $1,550 on account.
7	Purchased additional supplies for $475 cash.
16	Completed services for a customer and immediately collected $990.
20	Completed services for two customers and billed them a total of $4,500.
26	Paid $1,000 for the supplies purchased on account on November 6.
27	The telephone bill for November was $220. It will be paid in December.
27	Received a $750 cash advance from a customer for services to be provided in December.
29	Collected $2,800 from one of the customers billed on November 20.
30	Paid $60 interest on the note payable.

30   Paid the employee's monthly salary, $2,825.

30   Paid Haakon Kiersted $700 for his personal use.

30   Paid Sony Ltd. for a new sound system for Haakon's home, $1,150 cash.

Instructions

(a) Prepare journal entries to record the transactions.

(b) Post the journal entries to T accounts.

(c) Prepare a trial balance as at November 30, 2017.

TAKING IT FURTHER   Haakon asks if the change in his cash account balance from the beginning to the end of the month is equal to his profit or loss for the month. Explain to Haakon whether or not this is true and why.

Journalize transactions, post, and prepare trial balance.

(LO 2, 3, 4) AP

P2-7B   Highland Theatre is owned by Finnean Ferguson. At June 30, 2017, the ledger showed the following: Cash $6,000, Land $100,000, Buildings $80,000, Equipment $25,000, Accounts Payable $5,000, Mortgage Payable $125,000, and F. Ferguson, Capital $81,000. During July, the following events and transactions occurred:

July 2   Paid film rental of $800 on first movie to run in July.

      2   Paid advertising expenses, $620.

      3   Ordered two additional films at $750 each.

      5   Highland Theatre contracted with Seibert Company to operate a concession stand. Seibert agreed to pay Highland Theatre 20% of gross concession receipts, payable monthly, for the right to operate the concession stand.

   10   Received $1,950 cash from admissions.

   11   Paid $2,000 of the mortgage principal. Also paid $500 interest on the mortgage.

   12   Paid $350 cash to have the projection equipment repaired.

   16   Paid $2,800 of the accounts payable.

   19   Received one of the films ordered on July 3 and was billed $750. The film will be shown in July.

   29   Received $3,500 cash from customers for admissions.

   30   Paid Finnean Ferguson $1,200 for his personal use.

   30   Prepaid a $700 rental on a special film to be shown in August.

   31   Paid salaries, $1,900.

   31   Received a statement from Seibert. It shows gross concession receipts of $2,600 and a balance due to Highland Theatre of $520 ($2,600 × 20%) for July. Seibert paid one half of the balance due and will pay the rest on August 5.

In addition to the accounts identified above, Highland Theatre's ledger includes the following: Accounts Receivable; Prepaid Film Rental; F. Ferguson, Drawings; Admission Revenue; Concession Revenue; Advertising Expense; Film Rental Expense; Repairs Expense; Salaries Expense; and Interest Expense.

Instructions

(a) Journalize the July transactions.

(b) Enter the beginning balances in the ledger as at June 30. Use the ledger format provided in Illustration 2-6.

(c) Post the July journal entries to the ledger.

(d) Prepare a trial balance at the end of July 2017.

TAKING IT FURTHER   A friend of yours is considering buying Highland Theatre from the current owner. Using the information in the trial balance, comment on whether or not this may be a sound company for your friend to purchase.

Journalize transactions, post, and prepare trial balance.

(LO 2, 3, 4) AP

P2-8B   Lena Kuznetsova provides coaching and mentoring services to individuals and companies. She operates the business as a proprietorship, under the name LVK Coaching Services, which has a December 31 year end. On November 30, 2017, the company's general ledger included the following accounts (all accounts have normal balances):

Advertising expense	$ 1,265	L. Kuznetsova, drawings	$31,190
Accounts payable	4,245	Rent expense	5,775
Accounts receivable	2,110	Salaries expense	6,310
Cash	3,165	Service revenue	47,963
Equipment	17,730	Supplies	1,340
Insurance expense	3,388	Unearned revenue	765
L. Kuznetsova, capital	19,300		

December transactions were as follows:

Dec. 1 Paid December rent on her office space, $525.
   1 Purchased additional equipment with a manufacturer's suggested price of $3,270. After negotiations with the retailer, paid $1,270 cash and signed a note payable for $2,000.
   4 Collected $1,880 from customers in payment of their accounts.
   7 Paid the $308 monthly insurance premium.
   8 Purchased $135 of supplies on account.
   10 Paid $2,140 of the accounts payable from November.
   12 Finished a coaching contract with a client and earned $765. The client had paid her in November. (*Hint:* In November, Lena had recorded the $765 as a liability, Unearned Revenue. By finishing the coaching contract, she has "paid" this obligation.)
   20 Received $3,480 cash from clients for services provided in December.
   21 Paid monthly charges for maintaining a website advertising her services, $115.
   24 Withdrew $2,860 for personal use.
   28 Billed clients $2,280 for coaching services provided in December. These clients will pay in January.
   29 Received $560 cash advance from a client for a coaching contract that will start in January.
   30 Paid part-time office assistant $655 cash.
   31 Made a $170 payment on the note payable. Of this amount, $10 is interest and the remainder is a principal payment on the note payable.

Instructions

(a) Enter the November 30 balances in ledger accounts. Use T accounts.
(b) Journalize the December transactions.
(c) Post the December journal entries to the T accounts. Add new accounts if needed.
(d) Prepare a trial balance at December 31, 2017.

TAKING IT FURTHER Comment on the company's cash balance. What concerns and suggestions do you have for the company to consider in January?

P2-9B The following is an alphabetical list of accounts and balances for the J. Nikko proprietorship at November 30, 2017:

Prepare trial balance.
(LO 4) AP

Accounts Payable	$12,500	Notes Payable	$30,000
Accounts Receivable	10,250	Prepaid Expenses	3,000
Cash	8,000	Rent Expense	4,500
Equipment	18,250	Service Revenue	63,050
Interest Expense	500	Supplies	5,000
J. Nikko, Capital	28,000	Utilities Expense	550
J. Nikko, Drawings	12,000	Salaries Expense	7,500
Land	64,000		

Instructions

Prepare a trial balance at November 30, sorting each account into the debit or the credit column.

TAKING IT FURTHER J. Nikko believes that accounting would be more efficient if transactions were recorded directly in the ledger accounts. Explain to him the advantages of first recording transactions in the journal, and then posting them to the ledger.

P2-10B Refer to the trial balance prepared for Kiersted Financial Services in P2-6B, part (c).

Prepare financial statements.
(LO 4) AP

Instructions

(a) Prepare an income statement.
(b) Prepare a statement of owner's equity.
(c) Prepare a balance sheet.

TAKING IT FURTHER Discuss how well the company did in its first month of operations.

Journalize transactions, post, and prepare trial balance.
(LO 2, 3) AP

P2–11B Hobson Nolan is a human resources professional who operates a consulting practice under the name HN HR Consulting. The company had the following balances in its general ledger at February 28, 2017: Cash $3,500, Accounts Receivable $14,450, Equipment $15,100, Accounts Payable $18,750, and H. Nolan, Capital $14,300. The following events and transactions occurred during March 2017.

Mar.	1	Borrowed $12,000 cash from the bank, signing a note payable.
	2	Paid $13,000 to creditors on account.
	3	Paid the monthly insurance premium of $145.
	10	Paid the monthly charge of $550 for keeping the company's website up to date. The company uses the website to advertise its services.
	16	Collected accounts receivable of $8,000.
	18	Paid an additional $5,000 to creditors on account.
	30	Miscellaneous expenses were paid in cash, $580.
	31	Consulting services provided in March were for $2,000 cash and $5,000 on account.
	31	Paid salaries, $1,650.
	31	Paid the bank $555 on the note payable, of which $55 is interest and $500 is a partial payment of the note.
	31	Paid March and April's rent, which totalled $1,900 ($950 per month).
	31	Withdrew $1,000 cash for personal use.

Instructions

(a) Prepare journal entries to record each of the March transactions.
(b) Open the required ledger accounts for the transactions that were journalized, and enter the February 28, 2017, balances. Use T accounts.
(c) Post the journal entries to the accounts in the ledger.
(d) Prepare a trial balance as at the end of March.

TAKING IT FURTHER   Is the March 31 rent payment an asset or an expense? Explain.

Prepare financial statements.
(LO 4) AP

P2–12B   Refer to the trial balance prepared in part (d) of P2–11B for HN HR Consulting.

Instructions

Use the trial balance to do the following:

(a) Prepare an income statement.
(b) Prepare a statement of owner's equity.
(c) Prepare a balance sheet.

TAKING IT FURTHER   Hobson would like to close the business and retire. He has reviewed the financial statements, and thinks he will be able to take out cash equal to the balance in his capital account. Do you agree? Why or why not?

Prepare trial balance and financial statements.
(LO 4) AP

P2–13B   The ledger of Lazdowski Marketing Services has the following account balances at the company's year end, October 31, 2017:

Accounts payable	$ 4,403	Insurance expense	$ 2,020
Accounts receivable	6,010	Interest expense	2,445
Advertising expense	14,970	Notes payable	48,850
Cash	4,930	Prepaid rent	975
Equipment	25,970	Rent expense	11,700
Fees earned	?	Salaries expense	20,545
Furniture	56,685	Supplies	1,240
I. Lazdowski, capital	57,410	Supplies expense	5,000
I. Lazdowski, drawings	75,775	Unearned revenue	3,555

Instructions

(a) Prepare a trial balance, with the accounts arranged in ledger (financial statement) order, as illustrated in the chapter, and determine the missing amount for fees earned.
(b) Prepare an income statement, statement of owner's equity, and balance sheet.

TAKING IT FURTHER   The owner, Inga Lazdowski, is not sure how much cash she can withdraw from the company each year. After reviewing the financial statements, comment on the amount she withdrew this year.

P2–14B The bookkeeper for Shigeru's Dance Studio did the following in journalizing and posting:

Analyze errors and effects on trial balance. (LO 4) AN

1. A debit posting to Prepaid Insurance of $3,600 was not done.
2. A debit posting of $500 to Accounts Receivable was debited to Accounts Payable.
3. A purchase of supplies on account of $850 was debited to Supplies for $850 and credited to Accounts Payable for $850.
4. A credit to Salaries Payable for $1,200 was posted as a credit to Cash.
5. A credit posting of $250 to Cash was posted twice.
6. A debit side of the entry to record the payment of $1,200 for drawings was posted to Salaries Expense.
7. A credit to Unearned Revenue for $400 was posted as a credit to Service Revenue.
8. A credit to Accounts Payable of $375 was posted as a debit to Accounts Payable.
9. A purchase of equipment on account for $6,800 was posted as an $8,600 debit to Equipment and an $8,600 debit to Cash.
10. The provision of $950 of services on account was not recorded because the customer did not pay cash until the following month.

Instructions

(a) Indicate which of the above transactions are correct and which are incorrect.
(b) For each error identified in part (a), answer the following:
   1. Will the trial balance be in balance?
   2. Which account(s) will be incorrectly stated because of the error?
   3. For each account identified in (2) as being incorrect, is the account overstated or understated and by how much?
   4. Is the debit column total of the trial balance stated correctly? If not, does correcting the errors increase or decrease the total and by how much?
   5. Is the credit column total of the trial balance stated correctly? If not, does correcting the errors increase or decrease the total and by how much?

TAKING IT FURTHER Your best friend thinks it is a waste of time to correct all of the above errors. Your friend reasons that, as long as the trial balance is balanced, then there is no need to correct an error. Do you agree or disagree with your friend? Explain using at least two of the above errors to make your points.

P2–15B The trial balance that follows for Shawnee Slopes Company does not balance:

Prepare correct trial balance. (LO 4) AN

SHAWNEE SLOPES COMPANY
Trial Balance
June 30, 2017

	Debit	Credit
Cash	$ 5,875	
Accounts receivable		$ 3,620
Equipment	14,020	
Accounts payable	5,290	
Property tax payable		500
A. Shawnee, capital		17,900
Service revenue	7,027	
Advertising expense		1,132
Property tax expense	1,100	
Salaries expense	4,150	
Totals	$37,462	$23,152

Your review of the ledger reveals that each account has a normal balance. You also discover the following errors:

1. Property Tax Expense was understated by $500 and Property Tax Payable was overstated by $500.
2. A $650 credit to Service Revenue was incorrectly posted as a $560 credit.
3. A debit posting to Salaries Expense of $350 was not done.
4. A $750 cash withdrawal by the owner was debited to A. Shawnee, Capital, for $750 and credited to Cash for $750.
5. A $650 purchase of supplies on account was debited to Equipment for $650 and credited to Cash for $650.

6. A cash payment of $120 for advertising was debited to Advertising Expense for $210 and credited to Cash for $210.
7. A $385 collection from a customer was debited to Cash for $385 and debited to Accounts Receivable for $385.
8. A cash payment on account for $165 was recorded as a $165 credit to Cash and a $165 credit to Accounts Payable.
9. A $2,000 note payable was issued to purchase equipment. The transaction was neither journalized nor posted.

Instructions

Prepare a correct trial balance. (*Note:* You may need to add new accounts.)

TAKING IT FURTHER   After the trial balance is corrected for the above errors, could there still be errors? Explain why or why not.

CHAPTER 2: BROADENING YOUR PERSPECTIVE

⏵ Financial Reporting and Analysis

Financial Reporting Problem

BYP2–1   The financial statements of **Corus Entertainment** are shown in Appendix A at the back of this textbook. They contain the following selected accounts:

Interest Expense	Long-Term Debt
Cash and Cash Equivalents	Prepaid Expenses
Unearned Revenues	Sales
Inventories	Accounts Payable and
	Accrued Expenses

Instructions

(a) Answer the following questions:
　1. In which financial statement is each account included?
　2. Is it an asset, liability, revenue, or expense?
　3. What is the normal balance (debit or credit) for each of these accounts?
　4. What are the increase side and decrease side (debit or credit) for each of these accounts?
(b) Identify the probable other account(s) in the transaction, and the effect on that account(s), when:
　1. Accounts payable and accrued expenses are decreased.
　2. Long-term debt is increased.
　3. Sales are increased.
　4. Inventory is increased.
　5. Prepaid expenses are increased.

Interpreting Financial Statements

BYP2–2   **WestJet Airlines Ltd.**, a Canadian airline, was profitable in 2014. The following list of accounts and amounts was taken from its December 31, 2014, financial statements (in thousands):

Accounts payable and accrued liabilities	$ 502,432
Accounts receivable	54,950
Advance ticket sale liability	575,781
Aircraft fuel, leasing, and maintenance expense	1,466,465
Airport operations expense	507,743
Cash	1,416,220
Deferred income tax liability	296,892
Depreciation and amortization expense	226,740
Employee profit share expense	68,787
Flight operations and navigational charges	458,146
Guest revenues	3,599,157
Income tax expense	106,350
In flight expense	171,741
Intangibles	122,913
Inventory	36,658
Long-term debt	1,028,820
Maintenance provisions liability	191,768
Marketing, general, and administration expense	224,783
Non-operating expenses	85,164
Non-refundable guest credits liability	45,434
Other assets	78,306
Other liabilities	227,804
Other revenues	377,395
Prepaid expenses and deposits	144,192
Property and equipment	2,793,194
Sales and distribution expense	376,676
Shareholders' (owners') "drawings"	96,295
Shareholders' (owners') equity, Jan. 1, 2015	1,589,840

Instructions

(a) WestJet Airlines Ltd. is a corporation. Which of the items listed above are used only in corporations?
(b) Prepare a trial balance for WestJet with the accounts in financial statement order.

(c) WestJet has grouped several items together in its financial statements. For example, marketing, general, and administration expenses are shown as one amount. What are some possible reasons for doing this?

(d) In this chapter, you learned about unearned revenue. Would you expect a company like WestJet to have unearned revenue? If so, what account name has WestJet used for its unearned revenue?

▶ Critical Thinking

Collaborative Learning Activity

Note to instructor: Additional instructions and material for this group activity can be found on the Instructor Resource Site and in *WileyPLUS*.

BYP2–3 In this group activity, students will be given a trial balance and will be asked to work backwards to create a set of journal entries that would result in the trial balance.

Communication Activity

BYP2–4 White Glove Company offers home cleaning services. Three common transactions for the company are signing contracts with new customers, billing customers for services performed, and paying employee salaries. For example, on March 15 the company did the following:

1. Signed a contract with a new customer for $125 per week starting the first week in April.
2. Sent bills that totalled $6,000 to customers.
3. Paid $2,000 in salaries to employees.

Instructions

Write an e-mail to your instructor that explains if and how these transactions are recorded in the double-entry system. Include in your e-mail (a) whether, and why, the transaction should or should not be recorded, and (b) how the debit and credit rules are applied if the transaction is recorded.

"All About You" Activity

BYP2–5 The "All About You" feature shows the importance of good record-keeping for small businesses and students.

You are a first-year university student and very excited about moving away from home to go to university. Your parents have given you $4,000 and you have a $14,000 student loan. Your parents have told you that $4,000 is all you get for the school year and you are not to phone home for more money.

At September 1, you had $18,000 cash ($4,000 + $14,000), $1,000 worth of clothes, and a cell phone that cost $200. You have kept all of the receipts for all of your expenditures between September 1 and December 15. The following is a complete list of your receipts.

Receipts	Amount
Rent on furnished apartment ($400 per month)	$1,600
Damage deposit on apartment	400
Groceries	1,200
Tuition for September to December	2,800
Textbooks	600
Entertainment (movies, beverages, restaurants)	1,500
New clothes	1,500
Cell phone charges	250
Cable TV and Internet bill	200
Computer	1,000
Eight-month bus pass (September to April)	500
Airfare to go home at Christmas	450

PERSONAL TRIAL BALANCE December 15, 2017		
Account	**Debit**	**Credit**
Cash	$ 6,500	
Clothes	2,500	
Cell phone	200	
Computer	100	
Student loan		$14,000
Personal equity		5,200
Rent expense	2,000	
Groceries		1,200
Tuition for September to December	2,800	
Textbooks for September to December	600	
Entertainment expense	1,500	
Cell phone expense	250	
Cable TV and Internet expense	200	
Bus pass expense	500	
Airfare	540	
	$17,690	$20,400

On December 15, you checked the balance in your bank account and you only have $6,000 cash. You can't sleep, because you know there are some errors in your accounting records and that you will probably have to ask your parents for more money for the next semester.

Instructions

(a) Calculate your personal equity (deficit) at September 1, 2017.

(b) Prepare a corrected trial balance at December 15, 2017. For each error identified, describe the error.

(c) Calculate your total expenses for the semester and your personal equity (deficit) at December 15, 2017.

(d) Prepare a personal balance sheet at December 15, 2017.

(e) Assuming you will have the same expenses in the second semester, will you have enough cash to pay for them?

(f) Are there any expenses you might be able to avoid in the second semester to save cash?

(g) Are there any additional cash expenditures that will need to be made in the second semester?

(h) Will it be necessary for you to ask your parents for more money for the next semester? Explain.

 Santé Smoothie Saga

(*Note:* The Santé Smoothie Saga began in Chapter 1 and will continue in each chapter.)

BYP2-6   After researching the different forms of business organization, Natalie Koebel decides to operate Santé Smoothies as a proprietorship. She then starts the process of getting the business running. During the month of April 2017, the following activities take place:

Apr. 12   Natalie cashes her Canada Savings Bonds and receives $980, which she deposits in her personal bank account.

13   She opens a bank account under the name "Santé Smoothies" and transfers $900 from her personal account to the new account.

15   Natalie realizes that her initial cash investment is not enough. Her mother lends her $3,000 cash, for which Natalie signs a one-year, 3% note payable in the name of the business. Natalie deposits the money in the business bank account.

18   Natalie pays $325 to advertise in the April 20 issue of her community newspaper. Natalie hopes that this ad will generate revenue during the months of May and June.

20   She buys supplies, such as protein powder, cups, straws, and fresh fruit and vegetables, for $198 cash.

22   Natalie starts to investigate juicing machines for her business. She selects an excellent top-of-the-line juicer that costs $825. She pays for it using her own personal account.

23   Natalie prepares her first batch of smoothies to bring to the yoga studio. At the end of the first day, Natalie leaves an invoice for $300 with the studio owner. The owner says the invoice will be paid some time in May.

24   A $98 invoice is received for the use of Natalie's cell phone. The cell phone is used exclusively for the Santé Smoothies business. The invoice is for services provided in April and is due on April 30.

28   The yoga studio where Natalie sold her first smoothies orders smoothies for the next month. Natalie is thrilled! She receives $125 in advance as a down payment.

Instructions

(a) Prepare journal entries to record the transactions.

(b) Post the entries to T accounts.

(c) Prepare a trial balance as at April 30, 2017.

ANSWERS TO CHAPTER QUESTIONS

ANSWERS TO ACCOUNTING IN ACTION INSIGHT QUESTIONS

Business Insight, p. 66

Q: What are the issues involved in determining if a signing bonus is an asset or an expense?

A: Signing bonuses are paid because a company expects to benefit in the future from hiring the individual. Bonuses could be recorded as an asset at the time they are paid. A decision would be made by the team's management to treat the bonus as an expense once the benefit represented by this asset was used up. In the NHL, they would have to consider such things as the length of the contract, how well the player is performing, and whether or not the player is injured in order to decide when to record the bonus as an expense.

Ethics Insight, p. 79

Q: Who are the stakeholders in this situation and what impact will Vu's action have on them?

A: The stakeholders in this situation are Vu, internal and external users of Lim Company's financial statements, and Vu's supervisor, the chief accountant.

While it is important that financial information be prepared on a timely basis, it is also important that there are no material misstatements (errors that would make a difference to the users). While the net difference may be immaterial ($1,000), there may be more than one error and each error could have a material effect on the financial statements, leading the internal and external users to make decisions based on inaccurate information. If the amount of $1,000 is determined not to be significant, and the intent is not to commit fraud, Vu's action might not be considered unethical in the preparation of interim financial statements. However, she should disclose what she has done

to her supervisor. Otherwise, if Vu is violating a company accounting policy, then she is acting unethically.

All About You Insight, p. 80

Q: What categories of expenses do you have that a small business would also have?

A: Similar to a small business, you have expenses such as rent, utilities, phone and Internet, interest on loans (student loans, car loans, credit cards), taxes, and equipment (computers, printers).

ANSWERS TO SELF-STUDY QUESTIONS

1.b   2.d   3.d   4.b   5.d   6.a   7.c   8.d   9.a   10.c

3 ADJUSTING THE ACCOUNTS

CHAPTER PREVIEW

In Chapter 2, we learned the accounting cycle up to and including the preparation of the trial balance. In this chapter, we will learn that additional steps are usually needed before preparing the financial statements. These steps adjust accounts for timing mismatches, like what Maple Leaf Sports and Entertainment, in our feature story, does to account for advance ticket sales to games. In this chapter, we introduce the accrual accounting concepts that guide the adjustment process. The remainder of the accounting cycle is discussed in Chapter 4 and is illustrated here.

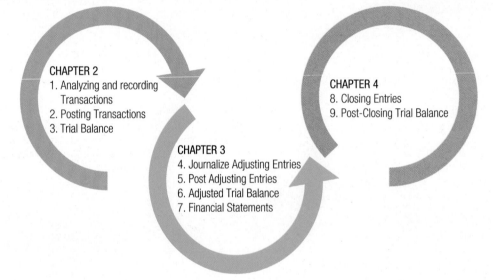

CHAPTER 2
1. Analyzing and recording Transactions
2. Posting Transactions
3. Trial Balance

CHAPTER 3
4. Journalize Adjusting Entries
5. Post Adjusting Entries
6. Adjusted Trial Balance
7. Financial Statements

CHAPTER 4
8. Closing Entries
9. Post-Closing Trial Balance

FEATURE STORY | ADVANCE SPORTS REVENUE IS JUST THE TICKET

TORONTO, Ont.—Professional sports teams sell millions of dollars worth of tickets before the players ever step onto the ice, court, or field. Some teams, such as the National Hockey League's Toronto Maple Leafs, have thousands of loyal season-ticket holders and a waiting list of season-ticket hopefuls.

Not only that, but the average price of a single ticket to a Leafs' game in the 2014–15 season was $373.50 on the resale market—the highest among all NHL teams.

Such strong ticket sales are good news to the Leafs' owner, Maple Leaf Sports and Entertainment Ltd. (MLSE), which also owns the Toronto Raptors National Basketball Association team, the Toronto FC professional soccer club, and the Toronto Marlies of the American Hockey League. MLSE also saw a revenue boost when the Raptors sold 3,000 season tickets for 2014–15.

How do these teams account for advance ticket sales, which are considered unearned revenue? MLSE is a private company (jointly owned by Rogers Communications Inc., BCE Inc., and Kilmer Sports Inc.) and so its financial statements are not made public. But teams typically record advance ticket sales as an increase in the liability account Unearned Revenue, because they are obligated to provide the service—the game—that customers have paid for.

However, sports ticket revenue is often received in a different accounting period than the games are held. Under the most common method of recognizing revenues and expenses—the accrual basis—transactions are recorded in the period in which they occur, not when the payment is received. That means that when preparing financial statements, sports teams need to make journal entries to adjust this mismatch in timing. These adjusting entries can be for very large amounts.

Abelimages/Getty Images

Based on the price of Leafs' tickets, an adjusting entry that MLSE might make for just one game held in a different accounting period could be for several million dollars.

Sources: Morgan Campbell, "Maple Leafs Won't Raise Prices on Season Tickets," *Toronto Star*, March 3, 2015; Brian Costello, "Toronto Maple Leafs Most Expensive Ticket in NHL; All Teams Listed 1 to 30," *The Hockey News*, October 7, 2014; Josh Rubin, "Toronto Raptors Ticket Sales Jump," *Toronto Star*, October 2, 2014; Grant Robertson and Tara Perkins, *The Globe and Mail*, "Rogers, Bell Agree to Deal for MLSE," BNN, December 10, 2011.

CHAPTER OUTLINE ⟩ LEARNING OBJECTIVES

1	Explain accrual basis accounting, and when to recognize revenues and expenses.	**Timing Issues** • Accrual versus cash basis accounting • Revenue and expense recognition	**DO IT 1** Accrual accounting	
2	Prepare adjusting entries for prepayments.	**The Basics of Adjusting Entries** • Adjusting entries for prepayments	**DO IT 2** Adjusting entries for prepayments	
3	Prepare adjusting entries for accruals.	• Adjusting entries for accruals	**DO IT 3** Adjusting entries for accruals	
4	Describe the nature and purpose of an adjusted trial balance, and prepare one.	**The Adjusted Trial Balance and Financial Statements** • Preparing the adjusted trial balance • Preparing financial statements	**DO IT 4** Trial balance	

Timing Issues

Accounting would be simple if we could wait until a company ended its operations before preparing its financial statements. As the following anecdote shows, if we waited until then, we could easily determine the amount of lifetime profit earned:

> A grocery store owner from the old country kept his accounts payable on a wire memo spike, accounts receivable on a notepad, and cash in a shoebox. His daughter, a CPA, chided her father: "I don't understand how you can run your business this way. How do you know what you've earned?"
>
> "Well," her father replied, "when I arrived in Canada 40 years ago, I had nothing but the pants I was wearing. Today, your brother is a doctor, your sister is a teacher, and you are a CPA. Your mother and I have a nice car, a well-furnished house, and a home by the lake. We have a good business and everything is paid for. So, you add all that together, subtract the pants, and there's your profit."

Although the grocer may be correct in his evaluation about how to calculate his profit over his lifetime, most companies need more immediate feedback on how they are doing. For example, management usually wants monthly financial statements. Investors want to view the results of publicly traded companies at least quarterly. The Canada Revenue Agency requires financial statements to be filed with annual income tax returns.

Consequently, **accountants divide the life of a business into artificial time periods, such as a month, a three-month quarter, or a year**. This is permitted by the **periodicity concept** explained in Chapter 1. Recall that this concept allows organizations to divide up their economic activities into distinct time periods.

An accounting time period that is one year long is called a **fiscal year**. Time periods of less than one year are called **interim periods**. The fiscal year used by many businesses is the same as the calendar year (January 1 to December 31). This is the case for many businesses. Illustration 3-1 is a timeline that shows when monthly, quarterly, and annual financial statements would be prepared for an entity with a December year end.

▶**ILLUSTRATION** **3-1**
Timeline of the preparation of December year end financial statements

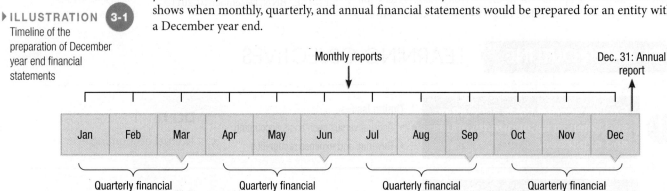

Corus's fiscal year is not the same as the calendar year, as its financial statements are dated August 31. Fiscal year ends can be different for other entities and businesses. For example, some retail companies use a 52-week period, instead of exactly one year, for their fiscal year. Lululemon does this, and has chosen the closest Sunday to January 31 as the end of its fiscal year. This usually results in a 52-week year, but occasionally may result in an additional week, resulting in a 53-week year. As another example, most governments use March 31 as their year end.

Because the life of a business is divided into accounting time periods, determining when to record transactions is important. Many business transactions affect more than one accounting time period. For example, many of Maple Leaf Sports and Entertainment's sports venues were constructed years ago, yet they are still in use today. We must consider the consequence of each business transaction to each specific accounting period. For example, how much does the cost of the arena contribute to operations this year?

ACCRUAL VERSUS CASH BASIS ACCOUNTING

There are two ways of deciding when to recognize or record revenues and expenses:

1. **Accrual basis accounting** means that transactions and other **events are recorded in the period when they occur, and not when the cash is paid or received.** For example, service revenue is recognized when it is earned, rather than when the cash is received. Expenses are recognized when services (e.g., salaries) or goods (e.g., supplies) are used or consumed, rather than when the cash is paid.

2. Under **cash basis accounting**, revenue is recorded when cash is received, and expenses are recorded when cash is paid. This sounds appealing due to its simplicity; however, it often leads to misleading financial statements. If a company fails to record revenue when it has performed the service because it has not yet received the cash, the company will not match expenses with revenues and therefore profits will be misrepresented.

Consider this simple example. Suppose you own a painting company and you paint a large building during year 1. In year 1, you pay $50,000 cash for the cost of the paint and your employees' salaries. Assume that you bill your customer $80,000 at the end of year 1, and that you receive the cash from your customer in year 2.

On an accrual basis, the revenue is reported during the period when the service is performed—year 1. Expenses, such as employees' salaries and the paint used, are recorded in the period in which the employees provide their services and the paint is used—year 1. Thus, your profit for year 1 is $30,000. No revenue or expense from this project is reported in year 2.

If, instead, you were reporting on a cash basis, you would report expenses of $50,000 in year 1 because you paid for them in year 1. Revenues of $80,000 would be recorded in year 2 because you received cash from the customer in year 2. For year 1, you would report a loss of $50,000. For year 2, you would report a profit of $80,000.

Illustration 3-2 summarizes this information and shows the differences between the accrual-based numbers and cash-based numbers.

▶ **ILLUSTRATION** **3-2**
Accrual versus cash basis accounting

	Year 1	Year 2
Activity	 Purchased paint, painted building, paid employees	 Received payment for work done in year 1
Accrual basis	Revenue $ 80,000 Expenses (50,000) Profit $ 30,000	Revenue $ 0 Expenses 0 Profit $ 0
Cumulative Profit		$30,000
Cash basis	Revenue $ 0 Expenses (50,000) Loss $(50,000)	Revenue $80,000 Expenses 0 Profit $80,000
Cumulative Profit		$30,000

Photo credits for Illustration 3-2 (From L-R): © istockphoto/mark wragg; © istockphoto/Arpad Benedek

Note that the total profit for years 1 and 2 is $30,000 for both the accrual and cash bases. However, the difference in when the revenues and expenses are recognized causes a difference in the amount of profit or loss each year. Which basis provides better information about how profitable your efforts were each year? It's the accrual basis, because it shows the profit earned on the job in the same year as when the work was performed.

Thus, accrual basis accounting is widely recognized as being significantly more useful for decision-making than cash basis accounting. **Accrual basis accounting is therefore in accordance with generally accepted accounting principles,** as mentioned in Chapter 1. In fact, it is assumed that all financial statements are prepared using accrual basis accounting. While accrual basis accounting provides better information, it is more complex than cash basis accounting. It is easy to determine when to recognize revenues or expenses if the only determining factor is when the cash is received or paid. But when using the accrual basis, it is necessary to have standards about when to record revenues and expenses.

REVENUE AND EXPENSE RECOGNITION

Recall that revenue is an increase in assets—or a decrease in liabilities—as the result of the company's business activities with its customers. It can be difficult to determine when to report revenues and expenses. The **revenue recognition principle** provides guidance about when revenue is to be recognized. **In general, revenue is recognized when the service has been performed or the goods have been sold and delivered, that is, when the performance obligation has been satisfied.** Both ASPE and IFRS include revenue recognition standards. Under ASPE, besides the requirement that performance be substantially complete, we also need to ensure that revenue can be reliably measured, and collection is reasonably certain. Under IFRS, a new revenue standard has been released (to be effective for years beginning on or after January 1, 2018). This new standard requires an entity to identify a contractual relationship with the customer as well as the performance obligation (the goods or services to be provided), to determine the transaction price and to allocate this price if multiple goods and services are to be provided. This will be discussed in more detail in Chapter 11.

Under both ASPE and IFRS, the revenue recognition principle follows the accrual basis of accounting—that is, revenue is recognized in the period when it is earned. Recall that in the painting example shown in Illustration 3-2, revenue was recorded in year 1 when the service was performed. At that point, there was an increase in the painting businesses assets—specifically Accounts Receivable—as the result of doing the work. At the end of year 1, the painting business would report the receivable on its balance sheet and revenue on its income statement for the service performed. In year 2, when the cash is received, the painting business records a reduction of its receivables, not revenue.

Recall from Chapter 1 that we introduced the **matching concept**. The matching concept often determines when we recognize expenses. Generally, when there is a direct association between the costs incurred and the earning of revenue, accounting attempts to match these costs and revenues. For example, as we saw with the painting business, under accrual basis accounting, the salaries and cost of the paint for the painting in year 1 are reported in the income statement for the same period in which the service revenue is recognized. Sometimes, however, there is no direct relationship between expenses and revenue. For example, we will see in the next section that long-lived assets may be used to help generate revenue over many years, but the use of the asset is not directly related to earning specific revenue. In these cases, we will see that expenses are recognized in the income statement over the life of the asset.

In other cases, the benefit from the expenditure is fully used in the current period, or there is a great deal of uncertainty about whether or not there is a future benefit. In these situations, the costs are reported as expenses in the period in which they occur.

ACCOUNTING IN ACTION
ETHICS INSIGHT

Allegations of abuse of the revenue recognition principle have become all too common in recent years. For example, it was alleged that Krispy Kreme sometimes doubled the number of doughnuts shipped to wholesale customers at the end of a quarter to boost quarterly results. The customers shipped the unsold doughnuts back after the beginning of the next quarter for a refund. One reason why companies want to accrue all possible revenues and defer as many expenses as possible is to smooth their earnings, to avoid a drop in share price that could make a public company a takeover target. For example, a pesticide manufacturer might have low sales in the year in which certain chemicals were banned by law. The company would want to record as much revenue as possible in the current year and defer as many expenses to the next year, when sales were expected to pick up with its new, environmentally friendly products.

© iStockphoto/Dean Turner

Q Who are the stakeholders when companies participate in activities that result in inaccurate reporting of revenues?

BEFORE YOU GO ON...DO IT **Accrual Accounting**

On January 1, 2017, customers owed Joma Company $30,000 for services provided in 2016. During 2017, Joma Co. received $125,000 cash from customers. On December 31, 2017, customers owed Joma $19,500 for services provided in 2017. Calculate revenue for 2017 using (a) cash basis accounting, and (b) accrual basis accounting.

Solution

(a) Revenue for 2017, using cash basis accounting $125,000

(b) Cash received from customers in 2017 $125,000
    Deduct: Collection of 2016 receivables   (30,000)
    Add: Amounts receivable at December 31, 2017   19,500
    Revenue for 2017, using accrual basis accounting $114,500

Related exercise material: BE3–1, E3–1, and E3–2.

Action Plan
- For cash basis accounting, revenue is equal to the cash received.
- For accrual basis accounting, revenue is recognized in the period in which it is earned, not when it is collected.
- Under accrual basis accounting, cash collected in 2017 for revenue earned in 2016 should not be included in the 2017 revenue.
- Under accrual basis accounting, amounts receivable at the end of 2017 for services provided in 2017 should be included in the 2017 revenue.

The Basics of Adjusting Entries

For revenues and expenses to be recorded in the correct period, adjusting entries are made at the end of the accounting period. **Adjusting entries** are needed to ensure that revenue is recorded when earned and expenses are recorded as incurred and that the correct amounts for assets, liabilities, and owner's equity are reported on the balance sheet.

Adjusting entries are needed every time financial statements are prepared. This may be monthly, quarterly, or annually. Companies reporting under IFRS must prepare quarterly financial statements and thus adjusting entries are required every quarter. Companies following ASPE must prepare annual financial statements and thus need only annual adjusting entries. For both public and private companies, if management wants monthly statements, then adjustments are prepared every month end.

You will recall that we learned the first four steps of the accounting cycle in Chapter 2. Adjusting entries are Step 5 of the accounting cycle, as shown in Illustration 3-3.

▶ILLUSTRATION **3-3**
The accounting cycle—
Steps 1 to 5

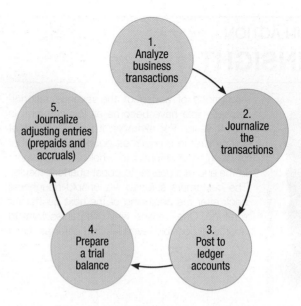

There are some common reasons why the trial balance—from Step 4 in the accounting cycle—may not contain complete and up-to-date data.

1. Some events are not recorded daily because it would not be efficient to do so. For example, companies do not record the daily use of supplies or the earning of wages by employees.
2. Some costs are not recorded during the accounting period because they expire with the passage of time rather than through daily transactions. Examples are rent and insurance.
3. Some items may be unrecorded. An example is a utility bill for services in the current accounting period that will not be received until the next accounting period.

Therefore, we must analyze each account in the trial balance and **prepare any required adjusting entries every time a company prepares financial statements** to see if the account is complete and up to date. The analysis requires a full understanding of the company's operations and the interrelationship of accounts. **Every adjusting entry will include one income statement and one balance sheet account.** Preparing adjusting entries is often a long process. For example, to accumulate the adjustment data, a company may need to count its remaining supplies.

Adjusting entries can be classified as prepayments or accruals, as follows:

PREPAYMENTS	ACCRUALS
1. **Prepaid Expenses** Expenses paid in cash and recorded as assets before they are used.	1. **Accrued Expenses** Expenses incurred but not yet paid in cash or recorded.
2. **Unearned Revenues** Cash received and recorded as a liability before revenue is earned.	2. **Accrued Revenues** Revenues earned but not yet received in cash or recorded.

Examples and explanations of each type of adjustment are given on the following pages. Each example is based on the October 31 trial balance of Lynk Software Services from Chapter 2, reproduced here in Illustration 3-4.

▶ILLUSTRATION 3-4
Trial balance

LYNK SOFTWARE SERVICES Trial Balance October 31, 2017	Debit	Credit
Cash	$14,250	
Accounts receivable	1,000	
Supplies	2,500	
Prepaid insurance	600	
Equipment	5,000	
Notes payable		$ 5,000
Accounts payable		1,750
Unearned revenue		1,200
T. Jacobs, capital		10,000
T. Jacobs, drawings	500	
Service revenue		10,800
Rent expense	900	
Salaries expense	4,000	
Totals	$28,750	$28,750

For illustration purposes, we assume that Lynk Software uses an accounting period of one month. Thus, monthly adjusting entries will be made and they will be dated October 31.

LEARNING OBJECTIVE 2 Prepare adjusting entries for prepayments.

ADJUSTING ENTRIES FOR PREPAYMENTS

Prepayments are either prepaid expenses or unearned revenues. Adjusting entries are used to record the portion of the prepayment used in the current accounting period and to reduce the asset account where the prepaid expense was originally recorded. This type of adjustment is necessary because the prepayment no longer has future benefit and consequently is no longer an asset—it has been used.

For unearned revenues, the adjusting entry records the revenue earned in the current period and reduces the liability account where the unearned revenue was originally recorded. This type of adjustment is necessary because the unearned revenue is no longer owed and so is no longer a liability—the service has been provided and the revenue earned.

Prepaid Expenses

Recall from Chapter 1 that costs paid in cash before they are used are called prepaid expenses. When such a cost is incurred, an asset (prepaid) account is debited to show the service or benefit that will be received in the future and cash is credited. Therefore, prepaid items such as prepaid expenses and supplies are assets on the balance sheet.

Prepaid expenses are assets that expire either with the passage of time (e.g., rent and insurance) or through use (e.g., supplies). It is not practical to record the use of these assets daily. Instead, companies record these entries when the financial statements are prepared. At each statement date, they make adjusting entries: (1) to expense the cost of an asset that has been used up in that period, and (2) to show an asset for the remaining amount (unexpired costs).

Before the prepaid expenses are adjusted, assets are overstated and expenses are understated. Therefore, an adjusting entry is required to reduce the amount of the asset used and to reflect the expense incurred.

As shown, **an adjusting entry for prepaid expenses results in an increase (debit) to an expense account and a decrease (credit) to an asset account.**

Helpful hint A cost can be an asset or an expense. If it has future benefits, it is an asset. If the benefits have expired or been used, it is an expense.

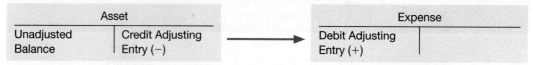

In the following section, we will look at three examples of adjusting prepaid expenses: supplies, insurance, and depreciation.

Supplies. The purchase of supplies, such as pens and paper, results in an increase (debit) to an asset account (Supplies). During the accounting period, the company uses the supplies. Rather than record the related supplies expense as the supplies are used, **an adjusting entry is recorded at the end of the accounting period to recognize the supplies used over the period**. This adjustment is determined when the company counts the supplies on hand at the end of the accounting period. The difference between the balance in the Supplies (asset) account and the cost of supplies actually remaining gives the supplies used (the expense).

Recall from Chapter 2 that Lynk Software Services purchased supplies costing $2,500 on October 4. The following journal entry was prepared:

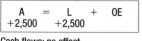

| Oct. 4 | Supplies | 2,500 | |
| | Accounts Payable | | 2,500 |

Cash flows: no effect

Now the Supplies account shows a balance of $2,500 in the October 31 trial balance. At the end of the accounting period, Tyler Jacobs, the proprietor, counts the supplies left at the end of the day on October 31. He determines that only $1,000 of supplies remain. This means that over the accounting period $1,500 ($2,500 − $1,000) of supplies were used and $1,000 of supplies remain on hand. An adjusting entry must now be prepared to reflect this usage. The adjusting entry will reduce the asset account (Supplies) and decrease the owner's equity as the Supplies Expense account increases by $1,500.

The following illustration outlines the analysis used to determine the adjusting journal entry to record and post. Note that the debit-credit rules you learned in Chapter 2 are also used for adjusting journal entries.

▶**ADJUSTMENT** ①
Prepaid expenses—
Supplies

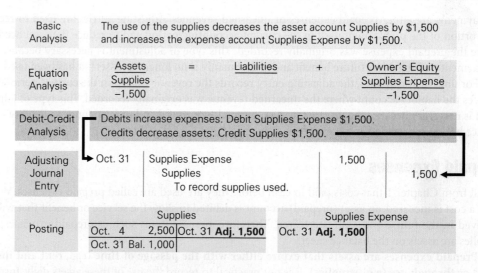

After the adjustment, the asset account Supplies now shows a balance of $1,000, which is equal to the cost of supplies remaining at the statement date. Supplies Expense shows a balance of $1,500, which equals the cost of supplies used in October. **If the adjusting entry is not made, October expenses will be understated and profit overstated by $1,500.** Also, **both assets and owner's equity will be overstated by $1,500 on the October 31 balance sheet.**

Insurance. Companies purchase insurance to protect themselves from losses caused by fire, theft, and unforeseen accidents. Insurance must be paid in advance, often for one year. Insurance payments (premiums) made in advance are normally charged to the asset account Prepaid Insurance when they are paid. At the financial statement date, **it is necessary to make an adjustment to debit (increase)**

Helpful hint
Summary journal entries for Supplies:
When purchased:
Supplies
   Cash/Accounts Payable
To adjust:
Supplies Expense
   Supplies

Insurance Expense and credit (decrease) Prepaid Insurance for the cost of insurance that has expired during the period.

On October 3, Lynk Software Services paid $600 for a one-year fire insurance policy. The starting date for the coverage was October 1. The premium was charged to Prepaid Insurance when it was paid. The following journal entry was prepared:

| Oct. 3 | Prepaid Insurance | 600 | |
| | Cash | | 600 |

A = L + OE
+600
−600

↓Cash flows: −600

This account shows a balance of $600 in the October 31 trial balance. An analysis of the policy reveals that $50 ($600 ÷ 12 months) expires each month. An adjusting entry must now be prepared to reflect this expiration over time. The adjusting entry will reduce the asset account (Prepaid Insurance) and decrease the owner's equity by increasing the Insurance Expense account by $50. The adjusting entry for Prepaid Insurance is made as follows:

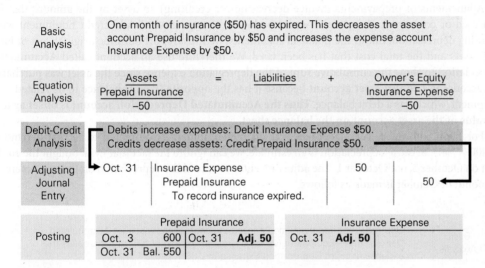

| Basic Analysis | One month of insurance ($50) has expired. This decreases the asset account Prepaid Insurance by $50 and increases the expense account Insurance Expense by $50. |

Equation Analysis	Assets = Liabilities + Owner's Equity
	Prepaid Insurance / Insurance Expense
	−50 / −50

| Debit-Credit Analysis | Debits increase expenses: Debit Insurance Expense $50. |
| | Credits decrease assets: Credit Prepaid Insurance $50. |

Adjusting Journal Entry	Oct. 31	Insurance Expense	50	
		Prepaid Insurance		50
		To record insurance expired.		

Posting	Prepaid Insurance		Insurance Expense	
	Oct. 3 600	Oct. 31 **Adj. 50**	Oct. 31 **Adj. 50**	
	Oct. 31 Bal. 550			

▶ **ADJUSTMENT** ②
Prepaid expenses—
Insurance

After the adjustment, the asset Prepaid Insurance shows a balance of $550. This amount represents the unexpired cost for the remaining 11 months of coverage (11 × $50). The $50 in the Insurance Expense account equals the insurance cost that expired in October. **If this adjustment is not made, October expenses will be understated by $50 and profit overstated by $50. Also, both assets and owner's equity will be overstated by $50 on the October 31 balance sheet.**

Helpful hint
Summary journal entries for Prepaid Insurance:
When purchased:
Prepaid Insurance
    Cash/Accounts Payable
To adjust:
Insurance Expense
    Prepaid Insurance

Depreciation. A business usually owns a variety of assets that have long lives, such as land, buildings, and equipment. These long-lived assets provide service for a number of years. The length of service is called the **useful life**. Companies record these assets at cost, as required by the historical cost principle explained in Chapter 1. A portion of the cost of a long-lived asset is recognized each period over the useful life of the asset. The process of allocating the cost of a long-lived asset over its useful life is called **depreciation**. From an accounting perspective, the purchase of a long-lived asset is basically a long-term prepayment for services. Similar to other prepaid expenses, an adjusting entry is necessary to recognize the cost that has been used up (the expense) during the period, and to report the unused cost (the asset) at the end of the period. Only assets with limited useful lives are depreciated; these are called depreciable assets. When an asset, such as land, has an unlimited useful life, it is not depreciated.

It is important to note that **depreciation is an allocation concept, not a valuation concept. Depreciation allocates an asset's cost over the periods it is used. Depreciation does not attempt to report the actual change in the value of an asset.**

Some companies use the term "amortization" instead of "depreciation," especially private companies following ASPE. The two terms mean the same thing—allocation of the cost of a long-lived asset to expense over its useful life. In Chapter 9, we will learn that the term "amortization" is also used under both ASPE and IFRS for the allocation of cost to expense for certain intangible long-lived assets.

Calculation of Depreciation. A common method of calculating depreciation expense is to divide the cost of the asset by its useful life. This is called the **straight-line depreciation method**. The useful life must be estimated because, at the time an asset is acquired, the company does not know exactly how long the asset will be used. Thus, depreciation is an estimate rather than a factual measurement of the expired cost.

Lynk Software Services purchased equipment that cost $5,000 on October 2. If its useful life is expected to be five years, annual depreciation is $1,000 ($5,000 ÷ 5). Illustration 3-5 shows the formula to calculate annual depreciation expense in its simplest form.

▶ **ILLUSTRATION 3-5**
Formula for straight-line depreciation

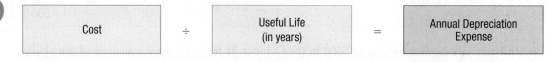

Of course, if you are calculating depreciation for partial periods, the annual expense amount must be adjusted for the relevant portion of the year. For example, if we want to determine the depreciation for one month, we would multiply the annual expense by $^1/_{12}$ as there are 12 months in a year.

Adjustments of prepayments involve decreasing (or crediting) an asset by the amount that has been used or consumed. Therefore, it would be logical to expect we should credit Equipment when recording depreciation. But in the financial statements, we must report both the original cost of long-lived assets and the total cost that has been used. We therefore use an account called **Accumulated Depreciation** to show the cumulative sum of the depreciation expense since the asset was purchased. This account is a **contra asset account** because it has the opposite (credit) balance to its related asset Equipment, which has a debit balance. **Thus the Accumulated Depreciation account is offset against the value of the asset account on the balance sheet.**

For Lynk Software Services, depreciation on the equipment is estimated to be $83 per month ($1,000 × $^1/_{12}$). Because depreciation is an estimate, we can ignore the fact that Lynk bought the equipment on October 2, not October 1. The adjusting entry to record the depreciation on the equipment for the month of October is made as follows:

Helpful hint To make the depreciation calculation easier to understand, we have assumed the asset has no value at the end of its useful life. In Chapter 9, we will show how to calculate depreciation when there is an estimated value at the end of the asset's useful life.

▶ **ADJUSTMENT 3**
Prepaid expenses—Depreciation

Helpful hint Increases, decreases, and normal balances of contra accounts are the opposite of the accounts they relate to.

Basic Analysis	One month of depreciation increases the contra asset account Accumulated Depreciation—Equipment (which decreases assets) by $83 and increases the expense account Depreciation Expense by $83.

Equation Analysis	Assets = Liabilities + Owner's Equity
	Accumulated Depreciation—Equipment −83 / Depreciation Expense −83

Debit-Credit Analysis	Debits increase expenses: Debit Depreciation Expense $83. Credits increase contra assets: Credit Accumulated Depreciation—Equipment $83.

Adjusting Journal Entry	Oct. 31	Depreciation Expense	83	
		Accumulated Depreciation—Equipment		83
		To record monthly depreciation.		

Posting	Equipment		Depreciation Expense
	Oct. 2 5,000		Oct. 31 **Adj. 83**
	Accumulated Depreciation—Equipment	
	Oct. 31 **Adj. 83**	

Helpful hint
To record depreciation:
Depreciation Expense
    Accumulated Depreciation

The balance in the Accumulated Depreciation account will increase by $83 each month and the balance in the Equipment account will remain unchanged until the asset is sold. We will learn in Chapter 9 that both the Accumulated Depreciation and Equipment accounts are reduced when the asset is sold. **If the adjusting entry is not made, expenses will be understated by $83. Total assets, total owner's equity, and profit will be overstated and expenses will be understated.**

Statement Presentation. As indicated, Accumulated Depreciation—Equipment is a contra asset account. It is offset against equipment on the balance sheet. In the financial statements, **the normal balance of a contra asset account is a credit; therefore, it always offsets against (is deducted from) its related**

asset account. Thus, on the balance sheet, Accumulated Depreciation—Equipment is deducted from Equipment, as follows:

	Oct.	Nov.	Dec.
Equipment	$5,000	$5,000	$5,000
Less: Accumulated depreciation—equipment	83	166	249
Carrying amount	$4,917	$4,834	$4,751

The difference between the cost of any depreciable asset and its accumulated depreciation is called the **carrying amount** of that asset. In the above chart, the carrying amount of the equipment at October 31, 2017, is $4,917. As demonstrated, as the asset is depreciated, the balance in the Equipment account does not change. However, the carrying amount is reduced every month by the increase to the contra asset account Accumulated Depreciation—Equipment. Also, remember that depreciation does not attempt to show what an asset is worth. The carrying amount and the fair value of the equipment (the price at which it could be sold) are generally two different amounts.

Alternative terminology An asset's carrying amount is also called its carrying value, net book value, or book value.

If a company owns both equipment and buildings, it calculates and records depreciation expense on each category. It can use one depreciation expense account but it must create separate accumulated depreciation accounts for each category.

Illustration 3-6 summarizes the accounting for prepaid expenses.

ACCOUNTING FOR PREPAID EXPENSES

Examples	Reason for Adjustment	Accounts Before Adjustment	Adjusting Entry
Insurance, supplies, advertising, rent, depreciation	Prepaid expenses recorded in asset accounts have been used.	Assets overstated. Expenses understated.	Dr. Expenses Cr. Assets or Contra Assets

▶ ILLUSTRATION 3-6
Accounting for prepaid expenses

Unearned Revenues

When companies receive cash before the services are performed, they record a liability by increasing (crediting) a liability account called Unearned Revenue. In other words, the company now has an obligation to provide one of its customers with a service. Examples include rent, magazine subscriptions, and customer deposits for future services. Airlines such as Air Canada treat receipts from the sale of tickets as unearned revenue until the flight service is provided. Similarly, as we saw in the feature story, advance ticket sales for sporting events such as Toronto Raptors and Toronto Maple Leafs games that are received before the game takes place are considered unearned revenue.

Alternative terminology Unearned revenues are sometimes referred to as deferred revenues or future revenues.

Unearned revenues are the opposite of prepaid expenses. Indeed, unearned revenue on the books of one company is likely to be a prepayment on the books of the company that has made the advance payment. For example, your landlord will have unearned rent revenue when you (the tenant) have prepaid rent.

Recall that, when a payment is received for services that will be provided in a future accounting period, Cash is debited (increased) and an Unearned Revenue account (a liability) should be credited (increased) to recognize the obligation that exists. The company subsequently recognizes revenues when the service is provided to the customer and the revenue is earned.

It may not be practical to make daily journal entries as the revenue is earned. Instead, recognition of earned revenue is normally delayed until the end of the accounting period. Then an adjusting entry is made to record the revenue that has been earned and to show the liability that remains at the end of the accounting period. Typically, prior to the adjustment, revenues are understated and profit and owner's equity are also understated. As shown below, **the adjusting entry for Unearned Revenue results in a decrease (debit) to a liability account and an increase (credit) to a revenue account.**

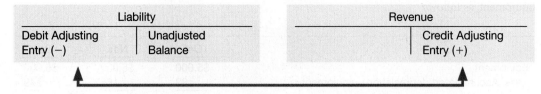

Unearned Revenue

In our Lynk Software Services example, the company received $1,200 on October 3 from R. Knox for advertising services that will be completed by December 31. The following journal entry was prepared:

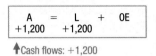

A = L + OE
+1,200 +1,200

↑Cash flows: +1,200

| Oct. 3 | Cash | 1,200 | |
| | Unearned Revenue | | 1,200 |

Now the Unearned Revenue account shows a credit balance of $1,200 in the October 31 trial balance. An evaluation of work performed by Lynk for Knox during October shows that $400 of work was done. The following adjusting entry is used to record earning this revenue:

▶ ADJUSTMENT **4**
Unearned Revenue

Basic Analysis	The liability account Unearned Revenue is decreased by $400 for the revenue earned and the revenue account Service Revenue is increased by $400.
Equation Analysis	<table><tr><td>Assets</td><td>=</td><td>Liabilities Unearned Revenue −400</td><td>+</td><td>Owner's Equity Service Revenue +400</td></tr></table>
Debit-Credit Analysis	Debits decrease liabilities: Debit Unearned Revenue $400. Credits increase revenues: Credit Service Revenue $400.

Adjusting Journal Entry	Oct. 31 Unearned Revenue 400
	          Service Revenue 400
	              To record revenue for services
	              provided in October.

Posting	**Unearned Revenue**
	Oct. 31 **Adj. 400** | Oct. 4 1,200
	                          Oct. 31 Bal. 800
	
	Service Revenue
	          Oct. 21 10,000
	          25 800
	          31 **Adj. 400**
	          Oct. 31 Bal. 11,200

Helpful hint
Summary journal entries for Unearned Revenue:
When cash received:
Cash
    Unearned Revenue
To adjust:
Unearned Revenue
    Service Revenue

The liability Unearned Revenue now shows a balance of $800. This amount represents the remaining advertising services to be performed in the future. At the same time, Service Revenue shows that revenue of $400 has been earned in October. **If this adjustment is not made, revenues and profit will be understated by $400 in the income statement. As well, liabilities will be overstated by $400 and owner's equity understated by that amount on the October 31 balance sheet.**

Illustration 3-7 summarizes the accounting for unearned revenues.

▶ ILLUSTRATION **3-7**
Accounting for unearned revenues

ACCOUNTING FOR UNEARNED REVENUES			
Examples	**Reason for Adjustment**	**Accounts Before Adjustment**	**Adjusting Entry**
Rent, magazine subscriptions, customer deposits for future service	Unearned revenues recorded in liability accounts are now recognized as revenue for services performed.	Liabilities overstated. Revenues understated.	Dr. Liabilities Cr. Revenues

ACCOUNTING IN ACTION
ACROSS THE ORGANIZATION INSIGHT

© iStockphoto/Skip ODonnell

Gift Card Sales

Gift cards are among the hottest marketing tools in merchandising today. Customers purchase gift cards and give them to someone for later use. Globally, gift card sales average about US$90 billion.

Although these programs are popular with marketing executives, they create accounting questions. Should revenue be recorded at the time the gift card is sold, or when it is exercised? How should expired gift cards be accounted for? Gift card sales can amount to millions of dollars for a company. For example, in 2014, Canadian Tire Corporation reported deferred revenue of $39.3 million, including unearned revenue relating to gift cards.

Sources: Canadian Tire Corporation 2014 annual report; "Gift Card Marketing," First Data Canada, https://www.firstdatacanada.ca/sell-more/gift-cards/, n.d.

Q Suppose that Sanjay Sharma purchases a $100 gift card at Canadian Tire on December 24, 2016, and gives it to his wife, Deepa, on December 25, 2016. On January 3, 2017, Deepa uses the card to purchase a $100 barbecue. When do you think Canadian Tire should recognize revenue and why?

BEFORE YOU GO ON...DO IT **Adjusting Entries for Prepayments**

The trial balance of Panos Co. on March 31, 2017, includes the following selected accounts before adjusting entries:

	Debit	Credit
Prepaid insurance	$ 1,200	
Supplies	2,800	
Equipment	24,000	
Accumulated depreciation—equipment		$2,200
Unearned revenue		9,300

An analysis of the accounts shows the following:

1. A one-year insurance policy for $1,200 was purchased on March 1, 2017.
2. Supplies on hand at March 31, 2017, total $800.
3. Equipment was purchased on April 1, 2016, and has an estimated useful life of 10 years.
4. One third of the unearned revenue was earned in March 2017.

Prepare the adjusting entries for the month of March.

Solution

1.	Mar. 31	Insurance Expense	100	
		Prepaid Insurance		100
		To record insurance expired: $1,200 ÷ 12.		
2.	31	Supplies Expense	2,000	
		Supplies		2,000
		To record supplies used: $2,800 previously on hand – $800 currently on hand = $2,000 used.		
3.	31	Depreciation Expense	200	
		Accumulated Depreciation—Equipment		200
		To record monthly depreciation: $24,000 ÷ 10 × $\frac{1}{12}$.		
4.	31	Unearned Revenue	3,100	
		Service Revenue		3,100
		To record revenue earned: $9,300 × $\frac{1}{3}$ = $3,100 earned.		

Action Plan
- Make sure you prepare adjustments for the correct time period.
- Adjusting entries for prepaid expenses require a debit to an expense account and a credit to an asset or contra asset account.
- Adjusting entries for unearned revenues require a debit to a liability account and a credit to a revenue account.

Related exercise material: BE3–2, BE3–3, BE3–4, BE3–5, BE3–6, BE3–7, BE3–8, BE3–9, E3–5, and E3–6.

ADJUSTING ENTRIES FOR ACCRUALS

The second category of adjusting entries is accruals. Unlike prepayments, which have already been recorded in the accounts, accruals are not recognized through transaction journal entries and thus are not included in the accounts. Accruals are required in situations where cash will be paid or received after the end of the accounting period.

Until an accrual adjustment is made, the revenue account (and the related asset account) is understated for accrued revenues. Similarly, the expense account (and the related liability account) is understated for accrued expenses. Thus, adjusting entries for accruals **increase both a balance sheet account and an income statement account**. We now look at each type of adjusting entry for accruals—accrued revenues and accrued expenses—in more detail.

ACCOUNTING IN ACTION
BUSINESS INSIGHT

At Western University in London, Ontario, as at campuses across the country, classes for most students start in September and end in April. Likewise, the university's fiscal year end is April 30. So essentially, the university closes its books at the same time the students do. This cohesion helps the university to satisfy the criteria needed to recognize revenues and expenses at the appropriate time when services are performed and expenses incurred, respectively.

However, many students at Western take intersession courses. They pay their course fees before the year end of April 30, but the courses don't start until May or later. The university defers the recognition of that revenue until the following accounting period, the one in which it provides the teaching services.

Getty Images/Archive Photos

Q When should a university like Western recognize the advance fees that students pay for residence admission to hold their spot for the coming year?

Accrued Revenues

Revenues for services performed but not yet recorded at the financial statement date are **accrued revenues**. Accrued revenues may accumulate (accrue) with the passage of time, as happens with interest revenue and rent revenue. These are unrecorded because the earning of interest does not involve daily transactions. Companies do not record interest revenue daily because this is often impractical. Accrued revenues may also result when services have been performed but the payment has not been billed or received, as can happen with commissions and fees.

Alternative terminology Accrued revenues are also called *accrued receivables*.

An adjusting entry is required for two purposes: (1) to show the receivable that exists at the balance sheet date, and (2) to record the revenue that has been earned during the period. Before the adjustment is recorded, both assets and revenues are understated. Accordingly, as shown below, **an adjusting entry for accrued revenues results in an increase (debit) to an asset account and an increase (credit) to a revenue account.**

Accrued Revenues

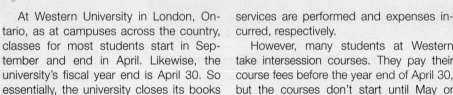

Asset		Revenue	
Debit Adjusting Entry (+)			Credit Adjusting Entry (+)

In October, Lynk Software Services earned $200 in fees for advertising services that were not billed to clients until November. Because these services have not been billed, they have not been recorded. An adjusting entry on October 31 is required as follows:

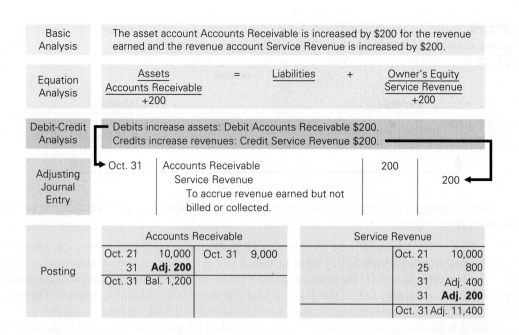

The asset Accounts Receivable shows that $1,200 is owed by clients at the balance sheet date. The balance of $11,400 ($10,000 + $800 + $400 + 200) in Service Revenue represents the total revenue earned during the month. Without the adjusting entry, **assets and owner's equity on the balance sheet, and revenues and profit on the income statement, will all be understated.**

On November 10, Lynk receives $200 cash for the services performed in October. The following entry is made:

Nov. 10	Cash	200	
	Accounts Receivable		200
	To record cash collected on account.		

The company records the collection of the receivables by a debit (increase) to Cash and a credit (decrease) to Accounts Receivable. Illustration 3-8 summarizes the accounting for accrued revenues.

Helpful hint
Summary journal entries for accrued revenues:
To adjust at end of period when revenue is earned but not recorded:
Accounts Receivable
    Service Revenue
When cash is collected:
Cash
    Accounts Receivable

A	=	L	+	OE
+200				
−200				

↑Cash flows: +200

ACCOUNTING FOR ACCRUED REVENUES			
Examples	**Reason for Adjustment**	**Accounts Before Adjustment**	**Adjusting Entry**
Interest, rent, services	Services performed but not yet paid for in cash or recorded.	Assets understated. Revenues understated.	Dr. Assets Cr. Revenues

▶ **ILLUSTRATION** ③-⑧
Accounting for accrued revenues

Accrued Expenses

Expenses incurred but not yet paid or recorded at the statement date are called **accrued expenses**. Interest, rent, property taxes, and salaries can be accrued expenses. Companies make adjustments for accrued expenses to record the obligations that exist at the end of the current accounting period. In fact, accrued expenses result from the same causes as accrued revenues; therefore, an accrued expense on the books of one company is an accrued revenue for another company. For example, the $200 accrual of revenue by Lynk is an accrued expense for the client that received the service.

Adjustments for accrued expenses are needed for two purposes: (1) to record the obligations that exist at the balance sheet date, and (2) to recognize the expenses that apply to the current accounting period. Before adjustment, both liabilities and expenses are understated. Profit and owner's equity are

Alternative terminology Accrued expenses are also called *accrued liabilities.*

overstated. Therefore, **an adjusting entry for accrued expenses results in an increase (debit) to an expense account and an increase (credit) to a liability account**, as follows.

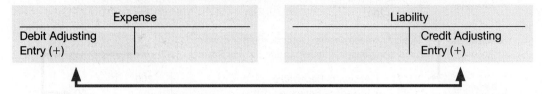

Accrued Expenses

There are many types of expenses that might need to be accrued at the end of an accounting period. Two of the most common are interest and salaries.

Interest. On October 2, Lynk Software Services signed a $5,000, three-month note payable, due January 2, 2018. The note requires interest to be paid at an annual rate of 6%. The amount of interest recorded is determined by three factors: (1) the principal amount of the note; (2) the interest rate, which is always expressed as an annual rate; and (3) the length of time that the note is outstanding (unpaid). The **principal** amount is the amount borrowed or the amount still owed on a loan, separate from interest.

Interest is sometimes due monthly, and sometimes when the principal is due. For Lynk, the total interest due on the $5,000 note at its due date three months later is $75 ($5,000 × 6% × $^3/_{12}$ months). Again note, interest rates are always expressed as an annual rate. Because the interest rate is for one year, the time period must be adjusted for the fraction of the year that the note is outstanding.

The formula for calculating interest and how it applies to Lynk Software Services for the month of October are shown in Illustration 3-9.

Helpful hint To make the illustration easier to understand, we have used a simplified method for calculating interest. In reality, interest is calculated using the exact number of days in the interest period and year.

▶ **ILLUSTRATION 3-9**
Formula for calculating interest

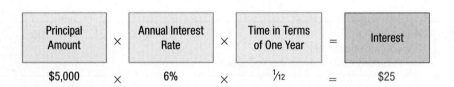

The accrued interest expense adjusting entry at October 31 follows:

▶ **ADJUSTMENT 6**
Accrued expenses—Interest

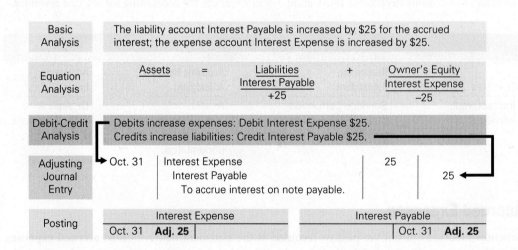

Interest Expense shows the interest charges for the month of October. The amount of interest owed at the statement date is shown in Interest Payable. It will not be paid until the note comes due, on January 2, 2018. The Interest Payable account is used instead of crediting Notes Payable in order to show the two types of obligations (interest and principal) in the accounts and statements. **Without this adjusting entry, liabilities and interest expense will be understated, and profit and owner's equity will be overstated.**

Since this is a three-month note, Lynk Software Services will also need to make identical adjustments at the end of November and at the end of December to accrue for interest expense incurred in each of these months. After the three adjusting entries have been posted, the balance in Interest Payable is $75 ($25 × 3). The following entry is made on January 2, 2018, when the note and interest are paid:

Jan. 2	Interest Payable	75	
	Notes Payable	5,000	
	Cash		5,075
	To record payment of note and interest.		

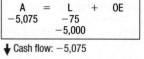

A	=	L	+	OE
−5,075		−75		
		−5,000		

↓ Cash flow: −5,075

This entry does two things: (1) it eliminates the liability for Interest Payable that was recorded in the October 31, November 30, and December 31 adjusting entries; and (2) it eliminates the note payable. Notice also that the Interest Expense account is not included in this entry, because the full amount of interest incurred was accrued in previous months.

Salaries. Some types of expenses, such as employee salaries and commissions, are paid after the work has been performed. At Lynk Software, employees began work on October 16. They are paid every two weeks and were last paid on October 27. The next payment of salaries will not occur until November 10. As shown on the calendar, in Illustration 3-10, there are two working days that remain unpaid at October 31 (October 30 and 31).

Helpful hint
Summary journal entries for accrued interest:
To adjust at end of each period when interest has accrued, but it is not recorded or due:
Interest Expense
    Interest Payable
When interest and principal are due and paid:
Interest expense (for time elapsed from last entry)
Interest Payable
Notes Payable
    Cash

▶ **ILLUSTRATION 3-10**
Lynk Software's pay periods

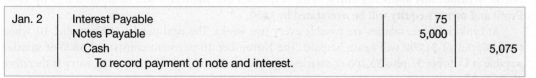

At October 31, the salaries for the last two working days (Monday, October 30, to Tuesday, October 31) represent an accrued expense and a related liability for Lynk Software because the employees have worked but have not been paid for this work as at October 31 (they will be paid November 10).

Recall from Chapter 2 that each of the four employees earns a salary of $500 for a five-day workweek, which is $100 per day. Thus, at October 31 the accrued salaries are $800 (4 employees × $100/day × 2 days). Lynk's accrued salaries expense adjusting entry follows:

Helpful hint Recognition of an accrued expense does not mean that a company is slow or bad at paying its debts. The accrued liability may not be payable until after the balance sheet date.

▶ **ADJUSTMENT 7**
Accrued expenses—
Salaries

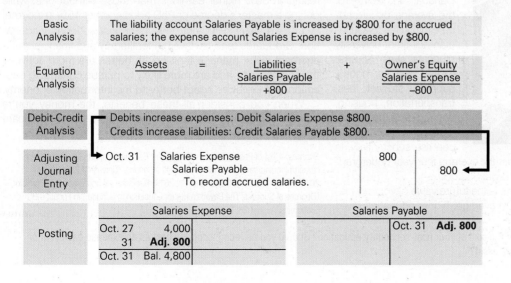

| Basic Analysis | The liability account Salaries Payable is increased by $800 for the accrued salaries; the expense account Salaries Expense is increased by $800. |

Helpful hint
Summary journal entries for accrued salaries:
To adjust at end of each period when employees have worked, but have not be paid:
Salaries Expense
    Salaries Payable
When salaries are paid the next pay period:
Salaries Payable
Salaries Expense (for days not recorded)
    Cash

A	=	L	+	OE
−4,000		−800		−3,200

↓ Cash flows: −4,000

After this adjustment, the balance in Salaries Expense of $4,800 (4 employees × $100/day × 12 days) is the actual salary expense for October. (The employees have worked 12 days in October).

The balance in Salaries Payable of $800 is the amount of the liability for salaries owed as at October 31. **Without this adjusting entry, Lynk's expenses and liabilities will be understated by $800. Profit and owner's equity will be overstated by $800.**

At Lynk Software, salaries are payable every two weeks. The next payday is November 10, when total salaries of $4,000 will again be paid. The November 10 payment consists of $800 of salaries payable at October 31 plus $3,200 of salaries expense for November. The following entry is therefore made on November 10:

Nov. 10	Salaries Payable	800	
	Salaries Expense	3,200	
	Cash		4,000
	To record November 10 payroll.		

This entry does two things: (1) it eliminates the liability for salaries payable that was recorded in the October 31 adjusting entry, and (2) it records the proper amount of salaries expense for the eight-day period from Wednesday, November 1, to Friday, November 10.

Illustration 3-11 summarizes the accounting for accrued expenses.

▶ **ILLUSTRATION 3-11**
Accounting for accrued expenses

ACCOUNTING FOR ACCRUED EXPENSES

Examples	Reason for Adjustment	Accounts Before Adjustment	Adjusting Entry
Interest, rent, salaries	Expenses have been incurred but not yet paid in cash or recorded.	Expenses understated. Liabilities understated.	Dr. Expenses Cr. Liabilities

ACCOUNTING IN ACTION
ALL ABOUT YOU INSIGHT

You are probably paying a lot for your education. According to Statistics Canada, in 2014–15, the average undergraduate tuition fee for Canadian full-time university students was $5,959. If the cost of books, supplies, student fees, transportation, housing, and other expenses is factored in, that amount can rise substantially. In 2010–11, it was estimated that the average four-year undergraduate degree in Canada cost about $58,000.

That is the cost, but what is the future value of your education? According to CIBC, "On average, higher education gives you a leg up in the job market." Post-secondary graduates are more likely to be employed, and typically earn more money over their lifetimes. The CIBC says that a bachelor's degree results in 30% higher earnings than those without one, while getting a master's degree or PhD adds another 15% in income.

There are also indirect benefits of post-secondary education. Graduates tend to have higher literacy and financial management skills, manage their health better, are more active in their community, and are more likely to pursue continuing education and therefore adapt better to the information economy.

When you consider all these benefits, the money you're spending now on your education should be a significant advantage to you in the future.

Sources: "Cost of Post-Secondary Education," CanLearn.ca, http://www.canlearn.ca/eng/planning/saving/cost.shtml; Statistics Canada, "University Tuition Fees 2014/2015," *The Daily*, September 11, 2014; Benjamin Tal and Emanuella Enenajor, "Degrees of Success: The Payoff to Higher Education in Canada," In Focus, CIBC Economics, August 26, 2013.

Q How should you account for the cost of your post-secondary education? Should you be recognizing the cost as an expense each year or should you recognize it as an asset?

Summary of Basic Relationships

The four basic types of adjusting entries are summarized in Illustration 3-12. Take some time to study and analyze the adjusting entries in the summary. Be sure to note that **each adjusting entry affects one balance sheet account and one income statement account**.

Type of Adjustment	Accounts Before Adjustment	Adjusting Entry
Prepaid expenses	Assets overstated. Expenses understated.	Dr. Expenses Cr. Assets or Cr. Contra Assets
Unearned revenues	Liabilities overstated. Revenues understated.	Dr. Liabilities Cr. Revenues
Accrued revenues	Assets understated. Revenues understated.	Dr. Assets Cr. Revenues
Accrued expenses	Expenses understated. Liabilities understated.	Dr. Expenses Cr. Liabilities

▶ ILLUSTRATION 3-12
Summary of adjusting entries

Note that adjusting entries never involve the Cash account (except for bank reconciliations, which we will study in Chapter 7). In the case of prepayments, cash has already been received or paid, and was already recorded in the original journal entry. The adjusting entry reallocates or adjusts amounts between a balance sheet account (e.g., prepaid assets or unearned revenues) and an income statement account (e.g., expenses or revenues). In the case of accruals, cash will be received or paid in the future and recorded then. The adjusting entry records the receivable or payable and the related revenue or expense.

Lynk Software Services Illustration

The journalizing and posting of adjusting entries for Lynk Software Services on October 31 are shown below and on the following pages. The title "Adjusting Entries" may be inserted in the general journal between the last transaction entry from Chapter 2 and the first adjusting entry so that the adjusting entries are clearly identified. As you review the general ledger, note that the adjustments are highlighted in colour.

	GENERAL JOURNAL			J2
Date	Account Titles and Explanation	Ref	Debit	Credit
2017	Adjusting Entries			
Oct. 31	Supplies Expense	740	1,500	
	Supplies	129		1,500
	To record supplies used.			
31	Insurance Expense	722	50	
	Prepaid Insurance	130		50
	To record insurance expired.			
31	Depreciation Expense	711	83	
	Accumulated Depreciation—Equipment	152		83
	To record monthly depreciation.			
31	Unearned Revenue	209	400	
	Service Revenue	400		400
	To record revenue for services provided in October.			
31	Accounts Receivable	112	200	
	Service Revenue	400		200
	To accrue revenue earned but not billed or collected.			
31	Interest Expense	905	25	
	Interest Payable	230		25
	To accrue interest on note payable.			
31	Salaries Expense	729	800	
	Salaries Payable	212		800
	To record accrued salaries.			

GENERAL LEDGER

	Cash			101				Interest Payable		230
Oct. 1	10,000	Oct. 3	900					Oct. 31 Adj.	25
3	1,200	3	600					Bal.	25
25	800	20	500						
31	9,000	24	4,000				T. Jacobs, Capital		301
		31	750					Oct. 1	10,000
Bal.	14,250							Bal.	10,000

	Accounts Receivable			112			T. Jacobs, Drawings		306
Oct. 21	10,000	Oct. 31	9,000		Oct. 20	500		
31 Adj.	200					Bal.	500	
Bal.	1,200							

	Supplies			129			Service Revenue		400
Oct. 4	2,500	Oct. 31 Adj.	1,500				Oct. 21	10,000
Bal.	1,000						25	800
							31 Adj.	400
							31 Adj.	200
							Bal.	11,400

	Prepaid Insurance			130					
Oct. 3	600	Oct. 31 Adj.	50			Depreciation Expense		711
Bal.	550				Oct. 31 Adj.	83		
					Bal.	83		

	Equipment		151			Insurance Expense		722
Oct. 2	5,000				Oct. 31 Adj.	50		
Bal.	5,000				Bal.	50		

Accumulated Depreciation—Equipment		152			Rent Expense		726
	Oct. 31 Adj.	83		Oct. 3	900		
	Bal.	83		Bal.	900		

	Notes Payable		200			Salaries Expense		729
	Oct. 2	5,000		Oct. 24	4,000		
	Bal.	5,000		31 Adj.	800		
				Bal.	4,800		

	Accounts Payable			201			Supplies Expense		740
Oct. 31	750	Oct. 4	2,500		Oct. 31 Adj.	1,500		
		Bal.	1,750		Bal.	1,500		

	Unearned Revenue			209			Interest Expense		905
Oct. 31 Adj.	400	Oct. 3	1,200		Oct. 31 Adj.	25		
		Bal.	800		Bal.	25		

	Salaries Payable		212
	Oct. 31 Adj.	800
	Bal.	800

BEFORE YOU GO ON…DO IT	3	**Adjusting Entries for Accruals**

Action Plan

- Remember that accruals are adjusting entries for revenues earned or expenses incurred that have not been recorded. The cash is received or paid after the end of the accounting period.

Amber Hobbs is the owner of the new company Pioneer Advertising Agency. At the end of August 2017, the first month of business, Amber is trying to prepare monthly financial statements. The following information is for August:

1. At August 31, Pioneer Advertising Agency owed its employees $800 in salaries that will be paid on September 2.
2. On August 1, Pioneer Advertising Agency borrowed $30,000 from a local bank on a five-year term loan. The annual interest rate is 5% and interest is paid monthly on the first of each month.
3. Service revenue earned in August but not yet billed or recorded at August 31 totalled $1,100.

(continued)

BEFORE YOU GO ON...DO IT Adjusting Entries for Accruals (continued)

Prepare the adjusting entries needed at August 31, 2017.

Solution

1.	Aug. 31	Salaries Expense	800	
		Salaries Payable		800
		To record accrued salaries.		
2.	31	Interest Expense	125	
		Interest Payable		125
		To record accrued interest:		
		$30,000 \times 5\% \times {}^{1}/_{12}$		
3.	31	Accounts Receivable	1,100	
		Service Revenue		1,100
		To accrue revenue earned but not billed or collected.		

Related exercise material: BE3–10, BE3–11, BE3–12, BE3–13, E3–7, E3–8 , E3–9, E3–10, E3–11, E3–12, and E3–13.

- Adjusting entries for accrued revenues increase a receivable account (an asset) and increase a revenue account.
- Remember that debits increase assets and credits increase revenues.
- Adjusting entries for accrued expenses increase a payable account (a liability) and increase an expense account.
- Remember that debits increase expenses and credits increase liabilities.

LEARNING OBJECTIVE **4**   Describe the nature and purpose of an adjusted trial balance, and prepare one.

The Adjusted Trial Balance and Financial Statements

After all adjusting entries have been journalized and posted, another trial balance is prepared from the general ledger accounts. This is called an **adjusted trial balance**. Financial statements are then prepared from the adjusted trial balance. Preparation of the adjusted trial balance and the financial statements are steps 6 and 7 of the accounting cycle, as shown in Illustration 3-13.

▸ILLUSTRATION 3-13
The accounting cycle

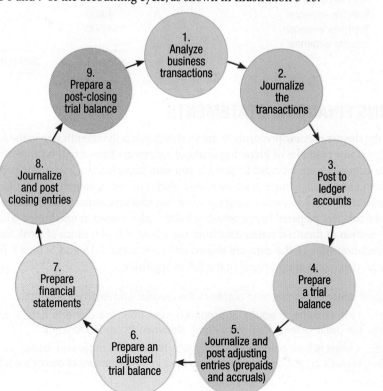

PREPARING THE ADJUSTED TRIAL BALANCE

The procedures for preparing an adjusted trial balance are the same as those described in Chapter 2 for preparing a trial balance. An adjusted trial balance, like a trial balance, only proves that the ledger is mathematically accurate. As discussed in Chapter 2, it does not prove that there are no mistakes in the ledger.

An adjusted trial balance proves that the total of the debit and credit balances in the ledger are equal after all adjustments have been posted. The adjusted trial balance is then used to prepare the financial statements.

The adjusted trial balance for Lynk Software Services is presented in Illustration 3-14. It has been prepared from the ledger accounts shown in the previous section. The amounts affected by the adjusting entries are highlighted in colour in the adjusted trial balance columns. Compare these amounts with those in the trial balance in Illustration 3-4.

▶ILLUSTRATION **3-14**
Adjusted trial balance

LYNK SOFTWARE SERVICES
Adjusted Trial Balance
October 31, 2017

	Debit	Credit
Cash	$14,250	
Accounts receivable	1,200	
Supplies	1,000	
Prepaid insurance	550	
Equipment	5,000	
Accumulated depreciation—equipment		$ 83
Notes payable		5,000
Accounts payable		1,750
Unearned revenue		800
Salaries payable		800
Interest payable		25
T. Jacobs, capital		10,000
T. Jacobs, drawings	500	
Service revenue		11,400
Depreciation expense	83	
Insurance expense	50	
Rent expense	900	
Salaries expense	4,800	
Supplies expense	1,500	
Interest expense	25	
	$29,858	$29,858

PREPARING FINANCIAL STATEMENTS

As shown in the chapter preview, preparing financial statements is the seventh step in the accounting cycle. In Chapter 2, you saw examples of preparing financial statements from a trial balance, without adjusting entries. Those examples were included to provide you with opportunities to practise preparing financial statements. But in reality, adjusting entries are almost always necessary to prepare financial statements on an accrual basis. Therefore, you should always prepare financial statements from an adjusted trial balance, never from trial balances prepared before adjusting entries (also known as unadjusted trial balances).

The preparation of financial statements from the adjusted trial balance of Lynk Software Services and the interrelationships of the data are shown in Illustrations 3-15 and 3-16. As Illustration 3-15 shows, financial statements are prepared in the following order:

1. The income statement is prepared first from the revenue and expense accounts.
2. The statement of owner's equity is prepared next from the owner's capital and drawings accounts. The profit (or loss) from the income statement is carried forward.
3. The balance sheet is then prepared (Illustration 3-16) from the asset and liability accounts and the ending owner's capital balance that is reported in the statement of owner's equity.

▶ ILLUSTRATION 3-15

Preparation of the income statement and statement of owner's equity from the adjusted trial balance

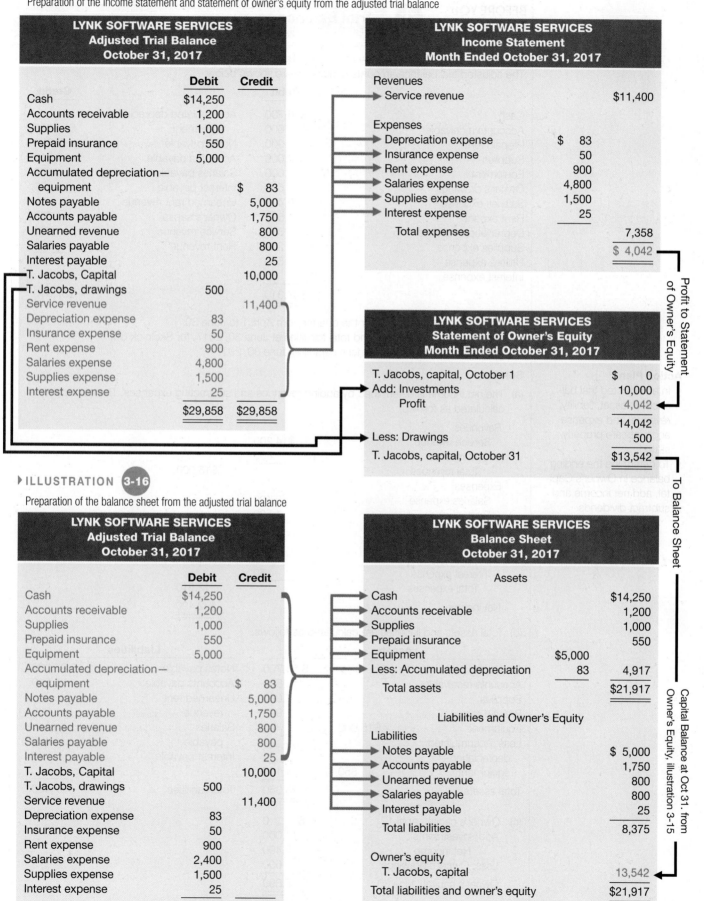

LYNK SOFTWARE SERVICES
Adjusted Trial Balance
October 31, 2017

	Debit	Credit
Cash	$14,250	
Accounts receivable	1,200	
Supplies	1,000	
Prepaid insurance	550	
Equipment	5,000	
Accumulated depreciation— equipment		$ 83
Notes payable		5,000
Accounts payable		1,750
Unearned revenue		800
Salaries payable		800
Interest payable		25
T. Jacobs, Capital		10,000
T. Jacobs, drawings	500	
Service revenue		11,400
Depreciation expense	83	
Insurance expense	50	
Rent expense	900	
Salaries expense	4,800	
Supplies expense	1,500	
Interest expense	25	
	$29,858	$29,858

LYNK SOFTWARE SERVICES
Income Statement
Month Ended October 31, 2017

Revenues		
Service revenue		$11,400
Expenses		
Depreciation expense	$ 83	
Insurance expense	50	
Rent expense	900	
Salaries expense	4,800	
Supplies expense	1,500	
Interest expense	25	
Total expenses		7,358
		$ 4,042

LYNK SOFTWARE SERVICES
Statement of Owner's Equity
Month Ended October 31, 2017

T. Jacobs, capital, October 1		$ 0
Add: Investments		10,000
Profit		4,042
		14,042
Less: Drawings		500
T. Jacobs, capital, October 31		$13,542

Profit to Statement of Owner's Equity

To Balance Sheet

▶ ILLUSTRATION 3-16

Preparation of the balance sheet from the adjusted trial balance

LYNK SOFTWARE SERVICES
Adjusted Trial Balance
October 31, 2017

	Debit	Credit
Cash	$14,250	
Accounts receivable	1,200	
Supplies	1,000	
Prepaid insurance	550	
Equipment	5,000	
Accumulated depreciation— equipment		$ 83
Notes payable		5,000
Accounts payable		1,750
Unearned revenue		800
Salaries payable		800
Interest payable		25
T. Jacobs, Capital		10,000
T. Jacobs, drawings	500	
Service revenue		11,400
Depreciation expense	83	
Insurance expense	50	
Rent expense	900	
Salaries expense	2,400	
Supplies expense	1,500	
Interest expense	25	
	$29,858	$29,858

LYNK SOFTWARE SERVICES
Balance Sheet
October 31, 2017

Assets		
Cash		$14,250
Accounts receivable		1,200
Supplies		1,000
Prepaid insurance		550
Equipment	$5,000	
Less: Accumulated depreciation	83	4,917
Total assets		$21,917

Liabilities and Owner's Equity		
Liabilities		
Notes payable		$ 5,000
Accounts payable		1,750
Unearned revenue		800
Salaries payable		800
Interest payable		25
Total liabilities		8,375
Owner's equity		
T. Jacobs, capital		13,542
Total liabilities and owner's equity		$21,917

Capital Balance at Oct 31, from Owner's Equity, illustration 3-15

Skolnick Co. was organized on April 1, 2017. The company prepares quarterly financial statements. The adjusted trial balance amounts at June 30 are shown below.

	Debit		Credit
Cash	$ 6,700	Accumulated depreciation—	
Accounts receivable	600	equipment	$ 850
Prepaid rent	900	Notes payable	5,000
Supplies	1,000	Accounts payable	1,510
Equipment	15,000	Salaries payable	400
Owner's drawings	600	Interest payable	50
Salaries expense	9,400	Unearned rent revenue	500
Rent expense	1,500	Owner's capital	14,000
Depreciation expense	850	Service revenue	14,200
Supplies expense	200	Rent revenue	800
Utilities expense	510		
Interest expense	50		
	$37,310		$37,310

(a) Determine the net income for the quarter from April 1 to June 30.
(b) Determine the total assets and total liabilities at June 30, 2017, for Skolnick Co.
(c) Determine the amount of owner's capital at June 30, 2017.

Action Plan

- In an adjusted trial balance, all asset, liability, revenue, and expense accounts are properly stated.
- To determine the ending balance in Owner's Capital, add net income and subtract dividends.

Solution

(a) The net income is determined by adding revenues and subtracting expenses. The net income is calculated as follows.

Revenues		
Service revenue	$14,200	
Rent revenue	800	
Total revenues		$15,000
Expenses		
Salaries expense	9,400	
Rent expense	1,500	
Depreciation expense	850	
Utilities expense	510	
Supplies expense	200	
Interest expense	50	
Total expenses		12,510
Net income		$ 2,490

(b) Total assets and liabilities are calculated as follows.

Assets			Liabilities	
Cash		$ 6,700	Notes payable	$5,000
Accounts receivable		600	Accounts payable	1,510
Supplies		1,000	Unearned rent	
Prepaid rent		900	revenue	500
Equipment	$15,000		Salaries	
Less: Accumulated			payable	400
depreciation—			Interest payable	50
equipment	850	14,150		
Total assets		$ 23,350	Total liabilities	$7,460

(c)
Owner's capital, April 1	$ 0
Add: Investments	14,000
Net income	2,490
Less: Owner's drawings	600
Owner's capital, June 30	$ 15,890

Related exercise material: BE3–14, BE3–15, BE 3–16, E3–14, E3–15, and E3–16.

Comparing IFRS and ASPE

Key Differences	International Financial Reporting Standards (IFRS)	Accounting Standards for Private Enterprises (ASPE)
Revenue	After Jan 1, 2018 in IFRS, there are five steps that must be met to recognize revenue. The entity must identify a contractual relationship with the customer as well as the performance obligation (the goods or services) to be provided, determine the transaction price and allocate this price if multiple goods and services are to be provided. When the performance obligation is satisfied (the goods and services have been provided), revenue may be recognized.	In ASPE, revenue is recorded when earned when the goods and services are provided to the customer, and the amount is measurable and collectible.
Timing of preparing adjusting journal entries	Public companies must prepare quarterly financial statements, so adjusting entries will have to be made at least four times a year.	Private companies must prepare annual financial statements, so adjusting entries are required only on an annual basis.
Terminology	In IFRS, the term "depreciation" is used for the allocation of the cost of long-lived assets such as buildings and equipment and the term "amortization" is used for intangible long-lived assets.	In ASPE, the term "amortization" is used for the allocation of the cost of buildings and equipment and for intangible long- lived assets. But private companies are allowed to use the term "depreciation" for buildings and equipment.

Demonstration Problem

Julie Szo opened Green Tree Lawn Care Company on April 1, 2017. At April 30, 2017, the trial balance is as follows:

GREEN TREE LAWN CARE COMPANY Trial Balance April 30, 2017		
	Debit	Credit
Cash	$10,950	
Prepaid insurance	3,600	
Supplies	850	
Equipment	28,000	
Notes payable		$20,000
Accounts payable		450
Unearned revenue		4,200
J. Szo, capital		18,000
J. Szo, drawings	650	
Service revenue		1,800
Rent expense	400	
Totals	$44,450	$44,450

Analysis reveals the following additional data for the month:

1. Prepaid insurance is the cost of a 12-month insurance policy that started April 1.
2. Supplies costing $225 were on hand on April 30.
3. The equipment is expected to have a useful life of four years.
4. The note payable is dated April 1. It is a six-month, 4% note with interest payable on the first of each month starting on May 1.
5. Seven customers paid for the company's six-month lawn service package of $600, beginning in April. These customers were served in April.
6. Lawn services performed for other customers but not billed or recorded at April 30 totalled $1,500.

Instructions
(a) Prepare the adjusting entries for the month of April. Show calculations.
(b) Prepare T accounts for the accounts affected by the adjusting entries. Post the adjusting entries to the T accounts.
(c) Prepare an adjusted trial balance at April 30, 2017.
(d) Prepare an income statement, statement of owner's equity, and balance sheet.

SOLUTION TO DEMONSTRATION PROBLEM

(a)

GENERAL JOURNAL

Date	Account Titles and Explanation	Debit	Credit
	Adjusting Entries		
Apr. 30	Insurance Expense	300	
	Prepaid Insurance		300
	To record insurance expired:		
	$3,600 \div 12 = $300 per month.		
30	Supplies Expense	625	
	Supplies		625
	To record supplies used: $850 - $225 = $625.		
30	Depreciation Expense	583	
	Accumulated Depreciation—Equipment		583
	To record monthly depreciation: $28,000 \div 4 =		
	$7,000 \times 1/12 = $583 per month.		
30	Interest Expense	67	
	Interest Payable		67
	To accrue interest on note payable:		
	$20,000 \times 4\% \times 1/12 = $67.		
30	Unearned Revenue	700	
	Service Revenue		700
	To record service revenue:		
	$600 \div 6 months = $100 per month;		
	$100 per month \times 7 customers = $700.		
30	Accounts Receivable	1,500	
	Service Revenue		1,500
	To accrue revenue earned but not billed or		
	collected.		

(b)

GENERAL LEDGER

Accounts Receivable		Accumulated Depreciation—Equipment	
Apr. 30 Adj. 1,500			Apr. 30 Adj. 583
Bal. 1,500			Bal. 583

Prepaid Insurance				Interest Payable		
Apr. 30 Bal.	3,600	Apr. 30 Adj.	300		Apr. 30 Adj.	67
Bal.	3,300				Bal.	67

Supplies				Unearned Revenue		
Apr. 30 Bal.	850	Apr. 30 Adj.	625	Apr. 30 Adj.	700	Apr. 30 Bal.	4,200
Bal.	225					Bal.	3,500

Service Revenue				Supplies Expense		
		Apr. 30 Bal.	1,800	Apr. 30 Adj.	625	
		30 Adj.	700	Bal.	625	
		30 Adj.	1,500			
		Bal.	4,000			

Depreciation Expense

		Interest Expense		
Apr. 30 Adj.	583	Apr. 30 Adj.	67	
Bal.	583	Bal.	67	

Insurance Expense

Apr. 30 Adj.	300
Bal.	300

(c)

GREEN TREE LAWN CARE COMPANY Adjusted Trial Balance April 30, 2017		
	Debit	Credit
Cash	$10,950	
Accounts receivable	1,500	
Prepaid insurance	3,300	
Supplies	225	
Equipment	28,000	
Accumulated depreciation—equipment		$ 583
Notes payable		20,000
Accounts payable		450
Interest payable		67
Unearned revenue		3,500
J. Szo, capital		18,000
J. Szo, drawings	650	
Service revenue		4,000
Depreciation expense	583	
Insurance expense	300	
Interest expense	67	
Rent expense	400	
Supplies expense	625	
Totals	$46,600	$46,600

Solution to Demonstration Problem *continued*

(d)

GREEN TREE LAWN CARE COMPANY Income Statement Month Ended April 30, 2017		
Revenues		
Service revenue		$4,000
Expenses		
Depreciation expense	$583	
Insurance expense	300	
Interest expense	67	
Rent expense	400	
Supplies expense	625	1,975
Profit		$2,025

GREEN TREE LAWN CARE COMPANY Statement of Owner's Equity Month Ended April 30, 2017		
J. Szo, capital, April 1		$ 0
Add: Investments	$18,000	
Profit	2,025	20,025
Less: Drawings		650
J. Szo, capital, April 30		$19,375

GREEN TREE LAWN CARE COMPANY Balance Sheet April 30, 2017		
Assets		
Cash		$10,950
Accounts receivable		1,500
Prepaid insurance		3,300
Supplies		225
Equipment	$28,000	
Less: Accumulated depreciation	583	27,417
Total assets		$43,392
Liabilities and Owner's Equity		
Liabilities		
Notes payable		$20,000
Accounts payable		450
Interest payable		67
Unearned revenue		3,500
Total liabilities		24,017
Owner's equity		
J. Szo, capital		19,375
Total liabilities and owner's equity		$43,392

▶ Summary of Learning Objectives

1. *Explain accrual basis accounting, and when to recognize revenues and expenses.* In order to provide timely information, accountants divide the life of a business into specific time periods. Therefore, it is important to record transactions in the correct time period. Under accrual basis accounting, events that change a company's financial statements are recorded in the periods in which the events occur, rather than in the periods in which the company receives or pays cash. The revenue recognition principle provides guidance about when to recognize revenues. Under ASPE, revenue is recognized when the service has been performed or the goods have been sold and delivered, the revenue can be reliably measured, and collection is reasonably certain. For IFRS, a contractual relationship to provide a performance obligation (goods or services) with the customer must exist. The transaction price must be determined and allocated if there are multiple goods and services to be provided. When the goods and services have been provided, the performance obligation is satisfied and revenue may be recognized. Expenses are recorded in the same period as revenue is recognized, if there is a direct association between the revenues and expenses. If there is no association between revenues and expenses, expenses are recorded in the period they are incurred.

2. *Prepare adjusting entries for prepayments.* Prepayments are either prepaid expenses or unearned revenues. Adjusting entries for prepayments record the portion of the prepayment that applies to the expense or revenue of the current accounting period. The adjusting entry for prepaid expenses debits (increases) an expense account and credits (decreases) an asset account. For a long-lived asset, the contra asset account Accumulated Depreciation is used instead of crediting the asset account directly. The adjusting entry for unearned revenues debits (decreases) a liability account and credits (increases) a revenue account.

3. *Prepare adjusting entries for accruals.* Accruals are either accrued revenues or accrued expenses. Adjusting entries for accruals record revenues and expenses that apply to the current accounting period and that have not yet been recognized through daily journal entries. The adjusting entry for accrued revenue debits (increases) a receivable account and credits (increases) a revenue account. The adjusting entry for an accrued expense debits (increases) an expense account and credits (increases) a liability account.

4. *Describe the nature and purpose of an adjusted trial balance, and prepare one.* An adjusted trial balance shows the balances of all accounts, including those that have been adjusted, at the end of an accounting period. It proves that the total of the accounts with debit balances is still equal to the total of the accounts with credit balances after the adjustments have been posted. Financial statements are prepared from an adjusted trial balance in the following order: (1) income statement, (2) statement of owner's equity, and (3) balance sheet.

▶ Glossary

Accrual basis accounting   A basis for accounting in which revenues are recorded when earned and expenses are recorded when incurred. (p. 117)

Accrued expenses   Expenses incurred but not yet paid in cash or recorded. (p. 129)

Accrued revenues   Revenues earned but not yet received in cash or recorded. (p. 128)

Accumulated depreciation   The cumulative sum of the depreciation expense since the asset was purchased. (p. 124)

Adjusted trial balance   A list of accounts and their balances after all adjustments have been posted. (p. 135)

Adjusting entries   Entries made at the end of an accounting period to ensure that the revenue and expense recognition criteria are followed. (p. 119)

Carrying amount   The difference between the cost of a depreciable asset and its accumulated depreciation; in other words, it is the unallocated or unexpired portion of the depreciable asset's cost. (p. 125)

Cash basis accounting   A basis for accounting in which revenue is recorded when cash is received and an expense is recorded when cash is paid. (p. 117)

Contra asset account   An account with the opposite balance (credit) compared with its related asset account, which has a debit balance. A contra asset is deducted from the related asset on the balance sheet. (p. 124)

Depreciation   The allocation of the cost of a long-lived asset to expense over its useful life in a rational and systematic manner. (p. 123)

Fiscal year   An accounting period that is one year long. It does not need to start and end on the same days as the calendar year. (p. 116)

Interim periods   Accounting time periods that are less than one year long, such as a month or a quarter of a year. (p. 116)

Matching concept   Dictates that efforts (expenses) must match results (revenues). (p. 118)

Principal   The amount borrowed or the amount still owed on a loan, separate from interest. (p. 130)

Revenue recognition principle   Provides guidance about when to record revenue. In general, it is recorded when the performance obligation has been satisfied, that is, the service has been performed or the goods sold and delivered. (p. 118)

Straight-line depreciation method   A depreciation method in which depreciation expense is calculated as the cost divided by the useful life. (p. 123)

Useful life   The length of service of a depreciable asset. (p. 123)

▶ Self-Study Questions

Answers are at the end of the chapter.

(LO 1) C **1.** The accrual basis of accounting is considered superior to the cash basis of accounting because it:
(a) is easier to use.
(b) provides better information about the activities of the business.
(c) records events in the period in which the cash is paid.
(d) is used by most businesses.

(LO 1) K **2.** Revenue should be recognized when:
(a) it is earned.
(b) there is an increase in assets or decrease in liabilities as the result of the company's business activities with its customers.
(c) the service is provided or the goods are sold and delivered.
(d) All of the above.

(LO 1) K **3.** Adjusting entries are made to ensure that:
(a) revenues and expenses are recorded in the correct accounting period.
(b) the accrual basis of accounting is used.
(c) assets and liabilities have up-to-date balances at the end of an accounting period.
(d) All of the above.

(LO 2) AP **4.** A company pays $1,140 for a one-year insurance policy effective April 1, 2017. The payment is recorded as Prepaid Insurance. On April 30, 2017, an adjusting entry is required to:
(a) increase the asset Prepaid Insurance by $95 and increase the expense Insurance Expense by $95.
(b) decrease the asset Prepaid Insurance by $95 and increase the expense Insurance Expense by $95.
(c) decrease the asset Prepaid Insurance by $1,045 and increase the expense Insurance Expense by $1,045.
(d) increase the asset Prepaid Insurance by $1,045 and increase the expense Insurance Expense by $1,045.

(LO 2) AP **5.** The trial balance shows Supplies $1,350 and Supplies Expense $0. If $600 of supplies are on hand at the end of the period, the adjusting entry is:

(a) Supplies	600	
Supplies Expense		600
(b) Supplies	750	
Supplies Expense		750
(c) Supplies Expense	750	
Supplies		750
(d) Supplies Expense	600	
Supplies		600

(LO 2) K **6.** Accumulated Depreciation is:
(a) an expense account.
(b) an owner's equity account.
(c) a liability account.
(d) a contra asset account.

(LO 2) AP **7.** Queenan Company calculates depreciation on its equipment of $1,000 for the month of June. The adjusting journal entry to record this depreciation expense is:

(a) Depreciation Expense	1,000	
Accumulated Depreciation—Equipment		1,000
(b) Depreciation Expense	1,000	
Equipment		1,000
(c) Equipment Expense	1,000	
Equipment		1,000
(d) Accumulated Depreciation—Equipment	1,000	
Equipment		1,000

(LO 2) K **8.** Adjustments for prepaid expenses:
(a) decrease assets and increase revenues.
(b) decrease expenses and increase assets.
(c) decrease assets and increase expenses.
(d) decrease revenues and increase assets.

(LO 2) K **9.** A company records all cash received in advance of providing a service as a liability. At the end of the accounting period, an adjustment for unearned revenues is required to:
(a) decrease liabilities and increase revenues.
(b) increase assets and increase revenues.
(c) decrease revenues and increase liabilities.
(d) decrease revenues and decrease assets.

(LO 3) AP **10.** A bank has a three-month, 4%, $6,000 note receivable, issued on November 1. Interest is due at maturity. What adjusting entry should the bank record on November 30?

(a) Cash	20	
Interest Revenue		20
(b) Interest Receivable	20	
Interest Revenue		20
(c) Interest Receivable	60	
Unearned Revenue		60
(d) Interest Receivable	60	
Interest Revenue		60

(LO 3) AP **11.** Kathy Kiska earned a salary of $400 in the last week of September. She will be paid for this in October. The adjusting entry for Kathy's employer at September 30 is:

(a) Salaries Expense	400	
Salaries Payable		400
(b) Salaries Expense	400	
Cash		400
(c) Salaries Payable	400	
Cash		400
(d) No entry is required.		

(LO 4) C **12.** Which of the following statements about the adjusted trial balance is incorrect?
(a) An adjusted trial balance proves that the total debit balances and the total credit balances in

the ledger are equal after all adjustments are
made.

(b) The adjusted trial balance is prepared after
preparing financial statements.

(c) The adjusted trial balance lists the account balances divided into assets and liabilities.

(d) The adjusted trial balance proves that the total
debits in the adjusting journal entries are equal
to the total credits in the adjusting journal
entries.

▶ Questions

(LO 1) K   1. (a) Why do accountants divide the life of a business
into specific time periods? (b) What is the difference
between a fiscal year and a calendar year?

(LO 1) C   2. Why is an accrual basis income statement more
useful than a cash basis income statement?

(LO 1) C   3. Pierce Dussault, a lawyer, accepts a legal engagement
in March, does the work in April, and is paid in May.
If Dussault's law firm prepares monthly financial
statements, when should it recognize revenue from
this engagement? Why?

(LO 1) C   4. In completing the engagement in question 3, Pierce
Dussault incurred $500 of salary expenses in March
that are specifically related to this engagement,
$2,500 in April, and none in May. How much
expense should be deducted from revenue in the
month(s) when the revenue is recognized? Why?

(LO 2) C   5. The name Prepaid Expense suggests that this account
is an expense and belongs on an income statement.
Instead the account appears on the balance sheet as
an asset. Explain why this is appropriate and why
prepaid expenses may need to be adjusted at the end
of each period.

(LO 2) K   6. What is the debit-credit effect of a prepaid expense
adjusting entry?

(LO 2) C   7. "Depreciation is a process of valuation that results in
the reporting of the fair value of the asset." Do you
agree? Explain.

(LO 2) K   8. Explain the difference between (a) depreciation
expense and accumulated depreciation, and
(b) cost and carrying amount.

(LO 2) C   9. Why do we credit the contra asset account Accumulated Depreciation—Equipment when recording
depreciation instead of crediting Equipment?

(LO 2) C   10. G. Phillips Company purchased equipment for
$18,000. By the current balance sheet date, $6,000
had been depreciated. Indicate the balance sheet
presentation of the data.

(LO 2) C   11. The name Unearned Revenue suggests that this type
of account is a revenue account and belongs on the
income statement. Instead the account appears on
the balance sheet as a liability. Explain why this is
appropriate and why unearned revenues may need to
be adjusted at the end of the period.

(LO 3) C   12. Waiparous General Store has a note receivable from
a customer. The customer pays the interest for the

previous month on the first day of each month.
Assuming Waiparous prepares monthly financial
statements, will it need to accrue for interest revenue
on the note at the end of each month? Why or why
not? When the interest payment is received each
month, what accounts will Waiparous increase and/
or decrease?

(LO 3) AP   13. A company makes an accrued expense adjusting
entry for $600. Which financial statement items were
overstated or understated before this entry? Explain.

(LO 2,3) C   14. For each of the following items, indicate (a) the type
of adjusting entry required (prepaid expense, unearned
revenue, accrued revenue, or accrued expense); and
(b) the name of the other account included in the
adjusting entry and whether that account is over- or
understated prior to the adjustment.
1. Accounts Receivable is understated.
2. Unearned Revenue is overstated.
3. Interest Payable is understated.
4. Supplies Expense is understated.
5. Prepaid Insurance is overstated.
6. Interest Revenue is understated.

(LO 2,3) K   15. One half of the adjusting entry is given below.
Indicate the title for the other half of the entry:
(a) Salaries Expense is debited.
(b) Depreciation Expense is debited.
(c) Interest Payable is credited.
(d) Supplies is credited.
(e) Accounts Receivable is debited.
(f) Unearned Revenue is debited.

(LO 2,3) K   16. Adjusting entries for accruals always involve the
Cash account, and adjusting entries for prepayments
never include the Cash account. Do you agree? Why
or why not?

(LO 2,3) C   17. "An adjusting entry may affect two balance sheet or
two income statement accounts." Do you agree? Why
or why not?

(LO 4) C   18. Identify the similarities and differences between a
trial balance and an adjusted trial balance. What is
the purpose of each one?

(LO 4) K   19. Is an adjusted trial balance up to date and complete?
Discuss.

(LO 4) C   20. Jeremiah is preparing a balance sheet. He includes
the amount shown in the adjusted trial balance for
the owner's capital account on the balance sheet. Will
the balance sheet balance? Why or why not?

▶ Brief Exercises

Determine profit using cash and accrual bases. (LO 1) AP

BE3–1   AA Lawn Care had the following transactions in May, its first month of business:
1. Collected $550 cash from customers for services provided in May.
2. Billed customers $725 for services provided in May.
3. Received $350 from customers for services to be provided in June.
4. Purchased $250 of supplies on account. All of the supplies were used in May but were paid for in June.
   (a) Calculate profit for May using cash basis accounting.
   (b) Calculate profit for May using accrual basis accounting.

Calculate missing data for supplies. (LO 2) AP

BE3–2   Calculate the missing information in each of the following independent situations:

	Red Co.	Blue Co.	Green Co.
Supplies on hand, May 31, 2016	$ 795	$ 985	$1,325
Supplies purchased during the year	3,830	3,070	2,395
Supplies on hand, May 31, 2017	665	?	1,700
Supplies used during the year	?	2,750	?

Identify the major types of adjusting entries. (LO 1, 2) C

BE3–3   Kee Company accumulates the following adjustment data at December 31. Indicate (a) the type of balance sheet account that requires adjustment (prepaid expense, accrued revenue, etc.); and (b) whether the identified balance sheet account is over- or understated before any adjustments are recorded.
1. Supplies of $100 are on hand. Kee Company started the year with $1,100 of supplies on hand.
2. Services were performed but not recorded.
3. Interest of $200 has accumulated on a note payable.
4. Rent collected in advance totalling $650 has been earned.

Prepare and post transaction and adjusting entries for supplies. (LO 2) AP

BE3–4   Hahn Consulting Company's general ledger showed $785 in the Supplies account on January 1, 2017. On May 31, 2017, the company paid $3,255 for additional supplies. A count on December 31, 2017, showed $1,035 of supplies on hand.
(a) Prepare the journal entry to record the purchase of supplies on May 31, 2017.
(b) Calculate the amount of supplies used in 2017.
(c) Prepare the adjusting entry required at December 31, 2017.

Prepare and post transaction and adjusting entries for insurance. (LO 2) AP

BE3–5   On March 1, 2017, Eire Co. paid $4,800 to Big North Insurance for a one-year insurance policy. Eire Co. has a December 31 fiscal year end and adjusts accounts annually. Complete the following for Eire Co.
(a) Prepare the March 1, 2017, journal entry for the purchase of the insurance.
(b) Calculate the amount of insurance that expired during 2017 and the unexpired cost at December 31, 2017.
(c) Prepare the adjusting entry required at December 31, 2017.

Prepare and post transaction and adjusting entries for insurance. (LO 2) AP

BE3–6   On July 1, 2017, Majors Co. buys a three-year insurance policy for $12,750. Majors Co. has a December 31 year end.
(a) Journalize the purchase of the insurance policy.
(b) Prepare the year-end adjusting entry for the amount of insurance expired.

Prepare transaction and adjusting entries for depreciation. (LO 2) AP

BE3–7   On July 1, 2017, Masood Company purchases equipment for $30,000. The company uses straight-line depreciation. It estimates the equipment will have a 10-year life. Masood Company has a December 31 year end.
(a) Record the purchase of the equipment.
(b) Calculate the amount of depreciation Masood Company should record for the year of the equipment purchase.
(c) Prepare the adjusting journal entry for the equipment at December 31, 2017.

Prepare transaction and adjusting entries for depreciation; show statement presentation. (LO 2) AP

BE3–8   Zhang Company paid $27,000 to purchase equipment on January 1, 2017. Zhang Company has a December 31 fiscal year end and uses straight-line depreciation. The company estimates the equipment will have a nine-year useful life.
(a) Prepare the journal entry to record the purchase of the equipment on January 1, 2017.
(b) Prepare the adjusting entries required on December 31, 2017 and 2018.
(c) Show the balance sheet and income statement presentation of the equipment at December 31, 2017 and 2018.

Prepare and post transaction and adjusting entries for unearned revenue. (LO 2) AP

BE3–9   On March 1, 2017, Big North Insurance received $4,800 cash from Eire Co. for a one-year insurance policy. Big North Insurance has an October 31 fiscal year end and adjusts accounts annually. Complete the following for Big North Insurance.
(a) Prepare the March 1, 2017, journal entry.
(b) Calculate the amount of revenue earned during 2017 and the amount unearned at October 31, 2017.

(c) Prepare the adjusting entry required on October 31, 2017.
(d) Using T accounts, post the entries for parts (a) and (c) above and indicate the adjusted balance in each account. It is not necessary to create a T account for Cash.

BE3–10 Vintage Clothing Co. is open for business six days a week. Weekly total salaries of $7,080 are paid every Monday morning to employees for salary earned during the previous six-day workweek (Monday through Satur-day). The company has a July 31 fiscal year end, which falls on Thursday this year. Salaries were last paid on Monday, July 28 (for July 21 to 26). The next payday is Monday, August 4 (for July 28 to August 2). Prepare the journal entries to record the following:
(a) the payment of salaries on July 28.
(b) the adjusting journal entry to accrue salaries at July 31.
(c) the payment of salaries on August 4.

Prepare adjusting and transaction entries for accruals. (LO 3) AP

BE3–11 Butternut Squash Company has the following two notes receivable at May 31, 2017, its fiscal year end:
1. $50,000 six-month, 6% note issued January 1, 2017
2. $20,000 three-month, 5% note issued April 30, 2017
   Interest is payable at maturity for both notes.
(a) Calculate the accrued interest on both notes at May 31, 2017.
(b) Prepare one adjusting journal entry to record the accrued interest on both notes.

Calculate and record accrued interest. (LO 3) AP

BE3–12 On July 31, 2016, a company purchased equipment for $150,000, paying $40,000 cash and signing a 5% note payable for the remainder. The interest and principal of the note are due on January 31, 2017. Prepare the journal entry to record the following:
(a) the purchase of the equipment on July 31, 2016.
(b) the accrual of the interest at year end, November 30, 2016, assuming interest has not previously been accrued.
(c) the repayment of the interest and note on January 31, 2017.

Prepare adjusting and transaction entries for interest. (LO 3) AP

BE3–13 The bookkeeper for Kwan Enterprises asks you to prepare the adjusting entries for the following items at December 31.
1. Interest on note payable of $400 is accrued.
2. Services performed but not recorded total $2,300.
3. Salaries earned by employees of $900 have not been recorded.

Use the following account titles: Service Revenue, Accounts Receivable, Interest Expense, Interest Payable, Salaries Expense, and Salaries Payable.

Identify effect of adjustment on elements of financial statements. (LO 2, 3) C

BE3–14 The account balances (after adjustments) from the general ledger of Winterholt Company at September 30, 2017, follow in alphabetical order. All accounts have normal balances.

Accounts payable	$ 2,890	Rent expense	$ 1,560
Accounts receivable	6,050	Salaries expense	12,215
Accumulated depreciation—equipment	6,400	Salaries payable	875
Cash	1,100	Service revenue	48,450
Depreciation expense	3,100	Unearned service revenue	840
Equipment	29,800	W. Winterholt, capital	16,150
Prepaid rent	780	W. Winterholt, drawings	21,000

(a) Prepare an adjusted trial balance.
(b) Beside each account, identify whether it is an asset (A), liability (L), capital (C), drawing (D), revenue (R), or expense (E).
(c) Beside each account, identify whether it should be included on the income statement (IS), statement of owner's equity (OE), or balance sheet (BS).

Prepare adjusted trial balance and identify financial statement. (LO 4) AP

BE3–15 The adjusted trial balance of Wildwood Company at December 31, 2017, includes the following accounts: D. Wood, Capital $15,600, D. Wood, Drawings $7,000, Service Revenue $39,000, Salaries Expense $1,500, Insurance Expense $2,000, Rent Expense $4,000, Supplies Expense $1,500, and Depreciation Expense $1,300. Prepare an income statement for the year.

Prepare an income statement from an adjusted trial balance. (LO 4) AP

BE3–16 The partial trial balance for Wildwood Company is presented in BE3–15. The balance in D. Wood, Capital is the balance as of January 1. Prepare a statement of owner's equity for the year assuming instead that net income is $14,200 for the year.

Prepare a statement of owner's equity from an adjusted trial balance. (LO 4) AP

▶ Exercises

Determine profit using cash and accrual bases and comment on usefulness. (LO 1) AP

E3–1   Cassist Enterprises began operations on January 1, 2017. During 2017 and 2018, the company entered into the following transactions:

	2017	2018
1. Cash collected from customers during the year for services provided that year.	$50,250	$55,430
2. Accounts receivable at year end for services provided on account during the year.	12,070	18,080
3. Cash collected from customers for services provided on account the previous year.	0	12,070
4. Cash collected from customers for services to be provided the following year.	4,580	1,760
5. Services provided to customers who had paid cash in advance the previous year.	0	4,580
6. Cash paid for operating expenses incurred during the year.	17,380	18,990
7. Accounts payable at year end for operating expenses incurred on account during the year.	2,199	3,120
8. Cash paid to creditors for operating expenses incurred on account during the previous year.	0	2,199

Instructions

(a) Calculate revenue, operating expenses, and profit for 2017 and 2018 using cash basis accounting.

(b) Calculate revenue, operating expenses, and profit for 2017 and 2018 using accrual basis accounting.

(c) Which basis of accounting (cash or accrual) gives more useful information for decision-makers? Explain.

Identify when revenue is recognized. (LO 1) AP

E3–2   For the following independent situations, use professional judgement to determine when the company should recognize revenue from the transactions:

1. **WestJet Airlines** sells you a nonrefundable airline ticket in September for your flight home at Christmas.
2. **Leon's Furniture** sells you a home theatre in January on a "no money down, no interest, and no payments for one year" promotional deal.
3. **The Toronto Blue Jays** sell season tickets to games in the Rogers Centre on-line. Fans can purchase the tickets at any time, although the season does not officially begin until April. It runs from April through October.
4. The **RBC Financial Group** lends you money at the beginning of August. The loan and the interest are repayable in full at the end of November.
5. In August, you order a sweater from **Amazon** on-line. Amazon ships the sweater to you in September and you charge it to your Visa credit card. In October, you receive your Visa bill and pay it.
6. You pay for a one-year subscription to *Canadian Business* magazine in May.
7. You purchase a gift card in December from **iTunes** to give to your friend for Christmas. Your friend uses the gift card in January.

Instructions

Identify when revenue should be recognized in each of the above situations.

Prepare basic analysis, debit-credit analysis, and adjusting journal entry. (LO 2, 3) AP

E3–3   Havanese Services Company records adjusting entries on an annual basis. The following information is available to be used in recording adjusting entries for the year ended December 31, 2017.

1. Prepaid insurance totalling $435 has expired.
2. Supplies of $425 have been used.
3. Annual depreciation on equipment is $1,240.
4. Unearned revenue of $320 has now been earned.
5. Salaries of $835 are unpaid.
6. Utility expenses for 2017 of $230 are unrecorded and unpaid.
7. Services provided but not collected in cash or recorded total $935.
8. Interest of $85 on a note payable has accrued.

Instructions

For each adjustment, prepare a basic analysis, a debit-credit analysis, and the adjusting journal entry. Use the following format, in which the first one has been done for you as an example.

Adjustment 1:

Basic Analysis	The asset Prepaid Insurance is decreased by $435. The expense Insurance Expense is increased by $435.		
Debit-Credit Analysis	Debits increase expenses: debit Insurance Expense $435. Credits decrease assets: credit Prepaid Insurance $435.		
Adjusting Journal Entry	Dec. 31	Insurance Expense	435	
		Prepaid Insurance		435
		To record insurance expired.		

E3–4   Grant's Graphics has a December 31 year end. Grant's Graphics records adjusting entries on an annual basis. Prepare the adjusting journal entries based on the following information.

Prepare adjusting entries. (LO 2, 3) AP

1. At the end of the year, the unadjusted balance in the Prepaid Insurance account was $3,200. Based on an analysis of the insurance policies, $2,800 had expired by year end.
2. At the end of the year, the unadjusted balance in the Unearned Revenue account was $2,000. During the last week of December, $500 of this amount had been earned.
3. On July 1, 2017, Grant signed a note payable for $10,000. The loan agreement stated that interest was 4%.
4. Depreciation for the computer and printing equipment was $2,150 for the year.
5. At the beginning of the year, Grant's had $950 of supplies on hand. During the year, $1,395 of supplies were purchased. A count at the end of the year indicated that $735 of supplies was left on December 31.
6. Between December 28 and December 31 inclusive, three employees worked eight-hour shifts at $15.25 per hour.
7. On December 31, it was determined that $5,000 of service revenue had been earned, but the bookkeeper did not record it.

E3–5   Action Quest Games adjusts its accounts annually. Assume that any prepaid expenses are initially recorded in asset accounts. Assume that any revenue collected in advance is initially recorded as liabilities. The following information is available for the year ended December 31, 2017:

Prepare transaction and adjusting entries for prepayments. (LO 2) AP

1. A $4,020 one-year insurance policy was purchased on April 1, 2017.
2. Paid $6,500 on August 31, 2017, for five months' rent in advance.
3. On September 27, 2017, received $3,600 cash from a corporation that sponsors games for the most improved students attending a nearby school. The $3,600 was for 10 games, worth $360 each, that are played on the first Friday of each month starting in October. (Use the Unearned Revenue account.)
4. Signed a contract for cleaning services starting December 1, 2017, for $500 per month. Paid for the first three months on November 30, 2017.
5. On December 15, 2017, sold $935 of gift certificates to a local game club. On December 31, 2017, determined that $545 of these gift certificates had not yet been redeemed. (Use the account Unearned Revenue.)

Instructions

(a) For each transaction, prepare the journal entry to record the initial transaction.
(b) For each transaction, prepare the adjusting journal entry required on December 31, 2017. Do both for each transaction before doing the next transaction.

E3–6   Jake's Mechanics owns the following long-lived assets:

Prepare adjusting entries for depreciation; calculate accumulated depreciation and carrying amount. (LO 2) AP

Asset	Date Purchased	Cost	Estimated Useful Life
Building	January 1, 2010	$68,000	25 years
Vehicles	December 31, 2013	28,000	7 years
Equipment	July 1, 2012	12,600	8 years

Instructions

(a) Prepare depreciation adjusting entries for Jake's Mechanics for the year ended December 31, 2017.
(b) For each asset, calculate its accumulated depreciation and carrying amount at December 31, 2017.

E3–7   Evan Watts opened a dental practice on January 1, 2017. During the first month of operations, the following transactions occurred.

Prepare adjusting entries. (LO 2, 3) AP

1. Watts performed services for patients totalling $2,400. These services have not yet been recorded.
2. Utility expenses incurred but not paid prior to January 31 totalled $400.
3. Purchased dental equipment on January 1 for $80,000, paying $20,000 in cash and signing a $60,000, three-year note payable. The equipment depreciates $500 per month. Interest is $600 per month.
4. Purchased a one-year malpractice insurance policy on January 1 for $12,000.
5. Purchased $2,600 of dental supplies. On January 31, determined that $900 of supplies were on hand.

Instructions

Prepare the adjusting entries on January 31.

E3–8   Blackice Coffeeshop began operations April 1. At April 30, the trial balance shows the following balances for selected accounts:

Prepare adjusting entries. (LO 2, 3) AP

Prepaid Insurance	$ 3,600
Equipment	28,000
Notes Payable	20,000
Unearned Service Revenue	4,200
Service Revenue	1,800

Analysis reveals the following additional data.

1. Prepaid insurance is the cost of a two-year insurance policy, effective April 1.
2. Depreciation on the equipment is $500 per month.
3. The note payable is dated April 1. It is a six-month, 6% note.
4. Services delivered to customers but not recorded at April 30 totalled $1,500.
5. Provided $600 of services to customers who had paid the previous month.

Instructions

Prepare the adjusting entries for the month of April. Show calculations.

Prepare adjusting and related transaction entries for accruals. (LO 2, 3) AP

E3-9 Plex Paintball records adjusting entries on an annual basis. The company has the following information available on accruals that must be recorded for the year ended May 31, 2017.

1. Plex Paintball has a 4% note payable with its bank for $48,000. Interest is payable on a monthly basis on the first of the month.
2. Plex Paintball is open seven days a week and employees are paid a total of $3,500 every Monday for a seven-day (Monday–Sunday) workweek. May 31, 2017, is a Wednesday so employees will have worked three days (Monday–Wednesday) before the year end that they have not been paid for as at May 31. Employees will be paid next on Monday, June 5, 2017.
3. Plex Paintball receives a commission from Pizza Shop next door for all pizzas sold to customers using the Plex Paintball facility. The amount owing for May is $520, which Pizza Shop will pay on June 7, 2017.
4. The May utility bill for $425 was unrecorded on May 31. Plex Paintball paid the bill on June 9, 2017.
5. Plex Paintball sold some equipment on May 1, 2017, in exchange for a $6,000, 6% note receivable. The principal and interest are due on August 1, 2017.

Instructions

(a) For each of the above items, prepare the adjusting entry required at May 31, 2017.
(b) For each of the above items, prepare the journal entry to record the related cash transaction in 2018. Assume all payments and receipts are made as indicated.

Prepare transaction and adjusting entries. (LO 2, 3) AP

E3-10 Nile Company had the following trial balance at June 30, 2017 (its year end):

	Debit	Credit
Cash	$ 5,840	
Accounts receivable	850	
Supplies	1,100	
Equipment	9,360	
Accumulated depreciation—equipment		$ 3,900
Unearned service revenue		1,500
R. Nile, capital		11,750
Totals	$17,150	$17,150

During the month of July, the following selected transactions took place:

July 2   Paid $750 cash for rent for July, August, and September.
     10   Purchased $200 of supplies for cash.
     14   Collected the full balance of accounts receivable.
     20   Received $700 cash from a customer for services to be provided in August.
     25   Provided $1,300 of services for a customer and immediately collected cash.

Additional information:

1. At July 31, the company had provided $800 of services for a customer that it had not billed or recorded.
2. Supplies on hand at July 31 were $800.
3. The equipment has a six-year useful life.
4. As at July 31, the company had earned $900 of revenue that had been paid in advance.

Instructions

(a) Record the July transactions.
(b) Prepare monthly adjusting entries at July 31.

Prepare adjusting entries. (LO 2, 3) AP

E3-11 The ledger of Bourque Rental Agency on March 31, 2017, includes the following selected accounts before preparing quarterly adjusting entries:

	Debit	Credit
Supplies	$14,400	
Prepaid insurance	3,600	
Equipment	37,800	
Accumulated depreciation—equipment		$ 9,450
Unearned rent revenue		9,300
Notes payable		30,000
Rent revenue		30,000
Salaries expense	14,000	

An analysis of the accounts shows the following:

1. The equipment has a four-year useful life.
2. One quarter of the unearned rent is still unearned on March 31, 2017.
3. The note payable has an interest rate of 6%. Interest is paid every June 30 and December 31.
4. Supplies on hand at March 31 total $850.
5. The one-year insurance policy was purchased on January 1, 2017.
6. As at March 31, a tenant owed Bourque $700 for the month of March.

Instructions

Prepare the quarterly adjusting entries required at March 31, 2017.

E3–12 During 2017, Aubergine Co. borrowed cash from Chartreuse Company by issuing notes payable as follows: *Prepare transaction and adjusting entries for notes and interest.* (LO 3) AP

1. July 1, 2017, issued an eight-month, 4% note for $75,000. Interest and principal are payable at maturity.
2. November 1, 2017, issued a three-month, 5% note for $42,000. Interest is payable monthly on the first day of the month. Principal is payable at maturity.

Aubergine has a December 31 fiscal year end and prepares adjusting entries on an annual basis.

Instructions

(a) Prepare all necessary journal entries for Aubergine Co. to record the notes.
(b) Prepare the necessary interest payment transactions for Aubergine in 2017 and 2018. Prepare separate adjusting entries for each note.

E3–13 Refer to the information provided in E3–12 for Aubergine Co. and Chartreuse Company. Chartreuse has *Prepare transaction and adjusting entries for notes and interest.* (LO 3) AP
a November 30 fiscal year end and prepares adjusting entries on an annual basis.

Instructions

(a) Prepare all necessary journal entries for Chartreuse to record the notes.
(b) Prepare all necessary adjusting entries for the interest for Chartreuse in 2017 and 2018. Prepare separate adjusting entries for each note.

E3–14 Trenton Company's fiscal year end is December 31. On January 31, 2017, the company's partial adjusted *Analyze adjusted data.* (LO 2, 3, 4) AN
trial balance shows the following:

TRENTON COMPANY Adjusted Trial Balance (Partial) January 31, 2017		
	Debit	Credit
Supplies	$ 700	
Prepaid insurance	1,600	
Equipment	7,200	
Accumulated depreciation—equipment		$3,660
Salaries payable		800
Unearned revenue		750
Service revenue		2,000
Depreciation expense	60	
Insurance expense	400	
Salaries expense	1,800	
Supplies expense	950	

Instructions

(a) If $1,600 was received in January for services performed in January, what was the balance in Unearned Revenue at December 31, 2016?
(b) If the amount in Depreciation Expense is the depreciation for one month, when was the equipment purchased?

(c) If the amount in Insurance Expense is the January 31 adjusting entry, and the original insurance premium was for one year, what was the total premium, and when was the policy purchased? (*Hint*: Assume the policy was purchased on the first day of the month.)

(d) If the amount in Supplies Expense is the January 31 adjusting entry, and the balance in Supplies on January 1 was $800, what was the amount of supplies purchased in January?

(e) If the balance in Salaries Payable on January 1, 2017, was $1,200, what was the amount of salaries paid in cash during January?

Prepare adjusting entries from analysis of trial balances. (LO 2, 3, 4) AP

E3–15 The trial balances before and after adjustment for Lane Company at October 31, 2017, which is the end of its fiscal year, are as follows:

	Before Adjustment		After Adjustment	
	Debit	Credit	Debit	Credit
Cash	$ 9,100		$ 9,100	
Accounts receivable	8,700		9,230	
Supplies	2,450		710	
Prepaid insurance	3,775		2,525	
Equipment	34,100		34,100	
Accumulated depreciation—equipment		$ 3,525		$ 5,800
Accounts payable		5,900		5,900
Notes payable		40,000		40,000
Salaries payable		0		1,125
Interest payable		0		500
Unearned service revenue		1,600		900
E. Lane, capital		5,600		5,600
E. Lane, drawings	10,000		10,000	
Service revenue		45,000		46,230
Depreciation expense	0		2,275	
Insurance expense	0		1,250	
Interest expense	1,500		2,000	
Rent expense	15,000		15,000	
Salaries expense	17,000		18,125	
Supplies expense	0		1,740	
Totals	$101,625	$101,625	$106,055	$106,055

Instructions

Prepare the adjusting entries that were made.

Prepare financial statements from adjusted trial balance. (LO 4) AP

E3–16 The adjusted trial balance for Lane Company is given in E3–15.

Instructions

Prepare Lane Company's income statement, statement of owner's equity, and balance sheet.

▶ Problems: Set A

Determine profit on cash and accrual bases; recommend method. (LO 1) AP

P3–1A Your examination of the records of Southlake Co. shows the company collected $85,500 cash from customers and paid $48,400 cash for operating costs during 2017. If Southlake followed the accrual basis of accounting, it would report the following year-end balances:

	2017	2016
Accounts payable	$ 1,310	$ 2,250
Accounts receivable	4,230	2,650
Accumulated depreciation	11,040	10,400
Prepaid insurance	1,580	1,250
Supplies	910	490
Unearned revenue	1,260	1,480

Instructions

(a) Determine Southlake's profit on a cash basis for 2017.

(b) Determine Southlake's profit on an accrual basis for 2017.

TAKING IT FURTHER Which method do you recommend that Southlake use? Why?

P3–2A Ouellette & Associates began operations on January 1, 2017. Its fiscal year end is December 31 and it prepares financial statements and adjusts its accounts annually. Selected transactions for 2017 follow:

1. On January 10, bought office supplies for $3,290 cash. A physical count at December 31, 2017, revealed $950 of supplies still on hand.
2. Paid cash for a $3,696, one-year insurance policy on February 1, 2017. The policy came into effect on this date.
3. On March 31, purchased equipment for $21,072 cash. The equipment has an estimated eight-year useful life.
4. Leased a truck on September 1 for a one-year period for $540 per month. Paid the full lease cost of $6,480 in cash.
5. On October 15, received a $1,749 advance cash payment from a client for accounting services expected to be provided in the future. As at December 31, one third of these services had not been performed.
6. On November 1, rented out unneeded office space for a six-month period starting on this date, and received a $1,794 cheque for the first three months' rent.

Instructions

(a) Prepare journal entries to record transactions 1 to 6. All prepaid costs should be recorded in asset accounts. All revenue collected in advance of providing services should be recorded as liabilities.
(b) An adjusting entry at December 31, 2017, is required for each of these transactions. Using the format shown in E3–3, prepare the following:
   1. A basic analysis and a debit-credit analysis of the required adjustment.
   2. The adjusting journal entry.

TAKING IT FURTHER Explain two generally accepted accounting principles that relate to adjusting the accounts.

Prepare and post prepayment transaction entries. Prepare basic analysis, debit-credit analysis, and journal entry. (LO 2) AP

P3–3A Demello & Associates records adjusting entries on an annual basis. The company has the following information available on accruals that must be recorded for the year ended December 31, 2017:

1. Demello has a $10,000, 8% note receivable with a customer. The customer pays the interest on a monthly basis on the first of the month. Assume the customer pays the correct amount each month.
2. Demello pays its employees a total of $6,500 every second Wednesday. Employees work a five-day week, Monday to Friday, and are paid for all statutory holidays. December 31, 2017, is a Sunday. Employees were paid on Wednesday, December 27, 2017 up to the Friday of the prior week.
3. Demello has a contract with a customer where it provides services prior to billing the customer. On December 31, 2017, this customer owed Demello $3,375. Demello billed the customer on January 7, 2018, and collected the full amount on January 18, 2018.
4. Demello received the $485 December utility bill on January 10, 2018. The bill was paid on its due date, January 22, 2018.
5. Demello has a $25,000, 5% note payable. Interest is paid every six months, on October 31 and April 30. Assume that Demello made the correct interest payment on April 30, 2017 and October 31, 2017.

Instructions

For each of the above items, do the following:
(a) Prepare the adjusting journal entries required on December 31, 2017.
(b) Prepare the journal entry to record the related cash transaction in 2018. Assume all payments and receipts are made as indicated.

TAKING IT FURTHER Indicate which elements in the financial statements (assets, liabilities, owner's equity, revenue, expenses, and profit) would be either understated or overstated at December 31, 2017, if the accounts were not adjusted.

Prepare entries for accrual adjustments and subsequent cash transactions. (LO 3) AP

P3–4A Logan Miller started her own accounting firm, Miller Accounting, on May 1, 2017. Logan Miller wants to prepare monthly financial statements, so adjusting journal entries are required on May 31. Selected transactions for May follow:

1. $900 of supplies were used during the month.
2. Utilities expense incurred but not yet recorded or paid on May 31, 2017, is $250.
3. Paid cash of $3,600 for a one-year insurance policy on May 1, 2017. The policy came into effect on this date.
4. On May 1, purchased office equipment for $11,400 cash. It is being depreciated at $190 per month for 60 months.
5. On May 1, Logan signs a note payable for $10,000, 6% interest.
6. May 31 is a Wednesday and employees are paid on Fridays. Miller Accounting has two employees, who are paid $920 each for a five-day workweek that ends on Friday.
7. On May 15, received a $1,000 advance cash payment from a client for accounting services expected to be provided in the future. As at May 31, one half of these services had not been performed.
8. Invoices representing $1,700 of services performed during the month of May have not been recorded as at May 31.

Prepare adjusting entries. (LO 2, 3) AP

Instructions

Prepare adjusting entries for the items above.

TAKING IT FURTHER   On June 4, Logan Miller receives and pays a utility bill for the month of May. Is it necessary to make an adjusting entry for May? Why or why not? If yes, specify the names and types of accounts that need to be adjusted and whether the accounts should be increased or decreased.

Prepare adjusting entries and subsequent cash payments.
(LO 2, 3) AP

P3–5A   Devin Wolf Company has the following balances in selected accounts on December 31, 2017. Devin has a calendar year end.

Accounts Receivable	$ 0
Accumulated Depreciation—Equipment	0
Equipment	7,000
Interest Payable	0
Notes Payable	10,000
Prepaid Insurance	2,100
Salaries Payable	0
Supplies	2,450
Unearned Revenue	30,000

All the accounts have normal balances. The information below has been gathered at December 31, 2017.

1. Devin Wolf Company borrowed $10,000 by signing a 4%, one-year note on September 1, 2017.
2. A count of supplies on December 31, 2017, indicates that supplies of $900 are on hand.
3. Depreciation on the equipment for 2017 is $1,000.
4. Devin Wolf Company paid $2,100 for 12 months of insurance coverage on June 1, 2017.
5. On December 1, 2017, Devin Wolf collected $32,000 for consulting services to be performed evenly from December 1, 2017, through March 31, 2018.
6. Devin Wolf performed consulting services for a client in December 2017. The client will be billed $4,200. Payment from the customer is expected on January 15, 2018.
7. Devin Wolf Company pays its employees total salaries of $9,000 every Wednesday for the preceding five-day week (Monday through Friday). On Wednesday, January 3, 2018, employees were paid for the last five weekdays of 2017.

Instructions

(a) Prepare adjusting entries for the seven items described above.
(b) Prepare the appropriate subsequent cash entries if applicable.

TAKING IT FURTHER   During the year, the employees at Devin Wolf did not track the supplies they used. Explain how the supply expense for the year can be determined even though detailed usage records were not kept.

Prepare transaction and adjusting entries.
(LO 2, 3) AP

P3–6A   The following independent items for Last Planet Theatre during the year ended December 31, 2017, may require a transaction journal entry, an adjusting entry, or both. The company records all prepaid costs as assets and all unearned revenues as liabilities and adjusts accounts annually.

1. Supplies on hand amounted to $875 on December 31, 2016. On June 10, 2017, additional supplies were purchased for $1,905 cash. On December 31, 2017, a physical count showed that supplies on hand amounted to $870.
2. Purchased equipment on August 1, 2017, for $43,500 cash. The equipment was estimated to have a useful life of 12 years.
3. Last Planet Theatre puts on eight plays each season. Season tickets sell for $500 each and 250 sold in July for the upcoming 2017–2018 season, which begins in September 2017 and ends in April 2018 (one play per month). Last Planet Theatre credited Unearned Revenue for the full amount received.
4. Every Wednesday, the total payroll is $5,400 for salaries earned during the previous workweek (Monday–Friday). Salaries were last paid on Wednesday, December 27. This year, December 31 falls on a Sunday.
5. Last Planet Theatre rents the theatre to a local children's choir, which uses the space for rehearsals twice a week at a rate of $800 per month. The choir was short of cash at the beginning of December and sent Last Planet Theatre a cheque for $550 on December 10, and a promise to pay the balance in January. On January 10, 2018, Last Planet Theatre received a cheque for the balance owing from December. At this time, the January rent was also paid.
6. On June 1, 2017, the theatre borrowed $25,000 from its bank at an annual interest rate of 4.5%. The principal and interest are to be repaid on May 31, 2018.
7. Upon reviewing its accounting records on December 31, 2017, the theatre noted that the telephone bill for the month of December had not yet been received. A call to the phone company determined that the December telephone bill was $573. The bill was paid on January 12, 2017.

Instructions

(a) Prepare the journal entries to record the 2017 transactions for items 1 through 6.

(b) Prepare the year-end adjusting entries for items 1 through 7.

(c) Prepare the journal entries to record:
   1. the payment of wages on Wednesday, January 3 (item 4).
   2. the receipt of the cheque from the children's choir on January 10 (item 5).
   3. the payment of the telephone bill on January 12 (item 7).
   4. the payment of the note and interest on May 30, 2018 (item 6).

TAKING IT FURTHER   There are three basic reasons why an unadjusted trial balance may not contain complete or up-to-date data. List these reasons and provide examples of each one using items 1 to 7 to illustrate your explanation.

P3–7A   Melody Lane Co. provides music lessons to many clients across the city. The following information is available to be used in recording annual adjusting entries at the company's September 30, 2017, year end:

Prepare adjusting entries.
(LO 2, 3) AP

1. On October 1, 2016, the company had a balance of $2,080 in its supplies account. Additional supplies were purchased during the year totalling $1,700. The supplies inventory on September 30, 2017, amounts to $810.
2. On November 1, 2016, Melody Lane purchased a one-year insurance policy for $3,200.
3. On January 2, 2017, a client paid $1,800 for six months of lessons starting April 2, 2017.
4. On February 1, 2017, Melody Lane purchased a grand piano (to be used in music lessons) for $24,000. The piano's estimated useful life is 12 years.
5. On May 1, 2017, Melody Lane borrowed $25,000 from the bank and signed a 10-month, 4% note payable. Interest and principal are to be paid at maturity.
6. On August 1, 2017, Melody Lane signed a contract with a neighbourhood school to provide weekly piano lessons to some of its students for a fee of $2,000 per month. The contract called for lessons to start on September 1, 2017. The school has not yet been sent an invoice for the month of September.
7. On August 15, 2017, the company paid $9,000 to Pinnacle Holdings to rent additional studio space for nine months starting September 1. Melody Lane recorded the full payment as Prepaid Rent.
8. Melody Lane's instructors have earned salaries of $3,500 for the last week of September 2017. This amount will be paid to the instructors on the next payday: October 6, 2017.
9. Music lessons were provided to a local church group for $1,500 on September 30, 2017. Melody Lane has not yet invoiced the group or recorded the transaction.
10. In early October 2017, Melody Lane received an invoice for $895 from the utility company for September utilities. The amount has not yet been recorded or paid.

Instructions

Prepare the adjusting journal entries.

TAKING IT FURTHER   Is it better to prepare monthly adjusting entries or annual adjusting entries as Melody Lane does? Why?

P3–8A   A review of the ledger of Greenberg Company at December 31, 2017, produces the following important data for the preparation of annual adjusting entries:

Prepare adjusting entries.
(LO 2, 3) AP

1. Prepaid Advertising, December 31, 2017, unadjusted balance, $15,600. This balance consists of payments on two advertising contracts for monthly advertising in two trade magazines. The terms of the contracts are as follows:

Contract	First Month	Amount	Number of Magazine Issues
A650	May 2017	$ 5,000	12
B974	October 2017	10,600	24
		$15,600	

2. Vehicles, December 31, 2017, balance, $70,000. The company owns two vehicles used for delivery purposes. The first, purchased for $30,000 on January 2, 2015, has an estimated seven-year useful life. The second, purchased for $40,000 on June 1, 2016, has an estimated eight-year useful life.
3. Notes Payable, December 31, 2017, balance, $85,000. This consists of an eight-month, 6.5% note, dated August 1. Interest is payable at maturity.
4. Salaries Payable, December 31, 2017, unadjusted balance, $0. There are nine salaried employees. Salaries are paid every following Monday for a six-day workweek (Monday–Saturday). Six employees receive a salary of $750 per week, and three employees earn $600 per week. December 31, 2017, is a Sunday.

5. Unearned Revenue, December 31, 2017, unadjusted balance, $270,000. Greenberg began renting office space to tenants in its new building on November 1. At December 31, Greenberg had the following rental contracts that were paid in full for the entire term of the lease:

Rental Term	Monthly Rent	Number of Tenants	Total Rent Paid
Nov. 1, 2017, to Apr. 30, 2018	$4,000	6	$144,000
Dec. 1, 2017, to May 31, 2018	7,000	3	126,000
			$270,000

Instructions

(a) Prepare the adjusting entries at December 31, 2017. Show all your calculations.

(b) For item 2, calculate the accumulated depreciation and carrying amount of each vehicle on December 31, 2017.

TAKING IT FURTHER   What is the purpose of recording depreciation? Why is land not depreciated?

Prepare transaction and adjusting entries for notes and interest. (LO 3) AP

P3-9A   During 2017, Cobalt Co. borrowed cash from Azores Enterprises by issuing notes payable as follows:

1. March 31, 2017, issued a one-year, 3.8% note for $107,900. Interest is payable quarterly, on June 30, September 30, and December 31, 2017, and March 31, 2018. Principal is payable at maturity.
2. June 1, 2017, issued a nine-month, 4.6% note for $75,000. Interest and principal are payable at maturity.
3. September 1, 2017, issued a three-month, 5% note for $24,400. Interest is payable monthly on the first day of the month. Principal is payable at maturity.

Both Cobalt and Azores prepare adjusting entries on an annual basis. Cobalt has a September 30 fiscal year end. Azores' fiscal year end is October 31.

Instructions

(a) Prepare all necessary journal entries for Cobalt in 2017 and 2018 regarding the notes and interest, including adjusting entries. Prepare separate adjusting entries for each note if an adjustment is required.

(b) Prepare all necessary journal entries for Azores in 2017 and 2018 regarding the notes and interest, including adjusting entries. Prepare separate adjusting entries for each note if an adjustment is required.

TAKING IT FURTHER   Is it appropriate for Cobalt to have interest payable on its September 30, 2017, balance sheet if the interest isn't payable until some point after the year end? Explain.

Prepare and post adjusting entries, and prepare adjusted trial balance. (LO 2, 3, 4) AP

P3-10A   Reyes Rides is owned by Jason Reyes. The company has an August 31 fiscal year end and prepares adjustments on an annual basis. The following is an alphabetical list of its accounts at August 31, 2017, before adjustments. All accounts have normal balances.

Accounts payable	$ 5,700	J. Reyes, drawings	$141,000
Accounts receivable	7,080	Notes payable	162,000
Accumulated depreciation—equipment	25,200	Prepaid insurance	12,660
Accumulated depreciation—vehicles	175,500	Rent expense	22,810
Cash	9,000	Salaries expense	140,625
Equipment	40,320	Service revenue	334,300
Fuel expense	23,972	Supplies	4,455
Interest expense	9,653	Unearned revenue	25,000
J. Reyes, capital	105,075	Vehicles	421,200

Additional information:

1. On August 31, a physical count shows $850 of supplies on hand.
2. The insurance policy has a one-year term that began on November 1, 2016.
3. The equipment has an estimated useful life of 10 years. The vehicles have an estimated useful life of 12 years.
4. The company collects cash in advance for any special services requested by customers. As at August 31, the company has provided all but $4,500 of these services.
5. The note payable has an annual interest rate of 4.5%. Interest is paid on the first day of each month.
6. Employees are paid a combined total of $545 per day. At August 31, 2017, five days of salaries are unpaid.
7. On August 31, the company provided $1,350 of services for a senior citizens' group. The group was not billed for the services until September 2.
8. Additional fuel costs of $620 have been incurred but not recorded. (Use the Accounts Payable account.)

Instructions

(a) Prepare T accounts and enter the unadjusted trial balance amounts.
(b) Journalize the annual adjusting entries at August 31, 2017.
(c) Post the adjusting entries.
(d) Prepare an adjusted trial balance at August 31, 2017.

TAKING IT FURTHER As at August 31, 2017, approximately how old are the equipment and vehicles?

P3-11A The Highland Cove Resort has a May 31 fiscal year end and prepares adjusting entries on a monthly basis. The following trial balance was prepared before recording the May 31 month-end adjustments:

Prepare and post adjusting entries, and prepare adjusted trial balance and financial statements. (LO 2, 3, 4) AP

HIGHLAND COVE RESORT		
Trial Balance		
May 31, 2017		
	Debit	Credit
Cash	$ 17,520	
Prepaid insurance	1,590	
Supplies	995	
Land	35,000	
Buildings	150,000	
Accumulated depreciation—buildings		$ 47,750
Furniture	33,000	
Accumulated depreciation—furniture		12,925
Accounts payable		8,500
Unearned revenue		15,000
Mortgage payable		96,000
K. MacPhail, capital		85,000
K. MacPhail, drawings	42,735	
Rent revenue		246,150
Depreciation expense	5,775	
Insurance expense	5,830	
Interest expense	5,720	
Repairs expense	14,400	
Salaries expense	156,710	
Supplies expense	4,450	
Utilities expense	37,600	
	$511,325	$511,325

Additional information:

1. The company pays $6,360 for its annual insurance policy on July 31 of each year.
2. A count shows $560 of supplies on hand on May 31, 2017.
3. The buildings have an estimated useful life of 50 years.
4. The furniture has an estimated useful life of 10 years.
5. Two thirds of the unearned revenue has been earned.
6. The mortgage interest rate is 6.5% per year. Interest has been paid to April 1, 2017.
7. Salaries accrued to the end of May were $1,450.
8. The May utility bill of $3,420 is unrecorded and unpaid.

Instructions

(a) Prepare T accounts and enter the unadjusted trial balance amounts.
(b) Prepare and post the monthly adjusting journal entries on May 31.
(c) Prepare an adjusted trial balance at May 31.
(d) Prepare an income statement and a statement of owner's equity for the year ended May 31, and a balance sheet as at May 31, 2017.

TAKING IT FURTHER Is the owner's capital account on the May 31, 2017, adjusted trial balance the same amount as shown in the May 31, 2017, balance sheet? Why or why not?

Journalize transactions, and adjusting entries, flow the entries through the accounting cycle to the preparation of the financial statements. (LO 2, 3, 4) AP

P3–12A On November 1, 2017, the account balances of Hamm Equipment Repair were as follows.

	Debit		Credit
Cash	$ 2,400	Accumulated Depreciation—Equipment	$ 2,000
Accounts Receivable	4,250	Accounts Payable	2,600
Supplies	1,800	Unearned Revenue	1,200
Equipment	12,000	Salaries Payable	700
		J. Hamm, Capital	13,950
	$20,450		$20,450

During November, the following summary transactions were completed.

Nov. 8 Paid $1,700 for salaries due employees, of which $700 is for October salaries.
  10 Received $3,620 cash from customers on account.
  12 Received $3,100 cash for services performed in November.
  15 Purchased equipment on account, $2,000.
  17 Purchased supplies on account, $700.
  20 Paid creditors on account, $2,700.
  22 Paid November rent of $400.
  25 Paid salaries of $1,700.
  27 Performed services on account and billed customers for these services, $2,200.
  29 Received $600 from customers for future service.

Adjustment data consist of:

1. Supplies on hand, $1,400
2. Accrued salaries payable, $350
3. Depreciation for the month is $200
4. Services related to unearned service revenue of $1,220 were performed

Instructions

(a) Enter the November 1 balances in the ledger accounts (use T accounts).
(b) Prepare and post the November transaction entries.
(c) Prepare a trial balance at November 30.
(d) Prepare and post the adjusting entries for the month.
(e) Prepare an adjusted trial balance.
(f) Prepare an income statement and a statement of owner's equity for November and a balance sheet at November 30.

TAKING IT FURTHER On Hamm Equipment Repair's trial balance, Accounts Payable is $2,600. After the adjusting entries have been posted, the balance in this account is still $2,600. Since there is no change, it is not necessary to include Accounts Payable on the adjusted trial balance. Do you agree? Why or why not?

P3–13A Fox Enterprises is owned by Edmund Fox and has a January 31 fiscal year end. The company prepares adjusting entries on an annual basis. The following trial balance was prepared before adjustments:

Prepare adjusting entries, adjusted trial balance, and financial statements. (LO 2, 3, 4) AP

FOX ENTERPRISES Trial Balance January 31, 2017	Debit	Credit
Cash	$ 4,970	
Accounts receivable	14,540	
Prepaid insurance	3,960	
Supplies	6,580	
Equipment	32,350	
Accumulated depreciation—equipment		$ 12,940
Accounts payable		7,760
Note payable		11,000
Unearned revenue		7,480
E. Fox, capital		18,320
E. Fox, drawings	119,000	
Service revenue		214,500
Rent expense	20,750	
Salaries expense	66,950	
Telephone expense	2,900	
	$272,000	$272,000

Additional information:

1. A one-year insurance policy was purchased on July 1, 2016.
2. A count of supplies on January 31, 2017, shows $920 of supplies on hand.
3. The equipment has an estimated useful life of five years.
4. An analysis of the Unearned Revenue account shows that $5,230 has been earned by January 31, 2017.
5. The eight-month, 6% note was issued on November 1, 2016. Interest and principal are due on the maturity date.
6. Salaries accrued to January 31, 2017, were $1,315.
7. On January 31, 2017, the company had earned but not billed or recorded consulting revenue of $2,675.
8. The telephone bill for January 2017 was $170. It has not been recorded or paid. (Use the Accounts Payable account.)

Instructions

(a) Prepare T accounts and enter the unadjusted trial balance amounts.
(b) Prepare and post the monthly adjusting journal entries on January 31.
(c) Prepare an adjusted trial balance at January 31.
(d) Prepare an income statement and a statement of owner's equity for the year ended January 31, and a balance sheet as at January 31, 2017.

TAKING IT FURTHER   Comment on the company's results of operations and its financial position. In your analysis, refer to specific items in the financial statements.

▶ Problems: Set B

P3-1B   Your examination of the records of Northland Co. shows the company collected $136,200 cash from customers and paid $108,700 cash for operating costs in 2017. If Northland followed the accrual basis of accounting, it would report the following year-end balances:

Determine profit on cash and accrual bases; recommend method. (LO 1) AP

	2017	2016
Accounts payable	$ 3,990	$ 1,460
Accounts receivable	6,100	13,200
Accumulated depreciation	18,250	15,000
Prepaid insurance	620	1,530
Supplies	550	2,350
Unearned revenue	7,400	1,560

Instructions

(a) Determine Northland's profit on a cash basis for 2017.
(b) Determine Northland's profit on an accrual basis for 2017.

TAKING IT FURTHER   Which method do you recommend that Northland use? Why?

P3-2B   Burke Bros. began operations on January 1, 2017. Its fiscal year end is December 31 and it prepares financial statements and adjusts its accounts annually. Selected transactions from 2017 follow:

Prepare and post prepayment transaction entries. Prepare basic analysis, debit-credit analysis, and journal entry, and post adjustments for the prepayments. (LO 2) AP

1. On January 9, bought office supplies for $2,950 cash. A physical count on December 31, 2017, revealed $715 of supplies still on hand.
2. Purchased a $4,920, one-year insurance policy for cash on March 1. The policy came into effect on this date.
3. On June 1, purchased equipment for $31,200 cash. The equipment has an estimated eight-year useful life.
4. Rented equipment from Abe's Rentals for a six-month period effective September 1, 2017, for $275 per month and paid cash for the full amount.
5. Rented unused office space to Negaar Madhany for an eight-month period effective October 1, 2017, for $325 per month and collected cash from Negaar for the full amount.
6. On November 15, received a $500 cash payment from each of five clients for services to be provided in the future (total = $2,500). As at December 31, services had been performed for three of the clients.

Instructions

(a) Prepare a journal entry to record transactions 1 to 6. All prepaid costs should be recorded in asset accounts. All revenue collected in advance of providing services should be recorded as liabilities.
(b) An adjusting entry is required for each of these transactions at December 31, 2017. Using the format shown in E3-3, prepare the following:
   1. A basic analysis and a debit-credit analysis of the required adjustment.
   2. The adjusting journal entry.
(c) Post the transactions and adjusting entries to T accounts and calculate the final balance in each account. (*Note:* Posting to the Cash account is not necessary.)

TAKING IT FURTHER   Could Burke Bros. avoid the need to record adjusting entries by originally recording items 1 through 4 as expenses, and items 5 and 6 as revenues? Explain.

Prepare entries for accrual adjustments and subsequent cash transactions. (LO 3) AP

P3–3B   Burke Bros. records adjusting entries on an annual basis. The company has the following information available on accruals that must be recorded for the year ended December 31, 2017:

1. Burke Bros. has a $40,000, 5.5% note payable. Interest is payable on a monthly basis on the first of the month. Assume that Burke Bros. made the correct interest payment on December 1, 2017, and January 1, 2018.
2. Burke Bros. pays its employees a total of $7,500 every second Monday for work completed the two preceding weeks. Employees work a five-day week, Monday to Friday, and are paid for all statutory holidays. December 31, 2017, is a Sunday. Employees were paid on Monday, December 18, 2017, and will be paid again on Tuesday, January 2, 2018.
3. Burke Bros. owns drilling equipment, which it rents to customers for $1,200 per day. On December 31, 2017, a customer has had the equipment for 10 days. Burke Bros. billed the customer for 15 days when the equipment was returned on January 5, 2018. The customer paid the full amount that day.
4. Burke Bros. received the $290 December telephone bill on January 5, 2018. The bill was paid on January 9, 2018.
5. Burke Bros. has a $10,000, 7% note receivable with a customer. Interest is receivable every six months on October 31 and April 30. Assume the customer makes the correct payment to Burke Bros. on October 31, 2017, and April 30, 2018.

Instructions

For each of the above items, do the following:

(a) Prepare the adjusting journal entry required on December 31, 2017.
(b) Prepare the journal entry to record the related cash transaction in 2018. Assume all payments and receipts are made as indicated.

TAKING IT FURTHER   Indicate which elements in the financial statements (assets, liabilities, owner's equity, revenue, expenses, and profit) would be either understated or overstated at December 31, 2017, if the accounts were not adjusted.

Prepare adjusting entries. (LO 2, 3) AP

P3–4B   Sam Buckley started his own cycle repair shop, Sam's Cycles, on September 1, 2017. Sam wants to prepare monthly financial statements, so adjusting journal entries are required on September 30. Selected transactions for September follow:

1. $1,100 of supplies were used during the month.
2. Utilities expense incurred but not yet recorded or paid on September 30, 2017, is $775.
3. Paid cash of $2,360 for a one-year insurance policy on September 1, 2017. The policy came into effect on this date.
4. On September 1, purchased repair equipment for $9,600 cash. It is being depreciated over 48 months.
5. On September 1, Sam signs a note payable for $15,000, 4.5% interest.
6. September 30 is a Saturday and employees are paid on Wednesdays for the preceding week. Sam's Cycles has three employees, who are paid $1,000 each for a five-day workweek that ends on Saturday.
7. Invoices representing $950 of services performed have not been recorded as at September 30.

Instructions

Prepare adjusting entries for the items above.

TAKING IT FURTHER   Sam has been reading about a recent accounting scandal where the company overstated its revenue on purpose. He now argues that it is never appropriate to make adjusting entries to accrue for revenue. Do you agree? Why or why not?

Prepare adjusting entries and subsequent cash payments. (LO 2, 3) AP

P3–5B   Kinder Company has the following balances in selected accounts on June 30, 2017, its fiscal year end.

Accounts Receivable	$ 0
Accumulated Depreciation—Equipment	0
Equipment	12,000
Interest Payable	0
Notes Payable	5,000
Prepaid Rent	900
Salaries Payable	0
Supplies	1,415
Unearned Revenue	2,590

All the accounts have normal balances. The information below has been gathered at June 30, 2017.

1. Kinder Company paid $900 for rent on June 1, 2017.
2. A count of supplies on June 30 indicates that supplies costing $900 are on hand.
3. The equipment, purchased on January 2, 2017, is being amortized over 36 months.
4. Kinder Company borrowed $5,000 by signing a 4.5%, one-year note on February 1, 2017.
5. Kinder Company performed consulting services for a client in June 2017. The client will be billed $3,650. Payment is expected in July.

6. Kinder Company pays its employees total salaries of $3,000 every Monday for the preceding five-day week (Monday through Friday). At the end of the year, five days remain unpaid.
7. $400 of the unearned revenue remains unearned at the end of the month.

Instructions

(a) Prepare adjusting entries for the seven items above.
(b) Prepare the appropriate subsequent cash entries if applicable.

TAKING IT FURTHER   "The amount included in an adjusted trial balance for a specific account will always be more than the amount that was included in the trial balance for the same account." Do you agree? Why or why not?

P3–6B   The following independent items for Théâtre Dupuis during the year ended November 30, 2017, may require a transaction journal entry, an adjusting entry, or both. The company records all prepaid costs as assets and all unearned revenues as liabilities and it adjusts accounts annually.

Prepare transaction and adjusting entries. (LO 2, 3) AP

1. Supplies on hand amounted to $950 on November 30, 2017. On January 31, 2017, additional supplies were purchased for $2,880 cash. On November 30, 2017, a physical count showed that supplies on hand amounted to $670.
2. Théâtre Dupuis puts on 10 plays each season. Season tickets sell for $200 each and 310 were sold in August for the upcoming 2017–2018 season, which starts in September 2017 and ends in June 2018 (one play per month). Théâtre Dupuis credited Unearned Revenue for the full amount received.
3. The total payroll for the theatre is $4,500 every Wednesday for employee salaries earned during the previous five-day week (Wednesday through Sunday). Salaries were last paid (and recorded) on Wednesday, November 29. In 2017, November 30 falls on a Thursday. The next payday is Wednesday, December 6, 2017.
4. Théâtre Dupuis rents the theatre to a local seniors' choir, which uses the space for rehearsals twice a week at a rate of $425 per month. The new treasurer of the choir accidentally sent a cheque for $245 on November 1. The treasurer promised to send a cheque in December for the balance when she returns from her vacation. On December 4, Théâtre Dupuis received a cheque for the balance owing from November plus all of December's rent.
5. On June 1, 2017, the theatre borrowed $11,000 from La caisse populaire Desjardins at an annual interest rate of 4.5%. The principal and interest are to be repaid on February 1, 2018.
6. Upon reviewing the books on November 30, 2017, it was noted that the utility bill for the month of November had not yet been received. A call to Hydro-Québec determined that the utility bill was for $1,420. The bill was paid on December 10.
7. Owned a truck during the year that had originally been purchased on December 1, 2013, for $37,975. The truck's estimated useful life is eight years.

Instructions

(a) Prepare the journal entries to record the original transactions for items 1 through 5.
(b) Prepare the year-end adjusting entries for items 1 through 7.
(c) Prepare the journal entries to record:
   1. the payment of wages on Wednesday, December 6 (item 3).
   2. the receipt of the cheque from the seniors' choir on December 4 (item 4).
   3. the payment of the utility bill on December 10 (item 6).
   4. the payment of the note and interest on February 1, 2015 (item 5).

TAKING IT FURTHER   There are three basic reasons why an unadjusted trial balance may not contain complete or up-to-date data. List these reasons and provide examples of each one using items 1 to 7 to illustrate your explanation.

P3–7B   Best First Aid offers first aid training to individuals and groups across the city. The following information is available to be used in recording annual adjusting entries for the company's October 31, 2017, year end:

Prepare adjusting entries. (LO 2, 3) AP

1. Best First Aid purchased equipment on November 1, 2013, for $9,000. The equipment was estimated to have a useful life of six years.
2. On November 1, 2016, the company had a balance of $1,000 in its Supplies account. Additional supplies were purchased during the year totalling $2,500. The supplies inventory on October 31, 2017, amounts to $980.
3. On July 1, 2017, Best First Aid borrowed $28,000 and signed a nine-month, 6% note payable. Interest and principal are payable at maturity.
4. On October 1, 2017, Best First Aid moved to new offices. Rent is $800 per month. Best First Aid paid the first three months' rent that day.
5. Best First Aid requires a $200 deposit from clients as an advance payment for first aid training courses when they are booked. As at October 31, 2017, Best First Aid has deposits for 15 training courses recorded as unearned revenue. A review of the company's records shows that the company has provided all but five of the 15 training courses.

6. On October 28, 2017, Best First Aid provided a first aid training course to MRC employees. Best First Aid was too busy to invoice MRC that day. Instead, it prepared the $1,550 invoice on November 2, 2017. MRC agreed to pay this amount on November 15, 2017.
7. Best First Aid has two employees, who are each paid $125 per day. On October 31, 2017, these employees had each worked three days since they were last paid.
8. In early November, Best First Aid received an invoice for $360 from BellTel for October telephone charges. The amount has not yet been recorded or paid.

Instructions

Prepare the adjusting journal entries.

TAKING IT FURTHER Is it better to prepare monthly adjusting entries or annual adjusting entries as Best First Aid does? Why?

Prepare adjusting entries. (LO 2, 3) AP

P3–8B A review of the ledger of Hashmi Company at July 31, 2017, produces the following data for the preparation of annual adjusting entries:

1. Prepaid Insurance, July 31, 2017, unadjusted balance, $15,840. The company has separate insurance policies on its buildings and its motor vehicles. Policy B4564 on the buildings was purchased on September 1, 2016, for $10,440. The policy has a term of two years. Policy A2958 on the vehicles was purchased on March 1, 2017, for $5,400. This policy has a term of one year.
2. Prepaid Rent, July 31, 2017, unadjusted balance, $6,350. The company has prepaid rental agreements for two pieces of equipment. The first one costs $335 per month and is for February 28, 2017, to December 31, 2017. The other costs $375 per month and is for December 1, 2016, to August 1, 2017. The company paid the full amount for each rental agreement at the start of the rental period.
3. Buildings, July 31, 2017, balance, $291,960. The first, purchased for $127,800 on September 1, 2001, has an estimated 30-year useful life. The second, purchased for $164,160 on May 1, 2003, has an estimated 40-year useful life.
4. Unearned Revenue, July 31, 2017, unadjusted balance, $46,550. The company began selling magazine subscriptions in 2016. The selling price of a subscription is $35 for 12 monthly issues. Customers start receiving the magazine in the month the subscription is purchased. A review of subscription contracts that customers have paid for prior to July 31 reveals the following:

Subscription Date	Number of Subscriptions
October 1	325
November 1	450
December 1	555

5. Salaries Payable, July 31, 2017, unadjusted balance, $0. There are nine salaried employees, each of whom is paid every Monday for the previous week (Monday to Friday). Six employees receive a salary of $650 each per week, and three employees earn $850 each per week. July 31 is a Monday.

Instructions

(a) Prepare the adjusting entries at July 31, 2017. Show all your calculations.
(b) For item 3, calculate the accumulated depreciation and carrying amount of each building on July 31, 2017.

TAKING IT FURTHER What is the purpose of recording depreciation? Why is land not depreciated?

Prepare transaction and adjusting entries for notes and interest. (LO 3) AP

P3–9B During 2017, Alabaster Co. borrowed cash from Fuchsia Enterprises by issuing notes payable as follows:

1. June 1, 2017, issued a seven-month, 4% note for $50,000. Interest and principal are payable at maturity.
2. September 30, 2017, issued a one-year, 3.5% note for $80,000. Interest is payable quarterly, on December 31, 2017, and March 31, June 30, and September 30, 2018. Principal is payable at maturity.
3. October 1, 2017, issued a three-month, 5.5% note for $45,000. Interest is payable monthly on the first day of the month. Principal is payable at maturity.

Both Alabaster and Fuchsia prepare adjusting entries on an annual basis. Alabaster has an October 31 fiscal year end. Fuchsia's fiscal year end is November 30.

Instructions

(a) Prepare all necessary journal entries for Alabaster in 2017 and 2018 regarding the notes and interest including adjusting entries. Prepare separate adjusting entries for each note if an adjustment is required.
(b) Prepare all necessary journal entries for Fuchsia in 2017 and 2018 regarding the notes and interest, including adjusting entries. Prepare separate adjusting entries for each note if an adjustment is required.

TAKING IT FURTHER Is it appropriate for Fuchsia to have interest receivable on its November 30, 2017, balance sheet if the interest isn't due until some point after the year end? Explain.

P3–10B   Red Bridges Towing is owned by Ken Cordial. The company has a June 30 fiscal year end and prepares adjustments on an annual basis. The following is an alphabetical list of its accounts at June 30, 2017, before adjustments. All accounts have normal balances.

Prepare and post adjusting entries, and prepare adjusted trial balance. (LO 2, 3, 4) AP

Accounts payable	$ 5,075	K. Cordial, drawings	$ 91,650
Accounts receivable	5,310	Notes payable	120,000
Accumulated depreciation—equipment	5,040	Prepaid insurance	9,480
Accumulated depreciation—vehicles	26,325	Rent expense	17,095
Cash	9,810	Salaries expense	101,400
Equipment	30,240	Service revenue	252,795
Fuel expense	17,980	Supplies	4,470
Interest expense	4,950	Unearned revenue	18,750
K. Cordial, capital	75,000	Vehicles	210,600

Additional information:

1. On June 30, a physical count of supplies shows $715 of supplies on hand.
2. The insurance policy has a one-year term that began on October 1, 2016.
3. The equipment has an estimated useful life of six years. The vehicles have an estimated useful life of eight years.
4. The company collects cash in advance for any special services requested by customers. As at June 30, the company has provided all but $2,250 of these services.
5. The note payable has an annual interest rate of 4.5%. Interest is paid on the first day of each month.
6. Employees are paid a combined total of $390 per day. At June 30, 2017, six days of salaries are unpaid.
7. On June 30, the company provided $1,100 of services at a local boat show. The group organizing the show was not billed for the services until July 2. They paid on July 5.

Instructions

(a) Prepare T accounts and enter the unadjusted trial balance amounts.
(b) Journalize the annual adjusting entries at June 30, 2017.
(c) Post the adjusting entries.
(d) Prepare an adjusted trial balance at June 30, 2017.

TAKING IT FURTHER   As at June 30, 2017, approximately how old are the equipment and vehicles?

P3–11B   Mountain Best Lodge has a May 31 fiscal year end and prepares adjusting entries on a monthly basis. The following trial balance was prepared before recording the May 31 month-end adjustments:

Prepare and post adjusting entries, and prepare adjusted trial balance and financial statements. (LO 2, 3, 4) AP

MOUNTAIN BEST LODGE
Trial Balance
May 31, 2017

	Debit	Credit
Cash	$ 12,365	
Prepaid insurance	3,080	
Supplies	1,050	
Land	80,000	
Buildings	180,000	
Accumulated depreciation—buildings		$ 76,125
Furniture	21,000	
Accumulated depreciation—furniture		12,250
Accounts payable		4,780
Unearned revenue		8,500
Mortgage payable		146,400
M. Rundle, capital		54,800
M. Rundle, drawings	18,750	
Rent revenue		102,100
Advertising expense	500	
Depreciation expense	7,975	
Salaries expense	49,304	
Supplies expense	5,410	
Interest expense	7,381	
Insurance expense	4,840	
Utilities expense	13,300	
	$404,955	$404,955

Additional information:

1. The company pays $5,280 for its annual insurance policy on November 30 of each year.
2. A count of supplies on May 31 shows $760 of supplies on hand.
3. The buildings were purchased on June 1, 2000, and have an estimated useful life of 40 years.
4. The furniture was purchased on June 1, 2014, and has an estimated useful life of five years.
5. Customers must pay a $50 deposit if they want to book a room in advance during peak times. An analysis of these bookings indicates that 170 deposits were received (all credited to Unearned Revenue) and 40 of the deposits have been earned by May 31, 2017.
6. The mortgage interest rate is 5.5% per year. Interest has been paid to May 1, 2017. The next payment is due on June 1.
7. Salaries accrued to the end of May were $1,025.
8. The May utility bill of $1,250 is unrecorded and unpaid.
9. On May 31, Mountain Best Lodge has earned $950 of rent revenue from customers who are currently using the rooms but will not pay the amount owing until they check out in June. This amount is in addition to any deposits earned in item 5 above.

Instructions

(a) Prepare T accounts and enter the unadjusted trial balance amounts.
(b) Prepare and post the monthly adjusting journal entries on May 31.
(c) Prepare an adjusted trial balance at May 31.
(d) Prepare an income statement and a statement of owner's equity for the year ended May 31, and a balance sheet as at May 31, 2017.

TAKING IT FURTHER   Is the owner's capital account on the May 31, 2017, adjusted trial balance the same amount as shown in the May 31, 2017, balance sheet? Why or why not?

Journalize transactions and follow through accounting cycle to adjusting entries and preparation of financial statements. (LO 2, 3, 4) AP

P3–12B   On November 1, 2017, the account balances of Pine Equipment Repair were as follows:

101	Cash	$ 2,790	154	Accumulated Depreciation—Equipment	$ 500
112	Accounts Receivable	2,510	201	Accounts Payable	2,100
126	Supplies	2,000	209	Unearned Revenue	1,400
153	Equipment	10,000	212	Salaries Payable	500
			301	S. Seed, Capital	12,800
		$17,300			$17,300

During November, the following summary transactions were completed.

Nov. 8   Paid $1,100 for salaries due employees, of which $600 is for November salaries.
     10   Received $1,200 cash from customers on account.
     12   Received $1,400 cash for services performed in November.
     15   Purchased equipment on account, $3,000.
     17   Purchased supplies on account, $500.
     20   Paid creditors on account, $2,500.
     22   Paid November rent of $300.
     25   Paid salaries of $1,300.
     27   Performed services on account and billed customers for services provided, $900.
     29   Received $550 from customers for future service.

Adjustment data consist of:

1. Supplies on hand, $1,000.
2. Accrued salaries payable, $500.
3. Depreciation for the month is $100.
4. Unearned service revenue of $1,150 is earned during the month.

Instructions

(a) Enter the November 1 balances in the ledger accounts (use T accounts).
(b) Journalize the November transactions.
(c) Post the November transactions.
(d) Prepare a trial balance at November 30.
(e) Journalize and post adjusting entries.
(f) Prepare an adjusted trial balance.
(g) Prepare an income statement and a statement of owner's equity for November and a balance sheet at November 30.

TAKING IT FURTHER   Comment on the company's results of operations and its financial position. In your analysis, refer to specific items in the financial statements.

P3–13B Shek Enterprises is owned by Memphis Shek and has a December 31 fiscal year end. The company prepares adjusting entries on an annual basis. Some additional information follows:

1. A one-year insurance policy was purchased on May 1, 2017.
2. A count of supplies on December 31, 2017, shows $1,290 of supplies on hand.
3. The equipment has an estimated useful life of six years.
4. An analysis of the Unearned Revenue account shows that $4,000 has been earned by December 31, 2017.
5. The three-year, 5% note payable was issued on April 1, 2017. Interest is payable every six months on April 1 and October 1 each year. The principal is payable at maturity.
6. Salaries accrued to December 31, 2017, were $915.
7. On December 31, 2017, the company had earned but not billed or recorded consulting revenue of $2,000.
8. The telephone bill for December 2017 was $210. It has not been recorded or paid. (Use the Accounts Payable account.)

The following trial balance was prepared before adjustments:

Prepare adjusting entries, adjusted trial balance, and financial statements.
(LO 2, 3, 4) AP

SHEK ENTERPRISES
Trial Balance
December 31, 2017

	Debit	Credit
Cash	$ 6,725	
Accounts receivable	10,915	
Prepaid insurance	5,940	
Supplies	8,680	
Equipment	24,240	
Accumulated depreciation—equipment		$ 10,100
Accounts payable		5,765
Note payable		14,000
Unearned revenue		5,550
M. Shek, capital		13,750
M. Shek, drawings	85,000	
Service revenue		160,875
Interest expense	350	
Rent expense	15,600	
Salaries expense	50,225	
Telephone expense	2,365	
	$210,040	$210,040

Instructions

(a) Prepare adjusting journal entries for the year ended December 31, 2017, as required.
(b) Prepare an adjusted trial balance at December 31, 2017.
(c) Prepare an income statement and statement of owner's equity for the year ended December 31, 2017, and a balance sheet at December 31, 2017.

TAKING IT FURTHER Comment on the company's results of operations and its financial position. In your analysis, refer to specific items in the financial statements.

▶ Cumulative Coverage—Chapters 1 to 3

On August 31, 2017, the account balances of Pitre Equipment Repair were as follows:

Prepare and post transaction and adjusting entries for prepayments. (LO 2, 4) AP

PITRE EQUIPMENT REPAIR
Trial Balance
August 31, 2017

	Debit	Credit
Cash	$ 1,880	
Accounts receivable	3,720	
Supplies	800	
Equipment	15,000	
Accumulated depreciation—equipment		$ 1,500
Accounts payable		3,100
Unearned revenue		400
Salaries payable		700
R. Pitre, capital		15,700
	$21,400	$21,400

During September, the following transactions were completed:

Sept.	1	Borrowed $10,000 from the bank and signed a two-year, 5% note payable.
	8	Paid $1,100 for employees' salaries, of which $400 is for September and $700 for August.
	10	Received $1,200 cash from customers on account.
	12	Received $3,400 cash for services performed in September.
	17	Purchased additional supplies on account, $1,500.
	20	Paid creditors $4,500 on account.
	22	Paid September and October rent, $1,000 ($500 per month).
	25	Paid salaries, $1,200.
	27	Performed services on account and billed customers for services provided, $900.
	29	Received $700 from customers for future services.
	30	Purchased additional equipment on account, $3,000.

The company adjusts its accounts on a monthly basis. Adjustment data consist of the following:

1. Supplies on hand at September 30 cost $1,280.
2. Accrued salaries payable at September 30 total $775.
3. Equipment has an expected useful life of five years.
4. Unearned service revenue of $450 is still not earned at September 30.
5. Interest is payable on the first of each month.

Instructions

(a) Enter the August 31 balances in the general ledger accounts.
(b) Journalize the September transactions.
(c) Post to the ledger accounts.
(d) Prepare a trial balance at September 30.
(e) Journalize and post adjusting entries.
(f) Prepare an adjusted trial balance.
(g) Prepare an income statement and a statement of owner's equity for September, and a balance sheet.

CHAPTER 3: BROADENING YOUR PERSPECTIVE

▶ Financial Reporting and Analysis

Financial Reporting Problem

BYP3–1 The financial statements of **Corus Entertainment** are presented in Appendix A at the end of this textbook.

Instructions

(a) What title does Corus use for its income statement? What title does Corus use for its balance sheet?
(b) How much depreciation on its property and equipment did Corus record in 2014 and 2013?

(c) Does Corus report profit or does it use another term for its financial results?
(d) Corus reports prepaid expenses on its balance sheet but does not provide any additional details in its notes to the financial statements. Provide two examples of expenses that Corus might have prepaid.

Interpreting Financial Statements

BYP3–2 **Rogers Communications Inc.** is a diversified Canadian communications and media company engaged in three primary lines of business: Wireless, Cable, and Media. The following is part of Rogers' revenue recognition policy note in its 2014 financial statements:

ROGERS COMMUNICATIONS INC.
Notes to the Financial Statements
December 31, 2014

Note 2 (d): Significant accounting policies—Revenue recognition

We recognize revenue when we can estimate its amount, have delivered on our obligations within the revenue generating arrangements, and are reasonably assured that we can collect it. Revenue is recorded net of discounts.

Source of revenue	How we recognize it
Monthly subscriber fees for wireless airtime and data services, cable, telephony and Internet services, network services, media subscriptions and rental of equipment	• Record revenue as the service is provided
Revenue from roaming, long-distance and other optional or non- subscription services, pay-per-use services and other sales of products	• Record revenue as the service is provided or product is delivered
Revenue from the sale of wireless and cable equipment	• Record revenue when the equipment is delivered and accepted by the independent dealer or subscriber in a direct sales channel
Equipment subsidies related to providing equipment to new and existing subscribers	• Record a reduction of equipment revenues when the equipment is activated
Installation fees charged to subscribers in Cable and Business Solutions	• These fees do not meet the criteria as a separate unit of accounting • In Cable, we defer and amortize these fees over the related service period, which is approximately three years • In Business Solutions we defer and amortize fees over the length of the customer contract
Activation fees charged to subscribers in Wireless	• These fees do not meet the criteria as a separate unit of accounting • We record these fees as part of equipment revenue
Advertising revenue	• Record revenue when the advertising airs on our radio or television stations, is featured in our publications or displayed on our digital properties
Monthly subscription revenues received by television stations for subscriptions from cable and satellite providers	• Record revenue when the services are delivered to cable and satellite providers' subscribers
Toronto Blue Jays' revenue from home game admission and concessions	• Recognize revenue when the related games are played during the baseball season and when goods are sold
Toronto Blue Jays' revenue from the Major League Baseball Revenue Sharing Agreement which redistributes funds between member clubs based on each club's relative revenues	• Recognize revenue when the amount can be determined
Revenue from Toronto Blue Jays, radio and television broadcast agreements	• Record revenue at the time the related games are aired
Revenue from sublicensing of program rights	• Record revenue over the course of the applicable season
Awards granted to customers through customer loyalty programs, which are considered a separately identifiable component of the sales transactions	• Estimate the portion of the original sale to allocate to the award credit based on the fair value of the future goods and services that can be obtained when the credit is redeemed • Defer the allocated amount until the awards are redeemed by the customer and we provide the goods or services • Recognize revenue based on the redemption of award credits relative to the award credits that we expect to be redeemed
Interest income on credit card receivables	• Record revenue as earned (i.e.- upon the passage of time) using the effective interest method

Rogers' balance sheet included a current liability of $443 million at December 31, 2014, called Unearned Revenue. Unearned revenue includes subscriber deposits, cable installation fees, and amounts received from subscribers related to services and subscriptions to be provided in future periods.

Instructions

(a) When does Rogers recognize its revenue from monthly subscriber fees?

(b) When should Rogers record unearned revenue from its subscription services? When should it record unearned revenue for its Blue Jays home game admission revenue?

(c) If Rogers (inappropriately) recorded these unearned revenues as revenue when the cash was received in advance, what would be the effect on the company's financial position? (Use the basic accounting equation and explain what elements would be overstated or understated.)

Critical Thinking

Collaborative Learning Activity

Note to instructor: Additional instructions and material for this group activity can be found on the Instructor Resource Site and in *WileyPLUS.*

BYP3-3   In this group activity, you will work in two different groups to improve your understanding of adjusting entries. First you will work in "expert" groups in which you will ensure that each group member thoroughly understands one type of adjusting journal entry. Then you will move to a second group consisting of one student from each of the different expert groups, and take turns teaching the different types of adjusting entries.

Communication Activity

BYP3-4   Some people believe that cash basis accounting is better than accrual basis accounting in predicting a company's future success. This idea became more popular after many reports of corporate financial scandals where management manipulated the timing of recognizing expenses and revenues in accrual accounting to influence profit. Others argue it is easier to manipulate profit using cash basis accounting.

Instructions

Write a memo discussing the following issues:

(a) What is the difference in calculating profit using accrual basis accounting versus cash basis accounting?

(b) Identify one way that management might be able to increase profit by manipulating the timing of revenue or expense recognition under accrual accounting.

(c) Identify one way that management might be able to increase profit using cash basis accounting.

(d) Which basis do you believe is more reliable for measuring performance and why?

"All About You" Activity

BYP3-5   A critical issue for accountants is the decision on whether an expenditure should be recorded as an asset or an expense. The distinction between asset and expense is not always clear. In certain instances, businesses have been forced to restate their financial statements because management has recorded an asset when an expense should be recorded. Let's apply this distinction to you. Post-secondary education results in higher earnings over an adult's working life and thus the money you are spending on your education today should be of significant future benefit. The question then is whether your education would meet the accounting definition of an asset or an expense.

Instructions

(a) Consider the nature of the cost of your education. What factors suggest that it should be considered an asset? What factors suggest that it should be considered an expense?

(b) Do you think the nature of the program you're taking should affect whether the cost of your education should be considered an asset or an expense? Explain.

(c) Economic theory suggests that people will always consider the benefit and cost of any expenditure and only incur the cost if the expected benefit is greater. Wouldn't this mean that every expenditure would meet the definition of an asset? Would you consider the cost of a vacation in Hawaii to be as valuable as a year of post-secondary education? Would you record them both as assets on a personal balance sheet? Why or why not?

(d) If you were applying for a loan, what might the potential effect be on the success of your application if you understated your assets? What might be the potential effect on the bank if your assets are overstated and expenses understated?

 Santé Smoothie Saga

(**Note:** This is a continuation of the Santé Smoothie Saga from Chapters 1 and 2. Use the information from the previous chapters and follow the instructions below using the ledger accounts you have already prepared.)

BYP3-6   It is the end of April and Natalie has been in touch with her mother. Her mother is curious to know if Natalie has been profitable and if Natalie requires another loan to help finance her business. Natalie too would like to know if she has been profitable during her first month of operation. Natalie realizes that, in order to determine Santé Smoothies' income, she must first make adjustments. Natalie puts together the following additional information:

1. A count reveals that $105 of supplies remain at the end of April.
2. Natalie was invited to deliver smoothies to a summer barbecue at her local community centre. At the end of the day, she left an invoice for $175 with the facility manager. Natalie had not had time to record this invoice in her accounting records.
3. Because there were so many guests expected to attend the barbecue in item 2, she asked a friend to help with making the smoothies and promised to pay her $12 an hour. The payment to her friend was made on May 4, 2017, for four hours of work.
4. Natalie estimates that all of her equipment will have a useful life of three years or 36 months. (Assume Natalie decides to record a full month's worth of depreciation, regardless of when the equipment was acquired by the business.)

5. Recall that Natalie's mother is charging 3% interest on the note payable extended on April 15. The loan plus interest is to be repaid in 12 months. (Calculate interest to the nearest month.)

Instructions

Using the information that you have gathered through Chapter 2, and based on the new information above, do and answer the following.

(a) Prepare and post the adjusting journal entries. Round all amounts to the nearest dollar.

(b) Prepare an adjusted trial balance.

(c) Prepare an income statement for the month ended April 30, 2017.

(d) Was Santé Smoothies profitable during the first month of operations? Why is it better for Santé Smoothies to measure profitability after the adjusting journal entries have been prepared and posted instead of before?

(e) How much cash is available to Natalie to operate her business? Why is the amount of cash different than the amount of profit that Santé Smoothies has earned? What is the most likely reason why Natalie may need to borrow additional money from her mother?

ANSWERS TO CHAPTER QUESTIONS

ANSWERS TO ACCOUNTING IN ACTION INSIGHT QUESTIONS

Ethics Insight, p. 119

Q: Who are the stakeholders when companies participate in activities that result in inaccurate reporting of revenues?

A: Stakeholders include customers (who may not want to purchase unordered merchandise), managers (whose bonuses may be tied to profits), regulators (who pass laws in the interest of the public, not necessarily companies), current shareholders (who may want to sell their shares if profits fall), and potential shareholders (who may want to buy shares if the share price falls).

Across the Organization Insight, p. 127

Q: Suppose that Sanjay Sharma purchases a $100 gift card at Canadian Tire on December 24, 2016, and gives it to his wife, Deepa, on December 25, 2016. On January 3, 2017, Deepa uses the card to purchase a $100 barbecue. When do you think Canadian Tire should recognize revenue and why?

A: According to the revenue recognition principle, companies should recognize revenue when the performance obligation is satisfied. In this case, revenue results when Canadian Tire provides the goods. Thus, when Canadian Tire receives cash in exchange for the gift card on December 24, 2016, it should recognize a liability, Unearned Revenue, for $100. On January 3, 2017, when Deepa Sharma exchanges the card for merchandise, Canadian Tire should recognize revenue and eliminate $100 from the balance in the Unearned Revenue account.

Business Insight, p. 128

Q: When should a university like Western recognize the advance fees that students pay for residence admission to hold their spot for the coming year?

A: Universities like Western defer recognition of revenue from advance accommodation fees until the start of the academic year in September, when the students move into the residences.

All About You Insight, p. 132

Q: How should you account for the cost of your post-secondary education? Should you be recognizing the cost as an expense each year or should you recognize it as an asset?

A: Expenses are recognized when there has been a decrease in an asset or an increase in a liability. Paying for an education will reduce assets such as cash and may also increase liabilities if you have to take out student loans. Therefore, most accountants would tell you that you should record the cost of your education as an expense as you incur those costs. On the other hand, it could be argued that your education is creating an asset—your increased future earning power. But then you would have to estimate the value of this asset. As with many situations in accounting, it is not easy to determine the correct answer.

ANSWERS TO SELF-STUDY QUESTIONS

1. b   2. d   3. d   4. b   5. c   6. d   7. a   8. c   9. a   10. b   11. a   12. b

4 COMPLETION OF THE ACCOUNTING CYCLE

CHAPTER PREVIEW In Chapter 3, we learned about the adjusting process and how to prepare financial statements from the adjusted trial balance. In this chapter, we will explain the remaining steps in the accounting cycle—the closing process—as shown in this illustration of the accounting cycle. Once again, we will use Lynk Software Services as an example. After that, we will look at correcting entries and end by discussing the classification and use of balance sheets.

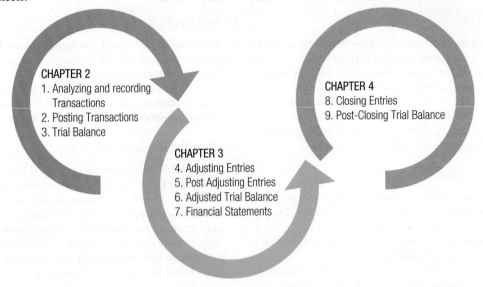

CHAPTER 2
1. Analyzing and recording Transactions
2. Posting Transactions
3. Trial Balance

CHAPTER 3
4. Adjusting Entries
5. Post Adjusting Entries
6. Adjusted Trial Balance
7. Financial Statements

CHAPTER 4
8. Closing Entries
9. Post-Closing Trial Balance

FEATURE STORY ## A "CUT ABOVE" IN BOOKKEEPING

OTTAWA, Ont.—With two busy businesses to run, a hair salon and a barber shop, Kristen Atkinson doesn't have much time to spend on bookkeeping. That's why she uses software to make sure her financial records are accurate and up to date. As the owner of Mint Hair Studio, which she opened in 2011 in Ottawa, and a barber shop that she opened down the street four years later, Ms. Atkinson needs to keep track of daily sales, biweekly payroll, quarterly sales taxes, and annual income taxes, among other things.

Instead of using a general ledger with accounts, Ms. Atkinson uses software designed for hair stylists called Rosy Salon Software, which records all revenues and expenses according to categories such as haircutting revenue, salaries expense for her four employees, commissions for her two commissioned stylists, and revenues from selling hair care products. At the end of every two-week period, she can generate reports to pay salaries and commissions. At the end of every quarter, she generates a

report to give to her accountant showing how much she owes in Harmonized Sales Tax—the proportion of the HST she collected from customers that she needs to remit to the government. "We charge HST on what we do. I pull up a screen in the software that tells me how much HST I owe."

At her fiscal year end, which is April 30, Ms. Atkinson generates a report for her accountant to close her books and calculate her income tax owed. He essentially takes the categories from the Rosy software and translates them into account titles such as Sales, Salaries Expense, and Cost of Goods Sold. He then in essence closes these accounts with the final amounts.

If Ms. Atkinson used a general ledger, one large account would be Merchandise Inventory—the various hair care products she buys wholesale and resells to customers. As part of closing her books at year end, she counts the amount of inventory on hand. "At any given time, I could have $10,000 in

stock in here, so it's good to know for the company's sake how much money is tied up in actual stock," she said.

In her several years of operation, Ms. Atkinson doesn't remember an account ever being out by any significant amount at year end—something that many businesses encounter when closing the books, requiring a correcting entry to balance out. In that sense, you could say that Mint Hair Studio is a cut above.

CHAPTER OUTLINE LEARNING OBJECTIVES

1 Prepare closing entries and a post-closing trial balance.

Closing the Books
- Preparing closing entries
- Posting closing entries
- Preparing a post-closing trial balance

DO IT 1
Closing entries

2 Explain the steps in the accounting cycle including optional steps and the preparation of correcting entries.

Summary of the Accounting Cycle
- Steps in the accounting cycle
- Correcting entries—an avoidable step

DO IT 2
Correcting entries

3 Prepare a classified balance sheet.

Classified Balance Sheet
- Standard balance sheet classifications
- Alternative balance sheet presentation

DO IT 3
Balance sheet classifications

4 Illustrate measures used to evaluate liquidity.

Using the Information in the Financial Statements
- Working capital
- Current ratio
- Acid-test ratio

DO IT 4
Ratios

5 Prepare a work sheet (Appendix 4A).

Appendix 4A: Work Sheets
- Steps in preparing a work sheet
- Preparing financial statements from a work sheet

DO IT 5
Work sheets

6 Prepare reversing entries (Appendix 4B).

Appendix 4B: Reversing Entries
- Accounting with and without reversing entries

DO IT 6
Reversing entries

LEARNING OBJECTIVE **1** ▶ **Prepare closing entries and a post-closing trial balance.**

Closing the Books

At the end of the accounting period, after the adjusting entries have been posted and the financial statements prepared, it is necessary to get the accounts in the general ledger ready for the next period. This is the next step in the accounting cycle and is called **closing the books**. This step involves bringing the balances in all revenue, expense, and drawings accounts to zero, and updating the balance in the Owner's Capital account.

Why is this necessary? Recall from Illustration 1-6 in Chapter 1 that revenues and investments by the owner increase owner's equity, and expenses and drawings decrease owner's equity. Also recall that investments by the owner are directly recorded in the Owner's Capital account, but that revenues, expenses, and drawings are all recorded in separate accounts. We use separate accounts for revenues, expenses, and drawings in order to create the information needed to prepare an income statement and a statement of owner's equity for the accounting period.

At the start of the next accounting period, we need to begin that period with zero in the revenue, expense, and drawings accounts. This will allow us to create the information to prepare the income statement and statement of owner's equity for the next accounting period. **This involves closing the temporary accounts—the accounts that relate to only one accounting period. All revenue, expense, and drawings accounts are considered temporary accounts** because they contain data for only a single accounting period and are closed at the end of the period. The journal entries to close the temporary accounts also update the balance in the Owner's Capital account.

In contrast, **permanent accounts relate to one or more accounting periods**. Therefore, **balance sheet accounts are considered permanent accounts because their balances are carried forward into the next accounting period**. These accounts are not closed at the end of the accounting period.

It is important to know the difference between temporary and permanent accounts. Temporary accounts are closed; permanent accounts are not closed. Illustration 4-1 summarizes temporary and permanent accounts.

▶**ILLUSTRATION** **4-1**
Temporary versus permanent accounts

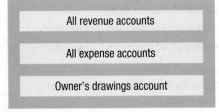

TEMPORARY These accounts are closed.	PERMANENT These accounts are not closed.
All revenue accounts	All asset accounts
All expense accounts	All liability accounts
Owner's drawings account	Owner's capital account

PREPARING CLOSING ENTRIES

The journal entries used to close the temporary accounts are called **closing entries**. Closing entries reduce the balance in the temporary accounts (revenues, expenses, and drawings) to zero and transfer the balances of these accounts to the permanent Owner's Capital account. **Closing entries therefore zero out the balance in each temporary account.** The temporary accounts are then ready to collect data in the next accounting period. Again, permanent accounts are not closed.

Before the closing entries are posted, the balance in the owner's equity account is the ending balance of the previous period. **After the closing entries are prepared and posted, the balance in the Owner's Capital account is equal to the end-of-period balance shown on the statement of owner's equity and**

the balance sheet. The statement of owner's equity shows users of financial statements the effect of that period's profit (or loss)—revenues minus expenses—and drawings on the Owner's Capital account. Therefore, **closing entries transfer the period's profit (or loss) and the Owner's Drawings to the Owner's Capital account.**

Journalizing and posting closing entries is a required step in the accounting cycle. This is done after the company prepares its financial statements. When closing entries are prepared, each income statement account could be closed directly to the Owner's Capital account. However, to do so would result in an excessive amount of detail in the Owner's Capital account. Instead, companies first close the revenue and expense accounts to another temporary account, **Income Summary.** The balance in the Income Summary account after closing revenues and expenses is equal to that period's profit or loss. Then the profit or loss is transferred from the Income Summary account to Owner's Capital.

The closing entry process is based on the expanded accounting equation shown in Illustration 1-8. Recall that the expanded accounting equation shows the relationship between revenues, expenses, profit (or loss), and owner's equity. Similarly, Illustration 4-2 shows the impact of the steps in the closing process on the Owner's Capital account. It also shows that the closing process does not affect the asset and liability accounts.

Helpful hint After the revenue and expense accounts have been closed, the balance in the Income Summary account must equal the profit or loss for the period.

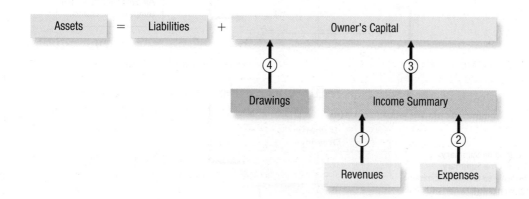

▶ **ILLUSTRATION 4-2**
Closing process

The four steps in Illustrations 4-2 and 4-3 represent four closing entries:

1. **Close Revenue accounts.** Debit each individual revenue account for its balance, and credit Income Summary for total revenues.
2. **Close Expense accounts.** Debit Income Summary for total expenses, and credit each individual expense account for its balance.
3. **Close Income Summary account.** Debit Income Summary for its balance (or credit it if there is a loss) and credit (debit) the Owner's Capital account.
4. **Close Drawings.** Debit the Owner's Capital account and credit the Owner's Drawings account for the balance in drawings.

Companies record closing entries in the general journal. The heading "Closing Entries," inserted in the journal between the last adjusting entry and the first closing entry, identifies these entries. Then the company posts the closing entries to the ledger accounts.

Helpful hint There are four steps to the closing process, which we can remember by the abbreviation R-E-I-D.

1. Revenue accounts are closed to the Income Summary.
2. Expense accounts are closed to the Income Summary.
3. Income Summary account is closed to Owner's Capital.
4. Drawings is closed to Owner's Capital.

Closing Entries Illustrated

To illustrate the journalizing and posting of closing entries, we will continue using the example of Lynk Software Services introduced in Chapters 2 and 3. In practice, companies generally prepare closing entries only at the end of the annual accounting period. Most companies, including Mint Hair Studio, introduced in the feature story, close their books once a year. However, to illustrate the process, we will assume that Lynk Software Services closes its books monthly.

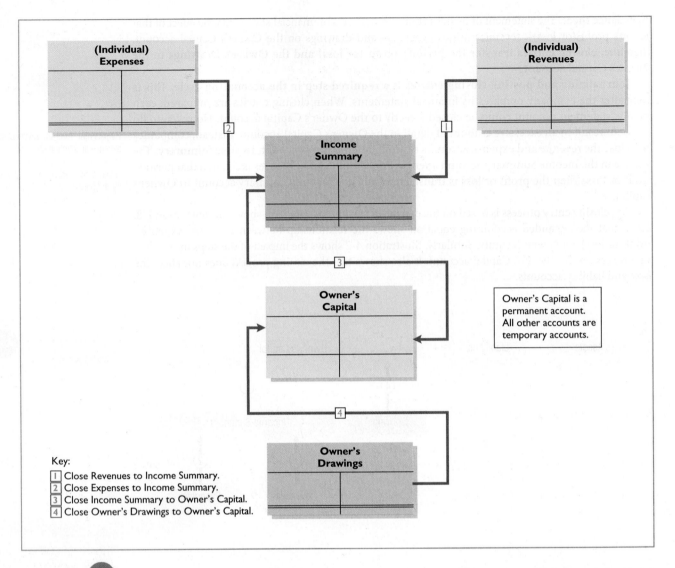

▶ ILLUSTRATION **4-3**
Closing process for
a proprietorship

Lynk Software's adjusted trial balance on October 31, 2017, first shown in Chapter 3 (Illustration 3-14), is shown again here in Illustration 4-4. The temporary accounts have been highlighted in green. T. Jacobs, Capital is a permanent account. It is highlighted in blue because it is used in the closing process, but it is not a temporary account.

Notice that the T. Jacobs, Capital account balance of $10,000 in the adjusted trial balance is the opening balance of $0 plus the $10,000 investment made by T. Jacobs during the period. It is not the ending balance of $13,542 that appears in the statement of owner's equity and balance sheet in Illustrations 3-15 and 3-16. This permanent account is updated to its ending balance by the closing entries as follows:

▶ CLOSING ENTRY **1**
Revenues to Income
Summary

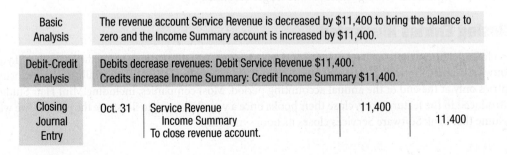

Basic Analysis	The revenue account Service Revenue is decreased by $11,400 to bring the balance to zero and the Income Summary account is increased by $11,400.		
Debit-Credit Analysis	Debits decrease revenues: Debit Service Revenue $11,400. Credits increase Income Summary: Credit Income Summary $11,400.		
Closing Journal Entry	Oct. 31	Service Revenue Income Summary To close revenue account.	11,400 11,400

ILLUSTRATION 4-4
Adjusted trial balance

LYNK SOFTWARE SERVICES
Adjusted Trial Balance
October 31, 2017

	Debit	Credit
Cash	$14,250	
Accounts receivable	1,200	
Supplies	1,000	
Prepaid insurance	550	
Equipment	5,000	
Accumulated depreciation—equipment		$ 83
Notes payable		5,000
Accounts payable		1,750
Unearned revenue		800
Salaries payable		800
Interest payable		25
T. Jacobs, capital		10,000
T. Jacobs, drawings	500	
Service revenue		11,400
Depreciation expense	83	
Insurance expense	50	
Rent expense	900	
Salaries expense	4,800	
Supplies expense	1,500	
Interest expense	25	
	$29,858	$29,858

This closing entry transfers revenue to the Income Summary account. If there are two or more revenue accounts, they are all closed in one entry with a separate debit to each revenue account and one credit to Income Summary for the total amount.

CLOSING ENTRY 2
Expenses to Income Summary

Basic Analysis	The expense accounts are decreased to bring the balance in each account to zero and the Income Summary account is decreased by the total of the expenses of $7,358.
Debit-Credit Analysis	Debits decrease Income Summary: Debit Income Summary $7,358. Credits decrease expenses: Credit each expense account by the balance in that account; the total of the credits is $7,358.

			Debit	Credit
Closing Journal Entry	Oct. 31	Income Summary	7,358	
		Depreciation Expense		83
		Insurance Expense		50
		Rent Expense		900
		Salaries Expense		4,800
		Supplies Expense		1,500
		Interest Expense		25
		To close expense accounts.		

This closing entry transfers the expenses to the Income Summary account. Notice that the closing entry includes **a separate credit to each of the expense accounts** but only one debit for the total amount to Income Summary.

As a result of these two closing entries, there is a credit balance of $4,042 ($11,400 − $7,358) in the Income Summary account. There is a credit balance because revenues were greater than expenses. The credit balance is equal to Lynk's profit for October as shown in Illustration 3-15. If expenses were greater than revenues, Lynk would have a loss and this would result in a debit balance in the Income Summary account after closing revenues and expenses.

▶ **CLOSING ENTRY 3**
Income Summary
to Owner's Capital

Basic Analysis	The Income Summary account is decreased by the balance in the account of $4,042 to bring it to zero and the owner's equity account T. Jacobs, Capital is increased by $4,042 because profit increases owner's equity.
Debit-Credit Analysis	Debits decrease Income Summary: Debit Income Summary $4,042. Credits increase owner's equity: Credit T. Jacobs, Capital $4,042.

Closing Journal Entry	Oct. 31 Income Summary 4,042
	          T. Jacobs, Capital 4,042
	          To close profit to capital.

This closing entry transfers the profit to the capital account. If Lynk had a loss, then it would have been necessary to credit the Income Summary account to bring it to zero and debit the Owner's Capital account. Since losses decrease owner's equity, it makes sense to debit the capital account when there is a loss.

▶ **CLOSING ENTRY 4**
Drawings to Owner's
Capital

Basic Analysis	The drawings account T. Jacobs, Drawings is decreased by $500 to bring the balance to zero and the owner's equity account T. Jacobs, Capital is decreased by $500 because drawings decrease owner's equity.
Debit-Credit Analysis	Debits decrease owner's equity: Debit T. Jacobs, Capital $500. Credits decrease drawings: Credit T. Jacobs, Drawings $500.

Closing Journal Entry	Oct. 31 T. Jacobs, Capital 500
	          T. Jacobs, Drawings 500
	          To close drawings account.

This closing entry transfers the drawings to the capital account. Always close drawings separately from revenues and expenses. Drawings are not an expense, and they are not a factor in determining profit. Remember, drawings are shown on the statement of owner's equity as a separate item and thus are also closed in a separate entry.

The closing entries are recorded in the general journal for Lynk Software Services as follows:

GENERAL JOURNAL				J3
Date	**Account Titles and Explanation**	**Ref.**	**Debit**	**Credit**
	Closing Entries			
2017	(1)			
Oct. 31	Service Revenue	400	11,400	
	Income Summary	350		11,400
	To close revenue account.			
	(2)			
31	Income Summary	350	7,358	
	Depreciation Expense	711		83
	Insurance Expense	722		50
	Rent Expense	726		900
	Salaries Expense	729		4,800
	Supplies Expense	740		1,500
	Interest Expense	905		25
	To close expense accounts.			
	(3)			
31	Income Summary	350	4,042	
	T. Jacobs, Capital	301		4,042
	To close profit to capital.			

Date	Account Titles and Explanation	Ref.	Debit	Credit
	(4)			
31	T. Jacobs, Capital	301	500	
	T. Jacobs, Drawings	306		500
	To close drawings account.			

Be careful when you prepare closing entries. Remember that the reason for making closing entries is to bring the temporary accounts to zero balances. Do not make the mistake of doubling the revenue, expense, drawings, and Income Summary account balances, rather than bringing them to zero.

ACCOUNTING IN ACTION
ACROSS THE ORGANIZATION

Technology has dramatically shortened the closing process. This is a good thing, because a 2014 survey of Canadian companies found that 41% had more than 500 active general ledger accounts. Other surveys have reported that the average U.S. company now takes only six to seven days to close, rather than the previous 20 days. But a few companies do much better. Cisco Systems can perform a "virtual close"—closing within 24 hours on any day in the quarter. The same is true at Lockheed Martin Corp., which improved its closing time by 85% in just a few years. Previously, it took 14 to 16 days. Managers at these companies emphasize that this increased speed has not reduced the accuracy and completeness of the data. It also means more staff time can be spent on analyzing data, mining data for business intelligence, and looking for new business opportunities.

The ability to close the books quickly is not just showing off. Knowing exactly where it is financially all of the time allows a company to respond faster than its competitors. Nova Scotia–based Clearwater Seafoods, for example, recently invested in a new financial information system. "We're focusing more of our effort on forecasting, because no matter how quickly you compile and release historic financial statements, you never make a decision off of them. You use forecasts for that," said Tyrone Cotie, Clearwater's treasurer.

Sources: Paul McDonald and Thomas Thompson, Jr., "2015 Benchmarking the Accounting & Finance Function," Robert Half International, 2015; "Reporting Practices: Few Do It All," *Financial Executive* (November 2003), p. 11.

Q **Who else benefits from a shorter closing process?**

POSTING CLOSING ENTRIES

The asset and liability accounts are never affected by the closing process. Thus we have not included them in Illustration 4-5 where the closing entries for Lynk Software are posted. The only accounts that change are the temporary accounts and the Owner's Capital account.

Note that after the closing entries have been posted, all of the temporary accounts have zero balances. Also, the balance in the Owner's Capital account represents the owner's total equity at the end of the accounting period. This is the balance that is presented on the balance sheet as the ending balance of the Owner's Capital account. Also note that Lynk Software uses the Income Summary account to close its accounts only at fiscal year end. It does not post entries to this account during the year. This is because during the year, the balances in the revenue and expense accounts are needed from one accounting period to the next to capture all year-to-date transactions.

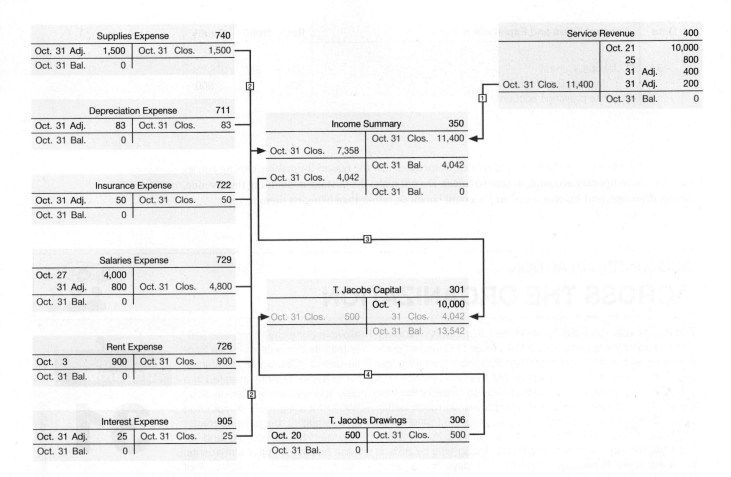

Key:
1 Close Revenues to Income Summary
2 Close Expenses to Income Summary
3 Close Income Summary to Owner's Capital
4 Close Owner's Drawings to Owner's Capital

▶ ILLUSTRATION 4-5
Posting of closing entries

Stop and check your work after the closing entries are posted:

1. The balance in Income Summary, immediately before the final closing entry to transfer the balance to the Owner's Capital account, should equal the profit (or loss).
2. All temporary accounts (revenues, expenses, Owner's Drawings, and Income Summary) should have zero balances.
3. The balance in the capital account should equal the ending balance reported in the statement of owner's equity and balance sheet.

PREPARING A POST-CLOSING TRIAL BALANCE

After all closing entries have been journalized and posted, another trial balance is prepared from the ledger. It is called a **post-closing trial balance**. The post- (or after-) closing trial balance lists permanent accounts and their balances after closing entries have been journalized and posted. The purpose of this trial balance is to prove the equality of the permanent account balances that are carried forward into the next accounting period. Because all temporary accounts have zero balances after closing, the post-closing trial balance contains only permanent—balance sheet—accounts.

The post-closing trial balance for Lynk Software Services is shown in Illustration 4-6. Note that the account balances are the same as the ones in the company's balance sheet. (Lynk Software's balance sheet is shown in Chapter 3, Illustration 3-16.)

Helpful hint Total debits in a post-closing trial balance will not equal total assets on the balance sheet if contra accounts, such as accumulated depreciation accounts, are present. Accumulated depreciation is deducted from assets on the balance sheet but added to the credit column in a trial balance.

LYNK SOFTWARE SERVICES
Post-Closing Trial Balance
October 31, 2017

	Debit	Credit
Cash	$14,250	
Accounts receivable	1,200	
Supplies	1,000	
Prepaid insurance	550	
Equipment	5,000	
Accumulated depreciation—equipment		$ 83
Notes payable		5,000
Accounts payable		1,750
Unearned revenue		800
Salaries payable		800
Interest payable		25
T. Jacobs, capital		13,542
	$22,000	$22,000

▶ILLUSTRATION 4-6
Post-closing
trial balance

A post-closing trial balance provides evidence that the journalizing and posting of closing entries has been completed properly. It also shows that the accounting equation is in balance at the end of the accounting period and the beginning of the next accounting period.

As in the case of the trial balance, the post-closing trial balance does not prove that all transactions have been recorded or that the ledger is correct. For example, the post-closing trial balance will still balance if a transaction is not journalized and posted, or if a transaction is journalized and posted twice.

Accounting software will automatically record and post closing entries when given instructions to prepare the accounting records for the next fiscal year. However, it is still very important to understand what is happening in the closing process and the impact that errors may have on the financial statements. You will find your understanding of adjusting entries is enhanced once you have mastered closing entries.

BEFORE YOU GO ON...DO IT **1** **Closing Entries**

The adjusted trial balance for Eng Company shows the following:

	Debit	Credit
Cash	$20,000	
Equipment	35,000	
Accounts payable		$10,000
L. Eng, capital		42,000
L. Eng, drawings	5,000	
Service revenue		18,000
Rent expense	2,000	
Salaries expense	7,500	
Supplies expense	500	
	$70,000	$70,000

Eng Company's statement of owner's equity for the year showed a profit of $8,000 and closing Owner's Capital of $45,000.

(a) Prepare the closing entries at December 31.
(b) Create T accounts for Income Summary and L. Eng, Capital, and post the closing entries to these accounts.

(continued)

Action Plan
• Debit each individual Revenue account for its balance and credit the total to Income Summary.
• Credit each individual Expense account for its balance and debit the total to Income Summary.
• Stop and check your work: Does the balance in Income Summary equal the reported profit?
• Debit the balance in Income Summary and credit the amount to the Owner's Capital account. (Do the opposite if the company had a loss.)

Action Plan (contd.)

- Credit the balance in the Drawings account and debit the amount to the Owner's Capital account. Do not close drawings with the expenses.
- Stop and check your work: Will your closing entries result in the temporary accounts having zero balances? Does the ending balance in the Owner's Capital account equal the closing owner's capital amount reported on the statement of owner's equity?

BEFORE YOU GO ON...DO IT   **Closing Entries** *(continued)*

Solution

Dec. 31	Service Revenue	18,000	
	Income Summary		18,000
	To close revenue account.		
31	Income Summary	10,000	
	Rent Expense		2,000
	Salaries Expense		7,500
	Supplies Expense		500
	To close expense accounts.		
31	Income Summary	8,000	
	L. Eng, Capital		8,000
	To close Income Summary.		
31	L. Eng, Capital	5,000	
	L. Eng, Drawings		5,000
	To close drawings.		

Income Summary			
Clos.	10,000	Clos.	18,000
		Bal.	8,000*
Clos.	8,000		
		Bal.	0

L. Eng, Capital			
		Bal.	42,000
Clos.	5,000	Clos.	8,000
		Bal.	45,000**

*Check if this equals profit.   **Check if this equals closing Owner's Capital.

Related exercise material: BE4–1, BE4–2, BE4–3, BE4–4, BE4–5, E4–1, E4–2, E4–3, E4–4, E4–5, E4–6, and E4–7.

Summary of the Accounting Cycle

In Chapter 2, we introduced the accounting cycle as a series of steps that accountants take to prepare financial statements. You have now learned all of the steps. In the following section, we review the cycle and discuss optional steps.

LEARNING OBJECTIVE 2   **Explain the steps in the accounting cycle including optional steps and the preparation of correcting entries.**

STEPS IN THE ACCOUNTING CYCLE

As introduced in Chapter 2, the cycle begins with the analysis and recording of business transactions (Steps 1, 2, and 3). This is followed by the preparation of a trial balance (Step 4), as also shown in Chapter 2. Chapter 3 covered the adjustment process and the preparation of financial statements (Steps 5, 6, and 7). In the first part of Chapter 4, the final steps of the accounting cycle—the closing process (Steps 8 and 9)—were covered. The full accounting cycle is reproduced here in Illustration 4-7.

The steps in the cycle are done in sequence (Steps 1 to 9). Once Step 9 is completed for an accounting period, the company can begin again with Step 1 in the next accounting period and repeat the steps for that accounting period and so on. Because the steps are repeated each accounting period, we show the full accounting cycle as a circle. Steps 1, 2, and 3 can occur every day during the accounting period, as explained in Chapter 2. Steps 4 through 7 are done periodically, such as monthly, quarterly, or annually. Steps 8 and 9, closing entries and a post-closing trial balance, are usually done only at the end of a company's annual accounting period.

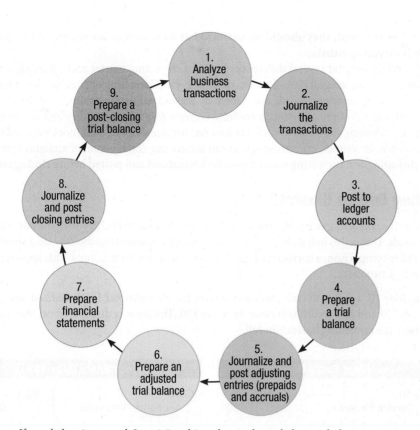

Optional steps: If a work sheet is prepared, Steps 4, 5, and 6 are done in the work sheet, and adjusting entries are journalized and posted after Step 7. If reversing entries are prepared, they occur between Steps 9 and 1.

There are also two optional steps in the accounting cycle: work sheets and reversing entries. These optional steps are explained in the following two sections.

Work Sheets—An Optional Step

Some accountants like to use an optional multiple-column form known as a **work sheet** to help them prepare adjusting entries and the financial statements. As its name suggests, the work sheet is a working tool. It is not a permanent accounting record; it is neither a journal nor a part of the general ledger. Companies generally computerize work sheets using an electronic spreadsheet program such as Excel.

Although using a work sheet is optional, it is useful. For example, a work sheet makes it easier to prepare interim (e.g., monthly or quarterly) financial information. The monthly or quarterly adjusting entries can be entered in the work sheet, and interim financial statements can then be easily developed.

As the preparation of a work sheet is optional, its basic form and the procedure for preparing it are explained in Appendix 4A at the end of the chapter.

Reversing Entries—An Optional Step

Some accountants prefer to reverse certain adjusting entries by making a reversing entry at the beginning of the next accounting period. A **reversing entry** is the exact opposite of the adjusting entry made in the previous period. Use of reversing entries is an optional bookkeeping procedure; **it is not a required step in the accounting cycle.** We have therefore chosen to explain this topic in Appendix 4B at the end of the chapter.

CORRECTING ENTRIES—AN AVOIDABLE STEP

Unfortunately, errors may happen in the recording process. The accounting cycle does not include a specific step for correcting errors because this step is not needed if the accounting records have no errors. But **if errors exist, they should be corrected** as soon as they are discovered by journalizing and posting **correcting entries**.

You should understand several differences between correcting entries and adjusting entries. First, adjusting entries are an integral part of the accounting cycle. Correcting entries, on the other hand, are unnecessary if the accounting records are error free. Second, adjustments are journalized and posted only at the end of an accounting period. In contrast, correcting entries are made whenever an error is discovered. Finally, adjusting entries always affect at least one balance sheet account (not Cash) and one income statement account. In contrast, correcting entries can involve any combination of accounts that need to be corrected. **Adjusting and correcting entries must be journalized and posted before closing entries.**

Correcting Entries Illustrated

To determine the correcting entry, it is useful to compare the incorrect entry with the entry that should have been made. Doing this helps identify the accounts and amounts that should—and should not—be corrected. After comparison, a correcting entry is made to correct the accounts. This approach is shown in the following two cases.

Case 1. On May 10, a $50 cash collection on account from a customer is journalized and posted as a debit to Cash $50 and as a credit to Service Revenue $50. The error is discovered on May 20 when the customer pays the remaining balance in full.

Incorrect Entry (May 10)			Correct Entry (May 10)		
Cash	50		Cash	50	
Service Revenue		50	Accounts Receivable		50

Comparison of the incorrect entry with the correct entry that should have been made (but was not) reveals that the debit to Cash of $50 is correct. However, the $50 credit to Service Revenue should have been credited to Accounts Receivable. As a result, both Service Revenue and Accounts Receivable are overstated in the ledger. The following correcting entry is needed:

		Correcting Entry		
May 20	Service Revenue		50	
	Accounts Receivable			50
	To correct May 10 entry.			

A = L + OE
−50   −50

Cash flows: no effect

Case 2. On May 18, equipment that costs $450 is purchased on account. The transaction is journalized and posted as a debit to Supplies $45 and as a credit to Accounts Payable $45. The error is discovered on June 3 when the monthly statement for May is received from the creditor.

Incorrect Entry (May 18)			Correct Entry (May 18)		
Supplies	45		Equipment	450	
Accounts Payable		45	Accounts Payable		450

A comparison of the two entries shows that three accounts are incorrect. Supplies is overstated by $45; Equipment is understated by $450; and Accounts Payable is understated by $405 ($450 − $45). The correcting entry is as follows:

A = L + OE
+450 +405
−45

Cash flows: no effect

		Correcting Entry		
June 3	Equipment		450	
	Supplies			45
	Accounts Payable			405
	To correct May 18 entry.			

ACCOUNTING IN ACTION
ETHICS INSIGHT

Getty Images/Justin Horrocks

Discovering errors in a company's previous financial statements can cause serious ethical issues. Let's say you are the controller of Select Cleaning Services and you find a significant error in the previous year's financial statements. Two journal entries for services provided on account were recognized in the previous fiscal year but should have been recognized this fiscal year. The incorrect financial statements were issued to banks and other creditors less than a month ago. You gather your courage to inform the president, Eddy Lieman, about this misstatement. Eddy says, "Hey! What they don't know won't hurt them. We have earned that revenue by now so it doesn't really matter when it was recorded. We can afford to have lower revenues this year than last year anyway! Just don't make that kind of mistake again."

Q Who are the stakeholders in this situation and what are the ethical issues?

Alternative Approach

Instead of preparing a correcting entry, many accountants simply reverse the incorrect entry and then record the correct entry. This approach will result in more entries and postings, but it is often easier and more logical. Note that entries posted in error should never be simply erased or removed from the accounting records. This compromises the paper trail that proves the financial records are complete and accurate.

Sometimes errors are not found until after the temporary accounts have been closed. A correcting entry that fixes an error from a previous accounting year is called a **prior period adjustment**. These correcting entries can be very complex, and will be covered in a later chapter.

BEFORE YOU GO ON...DO IT **2** ▷ **Correcting Entries**

The Chip 'N Dough Company made the following adjusting journal entry to record $5,200 of depreciation expense on a vehicle at year end:

Feb. 28	Depreciation Expense	520	
	Cash		520
	To record depreciation on a vehicle.		

Prepare the required correcting entry.

Solution

Feb. 28	Cash	520	
	Depreciation Expense ($5,200 − $520)	4,680	
	Accumulated Depreciation—Vehicles		5,200
	To correct depreciation adjustment.		

OR

Feb. 28	Cash	520	
	Depreciation Expense		520
	To reverse incorrect depreciation adjustment.		
28	Depreciation Expense	5,200	
	Accumulated Depreciation—Vehicles		5,200
	To record the correct depreciation entry.		

Related exercise material: BE4–6, BE4–7, E4–8, E4–9, E4–10, and E4–11.

Action Plan
- Determine the correct entry that should have been made.
- Compare it with the incorrect entry made and make the required corrections. Note that three accounts must be corrected.
- You could instead use the alternative approach of reversing the incorrect journal entry and recording the correct journal entry.

LEARNING OBJECTIVE **3** ▷ Prepare a classified balance sheet.

Classified Balance Sheet

The balance sheet presents a snapshot of a company's financial position at a point in time. The balance sheets that we have seen so far have all been very basic, with items classified simply as assets, liabilities, or owner's equity. To improve users' understanding of a company's financial position, companies often group similar assets and similar liabilities together.

STANDARD BALANCE SHEET CLASSIFICATIONS

A **classified balance sheet** groups together similar assets and similar liabilities, using standard classifications. This is useful as items within a group have similar characteristics. Generally the standard classifications are listed in Illustration 4-8.

▶ **ILLUSTRATION** **4-8**
Standard balance sheet classifications

Assets	Liabilities and Owner's Equity
Current assets	Current liabilities
Long-term investments	Non-current liabilities
Property, plant, and equipment	Owner's (shareholders') equity
Intangible assets	
Goodwill	

Alternative terminology The balance sheet is also known as the *statement of financial position.*

These groupings help readers determine such things as (1) whether the company has enough assets to pay its debts as they come due, and (2) the claims of short- and long-term creditors on total assets. These classifications are shown in the balance sheet of MacDonald Company in Illustration 4-9. In the sections that follow, we explain each of these groupings.

▶ **ILLUSTRATION** **4-9**
Classified balance sheet

MACDONALD COMPANY Balance Sheet November 30, 2017			
Assets			
Current assets			
Cash		$ 6,600	
Short-term investments		2,000	
Accounts receivable		7,000	
Inventories		4,000	
Supplies		2,100	
Prepaid insurance		400	
Total current assets			$ 22,100
Long-term investments			
Equity investment		5,200	
Debt investment		2,000	
Total long-term investments			7,200
Property, plant, and equipment			
Land		35,000	
Building	$75,000		
Less: Accumulated depreciation	15,000	60,000	
Equipment	24,000		
Less: Accumulated depreciation	5,000	19,000	
Total property, plant, and equipment			114,000
Licences			5,000
Goodwill			3,100
Total assets			$151,400

Liabilities and Owner's Equity		
Current liabilities		
Short-term notes payable	$11,000	
Accounts payable	2,100	
Unearned revenue	900	
Salaries payable	1,600	
Interest payable	450	
Current portion of long-term notes payable	1,000	
Total current liabilities		$ 17,050
Non-current liabilities		
Mortgage payable	9,000	
Long-term notes payable	1,300	
Total non-current liabilities		10,300
Total liabilities		27,350
Owner's equity		
J. MacDonald, capital		124,050
Total liabilities and owner's equity		$151,400

Current Assets

Current assets are normally cash and other assets that will be converted to cash, sold, or used up within one year from the balance sheet date, or its operating cycle, whichever is longer. The **operating cycle** of a company is the average time it takes to go from starting with cash to purchasing inventory, selling it on account, and then collecting the cash from its customers. Illustration 4-10 shows the basic steps involved in an operating cycle.

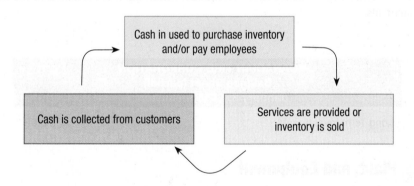

▸ **ILLUSTRATION** **4-10**
Steps in the operating cycle

For most businesses, this cycle is less than one year, so they use the one-year cut-off. But for other businesses, such as vineyards, construction contractors, or airplane manufacturers, this period may be longer than one year. **Except where noted, we will assume companies use one year to determine whether an asset is current or non-current.**

Common types of current assets are (1) cash; (2) short-term investments; (3) receivables, such as notes receivable, accounts receivable, and interest receivable; (4) inventories; (5) supplies; and (6) prepaid expenses, such as rent and insurance. Accounts receivable are current assets because they will be collected and converted to cash within one year. Inventory is a current asset because a company expects to sell it within one year. Supplies are a current asset because a company expects to use or consume supplies within one year. In Illustration 4-9, MacDonald Company had current assets of $22,100.

In Canada, companies generally list current assets in the order of their liquidity; that is, in the order in which they are expected to be converted into cash. Some international companies list current assets in reverse order of liquidity.

Current assets for Danier Leather Inc., one of Canada's premier retailers, are shown in Illustration 4-11. Note that Danier Leather lists its current assets in order of liquidity.

▶ILLUSTRATION  4-11
Current assets section

DANIER LEATHER Balance Sheet (partial) June 28, 2014 (in thousands)	
Current assets	
Cash	$13,507
Accounts receivable	638
Income tax recoverable	3,461
Inventories	21,721
Prepaid expenses	643

Alternative terminology Short-term investments are sometimes called *marketable securities, trading investments,* or *trading securities.*

The assets described in the next three sections are **non-current assets**. These are assets that are not expected to be converted to cash, sold, or used by the business within one year of the balance sheet date or its operating cycle. Basically that means that a non-current asset is anything that is not classified as a current asset.

Long-Term Investments

Long-term investments include (1) investments in stocks and bonds of other companies that management intends to hold over many years, (2) long-term notes receivable, and (3) assets such as land that the entity is not currently using in its operating activities but also plans to hold over the long term. These assets are classified as long-term because they are not readily marketable or expected to be converted into cash within one year. In Illustration 4-9, MacDonald Company reported long-term investments of $7,200 on its balance sheet.

Some companies have only one line on the balance sheet showing total long-term investments, and provide all of the details in the notes to the financial statements. If an item is simply called an "investment," without specifying if it is a short- or long-term investment, it is assumed to be a long-term investment.

Canadian Tire Corporation (as shown in the partial balance sheet in Illustration 4-12) presents its long-term investments on its balance sheet. Additional information is presented in the notes to the financial statements.

▶ILLUSTRATION  4-12
Long-term investments section

CANADIAN TIRE CORPORATION Balance Sheet (partial) January 3, 2015 (in millions)	
Long Term Investments	$176.00

Property, Plant, and Equipment

Alternative terminology Property, plant, and equipment are sometimes called *capital assets* or *fixed assets.*

Property, plant, and equipment are long-lived, tangible assets that are used in the business and are not intended for sale. This category includes land, buildings, equipment, vehicles, and furniture. In Illustration 4-9, MacDonald Company reported property, plant, and equipment of $114,000.

Although the order of property, plant, and equipment on the balance sheet can vary among companies, in Canada these assets have traditionally been listed in their order of permanency. That is, land is usually listed first, because it has an indefinite life, and is followed by the asset with the next longest useful life (normally buildings), and so on.

Since property, plant, and equipment benefit future periods, their cost is allocated to expense over their useful lives through depreciation, as we learned in Chapter 3. Assets that are depreciated are reported at their carrying amount (cost minus accumulated depreciation).

Indigo Books and Music Inc. reported the total carrying amount (or "net carrying value" as Indigo calls it) of $58,467 thousand for its property, plant, and equipment on its balance sheet. Indigo reports the cost, accumulated depreciation, and net carrying value of each category of property, plant, and equipment in a note to the financial statements, as shown in Illustration 4-13. This practice is very common among public companies because it keeps the balance sheet from looking too cluttered.

Note that, except for land (which has an unlimited useful life), all other property, plant, and equipment items are depreciated. This includes leasehold improvements, which are long-lived additions or renovations made to leased property. It also includes equipment under finance leases, which are assets leased by the entity but have the characteristics of ownership.

▶ILLUSTRATION **4-13**
Property, plant, and equipment section

INDIGO BOOKS AND MUSIC CO. Notes to the Financial Statements (excerpt) March 29, 2014 (in thousands)			
Note 8. Property, Plant and Equipment			
	Cost	Accumulated Amortization	Net Carrying Value
Furniture, Fixtures and Equipment	$ 62,118	$29,412	$32,706
Computer Equipment	11,080	5,029	6,051
Leasehold Improvements	54,329	35,407	18,922
Equipment under Finance Leases	2,824	2,027	797
	$130,351	$71,875	$58,476

Intangible Assets and Goodwill

Intangible assets are long-lived assets that do not have physical substance. They give a company rights and privileges and include such things as patents, copyrights, franchises, trademarks, trade names, and licences.

An asset that is similar to intangible assets is goodwill. **Goodwill** results from the acquisition of another company when the price paid for the company is higher than the fair value of the purchased company's net assets. In Illustration 4-9, MacDonald Company reported $5,000 of an intangible asset (licences) and $3,100 of goodwill.

Illustration 4-14 shows how TELUS Corporation reported intangible assets and goodwill in its balance sheet. The word "net" indicates that accumulated amortization has been deducted from the cost of the intangible assets. The notes to the financial statements explain that the intangible assets are composed of such things as brands, licences, and software. As required by IFRS, TELUS's balance sheet reports goodwill separately from intangible assets.

▶ILLUSTRATION **4-14**
Intangible assets and goodwill section

TELUS CORPORATION Statement of Financial Position (partial) December 31, 2014 (millions)	
Intangible assets, net (note 17)	$7,797
Goodwill (note 17)	3,757

Current Liabilities

Current liabilities are obligations that are expected to be settled within one year from the balance sheet date or in the company's operating cycle. As with current assets, companies use a period longer than one year if their operating cycle is longer than one year. In this textbook, we will always assume an operating cycle equal to, or shorter than, one year.

Common examples of current liabilities are notes payable, accounts payable, salaries payable, interest payable, sales taxes payable, unearned revenues, and current maturities of non-current liabilities (payments to be made within the next year on long-term debt). Corporations may also have income taxes payable included in the current liabilities section of the balance sheet. In Illustration 4-9, Mac-Donald Company reported six different types of current liabilities, for a total of $17,050.

Similar to current assets, North American companies often list current liabilities in order of liquidity. That is, the liabilities that will be due first are listed first. However, many companies simply list the items in their current liabilities section according to a company tradition. Some international companies list current liabilities in reverse order of liquidity, similar to current assets.

The current liabilities section from Tim Hortons Inc.'s balance sheet is shown in Illustration 4-15.

▶ ILLUSTRATION **4-15**
Current liabilities section

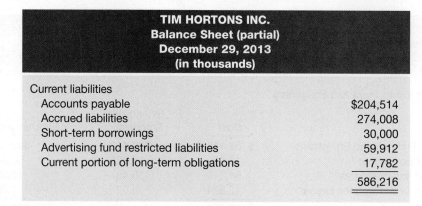

TIM HORTONS INC. Balance Sheet (partial) December 29, 2013 (in thousands)	
Current liabilities	
Accounts payable	$204,514
Accrued liabilities	274,008
Short-term borrowings	30,000
Advertising fund restricted liabilities	59,912
Current portion of long-term obligations	17,782
	586,216

Users of financial statements look closely at the relationship between current assets and current liabilities. This relationship is important in evaluating a company's ability to pay its current liabilities. We will talk more about this later in the chapter when we learn how to use the information in the financial statements.

Non-Current Liabilities

Alternative terminology Non-current liabilities are sometimes called *long-term liabilities, long-term obligations,* or *long-term debt.*

Obligations that are expected to be paid after one year or longer are classified as **non-current liabilities**. Liabilities in this category can include bonds payable, mortgages payable, notes payable, lease liabilities, and deferred income taxes (income taxes payable after more than one year), among others. In Illustration 4-9, MacDonald Company reported non-current liabilities of $10,300.

Illustration 4-16 shows the non-current liabilities that Saputo Inc., a Canadian-based dairy processor, reported on a recent balance sheet.

▶ ILLUSTRATION **4-16**
Non-current liabilities section

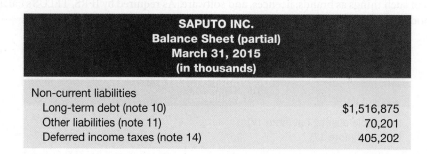

SAPUTO INC. Balance Sheet (partial) March 31, 2015 (in thousands)	
Non-current liabilities	
Long-term debt (note 10)	$1,516,875
Other liabilities (note 11)	70,201
Deferred income taxes (note 14)	405,202

The notes contain additional details about the liabilities, including how much must be paid during each of the next five years.

Equity

As introduced in Chapter 1, the name and specific accounts of the equity section vary with the form of business organization. In a proprietorship, there is one capital account under the heading "Owner's equity." In a partnership, there is a capital account for each partner under the heading "Partners' equity."

For a corporation, shareholders' equity always includes two parts: share capital and retained earnings. Amounts that are invested in the business by the shareholders are recorded as share capital. Profit that is kept for use in the business is recorded in the Retained Earnings account.

Some corporations may have other parts to the equity section, such as contributed surplus, which arises from the sale of shares, reserves, and accumulated other comprehensive income (or loss). We will learn more about corporation equity accounts in later chapters.

Illustration 4-17 shows how Husky Energy Inc., a corporation, reported its shareholders' equity section in its balance sheet.

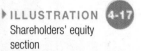

Alternative terminology Share capital is also commonly known as *capital stock* or *common shares.*

▶ILLUSTRATION **4-17**
Shareholders' equity section

HUSKY ENERGY INC. Consolidated Balance Sheet (partial) December 31, 2014 (in millions)	
Common shares	6,986
Preferred shares	534
Retained earnings	12,666
Other reserves	389
Shareholders' equity	$20,575

ALTERNATIVE BALANCE SHEET PRESENTATION

It is important to note that, when it comes to balance sheet presentation, both IFRS and ASPE allow for some choices. It is also interesting to note that, as different countries have adopted IFRS, where choices exist, companies have continued to follow the practices they used prior to adopting IFRS. Thus, the differences in balance sheet presentation when following IFRS, as compared with ASPE, are not necessarily that significant.

We will look at two differences that could arise.

Statement Name

IFRS uses "statement of financial position" and ASPE uses "balance sheet" in the written standards. But both sets of standards allow companies to use either of these titles. While "statement of financial position" more accurately describes the content of the statement, "balance sheet" has been much more widely used in Canada. As many Canadian companies, both public and private, continue to use "balance sheet," we also use that term in this textbook.

Classification of Assets

Both IFRS and ASPE require companies to separately present current assets; property, plant, and equipment; intangible assets; goodwill; and long-term investments, in the same way as in Illustration 4-9. The standards are designed to ensure separate presentation on the face of the balance sheet for items that are different in nature or function.

In practice, companies following IFRS typically include the heading "non-current assets" on the balance sheet, and group property, plant, and equipment; intangible assets; goodwill; and long-term investments under this heading.

ACCOUNTING IN ACTION
ALL ABOUT YOU INSIGHT

Getty Images/Peter Dazeley

Similar to a company's balance sheet, a personal balance sheet reports what you own and what you owe. What are the items of value that you own—your personal assets? Some of your assets are liquid—such as cash or short-term savings. Others, such as vehicles, real estate, and some types of investments, are less liquid. Some assets, such as real estate and investments, tend to increase in value, thereby increasing your personal equity. Other assets, such as vehicles, tend to fall in value, thereby decreasing your personal equity.

What are the amounts that you owe—your personal liabilities? Student loans? Credit cards? Your equity is the difference between your total assets and total liabilities. Financial planners call this your *net worth* or *personal equity*.

Each quarter, Statistics Canada reports on the national balance sheet accounts and net worth of households in Canada. At the end of 2014, Statscan reported that the net worth of Canadian households rose 7.5% from the end of 2013, to $233,000 per capita. The increase was largely due to a rise in the value of real estate and mutual fund holdings. However, Canadians are borrowing at a faster pace than disposable incomes—their after-tax incomes—are rising. In the fourth quarter of 2014, Canadian households' credit market debt—including credit card bills, mortgages, and other loans—reached a new high, at 163% of disposable income. This means that households had about $1.63 of credit market debt for every dollar of disposable income. How can you increase your net worth? As a student, you may not have a lot of assets now, but by learning to control your spending and using debt wisely, you will be better able to increase your net worth when you graduate and start working full-time.

Source: Statistics Canada, "National Balance Sheet and Financial Flow Accounts, Fourth Quarter, 2014" *The Daily*, March 12, 2015.

Q **How can preparing a personal balance sheet help you manage your net worth?**

BEFORE YOU GO ON...DO IT Balance Sheet Classifications

The following selected accounts were taken from a company's balance sheet:

Accounts payable	Merchandise inventories
Accounts receivable	Mortgage payable (due in 10 years)
Accumulated depreciation—buildings	Notes receivable (due in 5 years)
Current portion of notes payable	Other investments
Goodwill	Short-term investments
Intangibles	Unearned revenue
Interest payable	Vehicles

Classify each of the above accounts as current assets, non-current assets, current liabilities, or non-current liabilities.

Solution

Account	Balance Sheet Classification
Accounts payable	Current liabilities
Accounts receivable	Current assets
Accumulated depreciation—buildings	Non-current assets
Current portion of notes payable	Current liabilities
Goodwill	Non-current assets
Intangibles	Non-current assets
Interest payable	Current liabilities
Merchandise inventories	Current assets
Mortgage payable (due in 10 years)	Non-current liabilities
Notes receivable (due in 5 years)	Non-current assets
Other investments	Non-current assets
Short-term investments	Current assets
Unearned revenue	Current liabilities
Vehicles	Non-current assets

Action Plan

• Current assets include all assets that will be realized within one year.

• Current liabilities are obligations that are expected to be paid within one year.

• Non-current assets are all assets that are expected to be realized in more than one year.

• Obligations that are due after more than one year are classified as non-current liabilities.

Related exercise material: BE 4-8, BE4–9, BE4–10, BE4–11, BE4–12, E4–12, E4–13, and E4–14.

LEARNING OBJECTIVE 4 **Illustrate measures used to evaluate liquidity.**

Using the Information in the Financial Statements

In Chapter 1, we briefly discussed how the financial statements give information about a company's performance and financial position. In this chapter, we will begin to learn about a tool, called ratio analysis, that can be used to analyze financial statements in order to make a more meaningful evaluation of a company. Ratio analysis expresses the relationships between selected items in the financial statements.

As you study the chapters of this book, you will learn about three general types of ratios that are used to analyze financial statements: liquidity, profitability, and solvency ratios. Liquidity ratios measure a company's **liquidity**—the company's ability to pay its obligations as they come due within the next year and to meet unexpected needs for cash. As the name suggests, profitability ratios measure a company's profit or operating success for a specific period of time. Solvency ratios measure a company's ability to pay its total liabilities and survive over a long period of time. In this chapter, we introduce three liquidity ratios: working capital, the current ratio, and the acid-test ratio.

WORKING CAPITAL

When liquidity is being evaluated, an important relationship is the one between current assets and current liabilities. The difference between current assets and current liabilities is called **working capital**. **Working capital is important because it shows a company's ability to pay its short-term debts.** When current assets are more than current liabilities at the balance sheet date, the company will likely be able to pay its current liabilities. When the reverse is true, short-term creditors may not be paid.

Corus Entertainment's working capital is $41,669 thousand, as shown in Illustration 4-18, where amounts are in thousands.

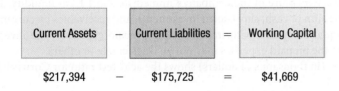

▶ ILLUSTRATION 4-18
Working capital

CURRENT RATIO

A second measure of short-term debt-paying ability is the **current ratio**, which is calculated by dividing current assets by current liabilities. The current ratio is a more dependable indicator of liquidity measures than working capital. Two companies with the same amount of working capital may have very different current ratios.

Illustration 4-19 (in thousands) shows the current ratio for Corus.

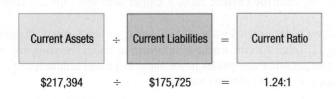

▶ ILLUSTRATION 4-19
Current ratio

This ratio tells us that on August 31, 2014, Corus had $1.24 of current assets for every dollar of current liabilities. As a general rule, a higher current ratio indicates better liquidity.

The current ratio is useful, but it does not take into account the composition of the current assets. For example, a satisfactory current ratio does not disclose the fact that a portion of current assets may be tied up in slow-moving inventory.

ACCOUNTING IN ACTION
BUSINESS INSIGHT

Generally, a higher current ratio is better as it indicates more liquidity—a company's ability to pay its short-term debts. But how high is too high? Some analysts argue that a current ratio of more than 3 or 4 is not good because it might mean that accounts receivable or inventory is building up. It could also mean that the company has too much cash and short-term investments that are not earning a greater rate of return or are not being put back into the business. But sometimes a high current ratio can be good, such as when a company is building up cash for strategic moves. For example, after Microsoft Corporation's current ratio reached 4, it paid shareholders its first dividend ever, made more acquisitions, and repurchased billions of dollars worth of shares. Afterwards, Microsoft's current ratio returned to a more moderate range of between 2 and 3. What is considered a desirable current ratio also varies by industry. For example, restaurants tend to have low current ratios because they usually have little or no accounts receivable.

Sources: "Current Ratio," Reuters Financial Glossary, retrieved from http://glossary.reuters.com/index.php/Current_Ratio; Joshua Kennon, "The Current Ratio," About.com; Bloomberg Businessweek, "Microsoft Corp.," retrieved from http://investing.businessweek.com/research/stocks/financials/ratios.asp?ticker5MSFT:US

Q Does a current ratio of less than 1 indicate that the company will have problems paying its obligations?

ACID-TEST RATIO

Alternative terminology The acid-test ratio is also known as the *quick ratio.*

The **acid-test ratio** is a measure of the company's immediate short-term liquidity. The ratio is calculated by dividing the sum of cash, short-term investments, and receivables by current liabilities. These assets are highly liquid compared with inventory and prepaid expenses. The inventory may not be readily saleable, and the prepaid expenses may not be transferable to others.

Illustration 4-20 (in thousands of dollars) shows the acid-test ratio for Corus at August 31, 2014.

▶ ILLUSTRATION **4-20**
Acid-test ratio

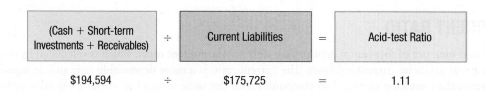

(Cash + Short-term Investments + Receivables)	÷	Current Liabilities	=	Acid-test Ratio
$194,594	÷	$175,725	=	1.11

This ratio tells us that on August 31, 2014, Corus had $1.11 of highly liquid assets for every dollar of current liabilities. As with the current ratio, a higher acid-test ratio generally indicates better liquidity.

Ratios should never be interpreted without considering certain factors: (1) general economic and industry conditions, (2) other specific financial information about the company over time, and (3) comparison with ratios for other companies in the same or related industries. We will have a longer discussion about how to interpret ratios in Chapter 18.

BEFORE YOU GO ON...DO IT **4**   **Ratios**

Selected financial information is available at December 31 for Dominic Co.

	2017	2016
Cash	$ 5,460	$ 6,645
Accounts receivable	3,505	3,470
Current assets	18,475	19,035
Current liabilities	18,860	17,305

(a) Calculate (1) working capital, (2) the current ratio, and (3) the acid-test ratio for 2016 and 2017.
(b) Indicate whether there was an improvement or deterioration in liquidity for Dominic in 2017.

Solution

(a)

	2017	2016
(1) Working capital	= $18,475 − $18,860 = $(385)	= $19,035 − $17,305 = $1,730
(2) Current ratio	= $18,475 ÷ $18,860 = 0.98 to 1	= $19,035 ÷ $17,305 = 1.1 to 1
(3) Acid-test ratio	= ($5,460 + $3,505) $18,860 = 0.48 to 1	= ($6,645 + $3,470) $17,305 = 0.58 to 1

(b) Working capital, the current ratio, and the acid-test ratio have all decreased in 2017 from 2016. This means that the company's liquidity has deteriorated during 2017.

Related exercise material: BE4–13, BE4–14, BE4–15, E4–15, and E4–16.

Action Plan
- Subtract current liabilities from current assets to calculate working capital.
- Divide current assets by current liabilities to calculate the current ratio.
- Divide cash plus accounts receivable by current liabilities to calculate the acid-test ratio.
- Recall if higher or lower ratios indicate if liquidity has improved or deteriorated.

APPENDIX 4A: WORK SHEETS

LEARNING OBJECTIVE **5**   Prepare a work sheet.

As discussed in the chapter, a work sheet is a multiple-column form that may be used in the adjustment process and in preparing financial statements. The work sheet is a working tool and it is not a permanent accounting record. It is neither a journal nor a general ledger. It is simply a device used to prepare adjusting entries and the financial statements and therefore its use is optional. The five steps for preparing a work sheet are described in the next section. They must be done in the order they are presented in.

STEPS IN PREPARING A WORK SHEET

We will use the October 31 trial balance and adjustment data for Lynk Software Services from Chapter 3 to show how to prepare a work sheet. Each step of the process is described below and is shown in Illustration 4A-1.

Step 1. Prepare a Trial Balance on the Work Sheet.

Enter all ledger accounts with balances in the account title space. Debit and credit amounts from the ledger are entered in the trial balance columns.

Step 2. Enter the Adjustments in the Adjustment Columns.

When a work sheet is used, all adjustments are entered in the adjustment columns. In entering the adjustments, relevant trial balance accounts should be used. If additional accounts are needed, they should be inserted on the lines immediately below the trial balance totals. A different letter identifies the debit and credit for each adjusting entry.

Year-end adjustments must still be recorded in the journal, but not until after the work sheet is completed and the financial statements have been prepared.

The adjustments on Lynk Software Services' work sheet in Illustration 4A-1 are the adjustments from the Lynk Software Services example in Chapter 3. They are recorded in the adjustment columns of the work sheet as follows:

(a) Debit Supplies Expense (an additional account) $1,500 for the cost of supplies used, and credit Supplies $1,500.

(b) Debit Insurance Expense (an additional account) $50 for the insurance that has expired, and credit Prepaid Insurance $50.

(c) Debit Unearned Revenue $400 for fees previously collected and now earned, and credit Service Revenue $400.

(d) Debit Accounts Receivable $200 for fees earned but not billed, and credit Service Revenue $200.

(e) Two additional accounts relating to interest are needed. Debit Interest Expense $25 for accrued interest, and credit Interest Payable $25.

(f) Debit Salaries Expense $800 for accrued salaries, and credit Salaries Payable (an additional account) $800.

(g) Two additional accounts are needed. Debit Depreciation Expense $83 for the month's depreciation, and credit Accumulated Depreciation—Equipment $83.

Note in the illustration that, after all the adjustments have been entered, the adjustment columns are totalled to prove the equality of the two adjustment column totals.

Step 3. Enter the Adjusted Balances in the Adjusted Trial Balance Columns.

The adjusted balance of an account is calculated by combining the amounts entered in the first four columns of the work sheet for each account. For example, the Prepaid Insurance account in the trial balance columns has a $600 debit balance and a $50 credit in the adjustment columns. These two amounts combine to result in a $550 debit balance in the adjusted trial balance columns. For each account on the work sheet, the amount in the adjusted trial balance columns is equal to the account balance that will appear in the ledger after the adjusting entries have been journalized and posted. The balances in these columns are the same as those in the adjusted trial balance in Illustration 4-4.

After all account balances have been entered in the adjusted trial balance columns, the columns are totalled to prove the equality of the two columns. If these columns do not agree, the financial statement columns will not balance and the financial statements will be incorrect. The total of each of these two columns in Illustration 4A-1 is $29,858.

Step 4. Enter the Adjusted Trial Balance Amounts in the Correct Financial Statement Columns.

Helpful hint Every adjusted trial balance amount must appear in one of the four statement columns.

The fourth step is to enter adjusted trial balance amounts in the income statement or balance sheet columns of the work sheet. Balance sheet accounts are entered in the correct balance sheet debit and credit columns. For instance, Cash is entered in the balance sheet debit column and Notes Payable is entered in the credit column. Accumulated Depreciation is entered in the credit column because it has a credit balance.

Because the work sheet does not have columns for the statement of owner's equity, the balance in Owner's Capital is entered in the balance sheet credit column. In addition, the balance in the Owner's Drawings account is entered in the balance sheet debit column because it is an owner's equity account with a debit balance.

The amounts in revenue and expense accounts such as Service Revenue and Salaries Expense are entered in the correct income statement columns. The last four columns of Illustration 4A-1 show where each account is entered.

▶ ILLUSTRATION 4A-1
Preparing a work sheet—Steps 1 to 5

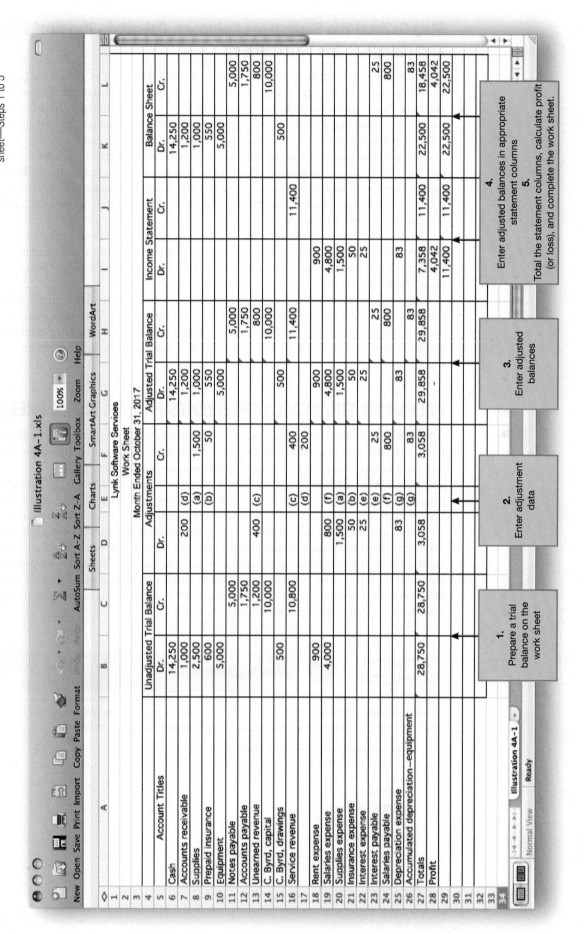

Step 5. Total the Statement Columns, Calculate the Profit (or Loss), and Complete the Work Sheet.

Each of the financial statement columns must be totalled. The profit or loss for the period is then found by calculating the difference between the totals of the two income statement columns. If total credits are more than total debits, profit has resulted. In such a case, as shown in Illustration 4A-1, the word "profit" is inserted in the account title space. The amount is then entered in the income statement debit column so that the totals of the two income statement columns are equal.

The profit or loss must also be entered in the balance sheet columns. If there is a profit, as is the case for Lynk Software, the amount is entered in the balance sheet credit column. The credit column is used because profit increases owner's equity. It is also necessary to enter the same amount in the credit column of the balance sheet as was entered in the debit column of the income statement so the financial statement columns will balance.

Conversely, if total debits in the income statement columns are more than total credits, a loss has occurred. In such a case, the amount of the loss is entered in the income statement credit column (to balance the income statement columns) and the balance sheet debit column (because a loss decreases owner's equity).

After the profit or loss has been entered, new column totals are determined. The totals shown in the debit and credit income statement columns will now match. The totals shown in the debit and credit balance sheet columns will also match. If either the income statement columns or the balance sheet columns are not equal after the profit or loss has been entered, there is an error in the work sheet.

PREPARING FINANCIAL STATEMENTS FROM A WORK SHEET

After a work sheet has been completed, all the data required to prepare the financial statements are at hand. The income statement is prepared from the income statement columns. The balance sheet and statement of owner's equity are prepared from the balance sheet columns.

Note that the amount shown for Owner's Capital in the work sheet is the account balance before considering drawings and profit (loss). When there have been no additional investments of capital by the owner during the period, this amount is the balance at the beginning of the period.

Using a work sheet, accountants can prepare financial statements before adjusting entries have been journalized and posted. However, the completed work sheet is not a substitute for formal financial statements. Data in the financial statement columns of the work sheet are not properly arranged for statement purposes. Also, as noted earlier, the financial statement presentation for some accounts differs from their statement columns on the work sheet. A work sheet is basically an accountant's working tool. It is not given to management or other parties.

BEFORE YOU GO ON...DO IT **5** **Work Sheets**

Susan Elbe is preparing a work sheet. Explain to Susan how she should extend the following adjusted trial balance accounts to the financial statement columns of the work sheet.

Accumulated Depreciation—Equipment
B. Sykes, Drawings
Cash
Equipment
Salaries Expense
Salaries Payable
Service Revenue

(continued)

BEFORE YOU GO ON...DO IT 5   **Work Sheets** *(continued)*

Solution

Account	Work Sheet Column
Accumulated Depreciation—Equipment	Balance sheet credit column
B. Sykes, Drawings	Balance sheet debit column
Cash	Balance sheet debit column
Equipment	Balance sheet debit column
Salaries Expense	Income statement debit column
Salaries Payable	Balance sheet credit column
Service Revenue	Income statement credit column

Related exercise material: *BE4–16, *BE4–17, *E4–17, and *E4–18.

Action Plan

- Assets and drawings belong in the balance sheet debit column.
- Liabilities, capital, and contra assets belong in the balance sheet credit column.
- Revenues belong in the income statement credit column.
- Expenses belong in the income statement debit column.

APPENDIX 4B: REVERSING ENTRIES

LEARNING OBJECTIVE 6   **Prepare reversing entries.**

After the financial statements are prepared and the books are closed, it can be helpful to reverse some of the adjusting entries before recording the regular transactions of the next period. Such entries are called reversing entries. A reversing entry is made at the beginning of the next accounting period and is the exact opposite of the adjusting entry that was made in the previous period. The recording of reversing entries is an optional step in the accounting cycle.

The purpose of reversing entries is to simplify the recording of future transactions that are related to an adjusting entry. As you may recall from Chapter 3, the payment of salaries on November 10 after an adjusting entry resulted in two debits: one to Salaries Payable and the other to Salaries Expense. With reversing entries, the entire later payment can be debited to Salaries Expense. You do not have to remember what has gone on before. The use of reversing entries does not change the amounts reported in the financial statements. It simply makes it easier to record transactions in the next accounting period.

ACCOUNTING WITH AND WITHOUT REVERSING ENTRIES

Reversing entries are used to reverse two types of adjusting entries: accrued revenues and accrued expenses. To illustrate the optional use of reversing entries for accrued expenses, we will use the salaries expense transactions for Lynk Software Services shown in Chapters 2, 3, and 4. The transaction and adjustment data were as follows:

1. October 27 (initial salary entry): Salaries of $4,000 earned between October 16 and October 27 are paid.
2. October 31 (adjusting entry): Salaries earned for October 30 and October 31 are $800. The company will pay the employees this amount in the November 10 payroll.
3. November 10 (subsequent salary entry): Salaries paid are $4,000. Of this amount, $800 applies to accrued salaries payable and $3,200 was earned between November 1 and November 7.

The comparative entries with and without reversing entries are as follows.

When Reversing Entries Are Not Used (as in the chapter)				When Reversing Entries Are Used (as in the appendix)			
Initial Salary Entry				**Initial Salary Entry**			
Oct. 27	Salaries Expense	4,000		Oct. 27	(Same Entry)		
	Cash		4,000				
Adjusting Entry				**Adjusting Entry**			
31	Salaries Expense	800		31	(Same Entry)		
	Salaries Payable		800				
Closing Entry				**Closing Entry**			
31	Income Summary	4,800		31	(Same Entry)		
	Salaries Expense		4,800				
Reversing Entry				**Reversing Entry**			
Nov. 1	No reversing entry is made.			Nov. 1	Salaries Payable	800	
					Salaries Expense		800
Subsequent Salary Entry				**Subsequent Salary Entry**			
10	Salaries Payable	800		10	Salaries Expense	4,000	
	Salaries Expense	3,200			Cash		4,000
	Cash		4,000				

The first three entries are the same whether or not reversing entries are used. The last two entries are different. The November 1 reversing entry eliminates the $800 balance in Salaries Payable that was created by the October 31 adjusting entry. The reversing entry also creates an $800 credit balance in the Salaries Expense account. As you know, it is unusual for an expense account to have a credit balance. The balance is correct in this instance, though, because it anticipates that the entire amount of the first salary payment in the new accounting period will be debited to Salaries Expense. This debit will eliminate the credit balance, and the resulting debit balance in the expense account will equal the actual salaries expense in the new accounting period ($3,200 in this example).

When reversing entries are made, all cash payments of expenses can be debited to the expense account. This means that on November 10 (and every payday), Salaries Expense can be debited for the amount paid without regard to any accrued salaries payable. Being able to make the same entry each time simplifies the recording process: future transactions can be recorded as if the related adjusting entry had never been made.

The posting of the entries with reversing entries is as follows, using T accounts.

Salaries Expense					Salaries Payable			
Oct. 27 Paid	4,000				Nov. 1 Rev.	800	Oct. 31 Adj.	800
31 Adj.	800						Nov. 1 Bal.	0
Oct. 31 Bal.	4,800	Oct. 31 Clos.	4,800					
Oct. 31 Bal.	0	Nov. 1 Rev.	800					
Nov. 10 Paid	4,000							
Nov. 10 Bal.	3,200							

Lynk Software could also have used reversing entries for accrued revenues. Recall that Lynk had accrued revenues of $200, which were recorded by a debit to Accounts Receivable and credit to Service Revenue. Thus, the reversing entry on November 1 is:

A	=	L	+	OE
−200				−200

Cash flows: no effect

Nov. 1	Service Revenue	200	
	Accounts Receivable		200
	To reverse Oct. 31 accrued revenue adjusting entry.		

Later in November, when Lynk collects the accrued revenue, it debits Cash and credits Service Revenue for the full amount collected. There would be no need to refer back to the October 31 adjusting entries to see how much relates to the prior month. Thus, as shown in the previous example with accrued expenses, the recording process is simplified.

BEFORE YOU GO ON...DO IT 6 | **Reversing Entries**

Pelican Company has a note receivable with a customer. On March 31, Pelican recorded an adjusting entry to accrue $300 of interest earned on the note. On April 30, Pelican collected $400 cash from the customer for interest earned from January 1 to April 30. Record Pelican's (a) March 31 adjusting entry, (b) April 1 reversing entry, and (c) April 30 entry.

Solution

(a) Mar. 31	Interest Receivable	300	
	Interest Revenue		300
	To record accrued interest.		
(b) Apr. 1	Interest Revenue	300	
	Interest Receivable		300
	To reverse Mar. 31 adjusting entry.		
(c) Apr. 30	Cash	400	
	Interest Revenue		400
	To record interest collected.		

Related exercise material: *BE4–18, *BE4–19, *E4–15, *E4–19, and *E4–20.

Action Plan

- Adjusting entries for accrued revenues are required when revenue has been earned but not yet received in cash or recorded.
- A reversing entry is the exact opposite of the adjusting entry.
- When a reversing entry has been recorded, it is not necessary to refer to the previous adjustment when recording the subsequent receipt of cash.

Comparing IFRS and ASPE

Key Differences	International Financial Reporting Standards (IFRS)	Accounting Standards for Private Enterprises (ASPE)
Statement name	Use "statement of financial position" but "balance sheet" is allowed.	Use "balance sheet" but "statement of financial position" is allowed.
Classification of assets	May group together property, plant, and equipment; intangibles; goodwill; and long-term investments under "non-current assets."	Typically do not use the subheading "non-current assets."
Order of presentation	May present assets, liabilities, and shareholders' equity in reverse order of liquidity.	Typically present assets and liabilities in order of liquidity.

Demonstration Problem

At the end of its first month of operations, Paquet Virtual Answering Service has the following unadjusted trial balance, with the accounts presented in alphabetical order rather than in financial statement order:

PAQUET VIRTUAL ANSWERING SERVICE
Trial Balance
August 31, 2017

	Debit	Credit
Accounts payable		$ 2,400
Accounts receivable	$ 2,800	
Accumulated depreciation—building		500
Accumulated depreciation—equipment		1,000
Advertising expense	400	
Building	150,000	
Cash	5,400	
Depreciation expense	1,500	
Equipment	60,000	
Insurance expense	200	
Interest expense	350	
Interest payable		1,350
Land	50,000	
Long-term debt investments	15,000	
Long-term equity investments	7,000	
Mortgage payable		140,000
Prepaid insurance	2,200	
R. Paquet, capital		155,000
R. Paquet, drawings	1,000	
Rent revenue		700
Salaries expense	3,200	
Service revenue		5,000
Short-term investments	4,800	
Supplies	1,000	
Supplies expense	300	
Utilities expense	800	
Totals	$305,950	$305,950

Instructions

(a) Calculate the profit or loss for the month.

(b) Calculate owner's equity at August 31, 2017.

(c) Prepare a classified balance sheet for Paquet Virtual Answering Service at August 31, 2017. Assume that $5,000 of the mortgage payable is due over the next year.

(d) Journalize the closing entries.

(e) Create T accounts for Income Summary and R. Paquet, Capital, and post the closing entries.

(f) Prepare a post-closing trial balance.

(g) Calculate working capital, current ratio, and acid-test ratio.

SOLUTION TO DEMONSTRATION PROBLEM

(a) Profit (loss) = Revenue − expenses

$$= \$700 + \$5,000 - \$400 - \$1,500 - \$200 - \$350 - \$3,200 - \$300 - \$800$$
$$= \$(1,050)$$

(b) Owner's equity at August 31, 2017 = Opening capital − loss − drawings

$$= \$155,000 - \$1,050 - \$1,000$$
$$= \$152,950$$

(c)

PAQUET VIRTUAL ANSWERING SERVICE
Balance Sheet
August 31, 2017

Assets

Current assets			
Cash			$ 5,400
Short-term investments			4,800
Accounts receivable			2,800
Prepaid insurance			2,200
Supplies			1,000
Total current assets			16,200
Long-term investments			
Equity investments		$ 7,000	
Debt investments		15,000	
Total long-term investments			22,000
Property, plant, and equipment			
Land		50,000	
Building	$150,000		
Less: Accumulated depreciation	500	149,500	
Equipment	60,000		
Less: Accumulated depreciation	1,000	59,000	258,500
Total assets			$296,700

Liabilities and Owner's Equity

Current liabilities		
Accounts payable		$ 2,400
Interest payable		1,350
Current portion of mortgage payable		5,000
Total current liabilities		8,750
Non-current liabilities		
Mortgage payable		135,000
Total liabilities		143,750
Owner's equity		
R. Paquet, capital		152,950
Total liabilities and owner's equity		$296,700

ACTION PLAN

- Identify which accounts are balance sheet accounts and which are income statement accounts.
- If revenues are more than expenses, this results in a profit; if expenses are more than revenues, this results in a loss.
- In preparing a classified balance sheet, know the contents of each section.
- In journalizing closing entries, remember that there are four entries. Revenues and expenses are closed to the Income Summary account; the Income Summary account and the drawings account are closed to Owner's Capital.
- Always check your work. Make sure the balance in Income Summary equals profit before closing the Income Summary account. Make sure that the balance in the Owner's Capital account after posting the closing entries equals the amount reported on the balance sheet.
- In preparing a post-closing trial balance, put the accounts in financial statement order. Remember that all temporary accounts will have a zero balance and do not need to be included.
- Use the formulas to calculate ratios.

(d)

			Debit	Credit
Aug. 31	Service Revenue		5,000	
	Rent Revenue		700	
	Income Summary			5,700
	To close revenue accounts.			
	Income Summary		6,750	
	Advertising Expense			400
	Depreciation Expense			1,500
	Insurance Expense			200
	Interest Expense			350
	Salaries Expense			3,200
	Supplies Expense			300
	Utilities Expense			800
	To close expense accounts.			
31	R. Paquet, Capital		1,050	
	Income Summary			1,050
	To close Income Summary.			
31	R. Paquet, Capital		1,000	
	R. Paquet, Drawings			1,000
	To close drawings.			

(e)

Income Summary					R. Paquet, Capital		
Clos.	6,750	Clos.	5,700			Bal.	155,000
Bal.	1,050				Clos.	1,050	
		Clos.	1,050		Clos.	1,000	
		Bal.	0			Bal.	152,950

(f)

PAQUET VIRTUAL ANSWERING SERVICE
Post-Closing Trial Balance
August 31, 2017

	Debit	Credit
Cash	$ 5,400	
Short-term investments	4,800	
Accounts receivable	2,800	
Prepaid insurance	2,200	
Supplies	1,000	
Long-term equity investments	7,000	
Long-term debt investments	15,000	
Land	50,000	
Building	150,000	
Accumulated depreciation—building		$ 500
Equipment	60,000	
Accumulated depreciation—equipment		1,000
Accounts payable		2,400
Interest payable		1,350
Mortgage payable		140,000
R. Paquet, capital		152,950
Totals	$298,200	$298,200

(g)

(1)	Working capital = Current assets − Current liabilities	= $16,200 − $8,750 = $7,450
(2)	Current ratio = Current assets ÷ Current liabilities	= $16,200 ÷ $8,750 = 1.85 to 1
(3)	Acid-test ratio (Cash + Short-term investments = $\dfrac{\text{+ Accounts receivable)}}{\text{Current liabilities}}$	= $\dfrac{(\$5,400 + \$4,800 + \$2,800)}{\$8,750}$ = 1.49 to 1

▶ Summary of Learning Objectives

1. **Prepare closing entries and a post-closing trial balance.** At the end of an accounting period, the temporary account balances (revenue, expense, Income Summary, and Owner's Drawings) are transferred to the Owner's Capital account by journalizing and posting closing entries. Separate entries are made to close revenues and expenses to Income Summary; then Income Summary to Owner's Capital; and, finally, Owner's Drawings to Owner's Capital. The temporary accounts begin the new period with a zero balance and the Owner's Capital account is updated to show its end-of-period balance. A post-closing trial balance has the balances in permanent accounts (i.e., balance sheet accounts) that are carried forward to the next accounting period. The purpose of this balance, as with other trial balances, is to prove the equality of these account balances.

2. **Explain the steps in the accounting cycle including optional steps and the preparation of correcting entries.** The steps in the accounting cycle are (1) analyze business transactions, (2) journalize the transactions, (3) post to ledger accounts, (4) prepare a trial balance, (5) journalize and post adjusting entries, (6) prepare an adjusted trial balance, (7) prepare financial statements, (8) journalize and post closing entries, and (9) prepare a post-closing trial balance. A work sheet may be used to help prepare adjusting entries and financial statements. Reversing entries are an optional step that may be used at the beginning of the next accounting period.

    Correcting entries are recorded whenever an error (an incorrect journal entry) is found. A correcting entry can be determined by comparing the incorrect entry with the journal entry that should have been recorded (the correct entry). The comparison will show which accounts need to be corrected and by how much. The correcting entry will correct the accounts. An equally acceptable alternative is to reverse the incorrect entry and then record the correct entry.

3. **Prepare a classified balance sheet.** In a classified balance sheet, assets are classified as current assets; long-term investments; property, plant, and equipment; intangible assets; and goodwill. Liabilities are classified as either current or non-current. Current assets are assets that are expected to be realized within one year of the balance sheet date. Current liabilities are liabilities that are expected to be paid from current assets within one year of the balance sheet date. The classified balance also includes an equity section, which varies with the form of business organization.

4. **Illustrate measures used to evaluate liquidity.** One of the measures used to evaluate a company's short-term liquidity is its working capital, which is the excess of current assets over current liabilities. This can also be expressed as the current ratio (current assets ÷ current liabilities). The acid-test ratio is a measure of the company's immediate short-term liquidity and is calculated by dividing the sum of cash, short-term investments, and receivables by current liabilities.

5. **Prepare a work sheet (Appendix 4A).** A work sheet is an optional multi-column form, used to assist in preparing adjusting entries and financial statements. The steps in preparing a work sheet are (1) prepare a trial balance on the work sheet; (2) enter the adjustments in the adjustment columns; (3) enter adjusted balances in the adjusted trial balance columns; (4) enter adjusted trial balance amounts in correct financial statement columns; and (5) total the statement columns, calculate profit (or loss), and complete the work sheet.

6. **Prepare reversing entries (Appendix 4B).** Reversing entries are optional entries used to simplify bookkeeping. They are made at the beginning of the new accounting period and are the direct opposite of the adjusting entry made in the preceding period. Only accrual adjusting entries are reversed. If reversing entries are used, then subsequent cash transactions can be recorded without referring to the adjusting entries prepared at the end of the previous period.

▶ Glossary

Acid-test ratio A measure of the company's immediate short-term liquidity. (p. 192)

Classified balance sheet A balance sheet that has several classifications or sections. (p. 184)

Closing entries Entries made at the end of an accounting period to transfer the balances of temporary accounts (revenues, expenses, Income Summary, and drawings) to the permanent owner's equity account, Owner's Capital. (p. 172)

Closing the books The process of journalizing and posting closing entries to update the capital account and prepare the temporary accounts for the next period's postings. (p. 172)

Correcting entries Entries to correct errors that were made when transactions were recorded. (p. 182)

Current assets Cash and other assets that will be converted to cash, sold, or used up within one year from the balance sheet date or in the company's normal operating cycle. (p. 185)

Current liabilities Obligations that are expected to be settled within one year from the balance sheet date or in the company's normal operating cycle. (p. 187)

Current ratio A measure of short-term debt-paying ability that is determined by dividing current assets by current liabilities. (p. 191)

Goodwill The amount paid to acquire another company that exceeds the fair value of the company's net identifiable assets. (p. 187)

Income Summary A temporary account that is used in closing revenue and expense accounts. (p. 173)

Intangible assets Long-lived assets that do not have physical substance and are rights and privileges that result from ownership. They include patents, copyrights, trademarks, trade names, and licences. (p. 187)

Liquidity The ability of a company to pay obligations as they come due within the next year and to meet unexpected needs for cash. (p. 191)

Long-term investments Investments in long-term debts that management intends to hold to earn interest or in equity of other companies that management plans to hold for many years as a strategic investment. (p. 186)

Non-current assets Assets that are not expected to be converted to cash, sold, or used by the business within one year of the balance sheet date or its operating cycle. (p. 186)

Non-current liabilities Obligations that are expected to be paid after one year or longer. (p. 188)

Operating cycle The time it takes to go from starting with cash to ending with cash in producing revenues. (p. 185)

Permanent accounts Balance sheet accounts, whose balances are carried forward to the next accounting period. (p. 172)

Post-closing trial balance A list of debit and credit balances of the permanent (balance sheet) accounts after closing entries have been journalized and posted. (p. 178)

Property, plant, and equipment Long-lived tangible assets that are used in the operations of the business and are not intended for sale. They include land, buildings, equipment, and furniture. (p. 186)

Reversing entry An entry made at the beginning of the next accounting period that is the exact opposite of the adjusting entry made in the previous period. (p. 181)

Temporary accounts Revenue, expense, Income Summary, and drawings accounts, whose balances are transferred to Owner's Capital at the end of an accounting period. (p. 172)

Work sheet A multiple-column form that may be used in the adjustment process and in preparing financial statements. (p. 181)

Working capital The difference between current assets and current liabilities. (p. 191)

Note: All questions, exercises, and problems below with an asterisk (*) relate to material in Appendices 4A and 4B.

▶ Self-Study Questions

Answers are at the end of the chapter.

(LO 1) K 1. When a loss has occurred, the journal entry to close the Income Summary account is:
   (a) debit Income Summary; credit Owner's Capital.
   (b) debit Owner's Capital; credit Income Summary.
   (c) debit Income Summary; credit Owner's Drawings.
   (d) debit Owner's Drawings; credit Income Summary.

(LO 1) K 2. After the closing entries have been posted, the balance in the Owner's Capital account should equal:
   (a) the profit or loss reported on the income statement.
   (b) the opening capital balance reported on the statement of owner's equity.

   (c) the ending capital balance reported on the statement of owner's equity and balance sheet.
   (d) the opening capital balance plus any investments made by the owner during the period.

(LO 1) K 3. Which accounts will appear in the post-closing trial balance?
   (a) Assets, liabilities, and Owner's Capital
   (b) Revenues, expenses, Owner's Drawings, and Owner's Capital
   (c) Assets, liabilities, revenues, and expenses
   (d) All accounts

(LO 2) K   4. The proper order of the following steps in the accounting cycle is:
(a) prepare unadjusted trial balance, journalize transactions, post to ledger accounts, journalize and post adjusting entries.
(b) journalize transactions, prepare unadjusted trial balance, post to ledger accounts, journalize and post adjusting entries.
(c) journalize transactions, post to ledger accounts, prepare unadjusted trial balance, journalize and post adjusting entries.
(d) prepare unadjusted trial balance, journalize and post adjusting entries, journalize transactions, post to ledger accounts.

(LO 2) C   5. All of the following are required steps in the accounting cycle, except:
(a) Journalizing and posting closing entries
(b) Preparing financial statements
(c) Analyzing transactions
(d) Preparing a work sheet

(LO 2) K   6. When Zander Company purchased supplies worth $500, it incorrectly recorded a credit to Supplies for $5,000 and a debit to Cash for $5,000. Before correcting this error:
(a) Cash is overstated and Supplies is overstated.
(b) Cash is understated and Supplies is understated.
(c) Cash is understated and Supplies is overstated.
(d) Cash is overstated and Supplies is understated.

(LO 2) AP   7. Cash of $100 is received at the time a service is provided. The transaction is journalized and posted as a debit to Accounts Receivable of $100 and a credit to Service Revenue of $100. The correcting entry is:

(a) Accounts Receivable	100	
Service Revenue		100
(b) Service Revenue	100	
Accounts Receivable		100
(c) Cash	100	
Service Revenue		100
(d) Cash	100	
Accounts Receivable		100

(LO 3) K   8. Which of the following statements about classifying assets is *correct*?
(a) Supplies are not current assets and should be included as part of property, plant, and equipment on the balance sheet.

(b) Current assets normally are cash and other assets that will be converted to cash, sold, or used up within one year from the balance sheet date.
(c) Some companies use a period shorter than one year to classify assets as current because they have an operating cycle that is shorter than one year.
(d) Prepaid expenses are considered non-current assets because they are intangible assets.

(LO 3) K   9. Non-current liabilities:
(a) are obligations that are expected to be paid before one year from the balance sheet date.
(b) cannot be called long-term liabilities.
(c) are sometimes listed on the balance sheet before current liabilities, if the company is following International Financial Reporting Standards.
(d) include accounts payable, salaries payable, and interest payable.

(LO 4) AP   10. A company reports current assets of $15,000 and current liabilities of $10,000. Its current ratio is:
(a) $5,000.
(b) 67%.
(c) 1.5:1.
(d) unknown without information about the amount of cash, short-term investments, and receivables, which is needed to calculate the ratio.

(LO 5) K *11. In a work sheet, profit is entered in the following columns:
(a) income statement (Dr.) and balance sheet (Dr.).
(b) income statement (Cr.) and balance sheet (Dr.).
(c) income statement (Dr.) and balance sheet (Cr.).
(d) income statement (Cr.) and balance sheet (Cr.).

(LO 6) AP *12. On December 31, 2017, Mott Company correctly made an adjusting entry to recognize $2,000 of accrued salaries payable. On January 8 of the next year, total salaries of $3,400 were paid. Assuming the correct reversing entry was made on January 1, the entry on January 8 will result in a credit to Cash of $3,400, and the following debit(s):
(a) Salaries Expense $3,400.
(b) Salaries Payable $1,400, and Salaries Expense $2,000.
(c) Salaries Payable $2,000, and Salaries Expense $1,400.
(d) Salaries Payable $3,400.

▶ Questions

(LO 1) C   1. What are permanent and temporary accounts? What is the relationship between them?

(LO 1) C   2. What are the two reasons for recording closing entries?

(LO 1) C   3. What is the purpose of using an Income Summary account? What types of summary data are posted to this account?

(LO 1, 2) C   4. Kathleen thinks that, after the financial statements have been prepared, it is necessary to prepare and post closing entries before starting to record transactions for the next accounting period. Explain to Kathleen why this is not always correct.

(LO 1) K   5. What are the content and purpose of a post-closing trial balance?

(LO 2)C　6. Balpreet thinks that analyzing business transactions is an optional step in the accounting cycle. Explain if this is correct or not.

(LO 2)C　7. Explain the differences between the three trial balances used in the accounting cycle and why it is important to prepare all three.

(LO 2)K　8. Which steps in the accounting cycle may be done daily? Which steps are done on a periodic basis (monthly, quarterly, or annually)? Which steps are usually done only at the company's fiscal year end?

(LO 2)C　9. How do correcting entries differ from adjusting entries?

(LO 2)C　10. Cristobal thinks that correcting entries are unnecessary. He suggests that, if an incorrect journal entry is found, it should be erased or removed and then the correct entry can be recorded in its place. Explain to Cristobal why this is not the correct thing to do.

(LO 2)C　11. Describe how to determine which accounts, and what amounts, to include in a correcting entry.

(LO 3)C　12. What are current assets and current liabilities? How are they different from non-current assets and non-current liabilities?

(LO 3)C　13. What is meant by the term "operating cycle"?

(LO 3)K　14. What standard classifications are used in preparing a classified balance sheet?

(LO 3)C　15. A Canadian company has the following current assets listed in alphabetical order: accounts receivable, cash, inventory, prepaid insurance, short-term investments, and supplies. In what order will they appear on the company's balance sheet and why?

(LO 3)C　16. What is the difference between long-term investments and property, plant, and equipment?

(LO 3)K　17. What are intangible assets and goodwill? Where are they reported on a classified balance sheet?

(LO 4)C　18. What is liquidity? Identify one measure of liquidity.

(LO 4)C　19. What factors need to be considered when interpreting ratios?

(LO 4)C　20. What are the differences between the current ratio and the acid-test ratio?

(LO 5)C *21. How is profit or loss calculated on a work sheet? How is this number entered on the work sheet if the company has profit? How is it entered if the company has a loss?

(LO 5)K *22. A work sheet is a permanent accounting record and it is a required step in the accounting cycle." Do you agree? Explain.

(LO 5)K *23. Why is it necessary to prepare formal financial statements if all the data are in the statement columns of the work sheet?

(LO 6)C *24. What are reversing entries and how are they related to adjusting entries? When are they prepared?

(LO 6)C *25. How is it helpful to use reversing entries? Explain if the use of reversing entries changes the amounts reported in the financial statements or not.

▶ Brief Exercises

Identify accounts to be closed. (LO 1) K

BE4–1　The following accounts were included on a company's adjusted trial balance. In the blank space, identify which accounts should be closed (C) or not closed (NC) at the year end.

_____ Accounts payable	_____ Notes payable
_____ Accounts receivable	_____ Rent revenue
_____ Depreciation expense	_____ Prepaid expenses
_____ Operating expenses	_____ Equipment
_____ Unearned revenue	_____ S. Young, drawings
_____ Interest expense	_____ Accumulated depreciation
_____ S. Young, capital	_____ Supplies

Prepare closing entries. (LO 1) AP

BE4–2　The income statement for Arbor Green Golf Club for the year ended July 31 shows Service Revenue of $16,400; Salary Expense $8,400; Rent Expense $2,500; profit $5,500; T. Arid, Capital $47,000; and T. Arid, Drawings $0. Prepare the closing entries.

Prepare and post closing entries. (LO 1) AP

BE4–3　Rizzo Company has the following year-end account balances on November 30, 2017: Service Revenue $38,500; Insurance Expense $2,750; Rent Expense $8,000; Supplies Expense $1,500; L. Wilfrid, Capital $42,000; and L. Wilfrid, Drawings $29,000. (a) Prepare the closing entries. (b) Calculate the balance in L. Wilfrid, Capital after the closing entries are posted.

BE4–4 The adjusted trial balance for Mosquera Golf Club at its October 31, 2017, year end included the following:

Prepare closing entries.
(LO 1) AP

	Debit	Credit
Cash	$ 7,500	
Prepaid expenses	3,000	
Equipment	65,000	
Accumulated depreciation—equipment		$ 15,000
Accounts payable		14,000
Unearned revenue		1,500
N. Mosquera, capital		65,000
N. Mosquera, drawings	45,000	
Service revenue		130,000
Maintenance expense	23,000	
Rent expense	10,000	
Salaries expense	72,000	

Prepare closing entries.

BE4–5 Refer to the information in BE4–4 for Mosquera Golf Club. Prepare a post-closing trial balance.

Prepare post-closing trial balance. (LO 1) AP

BE4–6 The required steps in the accounting cycle are listed below in random order. List the steps in the correct order by writing the numbers 1 to 9 in the blank spaces.

List steps in accounting cycle. (LO 2) K

(a) _____ Prepare a post-closing trial balance.
(b) _____ Prepare an adjusted trial balance.
(c) _____ Analyze business transactions.
(d) _____ Prepare a trial balance.
(e) _____ Journalize the transactions.
(f) _____ Journalize and post the closing entries.
(g) _____ Prepare the financial statements.
(h) _____ Journalize and post the adjusting entries.
(i) _____ Post to the ledger accounts.

BE4–7 At Hébert Company, the following errors were discovered after the transactions had been journalized and posted:

Identify impact of errors. (LO 2) AP

1. A collection of cash on account from a customer for $750 was recorded as a debit to Cash of $750 and a credit to Service Revenue of $750.
2. An invoice to a customer for $600 of services on account was recorded as a $600 debit to Accounts Receivable and a $600 credit to Unearned Revenue.
3. A $500 cash payment to the owner, Roch Hébert, was recorded as a debit to Salaries Expense of $500 and a credit to Cash of $500.

Prepare the correcting entries.

BE4–8 The following are the major balance sheet classifications.

Classify accounts on the balance sheet. (LO 3) K

Current assets (CA)   Current liabilities (CL)
Long-term investments (LTI)   Long-term liabilities (LTL)
Property, plant, and equipment (PPE)   Owner's equity (OE)
Intangible assets (IA)

Classify each of the following accounts taken from Faust Company's balance sheet.

_____ Accounts payable   _____ Accumulated depreciation—equipment
_____ Accounts receivable   _____ Buildings
_____ Cash   _____ Land (in use)
_____ L. Dawn, capital   _____ Notes payable (due in 2 years)
_____ Patents   _____ Supplies
_____ Salaries payable   _____ Equipment
_____ Merchandise inventory   _____ Prepaid expenses
_____ Short-term investments (to be
        sold in 7 months)

Prepare current assets section of balance sheet and classify other accounts. (LO 3) AP

BE4–9 The December 31, 2017, adjusted trial balance of Darius Company includes the following accounts:

Accounts receivable	$14,500	Patents	$ 3,900
Prepaid insurance	1,600	Unearned revenue	2,900
Goodwill	9,250	Cash	16,400
Supplies	4,200	Short-term investments	8,200
Vehicles	22,500	Merchandise inventory	9,000
Notes receivable (due February 1, 2019)	5,500		

(a) Determine which accounts are current assets and prepare the current assets section of the balance sheet as at December 31, 2017, with the accounts in order of decreasing liquidity.

(b) For each account that is not classified as a current asset, indicate how it would be classified on the balance sheet.

Classify balance sheet accounts. (LO 3) AP

BE4–10 The adjusted trial balance of Kaid Company includes the following accounts: Accounts Receivable $12,500, Prepaid Insurance $3,600, Cash $4,100, Supplies $5,200, and Short-Term Investments $6,700. Prepare the current assets section of the balance sheet, listing the accounts in proper sequence.

Classify balance sheet accounts. (LO 3) AP

BE4–11 The adjusted trial balance of Kaid Company includes the following accounts: Unearned Revenue $2,500, Mortgage Payable $50,800 (of which $5,000 is due in 6 months), Accounts Payable $8,500, Notes Payable $6,700 due in 10 months, and Interest Payable $750. Prepare the current liabilities section of the balance sheet.

Classify balance sheet accounts. (LO 3) AP

BE4–12 The December 31, 2017, adjusted trial balance of Odom Company includes the following accounts:

Supplies	$ 2,900	Land	$ 85,000
Notes payable (due March 1, 2019)	28,000	Buildings	125,000
Accumulated depreciation—equipment	25,800	Patents	12,300
Equipment	43,000	Goodwill	5,520
Accumulated depreciation—building	37,400	Merchandise inventory	14,000
Notes receivable (due April 1, 2018)	7,800		

Determine which accounts are non-current assets and prepare the non-current assets section of the balance sheet as at December 31, 2017.

Calculate working capital and current ratio and compare liquidity ratio measures. (LO 4) K

BE4–13 On December 31, 2017, Big River Company had $1 million of current assets and $900,000 of current liabilities. On the same day, Small Fry Company had $200,000 of current assets and $100,000 of current liabilities. Calculate the working capital and current ratio for both companies and compare the results. Which liquidity measure is more relevant?

Comment on liquidity. (LO 4) (AP)

BE4–14 Selected financial information is available for Jones Co.

	Year 1	Year 2	Year 3
Current assets	95,000	150,000	200,000
Current liabilities	65,000	100,000	95,000

(a) Calculate the working capital for Jones Co. for the three years

(b) Calculate the current ratio of Jones Co. for the three years and comment on it.

Calculate working capital, current ratio, and acid-test ratio, and comment on liquidity. (LO 4) AP

BE4–15 Selected financial information is available at July 31 for Drew Co.

	2017	2016
Cash and accounts receivable	$22,680	$20,430
Current assets	35,100	33,510
Current liabilities	24,460	24,800

(a) Calculate (1) working capital, (2) the current ratio, and (3) the acid-test ratio for 2016 and 2017.

(b) Indicate whether there was an improvement or deterioration in liquidity for Drew in 2017.

Complete work sheet. (LO 5) AP

*BE4–16 The accountant for Coulombe Company is almost finished preparing the work sheet for the year ended July 31, 2017. The totals of the accounts in the income statement and balance sheet columns are presented below. Calculate the profit or loss, write this number in the proper columns, and calculate the final totals for these columns. Clearly indicate whether the company had a profit or a loss.

	Income Statement		Balance Sheet	
	Dr.	Cr.	Dr.	Cr.
Totals	75,000	95,500	191,000	170,500
Profit or loss	———	———	———	———
Totals	≡≡≡	≡≡≡	≡≡≡	≡≡≡

*BE4–17 The accountant for Orange Line Company is almost finished preparing the work sheet for the year ended August 31, 2017. The totals of the accounts in the income statement and balance sheet columns are presented below. Calculate the profit or loss, write this in the proper columns, and calculate the final totals for these columns. Clearly indicate whether the company had a profit or loss.

Complete work sheet. (LO 5) AP

	Income Statement		Balance Sheet	
	Dr.	Cr.	Dr.	Cr.
Totals	53,875	43,425	55,550	66,000
Profit or loss	———	———	———	———
Totals	≡≡≡	≡≡≡	≡≡≡	≡≡≡

*BE4–18 At December 31, 2017, Giselle Company made an accrued expense adjusting entry of $1,700 for salaries. On January 4, 2018, it paid salaries of $3,000: $1,700 for December salaries and $1,300 for January salaries. (a) Prepare the December 31 adjusting entry. (b) Prepare the December 31 closing entry for salaries. (c) Prepare the January 1 reversing entry and the January 4 journal entry to record the payment of salaries. (d) Indicate the balances in Salaries Payable and Salaries Expense after posting these entries.

Prepare and post adjusting, closing, reversing, and subsequent entries. (LO 6) AP

*BE4–19 At December 31, 2017, Giselle Company had a five-month, 5%, $90,000 note receivable that was issued on October 1, 2017. Interest and principal are payable at maturity on March 1, 2018. (a) Prepare the December 31, 2017, adjusting entry for accrued interest. (b) Prepare the January 1, 2018, reversing entry. (c) Prepare the March 1, 2018, entry to record the receipt of cash at maturity for the note.

Prepare adjusting, reversing, and subsequent entries. (LO 6) AP

▶ Exercises

E4–1 Selected accounts for Lee's Salon at December 31, 2017 are presented below.

Prepare and post closing entries. (LO 1) AP

A. Lee, Capital			A. Lee, Drawings			Revenues		
Dr.		Cr.	Dr.		Cr.	Dr.		Cr.
		30,000	2,000					50,000

Salaries Expense			Rent Expense			Supplies Expense		
Dr.		Cr.	Dr.		Cr.	Dr.		Cr.
21,000			6,000			7,000		

Instructions

(a) Prepare closing entries to close the accounts.
(b) Post the entries.

E4–2 Selected T accounts for Victoire Esthetics on August 31, 2017, are as follows:

Prepare a statement of owner's equity and closing entries. (LO 1) AP

B. Victoire, Capital					B. Victoire, Drawings			
		Aug. 1	Bal.	9,000	Aug. 15		2,200	
		10		2,000	25		2,500	
		Aug. 31	Bal.	11,000	Aug. 31	Bal.	4,700	

Income Summary				
Aug. 31	8,000	Aug. 31		15,000
		Aug. 31	Bal.	7,000

Instructions

(a) Prepare a statement of owner's equity for August 2017.

(b) Prepare entries to close the Income Summary and drawings accounts. Post these entries.

Prepare closing entries.
(LO 1) AP

E4–3 At the end of its fiscal year, the adjusted trial balance of Donatello Company is as follows:

DONATELLO COMPANY Adjusted Trial Balance July 31, 2017		
	Debit	Credit
Cash	$ 4,650	
Accounts receivable	11,400	
Prepaid rent	500	
Supplies	750	
Debt investments	8,000	
Equipment	19,950	
Accumulated depreciation—equipment		$ 5,700
Patents	18,300	
Accounts payable		4,245
Interest payable		750
Unearned revenue		2,050
Notes payable (due on July 1, 2019)		45,000
B. Donatello, capital		28,285
B. Donatello, drawings	16,500	
Service revenue		75,000
Interest revenue		320
Depreciation expense	2,850	
Interest expense	3,000	
Rent expense	18,550	
Salaries expense	36,050	
Supplies expense	20,850	
	$161,350	$161,350

Instructions

Prepare the closing entries.

Prepare closing entries.
(LO 1) AP

E4–4 An alphabetical list of the adjusted account balances (all accounts have normal balances) at August 31, 2017, for Alpine Bowling Lanes is as follows:

Accounts payable	$ 8,200	Notes payable	$25,000
Accounts receivable	10,980	Prepaid insurance	820
Accumulated depreciation—equipment	18,600	Service revenue	35,900
Cash	17,940	Supplies	740
Depreciation expense	9,300	Supplies expense	7,845
Equipment	83,545	T. Williams, capital	85,500
Insurance expense	4,100	T. Williams, drawings	18,500
Interest expense	1,500	Unearned revenue	980

Instructions

Prepare the closing entries at August 31, 2017.

E4–5 The adjusted trial balance for Hercules Company is presented below.

Prepare and post closing entries and prepare post-closing trial balance. (LO 1) AP

HERCULES COMPANY
Adjusted Trial Balance
August 31, 2017

Account Titles	Debit	Credit
Cash	$10,900	
Accounts receivable	6,200	
Equipment	10,600	
Accumulated depreciation—equipment		$ 5,400
Accounts payable		2,800
Unearned revenue		1,200
S. Strong, capital		31,700
S. Strong, drawings	12,000	
Service revenue		42,400
Rent revenue		6,100
Depreciation expense	2,700	
Salaries expense	37,100	
Utilities expense	10,100	
	$89,600	$89,600

Instructions

(a) Prepare the closing entries.
(b) Prepare T accounts for the accounts affected by the closing entries. Post the closing entries.
(c) Prepare a post-closing trial balance at August 31, 2017.

E4–6 The adjusted trial balance for Victoria Lee Company for the year ended June 30, 2017, follows.

Prepare closing entries and prepare post-closing trial balance. (LO 1) AP

VICTORIA LEE COMPANY
Adjusted Trial Balance
June 30, 2017

Account Titles	Debit	Credit
Cash	$ 3,712	
Accounts receivable	3,904	
Supplies	480	
Accounts payable		$ 1,382
Unearned revenue		160
Salaries payable		460
V. Lee, capital		5,760
V. Lee, drawings	550	
Service revenue		4,300
Salaries expense	1,260	
Miscellaneous expense	256	
Supplies expense	1,900	
	$12,062	$12,062

Instructions

(a) Prepare closing entries at June 30, 2017.
(b) Prepare a post-closing trial balance.

Prepare adjusting and
closing entries.
(LO 1) AP

E4–7 The unadjusted trial balance for Garden Designs at its year end, April 30, 2017, is as follows:

GARDEN DESIGNS
Trial Balance
April 30, 2017

	Debit	Credit
Cash	$11,430	
Accounts receivable	8,780	
Prepaid rent	4,875	
Equipment	24,000	
Accumulated depreciation—equipment		$ 6,000
Accounts payable		5,650
Notes payable		12,000
Unearned revenue		1,500
T. Muzyka, capital		25,960
T. Muzyka, drawings	4,150	
Service revenue		15,400
Salaries expense	9,865	
Interest expense	660	
Depreciation expense	2,750	
	$66,510	$66,510

Additional information:

1. $500 of the unearned revenue has been earned by April 30, 2017.
2. The equipment has an estimated useful life of eight years.
3. Interest on the note payable is due on the first day of each month for the previous month's interest. The note payable has a 6% annual interest rate.

Instructions

(a) Graden Designs prepares adjusting entries monthly. Prepare adjusting entries for the month ended April 30, 2017.
(b) Post the adjusting entries.
(c) Prepare closing entries for the year ended.

Apply the steps in the
accounting cycle.
(LO 1, 2) AP

E4–8 Tim Sasse started Sasse Roof Repairs on April 2, 2017, by investing $4,000 cash in the business. During April, the following transactions occurred:

Apr. 6 Purchased supplies for $1,500 cash.
    15 Repaired a roof for a customer and collected $600 cash.
    25 Received $2,200 cash in advance from a customer for roof repairs to his house and garage.

On April 30, 2017, the following information was available:

1. Earned but unbilled revenue at April 30 was $600.
2. There is $800 of supplies on hand.
3. Of the $2,200 received on April 25, the company has earned $800 by completing repairs to the garage roof.

Instructions

(a) Journalize the transactions.
(b) Post to the ledger accounts. (Use T accounts.)
(c) Journalize and post any required adjusting entries.
(d) Prepare an adjusted trial balance.
(e) Assuming the company closes its books on a monthly basis, journalize and post closing entries.

E4–9 The unadjusted trial balance for Swift Creek Engineering at its year end, December 31, 2017, is as follows:

Prepare adjusting and closing entries. (LO 1, 2) AP

SWIFT CREEK ENGINEERING Trial Balance December 31, 2017		
	Debit	Credit
Cash	$ 8,450	
Accounts receivable	6,250	
Supplies	5,260	
Prepaid insurance	7,440	
Notes receivable	12,000	
Equipment	27,800	
Accumulated depreciation—equipment		$ 8,340
Accounts payable		4,560
H. Duguay, capital		34,900
H. Duguay, drawings	53,500	
Service revenue		112,300
Salaries expense	39,400	
	$160,100	$160,100

Additional information:

1. Revenue of $10,440 was earned but unrecorded and uncollected as at December 31, 2017.
2. On June 1, the company purchased a one-year insurance policy.
3. Depreciation on the equipment for 2017 is $2,780.
4. A count on December 31, 2017, showed $1,750 of supplies on hand.
5. The four-month, 4% note receivable was issued on October 1, 2017. Interest and principal are payable on the maturity date.

Instructions

(a) Prepare adjusting entries for the year ended December 31, 2017.
(b) Post the adjusting entries.
(c) Prepare closing entries.

E4–10 Choi Company has an inexperienced accountant. During the first two weeks on the job, the accountant made the following errors in journalizing transactions. All incorrect entries were posted.

Prepare correcting entries. (LO 2) AP

1. A payment on account of $750 to a creditor was debited $570 to Accounts Payable and credited $570 to Cash.
2. The purchase of supplies on account for $560 was not recorded.
3. A $500 withdrawal of cash for L. Choi's personal use was debited $500 to Salaries Expense and credited $500 to Cash.
4. Received $700 cash from a customer on account. Cash was debited $700 and Service Revenue was credited $700.
5. A customer was billed $350 for services provided. Accounts Receivable was debited $350 and Unearned Revenue was credited $350.

Instructions

Prepare the correcting entries.

E4–11 The owner of D'Addario Company has been doing all of the company's bookkeeping. When the accountant arrived to do the year-end adjusting entries, she found the following items:

Prepare correcting entries. (LO 2) AP

1. A payment of salaries of $700 was debited to Equipment and credited to Cash, both for $700.
2. The investment of $2,000 of cash by the owner, Toni D'Addario, was debited to Short-Term Investments and credited to Cash, both for $2,000.
3. The collection of an account receivable of $1,000 was debited to Cash and credited to Accounts Receivable, both for $1,000.
4. The company had purchased $440 of supplies on account. This entry was correctly recorded. When the account was paid, Supplies was debited $440 and Cash was credited $440.
5. Equipment costing $3,500 was purchased on account. Equipment Expense was debited and Accounts Payable was credited, both for $3,500.

Instructions

(a) Correct any errors by reversing the incorrect entry and preparing the correct entry.

(b) Correct any errors without reversing the incorrect entry.

Prepare financial statements.
(LO 3) AP

E4–12 The following items were taken from the financial statements of J. Parra Company on December 31, 2017. (All amounts are in thousands.)

Long-term debt	$ 1,000	Accumulated depreciation—equipment	$ 5,655
Prepaid insurance	880	Accounts payable	1,444
Equipment	11,500	Notes payable (due after 2018)	400
Long-term investments	264	J. Parra, capital	12,955
Short-term investments	3,690	Accounts receivable	1,696
Notes payable (due in 2018)	500	Merchandise inventory	1,256
Cash	2,668		

Instructions

Prepare a classified balance sheet in good form as at December 31, 2017.

Prepare financial statements.
(LO 3) AP

E4–13 The adjusted trial balance for Donatello Company is presented in E4–3.

Instructions

(a) Prepare an income statement and statement of owner's equity for the year. Mr. Donatello invested $5,000 cash in the business during the year.

(b) Prepare a classified balance sheet at July 31, 2017.

Prepare income statements, statement of owner's equity, and classified balance sheet.
(LO 3) AN

E4–14 These financial statement items are for Basten Company at year end, July 31, 2017.

Salaries payable	$ 2,080	Notes payable (long-term)	$ 1,800
Salaries expense	48,700	Cash	14,200
Utilities expense	22,600	Accounts receivable	9,780
Equipment	34,400	Accumulated depreciation—equipment	6,000
Accounts payable	4,100	D. Basten, drawings	3,000
Service revenue	63,000	Depreciation expense	4,000
Rent revenue	8,500	D. Basten, capital (beginning of the year)	51,200

Instructions

(a) Prepare an income statement and a statement of owner's equity for the year. The owner did not make any new investments during the year.

(b) Prepare a classified balance sheet at July 31.

Prepare classified balance sheet and comment on liquidity. (LO 3, 4) AN

E4–15 Selected financial information for JPC Enterprises as at December 31, 2017, follows:

Accounts payable	$105,600	Land	$105,600
Accounts receivable	197,000	Licences	98,300
Accumulated depreciation—building	79,900	Long-term equity investments	45,800
Building	306,300	Mortgage payable	230,000
Cash	16,500	Notes payable	55,000
Goodwill	36,000	Prepaid expenses	6,900
Interest payable	16,500	Salaries payable	28,700
J. Chrowder, capital	279,400	Supplies	10,100
		Unearned revenue	27,400

Additional information:

1. All accounts have normal balances.
2. $17,250 of the mortgage payable will be paid before December 31, 2018.
3. The notes payable are payable on May 17, 2018.

Instructions

(a) Prepare a classified balance sheet.

(b) Calculate working capital, the current ratio, and the acid-test ratio.

(c) Comment on the company's liquidity.

E4–16 Indigo Books & Music Inc. ("Indigo") is Canada's largest book, gift, and specialty toy retailer, operating stores in all ten provinces and one territory in Canada and offering online sales through its *indigo.ca* website. The following data (in thousands) were taken from Indigo's financial statements:

Calculate working capital, current ratio, and acid-test ratio, and comment on liquidity. (LO 4) AN

	March 28, 2015	March 29, 2014	March 30, 2013
Cash and cash equivalents	$203,162	$157,578	$210,562
Accounts receivable	4,896	5,582	7,126
Inventories	208,395	218,979	216,533
Income tax receivable	25	—	—
Prepaid expenses	5,477	5,184	4,153
Current assets	421,955	387,323	438,374
Current liabilities	223,239	197,627	214,031

Instructions

(a) Calculate the working capital, current ratio, and acid-test ratio for each year.

(b) Discuss Indigo's liquidity on March 28, 2015, compared with the two previous years.

*E4–17 The unadjusted trial balance at April 30, 2017, and adjustment data for the month of April 2017 for Garden Designs are presented in E4–7.

Prepare work sheet. (LO 5) AP

Instructions

Prepare the work sheet for the month ended April 30, 2017.

*E4–18 The unadjusted trial balance at December 31, 2017, and the year-end adjustment data for Swift Creek Engineering are presented in E4–9.

Prepare work sheet. (LO 5) AP

Instructions

Prepare the work sheet for the year ended December 31, 2017.

*E4–19 On December 31, the unadjusted trial balance of Masters Employment Agency shows the following selected data:

Prepare and post adjusting, closing, reversing, and subsequent entries. (LO 1, 6) AP

Accounts receivable	$24,000	Cash	$ 7,600
Interest expense	7,800	Service revenue	92,000
I. Masterson, capital	48,000	Interest payable	0

Analysis shows that adjusting entries are required to (1) accrue $6,900 of service revenue, and (2) accrue $1,250 of interest expense.

Instructions

(a) Prepare and post (1) the adjusting entries and (2) the closing entries for the temporary accounts at December 31.

(b) Prepare and post reversing entries on January 1.

(c) Prepare and post the entries to record:

   1. the collection of $8,200 of service revenue (including the accrued service revenue from December 31) on January 10, and
   2. the payment of $2,235 interest on January 31 (consisting of the accrued interest from December 31 plus January's interest).

*E4–20 Rosborough Company provides property management services to a variety of companies. At its fiscal year end on April 30, 2017, adjustments were required for the following items:

Prepare adjusting and reversing entries. (LO 6) AP

1. Service revenue of $600 was earned but not recorded or collected.
2. Of the balance in the Unearned Revenue account, $250 had been earned.
3. Depreciation expense for the year ended April 30, 2017, was $4,850.
4. Interest of $545 on a note payable had accrued.
5. Prepaid insurance of $385 had expired.
6. Property taxes for the calendar year are payable every year on June 30. The company estimated property taxes for 2017 to be $3,912.

Instructions

(a) Identify the adjustments for which it could be useful to prepare reversing entries.

(b) Prepare these reversing entries on May 1, 2017.

(c) Explain why and how the reversing entries are useful for these adjustments but not for the other adjustments.

▶ Problems: Set A

Prepare closing entries, and a
post-closing trial balance.
(LO 1) AP

P4-1A The adjusted trial balance columns of the work sheet for Thao Company, owned by D. Thao, are as follows.

<table>
<tr><td colspan="5" align="center">THAO COMPANY
Work Sheet
For the Year Ended December 31, 2017</td></tr>
<tr><td rowspan="2">Account
No.</td><td rowspan="2">Account Titles</td><td colspan="2" align="center">Adjusted
Trial Balance</td></tr>
<tr><td>Dr.</td><td>Cr.</td></tr>
<tr><td>101</td><td>Cash</td><td>5,300</td><td></td></tr>
<tr><td>112</td><td>Accounts receivable</td><td>10,800</td><td></td></tr>
<tr><td>126</td><td>Supplies</td><td>1,500</td><td></td></tr>
<tr><td>130</td><td>Prepaid insurance</td><td>2,000</td><td></td></tr>
<tr><td>157</td><td>Equipment</td><td>27,000</td><td></td></tr>
<tr><td>158</td><td>Accumulated depreciation—equipment</td><td></td><td>5,600</td></tr>
<tr><td>200</td><td>Notes payable</td><td></td><td>15,000</td></tr>
<tr><td>201</td><td>Accounts payable</td><td></td><td>6,100</td></tr>
<tr><td>212</td><td>Salaries payable</td><td></td><td>2,400</td></tr>
<tr><td>230</td><td>Interest payable</td><td></td><td>600</td></tr>
<tr><td>301</td><td>D. Thao, capital</td><td></td><td>13,000</td></tr>
<tr><td>306</td><td>D. Thao, drawings</td><td>7,000</td><td></td></tr>
<tr><td>400</td><td>Service revenue</td><td></td><td>61,000</td></tr>
<tr><td>610</td><td>Advertising expense</td><td>8,400</td><td></td></tr>
<tr><td>631</td><td>Supplies expense</td><td>4,000</td><td></td></tr>
<tr><td>711</td><td>Depreciation expense</td><td>5,600</td><td></td></tr>
<tr><td>722</td><td>Insurance expense</td><td>3,500</td><td></td></tr>
<tr><td>726</td><td>Salaries expense</td><td>28,000</td><td></td></tr>
<tr><td>905</td><td>Interest expense</td><td>600</td><td></td></tr>
<tr><td></td><td>Totals</td><td>103,700</td><td>103,700</td></tr>
</table>

Instructions

(a) Prepare closing entries.
(b) Use T accounts to post the closing entries and calculate the balance in each account. Income Summary is account No. 350. (Ignore the accounts not affected by the closing entries.)
(c) Prepare a post-closing trial balance.

TAKING IT FURTHER D. Thao does not understand why the Owner's Drawings account is not closed with the expense accounts and why a separate entry is required to close this account. Please explain to D. Thao why this is necessary.

Prepare financial statements,
closing entries, and a post-
closing trial balance.
(LO 1, 3) AP

P4-2A The completed financial statement columns of the work sheet for Bray Company are available.

Instructions

(a) Prepare an income statement, a statement of owner's equity, and a classified balance sheet. L. Bray did not make any additional investments during the year.
(b) Prepare the closing entries.
(c) Post the closing entries and calculate the balance in each account. (Use T accounts.) Income Summary is account No. 350.
(d) Prepare a post-closing trial balance.

TAKING IT FURTHER L. Bray has been told that, after the closing entries have been posted, he should stop and check his work. Explain to L. Bray what he should be checking for.

BRAY COMPANY
Work Sheet
For the Year Ended December 31, 2017

Account No.	Account Titles	Income Statement Dr.	Income Statement Cr.	Balance Sheet Dr.	Balance Sheet Cr.
101	Cash			8,800	
112	Accounts receivable			10,800	
130	Prepaid insurance			2,800	
157	Equipment			24,000	
158	Accumulated depreciation—equipment				4,200
201	Accounts payable				9,000
212	Salaries payable				2,400
301	L. Bray, capital				19,500
306	L. Bray, drawings			11,000	
400	Service revenue		60,000		
622	Maintenance expense	1,700			
711	Depreciation expense	2,800			
722	Insurance expense	1,800			
726	Salaries expense	30,000			
732	Utilities expense	1,400			
	Totals	37,700	60,000	57,400	35,100
	Net income	22,300			22,300
		60,000	60,000	57,400	57,400

P4-3A The adjusted trial balance for Marine Fishing Centre is as follows:

Prepare financial statements, closing entries, and post-closing trial balance.
(LO 1, 3) AP

MARINE FISHING CENTRE
Adjusted Trial Balance
March 31, 2017

	Debit	Credit
Cash	$ 7,720	
Interest receivable	750	
Supplies	1,425	
Debt investments	30,000	
Land	46,800	
Building	186,900	
Accumulated depreciation—building		$ 31,150
Equipment	36,200	
Accumulated depreciation—equipment		18,100
Accounts payable		5,875
Interest payable		990
Unearned revenue		2,190
Notes payable ($6,000 must be paid in 2018)		66,000
R. Falkner, capital		165,300
R. Falkner, drawings	46,200	
Service revenue		124,300
Interest revenue		1,500
Depreciation expense	9,850	
Interest expense	3,960	
Insurance expense	4,500	
Salaries expense	30,000	
Supplies expense	5,700	
Utilities expense	5,400	
	$415,405	$415,405

Instructions

(a) Prepare an income statement for the year ended March 31, 2017.

(b) Prepare a statement of owner's equity. The owner, Rachael Falkner, invested $2,300 cash in the business during the year. (*Note:* The investment has been recorded and it is included in the capital account.)

(c) Prepare a classified balance sheet.

(d) Prepare closing entries.

(e) Use T accounts to post the closing entries and calculate the balance in each account. (Ignore the accounts not affected by the closing entries.)

(f) Prepare a post-closing trial balance and compare the balance in the R. Falkner, Capital account with the information in the statement of owner's equity.

TAKING IT FURTHER   What alternatives should be considered when deciding on the presentation of information in the classified balance sheet?

Prepare adjusting entries, adjusted trial balance, financial statements, and closing entries. (LO 1, 3) AP

P4–4A   The following is Elbow Cycle Repair Shop's trial balance at January 31, 2017, the company's fiscal year end:

ELBOW CYCLE REPAIR SHOP Trial Balance January 31, 2017		
	Debit	Credit
Cash	$ 3,200	
Accounts receivable	6,630	
Prepaid insurance	6,420	
Supplies	5,240	
Land	50,000	
Building	190,000	
Accumulated depreciation—building		$ 11,000
Equipment	27,000	
Accumulated depreciation—equipment		4,500
Accounts payable		6,400
Unearned revenue		21,950
Mortgage payable		182,000
H. Dude, capital		61,000
H. Dude, drawings	101,100	
Service revenue		235,550
Salaries expense	115,200	
Utilities expense	12,000	
Interest expense	5,610	
	$522,400	$522,400

Additional information:

1. The 12-month insurance policy was purchased on June 1, 2016.
2. A physical count of supplies shows $1,310 on hand on January 31, 2017.
3. The building has an estimated useful life of 50 years. The equipment has an estimated useful life of 9 years.
4. The mortgage payable has a 5% interest rate. Interest is paid on the first day of each month for the previous month's interest.
5. By January 31, 2017, $1,300 of the unearned revenue has been earned.
6. During the next fiscal year, $4,500 of the mortgage payable is to be paid.

Instructions

(a) Prepare the adjusting entries.

(b) Prepare an adjusted trial balance.

(c) Prepare an income statement, statement of owner's equity, and classified balance sheet. The owner, Henry Dude, invested $5,000 cash in the business on November 17, 2016. (The investment has been recorded and it is included in the capital account).

(d) Prepare the closing entries.

TAKING IT FURTHER   Henry Dude is concerned that he had to invest cash in the business this year. Based on the information in the financial statements, what do you suggest to Henry?

P4–5A   Lee Chang opened Lee's Window Washing on July 1, 2017. In July, the following transactions were completed:

Complete all steps in the accounting cycle. (LO 1, 2) AP

July 1	Invested $20,000 cash in the business.
1	Purchased a used truck for $25,000, paying $5,000 cash and signing a note payable for the balance.
1	Paid $2,800 on a one-year insurance policy, effective July 1.
5	Billed customers $3,300 for cleaning services.
12	Purchased supplies for $2,100 on account.
18	Paid $3,000 for employee salaries.
25	Billed customers $8,900 for cleaning services.
28	Collected $3,300 from customers billed on July 5.
31	Paid $550 for fuel for the month on the truck.
31	Withdrew $2,600 cash for personal use.

Instructions

(a) Journalize and post the July transactions to the general ledger.
(b) Prepare a trial balance at July 31.
(c) Journalize and post the following July 31 adjustments:
   1. Earned but unbilled fees at July 31 were $1,500.
   2. The truck has an estimated useful life of five years.
   3. One twelfth of the insurance expired.
   4. An inventory count shows $700 of supplies on hand at July 31.
   5. Accrued but unpaid employee salaries were $800.
   6. The note payable has a 5.5% annual interest rate.
(d) Prepare an adjusted trial balance.
(e) Prepare the income statement and statement of owner's equity for July, and a classified balance sheet at July 31, 2017. Of the note payable, $5,000 must be paid by June 30, 2018.
(f) Journalize and post the closing entries.
(g) Prepare a post-closing trial balance at July 31.

TAKING IT FURTHER   Do companies need to make adjusting and closing entries at the end of every month?

P4–6A   Silver Ridge Plumbing's year end is October 31. The company's trial balance prior to adjustments follows:

Prepare adjusting entries, adjusted trial balance, financial statements, and closing entries.
(LO 1, 2, 3) AP

SILVER RIDGE PLUMBING Trial Balance October 31, 2017		
	Debit	Credit
Cash	$ 35,420	
Supplies	6,000	
Equipment	140,000	
Accumulated depreciation—equipment		$ 42,000
Vehicles	110,000	
Accumulated depreciation—vehicles		48,125
Accounts payable		7,950
Notes payable		60,000
H. Burke, capital		75,750
H. Burke, drawings	36,000	
Service revenue		200,525
Fuel expense	28,038	
Insurance expense	9,500	
Interest expense	3,392	
Rent expense	21,000	
Salaries expense	45,000	
	$434,350	$434,350

Additional information:

1. The equipment has an expected useful life of ten years. The vehicles' expected useful life is eight years.
2. A physical count showed $2,000 of supplies on hand at October 31, 2017.
3. Accrued salaries payable at October 31, 2017, were $2,550.
4. Interest on the 5.5% note payable is payable at the end of each month and $10,000 of the principal must be paid on December 31 each year. Interest payments are up to date as at September 30, 2017.
5. The owner, H. Burke, invested $2,000 cash in the business on December 28, 2016. (*Note:* This has been correctly recorded.)

Instructions

(a) Prepare the adjusting entries and an adjusted trial balance.
(b) Calculate profit or loss for the year.
(c) Prepare a statement of owner's equity and a classified balance sheet.
(d) Prepare the closing entries. Using T accounts, post to the Income Summary, Owner's Drawings, and Owner's Capital accounts. Compare the ending balance in the Owner's Capital account with the information in the statement of owner's equity.

TAKING IT FURTHER   Why do you need to know the amount the owner invested in the business this year if it has been correctly recorded?

Analyze errors and prepare corrections. (LO 2) AP

P4-7A   Casey Hartwig, CPA, was retained by Global Cable to prepare financial statements for the year ended April 30, 2017. Hartwig accumulated all the ledger balances per Global's records and found the following.

GLOBAL CABLE
Trial Balance
April 30, 2017

	Debit	Credit
Cash	$ 4,100	
Accounts receivable	3,200	
Supplies	800	
Equipment	10,600	
Accumulated depreciation—equipment		$ 1,350
Accounts payable		2,100
Salaries payable		700
Unearned revenue		890
S. Spade, capital		12,900
Service revenue		5,450
Salaries expense	3,300	
Advertising expense	600	
Miscellaneous expense	290	
Depreciation expense	500	
	$23,390	$23,390

Casey Hartwig reviewed the records and found the following errors.

1. Cash received from a customer on account was recorded as $950 instead of $590.
2. A payment of $75 for advertising expense was entered as a debit to Miscellaneous Expense $75 and a credit to Cash $75.
3. The first salary payment this month was for $1,900, which included $700 of salaries payable on March 31. The payment was recorded as a debit to Salaries Expense $1,900 and a credit to Cash $1,900. (No reversing entries were made on April 1.)
4. The purchase on account of a printer costing $310 was recorded as a debit to Supplies and a credit to Accounts Payable for $310.
5. A cash payment of repair expense on equipment for $96 was recorded as a debit to Equipment $69 and a credit to Cash $69.

Instructions

(a) Prepare an analysis of each error showing (1) the incorrect entry, (2) the correct entry, and (3) the correcting entry. Items 4 and 5 occurred on April 30, 2017.

(b) Prepare a correct trial balance.

TAKING IT FURTHER Explain how the company's financial statements would be incorrect if error 4 was not corrected and why it is important to correct this error.

P4-8A The following accounting items were found in the journal of Crossé Company:

Determine impact of errors on financial statements, and correct. (LO 2) AP

1. The payment of the current month's rent for $500 was recorded as a debit to Rent Payable and a credit to Cash, both for $500. (*Note:* This had not been previously accrued.)

2. The collection of an account receivable for $400 was debited to Cash and credited to Service Revenue, both for $400.

3. A payment for Utilities Expense of $230 was recorded as a debit to Utilities Expense and a credit to Cash, both for $320.

4. A customer was billed $850 for services provided on account. Accounts Receivable was debited and Unearned Revenue was credited, both for $850.

5. A $600 accrual of Interest Revenue was recorded as a debit to Interest Expense and a credit to Interest Receivable, both for $600.

6. A payment of a $250 account payable was recorded as a debit to Accounts Payable and a credit to Cash, both for $250.

7. A $300 advance from a customer was recorded as a debit to Cash and a credit to Service Revenue, both for $300.

8. The purchase of $2,000 of equipment on account was recorded as a debit to Repair Expense and a credit to Accounts Payable, both for $2,000.

Instructions

Correct any error by reversing the incorrect entry and then recording the correct entry.

TAKING IT FURTHER Explain why it is incorrect to record billing a customer for services provided on account, as described in error 4.

P4-9A Below is an alphabetical list of the adjusted accounts of Dunder Tour Company at its year end, December 31, 2017. All accounts have normal balances.

Calculate capital account balance; prepare classified balance sheet and calculate liquidity ratios. (LO 1, 3, 4) AP

Accounts payable	$ 7,300	Interest receivable	$ 100
Accounts receivable	3,500	Interest revenue	1,100
Accumulated depreciation—equipment	15,000	Notes payable	40,000
Cash	4,500	Notes receivable	18,400
Depreciation expense	10,000	Patents	15,000
Equipment	50,000	Prepaid insurance	2,900
F. Dunder, capital	17,300	Service revenue	65,000
F. Dunder, drawings	33,000	Short-term investments	2,700
Insurance expense	1,500	Supplies	3,100
Interest expense	2,800	Supplies expense	2,400
Interest payable	700	Unearned revenue	3,500

Additional information:

1. In 2018, $3,000 of the notes payable becomes due.

2. The note receivable is due in 2019.

3. On July 18, 2017, Fred Dunder invested $3,200 cash in the business.

Instructions

(a) Calculate the post-closing balance in F. Dunder, Capital on December 31, 2017.

(b) Prepare a classified balance sheet.

(c) On December 31, 2016, Dunder Tour Company had current assets of $17,400 and current liabilities of $22,300. Calculate the company's working capital and current ratio on December 31, 2016, and December 31, 2017.

(d) On December 31, 2016, the total of Dunder Tour Company's cash, short-term investments, and current receivables was $15,600. Calculate the company's acid-test ratio on December 31, 2016, and December 31, 2017.

TAKING IT FURTHER Has the company's ability to pay its debts improved or weakened over the year?

Calculate current assets and liabilities, working capital, current ratio, and acid-test ratio; comment on liquidity. (LO 4) AN

P4–10A   **Danier Leather Inc.** is one of the largest publicly traded specialty apparel leather retailers in the world. The following information (all amounts in thousands) can be found on its recent balance sheets:

	June 28, 2014	June 29, 2013	June 30, 2012
Cash	$13,507	$24,541	$ 34,332
Accounts receivable	638	1,197	517
Inventories	21,721	22,810	24,891
Income tax recoverable	3,461	358	426
Prepaid expenses	643	803	799
Property and equipment	16,826	16,034	150,124
Other long-term assets	3,833	3,306	2,635
Payables and accruals	9,185	10,101	10,161
Deferred revenue	1,511	1,548	1,463
Other current liabilities	94	99	124
Non-current liabilities	1,432	1,392	1,373
Shareholders' equity	48,407	55,909	65,491

Instructions

(a) Calculate Danier Leather's current assets and current liabilities for each period.

(b) Calculate Danier Leather's working capital, current ratio, and acid-test ratio for each period.

(c) What does each of the measures calculated in part (b) show? Comment on Danier's liquidity.

TAKING IT FURTHER   Why do you believe there is such a difference between the current and acid-test ratios? Is this normal?

Prepare work sheet. (LO 5) AP

*P4–11A   The unadjusted trial balance and adjustment data for Elbow Cycle Repair Shop are presented in P4–4A.

Instructions

Prepare a work sheet for the year ended January 31, 2017.

TAKING IT FURTHER   Is it still necessary to record the adjusting entries in the journal and post them to the ledger accounts when using a work sheet?

Prepare work sheet. (LO 5) AP

*P4–12A   The unadjusted trial balance and adjustment data for Silver Ridge Plumbing are presented in P4–6A.

Instructions

Prepare a work sheet for the year ended October 31, 2017.

TAKING IT FURTHER   Explain why preparing a work sheet is an optional step in the accounting cycle.

Prepare and post adjusting, closing, reversing, and cash transaction entries. (LO 1, 6) AP

*P4–13A   Bugatti Company has a September 30 fiscal year end and prepares adjusting entries on an annual basis. The trial balance included the following selected accounts:

Accumulated depreciation	$ 4,250
Depreciation expense	0
Interest expense	3,333
Interest payable	0
Interest receivable	0
Interest revenue	0
Salaries expense	153,000
Salaries payable	0

Additional information for its September 30, 2017, year-end adjustments:

1. Bugatti has a two-year, 3.5% note receivable for $50,000 that was issued on April 1, 2017. Interest is payable every six months, on October 1 and April 1. Principal is payable at maturity. Bugatti collected the correct amount on October 1, 2017.

2. Accrued salaries as at September 30, 2017, were $2,400. Payroll totalling $3,000 was paid on October 2, 2017.

3. Bugatti has a five-year, 5% note payable for $80,000 issued in 2015. Interest is payable quarterly on January 31, April 30, July 31, and October 31 each year. Bugatti paid the correct amounts in 2017.

4. Depreciation expense for the year ended September 30, 2017, was $4,250.

Instructions

(a) Prepare T accounts and record the September 30, 2017, balances.
(b) Prepare and post adjusting journal entries for items 1 to 4 above.
(c) Prepare entries to close these revenue and expense accounts. Post to the T accounts. (*Note:* Do not post to the Income Summary account.)
(d) Prepare and post reversing journal entries on October 1, 2017, as appropriate.
(e) Prepare and post the journal entry to record the cash transactions that occurred in October 2017.

TAKING IT FURTHER   Comment on the usefulness of reversing entries.

*P4–14A   The unadjusted trial balance for Veda's Video Arcade at its fiscal year end of May 31, 2017, is as follows:

Prepare adjusting, reversing, and subsequent cash entries.
(LO 6) AP

VEDA'S VIDEO ARCADE Trial Balance May 31, 2017		
	Debit	Credit
Cash	$ 5,940	
Supplies	2,910	
Equipment	115,000	
Accumulated depreciation—equipment		$ 46,000
Notes payable		60,000
Unearned revenue		1,500
V. Gupta, capital		32,200
V. Gupta, drawings	35,400	
Service revenue		81,250
Rent expense	12,600	
Salaries expense	45,800	
Interest expense	3,300	
	$220,950	$220,950

Additional information:

1. On May 31, 2017, Veda's Video Arcade had earned but not collected or recorded $750 of revenue. On June 19, it collected this amount plus an additional $1,150 for revenue earned in June.
2. There was $765 of supplies on hand on May 31, 2017.
3. The equipment has an estimated useful life of 10 years.
4. Accrued salaries to May 31 were $1,390. The next payday is June 2 and the employees will be paid a total of $1,980 that day.
5. The note payable has a 6% annual interest rate. Interest is paid monthly on the first day of the month.
6. As at May 31, 2017, there was $700 of unearned revenue.

Instructions

(a) Prepare adjusting journal entries for the year ended May 31, 2017, as required.
(b) Prepare reversing entries where appropriate.
(c) Prepare journal entries to record the June 2017 cash transactions.
(d) Now assume reversing entries were not prepared as in part (b) above. Prepare journal entries to record the June 2017 cash transactions.

TAKING IT FURTHER   Why is it not appropriate to use reversing entries for all of the adjusting entries?

 Problems: Set B

P4–1B   The adjusted trial balance for Unser Company, owned by J. Unser, is available.

Prepare closing entries, and a post-closing trial balance.
(LO 1) AP

UNSER COMPANY
Adjusted Trial Balance
For the year ended December 31, 2017

Account Titles	Debit	Credit
Cash	$ 5,300	
Accounts receivable	10,800	
Supplies	1,500	
Prepaid insurance	2,000	
Equipment	27,000	
Accumulated depreciation—equipment		$ 5,600
Notes payable		15,000
Accounts payable		6,100
Salaries payable		2,400
J. Unser, capital		13,600
J. Unser, drawings	7,000	
Service revenue		61,000
Advertising expense	8,400	
Supplies expense	4,000	
Depreciation expense	5,600	
Insurance expense	3,500	
Salaries expense	28,000	
Interest expense	600	
	$103,700	$103,700

Instructions

(a) Prepare closing entries.

(b) Use T accounts to post the closing entries and calculate the balance in each account. (Ignore the accounts not affected by the closing entries.)

(c) Prepare a post-closing trial balance.

TAKING IT FURTHER   Explain the standard classifications used in preparing a classified balance sheet.

Prepare financial statements, closing entries, and a post-closing trial balance.
(LO 1, 3) AP

P4–2B   The completed financial statement columns of the work sheet for Edgemont Entertainment Solutions are as follows:

EDGEMONT ENTERTAINMENT SOLUTIONS
Work Sheet
For the year ended December 31, 2017

Account Titles	Income Statement Dr.	Income Statement Cr.	Balance Sheet Dr.	Balance Sheet Cr.
Cash			6,200	
Accounts receivable			7,500	
Prepaid insurance			1,800	
Equipment			33,000	
Accumulated depreciation—equipment				8,600
Accounts payable				14,700
M. Edgemont, capital				34,000
M. Edgemont, drawings			7,200	
Service revenue		46,000		
Depreciation expense	2,800			
Insurance expense	1,200			
Salaries expense	39,600			
Utilities expense	4,000			
Totals	47,600	46,000	55,700	57,300
Net loss		1,600	1,600	
	47,600	47,600	57,300	57,300

Instructions

(a) Prepare an income statement, statement of owner's equity, and a classified balance sheet. M. Edgemont made an additional investment in the business of $4,000 during 2017. The investment has been recorded and it is included in the capital account.

(b) Prepare the closing entries.

(c) Post the closing entries.

(d) Prepare a post-closing trial balance.

TAKING IT FURTHER　Define current assets and explain how current assets are typically arranged within the current assets section of the balance sheet.

P4–3B　The adjusted trial balance for Boreal Rock Climbing Centre is as follows:

Prepare financial statements, closing entries, and post-closing trial balance.
(LO 1, 3) AP

BOREAL ROCK CLIMBING CENTRE Adjusted Trial Balance January 31, 2017		
	Debit	Credit
Cash	$ 9,650	
Short-term investment	9,375	
Supplies	1,780	
Equity investments (long-term)	20,000	
Land	58,500	
Building	165,000	
Accumulated depreciation—building		$ 27,500
Equipment	45,250	
Accumulated depreciation—equipment		22,625
Accounts payable		7,355
Salaries payable		1,250
Notes payable ($5,500 must be paid on May 1, 2017)		110,000
L. Massak, capital		150,700
L. Massak, drawings	52,500	
Service revenue		114,300
Depreciation expense	10,025	
Interest expense	4,950	
Insurance expense	5,625	
Salaries expense	37,200	
Supplies expense	7,125	
Utilities expense	6,750	
	$433,730	$433,730

Instructions

(a) Calculate profit or loss for the year. (*Note:* It is not necessary to prepare an income statement.)

(b) Prepare a statement of owner's equity. The owner, Lil Massak, invested $3,700 cash in the business during the year. (*Note:* This transaction has been correctly recorded.)

(c) Prepare a classified balance sheet.

(d) Prepare closing entries.

(e) Use T accounts to post the closing entries and calculate the balance in each account. (Ignore the accounts not affected by the closing entries.)

(f) Prepare a post-closing trial balance and compare the balance in the L. Massak, Capital account with the information in the statement of owner's equity.

TAKING IT FURTHER　What alternatives should be considered when deciding on the presentation of information in the classified balance sheet?

Prepare adjusting entries, adjusted trial balance, financial statements, and closing entries. (LO 1, 3) AP

P4–4B　The following is Edge Sports Repair Shop's trial balance at September 30, 2017, the company's fiscal year end:

EDGE SPORTS REPAIR SHOP Trial Balance September 30, 2017		
	Debit	Credit
Cash	$ 6,750	
Accounts receivable	11,540	
Prepaid insurance	4,140	
Supplies	3,780	
Land	55,000	
Building	100,000	
Accumulated depreciation—building		$ 19,150
Equipment	40,000	
Accumulated depreciation—equipment		11,500
Accounts payable		8,850
Unearned revenue		3,300
Mortgage payable		125,000
R. Brachman, capital		60,000
R. Brachman, drawings	103,525	
Service revenue		189,250
Interest expense	6,302	
Salaries expense	75,900	
Utilities expense	10,113	
	$417,050	$417,050

Additional information:

1. Service revenue earned but not recorded at September 30, 2017, was $5,350.
2. The 12-month insurance policy was purchased on February 1, 2017.
3. A physical count of supplies shows $560 on hand on September 30, 2017.
4. The building has an estimated useful life of 50 years. The equipment has an estimated useful life of eight years.
5. Salaries of $1,975 are accrued and unpaid at September 30, 2017.
6. The mortgage payable has a 4.5% interest rate. Interest is paid on the first day of each month for the previous month's interest.
7. On September 30, 2017, one quarter of the unearned revenue was still unearned.
8. During the next fiscal year, $5,400 of the mortgage payable is to be paid.

Instructions

(a) Prepare the adjusting entries.
(b) Prepare an adjusted trial balance.
(c) Prepare an income statement, statement of owner's equity, and classified balance sheet. The owner, Ralph Brachman, invested $4,000 cash in the business on November 21, 2016. The investment has been recorded and it is included in the capital account.
(d) Prepare the closing entries.

TAKING IT FURTHER　Ralph Brachman is concerned that he had to invest $4,000 cash in the business this year. Based on the information in the financial statements, what are your recommendations to Ralph?

P4–5B   Laura Eddy opened Eddy's Carpet Cleaners on March 1, 2017. In March, the following transactions were completed:

Complete all steps in accounting cycle.
(LO 1, 2) AP

Mar. 1	Laura invested $10,000 cash in the business.
1	Purchased a used truck for $6,500, paying $1,500 cash and signing a note payable for the balance.
3	Purchased supplies for $1,200 on account.
5	Paid $1,200 on a one-year insurance policy, effective March 1.
12	Billed customers $4,800 for cleaning services.
18	Paid $500 of amount owed on supplies.
20	Paid $1,800 for employee salaries.
21	Collected $1,400 from customers billed on March 12.
25	Billed customers $2,500 for cleaning services.
31	Paid $375 for fuel for the month on the truck.
31	Withdrew $900 cash for personal use.

Instructions

(a) Journalize and post the March transactions.
(b) Prepare a trial balance at March 31.
(c) Journalize and post the following adjustments:
   1. The truck has an estimated useful life of five years.
   2. One twelfth of the insurance expired.
   3. An inventory count shows $400 of supplies on hand at March 31.
   4. Accrued but unpaid employee salaries were $500.
   5. The note payable has a 4.5% annual interest rate.
   6. Earned but unbilled fees at March 31 were $500.
(d) Prepare an adjusted trial balance.
(e) Prepare the income statement and statement of owner's equity for March, and a classified balance sheet at March 31, 2017. Of the note payable, $2,000 must be paid by March 1, 2018.
(f) Journalize and post the closing entries.
(g) Prepare a post-closing trial balance at March 31.

TAKING IT FURTHER   Do companies need to make adjusting and closing entries at the end of every month?

P4–6B   Nazari Electrical Services has an August 31 fiscal year end. The company's trial balance prior to adjustments follows:

Prepare adjusting entries, adjusted trial balance, financial statements, and closing entries. (LO 1, 3) AP

NAZARI ELECTRICAL SERVICES Trial Balance August 31, 2017		
	Debit	Credit
Cash	$ 13,870	
Supplies	23,400	
Debt investments	18,000	
Equipment	108,000	
Accumulated depreciation—equipment		$ 38,250
Vehicles	98,000	
Accumulated depreciation—vehicles		42,875
Accounts payable		7,115
Unearned revenue		4,500
Notes payable		48,000
A. Nazari, capital		68,175
A. Nazari, drawings	32,400	
Service revenue		180,115
Interest revenue		360
Fuel expense	25,235	
Insurance expense	8,550	
Interest expense	2,535	
Rent expense	18,900	
Salaries expense	40,500	
	$389,390	$389,390

Additional information:

1. The equipment has an expected useful life of 12 years. The vehicles' expected useful life is eight years.
2. A physical count showed $1,500 of supplies on hand at August 31, 2017.
3. As at August 31, 2017, there was $2,500 of revenue received in advance that was still unearned.
4. Nazari Electrical Services has an investment in bonds that it intends to hold to earn interest until the bonds mature in 10 years. The bonds have an interest rate of 4% and pay interest on March 1 and September 1 each year.
5. Accrued salaries payable at August 31, 2017, were $1,850.
6. Interest on the 5% note payable is payable at the end of each month and $8,000 of the principal must be paid on December 31 each year. Interest payments are up to date as at August 31, 2017.
7. The owner, A. Nazari, invested $3,000 cash in the business on December 29, 2016. (*Note:* This has been correctly recorded.)

Instructions

(a) Prepare the adjusting entries and an adjusted trial balance.
(b) Calculate profit or loss for the year.
(c) Prepare a statement of owner's equity and a classified balance sheet.
(d) Prepare the closing entries. Using T accounts, post to the Income Summary, and Owner's Drawings and Owner's Capital accounts. Compare the ending balance in the Owner's Capital account with the information in the statement of owner's equity.

TAKING IT FURTHER   Why do you need to know the amount the owner invested in the business this year if it has been correctly recorded?

Analyze errors and prepare corrections. (LO 2) AP

P4-7B   Ilana Mathers, CPA, was hired by Interactive Computer Installations to prepare its financial statements for March 2017. Using all the ledger balances in the owner's records, Ilana put together the following trial balance:

INTERACTIVE COMPUTER INSTALLATIONS Trial Balance March 31, 2017		
	Debit	Credit
Cash	$ 6,680	
Accounts receivable	3,850	
Supplies	5,900	
Equipment	12,620	
Accumulated depreciation—equipment		$ 6,000
Accounts payable		5,330
Salaries payable	2,250	
Unearned revenue		4,955
M. Hubert, capital		15,375
Service revenue		7,800
Miscellaneous expense	3,360	
Salaries expense	4,800	
Totals	$39,460	$39,460

Ilana then reviewed the records and found the following items:

1. The purchase on account of equipment for $5,100 on March 1 was recorded as a debit to Supplies and a credit to Accounts Payable, both for $5,200.
2. March rent of $2,050 was paid on March 2. The company recorded this as a debit to Miscellaneous Expense and a credit to Cash, both for $2,050.
3. Cash of $1,735 was received from a customer on account. It was recorded as a debit to Cash and a credit to Service Revenue, both for $1,735.
4. A payment of a $575 account payable was entered as a debit to Cash and a credit to Accounts Receivable, both for $575.
5. The first salary payment made in March was for $3,000, which included $750 of salaries payable on February 28. The payment was recorded as a debit to Salaries Payable of $3,000 and a credit to Cash of $3,000. (No reversing entries were made on March 1.)
6. The owner, Maurice Hubert, paid himself $1,800 and recorded this as salary expense.
7. The depreciation expense for the month of March has not been recorded. All of the company's equipment is expected to have a five-year useful life.

Instructions

(a) Prepare an analysis of any errors and show (1) the incorrect entry, (2) the correct entry, and (3) the correcting entry.

(b) Prepare a correct trial balance.

TAKING IT FURTHER   Explain how the company's financial statements would be incorrect if error 6 was not corrected and why it is important to correct this error.

P4–8B   Fu Company is owned and operated by Jeremy Fu. The following errors were found in the company's journal:

1. The purchase of $700 of supplies on account was recorded as a debit to Supplies Expense and a credit to Accounts Payable, both for $700. (*Note:* The company records prepayments as assets.)
2. A $600 payment of an account payable was recorded as a debit to Cash and a credit to Accounts Payable, both for $600.
3. A cash advance of $575 from a customer was recorded as a debit to Service Revenue and a credit to Unearned Revenue, both for $350.
4. The depreciation adjusting entry was incorrectly recorded as $1,280. The amount should have been $1,820.
5. A customer was billed $650 for services provided on account. Unearned Revenue was debited and Service Revenue was credited, both for $650.
6. The accrual of $750 of interest expense was recorded as a debit to Interest Receivable and a credit to Interest Payable, both for $750.
7. A $500 collection of cash from a customer on account was recorded as a debit to Accounts Receivable and a credit to Cash, both for $500.
8. A $950 payment for rent for Jeremy Fu's (the company owner's) apartment was debited to Rent Expense and credited to Cash, both for $950.

Instructions

Correct each error by reversing the incorrect entry and then recording the correct entry.

TAKING IT FURTHER   Why it is incorrect to record the payment of the company owner's apartment rent as an expense, as described in error 8?

Determine impact of errors on financial statements, and correct. (LO 2) AP

P4–9B   Below is an alphabetical list of the adjusted accounts of Matrix Consulting Services at its year end, March 31, 2017. All accounts have normal balances.

Calculate capital account balance; prepare classified balance sheet and calculate liquidity ratios. (LO 1, 3, 4) AP

Accounts payable	$11,650	Interest revenue	$ 400
Accounts receivable	4,700	N. Anderson, capital	36,500
Accumulated depreciation—equipment	20,000	N. Anderson, drawings	57,700
Advertising expense	12,000	Notes payable	30,000
Cash	3,900	Notes receivable	10,000
Depreciation expense	8,000	Patents	16,000
Equipment	48,000	Prepaid insurance	4,400
Insurance expense	4,000	Service revenue	79,800
Interest expense	1,800	Short-term investments	3,000
Interest payable	150	Supplies	2,300
Interest receivable	200	Supplies expense	3,700
		Unearned revenue	1,200

Additional information:

1. Of the notes payable, $15,000 becomes due on July 1, 2017, and the rest on July 1, 2019.
2. The note receivable is due on June 1, 2020.
3. On September 20, 2016, Neil Anderson, the owner, invested $3,800 cash in the business.

Instructions

(a) Calculate the post-closing balance in N. Anderson, Capital, on March 31, 2017.
(b) Prepare a classified balance sheet.
(c) On March 31, 2016, Matrix Consulting Services had current assets of $30,700 and current liabilities of $15,950. Calculate the company's working capital and current ratio on March 31, 2016, and March 31, 2017.
(d) On March 31, 2016, the total of Matrix Consulting Services' cash, short-term investments, and current receivables was $25,500. Calculate the company's acid-test ratio on March 31, 2016, and March 31, 2017.

TAKING IT FURTHER   Has the company's short-term ability to pay its debts improved or weakened over the year?

Calculate current assets and liabilities, working capital, current ratio, and acid-test ratio; comment on liquidity.
(LO 4) AN

P4–10B   Big Rock Brewery Inc. brews and sells premium natural unpasteurized beer. The following information (all amounts in thousands) can be found on its recent balance sheets (or statements of financial position, as Big Rock calls them):

	December 30, 2014	December 30, 2013	December 30, 2012
Property, plant, and equipment	$38,332	$35,142	$35,277
Intangible assets	165	108	128
Inventories	3,813	2,983	3,892
Accounts receivable	1,473	1,353	2,358
Current taxes receivable	2,241	0	0
Prepaid expense	669	754	364
Cash	1,484	2,317	4,281
Accounts payable and accrued liabilities	3,583	4,100	3,978
Dividends payable	1,375	1,214	1,214
Current taxes payable	0	1,953	426
Current portion of long-term debt	0	0	700
Long-term liabilities and shareholders' equity	43,209	35,390	39,982

Instructions

(a) Calculate Big Rock's current assets and current liabilities for each year.

(b) Calculate Big Rock's working capital, current ratio, and acid-test ratio for each year.

(c) What does each of the measures calculated in part (b) show? Comment on Big Rock's liquidity.

TAKING IT FURTHER   At a specific point in time, a company will always have a larger current ratio than its acid-test ratio. Why? Would you expect this difference to be larger in a company like Big Rock Brewery than in a company like **WestJet Airlines**? Why or why not?

Prepare work sheet.
(LO 5) AP

*P4–11B   The unadjusted trial balance and adjustment data for Edge Sports Repair Shop are presented in P4–4B.

Instructions

Prepare a work sheet for the year ended September 30, 2017.

TAKING IT FURTHER   Is it still necessary to record the adjusting entries in the journal and post them to the ledger accounts?

Prepare work sheet.
(LO 5) AP

*P4–12B   The unadjusted trial balance and adjustment data for Nazari Electrical Services are presented in P4–6B.

Instructions

Prepare a work sheet for the year ended August 31, 2017.

TAKING IT FURTHER   Explain why preparing a work sheet is an optional step in the accounting cycle.

Prepare and post adjusting, closing, reversing, and cash transaction entries.
(LO 1, 6) AP

*P4–13B   Cypress Company has an October 31 fiscal year end and prepares adjusting entries on an annual basis. The October 31, 2017, trial balance included the following selected accounts:

Accumulated depreciation	$ 16,500
Depreciation expense	0
Interest expense	3,750
Interest payable	0
Interest receivable	0
Interest revenue	0
Salaries expense	156,000
Salaries payable	0

Additional information for its October 31, 2017, year-end adjustments:

1. Cypress has a two-year, 3.75% note receivable for $60,000 that was issued on May 1, 2017. Interest is payable every six months, on November 1 and May 1. Principal is payable at maturity. Cypress collected the correct amount on November 1, 2017.

2. Accrued salaries as at October 31, 2017, were $3,200. Payroll totalling $6,000 was paid on November 6, 2017.

3. Cypress has a five-year, 5% note payable for $90,000 issued in 2012. Interest is payable quarterly on March 1, June 1, September 1, and December 1 each year. Cypress paid the correct amounts during 2017.

4. Depreciation expense for the year ended October 31, 2017, was $5,500.

Instructions

(a) Prepare T accounts and record the October 31, 2017, balances.
(b) Prepare and post adjusting journal entries for items 1 to 4 above.
(c) Prepare entries to close these revenue and expense accounts. Post to the T accounts. (*Note:* Do not post to the Income Summary account.)
(d) Prepare and post reversing journal entries on November 1, 2017, as appropriate.
(e) Prepare and post the journal entry to record the cash receipts or payments that occurred in November and December 2017.

TAKING IT FURTHER   Comment on the usefulness of reversing entries.

*P4–14B   The unadjusted trial balance for Laurie's Laser Games at its fiscal year end of April 30, 2017, is as follows: Prepare adjusting, reversing, and subsequent cash entries. (LO 6) AP

LAURIE'S LASER GAMES
Trial Balance
April 30, 2017

	Debit	Credit
Cash	$ 3,800	
Supplies	4,270	
Equipment	130,000	
Accumulated depreciation—equipment		$ 39,000
Notes payable		90,000
Unearned revenue		1,965
L. Glans, capital		33,100
L. Glans, drawings	25,000	
Fees earned		70,180
Rent expense	13,200	
Salaries expense	53,850	
Interest expense	4,125	
	$234,245	$234,245

Additional information:

1. On April 30, 2017, Laurie's Laser Games had earned but not collected or recorded $1,550 of fees earned. On May 21, 2017, Laurie's Laser Games collected this amount plus an additional $2,750 for fees earned in May.
2. There was $880 of supplies on hand on April 30, 2017.
3. The equipment has an estimated useful life of 10 years.
4. On April 30, salaries earned but not paid or recorded were $2,150. The next payday is May 8 and the employees will be paid a total of $4,300 that day.
5. The note payable has a 4.5% annual interest rate. Interest is paid monthly on the first of the month. The next payment is due on May 1, 2017.
6. On April 30, $565 of the unearned revenue had been earned.

Instructions

(a) Prepare adjusting journal entries for the year ended April 30, 2017, as required.
(b) Prepare reversing entries where appropriate.
(c) Prepare journal entries to record the May 2017 cash transactions.
(d) Now assume reversing entries were not prepared as in part (b) above. Prepare journal entries to record the May 2017 cash transactions.

TAKING IT FURTHER   Why is it not appropriate to use reversing entries for all of the adjusting entries?

▶ Cumulative Coverage—Chapters 2 to 4

Alou Equipment Repair has a September 30 year end. The company adjusts and closes its accounts on an annual basis. On August 31, 2017, the account balances of Alou Equipment Repair were as follows:

ALOU EQUIPMENT REPAIR
Trial Balance
August 31, 2017

	Debit	Credit
Cash	$ 2,790	
Accounts receivable	7,910	
Supplies	8,500	
Equipment	9,000	
Accumulated depreciation—equipment		$ 1,800
Accounts payable		3,100
Unearned revenue		400
J. Alou, capital		21,200
J. Alou, drawings	15,600	
Service revenue		49,600
Rent expense	5,500	
Salaries expense	24,570	
Telephone expense	2,230	
	$76,100	$76,100

During September, the following transactions were completed:

Sept. 1   Borrowed $10,000 from the bank and signed a two-year, 5% note payable.
2   Paid September rent, $500.
8   Paid employee salaries, $1,050.
12   Received $1,500 cash from customers on account.
15   Received $5,700 cash for services performed in September.
17   Purchased additional supplies on account, $1,300.
20   Paid creditors $2,300 on account.
21   Paid September telephone bill, $200.
22   Paid employee salaries, $1,050.
27   Performed services on account and billed customers for services provided, $900.
29   Received $550 from customers for services to be provided in the future.
30   Paid J. Alou $800 cash for personal use.

Adjustment data consist of the following:

1. Supplies on hand at September 30 cost $1,000.
2. Accrued salaries payable at September 30 total $630.
3. The equipment has an expected useful life of five years.
4. Unearned revenue of $450 is still not earned at September 30.
5. Interest is payable on the first of each month.

Instructions

(a) Prepare T accounts and enter the August 31 balances.
(b) Journalize the September transactions.
(c) Post to T accounts.
(d) Prepare a trial balance at September 30.
(e) Journalize and post adjusting entries.
(f) Prepare an adjusted trial balance at September 30.
(g) Prepare an income statement and a statement of owner's equity, and a classified balance sheet.
(h) Prepare and post closing entries.
(i) Prepare post-closing trial balance at September 30.

CHAPTER 4: BROADENING YOUR PERSPECTIVE

▶ Financial Reporting and Analysis

BYP4-1 The financial statements and accompanying notes of **Corus Entertainment** are presented in Appendix A at the end of this book.

Instructions

(a) What classifications does Corus use in its balance sheet?
(b) In what order are Corus's current assets listed? Its non-current assets?

(c) What are Corus's total current assets at August 31, 2014?
(d) What are Corus's total current liabilities at August 31, 2014?
(e) Calculate Corus's working capital, current ratio, and acid-test ratio for the fiscal years 2014 and 2013. Compare and comment on the results.

Interpreting Financial Statements

BYP4-2 **The Gap, Inc.** reports its financial results for 52-week fiscal periods ending on a Saturday around the end of January each year. The following information (in US$ millions) was included in recent annual reports:

	Jan. 31, 2015	Feb. 1, 2014	Feb. 2, 2013	Jan. 28, 2012	Jan. 29, 2011
Working capital	2,083	1,985	1,788	$2,181	$1,831
Current ratio	1.93:1	1.81:1	1.76:1	2.02:1	1.87:1
Acid-test ratio	1.09:1	1.02:1	1.01:1	0.89:1	0.79:1
Cash and cash equivalents	1,515	1,510	1,460	$1,885	$1,561
Current liabilities	2,234	2,445	2,344	$2,128	$2,095

Instructions

(a) Comment on the changes in The Gap's liquidity over the five-year period. Which measure seems to give a better indication of its liquidity: working capital or the current ratio? Suggest a reason for the changes in The Gap's liquidity during the period.

(b) Do you believe that The Gap's creditors should be concerned about its liquidity?

▶ Critical Thinking

Collaborative Learning Activity

Note to instructor: Additional instructions and material for this group activity can be found on the Instructor Resource Site and in *WileyPLUS*.

BYP4–3 In this group activity, you will be provided with a skeleton classified balance sheet. Then, using the clues provided (including liquidity ratios) and the amounts from the statement, you will reconstruct the numbers on the balance sheet.

Communication Activity

BYP4–4 Your best friend is thinking about opening a business. He has never studied accounting and has no idea about the steps that must be followed in order to produce financial statements for his business.

Instructions

Write a memo to your friend that lists the steps in the accounting cycle in the order in which they should be completed. Include information on when each of these steps should be done and explain the purpose of the different types of journal entries and trial balances. Your memo should also discuss the optional steps in the accounting cycle.

"All About You" Activity

BYP4–5 As discussed in the "All About You" feature, in order to evaluate your personal financial position, you need to prepare a personal balance sheet. Complete the following table reflecting your current financial position:

Amount owed on student loan (long-term)
Balance in chequing account
Automobile
Balance on automobile loan (short-term)
Balance on automobile loan (long-term)
Computer and accessories
Clothes and furniture
Balance owed on credit cards
Other

Instructions

(a) Prepare a personal balance sheet using the format you have learned for a balance sheet for a proprietorship. For the Capital account, use Personal Equity (Deficit).

(b) Assume that, instead of borrowing to cover the cost of tuition, you earn $8,000 working during the summer and that after paying for your tuition you have $2,000 in your chequing account. What is the impact on your Personal Equity (Deficit) if the cost of the tuition is considered an expense?

 Santé Smoothie Saga

(*Note:* This is a continuation of the Santé Smoothie Saga from Chapters 1 through 3.)

BYP4–6 Natalie had a very busy May. At the end of the month, after Natalie has journalized and posted her adjusting and correcting entries, and has prepared an adjusted trial balance.

Instructions

Using the information in the adjusted trial balance, do the following:

(a) Prepare an income statement for the two months ended May 31, 2017.

(b) Prepare a statement of owner's equity for the two months ended May 31, 2017, and a classified balance sheet at May 31, 2017.

(c) Calculate Santé Smoothies' working capital, current ratio, and acid-test ratio. Comment on Santé Smoothies' liquidity.

(d) Natalie has decided that her year end will be May 31, 2017. Prepare closing entries.

(e) Prepare a post-closing trial balance.

(f) Natalie had reviewed her unadjusted trial balance prior to preparing the adjusting journal entries. When Natalie initially recorded the purchase of the equipment in May for $725, she thought the equipment should be recorded as "supplies expense." After posting the original transaction, Natalie reviewed her accounting textbook, and remembered that the purchase of equipment should be recorded as an asset. She then made an entry to correct this error. Had she not made a correcting entry, would the financial statements have been misstated? How?

SANTÉ SMOOTHIES
Adjusted Trial Balance
May 31, 2017

	Debit	Credit
Cash	$3,060	
Accounts receivable	675	
Supplies	95	
Equipment	1,550	
Accumulated depreciation—equipment		$ 66
Accounts payable		88
Unearned revenue		100
Interest payable		11
Notes payable, 3%, principal and interest due April 15, 2018		3,000
N. Koebel, capital		1,725
Revenue		1,225
Advertising expense	325	
Salaries expense	48	
Telephone expense	174	
Supplies expense	211	
Depreciation expense	66	
Interest expense	11	
	$6,215	$6,215

ANSWERS TO CHAPTER QUESTIONS

ANSWERS TO ACCOUNTING IN ACTION INSIGHT QUESTIONS

Across the Organization, p. 177

Q: Who else benefits from a shorter closing process?

A: Investors and analysts: Faster information means more timely decisions as to where best to invest and faster response time to financial trends.

Employees (particularly those in the accounting department): Traditionally, month end is a period requiring overtime to complete the closing process. A shorter close means fewer evenings requiring overtime.

Auditors: Often auditors are awaiting client information or for the client to close the books. A faster close means auditors can start or finish sooner.

Management: When faster information is available, management can react to the market and take corrective active faster.

Company analysts: A faster close means there is more time available to analyze the data, not just prepare them.

Ethics Insight, p. 183

Q: Who are the stakeholders in this situation and what are the ethical issues?

A: The stakeholders and ethical issues include:

You, as controller: You would be violating professional and ethical standards if you don't restate using the correct amounts. You could set a precedent where the president could again ask you to do unethical things in the future.

Eddy, as president: He wants to avoid risking the company's credit rating.

The banks and other creditors: They need to base their lending decisions on Select Cleaning Services' accurate financial information. If the company can't afford to repay its loans, lenders need to adjust their interest rates and credit lending terms to manage their risk.

Select Cleaning Services' employees: If banks and other creditors decide to stop lending to the company, it could go bankrupt.

All About You Insight, p. 190

Q: How can preparing a personal balance sheet help you manage your net worth?

A: In order to attain your financial objectives, you need to set goals early. A personal balance sheet provides a benchmark that allows you to measure your progress toward your financial goals.

Business Insight, p. 192

Q: Does a current ratio of less than 1 indicate that the company will have problems paying its obligations?

A: Not necessarily. A current ratio of less than 1 only indicates that at the balance sheet date the company would not have been able to pay off all of its current liabilities. But current liabilities don't have to be paid on the balance sheet date; a current liability is an obligation to pay an amount at some point over the following year. Therefore, as long as a company is able to generate cash quickly enough through its sales, it will have the cash available to pay the obligations as they come due.

ANSWERS TO SELF-STUDY QUESTIONS

1. b   2. c   3. a   4. c   5. d   6. d   7. d   8. b   9. c   10. c   *11. c   *12. a

5 ACCOUNTING FOR MERCHANDISING OPERATIONS

CHAPTER PREVIEW　The first four chapters of this text focused mostly on service companies, like the fictional Lynk Software Services. Other examples of service companies include Air Canada, Canada Post, College Pro Painters, and Scotiabank. Frank & Oak, as indicated in the feature story, sells goods instead of performing services to earn a profit.

FEATURE STORY　A "FRANK" LOOK AT TRACKING INVENTORY

MONTREAL, Que. Imagine being a retailer and having almost no goods to sell. That's what happened in the early days of Frank & Oak, a Montreal-based retailer of young men's clothing and accessories that started out in 2012 as a web-only store. "In the first, I would say, two or three months, our biggest problem was that people would come to the site and we had no inventory," said co-founder Hicham Ratnani. So Frank & Oak created waiting lists for customers to pre-order items to receive when they were back in stock. "After a couple of weeks, we had about a quarter of a million dollars' worth of waiting lists," Mr. Ratnani said. While most retailers would be doomed if they ran out of stock, Frank & Oak found that the high demand showed it had simply underestimated its popularity out of the starting gate. "It meant that the market was really there and people really wanted the product."

Keeping track of inventory is key to the success of merchandisers like Frank & Oak, which designs its own products and has them custom-manufactured in China. Frank & Oak releases a new collection every month, not just every season. Customers must sign up to become members in order to make a purchase; there are now more than 1.6 million members. Some 70% of sales are to the United States. In 2013 alone, the company sold more than 700,000 items.

In 2014, the retailer opened its first "bricks and mortar" store and now has locations in six cities across Canada, with plans to open six stores in the United States. These stores, along with temporary pop-up shops, typically carry only samples of Frank & Oak products. Customers can try these items on, order them, and have them delivered to their doors—without these stores carrying inventory. The stores, usually in established neighbourhoods, attract an older clientele than the website, along with a surprising number of women, so Frank & Oak has to ensure it carries enough stock in its warehouse to meet those customers' needs.

All of these inventory challenges mean that Frank & Oak most likely uses a perpetual inventory system, which keeps track of the quantity and cost of each item in stock perpetually, or in real time. It's all part of the fast world of fashion.

Sources: "Online Retailers Open Physical Stores to Boost Business," CBC news online, May 1, 2015; Murad Hemmadi, "How Frank & Oak Brings a Personal Touch to Digital Retail," *Canadian Business*, March 20, 2015; Hollie Shaw, "Digital Retail Heads Back to the Future with Old-Fashioned Stores," *Financial Post*, October 18, 2014; Lora Kolodny, "Frank & Oak Raises $15M to Make Menswear for Creative Professionals," *Wall Street Journal*, September 4, 2014; Joseph Czikk, "Video: Frank & Oak Cofounder Talks About the Jump from Employee to Entrepreneur," Betakit.com, April 11, 2014; Frank & Oak corporate website, https://ca.frankandoak.com/.

CHAPTER OUTLINE　LEARNING OBJECTIVES

　Describe the differences between service and merchandising companies.

Merchandising Operations
• Inventory systems

DO IT　1

Merchandising operations and inventory systems

2 Prepare entries for purchases under a perpetual inventory system.

Recording Purchases of Merchandise
- Subsidiary inventory records
- Freight costs
- Purchase returns and allowances
- Discounts
- Summary of purchase transactions

DO IT 2
Purchase transactions

3 Prepare entries for sales under a perpetual inventory system.

Recording Sales of Merchandise
- Freight costs
- Sales returns and allowances
- Discounts
- Summary of sales transactions
- Sales taxes

DO IT 3
Sales transactions

4 Perform the steps in the accounting cycle for a merchandising company.

Completing the Accounting Cycle
- Adjusting entries
- Closing entries
- Post-closing trial balance
- Summary of merchandising entries in a perpetual inventory system

DO IT 4
Closing entries

5 Prepare single-step and multiple-step income statements.

Merchandising Financial Statements
- Single-step income statement
- Multiple-step income statement
- Classified balance sheet

DO IT 5
Merchandising income statement

6 Calculate the gross profit margin and profit margin.

Using the Information in the Financial Statements
- Gross profit margin
- Profit margin

DO IT 6
Profitability ratios

7 Prepare the entries for purchases and sales under a periodic inventory system and calculate cost of goods sold (Appendix 5A).

Appendix 5A: Periodic Inventory System
- Recording purchases of merchandise
- Recording sales of merchandise
- Comparison of entries—perpetual vs. periodic
- Calculating cost of goods sold
- Multiple-step income statement
- Completing the accounting cycle

DO IT 7
Periodic inventory system

LEARNING OBJECTIVE **1** ▶ **Describe the differences between service and merchandising companies.**

Merchandising Operations

Merchandising involves purchasing products—also called merchandise inventory or just inventory—to resell to customers. Merchandising companies that purchase and sell directly to consumers—such as Best Buy, Aeropostale, lululemon, GAP, Mountain Equipment Co-op, and Toys "R" Us—are called **retailers**. Merchandising companies that sell to retailers are known as **wholesalers**.

The steps in the accounting cycle for a merchandising company are the same as the steps for a service company. However, merchandising companies need additional accounts and entries in order to record merchandising transactions. The calculations of profit for both a service and a merchandising company are shown in Illustration 5-1. As you can see, the items in the blue box are used only by a merchandising company because service companies do not sell goods.

▶ **ILLUSTRATION** **5-1**
Earnings measurement process for a service company and a merchandising company

Service company	Merchandising company
Revenue	Sales
− Operating expenses	− Cost of goods sold
= Profit (Loss)	= Gross profit
	− Operating expenses
	= Profit (Loss)

Measuring profit for a merchandising company is basically the same as for a service company. That is, profit (or loss) is equal to revenues less expenses. In a merchandising company, the main source of revenues is the sale of merchandise. These revenues are called **sales revenue**, or simply sales. Expenses for a merchandising company are divided into two categories: (1) cost of goods sold, and (2) operating expenses. A service company does not have a cost of goods sold because it provides services, not goods.

The **cost of goods sold** is the total cost of merchandise sold during the period. This expense is directly related to revenue from the sale of the goods. Sales revenue less cost of goods sold is called **gross profit**. For example, when a tablet that costs $150 is sold for $250, the gross profit is $100.

After gross profit is calculated, operating expenses are deducted to determine profit (or loss). **Operating expenses** are expenses that are incurred in the process of earning sales revenue or service revenue. The operating expenses of a merchandising company include the same basic expenses found in a service company, such as salaries, advertising, insurance, rent, and depreciation.

You learned about the operating cycle in Chapter 4. The operating cycle is the time that it takes to go from cash to cash in producing revenues. It is usually longer in a merchandising company than in a service company. The purchase of merchandise inventory and the lapse of time until it is sold lengthen the cycle. Illustrations 5-2 and 5-3 show the operating cycles of a service company and a merchandising company, respectively.

▶ **ILLUSTRATION** **5-2**
Operating cycle of a service company

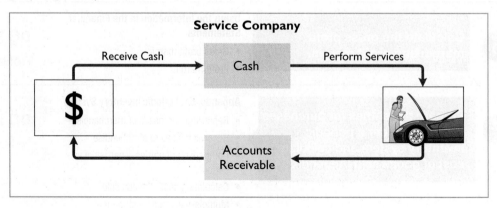

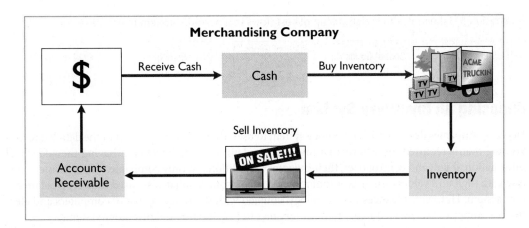

▶ILLUSTRATION 5-3
Operating cycle of a merchandising company

INVENTORY SYSTEMS

A merchandising company must keep track of its inventory to determine what is available for sale (inventory) and what has been sold (cost of goods sold). Companies use one of two kinds of systems to account for inventory: a perpetual inventory system or a periodic inventory system.

Perpetual Inventory System

In a **perpetual inventory system**, the company keeps detailed records of each inventory purchase and sale. This system continuously—perpetually—shows the quantity and cost of the inventory that should be on hand for every item. With the use of bar codes, optical scanners, and point-of-sale software, a store can keep a running record of every item that it buys and sells.

Illustration 5-4 shows the flow of costs in a perpetual inventory system, using T accounts to illustrate the inflows and outflows. When inventory is purchased under a perpetual system, the purchase is recorded by increasing (debiting) the Merchandise Inventory account. When inventory items are sold under a perpetual inventory system, the cost of the goods sold (the original purchase cost of the merchandise) is transferred from the Merchandise Inventory account (an asset) to the Cost of Goods Sold account (an expense). Under a perpetual inventory system, the company determines and records the cost of goods sold and the reduction in inventory **each time a sale occurs**.

Helpful hint "Flow of costs" in an inventory system refers to the manner in which the cost of an item of inventory moves through a company's records.

▶ILLUSTRATION 5-4
Flow of costs through a merchandising company using a perpetual inventory system

Merchandise Inventory (an asset)	
Debit	Credit
Beginning inventory	Cost of goods sold (each time a sale occurs)
Cost of goods purchased	
Ending inventory	

Cost of Goods Sold (an expense)	
Debit	Credit
Cost of Goods sold (each time a sale occurs)	

Periodic Inventory System

In a **periodic inventory system**, companies do not keep detailed inventory records of the goods on hand throughout the period. Instead, the cost of goods sold is determined **only at the end of the accounting period**; that is, periodically. At that point, the company takes a physical inventory count to determine the quantity and cost of the goods on hand.

To determine the cost of goods sold in a periodic inventory system, the following steps are necessary:

1. Determine the beginning inventory—the cost of goods on hand at the beginning of the accounting period. (This is the same amount as the previous period's ending inventory.)
2. Add the cost of goods purchased during the period.
3. Subtract the ending inventory—the cost of goods on hand at the end of the accounting period as determined from the physical inventory count.

Illustration 5-5 illustrates the relationship of cost flows in a periodic system in equation form.

▶ **ILLUSTRATION** **5-5**
Equation to determine
cost of goods sold in a
periodic inventory system

| Beginning Inventory | + | Cost of Goods Purchased | = | Cost of Goods Available for Sale | − | Ending Inventory | = | Cost of Goods Sold |

Choosing an Inventory System

How do companies decide which inventory system to use? They compare the cost of the detailed record keeping that is required for a perpetual inventory system with the benefits of having the additional information about, and control over, their inventory. Traditionally, only companies that sold merchandise with high unit values—such as automobiles or major home appliances—used the perpetual inventory system. However, advances in technology, coupled with the reduced cost of computers and electronic scanners, have enabled many more companies to install perpetual inventory systems.

A perpetual inventory system gives better control over inventories. Since the inventory records show the quantities that should be on hand, the goods can be counted at any time to see whether the amount of goods actually on hand agrees with the inventory records. Any shortages that are uncovered can be immediately investigated.

A perpetual inventory system also makes it easier to answer questions from customers about merchandise availability. Management can also maintain optimum inventory levels and avoid running out of stock, like what happened to Frank & Oak in our feature story when it first started business.

Some businesses find it unnecessary or uneconomical to invest in a computerized perpetual inventory system. Many small businesses, in particular, find that a perpetual inventory system costs more than it is worth. Managers of these businesses can control merchandise and manage day-to-day operations using a periodic inventory system.

A complete physical inventory count is always taken at least once a year under both the perpetual and periodic inventory systems. Companies using a periodic inventory system must count their merchandise to determine quantities on hand and establish the cost of the goods sold and the ending inventory for accounting purposes. In a perpetual inventory system, they must count their merchandise to verify that the accounting records are correct. We will learn more about how to determine the quantity and cost of inventory later in this chapter and in the next chapter.

In summary, no matter which system is chosen, the flow of costs for a merchandising company is as follows: Beginning inventory (inventory on hand at the beginning of the period) plus the cost of goods purchased is the cost of goods available for sale. As goods are sold, the cost of these goods becomes an expense (cost of goods sold). Those goods not sold by the end of the accounting period represent ending inventory. The ending inventory is reported as a current asset on the balance sheet. The cost of goods sold is an expense on the income statement.

Because the perpetual inventory system is widely used, we illustrate it in this chapter. The periodic system is described in Appendix 5A.

ACCOUNTING IN ACTION
BUSINESS INSIGHT

Perpetual inventory systems provide more accurate information than periodic inventory systems. However, perpetual inventory systems also increase the amount of time spent on inventory management. In the past, most retailers used a periodic inventory system to record and report inventory. The periodic system was easier to use but provided little in the way of timely information and was much less accurate, making management of inventory challenging. In 1986, the first commercially available point-of-sale (POS) system was introduced, making

perpetual inventory systems easier. Now retailers have an array of products to choose from that will instantaneously process inventory transactions from purchase to sale. For example, Lightspeed POS, a Montreal-based IT company, develops and sells POS systems for retail and restaurant markets. The products allow businesses to track inventory purchases, inventory levels, and sales in real time without sophisticated and expensive equipment. The system also provides a manager or owner with relevant analytics.

Benjamin Haas/Shutterstock

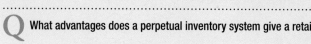

Q **What advantages does a perpetual inventory system give a retailer?**

BEFORE YOU GO ON...DO IT **1** **Merchandising Operations and Inventory Systems**

Indicate whether the following statements are true or false.

1. The primary source of revenue for a merchandising company results from performing services for customers.
2. The operating cycle of a service company is usually shorter than that of a merchandising company.
3. Sales revenue less cost of goods sold equals gross profit.
4. Ending inventory plus the cost of goods purchased equals cost of goods available for sale.

Solution

1. False. The primary source of revenue for a service company results from performing services for customers.
2. True.
3. True.
4. False. Beginning inventory plus the cost of goods purchased equals cost of goods available for sale.

Related exercise material: BE5–1, BE5–2, and E5–1.

Action Plan
- Review merchandising concepts.
- Recall the flow of costs in a merchandising company: Beginning inventory + cost of goods purchased – cost of ending inventory = cost of goods sold.

LEARNING OBJECTIVE **2** **Prepare entries for purchases under a perpetual inventory system.**

Recording Purchases of Merchandise

Companies purchase inventory using either cash or credit (on account). They normally record purchases when the goods are received from the seller. Every purchase should be supported by a document that provides written evidence of the transaction.

For example, there should be a cash receipt that indicates the items purchased and the amounts paid for each cash purchase. Cash purchases are recorded by an increase in Merchandise Inventory and a decrease in Cash.

Credit purchases should be supported by a purchase invoice showing the total purchase price and other relevant information. The purchaser uses a copy of the sales invoice sent by the seller as a purchase invoice. For example, in Illustration 5-6, Chelsea Electronics (the buyer) uses as a purchase invoice the sales invoice prepared by Highpoint Audio & TV Supply (the seller).

The buyer, Chelsea Electronics, makes the following entry to record the purchase of merchandise from Highpoint Audio & TV Supply. The entry increases (debits) Merchandise Inventory and increases (credits) Accounts Payable.

May 4	Merchandise Inventory	3,800	
	Accounts Payable		3,800
	To record goods purchased on account per invoice #731, terms 2/10, n/30.		

$$A = L + OE$$
$$+3,800 \quad +3,800$$

Cash flows: no effect

Only the goods purchased to sell to customers are recorded in the Merchandise Inventory account. Purchases of assets to use in the business—such as supplies or equipment—should be debited to the specific asset accounts.

▸ **ILLUSTRATION 5-6**
Sales/purchase invoice

Helpful hint To better understand the contents of this invoice, identify these items: 1. Seller; 2. Invoice date; 3. Purchaser; 4. Salesperson; 5. Credit terms; 6. Freight terms; 7. Goods sold: catalogue number, description, quantity, price per unit; 8. Total invoice amount.

INVOICE NO. 731

Highpoint Audio & TV Supply
277 Wellington Street, West
Toronto, Ontario, M5V 3H2

SOLD TO		
Firm name:	Chelsea Electronics	
Attention of:	James Hoover, Purchasing Agent	
Address:	21 King Street West	
	Hamilton	Ontario	L8P 4W7
	City	Province	Postal Code

Date: May 4, 2017	Salesperson: Malone	Terms 2/10, n/30	FOB shipping point		
Catalogue No.	Description		Quantity	Price	Amount
X572Y9820	70" 1080p 3D Smart TV		1	2,300	$2,300
A2547Z45	32" 1080p LED TV		5	300	1,500

IMPORTANT: ALL RETURNS MUST BE MADE WITHIN 10 DAYS		TOTAL	$3,800

SUBSIDIARY INVENTORY RECORDS

Imagine an organization like Frank & Oak recording purchases and sales of its inventory items in only one general ledger account—Merchandise Inventory. It would be almost impossible to determine the balance remaining of any particular inventory item at any specific time.

Instead, under a perpetual inventory system, a subsidiary ledger is used to organize and track individual inventory items. A **subsidiary ledger** is a group of accounts that share a common characteristic (for example, all inventory accounts). The subsidiary ledger frees the general ledger from the details of individual balances. In addition to having one for inventory, it is very common to have subsidiary ledgers for accounts receivable (to track individual customer balances), accounts payable (to track individual creditor balances), and payroll (to track individual employee pay records).

A subsidiary ledger is an addition to, and an expansion of, the general ledger, as Illustration 5-7 shows.

▸ **ILLUSTRATION 5-7**
Relationship of general ledger and subsidiary ledgers

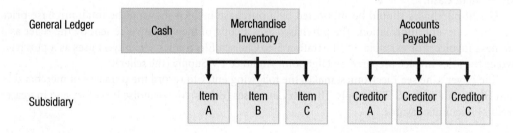

The general ledger account that summarizes the subsidiary ledger data is called a **control account**. In this illustration, the general ledger accounts Merchandise Inventory and Accounts Payable are control accounts with subsidiary ledgers. Cash is not a control account because there is no subsidiary ledger for this account.

Purchases and sales of each item of merchandise are recorded and posted to the individual inventory subsidiary ledger account. At any point in time, the inventory subsidiary ledger shows detailed information about the quantity and cost of each inventory item.

The detailed individual data from the inventory subsidiary ledger are summarized in the Merchandise Inventory control account in the general ledger. At all times, the control account balance must equal the total of all the individual inventory account balances.

Additional information about how to record and balance subsidiary and control account transactions can be found in Appendix C at the end of this textbook.

FREIGHT COSTS

The sales/purchase invoice should indicate when ownership of the goods transfers from the seller to the buyer. The company that owns the goods while they are being transported to the buyer's place of business pays the transportation charges and is responsible for any damage to the merchandise during transit. In North America, the point where ownership is transferred is called the FOB point and may be expressed as either "FOB destination" or "FOB shipping point." The letters FOB mean "free on board."

FOB is an enduring term in North America but is defined by the International Chamber of Commerce (ICC) as a term used for sea and inland waterway transport only. Alternative terms as defined by the ICC for general transport are FCA (free carrier) shipping point, which is similar to FOB shipping point, and DAP (delivered at place) destination, which is similar to FOB destination. For simplicity, we will use the terms "FOB destination" and "FOB shipping point" throughout the text.

FOB shipping point means:

1. Ownership changes from the seller to the buyer when the goods are placed on the carrier by the seller—the "shipping point."
2. The buyer pays the freight costs and is responsible for damages.

FOB destination means:

1. Ownership changes from the seller to the buyer when the goods are delivered by the carrier to the buyer's place of business—the "destination."
2. The seller pays the freight and is responsible for damages.

For example, the purchase invoice in Illustration 5-6 indicates that freight is FOB shipping point. The buyer (Chelsea Electronics) therefore pays the freight charges. Illustration 5-8 demonstrates these shipping terms.

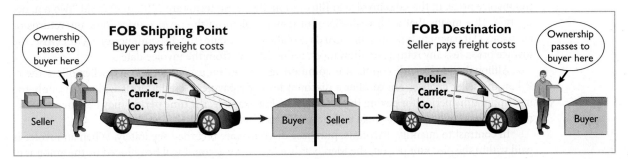

▶ ILLUSTRATION **5-8**
Terms of shipping

When the buyer pays for the freight costs, Merchandise Inventory is debited for the cost of the transportation. Why? Total merchandise inventory should include all costs incurred to purchase the merchandise, bring the goods to the buyer's location, and prepare the goods for resale. Freight charges represent one of the costs to bring the goods to the buyer's location.

For example, if upon delivery of the goods to Chelsea Electronics on May 4, Chelsea pays Public Carrier Co. $150 for freight charges, the entry on Chelsea Electronics' books is:

May 4	Merchandise Inventory	150	
	Cash		150
	To record payment of freight on goods purchased.		

A = L + OE
+150
−150

↓ Cash flows: −150

Thus, any freight costs incurred by the buyer are included in the cost of the merchandise.

PURCHASE RETURNS AND ALLOWANCES

A purchaser may be dissatisfied with the merchandise received if the goods are damaged or defective or of inferior quality, or if the goods do not meet the purchaser's specifications. In such cases, the purchaser may return the goods to the seller. This transaction is known as a **purchase return**. Alternatively, the purchaser may choose to keep the merchandise if the seller is willing to grant an allowance (deduction) from the purchase price. This transaction is known as a **purchase allowance**.

Assume that Chelsea Electronics returned goods costing $300 to Highpoint Audio & TV Supply on May 9. Highpoint will issue Chelsea a credit, which allows Chelsea to reduce its accounts payable. The entry by Chelsea Electronics for the returned merchandise is as follows:

A	=	L	+	OE
−300		−300		

Cash flows: no effect

May 9	Accounts Payable		300	
	Merchandise Inventory			300
	To record return of goods to Highpoint Audio & TV Supply.			

Because Chelsea Electronics increased Merchandise Inventory when the goods were purchased, Merchandise Inventory is decreased when Chelsea Electronics returns the goods. If Chelsea was given an allowance by Highpoint, the entry would be the same, reflecting that even though no merchandise was returned, Chelsea will not pay as much for the merchandise.

DISCOUNTS

Some events do not require a separate journal entry. For example, the terms of a credit purchase may include an offer of a **quantity discount** for a bulk purchase. A quantity discount gives a reduction in price according to the volume of the purchase. In other words, the larger the number of items purchased, the better the discount. Quantity discounts are not recorded or accounted for separately.

Quantity discounts are not the same as **purchase discounts**, which are offered to customers for early payment of the balance due. This incentive offers advantages to both parties: the purchaser saves money and the seller shortens its operating cycle by more quickly converting accounts receivable to cash.

Purchase discounts are noted on the invoice by the use of credit terms that specify the amount and time period for the purchase discount. They also indicate the length of time the buyer has to pay the full invoice price. In the sales invoice in Illustration 5-6, credit terms are 2/10, n/30 (read "two ten, net thirty"). This means that a 2% cash discount may be taken on the invoice price (less any returns or allowances) if payment is made within 10 days of the invoice date (the discount period). Otherwise, the invoice price, less any returns or allowances, is due 30 days from the invoice date.

Although purchase discounts are common in certain industries, not every seller offers them. When the seller chooses not to offer a discount for early payment, credit terms will specify only the maximum time period for paying the balance due. For example, the time period may be stated as n/30, meaning that the net amount must be paid in 30 days.

In contrast to quantity discounts, purchase discounts are recorded separately. When an invoice is paid within the discount period, the Merchandise Inventory account will be reduced by the amount of the discount because inventory is recorded at cost. By paying within the discount period, a company reduces the cost of its inventory.

To illustrate, assume that Chelsea Electronics pays the balance owing to Highpoint Audio & TV Supply on the last day of the discount period. Chelsea Electronics' entry to record its May 14 payment to Highpoint Audio & TV Supply is:

1. The balance owing to Highpoint Audio & TV Supply is $3,500, which is the result of the gross invoice price of $3,800 less purchase returns and allowances of $300.
2. The discount is $70 ($3,500 × 2%), reducing the Merchandise Inventory account to reflect the reduced cost of the merchandise.
3. The amount of cash paid by Chelsea Electronics to Highpoint Audio & TV Supply is $3,430 ($3,500 − $70).

A	=	L	+	OE
−70		−3,500		
−3,430				

↓ Cash flows: −3,430

May 14	Accounts Payable (1)		3,500	
	Merchandise Inventory (2)			70
	Cash (3)			3,430
	To record payment of invoice #731 within discount period.			

As a general rule, a company should usually take all available discounts. Not taking a discount is viewed as paying interest for use of the money not yet paid to the seller. For example, if Chelsea Electronics passed up the discount, it would have paid 2% for the use of $3,500 for 20 days. This equals an annual interest rate of 36.5% (2% × (365 ÷ 20)). Obviously, it would be better for Chelsea Electronics to borrow at bank interest rates than to lose the purchase discount.

If, contrary to best practices, Chelsea Electronics did not take advantage of the purchase discount and instead made full payment of $3,500 on June 3, the journal entry to record this payment would be:

June 3	Accounts Payable	3,500	
	Cash		3,500
	To record payment of invoice #731 with no discount.		

A	=	L	+	OE
−3,500		−3,500		

↓ Cash flows: −3,500

ACCOUNTING IN ACTION
ETHICS INSIGHT

Getty images/Daniel Grill

Even a company taking advantage of cash discounts can be subject to ethical issues. Consider the following hypothetical case as an example. Rita Pelzer was just hired as the assistant controller of Liu Stores. The company is a specialty retailer with nine stores in one city. Among other things, the payment of all invoices is centralized in one of the departments Rita will manage. Her main responsibilities are to maintain the company's high credit rating by paying all bills when they are due and to take advantage of all cash discounts.

Jamie Caterino, the former assistant controller, who has now been promoted to controller, is training Rita in her new duties. He instructs Rita to continue the practice of preparing all cheques for the amount due less the discount and to date the cheques the last day of the discount period. "But," Jamie continues, "we always hold the cheques at least four days beyond the discount period before mailing them. That way we get another four days of interest on our money. Most of our creditors need our business and don't complain. And, if they scream about our missing the discount period, we blame it on Canada Post. I think everybody does it. By the way, welcome to our team!"

 Q What are the ethical considerations in this case? Who are the stakeholders in this situation?

SUMMARY OF PURCHASE TRANSACTIONS

The following T account (with transaction descriptions) gives a summary of the effects of the transactions on Merchandise Inventory. Chelsea Electronics originally purchased $3,800 worth of inventory for resale. It paid $150 in freight charges. It then returned $300 worth of goods. And Chelsea Electronics received a discount of $70 by paying Highpoint Audio & TV Supply in the discount period. This results in a balance in Merchandise Inventory of $3,580.

		Merchandise Inventory			
Purchase	May 4	3,800	May 9	300	**Purchase return**
Freight	4	150	14	70	**Purchase discount**
	Bal.	3,580			

BEFORE YOU GO ON...**DO IT**	**2**	**Purchase Transactions**

Magnus Company had the following transactions in September:

Sept. 4   Bought merchandise on account from Perca Company for $1,500, terms 2/10, n/30, FOB destination.

     5   The correct company paid freight charges of $75.

     8   Returned $200 of the merchandise to Perca Company.

   14   Paid the total amount owing.

(continued)

BEFORE YOU GO ON...DO IT ② Purchase Transactions (continued)

(a) Record the transactions on Magnus Company's books.
(b) Post the transactions to the merchandise inventory account and determine the new balance.

Action Plan

- Purchases of goods for resale are recorded in the asset account Merchandise Inventory.
- Freight costs are paid by the seller when the freight terms are FOB destination.
- Freight charges paid by the buyer are debited to the Merchandise Inventory account and increase the cost of the merchandise inventory.
- The Merchandise Inventory account is reduced by the cost of merchandise returned.
- Calculate purchase discounts using the net amount owing.
- Reduce the Merchandise Inventory account by the amount of the purchase discount.

Solution

(a)

Magnus Company (buyer)

Sept. 4	Merchandise Inventory	1,500	
	Accounts Payable		1,500
	To record goods purchased on account.		
5	No journal entry. Terms FOB destination, therefore seller pays the freight.		
8	Accounts Payable	200	
	Merchandise Inventory		200
	To record return of goods.		
14	Accounts Payable ($1,500 – $200)	1,300	
	Merchandise Inventory ($1,300 × 2%)		26
	Cash ($1,300 – $26)		1,274
	To record cash payment within the discount period.		

(b)

Merchandise Inventory

Sept. 4		1,500	Sept. 8		200
			14		26
Sept. 30	Bal.	1,274			

Related exercise material: BE5–3, BE5–4, BE5–5, and E5–3.

LEARNING OBJECTIVE ③ ▶ **Prepare entries for sales under a perpetual inventory system.**

Recording Sales of Merchandise

Sales revenue, like service revenue, is recorded when there is an increase in assets (typically cash or accounts receivable) resulting from the company's business activities with its customers. For merchandising companies, this means that sales revenue is recorded (recognized) when the ownership of the goods is transferred from the seller to the buyer. This is typically when the goods have been sold and delivered. At this point, the sales transaction is completed and the sale price has been established.

There are two approaches to revenue recognition, 1) the contract-based approach and 2) the earnings approach. Both approaches may currently be used under IFRS and ASPE but as of January 1, 2018, only the contract-based approach may be used for companies following IFRS. We have chosen to demonstrate the earnings approach predominantly in this chapter because at the time of writing, the new revenue standard that mandates adoption of the contract-based approach is not yet in effect and the IASB is still working on clarification of the standard. In addition, although companies can adopt the contract-based approach earlier than January 1, 2018, it is not widely being used. The contract-based approach is discussed in more detail in Chapter 11.

Sales of merchandise may be made on credit or for cash. Every sales transaction should be supported by a business document that gives written evidence of the sale. Cash register tapes provide evidence of cash sales. A sales invoice, like the one shown in Illustration 5-6, provides support for a credit or cash sale. The seller prepares the invoice and gives a copy to the buyer.

Two entries are made for each sale in a perpetual inventory system:

1. **The first entry records the sales revenue:** Cash (or Accounts Receivable, if it is a credit sale) is increased by a debit, and the revenue account Sales is increased by a credit for the selling (invoice) price of the goods.
2. **The second entry records the cost of the merchandise sold:** the expense account Cost of Goods Sold is increased by a debit, and the asset account Merchandise Inventory is decreased by a credit for the cost of the goods. This entry ensures that the Merchandise Inventory account will always show the amount of inventory that should be on hand.

To illustrate a credit sales transaction, we will use the sales invoice shown in Illustration 5-6. Assuming that the merchandise cost Highpoint $2,400 when purchased, Highpoint Audio & TV Supply's $3,800 sale to Chelsea Electronics on May 4 is recorded as follows:

May 4	Accounts Receivable	3,800	
	Sales		3,800
	To record credit sale to Chelsea Electronics per invoice #731.		
4	Cost of Goods Sold	2,400	
	Merchandise Inventory		2,400
	To record cost of merchandise sold to Chelsea Electronics per invoice #731.		

A = L + OE
+3,800   +3,800
Cash flows: no effect

A = L + OE
−2,400   −2,400
Cash flows: no effect

For internal decision-making purposes, merchandisers may use more than one sales account, just as they use more than one inventory account. For example, Highpoint Audio & TV Supply may keep separate sales accounts for its televisions, car audio, and home theatre systems. By using separate sales accounts for major product lines, company management can monitor sales trends more closely and respond more strategically to changes in sales patterns. For example, if home theatre system sales are increasing while car audio systems are decreasing, the company can re-evaluate its advertising and pricing policies on each of these items.

On the income statement shown to outside investors, a merchandiser would normally give only a single sales figure—the sum of all of its individual sales accounts. This is done for two reasons. First, giving details on individual sales accounts would add too much length to the income statement and possibly make it less understandable. Second, companies do not want their competitors to know the details of their operating results.

FREIGHT COSTS

Recall that the freight terms FOB destination and FOB shipping point on the sales invoice indicate when ownership is transferred, and who is responsible for shipping costs. As explained earlier, if the term is FOB destination, the seller is responsible for getting the goods to their intended destination.

In Highpoint Audio & TV Supply's sale of electronic equipment to Chelsea Electronics, the freight terms (FOB shipping point) indicate that the purchaser, Chelsea Electronics, must pay the cost of shipping the goods from Highpoint Audio & TV Supply's location in Toronto to Chelsea Electronics' location in Hamilton. **Highpoint Audio & TV Supply, the seller, makes no journal entry to record the cost of shipping, since this is Chelsea's cost.**

If the freight terms on the invoice in Illustration 5-6 had been FOB destination, then Highpoint Audio & TV Supply would have paid the delivery charge. **Freight costs paid by the seller on merchandise sold are an operating expense to the seller** and are debited to a Freight Out account. Costs incurred to earn revenue are recorded as expenses. The following journal entry shows how Highpoint would have recorded the freight transaction if the terms had been FOB destination:

Alternative terminology The Freight Out account is also called *Delivery Expense* by some companies.

May 4	Freight Out	150	
	Cash		150
	To record payment of freight on goods sold.		

A = L + OE
−150   −150
↓ Cash flows: −150

When the seller pays the freight charges, it will usually establish a higher invoice price for the goods to cover the shipping expense.

SALES RETURNS AND ALLOWANCES

We now look at the opposite of purchase returns and allowances. When customers (buyers) return goods, or are given price reductions, the seller will either return cash to the buyer or reduce the buyer's accounts receivable if the goods were originally purchased on credit.

ACCOUNTING IN ACTION
BUSINESS INSIGHT

Returned goods can put a dent in a business's profits. When a customer returns a product, the business has to decide whether to scrap, liquidate, refurbish, return to seller, or return to stock. St. Catherines-based VDC Canada, has made a successful venture out of offering companies an opportunity to get some value out of unwanted products by liquidating them. It buys returned, discontinued, and excess

merchandise from retailers, distributors, and manufacturers and sells it to retailers across Canada at deep discounts. It's essentially a win-win situation for businesses and consumers: consumers get good value on a variety of quality goods, while manufacturers, wholesalers, and retailers have a place to dispose of unwanted merchandise.

Source: VDC website, www.vdccanada.com.

Q What accounting information would help a manager decide what to do with returned goods?

Under current IFRS and ASPE, the seller will need to record the reduction in cash or accounts receivable as well as the reduction in sales. But it is important for management to know about the amount of sales returns and allowances. If there is a large amount of returns and allowances, this suggests that there is inferior merchandise, inefficiencies in filling orders, errors in billing customers, and/ or mistakes in the delivery or shipment of goods. In order to provide information on **sales returns and allowances** to management, a **contra revenue account** called Sales Returns and Allowances is used. **Recall that a contra account is deducted from its related account in the financial statements.** By using a contra account, management can keep track of both the original sales and the amount of sales returns and allowances.

Helpful hint Remember that the increases, decreases, and normal balances of contra accounts are the opposite of the accounts they correspond to.

To illustrate, Highpoint Audio & TV Supply will make the following entry to record the goods returned on May 9 by Chelsea Electronics for a credit of $300:

A	=	L	+	OE
−300				−300

Cash flows: no effect

May 9	Sales Returns and Allowances	300	
	Accounts Receivable		300
	To record credit granted to Chelsea Electronics for returned goods.		

If the merchandise is not damaged and can be sold again, the seller will also need to record a second entry when goods are returned. Assuming this is the case with the goods returned by Chelsea, and assuming that the goods originally cost Highpoint $140, Highpoint Audio & TV Supply will record a second entry as follows:

A	=	L	+	OE
+140				+140

Cash flows: no effect

May 9	Merchandise Inventory	140	
	Cost of Goods Sold		140
	To record cost of returned goods.		

Notice that these two entries are basically the reverse of the entries recorded when the sale was originally made.

If the goods are damaged or defective and can no longer be sold, the second entry is not prepared. The second entry is also not required when the seller gives the buyer an allowance. If the goods have not been returned, or are defective and cannot be resold, the seller cannot increase its Merchandise Inventory and the original cost of goods sold recorded is still the correct amount.

DISCOUNTS

Sales are recorded at invoice price—whether it is the full retail price, a sales price, or a volume discount price. No separate entry is made to record a volume discount, or to show that the goods were sold at a special sales price.

Another type of discount, as discussed earlier in the chapter, is a cash discount for the early payment of the balance due. A seller may offer this to a customer to provide an incentive to pay early. From the seller's point of view, this is called a **sales discount** and is the opposite of a purchase discount.

A sales discount is a reduction in the selling price that a customer may or may not take advantage of. At the point of sale, it is not known if the customer will use the discount, so the revenue recorded at the point of sale is the full invoice price. If the customer subsequently decides to take advantage of the discount, then the seller must record the fact that revenue has been reduced.

As with sales returns and allowances, management will want to monitor if customers are taking advantage of the sales discounts. Thus, **a second contra revenue account, Sales Discounts, is used instead of directly reducing the Sales account.** The entry by Highpoint Audio & TV Supply to record the cash receipt from Chelsea Electronics on May 14 (within the discount period) is:

May 14	Cash	3,430	
	Sales Discounts	70	
	Accounts Receivable		3,500
	To record collection of invoice #731 within the		
	discount period.		

A	=	L	+	OE
+3,430				−70
−3,500				

↑Cash flows: +3,430

If the discount is not taken, and Chelsea Electronics instead pays the full amount on June 3, Highpoint Audio & TV Supply increases Cash and decreases Accounts Receivable by $3,500 at the date of collection, as shown below:

June 3	Cash	3,500	
	Accounts Receivable		3,500
	To record collection of invoice #731		
	with no discount.		

A	=	L	+	OE
+3,500				
−3,500				

↑Cash flows: +3,500

SUMMARY OF SALES TRANSACTIONS

Highpoint Audio & TV Supply sold merchandise for $3,800, with $300 of it later returned. A sales discount of $70 was given because the invoice was paid within the discount period. In contrast to the purchase transactions shown earlier in the chapter, which affected only one account, Merchandise Inventory, sales transactions are recorded in different accounts. A summary of these transactions is provided in the following T accounts:

Sales Revenue	Sales Returns and Allowances	Sales Discounts
3,800	300	70

These three accounts are combined to determine **net sales** as follows:

Sales		$3,800
Less: Sales returns and allowances	(300)	
Sales discounts	(70)	(370)
Net sales		$3,430

Total sales, before deducting the contra revenue accounts, is also known as **gross sales.**

SALES TAXES

We have now covered both the purchase of merchandise and the sale of merchandise in a merchandising company. There is one more topic that is related to both purchases and sales that is introduced here and discussed in more detail in Appendix B at the end of this textbook: sales taxes.

Sales taxes include the federal Goods and Services Tax (GST), the Provincial Sales Tax (PST), and in several provinces, the Harmonized Sales Tax (HST), which is a combination of GST and PST. The **GST or HST is paid by merchandising companies on the goods they purchase for resale**.

PST is not paid by a merchandiser—it is paid only by the final consumer. Therefore, retail businesses do not have to pay PST on any merchandise they purchase for resale.

GST and PST are collected by merchandising companies on the goods that they sell. When a company collects sales taxes on the sale of a good or service, these sales taxes are not recorded as revenue. The sales taxes are collected for the federal and provincial governments, and recorded as liabilities because the amounts are owed to these collecting authorities.

The accounting transactions described in this textbook are presented without the added complexity of sales taxes with the exception of those in Appendix B. That is why invoice number 731 shown in Illustration 5-6 did not include HST, which would normally be added to the invoice price for a business operating in Ontario.

BEFORE YOU GO ON...DO IT **3** | **Sales Transactions**

Record the following transactions for Perca Company:

Sept. 4 Sold merchandise for $1,500 on account to Magnus Company, terms 2/10, n/30, FOB destination. The original cost of the merchandise to Perca Company was $800.

     5 The correct company pays freight charges of $75.

     8 Magnus Company returned goods with a selling price of $200 and a cost of $80. The goods are restored to inventory.

    14 Received the correct payment from Magnus Company.

Action Plan

- Record both the sale and the cost of goods sold at the time of the sale.
- Freight costs are paid by the seller when the freight terms are FOB destination.
- Record sales returns in the contra account Sales Returns and Allowances and reduce Cost of Goods Sold when merchandise is returned to inventory.
- Calculate sales discounts using the net amount owing.
- Record sales discounts in the contra account Sales Discounts.

Solution

Perca Company (seller)

Sept.	4	Accounts Receivable	1,500	
		Sales		1,500
		To record credit sale.		
	4	Cost of Goods Sold	800	
		Merchandise Inventory		800
		To record cost of goods sold.		
	5	Freight Out	75	
		Cash		75
		To record freight paid on goods sold.		
	8	Sales Returns and Allowances	200	
		Accounts Receivable		200
		To record credit given for receipt of returned goods.		
	8	Merchandise Inventory	80	
		Cost of Goods Sold		80
		To record cost of goods returned.		
	14	Cash ($1,300 − $26)	1,274	
		Sales Discounts ($1,300 × 2%)	26	
		Accounts Receivable ($1,500 − $200)		1,300
		To record cash receipt within the discount period.		

Related exercise material: BE5–6, BE5–7, BE5–8, E5–4, E5–5, E5–6, and E5–7.

LEARNING OBJECTIVE **4** | Perform the steps in the accounting cycle for a merchandising company.

Completing the Accounting Cycle

Up to this point, we have shown the basic entries for recording transactions for purchases and sales in a perpetual inventory system. Now, it is time to consider the remaining steps in the accounting cycle for a merchandising company. All of the steps in the accounting cycle for a service company are also used for a merchandising company.

ADJUSTING ENTRIES

A merchandising company generally has the same types of adjusting entries as a service company. But a merchandiser that uses a perpetual inventory system may need one additional adjustment to make the accounting inventory records the same as the actual inventory on hand. This is necessary if errors in the accounting records have occurred, or if inventory has been stolen or damaged. **Even though the Merchandise Inventory account gives a record of the inventory on hand, it only indicates what** *should* **be there, not necessarily what actually** *is* **there.**

How does a company know if an adjustment is needed? The company will do a physical count of inventory on hand. As mentioned earlier in the chapter, a company must do a physical inventory count at least once a year.

If Highpoint Audio & TV Supply's accounting records show an ending inventory balance of $40,500 at the end of May and a physical inventory count indicates only $40,000 on hand, the following adjusting journal entry should be prepared.

May 31	Cost of Goods Sold	500	
	Merchandise Inventory		500
	To record difference between inventory records and physical units on hand.		

A	=	L	+	OE
−500				−500

Cash flows: no effect

The procedures involved in doing a physical count, and arriving at the total cost of the items counted, are covered in Chapter 6.

ACCOUNTING IN ACTION
ALL ABOUT YOU INSIGHT

© iStockphoto.com/Leah-Anne Thompson

Retailers around the world lost an estimated US$128.5 billion in 2013–14 to shrinkage—inventory loss due to theft and other reasons. This amounts to 1.29% of retail sales. Globally, the causes of shrinkage were shoplifters (thought to be responsible for about 38% of inventory loss), employee theft (28%), administration and non-crime losses (21%), and supplier fraud (13%). In Canada, shrinkage was around $4 billion in 2012, or about $10.8 million for every shopping day. Retailers are fighting back, spending billions of dollars on loss prevention measures. In Canada, for example, women's clothing chain Le Château became the first retailer to implement technology called

Fitting Room Central, which allows staff to scan and keep track of items as they go in and out of the fitting rooms—one of the most popular places for shoplifting to occur. Within eight months, Le Château's largest Montreal store, with 20 change rooms, reduced shrinkage by $30,000. Other loss prevention technology measures used by stores are radio frequency identification tags, magnetic tags, and surveillance cameras. Retailers also use low-tech methods to protect inventory, such as employing security guards; counting the number of items customers bring in and out of fitting rooms; publicizing anti-theft policies to customers, employees, and suppliers; and prosecuting those caught in the act of stealing to send a strong signal that theft will not be tolerated.

Sources: "Global Retail Theft Barometer 2013-14," accessed on June 18, 2015, at http://www.globalretailtheftbarometer.com/index.html; PricewaterhouseCoopers Canada, "Securing the Bottom Line: Canadian Retail Security Survey 2012"; Denise Deveau, "Out of Fitting Rooms, into the Profits," *Canadian Retailer*, September/October 2007.

Q Are there advantages to you as a customer when retailers increase theft prevention measures?

CLOSING ENTRIES

Using assumed data, an adjusted trial balance follows in Illustration 5-9 for Highpoint Audio & TV Supply at May 31, the company's year end. The accounts that are used only by a merchandising company are highlighted in green.

▶ILLUSTRATION 5-9
Adjusted trial balance

HIGHPOINT AUDIO & TV SUPPLY Adjusted Trial Balance May 31, 2017		
	Debit	**Credit**
Cash	$ 9,500	
Notes receivable	20,000	
Accounts receivable	7,900	
Merchandise inventory	40,000	
Equipment	70,000	
Accumulated depreciation—equipment		$ 24,000
Accounts payable		25,800
Notes payable		36,000
R. Lamb, capital		45,000
R. Lamb, drawings	15,000	
Sales		480,000
Sales returns and allowances	16,700	
Sales discounts	4,300	
Cost of goods sold	315,000	
Salaries expense	45,000	
Rent expense	19,000	
Utilities expense	17,000	
Advertising expense	16,000	
Depreciation expense	8,000	
Freight out	7,000	
Insurance expense	2,000	
Interest revenue		1,000
Rent revenue		2,400
Interest expense	1,800	
Totals	$614,200	$614,200

A merchandising company, like a service company, closes all accounts that affect profit to Income Summary. In journalizing, the company credits all temporary accounts with debit balances, and debits all temporary accounts with credit balances, as shown below for Highpoint Audio & TV Supply.

Helpful hint A merchandising company has more temporary accounts than a service company. Remember that Sales Returns and Allowances, Sales Discounts, Cost of Goods Sold, and Freight Out are temporary accounts with debit balances and must be closed to Income Summary.

May 31	Sales	480,000	
	Interest Revenue	1,000	
	Rent Revenue	2,400	
	Income Summary		483,400
	To close income statement accounts with credit balances.		
31	Income Summary	451,800	
	Sales Returns and Allowances		16,700
	Sales Discounts		4,300
	Cost of Goods Sold		315,000
	Salaries Expense		45,000
	Rent Expense		19,000
	Utilities Expense		17,000
	Advertising Expense		16,000
	Depreciation Expense		8,000
	Freight Out		7,000
	Insurance Expense		2,000
	Interest Expense		1,800
	To close income statement accounts with debit balances.		
31	Income Summary	31,600	
	R. Lamb, Capital		31,600
	To close income summary to capital.		
	R. Lamb, Capital	15,000	
	R. Lamb, Drawings		15,000
	To close drawings to capital.		

POST-CLOSING TRIAL BALANCE

After the closing entries are posted, all temporary accounts have zero balances. The R. Lamb, Capital account will have the same balance as is reported on the statement of owner's equity and balance sheet, and will be carried over to the next period. As with a service company, the final step in the accounting cycle is to prepare a post-closing trial balance. You will recall that the purpose of this trial balance is to ensure that debits equal credits in the permanent (balance sheet) accounts after all temporary accounts have been closed.

The post-closing trial balance is prepared in the same way as described in Chapter 4 and is not shown again here.

SUMMARY OF MERCHANDISING ENTRIES IN A PERPETUAL INVENTORY SYSTEM

Illustration 5-10 summarizes the entries for the merchandising accounts using a perpetual inventory system.

▶ ILLUSTRATION 5-10
Daily recurring, adjusting, and closing entries

	Transactions	Daily Recurring Entries	Debit	Credit
Purchases	Purchasing merchandise for resale.	Merchandise Inventory 　　Cash or Accounts Payable	XX	XX
	Paying freight costs on merchandise purchases, FOB shipping point.	Merchandise Inventory 　　Cash	XX	XX
	Receiving purchase returns or allowances from suppliers.	Cash or Accounts Payable 　　Merchandise Inventory	XX	XX
	Paying creditors on account within discount period.	Accounts Payable 　　Merchandise Inventory 　　Cash	XX	XX XX
	Paying creditors on account after the discount period.	Accounts Payable 　　Cash	XX	XX
Sales	Selling merchandise to customers.	Cash or Accounts Receivable 　　Sales Cost of Goods Sold 　　Merchandise Inventory	XX XX	XX XX
	Giving sales returns or allowances to customers.	Sales Returns and Allowances 　　Cash or Accounts Receivable Merchandise Inventory 　　Cost of Goods Sold	XX XX	XX XX
	Paying freight costs on sales, FOB destination.	Freight Out 　　Cash	XX	XX
	Receiving payment on account from customers within discount period.	Cash Sales Discounts 　　Accounts Receivable	XX XX	XX
	Receiving payment on account from customers after discount period.	Cash 　　Accounts Receivable	XX	XX

▶ILLUSTRATION **5-10**
(*continued*)

	Events	Daily Recurring Entries	Debit	Credit
Adjusting Entries	Determining, after a physical count, that inventory in general ledger is higher than inventory actually on hand.	Cost of Goods Sold Merchandise Inventory	XX	XX
Closing Entries	Closing temporary accounts with credit balances.	Sales Other Revenues Income Summary	XX XX	XX

	Closing temporary accounts with debit balances.	Income Summary
		    Sales Returns and Allowances
		    Sales Discounts
		    Cost of Goods Sold
		    Freight Out
		    Other expenses
			XX	XX
				XX
				XX
				XX
				XX

BEFORE YOU GO ON...DO IT **4** | **Closing Entries**

Action Plan

- Debit each temporary account with a credit balance and credit the total to the Income Summary account.
- Credit each temporary account with a debit balance and debit the total to the Income Summary account.
- Stop and check your work: Does the balance in the Income Summary account equal the reported profit?
- Debit the balance in the Income Summary account and credit the amount to the owner's capital account. (Do the opposite if the company had a loss.)
- Credit the balance in the drawings account and debit the amount to the owner's capital account. Do not close drawings with expenses.
- Stop and check your work: Does the balance in the owner's capital account equal the ending balance reported in the statement of owner's equity?

The trial balance of Yee Clothing Company at December 31 shows Merchandise Inventory $25,000; J. Yee, Capital $12,000; Sales $162,400; Sales Returns and Allowances $4,800; Sales Discounts $950; Cost of Goods Sold $110,000; Rental Revenue $6,000; Freight Out $1,800; Rent Expense $8,800; Salaries Expense $22,000; and J. Yee, Drawings $3,600. Yee Clothing Company's statement of owner's equity for the year showed profit of $20,050 and closing owner's capital of $28,450.

(a) Prepare the closing entries for the above accounts.
(b) Create T accounts for Income Summary and J. Yee, Capital, and post the closing entries to these accounts.

Solution

Dec. 31	Sales	162,400	
	Rental Revenue	6,000	
	Income Summary		168,400
	To close income statement accounts with credit balances.		
31	Income Summary	148,350	
	Sales Returns and Allowances		4,800
	Sales Discounts		950
	Cost of Goods Sold		110,000
	Freight Out		1,800
	Rent Expense		8,800
	Salaries Expense		22,000
	To close income statement accounts with debit balances.		
31	Income Summary	20,050	
	J. Yee, Capital		20,050
	To close Income Summary account.		
31	J. Yee, Capital	3,600	
	J. Yee, Drawings		3,600
	To close drawings account.		

Income Summary					J. Yee, Capital			
Clos.	148,350	Clos.	168,400				Bal.	12,000
		Bal.	20,050*		Clos.	3,600	Clos.	20,050
Clos.	20,050						Bal.	28,450**
		Bal.	0					

*Check = Profit   **Check = Closing owner's capital

Related exercise material: BE5–9, BE5–10, and E5–8.

Merchandising Financial Statements

Merchandisers widely use the classified balance sheet introduced in Chapter 4 and one of two forms of income statements. This section explains the use of these financial statements by merchandisers.

SINGLE-STEP INCOME STATEMENT

The income statement form used in previous chapters of this textbook is the **single-step income statement**. The statement is so named because only one step—subtracting total expenses from total revenues—is required in determining profit.

In a single-step income statement, all data are classified under two categories: (1) revenues and (2) expenses. A single-step income statement for Highpoint Audio & TV Supply, using the data from the adjusted trial balance in Illustration 5-9, is shown in Illustration 5-11.

ILLUSTRATION 5-11
Single-step income statement

HIGHPOINT AUDIO & TV SUPPLY Income Statement Year Ended May 31, 2017		
Revenues		
Net sales		$459,000
Interest revenue		1,000
Rent revenue		2,400
Total revenues		462,400
Expenses		
Cost of goods sold	$315,000	
Salaries expense	45,000	
Rent expense	19,000	
Utilities expense	17,000	
Advertising expense	16,000	
Depreciation expense	8,000	
Freight out	7,000	
Insurance expense	2,000	
Interest expense	1,800	
Total expenses		430,800
Profit		$ 31,600

Note that net sales was calculated by deducting sales returns and allowances and sales discounts from sales ($459,000 = $480,000 − $16,700 − $4,300). Revenue from investments, such as interest revenue, must be shown separately from other revenue. Cost of goods sold and interest expense (also income tax expense for corporations) must be reported separately on the income statement. Expenses that are not significant in themselves can be included separately in the income statement as shown above, or grouped with other similar items, with additional details in the notes to the financial statements.

Under ASPE, companies do not have to list their expenses in any particular order. Under IFRS, companies must classify operating and other expenses based on either the **nature** of the expenses or their **function** within the company. Classifying expenses by nature means that expenses are reported based on what the resources were spent on (e.g., employee costs, transportation, and advertising). Classifying expenses by function means that expenses are reported based on which business function the resources were spent on (e.g., costs of sales, administration, and selling). In Illustration 5-11, expenses are classified by nature.

There are two main reasons for using the single-step format: (1) a company does not realize any profit until total revenues exceed total expenses, so it makes sense to divide the statement into these two categories; and (2) the single-step format is simple and easy to read.

MULTIPLE-STEP INCOME STATEMENT

The **multiple-step income statement** is so named because it shows several steps in determining profit (or loss). This form is often considered more useful than a single-step income statement because the steps give additional information about a company's profitability and distinguish between the company's operating and non-operating activities as explained below.

Net Sales

The multiple-step income statement for a merchandising company begins by presenting sales revenue. The contra revenue accounts Sales Returns and Allowances and Sales Discounts are deducted from Sales to arrive at **net sales**. The sales revenue section for Highpoint Audio & TV Supply (using data from the adjusted trial balance in Illustration 5-9) is as follows:

Sales revenue		
Sales		$480,000
Less: Sales returns and allowances	$16,700	
Sales discounts	4,300	21,000
Net sales		**$459,000**

Many companies condense this information and report only the net sales figure in their income statement. This alternative was shown in the single-step income statement in Illustration 5-11.

Gross Profit

The next step is the calculation of gross profit. In Illustration 5-1, you learned that cost of goods sold is deducted from sales revenue to determine **gross profit**. For this calculation, companies use net sales as the amount of sales revenue. Based on the sales data above and the cost of goods sold in the adjusted trial balance in Illustration 5-9, the gross profit for Highpoint Audio & TV Supply is $144,000, calculated as follows:

Net sales	$459,000
Cost of goods sold	315,000
Gross profit	**$144,000**

Operating Expenses

Operating expenses are the next component in measuring profit for a merchandising company. They are the recurring expenses associated with the central operations of the company—other than cost of goods sold—that are incurred in the process of earning sales revenue. These expenses are similar in service and merchandising companies.

Highpoint Audio & TV Supply would classify the following items in its adjusted trial balance (as shown in Illustration 5-9) as operating expenses: Salaries Expense, $45,000; Rent Expense, $19,000; Utilities Expense, $17,000; Advertising Expense, $16,000; Depreciation Expense, $8,000; Freight Out, $7,000; and Insurance Expense, $2,000. This results in total operating expenses of $114,000.

Recall our discussion about classifying expenses by nature or function. Should a company choose to present their operating expenses by function, the expenses would be subdivided into selling expenses and administrative expenses. Selling expenses are associated with making sales. They include expenses for sales promotion, as well as the expenses involved to complete the sale (e.g., freight out or delivery expense). Administrative expenses relate to general operating activities such as management, accounting, and legal costs. This classification method can be used in both multiple- and single-step income statements.

Profit from Operations

Profit from operations, or the results of the company's normal operating activities, is determined by subtracting operating expenses from gross profit. Based on the gross profit and operating expenses data determined above, Highpoint Audio & TV Supply's profit from operations is $30,000, calculated as follows:

Gross profit	$144,000
Operating expenses	114,000
Profit from operations	**$ 30,000**

The purpose of showing profit from operations as a separate number from overall profit is to assist users of financial statements in understanding the company's main operations. The additional information helps users in making projections of future financial performance.

Non-operating Activities

Non-operating activities are other revenues and expenses not related to the company's main operations. Examples of other revenues include interest revenue, rental revenue (if earned from renting assets not needed for operations), and investment income. Examples of other expenses include interest expense.

Distinguishing between operating and non-operating activities is important to external users of financial statements. Non-operating activities are often short-term activities and are not expected to continue into the future as the company's main operating activities are. Separating the two in the income statement increases the predictive value of the statement.

Based on the data in Highpoint Audio & TV Supply's adjusted trial balance shown in Illustration 5-9, the company will show its non-operating activities as follows in its multiple-step income statement:

Net other non-operating revenues	**$1,600**

In this presentation, non-operating revenues of $3,400 (Interest and Rent revenue) are combined with non-operating expense (Interest expense) of $1,800 to give a net amount of revenue that equals $1,600. Companies may also choose to show separate line items for "Other Revenue" and "Other Expenses" as well as a net total.

Sometimes, as is the case in Corus's statement of income, these items are listed separately with no identifying heading.

Profit

Profit is the final outcome of all the company's operating and non-operating activities. Highpoint's profit is $31,600 after adding its net non-operating revenues of $1,600 to profit from operations as follows:

Profit from operations	$30,000
Net non-operating revenues	1,600
Profit	**$31,600**

If there are no non-operating activities, the company's profit from operations becomes its profit.

In Illustration 5-12, we bring together all of these steps in a comprehensive multiple-step income statement for Highpoint Audio & TV Supply.

Note that the profit amounts in Illustrations 5-11 (single-step) and 5-12 (multiple-step) are the same. The only differences between the two forms of income statements are the amount of detail shown and the order of presentation.

▶ILLUSTRATION 5-12
Multiple-step income statement

HIGHPOINT AUDIO & TV SUPPLY Income Statement Year Ended May 31, 2017			
Calculation of net sales and gross profit	Sales revenue		
	Sales		$480,000
	Less: Sales returns and allowances	$16,700	
	Sales discounts	4,300	21,000
	Net sales		459,000
	Cost of goods sold		315,000
	Gross profit		144,000
Calculation of operating expenses and profit from operations	Operating expenses		
	Salaries expense	$45,000	
	Rent expense	19,000	
	Utilities expense	17,000	
	Advertising expense	16,000	
	Depreciation expense	8,000	
	Freight out	7,000	
	Insurance expense	2,000	
	Total operating expenses		114,000
	Profit from operations		30,000
Calculation of non-operating activities and profit	Other revenues		
	Interest revenue	$ 1,000	
	Rent revenue	2,400	
	Total non-operating revenues	3,400	
	Other expenses		
	Interest expense	1,800	
	Net non-operating revenues		1,600
	Profit		$ 31,600

CLASSIFIED BALANCE SHEET

Recall from Chapter 4 that merchandise inventory is a current asset because we expect to sell it within one year of the balance sheet date. Also recall from Chapter 4 that items are typically listed under current assets in their order of liquidity. Merchandise inventory is less liquid than accounts receivable and short-term notes receivable because the goods must first be sold before revenue can be collected from the customer. Thus, in the balance sheet, merchandise inventory is reported as a current asset immediately below accounts receivable. Illustration 5-13 presents the assets section of a classified balance sheet for Highpoint Audio & TV Supply.

▶ILLUSTRATION 5-13

Assets section of a merchandising company's classified balance sheet

Helpful hint The $40,000 is the cost of the inventory on hand, not its expected selling price.

HIGHPOINT AUDIO & TV SUPPLY Balance Sheet (partial) May 31, 2017		
Current assets		
Cash		$ 9,500
Notes receivable		20,000
Accounts receivable		7,900
Merchandise inventory		40,000
Total current assets		77,400
Property, plant, and equipment		
Equipment	$70,000	
Less: Accumulated depreciation	24,000	46,000
Total assets		$123,400

The remaining two financial statements, the statement of owner's equity and cash flow statement (to be discussed in Chapter 17), are the same as those of a service company. They are not shown in this chapter.

BEFORE YOU GO ON...DO IT	**Merchandising Income Statement**

Silver Store reported the following information: Sales $620,000; Sales Returns and Allowances $32,000; Sales Discounts $10,200; Cost of Goods Sold $422,000; Depreciation Expense $10,000; Freight Out $5,000; Interest Expense $1,700; Rent Expense $15,000; and Salaries Expense $80,000.
   Calculate the following amounts: (a) net sales, (b) gross profit, (c) total operating expenses, (d) profit from operations, and (e) profit.

Solution

(a) Net sales: $620,000 − $32,000 − $10,200 = $577,800
(b) Gross profit: $577,800 − $422,000 = $155,800
(c) Total operating expenses: $10,000 + $5,000 + $15,000 + $80,000 = $110,000
(d) Profit from operations: $155,800 − $110,000 = $45,800
(e) Profit: $45,800 − $1,700 = $44,100

Related exercise material: BE5–11, BE5–12, E5–9, and E5–10.

Action Plan
- Deduct Sales Returns and Allowances and Sales Discounts from Sales to arrive at net sales.
- Deduct Cost of Goods Sold from net sales to arrive at gross profit.
- Identify which expenses are operating expenses and which are non-operating expenses.
- Deduct operating expenses from gross profit to arrive at profit from operations.
- Deduct any non-operating expenses from (and add any non-operating revenues to) profit from operations to arrive at profit.

LEARNING OBJECTIVE	**Calculate the gross profit margin and profit margin.**

Using the Information in the Financial Statements

In Chapter 4, we introduced a tool called ratio analysis that investors and creditors use to determine additional information about how a company is performing. In this chapter, we introduce two profitability ratios: gross profit margin and profit margin. **Profitability ratios** assess a company's ability to generate profit.

To demonstrate profitability ratios, we will use information provided in the annual financial statements for Dollarama Inc. for the year ended February 1, 2015.

(in thousands of dollars)	2015	2014
Sales	$2,330,805	$2,064,676
Gross profit	859,548	765,584
Net earnings for the year	295,410	250,094

GROSS PROFIT MARGIN

A company's gross profit may be expressed as a percentage, called the **gross profit margin**. This is calculated by dividing the amount of gross profit by net sales. Illustration 5-14 shows the gross profit margin for Dollarama Inc. for the year ended February 1, 2015 (dollars in millions).

Gross Profit	÷	Net Sales	=	Gross Profit Margin
$859,548	÷	$2,330,805	=	36.9%

▸ ILLUSTRATION 5-14
Gross profit margin

The gross profit *margin* is generally considered to be more useful than the gross profit *amount* because the margin shows the relative relationship between net sales and gross profit. For example, a gross profit amount of $1 million may sound impressive. But, if it is the result of net sales of $50 million, then the gross profit margin is only 2%, which is not so impressive.

The amount and trend of gross profit are closely watched by management and other interested parties. They compare current gross profit margin with past periods' gross profit margin. They also compare the company's gross profit margin with the margin of competitors and with industry averages. Such comparisons give information about the effectiveness of a company's purchasing and the soundness of its pricing policies. In general, a higher gross profit margin is seen as being more favourable than a lower gross profit margin.

Gross profit is important because inventory has a significant effect on a company's profitability. Cost of goods sold is usually the largest expense on the income statement. Gross profit represents a company's merchandising profit. It is not a measure of overall profitability, because operating expenses have not been deducted.

PROFIT MARGIN

Overall profitability is measured by examining profit. Profit is often expressed as a percentage of sales, similar to the gross profit margin. The **profit margin** measures the percentage of each dollar of sales that results in profit. It is calculated by dividing profit by net sales. Illustration 5-15 shows the profit margin for Dollarama for the year ended February 1, 2015 (dollars in thousands).

▶ **ILLUSTRATION 5-15**
Profit margin

Profit	÷	Net Sales	=	Profit Margin
$295,410	÷	$2,330,805	=	12.7%

How do the gross profit margin and profit margin differ? Gross profit margin measures the proportion of the selling price remaining after accounting for cost of goods sold. The profit margin measures the proportion of the selling price remaining after accounting for all expenses, including cost of goods sold. A company can improve its profit margin by increasing its gross profit margin (i.e., increasing sales or decreasing costs of goods sold), or by controlling its operating expenses (and non-operating activities), or by doing both.

BEFORE YOU GO ON...DO IT **6** **Profitability Ratios**

Selected financial information is available for two recent fiscal years for Antonia Co.

	2017	2016
Net sales	$550,000	$600,000
Cost of goods sold	300,000	350,000
Profit	50,000	25,000

(a) Calculate (1) gross profit, (2) gross profit margin, and (3) profit margin for 2016 and 2017.
(b) Comment on any changes in profitability.

Action Plan

- Gross profit is net sales minus cost of goods sold.
- Divide gross profit by net sales to calculate gross profit margin.
- Divide profit by net sales to calculate profit margin.
- Recall whether higher or lower ratios indicate improvement or deterioration in profitability.

Solution

(a)

	2017	2016
(1) Gross profit	= $550,000 − $300,000	= $600,000 − $350,000
	= $250,000	= $250,000
(2) Gross profit margin	= $250,000 ÷ $550,000	= $250,000 ÷ $600,000
	= 45.5%	= 41.7%
(3) Profit margin	= $50,000 ÷ $550,000	= $25,000 ÷ $600,000
	= 9.1%	= 4.2%

(b) The gross profit margin and profit margin have both increased in 2017 from 2016. In general, higher ratios indicate that the company's profitability has improved during 2017.

Related exercise material: BE5–13, E5–2, E5–11, and E5–12.

APPENDIX 5A: PERIODIC INVENTORY SYSTEM

LEARNING OBJECTIVE **7** | **Prepare the entries for purchases and sales under a periodic inventory system and calculate cost of goods sold.**

As described in this chapter, there are two basic systems of accounting for inventories: (1) the perpetual inventory system, and (2) the periodic inventory system. In the chapter, we focused on the characteristics of the perpetual inventory system. In this appendix, we discuss and illustrate the periodic inventory system.

One key difference between the two inventory systems is the timing for calculating the cost of goods sold. In a periodic inventory system, the cost of the merchandise sold is not recorded on the date of sale. Recall from the introduction to the periodic inventory system earlier in the chapter that the cost of goods sold during the period is calculated by taking a physical inventory count at the end of the period and deducting the cost of this inventory from the cost of the merchandise available for sale during the period. We will revisit this again later in this appendix.

There are other differences between the perpetual and periodic inventory systems. Under a periodic inventory system, **purchases of merchandise are recorded in the Purchases expense account**, rather than the Merchandise Inventory asset account. Also, under a periodic system, it is **customary to record purchase returns and allowances, purchase discounts, and freight in separate accounts.** That way, accumulated amounts are known for each.

To illustrate the recording of merchandise transactions under a periodic inventory system, we will use the purchase/sale transactions between Highpoint Audio & TV Supply (the seller) and Chelsea Electronics (the buyer) from earlier in this chapter.

RECORDING PURCHASES OF MERCHANDISE

Based on the sales invoice (Illustration 5-6) and receipt of the merchandise ordered from Highpoint Audio & TV Supply, if Chelsea Electronics uses a periodic inventory system, the following entry records the $3,800 purchase:

May 4	Purchases	3,800	
	Accounts Payable		3,800
	To record goods purchased on account per		
	invoice #731, terms 2/10, n/30.		

A = L + OE
      +3,800 −3,800
Cash flows: no effect

Purchases is an expense account whose normal balance is a debit.

Freight Costs

When the buyer pays for the freight costs, the account Freight In is debited. For example, Chelsea pays Public Carrier Co. $150 for freight charges on its purchase from Highpoint Audio & TV Supply. The entry on Chelsea's books is as follows:

May 4	Freight In	150	
	Cash		150
	To record payment of freight on goods purchased.		

A = L + OE
−150   −150
↓ Cash flows: −150

Like Purchases, Freight In is an expense account whose normal balance is a debit. Just as freight was a part of the cost of the merchandise inventory in a perpetual inventory system, Freight In is part of the cost of goods purchased in a periodic inventory system. The cost of goods purchased should include any freight charges for transporting the goods to the buyer.

Purchase Returns and Allowances

Chelsea Electronics returns $300 worth of goods and prepares the following entry to recognize the return:

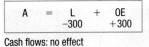

May 9	Accounts Payable	300	
	Purchase Returns and Allowances		300
	To record return of goods to Highpoint Audio & TV Supply.		

Purchase Returns and Allowances is a contra expense account whose normal balance is a credit and the balance will be subtracted from the Purchases account.

Purchase Discounts

Recall that the invoice terms were 2/10, n/30. On May 14, Chelsea Electronics pays the balance owing to Highpoint Audio & TV Supply of $3,500 ($3,800 less return of $300) less the 2% discount for payment within 10 days. Chelsea Electronics records the following entry:

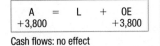

May 14	Accounts Payable ($3,800 − $300)	3,500	
	Purchase Discounts ($3,500 × 2%)		70
	Cash ($3,500 − $70)		3,430
	To record payment of invoice #731 within the discount period.		

Purchase Discounts is a contra expense account whose normal balance is a credit and the balance will be subtracted from the Purchases account.

In each of the above transactions, a temporary expense account was used to record the transactions related to purchases of merchandise rather than the Merchandise Inventory account that is used in a perpetual inventory system. A comparison of purchase transactions under the two inventory systems is shown later in the appendix.

RECORDING SALES OF MERCHANDISE

The seller, Highpoint Audio & TV Supply, records the sale of $3,800 of merchandise to Chelsea Electronics on May 4 (sales invoice in Illustration 5-6) as follows:

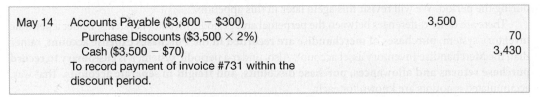

May 4	Accounts Receivable	3,800	
	Sales		3,800
	To record credit sale to Chelsea Electronics per invoice #731.		

Recall that in a periodic inventory system, there is no entry to record the cost of goods sold and reduction of inventory at the point of sale.

Freight Costs

There is no difference between the accounting for freight costs by the seller in a perpetual and a periodic inventory system. In both systems, freight costs paid by the seller are debited to Freight Out, an operating expense account. Recall that in this example the freight terms were FOB shipping point, so Highpoint did not incur freight costs.

Sales Returns and Allowances

The $300 return of goods on May 9 is recorded by Highpoint Audio & TV Supply as follows:

May 9	Sales Returns and Allowances	300	
	Accounts Receivable		300
	To record credit granted to Chelsea Electronics for returned goods.		

A = L + OE
−300   −300
Cash flows: no effect

Just as there is only one entry needed when sales are recorded in a periodic inventory system, one entry is also all that is needed to record a return. Different from the perpetual system, it doesn't matter if the inventory is damaged and discarded, or returned to inventory; no entry is needed in the periodic inventory system.

Sales Discounts

On May 14, Highpoint Audio & TV Supply receives a payment of $3,430 on account from Chelsea Electronics. Highpoint records this payment as follows:

May 14	Cash ($3,500 − $70)	3,430	
	Sales Discounts ($3,500 × 2%)	70	
	Accounts Receivable ($3,800 − $300)		3,500
	To record collection of invoice #731 within the discount period.		

A = L + OE
+3,430   −70
−3,500
↑ Cash flows: +3,430

COMPARISON OF ENTRIES—PERPETUAL VS. PERIODIC

Illustration 5A-1 summarizes the periodic inventory entries shown in this appendix and compares them with the perpetual inventory entries shown earlier in the chapter. Entries that are different in the two systems are shown in colour.

▶ ILLUSTRATION 5A-1
Comparison of journal entries under perpetual and periodic inventory systems

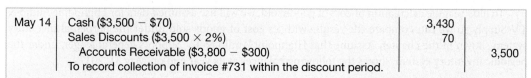

PURCHASES (ENTRIES MADE ON CHELSEA ELECTRONICS' BOOKS)

	Transaction	Perpetual Inventory System			Periodic Inventory System		
May 4	Purchase of merchandise on credit.	Merchandise Inventory	3,800		Purchases	3,800	
		Accounts Payable		3,800	Accounts Payable		3,800
4	Freight cost on purchases.	Merchandise Inventory	150		Freight In	150	
		Cash		150	Cash		150
9	Purchase returns and allowances.	Accounts Payable	300		Accounts Payable	300	
		Merchandise Inventory		300	Purchase Returns and Allowances		300
14	Payment on account with a discount.	Accounts Payable	3,500		Accounts Payable	3,500	
		Merchandise Inventory		70	Purchase Discounts		70
		Cash		3,430	Cash		3,430

SALES (ENTRIES ON HIGHPOINT AUDIO & TV SUPPLY'S BOOKS)

	Transaction	Perpetual Inventory System			Periodic Inventory System		
May 4	Sale of merchandise on credit.	Accounts Receivable	3,800		Accounts Receivable	3,800	
		Sales		3,800	Sales		3,800
		Cost of Goods Sold	2,400		No entry for cost of goods sold		
		Merchandise Inventory		2,400			
9	Return of merchandise sold.	Sales Returns and Allowances	300		Sales Returns and Allowances	300	
		Accounts Receivable		300	Accounts Receivable		300
		Merchandise Inventory	140		No entry for cost of goods sold		
		Cost of Goods Sold		140			
14	Cash received on account with a discount.	Cash	3,430		Cash	3,430	
		Sales Discounts	70		Sales Discounts	70	
		Accounts Receivable		3,500	Accounts Receivable		3,500

CALCULATING COST OF GOODS SOLD

In a periodic inventory system, the Merchandise Inventory account is not continuously updated for each purchase and sale. As we saw in the entries above, temporary accounts are used instead to accumulate the cost of the goods purchased throughout the period, and no entries are made to accumulate the cost of goods sold. Thus, the dollar amount of merchandise on hand at the end of the period and the cost of goods sold for the period are not known by looking at the general ledger accounts.

Instead, these amounts will have to be determined at the end of the accounting period in a periodic inventory system. The equation to calculate cost of goods sold was presented in Illustration 5-5 earlier in the chapter and is repeated below as Illustration 5A-2.

▶ ILLUSTRATION **5A-2**
Basic formula for
cost of goods sold

To illustrate the calculation of cost of goods sold, we will use assumed data for Highpoint Audio & TV Supply so we can compare the results with its cost of goods sold under the perpetual inventory system shown in the chapter. Assume that Highpoint Audio & TV Supply's general ledger, under the periodic inventory system, shows the following balances at its year end on May 31, 2017:

Merchandise Inventory	$ 35,000
Purchases	325,000
Purchase Returns and Allowances	10,400
Purchase Discounts	6,800
Freight In	12,200

Beginning Inventory

If Highpoint Audio & TV Supply uses the periodic inventory system, it will not record any transactions in the Merchandise Inventory account during the period, and the balance in this account will not have changed since the beginning of the year. Thus **the $35,000 balance in the general ledger—as shown above—is equal to beginning inventory.**

Cost of Goods Purchased

In a periodic inventory system, four accounts—Purchases, Purchase Returns and Allowances, Purchase Discounts, and Freight In—are used to record the purchase of inventory. These four accounts are combined to calculate the cost of goods purchased.

First, **net purchases** is calculated by subtracting purchase returns and allowances and purchase discounts (both credit balances) from purchases (a debit balance). This calculation for Highpoint for the year ended May 31, 2017, is $307,800, as shown in Illustration 5A-3.

▶ ILLUSTRATION **5A-3**
Formula for net
purchases

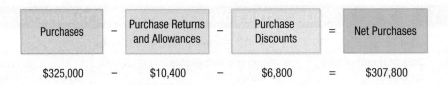

Then the **cost of goods purchased** is calculated by adding the balance in the Freight In account to net purchases. Highpoint's cost of goods purchased for the year ended May 31, 2017, is $320,000, as shown in Illustration 5A-4.

▶ ILLUSTRATION **5A-4**
Formula for cost of
goods purchased

Cost of Goods Available for Sale

As shown in Illustration 5A-2, the **cost of goods available for sale** is equal to the cost of the goods on hand at the beginning of the period (beginning inventory) plus the cost of goods purchased during the period. This is the total amount that the company could have sold during the period. Highpoint's cost of goods available for sale for the year ended May 31, 2017, is $355,000 ($35,000 + $320,000).

Ending Inventory

To determine the cost of the inventory on hand on May 31, 2017, Highpoint Audio & TV Supply must take a physical inventory. You will recall from earlier in this chapter that Highpoint determined that the cost of goods on hand or ending inventory on May 31, 2017, is $40,000. The inventory on hand is the same regardless of the inventory system used.

You will learn later in this appendix that the balance in the Merchandise Inventory account is adjusted from the beginning balance of $35,000 to the ending balance of $40,000 as part of the closing process.

Cost of Goods Sold

As shown in Illustration 5A-2, once the ending inventory is determined, the cost of goods sold is calculated by subtracting the ending inventory from the cost of goods available for sale. Highpoint's cost of goods sold is $315,000 ($355,000 − $40,000).

MULTIPLE-STEP INCOME STATEMENT

The only reporting difference in a multiple-step income statement is that the cost of goods sold section has more detail in a periodic inventory system—as shown in Illustration 5A-5—than in a perpetual inventory system, where only one line is reported for the cost of goods sold. Note that cost of goods sold, gross profit, and profit are the same amounts as shown in Illustration 5-12 in the chapter.

Most merchandising companies choose the multiple-step presentation for their income statement because it provides information about their gross profit. The single-step presentation was presented earlier in the chapter but, because it is not commonly used, it will not be presented here again.

Using the periodic inventory system does not affect the content of the balance sheet. As in the perpetual system, merchandise inventory is reported in the current assets section, and at the same amount.

COMPLETING THE ACCOUNTING CYCLE

After preparing the financial statements, closing entries and a post-closing trial balance complete the accounting cycle. For a merchandising company, as for a service company, all accounts that affect the determination of profit are closed to the Owner's Capital account.

It is also necessary to update the balance of the Merchandise Inventory account as part of the closing process in a periodic inventory system. During the year, no entries are made to this account when inventory is purchased or sold. Therefore, the Merchandise Inventory balance in the adjusted trial balance is its beginning balance, not its ending balance.

Two closing journal entries are used to update the Merchandise Inventory account from the beginning balance of $35,000 to the ending balance of $40,000. These two entries for Highpoint Audio & TV Supply are as follows:

May 31	Income Summary	35,000	
	Merchandise Inventory		35,000
	To close beginning inventory.		
31	Merchandise Inventory	40,000	
	Income Summary		40,000
	To record ending inventory.		

A	=	L	+	OE
−35,000				−35,000

Cash flows: no effect

A	=	L	+	OE
+40,000				+40,000

Cash flows: no effect

▶ILLUSTRATION 5A-5
Multiple-step income
statement—periodic
inventory system

HIGHPOINT AUDIO & TV SUPPLY			
Income Statement			
Year Ended May 31, 2017			
Sales revenue			
Sales			$480,000
Less: Sales returns and allowances		$ 16,700	
Sales discounts		4,300	21,000
Net sales			459,000
Cost of goods sold			
Inventory, June 1, 2016		$ 35,000	
Purchases	$325,000		
Less: Purchase returns and allowances	$10,400		
Purchase discounts	6,800	17,200	
Net purchases		307,800	
Add: Freight in		12,200	
Cost of goods purchased		320,000	
Cost of goods available for sale		355,000	
Inventory, May 31, 2017		40,000	
Cost of goods sold			315,000
Gross profit			144,000
Operating expenses			
Salaries expense		$ 45,000	
Rent expense		19,000	
Utilities expense		17,000	
Advertising expense		16,000	
Depreciation expense		8,000	
Freight out		7,000	
Insurance expense		2,000	
Total operating expenses			114,000
Profit from operations			30,000
Other revenues			
Interest revenue		$ 1,000	
Rent revenue		2,400	
Total non-operating revenues		3,400	
Other expenses			
Interest expense		1,800	
Net non-operating revenues			1,600
Profit			$ 31,600

The Income Summary account is used because beginning and ending inventory are used in the cost of goods sold calculation, which is then used to determine profit or loss for the period. After the closing entries are posted, the Merchandise Inventory account will show the following:

Merchandise Inventory					
June 1, 2016	Bal.	35,000	May 31, 2017	Clos.	35,000
May 31, 2017	Clos.	40,000			
May 31, 2017	Bal.	40,000			

The effect of the two closing journal entries on the Merchandise Inventory account is similar to the effect that the closing process has on the Owner's Capital account. The ending inventory and capital balances must be updated to agree with the amount reported on the balance sheet at the end of the period. The balance sheet reports these ending balances, not the amounts in the adjusted trial balance. The ending balance in Merchandise Inventory now becomes the beginning inventory amount for the next period.

The remaining closing entries are the same as those as we saw in prior chapters and are not shown here. The only difference between a merchandising company using the periodic inventory system and a service company is that there are several additional temporary accounts that must be closed.

After the closing entries are posted, a post-closing trial balance is prepared. The post-closing trial balance is prepared in the same way as described in earlier chapters and is not explained again here.

BEFORE YOU GO ON...DO IT 7 ▸ Periodic Inventory System

The following transactions occurred in August:

Aug. 1 Superior Seating Company buys merchandise on account from Cotton Company for $1,000, terms 2/10, n/30, FOB destination.
   1 The correct company pays freight charges of $70.
   3 Superior Seating Company returns $150 of the merchandise to Cotton Company and the goods are returned to inventory.
  10 Superior Seating Company pays the total amount owing.

Both companies use a periodic inventory system.

(a) Record Superior Seating Company's transactions.
(b) Record Cotton Company's transactions.

Solution

(a) Superior Seating Company (buyer)

Aug. 1	Purchases	1,000	
	Accounts Payable		1,000
	Goods purchased on account.		
1	No entry; seller pays for freight		
3	Accounts Payable	150	
	Purchase Returns and Allowances		150
	Returned goods.		
10	Accounts Payable ($1,000 − $150)	850	
	Purchase Discounts ($850 × 2%)		17
	Cash ($850 − $17)		833
	Cash payment within the discount period.		

(b) Cotton Company (seller)

Aug. 1	Accounts Receivable	1,000	
	Sales		1,000
	Credit sale of merchandise.		
1	Freight Out	70	
	Cash		70
	Payment of freight costs.		
3	Sales Returns and Allowances	150	
	Accounts Receivable		150
	Customer returned goods.		
10	Cash ($850 − $17)	833	
	Sales Discounts ($850 × 2%)	17	
	Accounts Receivable		850
	Cash received within the discount period.		

Related exercise material: *BE5–15, *BE5–16, *E5–13, *E5–14, *E5–15, and *E5–16.

Action Plan

- In a periodic system, purchases of inventory are recorded in the Purchases account.
- Examine freight terms to determine which company pays the freight charges.
- Calculate purchase discounts using the net amount owing and record in a Purchase Discounts account.
- In a periodic system, the cost of goods sold is not recorded at the time of the sale; it must be calculated at the end of the period after a physical inventory count.
- In a periodic system, inventory is not adjusted for returned merchandise.
- Calculate purchase/sales discounts using the net amount owing and record in a Purchase/Sales Discounts account.

Comparing IFRS and ASPE

Key Differences	International Financial Reporting Standards (IFRS)	Accounting Standards for Private Enterprises (ASPE)
Classification of expense in the income statement	Expenses must be classified by either nature or function.	Expenses can be classified in any manner the company finds useful.
Accounting for sales transactions.	Contract-based approach (effective January 1, 2018) covered in Chapter 11.	Contract-based approach or earnings approach.

Demonstration Problem 1

Fortuna Retailers and Bello Distributors had the following transactions in June. Both companies use a perpetual inventory system.

June 1 Fortuna Retailers purchased merchandise inventory for resale from Bello Distributors for $8,500. Terms of purchase were 2/10, n/30, FOB shipping point.

2 The correct company paid $175 cash for freight charges.

3 Fortuna noted that some of the goods were not exactly as ordered and returned the goods to Bello Distributors. Bello Distributors granted Fortuna a $500 purchase return.

10 Fortuna paid Bello Distributors the amount owing.

Additional information for Bello Distributors:

1. The cost of the merchandise sold on June 1 was $5,300.
2. The cost of the merchandise returned on June 3 was $300. The goods were returned to inventory.

Instructions

(a) Journalize the June transactions for Fortuna Retailers.
(b) Journalize the June transactions for Bello Distributors.

ACTION PLAN

- The Merchandise Inventory account is used for all transactions that affect the cost of the goods purchased.
- Cost of goods sold must be calculated and recorded at point of sale in a perpetual inventory system.
- A contra revenue account is used for sales allowances given to customers.
- A contra revenue account is used for sales discounts taken by customers.

SOLUTION TO DEMONSTRATION PROBLEM 1

(a) Fortuna Retailers (buyer)

Date	Account Titles and Explanation	Debit	Credit
June 1	Merchandise Inventory	8,500	
	Accounts Payable		8,500
	Purchased merchandise on account.		
2	Merchandise Inventory	175	
	Cash		175
	Paid freight charges on goods purchased.		
3	Accounts Payable	500	
	Merchandise Inventory		500
	Returned merchandise.		
10	Accounts Payable ($8,500 − $500)	8,000	
	Merchandise Inventory ($8,000 × 2%)		160
	Cash ($8,000 − $160)		7,840
	Paid for merchandise in the discount period.		

(b) Bello Distributors (seller)

Date	Account Titles and Explanation	Debit	Credit
June 1	Accounts Receivable	8,500	
	Sales		8,500
	Sold merchandise on account.		
	Cost of Goods Sold	5,300	
	Merchandise Inventory		5,300
	Record cost of goods sold.		
2	No entry. Purchaser pays freight.		
3	Sales Returns and Allowances	500	
	Accounts Receivable		500
	Customer returned merchandise.		
	Merchandise Inventory	300	
	Cost of Goods Sold		300
	Cost of goods returned.		
10	Cash	7,840	
	Sales Discount	160	
	Accounts Receivable		8,000
	Received payment in the discount period.		

Demonstration Problem 2

The adjusted trial balance data for the year ended December 31, 2017, for Dykstra Company are as follows:

DYKSTRA COMPANY
Adjusted Trial Balance
December 31, 2017

	Debit	Credit
Cash	$ 14,500	
Accounts receivable	15,100	
Merchandise inventory	29,000	
Prepaid insurance	2,500	
Land	150,000	
Building	500,000	
Accumulated depreciation—building		$ 40,000
Equipment	95,000	
Accumulated depreciation—equipment		18,000
Accounts payable		10,600
Property taxes payable		4,000
Mortgage payable—due before December 31, 2018		25,000
Mortgage payable—long-term		530,000
G. Dykstra, capital		81,000
G. Dykstra, drawings	12,000	
Sales		627,200
Sales returns and allowances	5,700	
Sales discounts	1,000	
Cost of goods sold	353,800	
Advertising expense	12,000	
Depreciation expense	29,000	
Freight out	7,600	
Insurance expense	4,500	
Property tax expense	24,000	
Salaries expense	61,000	
Utilities expense	18,000	
Interest revenue		2,500
Interest expense	3,600	
Totals	$1,338,300	$1,338,300

Instructions
(a) Prepare a single-step income statement for the year ended December 31, 2017.
(b) Prepare a multiple-step income statement for the year ended December 31, 2017.
(c) Prepare a statement of owner's equity for Dykstra Company for the year ended December 31, 2017. No additional investments were made by Mr. Dykstra during the year.
(d) Prepare a classified balance sheet as at December 31, 2017.
(e) Prepare closing entries.

ACTION PLAN

- Recall that in a single-step income statement, all revenues are together, then all of the expenses. Profit is the difference between the two subtotals.
- Remember that the major subtotal headings in the multiple-step income statement are net sales, gross profit, profit from operations, and profit (loss).
- Prepare the multiple-step income statement in steps:
  1. Sales less sales returns and allowances and sales discounts equals net sales.
  2. Net sales less cost of goods sold is equal to gross profit.
  3. Gross profit less operating expenses equals profit from operations.
  4. Profit from operations plus (minus) non-operating revenue (expense) items equals profit.
- Merchandise Inventory is a current asset in the classified balance sheet.
- Sales Returns and Allowances, Sales Discounts, and Cost of Goods Sold are temporary accounts with debit balances that must be closed.

SOLUTION TO DEMONSTRATION PROBLEM 2

(a)

DYKSTRA COMPANY
Income Statement
Year Ended December 31, 2017

Revenues		
Net sales		$620,500
Interest revenue		2,500
Total revenues		623,000
Expenses		
Cost of goods sold	$353,800	
Advertising expense	12,000	
Depreciation expense	29,000	
Freight out	7,600	
Insurance expense	4,500	
Interest expense	3,600	
Property tax expense	24,000	
Salaries expense	61,000	
Utilities expense	18,000	
Total expenses		513,500
Profit		$ 109,500

(b)

DYKSTRA COMPANY
Income Statement
Year Ended December 31, 2017

Sales revenue		
Sales		$627,200
Less: Sales returns and allowances	$ 5,700	
Sales discounts	1,000	6,700
Net sales		620,500
Cost of goods sold		353,800
Gross profit		266,700
Operating expenses		
Advertising expense	12,000	
Depreciation expense	29,000	
Freight out	7,600	
Insurance expense	4,500	
Property tax expense	24,000	
Salaries expense	61,000	
Utilities expense	18,000	
Total operating expenses		156,100
Profit from operations		110,600
Other revenues and expenses		
Interest revenue	2,500	
Interest expense	(3,600)	(1,100)
Profit		$109,500

(c)

DYKSTRA COMPANY
Statement of Owner's Equity
Year Ended December 31, 2017

G. Dykstra, capital, January 1, 2014	$ 81,000
Add: Profit	109,500
	190,500
Deduct: Drawings	12,000
G. Dykstra, capital, December 31, 2014	$178,500

(d)

DYKSTRA COMPANY
Balance Sheet
December 31, 2017

Assets

Current assets		
Cash		$ 14,500
Accounts receivable		15,100
Merchandise inventory		29,000
Prepaid insurance		2,500
Total current assets		61,100
Property, plant, and equipment		
Land		150,000
Building	$500,000	
Less: Accumulated depreciation	40,000	460,000
Equipment	$ 95,000	
Less: Accumulated depreciation	18,000	77,000
Total property, plant, and equipment		687,000
Total assets		$748,100

Liabilities and Owner's Equity

Current liabilities	
Accounts payable	$ 10,600
Property taxes payable	4,000
Current portion of mortgage payable	25,000
Total current liabilities	39,600
Non-current liabilities	
Mortgage payable	530,000
Total liabilities	569,600
Owner's equity	
G. Dykstra, capital	178,500
Total liabilities and owner's equity	$748,100

Solution to Demonstration Problem 2 *continued*

(e)

Dec. 31	Sales	627,200	
	Interest Revenue	2,500	
	Income Summary		629,700
	To close revenue accounts.		
31	Income Summary	520,200	
	Sales Returns and Allowances		5,700
	Sales Discounts		1,000
	Cost of Goods Sold		353,800
	Advertising Expense		12,000
	Depreciation Expense		29,000
	Freight Out		7,600
	Insurance Expense		4,500
	Property Tax Expense		24,000
	Salaries Expense		61,000
	Utilities Expense		18,000
	Interest Expense		3,600
	To close expense accounts.		
31	Income Summary ($629,700 − $520,200)	109,500	
	G. Dykstra, Capital		109,500
	To close Income Summary.		
31	G. Dykstra, Capital	12,000	
	G. Dykstra, Drawings		12,000
	To close drawings.		

▶ Summary of Learning Objectives

1. *Describe the differences between service and merchandising companies.* A service company performs services. It has service or fee revenue and operating expenses. A merchandising company sells goods. It has sales revenue, cost of goods sold, gross profit, and operating expenses. A merchandising company has a longer operating cycle than a service company. Merchandising companies must decide if they want to spend the extra resources to use a perpetual inventory system in which inventory records are updated with each purchase and sale. The benefit of the perpetual system is that it provides better information and control over inventory than a periodic system in which inventory records are updated only at the end of the accounting period.

2. *Prepare entries for purchases under a perpetual inventory system.* The Merchandise Inventory account is debited (increased) for all purchases of merchandise and freight, if freight is paid by the buyer. It is credited (decreased) for purchase returns and allowances and purchase discounts. Purchase discounts are cash reductions to the net invoice price for early payment.

3. *Prepare entries for sales under a perpetual inventory system.* When inventory is sold, two entries are required: (1) Accounts Receivable (or Cash) is debited and Sales is

credited for the selling price of the merchandise. (2) Cost of Goods Sold (an expense) is debited (increased) and Merchandise Inventory (a current asset) is credited (decreased) for the cost of the inventory items sold. Contra revenue accounts are used to record sales returns and allowances and sales discounts. When the returned merchandise can be sold again in the future, an additional entry is made to inventory and cost of goods sold. Freight costs paid by the seller are recorded as an operating expense.

4. *Perform the steps in the accounting cycle for a merchandising company.* Each of the required steps in the accounting cycle for a service company is also done for a merchandising company. An additional adjusting journal entry may be required under a perpetual inventory system. The Merchandise Inventory account must be adjusted to agree with the physical inventory count if there is a difference in the amounts. Merchandising companies have additional temporary accounts that must also be closed at the end of the accounting year.

5. *Prepare single-step and multiple-step income statements.* In a single-step income statement, all data are classified under two categories (revenues or expenses), and profit is

determined in one step. A multiple-step income statement shows several steps in determining profit. Net sales is calculated by deducting sales returns and allowances and sales discounts from sales. Next, gross profit is calculated by deducting the cost of goods sold from net sales. Profit (loss) from operations is then calculated by deducting operating expenses from gross profit. Total non-operating activities are added to (or deducted from) profit from operations to determine profit.

6. *Calculate the gross profit margin and profit margin.* The gross profit margin, calculated by dividing gross profit by net sales, measures the gross profit earned for each dollar of sales. The profit margin, calculated by dividing profit by net sales, measures the profit (total profit) earned for each dollar of sales. Both are measures of profitability that are closely watched by management and other interested parties.

7. *Prepare the entries for purchases and sales under a periodic inventory system and calculate cost of goods sold (Appendix 5A).* In a periodic inventory system, separate temporary expense and contra expense accounts are used to record (a) purchases, (b) purchase returns and allowances, (c) purchase discounts, and (d) freight costs paid by the buyer. Purchases − purchase returns and allowances − purchase discounts = net purchases. Net purchases + freight in = cost of goods purchased.

In a periodic inventory system, only one journal entry is made to record a sale of merchandise. Cost of goods sold is not recorded at the time of the sale. Instead, it is calculated as follows at the end of the period after the ending inventory has been counted: Beginning inventory + cost of goods purchased = cost of goods available for sale. Cost of goods available for sale − ending inventory = cost of goods sold.

▶ Glossary

Contra revenue account An account with the opposite balance (debit) compared with its related revenue account, which has a credit balance. The contra revenue account is deducted from the revenue account on the income statement. (p. 248)

Control account An account in the general ledger that summarizes the detail for a subsidiary ledger and controls it. (p. 242)

Cost of goods available for sale The cost of the goods on hand at the beginning of the period (beginning inventory) plus the cost of goods purchased during the period. (p. 265)

Cost of goods purchased Net purchases (purchases minus purchase returns and allowances and purchase discounts) plus freight in. (p. 264)

Cost of goods sold The total cost of merchandise sold during the period. In a perpetual inventory system, it is calculated and recorded for each sale. In a periodic inventory system, the total cost of goods sold for the period is calculated at the end of the accounting period by deducting ending inventory from the cost of goods available for sale. (p. 238)

FOB destination A freight term indicating that the buyer accepts ownership when the goods are delivered to the buyer's place of business. The seller pays the shipping costs and is responsible for damages to the goods during transit. (p. 243)

FOB shipping point A freight term indicating that the buyer accepts ownership when the goods are placed on the carrier by the seller. The buyer pays freight costs from the shipping point to the destination and is responsible for damages. (p. 243)

Function A method of classifying expenses on the income statement based on which business function the resources were spent on (e.g., cost of sales, administration, and selling). (p. 255)

Gross profit Sales revenue (net sales) less cost of goods sold. (p. 238)

Gross profit margin Gross profit expressed as a percentage of net sales. It is calculated by dividing gross profit by net sales. (p. 259)

Gross sales Total sales before deducting the contra revenue accounts. (p. 249)

Multiple-step income statement An income statement that shows several steps to determine profit or loss. (p. 256)

Nature A method of classifying expenses on the income statement based on what the resources were spent on (e.g., depreciation, employee costs, transportation, and advertising). (p. 255)

Net purchases Purchases minus purchase returns and allowances and purchase discounts. (p. 264)

Net sales Sales less sales returns and allowances and sales discounts. (p. 249)

Non-operating activities Other revenues and expenses that are unrelated to the company's main operations. (p. 257)

Operating expenses Expenses incurred in the process of earning sales revenue. They are deducted from gross profit in the income statement. (p. 238)

Periodic inventory system An inventory system where detailed inventory records are not updated whenever a transaction occurs. The cost of goods sold is determined only at the end of the accounting period. (p. 239)

Perpetual inventory system An inventory system where detailed records, showing the quantity and cost of each inventory item, are updated whenever a transaction occurs. The records continuously show the inventory that should be on hand. (p. 239)

Profit from operations Profit from a company's main operating activity, determined by subtracting operating expenses from gross profit. (p. 257)

Profit margin Profit expressed as a percentage of net sales. It is calculated by dividing profit by net sales. (p. 260)

Profitability ratios Measures of a company's profit or operating success (or shortcomings) for a specific period of time. (p. 259)

Purchase discount A discount, based on the invoice price less any returns and allowances, given to a buyer for early payment of a balance due. (p. 244)

Purchase return (allowance) The return, or reduction in price, of unsatisfactory merchandise that was purchased. They result in a debit to Cash or Accounts Payable. (p. 244)

Quantity discount A cash discount that reduces the invoice price and is given to the buyer for volume purchases. (p. 244)

Sales discount A reduction, based on the invoice price less any returns and allowances, given by a seller for early payment of a credit sale. (p. 249)

Sales returns (allowances) The return, or reduction in price, of unsatisfactory merchandise that was sold. They result in a credit to Cash or Accounts Receivable. (p. 248)

Sales revenue The main source of revenue in a merchandising company. (p. 238)

Single-step income statement An income statement that shows only one step (revenues less expenses) in determining profit (or loss). (p. 255)

Subsidiary ledger A group of accounts that give details for a control account in the general ledger. (p. 242)

Note: All questions, exercises, and problems below with an asterisk (*) relate to material in Appendix 5A.

▶ Self-Study Questions
Answers are at the end of the chapter.

(LO 1) C 1. Gross profit will result when:
    (a) Operating expenses are less than profit.
    (b) Sales revenues are greater than operating expenses.
    (c) Sales revenues are greater than cost of goods sold.
    (d) Operating expenses are greater than cost of goods sold.

(LO 1) K 2. Which of the following statements describes an advantage of a perpetual inventory system?
    (a) It is not necessary to calculate and record the cost of goods sold with each sale with a perpetual inventory system.
    (b) The perpetual inventory system provides better control over inventory because inventory shortages can be more easily identified.
    (c) It is not necessary to do a physical count of the inventory in a perpetual inventory system.
    (d) A perpetual inventory system results in less clerical work and is less costly than a periodic inventory system.

(LO 2) AP 3. A $750 purchase of merchandise inventory is made on June 13, terms 2/10, n/30. On June 16, merchandise costing $50 is returned. What amount will be the payment in full on June 22?
    (a) $686
    (b) $700
    (c) $735
    (d) $750

(LO 2, 3) K 4. When goods are shipped with the freight terms FOB shipping point in a perpetual inventory system:
    (a) the buyer pays the freight costs and debits Merchandise Inventory.
    (b) the buyer pays the freight costs and debits Freight In.
    (c) the seller pays the freight costs and debits Freight Out.
    (d) the seller pays the freight costs and debits Cost of Goods Sold.

(LO 2, 3) C 5. Discounts offered to customers for early payment of the balance due:
    (a) will reduce the cost of the merchandise for the purchaser and increase the cost of goods sold for the seller.
    (b) reduce the cash paid by the purchaser, and the cash received by the seller, by the same amount.

    (c) are required by provincial law.
    (d) benefit the seller but generally do not benefit the purchaser.

(LO 3) K 6. To record the sale of goods for cash in a perpetual inventory system:
    (a) only one journal entry is necessary to record the cost of goods sold and reduction of inventory.
    (b) only one journal entry is necessary to record the receipt of cash and the sales revenue.
    (c) two journal entries are necessary: one to record the receipt of cash and sales revenue, and one to record the cost of the goods sold and reduction of inventory.
    (d) two journal entries are necessary: one to record the receipt of cash and reduction of inventory, and one to record the cost of the goods sold and sales revenue.

(LO 3) AP 7. The adjusted trial balance of White Company reports a balance in Sales of $18,000, Sales Discounts has a balance of $400, and Sales Returns and Allowances has a balance of $1,500. White Company's net sales will be equal to:
    (a) $18,000
    (b) $17,600
    (c) $16,100
    (d) $16,500

(LO 4, 5) K 8. The steps in the accounting cycle for a merchandising company using the perpetual inventory system are the same as those for a service company *except*:
    (a) closing journal entries are not required for a merchandising company.
    (b) a post-closing trial balance is not required for a merchandising company.
    (c) an additional adjusting journal entry in the case of any inventory shortages may be needed in a merchandising company.
    (d) a multiple-step income statement is required for a merchandising company.

(LO 5) K 9. Which of the following appears on both a single-step and a multiple-step income statement for a merchandising company?
    (a) Merchandise inventory
    (b) Gross profit
    (c) Profit from operations
    (d) Cost of goods sold

(LO 6) AP10. Net sales are $400,000, cost of goods sold is $310,000, operating expenses are $60,000, and other revenues are $5,000. What are the gross profit margin and profit margin?
(a) 7.5% and 8.8%
(b) 22.5% and 7.4%
(c) 22.5% and 8.8%
(d) 77.5% and 8.8%

(LO 7) K *11. Under a periodic inventory system, when goods are purchased for resale by a company:
(a) purchases on account are debited to Merchandise Inventory.

(b) purchases on account are debited to Purchases.
(c) purchase returns are debited to Merchandise Inventory.
(d) freight costs are debited to Cost of Goods Sold.

(LO 7) AP *12. If beginning inventory is $60,000, purchases are $400,000, purchase returns and allowances are $25,000, freight in is $5,000, and ending inventory is $50,000, what is the cost of goods sold?
(a) $385,000
(b) $390,000
(c) $410,000
(d) $430,000

▶ Questions

(LO 1) C 1. What is the difference in determining profit for a merchandising company in comparison with a service company?

(LO 1) C 2. Explain the differences between a perpetual and a periodic inventory system. Include in your explanation why the words "perpetual" and "periodic" are used for the two systems.

(LO 1) C 3. Song Yee wonders why a physical inventory count is necessary in a perpetual inventory system. After all, the accounting records show how much inventory is on hand. Explain why a physical inventory count is required in a perpetual inventory system.

(LO 1) C 4. Describe the costs and the benefits of a perpetual inventory system compared with a periodic inventory system.

(LO 2) K 5. Describe what a subsidiary ledger is and what it is used for. Provide examples of common types of subsidiary ledgers that are used in companies.

(LO 3) C 6. Rosalee tells a friend in her introductory accounting class that they don't have to worry about how to account for sales taxes on inventory purchases because merchandising companies don't pay sales tax. Do you agree or disagree? Explain.

(LO 2, 3) C7. What are the differences between FOB shipping point and FOB destination? Explain the differences between how freight costs are recorded for inventory purchases as opposed to inventory sales.

(LO 2) K 8. Explain the difference between a purchase return and a purchase allowance. In a perpetual inventory system, what accounts would be affected by a purchase return and a purchase allowance?

(LO 2) C 9. Fukushima Company received an invoice for $16,000, terms 1/10, n/30. It will have to borrow from its bank in order to pay the invoice in 10 days. The interest rate Fukushima pays on its bank loans is 7.25%. Should Fukushima take advantage of the cash discount offered or not? Support your answer with calculations.

(LO 3) C 10. Shapiro Book Company sells a book that cost $50 for $75 cash. The accountant prepares a journal

entry with a debit to Cash for $75, a credit to Merchandise Inventory for $50, and a credit to Gross Profit for $25. What part of this is incorrect and why is it important to use the correct accounts? The company uses a perpetual inventory system.

(LO 2, 3) C 11. Explain the difference between a quantity discount, a purchase discount, and a sales discount. Explain how each of them is recorded.

(LO 3) K 12. What are the advantages of using multiple sales accounts to keep separate track of sales for major product lines? Would a merchandiser show individual sales accounts on its income statement? Why or why not?

(LO 3) C 13. Raymond is the accountant at an electronics retail store. He is friends with one of the salespeople, Geoff. Geoff tells Raymond to simply debit Sales whenever a customer returns an item that Geoff originally sold. Do you agree with Geoff's advice? What should Raymond do?

(LO 3) C 14. When the seller records a sales return or a sales allowance, sometimes they also adjust cost of goods sold and inventory. Explain when it is necessary to also record an entry in the cost of goods sold and inventory accounts, what is debited and credited, and what amount is used.

(LO 4) C 15. "The steps in the accounting cycle for a merchandising company are different from those in the accounting cycle for a service company." Do you agree or disagree? Explain.

(LO 4) C 16. Neptune Stores uses a perpetual inventory system and has just completed its annual physical inventory count. The accountant determines that the physical inventory count is higher than the accounting records. How could this be possible and what adjustment should be recorded, if any?

(LO 4) K 17. Compared with a service company, what additional accounts must be closed for a merchandising company using a perpetual inventory system? Include in your answer if the account should be debited or credited to close it.

(LO 5) K 18. Explain the differences between a single-step and a multiple-step income statement.

(LO 5) K 19. Explain the terms "net sales," "gross profit," "profit from operations," and "profit." Are these terms used only by merchandising companies or are they used by service companies also?

(LO 5) C 20. Why is interest expense reported as a non-operating expense instead of as an operating expense on a multiple-step income statement?

(LO 5) C 21. Is it possible for a company's profit from operations and its profit to be the same amount? If so, should any company bother to calculate both numbers?

(LO 5) AP 22. What are non-operating activities? Why is it important that these activities be distinguished from operating activities on the income statement?

(LO 6) C 23. What is the difference between gross profit and gross profit margin? Why is it useful to calculate a company's gross profit margin?

(LO 7) K *24. Explain the differences between how inventory purchases are recorded in a periodic system and in a perpetual system. Also explain the differences in recording sales between a periodic system and a perpetual system.

(LO 7) K *25. Identify the accounts that are added to or deducted from Purchases in a periodic system to determine the cost of goods purchased. For each account, indicate whether it is added or deducted.

(LO 7) C *26. In a periodic inventory system, closing entries are posted to the Merchandise Inventory account. What is the purpose of these entries?

▶ Brief Exercises

Calculate missing amounts in determining profit or loss. (LO 1) AP

BE5–1 The components in the income statements of companies A, B, C, and D follow. Determine the missing amounts.

	Sales	Cost of Goods Sold	Gross Profit	Operating Expenses	Profit/(Loss)
Company A	$350,000	$ (a)	$122,500	$105,000	$ (b)
Company B	735,000	367,500	(c)	(d)	73,500
Company C	525,000	315,000	(e)	115,500	(f)
Company D	(g)	346,500	148,500	188,100	(h)

Calculate missing amounts in determining cost of goods sold. (LO 1) AP

BE5–2 Presented below are the components in determining cost of goods sold. Determine the missing amounts.

	Beginning Inventory	Purchases	Cost of Goods Available for Sale	Ending Inventory	Cost of Goods Sold
1.	$250,000	$170,000	$ (a)	$50,000	$ (b)
2.	108,000	70,000	(c)	(d)	90,000
3.	75,000	(e)	130,000	(f)	38,000
4.	(g)	75,000	95,000	45,000	(h)

Record purchase transactions and indicate impact on assets, liabilities, and owner's equity. (LO 2) C

BE5–3 Novellus Electronics Store uses a perpetual inventory system. The company had the following transactions in March.

Mar. 16 Purchased $15,000 of merchandise from Venus Distributors, terms 2/10, n/30, FOB destination.
18 Novellus Electronics Store received an allowance of $750 for the merchandise purchased on March 16 because of minor damage to the goods.
25 Paid the balance due to Venus Distributors.

For each transaction, (a) prepare a journal entry to record the transaction and (b) indicate the amount by which the transaction increased or decreased total assets, total liabilities, and owner's equity. Indicate NE (no effect) if the transaction neither increased nor decreased any of these items.

Record purchase transactions—perpetual system. (LO 2) AP

BE5–4 Prepare the journal entries to record the following purchase transactions in Xiaoyan Company's books. Xiaoyan uses a perpetual inventory system.

Jan. 2 Xiaoyan purchased $20,000 of merchandise from Feng Company, terms n/30, FOB shipping point.
4 The correct company paid freight costs of $215.
6 Xiaoyan returned $1,500 of the merchandise purchased on January 2 because it was not needed.
Feb. 1 Xiaoyan paid the balance owing to Feng.

Record purchase transactions with a purchase discount—perpetual system. (LO 2) AP

BE5–5 Prepare the journal entries to record the following purchase transactions in Jarek Company's books. Jarek uses a perpetual inventory system.

Mar. 12   Jarek purchased $25,000 of merchandise from Dalibor Company, terms 2/10, n/30, FOB destination.
   13   The correct company paid freight costs of $265.
   14   Jarek returned $2,000 of the merchandise purchased on March 12 because it was damaged.
   21   Jarek paid the balance owing to Dalibor.

BE5–6   Central Paint Distributors uses a perpetual inventory system. The company had the following transactions in March.

Mar. 16   Sold $15,000 of merchandise to Fresh Look Paint Stores, terms 2/10, n/30, FOB destination. The merchandise had cost Central Paint Distributors $8,700.
   17   Paid freight costs of $170 for the March 16 sale.
   18   Gave Fresh Look Paint Stores an allowance of $750 for the March 16 sale. There was some minor damage to the goods.
   25   Collected the balance due from Fresh Paint Stores.

For each transaction, (a) prepare a journal entry to record the transaction and (b) indicate the amount by which the transaction increased or decreased total assets, total liabilities, and owner's equity. Indicate NE (no effect) if the transaction neither increased nor decreased any of these items.

Record sales transactions and indicate impact on assets, liabilities, and owner's equity. (LO 3) C

BE5–7   Prepare journal entries to record the following sales transactions in Feng Company's books. Feng uses a perpetual inventory system.

Jan. 2   Feng sold $20,000 of merchandise to Xiaoyan Company, terms n/30, FOB shipping point. The cost of the merchandise sold was $7,900.
   4   The correct company paid freight costs of $215.
   6   Xiaoyan returned $1,500 of the merchandise purchased on January 2 because it was not needed. The cost of the merchandise returned was $590, and it was restored to inventory.
Feb. 1   Feng received the balance due from Xiaoyan.

Record sales transactions— perpetual system. (LO 3) AP

BE5–8   Prepare journal entries to record the following sales transactions in Dalibor Company's books. Dalibor uses a perpetual inventory system.

Mar. 12   Dalibor sold $25,000 of merchandise to Jarek Company, terms 2/10, n/30, FOB destination. The cost of the merchandise sold was $13,250.
   13   The correct company paid freight costs of $265.
   14   Jarek returned $2,000 of the merchandise purchased on March 12 because it was damaged. The cost of the merchandise returned was $1,060. Dalibor examined the merchandise, decided it was no longer saleable, and discarded it.
   22   Dalibor received the balance due from Jarek.

Record sales transactions with a sales discount— perpetual system. (LO 3) AP

BE5–9   At year end, the perpetual inventory records of Guiterrez Company showed merchandise inventory of $98,000. The company determined, however, that its actual inventory on hand was $96,100. Record the necessary adjusting entry.

Prepare adjusting entry. (LO 4) AP

BE5–10   Home Goods Retail Company has the following merchandise account balances at its September 30 year end:

Prepare closing entries. (LO 4) AP

Cost of goods sold	$125,000	Sales	$218,750
Freight out	1,900	Sales discounts	950
Merchandise inventory	22,000	Sales returns and allowances	3,150
Salaries expense	40,000	Supplies	2,500

Prepare the entries to close the appropriate accounts to the Income Summary account.

BE5–11   Nelson Company provides the following information for the month ended October 31, 2017: sales on credit $280,000, cash sales $95,000, sales discounts $5,000, and sales returns and allowances $11,000. Prepare the sales section of the income statement based on this information.

Prepare sales section of income statement. (LO 5) AP

BE5–12   Chocolate Treats has the following account balances:

Calculate net sales, gross profit, operating expenses, profit from operations, and profit. (LO 5) AP

Cost of goods sold	$385,000	Rent expense	$ 44,000
Depreciation expense	13,200	Salaries expense	55,000
Insurance expense	3,300	Sales	561,000
Interest expense	11,000	Sales discounts	5,500
Interest revenue	8,800	Sales returns and allowances	16,500

Assuming Chocolate Treats uses a multiple-step income statement, calculate the following: (a) net sales, (b) gross profit, (c) operating expenses, (d) profit from operations, and (e) profit.

Calculate profitability ratios and comment. (LO 6) AP

BE5–13 GS Retail reported the following for the past two fiscal years:

	2017	2016
Net sales	$950,000	$800,000
Cost of goods sold	600,000	500,000
Profit	70,000	65,000

(a) Calculate the gross profit margin and profit margin for both years. (b) Comment on any changes in profitability.

Record purchase transactions—periodic system. (LO 7) AP

*BE5–14 Prepare the journal entries to record these transactions on Allied Company's books. Allied Company uses a periodic inventory system.

Feb. 5 Allied purchased $12,000 of merchandise from NW Wholesale Company, terms 2/10, n/30, FOB shipping point.
   6 The correct company paid freight costs of $110.
   8 Allied returned $1,000 of the merchandise purchased on February 5.
   11 Allied paid the balance due to NW Wholesale.

Record sales transactions— periodic system. (LO 7) AP

*BE5–15 Prepare the journal entries to record these transactions on NW Wholesale Company's books. NW Wholesale Company uses a periodic inventory system.

Feb. 5 NW Wholesale sells $12,000 of merchandise to Allied, terms 2/10, n/30, FOB shipping point.
   6 The correct company paid freight costs of $110.
   8 Allied returned $1,000 of the merchandise purchased on February 5. The inventory is not damaged and can be resold. NW Wholesale restores it to inventory.
   11 NW Wholesale collects the balance due from Allied.

Prepare the cost of goods sold section of the income statement. (LO 7) AP

*BE5–16 Sagina Stores uses a periodic inventory system and reports the following information for 2017:

Beginning inventory	$51,000	Net sales	$531,250
Ending inventory	68,000	Purchase discounts	6,800
Freight in	13,600	Purchase returns and allowances	9,350
Freight out	10,625	Purchases	340,000

Prepare the cost of goods sold section of the multiple-step income statement for Sagina Stores.

▶ Exercises

List the advantages and disadvantages of a perpetual inventory system and make a recommendation. (LO 1) C

E5–1 Jean-Pierre Paquet operates a pet supply store. Jean-Pierre has the opportunity to implement a new perpetual inventory system. The system would cost $50,000 for installation and training. The company's annual revenues are $850,000. Jean-Pierre is considering this option because as the business grows, maintaining inventory levels is getting more difficult and he must hire additional staff monthly to count the items on hand. Currently the company stocks approximately 2,000 separate inventory items. The company's bank requires up-to-date information on inventory levels and cost of goods sold. Projected revenue growth for the store over the next two years is 10%.

Instructions

(a) What would the benefits be for Jean-Pierre if a perpetual inventory system were implemented?
(b) Are there any drawbacks for the company in implementing a perpetual inventory system?
(c) What would you recommend for the pet supply store?

Match concepts with descriptions.

(LO 1, 2, 3, 4, 5, 6) K

E5–2 The following are some of the terms discussed in the chapter:

1. Gross profit
2. Perpetual inventory system
3. Cost of goods sold
4. Purchase returns
5. Freight out
6. FOB shipping point
7. Periodic inventory system
8. Subsidiary ledger

9. Sales discounts
10. FOB destination
11. Sales allowance
12. Non-operating activities
13. Profit margin
14. Contra revenue account
15. Merchandise inventory
16. Purchase discounts

Instructions

Match each term with the best description below. Each term may be used more than once, or may not be used at all.

(a) _____ An expense account that shows the cost of merchandise sold
(b) _____ A group of accounts that share a common characteristic, such as all inventory accounts
(c) _____ An account, such as Sales Discounts, that is deducted from a revenue account on the income statement
(d) _____ The return of unsatisfactory purchased merchandise
(e) _____ Freight terms where the seller will pay for the cost of shipping the goods
(f) _____ An inventory system where a physical inventory count is required to determine inventory on hand and establish cost of goods sold.
(g) _____ A reduction in price given to a customer for unsatisfactory inventory
(h) _____ Sales revenue less cost of goods sold
(i) _____ Revenues, expenses, gains, and losses that are not part of the company's main operations
(j) _____ Freight terms where the buyer will pay for the cost of shipping the goods
(k) _____ An inventory system where the cost of goods sold is calculated and recorded with every sales transaction
(l) _____ An asset that shows the cost of goods purchased for resale
(m) _____ Profit divided by net sales
(n) _____ A price reduction given by a seller for early payment on a credit sale

E5-3 Stellar Stores is a new company that started operations on March 1, 2017. The company has decided to use a perpetual inventory system. The following purchase transactions occurred in March:

Record purchase transactions. (LO 2) AP

Mar. 1   Stellar Stores purchases $9,000 of merchandise for resale from Octagon Wholesalers, terms 2/10, n/30, FOB shipping point.
2   The correct company pays $155 for the shipping charges.
3   Stellar returns $1,000 of the merchandise purchased on March 1 because it was the wrong colour. Octagon gives Stellar a $1,000 credit on its account.
21   Stellar Stores purchases an additional $13,000 of merchandise for resale from Octagon Wholesalers terms 2/10, n/30, FOB destination.
22   The correct company pays $170 for freight charges.
23   Stellar returns $400 of the merchandise purchased on March 21 because it was damaged. Octagon gives Stellar a $400 credit on its account.
30   Stellar pays Octagon the amount owing for the merchandise purchased on March 1.
31   Stellar pays Octagon the amount owing for the merchandise purchased on March 21.

Instructions
(a) Prepare Stellar Stores' journal entries to record the above transactions.
(b) Post the transactions to the Merchandise Inventory account. Compare the total in this account with the total of the cash paid during March by Stellar for the purchase of inventory. (*Note:* assume there were no sales of inventory in March.)

E5-4 Octagon Wholesalers uses a perpetual inventory system. Refer to the data in E5-3 regarding sales transactions with Stellar Stores and to the additional information below for Octagon.

Record sales transactions. (LO 3) AP

Mar. 1   Octagon's cost of the merchandise sold to Stellar was $3,960.
3   Octagon's cost of the merchandise returned by Stellar was $440. As the merchandise was not damaged, it was returned to Octagon's inventory.
21   Octagon's cost of the additional merchandise sold to Stellar Stores was $5,720.
23   Octagon's cost of the merchandise returned by Stellar was $176. As the merchandise was damaged, it was put in the recycling bin.

Instructions
(a) Prepare Octagon Wholesalers' journal entries to record the sales transactions with Stellar. Remember to record the freight and cash receipt transactions as appropriate.
(b) Calculate Octagon's net sales, cost of goods sold, and gross profit for these sales.

E5-5 The following transactions occurred in April and May. Both companies use a perpetual inventory system.

Record purchase and sales transactions—perpetual system. (LO 1, 2, 3) AP

Apr. 5   Olaf Company purchased merchandise from DeVito Company for $12,000, terms 2/10, n/30, FOB shipping point. DeVito had paid $8,500 for the merchandise.
6   The correct company paid freight costs of $300.
8   Olaf Company returned damaged merchandise to DeVito Company and was given a purchase allowance of $1,800. DeVito determined the merchandise could not be repaired and sent it to the recyclers. The merchandise had cost DeVito $1,275.
May 4   Olaf paid the amount due to DeVito Company in full.

Instructions

(a) Prepare the journal entries to record the above transactions for Olaf Company.
(b) Prepare the journal entries to record the above transactions for DeVito Company.
(c) Calculate the gross profit earned by DeVito on these transactions.

Record purchase and sales transactions—perpetual system. (LO 1, 2, 3) AP

E5–6 The following merchandise transactions occurred in December. Both companies use a perpetual inventory system.

Dec. 3   Pippen Company sold merchandise to Thomas Co. for $32,000, terms 2/10, n/30, FOB destination. This merchandise cost Pippen Company $18,000.
     4   The correct company paid freight charges of $650.
     8   Thomas Co. returned unwanted merchandise to Pippen. The returned merchandise had a sales price of $1,800 and a cost of $990. It was restored to inventory.
     13   Pippen Company received the balance due from Thomas Co.

Instructions

(a) Prepare the journal entries to record these transactions on the books of Pippen Company.
(b) Prepare the journal entries to record these transactions on the books of Thomas Co.
(c) Assuming that Thomas Co. had a balance in Merchandise Inventory on December 1 of $6,000, determine the balance in the Merchandise Inventory account at the end of December for Thomas Co.

Record correct inventory transactions—perpetual system. (LO 2, 3) AN

E5–7 The following transactions were recorded by an inexperienced bookkeeper during the months of June and July for JillyBean Company. JillyBean Company uses a perpetual inventory system.

June 10   A purchase of $4,000 of merchandise from DanDan Distributors was debited to Purchases and credited to Cash. The terms of the purchase were 2/10, n/30, FOB shipping point.
     11   The invoice for freight in the amount of $225 for the delivery of merchandise purchased from DanDan was paid and was debited to Delivery Expense
     12   Damaged goods totalling $200 were returned to DanDan Distributors for credit. The bookkeeper recorded a debit to Accounts Receivable and a credit to Sales Returns and Allowances.
     20   A payment was made to DanDan Distributors for the June 10 purchase. The payment was recorded as a debit to Purchases and a credit to Cash.
July 15   JillyBean sold goods for $9,275. Sales was credited and Cost of Goods Sold was debited for this amount. The cost of the inventory sold was $3,800. The terms of the sale were 1/15, n/30, FOB destination.
     15   Freight charges on the above transaction were debited to Accounts Receivable and credited to Cash for $175. The bookkeeper believed the customer had to pay for the freight charges.
     17   JillyBean's manager gave the customer from July 15 a $300 allowance. The entry made to record the allowance was a debit to Sales and a credit to Sales Returns and Allowances.

Instructions

(a) Review each transaction above and indicate whether you agree or disagree with how the bookkeeper accounted for the transaction.
(b) If you disagreed with any of the accounting, prepare the correct entry.

Prepare adjusting and closing entries—perpetual system. (LO 4) AP

E5–8 Presented below is information related to Hurly Co., owned by D. Flamont, for the month of January 2017.

Ending inventory per perpetual records	$ 21,600	Insurance expense	$ 12,000
Ending inventory actually on hand	21,000	Rent expense	20,000
Cost of goods sold	218,000	Salaries expense	55,000
Freight out	7,000	Sales discounts	10,000
		Sales returns and allowances	13,000
		Sales	380,000

Instructions

(a) Prepare the necessary adjusting entry for inventory.
(b) Prepare the necessary closing entries. D. Flamont did not withdraw any cash during the month of January.

Calculate missing amounts. (LO 5) AP

E5–9 Financial information follows for three different companies:

	Natural Cosmetics	Family Grocery	SE Footware
Sales	$215,000	$ (e)	$275,000
Sales returns and allowances	(a)	25,000	20,000
Net sales	201,000	335,000	(i)
Cost of goods sold	99,000	(f)	(j)
Gross profit	(b)	195,000	150,000
Operating expenses	45,000	(g)	95,000
Profit from operations	(c)	(h)	(k)
Other expenses	5,000	10,000	(l)
Profit	(d)	63,000	41,000

Instructions

Determine the missing amounts.

E5-10 The following is information from Crystal Company's adjusted trial balance at December 31, 2017:

	Debit	Credit
Cash	$ 75,700	
Notes receivable	100,000	
Merchandise inventory	70,000	
Equipment	450,000	
Accumulated depreciation—equipment		$ 135,000
Unearned revenue		8,000
Notes payable		175,000
L. Crystal, capital		235,000
L. Crystal, drawings	150,000	
Interest revenue		10,000
Rent revenue		24,000
Sales		1,980,000
Advertising expense	55,000	
Cost of goods sold	851,500	
Depreciation expense	45,000	
Freight out	25,000	
Insurance expense	15,000	
Interest expense	10,500	
Salaries expense	650,000	
Sales discounts	9,900	
Sales returns and allowances	59,400	
	$2,567,000	$2,567,000

Prepare single-step income statement, closing entries, and post-closing trial balance—perpetual system. (LO 4, 5) AP

Instructions

(a) Prepare a single-step income statement.
(b) Prepare closing entries and a post-closing trial balance.

E5-11 An alphabetical list of Rikards Company's adjusted accounts at its fiscal year end, August 31, 2017, follows. All accounts have normal balances.

Prepare financial statements and calculate ratios—perpetual system. (LO 5, 6) AP

Accounts payable	$ 15,500	Notes payable	$ 42,000
Accumulated depreciation—equipment	14,000	Prepaid insurance	575
Accumulated depreciation—furniture	17,500	R. Smistad, capital	65,750
Cash	15,450	R. Smistad, drawings	80,000
Cost of goods sold	271,500	Rent expense	24,000
Depreciation expense	7,000	Salaries expense	50,000
Equipment	35,000	Salaries payable	2,250
Furniture	42,000	Sales	465,000
Insurance expense	3,575	Sales returns and allowances	16,300
Interest expense	2,100	Supplies	950
Interest payable	525	Supplies expense	6,325
Merchandise inventory	70,350	Unearned revenue	2,600

Additional information:

1. Of the notes payable, $6,000 becomes due on February 17, 2018. The balance is due in 2019.
2. On July 18, 2017, R. Smistad invested $3,500 cash in the business.

Instructions

(a) Prepare a multiple-step income statement, statement of owner's equity, and classified balance sheet.
(b) Calculate the gross profit margin and profit margin.

E5-12 **lululemon athletica inc.** reported the following information (dollars in US thousands) for the three fiscal years ended:

Calculate profitability ratios. (LO 6) AN

	February 1, 2015	February 2, 2014	February 3, 2013
Net sales	$1,797,213	$1,591,188	$1,370,358
Cost of goods sold	883,033	751,112	607,532
Profit from operations	376,033	391,358	376,439
Profit	239,033	279,547	271,431

Instructions

(a) Calculate the gross profit margin and profit margin for lululemon for each of the three years.

(b) Recalculate profit margin using profit from operations as opposed to profit.

(c) Comment on whether the ratios improved or weakened over the three years.

Record purchase and sales transaction entries—periodic system. (LO 7) AP

*E5–13 Data for Olaf Company and DeVito Company are presented in E5–5.

Instructions

(a) Prepare the journal entries to record these transactions on the books of Olaf Company using a periodic inventory system instead of a perpetual system.

(b) Prepare the journal entries to record these transactions on the books of DeVito Company using a periodic inventory system instead of a perpetual system.

Record inventory transactions and calculate gross profit—periodic system. (LO 7) AP

*E5–14 Memories Company commenced operations on July 1. Memories Company uses a periodic inventory system. During July, Memories Company was involved in the following transactions and events:

July	2	Purchased $15,000 of merchandise from Suppliers Inc. on account, terms 2/10, n/30, FOB shipping point.
	3	Returned $1,200 of merchandise to Suppliers Inc. as it was damaged. Received a credit on account from Suppliers.
	4	Paid $500 of freight costs on July 2 shipment.
	8	Sold merchandise for $2,000 cash.
	11	Paid Suppliers Inc. the full amount owing.
	15	Sold merchandise for $6,000 on account, 1/10, n/30, FOB shipping point.
	25	Received full payment for the merchandise sold on July 15.
	31	Memories did a physical count and determined there was $10,500 of inventory on hand.

Instructions

(a) Record the transactions in Memories Company's books.

(b) What was Memories' gross profit for July?

Calculate various income statement items—periodic system. (LO 7) AP

*E5–15 On January 1, 2017, Casselberry Retailers had inventory of $50,000. On December 31, 2017, total inventory on hand was $66,000. Casselberry reported the following account balances on December 31:

Freight in	$ 4,000
Purchases	509,000
Purchase returns and allowances	2,000
Purchase discounts	6,000
Sales	840,000
Sales discounts	5,000
Sales returns and allowances	10,000

Instructions

(a) Calculate Casselberry Retailer's 2017 gross profit.

(b) Calculate Casselberry Retailer's 2017 operating expenses if profit is $130,000 and there are no non-operating activities.

Prepare multiple-step income statement and closing entries—periodic system. (LO 7) AP

*E5–16 The following selected information is for Okanagan Company for the year ended January 31, 2017:

Freight in	$ 6,500	Purchase discounts	$ 12,000
Freight out	7,000	Purchase returns and allowances	16,000
Insurance expense	12,000	Rent expense	20,000
Interest expense	6,000	Salaries expense	61,000
Merchandise inventory, beginning	61,000	Salaries payable	2,500
Merchandise inventory, ending	42,000	Sales	325,000
O. G. Pogo, capital	105,000	Sales discounts	14,000
O. G. Pogo, drawings	42,000	Sales returns and allowances	20,000
Purchases	210,000	Unearned revenue	4,500

Instructions

(a) Prepare a multiple-step income statement.

(b) Prepare closing entries.

▶ Problems: Set A

P5–1A AAA Dog 'n Cat Shop sells a variety of merchandise for the pet owner, including pet food, grooming supplies, toys, and kennels. Most customers use the option to purchase on account and take 60 days, on average, to pay their accounts. The owner of AAA Dog 'n Cat Shop, Adam Fleming, has decided the company needs a bank loan because the accounts payable need to be paid in 30 days. Adam estimates that it takes 45 days, on average, to sell merchandise from the time it arrives at his store. Since the company earns a good profit every year, the bank manager is willing to give AAA Dog 'n Cat Shop a loan but wants monthly financial statements.

Identify problems and recommend inventory system. (LO 1) C

　　Adam has also noticed that, while some of the merchandise sells very quickly, other items do not. Sometimes he wonders just how long he has had some of those older items. He has also noticed that he regularly seems to run out of some merchandise items. Adam is also concerned about preparing monthly financial statements. The company uses a periodic inventory system and Adam counts inventory once a year. He is wondering how he is going to calculate the cost of goods sold for the month without counting the inventory at the end of every month. He has come to you for help.

Instructions

(a) Explain to Adam what an operating cycle is and why he is having problems paying the bills.
(b) Explain to Adam how the periodic inventory system is contributing to his problems.

TAKING IT FURTHER Make a recommendation about what inventory system the company should use and why.

P5–2A At the beginning of the current tennis season, on April 1, 2017, Kicked-Back Tennis Shop's inventory consisted of 50 tennis racquets at a cost of $40 each. Kicked-Back uses a perpetual inventory system. The following transactions occurred in April:

Record and post inventory transactions—perpetual system. (LO 2, 3) AP

Apr. 2 Purchased 160 additional racquets from Roberts Inc. for $6,400, terms n/30.
　　 4 Determined that five of the racquets purchased on April 2 were damaged and returned them to Roberts Inc. Roberts Inc. credited Kicked-Back's account.
　　 5 Sold 45 racquets to Tennis Dome for $90 each, terms n/30.
　　 6 Tennis Dome returned 15 of the racquets after determining it had purchased more racquets than it needed. Kicked-Back gave Tennis Dome a credit on its account and returned the racquets to inventory.
　　 10 Sold 40 racquets at $90 each to cash customers.
　　 12 Ten of these racquets were returned for cash. The customers claimed they never play tennis and had no idea how they had been talked into purchasing the racquets. Refunded cash to these customers and returned the racquets to inventory.
　　 17 An additional 10 of the racquets sold on April 10 were returned because the racquets were damaged. The customers were refunded cash and the racquets were sent to a local recycler.
　　 25 Sold 60 racquets to the Summer Club for $90 each, terms n/30.
　　 29 Summer Club returned 25 of the racquets after the tennis pro had examined them and determined that these racquets were of inferior quality. Kicked-Back gave Summer Club a credit and decided to return the racquets to inventory with plans to sell them for the reduced price of $75 each.

Instructions

(a) Record the transactions for the month of April for Kicked-Back.
(b) Create T accounts for Sales, Sales Returns and Allowances, Cost of Goods Sold, and Merchandise Inventory. Post the opening balance and April's transactions, and calculate the April 30 balances.

TAKING IT FURTHER Assume that the owner of Kicked-Back hired an employee to run the store and is not involved in operating the business. The owner wants to know the amount of net sales and gross profit for the month. Will the owner be missing any important information by requesting only these two numbers? Explain.

P5–3A Presented below are selected transactions for Norlan Company during September and October of the current year. Norlan uses a perpetual inventory system.

Record inventory transactions—perpetual system. (LO 2, 3) AP

Sept. 1 Purchased merchandise on account from Hillary Company at a cost of $45,000, FOB destination, terms 1/15, n/30.
　　 2 The correct company paid $2,000 of freight charges to Trucking Company on the September 1 merchandise purchase.
　　 5 Returned for credit $3,000 of damaged goods purchased from Hillary Company on September 1.
　　 15 Sold the remaining merchandise purchased from Hillary Company to Irvine Company for $70,000, terms 2/10, n/30, FOB destination.
　　 16 The correct company paid $1,800 of freight charges on the September 15 sale of merchandise.

17 Issued Irvine Company a credit of $5,000 for returned goods. These goods had cost Norlan Company $3,000 and were returned to inventory.

25 Received the balance owing from Irvine Company for the September 15 sale.

30 Paid Hillary Company the balance owing for the September 1 purchase.

Oct. 1 Purchased merchandise on account from Kimmel Company at a cost of $52,000, terms 2/10, n/30, FOB shipping point.

2 The correct company paid freight costs of $1,100 on the October 1 purchase.

3 Obtained a purchase allowance of $2,000 from Kimmel Company to compensate for some minor damage to goods purchased on October 1.

10 Paid Kimmel Company the amount owing on the October 1 purchase.

11 Sold all of the merchandise purchased from Kimmel Company to Kieso Company for $83,500, terms 2/10, n/30, FOB shipping point.

12 The correct company paid $800 freight costs on the October 11 sale.

17 Issued Kieso Company a sales allowance of $1,500 because some of the goods did not meet Kieso's exact specifications.

31 Received a cheque from Kieso Company for the balance owing on the October 11 sale.

Instructions

Prepare journal entries to record the above transactions for Norlan Company.

TAKING IT FURTHER Explain why companies should always take advantage of purchase discounts even if they have to borrow from the bank. Refer to the two purchases made by Norlan Company in your answer.

Record inventory transactions and post to inventory account—perpetual system. (LO 2, 3) AP

P5-4A Travel Warehouse distributes suitcases to retail stores and extends credit terms of n/30 to all of its customers. Travel Warehouse uses a perpetual inventory system and at the end of June its inventory consisted of 25 suitcases purchased at $30 each. During the month of July, the following merchandising transactions occurred:

July 1 Purchased 50 suitcases on account for $30 each from Trunk Manufacturers, terms n/30, FOB destination.

2 The correct company paid $125 freight on the July 1 purchase.

4 Received $150 credit for five suitcases returned to Trunk Manufacturers because they were damaged.

10 Sold 45 suitcases that cost $30 each to Satchel World for $55 each on account.

12 Issued a $275 credit for five suitcases returned by Satchel World because they were the wrong colour. The suitcases were returned to inventory.

15 Purchased 60 additional suitcases from Trunk Manufacturers for $27.50 each, terms n/30, FOB shipping point.

18 The company paid $150 freight on the July 15 purchase.

21 Sold 54 suitcases that cost $30 each to Fly-By-Night for $55 each on account.

23 Gave Fly-By-Night a $110 credit for two returned suitcases. The suitcases had been damaged and were sent to the recyclers.

30 Paid Trunk Manufacturers for the July 1 purchase.

31 Received balance owing from Satchel World.

Instructions

(a) Record the transactions for the month of July for Travel Warehouse.

(b) Create a T account for Merchandise Inventory. Post the opening balance and July's transactions, and calculate the July 31 balance.

(c) Determine the number of suitcases on hand at the end of the month.

TAKING IT FURTHER Explain how freight terms can affect the selling price, and the cost, of merchandise. Use the transactions on July 1 and 15 between Travel Warehouse and Trunk Manufacturers as part of your explanation.

Record and post inventory transactions—perpetual system. Prepare partial income statement. (LO 2, 3, 5) AP

P5-5A At the beginning of June 2017, Willingham Distributing Company's ledger showed Cash $18,000, Merchandise Inventory $5,900, and D. Willingham, Capital, $23,900. During the month of June, the company had the following selected transactions:

June 1 Purchased $9,200 of merchandise inventory from Sun Supply Co., terms 1/15, n/30, FOB destination.

2 The correct company paid $250 cash for freight charges on the June 1 purchase.

5 Sold merchandise inventory to Moose Jaw Retailers for $12,000. The cost of the merchandise was $7,400 and the terms were 2/10, n/30, FOB destination.

6   Issued a $900 credit for merchandise returned by Moose Jaw Retailers. The merchandise originally cost $550 and was returned to inventory.

6   The correct company paid $300 freight on the June 5 sale.

7   Purchased $790 of supplies for cash.

10   Purchased $4,750 of merchandise inventory from Fey Wholesalers, terms 2/10, n/30, FOB shipping point.

10   The correct company paid $130 freight costs on the purchase from Fey Wholesalers.

12   Received a $250 credit from Fey Wholesalers for returned merchandise.

14   Paid Sun Supply Co. the amount due.

15   Collected the balance owing from Moose Jaw Retailers.

19   Sold merchandise for $7,200 cash. The cost of this merchandise was $4,600.

20   Paid Fey Wholesalers the balance owing from the June 10 purchase.

25   Made a $500 cash refund to a cash customer for merchandise returned. The returned merchandise had a cost of $315. The merchandise was damaged and could not be resold.

30   Sold merchandise to Bauer & Company for $4,100, terms n/30, FOB shipping point. Willingham's cost for this merchandise was $2,600.

Instructions

(a) Record the transactions assuming Willingham uses a perpetual inventory system.

(b) Set up general ledger accounts for Merchandise Inventory, Sales, Sales Returns and Allowances, Sales Discounts, and Cost of Goods Sold. Enter the beginning merchandise inventory balance, and post the transactions.

(c) Prepare a partial multiple-step income statement, up to gross profit, for the month of June 2017.

TAKING IT FURTHER   Assume that Willingham has a "no questions asked" policy in terms of accepting sales returns up to six months after the initial sale. What uncertainties does the company face in terms of calculating its gross profit for June?

P5-6A   Wolcott Warehouse Store has an August 31 fiscal year end and uses a perpetual inventory system. An alphabetical list of its account balances at August 31, 2017, follows. All accounts have normal balances.

Prepare adjusting and closing entries, and single-step income statement—perpetual system. Calculate ratios.
(LO 4, 5, 6) AP

Accounts payable	$ 29,180	Interest revenue	$ 960
Accounts receivable	19,000	Merchandise inventory	57,000
Accumulated depreciation—		Notes payable	38,990
equipment	26,280	Notes receivable	33,000
Cash	11,000	Rent expense	15,500
Cost of goods sold	575,500	Sales	704,000
Depreciation expense	6,750	Sales discounts	3,300
Equipment	65,700	Sales returns and allowances	14,700
Freight out	4,600	Supplies expense	5,600
Insurance expense	2,900	Unearned revenue	5,900
Interest expense	2,000	V. Wolcott, capital	72,700
Interest receivable	260	V. Wolcott, drawings	61,200

Additional information:

1. All adjustments have been recorded and posted except for the inventory adjustment. According to the inventory count, the company has $54,700 of merchandise on hand.

2. Last year Wolcott Warehouse Store had a gross profit margin of 20% and a profit margin of 9%.

Instructions

(a) Prepare any additional required adjusting entries and update account balances.

(b) Prepare a single-step income statement.

(c) Calculate gross profit margin and profit margin. Compare with last year's margins and comment on the results. (Hint: you will have to calculate the gross profit amount separately.)

(d) Prepare the closing entries. Post to the Income Summary account. Before closing the Income Summary account, check that the balance is equal to profit.

TAKING IT FURTHER   What would a company do if it wanted to improve gross profit margin and profit margin?

Prepare adjusting and closing entries, and single-step and multiple-step income statements—perpetual system. (LO 4, 5) AP

P5-7A   The unadjusted trial balance of World Enterprises for the year ended December 31, 2017, follows:

WORLD ENTERPRISES
Trial Balance
December 31, 2017

	Debit	Credit
Cash	$ 15,000	
Accounts receivable	19,200	
Merchandise inventory	37,050	
Prepaid insurance	3,000	
Supplies	2,950	
Equipment	150,000	
Accumulated depreciation—equipment		$ 35,000
Furniture	45,000	
Accumulated depreciation—furniture		18,000
Accounts payable		33,200
Unearned revenue		4,000
Mortgage payable		125,000
S. Kim, capital		46,200
S. Kim, drawings	48,000	
Sales		265,000
Sales returns and allowances	2,500	
Sales discounts	3,275	
Cost of goods sold	153,000	
Interest expense	6,875	
Salaries expense	35,450	
Utilities expense	5,100	
	$526,400	$526,400

Additional information:

1. There is $750 of supplies on hand on December 31, 2017.
2. The one-year insurance policy was purchased on March 1, 2017.
3. Depreciation expense for the year is $10,000 for the equipment and $4,500 for the furniture.
4. Accrued interest expense at December 31, 2017, is $675.
5. Unearned revenue of $975 is still unearned at December 31, 2017. On the sales that were earned, cost of goods sold was $1,750.
6. A physical count of merchandise inventory indicates $32,750 on hand on December 31, 2017.

Instructions

(a) Prepare the adjusting journal entries assuming they are prepared annually and update account balances.
(b) Prepare a multiple-step income statement.
(c) Prepare a single-step income statement.
(d) Prepare the closing entries.

TAKING IT FURTHER   Compare a single-step income statement and a multiple-step income statement for a merchandising company. How are they similar and different? Comment on the usefulness of each one.

Calculate ratios and comment. (LO 6) AN

P5-8A   Magna International Inc. is a leading global supplier of technologically advanced automotive components, systems, and modules. Selected financial information (dollars in US millions) follows:

	2014	2013	2012
Sales	$36,641	$34,835	$30,837
Cost of goods sold	31,623	30,287	27,019
Profit	1,882	1,561	1,433
Current assets	10,007	9,923	9,135
Current liabilities	7,611	7,309	6,684

Instructions

(a) Calculate the gross profit margin, profit margin, and current ratio for each year.
(b) Comment on whether the ratios have improved or deteriorated over the three years.

TAKING IT FURTHER   Assume you are thinking about investing in Magna International Inc. What other information would be useful in assessing these ratios?

*P5–9A   Data for Norlan Company are presented in P5–3A.

Instructions

Record the September and October transactions for Norlan Company, assuming a periodic inventory system is used instead of a perpetual inventory system.

TAKING IT FURTHER   Why might a periodic system be better than a perpetual system for Norlan Company?

Record inventory transactions—periodic system. (LO 7) AP

*P5–10A   Data for Travel Warehouse are presented in P5–4A.

Instructions

Record the July transactions for Travel Warehouse, assuming a periodic inventory system is used instead of a perpetual inventory system.

TAKING IT FURTHER   What are the costs and benefits for Travel Warehouse of using a perpetual, as opposed to a periodic, system?

Record inventory transactions—periodic system. (LO 7) AP

*P5–11A   Data for Willingham Distributing Company are presented in P5–5A. A physical inventory count shows $5,498 of inventory on hand on June 30, 2017.

Instructions

(a) Record the transactions assuming Willingham uses a periodic inventory system.
(b) Set up general ledger accounts for merchandise inventory and all of the temporary accounts used in the merchandising transactions. Enter beginning balances, and post the transactions.
(c) Prepare a partial multiple-step income statement, up to gross profit, for the month of June 2017.

TAKING IT FURTHER   Will gross profit be higher, lower, or the same amount, if using a periodic inventory system instead of a perpetual inventory system? Explain.

Record and post inventory transactions—periodic system. Prepare partial income statement. (LO 7) AP

*P5–12A   New West Company recently hired a new accountant whose first task was to prepare the financial statements for the year ended December 31, 2017. The following is what he produced:

Prepare correct multiple-step income statement, statement of owner's equity, and classified balance sheet—periodic system. (LO 7) AP

NEW WEST COMPANY
Income Statement
December 31, 2017

Sales		$395,000
Less: Unearned revenue	$ 5,500	
Purchase discounts	3,480	8,980
Total revenue		386,020
Cost of goods sold		
Purchases	$232,000	
Less: Purchase returns and allowances	4,000	
Net purchases	236,000	
Add: Sales returns and allowances	7,500	
Cost of goods available for sale	243,500	
Add: Freight out	9,500	
Cost of selling merchandise		253,000
Gross profit margin		133,020
Operating expenses		
Freight in	$ 4,500	
Insurance expense	10,500	
Interest expense	2,500	
Rent expense	18,000	
Salaries expense	42,000	
Total operating expenses		77,500
Profit margin		55,520
Other revenues		
Interest revenue	$ 1,500	
Investment by owner	3,500	5,000
Other expenses		
Depreciation expense	7,000	
Drawings by owner	48,000	55,000	(50,000)
Profit from operations		$ 5,520

NEW WEST COMPANY
Balance Sheet
Year Ended December 31, 2017

Assets

Cash		$16,780
Accounts receivable		7,800
Merchandise inventory, January 1, 2017		30,000
Merchandise inventory, December 31, 2017		24,000
Equipment	$70,000	
Less: loan payable (for equipment purchase)	50,000	20,000
Total assets		$98,580

Liabilities and Owner's Equity

Long-term investment	$50,000
Accumulated depreciation—equipment	21,000
Sales discounts	2,900
Total liabilities	73,900
Owner's equity	24,680
Total liabilities and owner's equity	$98,580

The owner of the company, Lily Oliver, is confused by the statements and has asked you for your help. She doesn't understand how, if her Owner's Capital account was $75,000 at December 31, 2016, owner's equity is now only $24,680. The accountant tells you that $24,680 must be correct because the balance sheet is balanced. The accountant also tells you that he didn't prepare a statement of owner's equity because it is an optional statement. You are relieved to find out that, even though there are errors in the statements, the amounts used from the accounts in the general ledger are the correct amounts.

Instructions

Prepare the correct multiple-step income statement, statement of owner's equity, and classified balance sheet. You determine that $5,000 of the loan payable on the equipment must be paid during 2018.

TAKING IT FURTHER If a company uses a periodic inventory system, does it have to show on its income statement all of the details as to how cost of goods sold was calculated? Why or why not?

Prepare financial statements and closing entries—periodic system. (LO 7) AP

P5-13A The following is an alphabetical list of Bud's Bakery's adjusted account balances at the end of the company's fiscal year on November 30, 2017:

Accounts payable	$ 32,310		Merchandise inventory	$ 34,360
Accounts receivable	13,770		Mortgage payable	106,000
Accumulated depreciation—building	61,200		Prepaid insurance	4,500
Accumulated depreciation—equipment	19,880		Property tax expense	3,500
B. Hachey, capital	104,480		Purchases	634,700
B. Hachey, drawings	12,000		Purchase discounts	6,300
Building	175,000		Purchase returns and allowances	13,315
Cash	8,500		Rent revenue	2,800
Depreciation expense	14,000		Salaries expense	122,000
Equipment	57,000		Salaries payable	8,500
Freight in	5,060		Sales	872,000
Freight out	8,200		Sales discounts	8,250
Insurance expense	9,000		Sales returns and allowances	9,845
Interest expense	5,300		Unearned revenue	3,000
Land	85,000		Utilities expense	19,800

Additional facts:

1. Bud's Bakery uses a periodic inventory system.
2. A physical count determined that merchandise inventory on hand at November 30, 2017, was $37,350.
3. Of the mortgage payable, $8,500 is due on March 31, 2018.

Instructions

(a) Prepare a multiple-step income statement, statement of owner's equity, and classified balance sheet for the November 30, 2017, year end.
(b) Prepare the closing journal entries.
(c) Post closing entries to the Merchandise Inventory and capital accounts. Check that the balances in these accounts are the same as the amounts on the balance sheet.

TAKING IT FURTHER If you had not been told that Bud's Bakery uses a periodic inventory system, how could you have determined that? What information is available in a periodic inventory system that is not available in a perpetual inventory system?

▶ Problems: Set B

P5–1B Home Décor Company sells a variety of home decorating merchandise, including pictures, small furniture items, dishes, candles, and area rugs. The company uses a periodic inventory system and counts inventory once a year. Most customers use the option to purchase on account and many take more than a month to pay. The owner of Home Décor, Rebecca Sherstabetoff, has decided that the company needs a bank loan because the accounts payable need to be paid long before the accounts receivable are collected. The bank manager is willing to give Home Décor a loan but wants monthly financial statements.

Identify problems and recommend inventory system. (LO 1) C

Rebecca has also noticed that, while some of her merchandise sells very quickly, other items do not. Sometimes she wonders just how long she has had some of those older items. She has also noticed that she regularly seems to run out of some merchandise. And she is wondering how she is going to find time to count the inventory every month so she can prepare the monthly financial statements for the bank. She has come to you for help.

Instructions

(a) Explain to Rebecca what an operating cycle is and why she is having problems paying her bills.
(b) Explain to Rebecca how her inventory system is contributing to her problems.

TAKING IT FURTHER Make a recommendation about what inventory system Rebecca should use and why.

P5–2B At the beginning of the current golf season, on April 1, 2017, Swing-Town Golf Shop's merchandise inventory included 20 specialty hybrid golf clubs at a cost of $160 each. Swing-Town uses a perpetual inventory system. The following transactions occurred in April:

Record and post inventory transactions—perpetual system. (LO 2, 3) AP

Apr. 2   Purchased 100 additional clubs from Weir Inc. for $16,000, terms n/30.
    4   Received credit from Weir for five returned damaged clubs purchased on April 2.
    5   Sold 20 clubs to Big Golf Practice Range for $265 each, terms n/30.
    6   Big Golf Practice Range returned eight of the clubs after determining it had purchased more clubs than it needed. Swing-Town gave Big Golf Practice Range a credit on its account and returned the clubs to inventory.
   10   Sold 30 clubs at $265 each to cash customers.
   12   Ten of these clubs were returned for cash. The customers claimed they never play golf and had no idea how they had been talked into purchasing the clubs. Refunded cash to these customers and returned the clubs to inventory.
   17   An additional 10 of the clubs sold on April 10 were returned because the clubs were damaged. The customers were refunded cash and the clubs were sent to a local recycler.
   25   Sold 45 clubs to Pro-Shop for $265 each, terms n/30.
   29   Pro-Shop returned 25 of the clubs after the golf pro had examined them and determined that these clubs were of inferior quality. Swing-Town gave Pro-Shop a credit and decided to return the clubs to inventory with plans to sell them for the reduced price of $185 each.

Instructions

(a) Record the transactions for the month of April for Swing-Town Golf.
(b) Create T accounts for Sales, Sales Returns and Allowances, Cost of Goods Sold, and Merchandise Inventory. Post the opening balance and April's transactions, and calculate the April 30 balances.

TAKING IT FURTHER Swing-Town's owner thinks that it is a waste of time and effort for the bookkeeper to use a Sales Returns and Allowances account and thinks that the bookkeeper should just reduce the Sales account for any sales returns or allowances. Explain to Swing-Town's owner how he would benefit from using a Sales Returns and Allowances account.

Record inventory transactions—perpetual system. (LO 2, 3) AP

P5–3B Transactions follow for Leeland Company during October and November of the current year. Leeland uses a perpetual inventory system.

Oct. 2   Purchased merchandise on account from Gregory Company at a cost of $35,000, terms 2/10, n/30, FOB destination.

     4   The correct company paid freight charges of $900 to Rail Company for shipping the merchandise purchased on October 2.

     5   Returned damaged goods having a gross invoice cost of $6,000 to Gregory Company. Received a credit for this.

   11   Paid Gregory Company the balance owing for the October 2 purchase.

   17   Sold the remaining merchandise purchased from Gregory Company to Kurji Company for $62,500, terms 2/10, n/30, FOB shipping point.

   18   The correct company paid Intermodal Co. $800 freight costs for the October 17 sale.

   19   Issued Kurji Company a sales allowance of $2,500 because some of the goods did not meet Kurji's exact specifications.

   27   Received the balance owing from Kurji Company for the October 17 sale.

Nov. 1   Purchased merchandise on account from Romeo Company at a cost of $60,000, terms 1/15, n/30, FOB shipping point.

     2   The correct company paid freight charges of $4,000.

     5   Sold the merchandise purchased from Romeo Company to Bear Company for $110,500, terms 2/10, n/30, FOB destination.

     6   The correct company paid freight charges of $2,600.

     7   Issued Bear Company a credit of $7,000 for returned goods. These goods had cost Leeland $4,050 and were returned to inventory.

   29   Received a cheque from Bear Company for the balance owing on the November 5 sale.

   30   Paid Romeo Company the amount owing on the November 1 purchase.

Instructions

Prepare journal entries to record the above transactions for Leeland Company.

TAKING IT FURTHER   Explain why companies should always take advantage of purchase discounts even if they have to borrow from the bank. Refer to the two purchases made by Leeland Company in your answer.

Record inventory transactions and post to inventory account—perpetual system. (LO 2, 3) AP

P5–4B Phantom Book Warehouse distributes hardcover books to retail stores and extends credit terms of n/30 to all of its customers. Phantom uses a perpetual inventory system and at the end of May had an inventory of 230 books purchased at $7 each. During the month of June, the following merchandise transactions occurred:

June 1   Purchased 170 books on account for $7 each from Reader's World Publishers, terms n/30, FOB destination.

     2   The correct company paid $85 freight on the June 1 purchase.

     3   Sold 190 books on account to Book Nook for $12 each.

     6   Received $70 credit for 10 books returned to Reader's World Publishers.

   18   Issued a $48 credit to Book Nook for the return of four damaged books. The books were determined to be no longer saleable and were destroyed.

   20   Purchased 140 books on account for $6.50 each from Reader's World Publishers, terms n/30, FOB shipping point.

   21   The correct company paid $70 freight for the July 20 purchase.

   27   Sold 100 books on account to Readers Bookstore for $12 each.

   28   Granted Readers Bookstore a $180 credit for 15 returned books. These books were restored to inventory.

   30   Paid Reader's World Publishers for the June 1 purchase.

   30   Received the balance owing from Book Nook.

Instructions

(a) Record the transactions for the month of June for Phantom Book Warehouse.

(b) Create a T account for Merchandise Inventory. Post the opening balance and June's transactions, and calculate the June 30 balance.

(c) Determine the number of books on hand at the end of the month and calculate the average cost per book of the inventory on hand at June 30.

TAKING IT FURTHER   Explain how freight terms can affect the selling price, and the cost, of merchandise. Use the transactions on June 1 and 20 between Phantom Book Warehouse and Reader's World Publishers as part of your explanation.

P5–5B At the beginning of September 2017, Stojanovic Distributing Company's ledger showed Cash $12,500, Merchandise Inventory $7,500, and D. Stojanovic, Capital, $20,000. During the month of September, the company had the following selected transactions:

Record and post inventory transactions—perpetual system. Prepare partial income statement.
(LO 2, 3, 5) AP

Sept. 2 Purchased $13,500 of merchandise inventory from Moon Supply Co., terms 1/15, n/30, FOB destination.
  4 The correct company paid $325 cash for freight charges on the September 2 purchase.
  5 Sold merchandise inventory to Brandon Retailers for $18,000. The cost of the merchandise was $11,310 and the terms were 2/10, n/30, FOB destination.
  6 Issued a $1,400 credit for merchandise returned by Brandon Retailers. The merchandise originally cost $890 and was returned to inventory.
  6 The correct company paid $420 freight on the September 5 sale.
  8 Purchased $900 of supplies for cash.
  10 Purchased $6,450 of merchandise inventory from Tina Wholesalers, terms 2/10, n/30, FOB shipping point.
  10 The correct company paid $150 freight costs on the purchase from Tina Wholesalers.
  12 Received a $450 credit from Tina Wholesalers for returned merchandise.
  15 Paid Moon Supply Co. the amount due.
  15 Collected the balance owing from Brandon Retailers.
  19 Sold merchandise for $10,875 cash. The cost of this merchandise was $6,855.
  20 Paid Tina Wholesalers the balance owing from the September 10 purchase.
  25 Made a $750 cash refund to a cash customer for merchandise returned. The returned merchandise had a cost of $470. The merchandise was damaged and could not be resold.
  30 Sold merchandise to Dragen & Company for $6,420, terms n/30, FOB shipping point. Stojanovic's cost for this merchandise was $4,050.

Instructions

(a) Record the transactions assuming Stojanovic uses a perpetual inventory system.
(b) Set up general ledger accounts for Merchandise Inventory, Sales, Sales Returns and Allowances, Sales Discounts, and Cost of Goods Sold. Enter the beginning Merchandise Inventory balance, post the transactions and calculate the balances for each account.
(c) Prepare a partial multiple-step income statement, up to gross profit, for the month of September 2017.

TAKING IT FURTHER Assume that Stojanovic has a "no questions asked" policy in terms of accepting sales returns up to six months after the initial sale. What uncertainties does the company face in terms of calculating its gross profit for September?

P5–6B Western Lighting Warehouse has a July 31 fiscal year end and uses a perpetual inventory system. An alphabetical list of its account balances at July 31, 2017, follows. All accounts have normal balances.

Prepare adjusting and closing entries, single-step income statement—perpetual system. Calculate ratios.
(LO 4, 5, 6) AP

A. Jamal, capital	$166,500	Interest expense	$ 2,300
A. Jamal, drawings	39,600	Interest revenue	3,000
Accounts payable	7,600	Merchandise inventory	41,250
Accounts receivable	38,900	Note payable	46,000
Accumulated depreciation—equipment	33,400	Notes receivable	75,000
Cash	30,875	Rent expense	62,000
Cost of goods sold	247,500	Salaries expense	45,000
Depreciation expense	8,350	Sales	450,000
Equipment	83,500	Sales discounts	4,500
Freight out	6,055	Sales returns and allowances	11,250
Insurance expense	3,195	Unearned revenue	4,800
Interest payable	575	Utilities expense	12,600

Additional information:

1. All adjustments have been recorded and posted except for the inventory adjustment. According to the inventory count, the company has $40,000 of merchandise on hand.
2. Last year Western Lighting Warehouse had a gross profit margin of 40% and a profit margin of 10%.

Instructions

(a) Prepare any additional required adjusting entries and update the account balances.
(b) Prepare a single-step income statement.
(c) Calculate gross profit margin and profit margin. Compare with last year's margins and comment on the results. (Hint: you will have to calculate gross profit separately.)
(d) Prepare the closing entries. Post to the Income Summary account. Check that the balance in the Income Summary account before closing it is equal to profit.

TAKING IT FURTHER What kind of information do the gross profit margin and profit margin provide to a user of the financial statements?

Prepare adjusting and closing entries, single-step and multiple step income statements—perpetual system. (LO 4, 5) AP

P5-7B The unadjusted trial balance of Global Enterprises for the year ended December 31, 2017, follows:

GLOBAL ENTERPRISES
Trial Balance
December 31, 2017

	Debit	Credit
Cash	$ 16,400	
Short-term investments	18,000	
Accounts receivable	15,700	
Merchandise inventory	37,500	
Supplies	1,650	
Furniture	26,800	
Accumulated depreciation—furniture		$ 10,720
Equipment	42,000	
Accumulated depreciation—equipment		8,400
Accounts payable		26,850
Unearned revenue		3,000
Notes payable		35,000
I. Rochefort, capital		45,500
I. Rochefort, drawings	35,500	
Sales		245,000
Sales returns and allowances	6,670	
Sales discounts	2,450	
Cost of goods sold	132,300	
Insurance expense	1,800	
Rent expense	9,300	
Salaries expense	28,400	
	$374,470	$374,470

Additional information:

1. There was $700 of supplies on hand on December 31, 2017.
2. Depreciation expense for the year is $5,360 on the furniture, and $4,200 on the equipment.
3. Accrued interest expense at December 31, 2017, is $1,750.
4. Accrued interest revenue at December 31, 2017, is $720.
5. Of the unearned revenue, $1,600 is still unearned at December 31, 2017. On the sales that were earned, the cost of goods sold was $755.
6. A physical count of merchandise inventory indicates $35,275 on hand on December 31, 2017.

Instructions

(a) Prepare the adjusting journal entries assuming they are prepared annually and update account balances.
(b) Prepare a multiple-step income statement.
(c) Prepare a single-step income statement.
(d) Prepare the closing entries.

TAKING IT FURTHER Compare the single-step and multiple-step income statements and comment on the usefulness of each. In your comments, refer to specific details provided on Global Enterprises' income statements.

P5-8B   The following information (dollars in thousands) is for **Danier Leather Inc.**:

Calculate ratios and comment. (LO 6) AN

	2014	2013	2012
Current assets	$ 33,970	$ 49,709	$ 60,965
Current liabilities	10,790	11,748	11,748
Net sales	141,930	154,995	148,219
Cost of goods sold	73,697	76,579	71,513
Profit (loss)	(7,663)	1,411	4,003

Instructions

(a) Calculate the gross profit margin, profit margin, and current ratio for Danier Leather for 2014, 2013, and 2012.

(b) Comment on whether the ratios have improved or deteriorated over the three years.

TAKING IT FURTHER   What other information would be useful when evaluating these ratios over the three-year period?

*P5-9B   Data for Leeland Company are presented in P5-3B.

Record inventory transactions—periodic system. (LO 7) AP

Instructions

Record the October and November transactions for Leeland Company, assuming a periodic inventory system is used instead of a perpetual inventory system.

TAKING IT FURTHER   Why might a periodic system be better than a perpetual system for Leeland Company?

*P5-10B   Data for Phantom Book Warehouse are presented in P5-4B.

Record inventory transactions—periodic system. (LO 7) AP

Instructions

Record the June transactions for Phantom Book Warehouse, assuming a periodic inventory system is used instead of a perpetual inventory system.

TAKING IT FURTHER   What are the costs and benefits for Phantom Book Warehouse of using a perpetual, as opposed to a periodic, inventory system?

*P5-11B   Data for Stojanovic Distributing Company are presented in P5-5B. A physical inventory count shows the company has $5,570 of inventory on hand at September 30, 2017.

Prepare financial statements and closing entries—periodic system. (LO 7) AP

Instructions

(a) Record the transactions assuming Stojanovic Distributing Company uses a periodic inventory system.

(b) Set up general ledger accounts for merchandise inventory and all of the temporary accounts used in the merchandising transactions. Enter beginning balances, post the transactions, and update the account balances.

(c) Prepare a partial multiple-step income statement, up to gross profit, for the month of September 2017.

TAKING IT FURTHER   Will Stojanovic Distributing Company's gross profit be higher, lower, or the same amount, if it uses a periodic inventory system instead of a perpetual inventory system? Explain.

Prepare correct multiple-step income statement, statement of owner's equity, and classified balance sheet—periodic system. (LO 7) AP

*P5–12B Up North Company recently hired a new accountant whose first task was to prepare the financial statements for the year ended December 31, 2017. The following is what she produced:

UP NORTH COMPANY
Income Statement
December 31, 2017

Sales			$474,000
Less: Unearned revenue		$ 6,600	
Purchase discounts		4,175	10,775
Total revenue			463,225
Cost of goods sold			
Purchases		$278,400	
Add: Purchase returns and allowances		4,800	
Net purchases		283,200	
Add: Sales returns and allowances		9,000	
Cost of goods available for sale		292,200	
Add: Freight out		11,400	
Cost of selling merchandise			303,600
Gross profit margin			159,625
Operating expenses			
Freight in		$ 5,400	
Insurance expense		12,600	
Interest expense		3,000	
Rent expense		21,600	
Salaries expense		50,400	
Total operating expenses			93,000
Profit margin			66,625
Other revenues			
Interest revenue	$ 1,800		
Investment by owner	4,200	6,000	
Other expenses			
Depreciation expense	$ 8,400		
Drawings by owner	57,600	66,000	(60,000)
Profit from operations			$ 6,625

UP NORTH COMPANY
Balance Sheet
Year Ended December 31, 2017

Assets

Cash		$ 20,135
Accounts receivable		9,360
Merchandise inventory, January 1, 2017		36,000
Merchandise inventory, December 31, 2017		28,800
Equipment	$84,000	
Less: loan payable (for equipment purchase)	60,000	24,000
Total assets		$118,295

Liabilities and Owner's Equity

Long-term investment		$ 60,000
Accumulated depreciation—equipment		25,200
Sales discounts		3,480
Total liabilities		88,680
Owner's equity		29,615
Total liabilities and owner's equity		$118,295

The owner of the company, James Prideaux, is confused by the statements and has asked you for your help. He doesn't understand how, if his Owner's Capital account was $90,000 at December 31, 2016, owner's equity is now only $29,615. The accountant tells you that $29,615 must be correct because the balance sheet is balanced. The accountant also tells you that she didn't prepare a statement of owner's equity because it is an optional statement. You are relieved to find out that, even though there are errors in the statements, the amounts used from the accounts in the general ledger are the correct amounts.

Instructions

Prepare the correct multiple-step income statement, statement of owner's equity, and classified balance sheet. You determine that $6,000 of the loan payable on the equipment must be paid during 2018.

TAKING IT FURTHER   Why do we not include both the beginning and the ending merchandise inventory amounts on the balance sheet?

*P5–13B   The following is an alphabetical list of Tse's Tater Tots' adjusted account balances at the end of the company's fiscal year on December 31, 2017:

Prepare financial statements and closing entries—periodic system. (LO 7) AP

Accounts payable	$ 86,300	Interest revenue	$ 1,050
Accounts receivable	44,200	Land	75,000
Accumulated depreciation—building	51,800	Merchandise inventory	40,500
Accumulated depreciation—equipment	42,900	Mortgage payable	155,000
Building	190,000	Property tax expense	4,800
Cash	17,000	Purchases	441,600
Depreciation expense	23,400	Purchase discounts	8,830
Equipment	110,000	Purchase returns and allowances	20,070
Freight in	5,600	Salaries expense	127,500
Freight out	7,500	Salaries payable	3,500
H. Tse, capital	143,600	Sales	642,800
H. Tse, drawings	14,450	Sales discounts	12,700
Insurance expense	9,600	Sales returns and allowances	11,900
Interest expense	11,345	Unearned revenue	8,300
Interest payable	945	Utilities expense	18,000

Additional information:

1. Tse's Tater Tots uses a periodic inventory system.
2. A physical inventory count determined that merchandise inventory on December 31, 2017, was $34,600.
3. Of the mortgage payable, $17,000 is to be paid April 30, 2018.

Instructions

(a) Prepare a multiple-step income statement, a statement of owner's equity, and a classified balance sheet.
(b) Prepare the closing journal entries.
(c) Post the closing entries to the inventory and capital accounts. Check that the balances in these accounts are the same as the amounts on the balance sheet.

TAKING IT FURTHER   If you had not been told that Tse's Tater Tots uses a periodic inventory system, how could you have determined that? What information is available in a periodic inventory system that is not available in a perpetual inventory system?

▶ Cumulative Coverage—Chapters 2 to 5

The Board Shop, owned by Andrew John, sells skateboards in the summer and snowboards in the winter. The shop has an August 31 fiscal year end and uses a perpetual inventory system. On August 1, 2017, the company had the following balances in its general ledger:

Cash	$21,385	A. John, drawings	$ 52,800
Merchandise inventory	64,125	Sales	485,500
Supplies	3,750	Rent revenue	1,200
Equipment	70,800	Sales returns and allowances	11,420
Accumulated depreciation—equipment	13,275	Cost of goods sold	301,010
Accounts payable	12,650	Salaries expense	68,200
Unearned revenue	4,680	Rent expense	18,150
Notes payable	42,000	Insurance expense	4,140
A. John, capital	58,400	Interest expense	1,925

During August, the last month of the fiscal year, the company had the following transactions:

Aug. 1   Paid $1,650 for August's rent.

     2   Paid $6,500 of the amount included in Accounts Payable.

     4   Sold merchandise costing $7,900 for $12,260 cash.

     5   Purchased merchandise on account from Orange Line Co., n/30, FOB shipping point, for $24,500.

     5   Paid freight charges of $500 on merchandise purchased from Orange Line Co.

     8   Purchased supplies on account for $345.

     9   Refunded a customer $425 cash for returned merchandise. The merchandise had cost $265 and was returned to inventory.

   10   Sold merchandise on account to Spider Company for $15,750, terms 2/10, n/30, FOB shipping point. The merchandise had a cost of $9,765.

   11   Paid Orange Line Co. for half of the merchandise purchased on August 5.

   12   Spider Company returned $750 of the merchandise it purchased. Board Shop issued Spider a credit to their account. The merchandise had a cost of $465 and was returned to inventory.

   15   Paid salaries, $3,100.

   19   Spider Company paid the amount owing.

   21   Purchased $9,900 of merchandise from Rainbow Option Co. on account, terms 2/10, n/30, FOB destination.

   23   Returned $800 of the merchandise to Rainbow Option Co. and received a credit on the account.

   24   Received $525 cash in advance from customers for merchandise to be delivered in September.

   30   Paid salaries, $3,100.

   30   Paid Rainbow Option Co. the amount owing.

   31   Andrew John withdrew $4,800 cash.

Adjustment and additional data:

1. A count of supplies on August 31 shows $755 on hand.
2. The equipment has an estimated eight-year useful life.
3. Of the notes payable, $6,000 must be paid on September 1 each year.
4. An analysis of the Unearned Revenue account shows that $3,750 has been earned by August 31. A corresponding entry of $2,325 for Cost of Goods Sold will also need to be recorded for these sales.
5. Interest accrued on the note payable to August 31 was $175.
6. A count of the merchandise inventory on August 31 shows $76,560 of inventory on hand.

Instructions

(a) Create a general ledger account for each of the above accounts and enter the August 1 balances.

(b) Record and post the August transactions. Update the balances in the general ledger accounts.

(c) Prepare a trial balance at August 31, 2017.

(d) Record and post the adjustments required at August 31, 2017 and update the account balances as required.

(e) Prepare an adjusted trial balance at August 31, 2017.

(f) Prepare a multiple-step income statement, statement of owner's equity, and classified balance sheet.

(g) Record and post closing entries.

(h) Prepare a post-closing trial balance at August 31, 2017.

CHAPTER 5: BROADENING YOUR PERSPECTIVE

▶ Financial Reporting and Analysis

Financial Reporting Problem

BYP5–1   Access the annual financial statements for **Indigo Books & Music Inc.** by going to www.sedar.com. Select your language preference, then choose "Company Profiles" and "I." Scroll down until you locate Indigo Books and Music Inc., then scroll down and click on "View this public company's documents." Scroll down to May 26, 2015, and click on the link "Audited Statements—English."

Instructions

Use these statements to answer the following questions.

(a) Read Note #2 on page 30. Is Indigo a service company or a merchandising company?

(b) Indigo does not disclose in its financial statements or notes if it uses a periodic or perpetual inventory system. Why do you think that readers of the financial statements do not need to know that information? What inventory system do you think it uses and why?

(c) On page 27 of the annual financial statements, Indigo presents the Consolidated Statements of Loss and Comprehensive Loss, which is the same as an income statement. Does Indigo use a single-step or multiple-step income statement format?

(d) What non-operating revenues and non-operating expenses are included in Indigo's income statement?

(e) Calculate Indigo's gross profit margin and profit margin for 2015 and 2014. What does a negative profit margin indicate?

(f) On page 26 of the annual financial statements, Indigo presents the Consolidated Balance Sheets. What amount does the company report for Inventory as at March 28, 2015?

(g) On the Consolidated Statements of Loss and Comprehensive Loss, Indigo reports one amount for operating and administrative expenses. On page 49, Note #15 provides additional information for this amount. List the items for which detailed amounts included in operating and administrative expenses are provided in the note.

(h) In Note # 4, on page 33, Indigo reports under the title "Inventories" that "Costs [of inventory] include all direct and reasonable expenditures that are incurred in bringing inventories to their present location and condition." Other than the purchase price of inventory, what additional costs might be included in the cost of Indigo's inventory? (Hint: refer to the summary of purchase transactions and adjusting entries required.)

Interpreting Financial Statements

BYP5-2 Selected information from Indigo Books & Music Inc.'s income statements for three recent years follows (dollars in thousands):

	2015	2014	2013
Revenue	$895,376	$867,668	$878,785
Cost of sales	503,059	493,955	495,099
Operating expense	398,031	403,693	383,319
Non-operating income	2,492	3,071	3,823
Profit (loss)	(3,534)	(30,999)	4,288

Instructions

(a) Calculate gross profit, and profit from operations, for each of the three years.

(b) Calculate the percentage change in revenue and profit from operations, from 2013 to 2015.

(c) Calculate the gross profit margin for each of the three years. Comment on any trend in this percentage.

(d) Calculate the profit margin for each of the three years. Comment on any trend in this percentage.

(e) Calculate profit margin again using profit from operations instead of profit for each of the three years. Comment on any trend in this percentage.

(f) Management often believes that profit from operations is a more meaningful basis of comparison than profit. Based on your findings in parts (d) and (e) above, do you agree or disagree with this statement? Explain.

▶ Critical Thinking

Collaborative Learning Activity

Note to instructor: Additional instructions and material for this group activity can be found on the Instructor Resource Site and in *WileyPLUS*.

BYP5-3 The purpose of this group activity is to improve your understanding of merchandising journal entries. You will be given a merchandising company's general ledger in T account format with missing transaction data. With your group, you will analyze these T accounts to determine the underlying journal entries and balance the general ledger.

Communication Activity

BYP5-4 Consider the following events listed in chronological order:

1. Dexter Maersk decides to buy a custom-made snowboard. He calls Great Canadian Snowboards and asks it to manufacture one for him.
2. The company e-mails Dexter a purchase order to fill out, which he immediately completes, signs, and sends back with the required 25% down payment.
3. Great Canadian Snowboards receives Dexter's purchase order and down payment, and begins working on the board.
4. Great Canadian Snowboards has its fiscal year end. At this time, Dexter's board is 75% completed.
5. The company completes the snowboard for Dexter and notifies him.
6. Dexter picks up his snowboard from the company and takes it home.
7. Dexter tries the snowboard out and likes it so much that he carves his initials in it.
8. Great Canadian Snowboards bills Dexter for the cost of the snowboard, less the 25% down payment.
9. The company receives partial payment (another 25%) from Dexter.
10. The company receives payment of the balance due from Dexter.

Instructions

In a memo to the president of Great Canadian Snowboards, answer these questions:

(a) When should Great Canadian Snowboards record the revenue and cost of goods sold related to the snowboard? Refer to the revenue and expense recognition criteria in your answer.

(b) Suppose that, with his purchase order, Dexter was required to pay for 100% of the board. Would that change your answer to part (a)?

"All About You" Activity

BYP5-5 In the "All About You" feature, you learned about inventory theft and a relatively new technology to help prevent theft. You have recently accepted a part-time sales position at a clothing store called College Fashions. The owner-manager of the store knows that you are enrolled in a business program and seeks your advice on preventing inventory shrinkage due to theft. The owner-manager is aware that average retail shrinkage rates are 1.29% of sales but does not know College Fashions' shrinkage rate.

Instructions

(a) Assume the store uses a perpetual inventory system. Explain to the owner-manager how she can determine the amount of inventory shrinkage.

(b) The owner-manager wants to know if she should implement some type of technology to prevent theft. What would you advise her to consider before making an expenditure on technology to prevent theft?

(c) Assume that College Fashions' sales revenues are $400,000 and the shrinkage rate is 4%. What is the dollar amount that College Fashions loses due to shrinkage?

(d) Some believe that great customer service is the best defence against shoplifting. Discuss why great customer service may help prevent shoplifting.

(e) You also learned in the All About You feature that employee inventory theft is a significant problem. What procedures might management implement to prevent or reduce employee theft of inventory?

(f) In your part-time sales position, you have observed a fellow employee whom you are friendly with provide unauthorized sales discounts to her friends when they purchase merchandise from the store. Is it appropriate for this employee to give her friends unauthorized sales discounts? Explain. What might be a consequence for you as an employee if you fail to inform management of these unauthorized sales discounts?

Santé Smoothie Saga

(**Note:** This is a continuation of the Santé Smoothie Saga from Chapters 1 through 4. From the information gathered in the previous chapters, follow the instructions below using the ledger account balances from Chapter 4.)

BYP5-6 Because Natalie has had such a successful first few months, she is considering other opportunities to develop her business. One opportunity is the sale of fine European juicing machines. The owner of Kzinski Supply Co. has approached Natalie to become the exclusive Canadian distributor of these fine juicers. The current cost of a juicer is approximately $525 Canadian, and Natalie would sell each one for $1,050. Natalie comes to you for advice on how to account for these juicers. Each juicer has a serial number and can be easily identified.

Natalie asks you the following questions:

1. "Would you consider these juicers to be inventory? Or should they be classified as supplies or equipment?"
2. "I've learned a little about keeping track of inventory using both the perpetual and the periodic systems of accounting for inventory. Which system do you think is better? Which one would you recommend for the type of inventory that I want to sell?"
3. "How often do I need to count inventory if I maintain it using the perpetual system? Do I need to count inventory at all?"

In the end, Natalie decides to use the perpetual inventory system. The following transactions happen during the month of June 2017:

June 6 Purchased and received three deluxe juicers on account from Kzinski Supply Co. for $1,575, FOB shipping point, terms n/30.
7 Paid $60 freight on the June 6 purchase.

8 Returned one of the juicers to Kzinski because it was damaged during shipping. Kzinski issued Santé Smoothies a credit note for the cost of the juicer plus $20 for the cost of freight that was paid on June 6 for one juicer.
9 Collected $500 of the accounts receivable from May 2017.
13 Two deluxe juicers were sold on account for $2,100, FOB destination, terms n/30. The juicers were sold to Koebel's Family Bakery, the bakery that is owned and operated by Natalie's mom and dad. Natalie expects that the juicers will be paid for in early August.
14 Paid the $75 of delivery charges for the two juicers that were sold on June 13.
14 Purchased and received four deluxe juicers on account from Kzinski Supply Co. for $2,100, FOB shipping point, terms n/30.
15 Received a deposit of $125 from another yoga studio for smoothies during the month of August.
20 Natalie was concerned that there was not enough cash available to pay for all of the juicers purchased. She invested an additional $1,000 cash in Santé Smoothies.
21 Paid $80 freight on the June 14 purchase.
21 Sold two deluxe mixers for $2,100 cash.
28 Issued a cheque to an assistant for 20 hours worked in June. The assistant earns $12 an hour.
29 Paid a $154 cellphone bill ($88 for the May 2017 account payable and $66 for the month of June). (Recall that the cellphone is only used for business purposes.)
29 Paid Kzinski all amounts due.

As at June 30, the following adjusting entry data are available:

1. A count of supplies reveals that none were used in June.
2. Another month's worth of depreciation needs to be recorded on the juicing equipment bought in April and May. (Recall that the equipment cost $1,550 and has a useful life of three years or 36 months.)
3. An additional month's worth of interest on her mother's loan needs to be accrued. (Recall that Santé Smoothies borrowed $3,000 and the interest rate is 3%.)
4. An analysis of the Unearned Revenue account reveals that no smoothies have been delivered during the month of June. As a result, the opening balance in Unearned Revenue is still unearned. Natalie has been in contact with the yoga studios that have provided deposits for early June.
5. An inventory count of juicers at the end of June reveals that Natalie has two juicers remaining.

Instructions

Using the information from previous chapters and the new information above, do the following:

(a) Answer Natalie's questions.
(b) Prepare and post to T accounts the June 2017 transactions.
(c) Prepare a trial balance.
(d) Prepare and post the adjusting journal entries required.
(e) Prepare an adjusted trial balance.
(f) Prepare a multiple-step income statement for the month ended June 30, 2017.
(g) Calculate gross profit margin and profit margin.

ANSWERS TO CHAPTER QUESTIONS

ANSWERS TO ACCOUNTING IN ACTION INSIGHT QUESTIONS

Business Insight, p. 240

Q: What advantages does a perpetual inventory system give a retailer?

A: A perpetual inventory system keeps track of all sales and purchases on a continuous basis. This provides a constant record of the number of units in the inventory which minimizes the risk of inventory shortages. Perpetual inventory systems—particularly computerized systems—provide information to management that is timely and accurate. Management can then use this information for organization planning and control.

Ethics Insight, p. 245

Q: What are the ethical considerations in this case? Who are the stakeholders in this situation?

A: Rita Pelzer, as a new employee, is placed in a position of responsibility and is pressured by her supervisor to continue delaying payments to creditors. Delaying payment is not an unethical practice. Companies can pay their bills late, but they risk incurring interest charges, impairing their credit ratings, or losing a discount. What is unethical is taking the discount for early payment even if the payment is made after the discount period, and lying by blaming the late payment on the post office.

Rita's dilemma is to decide whether to (1) delay payments and place inappropriate blame for these late payments on the mail room and/or post office, or (2) risk offending her boss and possibly lose the job she just assumed.

The stakeholders (affected parties) are:
Rita Pelzer, the assistant controller.
Jamie Caterino, the controller.
Liu Stores, the company.
Creditors of Liu Stores (suppliers).
Mail room/post office employees (those assigned the blame).

Business Insight, p. 248

Q: What accounting information would help a manager decide what to do with returned goods?

A: The manager would need to know the potential revenues and expenses for each alternative. For example, returning goods to stock and selling them again may provide the highest revenue but the cost of getting the goods ready for resale may also be high. The revenue earned from liquidating the returned goods may be much lower but the cost of doing this may also be very low. The manager should compare the estimated profit—not just the revenue earned—of each alternative when deciding what to do.

All About You Insight, p. 251

Q: Are there advantages to you as a customer when retailers increase theft prevention measures?

A: Many customers see theft prevention measures, such as locked fitting rooms, or having a store employee track the items they are taking into a fitting room, as a very annoying personal inconvenience. But there are benefits to the customers as well as the stores. Retailers have to be able to pass all of their costs on to customers in order to remain in business. When inventory theft increases, the selling price will also have to increase or the store will not be profitable. If customers are not willing to pay the increased prices, then the store may go out of business, resulting in less choice for consumers and fewer jobs. Inconveniences in using the fitting rooms may be a far smaller price to pay than the alternatives.

ANSWERS TO SELF-STUDY QUESTIONS

1. c   2. b   3. a   4. a   5. b   6. c   7. c   8. c   9. d   10. c   *11. b   *12. b

6 INVENTORY COSTING

CHAPTER PREVIEW In the previous chapter, we discussed accounting for merchandise transactions. In this chapter, we first explain the procedures for determining inventory quantities. We then discuss the three methods for determining cost of goods sold and the cost of inventory on hand: the specific identification method and the two cost formulas, FIFO (first-in, first-out) and weighted average. Next we see the effects of cost determination methods and inventory errors on a company's financial statements. We end by illustrating methods of reporting and analyzing inventory.

FEATURE STORY

A FRESH APPROACH TO COSTING INVENTORY

TORONTO, Ont.—For retailers, inventory accounts for a large share of their assets, so the method of recording the cost of inventory is important. Loblaw Companies Limited, Canada's largest retailer, recently spent millions of dollars overhauling its supply chain and upgrading its information technology to better move and track its hundreds of thousands of items—many of them perishable. The new inventory-tracking system had another benefit: allowing a more precise method to record inventory cost.

Before the second quarter of 2014, Loblaw used the retail method to estimate the cost of most of its inventory at its more than 2,300 stores across the country, which operate under banners such as the Loblaws, Independent, No Frills, and Provigo grocery chains; Joe Fresh apparel; and Shoppers Drug Mart. The company used the periodic inventory system to track inventory periodically. But the periodic inventory system makes it impractical for retailers such as Loblaw to determine the precise cost of each of many types of merchandise. So Loblaw used the retail method, which works backwards from the merchandise's selling price and uses a ratio that estimates the cost in relation to selling price.

But starting in the third quarter of 2014, thanks to its new inventory information technology system, Loblaw switched to a perpetual inventory system to track merchandise in real time. This meant it could also switch its method of determining inventory costs. Instead of the retail inventory method, which is an estimate, Loblaw now uses the weighted average cost formula, which uses the actual costs of the merchandise—in this case, an average of the items in its perpetual inventory system. "The implementation of a perpetual inventory system, combined with visibility to integrated costing information provided by the new IT systems, enables the Company to estimate the cost of inventory using a more precise system-generated average cost," Loblaw said in its 2014 annual report. The exception to using the weighted average cost formula is Shoppers Drug Mart, which Loblaw purchased in 2013. Shoppers' costs are determined using the first-in, first-out cost (FIFO) formula, again using actual costs of merchandise. FIFO assigns the cost of the first item purchased to the cost of the first item sold.

At year end, when reporting inventory on its financial statements, Loblaw values its merchandise inventory at the lower of cost and net realizable value. This means that, when inventory's realizable value is less than what it cost, the company writes down merchandise to its net realizable value.

Sources: "Helping Loblaw Achieve High Performance Through Supply Chain Transformation," Accenture case study, 2013; The Canadian Press, "Loblaws Claims Supply Chain Overhaul Successful," *Materials Management & Distribution,* March 1, 2012; Loblaw Companies Limited 2014 annual report; Loblaw Companies Limited corporate website, http://www.loblaw.ca/.

THE CANADIAN PRESS IMAGES/Ryan Remoirz

CHAPTER OUTLINE | LEARNING OBJECTIVES

1 Describe the steps in determining inventory quantities.

Determining Inventory Quantities
- Taking a physical inventory
- Determining ownership of goods

DO IT 1
Rules of ownership

2 Calculate cost of goods sold and ending inventory in a perpetual inventory system using the specific identification, FIFO, and weighted average methods of cost determination.

Inventory Cost Determination Methods
- Specific identification
- Cost formulas: FIFO and weighted average

DO IT 2
Cost formulas

3 Explain the financial statement effects of inventory cost determination methods.

Financial Statement Effects
- Choice of cost determination method

DO IT 3
Effect on financial information: FIFO vs. weighted average

4 Determine the financial statement effects of inventory errors.

Inventory Errors

DO IT 4
Inventory errors

5 Value inventory at the lower of cost and net realizable value.

Presentation and Analysis of Inventory
- Valuing inventory at the lower of cost and net realizable value

DO IT 5
Lower of cost and net realizable value

6 Demonstrate the presentation and analysis of inventory.

Reporting and Analyzing Inventory
- Presenting inventory in the financial statements

DO IT 6
Inventory turnover ratio and days sales in inventory

7 Calculate ending inventory and cost of goods sold in a periodic inventory system using FIFO and weighted average inventory cost formulas (Appendix 6A).

Appendix 6A: Inventory Cost Formulas in Periodic Systems
- Periodic system—First-in, first-out (FIFO)
- Periodic system—Weighted average

DO IT 7
Cost flow methods

8 Estimate ending inventory using the gross profit and retail inventory methods (Appendix 6B).

Appendix 6B: Estimating Inventories
- Gross profit method
- Retail inventory method

DO IT 8
Inventory estimation: Gross profit method

LEARNING OBJECTIVE 1   Describe the steps in determining inventory quantities.

Determining Inventory Quantities

Companies count their entire inventory at least once a year, whether they are using a perpetual or a periodic inventory system. This is called taking a physical inventory. If companies are using a perpetual system, they will use this information to check the accuracy of their perpetual inventory records. As we saw in Chapter 5, in a perpetual inventory system, the accounting records continuously—perpetually—show the amount of inventory **that should be on hand**, not necessarily the amount **that actually is on hand**. An adjusting entry is required if the physical inventory count does not match what was recorded in the general ledger.

In a periodic inventory system, inventory quantities are not continuously updated. Companies using a periodic inventory system must take a physical inventory to determine the amount on hand at the end of the accounting period. Once the ending inventory amount is known, this amount is then used to calculate the cost of goods sold for the period and to update the Merchandise Inventory account in the general ledger.

Inventory quantities are determined in two steps:

1. taking a physical inventory of goods on hand, and
2. determining the ownership of goods.

TAKING A PHYSICAL INVENTORY

Taking a physical inventory involves actually counting, weighing, or measuring each kind of inventory on hand. Taking a physical inventory can be an enormous task for many companies, especially for retailers such as Loblaw Companies Limited, which has thousands of product items. An inventory count is generally more accurate when goods are not being sold or received during the counting. This is why companies often count their inventory when they are closed or when business is slow.

To make fewer errors in taking the inventory, a company should ensure that it has a good system of internal control. **Internal control** is the process designed and implemented by management to help the company achieve reliable financial reporting, effective and efficient operations, and compliance with relevant laws and regulations. Some of the internal control procedures for counting inventory are as follows:

1. The counting should be done by employees who are not responsible for either custody of the inventory or keeping inventory records.
2. Each counter should establish that each inventory item actually exists, how many there are of it, and what condition each item is in. For example, does each box actually contain what it is supposed to contain?
3. There should be a second count by another employee or auditor. Counting should be done in teams of two.
4. Pre-numbered inventory tags should be used to ensure that all inventory items are counted and that no items are counted more than once.

ETHICS NOTE
In a famous fraud, a salad oil company filled its storage tanks mostly with water. The oil rose to the top, so auditors thought the tanks were full of oil.

We will revisit internal control procedures in Chapter 7.

After the physical inventory is taken, the quantity of each kind of inventory item is listed on inventory summary sheets. The second count by another employee or auditor helps ensure the count is accurate. In a large retailer like Loblaw Companies Limited, technology such as bar scanners and sophisticated software systems is used to make sure a minimum of errors and make sure the physical count can be completed in a timely manner. Unit costs are then applied to the quantities in order to determine the total cost of the inventory. This will be explained later in the chapter, when we discuss inventory costing.

DETERMINING OWNERSHIP OF GOODS

When we take a physical inventory, we need to consider the ownership of goods. To determine ownership of the goods, two questions need to be answered:

1. Do all of the goods included in the count belong to the company?
2. Does the company own any goods that were not included in the count?

Goods in Transit

An important aspect of determining ownership is the consideration of goods in transit (on board a public carrier such as a railway, airline, truck, or ship) at the end of the accounting period. Depending on the shipping terms, goods that are in transit at year end may be owned by the purchaser or seller.

Goods in transit should be included in the inventory of the company that has ownership (legal title) of the goods. Illustration 5-8 in Chapter 5 showed that ownership is determined by the terms of sale. This illustration is reproduced below in Illustration 6-1.

▶ ILLUSTRATION **6-1**
Terms of sale

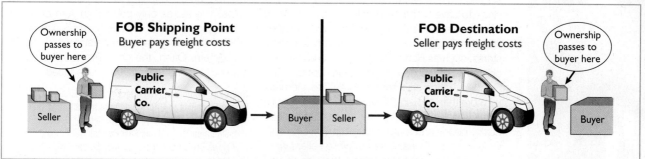

1. When the terms are FOB (free on board) shipping point, ownership (legal title) of the goods passes to the buyer when the public carrier accepts the goods from the seller.
2. When the terms are FOB destination, ownership (legal title) of the goods remains with the seller until the goods reach the buyer.

Inventory quantities may be seriously miscounted if goods in transit at the statement date are ignored. For example, assume that Hill Company has 20,000 units of inventory in its warehouse on December 31. It also has the following goods in transit on December 31:

1. 1,500 units shipped to a customer on December 31, FOB destination; and
2. 2,500 units purchased from a supplier shipped FOB shipping point on December 31.

Hill has legal title to both the units sold and the units purchased. If units in transit are ignored, inventory quantities would be understated by 4,000 units (1,500 + 2,500).

As we will see later in this chapter, inaccurate inventory quantities not only affect the inventory amount on the balance sheet, they also affect the cost of goods sold reported in the income statement.

Consigned Goods

For some businesses, it is customary to hold goods belonging to other parties and to sell them, for a fee, without ever taking ownership of the goods. These are called **consigned goods**. In such an arrangement, the consignee agrees to facilitate the sale of goods for the consignor. The consignee does not own the goods but will charge a fee or commission to sell the goods on the consignor's behalf.

For example, Amazon.com Inc. offers millions of items for sale to consumers on its various country websites, but not all the items are owned by the company. Some of the products the company sells are purchased and resold but some products are simply showcased for other companies and Amazon.com then facilitates the sale. In its annual report, Amazon refers to these companies as "third-party sellers" and the goods owned by these third-party sellers (consignors) are not included in Amazon's (consignee) inventory.

Other common examples of consignment arrangements can be seen in art galleries, craft stores, second-hand clothing and sporting goods stores, and antique dealers. Advantages of consignment arrangements for the consignee are lower inventory costs and avoiding the risk of purchasing an item it will not be able to sell.

Sometimes goods are not physically present at a company because they have been taken home *on approval* by a customer. Goods on approval should be added to the physical inventory count because they still belong to the seller. The customer will either return the item or decide to buy it.

ACCOUNTING IN ACTION
ALL ABOUT YOU INSIGHT

Have you ever shopped in or sold some things at a consignment store? Many students buy and sell second-hand items such as clothing and furniture to save money and help the environment. Parents who don't want to invest in kids' clothes that they'll outgrow also flock to consignment stores, such as Boomerang Kids, a chain of nine children's consignment stores in Ontario and Quebec, which saw same-store sales increase by more than 10% in the first half of 2013. Shoppers are attracted to lower prices for higher-quality goods and making long-term investments in designer and classic items, while sellers want to earn some cash for things they don't use anymore. The Internet has exposed people to designer brands and unique looks that consumers are eager to try out on a budget. For consignment store owners, the business model is attractive, too, because they have virtually no inventory costs. The stores only pay for an item once it's sold. Typically, stores give a commission of about 40% of the sale price to the person who brought in the item. Often, the commission will drop as time passes and the sale price is reduced.

Sources: "Boomerang Kids Becomes First Children's Resale Franchise to Offer Customers In-Store and Online Shopping," company news release, October 8, 2013; "Consignment Sales Up as Fashionistas Get Frugal," CTV News British Columbia on-line, January 26, 2012; Ed Stoddard and Tim Gaynor, "Second-Hand Retailers Score During Recession," Reuters, *The Globe and Mail,* October 5, 2009.

Q **What is one disadvantage of buying items on consignment?**

Action Plan

Apply the rules of ownership to goods held on consignment:

- Goods held on consignment *for* another company are not included in inventory.
- Goods held on consignment *by* another company are included in inventory.

Apply the rules of ownership to goods in transit:

- FOB shipping point: Goods sold or purchased and shipped FOB shipping point belong to the buyer when in transit.
- FOB destination: Goods sold or purchased and shipped FOB destination belong to the seller until they reach their destination.

BEFORE YOU GO ON...DO IT **1** ⟩ **Rules of Ownership**

Too Good to Be Threw Company completed its inventory count on June 30. It arrived at a total inventory value of $200,000, counting everything currently on hand in its warehouse. You have been given the information listed below. How will the following information affect the inventory count and cost?

1. Goods costing $15,000 that are being held on consignment for another company were included in the inventory.
2. Goods purchased for $10,000 and in transit at June 30 (terms FOB shipping point) were not included in the count.
3. Inventory sold for $18,000 that cost $12,000 when purchased and was in transit at June 30 (terms FOB destination) was not included in the count.

Solution

Original count	$200,000
1. Goods held on consignment from another company	(15,000)
2. Goods in transit purchased FOB shipping point	10,000
3. Goods in transit sold FOB destination	12,000
Adjusted count	$207,000

Related exercise material: BE6–1, BE6–2, E6–1, and E6–2.

Calculate cost of goods sold and ending inventory in a perpetual inventory system using the specific identification, FIFO, and weighted average methods of cost determination.

Inventory Cost Determination Methods

The physical inventory count we described in the last section is normally completed at a period end and gives management information about the **quantities** of the items on hand, but for accounting purposes, we need to determine the **cost of** the items on hand. In a perpetual inventory system, the cost of inventory items on hand and the cost of items that are sold are continuously updated. In a periodic inventory system, costs are assigned to items still on hand at the end of period and cost of goods sold is calculated. How do companies determine individual costs in either one of these inventory systems? The common methods used are specific identification, FIFO (first-in, first-out), and weighted average. This section will introduce these methods or techniques for assigning costs to units in ending inventory and units in cost of goods sold.

Retailers often purchase goods for resale in batches. Generally it is unwise to buy a long-term inventory of any product, because it may increase costs and increase the risk that the product won't sell or that a new, better version will be available before all the previous items can be sold. Instead, many retailers buy in smaller batches. Each time a retailer purchases the items, the cost of the goods may be exactly the same as the last purchase or different. Think about the last time you purchased your favourite chocolate bar. Was it the same price you paid the time before? Likely not, because costs and the resulting sales prices of consumer goods change regularly.

In an ideal world, identical inventory items would always cost the same amount and the accounting would be simple, because each item in ending inventory and cost of goods sold is assigned the same unit cost. Easy! However, when identical items have been purchased at different unit costs during the period, it is difficult to decide what the unit costs are of the items that have been sold and what the unit costs are of the items that remain in inventory.

In Chapter 5, you were introduced to the perpetual and periodic inventory systems. We learned how to account for inventory transactions. For each exercise, a dollar amount was provided for the cost of goods sold.

Recall that in a perpetual inventory system, when a sale is recorded, two entries are made as follows (using assumed dollar amounts):

Helpful hint The cost of inventory generally means the amount that a retailer pays to purchase it for later resale. The sales price is the amount a retailer charges a consumer to purchase the good for their own use.

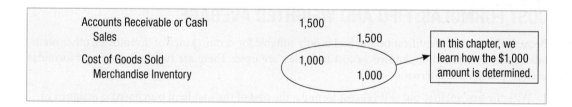

Accounts Receivable or Cash	1,500	
Sales		1,500
Cost of Goods Sold	1,000	
Merchandise Inventory		1,000

In this chapter, we learn how the $1,000 amount is determined.

In Chapter 6, we build on what you learned in Chapter 5. In this chapter, identical items will not be purchased for the same cost and you will have to determine the cost of the goods sold and the cost of the ending inventory.

SPECIFIC IDENTIFICATION

The **specific identification** method tracks the actual physical flow (movement) of the goods in a perpetual inventory system. Each item of inventory is marked, tagged, or coded with its specific unit cost. This means that, at any point in time, the cost of the goods sold and the cost of the ending inventory can be determined.

The specific identification method is used by companies that have large items or unique or custom products so that no two products are identical. For example, Katelyn's Kreations, a jewellery store that sells "one-of-a-kind" rings, would use specific identification. To illustrate, assume that Katelyn's Kreations had three rings available for sale in January with a total cost of $9,200 ($2,000 + $3,000 + $4,200).

As shown in Illustration 6-2, two rings are sold in January and the cost of the two rings sold is $6,200 ($2,000 + $4,200). The cost of the ring still on hand at the end of January is $3,000. Therefore, the cost of goods sold on the January income statement is $6,200 and the merchandise inventory on the January 31 balance sheet is $3,000. This determination is possible because it is easy to track the actual physical flow of the goods.

► **ILLUSTRATION 6-2**
Specific identification

ETHICS NOTE
A disadvantage of the specific identification method is that management may be able to manipulate profit. For example, it can boost profit by selling more units that were purchased at a low cost, or reduce profit by selling more units that were purchased at a high cost.

Specific identification **must be** used for goods that are not ordinarily interchangeable, or for goods that are produced for specific projects. In addition to the ring example, specific identification would be used for any other customized products, such as furniture and artistic works. Car manufacturers and dealerships also use specific identification for cars because each car has its own unique characteristics and vehicle identification number.

It may seem that specific identification is the ideal method for determining cost because it matches sales with the actual cost of the goods sold. But it can be time-consuming and expensive to apply.

COST FORMULAS: FIFO AND WEIGHTED AVERAGE

Because the specific identification method is only suitable for certain kinds of inventories, other methods of cost determination, known as cost formulas, are used. There are two inventory cost formulas used in Canada and internationally.

1. With the first-in, first-out (FIFO) cost formula, the cost of the first item purchased is assigned to the cost of the first item sold.
2. With the weighted average cost formula, the cost is determined using an average of the cost of the items purchased.

FIFO and weighted average are known as "cost formulas" because they assume a flow of costs that may not be the same as the actual physical flow of goods, unlike the specific identification method.

While specific identification is normally used only in a perpetual inventory system, FIFO and weighted average can be used in both the perpetual and periodic inventory systems. Recall from Chapter 5 that the two systems differ in determining when the cost of goods sold is calculated and recorded.

Under a perpetual inventory system, the cost of goods sold is determined as each item is sold. Under a periodic inventory system, the cost of goods available for sale (beginning inventory plus the cost of goods purchased) is allocated to ending inventory and to cost of goods sold at the end of the period. Recall that in a periodic system, the cost of goods sold is calculated by deducting the ending inventory from the cost of goods available for sale. How to calculate cost of goods sold and ending inventory in a periodic system using the FIFO and weighted average cost formulas is included in Appendix 6A.

To illustrate how the FIFO and weighted average cost formulas are applied, we will assume that Ingrid's Lighting Boutique reports the information shown in Illustration 6-3 for one of its products, the 23W compact fluorescent light bulb.

▶ILLUSTRATION 6-3
Inventory purchases, sales, and units on hand

| | INGRID'S LIGHTING BOUTIQUE | | | | |
| | 23W Compact Fluorescent Light Bulb | | | | |
Date	Explanation	Units	Unit Cost	Total Cost	Total Units in Inventory
Jan. 1	Beginning inventory	100	$10	$ 1,000	100
Apr. 15	Purchase	100	12	1,200	200
May 1	Sales	−125			75
Aug. 24	Purchase	300	14	4,200	375
Sept. 1	Sales	−350			25
Nov. 27	Purchase	400	15	6,000	425
				$12,400	

Perpetual Inventory System—First-In, First-Out (FIFO)

The **first-in, first-out (FIFO) cost formula** assumes that the earliest (oldest) goods purchased are the first ones to be sold. This does not necessarily mean that the oldest units are literally sold first; only that the cost of the oldest units is used first to determine cost of goods sold. It is used by a variety of companies including the Shoppers Drug Mart subsidiary of Loblaw. Although the cost formula chosen by a company does not have to match the actual physical movement of the inventory, it should correspond as closely as possible. FIFO often does match the actual physical flow of merchandise, because it generally is good business practice to sell the oldest units first, particularly if the goods are subject to spoilage or expiry.

We will use the information for Ingrid's Lighting Boutique's 23W compact fluorescent light bulbs as shown in Illustration 6-3 to prepare a perpetual inventory record using the FIFO cost formula. Perpetual inventory records are organized to show how the cost of goods sold for each sale is calculated. They also show the cost and number of units in inventory after each purchase and each sale. That is to say, the inventory record is continually updated.

Illustration 6-4 shows the completed inventory record. An explanation of each transaction is provided below corresponding to the number on the left in the illustration.

1. A perpetual inventory record starts with the inventory balance at the beginning of the year. On January 1, inventory consisted of 100 units costing $10.00 each for a total cost of $1,000.00.
2. On April 15, the company purchases 100 units costing $12.00 each for a total purchase cost of $1,200.00 Inventory now consists of two **tiers**: 100 units costing $10.00 each and 100 units costing $12.00 each. Total inventory is 200 units, at a total cost of $2,200 ($1,000.00 + $1,200.00). The FIFO cost formula requires costs in tiers to be tracked separately because the earliest costs are the first to be assigned to sales. In Chapter 5, we learned how to prepare the journal entry for a purchase in a perpetual system. As a reminder, the journal entry to record the purchase is:

Apr. 15	Merchandise Inventory	1,200	
	Accounts Payable or Cash		1,200

	A	B	C	D	E	F	G	H	I	J	K	L	M
1	FIFO												
2		Date	Purchases				Cost of goods sold				Inventory balance		
3			Units	Cost	Total		Units	Cost	Total		Units	Cost	Total
4	(1)	Jan. 1	Beginning inventory										
5			100	$10.00	$1,000.00						100	$10.00	$1,000.00
6	(2)	Apr. 15	100	12.00	1,200.00						100	10.00	1,000.00
7											100	12.00	1,200.00
8	(3)	May 1					100	$10.00	$1,000.00				
9							25	12.00	300.00		75	12.00	900.00
10	(4)	Aug. 24	300	14.00	4,200.00						75	12.00	900.00
11											300	14.00	4,200.00
12	(5)	Sept. 1					75	12.00	900.00				
13							275	14.00	3,850.00		25	14.00	350.00
14	(6)	Nov. 27	400	15.00	6,000.00						25	14.00	350.00
15											400	15.00	6,000.00
16													
17	(7)		900		$12,400.00		475		$6,050.00		425		$6,350.00
18													
19			Cost of goods available for sale			−	Cost of goods sold			=	Ending inventory		

After the purchase on April 15, the inventory balance consists of two tiers totalling $2,200.00

Total cost of goods sold for the units sold on May 1 is $1,300.00

Inventory after the sale on May 1 consists of only one tier – 75 units totalling $900.00

▶ILLUSTRATION 6-4
FIFO inventory record

3. On May 1, a sale of 125 units takes place. Recall that in a perpetual inventory system the cost of goods sold is calculated every time a sale is made. Therefore, on May 1, we apply FIFO to determine the cost of goods sold. The cost of the oldest goods on hand before the sale is allocated to the cost of goods sold. Accordingly, we start with the beginning inventory of 100 units costing $10.00 each. Since 125 units were sold on May 1, this means they sold the entire beginning inventory, and 25 of the $12.00 units. The total cost of goods sold is $1,300.00 ($1,000.00 + $300.00).

Assuming the company has a selling price for each bulb of $20, we can use our knowledge from Chapter 5 and prepare the journal entry to record the sale:

| May 1 | Accounts Receivable (125 units × $20) | 2,500 | |
| | Sales | | 2,500 |

| May 1 | Cost of Goods Sold | 1,300 | |
| | Merchandise Inventory | | 1,300 |

Finally, the number of units remaining consists of only one tier: 75 units costing $12.00 each, for a total inventory cost of $900.00.

4. Additional purchases are made on August 24. After updating the inventory record, the balance in inventory again consists of two tiers, 75 units costing $12.00 each and 300 units costing $14.00 each, which totals 375 units costing $5,100.00 ($900.00 + $4,200.00).

5. On September 1, when 350 units are sold, the cost of goods sold is determined using the remaining 75 units costing $12.00 each purchased on April 15 and 275 units costing $14.00 each from the August 24 purchase. The total cost of goods sold for this sale will be $4,750.00 ($900.00 + $3,850.00). Remaining inventory will consist of 25 units costing $14.00 each for a total cost of $350.00.

6. The purchase of 400 units on November 27 increases inventory to 425 units in total. Two tiers of inventory exist, 25 units costing $14.00 each from the August 24 purchase and 400 units costing $15.00 each purchased on November 27. Total inventory after the November 27 purchase will be 425 units, with a total cost of $6,350.00 ($350.00 + $6,000.00).

7. Recall the cost flow relationships illustrated in Chapter 5 as shown in Illustration 5-5. After the perpetual inventory record is complete for a period, we can use the cost flow relationships to check our work.

Beginning Inventory	+	Cost of Goods Purchased	=	Cost of Goods Available for Sale	−	Cost of Goods Sold	=	Ending Inventory
$1,000.00	+	$11,400.00	=	$12,400.00	−	$6,050.00	=	$6,350.00

In this case, we see that the record is balanced because the calculated inventory balance of $6,350.00 agrees with the inventory balance in the perpetual inventory record after the November 27 purchase transaction.

ACCOUNTING IN ACTION
BUSINESS INSIGHT

Technology has made it much easier for companies to maintain a perpetual inventory system. For example, more retailers are using radio-frequency identification (RFID), which involves putting special tags on merchandise with antennas and computer chips that track their movement through radio signals. Retailers used to count inventory once or twice a year because it was so laborious. But RFID tags allow merchandisers to switch to a perpetual inventory system, because the tags can keep a constant count of items.

The use of RFID is transforming inventory cost formulas, helping stores move to a specific identification method for goods that typically had to be valued based on their average cost. With an RFID tag, every item has a unique identifier, so retailers know what they paid for that particular item and how much they sold it for. They can know precisely the profit for that item, which they never could before.

Even the humble bar code and electronic scanners at checkouts can improve inventory counting. Montreal-based Dollarama Inc., Canada's largest chain of dollar stores, recently moved from a periodic to a perpetual inventory system when it transformed its manual inventory counting system to an electronic one. It used to take 27 days for each store to count its approximately 4,000 items. Moving to bar codes and checkout scanners means it now knows instantly what its stock levels are.

Sources: Paula Rosenblum, "How Walmart Could Solve Its Inventory Problem and Improve Earnings," *Forbes*, May 22, 2014; John Daly, "A Man and His Merchandise," *Globe and Mail Report on Business*, April 2012, pp. 25–30; Dollarama 2012 annual report.

Q Retailers used to count inventory once a year for financial reporting purposes. What is the advantage of moving to a periodic inventory system that goes beyond accounting?

Perpetual Inventory System—Weighted Average

The **weighted average cost formula** recognizes that it is not possible to measure a specific physical flow of inventory when the goods available for sale are homogeneous and non-distinguishable. Under this cost formula, the allocation of the cost of goods available for sale is based on the weighted average unit cost. The formula of the **weighted average unit cost** is presented in Illustration 6-5.

Cost of Goods Available for Sale	÷	Total Units Available for Sale	=	Weighted Average Unit Cost

▶ **ILLUSTRATION** 6-5
Calculation of weighted average unit cost

Note that the weighted average unit cost is **not** calculated by taking a simple average of the costs of each purchase. Rather, it is calculated by weighting the quantities purchased at each unit cost. This is done by dividing the cost of goods available for sale by the units available for sale at the date of each purchase.

We will again use the information for Ingrid's Lighting Boutique, in Illustration 6-3, to prepare a perpetual inventory record with the weighted average cost formula. You can then see the similarities and differences between the weighted average and FIFO cost formulas.

Illustration 6-6 shows the completed inventory record. An explanation of each transaction is provided below corresponding to the number on the left of the illustration.

WA

> Inventory on hand after the sale on May 1 consists of only one tier of inventory totalling $825.00

> The weighted average cost per unit of $11.00 calculated on April 15 is used to assign a cost to the units sold on May 1

	Date	Purchases			Cost of goods sold			Inventory balance			Weighted Average Calculations		
		Units	Cost	Total	Units	Cost	Total	Units	Cost	Total	Units (A)	Total cost (B)	WA cost per unit (B ÷ A)
(1)	Jan. 1	Beginning inventory						100	$10.00	$1,000.00	100	$1,000.00	
		100	$10.00	$1,000.00									
(2)	Apr. 15	100	12.00	1,200.00				200	11.00	2,200.00	100	1,200.00	
											200	2,200.00	$11.00
(3)	May 1				125	$11.00	$1,375.00	75	11.00	825.00	200	2,200.00	
											−125	−1,375.00	
											75	825.00	$11.00
(4)	Aug. 24	300	14.00	4,200.00				375	13.40	5,025.00	75	825.00	
											300	4,200.00	
											375	5,025.00	$13.40
(5)	Sept. 1				350	13.40	4,690.00	25	13.40	335.00	375	5,025.00	
											−350	−4,690.00	
											25	335.00	$13.40
(6)	Nov. 27	400	15.00	6,000.00				425	14.91	6,335.00	25	335.00	
											400	6,000.00	
											425	$6,335.00	$14.91
(7)		900		$12,400.00	475		$6,065.00	425		$6,335.00			
		Cost of goods available for sale	−		Cost of goods sold		=	Ending inventory					

1. The record again starts with beginning inventory of 100 units with a weighted average cost of $10 each for a total of $1,000.00. This time we assume the $10 unit price is the weighted average cost per unit determined in the previous period.

2. The April 15 purchase of $1,200.00 and the beginning inventory of $1,000.00 are combined to show a total cost of goods available for sale of $2,200.00, and the 100 units in beginning inventory and the 100 units purchased on April 15 are combined to show a total of 200 units. Using the formula in Illustration 6-5, the weighted average unit cost on April 15 is $11.00 per unit ($2,200.00 ÷ 200).

3. On May 1, the cost of goods sold is calculated using the $11.00 weighted average unit cost determined after the April 15 purchase. Refer to Illustration 6-6 and notice that the inventory balance is determined by subtracting the calculated cost of goods sold of $1,375.00 from $2,200.00 to arrive at a new inventory balance of $825.00 for all 75 units remaining. Once again, a calculation is required to calculate the weighted average cost per unit. The weighted average cost per unit is still $11.00 ($825.00 ÷ 75).

4. On August 24, when 300 units costing $14 each are purchased, it is necessary to calculate a new weighted average unit cost. Cost of goods available for sale is now $5,025.00 ($825.00 + $4,200.00) and total units available for sale is now 375 (75 + 300). The new weighted average cost per unit is $13.40 ($5,025.00 ÷ 375).

5. On September 1, the sale of 350 units is assigned a cost of $13.40 per unit. Total cost of goods sold for this sale is $4,690.00. The inventory balance is updated by subtracting $4,690.00 from $5,025.00 to arrive at $335.00. There are now 25 units remaining in inventory (375 – 350) with a total cost of $335.00.

It is important to note here that the **correct technique of calculating ending inventory when using the weighted average cost formula is to subtract the calculated cost of goods sold from the previous total inventory cost and then update the weighted average unit cost.** Most often after a sale, the weighted average unit cost will not change, as in Illustration 6-6, but occasionally, because we round the unit cost to two decimal places to calculate cost of goods sold, the unit cost might change by a few cents. In a manual accounting system, this is perfectly normal. Any rounding differences are essentially recorded in cost of goods sold. In a computerized system, the weighted average unit costs are calculated with sufficient decimal places to eliminate rounding issues but this becomes cumbersome in a manual system. For our purposes, we will always round the weighted average unit cost to two decimal places and any rounding differences will flow through cost of goods sold.

If instead, the remaining units on hand are multiplied by the weighted average unit cost, these rounding issues will affect the inventory balance and consequently the perpetual record will not agree to the inventory control account in the general ledger. Remember that preparing the inventory record is only one step in the process. A journal entry is still required to record a sale and to update ending inventory.

6. On November 27, after purchasing 400 units at $15.00 each, a new weighted average unit cost of $14.91 is determined ($6,335.00 ÷ 425).

7. As with FIFO, it is important to check our work. We can use the cost flow relationships and equation to ensure that the amount of cost of goods available for sale less cost of goods sold is equal to ending inventory.

Beginning Inventory	+	Cost of Goods Purchased	=	Cost of Goods Available for Sale	–	Cost of Goods Sold	=	Ending Inventory
$1,000.00	+	$11,400.00	=	$12,400.00	–	$6,065.00	=	$6,335.00

In summary, this cost formula uses the weighted average unit cost of the goods that are available for sale to determine the cost of goods sold. When a perpetual inventory system is used, an updated weighted average unit cost is determined after each purchase. This amount is then used to record the cost of goods sold on subsequent sales until another purchase is made and a new weighted average unit cost is calculated. Because the weighted average unit cost changes with each purchase, this cost formula is sometimes called the moving weighted average cost formula.

Action Plan
- For FIFO, allocate the earliest unit costs to the cost of goods sold at the date of each sale. The latest costs will be allocated to the remaining inventory.
- For weighted average, determine the weighted average unit cost (cost of goods available for sale ÷ number of units available for sale) after each purchase. Multiply this cost by the number of units sold to determine the cost of goods sold. Subtract the total cost of goods sold from the cost of goods available for sale prior to the purchase to determine the cost of the remaining inventory.
- Prove that cost of goods available for sale − cost of goods sold = ending inventory.
- Use the information in the perpetual inventory records (purchases and cost of goods sold columns) when preparing the journal entries.

Wynneck Marlon Sports Company uses a perpetual inventory system. All inventory items are sold for $10 per unit and all sales and purchases are on account. The company's accounting records show the following:

Date		Explanation	Units	Unit Cost	Total Cost
Mar.	1	Beginning inventory	4,000	$3	$12,000
	10	Purchase	6,000	4	24,000
	19	Sales	(8,000)		
	22	Purchase	5,000	5	25,000
	28	Sales	(5,500)		
					$61,000

(a) Assume Wynneck Marlon uses FIFO. (1) Prepare a perpetual inventory record and determine the cost of goods sold and ending inventory. (2) Prepare journal entries to record the March 10 purchase and the March 19 sale.

(b) Assume Wynneck Marlon uses the weighted average cost formula. (1) Prepare a perpetual inventory record and determine the cost of goods sold and ending inventory. (2) Prepare journal entries to record the March 10 purchase and the March 19 sale.

Solution

(a) FIFO—perpetual
1. Perpetual inventory record

	A	B	C	D	E	F	G	H	I	J	K	L	M
1	**FIFO**												
2		**Date**	**Purchases**				**Cost of goods sold**				**Inventory balance**		
3			Units	Cost	Total		Units	Cost	Total		Units	Cost	Total
4		Mar. 1	Beginning inventory										
5			4,000	$3	$12,000						4,000	$3	$12,000
6		Mar. 10	6,000	4	24,000						4,000	3	12,000
7											6,000	4	24,000
8		Mar. 19					4,000	$3	$12,000				
9							4,000	4	16,000		2,000	4	8,000
10		Mar. 22	5,000	5	25,000						2,000	4	8,000
11											5,000	5	25,000
12		Mar. 28					2,000	4	8,000				
13							3,500	5	17,500		1,500	5	7,500
14													
15			15,000		$61,000		13,500		$53,500		1,500		$7,500
16													
17			Cost of goods available for sale			−	Cost of goods sold			=	Ending inventory		

2. Journal entries

Mar. 10	Merchandise Inventory	24,000	
	Accounts Payable		24,000
	To record goods purchased on account.		
19	Accounts Receivable	80,000	
	Sales		80,000
	To record credit sale ($10 × 8,000).		
	Cost of Goods Sold	28,000	
	Merchandise Inventory		28,000
	To record cost of goods sold ($12,000 + $16,000).		

(continued)

BEFORE YOU GO ON...DO IT ❯ **Cost Formulas** *(continued)*

(b) Weighted average—perpetual
   1. Perpetual inventory record

	A	B	C	D	E	F	G	H	I	J	K	L	M	N	O	P	Q
1															**Weighted Average Calculations**		
2	**Date**	**Purchases**				**Cost of goods sold**				**Inventory balance**					**Total**		**WA cost**
3		**Units**	**Cost**	**Total**		**Units**	**Cost**	**Total**		**Units**	**Cost**	**Total**	**Units**		**cost**		**per unit**
4	Mar. 1	Beginning inventory											A		B		B÷A
5		4,000	$3.00	$12,000						4,000	$3.00	$12,000					
6	Mar. 10	6,000	4.00	24,000						10,000	3.60	36,000	4,000		$12,000.00		
7													6,000		24,000.00		
8													10,000		36,000.00		$3.60
9	Mar. 19					8,000	$3.60	$28,800.00		2,000	3.60	7,200	10,000		$36,000.00		
10													−8,000		−28,800.00		
11													2,000		7,200.00		$3.60
12	Mar. 22	5,000	5.00	25,000						7,000	4.60	32,200	2,000		$7,200.00		
13													5,000		25,000.00		
14													7,000		32,200.00		$4.60
15	Mar. 28					5,500	4.60	25,300.00		1,500	4.60	6,900	7,000		$32,200.00		
16													−5,500		−25,300.00		
17													1,500		$6,900.00		$4.60
18																	
19		15,000		$61,000		550		$54,100.00		1,500		$6,900					
20																	
21		Cost of goods available for sale			−	Cost of goods sold			=	Ending inventory							
22																	

2. Journal entries:

Mar. 10	Merchandise Inventory		24,000	
		Accounts Payable		24,000
	To record goods purchased on account.			
19	Accounts Receivable		80,000	
		Sales		80,000
	To record credit sale ($10 × 8,000).			
	Cost of Goods Sold		28,800	
		Merchandise Inventory		28,800
	To record cost of goods sold.			

Related exercise material: BE6–3, BE6–4, BE6–5, BE6–6, BE6–7, BE6–8, *BE6–18, E6–3, E6–4, E6–5, E6–6, E6–7, *E6–15, and *E6–16.

Financial Statement Effects

Inventory affects both the income statement and the balance sheet. The ending inventory is included as a current asset on the balance sheet and cost of goods sold is an expense on the income statement. Cost of goods sold will affect profit, which in turn will affect owner's equity on the balance sheet. Thus, the choice of cost determination method can have a significant impact on the financial statements.

Errors can occur when a physical inventory is being taken or when the cost of the inventory is being determined. The effects of these errors on financial statements can be significant. We will address these topics in the next two sections.

LEARNING OBJECTIVE 3 > Explain the financial statement effects of inventory cost determination methods.

CHOICE OF COST DETERMINATION METHOD

If companies have goods that are not ordinarily interchangeable, or goods that have been produced for specific projects, they must use the specific identification method to determine the cost of their inventory. Otherwise, they must use either FIFO or weighted average.

We learned in our feature story that Loblaw Companies Limited uses the weighted average cost formula for most of its merchandise, and the FIFO cost formula for Shoppers Drug Mart. How should a company such as Loblaw choose between FIFO and weighted average? It should consider the following factors when choosing a cost determination method:

1. Choose the method that corresponds as closely as possible to the physical flow of goods.
2. Report an inventory cost on the balance sheet that is close to the inventory's recent costs.
3. Use the same method for all inventories having a similar nature and use in the company.

After a company chooses a method of determining the cost of its inventory, this method should be used consistently from one period to the next. Consistency is what makes it possible to compare financial statements from one period to the next. Using FIFO in one year and weighted average in the next year would make it difficult to compare the profits for the two years.

This is not to say that a company can never change from one method to another. However, a change in the method of cost determination can only occur if the physical flow of inventory changes and a different method would result in more relevant information in the financial statements.

In Chapter 11, we will expand on the concepts of comparability and relevance. For now, it is important to note that a company should choose a cost determination method that best matches the factors mentioned above. The approach used when a change must be made is beyond the scope of this course and will be covered in depth in more advanced accounting courses.

Income Statement Effects

To understand the impact of the FIFO and weighted average cost formulas on the income statement, let's look at Ingrid's Lighting Boutique's cost of goods sold and operating expenses on the 23W compact fluorescent light bulb. The condensed income statements in Illustration 6-7 assume that Ingrid's Lighting Boutique sold 475 such light bulbs for $9,500 ($20 selling price) and that operating expenses were $2,000. The cost of goods sold was previously calculated in Illustrations 6-4 and 6-6.

> ►**ILLUSTRATION 6-7**
> Comparative effects of inventory cost formulas

INGRID'S LIGHTING BOUTIQUE Condensed Income Statements		
	FIFO	**Weighted Average**
Sales	$9,500	$9,500
Cost of goods sold	6,050	6,065
Gross profit	3,450	3,435
Operating expenses	2,000	2,000
Profit	$1,450	$1,435

The sales and the operating expenses are the same under both FIFO and weighted average. But the cost of goods sold amounts are different. This difference is the result of how the unit costs are allocated under each cost formula. Each dollar of difference in cost of goods sold results in a corresponding dollar difference in profit. For Ingrid's Lighting Boutique, there is a $15 difference in cost of goods sold and in profit between FIFO and weighted average.

In periods of changing prices, the choice of inventory cost formula can have a significant impact on profit. In a period of rising prices, as is the case here, FIFO produces a higher profit. This happens because the lower unit costs will be included in cost of goods sold. As shown in Illustration 6-7, FIFO reports the higher profit ($1,450) and weighted average reports the lower profit ($1,435).

If prices are decreasing, the results from the use of FIFO and weighted average are reversed. FIFO will report the lower profit and weighted average will report the higher profit. If prices are stable, both cost formulas will report the same results.

An advantage of using the weighted average formula is that it results in more recent costs being reflected in cost of goods sold. This will better match current costs with current revenues and provide a better income statement valuation. An advantage of using FIFO is that it results in a better merchandise inventory valuation on the balance sheet, which we discuss next.

Balance Sheet Effects

The choice of inventory cost formula will also have an impact on the balance sheet; both merchandise inventory and owner's equity will be affected. In our example for Ingrid's Lighting Boutique, profit is $15 higher under FIFO. Therefore, owner's equity is also $15 higher under FIFO. Similarly, merchandise inventory is $15 higher under FIFO. As shown in Illustrations 6-4 and 6-6, the merchandise inventory balance at the end of the period is $6,350 using FIFO and $6,335 using weighted average.

In terms of the balance sheet, one advantage of FIFO is that the costs allocated to ending inventory will approximate the inventory item's current (replacement) cost. For example, for Ingrid's Lighting Boutique, 400 of the 425 units in the inventory are assigned a cost on November 27 of $15.00, the most recent cost of the 23W compact fluorescent light bulb. FIFO provides a more relevant asset amount for users.

By extension, a limitation of the weighted average formula is that in a period of inflation the costs allocated to inventory may be understated (too low) in terms of the current cost of the inventory. That is, the weighted average cost formula results in older costs being included in inventory.

Summary of Effects

When prices are constant, the cost of goods sold and ending inventory will be the same for all three cost determination methods. In specific identification, cost of goods sold and ending inventory depend on which specific units are sold and which remain in inventory. Thus we cannot make any general comments about how it will compare with FIFO and weighted average.

We have seen that both inventory on the balance sheet and profit on the income statement are higher when FIFO is used in a period of rising prices. The reverse will happen in a period of falling prices. The key differences between the two cost formulas are summarized in Illustration 6-8.

	Rising Prices		Falling Prices	
Income statement	FIFO	Weighted Average	FIFO	Weighted Average
Cost of goods sold	Lower	Higher	Higher	Lower
Gross profit and profit	Higher	Lower	Lower	Higher
Balance sheet				
Cash flow	Same	Same	Same	Same
Ending inventory	Higher	Lower	Lower	Higher
Owner's equity	Higher	Lower	Lower	Higher

▶ ILLUSTRATION 6-8
A comparison of the FIFO and weighted average cost flow formulas when prices are rising or falling

Notice in Illustration 6-8 that cash flow is the same with both cost formulas. In fact, all three methods of cost determination—specific identification, FIFO, and weighted average—produce exactly the same cash flow. Sales and purchases are not affected by the methods of cost determination. The only thing that is affected is the allocation between inventory and cost of goods sold, which does not involve cash.

It is also worth remembering that all three cost determination methods will give exactly the same results over the life cycle of the business or its product. That is, the allocation between cost of goods sold and ending inventory may vary within a period, but will produce the same cumulative results over time.

Effect on Financial Information: FIFO vs. Weighted Average

CJ Games reported sales of $15,000 and operating expenses of $3,500. If CJ Games uses FIFO, cost of goods sold is $4,700. If the weighted average formula is used, cost of goods sold is $4,550.

(a) Prepare comparative income statements for each cost formula: FIFO and weighted average.
(b) Which cost formula will result in higher owner's equity?
(c) Which cost formula should CJ Games use?
(d) Are prices rising or falling? Explain.

Action Plan

- In preparing comparative income statements, note that sales and operating expenses are the same for both cost formulas. Cost of goods sold, gross profit, and profit are different.
- Recall that profit is added to owner's equity.
- Review the objectives that should be considered in determining the correct inventory cost formula.
- Recall that FIFO uses the oldest costs in determining cost of goods sold.

Solution

(a)

CJ GAMES
Condensed Income Statements

	FIFO	Weighted Average
Sales	$15,000	$15,000
Cost of goods sold	4,700	4,550
Gross profit	10,300	10,450
Operating expenses	3,500	3,500
Profit	$ 6,800	$ 6,950

(b) Because profit is $150 ($6,950 − $6,800) higher using weighted average, owner's equity will also be $150 higher using weighted average.
(c) The cost formula that should be used would be the one that best matches the physical flow of goods.
(d) Because FIFO has the higher cost of goods sold, prices must be falling. FIFO has the oldest costs in its cost of goods sold; weighted average will have a combination of older and more recent costs in its cost of goods sold.

Related exercise material: BE6–9, BE6–10, E6–6, and E6–7.

LEARNING OBJECTIVE **4** ▷ **Determine the financial statement effects of inventory errors.**

Inventory Errors

Some inventory errors are caused by mistakes in counting or assigning cost to the inventory. Other inventory errors are because of mistakes in recognizing the timing of the transfer of legal title for goods in transit. These mistakes can result in errors in determining:

- beginning inventory
- cost of goods purchased
- ending inventory

Any errors in determining these items can also cause an error in cost of goods sold. Once again, we revisit the cost flow relationships in a merchandising company, which was first introduced in Chapter 5. The illustration is reproduced in Illustration 6-9. Errors in any of the above-mentioned amounts will affect ending inventory and cost of goods sold.

▶ **ILLUSTRATION** **6-9**
Flow of inventory costs for a merchandising company

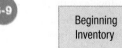

Beginning Inventory + Cost of Goods Purchased = Cost of Goods Available for Sale − Ending Inventory = Cost of Goods Sold

Errors in cost of goods sold will affect the income statement. If there is an error in ending inventory, it will affect the balance sheet, both in ending inventory and in owner's capital. In the following sections, we will illustrate these effects.

Income Statement Effects

Cost of goods sold will be incorrect if there is an error in any one of beginning inventory, cost of goods purchased, or ending inventory. The following simplified demonstration shows how this will occur.

Using assumed **correct** information:

Beginning inventory + cost of goods purchased = cost of goods available for sale

$1,000 + 5,000 = $6,000

Cost of goods available for sale − ending inventory = cost of goods sold

$6,000 − $500 = $5,500

Cost of goods sold should correctly amount to $5,500. If we now change the ending inventory to an **incorrect** amount of $600, the effect will be as follows:

Cost of goods available for sale − ending inventory = cost of goods sold

$6,000 − $600 = $5,400

In this case, a $100 overstatement of ending inventory will understate cost of goods sold by $100. To appreciate how the relationships work, use the above equations and change the numbers to see the impact on each of the components.

A summary of the impact of errors in these components on cost of goods sold is shown in Illustration 6-10 by using the cost of goods sold formula. U stands for understatement, O for overstatement, and NE for no effect.

▶ ILLUSTRATION 6-10
Effects of inventory errors on cost of goods sold

Impact on Cost of Goods Sold	Error in Beginning Inventory		Error in Cost of Goods Purchased		Error in Ending Inventory	
Beginning Inventory	O	U				
+ Cost of Goods Purchased			O	U		
− Ending Inventory					O	U
= Cost of Goods Sold	O	U	O	U	U	O

Notice that errors in beginning inventory and cost of goods purchased have the same impact on cost of goods sold. That is, if beginning inventory or cost of goods purchased is overstated, in both cases, cost of goods sold will be overstated. And if beginning inventory or cost of goods purchased is understated, in both cases, cost of goods sold is understated.

On the other hand, an overstatement of ending inventory has the opposite impact on cost of goods sold. If ending inventory is overstated (as in the demonstration example above), this results in an understatement of cost of goods sold. If ending inventory is understated, this results in an overstatement of cost of goods sold. This is because ending inventory is deducted when determining cost of goods sold.

Once the impact of an error on cost of goods sold is determined, then we can determine the effect of this error on the income statement. These results are summarized below in Illustration 6-11. U stands for understatement, O for overstatement, and NE for no effect.

▶ ILLUSTRATION 6-11
Effects of inventory errors on income statement

Nature of Error	Net Sales	−	Cost of Goods Sold	=	Gross Profit	−	Operating Expenses	=	Profit
Overstate beginning inventory or cost of goods purchased	NE		O		U		NE		U
Understate beginning inventory or cost of goods purchased	NE		U		O		NE		O
Overstate ending inventory	NE		U		O		NE		O
Understate ending inventory	NE		O		U		NE		U

Notice that an error in cost of goods sold has the opposite impact on gross profit and profit. If cost of goods sold is overstated, then gross profit and profit are understated. If cost of goods sold is understated, then gross profit and profit are overstated. This is because cost of goods sold is deducted from net sales when calculating gross profit.

Since the ending inventory of one period becomes the beginning inventory of the next period, **an error in ending inventory of the current period will have a reverse effect on the profit of the next period**. To illustrate, assume that on December 31, 2017, inventory is overstated by $3,000. The following T accounts show the impact of this error on the Merchandise Inventory account, and thus on cost of goods sold, over two years.

Merchandise Inventory (incorrect Dec. 31, 2017, inventory amount)					Merchandise Inventory (correct Dec. 31, 2017, inventory amount)				
Jan. 1/17		20,000			Jan. 1/17		20,000		
Purchases		40,000	Cost of goods sold	42,000	Purchases		40,000	Cost of goods sold	45,000
Dec. 31/17	Bal.	18,000			Dec. 31/17	Bal.	15,000		
Purchases		40,000	Cost of goods sold	48,000	Purchases		40,000	Cost of goods sold	45,000
Dec. 31/18	Bal.	10,000			Dec. 31/18	Bal.	10,000		

Assuming ending inventory in 2018 is correct, the error will correct itself. But over the two-year period it will affect profit, as shown in Illustration 6-12.

▶ **ILLUSTRATION 6-12**
Effects of inventory errors on income statements of two successive years

	2017		2018	
	Incorrect	Correct	Incorrect	Correct
Sales	$80,000	$80,000	$80,000	$80,000
Cost of goods sold	42,000	45,000	48,000	45,000
Gross profit	38,000	35,000	32,000	35,000
Operating expenses	10,000	10,000	10,000	10,000
Profit	$28,000	$25,000	$22,000	$25,000

($3,000) $3,000

Profit overstated   Profit understated

The combined profit for two years is correct because the errors cancel each other out.

Note that in 2017, the $3,000 understatement of cost of goods sold results in a $3,000 overstatement of profit ($28,000 instead of $25,000). In 2018, the opposite occurs and profit is understated by $3,000 ($22,000 instead of $25,000).

Over the two years, total profit is correct. The errors offset one another. Notice that combined profit over the two years using incorrect data is $50,000 ($28,000 + $22,000). This is the same as the combined profit of $50,000 ($25,000 + $25,000) using correct data. Nevertheless, the distortion of the year-by-year results can have a serious impact on financial analysis and management decisions.

Note that an error in the beginning inventory does not result in a corresponding error in the ending inventory. The accuracy of the ending inventory depends entirely on correctly taking and costing the inventory at the balance sheet date.

Balance Sheet Effects

The effects of inventory errors on the balance sheet can be determined by using the basic accounting equation: assets = liabilities + owner's equity. These results are summarized in Illustration 6-13. U is for understatement, O is for overstatement, and NE is for no effect.

Nature of Error	Assets	=	Liabilities	+	Owner's Equity
Understate ending inventory	U		NE		U
Overstate ending inventory	O		NE		O

▶ **ILLUSTRATION 6-13**
Effects of inventory errors on balance sheet

When ending inventory is understated, total assets are understated. As discussed in the previous section, understating ending inventory will also overstate cost of goods sold, which results in understated profit. If profit is understated, then owner's equity will also be understated, because profit is part of owner's equity.

An error in ending inventory in one period will result in an error in beginning inventory in the next period. An example of this type of error was shown in Illustration 6-12. As previously noted, total profit for the two periods is correct. Thus, total assets and owner's equity reported on the balance sheet at the end of 2018 will also be correct. In other words, errors in beginning inventory have no impact on the balance sheet if ending inventory is correctly calculated at the end of that period.

Errors in the **cost of goods purchased** may also have an effect on the balance sheet. For example, if a company records a purchase of inventory on account in 2017 that should have been recorded in 2018, accounts payable and ending inventory will be overstated at December 31, 2017. Recall that when ending inventory is overstated in one period, cost of goods sold will be understated. Understating cost of goods sold understates profit and owner's equity.

You should also note that inventory errors can occur in either a perpetual or a periodic inventory system and that the errors have the same impact on the income statement and balance sheet regardless of which system is used. But one of the major benefits of a perpetual inventory system is that many inventory mistakes are much more likely to be found, and corrected, when the accounting records are compared with the results of the inventory count.

ACCOUNTING IN ACTION
ETHICS INSIGHT

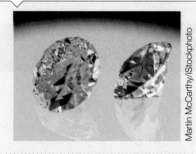

Martin McCarthy/iStockphoto

Discount Diamonds carries a variety of brands and sizes of diamonds. The company resells the diamonds to jewellery craftspeople. The diamonds are purchased in batches of like size and quality. Each batch of diamonds that is purchased is carefully coded and marked with its purchase cost. The company currently uses the specific identification cost determination method to cost inventory. A potential investor has been looking at the records for Discount Diamonds and is concerned that management may be able to manipulate gross profit by using the specific identification method.

 Q Is it unethical to use the specific identification method in this situation?

BEFORE YOU GO ON...DO IT (4) Inventory Errors

On December 31, PEL Company counted and recorded $600,000 of inventory. This count did not include $90,000 of goods in transit, shipped to PEL Company on December 29, FOB shipping point. PEL Company recorded the purchase correctly on December 29 when the goods were shipped.
(a) Determine the correct December 31 inventory balance. (b) Identify any accounts that are in error, and state the amount and direction (that is, overstatement or understatement) of the error.

Solution

(a) The correct inventory count should have included the goods in transit. The correct December 31 inventory balance was $690,000 ($600,000 + $90,000).

(continued)

Action Plan
- Use the cost flow relationships to determine the impact of an error on the income statement.
- Use the accounting equation to determine the impact of an error on the balance sheet.

(b) *Income statement accounts:* Because the purchase had been recorded, the cost of goods purchased is correctly stated, but because the inventory had not been included in the inventory count, the ending inventory is understated. Thus, as shown below, the cost of goods sold is overstated.

Beginning inventory	No effect
Plus: Cost of goods purchased	No effect
Cost of goods available for sale	No effect
Less: Ending inventory	U $90,000
Cost of goods sold	O $90,000

Balance sheet accounts: Merchandise Inventory is understated

Assets	=	Liabilities	+	Owner's equity
U $90,000	=	No effect	+	U $90,000

Related exercise material: BE6–11, BE6–12, E6–8, and E6–9.

Presentation and Analysis of Inventory

Presenting inventory on the financial statements is important because inventory is usually the largest current asset (Merchandise Inventory) on the balance sheet and the largest expense (Cost of Goods Sold) on the income statement. In addition, these reported numbers are critical for analyzing how well a company manages its inventory. In the next sections, we will discuss the presentation and analysis of inventory.

LEARNING OBJECTIVE **5**   **Value inventory at the lower of cost and net realizable value.**

VALUING INVENTORY AT THE LOWER OF COST AND NET REALIZABLE VALUE

Before reporting inventory on the financial statements, we must first ensure that it is properly valued. The value of inventory items sometimes falls due to changes in technology or changes in consumer preferences. For example, suppose you manage a retail store that sells computers, and at the end of the year the computers' value has dropped almost 25%. Do you think inventory should be stated at cost, in accordance with the cost measurement model, or at its lower value?

As you probably reasoned, this situation requires an exception to following the cost basis of accounting. When the realizable value of inventory is lower than its cost, the inventory is written down to its net realizable value at the end of the period. This is called the **lower of cost and net realizable value (LCNRV)** valuation standard. **Net realizable value (NRV)** is defined as:

Selling price less any costs required to make the goods ready for sale.

The lower of cost and NRV rule is applied to the items in inventory at the end of the accounting period. To apply this rule, four steps are followed:

Helpful hint In accounting, realizable value generally refers to the amount that a company could reasonably expect to receive (or realize) from the asset in the near future. Net realizable value is the same except it includes any additional costs that have to be incurred.

1. Determine the cost of the items in ending inventory using the appropriate cost determination method: specific identification, FIFO, or weighted average.
2. Determine the net realizable value of the items in ending inventory.
3. Compare the values determined in steps 1 and 2.
4. Use the lower value to report inventory on the balance sheet.

To illustrate, assume that on March 31, 2017, Très Chic Fashion has the following lines of merchandise with costs and net realizable values as indicated. The lower of cost and NRV produces the following results:

	Cost	NRV	Lower of Cost and NRV
Accessories			
Silk scarves	$ 60,000	$ 55,000	$ 55,000
Leather belts	45,000	52,000	45,000
	105,000	107,000	100,000
Designer shoes			
Ladies' leather pumps	48,000	45,000	45,000
Men's leather dress shoes	15,000	14,000	14,000
	63,000	59,000	59,000
Total inventory	$168,000	$166,000	$159,000

This means Très Chic Fashion will report $159,000 for merchandise inventory on its balance sheet. The lower of cost and net realizable value rule is applied to individual inventory items, not total inventory. For instance, in the above example, all of the company's different types of silk scarves were grouped together and we compared the cost of the scarves with their total net realizable value.

If Très Chic Fashion uses a perpetual inventory system, the entry to adjust inventory from cost to net realizable value will be the following:

Mar. 31	Cost of Goods Sold	9,000	
	Merchandise Inventory		9,000
	To record decline in inventory value from original cost of $168,000 to net realizable value of $159,000.		

A	=	L	+	OE
−9,000				−9,000

Cash flows: no effect

The Cost of Goods Sold account is debited directly for the loss because a decline in the value of inventory is considered to be part of the overall cost of buying and selling inventory. The amount of the loss must be separately reported and most companies do this in the notes to the financial statements. Thus, some companies may choose to debit a separate expense account to make it easier to keep track of the amount. Alternative methods of recording a decline in inventory value are covered in an intermediate accounting course.

In certain cases, the lower of cost and net realizable value rule can be applied to groups of similar items. For instance, we could compare the total cost of all accessories ($105,000) with the total NRV of the accessories ($107,000). We could also compare the total cost of the designer shoes ($63,000) with the total NRV of the designer shoes ($59,000). If this approach were used, total ending inventory would be adjusted to $164,000 ($105,000 + $59,000). The journal entry to record the writedown using this approach would be:

Mar. 31	Cost of Goods Sold	4,000	
	Merchandise Inventory		4,000
	To record decline in inventory value from original cost of $168,000 to net realizable value of $164,000.		

A	=	L	+	OE
−4,000				−4,000

Cash flows: no effect

Either approach can be used by companies based on their inventory characteristics. We recommend that you use the item-by-item approach unless otherwise advised in your assignments.

When there is clear evidence of an increase in net realizable value, because of changed economic circumstances, the amount of the writedown is reversed. The evidence required for this reversal would generally be an increase in selling prices. If the item of inventory that was previously written down to net realizable value is still on hand, and the selling price has increased, then a reversal is recorded. The reversing entry will consist of a debit to merchandise inventory and a credit to cost of goods sold.

If there is a recovery in the value of the inventory, the write-up can never be larger than the original writedown. The lower of cost and net realizable value rule will still be applied to the inventory. This ensures that the inventory is never reported at an amount greater than its original cost.

ACCOUNTING IN ACTION
BUSINESS INSIGHT

Bloomberg/Getty Images

If you read the U.S. business press, financial statements from U.S. companies, or Canadian companies that report using U.S. GAAP, then you may have heard of LIFO. The last-in, first-out inventory method is allowed under U.S. GAAP but is not allowed under IFRS or Canadian ASPE. The use of LIFO in the United States is controversial, however. ExxonMobil Corporation, like many U.S. companies, uses LIFO to value its inventory at current prices for financial reporting and tax purposes. In one recent year, this resulted in a cost of goods sold figure that was $5.6 billion higher than it would have been under FIFO. By increasing cost of goods sold, ExxonMobil reduces net income, which reduces taxes. Critics say that LIFO provides an unfair "tax dodge." The administration of U.S. President Barack Obama has lobbied

Congress since 2011 to eliminate the use of LIFO and discussions were ongoing in 2015. The U.S. Treasury Department estimated that eliminating LIFO would have increased federal tax revenue by US$53 billion by 2016 if it had been done back in 2011. Bloomberg News estimated that ExxonMobil's tax bill would rise by $7.5 billion over 10 years if LIFO were disallowed. Supporters of LIFO argue that the method is conceptually sound because it matches current costs with current revenues. In addition, they point out that this matching provides protection against inflation.

Because IFRS does not allow the use of LIFO, the net income of foreign oil companies such as BP and Royal Dutch Shell is not directly comparable to that of U.S. companies, which makes analysis difficult.

Sources: Katherine Arline, "FIFO vs. LIFO: What Is the Difference?," *Business News Daily*, February 20, 2015; "LIFO Should Be First Tax Reducer to Go in a Budget Fix: View," The Editors of BloombergView.com, July 15, 2011; David Reilly, "Big Oil's Accounting Methods Fuel Criticism," *Wall Street Journal*, August 8, 2006, p. C1.

Q What are the arguments for and against the use of LIFO?

BEFORE YOU GO ON...DO IT **5** **Lower of Cost and Net Realizable Value**

Tanguay's Jersey Store uses a perpetual inventory system and has the following items in its inventory at December 31, 2017:

Product	Quantity	Per Unit Cost	Per Unit Net Realizable Value
Jerseys	95	$50	$45
Socks	155	5	6

(a) What amount for inventory should Tanguay's Jersey Store report on its balance sheet?
(b) Record any necessary adjustments.

Solution

(a)

	Cost		Net Realizable Value		Lower of Cost and Net Realizable Value
Jerseys	(95 × $50)	$4,750	(95 × $45)	$4,275	$4,275
Socks	(155 × $5)	775	(155 × $6)	930	775
Total inventory		$5,525		$5,205	$5,050

(continued)

Action Plan

• Calculate the cost of the inventory.
• Calculate the net realizable value of the inventory.
• For each inventory item, determine which number is lower—cost or net realizable value.
• Record a journal entry to adjust the inventory account to net realizable value if required.

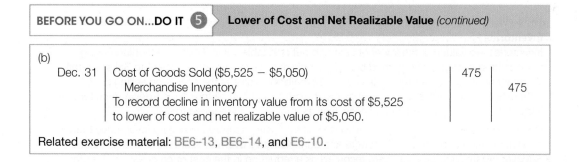

(b)

Dec. 31	Cost of Goods Sold ($5,525 − $5,050)	475	
	⠀⠀Merchandise Inventory		475
	⠀⠀To record decline in inventory value from its cost of $5,525		
	⠀⠀to lower of cost and net realizable value of $5,050.		

Related exercise material: BE6–13, BE6–14, and E6–10.

LEARNING OBJECTIVE **6** ⟩ **Demonstrate the presentation and analysis of inventory.**

Reporting and Analyzing Inventory

PRESENTING INVENTORY IN THE FINANCIAL STATEMENTS

How a company classifies its inventory depends on whether the company is a merchandiser or a manufacturer. A merchandiser **buys** its inventory. A manufacturer **produces** its inventory. In a merchandising company, inventory consists of many different items. Textbooks, paper, and pens, for example, are just a few of the inventory items on hand in a bookstore. These items have two common characteristics: (1) they are owned by the company, and (2) they are in a form ready for sale to customers. Only one inventory classification, merchandise inventory, is needed to describe the many different items that make up the total inventory.

In a manufacturing company, some goods may not yet be ready for sale. As a result, inventory is usually classified into three categories: raw materials, work in process, and finished goods. For example, an automobile manufacturer classifies the steel, fibreglass, upholstery material, and other components that are on hand waiting to be used in production as raw materials. Partially completed automobiles on an assembly line are classified as work in process. Automobiles completed and ready for sale are identified as finished goods.

As discussed in the previous section, inventory is reported on the balance sheet at the lower of cost and net realizable value. Inventory is typically recorded as a current asset because management expects to sell it within the next year. But if part of the inventory will not be sold for more than a year, this inventory should be reported as a non-current asset. For example, if inventory is being stockpiled because of concerns about future prices, then it may be appropriate to classify this inventory as a non-current asset.

A company should disclose the following information in its financial statements or the notes to the statements:

1. the total amount of inventory;
2. the cost determination method (specific identification, FIFO, or weighted average);
3. the cost of goods sold;
4. the amount of any writedown to net realizable value; and
5. the amount of any reversals of previous writedowns, including the reason why the writedown was reversed.

To illustrate inventory reporting requirements, some excerpts from Hudson's Bay Company's January 31, 2015, financial statements are reproduced in Illustration 6-14. Hudson's Bay Company is Canada's leading department store offering a wide assortment of merchandise ranging from apparel to home merchandise. The company's shares trade on the Toronto Stock Exchange and it reports according to IFRS.

Publicly traded companies (like Hudson's Bay Company) and private companies value and report inventory in a similar manner. There are no significant differences in this regard at the introductory accounting level between International Financial Reporting Standards and Accounting Standards for Private Enterprises. The inventory and cost of goods sold information reported in the financial statements is also used to analyze how effectively the company is managing its inventory.

▶ ILLUSTRATION 6-14

Notes to the financial statements of Hudson's Bay Company

Note 2(i)

Inventories

Inventories are valued at the lower of cost and net realizable value. Cost is determined using the weighted average cost method based on individual items and, with respect to Saks, a retail inventory method that approximates cost. Net realizable value is the estimated selling price determined at the item level using gross profit expectation and historical markdown rates for similar items in the ordinary course of business, less estimated costs required to sell.

Costs comprise all variable costs, and certain fixed costs, incurred in bringing inventories to their present location and condition. Storage and administrative overheads are expensed as incurred. Supplier rebates and discounts are recorded as a reduction in the cost of purchases unless they relate to a reimbursement of specific incremental expenses.

Merchandise that is subject to consignment or licensee (concession) agreements is not included in inventories.

Note 3

Inventory valuation

Inventory is valued at the lower of cost and net realizable value. Current selling price and historical trends for estimating future markdowns are utilized to estimate net realizable value. Inventory valuation also incorporates a write-down to reflect future losses on the disposition of obsolete merchandise.

Inventory is adjusted to reflect estimated losses ("shortage") incurred since the last inventory count. Shortage is estimated based on historical experience as a percentage of sales for the period from the date of the last inventory count to the end of the fiscal year.

Note 10

Inventories

Inventories on hand at January 31, 2015 and February 1, 2014 were available for sale. The cost of merchandise inventories related to continuing operations recognized as expense for fiscal 2014 was $4,893 million (2013: $3,217 million). The write-down of merchandise inventories below cost to net realizable value relating to continuing operations as at January 31, 2015 was $48 million (February 1, 2014: $47 million). There was no reversal of write-downs previously taken on merchandise inventories that are no longer estimated to sell below cost. Inventory has been pledged as security for certain borrowing agreements as described in note 14.

In the following illustrations, we will once again use the financial statements of Hudson's Bay Company. The asset section of the consolidated balance sheet and partial consolidated statements of loss are reproduced in Illustrations 6-15 and 6-16, respectively.

▶ ILLUSTRATION 6-15

Partial consolidated balance sheet for Hudson's Bay Company

HUDSON'S BAY COMPANY CONSOLIDATED BALANCE SHEETS For the 52 weeks ended January 31, 2015 and February 1, 2014 (millions of Canadian dollars)			
	Notes	**2015** **$**	**2014** **$**
ASSETS			
Cash	8	**168**	21
Trade and other receivables	9	**212**	137
Inventories	10	**2,349**	2,048
Financial assets	18	**24**	8
Income taxes recoverable		**7**	23
Other current assets		**69**	71
Assets of discontinued operations	29	**—**	2
Total current assets		**2,829**	2,310
Property, plant and equipment	11	**4,606**	4,110
Intangible assets	12	**1,076**	980
Goodwill	12	**237**	208
Pensions and employee benefits	17	**69**	72
Deferred tax assets	7	**240**	249
Other assets		**15**	13
Total assets		**9,072**	7,942

▶ ILLUSTRATION 6-16
Partial consolidated
statements of earnings (loss)
for Hudson's Bay Company

HUDSON'S BAY COMPANY
CONSOLIDATED STATEMENTS OF EARNINGS (LOSS)
For the 52 weeks ended January 31, 2015 and February 1, 2014
(millions of Canadian dollars)

	Notes	2015 $	2014 $
Retail sales		8,169	5,223
Cost of sales	10	(4,893)	(3,217)
Selling, general and administrative expenses		(2,759)	(1,826)
Depreciation and amortization	5	(344)	(175)
Gain on sale and leaseback transaction	28	308	—
Operating income		**481**	**5**

Inventory Turnover

A delicate balance must be kept between having too little inventory and too much inventory. On one hand, management wants to have a variety and quantity of merchandise available so that customers will find a wide selection of items in stock. But having too much inventory on hand can cost the company money in storage costs, interest costs (on money tied up in inventory), and costs due to high-tech goods becoming obsolete, or changing fashions. On the other hand, low inventory levels can result in stockouts (item unavailability), lost sales, and unhappy customers.

How quickly a company sells its inventory, or turns it over, is one way to determine whether the company has too much or too little inventory. In Chapter 4, we introduced the current and acid-test ratios, which are measures of liquidity. Inventory is a significant component of the current ratio and a high level of inventory will result in a high current ratio. But if the inventory is not turning over very quickly, this may be a problem. In this section, we add another liquidity ratio that is commonly used to evaluate inventory levels: the inventory turnover ratio. We also present a related measure: the average days to sell the inventory.

Inventory Turnover Ratio. The **inventory turnover** ratio measures the number of times, on average, inventory is sold (turned over) during the period. It is calculated by dividing the cost of goods sold by average inventory.

Whenever a ratio compares a balance sheet figure (e.g., inventory) with an income statement figure (e.g., cost of goods sold), the balance sheet figure must be averaged. Average balance sheet figures are determined by adding beginning and ending balances together and dividing by two. Averages are used to ensure that the balance sheet figures (which represent end-of-period amounts) cover the same period of time as the income statement figures (which represent amounts for the entire period). Illustration 6-17 shows the formula for calculating the inventory turnover ratio and the data used are for Hudson's Bay Company presented in Illustrations 6-15 and 6-16 (dollars in thousands).

▶ ILLUSTRATION 6-17
Inventory turnover

Cost of Goods Sold	÷	Average Inventory	=	Inventory Turnover
$4,893	÷	$\dfrac{(\$2,349 + \$2,048)}{2}$	=	2.2 times

Generally, the more times that inventory turns over each year, the more efficiently sales are being made.

Days Sales in Inventory. The inventory turnover ratio is complemented by the **days sales in inventory** ratio. It converts the inventory turnover ratio into a measure of the average age of the inventory on hand.

This ratio is calculated by dividing 365 days by the inventory turnover ratio, as in Illustration 6-18. Again we will use data from Illustrations 6-15 and 6-16 for Hudson's Bay Company in the demonstration in Illustration 6-18.

▸ILLUSTRATION
Days sales in inventory

Days in Year	÷	Inventory Turnover	=	Days Sales in Inventory
365 days	÷	2.2	=	166 days

This means that Hudson's Bay Company's inventory, on average, is in stock for 166 days. This ratio must be interpreted carefully: it should be compared with the company's ratio in previous years, and with the industry average. What we see here is a total average only.

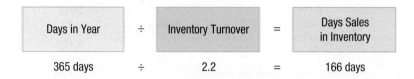

BEFORE YOU GO ON...DO IT ⑥ **Inventory Turnover Ratio and Days Sales in Inventory**

Action Plan

- Calculate average inventory using the inventory balance at the beginning and end of the year.
- Divide cost of goods sold by the average inventory for that year to calculate inventory turnover.
- Divide 365 by the inventory turnover to calculate days sales in inventory.
- Recall if it is better for inventory turnover to increase or decrease.

The following information is available for Sanchez Company for three recent years:

	2017	2016	2015
Inventory	$ 40,000	$ 42,000	$ 46,000
Cost of goods sold	123,000	125,000	130,000

Calculate the inventory turnover ratio and days sales in inventory for Sanchez Company for 2017 and 2016 and comment on any trends.

Solution

	2017	2016
Inventory turnover	$3.00 \text{ times} = \dfrac{\$123{,}000}{[(\$40{,}000 + 42{,}000) \div 2]}$	$2.84 \text{ times} = \dfrac{\$125{,}000}{[(\$42{,}000 + 46{,}000) \div 2]}$
Days sales in inventory	122 days = 365 ÷ 3.00	129 days = 365 ÷ 2.84

The inventory turnover ratio has increased in 2017 and decreased the number of days sales in inventory. In general, the higher the inventory turnover and the lower the number of days sales in inventory, the better. Sanchez has improved its inventory management in 2017 compared with 2016.

Related exercise material: BE6–15, BE6–16, E6–11, and E6–12.

APPENDIX 6A: INVENTORY COST FORMULAS IN PERIODIC SYSTEMS

LEARNING OBJECTIVE Calculate ending inventory and cost of goods sold in a periodic inventory system using FIFO and weighted average inventory cost formulas.

Both of the inventory cost formulas described in the chapter for a perpetual inventory system can be used in a periodic inventory system. To show how to use FIFO and weighted average in a periodic system, we will use the data below for Ingrid's Lighting Boutique.

INGRID'S LIGHTING BOUTIQUE 23W Compact Fluorescent Light Bulb					
Date	Explanation	Units	Unit Cost	Total Cost	Total Units in Inventory
Jan. 1	Beginning inventory	100	$10	$ 1,000	100
Apr. 15	Purchase	100	12	1,200	200
Aug. 24	Purchase	300	14	4,200	375
Nov. 27	Purchase	400	15	6,000	425
				$12,400	

These data are the same as those shown earlier in the chapter, except that the sales information has been omitted. In the periodic inventory system, we don't keep track of the number or cost of units sold during the year. Instead we wait until the end of the period to allocate the cost of goods available for sale to ending inventory and cost of goods sold.

Ingrid's Lighting Boutique had a total of 900 units available for sale during the year. The total cost of these units was $12,400. A physical inventory count at the end of the year determined that 425 units remained on hand. Using these data, Illustration 6A-1 shows the formula for calculating cost of goods sold that we first learned in Chapter 5.

Beginning Inventory	+	Cost of Goods Purchased	=	Cost of Goods Available for Sale	−	Ending Inventory	=	Cost of Goods Sold
100 units $1,000	+	800 units $11,400	=	900 units $12,400	−	425 units ?	=	475 units ?

▶ILLUSTRATION 6A-1
Formula for cost of goods sold

If we apply this formula to the unit numbers, we can determine that 475 units must have been sold during the year. The total cost of the 900 units available for sale was $12,400. We will demonstrate the allocation of the total cost using FIFO and weighted average in the next sections.

PERIODIC SYSTEM—FIRST-IN, FIRST-OUT (FIFO)

Similar to perpetual FIFO, the cost of the oldest goods on hand is allocated to the cost of goods sold. This means that the cost of the most recent purchases is assumed to remain in ending inventory. The allocation of the cost of goods available for sale at Ingrid's Lighting Boutique under FIFO is shown in Illustration 6A-2.

▶ILLUSTRATION 6A-2
Periodic system—FIFO

COST OF GOODS AVAILABLE FOR SALE				
Date	Explanation	Units	Unit Cost	Total Cost
Jan. 1	Beginning inventory	100	$10	$ 1,000
Apr. 15	Purchase	100	12	1,200
Aug. 24	Purchase	300	14	4,200
Nov. 27	Purchase	400	15	6,000
	Total	900		$12,400

Step 1: Ending Inventory				Step 2: Cost of Goods Sold	
Date	Units	Unit Cost	Total Cost		
Nov. 27	400	$15	$6,000	Cost of goods available for sale	$12,400
Aug. 24	25	14	350	Less: Ending inventory	6,350
Total	425		$6,350	Cost of goods sold	$ 6,050

The cost of the ending inventory is determined by taking the unit cost of the most recent purchase and working backward until all units of inventory have been assigned a cost. In this example, the 425 units of ending inventory are assigned costs as follows:

1. November 27 purchase, 400 units are assigned a $15 per-unit cost so that 400 units have an ending inventory value of $6,000.
2. August 24 purchase, 25 units are assigned a $14 per-unit cost so that 25 units have an ending inventory value of $350.

Once the cost of the ending inventory is determined, the cost of goods sold is calculated by subtracting the cost of the ending inventory from the cost of the goods available for sale.

PERIODIC SYSTEM—WEIGHTED AVERAGE

The weighted average unit cost is calculated in the same manner as we calculated it in a perpetual inventory system: by dividing the cost of the goods available for sale by the units available for sale. The key difference between this calculation in a periodic system and in a perpetual system is that this calculation is done after every purchase in a perpetual system. In a periodic system, it is done only at the end of the period, as shown in Illustration 6A-3.

▶ **ILLUSTRATION**
Calculation of
weighted average unit cost

The weighted average unit cost, $13.78 in this case, is then applied to the units on hand to determine the cost of the ending inventory. The allocation of the cost of goods available for sale at Ingrid's Lighting Boutique using the weighted average cost formula is shown in Illustration 6A-4.

▶ **ILLUSTRATION** 6A-4
Periodic system—
average

COST OF GOODS AVAILABLE FOR SALE				
Date	**Explanation**	**Units**	**Unit Cost**	**Total Cost**
Jan. 1	Beginning inventory	100	$10	$ 1,000
Apr. 15	Purchase	100	12	1,200
Aug. 24	Purchase	300	14	4,200
Nov. 27	Purchase	400	15	6,000
	Total	900		$12,400

Step 1: Ending Inventory	Step 2: Cost of Goods Sold
Calculate unit cost: $12,400 ÷ 900 = $13.78	Cost of goods available for sale $ 12,400.00
Units × Unit cost = Total Cost	Less: Ending inventory 5,856.50
425 $13.78 **$5,856.50**	Cost of goods sold **$6,543.50**

Illustration 6A-5 shows a comparison between FIFO and weighted average in both a perpetual and a periodic inventory system. The data presented for the perpetual system come from Illustrations 6-4 and 6-6 earlier in the chapter.

Some important points to note about the comparison:

1. FIFO will always result in the **same** allocation of cost of goods available for sale to cost of goods sold and ending inventory. The results are the same because under both inventory systems, the first costs are the ones assigned to cost of goods sold regardless of when the sales actually happened.
2. Weighted average cost will result in **different** amounts being allocated to cost of goods sold and ending inventory. This is because in a perpetual inventory system, a new moving weighted average is calculated with each purchase. In a periodic inventory system, the same weighted average is used to calculate the cost of goods sold and ending inventory for all the units regardless of when purchases or sales were made.

	FIFO		Weighted Average	
	Perpetual	Periodic	Perpetual	Periodic
Cost of goods sold	$ 6,050	$ 6,050	$ 6,065	$ 6,543.50
Ending inventory balance	6,350	6,350	6,335	5,856.50
Cost of goods available for sale	$12,400	$12,400	$12,400	$12,400.00

▶ILLUSTRATION 6A-5
Comparison of FIFO and weighted average in perpetual and periodic inventory systems

As you can see, regardless of whether you use the FIFO or weighted average cost formula using either a perpetual or periodic system, adding the cost of goods sold to the ending inventory balance will equal the goods available for sale of $12,400.

BEFORE YOU GO ON...DO IT ⑦ | **Cost Flow Methods**

Cookie Cutters Company uses the periodic inventory system. All purchases and sales are on account. The accounting records of Cookie Cutters Company show the following data:

Beginning inventory, June 1	4,000 units at $3
Purchases, June 13	6,000 units at $4
Sales, June 25	$64,000

The physical inventory count at June 30 showed 2,000 units on hand.

(a) Determine the cost of goods available for sale and the number of units sold.
(b) Assume Cookie Cutters uses FIFO. (1) Calculate cost of goods sold and ending inventory.
    (2) Prepare journal entries to record the June 13 purchase and the June 25 sale.
(c) Assume Cookie Cutters uses weighted average. (1) Calculate cost of goods sold and ending inventory.
    (2) Prepare journal entries to record the June 13 purchase and the June 25 sale.

Solution

(a) The cost of goods available for sale is $36,000, calculated as follows:

Beginning inventory, June 1	4,000	units at $3.00	$12,000
Purchases, June 13	6,000	units at $4.00	24,000
	10,000		$36,000

Total units available for sale	10,000
Minus: units in ending inventory	2,000
Units sold	8,000

(b) FIFO—periodic
   1. Calculations:

Ending inventory:

Date	Units	Unit Cost	Total Cost
June 13	2,000	$4.00	$8,000

Cost of goods sold: $36,000 − $8,000 = $28,000

Check of cost of goods sold:

Date	Units	Unit Cost	Total Cost
June 1	4,000	$3.00	$12,000
13	4,000	4.00	16,000
	8,000		$28,000

Check: $8,000 + $28,000 = $36,000
   2. Journal entries

June 13	Purchases	24,000	
	Accounts Payable		24,000
	To record goods purchased on account.		
25	Accounts Receivable	64,000	
	Sales		64,000
	To record credit sale.		

(continued)

Action Plan
- Calculate the cost of goods available for sale.
- Determine the cost of ending inventory first. Then calculate cost of goods sold by subtracting ending inventory from the cost of goods available for sale.
- For FIFO, allocate the most recent costs to the goods on hand. (The first costs will be allocated to the cost of goods sold.)
- For weighted average, determine the weighted average unit cost (cost of goods available for sale ÷ number of units available for sale). Multiply this cost by the number of units on hand.
- Recall that in a periodic inventory system, the cost of goods sold is not recorded at the date of sale.

BEFORE YOU GO ON...DO IT **7** **Cost Flow Methods** *(continued)*

(c) Weighted average—periodic
1. Calculations:

Weighted average unit cost:	$36,000 ÷ 10,000 units = $3.60 per unit
Ending inventory:	2,000 units × $3.60 = $7,200
Cost of goods sold:	$36,000 − $7,200 = $28,800
Check of cost of goods sold:	8,000 units × $3.60 = $28,800
Check:	$7,200 + $28,800 = $36,000

2. Journal entries

June 13	Purchases	24,000	
	Accounts Payable		24,000
	To record goods purchased on account.		
25	Accounts Receivable	64,000	
	Sales		64,000
	To record credit sale.		

Related exercise material: *BE6–17, *BE6–18, *E6–13, *E6–14, *E6–15, and *E6–16.

APPENDIX 6B: ESTIMATING INVENTORIES

LEARNING OBJECTIVE **8** Estimate ending inventory using the gross profit and retail inventory methods.

When a company uses a periodic inventory system, it must be able to do a physical count of its inventory in order to determine the cost of its ending inventory and the cost of goods sold. But what if a company cannot do a physical count? It may be impractical or impossible to count the inventory. Fortunately, it is possible to do an estimate.

There are three reasons for sometimes needing to estimate inventories.

1. Management may want monthly or quarterly financial statements but does not have the time for, or want the expense of, doing a physical inventory count every month or quarter.
2. A casualty such as a fire or flood may make it impossible to take a physical inventory.
3. The company may want to check the reasonableness of the actual inventory count.

There are two widely used methods of estimating inventories: (1) the gross profit method, and (2) the retail inventory method.

GROSS PROFIT METHOD

The **gross profit method** estimates the cost of ending inventory by applying the gross profit margin to net sales. It is commonly used to prepare interim (e.g., monthly) financial statements in a periodic inventory system. This method is relatively simple but effective.

To use this method, a company needs to know its net sales, cost of goods available for sale (beginning inventory + cost of goods purchased), and gross profit margin. Recall that we learned how to calculate gross profit margin in Chapter 5. Gross profit for the period is estimated by multiplying net sales by the gross profit margin. The estimated gross profit is then used to calculate the estimated cost of goods sold and the estimated ending inventory.

The formulas for using the gross profit method are given in Illustration 6B-1.

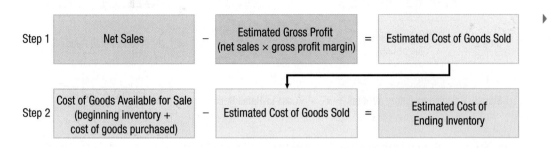

▶ **ILLUSTRATION** 6B-1
Gross profit method formulas

To illustrate, assume that Lalonde Company wants to prepare an income statement for the month of January. Its records show net sales of $200,000, beginning inventory of $40,000, and cost of goods purchased of $120,000. In the preceding year, the company had a 30% gross profit margin. It expects to earn the same margin this year. Given these facts and assumptions, Lalonde can calculate the estimated cost of the ending inventory at January 31 under the gross profit method as follows:

Step 1:	Net sales	$200,000
	Less: Estimated gross profit ($200,000 × 30%)	60,000
	Estimated cost of goods sold	$140,000
Step 2:	Beginning inventory	$ 40,000
	Cost of goods purchased	120,000
	Cost of goods available for sale	160,000
	Less: Estimated cost of goods sold	140,000
	Estimated cost of ending inventory	$ 20,000

The gross profit method is based on the assumption that the gross profit margin will remain constant from one year to the next. But it may not remain constant, because of a change in merchandising policies or in market conditions. In such cases, the margin should be adjusted to reflect the current operating conditions. In some cases, a better estimate can be had by applying this method to a department or product line as a whole.

The gross profit method should not be used in preparing a company's financial statements at the end of the year. These statements should be based on a physical inventory count.

RETAIL INVENTORY METHOD

A retail organization, such as Hudson's Bay Company, has thousands of types of merchandise. In such cases, determining the cost of each type of merchandise can be difficult and time-consuming if the company uses a periodic inventory system. For these retail companies, it can be easier to calculate the selling price, or retail price, of the total inventory than to look at the purchase invoices to find the cost of each individual inventory item. Most retail businesses can establish a relationship between cost and selling price—called the cost-to-retail percentage or ratio. The cost-to-retail percentage is then applied to the ending inventory at retail prices to determine the estimated cost of the inventory. This is called the **retail inventory method** of estimating the cost of inventory.

To use the retail inventory method, a company's records must show both the cost and the retail value of the goods available for sale. The formulas for using the retail inventory method are given in Illustration 6B-2.

Helpful hint In determining inventory at retail, selling prices of individual units are used. Tracing actual unit costs to invoices is unnecessary.

▶ ILLUSTRATION 6B-2
Retail inventory
method formulas

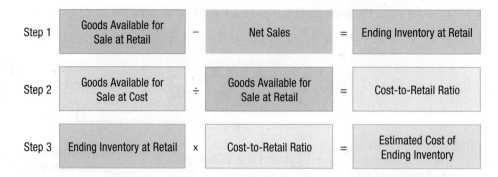

The following example shows how to apply the retail method, using assumed data for Janas Co.:

	At Cost	At Retail
Beginning inventory	$14,000	$ 21,500
Goods purchased	61,000	78,500
Goods available for sale	$75,000	100,000
Net sales		70,000
Step 1: Ending inventory at retail		$ 30,000

Step 2: Cost-to-retail ratio = $75,000 ÷ $100,000 = **75%**
Step 3: Estimated cost of ending inventory **$30,000 × 75%** = $22,500

Using the retail inventory method also makes it easier to take a physical inventory at the end of the year. The goods on hand can be valued at the prices marked on the merchandise. The cost-to-retail ratio is then applied to the goods on hand at retail to determine the ending inventory at cost. This value can be used for reporting purposes in the year-end financial statements if the results are similar to using cost.

The retail inventory method is also useful for estimating the amount of shrinkage due to breakage, loss, or theft. For example, assume that the retail value of Janas Co's physical inventory count is $29,400. When this amount is compared with the estimated retail value of $30,000 that was calculated above, it reveals a $600 estimated inventory shortage at retail. The estimated inventory shortage at cost is $450 ($600 × 75%).

The major disadvantage of the retail method is that it is an averaging technique. It may produce an incorrect inventory valuation if the mix of the ending inventory is not representative of the mix in the goods available for sale. Assume, for example, that the cost-to-retail ratio of 75% in the Janas Co. illustration consists of equal proportions of inventory items that have cost-to-retail ratios of 70%, 75%, and 80%, respectively. If the ending inventory contains only items with a 70% ratio, an incorrect inventory cost will result. This problem can be lessened by applying the retail method to a department or product line as a whole.

BEFORE YOU GO ON...DO IT **Inventory Estimation: Gross Profit Method**

At May 31, Purcell Company has net sales of $330,000 and cost of goods available for sale of $230,000. Last year, the company had a gross profit margin of 35%. Calculate the estimated cost of the ending inventory.

Action Plan
- Calculate the estimated cost of goods sold.
- Deduct the estimated cost of goods sold from cost of goods available for sale.

Solution

Net Sales	$ 330,000
Less: Estimated gross profit ($330,000 × 35%)	115,500
Estimated cost of goods sold	$ 214,500
Cost of goods available for sale	$ 230,000
Less: Estimated cost of goods sold	214,500
Estimated cost of ending inventory	$ 15,500

Related exercise material: *BE6–19, *BE6–20, *E6–17, and *E6–18.

Comparing IFRS and ASPE

Key Differences	International Financial Reporting Standards (IFRS)	Accounting Standards for Private Enterprises (ASPE)
No significant differences		

Demonstration Problem 1 (Perpetual Inventory System)

Jonah Company uses a perpetual inventory system. All sales and purchases are on account. The selling price is $9 per unit. The company has the following inventory data for the month of March:

Date	Explanation	Units	Unit Cost	Total Cost
Mar. 1	Beginning inventory	200	$4.30	$ 860
10	Purchase	500	4.50	2,250
15	Sales	(500)		
20	Purchase	400	4.75	1,900
25	Sales	(400)		
30	Purchase	300	5.00	1,500
		500		$6,510

Instructions

(a) Determine the cost of ending inventory at March 31 and cost of goods sold for March under (1) FIFO, and (2) weighted average.

(b) Prepare journal entries for the March 25 sale and the March 30 purchase under (1) FIFO, and (2) weighted average.

SOLUTION TO DEMONSTRATION PROBLEM 1

(a) 1. FIFO—perpetual

	A	B	C	D	E	F	G	H	I	J	K	L
1	Date	Purchases				Cost of goods sold				Inventory balance		
2		Units	Cost	Total		Units	Cost	Total		Units	Cost	Total
3	Mar. 1	Beginning inventory										
4		200	$4.30	$ 860						200	$4.30	$ 860
5	Mar. 10	500	4.50	2,250						200	4.30	860
6										500	4.50	2,250
7	Mar. 15					200	$4.30	$ 860				
8						300	4.50	1,350		200	4.50	900
9	Mar. 20	400	4.75	1,900						200	4.50	900
10										400	4.75	1,900
11	Mar. 25					200	4.50	900				
12						200	4.75	950		200	4.75	950
13	Mar. 30	300	5.00	1,500						200	4.75	950
14										300	5.00	1,500
15												
16		1,400		$6,510		900		$4,060		500		$2,450
17												
18		Cost of goods available for sale			−	Cost of goods sold			=	Ending inventory		

ACTION PLAN

- In a perpetual inventory system, cost of goods sold is calculated for each sale and a running balance of the ending inventory on hand is maintained.
- For FIFO, allocate the first costs to the cost of goods sold at the date of each sale. The latest costs will be allocated to the goods on hand (ending inventory).
- For weighted average, determine the weighted average unit cost (cost of goods available for sale ÷ number of units available for sale) after each purchase. Multiply this cost by the number of units sold to determine the cost of goods sold. Subtract the cost of goods sold for each sale from the previous ending inventory balance to arrive at the updated ending inventory balance.

(a) 2. Weighted average—perpetual

	A	B	C	D	E	F	G	H	I	J	K	L	M	N	O	P	Q
1															Weighted Average Calculations		
2	Date	Purchases				Cost of goods sold				Inventory balance					Total		WA cost
3		Units	Cost	Total		Units	Cost	Total		Units	Cost	Total	Units		cost		per unit
4	Mar. 1	Beginning inventory											A		B		B÷A
5		200	4.30	860						200	4.30	860					
6	Mar. 10	500	4.50	2,250						700	4.44	3,110	200		860.00		
7													500		2,250.00		
8													700		3,110.00		4.44
9	Mar. 15					500	4.44	2,220		200	4.45*	890	700		3,110.00		
10													−500		−2,220.00		
11													200		890.00		4.45
12	Mar. 20	400	4.75	1,900						600	4.65	2,790	200		890.00		
13													400		1,900.00		
14													600		2,790.00		4.65
15	Mar. 25					400	4.65	1,860		200	4.65	930	600		2,790.00		
16													−400		−1,860.00		
17													200		930.00		4.65
18	Mar. 30	300	5.00	1,500						500	4.86	2,430	200		930.00		
19													300		1,500.00		
20													500		2,430.00		4.86
21																	
22		1,400		6,510		900		4,080		500		2,430					
23																	
24		Cost of goods available for sale		−		Cost of goods sold				= Ending inventory							
25																	
26	*rounding																

(b) 1. & 2. FIFO and weighted average perpetual journal entries

			FIFO—Perpetual		Weighted Average—Perpetual	
Mar. 25	Accounts Receivable		3,600		3,600	
	Sales			3,600		3,600
	To record credit sale ($9 × 400).					
	Cost of Goods Sold		1,850		1,860	
	Merchandise Inventory			1,850		1,860
	To record cost of goods sold.					
30	Merchandise Inventory		1,500		1,500	
	Accounts Payable			1,500		1,500
	To record goods purchased on account.					

- Check your work: do an independent calculation of cost of goods sold and check that cost of goods available for sale − cost of goods sold = ending inventory.
- Recall that the journal entries required to record sales and purchases are the same no matter what cost determination method is being used.
- Use the information in the FIFO and weighted average inventory records to prepare the journal entries for cost of goods sold.

Demonstration Problem 2 (Periodic Inventory System)

Assume instead that Jonah Company uses a periodic inventory system. All sales and purchases are made on account. The company has the following inventory data for the month of March:

Inventory	March 1	200 units @ $4.30		$ 860
Purchases	March 10	500 units @ $4.50		2,250
	20	400 units @ $4.75		1,900
	30	300 units @ $5.00		1,500
Sales	March 15	500 units @ $9.00		4,500
	25	400 units @ $9.00		3,600

The physical inventory count on March 31 shows 500 units on hand.

Instructions

(a) Determine the cost of ending inventory at March 31 and cost of goods sold for March under (1) FIFO, and (2) weighted average.

(b) Prepare journal entries for the March 25 sale and the March 30 purchase under (1) FIFO, and (2) weighted average.

SOLUTION TO DEMONSTRATION PROBLEM 2

The cost of goods available for sale is $6,510, calculated as follows:

Inventory	March	1	200	units @ $4.30	$ 860
Purchases	March	10	500	units @ $4.50	2,250
		20	400	units @ $4.75	1,900
		30	300	units @ $5.00	1,500
			1,400		$6,510

The physical inventory count on March 31 shows 500 units on hand.

The number of units sold is 900 (1,400 units available for sale – 500 units on hand).

(a) 1. FIFO—periodic

Ending inventory:	Date	Units	Unit Cost	Total Cost
	Mar. 30	300	$5.00	$1,500
	20	200	4.75	950
		500		$2,450

Cost of goods sold: $6,510 – $2,450 = $4,060

Check of cost of goods sold:	Date	Units	Unit Cost	Total Cost
	Mar. 1	200	$4.30	$ 860
	10	500	4.50	2,250
	20	200	4.75	950
		900		$4,060

Check: $4,060 + $2,450 = $6,510

2. Weighted average—periodic

Weighted average unit cost:	$6,510 ÷ 1,400 units = $4.65 per unit
Ending inventory:	500 units × $4.65 = $2,325
Cost of goods sold:	$6,510 – $2,325 = $4,185
Check of cost of goods sold:	900 units × $4.65 = $4,185
Check:	$4,185 + $2,325 = $6,510

(b) 1. & 2. FIFO and weighted average periodic journal entries

		FIFO—Periodic		Weighted Average—Periodic	
Mar. 25	Accounts Receivable	3,600		3,600	
	Sales		3,600		3,600
	To record credit sale ($9 × 400).				
30	Purchases	1,500		1,500	
	Accounts Payable		1,500		1,500
	To record goods purchased on account.				

ACTION PLAN

- In a periodic system, cost of ending inventory and cost of goods sold are determined at the end of the period.
- Calculate cost of goods available for sale, then allocate costs to ending inventory and cost of goods sold.
- For FIFO, allocate the most recent costs to the goods on hand. (The first costs will be allocated to the cost of goods sold.)
- For weighted average, calculate the weighted average unit cost (cost of goods available for sale divided by the total units available for sale). Multiply this cost by the number of units on hand to determine ending inventory.
- Subtract ending inventory from the cost of goods available for sale to determine the cost of goods sold for each cost formula.
- Check your work: check that cost of goods available for sale – cost of goods sold = ending inventory.
- Recall that in a periodic inventory system, cost of goods sold is not recorded at the point of sale.

▶ Summary of Learning Objectives

1. *Describe the steps in determining inventory quantities.* The steps in determining inventory quantities are (1) taking a physical inventory of goods on hand, and (2) determining the ownership of goods in transit, on consignment, and in similar situations.

2. *Calculate cost of goods sold and ending inventory in a perpetual inventory system using the specific identification, FIFO, and weighted average methods of cost determination.* Costs are allocated to the Cost of Goods Sold account each time a sale occurs in a perpetual inventory system. The cost is determined by specific identification or by one of two cost formulas: FIFO (first-in, first-out) and weighted average.

   Specific identification is used for goods that are not ordinarily interchangeable. This method tracks the actual physical flow of goods, allocating the exact cost of each merchandise item to cost of goods sold and ending inventory.

   The FIFO cost formula assumes a first-in, first-out cost flow for sales. Cost of goods sold consists of the cost of the earliest goods purchased. Ending inventory is determined by allocating the cost of the most recent purchases to the units on hand.

   The weighted average cost formula is used for goods that are homogeneous or non-distinguishable. Under weighted average, a new weighted (moving) average unit cost is calculated after each purchase and applied to the number of units sold. Inventory is updated by subtracting cost of goods sold for each sale from the previous ending inventory balance.

3. *Explain the financial statement effects of inventory cost determination methods.* Specific identification results in the best match of costs and revenues on the income statement. When prices are rising, weighted average results in a higher cost of goods sold and lower profit than FIFO. Weighted average results in a better match on the income statement because it results in an expense amount made up of more current costs. On the balance sheet, FIFO results in an ending inventory that is closest to the current (replacement) value and the best balance sheet valuation. All three methods result in the same cash flow.

4. *Determine the financial statement effects of inventory errors.* An error in beginning inventory will have a reverse effect on profit in the current year (e.g., an overstatement of beginning inventory results in an overstatement of cost of goods sold and an understatement of profit). An error in the cost of goods purchased will have a reverse effect on profit (e.g., an overstatement of purchases results in an overstatement of cost of goods sold and an understatement of profit). An error in ending inventory will have a similar effect on profit (e.g., an overstatement of ending inventory results in an understatement of cost of goods sold and an overstatement of profit). If ending inventory errors are not corrected in the following period, their effect on profit for the second period is reversed and total profit for the two years will be correct. On the balance sheet, ending inventory errors will have the same effects on total assets and total owner's equity, and no effect on liabilities.

5. *Value inventory at the lower of cost and net realizable value.* The cost of the ending inventory is compared with its net realizable value. If the net realizable value is lower, a writedown is recorded, which results in an increase in cost of goods sold, and a reduction in inventory. The writedown is reversed if the net realizable value of the inventory increases, but the value of the inventory can never be higher than its original cost.

6. *Demonstrate the presentation and analysis of inventory.* Ending inventory is reported as a current asset on the balance sheet at the lower of cost and net realizable value. Cost of goods sold is reported as an expense on the income statement. Additional disclosures include the cost determination method.

   The inventory turnover ratio is a measure of liquidity. It is calculated by dividing the cost of goods sold by average inventory. It can be converted to days sales in inventory by dividing 365 days by the inventory turnover ratio.

7. *Calculate ending inventory and cost of goods sold in a periodic inventory system using FIFO and weighted average inventory cost formulas (Appendix 6A).* Under the FIFO cost formula, the cost of the most recent goods purchased is allocated to ending inventory. The cost of the earliest goods on hand is allocated to cost of goods sold. Under the weighted average cost formula, the total cost available for sale is divided by the total units available to calculate a weighted average unit cost. The weighted average unit cost is applied to the number of units on hand at the end of the period to determine ending inventory. Cost of goods sold is calculated by subtracting ending inventory from the cost of goods available for sale.

   The main difference between applying cost formulas in a periodic inventory system and applying cost formulas in a perpetual inventory system is the timing of the calculations. In a periodic inventory system, the cost formula is applied at the end of the period. In a perpetual inventory system, the cost formula is applied at the date of each sale to determine the cost of goods sold.

8. *Estimate ending inventory using the gross profit and retail inventory methods (Appendix 6B).* Two methods of estimating inventories are the gross profit method and the retail inventory method. Under the gross profit method, the gross profit margin is applied to net sales to determine the estimated cost of goods sold. The estimated cost of goods sold is subtracted from the cost of goods available for sale to

determine the estimated cost of the ending inventory. Under the retail inventory method, a cost-to-retail ratio is calculated by dividing the cost of goods available for sale by the retail value of the goods available for sale. This ratio is then applied to the ending inventory at retail to determine the estimated cost of the ending inventory.

▶ Glossary

Consigned goods   Goods held for sale that belong to another party. The party holding the goods is called the consignee, and the party that owns the goods is called the consignor. (p. 303)

Days sales in inventory   A liquidity measure of the average number of days that inventory is held. It is calculated as 365 days divided by the inventory turnover ratio. (p. 325)

First-in, first-out (FIFO) cost formula   An inventory cost formula that assumes that the costs of the earliest (oldest) goods purchased are the first to be recognized as the cost of goods sold. The costs of the latest goods purchased are assumed to remain in ending inventory. (p. 307)

Gross profit method   A method for estimating the cost of the ending inventory by applying the gross profit margin to net sales. (p. 330)

Internal control   The process designed and implemented by management to help the company achieve reliable financial reporting, effective and efficient operations, and compliance with relevant laws and regulations. (p. 302)

Inventory turnover   A liquidity measure of the number of times, on average, that inventory is sold during the period. It is calculated by dividing cost of goods sold by average inventory. Average inventory is calculated by adding beginning inventory and ending inventory balances and dividing the result by two. (p. 325)

Lower of cost and net realizable value (LCNRV)   A basis for stating inventory at the lower of its original cost and the net realizable value at the end of the period. (p. 320)

Net realizable value (NRV)   The selling price of an inventory item, less any estimated costs required to make the item saleable. (p. 320)

Retail inventory method   A method for estimating the cost of the ending inventory by applying a cost-to-retail ratio to the ending inventory at retail prices. (p. 331)

Specific identification   An inventory costing method used when goods are distinguishable and not ordinarily interchangeable. It follows the actual physical flow of goods and items are specifically costed to arrive at the cost of goods sold and the cost of the ending inventory. (p. 305)

Weighted average cost formula   An inventory cost formula that assumes that the goods available for sale are homogeneous or non-distinguishable. The cost of goods sold and the ending inventory are determined using a weighted average cost, calculated by dividing the cost of the goods available for sale by the units available for sale. (p. 309)

Weighted average unit cost   The average cost of inventory weighted by the number of units purchased at each unit cost. It is calculated by dividing the cost of goods available for sale by the number of units available for sale. (p. 309)

Note: All questions, exercises, and problems below with an asterisk (*) relate to material in Appendices 6A and 6B.

▶ Self-Study Questions
Answers are at the end of the chapter.

(LO 1) K   1. Which of the following should not be included in a company's physical inventory?
(a) Goods held on consignment from another company
(b) Goods shipped on consignment to another company
(c) Goods in transit that were purchased from a supplier and shipped FOB shipping point
(d) Goods in transit that were sold to a customer and shipped FOB destination

(LO 1) AP   2. As a result of a physical inventory count, Atlantic Company determined that it had inventory worth $180,000 at December 31, 2017. This count did not take into consideration the following: Rogers Consignment store currently has goods that cost $35,000 on its sales floor that belong to Atlantic but are being sold on consignment by Rogers. The selling price of these goods is $50,000. Atlantic purchased $13,000 of goods that were shipped on December 27,

FOB destination, and they were received by Atlantic on January 3. Determine the correct amount of inventory that Atlantic should report.
(a) $230,000
(b) $215,000
(c) $228,000
(d) $193,000

(LO 2) AP   3. Peg City Brews uses a perpetual inventory system and has the following beginning inventory, purchases, and sales of inventory in April:

	Units	Unit Cost	Total Cost
Inventory, Apr. 1	6,000	$9	$ 54,000
Purchase, Apr. 9	18,000	10	180,000
Sale, Apr. 12	(20,000)		
Purchase, Apr. 18	16,000	11	176,000

What was the moving weighted average unit cost after the last purchase on April 18?
(a) $9.75
(b) $10.75
(c) $11.00
(d) $10.00

(LO 2) AP 4. Using the data in question 3 above, the cost of goods sold in a perpetual inventory system under FIFO is:
(a) $174,000.
(b) $180,000.
(c) $195,000.
(d) $194,000.

(LO 3) K 5. Using FIFO, the current asset Merchandise Inventory will report:
(a) the most recent cost of purchases.
(b) the oldest cost of purchases.
(c) the average cost of all purchases.
(d) the exact amount of each inventory unit on hand.

(LO 4) C 6. In Fran Company, ending inventory is overstated by $4,000. The effects of this error on the current year's cost of goods sold and profit, respectively, are:
(a) understated, overstated.
(b) overstated, understated.
(c) overstated, overstated.
(d) understated, understated.

(LO 5) C 7. Rickety Company purchased 1,000 units of inventory at a cost of $15 each. There are 200 units left in ending inventory. The net realizable value of these units is $12 each. The ending inventory under the lower of cost and net realizable value rule is:
(a) $2,400.
(b) $3,000.
(c) $600.
(d) $12,000.

(LO 5) K 8. The inventory turnover ratio provides an indication of:
(a) how much profit the company has per dollar of sales.
(b) whether the company consistently has too much or too little inventory.
(c) the number of days inventory is held in stock.
(d) the company's cash flow position.

(LO 6) AP 9. If a company's cost of goods sold is $240,000, its beginning inventory is $50,000, and its ending inventory

is $30,000, what are its inventory turnover and days sales in inventory?
(a) 3 times and 122 days
(b) 6 times and 61 days
(c) 4.8 times and 76 days
(d) 8 times and 46 days

(LO 7) AP *10. Kam Company uses a periodic inventory system and has the following:

	Units	Unit Cost
Inventory, Jan. 1	8,000	$11
Purchase, June 19	13,000	12
Purchase, Nov. 8	5,000	13
	26,000	

If 9,000 units are on hand at December 31, what is the cost of the goods sold using weighted average? Round cost per unit to two decimal places.
(a) $106,962
(b) $108,000
(c) $180,000
(d) $202,038

(LO 7) AP *11. Using the data in question 10 above, the ending inventory using a periodic inventory system and FIFO is:
(a) $100,000.
(b) $108,000.
(c) $113,000.
(d) $117,000.

(LO 8) AP *12. Filman Company has sales of $200,000 and a cost of goods available for sale of $156,000. If the gross profit margin is 30%, the estimated cost of the ending inventory under the gross profit method is:
(a) $16,000.
(b) $60,000.
(c) $37,200.
(d) $76,000.

(LO 8) AP *13. Deko Company reports the following selected information: cost of goods available for sale at cost, $60,000; at retail, $100,000; and net sales at retail, $70,000. What is the estimated cost of Deko Company's ending inventory under the retail method?
(a) $18,000
(b) $21,000
(c) $30,000
(d) $42,000

▶ Questions

(LO 1) C 1. Your friend Tom Wetzel has been hired to help take the physical inventory in Kikujiro's Hardware Store. Explain to Tom what this job will involve.

(LO 1) C 2. Explain to Janine Company whether the buyer or the seller should include goods in transit in their inventory.

(LO 1) C 3. What are consigned goods? Which company, the consignee or the consignor, should include consigned goods in its inventory balance? Explain why.

(LO 2) C 4. Explain circumstances in which the specific identification method is used.

(LO 2) C 5. Differentiate between the three methods of determining cost for inventories: specific identification, FIFO, and weighted average. Give an example of a type of inventory for which each method might be used.

(LO 2) C 6. Jenny believes that, when the perpetual system is used, the weighted average cost per unit changes with *every* purchase and *every* sale. Do you agree or disagree with Jenny? Explain.

(LO 3) C   7. Compare the financial statement effects of using the FIFO and weighted average cost formulas during a period of rising prices on (a) cash, (b) ending inventory, (c) cost of goods sold, and (d) profit.

(LO 3) C   8. Which inventory cost formula—FIFO or weighted average—provides a better match between sales and cost of goods sold? The better inventory valuation? Explain.

(LO 3) K   9. What factors should a company consider when it is choosing between the two inventory cost formulas—FIFO and weighted average?

(LO 4) C   10. Mila Company discovers in 2017 that its ending inventory at December 31, 2016, was overstated by $5,000. What effect will this error have on (a) 2016 profit, (b) 2017 profit, and (c) the combined profit for the two years?

(LO 4) K   11. List the common kinds of errors that can happen related to inventory.

(LO 5) C   12. Lucy Ritter is studying for the next accounting exam. What should Lucy know about (a) when not to use the cost basis of accounting for inventories, and (b) the meaning of "net realizable value" in the lower of cost and net realizable value method?

(LO 5) K   13. How is net realizable value calculated?

(LO 5) C   14. A company must record a loss (or an increase in cost of goods sold) when net realizable value is lower than cost. Should a company record a gain when net realizable value is higher than cost? Explain.

(LO 6) K   15. An item must possess two characteristics to be classified as inventory by a merchandiser. What are these two characteristics?

(LO 6) K   16. Leo Company's balance sheet shows Inventory of $162,800. What additional disclosures must be made?

(LO 6) AN   17. If a company's days sales in inventory ratio decreases from one year to the next, would this be viewed as a sign that the company's inventory management has improved or deteriorated? Explain.

(LO 6) C   18. Describe what information an inventory turnover ratio can provide about a company.

(LO 7) C *19. Why is it necessary to calculate cost of goods available for sale when applying FIFO or weighted average in a periodic inventory system?

(LO 7) K *20. Inventory cost flow relationships are used in a variety of ways to account for inventory in a business. Show how the relationships can be translated into equations for practical purposes.

(LO 7) C *21. Explain why ending inventory and cost of goods sold under the weighted average cost formula are not the same amounts in a periodic inventory system as they are in a perpetual inventory system.

(LO 8) K *22. When is it necessary to estimate the cost of inventories?

(LO 8) C *23. In order to save the cost of counting inventory at year end, it is acceptable to use the gross profit method to determine ending inventory for the year-end financial statements. Do you agree or disagree? Explain.

(LO 8) C *24. Explain the major weakness of the retail method and when it is not appropriate to use it.

▶ Brief Exercises

BE6–1 Helgeson Company has identified the following items to include or exclude when it takes its physical inventory. Indicate whether each item should be included or excluded.
(a) Goods shipped on consignment by Helgeson to another company
(b) Goods in transit to Helgeson from a supplier, shipped FOB destination
(c) Goods sold to a customer but being held for delivery
(d) Goods from another company held on consignment by Helgeson
(e) Goods in transit to a customer, shipped FOB shipping point

Identify items in inventory.
(LO 1) K

BE6–2 The merchandise inventory in Claire's Clothing Store was counted after the close of business on December 31, 2017, the company's year end. It was determined that the total cost of this inventory was $55,500. Claire wants to know if this is the correct amount that should be reported on the company's December 31, 2017, balance sheet or if an adjustment needs to be made for any of the following items:
(a) The count included items costing $1,500 that had been sold but are being held for alterations. The customers have paid in full for these items.
(b) Claire's Clothing Store has $4,250 of merchandise held on consignment for a local designer. These items were included in the inventory count.
(c) A shipment of inventory costing $2,875 was received on January 2, 2017. It had been shipped by the seller on December 30, FOB shipping point. Freight charges are $310. These items were not included in the inventory count.
(d) A second shipment of inventory costing $4,350 was received on January 3, 2017. It had been shipped by the seller on December 31, FOB destination. Freight charges are $390. These items were also not included in the inventory count.
Determine the correct amount of Claire's Clothing Store's merchandise inventory at December 31, 2017.

Calculate inventory balance.
(LO 1) AP

Apply specific identification cost determination method. (LO 2) AP

BE6-3 In October, Courtney's Gallery purchased four original paintings for resale for the following amounts: Painting 1, $500; Painting 2, $2,500; Painting 3, $2,900; and Painting 4, $3,900. Paintings 3 and 4 were sold during October for $6,500 each. Calculate the cost of goods sold for the month and the ending inventory balance on October 31 using specific identification.

Recommend cost determination method. (LO 2) AP

BE6-4 The following are three inventory cost determination methods:

1. Specific identification
2. FIFO
3. Weighted average

Below is a list of different types of companies and their main inventory item. Beside each one, insert the number of the inventory cost determination method above that the company would most likely use.

(a) _____ Grocery store (food)
(b) _____ Car dealership (automobiles)
(c) _____ Clothing store (clothing)
(d) _____ Car dealership (parts)

(e) _____ Gas station (fuel)
(f) _____ Jewellery store (custom-made jewellery)
(g) _____ Consignment clothing store (clothing)

Apply perpetual FIFO. (LO 2) AP

BE6-5 First Choice Company uses the FIFO cost formula in a perpetual inventory system. Fill in the missing amounts for items (a) through (k) in the following perpetual inventory record:

Date	Purchases Units	Cost	Total	Cost Of Goods Sold Units	Cost	Total	Inventory Balance Units	Cost	Total
June 1	Beginning Inventory								
	200	$25.00	$5,000.00				200	$25.00	$5,000.00
7	400	$22.00	$8,800.00				(a)	(b)	(c)
18				350	(d)	(e)	(f)	(g)	(h)
26	350	$20.00	$7,000.00				(i)	(j)	(k)

Apply perpetual weighted average. (LO 2) AP

BE6-6 Average Joe Company uses the weighted average cost formula in a perpetual inventory system. Fill in the missing amounts for items (a) through (k) in the following perpetual inventory record (round the weighted average cost to two decimal places):

Date	Purchases Units	Cost	Total	Cost Of Goods Sold Units	Cost	Total	Inventory Balance Units	Cost	Total
June 1	Beginning Inventory								
	400	$25.00	$10,000				400	$25.00	$10,000
7	600	$22.00	$13,200				(a)	(b)	(c)
18				550	(d)	(e)	(f)	(g)	(h)
26	450	$20.00	$9,000				(i)	(j)	(k)

Apply perpetual FIFO and weighted average. (LO 2) AP

BE6-7 Jordy & Company uses a perpetual inventory system. The following information is available for November:

		Units	Purchase Price	Sales Price
Nov. 1	Balance	10	$5.00	
4	Purchase	20	$5.50	
7	Purchase	20	$6.00	
10	Sale	(10)		$8.00
12	Sale	(30)		$8.00

Calculate the cost of goods sold and ending inventory under (a) FIFO and (b) weighted average. (Round the weighted average cost per unit to two decimal places.)

Record journal entries using perpetual FIFO and weighted average. (LO 2) AP

BE6-8 Refer to the data in BE6-7 for Jordy & Company. Prepare journal entries to record the November 4 purchase and the November 12 sale using (a) FIFO and (b) weighted average. Assume all sales and purchases are on credit.

BE6–9 For each statement that follows, identify the inventory cost formula that best fits the description, assuming a period of rising prices:

Identify inventory cost formula. (LO 3) C

(a) It results in a balance sheet inventory amount that is closer to the replacement cost.
(b) It does a better job of matching recent costs against revenue.
(c) It understates the value of the inventory on the balance sheet.
(d) It may overstate gross profit.

BE6–10 Interactive Tech Company just started business and is trying to decide which inventory cost formula to use. Assuming prices are falling, as they often do in the information technology sector, answer the following questions for Interactive Tech:

Compare impact of inventory cost formulas. (LO 3) C

(a) Which formula will result in the higher ending inventory? Explain.
(b) Which formula will result in the higher cost of goods sold? Explain.
(c) Which formula will result in the higher cash flow? Explain.
(d) What factors are important for Interactive Tech to consider as it tries to choose the most appropriate inventory cost formula?

BE6–11 Collie Company incorrectly included $23,000 of goods held on consignment for Retriever Company in Collie's beginning inventory for the year ended December 31, 2016. The ending inventory for 2016 and 2017 was correctly counted. (a) What is the impact on the 2016 financial statements? (b) What is the impact on the 2017 financial statements?

Determine effect of beginning inventory error. (LO 4) AN

BE6–12 FirstIn Company reported profit of $90,000 in 2016. When counting its inventory on December 31, 2016, the company forgot to include items stored in a separate room in the warehouse. As a result, ending inventory was understated by $7,000.

Determine effects of inventory error over two years. (LO 4) AN

(a) What is the correct profit for 2016?
(b) What effect, if any, will this error have on total assets and owner's equity reported on the balance sheet at December 31, 2016?
(c) Assuming the inventory is correctly counted on December 31, 2017, what effect, if any, will this error have on the 2017 financial statements?

BE6–13 Smart Information Technology Company has the following cost and net realizable value data at December 31, 2017:

Determine LCNRV valuation and prepare adjustment. (LO 5) AP

Inventory Categories	Cost	Net Realizable Value
Personal computers	$27,000	$21,500
Servers	18,000	19,500
Total solution printers	10,000	8,500

(a) Calculate the lower of cost and net realizable value valuation assuming Smart Information Technology Company applies LCNRV to individual products.
(b) What adjustment should the company record if it uses a perpetual inventory system?

BE6–14 Refer to the data in BE6–13 for Smart Information Technology Company. Prior to making the adjustment in BE6–13 part (b), cost of goods sold for 2017 was $418,500. What is the correct ending inventory that should be reported on the balance sheet on December 31, 2017? What is the correct cost of goods sold that should be reported on the income statement for the year ended December 31, 2017?

Apply LCNRV. (LO 5) AP

BE6–15 Reynold's Company had net sales of $2,500,000, cost of goods sold of $1,150,000, and profit of $500,000 in 2017. The company had a January 1, 2017, inventory balance of $132,000 and a December 31, 2017, inventory balance of $143,000. Calculate the inventory turnover and days sales in inventory ratios for 2017.

Calculate inventory ratios. (LO 6) AP

BE6–16 Refer to the data in BE6–15 for Reynold's Company. Assume for 2016 the company had an inventory turnover ratio of 9.1 and 40.1 days sales in inventory. Has the company's inventory management improved or deteriorated in 2017? Explain.

Compare inventory ratios. (LO 6) C

*BE6–17 In its first month of operations, Panther Company made three purchases of merchandise in the following sequence: 200 units at $8; 250 units at $7; and 300 units at $6. There are 400 units on hand at the end of the period. Panther uses a periodic inventory system. Calculate the cost of the ending inventory and cost of goods sold under (a) FIFO, and (b) weighted average. (*Hint:* Round to two decimal places for the weighted average cost per unit.)

Apply periodic FIFO and weighted average. (LO 7) AP

Record transactions using periodic FIFO and weighted average. (LO 2, 7) AP

*BE6–18   At the beginning of the year, Cully Company had 400 units with a cost of $4 per unit in its beginning inventory. The following inventory transactions occurred during the month of January:

Jan. 3   Purchased 1,000 units on account for $4.50 per unit.
    9   Sold 550 units on account for $10 each.
  15   Sold 850 units for cash for $10 each.

Prepare journal entries to record the January transactions assuming that Cully Company uses a periodic inventory system under (a) FIFO and (b) weighted average.

Apply gross profit method. (LO 8) AP

*BE6–19   Jared Company had beginning inventory of $40,000; net sales of $275,000; and cost of goods purchased of $160,000. In the previous year, the company had a gross profit margin of 45%. Calculate the estimated cost of the ending inventory using the gross profit method.

Apply retail inventory method. (LO 8) AP

*BE6–20   On July 31, Melodie's Fabric Store had the following data related to the retail inventory method: goods available for sale at cost $35,000; at retail $50,000; and net sales of $40,000. Calculate the estimated cost of the ending inventory using the retail inventory method.

▶ Exercises

Identify items in inventory. (LO 1) K

E6–1   Sam's Surplus Supply had the following inventory situations to consider at January 31, its year end:

1. Goods held on consignment for MailBoxes Etc. since December 22
2. Goods that are still in transit and were shipped to a customer, FOB destination, on January 28
3. Goods that are still in transit and were purchased from a supplier, FOB destination, on January 25
4. Goods that are still in transit and were purchased from a supplier, FOB shipping point, on January 29
5. Freight costs due on goods in transit from item 4 above
6. Freight costs due on goods in transit from item 2 above

Instructions

Which of the above items should Sam's Surplus Supply include in its inventory? Provide an explanation.

Determine correct inventory amount. (LO 1) AP

E6–2   First Bank is considering giving Moghul Company a loan. First, however, it decides that it would be a good idea to have further discussions with Moghul's accountant. One area of particular concern is the inventory account, which has a December 31 balance of $281,000. Discussions with the accountant reveal the following:

1. The physical count of the inventory did not include goods that cost $95,000 that were shipped to Moghul, FOB shipping point, on December 27 and were still in transit at year end.
2. Moghul sold goods that cost $35,000 to Novotna Company, FOB destination, on December 28. The goods are not expected to arrive at their destination in India until January 12. The goods were not included in the physical inventory because they were not in the warehouse.
3. On December 31, Board Company had $30,500 of goods held on consignment for Moghul. The goods were not included in Moghul's ending inventory balance.
4. Moghul received goods that cost $28,000 on January 2. The goods were shipped FOB shipping point on December 26 by Cellar Co. The goods were not included in the physical count.

Instructions

Determine the correct inventory amount at December 31.

Apply specific identification. (LO 2) AP

E6–3   In December, Carrie's Car Emporium purchased the following items:

Date Purchased	Description	Cost
Dec. 12	2014 Red Jeep	$15,000
5	2015 Blue Honda	12,000
10	2016 Black Audi	25,000
19	2013 Grey Toyota	18,000
20	2013 Green Range Rover	10,000

On December 22, the 2015 Honda and 2014 Jeep were sold for $16,500 each.

Instructions

(a) Should Carrie's Car Emporium use specific identification or one of the two cost formulas (FIFO or weighted average) instead? Explain.

(b) Calculate ending inventory and cost of goods sold using specific identification.
(c) Prepare the journal entry to record the December 22 sale.

E6–4   On May 1, Black Bear Company had 400 units of inventory on hand, at a cost of $4.00 each. The company uses a perpetual inventory system. All purchases and sales are on account. A record of inventory transactions for the month of May for the company is as follows:

Apply perpetual FIFO, record journal entries, and calculate gross profit. (LO 2) AP

Purchases			Sales		
May 4	1,300 @ $4.10		May 3	300 @ $7.00	
14	700 @ $4.40		16	1,000 @ 7.00	
29	500 @ $4.75		18	400 @ 7.50	

Instructions
(a) Calculate the cost of goods sold and ending inventory using FIFO.
(b) Prepare journal entries to record the May 4 purchase and the May 3 and 16 sales.
(c) Calculate gross profit for May.

E6–5   Top Light Company uses a perpetual inventory system. The company began 2017 with 1,000 lamps in inventory at a cost of $12 per unit. During 2017, Top Light had the following purchases and sales of lamps:

Apply perpetual weighted average, record journal entries, and calculate gross profit. (LO 2) AP

February 15	Purchased	2,000 units @ $18 per unit
April 24	Sold	2,500 units @ $30 per unit
June 6	Purchased	3,500 units @ $23 per unit
October 18	Sold	2,000 units @ $33 per unit
December 4	Purchased	1,400 units @ $26 per unit

All purchases and sales are on account.

Instructions
(a) Calculate the cost of goods sold and ending inventory using weighted average. (*Hint:* Round the weighted average cost per unit to two decimal places.)
(b) Prepare journal entries to record the June 6 purchase and the October 18 sale.
(c) Calculate gross profit for the year.

E6–6   Dene Company uses a perpetual inventory system and reports the following inventory transactions for the month of July:

Apply perpetual FIFO and weighted average. Answer questions about results. (LO 2, 3) AP

		Units	Unit Cost	Total Cost
July 1	Inventory	150	$5	$ 750
12	Purchases	230	6.75	1,552.50
20	Sale	(250)		
28	Purchases	490	7	3,430

Instructions
(a) Calculate the cost of goods sold and ending inventory under (1) FIFO and (2) weighted average. (Round the weighted average cost per unit to two decimal places.)
(b) Which cost formula gives the higher ending inventory? Why?
(c) Which cost formula results in the higher cost of goods sold? Why?

E6–7   Sun Care Company uses a perpetual inventory system. The following information is provided for cost of goods sold and ending inventory under FIFO and weighted average.

Apply perpetual FIFO and weighted average. Answer questions about results. (LO 2, 3) AP

	FIFO	Weighted Average
Cost of goods sold	$8,060	$7,787
Ending inventory	$1,375	$1,648

Instructions
(a) Assuming 1,180 units are sold for $15 per unit, and the product costs are decreasing, calculate gross profit under (1) FIFO and (2) weighted average. Comment on why gross profit is not the same under the two cost formulas.
(b) What impact, if any, does the choice of cost formula have on cash flow? Explain.

E6–8   Glacier Fishing Gear reported the following amounts for its cost of goods sold and ending inventory:

Determine effects of inventory errors. (LO 4) AN

	2017	2016
Cost of goods sold	$170,000	$175,000
Ending inventory	30,000	30,000

Glacier made two errors: (1) 2016 ending inventory was overstated by $5,500, and (2) 2017 ending inventory was understated by $4,000.

Instructions

(a) Calculate the correct cost of goods sold and ending inventory for each year.

(b) Describe the impact of the errors on profit for 2016 and 2017 and on owner's equity at the end of 2016 and 2017.

(c) Explain why it is important that Glacier Fishing Gear correct these errors as soon as they are discovered.

Correct partial income statements and calculate gross profit margin. (LO 4) AN

E6-9   Marrakesh Company reported the following income statement data for the years ended December 31:

	2017	2016
Sales	$500,000	$500,000
Cost of goods sold	410,000	410,000
Gross profit	$ 90,000	$ 90,000

The inventories at January 1, 2016, and December 31, 2017, are correct. However, the ending inventory at December 31, 2016, was understated by $20,000.

Instructions

(a) Prepare the correct income statement up to gross profit for the two years.

(b) What is the combined effect of the inventory error on total gross profit for the two years?

Determine LCNRV valuation. (LO 5) AP

E6-10   Gloria's Gift Shop uses a perpetual inventory system and the FIFO cost formula for valuing inventory. The company is now in the process of comparing the cost of its inventory with its net realizable value. The following data are available at Gloria's Gift Shop's year end, December 31:

	Units	Unit Cost	Net Realizable Value per Unit
Clothing	95	$ 7	$ 6
Jewellery	72	20	28
Greeting cards	47	1	2
Stuffed toys	56	12	39

Instructions

(a) Determine the lower of cost and net realizable value of the ending inventory assuming Gloria's Gift Shop applies LCNRV on individual items.

(b) Prepare the journal entry required, if any, to record the adjustment from cost to net realizable value.

Determine LCNRV valuation and note disclosures. (LO 5, 6) AP

E6-11   Picture Perfect Camera Shop is determining the lower of cost and net realizable value of its inventory. The following data are available at December 31:

		Units	Unit Cost	Net Realizable Value
Cameras:	Nikon	15	$675	$600
	Canon	17	400	425
Lenses:	Sony	22	135	124
	Sigma	20	215	220

Instructions

(a) Determine the lower of cost and net realizable value of the ending inventory assuming Picture Perfect Camera Shop applies LCNRV to major categories of items.

(b) Prepare the journal entry required, if any, to record the adjustment from cost to net realizable value assuming Picture Perfect Camera Shop uses a perpetual inventory system.

(c) What information regarding its inventory will Picture Perfect Camera Shop need to report in the notes to its financial statements?

Calculate inventory turnover, days sales in inventory, and gross profit margin. (LO 6) AP

E6-12   Dartmouth Games reported the following information for a three-year period:

	2017	2016	2015
Ending inventory	$ 20,000	$ 30,000	$ 34,000
Sales	125,000	128,000	115,000
Cost of goods sold	50,000	51,200	46,000
Profit	30,000	42,000	40,000

Instructions

(a) Calculate the inventory turnover, days sales in inventory, and gross profit margin for 2017 and 2016.

(b) Based on this information, does the company's liquidity appear to be improving or deteriorating?

*E6–13 Lombart Company uses a periodic inventory system. Its records show the following for the month of April, with 25 units on hand at April 30:

Apply periodic FIFO and weighted average. (LO 7) AP

		Units	Unit Cost	Total Cost
April 1	Inventory	30	$ 8	$240
12	Purchases	45	11	495
16	Purchases	15	12	180
	Total	90		$915

Instructions

(a) Calculate the ending inventory and cost of goods sold at April 30 using the FIFO and weighted average cost formulas.
(b) Prove the cost of goods sold calculations.

*E6–14 Dene Company uses a periodic inventory system and its accounting records include the following inventory information for the month of July:

Apply periodic FIFO and weighted average. (LO 7) AP

		Units	Unit Cost	Total Cost
July 1	Inventory on hand	150	$5.00	$ 750.00
12	Purchase	230	6.75	1,552.50
20	Sale	(250)		.00
28	Purchase	490	7.00	3,430.00

A physical inventory count determined that 620 units were on hand at July 31.

Instructions

(a) Calculate the ending inventory and the cost of goods sold under (1) FIFO and (2) weighted average.
(b) For item 2 of part (a), explain why the weighted average unit cost is not $6.25.
(c) How do the results for part (a) differ from E6–6, where the same information for Dene Company was used in a perpetual inventory system?

*E6–15 Xpert Snowboards sells an ultra-lightweight snowboard that is considered to be one of the best on the market. Information follows for Xpert's purchases and sales of the ultra-lightweight snowboard in October:

Apply periodic and perpetual FIFO and weighted average. (LO 2, 7) AP

Date	Transaction	Units	Unit Purchase Price	Unit Sales Price
Oct. 1	Beginning inventory	25	$295	
10	Purchase	30	300	
12	Sale	(42)		$450
13	Purchase	35	305	
25	Sale	(45)		460
27	Purchase	20	310	

Instructions

(a) Calculate the cost of goods sold and the ending inventory using FIFO and weighted average, assuming Xpert uses a perpetual inventory system. (Round the weighted average cost per unit to two decimal places.)
(b) What would be the ending inventory and cost of goods sold if Xpert used FIFO and weighted average in a periodic inventory system? (Round the weighted average cost per unit to two decimal places.)

*E6–16 Refer to the data for Xpert Snowboards in E6–15. Assume that all of Xpert's sales are for cash and all of its purchases are on account.

Record transactions in perpetual and periodic inventory systems. (LO 2, 7) AP

Instructions

(a) Record the purchase on October 10 and sale on October 12 for Xpert Snowboards in a perpetual inventory system under (1) FIFO and (2) weighted average.
(b) Record the purchase on October 13 and sale on October 25 for Xpert Snowboards in a periodic inventory system under (1) FIFO and (2) weighted average.

*E6–17 The inventory of Marshall's Merchandise Company was destroyed by fire on June 1. From an examination of the accounting records, the following data for the first five months of the year were obtained: Sales $90,000; Sales Returns and Allowances $1,500; Sales Discounts $700; Freight Out $2,500; Purchases $51,200; Freight In $2,200; Purchase Returns and Allowances $2,400; and Purchase Discounts $1,300.

Estimate inventory loss using gross profit method. (LO 8) AP

Instructions

Determine the inventory lost by fire, assuming a beginning inventory of $25,000 and a gross profit margin of 40%.

Estimate cost of ending inventory using retail method. (LO 8) AP

*E6–18   Zhang Shoe Store uses the retail inventory method for its two departments: men's shoes and women's shoes. The following information is obtained for each department:

Item	Men's Shoes	Women's Shoes
Beginning inventory at cost	$ 36,000	$ 45,000
Beginning inventory at retail	58,050	95,750
Cost of goods purchased	216,000	315,000
Retail price of goods purchased	348,400	670,200
Net sales	365,000	635,000

Instructions

Calculate the estimated cost of the ending inventory for each shoe department under the retail inventory method.

▶ Problems: Set A

Identify items in inventory. (LO 1) AP

P6–1A   Carberry Company is trying to determine the value of its ending inventory as at February 28, 2017, the company's year end. The accountant counted everything that was in the warehouse as at February 28, which resulted in an ending inventory valuation of $65,000. However, he was not sure how to treat the following transactions, so he did not include them in inventory:

1. Carberry Company shipped $875 of inventory on consignment to Morden Company on February 20. By February 28, Morden Company had sold $365 of this inventory for Carberry.
2. On February 28, Carberry was holding merchandise that had been sold to a customer on February 25 but needed some minor alterations. The customer has paid for the goods and will pick them up on March 3 after the alterations are complete. This inventory cost $490 and was sold for $880.
3. In Carberry's warehouse on February 28 is $400 of inventory that Craft Producers shipped to Carberry on consignment.
4. On February 27, Carberry shipped goods costing $950 to a customer and charged the customer $1,300. The goods were shipped FOB destination and the receiving report indicates that the customer received the goods on March 3.
5. On February 26, Teulon Company shipped goods to Carberry, FOB shipping point. The invoice price was $375 plus $30 for freight. The receiving report indicates that the goods were received by Carberry on March 2.
6. Carberry had $630 of inventory put aside in the warehouse. The inventory is for a customer who has asked that the goods be shipped on March 10.
7. On February 26, Carberry issued a purchase order to acquire goods costing $750. The goods were shipped FOB destination. The receiving report indicates that Carberry received the goods on March 2.
8. On February 26, Carberry shipped goods to a customer, FOB shipping point. The invoice price was $350 plus $25 for freight. The cost of the items was $280. The receiving report indicates that the goods were received by the customer on March 4.

Instructions

(a) For each of the above transactions, specify whether the item should be included in ending inventory, and if so, at what amount. Explain your reasoning.
(b) What is the revised ending inventory valuation?

TAKING IT FURTHER   If the accountant of Carberry Company is paid a bonus based on profit, which of these errors might he consider overlooking and not correcting? Explain.

Apply specific identification. (LO 2) AP

P6–2A   EastPoint Toyota, a small dealership, has provided you with the following information with respect to its vehicle inventory for the month of November. The company uses the specific identification method.

Date	Explanation	Model	Serial #	Unit Cost	Unit Selling Price
Nov. 1	Inventory	Corolla	C63825	$15,000	
		Corolla	C81362	20,000	
		Camry	G62313	26,000	
		Venza	X3892	27,000	
		Tundra	F1883	22,000	
		Tundra	F1921	25,000	
8	Sales	Corolla	C81362		$22,000
		Camry	G62313		28,000

Date	Explanation	Model	Serial #	Unit Cost	Unit Selling Price
Nov. 12	Purchases	Camry	G71811	$27,000	
		Camry	G71891	25,000	
		Venza	X4212	28,000	
		Venza	X4214	31,000	
18	Sales	Camry	G71891		$27,000
		Venza	X3892		31,000
		Tundra	F1921		29,000
23	Purchases	Tundra	F2182	23,000	
		Camry	G72166	30,000	

Instructions

Determine the cost of goods sold and the ending inventory for the month of November.

TAKING IT FURTHER   Should EastPoint Toyota use the specific identification cost determination method or one of the cost formulas? Explain.

P6–3A   You are given the following information for Churchill Company for the month ended November 30, 2017:

Date	Description	Units	Unit Price
Nov. 1	Beginning inventory	60	$50
9	Purchase	100	46
15	Sale	(120)	
22	Purchase	150	44
29	Sale	(160)	
30	Purchase	45	42

Apply perpetual FIFO. Record sales and inventory adjustment, calculate gross profit, and answer questions. (LO 2, 4) AP

Churchill Company uses a perpetual inventory system. All sales and purchases are on account.

Instructions

(a) Calculate the cost of goods sold and the ending inventory using FIFO.

(b) Assume the sales price was $66 per unit for the goods sold on November 15, and $60 per unit for the sale on November 29. Prepare journal entries to record the November 22 purchase and the November 29 sale.

(c) Calculate gross profit for November.

(d) Assume that at the end of November, the company counted its inventory. There are 73 units on hand. What journal entry, if any, should the company make to record the shortage?

(e) If the company had not discovered this shortage, what would be overstated or understated on the balance sheet and income statement and by what amount?

TAKING IT FURTHER   In what respects does FIFO provide more useful information than weighted average?

P6–4A   Information for Churchill Company is presented in P6–3A. Assume the same inventory data and that the company uses a perpetual inventory system. Ignore the inventory shortage in P6–3A part (d).

Apply perpetual weighted average and answer questions. (LO 2, 3) AP

Instructions

(a) Calculate the cost of goods sold and the ending inventory using weighted average. (Round the weighted average cost per unit to two decimal places.)

(b) Prepare the journal entry to record the November 15 sale.

(c) If the company changes from weighted average to FIFO and prices continue to fall, would you expect the cost of goods sold and ending inventory amounts to be higher or lower?

TAKING IT FURTHER   If Churchill Company wishes to change from weighted average to the FIFO cost formula, what factors must it consider before making this change?

P6–5A   Fly-Buy Frisbees sells a wide variety of frisbees and uses a perpetual inventory system. On June 1, Fly-Buy Frisbees had five Fast Flying Frisbees on hand at a unit cost of $105. During June and July, the company had the following purchases and sales for this frisbee (all for cash):

Apply perpetual FIFO and weighted average. Answer question about financial statement effects. (LO 2, 3) AP

	Purchases		Sales	
	Units	Unit Cost	Units	Unit Price
June 4			2	$210
18	5	$115		
30			6	235
July 5	5	120		
12			3	255
25			2	255

Instructions

(a) Determine the cost of goods sold and ending inventory under a perpetual inventory system using (1) FIFO and (2) weighted average. (*Hint:* Round the weighted average cost per unit to two decimal places.)
(b) Calculate gross profit using (1) FIFO and (2) weighted average.

TAKING IT FURTHER What factors should the owner of Fly-Buy Frisbees consider when choosing a cost formula?

Record transactions using perpetual weighted average. Apply LCNRV. (LO 2, 5) AP

P6–6A You are given the following information for Amelia Company. All transactions are settled in cash. Amelia uses a perpetual inventory system and the weighted average cost formula. Increased competition has reduced the price of the product.

Date	Transaction	Units	Unit Price
July 1	Beginning inventory	25	$10
5	Purchase	55	9
8	Sale	(70)	15
15	Purchase	55	8
20	Sale	(55)	12
25	Purchase	10	7

Instructions

(a) Prepare the required journal entries for the month of July for Amelia Company. (Round the weighted average cost per unit to two decimal places.)
(b) Determine the ending inventory for Amelia.
(c) On July 31, Amelia Company learns that the product has a net realizable value of $8 per unit. Prepare the journal entry, if required, to recognize the decrease in value of this product. If no entry is required, explain why.
(d) What amount should the ending inventory be valued at on the July 31 balance sheet? What amount should the cost of goods sold be valued at on the July income statement?

TAKING IT FURTHER What if Amelia had used FIFO instead of weighted average? How would this affect the July 31 ending inventory on the balance sheet compared with weighted average?

Determine effects of inventory errors. (LO 1, 4) AN

P6–7A The records of Alyssa Company show the following amounts in its December 31 financial statements:

	2017	2016	2015
Total assets	$925,000	$900,000	$850,000
Owner's equity	750,000	700,000	650,000
Cost of goods sold	550,000	550,000	500,000
Profit	90,000	80,000	70,000

Alyssa Company made the following errors in determining its ending inventory:

1. The ending inventory account balance at December 31, 2015, included $20,000 of goods held on consignment for Gillies Company.
2. The ending inventory account balance at December 31, 2016, did not include goods sold and shipped on December 30, 2016, FOB destination. The selling price of these goods was $40,000 and the cost of these goods was $32,000. The goods arrived at the destination on January 4, 2017.

All purchases and sales of inventory were recorded in the correct fiscal year.

Instructions

(a) Calculate the correct amount for each of the following for 2017, 2016, and 2015:
   1. Total assets
   2. Owner's equity
   3. Cost of goods sold
   4. Profit
(b) Indicate the effect of these errors (overstated, understated, or no effect) on cash at the end of 2015, 2016, and 2017.

TAKING IT FURTHER As long as the merchandise inventory balance is correct as at December 31, 2017, is it necessary to correct the errors in the previous years' financial statements? Explain.

P6–8A Harrison Company has a July 31 fiscal year end and uses a perpetual inventory system. The records of Harrison Company show the following data:

	2017	2016	2015
Income statement:			
Sales	$350,000	$330,000	$310,000
Cost of goods sold	245,000	235,000	225,000
Operating expenses	76,000	76,000	76,000
Balance sheet:			
Merchandise inventory	55,000	45,000	35,000

Determine effects of inventory errors. Calculate inventory turnover.
(LO 4, 6) AN

After its July 31, 2017, year end, Harrison discovered two errors:

1. At July 31, 2016, Harrison had $10,000 of goods held on consignment at another company that were not included in the physical count.
2. In July 2016, Harrison recorded a $15,000 inventory purchase on account that should have been recorded in August 2016.

Instructions

(a) Prepare corrected income statements for Harrison for the years ended July 31, 2015, 2016, and 2017.
(b) What is the impact of these errors on the owner's equity at July 31, 2017?
(c) Calculate the incorrect and correct inventory turnover ratios for 2016 and 2017.

TAKING IT FURTHER Compare the trends in the incorrectly calculated annual profits with the trends in the correctly calculated annual profits. Does it appear that management may have deliberately made these errors, or do they appear to be honest errors? Explain.

P6–9A Copperhead Company has provided you with the following information regarding its inventory of copper for September and October. Copperhead uses a perpetual inventory system.

Apply LCNRV and prepare adjustment. (LO 5) AP

	September 30	October 31
Copper inventory (in tonnes)	2,500	2,000
Cost per tonne	$505	$535
NRV per tonne	$540	$520

Instructions

(a) Calculate the cost, the net realizable value, and the amount to be reported on the balance sheet for Copperhead's inventory at (1) September 30 and (2) October 31.
(b) Prepare any journal entries required to record the LCNRV of the copper inventory at (1) September 30 and (2) October 31.
(c) Assume that during the month of November the company did not purchase or sell any copper inventory and that the NRV per tonne was $530 on November 30. Is an adjusting entry required at November 30? Explain. If so, prepare the adjusting entry.
(d) What will have to be disclosed in Copperhead's notes to the financial statements with regard to its copper inventory?

TAKING IT FURTHER Do all companies have to report inventory at the LCNRV on the balance sheet?

P6–10A The following financial information (in US$ millions) is for two major corporations for the three years ended December 31:

Calculate ratios. (LO 6) AN

PepsiCo Inc.	2014	2013	2012
Net sales	$66,683	$66,415	$65,492
Cost of sales	30,884	31,243	31,291
Profit	6,558	6,787	6,214
Inventory	3,143	3,409	3,581
Coca-Cola Company			
Net sales	$45,998	$46,854	$48,017
Cost of sales	17,889	18,421	19,053
Profit	7,124	8,626	9,086
Inventory	3,100	3,277	3,264

Instructions

(a) Calculate the inventory turnover, days sales in inventory, and gross profit margin for each company for 2014 and 2013.
(b) Comment on your findings.

TAKING IT FURTHER   Companies are required to disclose in a significant accounting policies note how they determine the cost of their inventory. Both Pepsi and Coca-Cola state that they use weighted average and FIFO. Under what circumstances would it make sense for a company to use both cost formulas?

Apply periodic FIFO and weighted average. (LO 7) AP

*P6–11A   The Baby Store had a beginning inventory on January 1 of 200 full-size strollers at a cost of $110 per unit. During the year, the following purchases were made:

	Units	Unit Cost
Mar. 15	80	$111
July 20	60	110
Sept. 4	25	108
Dec. 2	10	103

At the end of the year, there were 35 units on hand. The Baby Store uses a periodic inventory system.

Instructions

(a) Determine the cost of goods available for sale.
(b) During the year, The Baby Store sold the strollers for $290 per unit. Calculate the number of units sold during the year and total sales revenue.
(c) Determine the cost of the ending inventory and the cost of goods sold using (1) FIFO and (2) weighted average. (Round the weighted average cost per unit to two decimal places.)
(d) Calculate gross profit using (1) FIFO and (2) weighted average.

TAKING IT FURTHER   The owner of The Baby Store would like to minimize profit. Last year, prices were rising and The Baby Store used the weighted average cost formula. This year, the owner would like to use FIFO. Should the company change to FIFO? Explain.

Apply periodic and perpetual FIFO. (LO 2, 7) AP

*P6–12A   Meesha Novelty had a beginning inventory balance on July 1 of 400 units at a cost of $3 each. During the month, the following inventory transactions took place:

Purchases			Sales		
Date	Units	Cost per unit	Date	Units	Price per unit
July 10	1,300	3.10	July 2	300	$6.00
13	700	3.40	11	1,000	6.00
27	600	3.75	28	400	6.50

Instructions

(a) Calculate the cost of goods available for sale and the number of units of ending inventory.
(b) Assume Meesha uses FIFO periodic. Calculate the cost of ending inventory, cost of the goods sold, and gross profit.
(c) Assume Meesha uses FIFO perpetual. Calculate the cost of ending inventory, cost of goods sold, and gross profit.
(d) Prepare journal entries to record the July 10 purchase and the July 11 sale using (1) FIFO periodic and (2) FIFO perpetual. Assume both the sale and purchase were for cash.
(e) Compare the results of parts (b) and (c) above and comment.

TAKING IT FURTHER   Companies are required to disclose their cost determination method, but not the inventory system (periodic or perpetual). Provide an explanation as to why.

Apply periodic and perpetual weighted average. (LO 2, 7) AP

*P6–13A   Aldor Corporation opened a new store on January 1, 2017. During 2017, the first year of operations, the following purchases and sales of inventory were made:

Purchases			Sales		
Date	Units	Cost per unit	Date	Units	Price per unit
Jan. 5	10	$1,000	July 4	15	$2,000
June 11	10	1,200	Dec. 29	35	$2,000
Oct. 18	15	1,300			
Dec. 20	20	1,500			

Instructions

(a) Calculate the cost of goods available for sale and the number of units of ending inventory.
(b) Assume Aldor uses weighted average periodic. Calculate the cost of ending inventory, cost of the goods sold, and gross profit.

(c) Assume Aldor uses weighted average perpetual. Calculate the cost of ending inventory, cost of the goods sold, and gross profit.

(d) Prepare journal entries to record the December 20 purchase and the December 29 sale using (1) weighted average periodic and (2) weighted average perpetual. Assume both the sale and purchase were for cash.

(e) Compare the results of parts (b) and (c) above and comment.

TAKING IT FURTHER   If a company uses the weighted average cost formula, are there any benefits to using weighted average in a perpetual inventory system compared with using weighted average in a periodic inventory system? Explain.

*P6–14A   Westor Company lost all of its inventory in a fire on December 28, 2017. The accounting records showed the following gross profit data for November and December:

Determine inventory loss using gross profit method. (LO 8) AP

	November	December (to Dec. 28)
Sales	$674,000	$965,390
Sales returns and allowances	14,000	26,600
Purchases	441,190	621,660
Purchase returns and allowances	17,550	22,575
Freight in	6,860	12,300
Beginning inventory	34,050	39,405
Ending inventory	39,405	?

Westor is fully insured for fire losses but must prepare a report for the insurance company.

Instructions

Determine the amount of inventory lost by Westor as a result of the fire using the gross profit method.

TAKING IT FURTHER   The insurance adjustor is concerned that this method of calculating the cost of the inventory destroyed might not be accurate. What factors contribute to the accuracy of the ending inventory amount when using the gross profit method?

*P6–15A   Brandon Shoe Store uses the retail inventory method to estimate its monthly ending inventories. The following information is available at November 30, 2017:

Determine ending inventory using retail method. (LO 8) AP

	Women's Shoes		Men's Shoes	
	Cost	Retail	Cost	Retail
Beginning inventory	$ 276,000	$ 424,000	$ 191,000	$ 323,000
Purchases	1,181,000	1,801,000	1,046,000	1,772,000
Purchase returns and allowances	24,600	37,000	21,900	36,400
Freight in	6,000		7,200	
Sales		1,826,000		1,651,000
Sales returns and allowances		28,000		25,000

At November 30, Brandon Shoe Store takes a physical inventory count at retail. The actual retail values of the inventories in each department on November 30, 2017, are as follows: Women's Shoes $381,250, and Men's Shoes $426,100.

Instructions

Determine the estimated cost of the ending inventory at November 30, 2017, using the retail inventory method.

TAKING IT FURTHER   Calculate the store's loss on November 30, 2017, from theft and other causes, at retail and at cost.

▶ Problems: Set B

P6–1B   Morden Company is trying to determine the value of its ending inventory as at February 28, 2017, the company's year end. The accountant counted everything that was in the warehouse as at February 28, which resulted in an ending inventory cost of $56,000. However, she was not sure how to treat the following transactions, so she did not include them in inventory:

Identify items in inventory. (LO 1) AP

1. On February 20, Morden Company had received $875 of inventory on consignment from Carberry Company. By February 28, Morden Company had sold $365 of this inventory for Carberry Company.

2. On February 25, Morden ordered goods costing $750. The goods were shipped FOB shipping point on February 27. The receiving report indicates that Morden received the goods on March 1.
3. On February 26, Morden shipped goods costing $800 to a customer. The goods were shipped FOB shipping point. The receiving report indicates that the customer received the goods on March 1.
4. On February 27, Stony Mountain Company shipped goods to Morden, FOB destination. The invoice price was $350 plus $25 for freight. The receiving report indicates that the goods were received by Morden on March 2.
5. On February 28, Morden packaged goods and moved them to the shipping department for shipping to a customer, FOB destination. The invoice price was $425 plus $20 for freight. The cost of the items was $360. The receiving report indicates that the goods were received by the customer on March 2.
6. Morden had damaged goods set aside in the warehouse because they were not saleable. These goods originally cost $400. Morden had expected to sell these items for $600 before they were damaged.
7. On February 28, Morden was holding merchandise that had been sold to a customer on February 25. The customer has paid for the goods and will pick them up on March 3. This inventory cost $940 and was sold for $1,340.
8. Morden had $620 of inventory at a customer's warehouse "on approval." The customer was going to let Morden know whether it wanted the merchandise by the end of the week, March 7.

Instructions

(a) For each of the above transactions, specify whether the item in question should be included in ending inventory, and if so, at what amount. Explain your reasoning.
(b) What is the revised ending inventory cost?

TAKING IT FURTHER If the owner of Morden Company wants to minimize the amount of income taxes he or she will have to pay, what errors might the owner tell the accountant not to correct? Explain.

Apply specific identification. (LO 2) AP

P6–2B EastPoint Honda, a small dealership, has provided you with the following information with respect to its vehicle inventory for the month of July. The company uses the specific identification method.

Date	Explanation	Model	Serial #	Unit Cost	Unit Selling Price
July 1	Inventory	Fit	YH6318	$26,500	
		Civic	SZ5824	26,700	
		Civic	SZ5828	26,600	
		Accord	ST0815	26,200	
		Accord	ST8411	27,600	
		Accord	ST0944	27,200	
10	Sales	Civic	SZ5828		$29,800
12	Purchases	Fit	YH4418	26,300	
		Fit	YH5632	26,600	
13	Sales	Fit	YH4418		28,900
		Accord	ST0944		28,700
		Civic	SZ5824		29,850
25	Purchases	Civic	SZ6132	26,800	
		Civic	SZ6148	26,600	
27	Sales	Civic	SZ6132		28,800
		Accord	ST0815		27,000
		Fit	YH6318		29,500

Instructions

Determine the cost of goods sold and the ending inventory for the month of July.

TAKING IT FURTHER Should EastPoint Honda use the specific identification cost determination method or one of the cost formulas? Explain.

Apply perpetual weighted average. Record sales and inventory adjustment, calculate gross profit, and answer questions. (LO 2) AP

P6–3B You are given the following information for Swan Valley Company for the month ended June 30, 2017:

Date	Description	Units	Unit Price
June 1	Beginning inventory	20	$50
4	Purchase	85	55
10	Sale	(90)	
18	Purchase	35	58
25	Sale	(30)	
28	Purchase	15	60

Swan Valley Company uses a perpetual inventory system. All sales and purchases are on account.

Instructions

(a) Calculate the cost of goods sold and the ending inventory using weighted average. (Round the weighted average cost per unit to two decimal places.)

(b) Assume the sales price was $90 per unit for the goods sold on June 10, and $95 per unit for the sale on June 25. Prepare journal entries to record the June 10 sale and the June 18 purchase.

(c) At the end of June, the company counted its inventory. There were 32 units on hand. What journal entry, if any, should the company make to record the difference?

(d) If the company had not discovered this shortage, what would be overstated or understated on the balance sheet and income statement and by what amount?

TAKING IT FURTHER   In what respects does weighted average provide more useful information than FIFO?

P6–4B   Information for Swan Valley Company is presented in P6–3B. Assume the same inventory data and that the company uses a perpetual inventory system. Ignore the inventory difference from P6–3B part (c). | *Apply perpetual FIFO and answer questions.* *(LO 2, 3) AP*

Instructions

(a) Calculate the cost of goods sold and the ending inventory at June 30 using FIFO.

(b) Prepare the journal entries to record the June 25 sale.

(c) If the company changes from FIFO to weighted average and prices continue to rise, would you expect the cost of goods sold and ending inventory amounts to be higher or lower than these amounts?

TAKING IT FURTHER   If Swan Valley Company wishes to change from FIFO to the weighted average cost formula, what factors must it consider before making this change?

P6–5B   Bennett Basketball sells a variety of basketballs and accessories. Information follows for Bennett Basketball's purchases and sales during February and March for Up-Snap, one of its top brands of basketballs: | *Apply perpetual FIFO and weighted average. Answer question about financial statement effects.* *(LO 2, 3) AP*

	Purchases		Sales	
	Units	Unit Cost	Units	Unit Price
Feb. 7			18	$32
23	50	$20		
26			50	30
Mar. 10	24	19		
23			32	29

Bennett uses a perpetual inventory system. On February 1, Bennett had 36 units on hand at a cost of $21 each. All purchases and sales during February and March were on account.

Instructions

(a) Determine the cost of goods sold and ending inventory under a perpetual inventory system using (1) FIFO and (2) weighted average. (Round the weighted average cost per unit to two decimal places.)

(b) Calculate gross profit using (1) FIFO and (2) weighted average.

TAKING IT FURTHER   What factors should Bennett's owner consider when choosing a cost formula?

P6–6B   You are given the following information for transactions by Schwinghamer Co. All transactions are settled in cash. Schwinghamer uses a perpetual inventory system and the FIFO cost formula. | *Record transactions using perpetual FIFO. Apply LCNRV. (LO 2, 5) AP*

Date	Transaction	Units	Unit Cost/ Selling Price
Oct. 1	Beginning inventory	60	$14
5	Purchase	110	13
8	Sale	(140)	20
15	Purchase	52	12
20	Sale	(70)	16
25	Purchase	15	11

Instructions

(a) Prepare the required journal entries for the month of October for Schwinghamer Co.

(b) Determine the ending inventory for Schwinghamer.

(c) On October 31, Schwinghamer determines that the product has a net realizable value of $10 per unit. What amount should the inventory be valued at on the October 31 balance sheet? Prepare any required journal entries.

(d) Considering your answer from part (c), what amount will be reported on the October income statement for cost of goods sold?

TAKING IT FURTHER   What if Schwinghamer had used weighted average instead of FIFO? How would this affect the October 31 ending inventory on the balance sheet compared with FIFO?

Determine effects of inventory errors.
(LO 1, 4) AN

P6–7B   The records of Khanna Company show the following amounts in its December 31 financial statements:

	2017	2016	2015
Total assets	$600,000	$575,000	$525,000
Owner's equity	280,000	275,000	250,000
Cost of goods sold	315,000	335,000	300,000
Profit	60,000	50,000	40,000

Khanna made the following errors in determining its ending inventory:

1. The ending inventory account balance at December 31, 2015, included $20,000 of goods held on consignment for Leblanc Company.
2. The ending inventory account balance at December 31, 2016, did not include goods that were purchased for $30,000 and shipped on December 30, 2016, FOB shipping point.

All purchases and sales of inventory were correctly recorded each year.

Instructions

(a) Calculate the correct amount for each of the following for 2015, 2016, and 2017:
   1. Total assets
   2. Owner's equity
   3. Cost of goods sold
   4. Profit
(b) Indicate the effect of these errors (overstated, understated, or no effect) on cash at the end of 2015, 2016, and 2017.

TAKING IT FURTHER   If the merchandise inventory balance is correct as at December 31, 2017, is it necessary to correct the errors in the previous years' financial statements? Explain.

Determine effects of inventory errors. Calculate inventory turnover.
(LO 4, 6) AN

P6–8B   The records of James Company show the following data:

	2017	2016	2015
Income statement:			
Sales	$648,000	$624,000	$600,000
Cost of goods sold	540,000	510,000	480,000
Operating expenses	100,000	100,000	100,000
Balance sheet:			
Merchandise inventory	40,000	60,000	70,000

After its July 31, 2017, year end, James Company discovered two errors:

1. In August 2015, James recorded a $30,000 inventory purchase on account for goods that had been received in July 2015. The physical inventory account correctly included this inventory, and $70,000 is the correct amount of inventory at July 31, 2015.
2. Ending inventory in 2016 was overstated by $20,000. James included goods held on consignment for another company in its physical count.

Instructions

(a) Prepare incorrect and corrected income statements for the years ended July 31, 2015, 2016, and 2017.
(b) What is the combined effect of the errors on owner's equity at July 31, 2017, before correction?
(c) Calculate the incorrect and correct inventory turnover ratios for each of the years 2016 and 2017.

TAKING IT FURTHER   Compare the trends in the incorrectly calculated annual profits with the trends in the correctly calculated annual profits. Does it appear that management may have deliberately made these errors, or do they appear to be honest errors? Explain.

P6–9B   Vasquez Paper Company has provided you with the following information regarding its inventory of paper for June and July. Vasquez uses a perpetual inventory system.

Apply LCNRV and prepare adjustment. (LO 5) AP

	June 30	July 31
Paper inventory (in tonnes)	4,500	6,200
Cost per tonne	$560	$680
NRV per tonne	$650	$615

Instructions

(a) Calculate the cost, the net realizable value, and the amount to be reported on the balance sheet for Vasquez Paper Company's inventory at (1) June 30 and (2) July 31.

(b) Prepare any journal entries required to record the LCNRV of the paper inventory at (1) June 30 and (2) July 31.

(c) Assume that during the month of August, the company did not purchase any additional paper inventory. Assume also that on August 31 it had 5,000 tonnes in inventory and the NRV per tonne was $720. Is an adjusting entry required at August 31? Explain. If so, prepare the adjusting entry.

(d) What is Vasquez Paper Company required to disclose in its notes to the financial statements with regard to LCNRV?

TAKING IT FURTHER   Why is it important to report inventory at the LCNRV on the balance sheet?

P6–10B   The following financial information (in US$ millions) is for two major corporations for the three fiscal years ending as follows:

Calculate ratios. (LO 6) AN

Home Depot, Inc.	February 1, 2015	February 2, 2014	February 3, 2013
Net sales	$83,176	$78,812	$74,754
Cost of sales	54,222	51,422	48,912
Profit	6,345	5,385	4,535
Inventory	11,079	11,057	10,710

Lowe's Companies, Inc.	January 30, 2015	January 31, 2014	February 1, 2013
Net sales	$56,223	$53,417	$50,521
Cost of sales	36,665	34,941	33,194
Profit	2,698	2,286	1,959
Inventory	8,911	9,127	8,600

Instructions

(a) Calculate the inventory turnover, days sales in inventory, and gross profit margin, for each company for fiscal 2015 and 2014.

(b) Comment on your findings.

TAKING IT FURTHER   Home Depot reports that approximately 74% of its inventory is valued under the retail inventory method (inventory estimation method) and the remainder is valued at cost. Lowe's reports that all of its inventory is valued at cost. Does the use of the retail inventory method affect the comparison between companies? Explain.

*P6–11B   On January 1, The Big Kids Store had a beginning inventory of 150 units of the RC Spitfire-MK IIB model airplane at a cost of $65 per unit. During the year, purchases were as follows:

Apply periodic FIFO and weighted average. (LO 7) AP

	Units	Unit Cost
Feb. 17	70	$65
Apr. 12	40	66
July 10	30	68
Oct. 26	25	70

The Big Kids Store uses a periodic inventory system. At the end of the year, there were 20 units on hand.

Instructions

(a) Determine the cost of goods available for sale.

(b) During the year, The Big Kids Store sold the RC Spitfire for $135 per unit. Calculate the number of units sold during the year and total sales revenue.

(c) Determine the ending inventory and the cost of goods sold using (1) FIFO and (2) weighted average.

(d) Calculate gross profit using FIFO and weighted average.

TAKING IT FURTHER   The owner of The Big Kids Store would like to minimize profit. Last year, prices were falling and The Big Kids Store used FIFO. This year she would like to switch to weighted average. Do you recommend this change or not? Explain.

Apply periodic and perpetual weighted average.
(LO 2, 7) AP

*P6–12B   You are given the following information about Sasha Company's inventory for the month of April.

Purchases			Sales		
Date	Units	Cost per unit	Date	Units	Price per unit
April 1	400	$4.00	April 2	300	$7.00
10	1,300	4.10	11	1,000	7.00
25	1,200	4.50	29	1,400	7.50
27	600	4.75			

Instructions

(a) Calculate the cost of goods available for sale and the number of units of ending inventory.

(b) Assume Sasha uses weighted average periodic. Calculate the cost of ending inventory, cost of goods sold, and gross profit. (*Note:* Round the weighted average cost per unit to two decimal places.)

(c) Assume Sasha uses weighted average perpetual. Calculate the cost of ending inventory, cost of goods sold, and gross profit. (*Note:* Round the weighted average cost per unit to two decimal places.)

(d) Prepare journal entries to record the April 25 purchase and the April 29 sale using (1) weighted average periodic and (2) weighted average perpetual.

(e) Compare the results of parts (b) and (c) above and comment.

TAKING IT FURTHER   Companies are required to disclose their cost determination method, but not the inventory system (periodic or perpetual). Provide an explanation as to why.

Apply periodic and perpetual FIFO. (LO 2, 7) AP

*P6–13B   Una Company opened a new store in February this year. During the first year of operations, the company made the following purchases and sales:

Purchases			Sales		
Date	Units	Cost	Date	Units	Price
Feb. 7	20	$100	Apr. 30	35	$120
Apr. 12	20	$120	Nov. 12	50	$160
July 18	25	$130			
Oct. 26	40	$150			

Instructions

(a) Calculate the cost of goods available for sale and the number of units of ending inventory.

(b) Assume Una uses FIFO periodic. Calculate the cost of ending inventory, cost of goods sold, and gross profit.

(c) Assume Una uses FIFO perpetual. Calculate the cost of ending inventory, cost of goods sold, and gross profit.

(d) Prepare journal entries to record the April 12 purchase and the April 30 sale using (1) FIFO periodic and (2) FIFO perpetual. Assume all transactions were on account.

(e) Compare the results of parts (b) and (c) above and comment.

TAKING IT FURTHER   If a company uses the FIFO cost formula, are there any benefits to using FIFO in a perpetual inventory system compared with using FIFO in a periodic inventory system? Explain.

Determine inventory loss using gross profit method.
(LO 8) AP

*P6–14B   Merrett Company lost 80% of its inventory in a fire on March 23, 2017. The accounting records showed the following gross profit data for February and March:

	February	March (to Mar. 23)
Sales	$310,000	$293,500
Sales returns and allowances	7,000	6,800
Purchases	204,000	197,000
Purchase returns and allowances	5,300	4,940
Freight in	4,000	3,940
Beginning inventory	18,500	26,200
Ending inventory	26,200	?

Merrett is fully insured for fire losses but must prepare a report for the insurance company.

Instructions

Determine the amount of inventory lost by Merrett as a result of the fire using the gross profit method.

TAKING IT FURTHER   The insurance adjustor is concerned that this method of calculating the cost of the inventory destroyed might not be accurate. What factors contribute to the accuracy of the ending inventory amount when using the gross profit method?

*P6–15B   Hakim's Department Store uses the retail inventory method to estimate its monthly ending inventories. The following information is available for two of its departments at August 31, 2017:

	Clothing		Jewellery	
	Cost	Retail	Cost	Retail
Sales		$1,300,000		$850,000
Sales returns and allowances		32,000		10,400
Purchases	$775,000	1,445,000	$565,000	923,000
Purchase returns and allowances	41,000	71,500	17,200	25,700
Freight in	8,900		6,700	
Beginning inventory	55,600	98,000	34,000	54,000

On August 31, Hakim's Department Store takes a physical inventory count at retail. The actual retail values of the inventories in each department on August 31, 2017, are as follows: Clothing $100,750, and Jewellery $40,300.

Instructions

Determine the estimated cost of the ending inventory for each department on August 31, 2017, using the retail inventory method.

TAKING IT FURTHER   Calculate the store's loss on August 31, 2017, from theft and other causes, at retail and at cost.

Determine ending inventory using retail method.
(LO 8) AP

CHAPTER 6: BROADENING YOUR PERSPECTIVE

▶ Financial Reporting and Analysis

Financial Reporting Problem

BYP6–1   Refer to the financial statements and notes to consolidated financial statements for **Hudson's Bay Company**, whose partial financial information is presented in Illustrations 6-14 to 6-16.

Instructions

(a) How does Hudson's Bay Company value its inventory?
(b) Which inventory cost formula does Hudson's Bay Company use?
(c) Would using the specific identification cost determination method be appropriate for an organization like Hudson's Bay Company? Explain.
(d) For 2015 and 2014, calculate Hudson's Bay Company's inventory as a percentage of current assets and its cost of sales as a percentage of total revenue. Comment on the results.
(e) Hudson's Bay Company's inventory turnover and days sales in inventory were calculated for 2015 in this chapter in Illustrations 6-17 and 6-18, respectively. Calculate these same two ratios for 2014. The balance in inventory on February 2, 2013, was $994. Comment on whether Hudson's Bay Company's management of its inventory improved or weakened in 2015.

Interpreting Financial Statements

BYP6–2   Headquartered in Toronto, **Indigo Books & Music Inc.** is Canada's largest book retailer and the third largest in North America. The following information was taken from the management discussion and analysis section of the company's March 28, 2015, annual report (in thousands):

	2015	2014	2013
Cost of sales (cost of goods sold)	$503,059	$493,955	$495,099
Inventories	$208,395	$218,979	$216,533

Additional information from the company's annual report:

1. Inventories are valued at the lower of cost, determined using a moving weighted average cost formula, and market, being net realizable value. Under weighted average, inventory is recorded at the level of the individual article (stock-keeping unit or SKU).
2. Costs include all direct and reasonable expenditures that are incurred in bringing inventories to their present location and condition. Vendor rebates are recorded as a reduction in the price of the products and corresponding inventory is recorded net of vendor rebates.
3. The weighted average cost of an article is continually updated based on the cost of each purchase recorded in inventory. When the company permanently reduces the retail price of an item,

there is a corresponding reduction in inventory recognized in the period if the markdown incurred brings the retail price below the cost of the item.

4. The amount of inventory writedowns as a result of net realizable value lower than cost was $9.4 million in 2015 ($8.6 million in fiscal 2014), and there were no reversals of inventory writedowns that were recognized in 2015 or 2014. The amount of inventory at March 28, 2015 with net realizable value equal to cost was $1.8 million ($1.8 million at March 30, 2014).

Instructions

(a) Calculate the company's inventory turnover and days sales in inventory ratios for 2015 and 2014. Comment on whether Indigo's management of its inventory improved or weakened in fiscal 2015.

(b) Does Indigo follow the lower of cost and net realizable value rule? Did the application of this rule have any effect on 2015 results? Explain.

(c) Indigo uses the moving weighted average cost formula to account for its inventories. A major competitor, **Amazon.com, Inc.**, uses the FIFO cost formula to account for its inventories. What difficulties would this create in comparing Indigo's financial results with those of Amazon.com? Explain.

● Critical Thinking

Collaborative Learning Activity

Note to instructor: Additional instructions and material for this group activity can be found on the Instructor Resource Site and in *WileyPLUS*.

BYP6–3 In this group activity, you will work in two different groups to improve your understanding of inventory cost determination methods using a perpetual inventory system. First, you will work in an "expert" group in which you will ensure that each group member thoroughly understands one of the inventory cost determination methods. Then you will pair up with a member from the other group and take turns teaching your inventory cost determination methods to each other.

Communication Activity

BYP6–4 You are the controller of Small Toys Inc. Mutahir Kazmi, the president, recently mentioned to you that he found an error in the 2016 financial statements that he believes has now corrected itself. In discussions with the purchasing department, Mutahir determined that the 2016 ending inventory was understated by $1 million. However, the 2017 ending inventory is correct. Mutahir assumes that 2017 profit is correct and comments to you, "What happened has happened—there's no point in worrying about it now."

Instructions

You conclude that Mutahir is wrong. Write a brief, tactful e-mail to him that clarifies the situation.

"All About You" Activity

BYP6–5 In the "All About You" feature, you read about consignment shops and how they provide an alternative to paying full price for quality goods. As a student living on a tight budget, you have decided to sell some of your textbooks after you have finished the courses. You are considering two options: selling the textbooks yourself or taking them to the second-hand bookstore that sells used textbooks on consignment.

Instructions

(a) What is selling on consignment? If you sell your books on consignment, will you be the consignor or the consignee?

(b) What are the advantages and disadvantages of selling your textbooks on consignment?

(c) It is suggested that there should be a written agreement between the consignor and consignee. If you decide to sell your textbooks on consignment, what should be agreed to in writing?

(d) Assume you decide to sell your books on consignment through a second-hand bookstore. What are the risks to you of doing this?

(e) Should you keep your accounting textbook forever?

Santé Smoothie Saga

(**Note:** This is a continuation of the Santé Smoothie Saga from Chapters 1 through 5.)

BYP6–6 Natalie is busy establishing both divisions of her business (smoothie making and juicer sales) and completing her business diploma. Her goals for the next 11 months are to sell one juicer per month and to sell smoothies at two to three studios per week.

The cost of the fine European juicers is expected to increase. Natalie has just negotiated new terms with Kzinski that include shipping costs in the negotiated purchase price. (Juicers will be shipped FOB destination.)

Recall that Natalie has two juicers in inventory: juicer #1 (serial number 12459) and juicer #2 (serial number 23568). Inventory cost for each of these units is $545.

The following juicer purchase and sale transactions occur in July and August 2017:

July	3	Natalie orders three juicers on account from Kzinski Supply Co. for $1,650 ($550 each), FOB destination, terms n/30.
	14	Natalie receives juicer #3 (serial number 49295), juicer #4 (serial number 56204), and juicer #5 (serial number 62897).
	19	Natalie sells one deluxe juicer, juicer #4, for $1,050 cash.
Aug.	3	Natalie orders two deluxe juicers on account from Kzinski Supply Co. for $1,142, FOB destination, terms n/30.
	17	Natalie receives juicer #6 (serial number 69896) and juicer #7 (serial number 72531).
	18	Natalie returns juicer #6. It is not the one ordered.
	27	Natalie sells two deluxe juicers, juicer #2 and juicer #5, for a total of $2,100 cash.

All of the juicers Natalie has purchased and sold are identical. Natalie has accounted for all of these transactions by juicer number to ensure that she does not lose track of juicers on hand and juicers that have been sold. Natalie wonders if she is accounting for the costs of these juicers correctly.

Instructions

(a) Answer Natalie's concerns. Is Natalie accounting for these transactions correctly? Why or why not? What are the alternatives that Natalie could use in accounting for her juicer inventory?

(b) Given that Natalie has accounted for all of these transactions by juicer number, what is the total cost of goods sold for July and August, and the inventory balance at the end of August in Santé Smoothies' accounting records?

(c) Using the moving weighted average cost formula in a perpetual inventory system, prepare a record to track the purchases and sales of juicers, and the balance in the juicers inventory account. Use the format from Illustration 6-6.

(d) Prepare a journal entry to correct the August 31 inventory balance from the amount calculated in part (b) to the amount

determined in part (c) assuming Natalie decided to use the weighted average cost formula in a perpetual inventory system (instead of recording cost by specific juicer).

(e) Assume instead that Natalie had used the weighted average cost formula to record all of the July and August transactions. Using the information prepared in part (c) above, prepare the journal entries that would be required had Natalie used this cost formula.

ANSWERS TO CHAPTER QUESTIONS

ANSWERS TO ACCOUNTING IN ACTION INSIGHT QUESTIONS

All About You Insight, p. 304

Q: What is one disadvantage of buying items on consignment?

A: Consignment stores do not typically allow you to return goods, so you need to be very careful when purchasing items.

Business Insight, p. 309

Q: Retailers used to count inventory once a year for financial reporting purposes. What is the advantage of moving to a periodic inventory system that goes beyond accounting?

A: Retailers that move to a periodic inventory system thanks to technology such as RFID tags and bar-code scanners know in real time how much inventory they have. This means they can more easily reorder items to avoid stockouts and lost sales and unhappy customers.

Ethics Insight, p. 319

Q: Is it unethical to use the specific identification method in this situation?

A: The investor is correct, the company could maximize gross profit by selecting the lowest-cost inventory to sell in a particular

month or conversely it could minimize gross profit by selecting the highest-cost inventory to sell during the course of a month.

Specific identification is not an appropriate method for this type of business, because all of the diamonds are interchangeable. Choosing which diamonds to sell in a month is unethical because it enables the company to manipulate its profit. A more appropriate method to use would be the weighted average cost formula. This method will result in reasonable values for both the income statement and balance sheet and is less susceptible to income manipulation.

Business Insight, p. 322

Q: What are the arguments for and against the use of LIFO?

A: Proponents of LIFO argue that it is conceptually superior because it matches the most recent cost with the most recent selling price. Critics contend that it artificially understates the company's net income and consequently reduces tax payments. Also, because most foreign companies are not allowed to use LIFO, its use by U.S. companies reduces the ability of investors to compare U.S. companies with foreign companies.

ANSWERS TO SELF-STUDY QUESTIONS

1. a   2. b   3. b   4. d   5. a   6. a   7. a   8. b   9. b   *10. d   *11. c   *12. a   *13. a

7 INTERNAL CONTROL AND CASH

CHAPTER PREVIEW ▸ As the feature story about Beanz Espresso Bar shows, control of cash is important. Business owners and managers are responsible for safeguarding cash and other assets and for making sure that financial information is reliable. In this chapter, we explain the important features of an internal control system and how it helps to prevent fraud and errors. We also describe how internal controls apply to cash. Then we describe the use of a bank account and explain how cash is reported on the balance sheet.

FEATURE STORY ▸

KEEPING TRACK OF THE CASH

CHARLOTTETOWN, P.E.I.—Located right in the heart of downtown Charlottetown, Beanz Espresso Bar is bustling with activity on weekdays. Scores of customers stop by each day for its selection of specialty coffees, homemade soups, sandwiches, and baked goods.

Lunch is the busiest time for Beanz. The two cash registers are shared by the six staff members working behind the counter on any given shift. "In an ideal situation, one or two people would be designated to ring in orders, but when we get swamped, we all have to work together to keep things running smoothly," says owner Lori Kays, who launched the business back in 1995.

The prices of most items are preprogrammed in the machines, which reduces the chances of entry errors. Each register generates a sales report at the end of the day. Ms. Kays checks the day's cash receipts against the report to make sure they match. She also verifies the closing balances for the two floats—$250 for each till. "I tend to allow a few dollars' leeway since we round down amounts here and there when customers are short a few cents."

If the difference is larger, she goes through the register's internal tape to trace the source. "I will backtrack and try to make sure there weren't any payouts for which a receipt should have been turned in—we often make a run to the grocery store for something we need using cash from the till," she explains. For these petty cash items, staff use the Paid Out button on the till and have a receipt/invoice to match the payout. She prefers to keep track of these small purchases with the till than to have a petty cash box, which would be "just another thing that someone has to check every day to make sure it balances out," she says.

Ms. Kays deposits cash from sales in the bank at the end of the day. She does all of her bookkeeping herself using Simply Accounting software. "I post my sales totals each day and reconcile everything with my bank statements once a month," she says. "At the end of every year, I do everything except the last few adjusting entries before sending things off to the accountants." Careful cash control throughout the year helps ensure that everything adds up every time!

© Heather Taweel/The Guardian

CHAPTER OUTLINE   LEARNING OBJECTIVES

1 Define cash and internal control.

Cash and Internal Control
- What is cash?
- Internal control
- Control activities
- Limitations of internal control

DO IT 1
Control activities

2 Apply control activities to cash receipts and cash payments.

Cash Controls
- Internal control over cash receipts
- Internal control over cash payments

DO IT 2
Recording cash receipts and cash payments

3 Describe the operation of a petty cash fund.

Petty Cash Fund
- Establishing the fund
- Making payments from the fund
- Replenishing the fund

DO IT 3
Petty cash fund

4 Describe the control features of a bank account and prepare a bank reconciliation.

Bank Accounts
- Use of a bank account
- Reconciling the bank account

DO IT 4
Bank reconciliation

5 Report cash on the balance sheet.

Reporting Cash

DO IT 5
Balance sheet reporting

LEARNING OBJECTIVE ❶ ▸ Define cash and internal control.

Cash and Internal Control

In the following sections of this chapter, we define cash, and explain internal control features. Internal controls are important for all companies, including businesses such as Beanz Espresso Bar described in the feature story, to prevent one of the biggest risks associated with cash, fraud.

WHAT IS CASH?

Cash is generally an asset in high demand, but what is cash? Most of us think of coins and paper bills when we hear the word "cash." However, from an accounting perspective, **cash** consists of coins, currency (paper money), cheques, money orders, travellers' cheques, and money on deposit in a bank or similar depository. Cash does not include cheques that are postdated (payable in the future), stale-dated (more than six months old), or returned (NSF—not sufficient funds).

Many companies also combine cash with cash equivalents. **Cash equivalents** are short-term, highly liquid (easily sold) investments that are not subject to significant risk of changes in value, such as term deposits, treasury bills, and guaranteed investment certificates (GICs). To be considered a cash equivalent, an investment typically has a maturity of three months or less from the date it is purchased.

Risks Associated with Cash

Besides being highly desirable, cash is easily concealed and transported, and lacks ownership. It is also the one asset that is readily convertible into any other type of asset. These features, as well as the large volume of cash transactions, mean fraud and errors may easily happen when handling and recording cash. Therefore, safeguarding cash and ensuring the accuracy of the accounting records are critical. This safeguarding is done through internal controls.

Fraud refers to a crime where dishonest schemes are used to take something of value. The three main factors that contribute to fraud are shown by the **fraud triangle** depicted here:

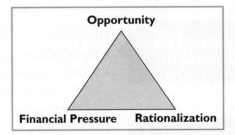

The most important element that makes up the fraud triangle is opportunity. For an employee to commit fraud, there must be an opportunity to do so in the workplace. Opportunities occur when the workplace lacks sufficient controls to deter and detect fraud. For example, employees may be more likely to commit a fraud if they are not properly monitored and think they will not be caught.

A second factor that contributes to fraud is financial pressure. Employees sometimes commit fraud because of personal financial problems such as too much debt. Excessive lifestyles and drug or gambling addictions may also increase the likelihood that an employee will commit fraud.

The third factor that contributes to fraud is rationalization. In order to justify their fraud, employees rationalize their dishonest actions. For example, employees may believe they are underpaid and deserve to be paid more.

INTERNAL CONTROL

In order to minimize the risk of fraud and error, most companies implement some level of internal control. **Internal controls** consist of all of the related methods and measures that management designs and implements to help an organization achieve the following:

1. reliable financial reporting,
2. effective and efficient operations, and
3. compliance with relevant laws and regulations.

Internal control has received increased attention in recent years. For example, the Sarbanes-Oxley Act governing publicly traded companies was created in the United States to help restore confidence in financial reporting after a series of high-profile fraud cases, including the downfall of large corporations such as Enron and WorldCom. In Canada, similar legislation requires senior executives, such as chief financial officers and chief executive officers, of publicly traded companies to formally certify the effectiveness of their company's internal controls.

Helpful hint Errors are unintentional mistakes. Irregularities are intentional mistakes and misrepresentations.

CONTROL ACTIVITIES

While there are various aspects to internal control, we will focus here on control activities. The reason? These activities are the backbone of the company's efforts to address the risks it faces, such as fraud. The specific control activities used by a company will vary, depending on management's assessment of the risks faced. This assessment is heavily influenced by the size and nature of the company.

Control activities are the policies and procedures that address the specific risks faced by a company. Control activities include:

- establishment of responsibility,
- segregation of duties,
- documentation procedures,
- physical and IT controls,
- independent checks of performance, and
- human resource controls.

Each of these control activities is explained in the following sections.

Establishment of Responsibility

An essential characteristic of internal control is assigning responsibility to specific individuals. **Control is most effective when only one person is responsible for a task**.

To illustrate, assume that the cash in the cash register at the end of the day at Beanz Espresso Bar in the feature story is $50 less than it should be according to the cash register tape. If only one person at the restaurant has operated the register, that person is probably responsible for the shortage. If two or more individuals have worked the register, however, as happens at Beanz Espresso Bar when the restaurant is busy, it may be impossible to determine who is responsible for the error.

Establishing responsibility is easier when there is a system for proper authorization of an activity. For example, computerized systems often require a passcode that keeps track of who rang up a sale, or who made a journal entry, or who entered an inventory stockroom at a particular time. Using identifying passcodes enables the company to establish responsibility by identifying the particular employee who carried out the activity.

Segregation of Duties

Segregation of duties is essential in a system of internal control. Duties should be divided up so that one person cannot both commit a fraud and cover it up.

There are two common ways of applying this control activity:

1. Different individuals should be responsible for related activities.
2. The responsibility for accounting or record keeping for an asset should be separate from the responsibility for physical custody of that asset.

The rationale for segregation of duties is this: the work of one employee should, without a duplication of effort, provide a reasonable basis for evaluating the work of another employee.

Segregation of Related Activities. **When one person is responsible for all related activities, the potential for errors and irregularities increases.** As a general rule, the duties of custody, authorization, and recording should be performed by different people.

For example, related sales activities should be done by different individuals. Related selling activities include making a sale, shipping (or delivering) the goods to the customer, billing the customer, and receiving payment. Various frauds are possible when one person handles related sales transactions, as the following examples show.

- If a salesperson can make a sale without obtaining supervisory approval, he or she can make sales at unauthorized prices to increase sales commissions.
- A billing clerk who handles billing and receipt could understate the amount that is billed in sales to friends and relatives.
- A shipping clerk who has access to the accounting records could ship goods to himself.

These abuses are less likely to occur when companies divide the sales tasks: salespersons make the sale, shipping department employees ship the goods based on the sales order, and billing department employees prepare the sales invoice after comparing the sales order with the report of goods shipped.

Segregation of selling duties in a small business can be difficult, because there are fewer people. In these situations, the owner must be more involved to reduce the risk of fraud.

Anatomy of a Fraud

Marie Francis worked as an accounting manager for a large logistics company. One of Marie's responsibilities was to set up new suppliers in the accounts payable system. She also had the authority to approve invoices. Marie created several fictitious companies, created fake suppliers in the accounts payable system, and approved several bogus invoices. Marie cashed the cheques issued for the phony invoices and pocketed the cash.

The Missing Control

Segregation of related activities: The logistics company did not segregate the responsibility for creating suppliers and approving invoices. This allowed Marie to set up fictitious suppliers and approve bogus invoices to commit fraud.

Segregation of Record Keeping from Physical Custody. If the same person has physical custody (the custodian) of an asset and keeps the accounting records for that asset, then errors or theft could be hidden by changing the accounting records. When the employee who keeps the records of an asset is a different person from the employee who keeps the asset itself, the employee who keeps the asset is unlikely to use it dishonestly. The separation of accounting responsibility from the custody of assets is especially important for cash and inventories because these assets are vulnerable to unauthorized use or theft.

Documentation Procedures

Documents give evidence that transactions and events have happened. At Beanz Espresso Bar, the cash register sales report is the restaurant's documentation for a sale and the amount of cash received. Similarly, a shipping document indicates that goods have been shipped, and a sales invoice indicates that the customer has been billed for the goods. By adding signatures (or initials) to a document, it also becomes possible to identify the individual(s) responsible for the transaction or event.

Procedures should be established for documents. First, whenever possible, **documents should be pre-numbered and all documents should be accounted for**. Pre-numbering helps to prevent a transaction from being recorded more than once, or not at all. Second, only original documents (such as original receipts) for accounting entries should be promptly sent to the accounting department to help the transaction be recorded in a timely way. Photocopies of documents should not be used to reduce the likelihood of making duplicate payments for invoices already paid.

Anatomy of a Fraud

For more than 13 years, François Martin was the sole clerk in charge of a sales program that sold liquor to accredited diplomats at a discount. He ran the program based on an honour system. Sales and cash receipts were handwritten in a notebook. Mr. Martin often accepted payments for legitimate sales and then deleted the sales records and pocketed the cash receipts. When the fraud was investigated, it was found that he had defrauded the liquor control board of more than $2 million.

The Missing Control

Documentation procedures: There were no formal documentation procedures for the sales program. If there had been a requirement that sales be recorded on pre-numbered sequential invoices, the deletion of sales and the related cash receipts would have been detected.

Documentation as a control procedure also includes ensuring that all controls are written down and kept updated. Well-maintained documentation procedures ensure that the control activities are not forgotten and can make it easier to train new employees.

Physical and IT Controls

Physical and information technology (IT) controls relate to the safeguarding (protecting) of assets and enhancing the accuracy and reliability of the accounting records. Examples of these controls are shown in Illustration 7-1.

▶ ILLUSTRATION **7-1**
Physical and IT controls

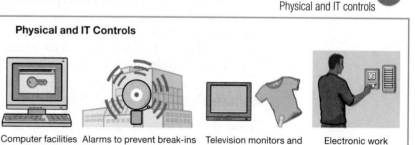

Physical and IT Controls

| Safes, vaults, and safety deposit boxes for cash and business papers | Locked warehouses and storage cabinets for inventories and records | Computer facilities that require a password, fingerprint, or eyeball scan. | Alarms to prevent break-ins | Television monitors and garment sensors to discourage theft | Electronic work monitoring |

Independent Checks of Performance

Most internal control systems include **independent internal and/or external reviews of performance and records**. This means having an independent person verify that the company's control activities are being correctly followed. To get the most from a performance review:

1. The review should be done periodically or by surprise.
2. The review should be done by someone who is independent of the employee who is responsible for the information.
3. Discrepancies and exceptions should be reported to a management level that can do whatever is necessary to correct the situation.

Internal Review. Segregating the physical custody of assets from accounting record keeping is not enough to ensure that nothing has been stolen. An independent review still needs to be done. In such a review, the accounting records are compared with existing assets or with external sources of information. The reconciliation of the cash register sales report with the cash in the register by Beanz Espresso Bar owner Lori Kays in the feature story is an example of comparing records with assets. When the person who does the review works for the organization, we call this an internal review.

In large companies, control activities, including independent internal reviews, are often monitored by internal auditors. **Internal auditors** are company employees who evaluate the effectiveness of the company's system of internal control. They periodically review the activities of departments and individuals to determine whether the correct control activities are being followed.

Anatomy of a Fraud

Jag Brar owned several retail stores across the country that sold fitness clothes and products. Every location had a store manager who was responsible for the daily operations. Part of the manager's daily responsibilities was to deposit the cash sales at a nearby bank at the end of the day. The accounting clerk at head office would print off a daily sales report from the point-of-sale system for each location and file it in a folder labelled "daily sales." Bank statements from the local banks were sent to head office and filed by the receptionist.

Jag could never understand why the locations' sales reports showed strong daily sales yet the locations were always short of cash. What he did not realize was that the store managers were depositing only a portion of the cash sales and pocketing the rest.

The Missing Control

Internal review: There was no independent review of the cash deposited and the sales reported. If the accounting clerk had compared the daily sales with the amount deposited in the bank and reported these discrepancies to Jag, this fraud would have been detected.

External Review. It is useful to contrast independent *internal* reviews with independent *external* reviews. **External auditors** are independent of the company. They are professional accountants hired by a company to report on whether or not the company's financial statements present fairly the company's financial position and results of operations.

All public companies, including Corus Entertainment, are required to have an external audit. A copy of Corus's auditors' report is included in Appendix A. As you will see in the report, external auditors plan and perform an audit that will allow them to be reasonably sure that the financial statements do not contain any significant errors.

Human Resource Controls

Human resource control measures include the following:

1. **Bonding of employees who handle cash. Bonding** involves getting insurance protection against the theft of assets by dishonest employees. This measure also helps safeguard cash in two ways: First, the insurance company carefully screens all individuals before adding them to the policy and it may reject risky applicants. Second, bonded employees know that the insurance company will prosecute all offenders.
2. **Rotating employees' duties and requiring employees to take vacations.** These measures discourage employees from attempting any thefts since they will not be able to permanently hide their improper actions. Many banks, for example, have discovered employee thefts when the guilty employee was on vacation or assigned to a new position.
3. **Conducting thorough background checks.** Many people believe that the most important, and the least expensive, measure a company can take to reduce employee theft and fraud is to conduct thorough background checks.

Anatomy of a Fraud

Joseph Chan worked for a small retail store. Management often described Joseph as a reliable, dedicated employee who never took sick time or holidays. He was often the only person minding the store. Joseph felt he was underpaid and found a way to "compensate" himself. When ringing in sales, he would charge the customer the full retail amount but he would ring in the sale as if the customer received a discount. He would then pocket the difference. When Joseph's mother became ill, he had to take two months off to care for her. During this time, management noticed a significant increase in sales. They investigated and discovered Joseph's discount scheme.

The Missing Control

Human resource controls: The retailer did not do a background check before hiring Joseph. If it had, management would have discovered he had been fired from a past position for committing the same scheme. Furthermore, the fraud might have been discovered sooner if the entity had a policy of mandatory vacations and days off.

LIMITATIONS OF INTERNAL CONTROL

No matter how well it is designed and operated, a company's system of internal control can give only *reasonable assurance* that assets are properly safeguarded and that accounting records are reliable—it cannot make any *guarantees*. The concept of reasonable assurance is based on the belief that the cost of control activities should not be more than their expected benefit.

To illustrate, consider shoplifting losses in retail stores. Such losses could be eliminated by having a security guard stop and search customers as they leave the store. Store managers have concluded, however, that the negative effects of doing this cannot be justified. Instead, stores have tried to control shoplifting losses by using less costly and intrusive procedures such as posting signs that state "We reserve the right to inspect all packages" and "All shoplifters will be prosecuted," using hidden TV cameras and store detectives to watch customer activity, and using sensor equipment at exits.

The human factor is an important limit in every system of internal control. A good system can become ineffective as a result of employee fatigue, carelessness, indifference, or lack of proper training. For example, a receiving clerk may not bother to count goods received, or may alter or "fudge" the counts. Occasionally, two or more individuals may work together to get around controls, which eliminates the protection offered by segregating duties. This is often referred to as collusion.

The size of the business may also limit internal control. As mentioned earlier, in small companies it may be difficult to segregate duties or have independent checks of performance.

> **Helpful hint** Controls may vary with the risk level of the item. For example, management may consider the loss of cash to be a higher risk than loss of equipment; therefore, management may implement stronger controls over cash.

ACCOUNTING IN ACTION
ALL ABOUT YOU INSIGHT

istockphoto.com/Peter Garbet

Protect your identity. Personal information, such as your name, date of birth, address, credit card number, and social insurance number (SIN), can be used to steal money from your bank account, make purchases, or even get a job. Are you a victim? According to a report by the Canadian Anti-Fraud Centre (a joint forces operation of the RCMP, Competition Bureau of Canada, and Ontario Provincial Police), there were nearly 19,500 reported cases of identity theft in 2013. These victims reported total dollar losses of over $11.0 million. However, it's estimated that far more identity theft occurs than what is reported to police. A 2014 survey by the Chartered Professional Accountants of Canada found that 7% of respondents had been victims of identity theft in the past. Many respondents said they take several measures to prevent identity theft, such as always shredding banking and credit card statements (72% of respondents), always covering their personal identification number when using a bank or credit card in a retailer (59%), or being very reluctant to use their SIN as identification (49%). The SIN is a key piece of information that identity thieves use to obtain personal data, to receive government benefits and tax refunds, or to get a job. To help protect Canadians, the federal government in April 2014 stopped issuing SIN cards, instead assigning the numbers via personal letters.

Sources: Canadian Anti-Fraud Centre, "Annual Statistical Report 2013: Mass Marketing Fraud & ID Theft Activities"; "Government of Canada Helps Protect Canadians and Reduces Costs: Social Insurance Number Program Modernized," Employment and Social Development Canada news release, April 1, 2014; "Canadians Must Remain on Guard against Fraud, Identity Theft: CPA Canada Survey," CPA Canada news release, February 28, 2014.

 Who is responsible for losses due to unauthorized credit card use?

Control Activities

In each of the following situations, identify the appropriate control activity and state whether it has been supported or violated.

(a) The purchasing department orders, receives, and pays for merchandise.
(b) All cheques are pre-numbered and accounted for.
(c) Management performs surprise cash account checks.
(d) Extra cash is kept locked in a safe that can be accessed only by the head cashier.
(e) Each cashier has his or her own cash drawer.
(f) The company's controller received a plaque for distinguished service because he had not taken a vacation in five years.

Solution

(a) Violation of segregation of duties
(b) Support of documentation procedures
(c) Support of independent checks of performance
(d) Support of physical and IT controls
(e) Support of establishment of responsibility
(f) Violation of human resource controls (employees should take vacations)

Related exercise material: BE7–1 and E7–1.

Action Plan

• Understand each of the control activities: establishment of responsibility, segregation of duties, documentation procedures, physical and IT controls, independent checks of performance, and human resource controls.

LEARNING OBJECTIVE 2   **Apply control activities to cash receipts and cash payments.**

Cash Controls

As previously stated, cash is very susceptible to fraudulent activities; therefore, strong controls over cash receipts and disbursements are critical. We will now consider specific controls over cash receipts and payments.

INTERNAL CONTROL OVER CASH RECEIPTS

Cash receipts come from a variety of sources: cash sales; collections on account from customers; the receipt of interest, dividends, and rents; investments by owners; bank loans; and proceeds from the sale of property, plant, and equipment. Generally, internal control over cash receipts is more effective when all cash receipts are deposited intact in the bank account every day. Illustration 7-2 shows examples of how the control activities explained earlier apply to cash receipt transactions.

As might be expected, companies vary considerably in how they apply these principles. To illustrate internal control over cash receipts, we will discuss useful control activities for a retail store with over-the-counter, mail-in, and electronic receipts.

Over-the-Counter Receipts

Control of over-the-counter receipts in retail businesses is centred on cash registers that are visible to customers. All sales must be entered into the cash register through point-of-sale software that records the sale and updates the inventory records. The amount of the sale should be visible to the customer to prevent the cashier from entering a lower amount and pocketing the difference. Each customer should receive an itemized receipt to ensure all cash sales are entered into the point-of-sale system.

Today, sales settled with coins and paper currency are becoming rarer. Most customers pay by debit or bank credit card. Although banks charge retailers when these cards are used, debit and credit cards strengthen internal control because employees handle less cash.

Control Activities over Cash Receipts

Establishment of Responsibility

Only designated personnel (cashiers) are authorized to handle cash receipts.

Physical and IT Controls

Store cash in safes and bank vaults; limit access to storage areas; use cash registers; deposit all cash in a bank daily.

Segregation of Duties

Different individuals receive cash, record cash receipts, and handle cash.

Independent Checks of Performance

Supervisors count cash receipts daily; controller's office compares total receipts with bank deposits daily.

Documentation Procedures

Use remittance advices (mail receipts), cash register tapes, and deposit slips.

Human Resource Controls

Bond personnel who handle cash; require employees to take vacations; conduct background checks.

▶ILLUSTRATION **7-2**
Application of control activities to cash receipts

Regardless of payment method, controls should still be in place over cash receipts. While procedures may vary from company to company, the basic internal control principles should be the same. Cashiers should sign for a cash float at the beginning of each shift and no other employees should have access to this float. At the end of his or her shift, the cashier should count the cash in the register, record the amount, and turn the cash and the recorded amount over to either a supervisor or the person responsible for making the bank deposit. The person handling the cash and making the bank deposit should not be able to make changes to the sales recorded in the point-of-sale system or the accounting records. Employees must also make sure there are receipts on hand for debit or credit card sales and that these match the amounts recorded for each type of payment by the point-of-sale system. Deposits should be made daily to reduce the amount of accessible cash on hand.

Sales using debit and credit cards are considered cash transactions. Debit cards allow customers to spend only what is in their bank account. When a debit card sale occurs, the bank immediately deducts the cost of the purchase from the customer's bank account. Therefore, the major advantage of debit cards is that the retailer knows immediately if the customer has enough money in the bank to pay for the purchase. With bank credit card sales, such as Visa and MasterCard, the customer has access to money made available by a bank or other financial institution (essentially a short-term loan that has to be repaid). When a customer uses a bank credit card, the bank transfers the amount of the sale to the retailer's bank.

For both types of transactions, the retailer has a choice about how often the proceeds from the debit and credit card transactions are electronically transferred into the retailer's bank account. Some retailers ask the bank to make one deposit at the end of each business day; other retailers wait and have several days of transactions deposited together. Banks usually charge the retailer a transaction fee for each debit or credit card transaction and deduct this fee from the amount deposited in the retailer's bank account.

The fees for bank credit cards are generally higher than debit card fees. Why? With a debit card, the bank is charging only for transferring the customer's money to the retailer. With a credit card, the bank is taking the risk that the customer may never repay it for the loan. Also, the rates charged by credit card companies to retailers vary greatly depending on such factors as the type of card used, the method of processing the transaction, and the volume of transactions. Retailers with a high number of transactions usually get a lower rate; those with a small number of transactions often have a higher rate. Except for the higher bank charges, recording of bank credit card sales is similar to recording a debit card sale.

To illustrate, suppose that on March 21, 10 customers use debit cards to purchase merchandise totalling $800 from Lee Company. Assuming the bank charges Lee Company $0.50 per debit card transaction, the entry made to record these transactions by Lee Company is as follows:

A	=	L	+	OE
+795				−5
				+800

↑ Cash flows: +795

Mar. 21	Debit Card Expense (10 × $0.50)	5	
	Cash ($800 − $5)	795	
	Sales		800
	To record debit card sales.		

In addition to the service charge for each transaction, Lee Company will also pay a monthly rental charge for the point-of-sale equipment that it uses for debit and credit card transactions.

Similarly, suppose that on March 21, Lee Company sells $800 of merchandise to customers who use bank credit cards. The banks charge Lee Company a service fee of 3.5% for credit card sales. The entry made to record these transactions by Lee Company is:

A	=	L	+	OE
+772				−28
				+800

↑ Cash flows: +772

Mar. 21	Credit Card Expense ($800 × 3.5%)	28	
	Cash ($800 − $28)	772	
	Sales		800
	To record bank credit card sales.		

In addition to accepting bank credit cards, many large department stores and gasoline retailers have their own credit cards. Sales using the retailer's own credit cards are credit sales; they result in accounts receivable, not cash, at the point of sale.

Mail-In Receipts

Helpful hint When billing customers, many companies state "Pay by cheque; do not send cash through the mail." This is done to reduce the risk of cash receipts being misappropriated by employees when they are received.

Although the use of cheques has decreased, many companies still receive payment from their customers via cheques. In particular for high-value purchases, this reduces the service charges paid by the business as compared with credit card sales.

When a cheque is received in the mail, it is usually accompanied by a remittance slip showing the details of payment. All mail-in receipts should be opened in the presence of two mail clerks and the remittance slip compared with the cheque. The remittance slips are sent to the accounting department for recording and the cheques are stamped for deposit only and sent to the person responsible for making the bank deposits. Persons handling the cheques must not be able to alter the accounting records. An independent person should compare the deposit recorded by the bank with the amount recorded in the accounting records. In a small company, where it is not possible to have the necessary segregation of duties, the owner should be responsible for cash receipts.

Electronic Receipts

Electronic funds transfer (EFT) is the electronic exchange or transfer of money from one account to another, either within a single financial institution or across multiple institutions, through computer-based systems. Examples of transactions covered by the term "EFT" include:

- debit and credit card transactions,
- pre-authorized debits,
- electronic bill payments using on-line banking,
- bank machine withdrawals, and
- prepaid smart cards.

EFT transactions have grown dramatically while cheques and cash transactions have decreased. There has also been a rapid growth in the different types of EFTs. Some EFTs are initiated by the customer, such as on-line electronic bill payments. Others are initiated by the company, such as pre-authorized debits. Electronic funds transfers normally result in better internal control because no cash or cheques are handled by company employees. But it is still important to have proper authorization and segregation of duties to ensure an employee cannot divert a customer payment to a personal bank account and then cover it up through fraudulent accounting entries.

ACCOUNTING IN ACTION
ACROSS THE ORGANIZATION INSIGHT

Getty Images/Markus Bernard

Will that be cash, cheque, or smart phone? Canada has begun the rollout of widescale mobile payment—the ability to swipe a mobile phone to pay for everything from a cup of coffee to bus fare. Mobile payment is seen as a boon to consumers and business alike, as it offers unparalleled convenience, especially for purchases of low dollar value. A federal government task force on payments systems estimated that businesses can reduce invoicing costs by up to 80%. Mobile payments also cut down on transaction processing time and reduce cash handling costs. But many Canadians have been sceptical of the technology. One survey found that 4 in 10 Canadians considering using their smart phone to make payments were most concerned about security, and 1 in 3 said they would never use the technology. In another survey, roughly 8 in 10 Canadian businesses thought that consumers would worry that hackers could steal their financial or other personal information from their smart phone. The government task force says the reality is quite different, because mobile payments are safer and more secure than the existing payment system. In early 2015, the government extended its code of conduct for the credit and debit card industry to include mobile payments, further protecting businesses and consumers.

Sources: Robin Arnfield, "Canadian Government Extends Code of Conduct to Mobile Payments," MobilePaymentsToday.com, April 21, 2015; Scott Simpson, "Canada Needs Quicker Shift to Mobile Payments, Task Force Says," *Financial Post*, March 27, 2012; Brian Jackson, "Canadians Cautious About Mobile Payment Security," ITBusiness.ca, October 6, 2011; KPMG, "Mobile Payments: Is Canada Ready? Insights from our Global Survey on Mobile Payments," October 2011.

 Q How might an organization's marketing department assist in, and benefit from, the implementation of a mobile payments system?

INTERNAL CONTROL OVER CASH PAYMENTS

Cash is disbursed for a variety of reasons, such as to pay expenses and liabilities, or to purchase assets. **Generally, internal control over cash payments is better when payments are made by cheque or EFT, rather than in cash.** Payment by cheque should occur only after specified control procedures have been followed. The paid cheque gives proof of payment. Illustration 7-3 shows examples of how the control activities explained earlier apply to cash payments.

Cheques

Good control over cheques includes having them signed by at least two authorized people. The cheque signers should carefully review the supporting documentation for the payment before signing the cheque. There should be a clear segregation of duties between the cheque-signing function and the accounts payable function. Cheques should be pre-numbered, and all cheque numbers must be accounted for in the payment and recording process. Cheques should never be pre-signed, and blank (unissued) cheques should be physically controlled.

Control Activities over Cash Payments

Establishment of Responsibility

Only designated personnel are authorized to sign cheques or approve electronic payments.

Physical and IT Controls

Store cash in safes, limit access to blank cheques and signing machines, and use electronic payments when possible.

Segregation of Duties

Different individuals approve and make payments; cheque signers do not record disbursements.

Independent Checks of Performance

Compare cheques with invoices; reconcile bank statement monthly.

Documentation Procedures

Use pre-numbered cheques and account for them in sequence; each cheque must have an approved invoice.

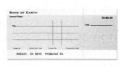

Human Resources

Bond personnel who handle cash, require employees to take vacations, and conduct background checks.

▶ ILLUSTRATION **7-3**
Application of control activities over cash payments

Electronic Payments

Just as a company may use electronic funds transfer systems to receive cash, it can also use those systems to make payments to suppliers and employees. For example, when a company pays its employees' salaries using a direct deposit option, the cash is instantly transferred from the company's bank account to each employee's bank account. Electronic pre-authorized payments are often made for things paid on a recurring basis like insurance or loans and interest.

The use of EFT for cash payments will result in better internal control as long as there is proper authorization and segregation of duties. EFT payments also reduce the extra costs of making payments by cheque, such as postage and envelope costs.

BEFORE YOU GO ON...DO IT	②	Recording Cash Receipts and Cash Payments

Prepare journal entries to record the following selected debit and credit card transactions for Bulk Department Store:

July 18 A customer used her debit card to pay for a $650 purchase. Bulk Department Store was charged a $2 service fee.

22 A customer paid for a $1,200 purchase with her Visa credit card. The bank charges Bulk Department Store a service fee of 3.0%.

26 A customer paid for a $500 purchase with his Bulk Department Store credit card.

27 A customer sends a $5,000 cheque for goods previously purchased.

Action Plan
- Debit cards are recorded as cash sales, less the service charge.
- Bank credit cards are recorded as cash sales, less the service charge.
- Nonbank credit cards are recorded as receivables. There is no bank service charge when a customer uses a company credit card.

Solution

July 18	Debit Card Expense	2	
	Cash ($650 − $2)	648	
	Sales		650
	To record debit card sale.		

(continued)

BEFORE YOU GO ON...DO IT   Recording Cash Receipts and Cash Payments *(continued)*

22	Credit Card Expense ($1,200 × 3.0%)	36	
	Cash ($1,200 − $36)	1,164	
	Sales		1,200
	To record Visa credit card sale.		
26	Accounts Receivable	500	
	Sales		500
	To record company credit card sale.		
27	Cash	5,000	
	Accounts Receivable		5,000
	To record a customer cheque received.		

Related exercise material: BE7–2, BE7–3, BE7–4, BE7–5, BE7–6, E7–2, E7–3, and E7–4.

LEARNING OBJECTIVE 3 ▸ Describe the operation of a petty cash fund.

Petty Cash Fund

While making payments by EFT and cheques results in better internal control than using cash, it can be both impractical and a nuisance to use cheques or EFT to pay for small amounts. For example, a company may not want to write cheques to pay for postage, couriers, or small purchases of supplies. A common way to handle such payments, while maintaining satisfactory control, is to use a **petty cash fund**. A petty cash fund maintains internal controls over small cash disbursements by ensuring that all amounts are accounted for and all transactions are recorded. The operation of a petty cash fund, also called an imprest system, involves three steps: (1) establishing the fund, (2) making payments from the fund, and (3) replenishing the fund.

ESTABLISHING THE FUND

Two essential steps are required to establish a petty cash fund: (1) appoint a petty cash custodian to be responsible for the fund, and (2) determine the size of the fund. Ordinarily, the amount is expected to be enough for likely payments in a three- to four-week period.

To establish the fund, a cheque payable to the petty cash custodian is issued for the determined amount. For example, if Lee Company decides to establish a $100 petty cash fund on March 1, the general journal entry is as follows:

Mar. 1	Petty Cash	100	
	Cash		100
	To establish a petty cash fund.		

A   =   L   +   OE
+100
−100

Cash flows: no effect

ETHICS NOTE
Petty cash funds are authorized and legitimate. In contrast, "slush" funds are unauthorized and hidden (under the table).

There is no effect on cash flows because the company's total cash has not changed. There is $100 less in the bank account but $100 more cash on hand. The custodian cashes the cheque and places the proceeds in a locked petty cash box or drawer. No other entries are made to the Petty Cash account unless the size of the fund is increased or decreased. For example, if Lee Company decides on March 15 to increase the size of the fund to $250, it will debit Petty Cash and credit Cash $150 ($250 − $100).

MAKING PAYMENTS FROM THE FUND

The petty cash custodian has the authority to make payments from the fund in accordance with management policies. Usually, management limits the size of expenditures that may be made. Likewise, it may not allow the fund to be used for certain types of transactions (such as making short-term loans to employees).

Helpful hint For internal control, the receipt satisfies two principles: (1) establishment of responsibility (signature of the custodian), and (2) documentation procedures.

Each payment from the fund should be documented on a pre-numbered petty cash receipt, signed by both the custodian and the person who receives the payment. If other supporting documents, such as a freight bill or invoice, are available, they should be attached to the petty cash receipt. The receipts are kept in the petty cash box until the fund runs low and the cash needs to be replenished. The sum of the petty cash receipts and money in the fund should equal the established total at all times. Surprise counts should be made by an independent person, such as a supervisor or internal auditor, to determine whether the fund is being properly administered.

An accounting entry is not recorded when a payment is made from the petty cash fund. Instead, it is recorded when the fund is replenished.

REPLENISHING THE FUND

Helpful hint Replenishing involves three internal control procedures: (1) segregation of duties, (2) documentation procedures, and (3) independent checks of performance.

When the money in the petty cash fund reaches a minimum level, the company replenishes the fund. The request for reimbursement is made by the petty cash custodian. This individual prepares a schedule (or summary) of the payments that have been made and sends the schedule, supported by petty cash receipts and other documentation, to the controller's office. The receipts and supporting documents are examined in the controller's office to verify that they were proper payments from the fund. The request is approved and a cheque is issued to restore the fund to its established amount. At the same time, all supporting documentation is stamped "Paid" so that it cannot be submitted again for payment.

To illustrate, assume that on March 15, Lee's petty cash fund has $13 cash and petty cash receipts for postage $44, freight in $38 (assume a perpetual inventory system is used), and miscellaneous expenses $5. The petty cash custodian will request a cheque for $87 ($100 − $13). The entry to record the cheque is as follows:

A	=	L	+	OE
+38				−44
−87				−5

↓Cash flows: −87

Mar. 15	Postage Expense	44	
	Merchandise Inventory	38	
	Miscellaneous Expense	5	
	Cash		87
	To replenish petty cash.		

Note that the Petty Cash account is not affected by the reimbursement entry. Replenishment changes what's in the fund by replacing the petty cash receipts with cash. It does not change the balance in the fund.

Occasionally, when replenishing a petty cash fund, the company may need to recognize a cash shortage or overage. This results when the receipts plus cash in the petty cash box do not equal the established amount of the petty cash fund. To illustrate, assume in the example above that the custodian had only $12 in cash in the fund, plus the receipts as listed. The request for reimbursement would, therefore, have been for $88 ($100 − $12). The following entry would be made:

A	=	L	+	OE
+38				−44
−88				−5
				−1

↓Cash flows: −88

Mar. 15	Postage Expense	44	
	Merchandise Inventory	38	
	Miscellaneous Expense	5	
	Cash Over and Short	1	
	Cash		88
	To replenish petty cash.		

Helpful hint Cash over and short results from mathematical errors or from failure to keep accurate records.

Conversely, if the custodian had $14 in cash, the reimbursement request would have been for $86 ($100 − $14) and Cash Over and Short would have been credited for $1. A debit balance in Cash Over and Short is reported in the income statement as miscellaneous expense. A credit balance in the account is reported as miscellaneous revenue.

If the petty cash fund is not big enough, it is often increased (or decreased if the amount is too large) when the fund is replenished. Assume that Lee Company decides to increase the size of its petty cash fund from $100 to $125 on March 15 when it replenishes the fund. The entry to record the reimbursement and change in fund size is as follows:

Mar. 15	Petty Cash	25	
	Postage Expense	44	
	Merchandise Inventory	38	
	Miscellaneous Expense	5	
	Cash Over and Short	1	
	Cash		113
	To replenish petty cash and increase the fund size by $25.		

A	=	L	+	OE
+25				−44
+38				−5
−113				−1

↓ Cash flows: −88

In this entry, the Petty Cash account is affected because of the change in size of the fund. After this entry, the general ledger account shows a balance of $125 and the custodian must ensure that cash and paid-out receipts now total $125. Although a $113 cheque has been written, total cash is decreased by only $88 as $25 is added to Petty Cash.

A petty cash fund should be replenished at the end of the accounting period regardless of how much cash is in the fund. Replenishment at this time is needed to recognize the effects of the petty cash payments on the financial statements.

 BEFORE YOU GO ON...DO IT **3** > **Petty Cash Fund**

Bateer Company established a $50 petty cash fund on July 1. On July 30, the fund had $12 cash remaining and petty cash receipts for postage $14, supplies $10, and delivery expense $15. Prepare the journal entries to establish the fund on July 1 and replenish the fund on July 30.

Solution

July 1	Petty Cash	50	
	Cash		50
	To establish a petty cash fund.		
30	Postage Expense	14	
	Supplies	10	
	Delivery Expense	15	
	Cash Over and Short ($39 − $38)		1
	Cash ($50 − $12)		38
	To replenish petty cash.		

Related exercise material: BE7–7, BE7–8, E7–5, E7–6, and E7–7.

Action Plan
- Set up a separate general ledger account when the fund is established.
- Determine how much cash is needed to replenish the fund—subtract the cash remaining from the petty cash fund balance.
- Total the petty cash receipts. Determine any cash over or short—the difference between the cash needed to replenish the fund and the total of the petty cash receipts.
- Record the expenses incurred according to the petty cash receipts when replenishing the fund.

 LEARNING OBJECTIVE **4** > **Describe the control features of a bank account and prepare a bank reconciliation.**

Bank Accounts

USE OF A BANK ACCOUNT

The use of a bank contributes significantly to good internal control over cash. A company can safeguard its cash by using a bank as a depository and reduce the amount of currency that must be kept on hand. In addition, using a bank increases internal control, because it creates a double record of all bank transactions—one by the business and the other by the bank. The asset account Cash, maintained by the company, should have the same balance as the bank's liability account for that company. A **bank reconciliation** compares the bank's balance with the company's balance and explains any differences.

Many companies have more than one bank account. For efficiency of operations and better control, national retailers like Walmart Inc. and Best Buy may have local bank accounts. Similarly, a company may have a payroll bank account, as well as one or more general bank accounts. A company may also have accounts with different banks in order to have more than one source for short-term loans when needed.

ACCOUNTING IN ACTION
ETHICS INSIGHT

Getty Images/DNY59

You are the assistant controller in charge of general ledger accounting at Barn Bottling Company. Your company has a large bank loan. The loan agreement requires that the company's cash account balance be maintained at $200,000 or more, as reported monthly.

At June 30, the cash balance is $80,000, which you report to McKenna Amlani, the chief financial officer. McKenna excitedly instructs you to keep the cash receipts book open for one additional day

for purposes of the June 30 report to the bank. McKenna says, "If we don't get that cash balance over $200,000, we'll default on our loan agreement. They could close us down, put us all out of our jobs!" McKenna continues, "I talked to Oconto Distributors (one of Barn's largest customers) this morning. They said they sent us a cheque for $150,000 yesterday. We should receive it tomorrow. If we include just that one cheque in our cash balance, we'll be in the clear. It's in the mail!"

Q What are the ethical considerations in this case and who will suffer if you do or do not follow McKenna Amlani's instructions?

Bank Deposits and Cheques

Bank deposits should be made by an authorized employee, such as the head cashier. Each deposit must be documented by a deposit slip, as shown in Illustration 7-4. Both the company and the bank will need a copy of the deposit slip.

While bank deposits increase the bank account balance, cheques decrease it. A cheque is a written order instructing the bank to pay a specific sum of money to a designated recipient. There are three parties to a cheque: (1) the maker (or drawer) who issues the cheque, (2) the bank (or payer) on which the cheque is drawn, and (3) the payee to whom the cheque is payable. A cheque is a negotiable instrument that can be transferred to another party by endorsement.

Each cheque should clearly explain its purpose. The purpose of a cheque can be detailed on the cheque stub, as shown in Illustration 7-5. The purpose of the cheque should also be clear for the payee, either by referencing the invoice directly on the cheque—see the reference to invoice #27662 on the "For" line of the cheque in the illustration—or by attaching a copy of the invoice to the cheque.

Automated teller machine cash withdrawals are not allowed on a business bank account where two signatures are required on cheques. There is no way of knowing if both of the authorized individuals are present when the withdrawal is made. The same principle applies to EFT payments on business bank accounts. When two signatures are required, the only way to maintain internal control is to make all payments by cheque or pre-authorized EFT.

How does cash actually flow through the banking system? When cheques, debit cards, and pre-authorized or other payments occur, they may result in one financial institution owing money to another. For example, if a company (the maker) writes a cheque to a supplier (the payee), the payee deposits the cheque in its own bank account.

▶ ILLUSTRATION 7-4
Deposit slip (reproduced with permission of BMO Bank of Montreal)

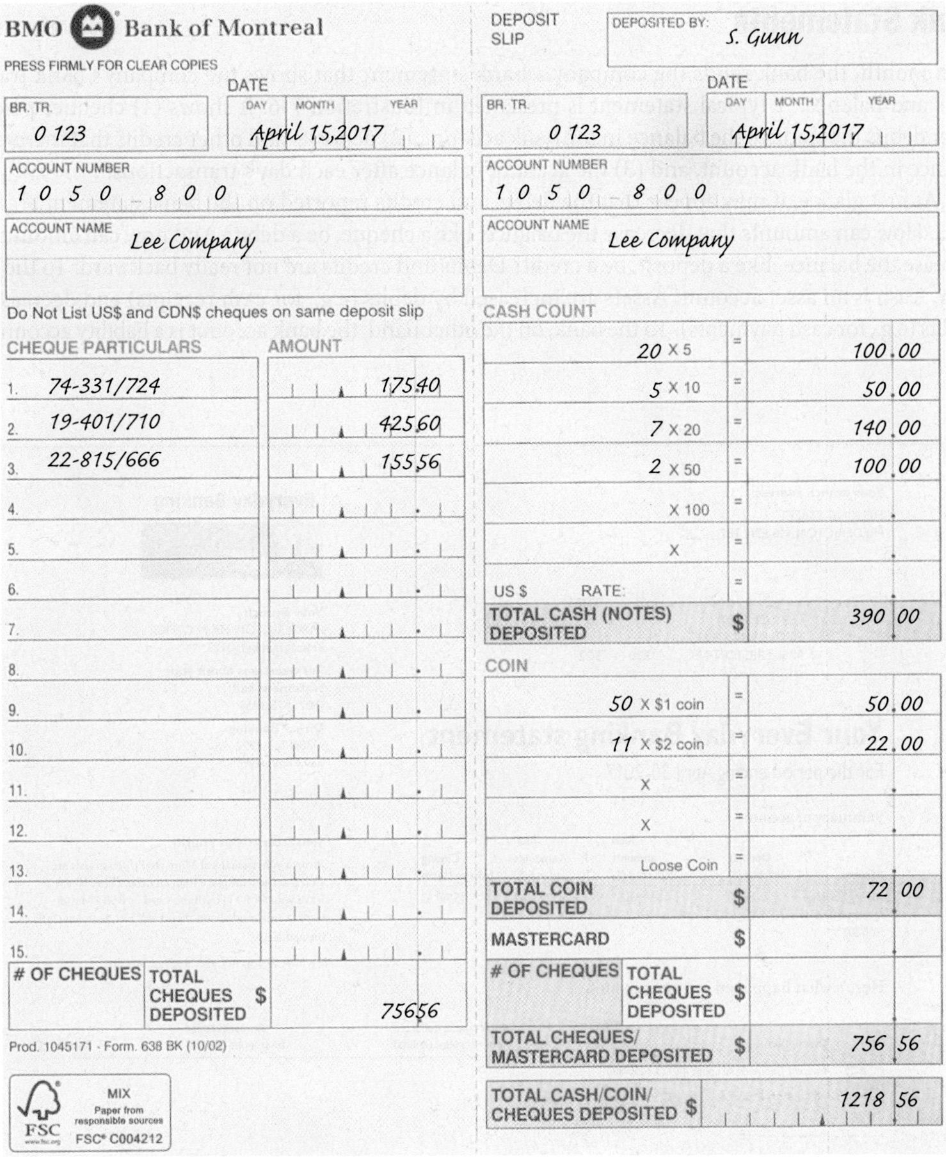

BMO Bank of Montreal

PRESS FIRMLY FOR CLEAR COPIES

DEPOSIT SLIP — DEPOSITED BY: S. Gunn

BR. TR.	DATE (DAY / MONTH / YEAR)
0 123	April 15, 2017

ACCOUNT NUMBER: 1 0 5 0 8 0 0

ACCOUNT NAME: Lee Company

Do Not List US$ and CDN$ cheques on same deposit slip

CHEQUE PARTICULARS	AMOUNT
1. 74-331/724	175.40
2. 19-401/710	425.60
3. 22-815/666	155.56
4.	
5.	
6.	
7.	
8.	
9.	
10.	
11.	
12.	
13.	
14.	
15.	
# OF CHEQUES / TOTAL CHEQUES DEPOSITED $	756.56

CASH COUNT

20 X 5 =	100.00
5 X 10 =	50.00
7 X 20 =	140.00
2 X 50 =	100.00
X 100 =	
X =	
US $ RATE: =	
TOTAL CASH (NOTES) DEPOSITED $	390.00

COIN

50 X $1 coin =	50.00
11 X $2 coin =	22.00
X =	
X =	
Loose Coin =	
TOTAL COIN DEPOSITED $	72.00
MASTERCARD $	
# OF CHEQUES / TOTAL CHEQUES DEPOSITED $	
TOTAL CHEQUES/ MASTERCARD DEPOSITED $	756.56
TOTAL CASH/COIN/ CHEQUES DEPOSITED $	1218.56

Prod. 1045171 · Form. 638 BK (10/02)

MIX Paper from responsible sources FSC FSC® C004212

▶ ILLUSTRATION 7-5
Cheque (reproduced with permission of BMO Bank of Montreal)

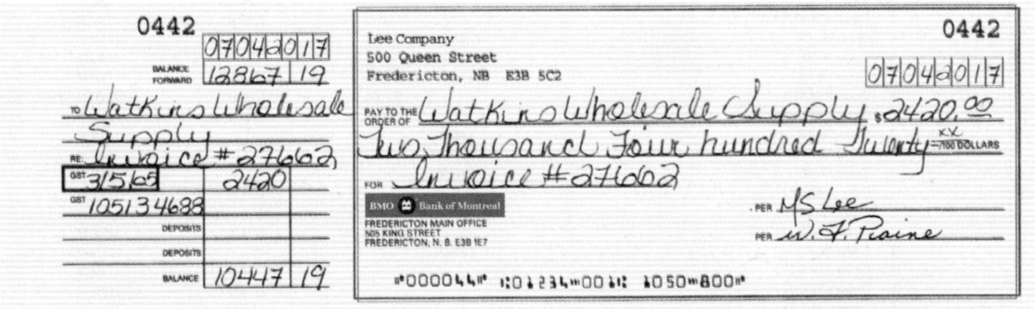

0442 — 07 04 2017
BALANCE FORWARD 12867.19
TO Watkins Wholesale Supply
RE: Invoice #27662
GST 315.65 — 2420
GST 105134683
DEPOSITS
DEPOSITS
BALANCE 10447.19

Lee Company
500 Queen Street
Fredericton, NB E3B 5C2
0442
07 04 2017
PAY TO THE ORDER OF Watkins Wholesale Supply $2420.00
Two Thousand Four hundred Twenty — xx/100 DOLLARS
FOR Invoice #27662
BMO Bank of Montreal
FREDERICTON MAIN OFFICE
505 KING STREET
FREDERICTON, N. B. E3B 1E7
PER M S Lee
PER W. F. Raine
⑈000044⑈ ⑆01234⑉001⑆ 1050⑉800⑈

When the cheque is deposited, it is sent to a regional data centre for processing, usually the same day. When the cheque arrives at the regional data centre, it is "presented" to the maker's financial institution, where it is determined whether the cheque will be honoured or returned. Examples are if there are insufficient funds in the account to cover the amount of the cheque, or if a stop payment order has been placed on the cheque by the maker, which stops the money from being paid by the cheque. This process is automated and happens very quickly. In most cases, the cheque will clear the maker's bank account before the next day. **Clearing** is what occurs when a cheque or deposit is accepted by the maker's bank. It results in a transfer of funds from the maker's bank to the payee's bank.

Bank Statements

Each month, the bank sends the company a **bank statement** that shows the company's bank transactions and balance. A typical statement is presented in Illustration 7-6. It shows (1) cheques paid and other debits that reduce the balance in the bank account, (2) deposits and other credits that increase the balance in the bank account, and (3) the account balance after each day's transactions.

At first glance, it may appear that the debits and credits reported on the bank statement are backward. How can amounts that decrease the balance, like a cheque, be a debit? And how can amounts that increase the balance, like a deposit, be a credit? Debits and credits are not really backward. To the company, Cash is an asset account. Assets are increased by debits (e.g., for cash receipts) and decreased by credits (e.g., for cash payments). To the bank, on the other hand, the bank account is a liability account—an

Helpful hint Every deposit received by the bank is credited to the customer's account. The reverse happens when the bank "pays" a cheque issued by a company on the company's chequing account balance. Because payment reduces the bank's liability, the amount is debited to the customer's account with the bank.

▶ **ILLUSTRATION 7-6**
Bank statement
(reproduced with permission of BMO Bank of Montreal)

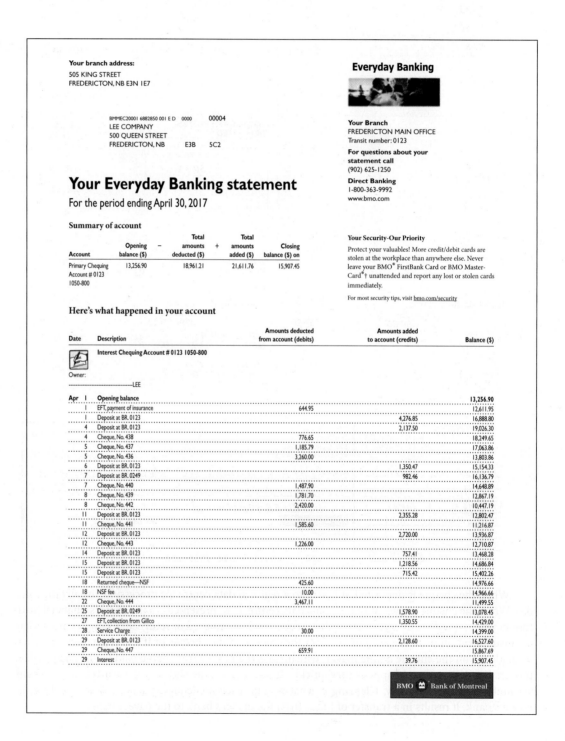

amount it must repay to you upon request. Liabilities are increased by credits and decreased by debits. When you deposit money in your bank account, the bank's liability to you increases. That is why the bank shows deposits as credits. When you write a cheque on your account, the bank pays out this amount and decreases (debits) its liability to you.

The bank will include a **debit memorandum** with the bank statement when additional information is needed to explain a charge on the bank statement. The symbol DM (debit memo) is often used on the bank statement for such charges. For example, a debit memorandum is used by the bank when a deposited cheque from a customer "bounces" because of insufficient funds. In such a case, the cheque is marked **NSF (not sufficient funds)** or RT (returned item) by the customer's bank, and is returned to the depositor's bank. The bank then debits the depositor's account, as shown by the April 18 entry "Returned cheque—NSF" on the bank statement in Illustration 7-6. Note that this cheque for $425.60 was originally included in the deposit made on April 15, detailed in Illustration 7-4. Because the deposit was credited (added) to the bank account on April 15 and the cheque was not honoured, it must be debited (deducted) by the bank on April 18.

The company's bank may also charge the company a service charge of $10 or more for processing the returned cheque. In Illustration 7-6 we can see that BMO writes the entry "NSF fee" on the customer's statement for these charges. The company (depositor) then advises the customer who wrote the NSF cheque that their cheque was returned NSF and that a payment is still owed on the account. The company also usually passes the bank charges on to the customer by adding them to the customer's account balance. In summary, the overall effect of an NSF cheque on the depositor is to create an account receivable, and to reduce cash in the bank account. The customer's own bank will also charge the customer an NSF fee of $40 or more for writing an NSF cheque.

Recording an account receivable assumes that the customer will honour the account due by replacing the bounced cheque with a valid cheque or with cash. This happens in most cases. In the next chapter, we will discuss how to account for uncollectible accounts receivable when customers are unable to pay their accounts.

The bank uses **credit memoranda (CM)** to identify and explain miscellaneous amounts added to the bank account for items such as interest earned on the bank account, and electronic funds transfers into the depositor's account. For example, as explained earlier in the chapter, some retailers accept electronic payments for merchandise sold on account. Funds are electronically transferred from the customer's account to the retailer's account in payment of the bill. In Illustration 7-6, Lee Company collected an electronic payment from a customer for $1,350.55 on April 27, as indicated by the symbol EFT. Also note that in Illustration 7-6, interest of $39.76 has been added to Lee Company's bank balance.

RECONCILING THE BANK ACCOUNT

You might assume that the balances you and the bank have for your account will always agree. In fact, the two balances are almost never the same at any specific time. It is necessary to make the balance per books (the balance recorded in a company's general ledger cash account) agree with the balance per bank (the balance recorded on the bank statement)—a process called **reconciling the bank account**.

The lack of agreement between the two balances is due to the following:

- time lags that prevent one of the parties from recording a transaction in the same period as the other or
- errors by either party in recording transactions.

Except in electronic banking applications, time lags happen often. For example, several days pass between the time a cheque is mailed to a payee and the date the cheque is presented to, and cleared (paid) by, the bank. Cheques recorded by a company that have not yet cleared the bank are called **outstanding cheques.**

Similarly, when a company uses the bank's night depository to make deposits, there will be a difference of one day (or more if it's the weekend or a holiday) between the day the receipts are recorded by the company and the day they are recorded by the bank. Deposits recorded by the company that have not yet been recorded by the bank are called **deposits in transit**.

While bank errors are not common, they can still occur. The frequency of errors by the company in its cash account depends on the effectiveness of its internal controls. For example, either party could unintentionally record a $450 cheque as $45 or $540. Or the bank might mistakenly charge a cheque to the wrong account if the proper coding is missing or if the cheque cannot be scanned.

Reconciliation Procedure

The bank reconciliation should be prepared by an employee who has no other responsibilities related to cash, or by the owner of the company. In the feature story about Beanz, the owner prepares the bank reconciliation. If the control activities of segregation of duties and independent checks of performance are not followed when the reconciliation is prepared, cash embezzlements may go unnoticed. For example, a cashier who prepares the reconciliation can steal cash and conceal the theft by misstating the reconciliation. In this way, the bank accounts would appear to reconcile with the company account and the theft would not be discovered.

In reconciling the bank account, it is customary to reconcile the balance per books (found in the Cash account in the general ledger) and the balance per bank (found on the bank statement provided by the bank) to their adjusted (correct) cash balances. The starting point when preparing the reconciliation is to enter the balance per bank statement and balance per books on the schedule. Adjustments are then made to each section, as shown in Illustration 7-7.

▶ILLUSTRATION **7-7**
Bank reconciliation procedures

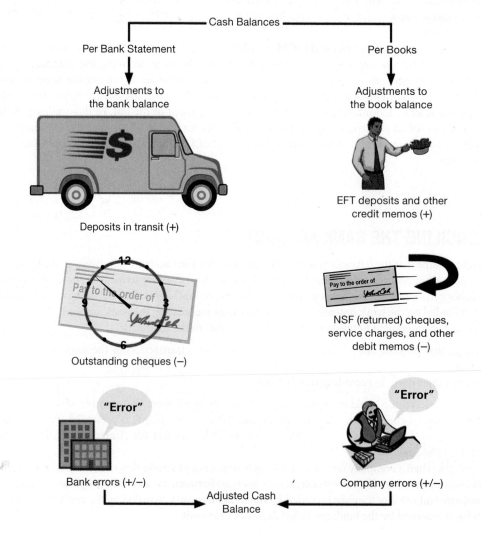

Reconciling Items per Bank. On the bank side of the reconciliation, the items to include are deposits in transit, outstanding cheques, and bank errors.

Step 1: Deposits in Transit. Compare the individual deposits on the bank statement with (1) the deposits in transit from the preceding bank reconciliation, and (2) the deposits recorded in the company's books. **Deposits in transit have been recorded on the company's books but have not yet been recorded by the bank.** Add these deposits to the balance per the bank.

Step 2: Outstanding Cheques. Compare the paid cheques shown on the bank statement or returned with the bank statement with (1) cheques that are outstanding from the preceding bank reconciliation, and (2) cheques that have been issued by the company during the month. **Cheques are "outstanding" if they have been recorded on the company's books but have not cleared the bank account yet.** Deduct outstanding cheques from the balance per the bank.

If a cheque that was outstanding in the previous period has been paid by the bank in the current period, the cheque is no longer outstanding and will **not** be included in the current month's bank reconciliation. If the cheque has still not been paid by the bank, it will continue to be outstanding and needs to be included with the outstanding cheques and deducted from the bank balance on the current month's bank reconciliation.

Helpful hint Deposits in transit and outstanding cheques are reconciling items because of time lags.

Step 3: Bank Errors. Note any errors that are discovered in the previous steps. Errors can be made by either the bank or the company and can be in both directions (increases or decreases). Include only errors made by the bank as reconciling items when calculating the adjusted cash balance per bank. For example, if the bank processed a deposit of $1,693 as $1,639 in error, the difference of $54 is added to the balance per bank on the bank reconciliation.

Reconciling Items per Books. Reconciling items on the book side include adjustments from any unrecorded credit memoranda (amounts added) and debit memoranda (amounts deducted), and company errors.

Step 1: Credit Memoranda and Other Deposits. Compare the credit memoranda and other deposits on the bank statement with the company records. Any amounts not recorded in the company's records should be added to the balance per books. For example, if the bank statement shows electronic funds transfers from customers paying their accounts on-line, these amounts will be added to the balance per books on the bank reconciliation, unless they had been previously recorded by the company. This makes the company's records agree with the bank's records.

Step 2: Debit Memoranda and Other Payments. Similarly, any unrecorded debit memoranda should be deducted from the balance per books. If the bank statement shows a debit memorandum for bank service charges, this amount is deducted from the balance per books on the bank reconciliation to make the company's records agree with the bank's records. Frequently, electronic payments have already been recorded by the company. If not, they must also be deducted from the balance per books on the bank reconciliation.

Step 3: Company Errors. Errors discovered in the company's records must also be included in the bank reconciliation. For example, we will see below that Lee Company wrote a cheque for $1,226 and mistakenly recorded it as $1,262. The error of $36 is added to the balance per books because Lee Company reduced the balance per books by $36 too much when it recorded the cheque as $1,262 instead of $1,226. Make sure you include only errors made by the company as reconciling items when calculating the adjusted cash balance per books.

Bank Reconciliation Illustrated

The bank statement for Lee Company was shown in Illustration 7-6. It shows a balance per bank of $15,907.45 on April 30, 2017. On this date, the balance of cash per books is $11,244.14. Using the above steps, the following reconciling items are determined:

Reconciling items per bank:

1. **Deposits in transit:** After comparing the deposits recorded in the books with the deposits listed in the bank statement, it was determined that the April 30 deposit was not recorded by the bank until May 1. $2,201.40

2. **Outstanding cheques:** After comparing the cheques recorded in the books with the cheques listed on the bank statement, it was determined that three cheques were outstanding:

No. 445	$3,000.00	
No. 446	1,401.30	
No. 448	1,502.70	5,904.00

3. **Bank errors:** None

Reconciling items per books:

1. **Credit memoranda and other deposits:**

Electronic receipt from customer on account	$1,350.55
Interest earned	39.76

2. **Debit memoranda and other payments:**

NSF cheque from J. R. Baron	425.60
Bank service charge for NSF cheque	10.00
Bank service charge	30.00

3. **Company errors:** Cheque No. 443 was correctly written by Lee for $1,226.00 and was correctly paid by the bank. However, it was recorded as $1,262.00 by Lee.   36.00

The bank reconciliation follows:

LEE COMPANY
Bank Reconciliation
April 30, 2017

Cash balance per bank statement		$15,907.45
Add: Deposit in transit		2,201.40
		18,108.85
Less: Outstanding cheques		
No. 445	$3,000.00	
No. 446	1,401.30	
No. 448	1,502.70	5,904.00
Adjusted cash balance per bank		$12,204.85
Cash balance per books		$11,244.14
Add: Electronic receipt from customer on account	$1,350.55	
Interest earned	39.76	
Error: cheque No. 443 for Accounts Payable		
($1,262.00 − $1,226.00)	36.00	1,426.31
		12,670.45
Less: Returned NSF cheque and bank charge		
($425.60 + $10.00)	$ 435.60	
Bank service charge	30.00	465.60
Adjusted cash balance per books		$12,204.85

The adjusted cash balances are now both equal to $12,204.85, which means the bank account has been reconciled.

Entries from Bank Reconciliation

After preparing the bank reconciliation, the company must prepare adjusting journal entries to record each reconciling item used to determine the **adjusted cash balance per books. If these items are not journalized and posted, the Cash account will not show the correct balance.** Lee Company would record the following entries on April 30.

EFT Receipt from Customer on Account. When a customer pays their account, the journal entry is the same regardless of whether the customer pays by cash, by cheque, or by EFT. The entry is:

Apr. 30	Cash	1,350.55	
	Accounts Receivable		1,350.55
	To record electronic receipt from customer on account.		

A = L + OE
+1,350.55
−1,350.55

▲Cash flows: +1,350.55

This entry is only required when the company has not already recorded the EFT receipt during the month. If that had been the case, then this item would not have been a reconciling item and would not have appeared on the bank reconciliation and thus would not have needed an adjustment.

Interest Revenue. Assuming the company had not already recorded an accrual, the interest earned is credited to the Interest Revenue account. The entry is:

Apr. 30	Cash	39.76	
	Interest Revenue		39.76
	To record interest earned.		

A = L + OE
+39.76   +39.76

▲Cash flows: +39.76

Company Error. The journal shows that cheque No. 443 had been issued to pay an account payable. The entry is:

Apr. 30	Cash	36.00	
	Accounts Payable		36.00
	To correct error in recording cheque No. 443.		

A = L + OE
+36.00   +36.00

▲Cash flows: +36.00

NSF Cheque. As explained earlier, a customer cheque returned for not sufficient funds and any related bank service charges become an account receivable to the depositor. The entry is:

Apr. 30	Accounts Receivable ($425.60 + $10.00)	435.60	
	Cash		435.60
	To record NSF cheque from J. R. Baron plus bank charge.		

A = L + OE
+435.60
−435.60

▼Cash flows: −435.60

Bank Service Charges. Bank service charges are normally debited to Bank Charges expense. The entry is:

Apr. 30	Bank Charges Expense	30.00	
	Cash		30.00
	To record bank service charge expense for April.		

A = L + OE
−30.00   −30.00

▼Cash flows: −30.00

The five journal entries shown above could also be combined into one compound entry.
After the entries above are posted, the Cash account will show the following:

		Cash		
Apr. 30	Bal.	11,244.14	Apr. 30	435.60
30		1,350.55	30	30.00
30		39.76		
30		36.00		
Apr. 30	Bal.	**12,204.85**		

The adjusted cash balance in the general ledger should agree with the adjusted cash balance per books in the bank reconciliation shown earlier.

What entries does the bank make? If any bank errors are discovered in preparing the reconciliation, the bank should be notified. The bank can then make the necessary corrections on its records. The bank does not correct your errors on its books, and you do not correct the bank's errors on your books. The bank does not make any entries for deposits in transit or outstanding cheques. The bank will record these items when they reach it.

BEFORE YOU GO ON...DO IT **4**   **Bank Reconciliation**

The Cash account of Kist Company showed a balance of $16,333 on December 31, 2017. The bank statement as at that date showed a balance of $18,084. After comparing the bank statement with the cash records, the following information was determined:

1. The bank returned an NSF cheque in the amount of $239 that Kist had deposited on December 20. The cheque was a payment on a customer's account.
2. Electronic receipts from customers on account totalled $2,300. These receipts have not yet been recorded by the company.
3. The bank issued a credit memo for $9 of interest earned on Kist's account.
4. The bank issued a debit memo for bank service charges of $37. This amount included $10 for processing the NSF cheque (see #1 above).
5. The company made an error in recording a customer's deposit. The company recorded the payment on account as $209 when it should have been $290. The bank correctly recorded the deposit as $290.
6. Deposits in transit as at December 31 amounted to $3,643.
7. Outstanding cheques written in the month of December amounted to $3,000. Cheques still outstanding from the month of November totalled $280.

Prepare a bank reconciliation and any required journal entries for Kist Company at December 31, 2017. Post the entries to the Cash account.

Solution

Action Plan

- Prepare the bank reconciliation in two sections: one for the bank and one for the company.
- Determine which reconciling items each side has already recorded and adjust the other side accordingly.
- Be careful when you determine the direction of an error correction; think about how the error has affected the bank balance or the cash account balance.
- Prepare journal entries only for reconciling items to the book side, not the bank side.
- The adjusted cash balances must agree with each other when complete, and with the general ledger account after the journal entries are posted.

<table>
<tr><td colspan="3" align="center">**KIST COMPANY**
Bank Reconciliation
December 31, 2017</td></tr>
<tr><td>Cash balance per bank statement</td><td></td><td>$18,084</td></tr>
<tr><td>Add: Deposits in transit</td><td></td><td>3,643</td></tr>
<tr><td></td><td></td><td>21,727</td></tr>
<tr><td>Less: Outstanding cheques ($3,000 + $280)</td><td></td><td>3,280</td></tr>
<tr><td>Adjusted cash balance per bank</td><td></td><td>$18,447</td></tr>
<tr><td>Cash balance per books</td><td></td><td>$16,333</td></tr>
<tr><td>Add:</td><td></td><td></td></tr>
<tr><td> Electronic receipts from customers on account</td><td>$2,300</td><td></td></tr>
<tr><td> Interest earned</td><td>9</td><td></td></tr>
<tr><td> Error in deposit of Accounts Receivable ($290 − $209)</td><td>81</td><td>2,390</td></tr>
<tr><td></td><td></td><td>18,723</td></tr>
<tr><td>Less: Returned NSF cheque</td><td>$ 239</td><td></td></tr>
<tr><td>   Bank service charges</td><td>37</td><td>276</td></tr>
<tr><td>Adjusted cash balance per books</td><td></td><td>$18,447</td></tr>
</table>

(continued)

Dec. 31	Cash	2,300	
	Accounts Receivable		2,300
	To record electronic receipts on account.		
31	Cash	9	
	Interest Revenue		9
	To record interest earned on bank account.		
31	Cash	81	
	Accounts Receivable ($290 – $209)		81
	To correct deposit error.		
31	Accounts Receivable ($239 + $10)	249	
	Cash		249
	To re-establish accounts receivable for NSF cheque and related service charge.		
31	Bank Charges Expense ($37 – $10)	27	
	Cash		27
	To record bank service charges.		

Cash

Dec. 31	Bal.	16,333	Dec. 31		249
	31	2,300	31		27
	31	9			
	31	81			
Dec. 31	Bal.	18,447			

Related exercise material: BE7–9, BE7–10, BE7–11, BE7–12, BE7–13, BE7–14, BE7–15, BE7–16, BE7–17, BE7–18, BE7–19, BE7–20, E7–8, E7–9, E7–10, E7–11, E7–12, E7–13, E7–14, and E7–15.

LEARNING OBJECTIVE **Report cash on the balance sheet.**

Reporting Cash

Companies report cash in two different statements: the balance sheet and the cash flow statement. The balance sheet reports the amount of cash available at a point in time (the date of the balance sheet). The cash flow statement shows the sources and uses of cash during a period of time. The cash flow statement was introduced in Chapter 1 and will be discussed in much more detail in Chapter 17.

When presented on the balance sheet, cash on hand, cash in banks, and petty cash are normally combined and reported simply as cash. Because cash is the most liquid asset owned by a company, Canadian companies have traditionally listed cash first in the current assets section of the balance sheet. A company may have cash that is not available for general use because it is restricted for a special purpose. An example is funds held on deposit until completion of an offer to buy real estate. Cash that has a restricted use—and is in a significant amount—should be reported separately on the balance sheet as **restricted cash**. If the restricted cash is expected to be used within the next year, the amount should be reported as a current asset. When restricted funds will not be used in that time, they should be reported as a non-current asset.

Illustration 7-8 shows how Canadian National Railway Co. (CN) presents its cash and cash equivalents and restricted cash on its balance sheet.

ETHICS NOTE
Recently, some companies were forced to restate their financial statements because they had too broadly interpreted which types of investments could be treated as cash equivalents. By reporting these items as cash equivalents, the companies made themselves look more liquid.

▶ ILLUSTRATION **7-8**
Presentation of cash

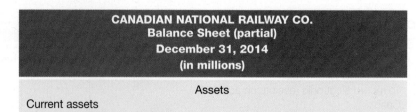

Assets	
CANADIAN NATIONAL RAILWAY CO.	
Balance Sheet (partial)	
December 31, 2014	
(in millions)	
Current assets	
Cash and cash equivalents	$ 52
Restricted cash and cash equivalents	463

In the notes to its financial statements, CN states that the company considers short-term investments that are highly liquid and have original maturities of three months or less as cash equivalents. The restricted cash and cash equivalents are related to collateral for letters of credit. Letters of credit are common for companies that are involved in international trade. In this case, CN has entered into agreements with various banks to restrict a guaranteed cash balance. In return, the bank holding the letter of credit guarantees payment to CN's suppliers.

Some companies may be in a cash deficit or negative position at year end. This can happen when the company is in an overdraft position at the bank. A **bank overdraft** occurs when withdrawals or payments are more than the amount in the bank account. This becomes a short-term loan from the bank, assuming that the bank does not reject the withdrawal or payment. Most companies have overdraft protection up to a certain amount with their banks. In an overdraft situation, the Cash account shows a credit balance in the general ledger and is reported as a current liability called bank indebtedness.

BEFORE YOU
GO ON...DO IT   **Balance Sheet Reporting**

On December 31, Ranchero Company has the following items: $12,250 in its bank chequing account, $6,400 in its bank savings account, a $250 petty cash fund, $4,300 of postdated cheques from customers, $8,800 in highly liquid short-term investments purchased with maturity dates of less than 90 days, $10,600 of short-term investments with maturity dates of 100 to 365 days, and $5,200 in a bank account restricted for use in settling advance ticket sales. How will each of these items be reported on the balance sheet?

Solution

The following items are reported as current assets on the balance sheet:

Action Plan
- Review which items are included in cash and cash equivalents.
- Determine the difference between cash equivalents and short-term investments.
- Recall that restricted cash balances must be reported separately.

1. Cash and cash equivalents		
Bank chequing account	$12,250	
Bank savings account	6,400	
Petty cash fund	250	
Highly liquid investments < 90 days	8,800	
Cash and cash equivalents		$27,700
2. Restricted cash		5,200
3. Short-term investments		10,600

Related exercise material: BE7–21, BE7–22, E7–16, and E7–17.

Comparing IFRS and ASPE

Key Differences	International Financial Reporting Standards (IFRS)	Accounting Standards for Private Enterprises (ASPE)
No significant differences		

Demonstration Problem

On the April 30, 2017, bank reconciliation for Gurjot Imports, there were three outstanding cheques: #286 for $217, #289 for $326, and #290 for $105. There were no deposits in transit as at April 30, 2017. The bank balance at April 30 was $4,261. The adjusted cash balance was $3,613. On May 31, the unadjusted bank balance was $8,885 and the unadjusted book balance was $5,657. The following is selected information from the May bank statement:

Cheques Cleared				Other Bank Account Transactions		
Date	Cheque No.	Amount		Date	Amount	Transaction
May 1	286	$ 217		May 8	$2,620+	Deposit
8	305	402		12	4,718+	Deposit
20	306	105		24	3,190+	Deposit
22	308	1,648		25	280−	NSF cheque
22	289	326		28	28−	Service charge
23	304	2,735		31	12+	Interest
31	309	175				
Total		$5,608				

The NSF cheque was originally received from a customer, R. Siddiqi, in payment of his account of $265. The bank included a $15 service charge for a total of $280. Information from the company's accounting records for May follows:

Cash Receipts			Cash Payments		
Date	Amount		Date	Cheque No.	Amount
May 5	$ 2,260		May 5	304	$2,735
12	4,718		5	305	402
23	3,190		19	306	150
31	1,004		19	307	3,266
Total	$11,172		31	309	175
			31	310	2,400
			Total		$9,128

Investigation reveals that cheque #306 was issued to pay the telephone bill and cheque #308 was issued to pay rent. All deposits are for collections of accounts receivable. The bank made no errors.

Instructions
(a) Prepare a bank reconciliation at May 31.
(b) Prepare the necessary adjusting entries at May 31.
(c) Post the adjustments to the Cash account. What balance would Gurjot Imports report as cash in the current assets section of its balance sheet on May 31, 2017?

ACTION PLAN

- Compare the deposits on the May bank statement with the May cash receipts on the company's records and note any differences. Cash receipts recorded by the company and not by the bank are deposits in transit.
- Compare the outstanding cheques at the end of April plus the cash payments in May in the company records with the cheques that cleared the bank in May to determine which cheques are outstanding at the end of May.
- Identify any items recorded by the bank but not by the company as reconciling items per books.
- If an item is recorded by both the company and the bank, but the amount is not exactly the same, determine if it is the bank or the company that made the error.
- All the reconciling items per books require adjusting journal entries.
- Post the adjustments to the Cash ledger account balance, and ensure the adjusted May 31 balance agrees with the adjusted cash balance per books on the bank reconciliation.

SOLUTION TO DEMONSTRATION PROBLEM

(a)

GURJOT IMPORTS
Bank Reconciliation
May 31, 2017

Unadjusted cash balance per bank balance		$8,885
Add: Deposits in transit		1,004
		9,889
Less: Outstanding cheques		
No. 290	$ 105	
No. 307	3,266	
No. 310	2,400	
		5,771
Adjusted cash balance per bank		$4,118
Unadjusted cash balance per books		$5,657
Add: Interest	$ 12	
Error: cheque #306 ($150 − $105)		
[Telephone expense]	45	
Error: May 5 deposit ($2,620 − $2,260)		
[Accounts receivable]	360	417
		6,074
Less: NSF cheque returned ($265 + $15)	$ 280	
Error: cheque #308 not recorded [Rent expense]	1,648	
Bank service charges	28	1,956
Adjusted cash balance		$4,118

(b)

May 31	Cash	12	
	Interest Revenue		12
	To record bank interest earned.		
31	Cash	45	
	Telephone Expense		45
	To correct error in recording cheque #306.		
31	Cash	360	
	Accounts Receivable		360
	To correct error in May 5 deposit.		
31	Accounts Receivable—R. Siddiqi	280	
	Cash		280
	To re-establish accounts receivable for NSF cheque and related service charge.		
31	Bank Charges Expense	28	
	Cash		28
	To record bank service charges.		
31	Rent Expense	1,648	
	Cash		1,648
	To record cheque #308 not recorded in error.		

(c)

	Cash		
May 31 Bal.	5,657	May 31	280
31	12	31	28
	45	31	1,648
	360		
May 31 Bal.	4,118*		

*Check that the balance is equal to the adjusted cash balance on the bank reconciliation.
The reported cash balance on the May 31, 2017, balance sheet is $4,118.

▶ Summary of Learning Objectives

1. **Define cash and internal control.** Cash not only includes coins and paper currency, it may also include cash equivalents. Cash equivalents are short-term, highly liquid (easily sold) investments that are not subject to significant risk of changes in value. Internal control consists of all the related methods and measures that management implements in order to achieve reliable financial reporting, effective and efficient operations, and compliance with relevant laws and regulations. Control activities include (a) establishment of responsibility, (b) segregation of duties, (c) documentation procedures, (d) physical and IT controls, (e) independent checks of performance, and (f) human resource controls.

2. **Apply control activities to cash receipts and cash payments.** Internal controls over cash receipts include (a) designating only personnel such as cashiers to handle cash; (b) assigning the duties of handling or receiving cash, and recording cash to different individuals; (c) using remittance advices for mail receipts, cash register tapes (or point-of-sale computerized systems) for over-the-counter receipts, and deposit slips for bank deposits; (d) using company safes and bank vaults to store cash, with only authorized personnel having access, and using cash registers; (e) depositing all cash intact daily; (f) making independent daily counts of register receipts and daily comparisons of total receipts with total deposits; and (g) bonding personnel who handle cash. Debit and credit card transactions increase internal control but have related bank charges. Electronic funds transfer receipts also increase internal control over cash receipts.

    Internal controls over cash payments include (a) authorizing only specified individuals such as the controller to sign cheques and authorize electronic funds transfer payments; (b) assigning the duties of approving items for payment, paying for the items, and recording the payment

to different individuals; (c) using pre-numbered cheques and accounting for all cheques, with each cheque supported by an approved invoice; (d) storing blank cheques and signing machines in a safe or vault, with access restricted to authorized personnel; (e) comparing each cheque with the approved invoice before issuing the cheque and making monthly reconciliations of bank and book balances; and (f) stamping each approved invoice "Paid" after payment.

3. **Describe the operation of a petty cash fund.** Companies operate a petty cash fund to pay relatively small amounts of cash. They must establish the fund, make payments from the fund, and replenish the fund. Journal entries are made only when the fund is established and replenished.

4. **Describe the control features of a bank account and prepare a bank reconciliation.** A bank account contributes to good internal control by giving physical and IT controls for the storage of cash, reducing the amount of currency that must be kept on hand, and creating a double record of a depositor's bank transactions.

    It is customary to reconcile the balance per books and balance per bank to their adjusted balance. Reconciling items include deposits in transit, outstanding cheques, errors by the bank, unrecorded bank memoranda, and errors by the company. Adjusting entries must be made for any errors made by the company and unrecorded bank memoranda (e.g., interest).

5. **Report cash on the balance sheet.** Cash is usually listed first in the current assets section of the balance sheet. Cash may be reported together with highly liquid, very short-term investments called cash equivalents. Cash that is restricted for a special purpose is reported separately as a current asset or a non-current asset, depending on when the cash is expected to be used.

▶ Glossary

Bank overdraft   What occurs when withdrawals are more than the amount available in the bank account. (p. 386)

Bank reconciliation   A comparison of the balance in a company's bank account with the balance in the cash account at a point in time that explains any differences. (p. 376)

Bank statement   A statement received monthly from the bank that shows the depositor's bank transactions and balances. (p. 378)

Bonding   Obtaining insurance protection against theft by employees. (p. 366)

Cash   Resources such as coins, currency (paper money), cheques, money orders, travellers' cheques, and money on deposit in a bank or similar depository. (p. 362)

Cash equivalents   Highly liquid, short-term investments with maturities of three months or less that are subject to an insignificant risk of changes in value. (p. 362)

Clearing   What occurs when a cheque or deposit is accepted by the maker's bank. Clearing results in a transfer of funds from the maker's bank to the payee's bank. (p. 377)

Credit memoranda (CM)   Supporting documentation for increases to a bank account that appear on a bank statement. (p. 379)

Debit memoranda (DM)   Supporting documentation for decreases to a bank account that appear on a bank statement. (p. 379)

Deposits in transit   Deposits recorded by the depositor that have not been recorded by the bank. (p. 379)

Electronic funds transfer (EFT)   The electronic exchange or transfer of money from one account to another, either within a single financial institution or across multiple institutions, through computer-based systems. (p. 370)

External auditors   Auditors who are independent of the organization. They report on whether or not the financial statements fairly present the financial position and performance of an organization. (p. 366)

Fraud   An intentional dishonest act that results in a personal financial benefit by misappropriating (stealing) assets or misstating financial statements. (p. 362)

Fraud triangle   The three factors that contribute to fraudulent activity by employees: opportunity, financial pressure, and rationalization. (p. 362)

Internal auditors   Company employees who evaluate the effectiveness of the company's system of internal control. (p. 366)

Internal control   The related methods and measures that management designs and implements to help an organization achieve reliable financial reporting, effective and efficient operations, and compliance with relevant laws and regulations. (p. 363)

NSF (not sufficient funds) cheque   A cheque that is not paid by the customer's bank and is returned to the depositor's bank because of insufficient funds in the customer's account. (p. 379)

Outstanding cheques   Cheques issued and recorded by a company that have not been paid by the bank. (p. 379)

Petty cash fund   A cash fund that is used for paying relatively small amounts. (p. 373)

Reconciling the bank account   The process of making the balance in a company's general ledger cash account agree with the balance per bank. (p. 379)

Restricted cash   Cash that is not available for general use, but instead is restricted for a particular purpose. (p. 385)

▶ Self-Study Questions

Answers are at the end of the chapter.

(LO 1) K   1. Which of the following factors could limit a company's system of internal control?
   (a) Collusion by two or more employees
   (b) The cost of internal control being greater than the benefit
   (c) Difficulty in segregating duties in small businesses
   (d) All of the above

(LO 1) K   2. The principles of internal control do *not* include:
   (a) establishment of responsibility.
   (b) documentation procedures.
   (c) management responsibility.
   (d) independent internal verification.

(LO 1) C   3. Permitting only designated personnel to handle cash receipts is an application of the concept of:
   (a) segregation of duties.
   (b) establishment of responsibility.
   (c) independent checks of performance.
   (d) human resource controls.

(LO 2) AP   4. The use of pre-numbered cheques in disbursing cash is an application of the principle of:
   (a) establishment of responsibility.
   (b) segregation of duties.
   (c) physical controls.
   (d) documentation procedures.

(LO 2) C   5. Authorizing only designated personnel to sign cheques is an application of the principle of:
   (a) establishment of responsibility.
   (b) segregation of duties.
   (c) independent checks of performance.
   (d) documentation procedures.

(LO 3) AP   6. A cheque is written to replenish a $150 petty cash fund when the fund has receipts of $148 and $7 in cash. In recording the cheque:
   (a) Cash Over and Short should be debited for $5.
   (b) Cash Over and Short should be credited for $5.
   (c) Petty Cash should be debited for $148.
   (d) Cash should be credited for $148.

(LO 4) K   7. Bank accounts improve control over cash by:
(a) safeguarding cash by using a bank as a depository.
(b) minimizing the amount of cash that must be kept on hand.
(c) giving a double record of all bank transactions.
(d) all of the above.

(LO 4) AP   8. Suzanne Terriault has a balance of $410 in her chequebook (her Cash account) at the end of the month. The balance on her bank statement is $500. Reconciling items include deposits in transit of $250, outstanding cheques of $350, and service charges of $10. What is Suzanne's adjusted cash balance?
(a) $390
(b) $400
(c) $410
(d) $500

(LO 4) AP   9. A company mistakenly recorded a $348 cheque written in payment of an account as $384. The journal entry required to correct this would be:
(a) debit Accounts Payable $36; credit Cash $36.
(b) debit Cash $36; credit Accounts Payable $36.
(c) debit Accounts Payable $348; credit Cash $348.
(d) debit Cash $384; credit Accounts Payable $384.

(LO 5) K   10. Which of the following correctly describes the reporting of cash?
(a) Petty cash must be reported separately from cash on the balance sheet.
(b) Restricted cash funds are always reported as a current asset.
(c) Cash equivalents may be combined with cash on the balance sheet.
(d) Postdated cheques from customers are included in the Cash account balance.

Questions

(LO 1) K   1. Define cash and cash equivalents. Give an example of each.

(LO 1) C   2. "Internal control can help organizations achieve efficiency of operations." Do you agree? Explain.

(LO 1) K   3. In an ice cream shop, all employees make change out of the same cash register drawer. Is this a violation of internal control? Why or why not?

(LO 1) C   4. Trushi Miyamura is questioning why independent checks of performance are important if the company also segregates duties. Respond to Trushi's question.

(LO 1) K   5. What are documentation procedures? Provide an example and explain how it contributes to good internal control.

(LO 1) C   6. Joan Trainer is trying to design internal control activities so that there is no possibility of errors or theft. Explain to Joan why this may be impractical, and may even be impossible.

(LO 2) K   7. What are the similarities and differences between a debit card sale and a bank credit card sale to a retailer? To the customer?

(LO 2) C   8. Over-the-counter cash receipts require special care. Explain the procedures that should be followed at the end of the day (or shift) to ensure proper internal control.

(LO 2) C   9. Best Books has just installed electronic cash registers with scanners in its stores. How do cash registers such as these improve internal control over cash receipts?

(LO 2) C   10. Describe appropriate internal control procedures for handling cheques received by mail.

(LO 2) C   11. Sanjeet argues that no special internal controls are required for electronic funds transfer (EFT) cash receipts because employees are not handling cash or cheques. Is Sanjeet correct? Explain.

(LO 2) C   12. "Use of cash for payments should be avoided. Effective internal control over cash payments can only be achieved by the use of cheques or electronic funds transfer." Is this true? Explain.

(LO 2) C   13. Walter's Watches is a small retail store. Walter, the owner of the company, has recently hired a new employee, Wanda, who will be responsible for selling and shipping merchandise to customers, invoicing the customer, and receiving and recording the customer's payment. Describe the various ways Wanda could commit a fraud with this arrangement.

(LO 3) K   14. Identify the three activities that pertain to a petty cash fund, and indicate an internal control principle that applies to each activity.

(LO 3) K   15. When are journal entries required in the operation of a petty cash fund?

(LO 4) K   16. Opening a bank account is a simple procedure. Give four examples of how a bank account improves a company's internal controls.

(LO 4) C   17. What is the purpose of a bank reconciliation? Who should prepare it? Why is it important to have the appropriate person prepare it?

(LO 4) K   18. What are the four steps involved in finding differences between the balance per books and balance per bank?

(LO 4) K   19. Nicholas Kerpatrick asks for your help concerning an NSF cheque. Explain to Nicholas (a) what an NSF cheque is, (b) how it is treated in a bank reconciliation, and (c) whether it will require an adjusting entry.

(LO 4) K   20. Paul Reimer does not keep a personal record of his bank account and does not see the need to do a bank reconciliation. He says he can always use on-line banking to look up the balance in his bank account before writing a cheque. Explain why Paul should keep his own records and do regular bank reconciliations.

(LO 4) C   21. Jayne is reviewing her June 30 bank statement and notices an entry for $32 regarding monthly interest. Jayne is not sure if she should include this in her bank reconciliation or not. If it is included, then she believes it should be in the bank section of the

reconciliation because it is on the bank statement. Explain to Jayne how to handle this item.

(LO 5) C   22. "Since cash is an asset, the Cash account must always have a debit balance. If it has a credit balance, that means there is an error in the account." Do you agree? Explain.

(LO 5) K   23. What is restricted cash? How should it be reported on the balance sheet?

▶ Brief Exercises

Determine the cash balance. (LO 1) C

BE7–1   Riverside Fertilizer Co. owns the following items:

Cash in bank savings account	$ 8,000
Cash on hand	850
Cash refund due from the Canada Revenue Agency	1,000
Chequing account balance	14,000
Postdated cheques	500

What amount should Riverside report as cash?

Identify control activities. (LO 1) C

BE7–2   Nathan McPhail is the new owner of Liberty Parking, a parking garage. He has heard about internal control but is not clear about its importance for his business. Explain to Nathan the six types of control activities. Give him an example of how each type of activity might apply to his business.

Identify control activities applicable to cash receipts. (LO 2) C

BE7–3   Miramichi Company has the following internal controls over cash receipts. Identify the control activity that is applicable to each of the following.

1. The company conducts thorough background checks on all cashiers when they are hired.
2. All sales must be entered into the cash register through a scanner and point-of-sale software.
3. Surprise cash counts are made by the department supervisors.
4. The duties of receiving cash, recording cash, and maintaining custody of cash are assigned to different individuals.
5. At the end of his or her shift, the cashier ensures there are receipts on hand for all debit or credit card sales.
6. Each cashier uses a different cash register and uses a separate password.

Identify control activities applicable to cash payments. (LO 2) C

BE7–4   Bujold Company has the following internal controls over cash payments. Identify the control activity that is applicable to each of the following.

1. Company cheques are pre-numbered.
2. Blank cheques are stored in a safe in the controller's office.
3. All employees in the accounting department are required to take vacations each year.
4. The bank statement is reconciled monthly by the assistant controller.
5. Both the controller and the treasurer are required to sign cheques or authorize EFT.
6. Cheque signers are not allowed to record cash payments.

Record debit card transactions. (LO 2) AP

BE7–5   On September 12, five customers use debit cards to purchase merchandise totalling $500 from Triomedia Company. The bank charges Triomedia Company $0.70 per debit card transaction. Prepare the entry to record the transactions by Triomedia Company.

Record credit card transactions. (LO 2) AP

BE7–6   On April 16, Triomedia Company made sales of $12,950 to customers using credit cards for payment. The credit card company charges Triomedia a service fee of 2.5% for credit card transactions. Prepare the entry to record the credit card sales. Round to the nearest dollar.

Record entries to establish and replenish a petty cash fund. (LO 3) AP

BE7–7   On March 2, Pugh Company established a petty cash fund of $100. On March 27, the fund was replenished when it had $18 in cash and receipts for supplies $20, postage for $27, and repairs expense $35.

(a) Prepare the journal entries to establish the petty cash fund on March 2.
(b) Prepare the journal entry to replenish the petty cash fund on March 27.

Record entry to replenish a petty cash fund. (LO 3) AP

BE7–8   Carla's Snack Shop has a petty cash fund of $100. On November 30, the fund contained $10 in cash and receipts for postage of $31, supplies of $42, and travel expenses of $16. Make the journal entry to replenish the fund.

BE7–9 Lance Bachman is uncertain about the control features of a bank account. Explain the control benefits of (a) a cheque and (b) a bank statement.

BE7–10 How would each of the following items be recorded on a bank reconciliation? Next to each item, record the correct letter from this list: (a) increase to bank balance, (b) decrease to bank balance, (c) increase to company cash balance, (d) decrease to company cash balance, or (e) not included in the bank reconciliation.

1. _____ EFT payment made by a customer
2. _____ Bank debit memorandum for service charges
3. _____ Outstanding cheques from the current month
4. _____ Bank error in recording a $1,779 deposit as $1,977
5. _____ Outstanding cheques from the previous month that are still outstanding
6. _____ Outstanding cheques from the previous month that are no longer outstanding
7. _____ Bank error in recording a company cheque made out for $160 as $610
8. _____ Bank credit memorandum for interest revenue
9. _____ Company error in recording a deposit of $160 as $1,600
10. _____ Bank debit memorandum for a customer's NSF cheque
11. _____ Deposit in transit from the current month
12. _____ Company error in recording a cheque made out for $630 as $360

BE7–11 Referring to BE7–10, indicate (a) the items that will result in an adjustment to the company's records, and (b) why the other items do not require an adjustment.

BE7–12 Jayden Randolph owns Randolph Electric. Jayden asks you to explain how he should treat the following items when reconciling the company's bank account:

(a) Outstanding cheques of $1,200
(b) Deposits in transit of $5,250
(c) Debit memorandum for bank service charge of $25
(d) EFT of $1,970 from a customer for goods received

BE7–13 Referring to Randolph Electric in BE7–12, Jayden indicates on December 31 the unadjusted balance per his books is $8,758 and the unadjusted balance on his bank statement is $6,653. Prepare a bank reconciliation.

BE7–14 Refer to the bank reconciliation for Randolph Electric prepared in BE7–13. Prepare the adjusting journal entries.

BE7–15 At July 31, Ramirez Company has the following bank information: cash balance per bank $7,420, outstanding cheques $762, deposits in transit $1,620, and a bank service charge $20. Determine the adjusted cash balance per bank at July 31.

BE7–16 At August 31, Pratt Company has a cash balance per books of $9,500 and the following additional data from the bank statement: charge for printing Pratt Company cheques $35, interest earned on chequing account balance $40, and outstanding cheques $800.

Determine the adjusted cash balance per books at August 31.

BE7–17 On August 31, Howel Company had an unadjusted cash balance of $10,050. An examination of the August bank statement shows a balance of $8,370 on August 31, bank service charges of $40, deposits in transit of $3,005, interest earned of $22, outstanding cheques of $1,623, and an NSF cheque of $280. Prepare a bank reconciliation at August 31.

BE7–18 Refer to the bank reconciliation prepared in BE7–17. Prepare the adjusting journal entries for Howel Company on August 31.

BE7–19 The following errors were found when the controller at Westshore Hotel was doing the March 31 bank reconciliation.

1. On March 5, Westshore recorded a payment of an account payable as $2,270. The correct amount was $1,270. It was correctly recorded by the bank.
2. On March 19, Westshore recorded a deposit as $2,450. The correct amount was $4,250. The deposit was for the collection of an account receivable and the bank recorded it correctly.
3. On March 31, the bank recorded a deposit as $5,750. The correct amount was $2,720. This error was corrected by the bank on April 1. Westshore had correctly recorded the deposit.

For each of these errors, (a) indicate if and how it would be shown on the bank reconciliation, and (b) prepare an adjusting entry for Westshore if required.

Analyze errors. (LO 4) AP

BE7–20   The following errors were found when the controller at East Mountain Motel was doing the June 30 bank reconciliation.

1. On June 7, East Mountain recorded a payment of an account payable as $2,810. The correct amount was $1,810. It was correctly recorded by the bank.
2. On June 20, East Mountain recorded a deposit as $2,222. The correct amount was $3,333. The deposit was for the collection of an account receivable and the bank recorded it correctly.
3. On June 25, the bank posted a cheque in the amount of $825 to East Mountain's bank account. The cheque had been written by another company, East Mountainside Company.

For each of these errors, (a) indicate if and how it would be shown on the bank reconciliation, and (b) prepare an adjusting entry for East Mountain if required.

Calculate cash. (LO 5) AP

BE7–21   Sirois Company owns the following assets at the balance sheet date:

Cash in bank—savings account	$ 5,500
Cash on hand	750
Cash refund due from the Canada Revenue Agency	1,000
Cash in bank—chequing account	10,000
Stale-dated cheques from customers	250
Postdated cheques from customers	500
60-day treasury bill	3,500

What amount should be reported as cash and cash equivalents in the balance sheet?

Explain statement presentation. (LO 5) C

BE7–22   Dupré Company has the following items: cash in bank $17,500, payroll bank account $6,000, store cash floats $1,500, petty cash fund $250, short-term, highly liquid investments with maturity dates of less than 90 days $15,000, short-term investments with maturity dates of 100 to 365 days $40,000, and plant expansion fund cash $25,000. The plant expansion will begin in three years. Explain how each item should be reported on the balance sheet.

▶ Exercises

Identify internal control strengths and weaknesses and suggest improvements. (LO 1) C

E7–1   The following situations suggest either a strength or a weakness in internal control.

1. At Frederico's, Amanda and Long work alternate lunch hours. Normally Amanda works the cash register at the checkout counter, but during her lunch hour Long takes her place. They both use the same cash drawer and count cash together at the end of the day.
2. Sandeep is a very hard-working employee at Stan's Hardware. Sandeep does such a good job that he is responsible for most of the company's office and accounting tasks. The only thing the owner has to do is sign cheques.
3. At Half Pipe Skate, they are very concerned about running an efficient, low-cost business. Consequently, the manager has assigned the same individual to do the purchasing and prepare the receiving reports when the merchandise is delivered.
4. At Traction Tires, most of the tires are stored in a fenced outdoor storage area. One of the employees noticed a place where the fence needed to be repaired and reported this to the manager. The fence was fixed before the close of business that night.
5. The internal auditors at Humber Manufacturing regularly report their findings to senior management, who get the accounting department to investigate and resolve any problems.
6. All employees at Vincent Travel take a vacation every year. During that time, with the exception of the controller's position, the employees' duties are assigned to another individual while they are on vacation.

Instructions

(a) State whether each situation above is a strength or a weakness in internal control.
(b) For each weakness, suggest an improvement.

Identify weaknesses in internal control over cash receipts and suggest improvements. (LO 1, 2) C

E7–2   The following control procedures are used in Sheridan Company for cash receipts.

1. To minimize the risk of robbery, cash in excess of $200 is stored in a locked metal box in the office manager's office until it is deposited in the bank. All employees know where the office manager keeps the key to the box.
2. The company has one cash register with a single cash drawer. Any one of three employees may operate the cash register.
3. All employees handling cash receipts are experienced and therefore are not bonded.
4. In order to increase efficiency, the assistant controller opens all of the mail, prepares the bank deposit, and prepares the journal entries to record the cash receipts.
5. Due to a lack of storage space, all remittance advices and debit or credit card sales receipts are destroyed each weekend.

Instructions

(a) For each procedure, explain the weaknesses in internal control, and identify the control activity that is violated.

(b) For each weakness, suggest a change in procedure that will result in good internal control.

E7–3 Presented below are three independent situations.

1. On March 15, 40 customers used debit cards to purchase merchandise for a total of $8,740 from Hockey Town. Hockey Town pays a $1.35 debit card fee for each transaction.
2. On June 21, Circle Creations Gallery sells a painting to Constance Furrow for $1,960. Constance uses her Visa bank credit card to pay for the purchase. The bank charges Circle Creations a 4.0% fee for all credit card transactions. On July 17, Constance receives her Visa bill and pays for this purchase. Round to the nearest dollar.
3. On October 7, A. Ramos uses his store credit card to purchase merchandise from The Bay for $550. On November 10, Ramos receives his credit card bill from The Bay and pays for this purchase.

Prepare entries for debit and credit card sales. (LO 2) AP

Instructions

(a) Prepare Hockey Town's journal entries for the transactions in part (1).
(b) Prepare Circle Creations' journal entries for the transactions in part (2).
(c) Prepare The Bay's journal entries for the transactions in part (3).

E7–4 The following control procedures are used in Centennial Bay General Merchandise for cash payments.

Identify weaknesses in internal control over cash payments, and suggest improvements. (LO 1, 2) AP

1. Company cheques are not pre-numbered and are kept in an unlocked file cabinet in the controller's office.
2. Cheques must be signed by the controller.
3. The purchasing agent verifies that the goods have been received, verifies the accuracy of the invoice, and authorizes the controller to issue a cheque for the purchase.
4. After the controller prepares and signs the cheque, she stamps the invoice "paid" and files it. She then records the cheque in the journal.
5. The controller prepares the bank reconciliation on a monthly basis and gives it to the company owner. As the company owner trusts the controller, he doesn't bother checking the bank reconciliations.
6. Background checks are not conducted on personnel hired for senior positions such as the purchasing agent or controller.
7. The company owner is impressed with how hard the purchasing agent works. He hasn't taken a vacation in two years.

Instructions

(a) For each procedure, explain the weaknesses in internal control, and identify the control activity that is violated.
(b) For each weakness, suggest a change in procedure that will result in good internal control.

E7–5 Bulyea Boxes uses a petty cash imprest system. The fund was established on February 14 with a balance of $100. On February 28, there were $5 cash and the following petty cash receipts in the petty cash box:

Record petty cash transactions. (LO 3) AP

Date	Receipt No.	For	Amount
Feb. 15	1	Supplies	$10
18	2	Miscellaneous expense	7
20	3	Freight in (assume perpetual inventory system)	30
21	4	Supplies	13
22	5	Delivery charges on outgoing freight	17
27	6	Supplies	23

Instructions

(a) Record the journal entry on February 14 to establish the petty cash fund.
(b) Record the journal entry on February 28 to replenish the fund and increase the balance to $175.

E7–6 Brooklyn Buttons uses a petty cash imprest system. The fund was established on September 4 with a balance of $200. On September 30, there were $50 cash and the following petty cash receipts in the petty cash box:

Record petty cash transactions. (LO 3) AP

Date	Receipt No.	For	Amount
Sept. 5	1	Freight in (assume perpetual inventory system)	$25
9	2	Delivery charges on outgoing freight	15
14	3	Freight in	30
16	4	Supplies	10
20	5	Delivery charges on outgoing freight	20
29	6	Freight in	40

Instructions

(a) Record the journal entry on September 4 to establish the petty cash fund.

(b) Record the journal entry on September 30 to replenish the fund and decrease the balance to $150.

Record petty cash transactions. (LO 3) AP

E7-7   Kris Allen Company established a petty cash fund on May 1, cashing a cheque for $150. The company reimbursed the fund on June 1 and July 1 with the following results.

	June 1:	Cash in fund, $4.75	
		Receipts:	
		Delivery expense	$31.25
		Postage expense	39.00
		Travel expense	62.00
	July 1:	Cash in fund, $3.25	
		Receipts:	
		Delivery expense	$31.00
		Entertainment expense	71.00
		Supplies	44.75

On July 10, Kris Allen increased the fund from $150 to $200.

Instructions

Prepare journal entries for Kris Allen Company for May 1, June 1, July 1, and July 10.

Prepare bank reconciliation and related entries. (LO 4) AP

E7-8   The following information is for Tindall Company in September:

1. Cash balance per bank, September 30, $7,100.
2. Cash balance per books, September 30, $5,470.
3. Outstanding cheques, $3,120.
4. Bank service charge, $22.
5. NSF cheque from customer, $220.
6. Deposits in transit, $1,380.
7. EFT receipts from customers in payment of their accounts, $78.
8. Cheque #212 was correctly written and posted by the bank as $428. Tindall Company had recorded the cheque as $482 in error. The cheque was written for the purchase of supplies.

Instructions

(a) Prepare a bank reconciliation at September 30, 2017.

(b) Journalize the adjusting entries at September 30, 2017, on Tindall Company's books.

Prepare bank reconciliation and related entries. (LO 4) AP

E7-9   Don Wyatt is unable to reconcile the bank balance at January 31. Don's reconciliation is as follows.

Cash balance per bank	$3,560.20
Add: NSF cheque	490.00
Less: Bank service charge	25.00
Adjusted balance per bank	$4,025.20
Cash	$3,875.20
Less: Deposits in transit	530.00
Add: Outstanding cheques	730.00
Adjusted balance per books	$4,075.20

Instructions

(a) Prepare a correct bank reconciliation.

(b) Journalize the entries required by the reconciliation.

Prepare bank reconciliation and related entries. (LO 4) AP

E7-10   The following information is for Crane Video Company:

1. Cash balance per bank, July 31, $7,263.
2. July bank service charge not recorded by the depositor, $28.
3. Cash balance per books, July 31, $7,284.
4. Deposits in transit, July 31, $1,300.
5. Bank collected $700 note for Crane in July, plus interest $36, less fee $20. The collection has not been recorded by Crane, and no interest has been accrued.
6. Outstanding cheques, July 31, $591.

Instructions

(a) Prepare a bank reconciliation at July 31.

(b) Journalize the adjusting entries at July 31 on the books of Crane Video Company.

E7–11 The following information is for Brad's Burger Company:

1. Cash balance per bank, July 31, $7,363.
2. July bank service charge not recorded by the depositor, $22.
3. The bank erroneously charged another company's $700 cheque against Brad's Burger's account.
4. Cash balance per books, July 31, $8,784.
5. The bank charged Brad's Burger's account $350 for a customer's NSF cheque.
6. Deposits in transit, July 31, $2,200.
7. Brad's Burger recorded a cash receipt from a cash sale from a customer as $32. The bank correctly recorded it as $23.
8. The bank collected a $1,250 note for Brad's Burger in July, plus interest of $36, less a fee of $20. The collection has not been recorded by Brad's Burger and no interest has been accrued.
9. Outstanding cheques, July 31, $594.

Prepare bank reconciliation and related entries. (LO 4) AP

Instructions

(a) Prepare a bank reconciliation for July 31.
(b) Journalize the adjusting entries for July 31 on the books of Brad's Burger Company.

E7–12 On April 30, the bank reconciliation of Hidden Valley Company shows a deposit in transit of $1,437. The May bank statement and the general ledger Cash account in May show the following:

Determine deposits in transit and other reconciling items. (LO 4) AP

HIDDEN VALLEY COMPANY Bank Statement (partial) Deposits/Credits		
Date	Description	Amount
May 1	Deposit	$1,437
5	Deposit	2,255
12	Deposit	3,281
20	Deposit	945
26	Deposit	1,298
30	EFT	956
30	Interest Earned	32

HIDDEN VALLEY COMPANY Cash Account (partial) Deposits Made	
Date	Amount
May 2	$2,255
9	3,218
16	945
23	1,298
30	1,353

Additional information:

1. The bank did not make any errors in May.
2. EFT is an electronic on-line payment from a customer.

Instructions

(a) List the deposits in transit at May 31.
(b) List any other items that must be included in the bank reconciliation. Describe the impact of each item on the bank reconciliation.

E7–13 On April 30, the bank reconciliation of Hidden Valley Company shows three outstanding cheques: No. 254 for $560, No. 255 for $262, and No. 257 for $620. The May bank statement and the general ledger Cash account in May show the following:

Determine outstanding cheques and other reconciling items. (LO 4) AP

HIDDEN VALLEY COMPANY Bank Statement (partial) Cheques Paid/Debits		
Date	Cheque No.	Amount
May 2	254	$560
5	258	159
12	257	620
15	259	275
20	260	500
22	NSF	395
28	263	440
30	262	750
30	SC	54

HIDDEN VALLEY COMPANY Cash Account (partial) Cheques Written		
Date	Cheque No.	Amount
May 2	258	$159
5	259	275
9	260	50
15	261	786
22	262	750
23	263	440
29	264	680

Additional information:

1. The bank did not make any errors in May.
2. NSF is a customer's cheque that was returned because the customer did not have sufficient funds.
3. SC stands for service charge.

Instructions

(a) List the outstanding cheques at May 31.
(b) List any other items that must be included in the bank reconciliation. Describe the impact of each item on the bank reconciliation.

Analyze errors. (LO 4) AP

E7–14   The following errors were found when the controller at Country Lane Camping was doing the July 31 bank reconciliation.

1. On July 9, Country Lane recorded a deposit as $2,050. The correct amount was $2,090. The deposit was for the collection of an account receivable and the bank recorded it correctly.
2. On July 14, Country Lane recorded a payment on account as $1,060. The correct amount was $610. It was correctly recorded by the bank.
3. On July 16, Country Lane recorded a payment for the purchase of supplies as $360. The correct amount was $630. It was correctly recorded by the bank.
4. On July 22, the bank recorded a deposit as $940. The correct amount was $490. This error was corrected by the bank on July 23. Country Lane had correctly recorded the deposit.
5. On July 25, Country Lane recorded a deposit as $670. The correct amount was $970. The deposit was for the collection of an account receivable. This deposit was correctly recorded by the bank on July 28.
6. On July 31, the bank debited Country Lane's account $200 for a cheque written by another company, Country Land, because the account number on the cheque had been damaged. The bank employee who looked up the account number made a mistake.

Instructions

(a) Describe the impact of each of these items on the bank reconciliation.
(b) Prepare any adjusting entries that Country Lane will need to record.

Prepare a bank reconciliation. (LO 4) AP

E7–15   On August 31, 2017, Claresview Company had a cash balance per its books of $26,030. The bank statement on that date showed a balance of $17,100. A comparison of the bank statement with the Cash account revealed the following.

1. The August 31 deposit of $17,050 was not included on the August bank statement.
2. The bank statement shows that Claresview received EFT deposits from customers on account totalling $2,050 in August. Claresview has not recorded any of these amounts.
3. Cheque #673 for $1,490 was outstanding on July 31. It did not clear the bank account in August. All of the cheques written in August have cleared the bank by August 31, except for cheque #710 for $2,550, and #712 for $2,480.
4. The bank statement showed on August 29 an NSF charge of $416 for a cheque issued by R. Dubai, a customer, in payment of their account. This amount included an $11 service charge by Claresview's bank.
5. Bank service charges of $25 were included on the August statement.
6. The bank recorded cheque #705 for $189 as $198. The cheque had been issued to pay for freight out on a sale. Claresview had correctly recorded the cheque.

Instructions

(a) Prepare a bank reconciliation at August 31.
(b) Prepare the necessary adjusting entries on August 31.

Calculate cash balance and report other items. (LO 5) AP

E7–16   A new accountant at Magenta Company is trying to identify which of the following amounts should be reported as the current asset Cash in the year-end balance sheet, as at June 30, 2017:

1. Currency and coins totalling $76 in a locked box used for petty cash transactions.
2. A 60-day, $12,900 guaranteed investment certificate, due July 31, 2017.
3. June-dated cheques worth $375 that Magenta has received from customers but not yet deposited.
4. A $104 cheque received from a customer in payment of her June account, but postdated to July 1.
5. A balance of $2,360 in the Royal Bank chequing account.
6. A balance of $4,160 in the Royal Bank savings account.
7. Prepaid postage of $52 in the postage meter.
8. A $110 IOU from the company receptionist.
9. Cash register floats of $330.
10. Over-the-counter cash receipts for June 30 consisting of $540 of currency and coins, $90 of cheques from customers, $550 of debit card slips, and $740 of bank credit card slips. These amounts were processed by the bank and posted to the bank account on July 1.

Instructions

(a) What amount should Magenta report as its cash and cash equivalents balance at June 30, 2017?

(b) In which financial statement and in which account should the items not included as cash and cash equivalents be reported?

E7–17 Wynn Company has recorded the following items in its financial records:

Cash in bank	$ 42,000
Cash in plant expansion fund	100,000
Cash on hand	12,000
Highly liquid investments	34,000
Petty cash	500
Receivables from customers	89,000
Stock investments	61,000

Calculate cash balance and report other items. (LO 5) AP

The highly liquid investments had maturities of three months or less when they were purchased. The stock investments will be sold in the next six to 12 months. The plant expansion project will begin in three years.

Instructions

(a) What amount should Wynn report as "Cash and cash equivalents" on its balance sheet?

(b) Where should the items not included in part (a) be reported on the balance sheet?

▶ Problems: Set A

P7–1A Seegall Supply Company recently changed its system of internal control over its purchasing operations and cash payments to make the system more efficient. One employee is now responsible for both purchasing and receiving. For each purchase, that individual matches the purchase order with the receiving report and the supplier's invoice. The invoice is approved for payment by this individual and sent to the accounting department.

Identify internal control activities related to cash payments. (LO 1, 2) C

All cheques are pre-numbered and kept in a safe in the controller's office. The combination to the safe is known only by the controller, his assistant, and the company owner. Since the bank has never made a mistake with the account, the cheque numbers are not tracked.

The controller prepares all of the cheques and all of the journal entries. All cheques must be signed by the company owner, Stephanie Seegall. After the owner has signed the cheque, the controller stamps the invoice paid and has his assistant file the invoice and post the journal entry. Whenever the owner is going to be away for several days, she will leave signed blank cheques in the safe for the controller.

The controller prepares the monthly bank reconciliation. Every month he finds at least three cheques that have cleared the bank but have not been recorded by the company. These cheques are always properly signed by the owner. When the controller first started working for the company, he would ask the owner about the cheques. These cheques were always for the owner's personal expenses, so now he always records these cheques as owner's drawings when doing the bank reconciliation.

Instructions

(a) Identify the control weaknesses over cash payments.

(b) What changes should be made to improve the internal control over cash payments?

TAKING IT FURTHER Often people think internal control activities are too much work and not necessary. Explain how an improved system of internal control could help protect the individuals working for this company from being falsely accused of fraud.

P7–2A Each of the following independent situations has one or more internal control weaknesses.

Identify internal control weaknesses for cash receipts and cash payments. (LO 1, 2) C

1. Board Riders is a small snowboarding club that offers specialized coaching for teenagers who want to improve their skills. Group lessons are offered every day. Members who want a lesson pay a $15 fee directly to the teacher at the start of the lesson that day. Most members pay cash. At the end of the lesson, the teacher reports the number of students and turns over the cash to the office manager.

2. Coloroso Agency offers parenting advice to young single mothers. Most of the agency's revenues are from government grants. The general manager is responsible for all of the accounting work, including approving invoices for payment, preparing and posting all entries into the accounting system, and preparing bank reconciliations.

3. At Nexus Company, each salesperson is responsible for deciding on the correct credit policies for his or her customers. For example, the salesperson decides if Nexus should sell to the customer on credit and how high the credit limit should be. Salespeople receive a commission based on their sales.

4. Algorithm Company is a software company that employs many computer programmers. The company uses accounting software that was created by one of the employees. In order to be more flexible and share the workload, all of the programmers have access to the accounting software program in case changes are needed.

5. The warehouse manager at Orange Wing Distributors is well known for running an efficient, cost-saving operation. He has eliminated the requirement for staff to create receiving reports and purchase orders because it was taking staff too long to prepare them.

Instructions

(a) Identify the internal control weaknesses in each situation.

(b) Explain the problems that could occur as a result of these weaknesses.

TAKING IT FURTHER Make recommendations for correcting each situation.

Identify internal control weaknesses over cash receipts and cash payments and suggest improvements. (LO 1, 2) C

P7–3A Cedar Grove Middle School wants to raise money for a new sound system for its auditorium. The main fundraising event is a dance at which the famous disc jockey Obnoxious Al will play classic and not-so-classic dance tunes. Roger DeMaster, the music teacher, has been given the responsibility for coordinating the fundraising efforts. This is Roger's first experience with fundraising. He asks the Student Representative Council (SRC) to help him with the event.

Roger had 500 unnumbered tickets printed for the dance. He left the tickets in a box on his desk and told the SRC students to take as many tickets as they thought they could sell for $5 each. In order to ensure that no extra tickets would be floating around, he told them to dispose of any unsold tickets. When the students received payment for the tickets, they were to bring the cash back to Roger. He then put it in a locked box in his desk drawer.

Some of the students were responsible for decorating the gymnasium for the dance. Roger gave each of them a key to the cash box. He told them that if they took money out to buy materials, they should put a note in the box saying how much they took and what it was used for. After two weeks, the cash box appeared to be getting full, so Roger asked Freda Stevens to count the money, prepare a deposit slip, and deposit the money in a bank account Roger had opened.

The day of the dance, Roger wrote a cheque from the account to pay Obnoxious Al. Al said that he accepted only cash and did not give receipts. So Roger took $200 out of the cash box and gave it to Al. At the dance, Roger had Sara Billings working at the entrance to the gymnasium. She collected tickets from students and sold tickets to those who had not prepurchased them. Roger estimated 400 students attended the dance.

The following day, Roger closed out the bank account, which had $250 in it. He gave that amount plus the $180 in the cash box to Principal Skinner. Principal Skinner seemed surprised that, after generating roughly $2,000 in sales, the dance netted only $430 in cash. Roger did not know how to respond.

Instructions

(a) Identify the weaknesses in internal control over cash receipts and cash payments.

(b) What improvements in internal control should the school consider?

TAKING IT FURTHER Often people think internal control activities are too much work and not necessary. Explain how an improved system of internal control could help protect the individuals involved in this situation from being falsely accused of fraud.

Record petty cash transactions and identify internal controls. (LO 1, 2, 3) AP

P7–4A Forney Company maintains a petty cash fund for small expenditures. The following transactions occurred over a two-month period:

Feb. 1 Established petty cash fund by writing a cheque on Algonquin Bank for $200.

Feb. 15 Replenished the petty cash fund by writing a cheque for $195.00. On this date the fund consisted of $5.00 in cash and the following petty cash receipts:

Freight out	$82.00
Postage expense	72.50
Entertainment expense	36.60

Feb. 28 Replenished the petty cash fund by writing a cheque for $152.00. At this date, the fund consisted of $48.00 in cash and the following petty cash receipts:

Freight out	$42.50
Contributions expense	25.00
Repairs expense	41.90
Supplies	45.00

Mar. 15 Replenished the petty cash fund by writing a cheque for $187.00. On this date, the fund consisted of $13.00 in cash and the following petty cash receipts:

Freight out	$37.60
Entertainment expense	53.75
Postage expense	33.25
Supplies	67.00

Mar. 16   Increased the amount of the petty cash fund to $250 by writing a cheque for $50.
Mar. 31   Replenished the petty cash fund by writing a cheque for $234.00. On this date, the fund consisted of $16 in cash and the following petty cash receipts:

Postage expense	$40.00
Travel expense	75.60
Freight out	47.10
Entertainment expense	68.50

Instructions

(a) Journalize the petty cash transactions.
(b) What internal control features exist in a petty cash fund?

TAKING IT FURTHER   Forney Company established a petty cash fund to pay for a variety of low-value items. Su Ma, the petty cash custodian, regularly borrows cash from the fund to pay for personal expenses. Su Ma has always repaid these amounts. Is this a problem for Forney Company? If it is, explain what the company could do to strengthen internal control.

P7-5A   Malik Retail Shop allows customers to use debit and bank credit cards as well as cash for purchases of merchandise. The company does not accept personal cheques.

Malik's bank charges $1.25 for every debit card transaction and 2.0% for bank credit card transactions.

On July 1, the company established a petty cash fund. Before it created the petty cash fund, cash was taken from the cash register whenever someone needed cash to pay for a small expense.

The following transactions happened in July:

Record debit and bank credit card and petty cash transactions, and identify internal controls. (LO 1, 2, 3) AP

July 1   Established the petty cash fund by cashing a cheque for $300.
    8   Total sales for the week were $32,750. Customers paid for these purchases as follows: $12,081 in cash, $8,943 on debit cards (134 transactions), and the balance using bank credit cards.
    8   Replenished the petty cash fund. On this date, the fund consisted of $87 in cash and the following petty cash receipts:

Freight out	$69
Supplies	35
Advertising in local paper	46
Personal withdrawal by owner, R. Malik	58

    15   Total sales for the week were $29,050. Customers paid for these purchases as follows: $10,912 in cash, $9,832 on debit cards (156 transactions), and the balance using bank credit cards.
    25   Replenished the petty cash fund and decreased the balance to $250. On this date, the fund consisted of $16 in cash and the following petty cash receipts:

Postage	$79
Advertising in local newspaper	93
Supplies	98

Instructions

(a) Record the transactions. Round to the nearest dollar.
(b) What are the benefits of having a petty cash fund instead of paying small expenses from the cash register receipts? What policies and procedures should Malik follow to ensure there is good internal control over its petty cash fund?

TAKING IT FURTHER   What are the advantages and disadvantages of accepting debit and credit card transactions as opposed to accepting personal cheques from customers? Consider both the internal control and business reasons.

P7-6A   You are the accountant for Reliable Snow Removal Services. The company decided to establish a petty cash fund for small expenditures on November 1. Your responsibility is to oversee the fund, which includes collecting receipts, paying out the cash, and replenishing the fund. You completed the following transactions in November with regard to the petty cash fund:

Record petty cash transactions, and identify impact on financial statements. (LO 3, 4) AP

Nov. 1   Cashed a cheque for $150 and put the cash in the petty cash box.
    3   Paid $16 for windshield fluid for the company trucks.
    5   Paid $26 for repairs to a tire on a company truck.
    7   Paid $51 to advertise in a community newsletter.
    9   Gave the company owner, Roberta Hayes, $38 cash for personal expenses. Noted this on a piece of paper and put it in the petty cash box.

14   Paid $9 for miscellaneous expenses.

15   Determined that there was $11 cash and that the fund needed to be replenished. Removed the receipts from the petty cash box for the above expenditures and filed them as documentation for the reimbursement. Cashed the cheque and put the cash in the petty cash box.

17   Paid $30 for repairs to the windshield of a company truck.

19   Paid $11 for oil for a company truck.

24   Paid $44 for supplies.

28   Gave the company owner, Roberta Hayes, $44 cash for personal expenses. Noted this on a piece of paper and put it in the petty cash box.

29   Paid $7 for miscellaneous expenses.

30   Determined that there was $11 cash and that the fund needed to be replenished. Removed the receipts from the petty cash box for the above expenditures and filed them as documentation for the reimbursement. Cashed the cheque and put the cash in the petty cash box.

Note: Use Repairs Expense for any expenditures related to the company trucks.

Instructions

(a) Record the November petty cash transactions as appropriate.

(b) Assume the company has a November 30 fiscal year end and that you did not have time to replenish the fund until early December. What impact, if any, would this have on the financial statements?

TAKING IT FURTHER   What things should the company owner check to ensure the fund is being properly administered?

Prepare bank reconciliation and related entries. (LO 4) AP

P7–7A   On October 31, 2017, Lisik Company had a cash balance per books of $8,946. The bank statement on that date showed a balance of $10,155. A comparison of the statement with the Cash account revealed the following:

1. The statement included debit memos of $35 for the printing of additional company cheques and $30 for bank service charges.

2. Cash sales of $417 on October 12 were deposited in the bank. The journal entry to record the cash receipt and the deposit slip were incorrectly made out and recorded by Lisik as $741. The bank detected the error on the deposit slip and credited Lisik Company for the correct amount.

3. The September 30 deposit of $985 was included on the October bank statement. The deposit had been placed in the bank's night deposit vault on September 30.

4. The October 31 deposit of $960 was not included on the October bank statement. The deposit had been placed in the bank's night deposit vault on October 31.

5. Cheques #1006 for $415 and #1072 for $975 were outstanding on September 30. Of these, #1072 cleared the bank in October. All the cheques written in October except for #1278 for $555, #1284 for $646, and #1285 for $315 had cleared the bank by October 31.

6. On October 18, the company issued cheque #1181 for $457 to Helms & Co., on account. The cheque, which cleared the bank in October, was incorrectly journalized and posted by Lisik Company for $574.

7. A review of the bank statement revealed that Lisik Company received electronic payments from customers on account of $1,875 in October. The bank had also credited the account with $25 of interest revenue on October 31. Lisik had no previous notice of these amounts.

8. Included with the cancelled cheques was a cheque issued by Lasik Company for $585 that was incorrectly charged to Lisik Company by the bank.

9. On October 31, the bank statement showed an NSF charge of $805 for a cheque issued by W. Hoad, a customer, to Lisik Company on account. This amount included a $16 service charge by the bank. The company's policy is to pass on all NSF fees to the customer.

Instructions

(a) Prepare the bank reconciliation at October 31.

(b) Prepare the necessary adjusting entries at October 31.

TAKING IT FURTHER   What are the risks of not performing bank reconciliations? Why not just rely on the bank records?

Prepare bank reconciliation and related entries. (LO 4) AP

P7–8A   On May 31, 2017, Forester Theatre's cash account per its general ledger showed the following balance:

CASH					No. 101
Date	**Explanation**	**Ref**	**Debit**	**Credit**	**Balance**
May 31	Balance				6,841

The bank statement from Canada Bank on that date showed the following balance:

CANADA BANK		
Cheques and Debits	**Deposits and Credits**	**Daily Balance**
XXX	XXX	5/31 6,804

A comparison of the details on the bank statement with the details in the Cash account revealed the following facts.

1. The statement included a debit memo of $45 for the monthly bank service charges.
2. Cash sales of $836 on May 12 were deposited in the bank. The bookkeeper recorded the deposit in the cash journal as $846.
3. Outstanding cheques on May 31 totalled $515 and deposits in transit were $1,436.
4. On May 18, the company issued cheque #1581 for $685 to M. Datz on account. The cheque, which cleared the bank in May, was incorrectly journalized and posted by Forester Theatre for $658.
5. A $2,500 note receivable was wired to the bank account of Forester Theatre on May 31. Interest was not collected for the note.
6. Included with the cancelled cheques was a cheque issued by Bohr Theatre for $600 that was incorrectly charged to Forester Theatre by the bank.
7. On May 31, the bank statement showed an NSF charge of $934 for a cheque issued by Tyler Bickell, a customer, to Forester Theatre on account.

Instructions

(a) Prepare the bank reconciliation at May 31.
(b) Prepare the necessary adjusting entries at May 31.

TAKING IT FURTHER   Sue Forester is contemplating implementing an EFT process for all supplier payments as she believes EFT is less expensive for a company because there is a reduced need for internal control as compared with writing cheques. Is Sue correct? Why or why not?

P7-9A   The March bank statement showed the following for Yap Co.:

Prepare bank reconciliation and related entries. (LO 4) AP

	YAP CO.			
	Bank Statement			
	March 31, 2017			
	Cheques and Other Debits			
Date	Number	Amount	Deposits	Amount
Feb. 28				$12,742
Mar. 3	3470	$1,535	$2,530	13,737
4	3471	845		12,892
6	3472	1,427	1,221	12,686
7	3473	275		12,411
10	NSF	595		11,816
11	3475	487	1,745	13,074
14	3477	915		12,159
17	3476	1,828	2,283	12,614
20			1,832	14,446
21	3474	2,330		12,116
26	3478	1,080	2,657	13,693
31	LN	1,125		12,568
31	3480	1,679		10,889
31	SC	49	IN 23	10,863

Additional information:

1. The bank statement contained three debit memoranda:
   - An NSF cheque of $595 that Yap had deposited was returned due to insufficient funds in the maker's bank account. This cheque was originally given to Yap by Mr. Jordan, a customer, in payment of his account. Yap believes it will be able to collect this amount from Mr. Jordan.
   - A bank loan payment (LN), which included $125 of interest and a $1,000 payment on the principal.
   - A service charge (SC) of $49 for bank services provided throughout the month.
2. The bank statement contained one credit memorandum for $23 of interest (IN) earned on the account for the month.

3. The bank made an error processing cheque #3478. No other errors were made by the bank.

Yap's unadjusted cash balance per its general ledger on March 31 is $8,495. Yap's list of cash receipts and cash payments showed the following for March:

Cash Receipts				Cash Payments		
Date	Amount		Date	Cheque No.	Amount	
Mar. 5	$ 1,221		Mar. 3	3472	$ 1,427	
10	1,745		4	3473	725	
14	2,283		6	3474	2,330	
20	1,832		7	3475	487	
25	2,675		13	3476	1,828	
31	1,025		14	3477	915	
Total	$10,781		19	3478	1,380	
			21	3479	159	
			28	3480	1,679	
			31	3481	862	
			31	3482	1,126	
			Total		$12,918	

The bank portion of the previous month's bank reconciliation for Yap Co. at February 28, 2017, was as follows:

YAP CO.
Bank Reconciliation
February 28, 2017

Cash balance per bank		$12,742
Add: Deposits in transit		2,530
		15,272
Less: Outstanding cheques		
#3451	$2,260	
#3470	1,535	
#3471	845	4,640
Adjusted cash balance per bank		$10,632

Instructions

(a) Prepare a bank reconciliation at March 31.

(b) Prepare the necessary adjusting entries at March 31. (*Note:* The correction of any errors in the recording of cheques should be made to Accounts Payable. The correction of any errors in the recording of cash receipts should be made to Accounts Receivable.)

TAKING IT FURTHER The company will prepare entries to record items found in the above bank reconciliation (see part [b] in the instructions). Describe any other follow-up actions required regarding the other reconciling items in Yap Co.'s bank reconciliation.

Prepare bank reconciliation and related entries. (LO 4) AP

P7–10A The bank portion of the bank reconciliation for Maloney Company at October 31, 2017, was as follows:

MALONEY COMPANY
Bank Reconciliation
October 31, 2017

Cash balance per bank		$11,545
Add: Deposits in transit		1,530
		13,075
Less: Outstanding cheques		
#2451	$1,260	
#2470	920	
#2471	845	
#2472	504	
#2474	1,050	4,579
Adjusted cash balance per bank		$ 8,496

The adjusted cash balance per bank agreed with the cash balance per books at October 31. The November bank statement showed the following:

MALONEY COMPANY
Bank Statement
November 30, 2017

Date		Number	Amount	Deposits	Amount
		Cheques and Other Debits			
		Number	Amount	Deposits	Amount
Oct.	31				$11,545
Nov.	3	2470	$ 920	$1,530	12,155
	4	2471	845		11,310
	5	2475	1,641	1,212	10,881
	6	2474	1,050		9,831
	7	2476	2,830	990	7,991
	10	2477	600		7,391
	13			2,575	9,966
	14	2479	1,750		8,216
	18	2480	1,330	1,473	8,359
	21			2,966	11,325
	25	NSF	260	2,567	13,632
	26	2481	695		12,937
	27			1,650	14,587
	28	2486	900	EFT 2,479	16,166
	28	2483	575	1,186	16,777
	30	LN	2,250		14,527

Additional information from the bank statement:

1. The EFT of $2,479 is an electronic transfer from a customer in payment of its account. The amount includes $49 of interest that Maloney Company had not previously accrued.
2. The NSF for $260 is a $245 cheque from a customer, Pendray Holdings, in payment of its account, plus a $15 processing fee.
3. The LN is a payment of a note payable with the bank and consists of $250 interest and $2,000 principal.
4. At October 31, the cash balance per books was $10,160. The bank did not make any errors.
   The cash records per books for November follow. Three errors were made by Maloney Company.

		Cash Payments							Cash Receipts	
Date	Number	Amount	Date	Number	Amount			Date	Amount	
Nov. 3	2475	$1,641	Nov. 18	2482	$ 612			Nov. 3	$ 1,212	
3	2476	2,380	20	2483	575			7	990	
4	2477	600	21	2484	830			12	2,575	
6	2478	538	24	2485	975			17	1,473	
8	2479	1,750	26	2486	900			20	2,699	
10	2480	1,330	28	2487	1,200			24	2,567	
14	2481	695	Total		$14,026			27	1,650	
								28	1,186	
								30	1,338	
								Total	$15,690	

Instructions

(a) Prepare a bank reconciliation at November 30.
(b) Prepare the necessary adjusting entries at November 30. (*Note:* The correction of any errors in the recording of cheques should be made to Accounts Payable. The correction of any errors in the recording of cash receipts should be made to Accounts Receivable.)

TAKING IT FURTHER   When there is an error, how does a company determine if it was a bank error or a company error? How would you know if the bank has made an error in your account?

Prepare bank
reconciliation and related
entries. (LO 4) AP

P7-11A   When the accountant of Trillo Company prepared the bank reconciliation on May 31, 2017, there were three outstanding cheques: #690 for $307, #693 for $179, and #694 for $264. There were no deposits in transit as at May 31, 2017. The bank balance at May 31 was $17,690. The balance in the Cash account on the May 31, 2017, adjusted trial balance was $16,940. The following is selected information from the June bank statement:

Cheques Cleared				Other Bank Account Transactions		
Date	Cheque No.	Amount		Date	Amount	Transaction
June 1	690	$ 307		June 3	$3,325	Deposit
5	709	3,257		10	5,391	Deposit
6	693	179		17	3,180	Deposit
13	710	1,492		24	2,156	Deposit
20	712	3,266		25	−175	NSF cheque
23	119	467		27	−500	EFT insurance payment
24	711	1,780		30	−12	Service charge
				30	35	Interest

The NSF cheque was originally received from a customer, Massif Co., in payment of its account of $165. The bank included a $10 service charge for a total of $175. Information from the company's accounting records follows:

Cash Receipts			Cash Payments		
Date	Amount		Date	Cheque No.	Amount
June 2	$3,325		June 5	708	$2,910
9	5,391		5	709	3,257
16	3,810		19	711	1,780
23	2,156		19	712	3,626
30	3,127		27	713	3,058
			27	714	3,860

Investigation reveals that cheque #712 was issued to purchase equipment and cheque #710 was issued to pay an account payable. All deposits are for collections of accounts receivable. The bank made one error: cheque #119 for Trillo Co. Ltd. was charged to Trillo's bank account.

Instructions

(a) Calculate the balance per bank statement at June 30 and the unadjusted Cash balance per company records at June 30.

(b) Prepare a bank reconciliation at June 30.

(c) Prepare the necessary adjusting entries at June 30.

(d) What balance would Trillo Company report as cash in the current assets section of its balance sheet on June 30, 2017?

TAKING IT FURTHER   Will the bank be concerned if it looks at Trillo Company's balance sheet and sees a different number than the one on the bank statement? Why or why not?

Prepare bank
reconciliation and
adjusting entries.
(LO 4) AP

P7-12A   Sally's Sweet Shop's August 31 bank balance was $11,135. The company's cash balance at August 31 was $10,805. Other information follows:

1. Outstanding cheques were #421 for $165, #485 for $265, #492 for $175, and #494 for $1,165. Cheque #421 was also outstanding on July 31 and was included on July's bank reconciliation.

2. Included with the statement were EFT deposits totalling $1,735 during August in payment of accounts receivable. These deposits have not been recorded by the company.

3. Cheque #490 was correctly written and paid by the bank for $206. The cheque had been issued to pay accounts payable and the company had recorded it as $266.

4. The bank statement showed a cheque #4832 for $795, which did not appear on the company's books. Investigation revealed that the cheque was actually issued by Wally's Water Works and was charged to Sally's Sweet Shop's account in error.

5. The bank returned an NSF cheque from a customer for $385.

6. The bank statement showed two debit memoranda for service charges: one for $25 related to the NSF cheque (see item [5] above) and one for $45 for cheque printing charges.

7. The company's records showed the August 15 deposit as $4,690. On the bank statement, it was correctly recorded as $4,990. The deposit was for cash sales.
8. The company has a pre-authorized EFT payment for its monthly utilities for $245 scheduled for the last day of each month. As August 31 was a Sunday this year, the bank posted it on September 1. The company recorded it in August.
9. The $1,355 July 31 bank deposit was recorded on August 1 on the bank statement. The August 31 bank deposit of $2,530 was not included on the August bank statement.

Instructions

(a) Prepare a bank reconciliation.
(b) Prepare any necessary adjusting journal entries.
(c) What amount should be reported as cash on the August 31 balance sheet?

TAKING IT FURTHER Why is it important that the person who prepares the bank reconciliation shouldn't also be able to write and sign cheques? In what ways would that increase the opportunity for employee fraud?

P7–13A   A first-year co-op student is trying to determine the amount of cash and cash equivalents that should be reported on a company's balance sheet. The following information was given to the student at year end.

Calculate cash balance and report other items. (LO 5) AP

1. The cash float for the cash registers totals $530.
2. The balance in the Petty Cash account is $300. At year end, the fund had $125 cash and receipts totalling $175.
3. The balance in the company's chequing account is $24,500. The company also has a U.S. bank account, which contained the equivalent of $16,300 Canadian at year end.
4. The company has overdraft protection of $10,000 on its chequing account.
5. The company has a separate bank account with a balance of $4,250. This consists of cash deposits paid by tenants who lease office space from the company. The deposits will be refunded to the tenants at the end of their leases.
6. The company has $14,800 of postdated cheques from customers for payment of accounts receivable.
7. The company has the following short-term investments:
   - $25,000 in treasury bills with a maturity date of less than 90 days.
   - $36,000 in shares of Reitmans (Canada) Limited.
   - $12,000 in a guaranteed investment certificate that matures in six months.
8. The balance in the company owner's personal bank account is $2,150.
9. The company has NSF cheques from customers totalling $875 that were returned by the bank.

Instructions

(a) Calculate the amount of cash and cash equivalents that should be reported on the year-end balance sheet as a current asset.
(b) Identify where any items that were not reported as cash and cash equivalents in part (a) should be reported.

TAKING IT FURTHER Why are restricted cash balances presented separately from cash?

▶ Problems: Set B

P7–1B   Strivent Theatre's cashier's booth is located near the entrance to the theatre. Two cashiers are employed. One works from 3:00 p.m. to 7:00 p.m., the other from 7:00 p.m. to 11:00 p.m. Each cashier is bonded. The cashiers receive cash from customers and operate a machine that ejects serially numbered tickets. The rolls of tickets are inserted and locked into the machine by the theatre manager at the beginning of each cashier's shift.

Identify internal control weaknesses over cash receipts and suggest improvements. (LO 1, 2) C

After purchasing a ticket, which may cost different prices depending on the customer's age group, the customer takes the ticket to an usher stationed at the entrance of the theatre lobby, about 10 metres from the cashier's booth. The usher tears the ticket in half, admits the customer, and returns the ticket stub to the customer. The other half of the ticket is dropped into a locked box by the usher.

At the end of each cashier's shift, the theatre manager removes the ticket rolls from the machine and makes a cash count. The cash count sheet is initialled by the cashier. At the end of the day, the manager deposits the receipts in total in a bank night deposit vault located in the mall. The manager also sends copies of the deposit slip and the initialled cash count sheets to the theatre company controller for verification, and to the company's accounting department. Receipts from the first shift are stored in a safe located in the manager's office.

Instructions

Identify the internal control activities and how they apply to cash receipts at Strivent Theatre.

TAKING IT FURTHER If the usher and the cashier decide to collaborate to steal cash, how might they do this?

Identify internal control weaknesses over cash receipts and suggest improvements.
(LO 1, 2) C

P7-2B   The board of trustees of a local church has asked for your help with the controls activities for the offering collections made at weekly services. At a board meeting, you learn the following.

1. The board has made the finance committee responsible for the financial management and audit of the financial records. This group prepares the annual budget and approves major payments but is not involved in collections or record keeping. No audit has been done in recent years, because the same trusted employee has kept church records and served as financial secretary for 15 years. None of the church employees, or members of the board of trustees, are bonded.
2. The collection at the weekly service is taken by a team of ushers who volunteer to serve for one month. The ushers take the collection plates to a basement office at the rear of the church. They hand their plates to the head usher and return to the church service. After all plates have been turned in, the head usher counts the cash collected. The head usher then places the cash in the unlocked church safe and includes a note that states the amount counted. The head usher volunteers to serve for three months.
3. The next morning, the financial secretary opens the safe and recounts the collection. The secretary withholds between $150 and $200 in cash, depending on the cash expenditures expected for the week, and deposits the remainder of the collections in the bank. To make the deposit easier, church members who contribute by cheque are asked to make their cheques payable to Cash.
4. Each month, the financial secretary reconciles the bank statement and submits a copy of the reconciliation to the board of trustees. The reconciliations have rarely contained any bank errors and have never shown any errors per books.

Instructions

(a) Indicate the weaknesses in internal control in the handling of collections.
(b) List the improvements in internal control that should be recommended with regard to (1) the ushers, (2) the head usher, and (3) the financial secretary.

TAKING IT FURTHER   Under what circumstances might these internal control weaknesses lead to fraud?

Identify internal control weaknesses over cash receipts and cash payments.
(LO 1, 2) C

P7-3B   Each of the following independent situations has an internal control weakness.

1. Henry's Lawn Care Service provides residential grass cutting services for a large number of clients who all pay cash. Henry collects the cash and keeps it in the glove compartment of his car until the end of the week, when he has time to count it and prepare a bank deposit.
2. Tasty Treats sells a variety of items, including ice cream, pop, and other snack foods. A long-term employee is responsible for ordering all merchandise, checking all deliveries, and approving invoices for payment.
3. At Pop's Pizza, there are three sales clerks on duty during busy times. All three of them use the same cash drawer.
4. Most customers at Ultimate Definition TVs use the option to pay for their televisions in 24 equal payments over two years. These customers send the company cheques or cash each month. The office manager opens the mail each day, makes a bank deposit with the cheques received in the mail that day, and prepares and posts an entry in the accounting records.
5. Trends Incorporated manufactures celebrity posters for teenagers. Naiara Mann is the custodian of the company's $500 petty cash fund. The fund is replenished every week. Frequently people do not have a receipt for their expenses because of things like parking meter expenses. In this case, Naiara just creates a receipt for that person and gives them their cash. Naiara has been with the company for 15 years and is good friends with many of the employees. Naiara is very hard-working and never takes a vacation.

Instructions

(a) Identify the internal control weaknesses in each situation.
(b) Explain the problems that could occur as a result of these weaknesses.

TAKING IT FURTHER   Make recommendations for correcting each situation.

Record petty cash transactions and identify internal controls.
(LO 1, 2, 3) AP

P7-4B   Cheema Company maintains a petty cash fund for small expenditures. The following transactions occurred over a two-month period:

July 1   Established petty cash fund by writing a cheque on Haida Bank for $200.
July 15   Replenished the petty cash fund by writing a cheque for $194.30. On this date the fund consisted of $5.70 in cash and the following petty cash receipts:

Freight out	$94.00
Postage expense	42.40
Entertainment expense	45.90
Supplies	10.70

July 31 Replenished the petty cash fund by writing a cheque for $192.00. At this date, the fund consisted of $8.00 in cash and the following petty cash receipts:

Freight out	$82.10
Contributions expense	30.00
Postage expense	47.80
Repairs expense	32.10

Aug. 15 Replenished the petty cash fund by writing a cheque for $188.00. On this date, the fund consisted of $12.00 in cash and the following petty cash receipts:

Freight out	$77.60
Entertainment expense	30.00
Postage expense	47.80
Supplies	32.10

Aug. 16 Increased the amount of the petty cash fund to $300 by writing a cheque for $100.

Aug. 31 Replenished the petty cash fund by writing a cheque for $283.00. On this date, the fund consisted of $17.00 in cash and the following petty cash receipts:

Postage expense	$145.00
Travel expense	90.60
Freight out	46.00

Instructions

(a) Journalize the petty cash transactions.
(b) What internal control features exist in a petty cash fund?

TAKING IT FURTHER Frank Cheema believes that because a petty cash fund is established, there will no longer be a need to record any journal entries for the expenses paid using the fund. Is Frank correct? Why or why not?

P7–5B Ramesh & Company allows customers to use debit and bank credit cards and cash for purchases of merchandise. The company does not accept personal cheques from customers. Ramesh's bank charges $1.05 for every debit card transaction and 4% for credit card transactions.

> Record debit and bank credit card and petty cash transactions and identify internal controls.
> (LO 1, 2, 3) AP

On May 1, the company established a petty cash fund. Before it created the petty cash fund, cash was taken from the cash register whenever someone needed cash to pay for a small expense.

The following transactions happened in the first two weeks of May:

May 1 Established the petty cash fund by cashing a cheque for $250.

8 Total sales for the week were $35,000. Customers paid for these purchases as follows: $12,912 in cash, $9,558 on debit cards (122 transactions), and the balance using bank credit cards.

8 Replenished the petty cash fund. On this date, the fund consisted of $75 in cash and the following petty cash receipts:

Delivery of merchandise to customers	$60
Postage	30
Advertising in local paper	40
Miscellaneous expense	49

15 Total sales for the week were $16,380. Customers paid for these purchases as follows: $3,690 in cash, $7,390 on debit cards (85 transactions), and the balance using bank credit cards.

15 Replenished the petty cash fund and increased the balance to $300. On this date, the fund consisted of $5 in cash and the following petty cash receipts:

B. Ramesh's personal withdrawal	$98
Supplies	36
Delivery of merchandise to customers	60

Instructions

(a) Record the transactions. Round to the nearest dollar.
(b) What are the advantages and disadvantages of accepting debit and bank credit card transactions as opposed to accepting only cash and personal cheques from customers? Consider both the internal control and business reasons.

TAKING IT FURTHER What are the benefits of having a petty cash fund instead of paying small expenses from the cash register receipts? What policies and procedures should Ramesh & Company follow to ensure there is good internal control over its petty cash fund?

Record petty cash transactions, and identify impact on financial statements. (LO 3) AP

P7-6B   You are the accountant for Lakeside Sweetshop. The company has decided to establish a petty cash fund for small expenditures on June 1. Your responsibility is to oversee the fund, which includes collecting receipts, paying out the cash, and replenishing the fund. You completed the following transactions in June with regard to the petty cash fund:

June 1   Cashed a cheque for $200 and put the cash in the petty cash box.

3   Paid $35 for supplies.

5   Paid $48 for repairs to the cash register.

7   Paid $55 to advertise in a community newsletter.

9   Gave the company owner, Elliott Bender, $40 cash for personal expenses. Noted this on a piece of paper and put it in the petty cash box.

14   Paid $19 for miscellaneous expenses.

15   Determined that there was $1 cash and that the fund needed to be replenished. Removed the receipts from the petty cash box for the above expenditures and filed them as documentation for the reimbursement. Cashed the cheque and put the cash in the petty cash box.

17   Paid $10 to one of the neighbourhood children for delivering merchandise to a customer who had a broken leg and was unable to walk to the shop.

19   Paid $54 for supplies.

24   Paid $48 for a sign advertising the store hours of operation.

28   Gave the company owner, Elliott Bender, $45 cash for personal expenses. Noted this on a piece of paper and put it in the petty cash box.

29   Paid $18 for miscellaneous expenses.

30   Determined that there was $29 cash in the fund. Prepared a cheque to reimburse the fund. Removed the receipts from the petty cash box for the above expenditures and filed them as documentation for the reimbursement. Cashed the cheque and put the cash in the petty cash box.

Instructions

(a) Record the June petty cash transactions as appropriate.

(b) Assume the company has a June 30 fiscal year end and that you did not replenish the fund until early in July when almost all of the cash had been used. What impact, if any, would this have on the financial statements?

TAKING IT FURTHER   It was stated in the chapter that "internal control over cash payments is better when payments are made by cheque." Why, then, would a company choose to make some payments from petty cash rather than by cheque? What should a company do to maintain good internal control over the petty cash fund?

Prepare bank reconciliation and related entries. (LO 4) AP

P7-7B   The Agricultural Genetics Company's Cash account in its general ledger reported a balance of $6,782 on May 31, 2017. The company's bank statement from Western Bank reported a balance of $6,405 on the same date.

    A comparison of the details in the bank statement with the details in the Cash account revealed the following facts.

1. The bank statement included a debit memo of $40 for bank service charges.

2. Cash sales of $836 on May 18 were deposited in the bank. The journal entry to record the cash sales and the deposit slip to deposit the cash were incorrectly made out for $886. The bank correctly credited Agricultural Genetics Company for the correct amount.

3. The April 30 deposit of $2,190 was included on the May bank statement. The deposit had been placed in the bank's night deposit vault on April 30.

4. The May 31 deposit of $2,416 was not included on the May bank statement. The deposit had been placed in the bank's night deposit vault on May 31.

5. Cheques #928 for $180 and #1014 for $236 were outstanding on April 30. Of these, #928 cleared the bank in May. All of the cheques written in May except for #1127 for $105 and #1195 for $235 had cleared the bank by May 31.

6. On May 18, the company issued cheque #1151 for $685 to L. Kingston, on account. The cheque, which cleared the bank in May, was incorrectly journalized and posted by Agricultural Genetics Company for $658.

7. A review of the bank statement revealed that Agricultural Genetics Company received $2,200 of electronic payments from customers on account in May. The bank had also credited the company's account with $80 of interest revenue on May 31. The bank charged a $20 collection fee. Agricultural Genetics Company had no previous notice of these amounts.

8. On May 31, the bank statement showed an NSF charge of $680 for a cheque issued by Pete Dell, a customer, to Agricultural Genetics Company on account.

Instructions

(a) Prepare the bank reconciliation at May 31.

(b) Prepare the necessary adjusting entries at May 31.

TAKING IT FURTHER   What would you say to the Agricultural Genetics Company's bank manager, who is concerned that the company's May 31 Cash account balance shows a different amount than the May 31 bank statement?

P7–8B   On June 30, 2017, EZ Fertilizer's cash account per its general ledger showed the following balance:

Prepare bank reconciliation and related entries. (LO 4) AP

CASH					No. 101
Date	Explanation	Ref	Debit	Credit	Balance
June 30	Balance				6,925

The bank statement from Canada Bank on that date showed the following balance:

CANADA BANK		
Cheques and Debits	Deposits and Credits	Daily Balance
XXX	XXX	6/30 6,776

A comparison of the details on the bank statement with the details in the Cash account revealed the following facts.

1. The statement included a debit memo of $40 for printing of additional company cheques.
2. Cash sales of $624 on June 21 were deposited in the bank. The bookkeeper recorded the deposit in the cash journal as $642.
3. Outstanding cheques on June 30 totalled $946 and deposits in transit were $1,587.
4. On June 18, the company issued cheque #1924 for $356 to D. Katz on account. The cheque, which cleared the bank in June, was incorrectly journalized and posted by EZ Fertilizer for $536.
5. A $1,550 note receivable was wired to the bank account of EZ Fertilizer on June 30 plus $45 interest. The bank charged a $25 collection fee. No interest has been accrued on the note.
6. Included with the cancelled cheques was a cheque issued by EZ Company for $234 that was incorrectly charged to EZ Fertilizer by the bank.
7. On June 30, the bank statement showed an NSF charge of $966 for a cheque issued by Amanda Vallee, a customer, to EZ Fertilizer on account.

Instructions

(a) Prepare the bank reconciliation at June 30.
(b) Prepare the necessary adjusting entries at June 30.

TAKING IT FURTHER   The owner of EZ Fertilizer has advised the bookkeeper to prepare the company's bank reconciliation only at year end. Explain to the owner the benefits of preparing a monthly bank reconciliation.

P7–9B   The bank portion of the bank reconciliation for Katsaris Company at August 31, 2017, was as follows:

Prepare bank reconciliation and related entries. (LO 4) AP

KATSARIS COMPANY		
Bank Reconciliation		
August 31, 2017		
Cash balance per bank		$13,229
Add: Deposits in transit		2,350
		15,579
Less: Outstanding cheques		
#4451	$1,740	
#4460	549	
#4461	723	
#4462	1,840	
#4464	620	5,472
Adjusted cash balance per bank		$10,107

The unadjusted cash balance per books on September 30, 2017, was $10,228. The September bank statement showed the following:

KATSARIS COMPANY				
Bank Statement				
September 30, 2017				

| Date | Cheques and Other Debits | | Deposits | Amount |
	Number	Amount		
Aug. 31				$13,229
Sept. 1	4460	$ 549	$2,350	15,030
2	4461	723		14,307
5	4465	1,459	1,212	14,060
7	4462	1,840		12,220
8	4466	1,180	2,365	13,405
9	4467	2,268		11,137
15	4468	554	3,145	13,728
16			2,673	16,401
20			1,967	18,368
23	NSF	1,027	3,126	20,467
26	4470	3,040		17,427
27	4474	1,439	1,940	17,928
27	4472	488	1,070	18,510
30	4475	535		17,975
30	SC	45		17,930

Additional information:

1. The deposit of $3,145 on September 15 is an electronic transfer from a customer in payment of its account. The amount includes $65 of interest, which Katsaris Company had not previously accrued.
2. The NSF for $1,027 is for a $1,015 cheque from a customer, Hopper Holdings, in payment of its account, plus a $12 processing fee.
3. SC represents bank service charges for the month.

The bank made one error: it recorded cheque #4475 incorrectly. Any other errors were made by Katsaris Company. The cash records per the company's books for September showed the following:

| Cash Payments | | | | | | Cash Receipts | |
Date	Number	Amount	Date	Number	Amount	Date	Amount
Sept. 1	4465	$1,459	Sept. 23	4474	$ 1,439	Sept. 2	$ 1,212
2	4466	1,180	24	4475	553	7	2,365
2	4467	2,268	30	4476	1,280	15	2,763
5	4468	554	Total		$15,076	20	1,967
8	4469	600				26	3,126
12	4470	3,400				28	1,940
17	4471	621				30	1,070
20	4472	488				30	754
22	4473	1,234				Total	$15,197

Instructions

(a) Prepare a bank reconciliation at September 30.
(b) Prepare the necessary adjusting entries at September 30. (*Note:* The correction of any errors in the recording of cheques should be made to Accounts Payable. The correction of any errors in the recording of cash receipts should be made to Accounts Receivable.)

TAKING IT FURTHER   The company will prepare entries to record items found in the above bank reconciliation (see part [b] in the instructions). Describe any other follow-up actions required regarding the other reconciling items in Katsaris Company's bank reconciliation.

P7–10B   You are given the following information for River Adventures Company:

Prepare bank reconciliation and related entries. (LO 4) AP

RIVER ADVENTURES COMPANY
Bank Reconciliation
April 30, 2017

Cash balance per bank		$9,009
Add: Deposits in transit		846
		9,855
Less: Outstanding cheques		
#526	$1,358	
#533	279	
#541	363	
#555	79	2,079
Adjusted cash balance per bank		$7,776

The unadjusted cash balance at May 31 was $1,075. The May bank statement showed the following:

RIVER ADVENTURES COMPANY
Bank Statement
May 31, 2017

	Cheques and Other Debits			
Date	Number	Amount	Deposits	Amount
Apr. 30				$9,009
May 1	526	$1,358	$ 846	8,497
2	541	363		8,134
6	556	223		7,911
6	557	1,800	1,250	7,361
9			980	8,341
12	559	1,650		6,691
13			426	7,117
13			1,650	8,767
14	561	799		7,968
16	562	2,045		5,923
20			222	6,145
21	563	2,487		3,658
22	564	603		3,055
23	565	1,033		2,022
27			980	3,002
28	NSF	440	1,771	4,333
31	SC	25		4,308

Additional information from the bank statement:

1. The deposit of $1,650 on May 13 is an electronic transfer from a customer in payment of its account. The amount includes $35 of interest, which River Adventures Company had not previously accrued.
2. The NSF for $440 is for a $425 cheque from a customer, Ralph King, in payment of his account, plus a $15 processing fee.
3. SC represents bank service charges for the month.
4. The bank made an error when processing cheque #564. The company also made two errors in the month. All cheques were written to pay accounts payable; all cash receipts were collections of accounts receivable.

The company's recorded cash payments and cash receipts for the month were as follows:

Cash Receipts			Cash Payments		
Date	Amount		Date	Cheque No.	Amount
May 5	$1,250		May 2	556	$ 223
8	980		5	557	1,800
12	426		7	558	943
18	222		7	559	1,650
25	890		8	560	890
28	1,771		12	561	799
31	1,286		15	562	2,045
Total	$6,825		16	563	2,887
			20	564	306
			23	565	1,033
			30	566	950
			Total		$13,526

Instructions

(a) Prepare a bank reconciliation.
(b) Prepare the necessary adjusting journal entries at May 31.

TAKING IT FURTHER How would you know if the bank has made an error in your account? Does this require an adjustment to your books?

Prepare bank reconciliation and related entries. (LO 4) AP

P7-11B In the November 30, 2017, bank reconciliation at Kiran's Kayaks, there were two outstanding cheques: #165 for $812 and #169 for $529. There was a $1,128 deposit in transit as at November 30, 2017. The bank balance at November 30 was $7,181; the adjusted cash balance was $6,968. The December bank statement had the following selected information:

Cheques Cleared			Other Bank Account Transactions		
Date	Cheque No.	Amount	Date	Amount	Transaction
Dec. 1	169	$ 529	Dec. 1	$1,128 +	Deposit
8	184	592	4	2,321 +	Deposit
17	186	3,491	11	3,991 +	Deposit
22	187	833	18	3,007 +	Deposit
23	183	2,955	23	520 −	NSF cheque
31	188	341	29	1,504 +	Deposit
			31	48 −	Service charge

The NSF cheque was originally received from a customer, M. Sevigny, in payment of her account of $500. The bank included a $20 service charge for a total of $520.

Information from the company's accounting records follows:

Cash Receipts			Cash Payments		
Date	Amount		Date	Cheque No.	Amount
Dec. 3	$2,321		Dec. 5	183	$2,955
10	3,991		5	184	592
17	3,707		12	185	1,165
24	1,504		12	186	3,941
31	2,218		16	187	833
			31	188	341
			31	189	1,721

Investigation reveals that cheque #186 was issued to buy equipment. All deposits are for collections of accounts receivable. The bank made no errors.

Instructions

(a) Calculate the balance per bank statement at December 31 and the unadjusted cash balance per company records at December 31.

(b) Prepare a bank reconciliation for Kiran's Kayaks at December 31.

(c) Prepare the necessary adjusting entries at December 31.

(d) What balance would Kiran's Kayaks report as cash in the current assets section of its balance sheet on December 31, 2017?

TAKING IT FURTHER   Explain why it is important for Kiran's Kayaks to complete the above bank reconciliation before preparing closing entries.

P7-12B   South Hampton Pool Supplies' May 31, 2017, bank balance was $7,350. The company's cash balance at May 31 was $8,210. Other information follows:

Prepare bank reconciliation and adjusting entries.
(LO 4) AP

1. Outstanding cheques were #321 for $653, #371 for $238, #375 for $281, and #376 for $958. Cheque #321 was also outstanding on April 30 and was included on April's bank reconciliation.

2. Included with the statement were EFT deposits totalling $975 during May in payment of accounts receivable. These deposits have not been recorded by the company.

3. Cheque #370 was correctly written and paid by the bank for $488. The cheque had been issued to pay accounts payable and the company had recorded it as $408.

4. The bank statement showed a cheque #3723 for $600, which did not appear on the company's books. Investigation revealed that the cheque was actually issued by South Hampton Pizzeria and was charged to South Hampton Pool Supplies' account in error.

5. The bank returned an NSF cheque from a customer for $249.

6. The bank statement showed two debit memoranda for service charges: one for $17 related to the NSF cheque (see item [5] above) and one for $44 for monthly bank charges.

7. The company's records showed the May 15 deposit as $2,850. On the bank statement it was correctly recorded as $2,580. The deposit was for cash sales.

8. The company has a pre-authorized EFT payment for its monthly utilities for $225 scheduled for the last day of each month. As May 31 was a Saturday this year, the bank posted it on June 2. The company recorded it in May.

9. The $1,370 April 30 bank deposit was recorded on May 1 on the bank statement. The May 31 bank deposit of $2,930 was not included on the May bank statement.

Instructions

(a) Prepare a bank reconciliation.

(b) Prepare any necessary adjusting journal entries.

(c) What amount should be reported as cash on the May 31 balance sheet?

TAKING IT FURTHER   Explain how the bank reconciliation process can strengthen internal control.

P7-13B   Sunil's Supplies has hired a new junior accountant and has given her the task of identifying what should be reported as cash as at February 28, 2017, on the company's balance sheet. The following information is available.

Calculate cash balance and report other items. (LO 5) AP

1. Cash on hand in the cash registers on February 28 totals $2,339. Of this amount, $250 is kept on hand as a cash float.

2. The balance in the petty cash fund is $275. Actual petty cash on hand at February 28 is $69. Receipts total $206.

3. The balance in the bank chequing account at February 28 is $7,460.

4. The company has two short-term investments: (1) $5,000 in a 60-day treasury bill, and (2) $3,000 in a six-month term deposit.

5. The company has a stale-dated cheque for $840 from a customer for the purchase of merchandise. The customer made a mistake on the date of the cheque and the company's bank wouldn't let it deposit the cheque. The customer has promised to fix the cheque on March 2.

6. The company has a U.S. dollar bank account. At February 28, its U.S. funds were worth the equivalent of $8,555 Canadian.

7. The company received $10,500 of cash on February 28 as an advance deposit in trust on a property sale.

8. In order to hook up utilities, the company is required to deposit $500 in trust with Ontario Hydro. This amount must remain on deposit until a satisfactory credit history has been established. The company expects to have this deposit back within the year.

Instructions

(a) Calculate the amount of cash and cash equivalents that should be reported on the year-end balance sheet as a current asset.

(b) Identify where any items that were not reported in the balance for cash in part (a) should be reported.

TAKING IT FURTHER   Under certain circumstances, cash may have to be presented as non-current. Why is this important information for users of the financial statements?

CHAPTER 7: BROADENING YOUR PERSPECTIVE

▶ Financial Reporting and Analysis

Financial Reporting Problem

BYP7-1   **Corus Entertainment's** financial statements are presented in Appendix A of this book.

Instructions

(a) Based on the information contained in these financial statements, determine each of the following:

1. Cash and cash equivalents balance at August 31, 2014, and the prior year, August 31, 2013.

2. Increase (decrease) in cash and cash equivalents from 2013 to 2014.

3. Cash provided by operating activities during the year ended August 31, 2014 (from statement of cash flows).

(b) What conclusions concerning the management of cash can you draw from these data?

Interpreting Financial Statements

BYP7-2   **Avigilon Corporation** sells security solutions. Its security cameras and surveillance software are sold to a variety of users and locations around the world, including airports, casinos, factories, and prisons. The company is headquartered in Vancouver and its security solutions are assembled and tested in its Richmond, B.C., facility. Selected information from Avigilon's comparative balance sheet follows.

AVIGILON CORPORATION Consolidated Balance Sheet (partial) December 31 (in Canadian dollars)		
	Dec. 31, 2014	Dec. 31, 2013
Current assets		
Cash	73,141	104,875
Trade and other receivables	48,977	31,316
Inventories	37,691	19,444
Prepaid expenses	5,122	1,467
Total current assets	164,931	157,102
Non-current assets		
Property, plant and equipment	12,987	8,568
Intangible assets	129,669	14,791
Goodwill	17,040	6,558
Deposits	747	586
Deferred tax assets	9,253	1,334
Total assets	$334,627	$188,939
Total current liabilities	32,677	20,818

Instructions

(a) In the financial statement notes, the company explains that cash consists of cash on hand and cash equivalents. What is a cash equivalent?

(b) Calculate (1) working capital and (2) the current ratio for each year. Comment on your results.

(c) Should the inventory be included in an acid-test ratio calculation? Why or why not?

▶ Critical Thinking

Collaborative Learning Activity

Note to instructor: Additional instructions and material for this group activity can be found on the Instructor Resource Site and in *WileyPLUS*.

BYP7–3 In this group activity, you will identify the strengths and weaknesses of a small coffee shop's processes for sales or purchases and make recommendations for processes that will improve internal control.

Communication Activity

BYP7–4 Tenacity Corporation is a medium-sized private company that sells auto parts. Blake Pike has been with the company from the beginning, ordering the auto parts, taking delivery of the parts, and authorizing payments for them. Blake often signs cheques and prepares the bank reconciliation if the controller is on vacation. The company has grown in size from five employees to 25. Annual sales have increased tenfold. Blake is still performing the same tasks as he was when the company was small and he says that he does not need any help.

Instructions

Write a letter to L. S. Osman, owner of Tenacity Corporation, which outlines a plan to improve internal control within the organization given its recent increase in size. Highlight in your letter any weaknesses you are currently aware of and suggest specific recommendations.

"All About You" Activity

BYP7–5 In the "All About You" feature, you learned about the dangers of identity theft. To protect yourself from identity theft, you should understand how it can happen and learn what you can do to prevent it.

Instructions

(a) Go to the Ontario Ministry of Government and Consumer Services website and search for the page "How to avoid or recover from identity theft." On that page, look under the heading "Types of ID fraud." What is identity theft? Identify the key types of information that thieves use.

(b) On the same web page as in part (a), look under the heading "How identity is stolen." Identify how identity thieves can get your personal information.

(c) On the same web page as in part (a), look under the heading "Signs of identity theft." What are some of the signs that may indicate that your identity has been stolen?

(d) Just as a business should implement internal control systems to protect its assets, an individual should also implement controls to prevent and recognize identity theft. On the same web page as in part (a), look under the heading "Protect your identity."

1. Identify the physical and IT controls that can be implemented to safeguard your identity.
2. Identify the checks that you can do to recognize identity theft and prevent it from continuing.

 Santé Smoothie Saga

(*Note:* This is a continuation of the Smoothie Saga from Chapters 1 through 6.)

BYP7–6 Natalie is struggling to keep up with the recording of her accounting transactions. She is spending a lot of time marketing and selling smoothies and juicers. Her friend John is an accounting student who runs his own accounting service. He has asked Natalie if she would like to have him do her accounting.

John and Natalie meet and discuss her business. John suggests that he could perform the following procedures for Natalie:

1. Take the deposits to the bank every Friday. All cheques and cash received would be kept in a locked box at Natalie's house.
2. Write and sign all of the cheques. He would review the invoices and send out cheques as soon as the invoices are received.
3. Record all of the deposits in the accounting records.
4. Record all of the cheques in the accounting records.
5. Prepare the monthly bank reconciliation.
6. Transfer Natalie's manual accounting records to his computer accounting program. John maintains the accounting information that he keeps for his clients on his laptop computer.
7. Prepare monthly financial statements for Natalie to review.
8. Write himself a cheque every month for the work he has done for Natalie.

Instructions

(a) Identify the weaknesses in internal control that you see in the system John is recommending. Can you suggest any improvements if Natalie hires John to do the accounting?

(b) Natalie would like you to help her. She asks you to prepare a bank reconciliation for October 31, 2017, and any necessary journal entries using the following information.

		GENERAL LEDGER—Santé Smoothies				
		Cash				
Date	**Explanation**	**Ref**	**Debit**	**Credit**	**Balance**	
2017						
Oct 1	Balance				2,657	
1			750		3,407	
3	Cheque #600			625	2,782	
3	Cheque #601			95	2,687	
8	Cheque #602			56	2,631	
9			1,050		3,681	
13	Cheque #603			425	3,256	
20			155		3,411	
28	Cheque #604			297	3,114	
28			110		3,224	

	PREMIER BANK			
	Statement of Account—Santé Smoothies			
	Oct 31, 2017			
Date	**Explanation**	**Cheques**	**Deposits**	**Balance**
Sept 30	Balance			3,256
Oct 1	Deposit		750	4,006
6	Cheque #600	625		3,381
6	Cheque #601	95		3,286
8	Cheque #602	56		3,230
9	Deposit		1,050	4,280
10	NSF cheque	100		
10	NSF Cheque fee	35		4,145
14	Cheque #603	452		3,693
20	Deposit		125	3,818
23	EFT—Telus	85		3,733
28	Cheque #599	361		3,372
30	Bank charges	13		3,359

Additional information:

1. On September 30, there were two outstanding cheques: #595 for $238 and #599 for $361.
2. Premier Bank made a posting error to the bank statement: cheque #603 was issued for $425, not $452.
3. The deposit made on October 20 was for $125 that Natalie received for selling smoothies. Natalie made an error in recording this transaction.

4. Natalie decided to set up an automatic payment to Telus for her cell phone invoice every month. Remember that she uses this phone only for business.
5. The NSF cheque was from Ron Black. Natalie received this cheque for selling smoothies to Ron and his children. Natalie contacted Ron, and he assured her that she will receive a cheque in the mail for the outstanding amount of the invoice and the NSF bank charge.

ANSWERS TO CHAPTER QUESTIONS

ANSWERS TO ACCOUNTING IN ACTION INSIGHT QUESTIONS

All About You, p. 367

Q: Who is responsible for losses due to unauthorized credit card use?

A: Most major credit card companies offer zero liability for credit card fraud, which protects the cardholder from losses due to fraud. You should find out if your cardholder agreement for any credit cards that you have offers protection from credit card fraud so that you can avoid taking on the identity thief's debts.

Across the Organization Insight, p. 371

Q: How might an organization's marketing department assist in, and benefit from, the implementation of a mobile payments system?

A: As you read in the Accounting in Action box, many consumers are worried about security in using their smart phones to make mobile payments. The marketing department could help in creating awareness of the benefits to consumers through social media and other more traditional advertising methods. In doing so, it would also be an opportunity to promote the business.

Ethics Insight, p. 376

Q: What are the ethical considerations in this case and who will suffer if you do or do not follow McKenna Amlani's instructions?

A: As assistant controller, you have to decide if you will follow your boss's instructions and include the cheque in transit in the cash balance or not. Including the cheque will fraudulently overstate the cash balance by $150,000 but the bank's loan requirements will be met. This will ensure Barn Bottling will not default on the loan.

You, as assistant controller, may suffer some negative effects from McKenna Amlani, the chief financial officer, if you don't follow her instructions. If you comply and falsify the June 30 cash balance, you will suffer personally by sacrificing your integrity. If you are found out, your reputation would be harmed. There could be other negative consequences from senior management and others in the accounting profession.

The bank, as the lender and creditor, is deceived.

Holding the cash receipts book open in order to overstate the cash balance is a deceitful, unethical action. The chief financial officer should not encourage such behaviour and an assistant controller should not follow such instructions.

ANSWERS TO SELF-STUDY QUESTIONS

1. d   2. c   3. b   4. d   5. a   6. b   7. d   8. b   9. b   10. c

8 ACCOUNTING FOR RECEIVABLES

CHAPTER PREVIEW As indicated in our feature story, management of receivables is important for any company that sells on credit, as Rogers Communications does. In this chapter, we will first review the journal entries that companies make when goods and services are sold on account and when cash is collected from those sales. Next, we will learn how companies estimate, record, and then, in some cases, collect their uncollectible accounts. We will also learn about notes receivable, the statement presentation of receivables, and management of receivables.

FEATURE STORY   LAST CALL FOR CUSTOMER PAYMENTS

The cable and phone bill is one that most Canadians pay in full every month. But what happens when customers fall behind in their accounts?

One of Canada's top communications companies, Rogers Communications, has accounts receivable in the hundreds of millions of dollars every month, from both residential and business customers. Its revenues, which were $12.9 billion in 2014, include fees for home and business telephone service, cellular service, high-speed Internet, television, and magazines, along with advertising revenues from businesses that advertise in its TV channels (such as Sportsnet), radio stations, and publishing ventures (such as *Maclean's* magazine).

Some of Rogers' billing terms are regulated by the federal Canadian Radio-television and Telecommunications Commission (CRTC). The company bills monthly for services in advance, and payments are due within about three weeks of the billing date. Late payment charges begin to accrue at 30 days from the billing date. Most companies intend late payment charges to be punitive, to encourage customers to pay on time. Rogers charges 2% per month for overdue accounts. "We use various internal controls, such as credit checks, deposits on account and billing in advance, to mitigate credit risk," Rogers says in its annual report.

If a customer's bill does not get paid on time, companies such as Rogers will start making calls, sending reminder notices, and perhaps negotiating new payment terms. If there is still no payment, telecom companies will typically suspend the account for 21 days, then reconnect for one day, and contact the client again. If there is still no payment, they will permanently disconnect the customer. The company then would send final notices to the client, and finally the bill goes to a collection agency. "We monitor and take appropriate action to suspend services when customers have fully used their approved credit limits or violated established payment terms," Rogers says in its annual report.

As at December 31, 2014, Rogers reported accounts receivable of $1.6 billion. While having significant accounts receivable can be a credit risk, many companies, including Rogers, capitalize on their accounts receivable. In 2013, Rogers announced that it would, for the first time, sell part of its accounts receivable to an unnamed financial institution, borrowing against the expected revenue to raise money. This is a strategy known as securitization. In 2014, Rogers received funding of $192 million, net of repayments, under its accounts receivable securitization program.

Sources: Barry Critchley, "Rogers Communications Enters the World of Securitizing Accounts Receivables, Makes an Initial $400-Million Draw," *Financial Post*, March 18, 2013; Rogers Communications 2014 annual report; "Rogers Terms of Service, Acceptable Use Policy and Privacy Policy," 2015.

The Canadian Press/Darren Calabrese

1	**Prepare journal entries for accounts receivable transactions.**	**Accounts Receivable** • Recognizing accounts receivable	**DO IT** ① Preparing journal entries to recognize accounts receivable
2	**Demonstrate how to value accounts receivable and prepare adjusting journal entries for uncollectible accounts.**	• Valuing accounts receivable	**DO IT** ② Uncollectible accounts receivable
3	**Prepare journal entries for notes receivable transactions.**	**Notes Receivable** • Recognizing notes receivable • Disposing of notes receivable	**DO IT** ③ Accounting for notes receivable
4	**Demonstrate the presentation, analysis, and management of receivables.**	**Statement Presentation and Management of Receivables** • Presentation • Analysis • Accelerating cash receipts from receivables	**DO IT** ④ Analysis of receivables

Accounts Receivable

The term "receivables" refers to amounts due to a company from individuals and other companies. They are claims that are expected to be collected in cash. The two most common types of receivables are accounts receivable and notes receivable.

Accounts receivable are amounts owed by customers on account. They result from the sale of goods and services. These receivables are generally expected to be collected within 30 days or so and are classified as current assets. **Notes receivable** are claims for which formal instruments of credit (a written note) are issued as proof of the debt. A note normally requires the debtor to pay interest and extends for longer than the company's normal credit terms. Accounts and notes receivable that result from sale transactions are often called **trade receivables**. In this section, we will learn about accounts receivable. Notes receivable will be covered later in the chapter.

Accounts receivable are usually the most significant type of claim held by a company. Two important accounting issues—recognizing accounts receivable and valuing accounts receivable—will be discussed in this section. A third issue—accelerating cash receipts from receivables—is introduced later in the chapter.

| LEARNING OBJECTIVE | **1** | **Prepare journal entries for accounts receivable transactions.** |

RECOGNIZING ACCOUNTS RECEIVABLE

Recognizing accounts receivable is relatively straightforward. Recall from Chapter 2 that for a service company, an account receivable (an asset) is recorded when a service performance obligation is completed, the revenue is recognized, and the customer is given credit terms. The asset will provide future economic benefit from the receipt of cash in the future. Recall in Chapter 5 that, for a merchandising company, a receivable is recorded when the performance obligation is complete—when the product is delivered to the customer. We also saw how accounts receivable are reduced by sales returns and allowances and sales discounts. The asset is reduced because the returns and discounts will result in less cash being received from the customer.

To review, assume that Adorable Junior Garment sells merchandise on account to MegaMart on July 1 for $1,000 with payment terms of 2/10, n/30. On July 4, MegaMart returns merchandise worth $100 to Adorable Junior Garment. On July 10, Adorable Junior Garment receives payment from MegaMart for the balance due. The journal entries to record these transactions on the books of Adorable Junior Garment are as follows:

A	=	L	+	OE
+1,000				+1,000

Cash flows: no effect

A	=	L	+	OE
−100				−100

Cash flows: no effect

A	=	L	+	OE
+882				−18
−900				

 Cash flows: +882

July 1	Accounts Receivable—MegaMart	1,000	
	Sales		1,000
	To record sale of merchandise on account.		
4	Sales Returns and Allowances	100	
	Accounts Receivable—MegaMart		100
	To record merchandise returned.		
10	Cash [($1,000 − $100) × 98%]	882	
	Sales Discounts [($1,000 − $100) × 2%]	18	
	Accounts Receivable—MegaMart ($1,000 − $100)		900
	To record collection of accounts receivable.		

As we learned in Chapter 5, if Adorable Junior Garment uses a perpetual inventory system, a second journal entry to record the cost of the goods sold (and the cost of the goods returned) would be required for the July 1 and July 4 transactions. We have chosen not to include these entries here.

Subsidiary Accounts Receivable Ledger

Adorable Junior Garment does not have only MegaMart as a customer. It has hundreds of customers. If it recorded the accounts receivable for each of these customers in only one general ledger account, as we did above in Accounts Receivable, it would be hard to determine the balance owed by a specific customer, such as MegaMart, at a specific point in time. It is critical that a company know what each customer owes so that it can collect that cash from them.

Most companies that sell on account use a subsidiary ledger to keep track of individual customer accounts. As we learned in Chapter 5, a subsidiary ledger gives supporting detail to the general ledger. The company's Accounts Receivable account in the general ledger is the control account that provides the balance in accounts receivable reported on the balance sheet. Illustration 8-1 shows the information included in Adorable Junior Garment's accounts receivable subsidiary ledger and the general ledger (using assumed dollar amounts).

▶ ILLUSTRATION 8-1
Accounts Receivable general ledger control account and subsidiary ledger

GENERAL LEDGER

Accounts Receivable is a control account.

Accounts Receivable — No. 112

Date	Explanation	Ref.	Debit	Credit	Balance
2017 July 4				100	(100)
31			10,000		9,900
31				5,900	4,000

ACCOUNTS RECEIVABLE SUBSIDIARY LEDGER

The subsidiary ledger is separate from the general ledger.

Kids Online — No. 112-203

Date	Explanation	Ref.	Debit	Credit	Balance
2017 July 11	Invoice 1310		6,000		6,000
19	Payment			4,000	2,000

Snazzy Kids Co. — No. 112-413

Date	Explanation	Ref.	Debit	Credit	Balance
2017 July 12	Invoice 1318		3,000		3,000
21	Payment			1,000	2,000

MegaMart — No. 112-581

Date	Explanation	Ref.	Debit	Credit	Balance
2017 July 1	Invoice 1215		1,000		1,000
4	Credit Memo 1222			100	900
10	Payment			900	0

Note that the balance of $4,000 in the control account in the general ledger agrees with the total of the balances in the individual accounts receivable accounts in the subsidiary ledger (Kids Online $2,000 + Snazzy Kids $2,000 + MegaMart $0). There is more information about how subsidiary ledgers work in Appendix C at the end of this textbook.

Today, most businesses use computerized accounting systems that automatically update the subsidiary ledger and general ledger when a journal entry is recorded. Regardless of whether the accounting system is computerized or manual, the accounting records must provide accurate, up-to-date information for each customer account. As well, the total of the customer account balances must equal the total in the general ledger control account.

Credit Card Receivables

In Chapter 7, we learned that debit and bank credit card sales are typically treated as cash sales. Some retailers issue their own credit cards; for example, Home Depot and The Brick. In many cases, these companies have their own financial divisions that will process the billings to and collections from customers. For these retailers, the credit card sale becomes a type of account receivable and the accounting is similar to the accounts receivable transactions demonstrated earlier in the chapter.

To illustrate, assume that you use your Home Depot credit card to purchase a new patio set with a sales price of $400 on June 1, 2017. Home Depot will record the sale as follows (cost of goods sold entry omitted):

A	=	L	+	OE
+400				+400

Cash flows: no effect

June 1	Credit Card Receivable	400	
	Sales		400
	To record sale of merchandise.		

Interest Revenue

At the end of each month, the company can use the subsidiary ledger to easily determine the transactions that occurred in each customer's account during the month and then send the customer a statement of transactions for the month. If the customer does not pay in full within a specified period (usually 30 days), most retailers add an interest (financing) charge to the balance due.

When financing charges are added, the seller increases the accounts receivable and recognizes interest revenue.

For example, if Kids Online still owes $2,000 at the end of the next month, August 31, and Adorable Junior Garment charges 18% on the balance due, the entry that Adorable Junior Garment will make to record interest revenue of $30 ($2,000 \times 18\% \times \frac{1}{12}$) is as follows:

A	=	L	+	OE
+30				+30

Cash flows: no effect

Aug. 31	Accounts Receivable—Kids Online	30	
	Interest Revenue		30
	To record interest on amount due.		

When you use a retailer's credit card, the retailer charges interest on the balance due if not paid within a specified period (usually 25–30 days). For example, assuming that you still owe $400 at the end of June on your Home Depot credit card and Home Depot charges 18% interest, the adjusting entry to record interest revenue of $6.00 ($400 \times 18\% \times \frac{1}{12}$) on June 30 is as follows:

A	=	L	+	OE
+6				+6

Cash flows: no effect

June 30	Credit Card Receivable	6	
	Interest Revenue		6
	To record interest on amount due.		

ACCOUNTING IN ACTION
ALL ABOUT YOU INSIGHT

© istockphoto.com/Marcus Clackson

Interest rates on bank credit cards can vary depending on the card's various features; recently, the interest rates on Canadian bank credit cards were around 19.99%. Credit cards with lower interest rates usually have annual fees and may only be available to those with an excellent credit rating. Nonbank cards can charge significantly higher interest rates, such as retailer HBC's interest rate of 29.9%. At the same time, the Canadian banks' prime lending rate was 2.85%. The prime lending rate, the rate banks charge their best customers, changes depending on the supply and demand for money. Credit card interest rates, on the other hand, hardly budge at all. Why are credit card rates so much higher than other interest rates?

The higher rate is due to the risk involved. A bank loan, such as a mortgage, is a secured loan because the loan is backed by a tangible asset: a house. Using a credit card is essentially taking out an unsecured loan because nothing physical is used as security for the lender. In addition, credit cards are much more susceptible to fraud, and thus require a consistently high interest rate.

Sources: Credit Cards Canada website, www.creditcardscanada. ca; "HBC Account Agreement," available at http://financial.hbc. com/en/credit/terms.shtml; Bank of Canada website, www. bankofcanada.ca/rates/daily-digest/.

 Should you use credit cards or not?

Rogers Communications in our feature story starts to accrue interest if payment is not received from the customer within 30 days of the billing date. The interest charges are meant to be punitive and the customer charges are 2% per month. As discussed in Chapter 5, interest revenue is included in other revenues in the non-operating section of the income statement.

| BEFORE YOU GO ON...DO IT | | Preparing Journal Entries to Recognize Accounts Receivable |

On May 1, Wilton sold merchandise on account to Bates for $50,000, terms 2/15, net 30. On May 4, Bates returned merchandise with a sales price of $2,000. On May 16, Wilton received payment from Bates for the balance due.

Prepare journal entries to record the transactions for Wilton.

Solution

May	1	Accounts Receivable—Bates	50,000	
		Sales Revenue		50,000
	4	Sales Returns and Allowances	2,000	
		Accounts Receivable—Bates		2,000
	16	Cash ($48,000 − $960)	47,040	
		Sales Discounts ($48,000 × .02)	960	
		Accounts Receivable—Bates		48,000

Related exercise material: BE8–1, BE8–2, BE8–3, BE8–4, E8–1, E8–2, and E8–3.

Action Plan
- Prepare the journal entry to record the sale on May 1.
- Record the return of goods on May 4.
- Calculate the amount of cash that will be received considering the goods returned and the discount that the customer is entitled to take.
- Record the journal entry for the cash received.

| LEARNING OBJECTIVE | | Demonstrate how to value accounts receivable and prepare adjusting journal entries for uncollectible accounts. |

VALUING ACCOUNTS RECEIVABLE

After receivables are recorded in the accounts, the next question is how these receivables should be reported on the balance sheet. In Chapter 3, we studied the adjusting process. Recall that at the end of a period, before financial statements are prepared, adjusting journal entries are required to ensure revenues and expenses are recorded in the proper period and that assets, liabilities, and owner's equity are correct on the balance sheet. Receivables are assets, but determining the amount to report as an asset is sometimes difficult because some receivables will become uncollectible. A receivable can be reported as an asset only if it will give a future benefit. **This means that only** *collectible* **receivables can be reported as assets in the financial statements.** This collectible amount is called the receivables' **net realizable value**. Reporting accounts receivable at net realizable value provides information to investors and creditors on the company's ability to generate cash.

In order to minimize the risk of uncollectible accounts, companies consider the creditworthiness of potential credit customers. But even if a customer satisfies the company's credit requirements, inevitably, some accounts receivable still become uncollectible. For example, a usually reliable customer may suddenly not be able to pay because of an unexpected decrease in its revenues or because it is faced with unexpected bills.

Why do companies still decide to sell goods or services on credit if there is always a risk of not collecting the receivable? Customers like the convenience and flexibility of purchasing goods and services on credit. By offering credit terms, companies hope to increase the number and size of sales and therefore increase revenues and profit. Generally, these companies expect that the increase in revenues and profit from selling on credit will be greater than any uncollectible accounts or credit losses. Such losses are considered a normal and necessary risk of extending credit to customers.

When receivables are adjusted to net realizable value because of expected credit losses, owner's equity must also be reduced so that assets remain equal to liabilities plus owner's equity. As we learned in Chapter 1, a decrease in an asset that results in a decrease in owner's equity (excluding withdrawals by owners) is an expense. The expense for credit losses is called **bad debt expense**.

Alternative terminology Bad debt expense is also sometimes called *uncollectible account expense*.

The key issue in valuing accounts receivable is to estimate the amount of accounts receivable that will not be collected. If the company waits until it knows for sure that a specific account will not be collected, it could end up overstating the asset accounts receivable on the balance sheet and understating expenses.

Consider the following example. Assume that in 2017, Quick Buck Computer Company decides it could increase its revenues by offering computers to students without requiring any money down and with no credit approval process. On campuses across the country, it sells 100,000 computers with a selling price of $400 each. This increases Quick Buck's receivables and revenues by $40 million. The promotion is a huge success! In 2017, the financial statements will portray a very successful company. Unfortunately, in 2018, nearly 40% of the student customers **default** on (do not pay) their accounts. The 2018 financial statements now portray a company struggling. Illustration 8-2 shows that the promotion in 2017 was not such a great success after all.

▶ **ILLUSTRATION 8-2**
Effect of overstating accounts receivable and understating expenses

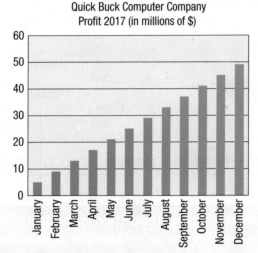

Quick Buck Computer Company
Profit 2017 (in millions of $)

Huge sales promotion. Accounts receivable increase dramatically. Profit increases dramatically.

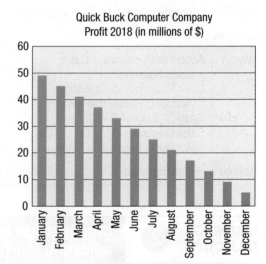

Quick Buck Computer Company
Profit 2018 (in millions of $)

Customers default on amounts owed. Accounts receivable drop dramatically. Bad debt expense increases and profit decreases dramatically.

If credit losses are not recorded until they occur, the accounts receivable in the balance sheet are not reported at the amount that is actually expected to be collected. Quick Buck Computer's receivables were overstated at the end of 2017, which misrepresented the amount that should have been reported as an asset.

To avoid overstating assets and profit, we cannot wait until we know exactly which receivables are uncollectible. Because we do not know which specific accounts receivable will need to be written off, we use what is known as the **allowance method** in which we estimate uncollectible accounts at the end of each accounting period. In this method, the estimated uncollectible accounts are recorded as a credit balance in a contra asset account, **Allowance for Doubtful Accounts**. The allowance is deducted from Accounts Receivable on the balance sheet to report the net realizable value of the receivables.

The allowance method also ensures better matching of expenses with revenues on the income statement because credit losses that are expected to happen from sales or service revenue in that accounting period are recorded in the same accounting period as the revenue recognized. The allowance method is required for financial reporting purposes and has three essential features:

1. **Recording estimated uncollectibles:** The amount of uncollectible accounts receivable is estimated at the end of an accounting period and an adjusting journal entry is recorded.
2. **Writing off uncollectible accounts:** In the next accounting period, actual uncollectible accounts are written off when the specific account is determined to be uncollectible.
3. **Collection of a previously written-off account:** If an account that was previously written off is later collected, the original write off is reversed and the collection is recorded.

We explain these features of the allowance method in the following sections.

Helpful hint A "write off" is what occurs when recognizing the reduced value of an element of the financial statements.

1. Recording Estimated Uncollectibles

The first step is to estimate the Allowance for Doubtful Accounts. To illustrate the allowance method, we return to the example for Adorable Junior Garment. Assume that the company has accounts receivable of $200,000 at December 31, 2017. Not all of these receivables will be collected. As it is not known at December 31, 2017, which specific accounts are uncollectible, the amount of uncollectibles must be estimated. How is this amount estimated? There are two approaches that most companies use to determine this amount: (1) percentage of receivables, and (2) percentage of sales.

Percentage of Receivables Approach. Under the **percentage of receivables approach**, management uses experience to estimate the percentage of receivables that will become uncollectible accounts. The easiest way to do this is to multiply the total amount of accounts receivable by management's estimate of the percentage of accounts that will become uncollectible. The problem with this simple approach is that it doesn't take into consideration that the longer a receivable is past due or outstanding, the less likely it is to be collected.

Therefore, the more common practice is to use different percentages depending on how long individual accounts receivable have been outstanding. This variation of the percentage of receivables approach is more sensitive to the actual status of the accounts receivable.

A schedule must be prepared, called an **aging schedule**, which places each accounts receivable amount into a category depending on how many days outstanding the account is. After the age of each account receivable is determined and included in a category, the loss from uncollectible accounts is estimated. This is done by applying percentages, based on experience, to the totals in each category. The estimated percentage of uncollectible accounts increases as the number of days outstanding increases. An aging schedule for Adorable Junior Garment is shown in Illustration 8-3.

Alternative terminology The percentage of receivables approach is sometimes referred to as the *balance sheet approach*.

▶ **ILLUSTRATION** 8-3
Aging schedule

Customer	Total	Number of Days Outstanding				
		0–30	31–60	61–90	91–120	Over 120
Bansal Garments	$ 6,000		$ 3,000	$ 3,000		
Bortz Clothing	3,000	$ 3,000				
Kids Online	4,500				$ 2,000	$ 2,500
Snazzy Kids Co.	17,000	2,000	5,000	5,000	5,000	
Tykes n' Tots	26,500	10,000	10,000	6,000	500	
MegaMart	42,000	32,000	10,000			
Walmart	61,000	48,000	12,000	1,000		
Others	40,000	5,000	10,000	10,000	5,000	10,000
	$200,000	$100,000	$50,000	$25,000	$12,500	$12,500
Estimated percentage uncollectible		5%	10%	20%	30%	50%
Estimated uncollectible accounts	**$25,000**	$ 5,000	$ 5,000	$ 5,000	$ 3,750	$ 6,250

The $25,000 total for estimated uncollectible accounts is the amount of existing receivables that are expected to become uncollectible in the future. This also means that Adorable Junior Garment expects to collect the remaining accounts receivable of $175,000 ($200,000 of accounts receivable in total less the estimated uncollectible accounts of $25,000).

As previously explained, since Adorable Junior Garment doesn't know specifically which accounts receivable it will not collect, we do not know which specific accounts to credit in the subsidiary ledger. The problem is solved by using the contra asset account, Allowance for Doubtful Accounts, instead of crediting Accounts Receivable. Remember that the balance of a contra asset account (a credit) is deducted from the related asset on the balance sheet (a debit). The difference between Adorable Junior Garment's **gross accounts receivable** and its allowance for doubtful accounts is the net realizable value (the collectible amount) of its accounts receivable. This can be represented by the formula shown in Illustration 8-4.

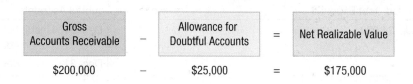

Gross Accounts Receivable	−	Allowance for Doubtful Accounts	=	Net Realizable Value
$200,000	−	$25,000	=	$175,000

▶ **ILLUSTRATION** 8-4
Formula for calculating net realizable value

In the current assets section of the balance sheet, Accounts Receivable, the Allowance for Doubtful Accounts, and the net realizable value are reported as follows (using assumed data for the other current asset accounts):

ADORABLE JUNIOR GARMENT		
Balance Sheet (partial)		
December 31, 2017		
Current assets		
Cash		$ 14,800
Accounts receivable	$200,000	
Less: Allowance for doubtful accounts	25,000	175,000
Merchandise inventory		310,000
Prepaid expenses		25,000
Total current assets		$524,800

How do we record estimated uncollectible amounts? We now have an estimate of the amounts that will be uncollectible in the future. The next step is to prepare an adjusting journal entry to record bad debt expense and update the allowance for doubtful accounts.

It is important to remember that, when using the percentage of receivables approach, the goal is to estimate the *required* balance in the Allowance for Doubtful Accounts. Recall that assets, liabilities, and owner's equity accounts are permanent accounts; the allowance is a contra asset but still a type of asset. That means the balance in a contra asset account is carried forward to the next accounting period. We need to know the unadjusted balance in the Allowance for Doubtful Accounts in order to **adjust** the account to its required balance of $25,000. This adjusting entry also records bad debt expense. Since Bad Debt Expense is a temporary account, it starts each accounting period with a zero balance.

To illustrate, let us assume that Adorable Junior Garment has an unadjusted credit balance of $1,000 in its Allowance for Doubtful Accounts. Because the account already has a credit balance, it needs to be adjusted by only the difference between the required balance of $25,000 and the existing balance of $1,000. Thus the amount of the adjusting entry is $24,000, as shown in Illustration 8-5.

▶ILLUSTRATION 8-5
Calculation of bad debt expense using the percentage of receivables approach—unadjusted credit balance in allowance

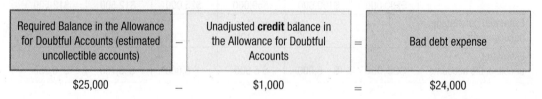

Required Balance in the Allowance for Doubtful Accounts (estimated uncollectible accounts)	−	Unadjusted **credit** balance in the Allowance for Doubtful Accounts	=	Bad debt expense
$25,000	−	$1,000	=	$24,000

Note that when we use the above equation, the result will also give us the balance in the Bad Debt Expense account for the period.

The adjusting entry for $24,000 is as follows:

A	=	L	+	OE
−24,000				−24,000

Cash flows: no effect

Dec. 31	Bad Debt Expense	24,000	
	Allowance for Doubtful Accounts		24,000
	To record estimate of uncollectible accounts.		

After the adjusting entry is posted, the balance in the Allowance for Doubtful Accounts will be equal to the estimated uncollectible accounts calculated in Illustration 8-3. This is shown in Adorable Junior Garment's accounts:

Bad Debt Expense		Allowance for Doubtful Accounts		
Dec. 31 Adj. 24,000			Dec. 31 Unadj. bal.	1,000
			31 Adj.	24,000
			Dec. 31 Bal.	25,000

Bad debt expense of $24,000 is reported in the income statement in the period when the sales are recognized. Notice this is less than the balance in the Allowance for Doubtful Accounts. This will always be the case when there is a credit amount in the unadjusted balance of the allowance account.

Occasionally, the allowance account will have a debit balance before recording the adjusting entry. This happens when write offs in the year are higher than the previous estimates for bad debts. (We will discuss write offs in the next section.) If there is a debit balance prior to recording the adjusting entry, the debit balance is added to the required balance when the adjusting entry is made. For example, if there had been a $500 debit balance in the Adorable Junior Garment allowance account before adjustment, the adjusting entry would have been for $25,500, to arrive at a credit balance in the allowance account of $25,000. The calculation of the adjusting entry is shown in Illustration 8-6.

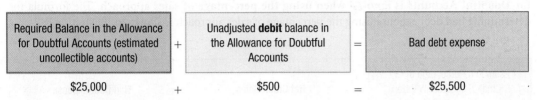

Required Balance in the Allowance for Doubtful Accounts (estimated uncollectible accounts)	+	Unadjusted **debit** balance in the Allowance for Doubtful Accounts	=	Bad debt expense
$25,000	+	$500	=	$25,500

▶ILLUSTRATION **8-6**
Calculation of bad debt expense using the percentage of receivables approach—unadjusted debit balance in the allowance

In this case, the adjusting entry is for $25,500 as follows:

Dec. 31	Bad Debt Expense	25,500	
	Allowance for Doubtful Accounts		25,500
	To record estimate of uncollectible accounts.		

A	=	L	+	OE
−25,500				−25,500

Cash flows: no effect

After the adjusting entry is posted, the balance in the Allowance for Doubtful Accounts is equal to the estimated uncollectible accounts calculated in Illustration 8-3. This is shown in Adorable Junior Garment's accounts:

Bad Debt Expense		Allowance for Doubtful Accounts	
Dec. 31 Adj. 25,500		Dec. 31 Unadj. bal. 500	
			31 Adj. 25,500
			Dec. 31 Bal. **25,000**

Notice that, although the adjusted balance in the Allowance for Doubtful Accounts is the same amount in the two examples shown, the Bad Debt Expense is different. In this case, it is higher than the balance in the allowance in order to compensate for the fact that Adorable Junior Garment underestimated its uncollectible accounts in the previous year.

Percentage of Sales Approach. The **percentage of sales approach** estimates the amount of bad debt expense as a percentage of net credit sales. This amount is also recorded in the Allowance for Doubtful Accounts, as illustrated below. Management determines the percentage based on experience and the company's credit policy.

To illustrate, assume that Adorable Junior Garment concludes that 2% of net credit sales will become uncollectible and net credit sales for the calendar year 2017 are $1.2 million. Estimated bad debt expense using the percentage of sales approach is $24,000 (2% × $1,200,000). The adjusting entry is:

Dec. 31	Bad Debt Expense	24,000	
	Allowance for Doubtful Accounts		24,000
	To record estimate of uncollectible accounts.		

A	=	L	+	OE
−24,000				−24,000

Cash flows: no effect

Assume again that the Allowance for Doubtful Accounts has a credit balance of $1,000 before the adjustment. After the adjusting entry is posted, the accounts will show the following:

Bad Debt Expense		Allowance for Doubtful Accounts	
Dec. 31 Adj. 24,000		Dec. 31 Unadj. bal. 1,000	
		31 Adj. 24,000	
		Dec. 31 Bal. 25,000	

Helpful hint Because the income statement is emphasized in the percentage of sales approach, the balance in the allowance account is not involved in calculating the bad debt expense in the adjusting entry.

When calculating the amount in the adjusting entry ($24,000), **the existing balance in Allowance for Doubtful Accounts is ignored when using the percentage of sales approach**. The formula for determining bad debt expense using the percentage of sales approach is shown in Illustration 8-7.

▶ **ILLUSTRATION 8-7**
Calculation of bad debt expense using the percentage of sales approach

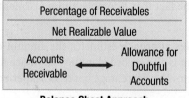

Estimated Percentage of Net Credit Sales That Will Be Uncollectible	×	Net Credit Sales	=	Bad Debt Expense
2%	×	$1.2 million	=	$24,000

This approach to estimating uncollectibles results in better matching of expenses with revenues because the bad debt expense is related to the sales recorded in the same period. Because an income statement account (Sales) is used to calculate another income statement account (Bad Debt Expense), and because any balance in the balance sheet account (Allowance for Doubtful Accounts) is ignored, this approach is often called the **income statement approach**.

Both the percentage of receivables and the percentage of sales approaches are generally accepted. Current accounting standards emphasize the balance sheet and valuation of assets, liabilities, and equity as primary measurements. Therefore, **the percentage of accounts receivable approach is most appropriate for reporting accounts receivable assets at a reporting date**. However, the percentage of sales approach is quick and easy to use so companies will often use a mix of the two approaches. The percentages of sales approach can be used monthly to estimate uncollectible amounts and the percentage of accounts receivable can then be used as the final period-end adjustment for financial reporting purposes. Both approaches use the Allowance for Doubtful Accounts. You should note that, unlike in our example with Adorable Junior Garment, the two approaches normally result in different amounts in the adjusting entry.

Illustration 8-8 compares the percentage of receivables approach with the percentage of sales approach.

▶ **ILLUSTRATION 8-8**
Comparison of approaches for estimating uncollectibles

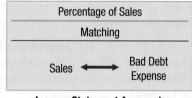

Percentage of Receivables
Net Realizable Value
Accounts Receivable ⟷ Allowance for Doubtful Accounts

Balance Sheet Approach

Percentage of Sales
Matching
Sales ⟷ Bad Debt Expense

Income Statement Approach

2. Writing Off Uncollectible Accounts

Companies use various methods for collecting past-due accounts, including letters, calls, and legal actions. As mentioned in our feature story, telecom companies typically classify customers by risk levels, which they use to determine how large and how far in arrears they will allow the bill to get before taking action. They then follow up on late accounts with letters and calls, and will cut back or suspend service if the customer does not negotiate new payment terms. If there is still no payment from the customer, service is permanently cut off. The final step involves sending the account to a collection agency.

When all the ways of collecting a past-due account have been tried and collection appears impossible, the account should be written off. It is at this point that any future benefit is unlikely or impossible. To prevent premature write offs, each write off should be approved in writing by management. To keep good internal control, the authorization to write off accounts should not be given to someone who also has responsibilities related to cash or receivables.

Note that the journal entries required to write off specific accounts receivable will be the same whether the company uses the percentage of receivables or percentage of sales approach to estimate uncollectible amounts.

To illustrate a receivables write off, assume that the vice-president of finance of Adorable Junior Garment authorizes the write off of a $4,500 balance owed by a delinquent customer, Kids Online, on March 1, 2018. The entry to record the write off is as follows:

Mar. 1	Allowance for Doubtful Accounts	4,500	
	Accounts Receivable—Kids Online		4,500
	Write off of uncollectible account.		

A = L + OE
+4,500
−4,500

Cash flows: no effect

Bad Debt Expense is not increased (debited) when the write off occurs. Under the allowance method, every account write off is debited to the allowance account rather than to Bad Debt Expense. A debit to Bad Debt Expense would be incorrect because the expense was already recognized when the adjusting entry was made for uncollectible accounts at the end of the previous year.

Instead, the entry to record the write off of an uncollectible account reduces both Accounts Receivable and Allowance for Doubtful Accounts. Assuming a balance of $230,000 in Accounts Receivable on February 28, 2018, the general ledger accounts will appear as follows after the March 1, 2018, entry is posted:

Accounts Receivable					Allowance for Doubtful Accounts			
Feb. 28 Bal.	230,000	Mar. 1	4,500		Mar. 1	4,500	Jan. 1 Bal.	25,000
Mar. 1 Bal.	225,500						Mar. 1 Bal.	20,500

A write off affects only balance sheet accounts. The write off of the account reduces both Accounts Receivable and Allowance for Doubtful Accounts. Net realizable value in the balance sheet remains the same, as shown below:

	Before Write Off	After Write Off
Accounts receivable	$230,000	$225,500
Less: Allowance for doubtful accounts	25,000	20,500
Net realizable value	$205,000	$205,000

As mentioned earlier, the allowance account can sometimes end up in a debit balance position after the write off of an uncollectible account. This can happen if the write offs during the period are more than the opening balance of the allowance. It means the actual credit losses were greater than the estimated credit losses. The balance in Allowance for Doubtful Accounts will be corrected when the adjusting entry for estimated uncollectible accounts is made at the end of the period.

3. Collection of a Previously Written-Off Uncollectible Account

Occasionally, a company collects cash from a customer after its account has been written off. Two entries are required to record the collection of a previously written-off account: (1) the entry previously made when the account was written off is reversed to restore the customer's account; and (2) the collection is recorded in the usual way. The journal entries required for a previously written-off uncollectible account demonstrated below will be the same when using the percentage of receivables approach or the percentage of sales approach.

To illustrate, assume that on July 1, 2018, Kids Online pays the $4,500 amount that had been written off on March 1. The entries are as follows:

A	=	L	+	OE
+4,500				
−4,500				

Cash flows: no effect

A	=	L	+	OE
+4,500				
−4,500				

⬆Cash flows: +4,500

	(1)		
July 1	Accounts Receivable—Kids Online	4,500	
	Allowance for Doubtful Accounts		4,500
	To reverse write off of Kids Online account.		
	(2)		
July 1	Cash	4,500	
	Accounts Receivable—Kids Online		4,500
	To record collection from Kids Online.		

Note that the collection of a previously written-off account, like the write off of a bad debt, affects only balance sheet accounts. The net effect of the two entries is a debit to Cash and a credit to Allowance for Doubtful Accounts for $4,500. Accounts Receivable is debited and later credited for two reasons. First, the company must reverse the write off. Second, Kids Online did pay, so the Accounts Receivable account in the general ledger and Kids Online's account in the subsidiary ledger should show this payment because it will need to be considered in deciding what credit to give to Kids Online in the future.

Summary of Allowance Method

In summary, there are three types of transactions that may be recorded when valuing accounts receivable using the allowance method:

1. Estimate uncollectible accounts using either the percentage of accounts receivable approach or the percentage of sales approach. Record a debit to Bad Debt expense and a credit to Allowance for Doubtful Accounts for the appropriate amount. Remember when using the percentage of accounts receivable approach that the amount of the adjustment is the difference between the required balance in the allowance account and the existing balance in the allowance account.
2. Write offs of actual uncollectible accounts are recorded in the next accounting period by debiting Allowance for Doubtful Accounts and crediting Accounts Receivable.
3. Later collections of previously written-off accounts, if any, are recorded in two separate entries.
   (a) The first reverses the write off by debiting Accounts Receivable and crediting Allowance for Doubtful Accounts.
   (b) The second records the normal collection of the account by debiting Cash and crediting Accounts Receivable.

These entries are summarized below:

Entry description	Accounts	Debit	Credit
Recording estimated uncollectibles	Bad Debt Expense	xxx	
	Allowance for Doubtful Accounts		xxx
Recording a write off of uncollectible account	Allowance for Doubtful Accounts	xxx	
	Accounts Receivable		xxx
Collection of previously written off accounts receivable (entry 1)	Accounts Receivable	xxx	
	Allowance for Doubtful Accounts		xxx
Collection of previously written off accounts receivable (entry 2)	Cash	xxx	
	Accounts Receivable		xxx

BEFORE YOU GO ON...DO IT 2

Uncollectible Accounts Receivable

The following information for Zhang Wholesalers Co.'s accounts receivable is available at December 31. Zhang Wholesalers uses the percentage of receivables approach for estimating uncollectible accounts.

Number of Days Outstanding	Accounts Receivable	Estimated Percentage Uncollectible
0–30 days	$ 85,000	5%
31–60 days	25,000	15%
Over 60 days	10,000	25%
Total	$120,000	

(a) Calculate the estimated uncollectible accounts and the net realizable value of Zhang's accounts receivable at December 31.

(b) Prepare the adjusting journal entry to record bad debt expense for each of the following independent situations:
  1. The Allowance for Doubtful Accounts has an unadjusted $2,000 credit balance.
  2. The Allowance for Doubtful Accounts has an unadjusted $1,200 debit balance.

(c) Prepare the required journal entry if Zhang learns that its $1,500 receivable from Rutger Retailers is not collectible.

(d) Prepare the required journal entries if Zhang subsequently collects the $1,500 receivable from Rutger Retailers that was previously written off.

(e) Assume instead that Zhang uses the percentage of sales approach to estimate uncollectible accounts and management concludes that 1% of net credit sales should be used. Net credit sales are $800,000 for the period ended December 31 and the Allowance for Doubtful Accounts has an unadjusted credit balance of $2,000. Calculate the bad debt expense and the net realizable value of Zhang's accounts receivable at December 31.

Solution

(a) Estimated uncollectible accounts = ($85,000 × 5%) + ($25,000 × 15%) + ($10,000 × 25%)
$$= \$10,500$$
$$\text{Net Realizable Value} = \$120,000 - \$10,500$$
$$= \$109,500$$

(b) 1. Bad Debt Expense ($10,500 − $2,000) 8,500
    Allowance for Doubtful Accounts 8,500
    To record estimate of uncollectible accounts.

2. Bad Debt Expense ($10,500 + $1,200) 11,700
    Allowance for Doubtful Accounts 11,700
    To record estimate of uncollectible accounts.

(c) Allowance for Doubtful Accounts 1,500
    Accounts Receivable—Rutger Retailers 1,500
    To record write off of account receivable.

(d) Accounts Receivable—Rutger Retailers 1,500
    Allowance for Doubtful Accounts 1,500
    To reverse write off of Rutger Retailers' account receivable.

Cash 1,500
    Accounts Receivable 1,500
    To record collection from Rutger Retailers.

(e) Estimated uncollectible accounts = $800,000 × 1%
$$= \$8,000$$
$$\text{Net realizable value} = \$120,000 - (\$2,000 + \$8,000)$$
$$= \$110,000$$

Related exercise material: BE8–5, BE8–6, BE8–7, BE8–8, BE8–9, BE8–10, E8–4, E8–5, E8–6, E8–7, and E8–12.

Action Plan

- Apply percentages to the receivables in each age category to determine total estimated uncollectible accounts using the percentage of receivables approach. This is the ending balance required in the allowance account.
- Net realizable value using the percentage of receivables approach is equal to the balance in Accounts Receivable minus the required balance in Allowance for Doubtful Accounts.
- Use the unadjusted balance in the allowance account to determine the adjusting entry. If the unadjusted balance in the allowance account is a credit, the amount of the adjustment is equal to the required balance minus the unadjusted credit balance. If the unadjusted balance is a debit, the amount of the adjustment is equal to the required balance plus the unadjusted debit balance.
- Record the write offs of accounts and subsequent collection of accounts written off only in the balance sheet accounts, Accounts Receivable and Allowance for Doubtful Accounts.
- Apply the percentage estimated by management to net credit sales to determine bad debt expense using the percentage of sales approach. This is the adjusting entry amount.
- Net realizable value is equal to the balance in Accounts Receivable minus the balance in Allowance for Doubtful Accounts after the journal entry to record bad debt expense has been recorded.

ACCOUNTING IN ACTION
ETHICS INSIGHT

The controller of Proust Company has completed draft financial statements for the year just ended and is reviewing them with the president. As part of the review, he has summarized an aging schedule showing the basis of estimating uncollectible accounts using the following percentages: 0–30 days, 5%; 31–60 days, 10%; 61–90 days, 30%; 91–120 days, 50%; and over 120 days, 80%.

The president of the company, Suzanne Bros, is nervous because the bank expects the company to sustain a growth rate for profit of at least 5% each year over the next two years—the remaining term of its bank loan. The profit growth for the past year was much more than 5% because of certain special orders with high margins, but those orders will not be repeated next year, so it will be very hard to achieve even the same profit next year, and even more difficult to grow it another 5%. It would be easier to show an increase next year if the past year's reported profit had been a little lower. President Bros recalls from her college accounting course that bad debt expense is based on certain estimates subject to judgement. She suggests that the controller increase the estimate percentages, which will increase the amount of the required bad debt expense adjustment and therefore lower profit for last year so that it will be easier to show a better growth rate next year.

Q   Should the controller be concerned with Proust Company's reported growth rate in estimating the allowance?

LEARNING OBJECTIVE 3   **Prepare journal entries for notes receivable transactions.**

Notes Receivable

Credit may also be granted in exchange for a formal credit instrument known as a promissory note. A **promissory note** is a written promise to pay a specified amount of money on demand or at a definite time. Promissory notes may be used (1) when individuals and companies lend or borrow money, (2) when the amount of the transaction and the credit period are longer than normal limits, or (3) in the settlement of accounts receivable.

In a promissory note, the party making the promise to pay is called the **maker**. The party to whom payment is to be made is called the **payee**. In the note shown in Illustration 8-9, Higly Inc. is the maker and Wolder Company is the payee. To Wolder Company, the promissory note is a note receivable. To Higly Inc., it is a note payable.

▶ **ILLUSTRATION 8-9**
Promissory note

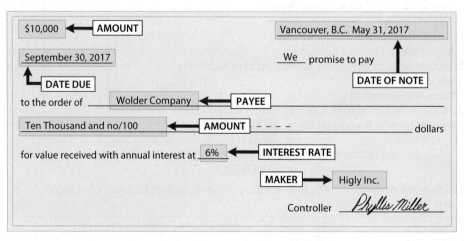

A promissory note might also contain other details such as whether any security is pledged as collateral for the loan and what happens if the maker defaults.

A note receivable is a **formal** promise to pay an amount that bears interest from the time it is issued until it is due. An account receivable is an **informal** promise to pay that bears interest only after its due date. Because it is less formal, it does not have as strong a legal claim as a note receivable. Most accounts receivable are due within a short period of time, usually 30 days, while a note can extend over longer periods of time.

There are also similarities between notes and accounts receivable. Both extend credit to customers, can be sold to another party, and are valued at their net realizable values.

RECOGNIZING NOTES RECEIVABLE

Like accounts receivable, a note receivable is an asset; it will provide future benefit as the company will collect cash in the future. To illustrate the basic entries for notes receivable, we will use the $10,000, four-month, 6% promissory note shown in Illustration 8-9. Assuming that Higly Inc. wrote the note in settlement of an account receivable, Wolder Company makes the following entry for the receipt of the note:

May 31	Notes Receivable—Higly	10,000	
	Accounts Receivable—Higly		10,000
	To record acceptance of Higly note.		

A = L + OE
+10,000
−10,000

Cash flows: no effect

If a note is exchanged for cash instead of an account receivable, the entry is a debit to Notes Receivable and a credit to Cash for the amount of the loan.

The note receivable is recorded at its principal amount (the value shown on the face of the note). No interest revenue is reported when the note is accepted because interest revenue is recognized as time passes. As each month passes and the note is not repaid, the payee is entitled to receive interest as a payment for giving the maker the use of the borrowed funds.

Recording Interest

As we learned in Chapter 3, the basic formula for calculating interest on an interest-bearing note is shown in Illustration 8-10.

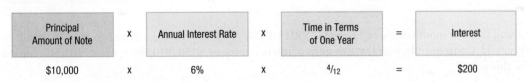

Principal Amount of Note	X	Annual Interest Rate	X	Time in Terms of One Year	=	Interest
$10,000	X	6%	X	$4/12$	=	$200

▶ ILLUSTRATION **8-10**
Formula for calculating interest

Recall from Chapter 3 that the principal amount is the amount borrowed, or the amount still outstanding on a loan, separate from interest. This is also the balance in the Notes Receivable account in Wolder's accounting records.

The interest rate specified in a note is an annual rate of interest. There are many factors that affect the interest rate. You will learn more about that in a finance course. Interest rates may also be fixed for the term of the note or may change over the term. In this textbook, we will always assume that the rate remains fixed for the term.

The time factor in the above formula gives the fraction of the year that interest has been earned. As we did in past chapters, to keep it simple we will assume that interest is calculated in months rather than days. Illustration 8-10 shows the calculation of interest revenue for Wolder Company and interest expense for Higly Inc. for the term of the note.

In Chapter 3, we illustrated an adjusting journal entry for accrued revenue. If Wolder Company's year end was June 30, the following adjusting journal entry for accrued revenue would be required to accrue interest for the month of June:

June 30	Interest Receivable	50	
	Interest Revenue ($10,000 × 6% × $1/12$)		50
	To accrue interest on Higly note receivable.		

A = L + OE
+50   +50

Cash flows: no effect

Notice that interest on a note receivable is not debited to the Notes Receivable account. Instead, a separate asset account for the interest receivable is used. The Notes Receivable account balance must be equal to the amount still outstanding on the note, in order to correctly calculate interest.

Valuing Notes Receivable

Like accounts receivable, notes receivable are reported at their net realizable value. Each note must be analyzed to determine how likely it is to be collected. If eventual collection is doubtful, bad debt expense and an allowance for doubtful notes must be recorded using the allowance method in the same way as for accounts receivable. Some companies use only one allowance account for both accounts and notes, and call it Allowance for Doubtful Accounts. In the discussion and end-of-chapter material that follow, we will use only one account to recognize uncollectible accounts for both accounts receivable and notes receivable: Allowance for Doubtful Accounts.

DISPOSING OF NOTES RECEIVABLE

Notes are normally held to their maturity date, at which time the principal plus any unpaid interest is collected. This is known as honouring (paying) the note. Sometimes, the maker of the note defaults and an adjustment to the accounts must be made. This is known as dishonouring (not paying) the note.

Honouring of Notes Receivable

A note is honoured when it is paid in full at its maturity date. The amount due at maturity is the principal of the note plus interest for the length of time the note is outstanding (assuming interest is due at maturity rather than monthly). If Higly Inc. honours the note when it is due on September 30—the maturity date—the entry by Wolder Company to record the collection is:

```
A    =   L   +   OE
+10,200          +150
−10,000
   −50
```
↑ Cash flows: +10,200

Sept. 30	Cash	10,200	
	Notes Receivable—Higly		10,000
	Interest Revenue		150
	Interest Receivable		50
	To record collection of Higly note.		

Recall that one month of interest revenue, $50 ($10,000 \times 6\% \times {}^1/_{12}$), was accrued on June 30, Wolder's year end. Consequently, only three months of interest revenue, $150 ($10,000 \times 6\% \times {}^3/_{12}$), is recorded in this period.

Dishonouring of Notes Receivable

A **dishonoured note** is a note that is not paid in full at maturity. Since a dishonoured note receivable is no longer negotiable, the Notes Receivable account must be reduced to zero. The payee still has a claim against the maker of the note for both the principal and any unpaid interest. The payee will transfer the amount owing to an Accounts Receivable account if there is hope that the amount will eventually be collected.

To illustrate, assume that on September 30, Higly Inc. says that it cannot pay at the present time but Wolder Company expects eventual collection. Wolder would make the following entry at the time the note is dishonoured:

Helpful hint A promissory note that is no longer negotiable cannot be transferred to another party for any value and is therefore no longer liquid.

```
A    =   L   +   OE
+10,200          +150
−10,000
   −50
```
Cash flows: no effect

Sept. 30	Accounts Receivable—Higly	10,200	
	Notes Receivable—Higly		10,000
	Interest Revenue		150
	Interest Receivable		50
	To record dishonouring of Higly note where collection is expected.		

Note that the amount recorded in the accounts receivable is the total amount owed (interest and principal) by Higly.

Wolder will continue to follow up with Higly. If the amount owing is eventually collected, Wolder will simply debit Cash and credit Accounts Receivable. If Wolder decides at a later date that it will never collect this amount from Higly, Wolder will write off the account receivable in the same way we learned earlier in the chapter—debit Allowance for Doubtful Accounts and credit Accounts Receivable.

On the other hand, Wolder could directly write the note off on September 30 if it decided there was no hope of collection. Assuming Wolder uses one allowance account for both accounts and notes, it would record the following:

Sept. 30	Allowance for Doubtful Accounts	10,050	
	Notes Receivable—Higly		10,000
	Interest Receivable		50
	To record dishonouring of Higly note where collection is not expected.		

A	=	L	+	OE
+10,050				
−10,000				
−50				

Cash flows: no effect

No interest revenue is recorded, because collection will not occur. The interest receivable that previously had been accrued is also written off and the Allowance for Doubtful Accounts is debited for both the principal amount owed and the interest receivable.

BEFORE YOU GO ON...DO IT **Accounting for Notes Receivable**

On May 1, Griffith Company accepts from S. Drummond a $3,400, three-month, 5% note in settlement of Drummond's overdue account. Interest is due at maturity. Griffith has a June 30 year end.

(a) Prepare the required journal entry to record the issue of the note on May 1, the adjusting journal entry on June 30, and the settlement of the note on August 1 assuming Drummond honours the note.

(b) Prepare the required journal entry on August 1 if Drummond does not pay the note and collection is not expected in the future.

Solution

(a)	May 1	Notes Receivable—S. Drummond	3,400	
		Accounts Receivable—S. Drummond		3,400
		To replace account receivable with 5% note receivable, due August 1.		
	June 30	Interest Receivable	28	
		Interest Revenue ($3,400 × 5% × $^2/_{12}$)		28
		To record interest earned to June 30.		
	Aug. 1	Cash	3,442	
		Interest Receivable		28
		Notes Receivable—S. Drummond		3,400
		Interest Revenue ($3,400 × 5% × $^1/_{12}$)		14
		To record collection of Drummond note plus interest.		
(b)	Aug. 1	Allowance for Doubtful Accounts	3,428	
		Interest Receivable		28
		Notes Receivable—S. Drummond		3,400
		To record dishonouring of Drummond note because collection is not expected.		

Related exercise material: BE8–11, BE8–12, BE8–13, BE8–14, E8–8, E8–9, E8–10, and E8–11.

Action Plan
- Calculate the accrued interest. The formula is: Principal × annual interest rate × time in terms of one year.
- Record the interest accrued on June 30 to follow revenue recognition criteria. Use Interest Receivable, not Notes Receivable, for accrued interest.
- If the note is honoured, calculate the interest accrued after June 30 and the total interest on the note. Record the interest accrued and the collection of the note and the total interest.
- If the note is dishonoured, record the transfer of the note and any interest earned to an accounts receivable account if eventual collection is expected or to an allowance account if collection is not expected.

Statement Presentation and Management of Receivables

The way receivables are presented in the financial statements is important because receivables are directly affected by how a company recognizes its revenue and bad debt expense. In addition, these reported numbers are critical for analyzing a company's liquidity and how well it manages its receivables. In the next sections, we will discuss the presentation, analysis, and management of receivables.

PRESENTATION

Each of the major types of receivables should be identified in the balance sheet or in the notes to the financial statements. Other receivables include interest receivable, loans or advances to employees, and recoverable sales and income taxes. These receivables are generally classified and reported as separate items in the current or noncurrent sections of the balance sheet, according to their due dates. Notes receivable may also be either current assets or long-term assets, depending on their due dates.

In addition to the net realizable value of the receivables shown on the balance sheet, both the gross amount of receivables and the allowance for doubtful accounts must be disclosed in either the balance sheet or the notes to the financial statements.

Bad debt expense is reported in the operating expenses section of the income statement.

Illustration 8-11 shows a partial balance sheet and an associated note disclosure for Rogers Communications Inc., which provides wireless, cable, and other media services.

▶ILLUSTRATION 8-11
Presentation of receivables

CONSOLIDATED STATEMENTS OF FINANCIAL POSITION (partial) (In millions of Canadian dollars)			
As at December 31	Note	2014	2013
Assets			
Current assets:			
Cash and cash equivalents		176	2,301
Accounts receivable	16	1,591	1,509
Inventories	15	251	276
Other current assets		191	162
Current portion of derivative instruments	16	136	73
Total current assets		2,345	4,321

At December 31, 2014, Rogers reports accounts receivable on the consolidated statements of financial position (balance sheet). The company also discloses additional information about the total accounts receivable reported on the statement of financial position in Note 16 as follows:

The table below provides an aging of our customer accounts receivable as at December 31 and additional information related to the allowance for doubtful accounts.

(In millions of dollars)	2014	2013
Customer accounts receivables (net of allowance for doubtful accounts)		
Less than 30 days past billing date	713	695
30-60 days past billing date	326	291
61-90 days past billing date	108	94
Greater than 90 days past billing date	62	68
Total	1,209	1,148

The activity related to our allowance for doubtful accounts is as follows:

(In millions of dollars)	**2014**	2013
Balance, beginning of the year	**104**	119
Allowance for doubtful accounts expense	**77**	111
Net use	**(83)**	(126)
Balance, end of the year	**98**	104

Rogers also reports in its notes to the financial statements that its allowance for doubtful accounts is determined by considering the company's experience in collections and write offs, the number of days the account is past due, and the status of the account.

ANALYSIS

Management of accounts receivable is critical to a business's success. Accounts receivable are generally the most important source of cash for business. If sales increase, then accounts receivable are also expected to increase. On the other hand, an increase in accounts receivable might signal trouble. Perhaps the company increased its sales by loosening its credit policy, and these receivables may be difficult or impossible to collect. The company could also end up with higher costs because of the increase in sales since it may need more cash to pay for inventory and salaries.

Recall that the ability to pay obligations as they come due is measured by a company's liquidity. How can we tell if a company's management of its receivables is helping or hurting the company's liquidity? One way of doing this is to calculate a ratio called the **receivables turnover ratio**. This ratio measures the number of times, on average, that receivables are collected during the period. It is calculated by dividing net credit sales by average gross receivables during the year.

Unfortunately, companies rarely report the amount of net sales made on credit in their financial statements. As a result, net sales (including both cash and credit sales) are used as a substitute. As long as net sales are used to calculate the ratio for all companies being compared, the comparison is fair.

In Illustration 8-12 the amounts for total sales and trade and other receivables were used to calculate Corus Entertainment's 2014 accounts receivable turnover.

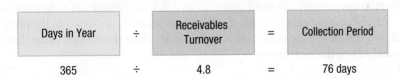

$$\text{Net Credit Sales} \div \text{Average Gross Accounts Receivable} = \text{Receivables Turnover}$$

$$\$833,016 \div \frac{(\$183,009 + \$164,302)}{2} = 4.8 \text{ times}$$

▶ **ILLUSTRATION 8-12**
Receivables turnover

The result indicates an accounts receivable turnover ratio of 4.8 times per year for Corus. The higher the turnover ratio, the more liquid the company's receivables are.

A popular variation of the receivables turnover ratio is to convert it into the number of days it takes the company to collect its receivables. This ratio, called the **collection period**, is calculated by dividing 365 days by the receivables turnover, as shown for Corus in Illustration 8-13.

$$\text{Days in Year} \div \text{Receivables Turnover} = \text{Collection Period}$$

$$365 \div 4.8 = 76 \text{ days}$$

▶ **ILLUSTRATION 8-13**
Collection period

This means that in fiscal 2014, Corus collected its receivables, on average, in approximately 76 days. Generally a company will provide customers with 30 days to pay a trade invoice. This is true in many industries, such as basic service or retail industries. However, Corus Entertainment is in the broadcasting industry and unlike a retailer, its operating cycle may be measured by determining the average time it takes to prepare programming, sell it on account, and collect cash from customers. The operating cycle for Corus is likely longer because of the nature of selling advertising and subscriptions, and preparing programming. So while 76 days, on average, to collect accounts receivable seems high, the broadcasting industry average is approximately 138 days, which means that Corus is actually doing better than average in its collection efforts. It is important to remember that ratios can and do provide insight into a company only when used in conjunction with historical information, industry information, and specific business operating environments.

The collection period is often used to judge how effective a company's credit and collection policies are. The general rule is that the collection period should not be much longer than the credit term period (that is, the time allowed for payment). Accounts receivable are basically an interest-free loan to the customer, so the faster they are collected, the better.

Both the receivables turnover and the collection period are useful for judging how efficiently a company converts its credit sales to cash. Remember that these measures should also be compared with industry averages, and with previous years.

In addition, these measures should be analyzed along with other information about a company's liquidity, including the current ratio and inventory turnover. For example, low receivables may result in a low current ratio, which might make the company look like it has poor liquidity. But the receivables may be low because they are turning over quickly. In general, the faster the turnover, the more reliable the current ratio is for assessing liquidity.

The collection period can also be used to assess the length of a company's operating cycle. Recall from Chapter 4 that the operating cycle is the time it takes to go from cash to cash in producing revenues. In a merchandising company, the operating cycle may be measured by determining the average time that it takes to purchase inventory, sell it on account, and then collect cash from customers. In a service company, such as Corus, the operating cycle is the time it takes to offer a service, complete the service, and collect cash.

In Chapter 6, we learned how to calculate days sales in inventory, which is the average age of the inventory on hand. The combination of the collection period and days sales in inventory is a useful way to measure the length of a company's operating cycle.

For example, Boomlet Company purchases and resells designer jeans. At the fiscal year end of September 30, 2017, the company calculated days sales in inventory at 43 days and the collection period at 35 days. Using both of these ratios, we can estimate Boomlet's operating cycle in days as shown in Illustration 8-14.

▶ **ILLUSTRATION 8-14**
Operating cycle

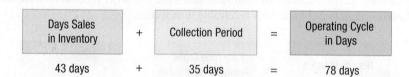

Days Sales in Inventory	+	Collection Period	=	Operating Cycle in Days
43 days	+	35 days	=	78 days

This means that in fiscal 2017, it took 78 days on average from the time Boomlet purchased its inventory until it collected cash.

ACCELERATING CASH RECEIPTS FROM RECEIVABLES

If a company sells on credit, it has to wait until the customer pays the receivable before it has cash available to pay for such items as inventory and operating expenses. As credit sales and receivables increase in size and significance, waiting for receivables to be collected increases costs because the company cannot use the revenue from the sale until cash is collected. If a company can collect cash more quickly from its receivables, it can shorten the cash-to-cash operating cycle discussed in the previous section.

There are two typical ways to collect cash more quickly from receivables: using the receivables to secure a loan and selling the receivables.

Loans Secured by Receivables

One of the most common ways to speed up cash flow from accounts receivable is to go to a bank and borrow money using accounts receivable as collateral. While this does have a cost (interest has to be paid to the bank on the loan), the cash is available for the company to use earlier. The loan can then be repaid as the receivables are collected. Generally, depending on the industry, banks are willing to give financing of up to 75% of receivables that are less than 90 days old. Quite often, these arrangements occur through an operating line of credit, which we will discuss in Chapter 10.

Sale of Receivables

Companies also frequently sell their receivables to another company because it provides an immediate source of cash. There are two other reasons for the sale of receivables. The first is their size. To be competitive, sellers often give financing to purchasers of their goods to encourage the sale of the product. But the companies may not want to hold large amounts of receivables. As a result, many major companies in the automobile, truck, equipment, computer, and appliance industries have created wholly owned finance companies that accept responsibility for accounts receivable financing. An example is Ford Credit Canada, owned by the Ford Motor Company of Canada.

Another reason for selling receivables is to reduce the costs of monitoring and collecting receivables. For example, it is often more cost-effective for a retailer to sell its receivables to credit card companies, such as Visa and MasterCard, which specialize in billing and collecting accounts receivable.

The processes involved in the sale of receivables will be covered in intermediate accounting courses.

ACCOUNTING IN ACTION

ACROSS THE ORGANIZATION

Andy Dean/iStockphoto

For a bank and other types of financial institutions, one of the biggest receivables is outstanding loans to customers. Lenders must manage the risk that customers won't be able to pay back their loans. When that risk isn't adequately managed, it can cause financial ruin to not only lenders but the economy at large. That's what happened in 2008, when the financial crisis started in the United States and circled the globe in a ripple effect. Several lenders failed to investigate loan customers sufficiently. For example, a U.S. company called Countrywide Financial Corporation wrote many loans under its "Fast and Easy" loan program. The program allowed borrowers to provide little or no proof of their income or assets. A study of

similar programs found that 60% of applicants overstated their incomes by more than 50% in order to qualify for a loan. As you might imagine, many of the customers couldn't make their loan payments, such as mortgages, and they defaulted on their loans in huge numbers, which resulted in home foreclosures and a credit crunch. Critics of the banking industry say that, because loan officers were compensated for loan volume and because banks were selling the loans to investors rather than holding them, the lenders had little incentive to investigate the borrowers' creditworthiness. The situation was less dire in Canada, where the banking industry is heavily regulated and banks tend to be more conservative, but the lesson was clear: lenders need to be stricter when choosing who to lend money to.

Sources: Timothy Lane, Deputy Governor, Bank of Canada, "Financial Stability in One Country?," speech to Harvard University, February 11, 2013; Glenn R. Simpson and James R. Hagerty, "Countrywide Loss Focuses Attention on Underwriting," *The Wall Street Journal*, April 30, 2008, p. B1; Michael Corkery, "Fraud Seen as Driver in Wave of Foreclosures," *The Wall Street Journal*, December 21, 2007, p. A1.

BEFORE YOU GO ON...DO IT **4** > **Analysis of Receivables**

The following information is available for Jupiter Company.

	2017	2016	2015
Net credit sales	$1,500,000	$1,300,000	$1,350,000
Gross accounts receivable	127,000	124,000	118,000
Days sales in inventory	44.5 days	43 days	

Calculate the accounts receivable turnover ratio, collection period, and operating cycle in days for 2016 and 2017 and comment on any trends.

(continued)

Action Plan

- Calculate the average gross accounts receivable using the accounts receivable balance at the beginning and ending of the year.
- Divide net credit sales by the average accounts receivable for that year to calculate receivables turnover.
- Divide 365 by the receivables turnover to calculate collection period.
- Add the collection period to days sales in inventory to calculate operating cycle in days.

BEFORE YOU GO ON...DO IT **4**   **Analysis of Receivables** (continued)

Solution

	2017	2016
Receivables turnover	$11.95 \text{ times} = \dfrac{\$1,500,000}{[(\$127,000 + \$124,000) \div 2]}$	$10.74 \text{ times} = \dfrac{\$1,300,000}{[(\$124,000 + \$118,000) \div 2]}$
Collection period	$30.54 \text{ days} = \dfrac{365 \text{ days}}{11.95 \text{ times}}$	$34 \text{ days} = \dfrac{365 \text{ days}}{10.74 \text{ times}}$
Operating cycle in days	$75 \text{ days} = 30.54 + 44.5$	$77 \text{ days} = 34 + 43$

The accounts receivable turnover has increased and the collection period decreased. In general, it is better to have a higher accounts receivable turnover and a lower collection period. Even though the days sales in inventory has increased, the operating cycle has decreased, which generally is better for the company.

Related exercise material: BE8–6, BE8–14, BE8–15, BE8–16, E8–3, E8–11, E8–12, and E8–13.

▉Comparing IFRS and ASPE ▉

Key Differences	International Financial Reporting Standards (IFRS)	Accounting Standards for Private Enterprises (ASPE)
No significant differences		

Demonstration Problem

On February 28, Dylan Co. had the following balances in select accounts:

Accounts Receivable	$200,000
Allowance for Doubtful Accounts (credit)	12,500

Selected transactions for Dylan Co. follow. Dylan's year end is June 30.

Mar. 1   Sold $20,000 of merchandise to Potter Company, terms n/30.
    1   Accepted Juno Company's $16,500, six-month, 6% note for the balance due on account.
   11   Potter Company returned $600 worth of goods.
   13   Sold $13,200 of merchandise to Henry Company, terms n/30.
   30   Received payment in full from Potter Company.
Apr. 13   Recorded interest on the balance owing from Henry Company's overdue account. Dylan Co. charges 24% interest on overdue accounts.
May 10   Wrote off as uncollectible $15,000 of accounts receivable.
   11   Received payment in full from Henry Company.
June 30   Estimated uncollectible accounts are determined to be $20,000 at June 30.
   30   Recorded the interest accrued on the Juno Company note.
July 16   Received payment in full, $4,000, on an account that was previously written off in May.
Sept. 1   Collected cash from Juno Company in payment of the March 1 note receivable.

Dylan uses the percentage of receivables approach to estimate uncollectible accounts.

Instructions

(a) Prepare the journal entries for the transactions. Ignore cost of goods sold entries for purposes of this question.
(b) Open T accounts for Accounts Receivable and the Allowance for Doubtful Accounts, and post the relevant journal entries to these accounts. Calculate the balance in these accounts at June 30 and at September 1.
(c) Calculate the net realizable value of the accounts receivable at June 30 and September 1.

SOLUTION TO DEMONSTRATION PROBLEM

(a)

Mar. 1	Accounts Receivable—Potter	20,000	
	Sales		20,000
	To record sale on account.		
1	Notes Receivable—Juno	16,500	
	Accounts Receivable—Juno		16,500
	To record acceptance of Juno Company note.		
11	Sales Returns and Allowances	600	
	Accounts Receivable—Potter		600
	To record return of goods.		
13	Accounts Receivable—Henry Company	13,200	
	Sales		13,200
	To record sale on account.		
30	Cash ($20,000 − $600)	19,400	
	Accounts Receivable—Potter		19,400
	To record collection of account receivable.		
Apr. 13	Accounts Receivable—Henry Company	264	
	($13,200 \times 24\% \times \frac{1}{12}$)		
	Interest Revenue		264
	To record interest on overdue account.		
May 10	Allowance for Doubtful Accounts	15,000	
	Accounts Receivable		15,000
	To record write off of accounts receivable.		
11	Cash (13,200 + 264)	13,464	
	Accounts Receivable—Henry Company		13,464
	To record payment received from Henry Company.		
June 30	Bad Debt Expense ($20,000 + $2,500)	22,500	
	Allowance for Doubtful Accounts		22,500
	To record estimate of uncollectible accounts.		
30	Interest Receivable ($16,500 \times 6\% \times \frac{4}{12}$)	330	
	Interest Revenue		330
	To record interest earned.		
July 16	Accounts Receivable	4,000	
	Allowance for Doubtful Accounts		4,000
	To reverse write off of account receivable.		
16	Cash	4,000	
	Accounts Receivable		4,000
	To record collection of account receivable.		
Sept. 1	Cash [$16,500 + ($16,500 \times 6\% \times \frac{6}{12}$)]	16,995	
	Interest Revenue ($16,500 \times 6\% \times \frac{2}{12}$)		165
	Interest Receivable		330
	Note Receivable		16,500
	To record collection of note receivable plus interest.		

ACTION PLAN

- Record receivables at the invoice price.
- Recognize that sales returns and allowances reduce the amount received on accounts receivable.
- Calculate interest by multiplying the principal by the interest rate by the part of the year that has passed.
- Record write offs of accounts and collection of previously written-off accounts only in balance sheet accounts.
- Consider any existing balance in the allowance account when making the adjustment for uncollectible accounts.
- Recognize any remaining interest on notes receivable when recording the collection of a note.

(b)

Accounts Receivable

Feb. 28	Bal.	200,000		16,500
		20,000		600
		13,200		19,400
		264		15,000
				13,464
June 30	Bal.	168,500		
July 16		4,000	July 16	4,000
Sept. 1	Bal.	168,500		

Allowance for Doubtful Accounts

May 10		15,000	Feb. 28	Bal.	12,500
June 30	Bal.	2,500			
			June 30	Adj.	22,500
			June 30	Bal.	20,000
			July 16		4,000
			Sept. 1	Bal.	24,000

(c)

	June 30	Sept. 1
Accounts receivable	$168,500	$168,500
Less: Allowance for doubtful accounts	20,000	24,000
Net realizable value	$148,500	$144,500

▶ Summary of Learning Objectives

1. **Prepare journal entries for accounts receivable transactions.** Accounts receivable are recorded at the invoice price. They are reduced by sales returns and allowances and sales discounts. Accounts receivable subsidiary ledgers are used to keep track of individual account balances. When interest is charged on a past-due receivable, this interest is added to the accounts receivable balance and is recognized as interest revenue. Some retailers issue their own credit cards and these are accounted for as a type of accounts receivable transaction.

2. **Demonstrate how to value accounts receivable and prepare adjusting journal entries for uncollectible accounts.** Accounts receivable must be reported at their net realizable value on the balance sheet. The allowance method is used to record the estimated uncollectible accounts in the Allowance for Doubtful Accounts. The net realizable value of the receivables is equal to the gross accounts receivable minus the allowance. There are two approaches that can be used to estimate uncollectible accounts: (a) percentage of receivables, or (b) percentage of sales. The percentage of receivables approach emphasizes determining the correct net realizable value of the accounts receivable. An aging schedule is usually used with the percentage of receivables approach where percentages are applied to different categories of accounts receivable to determine the allowance for doubtful accounts. The percentage of sales approach emphasizes achieving the most accurate matching of expenses to revenues. A percentage is applied to credit sales to determine the bad debt expense.

When a specific account receivable is determined to be uncollectible, the account is written off and the allowance is reduced. When a previously written-off account is collected, the entry previously made to write off the account is reversed and the collection is recorded.

3. **Prepare journal entries for notes receivable transactions.** Notes receivable are recorded at their principal amount. Interest is earned from the date the note is issued until it matures and must be recorded in the correct accounting period. Interest receivable is recorded in a separate account from the note. Like accounts receivable, notes receivable are reported at their net realizable value.

Notes are normally held to maturity. At that time, the principal plus any unpaid interest is due and the note is removed from the accounts. If a note is not paid at maturity, it is said to be dishonoured. If eventual collection is still expected, an account receivable replaces the note receivable and any unpaid interest. Otherwise, the note must be written off.

4. **Demonstrate the presentation, analysis, and management of receivables.** Each major type of receivable should be identified in the balance sheet or in the notes to the financial statements. Both the gross amount of receivables and the allowance for doubtful accounts/notes is required to be reported in the balance sheet or the notes to the financial statements. Bad debt expense is reported in the income statement as an operating expense.

The liquidity of receivables can be evaluated by calculating the receivables turnover and collection period ratios.

The receivables turnover is calculated by dividing net credit sales by average gross accounts receivable. This ratio measures how efficiently the company is converting its receivables into sales. The collection period converts the receivables turnover into days, dividing 365 days by the receivables turnover ratio. It shows the number of days, on average, it takes a company to collect its accounts receivable. The combination of the collection period and days sales in inventory is a useful way to measure the length of a company's operating cycle.

Companies may accelerate the collection of cash by using the receivables to secure a loan or by selling the receivables.

▶ Glossary

Accounts receivable Amounts owed by customers on account. (p. 422)

Aging schedule A list of accounts receivable organized by the length of time they have been unpaid. (p. 427)

Allowance for Doubtful Accounts A contra asset account that is deducted from gross accounts receivable to report receivables at their net realizable value. (p. 426)

Allowance method The method of accounting for bad debts that involves estimating uncollectible accounts at the end of each period. (p. 426)

Bad debt expense An expense account to record uncollectible receivables. (p. 425)

Collection period The average number of days that receivables are outstanding. It is calculated by dividing 365 days by the receivables turnover. (p. 439)

Default What happens when the maker of the note does not pay the note in full. Also referred to as dishonouring the note. (p. 426)

Dishonoured note A note that is not paid in full at maturity. (p. 436)

Gross accounts receivable The total accounts receivable in the control account in the general ledger; includes both collectible and uncollectible accounts. (p. 427)

Maker The party making the promise to pay a promissory note. (p. 434)

Net realizable value The net amount of receivables expected to be collected. (p. 425)

Notes receivable Claims for which formal instruments (written instruments) of credit are issued as evidence of the debt. (p. 422)

Payee The party to whom payment is to be made. (p. 434)

Percentage of receivables approach The approach used to estimate uncollectible accounts where the allowance for doubtful accounts is calculated as a percentage of receivables. (p. 427)

Percentage of sales approach An approach to estimating uncollectible accounts where bad debt expense is calculated as a percentage of net credit sales. (p. 429)

Promissory note A written promise to pay a specified amount of money on demand or at a definite time. (p. 434)

Receivables turnover ratio A measure of the liquidity of receivables, calculated by dividing net credit sales by average gross accounts receivable. (p. 439)

Trade receivables Accounts and notes receivable that result from sales transactions. (p. 422)

▶ Self-Study Questions
Answers are at the end of the chapter.

(LO 1) C 1. Creative Corporation reports the following balances in its accounts receivable subledger:

T. L. Jones	$1,500
M. McLean	$6,800
B. Patel	$950

What is the balance in the accounts receivable control account?

(a) $9,250   (c) $6,800
(b) $1,500   (d) $8,300

(LO 1) AP 2. On June 1, Jade Company sells merchandise on account to Ruby Enterprises for $22,000, terms 2/10, n/30. On June 3, Ruby returns merchandise worth $4,000 to Jade. On June 11, payment is received from Ruby for the balance due. What is the amount of cash received?
(a) $18,000
(b) $17,640
(c) $21,560
(d) $22,000

(LO 1) AP 3. Jasper Company sold merchandise on account to Opal Co. for $1,000, terms 2/10, n/30 on June 15. On June 24, payment was received from Opal Co. for the balance due. What is the amount of cash received?
(a) $1,000
(b) $980
(c) $1,020
(d) $0

(LO 2) AP 4. Kartik Company's accounts receivable are $200,000 at the end of the year. The allowance for doubtful accounts has a credit balance of $4,000 before any adjustments have been made. The company estimates that 5% of accounts receivable will not be collected. What is the net realizable value of the accounts receivable at the end of the year?
(a) $196,000
(b) $200,000
(c) $186,000
(d) $190,000

(LO 2) AP 5. Net sales for the month are $800,000 and bad debts are expected to be 1.5% of net sales. The company uses the percentage of sales approach. If Allowance for Doubtful Accounts has a credit balance of $15,000 before adjustment, what is the balance in the allowance account after adjustment?
(a) $15,000
(b) $23,000
(c) $27,000
(d) $12,000

(LO 2) AP 6. On December 31, 2017, the Allowance for Doubtful Accounts has an unadjusted debit balance of $8,000. An aging schedule indicates that uncollectible accounts are $20,000 at the end of 2017. What is the required bad debt expense adjustment to the Allowance for Doubtful Accounts at December 31, 2017?
(a) $8,000
(b) $12,000
(c) $20,000
(d) $28,000

(LO 2) AP 7. On January 1, 2017, Allowance for Doubtful Accounts had a credit balance of $40,000. In 2017, $30,000 of uncollectible accounts receivable were written off. On December 31, 2017, the company had accounts receivable of $900,000. Experience indicates that 4% of total receivables will become uncollectible. The adjusting journal entry that would be recorded on December 31, 2017, would be:

(a) Allowance for Doubtful Accounts	26,000	
Accounts Receivable		26,000
(b) Bad Debt Expense	36,000	
Accounts Receivable		36,000
(c) Bad Debt Expense	26,000	
Allowance for Doubtful Accounts		26,000
(d) Bad Debt Expense	36,000	
Allowance for Doubtful Accounts		36,000

(LO 3) C 8. Which of the following statements about promissory notes is **incorrect**?
(a) A promissory note is a written promise to pay a specified amount of money on demand.
(b) Promissory notes are used when individuals lend or borrow money.
(c) The party making the promise to pay is called the payee.
(d) Promissory notes are used in settlement of accounts receivable.

(LO 3) AP 9. On June 1, Sorenson Co. accepts a $2,000, four-month, 6% promissory note in settlement of an account with Parton Co. Sorenson has a July 31 fiscal year end. The adjusting entry to record interest on July 31 is:

(a) Interest Receivable	20	
Interest Revenue		20
(b) Interest Receivable	120	
Interest Revenue		120
(c) Notes Receivable	120	
Unearned Interest Revenue		120
(d) Interest Receivable	40	
Interest Revenue		40

(LO 3) AP 10. Pawar Company holds Abbott Retailers' $10,000, four-month, 9% note. If no interest has been previously accrued when the note is collected, the entry made by Pawar Company is:

(a) Cash	10,300	
Notes Receivable		10,300
(b) Cash	10,900	
Interest Revenue		900
Notes Receivable		10,000
(c) Accounts Receivable	10,300	
Notes Receivable		10,000
Interest Revenue		300
(d) Cash	10,300	
Notes Receivable		10,000
Interest Revenue		300

(LO 4) C 11. The allowance for doubtful accounts is presented in the financial statements as:
(a) a current liability in the balance sheet.
(b) a deduction from accounts receivable in the balance sheet.
(c) a contra revenue account in the income statement.
(d) an operating expense in the income statement.

(LO 4) AP 12. Moore Company had net credit sales of $800,000 in the year and a cost of goods sold of $500,000. The balance in Accounts Receivable at the beginning of the year was $100,000 and at the end of the year it was $150,000. What were the receivables turnover and collection period ratios, respectively?
(a) 4.0 and 91 days
(b) 5.3 and 69 days
(c) 6.4 and 57 days
(d) 8.0 and 46 days

▶ Questions

(LO 1) C 1. When should a receivable be recorded for a service company? For a merchandising company?

(LO 1) K 2. What is the difference between an account receivable and a note receivable?

(LO 1) C 3. (a) What information does a company need to manage its accounts receivable? (b) How is this information tracked in an accounting system?

(LO 1) K 4. Under what circumstances is interest normally recorded for an account receivable?

(LO 2) C 5. Why would a company decide to sell goods or services on credit if there is always a risk of not collecting amounts owed?

(LO 2) C 6. Access Company has had significant bad debts in previous years. To eliminate the risk of bad debts, the accounting manager of Access Company has recommended to the sales manager to make only cash sales. The sales manager does not think this is the best business decision. Do you agree or disagree with the sales manager? What do you recommend the company do to reduce the risk of bad debts?

(LO 2) C 7. What is the net realizable value of accounts receivable? Why are accounts receivable reported at net realizable value on the balance sheet?

(LO 2) K 8. Explain the allowance method of accounting for bad debts. How does this method result in assets not being overstated?

(LO 2) C 9. Explain the difference between the percentage of receivables and the percentage of sales approaches for estimating uncollectible accounts.

(LO 2) C 10. Matthew doesn't understand why the bad debt expense reported in the income statement is usually not equal to the allowance for doubtful accounts reported in the balance sheet. Explain why this happens.

(LO 2) C 11. Zahra doesn't understand why bad debt expense is not increased when a specific customer account is determined to be uncollectible and written off. Explain.

(LO 2) C 12. Describe the components of an aging schedule. How is the aging schedule used to estimate the amount of uncollectibles?

(LO 2) K 13. When an account receivable that was written off is later collected, two journal entries are usually made. What are the journal entries?

(LO 3) C 14. Why will a company take a note receivable from a customer in settlement of a late account receivable?

(LO 3) C 15. What does it mean if a note is dishonoured?

(LO 3) K 16. Deidre does not understand the difference between an account receivable and a note receivable. Explain the differences to Deidre and include in your explanation appropriate terminology used to describe a note receivable.

(LO 4) C 17. Mac Leonard is preparing the financial statements and has reported the Allowance for Doubtful Accounts in the current liabilities section of the balance sheet because the normal balance of the allowance is a credit. Do you agree with this treatment? Explain.

(LO 4) C 18. Saucier Company has accounts receivable, notes receivable due in three months, notes receivable due in two years, an allowance for doubtful accounts, sales taxes recoverable, and income tax receivable. Show how these amounts would be reported on the balance sheet at the company's year end.

(LO 4) C 19. The president of Unlimited Enterprises proudly announces that her company's liquidity has improved. Its current ratio increased substantially this year. Does an increase in the current ratio always indicate improved liquidity?

(LO 4) C 20. Refer to Question 19. What other ratio(s) of Unlimited Enterprises might you review to determine whether or not the increase in the current ratio represents an improvement in the company's financial health?

(LO 4) C 21. Canadian Worldwide Communications Co.'s receivables turnover was 6.5 times in 2016 and 5.9 times in 2017. Has the company's receivables management improved or worsened?

(LO 4) K 22. Why do companies sometimes sell their receivables?

▶ Brief Exercises

BE8–1 Six transactions follow. For each transaction, indicate if the transaction increases, decreases, or has no effect on (a) accounts receivable, (b) notes receivable, (c) total assets, (d) total liabilities, and (e) owner's equity. Use the following format, in which the first transaction is given as an example.

Identify impact of transaction on receivables, total assets, liabilities, and owner's equity.
(LO 1) K

Transaction:	(a) Accounts Receivable	(b) Notes Receivable	(c) Total Assets	(d) Total Liabilities	(e) Owner's Equity
1. Performed services on account for a customer.	Increase	No effect	Increase	No effect	Increase
2. A customer paid cash for services to be provided next month.					
3. Performed services for a customer in exchange for a note.					
4. Collected cash from the customer in transaction 1. above.					
5. Extended a customer's account for three months by accepting a note in exchange for it.					
6. Performed services for a customer who had paid in advance.					

Record accounts receivable transactions. (LO 1) AP

BE8–2   Record the following transactions on the books of Diaz Computer Company:
(a) On September 1, Diaz provided services on account to Thomas & Perez Law Office for $16,000, terms 2/10, n/30.
(b) On September 10, Thomas & Perez paid the amount owing.

Record accounts receivable transactions. (LO 1) AP

BE8–3   Record the following transactions on the books of Fowler Co.:
(a) On May 1, Fowler Co. sold merchandise on account to Kaneva Inc. for $30,000, terms 2/10, n/30. Ignore any entries that affect inventory and cost of goods sold for purposes of this question.
(b) On June 30, Fowler Co. charged Kaneva Inc. one month's interest for the overdue account. Fowler charges 10% on overdue accounts.
(c) On July 5, Kaneva paid the amount owing to Fowler Co.

Record credit card transactions. (LO 1) AP

BE8–4   On August 7, Imports to You Co. sold merchandise with a cost of $250 for $600 to Jade Biggs, who used an Imports to You Co. credit card for payment. On August 15, Jade returned $100 of merchandise that was damaged and the goods were scrapped. On September 7, Imports to You Co. recorded interest on the credit card balance owing on Jade Biggs's account. Imports to You Co. charges 18% on any balance owing on its credit cards. Prepare journal entries to record the above transactions. (Round answer to the nearest cent.)

Complete aging schedule and determine the allowance and net realizable value. (LO 2) AP

BE8–5   Gourdeau Co. uses an aging schedule to determine its estimated uncollectible accounts at December 31. Complete the following schedule and determine the required balance in the Allowance for Doubtful Accounts and the net realizable value of the accounts receivable.

Number of Days Outstanding	Accounts Receivable	Estimated % Uncollectible	Estimated Uncollectible Accounts
0–30 days	$265,000	1%	
31–60 days	70,000	4%	
61–90 days	45,000	10%	
Over 90 days	20,000	20%	
Total	$400,000		

Determine the allowance and prepare partial balance sheet. (LO 2, 4) AP

BE8–6   Refer to the data in BE8–5 for Gourdeau Co.
(a) Assuming the allowance for doubtful accounts has an unadjusted credit balance of $4,500 at December 31, what is the bad debt expense for the year?
(b) Prepare the current assets section of the balance sheet for Gourdeau Co. Assume that, in addition to the receivables, it has cash of $90,000, merchandise inventory of $130,000, and prepaid insurance of $7,500.

BE8-7 Qinshan Co. uses the percentage of sales approach to record bad debt expense. It estimates that 1.5% of net credit sales will become uncollectible. Credit sales are $950,000 for the year ended April 30, 2017; sales returns and allowances are $60,000; sales discounts are $20,000; accounts receivable are $310,000; and the allowance for doubtful accounts has a credit balance of $6,000.
(a) Prepare the adjusting entry to record bad debt expense in 2017.
(b) Calculate the net realizable value of accounts receivable on April 30, 2017.

Determine the allowance and net realizable value and record bad debts using the percentage of sales approach. (LO 2) AP

BE8-8 Stilton Company reported the following in its general ledger. Using your knowledge of receivables transactions, match each of the transactions (a) to (f) with the best description of the economic event.

Analyze accounts receivable transactions. (LO 2) AP

Accounts Receivable			
Jan. 1	20,000	(b)	80,000
(a)	120,000	(c)	500
Dec. 31	59,500		
(e)	500	(f)	500

Service Revenue	
	120,000 (a)

Allowance for Doubtful Accounts			
		Jan. 1	2,000
(c)	500	(d)	900
		Dec. 31	2,400
		(e)	500

Bad Debt Expense	
(d) 900	

1. Collect previously written-off account _____
2. Provide service on account _____
3. Write off uncollectible account _____
4. Collect accounts receivable _____
5. Record bad debt expense _____
6. Reverse previously written-off account _____

BE8-9 At the end of 2016, Perry Co. has an allowance for doubtful accounts of $28,000. On January 31, 2017, when it has accounts receivable of $575,000, Perry Co. learns that its $5,500 receivable from Tokarik Inc. is not collectible. Management authorizes a write off.
(a) Record the write off.
(b) What is the net realizable value of the accounts receivable (1) before the write off, and (2) after the write off?

Record write off and compare net realizable value. (LO 2) AP

BE8-10 Assume the same information as in BE8-9. Tokarik Inc.'s financial difficulties are over. On June 4, 2017, Perry Co. receives a payment in full of $5,500 from Tokarik Inc. Record this transaction.

Record collection of account previously written off. (LO 2) AP

BE8-11 Yamada Co. has three outstanding notes receivable at its December 31, 2017, fiscal year end. For each note, calculate (a) total interest revenue, (b) interest revenue to be recorded in 2017, and (c) interest revenue to be recorded in 2018.

Calculate interest on notes receivable. (LO 3) AP

Issue Date	Term	Principal	Interest Rate
1. August 31, 2017	9 months	$15,000	6%
2. November 1, 2017	6 months	44,000	8%
3. October 1, 2017	15 months	30,000	7%

BE8-12 On January 10, 2017, Kato Kreations sold merchandise on account to Lechner & Associates for $15,600, n/30. On February 9, Lechner gave Kato a 10% promissory note in settlement of this account. Prepare the journal entries to record the sale and the settlement of the accounts receivable.

Record notes receivable transactions. (LO 3) AP

BE8-13 Lee Company accepts a $27,000, four-month, 6% note receivable in settlement of an account receivable on June 1, 2017. Interest is to be paid at maturity. Lee Company has a December 31 year end and adjusts its accounts annually.
(a) Record (1) the issue of the note on June 1 and (2) the settlement of the note on October 1, assuming the note is honoured.
(b) Assume instead that the note is dishonoured but eventual collection is expected. Record the October 1 journal entry.
(c) Assume instead that the note is dishonoured and eventual collection is not expected. Record the October 1 journal entry.

Record notes receivable transactions. (LO 3) AP

Record notes receivable transactions and indicate statement presentation. (LO 3, 4) AP

BE8–14 Demir Financial Services loaned Sharp Inc. $100,000 cash in exchange for a one-year, 4% note on July 1, 2017. Interest is payable quarterly beginning on October 1, 2017. Demir has a December 31 year end and records adjusting entries annually.
(a) Record Demir's entries related to the note on July 1 and October 1, 2017.
(b) Prepare the adjusting journal entry for accrued interest on December 31, 2017.
(c) Indicate what amounts will be reported on Demir's December 31, 2017, balance sheet related to the note receivable.

Calculate ratios. (LO 4) AP

BE8–15 The financial statements of Clark & Powell report net credit sales of $2 million. Accounts receivable are $270,000 at the beginning of the year and $280,000 at the end of the year. Calculate Clark & Powell's accounts receivable turnover and average collection period for accounts receivable in days.

Calculate ratios to analyze receivables. (LO 4) AN

BE8–16 The financial statements of **Maple Leaf Foods Inc.** reported the following for the years ended December 31, 2014, 2013, and 2012.

Financial Statement Data (in thousands of dollars)			
	2014	2013	2012
Sales	$3,157,241	$2,954,777	$4,551,828
Accounts receivable	60,396	111,034	117,533

(a) Calculate Maple Leaf's receivables turnover and collection period for 2014 and 2013.
(b) Has the company's liquidity improved or weakened?

▶ Exercises

Record accounts receivable transactions. (LO 1) AP

E8–1 Transactions follow for the Extreme Sports Ltd. store and four of its customers in the company's first month of business:

June	3	Ben Kidd used his Extreme Sports credit card to purchase $1,050 of merchandise.
	6	Biljana Pavic used her MasterCard credit card to purchase $840 of merchandise. MasterCard charges a 2.5% service fee.
	9	Nicole Montpetit purchased $421 of merchandise on account, terms 2/10, n/30.
	19	Bonnie Cutcliffe used her debit card to purchase $230 of merchandise. There is a $0.50 service charge on all debit card transactions.
	20	Ben Kidd made a $315 payment on his credit card account.
	23	Nicole Montpetit purchased an additional $498 of merchandise on account, terms 2/10, n/30.
	25	Nicole Montpetit paid the amount owing on her June 9 purchase.
	30	Biljana Pavic used her MasterCard to purchase $420 of merchandise. MasterCard charges a 2.5% service fee.

Instructions

Record the above transactions. Round dollar amounts to the nearest cent. Ignore any inventory or cost of goods sold entries for purposes of this question.

Record accounts receivable transactions. (LO 1) AP

E8–2 Presented below are two independent situations. Assume each company uses a periodic inventory system.

1. On January 6, Bow Co. sells merchandise on account to Pryor Company for $7,000, terms 2/10, n/30. On January 16, Pryor Company pays the amount due.
2. On January 10, D. Laskowski purchases $9,000 of merchandise from Paltrow Co., terms 2/10, n/30. D. Laskowski returns $600 of merchandise to Paltrow on January 15. Paltrow Co. charges its customers 1% per month on overdue amounts. On March 10, Paltrow records interest on D. Laskowski's past due account. On March 31, D. Laskowski pays his account in full.

Instructions

(a) For item 1, prepare the entries on January 6 and January 16 on Bow Co.'s books.
(b) For item 2, prepare the entries required on January 10, January 15, March 10, and March 31 on Paltrow Company's books.

Record sales transactions and indicate statement presentation. (LO 1, 4) AP

E8–3 Casa Garage Co. accepts the following forms of payment: Visa, MasterCard, the Casa Garage Co. credit card, and debit. Casa is charged 3.5% for all bank credit card transactions and $0.50 per transaction for all debit card transactions. Casa charges 14.25% interest on balances owing on the Casa Garage Co. credit card. In October and November 2017, the following summary transactions occurred:

Oct.	15	Performed services totalling $15,000 for customers who used the Casa Garage Co. credit card for payment.
	20	Performed services totalling $7,500 to customers who used Visa credit cards.

30   Performed services totalling $2,000 on account, terms, n/30.

31   Performed services totalling $5,000 for customers who used debit cards (100 transactions).

Nov. 15   Collected amounts owing from October 15 transactions.

Instructions

(a) Record the above transactions for Casa Garage Co.

(b) In addition to these transactions, Casa had rent expense of $4,000, supplies expense of $500, and salary expense of $5,000 for the months of October and November. Prepare a single-step income statement for Casa Garage Co. for the two months ended November 30.

E8–4   The account balances of Assen Company at December 31, 2017, the end of the current year, show Accounts Receivable $180,000; Allowance for Doubtful Accounts $2,200 (credit); Sales $1,420,000; Sales Returns and Allowances $50,000; and Sales Discounts $20,000.

Calculate net realizable value and record bad debts using two approaches. (LO 2) AP

Instructions

(a) Record the adjusting entry at December 31, 2017, assuming bad debts are estimated to be (1) 10% of accounts receivable, and (2) 1.5% of net sales.

(b) Calculate the net realizable value of the accounts receivable for each approach to estimating uncollectible accounts in part (a) above.

(c) Assume instead that the Allowance for Doubtful Accounts had a debit balance of $2,600 at December 31, 2017. What is bad debt expense for 2017, and what is the net realizable value of the accounts receivable at December 31, 2017, assuming bad debts are estimated to be (1) 10% of accounts receivable, and (2) 1.5% of net sales?

E8–5   Rowen Company has accounts receivable of $241,000 at September 30, 2017. An analysis of the accounts shows the following:

Prepare aging schedule and record bad debts. (LO 2) AP

Month of Sale	Balance
September	$170,000
August	35,700
July	20,000
April, May, and June	15,300
	$241,000

Credit terms are 2/10, n/30. The unadjusted balance in the Allowance for Doubtful Accounts on September 30, 2017, is $1,400 debit. The company uses an aging schedule to estimate uncollectible accounts. The company's percentage estimates of bad debts are as follows:

Number of Days Outstanding	Estimated % Uncollectible
0–30	1%
31–60	10%
61–90	25%
Over 90	60%

Instructions

(a) Prepare an aging schedule to determine the total estimated uncollectible accounts at September 30, 2017.

(b) What is the net realizable value of the accounts receivable at September 30, 2017?

(c) Prepare the adjusting entry at September 30 to record bad debt expense.

E8–6   Chelsea Corporation reported the following information in its general ledger at December 31.

Determine missing amounts and describe the accounts receivable transactions. (LO 1, 2) AP

Accounts Receivable				Sales	
Beg.	bal.	15,000	35,200		45,000
		(a)	(b)		
End.	bal.	(c)			

Allowance for Doubtful Accounts				Bad Debt Expense	
		Beg.	bal. 1,200	(d)	
	800		(d)		
		End.	bal. (e)		

All sales were on account. At the end of the year, uncollectible accounts were estimated to be 10% of accounts receivable.

Instructions

(a) Using your knowledge of receivables transactions, determine the missing amounts. (*Hint:* You may find it helpful to reconstruct the journal entries.)

(b) Describe each transaction that has been recorded.

(c) What is the amount of cash collected?

Record bad debts, write off, and collection of previously written-off account; calculate net realizable value. (LO 2) AP

E8–7   Accounts receivable transactions are provided below for J Looney Co.

Dec. 31, 2016	The company estimated that 5% of its accounts receivable would become uncollectible. The balances in the Accounts Receivable account and Allowance for Doubtful Accounts were $650,000 and $2,300 (debit), respectively.
Mar. 5, 2017	The company determined that R. Mirza's $3,700 account and D. Wight's $6,900 account were uncollectible. The company's accounts receivable were $685,000 before the accounts were written off.
June 6, 2017	Wight paid the amount that had been written off on March 5. The company's accounts receivable were $641,000 prior to recording the cash receipt for Wight.

Instructions

(a) Prepare the journal entries on December 31, 2016, March 5, 2017, and June 6, 2017.

(b) Post the journal entries to Allowance for Doubtful Accounts and calculate the new balance after each entry.

(c) Calculate the net realizable value of the accounts receivable both before and after recording the cash receipt from Wight on June 6, 2017.

Calculate interest. (LO 3) AN

E8–8   Data on three promissory notes accepted by Levin Ltd. during 2017 follow.

Date of Note	Term in Months	Principal	Interest Rate	Total Interest	Interest Revenue to Record for Year Ended December 31
Oct. 1	3	$180,000	10%	(c)	(d)
Aug. 1	6	120,000	(b)	$4,800	(e)
Nov. 1	24	(a)	6%	12,000	(f)

Instructions

Determine the missing amounts.

Calculate interest. (LO 3) AN

E8–9   Data on four promissory notes accepted by Dryer Interiors during 2017 follow.

Note #	Principal	Annual Interest Rate	Time	Total Interest
1	(a)	9%	4 months	$ 450
2	$30,000	10%	6 months	(c)
3	$60,000	(b)	5 months	$1,500
4	$45,000	8%	4 months	(d)

Instructions

Determine the missing amounts.

Record notes receivable transactions. (LO 3) AP

E8–10   Passera Supply Co. has the following transactions:

Nov. 1	Loaned $60,000 cash to A. Morgan on a one-year, 8% note.
15	Sold goods to H. Giorgi on account for $12,000, terms n/30. The goods cost Passera $7,500. Passera uses the perpetual inventory system.
Dec. 1	Sold goods to Wrightman, Inc., receiving a $21,000, three-month, 6% note. The goods cost Passera $14,000.
15	H. Giorgi was unable to pay her account. Giorgi gave Passera a six-month, 7% note in settlement of her account.
31	Accrued interest revenue on all notes receivable. Interest is due at maturity.
Mar. 1	Collected the amount owing on the Wrightman note.
June 15	H. Giorgi defaulted on the note. Future payment is expected.

Instructions

Record the transactions for Passera Supply Co.

Record notes receivable transactions. (LO 3) AP

E8–11   The following are notes receivable transactions for Rather Co.:

May 1	Received a $15,000, six-month, 6% note from Jioux Company in settlement of an account receivable. Interest is due at maturity.

June 30   Accrued interest on the Jioux note, at Rather's year end. Adjustments are recorded annually.

July 31   Lent $2,000 cash to an employee, Noreen Irvine, receiving a two-month, 5% note. Interest is due at the end of each month.

Aug. 31   Received the interest due from Ms. Irvine.

Sept. 30   Received payment in full from Ms. Irvine.

Nov. 1   Jioux Company defaulted on its note. Rather does not expect to collect on the note.

Instructions

Record the transactions for Rather Co. (Round calculations to the nearest dollar.)

E8–12   Ni Co. has the following notes receivable outstanding at December 31, 2017:

Issue Date	Term	Principal	Interest Rate
1. August 31, 2017	5 months	$15,000	4%
2. February 1, 2017	12 months	32,000	4%
3. October 31, 2017	6 months	9,000	5%

Record notes receivable transactions and indicate statement presentation. (LO 3, 4) AP

Interest on each of the above notes is payable at maturity.

Instructions

(a) Calculate the interest revenue that Ni Co. will report on its income statement for the year ended December 31, 2017. Indicate where this will be presented on a multiple-step income statement. (Round calculations to the nearest dollar.)

(b) Calculate the amounts related to these notes that will be reported on Ni Co.'s balance sheet at December 31, 2017. Indicate where they will be presented. (Round calculations to the nearest dollar.)

E8–13   At December 31, 2017, Nicholay Industries reports the following selected accounts from the unadjusted trial balance for its first year of operations:

Record bad debts, prepare partial balance sheet, and calculate ratios. (LO 2, 4) AP

Account	Debit	Credit
Accounts receivable	$ 700,000	
Accounts payable		$ 350,000
Cash	40,000	
Cost of goods sold	1,750,000	
Interest receivable	1,125	
Interest revenue		2,250
Merchandise inventory	325,000	
Notes receivable, due April 10, 2018	45,000	
Prepaid insurance	8,000	
Short-term investments	50,000	
Sales		4,000,000
Sales returns and allowances	100,000	
Unearned revenue		25,000

Instructions

(a) Prepare the journal entry to record the bad debt expense on December 31, 2017, assuming the credit manager estimates that 4% of the accounts receivable will become uncollectible.

(b) Prepare the current assets section of the balance sheet for Nicholay Industries on December 31, 2017.

(c) Calculate the receivables turnover and collection period. (Remember that this is the end of the first year of business.)

E8–14   The following information (in millions) was taken from the December 31 financial statements of **Canadian National Railway Company**:

Calculate ratios and comment. (LO 4) AN

	2014	2013	2012
Accounts receivable, gross	$ 937	$ 822	$ 841
Allowance for doubtful accounts	9	7	10
Accounts receivable, net	928	815	831
Revenues	12,134	10,575	9,920
Total current assets	2,066	1,977	1,869
Total current liabilities	2,201	2,498	2,203

Instructions

(a) Calculate the 2014 and 2013 current ratios.

(b) Calculate the receivables turnover and average collection period for 2014 and 2013.

(c) Comment on any improvement or weakening in CN's liquidity and its management of accounts receivable.

▶ Problems: Set A

Record accounts receivable transactions. Post to subsidiary and general ledgers and prepare adjusting entry. (LO 1, 2) AP

P8–1A At December 31, 2017, the general ledger and subsidiary ledger for Albert's, a small auto parts store, showed the following:

General Ledger		Accounts Receivable Subsidiary Ledger	
Accounts receivable	$75,000	Best Auto Repair	$ 3,800
Allowance for doubtful accounts	3,750	Brown's Repair	23,000
		Custom Repair	0
		Jen's Auto Body	35,000
		Luxury Autos	13,200
		Total	$75,000

Jan.	3	Brown's Repair paid $18,000 on its account.
	4	Custom Repair paid $1,400 on its account that had previously been written off.
	8	Jen's Auto Body purchased $3,800 of merchandise on account.
	9	Antique Auto Repair paid cash for $1,500 of merchandise.
	18	Jen's Auto Body returned $800 of merchandise.
	19	Luxury Autos paid $13,200 on its account.
	20	Jen's Auto Body paid $25,000 on its account.
	23	Brown's Repair purchased $5,600 on account.
	25	Custom Repair purchased $10,000 of merchandise on Visa.
	26	Luxury Autos purchased $18,000 of merchandise on account.
	31	Albert's determined that the Best Auto Repair account receivable was not collectible.

Instructions

(a) Record the above transactions. Ignore credit card fees and any entries to the Inventory or Cost of Goods Sold accounts for purposes of this question.

(b) Set up T accounts for the Accounts Receivable general ledger (control) account, the Allowance for Doubtful Accounts general ledger account, and the Accounts Receivable subsidiary ledger accounts. Post the journal entries to these accounts.

(c) Albert's estimated that 10% of accounts receivable is not collectible. Record the required adjustment to the Allowance for Doubtful Accounts.

(d) Prepare a list of customers and the balances of their accounts from the subsidiary ledger. Prove that the total of the subsidiary ledger is equal to the control account balance.

TAKING IT FURTHER   Albert Erickson, the owner of Albert's, is considering changing his customer payment policy. He wants to discontinue offering credit to his customers and accept only bank credit and debit cards as well as cash. Provide Albert with a list of advantages and disadvantages for the proposed policy change.

Identify impact of accounts receivable and bad debt transactions; determine statement presentation. (LO 1, 2, 4) AP

P8–2A   Cotton Company uses the percentage of sales approach to record bad debt expense for its monthly financial statements and the percentage of receivables approach for its year-end financial statements. Cotton Company has an October 31 fiscal year end, closes temporary accounts annually, and uses a perpetual inventory system.

On August 31, 2017, after completing its month-end adjustments, it had accounts receivable of $74,500, a credit balance of $2,980 in Allowance for Doubtful Accounts, and bad debt expense of $9,860. In September and October, the following occurred:

September

1. Sold $56,300 of merchandise on account; the cost of the merchandise was $25,335.
2. A total of $900 of the merchandise sold on account was returned. These customers were issued credit memos. The cost of the merchandise was $400 and it was returned to inventory.
3. Collected $59,200 cash on account from customers.
4. Interest charges of $745 were charged to outstanding accounts receivable.
5. As part of the month-end adjusting entries, recorded bad debt expense of 2% of net credit sales for the month.

October

1. Credit sales in the month were $63,900; the cost of the merchandise was $28,700.
2. Received $350 cash from a customer whose account had been written off in July.
3. Collected $58,500 cash, in addition to the cash collected in transaction 2. above, from customers on account.
4. Wrote off $7,500 of accounts receivable as uncollectible.

5. Interest charges of $710 were charged to outstanding accounts receivable.
6. Recorded the year-end adjustment for bad debts. Uncollectible accounts were estimated to be 4% of accounts receivable. (Round answer to the nearest dollar.)

Instructions

(a) For each of these transactions, indicate if the transaction has increased (+) or decreased (−) Cash, Accounts Receivable, Allowance for Doubtful Accounts, Inventory, Total Assets, and Owner's Equity, and by how much. If the item is not changed, write NE to indicate there is no effect. Use the following format, in which the first one has been done for you as an example.

Transaction	Cash	Accounts Receivable	Allowance for Doubtful Accounts	Inventory	Total Assets	Owner's Equity
Sept. 1	NE	+$56,300	NE	−$25,335	+$30,965	+$30,965

(b) Show how accounts receivable will appear on the October 31, 2017, balance sheet.
(c) What amount will be reported as bad debt expense on the income statement for the year ended October 31, 2017?

TAKING IT FURTHER   Discuss the appropriateness of Cotton using the percentage of sales approach to estimating uncollectible accounts for its monthly financial statements and the percentage of receivables approach for its year-end financial statements. The monthly financial statements are used by Cotton's management and are not distributed to anyone outside of the company.

P8–3A   At the beginning of the current period, Huang Co. had a balance of $100,000 in Accounts Receivable and a $7,000 credit balance in Allowance for Doubtful Accounts. In the period, it had net credit sales of $400,000 and collections of $361,500. It wrote off accounts receivable of $10,500 as uncollectible. After a $1,750 account was written off as uncollectible, it was subsequently collected. This is in addition to the other cash collections. Based on an aging schedule, uncollectible accounts are estimated to be $8,000 at the end of the period.

Record accounts receivable and bad debt transactions; show financial statement presentation. (LO 1, 2, 4) AP

Instructions

(a) Record sales and collections in the period.
(b) Record the write off of uncollectible accounts in the period.
(c) Record the collection of the account previously written off as uncollectible.
(d) Record the bad debt expense adjusting entry for the period.
(e) Show the balance sheet presentation of the receivables at the end of the period.
(f) What is the amount of bad debt expense on the income statement for the period?

TAKING IT FURTHER   Why is bad debt expense not increased when an account receivable is written off because it is determined to be uncollectible?

P8–4A   Information on Hohenberger Company for 2017 follows:

Total credit sales	$1,000,000
Accounts receivable at December 31	400,000
Uncollectible accounts written off	17,500
Amount collected on accounts previously written off (after write off but before year end)	2,500

Calculate bad debt amounts and answer questions. (LO 2) AP

Instructions

(a) Assume that Hohenberger Company decides to estimate its uncollectible accounts using the allowance method and an aging schedule. Uncollectible accounts are estimated to be $24,000. What amount of bad debt expense will Hohenberger Company record if Allowance for Doubtful Accounts had an opening balance of $20,000 on January 1, 2017?
(b) Assume that Hohenberger Company decides to estimate its uncollectible accounts using the allowance method and estimates its bad debt expense at 2.25% of credit sales. What amount of bad debt expense will Hohenberger Company record if Allowance for Doubtful Accounts had an opening balance of $20,000 on January 1, 2017?
(c) Assume the same facts as in part (a) except that the Allowance for Doubtful Accounts had a $12,000 balance on January 1, 2017. What amount of bad debt expense will Hohenberger record on December 31, 2017?
(d) How does the amount of accounts written off during the period affect the amount of bad debt expense recorded at the end of the period when using the percentage of receivables approach?
(e) How does the collection of an account that had previously been written off affect the net realizable value of accounts receivable?

TAKING IT FURTHER   Hohenberger would like to speed up the collection of accounts receivable balances. What are two ways a company could do this? What are the advantages and disadvantages of each?

Prepare aging schedule and record bad debts and explain method. (LO 2) AP

P8-5A   Pearson Company uses the allowance method to estimate uncollectible accounts receivable. The company produced the following information from aging its accounts receivable at year end:

	Total	0–30	31–60	61–90	91–120
		Number of Days Outstanding			
Accounts receivable	$640,000	$360,000	$140,000	$100,000	$40,000
Estimated % uncollectible		2%	5%	10%	30%
Estimated uncollectible accounts					

The unadjusted balance in Allowance for Doubtful Accounts is a debit of $3,000.

Instructions

(a) Complete the aging schedule and calculate the total estimated uncollectible accounts.

(b) Record the bad debt adjusting entry using the information determined in part (a).

(c) In the following year, $18,000 of the outstanding accounts receivable is determined to be uncollectible. Record the write off of the uncollectible accounts.

(d) The company collects $4,500 of the $18,000 of accounts that was determined to be uncollectible in part (c). The company also expects to collect an additional $1,000. Record the journal entry (or entries) to restore the accounts receivable and the cash collected. Collection of the $1,000 is expected in the near future.

(e) Explain how using the allowance method matches expenses with revenues.

(f) Explain how using the allowance method values Accounts Receivable at net realizable value on the balance sheet.

TAKING IT FURTHER   What are the advantages and disadvantages to the company of using an aging schedule to estimate uncollectible accounts, as compared with estimating uncollectible accounts as 10% of total accounts receivable?

Prepare aging schedule and record bad debts. (LO 2) AP

P8-6A   An aging analysis of Hagiwara Company's accounts receivable at December 31, 2016 and 2017, showed the following:

Number of Days Outstanding	Estimated % Uncollectible	Accounts Receivable	
		2017	2016
0–30 days	3%	$115,000	$145,000
31–60 days	6%	35,000	63,000
61–90 days	12%	45,000	38,000
Over 90 days	25%	80,000	24,000
Total		$275,000	$270,000

Additional information:

1. At December 31, 2016, the unadjusted balance in Allowance for Doubtful Accounts was a credit of $6,600.

2. In 2017, $23,500 of accounts was written off as uncollectible and $2,200 of accounts previously written off was collected.

Instructions

(a) Prepare an aging schedule to calculate the estimated uncollectible accounts at December 31, 2016, and at December 31, 2017.

(b) Calculate the net realizable value of Hagiwara's accounts receivable at December 31, 2016, and December 31, 2017.

(c) Record the following:
   1. The adjusting entry on December 31, 2016
   2. The write off of uncollectible accounts in 2017
   3. The collection in 2017 of accounts previously written off
   4. The adjusting entry on December 31, 2017

TAKING IT FURTHER   What are the implications of the changes in the age of the receivables from 2016 to 2017?

P8–7A The following information was reported in Nenshi Company's general ledger at September 30:

Determine missing amounts.
(LO 2) AN

Accounts Receivable			
Beg.	bal.	845,000	(b)
		(a)	(c)
		4,200	(d)
End.	bal.	927,500	

Sales	
	5,370,000

Allowance for Doubtful Accounts			
		Beg. bal.	76,050
50,400			(b)
			(e)
		End. bal.	83,550

Bad Debt Expense	
(e)	

All sales were made on account. Bad debt expense is estimated to be 1% of sales.

Instructions

Determine the missing amounts in Nenshi Company's accounts. State what each of these amounts represents. You will not be able to determine the missing items in alphabetical order. (To solve this problem, it might help if you reconstruct the journal entries.)

TAKING IT FURTHER   Explain the differences between bad debt expense and the allowance for doubtful accounts.

P8–8A   Presented below is an aging schedule for Kimler Company on December 31, 2017. Kimler sells all of its goods on account with terms n/30.

Record bad debt expense and show balance sheet presentation. (LO 1, 2, 4) AP

Customer	Total	Not yet Due	Number of Days Past Due			
			1–30	31–60	61–90	Over 90
Akers	$ 20,000		$ 9,000	$11,000		
Barrett	30,000	$ 30,000				
Corner	50,000	15,000	5,000		$30,000	
DeJong	38,000					$38,000
Other	126,000	92,000	15,000	13,000		6,000
	$264,000	$137,000	$29,000	$24,000	$30,000	$44,000
Estimated percentage uncollectible		2%	5%	10%	24%	50%
Total estimated bad debts						

At December 31, 2017, the unadjusted balance in Allowance for Doubtful Accounts is a credit of $10,000.

Instructions

(a) Using the above aging schedule, determine the total estimated uncollectible accounts at December 31, 2017.
(b) Prepare the adjusting journal entry to record bad debt expense.
(c) Show how accounts receivable would be presented on the balance sheet on December 31, 2017.

TAKING IT FURTHER   If Kimler's credit manager increases the amount of credit checking the company does before granting credit on all of its customers, will that eliminate the bad debts? Explain.

P8–9A   Schneider Company has a May 31 fiscal year end and adjusts accounts annually. Selected transactions in the year included the following:

Record receivables transactions. (LO 1, 3) AP

Jan. 2   Sold $24,000 of merchandise to Sapounas Company, terms n/30. The cost of the goods sold was $14,400. Schneider uses the perpetual inventory system.

Feb. 1   Accepted a $24,000, five-month, 5% promissory note from Sapounas Company for the balance due. (See January 2 transaction.) Interest is payable at maturity.

 15   Sold $15,000 of merchandise costing $9,000 to Garrison Company and accepted Garrison's three-month, 5% note in payment. Interest is payable at maturity.

Mar. 15   Sold $12,000 of merchandise to Hoffman Co., terms n/30. The cost of the merchandise sold was $7,200.

April 15   Collected the amount owing from Hoffman Co. in full.

May 15   Collected the Garrison note in full. (See February 15 transaction.)

 31   Accrued interest at year end.

July 1   Sapounas Company dishonoured its note of February 1. The company is bankrupt and there is no hope of future settlement.

      13   Sold $6,000 merchandise costing $3,600 to Weber Enterprises and accepted Weber's $6,000, three-month, 7% note for the amount due, with interest payable at maturity.

Oct. 13   The Weber Enterprises note was dishonoured. (See July 13 transaction.) It is expected that Weber will eventually pay the amount owed.

Instructions

Record the above transactions. (Round calculations to the nearest dollar.)

TAKING IT FURTHER   What are the advantages and disadvantages of Schneider Company accepting notes receivable from its customers?

Record notes receivable transactions; show balance sheet presentation. (LO 3, 4) AP

P8–10A   Farwell Company adjusts its accounting records monthly in order to prepare monthly financial statements. On September 30, 2017, selected general ledger account balances are:

Notes receivable	$37,000
Interest receivable	228

Notes Receivable include the following:

Issue Date	Maker	Principal	Interest	Term
Aug. 1, 2017	K. Leroy Co.	$12,000	8.0%	3 months
Aug. 31, 2017	Fournier Co.	9,000	9.0%	2 months
Sept. 30, 2017	Nesbitt Co.	16,000	7.0%	18 months

Interest is payable on the first day of each month for notes with terms of one year or longer. Interest is payable at maturity for notes with terms of less than one year. In October, the following transactions were completed:

Oct. 31   Received notice that the Fournier Co. note had been dishonoured. (Assume that Fournier is expected to pay in the future.)

      31   Collected the amount owing from K. Leroy Co.

Instructions

(a) Record the transactions on October 31 and the October 31 adjusting entry to accrue interest revenue. (Round to the nearest dollar.)

(b) Create general ledger accounts for Notes Receivable and Interest Receivable and enter the opening balances on October 1. Post the entries from October 31 to Notes Receivable and Interest Receivable and update the balances.

(c) Show the balance sheet presentation of the interest and notes receivable accounts at October 31.

(d) How would the journal entry on October 31 be different if Fournier were not expected to pay in the future?

TAKING IT FURTHER   The interest rate for the Fournier note is higher than for the other notes. Why might that have been the case?

Prepare assets section of balance sheet; calculate and interpret ratios. (LO 4) AN

P8–11A   Jensen Company's general ledger included the following selected accounts (in thousands) at December 31, 2017:

Accounts payable	$1,077.3
Accounts receivable	590.4
Accumulated depreciation—equipment	858.7
Allowance for doubtful accounts	35.4
Bad debt expense	91.3
Cash	395.6
Cost of goods sold	660.4
Equipment	1,732.8
Interest revenue	19.7
Merchandise inventory	630.9
Notes receivable—due in 2018	96.0
Notes receivable—due in 2021	191.1
Prepaid expenses	20.1
Sales	4,565.5
Sales discounts	31.3
Short-term investments	194.9
Supplies	21.7
Unearned revenue	56.3

Additional information:

1. On December 31, 2016, Accounts Receivable was $611.1 thousand and the Allowance for Doubtful Accounts was $36.6 thousand.
2. The receivables turnover was 8.3 the previous year.

Instructions

(a) Prepare the assets section of the balance sheet.
(b) Calculate the receivables turnover and average collection period. Compare these results with the previous year's results and comment on any trends.

TAKING IT FURTHER   What other information should Jensen consider when analyzing its receivables turnover and average collection period?

P8–12A   Presented here is selected financial information (in millions) from the 2014 financial statements of **Rogers Communications Inc.** and **Shaw Communications Inc.**:

Calculate and interpret ratios. (LO 4) AN

	Rogers	Shaw
Sales	$12,850	$5,241
Allowance for doubtful accounts, beginning of year	104	27
Allowance for doubtful accounts, end of year	98	32
Accounts receivable balance (net), beginning of year	1,509	486
Accounts receivable balance (net), end of year	1,591	493

Instructions

(a) Calculate the receivables turnover and average collection period for both companies.
(b) Comment on the difference in their collection experiences.

TAKING IT FURTHER   If Rogers or Shaw sells its accounts receivable to speed up cash flows, what impact would you expect that to have on its ratios? Would a comparison between the two companies still be appropriate?

P8–13A   The following ratios are available for Satellite Mechanical:

Evaluate liquidity. (LO 4) AN

	2017	2016	2015
Current ratio	2.0 to 1	1.6 to 1	1.4 to 1
Acid-test ratio	1.1 to 1	0.8 to 1	0.7 to 1
Receivables turnover	7.3 times	10.1 times	10.3 times
Inventory turnover	6.3 times	6.1 times	6.4 times

Instructions

(a) Calculate the collection period, days sales in inventory, and operating cycle in days for each year.
(b) Has Satellite Mechanical's liquidity improved or weakened over the three-year period? Explain.
(c) Do changes in turnover ratios affect profitability? Explain.

TAKING IT FURTHER   At the beginning of 2017, the owner of Satellite Mechanical decided to eliminate sales discounts because she thought it was costing the company too much money. The terms of credit sales were changed from 2/10, n/30 to n/30. Evaluate this decision.

▶ Problems: Set B

P8–1B   At December 31, 2017, the general ledger and subsidiary ledger for Wow's, a small beauty supply company, showed the following:

Record accounts receivable transactions. Post to subsidiary and general ledgers and prepare adjusting entry. (LO 1, 2) AP

General Ledger	
Accounts receivable	$35,000
Allowance for doubtful accounts	3,500

Accounts Receivable Subsidiary Ledger	
Hair Designs	$ 8,000
Great Looks	11,000
Ken's Salon	9,000
Luxury Spa	7,000
New Do	0
Total	$35,000

Jan. 3   Hair Designs paid $8,000 on its account.

    4   New Do paid $900 on its account that had previously been written off.

    8   Great Looks purchased $3,000 of merchandise on account.

    9   Your Spa paid cash for $2,000 of merchandise.

   18   Great Looks returned $500 of merchandise.

   19   Luxury Spa paid $5,000 on its account.

   20   Great Looks paid $10,000 on is account.

   23   Hair Designs purchased $9,000 on account.

   24   Ken's Salon paid $3,000 on account.

   25   New Do purchased $5,000 of merchandise on Visa.

   26   Luxury Spa purchased $12,000 of merchandise on account.

   31   Wow determined that the Ken's Salon account receivable was not collectible.

Instructions

(a) Record the above transactions. Ignore credit card fees and inventory and cost of goods sold entries for purposes of this question.

(b) Set up T accounts for the Accounts Receivable general ledger (control) account, the Allowance for Doubtful Accounts general ledger account, and the Accounts Receivable subsidiary ledger accounts. Post the journal entries to these accounts.

(c) Wow estimated that 6% of accounts receivable is not collectible. Record the required adjustment to the Allowance for Doubtful Accounts.

(d) Prepare a list of customers and the balances of their accounts from the subsidiary ledger. Prove that the total of the subsidiary ledger is equal to the control account balance.

TAKING IT FURTHER What types of errors could result if the total of the account balances in the subsidiary ledger did not agree with the general ledger control account?

Identify impact of accounts receivable and bad debts transactions; determine statement presentation. (LO 1, 2, 4) AP

P8-2B Rayon Co. uses the percentage of sales approach to record bad debt expense for its monthly financial statements and the percentage of receivables approach for its year-end financial statements. Rayon Co. has a May 31 fiscal year end, closes temporary accounts annually, and uses the perpetual inventory system.

On March 31, 2017, after completing its month-end adjustments, it had accounts receivable of $89,200, a credit balance of $4,930 in Allowance for Doubtful Accounts, and a debit balance in Bad Debt Expense of $19,880. In April and May, the following transactions occurred:

April

1. Sold $64,600 of merchandise on credit. The cost of the merchandise was $35,530.
2. Accepted $800 of returns on the merchandise sold on credit. These customers were issued credit memos. The merchandise had a cost of $440 and was discarded because it was damaged.
3. Collected $69,200 cash on account from customers.
4. Interest charges of $1,645 were charged to outstanding accounts receivable.
5. As part of the month-end adjusting entries, recorded bad debt expense of 3% of net credit sales for the month.

May

1. Credit sales were $76,600. The cost of the merchandise was $42,130.
2. Received $450 cash from a customer whose account had been written off in March.
3. Collected $78,500 cash, in addition to the cash collected in transaction 2. above, from customers on account.
4. Wrote off $9,580 of accounts receivable as uncollectible.
5. Interest charges of $1,570 were charged to outstanding accounts receivable.
6. Recorded the year-end adjustment for bad debts. Uncollectible accounts were estimated to be 6% of accounts receivable.

Instructions

(a) For each of these transactions, indicate if the transaction has increased (+) or decreased (−) Cash, Accounts Receivable, Allowance for Doubtful Accounts, Inventory, Total Assets, and Owner's Equity, and by how much. If the item is not changed, write NE to indicate there is no effect. Use the following format, in which the first one has been done for you as an example.

Transaction	Cash	Accounts Receivable	Allowance for Doubtful Accounts	Inventory	Total Assets	Owner's Equity
April 1	NE	+$64,600	NE	−$35,530	+$29,070	+$29,070

(b) Show how accounts receivable will appear on the May 31, 2017, balance sheet.

(c) What amount will be reported as bad debt expense on the income statement for the year ended May 31, 2017?

TAKING IT FURTHER Discuss the possible reasons that Rayon Co. uses a mix of two approaches to estimate uncollectible accounts.

P8-3B At the beginning of the current period, Fassi Co. had a balance of $800,000 in Accounts Receivable and a $44,000 credit balance in Allowance for Doubtful Accounts. In the period, it had net credit sales of $1,900,000 and collections of $2,042,000. It wrote off accounts receivable of $58,000. After a $4,000 account was written off as uncollectible, it was subsequently collected. This is in addition to the other cash collections. Based on an aging schedule, uncollectible accounts are estimated to be $36,000 at the end of the period.

Record accounts receivable and bad debt transactions; show financial statement presentation. (LO 1, 2, 4) AP

Instructions

(a) Record sales and collections in the period.

(b) Record the write off of uncollectible accounts in the period.

(c) Record the collection of the account previously written off.

(d) Record the bad debt expense adjusting entry for the period.

(e) Show the balance sheet presentation of the accounts receivable at the end of the period.

(f) What is the bad debt expense on the income statement for the period?

TAKING IT FURTHER Why is bad debt expense not reduced when a previously written-off account is collected?

P8-4B Information for Jager Company in 2017 follows:

Calculate bad debt amounts and answer questions. (LO 2) AP

Total net credit sales	$3,300,000
Accounts receivable at December 31	1,250,000
Accounts receivable written off	48,000
Amount collected on accounts previously written off (after write off but before year end)	8,000

Instructions

(a) Assume that Jager Company decides to use the allowance method and estimates its uncollectible accounts to be $52,000 based on an aging schedule. What amount of bad debt expense will Jager record if Allowance for Doubtful Accounts had an opening credit balance of $30,000 on January 1, 2017?

(b) Assume the same facts as in part (a), except that the Allowance for Doubtful Accounts had a $42,250 credit balance on January 1, 2017. What amount of bad debt expense will Jager record on December 31, 2017?

(c) Assume instead that Jager Company decides to estimate its uncollectible accounts using 1.5% of net credit sales. What amount of bad debt expense will Jager record if Allowance for Doubtful Accounts had an opening creidt balance of $30,000 on January 1, 2017?

(d) How does the amount of accounts written off during the period affect the amount of bad debt expense recorded at the end of the period when using the percentage of receivables approach?

(e) How does the collection of an account that had previously been written off affect the net realizable value of accounts receivable?

TAKING IT FURTHER Why can a company not be certain what accounts are not collectible?

P8-5B Creative Co. uses the allowance method to estimate uncollectible accounts receivable. The computer produced the following aging of the accounts receivable at year end:

Prepare aging schedule and record bad debts and comment. (LO 2) AP

		Number of Days Outstanding			
	Total	0–30	31–60	61–90	91–120
Accounts receivable	$210,000	$120,000	$55,000	$20,000	$15,000
Estimated % uncollectible		1%	7%	12%	25%
Estimated uncollectible accounts					

The unadjusted balance in Allowance for Doubtful Accounts is a credit of $5,000.

Instructions

(a) Complete the aging schedule and calculate the total estimated uncollectible accounts from the above information.

(b) Record the bad debt adjusting entry using the above information.

(c) In the following year, $12,200 of the outstanding accounts receivable is determined to be uncollectible. Record the write off of the uncollectible accounts.

(d) The company collects $3,400 of the $12,200 of accounts receivable that were determined to be uncollectible in part (c). No further amounts are expected to be collected. Prepare the journal entry (or entries) to record the collection of this amount.

(e) Comment on how your answers to parts (a) to (d) would change if Creative Co. used a percentage of total accounts receivable of 8% instead of aging the accounts receivable.

TAKING IT FURTHER   What are the advantages for the company of aging the accounts receivable rather than applying a percentage to total accounts receivable?

Prepare aging schedule and record bad debts. (LO 2) AP

P8-6B   An aging analysis of Hake Company's accounts receivable at November 30, 2016 and 2017, showed the following:

Number of Days Outstanding	Estimated % Uncollectible	November 30 2017	November 30 2016
0–30 days	2.5%	$190,000	$220,000
31–60 days	6%	40,000	105,000
61–90 days	18%	65,000	40,000
Over 90 days	25%	75,000	25,000
Total		$370,000	$390,000

Additional information:

1. At November 30, 2016, the unadjusted balance in Allowance for Doubtful Accounts was a debit of $3,400.
2. In 2017, $22,300 of accounts was written off as uncollectible and $2,500 of accounts previously written off was collected.

Instructions

(a) Prepare an aging schedule to calculate the estimated uncollectible accounts at November 30, 2016, and November 30, 2017.

(b) Calculate the net realizable value of Hake's accounts receivable at November 30, 2016, and November 30, 2017.

(c) Record the following:
   1. The adjusting entry on November 30, 2016
   2. The write off of uncollectible accounts in 2017
   3. The collection in 2017 of accounts previously written off
   4. The adjusting entry on November 30, 2017

TAKING IT FURTHER   What are the implications of the changes in the age of accounts receivable from 2016 to 2017?

Determine missing amounts. (LO 2) AN

P8-7B   The following information was reported in Beckford Company's general ledger at August 31:

Accounts Receivable				Sales	
Beg. bal. 360,000		2,545,000			(a)
(a)		(d)			
(b)		5,520			
End. bal. (c)					

Allowance for Doubtful Accounts			Bad Debt Expense
	Beg. bal. (e)		(f)
28,540	(b)		
	(f)		
End. bal. 29,400			

All sales were made on account. At the beginning of the year, uncollectible accounts were estimated to be 6% of accounts receivable. At the end of the year, uncollectible accounts were estimated to be 7% of accounts receivable.

Instructions

Determine the missing amounts in Beckford Company's accounts. State what each of these amounts represents. You will not be able to determine the missing items in alphabetical order. (To solve this problem, it might help if you reconstruct the journal entries.)

TAKING IT FURTHER   Explain the difference between bad debt expense and the allowance for doubtful accounts.

P8-8B   Presented below is an aging schedule for Bravo Wholesale Food Company on December 31, 2017. Bravo sells all its goods on account with terms n/7.

Record bad debt expense and show financial statement presentation. (LO 1, 2, 4) AP

Customer	Total	Number of days outstanding				
		1-7	8-30	31-60	61-90	Over 90
Aaron	$ 18,000	$ 3,000	$10,000	$ 5,000		
Bosch	60,000		40,000	20,000		
Clever	26,000	16,000	5,000		$ 5,000	
DuPont	5,500					$ 5,500
Other	119,000	55,000	15,000		32,000	17,000
	$228,500	$74,000	$70,000	$25,000	$37,000	$22,500
Estimated percentage uncollectible		1%	4%	8%	18%	40%
Total estimated bad debts						

At December 31, 2017, the unadjusted balance in Allowance for Doubtful Accounts is a debit of $6,500.

Instructions

(a) Using the above aging schedule, determine to the total estimated uncollectible accounts at December 31, 2017.

(b) Prepare the adjusting journal entry to record bad debt expense.

(c) Show how accounts receivable would be presented on the balance sheet on December 31, 2017.

(d) What amount will be reported on the income statement for the year ended December 31, 2017, for bad debt expense?

TAKING IT FURTHER   To eliminate bad debt expense, should Bravo Wholesale Food Company require all of its customers to pay cash? Explain.

P8-9B   On January 2, 2017, Durand Co. had a $20,000, five-month, 6% note receivable from Vincent Company dated October 31, 2016. Interest receivable of $200 was accrued on the note on December 31, 2016. Interest on the note is due at maturity. Durand Co. has a December 31 fiscal year end and adjusts its accounts annually. In 2017, the following selected transactions occurred:

Record receivables transactions. (LO 1, 3) AP

Jan.   2   Sold $25,000 of merchandise costing $13,750 to Braun Company, terms 2/10, n/30. Durand Co. uses the perpetual inventory system.

Feb.   1   Accepted Braun Company's $25,000, three-month, 6% note for the balance due. (See January 2 transaction.) Interest is due at maturity.

Mar. 31   Received payment in full from Vincent Company for the amount due.

May   1   Collected Braun Company note in full. (See February 1 transaction.)

       25   Accepted Noah Inc.'s $12,000, two-month, 6% note in settlement of a past-due balance on account. Interest is payable monthly.

June 25   Received one month's interest from Noah Inc. on its note. (See May 25 transaction.)

July 25   The Noah Inc. note was dishonoured. (See May 25 transaction.) Future payment is not expected.

Nov. 30   Gave UOA Corp. a $10,000 cash loan and accepted UOA's four-month, 4.5% note. Interest is due at maturity.

Dec 31   Accrued interest is recorded on any outstanding notes at year end.

Instructions

Record the above transactions.

TAKING IT FURTHER   Noah Inc. has recovered some of its financial health and would like to do business with Durand Co. once again; that is, by purchasing goods on credit. What should Durand Co. do? What conditions might Durand Co. put in its future agreements with Noah?

P8-10B   Ouellette Co. adjusts its books monthly. On June 30, 2017, notes receivable include the following:

Record notes receivable transactions; show balance sheet presentation. (LO 3, 4) AP

Issue Date	Maker	Principal	Term	Interest
May 1, 2016	ALD Inc.	$ 6,000	3 years	4.0%
October 31, 2016	Kabam Ltd.	10,000	15 months	5.0%
January 31, 2017	Best Foot Forward Shoe Co.	15,000	6 months	5.5%
May 31, 2017	DNR Co.	4,800	2 months	8.75%
June 30, 2017	M&J Hardware Corp.	9,000	8 months	5.0%

Interest is payable on the first day of each month for notes with terms of one year or longer. Interest is payable at maturity for notes with terms of less than one year. In July, the following transactions were completed:

July 1   Received payment of the interest due from ALD Inc.
    2   Received the interest due from Kabam Ltd.
    31   Collected the full amount on the Best Foot Forward Shoe Co. note.
    31   Received notice that the DNR Co. note had been dishonoured. Assume that DNR Co. is expected to pay in the future.

Instructions

(a) Calculate the balance in the Interest Receivable and Notes Receivable accounts at June 30, 2017.
(b) Record the July transactions and the July 31 adjusting entry for accrued interest receivable.
(c) Enter the balances at July 1 in the receivables accounts. Post the entries to the receivables accounts.
(d) Show the balance sheet presentation of the receivables accounts at July 31, 2017.
(e) How would the journal entry on July 31 be different if DNR Co. were not expected to pay in the future?

TAKING IT FURTHER   The interest rate for the DNR note is higher than for the other notes. Why might that be the case?

Prepare assets section of balance sheet; calculate and interpret ratios. (LO 4) AN

P8–11B   Norlandia Saga Company's general ledger included the following selected accounts (in thousands) at November 30, 2017:

Accounts payable	$ 546.2
Accounts receivable	311.4
Accumulated depreciation—equipment	471.7
Allowance for doubtful accounts	14.8
Bad debt expense	43.6
Cash	417.1
Cost of goods sold	353.0
Equipment	924.2
Interest revenue	10.7
Merchandise inventory	336.5
Notes receivable—due in June 2018	51.2
Notes receivable—due in 2021	101.9
Prepaid expenses	19.3
Sales	2,823.8
Sales discounts	18.5
Short-term investments	224.6
Supplies	15.9
Unearned revenue	40.2

Additional information:

1. On November 30, 2016, Accounts Receivable was $271.7 thousand and the Allowance for Doubtful Accounts was $13.6 thousand.
2. The receivables turnover was 9.1 the previous year.

Instructions

(a) Prepare the assets section of the balance sheet.
(b) Calculate the receivables turnover and average collection period. Compare these results with the previous year's results and comment on any trends.

TAKING IT FURTHER   What other information should Norlandia Saga consider when analyzing its receivables turnover and average collection period?

Calculate and interpret ratios. (LO 4) AN

P8–12B   Presented here is selected financial information from the 2014 financial statements of **Nike** (in US$ millions) and **Adidas** (in euro millions):

	Nike	Adidas
Sales	$27,799	€14,534
Allowance for doubtful accounts, beginning	104	120
Allowance for doubtful accounts, ending	78	139
Accounts receivable balance (net), beginning	3,117	1,809
Accounts receivable balance (net), ending	3,434	1,946

Instructions

Calculate the receivables turnover and average collection period for both companies and compare the two companies. Comment on the difference in the two companies' collection experiences.

TAKING IT FURTHER　Adidas's financial statements are prepared using euros, while Nike uses U.S. dollars. How does this affect our ability to compare sales for the two companies? To compare the receivables turnover and collection period?

P8–13B　The following ratios are available for Western Roofing:　　　　　　　Evaluate liquidity. (LO 4) AN

	2017	2016	2015
Current ratio	1.6 to 1	2.0 to 1	1.9 to 1
Acid-test ratio	0.8 to 1	1.3 to 1	1.2 to 1
Receivables turnover	10.6 times	8.9 times	9.0 times
Inventory turnover	7.3 times	7.6 times	7.5 times

Instructions

(a) Calculate the collection period, days sales in inventory, and operating cycle for each year.
(b) Has Western Roofing's liquidity improved or weakened over the three-year period? Explain.
(c) Do changes in turnover ratios affect profitability? Explain.

TAKING IT FURTHER　At the beginning of 2017, the owner of Western Roofing decided to start offering customers a sales discount for early payment. The terms of credit sales were changed from n/30 to 2/10, n/30. Evaluate this decision.

CHAPTER 8: BROADENING YOUR PERSPECTIVE

▶ Financial Reporting and Analysis

Financial Reporting Problem

BYP8–1　The receivables turnover and collection period for **Corus Entertainment Inc.** were calculated in this chapter, based on the company's financial statements for the 2014 fiscal year. These financial statements are presented in Appendix A.

Instructions

(a) Calculate Corus's receivables turnover and collection period for the 2013 fiscal year.
(b) Comment on any significant differences you observe between the ratios for 2014 (as calculated in the chapter) and 2013 (as calculated by you above).
(c) Note 4 to the Corus Entertainment Inc. financial statements reports additional detail about accounts receivable. Identify the amount of gross accounts receivable on August 31, 2014. Identify the net realizable value of accounts receivable on August 31, 2014.
(d) Note 23 to the Corus Entertainment Inc. financial statements reports additional detail about the company's financial

instruments. (Accounts receivable is considered a financial instrument.) Identify the amount of accounts receivable that was over three months past due. Identify the amount of accounts receivable that was written off as uncollectible during the year.

Interpreting Financial Statements

BYP8–2　**Shaw Communications Inc.** is a diversified Canadian communications company whose core operating business is providing broadband cable television services, Internet, telecommunications services, satellite services, and programming content. Shaw reported the following information (in millions) in its financial statements for the fiscal years 2012 to 2014:

	2014	2013	2012
Operating revenues (assume all credit)	$5,241	$5,142	$4,998
Cash	637	422	427
Accounts receivable (gross)	525	513	461
Allowance for doubtful accounts	32	27	28
Inventories	119	96	102
Other current assets	73	72	89
Total current liabilities	1,396	2,205	1,595

Additional details about Shaw's receivables include the following:

Bad debt expense (or provision for doubtful accounts, as Shaw calls it) of $38 (2013, $26; 2012, $30) is included in operating, general, and administrative expenses. Shaw writes off uncollectible accounts receivable against the allowance account based on the age of the account and payment history.

Instructions

(a) Calculate the current ratios, acid-test ratios, receivables turnover ratios, and average collection periods for fiscal 2014 and 2013. Comment on Shaw's liquidity for each of the years.

(b) Based on the information provided, calculate the amount of accounts receivable that was written off in 2014.

(c) Shaw indicates in its notes to the financial statements that it reduces the risk of uncollectible accounts by billing in advance of providing service. How does billing in advance of providing service reduce the risk of uncollectible accounts?

▶ Critical Thinking

Collaborative Learning Activity

Note to instructor: Additional instructions and material for this group activity can be found on the Instructor Resource Site and in *WileyPLUS*.

BYP8-3 In this group activity, you will prepare the year-end adjustment for bad debt expense and finalize the financial statements, using company information given to you by your instructor. You will be required to use professional judgement to determine the amount of the adjustment and explain your rationale. Your instructor will assume the role of the company's external auditor and will judge you on the appropriateness of the amount and your rationale.

Communication Activity

BYP8-4 Toys for Big Boys sells snowmobiles, personal watercraft, ATVs, and the like. Recently, the credit manager of Toys for Big Boys retired. The sales staff threw him a big retirement party—they were glad to see him go because they felt his credit policies restricted their selling ability. The sales staff convinced management that there was no need to replace the credit manager since they could handle this responsibility in addition to their sales positions.

Management was thrilled at year end when sales doubled. However, accounts receivable quadrupled and cash flow halved. The company's average collection period increased from 30 days to 120 days.

Instructions

In a memo to management, explain the financial impact of allowing the sales staff to manage the credit function. Has the business assumed any additional credit risk? What would you recommend the company do to better manage its increasing accounts receivable?

"All About You" Activity

BYP8-5 In the "All About You" feature, you learned about interest rates charged on credit cards and some of the advantages and disadvantages of credit cards. To get the most from your credit card and

to save money, you need to understand the features of your credit card and how interest is charged on credit cards.

Instructions

Go to the Financial Consumer Agency of Canada at **www.fcac-acfc. gc.ca/Eng/forConsumers/Pages/home-accueil.aspx** and answer the following questions:

(a) Search for the document, "Be Smart with Your Credit Card: Tips to Help You Use Your Credit Card Wisely." What are the tips?

(b) Go to "Credit Cards: Understanding Your Rights and Your Responsibilities" and then go to "Understanding Your Credit Card Payment Terms." Credit cards provide interest-free loans on the purchase of goods, as long as you pay your bill in full by the end of the grace period. What is the required minimum grace period? Assume you used a credit card to purchase your textbooks on September 15, and the last date covered by your statement is October 7 and the grace period is 21 days. How many days is the interest-free period?

(c) There is no interest-free period on cash advances or balance transfers on credit cards. What is a cash advance? What is a balance transfer?

(d) Suppose you have one month left in the semester and you take a $1,000 cash advance on your credit card on April 1 to cover your living expenses until you get your first paycheque from your summer job on May 15. The interest rate on your credit card is 19%. Assuming that is the only charge on your credit card, calculate the interest you will be charged assuming you pay your bill in full on May 15. (*Hint:* Go to "How Interest Charges Are Calculated" on the website under "Credit Cards: Understanding Your Rights and Responsibilities: Credit Card Payment Terms.")

(e) Go to the Financial Consumer Agency of Canada's interactive tool "Credit Card Payment Calculator." (*Hint:* To find the Credit Card Payment Calculator, go to **www.fcac-acfc.gc.ca/Eng/ forConsumers/Pages/home-accueil.aspx** and in the search box, type in "credit card payment calculator.")

1. For option A, assume you have a credit card balance of $1,000, the interest rate is 19%, and the minimum monthly payment is $10 or 3%, whichever is greater.

2. For option B, assume the same information as in part 1, but you make an additional monthly payment of $10.

3. For option C, assume the same information as in part 1, but you make a monthly payment of $100.

For each of the options A, B, and C, calculate how long it will take to pay off the credit card, assuming there are no additional purchases made, and calculate the total amount of interest paid.

 Santé Smoothie Saga

(*Note:* This is a continuation of the Santé Smoothie Saga from Chapters 1 through 7.)

BYP8-6 Natalie has been approached by one of her friends, Curtis Lesperance. Curtis runs a coffee shop where he sells specialty coffees and prepares and sells muffins and cookies. He is very anxious to buy one of Natalie's juicers because he would then be able to prepare and sell smoothies as well. Curtis, however, cannot afford to pay for the juicer for at least 30 days. He has asked Natalie if she would be willing to sell him the juicer on credit.

Natalie comes to you for advice and asks the following questions.

1. "Curtis has given me a set of his most recent financial statements. What calculations should I do with the data from these statements? What questions should I ask him after I have analyzed the statements? How will this information help me decide if I should extend credit to Curtis?"

2. "If, instead of extending credit to Curtis for 30 days, I have Curtis sign a promissory note and he is unable to pay at the end of the agreement term, will having that signed promissory note really make any difference?"

The following transactions occur in November and December 2017:

Nov. 1   After much thought, Natalie sells a juicer to Curtis for

$1,050. (The cost of the juicer was $553.) Curtis signs a two-month, 7.5% promissory note. Curtis can repay the note at any time before the due date, with interest accruing to the date of payment.

30   Curtis calls Natalie. He expects to pay the amount outstanding in the next week or so.

Dec. 15   Natalie receives a cheque from Curtis in payment of his balance owing plus interest that has accrued.

Instructions

(a) Answer Natalie's questions.

(b) Prepare journal entries for the transactions that occurred in November and December.

ANSWERS TO CHAPTER QUESTIONS

ANSWERS TO ACCOUNTING IN ACTION INSIGHT QUESTIONS

All About You Insight, p. 424

Q: Should you use credit cards or not?

A: Credit cards can make your life easier, as long as they are used properly. They certainly have advantages: (1) they provide interest-free loans on the purchase of goods, as long as you pay your bill in full by the end of the grace period; (2) monthly credit card statements provide detailed records of all transactions, payments, and returned merchandise; and (3) many transactions, such as Internet purchases, are difficult or impossible to carry out without a credit card.

However, credit cards also have disadvantages: (1) if you do not pay your bill in full every month, expect to pay a very high interest rate on the unpaid balance; (2) they are so easy to use that you might start buying items without thinking about whether you really need them—and can afford them; and (3) credit cards can be stolen, which might damage your credit rating.

Ethics Insight, p. 434

Q: Should the controller be concerned with Proust Company's reported growth rate in estimating the allowance?

A: Proust Company's growth rate should be a product of fair and accurate financial statements. One should not prepare financial statements with the objective of achieving or sustaining a predetermined growth rate. The growth rate should be a product of management and operating results, not of "creative accounting."

Across the Organization Insight, p. 441

Q: What steps should the banks have taken to ensure the accuracy of financial information provided on loan applications?

A: The banks should have asked for supporting documentation about an applicant's income and assets. The supporting documentation should then have been verified as accurate by bank employees. The banks should not have made compensation of loan officers based on loan volume but rather on overall profitability of the organization, something the loan officers have less ability to directly influence. Compensation could also take the form of share options, giving the loan officers a vested interest in the well-being of the company.

ANSWERS TO SELF-STUDY QUESTIONS

1. a   2. b   3. b   4. d   5. c   6. d   7. c   8. c   9. a   10. d   11. b   12. c

9

LONG-LIVED ASSETS

CHAPTER PREVIEW ➤ Under International Financial Reporting Standards, companies have two models they can choose between to account for their long-lived assets: the cost model or the revaluation model. The cost model is the more commonly used method, and is the only model allowed under ASPE. We will cover the cost model in the following sections of the chapter and refer briefly to the revaluation model in a later section.

The **cost model** records long-lived assets at cost of acquisition. After acquisition, depreciation (when applicable) is recorded each period and the assets are carried at cost less accumulated depreciation.

For organizations such as Red River College, making the right decisions about long-lived assets is critical because these assets represent huge investments. Organizations must make decisions about what assets to acquire, how to account for them, and when to dispose of them.

In this chapter, we address these and other issues surrounding long-lived assets. Our discussions will focus on three types of long-lived assets: (1) property, plant, and equipment; (2) natural resources; and (3) intangible assets.

FEATURE STORY ➤ CAPITALIZING ON EDUCATION

WINNIPEG, Man.—Chances are that your college or university does not consist of one big building—it's likely a sprawling campus, perhaps with several locations around the city or region. That's certainly the case for Red River College—Manitoba's largest institute of applied learning, with more than 30,000 students—which has eight campuses in Winnipeg and several other communities in the province. Its largest campus, Notre Dame campus in Winnipeg, has 1.3 million square feet (120,000 square metres) of building space spread over 100 acres (40 hectares).

How does a post-secondary institution account for all these buildings, which are usually the largest asset on its books? The accounting treatment varies depending on the ownership. Until 1992, community colleges in Manitoba were part of a provincial government department. After that, they became not-for-profit entities operated by a board of governors, and the colleges started renting their buildings from the province, recording the rent as an operating expense. Gradually, the province has been transferring ownership of campus buildings to the colleges, which record the buildings as capital assets. Red River College expected the transfer of the remainder of its buildings to be completed in 2016, said Ted Maciurzynski, Director of Campus Planning. "We will have the keys to the campus," he said.

For the buildings it owned in 2014, Red River College recorded a net book value (carrying amount) in its financial statements of $97.3 million—by far the largest asset—while its assets under capital leases had a net book value of $2.7 million. The college depreciates the buildings it owns using the straight-line method: a constant rate of depreciating value of 2.5% per year for 40 years. Assets under capital leases are depreciated on a straight-line basis over their expected useful lives.

Red River College has another long-lived asset with an interesting accounting treatment. It recently acquired an unused school in Portage la Prairie, west of Winnipeg, from the local school district. "Essentially, we got the building for $1," said Mr. Maciurzynski. But the college doesn't record the building's value as $1, because it spent about $2.5 million renovating the school for use as college classrooms and offices, he said. The college depreciates the cost of the renovated building at a straight-line rate of 2.5% per year.

What about all the equipment, furniture, and computers inside these buildings? They're not considered long-lived assets, the way buildings are. Their depreciation rates vary depending on their estimated useful lives. Red River College depreciates the cost of equipment and furniture at a rate between 10% and 20% per year, while it depreciates computers and software—which can become obsolete very quickly—at up to 33% per year, according to its financial statements.

CHAPTER OUTLINE ▸ LEARNING OBJECTIVES

1 Calculate the cost of property, plant, and equipment.

Property, Plant, and Equipment
- Determining the cost of property, plant, and equipment

DO IT 1
Cost of plant assets

---

2 Apply depreciation methods to property, plant, and equipment.

- Depreciation

DO IT 2
Methods of depreciation

---

3 Explain the factors that cause changes in periodic depreciation and calculate revised depreciation for property, plant, and equipment.

- Revising periodic depreciation

DO IT 3
Revised depreciation

---

4 Demonstrate how to account for property, plant, and equipment disposals.

- Disposal of property, plant, and equipment

DO IT 4
Plant asset disposal

---

5 Record natural resource transactions and calculate depletion.

Natural Resources
- Cost
- Depletion
- Disposal

DO IT 5
Calculating depletion for natural assets

---

6 Identify the basic accounting issues for intangible assets and goodwill.

Intangible Assets and Goodwill
- Accounting for intangible assets
- Intangible assets with finite lives
- Intangible assets with indefinite lives
- Goodwill

DO IT 6
Accounting for intangible assets

---

7 Illustrate the reporting and analysis of long-lived assets.

Statement Presentation and Analysis
- Presentation
- Analysis

DO IT 7
Asset turnover and return on assets

Property, Plant, and Equipment

Property, plant, and equipment are long-lived assets that the company owns and uses for the production and sale of goods or services to consumers. They have three characteristics. They (1) have a physical substance (a definite size and shape); (2) are held for use in the production or supply of goods or services, for rental to others, or for administrative purposes; and (3) are not intended for sale to customers. Unlike current assets, these assets are expected to provide services to a company for a number of years.

LEARNING OBJECTIVE 1   Calculate the cost of property, plant, and equipment.

DETERMINING THE COST OF PROPERTY, PLANT, AND EQUIPMENT

The cost of an item of property, plant, and equipment includes the following:

1. The purchase price, plus any non-refundable taxes, less any discounts or rebates;
2. The expenditures necessary to bring the asset to the required location and make it ready for its intended use;
3. If there are obligations to dismantle, remove, or restore the asset when it is retired, an estimate of these costs is also included in the cost of the long-lived asset. We will assume that these costs, known as **asset retirement costs**, are equal to zero in the examples in this text. (Accounting for these costs will be covered in more advanced courses.)

All of the above-mentioned expenditures are **capitalized** (recorded as property, plant, and equipment), rather than expensed, if it is probable that the company will receive an economic benefit in the future from the asset. Determining which costs to include in a long-lived asset account and which costs not to include is very important. Costs that benefit only the current period are expensed. Such costs are called **operating expenditures**. Costs that benefit future periods are included in a long-lived asset account. These costs are called **capital expenditures**.

Consider the following example:

JJ & Company purchased equipment for its factory; the equipment is expected to be used for 10 years. The following costs were incurred:

Description of expenditure	Amount	Expenditure type
Purchase price	$100,000	Capital expenditure
Shipping	8,000	Capital expenditure
Insurance while the equipment was in transit	1,200	Capital expenditure
Installation in factory	3,500	Capital expenditure
Total	$112,700	

In the above example, JJ & Company would record each of the expenditures as an addition to the Equipment account. The total cost of the equipment is $112,700. All of these costs were necessary to get the equipment to its required location and ready for use.

Continuing with this example, assume that JJ & Company begins using the equipment on July 1. Over the next six months, the following expenditures are made related to the equipment:

Description of expenditure	Amount	Expenditure type
Oil and lubrication	$ 160	Operating expenditure
Repairs required because of normal wear and tear	1,600	Operating expenditure
Total	$1,760	

The above costs are incurred after the equipment is put into use and will only benefit the current period, so JJ & Company would record these costs as Repairs Expense.

However, it is also important to note that companies will expense, rather than capitalize, low-cost long-lived assets. For example, JJ & Company might purchase several stools for its employees while they are working in the factory. The stools cost $500 in total. JJ & Company has a policy that costs incurred below $1,000 for long-lived assets will be recognized as operating expenditures and included in an expense account rather than an asset account. This is an application of a concept known as materiality, which you will learn more about in Chapter 11. It allows companies to immediately record immaterial expenditures as an expense.

Subsequent to acquisition, the same distinction exists between capital and operating expenditures. For example, once the asset is in use, having an insurance policy benefits only the current period and is treated as an expense. But major expenditures that are incurred once the asset is in use that **increase the life of the asset or its productivity are capitalized**. We will discuss expenditures subsequent to acquisition in more depth later in the chapter.

Property, plant, and equipment are often subdivided into four classes:

1. **Land**, such as a building site
2. **Land improvements**, such as driveways, parking lots, fences, and underground sprinkler systems
3. **Buildings**, such as stores, offices, factories, and warehouses
4. **Equipment**, such as store checkout counters, cash registers, office furniture, computer equipment, factory equipment, and delivery equipment

Determining the cost of each of the major classes of property, plant, and equipment is explained in the following sections.

Land

The cost of land includes (1) the purchase price, (2) closing costs such as surveying and legal fees, and (3) the costs of preparing the land for its intended use, such as the removal of old buildings, clearing, draining, filling, and grading. All of these costs (less any proceeds from salvaged materials) are debited to the Land account.

To illustrate, assume that JJ & Company purchases property for $200,000 cash. An old warehouse stood on the property and was removed at a cost of $7,500. Parts of the old warehouse are salvaged and sold for $1,500 cash. Additional expenditures include legal fees of $3,000. The cost of the land is $209,000, calculated as follows:

Land	
Cash price of property	$200,000
Cost of removing warehouse	7,500
Proceeds from salvaged material	(1,500)
Legal fees	3,000
Cost of land	$209,000

When recording the acquisition, Land is debited for $209,000 and Cash is credited for $209,000 (assuming the costs were paid in cash). Land is a unique long-lived asset. Its cost is not depreciated because land has an unlimited useful life.

Land Improvements

Land improvements are structural additions made to land, such as driveways, sidewalks, fences, and parking lots. Land improvements, unlike land, decline in service potential over time, and require maintenance and replacement. Because of this, land improvements are recorded separately from land and are depreciated over their useful lives.

When classifying costs, **it is important to remember that one-time costs required for getting the land ready to use are always charged to the Land account, not the Land Improvements account.**

Buildings

All costs that are directly related to the purchase or construction of a building are debited to the Buildings account. When a building is purchased, these costs include the purchase price and closing costs (such as legal fees). The costs of making a building ready to be used as intended can include expenditures for remodelling, and for replacing or repairing the roof, floors, electrical wiring, and plumbing. These costs are also debited to Buildings. **As noted above, any costs incurred to remove or demolish existing buildings are debited to the Land account and should not be included in the Building account.**

When a new building is built, its cost includes the contract price plus payments for architects' fees, building permits, and excavation costs. The interest costs of financing the construction project are also included in the asset's cost but only the interest costs incurred during the construction phase. In these circumstances, interest costs are considered to be as necessary as materials and labour are. When the building is ready for use, interest costs are once again included in Interest Expense.

Equipment

The "equipment" classification is a broad one that can include delivery equipment, office equipment, computers, machinery, vehicles, furniture and fixtures, and other similar assets. The cost of these assets includes the purchase price; freight charges and insurance during transit paid by the purchaser; and the costs of assembling, installing, and testing the equipment. These costs are treated as capital expenditures because they benefit future periods and are necessary to bring the asset to its required location and make it ready for use.

Annual costs such as motor vehicle licences and insurance on company trucks and cars are treated as operating expenditures because they are recurring expenditures that do not benefit future periods.

To illustrate, assume that JJ & Company purchases a used delivery truck on January 2, 2017, for $24,500 cash. Related expenditures include painting and lettering, $500; a motor vehicle licence, $80; and a one-year insurance policy, $2,600. The cost of the delivery truck is $25,000, calculated as follows:

Delivery Truck	
Cash price	$24,500
Painting and lettering	500
Cost of delivery truck	$25,000

The cost of the motor vehicle licence is recorded as an expense and the cost of the insurance policy is recorded as a prepaid asset. The entry to record the purchase of the truck and related expenditures, assuming they were all paid for in cash, is as follows:

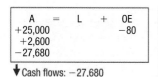

A = L + OE
+25,000   −80
+2,600
−27,680

↓ Cash flows: −27,680

Jan. 2	Vehicles	25,000	
	Licence Expense	80	
	Prepaid Insurance	2,600	
	Cash		27,680
	To record purchase of delivery truck and related expenditures.		

Allocating Cost to Multiple Assets or Significant Components

Alternative terminology A basket purchase is also known as a *lump sum purchase.*

Multiple Assets. Property, plant, and equipment are often purchased together for a single price. This is known as a **basket purchase.** Each asset will have a different useful life (number of years the asset is expected to provide benefit). We need to know the cost of each individual asset in order to journalize the purchase, and later calculate the depreciation of each asset. When a basket purchase occurs, we determine individual asset costs by allocating the total price paid for the group of assets to each individual asset based on its relative fair value.

To illustrate, assume Paradise Manufacturing Company purchased land, a building, and some equipment on July 31 for $400,000 cash. The land was appraised at $135,000, the building at $270,000, and the equipment at $45,000. The $400,000 cost should be allocated based on fair values (i.e., appraised values), as shown in Illustration 9-1.

Asset	Appraised Value (Fair Value)	Percent of Total Fair Value			Total Purchase Price		Cost of Each Asset
Land	$135,000	30%	($135,000 ÷ $450,000)	×	$400,000	=	$120,000
Building	270,000	60%	($270,000 ÷ $450,000)	×	$400,000	=	240,000
Equipment	45,000	10%	($ 45,000 ÷ $450,000)	×	$400,000	=	40,000
Totals	$450,000	100%					$400,000

▶ ILLUSTRATION 9-1
Allocating cost in a basket purchase

The journal entry to record this purchase is as follows:

July 31	Land	120,000	
	Building	240,000	
	Equipment	40,000	
	Cash		400,000
	To record purchase of land, building, and equipment.		

A	=	L	+	OE
+120,000				
+240,000				
+40,000				
−400,000				

▼ Cash flows: −400,000

Significant Components. When an item of property, plant, and equipment includes individual components that have different useful lives, the cost of the item should be allocated to each of its significant components. This allows each component to be depreciated separately over the different useful lives or possibly by using different depreciation methods. For example, an aircraft and its engine may need to be treated as separate depreciable assets if they have different useful lives.

Further discussion of calculating depreciation for the different component parts of an asset will be covered in advanced accounting courses. For simplicity, we will assume in this text that all of the components of a depreciable asset have the same useful life, and we will depreciate assets as a whole.

BEFORE YOU GO ON...DO IT **1** **Cost of Plant Assets**

Assume that factory equipment is purchased on November 6 for $10,000 cash and a $40,000 note payable. Related cash expenditures include insurance during shipping, $500; the annual insurance policy, $750; and installation and testing, $1,000. (a) What is the cost of the equipment? (b) Record these expenditures.

Solution

Factory Equipment

Purchase price	$50,000
Insurance during shipping	500
Installation and testing	1,000
Cost of equipment	$51,500

The entry to record the purchase and related expenditures is:

Nov. 6	Equipment	51,500	
	Prepaid Insurance	750	
	Cash ($10,000 + $500 + $750 + $1,000)		12,250
	Note Payable		40,000
	To record purchase of factory equipment and related expenditures.		

Related exercise material: BE9–1, BE9–2, BE9–3, BE9–4, E9–1, E9–2, E9–3, and E9–12.

Action Plan
- Capitalize expenditures that are made to get the equipment ready for its intended use.
- Expense operating expenditures that benefit only the current period, or are recurring costs.

Apply depreciation methods to property, plant, and equipment.

DEPRECIATION

As we learned in Chapter 3, depreciation is the systematic allocation of the cost of a long-lived asset, such as property, plant, and equipment, over the asset's useful life. The cost is allocated to expense over the asset's useful life to recognize the cost that has been used up (the expense) during the period, and report the unused cost (the asset) at the end of the period.

You will recall that depreciation is recorded through an adjusting journal entry that debits Depreciation Expense and credits Accumulated Depreciation. Depreciation Expense is an operating expense on the income statement. Accumulated Depreciation appears on the balance sheet as a contra account to the related long-lived asset account. The resulting balance, cost less accumulated depreciation, is the carrying amount of the depreciable asset, as defined in Chapter 4.

It is important to understand that **depreciation is a process of cost allocation, not a process of determining an asset's real value**. Illustration 9-2 shows this. Under the cost model, an increase in an asset's fair value is not relevant because property, plant, and equipment are not for resale. As a result, the carrying amount of property, plant, or equipment (cost less accumulated depreciation) may be very different from its fair value.

Alternative terminology An asset's *carrying amount* is also called its *carrying value, book value,* or *net book value.*

▶**ILLUSTRATION** **9-2**
Depreciation as an allocation concept

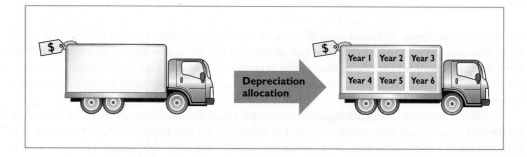

It is also important to understand that **depreciation neither uses up nor provides cash to replace the asset**. The balance in Accumulated Depreciation only represents the total amount of the asset's cost that has been allocated to expense so far. It is not a cash fund. Cash is neither increased nor decreased by the adjusting entry to record depreciation.

During a depreciable asset's useful life, its revenue-producing ability declines because of physical factors such as wear and tear, and economic factors such as obsolescence. For example, a company may replace a truck because it is physically worn out. On the other hand, companies replace computers long before they are physically worn out because improvements in hardware and software have made the old computers obsolete.

Factors in Calculating Depreciation

In Chapter 3, we learned that depreciation expense was calculated by dividing the cost of a depreciable asset by its useful life. At that time, we assumed the asset's residual value was zero. In this chapter, we will now include a residual value when calculating depreciation. Consequently, there are now three factors that affect the calculation of depreciation: (1) cost, (2) useful life, and (3) residual value.

Cost. The factors that affect the cost of a depreciable asset were explained earlier in this chapter. Remember that the cost of property, plant, and equipment includes the purchase price plus all costs necessary to get the asset ready for use. Cost includes an initial estimate of the retirement costs, if there are any.

Useful Life. **Useful life** is either (1) the period of time over which an asset is expected to be available for use or (2) the number of units of production (such as machine hours) or units of output that are expected to be obtained from an asset. Useful life is an estimate based on such factors as the asset's intended use, its expected need for repair and maintenance, and how vulnerable it is to wearing out or becoming obsolete. The company's past experience with similar assets often helps in estimating the expected useful life. Red River College, in the feature story, uses a five- to 10-year useful life for most of its equipment, but only three years for computers because computer equipment can quickly become technologically obsolete.

Residual Value. Residual value is the estimated amount that a company would obtain from disposing of the asset at the end of its useful life. Residual value is not depreciated, because the amount is expected to be recovered at the end of the asset's useful life.

Alternative terminology Residual value is sometimes called salvage value.

Illustration 9-3 summarizes these three factors in calculating depreciation.

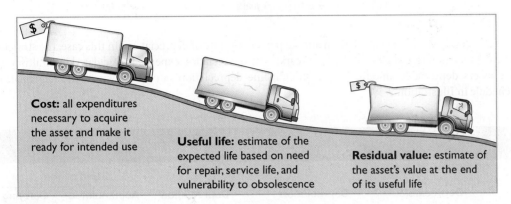

▶ ILLUSTRATION **9-3**
Three factors in calculating depreciation

Cost: all expenditures necessary to acquire the asset and make it ready for intended use

Useful life: estimate of the expected life based on need for repair, service life, and vulnerability to obsolescence

Residual value: estimate of the asset's value at the end of its useful life

The difference between an asset's cost and its residual value is called the **depreciable amount**, which is the total amount to be depreciated over the useful life. As we learned in Chapter 3, companies reporting under ASPE may use the term "amortization" instead of "depreciation." Because of this, the depreciable amount is often called the "amortizable cost."

Depreciation Methods

Depreciation is generally calculated using one of the following methods:

1. Straight-line
2. Diminishing-balance
3. Units-of-production

The straight-line method of depreciation is used by the majority of publicly traded companies. But how do companies decide which of the three depreciation methods to use? Management must choose the method that best matches the estimated pattern in which the asset's future economic benefits are expected to be consumed. The depreciation method must be reviewed at least once a year. If the expected pattern of consumption of the future economic benefits has changed, the depreciation method must be changed, and the change disclosed in the notes to the financial statements.

To learn how to calculate the three depreciation methods and to compare them, we will use the following data for the small delivery truck bought by JJ & Company on January 2, 2017:

Cost (as shown earlier in the chapter)	$25,000
Estimated residual value	$2,000
Estimated useful life (in years)	5
Estimated useful life (in kilometres)	200,000

Straight-Line. The straight-line method was first defined in Chapter 3. We will define it again here, this time including the impact of a residual value on the calculation. The **straight-line method** of calculating depreciation has two steps. First, residual value is deducted from the asset's cost to determine an asset's depreciable amount. Second, the depreciable amount is divided by the asset's useful life to calculate the annual depreciation expense.

The depreciation expense will be the same for each year of the asset's useful life if the cost, the useful life, and the residual value do not change. The calculation of depreciation expense in the first year for JJ & Company's delivery truck is shown in Illustration 9-4.

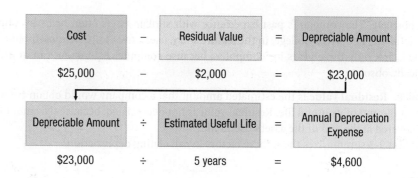

Alternatively, we can calculate an annual percentage rate of depreciation. In this case, the straight-line depreciation rate is 20% (100% ÷ 5 years). The depreciation expense is calculated by multiplying the asset's depreciable amount by the straight-line depreciation rate as shown in the depreciation schedule in Illustration 9-5.

▶ **ILLUSTRATION** **9-5**
Straight-line depreciation schedule

Carrying amount = Cost − Accumulated depreciation

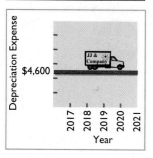

		JJ & COMPANY				
		Straight-Line Depreciation Schedule				
					End of Year	
Year	**Depreciable Amount**	**×** **Depreciation Rate**	**=**	**Depreciation Expense**	**Accumulated Depreciation**	**Carrying Amount**
						$25,000
2017	$23,000	20%		$ 4,600	$ 4,600	20,400
2018	23,000	20%		4,600	9,200	15,800
2019	23,000	20%		4,600	13,800	11,200
2020	23,000	20%		4,600	18,400	6,600
2021	23,000	20%		4,600	23,000	2,000
				$23,000		

Note that the depreciation expense of $4,600 is the same each year. Also note that the column total for depreciation expense is equal to the asset's depreciable amount, and that the carrying amount at the end of the useful life is equal to the estimated $2,000 residual value. The journal entry to record depreciation expense in 2017 is:

A = L + OE
−4,600   −4,600

Cash flows: no effect

2017			
Dec. 31	Depreciation Expense	4,600	
	Accumulated Depreciation—Vehicles		4,600
	To record depreciation expense for delivery truck.		

Straight-line is the most appropriate method of depreciation when the asset is used quite uniformly throughout its useful life. Examples of assets that deliver their benefit primarily as a function of time include office furniture and fixtures, buildings, warehouses, and garages for motor vehicles. Red River College, in the feature story, uses straight-line depreciation for its buildings.

Diminishing-Balance. The **diminishing-balance method** produces a decreasing annual depreciation expense over the asset's useful life. This method is so named because the periodic depreciation is based on a diminishing carrying amount (cost less accumulated depreciation) of the asset. Annual depreciation expense is calculated by multiplying the carrying amount at the beginning of the year by the depreciation rate. **The depreciation rate remains constant from year to year, but the rate is applied to a carrying amount that declines each year.**

The carrying amount for the first year is the asset's cost, because the balance in Accumulated Depreciation at the beginning of the asset's useful life is zero. In the following years, the carrying

Alternative terminology The diminishing-balance method is sometimes called the *declining-balance method*.

amount is the difference between the cost and the accumulated depreciation at the beginning of the year. Unlike the other depreciation methods, the diminishing-balance method does not use a depreciable amount in calculating annual depreciation expense. **Residual value is not included in the calculation of either the depreciation rate or the depreciation expense.** Residual value does, however, limit the total depreciation that can be recorded. Depreciation expense entries stop when the asset's carrying amount equals its estimated residual value.

A common diminishing-balance method is double the straight-line rate and is referred to as the **double diminishing-balance method**. Other variations include one time (single) and even three times (triple). In this textbook, we will use the double diminishing-balance method.

If JJ & Company uses the double diminishing-balance method, the depreciation rate is 40%, as shown in Illustration 9-6.

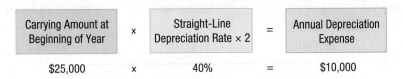

200%	÷	Useful life in years	= Depreciation rate
200%	÷	5	= 40%

▸ **ILLUSTRATION** 9-6
Formula for depreciation rate—double-diminishing-balance method

The rate can also be determined by multiplying the straight-line rate by 2. Illustration 9-7 shows the calculation of depreciation on the delivery truck for the first year.

Carrying Amount at Beginning of Year	x	Straight-Line Depreciation Rate × 2	=	Annual Depreciation Expense
$25,000	x	40%	=	$10,000

▸ **ILLUSTRATION** 9-7
Formula for double diminishing-balance method

The depreciation schedule under this method is given in Illustration 9-8.

▸ **ILLUSTRATION** 9-8
Double diminishing-balance depreciation schedule

JJ & COMPANY
Double Diminishing-Balance Depreciation Schedule

					End of Year	
Year	Carrying Amount Beginning Year	× Depreciation Rate	=	Depreciation Expense	Accumulated Depreciation	Carrying Amount
						$25,000
2017	$25,000	40%		$10,000	$10,000	15,000
2018	15,000	40%		6,000	16,000	9,000
2019	9,000	40%		3,600	19,600	5,400
2020	5,400	40%		2,160	21,760	3,240
2021	3,240	40%		1,240*	23,000	2,000
				$23,000		

*The calculation of $1,296 ($3,240 × 40%) is adjusted to $1,240 so that the carrying amount will equal the residual value.

Carrying amount = Cost − Accumulated depreciation to date

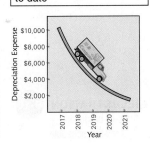

Returning to Illustration 9-8, you can see that the delivery truck is 70% depreciated ($16,000 ÷ $23,000) at the end of the second year. Under the straight-line method, it would be 40% depreciated ($9,200 ÷ $23,000) at that same time. Because the diminishing-balance method produces higher depreciation expense in the early years than in the later years, it is considered an *accelerated* depreciation method. In later years, its depreciation expense will be less than the straight-line depreciation expense. Regardless of the method that is used, the total amount of depreciation over the life of the delivery truck is $23,000—the depreciable amount. The journal entry to record depreciation Expense in 2017 is:

2017 Dec. 31	Depreciation Expense	10,000	
	Accumulated Depreciation—Vehicles		10,000
	To record depreciation expense for delivery truck.		

A	=	L	+	OE
−10,000				−10,000

Cash flows: no effect

Helpful hint The straight-line rate is determined by dividing 100% by the estimated useful life. In JJ & Company's case, it is 100% ÷ 5 = 20%.

The diminishing-balance method, or another accelerated method, should be used if the company receives more economic benefit in the early years of the asset's useful life than in the later years. Examples of assets that deliver more economic benefit in the early years of the asset's useful life are motor vehicles and computer systems.

Units-of-Production. Useful life can be expressed in ways other than time. In the **units-of-production method**, useful life is either the estimated total units of production or total expected use of the asset, not the number of years that the asset is expected to be used. The units-of-production method is ideal for equipment whose activity can be measured in units of output, such as kilometres driven or hours in use. The units-of-production method is generally not suitable for buildings or furniture, because depreciation of these assets is more a result of time than of use.

Alternative terminology The units-of-production method is often called the *units-of-activity method*.

In this method, the total units of production for the entire useful life are estimated. This amount is divided into the depreciable amount (cost – residual value) to determine the depreciable amount per unit. The depreciable amount per unit is then multiplied by the actual units of production during the year to calculate the annual depreciation expense.

To illustrate, assume that JJ & Company's delivery truck has a total estimated life of 200,000 km and that in the first year of the truck's use it is driven 30,000 km. Illustration 9-9 shows the steps involved to calculate depreciation expense in the first year.

▶ **ILLUSTRATION 9-9**
Formula for units-of-production method

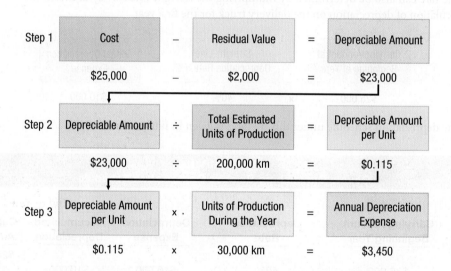

Illustration 9-10 shows the units-of-production depreciation schedule, using assumed units of production (kilometres driven) for the later years.

▶ **ILLUSTRATION 9-10**
Units-of-production depreciation schedule

Carrying amount = Cost − Accumulated depreciation to date

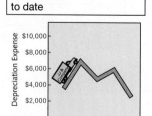

JJ & COMPANY
Units-of-Production Depreciation Schedule

Year	Units of Production	×	Depreciation Cost/Unit	=	Depreciation Expense	Accumulated Depreciation (End of Year)	Carrying Amount (End of Year)
							$25,000
2017	30,000		$0.115		$ 3,450	$ 3,450	21,550
2018	60,000		$0.115		6,900	10,350	14,650
2019	40,000		$0.115		4,600	14,950	10,050
2020	50,000		$0.115		5,750	20,700	4,300
2021	20,000		$0.115		2,300	23,000	2,000
	200,000				$23,000		

In the example in Illustration 9-10, the total actual units of production equals the original estimated total units of production of 200,000 km. But in most real-life situations, the total actual units of production do not exactly equal the total estimated units of production. This means that the final year's depreciation will have to be adjusted—as we saw in the double diminishing-balance method in Illustration 9-8—so that the ending carrying amount is equal to the estimated residual value. The journal entry to record depreciation expense in 2017 is:

2017			
Dec. 31	Depreciation Expense	3,450	
	Accumulated Depreciation—Vehicles		3,450
	To record depreciation expense for delivery truck.		

A	=	L	+	OE
−3,450				−3,450

Cash flows: no effect

The units-of-production method is used for assets whose activity can be measured in units of output. But it can only be used if it is possible to make a reasonable estimate of total activity. Later in this chapter, we will see that this method is widely used to depreciate natural resources. The units-of-production method results in the best matching of expenses with revenues when the asset's productivity varies significantly from one period to another.

Comparison of Depreciation Methods

Illustration 9-11 represents a comparison of annual and total depreciation expense for JJ & Company under each of the three depreciation methods. In addition, if we assume for simplicity that profit before deducting depreciation expense is $50,000 for each of the five years, we can clearly see the impact that the choice of method has on profit.

▶ ILLUSTRATION 9-11
Comparison of depreciation methods

	Straight-Line		Double Diminishing-Balance		Units-of-Production	
Year	Depreciation Expense	Profit	Depreciation Expense	Profit	Depreciation Expense	Profit
2017	$ 4,600	$ 45,400	$10,000	$ 40,000	$ 3,450	$ 46,550
2018	4,600	45,400	6,000	44,000	6,900	43,100
2019	4,600	45,400	3,600	46,400	4,600	45,400
2020	4,600	45,400	2,160	47,840	5,750	44,250
2021	4,600	45,400	1,240	48,760	2,300	47,700
	$23,000	$227,000	$23,000	$227,000	$23,000	$227,000

Recall that straight-line depreciation results in the same amount of depreciation expense and therefore profit each year. Diminishing-balance depreciation results in a higher depreciation expense in early years, and therefore lower profit, and a lower depreciation expense and higher profit in later years. Results with the units-of-production method vary, depending on how much the asset is used each year. While the depreciation expense and profit will be different each year for each method, *total* depreciation expense and *total* profit after the five-year period are the same for all three methods.

The balance sheet is also affected by the choice of depreciation method because accumulated depreciation is increased by depreciation expense and owner's equity is increased by profit. There is no impact on cash flow because depreciation does not involve cash.

Partial Period Depreciation

All of the examples so far portray a situation where a property, plant, and equipment asset is purchased on the first day of a fiscal period. Depreciation expense is then calculated for an entire year. But what happens when an asset is purchased part way through the fiscal period? In that case, depending on the depreciation method used, it is necessary to **pro-rate the annual depreciation for the part of the year that the asset was used**. Note that depreciation is normally rounded to the nearest month. Since depreciation is an estimate, calculating it to the nearest day gives a false sense of accuracy.

To keep things simple, some companies establish a policy for partial-period depreciation rather than calculating depreciation monthly. Some other common policies that companies use are:

- Full first year policy: This method records a full year of depreciation expense in the year of acquisition regardless of what point in the year the asset was purchased and put into use and none in the final year of the asset's life.
- Half-year policy: This method records a half year of depreciation expense in the year of acquisition and a half year of depreciation expense in the final year of the asset's life.

Whatever policy is chosen for partial-year depreciation, the impact is not significant in the long run if the policy is used consistently.

To illustrate the techniques used for partial period depreciation, we return to JJ & Company and the purchase of the small delivery truck. The relevant factors for depreciation calculations are reproduced below. This time, let's assume that the truck was purchased on April 1, 2017, and JJ & Company uses the nearest month policy for partial period depreciation calculations.

Cost	$25,000
Estimated residual value	$2,000
Estimated useful life (in years)	5
Estimated useful life (in kilometres)	200,000

Straight-Line Depreciation for a Partial Year. If the delivery truck was ready to be used on April 1, 2017, the truck would be depreciated for nine months in 2017 (April through December). The depreciation for 2017 would be $3,450 ($23,000 × 20% × 9/12).

The new depreciation schedule is shown in Illustration 9-12.

▶**ILLUSTRATION 9-12**
Straight-line
depreciation schedule—
partial year

JJ & COMPANY
Straight-Line Depreciation Schedule

Year	Depreciable Amount	×	Depreciation Rate	×	Fraction of a year	=	Depreciation Expense	End of Year Accumulated Depreciation	Carrying Amount
2017	$23,000		20.00%		9/12		$ 3,450	$ 3,450	$21,550
2018	23,000		20.00%		-		4,600	8,050	16,950
2019	23,000		20.00%		-		4,600	12,650	12,350
2020	23,000		20.00%		-		4,600	17,250	7,750
2021	23,000		20.00%				4,600	21,850	3,150
2022	23,000		20.00%		3/12		1,150	23,000	2,000
							23,000		

Note that when a partial year is used in the year of acquisition of the asset, a partial year is also used in the final year of the asset's life. This ensures that five full years of depreciation are recorded and the carrying amount is equal to the residual value at the end of the asset's life. The journal entry to record depreciation expense in 2017 would include a debit to Depreciation Expense for $3,450 and a credit to Accumulated Depreciation—Vehicles for $3,450.

Diminishing-Balance Depreciation for a Partial Year. Similar to straight-line, when using diminishing-balance it is also necessary to pro-rate depreciation expense in the year of acquisition.

If JJ & Company uses double diminishing-balance depreciation, depreciation expense in 2017 would be $7,500 ($25,000 × 40% × 9/12) if depreciation is calculated monthly. The carrying amount for calculating depreciation in 2018 would then become $17,500 ($25,000 – $7,500) and so on as shown in Illustration 9-13.

	Carrying Amount Beginning Year	×	Depreciation Rate	×	Fraction of a Year	=	Depreciation Expense	End of Year	
Year								Accumulated Depreciation	Carrying Amount
2017	$25,000		40%		$^9/_{12}$		$ 7,500	$ 7,500	$17,500
2018	17,500		40%				7,000	14,500	10,500
2019	10,500		40%				4,200	18,700	6,300
2020	6,300		40%				2,520	21,220	3,780
2021	3,780		40%				1,512	22,732	2,268
2022	2,268		40%		$^3/_{12}$		268*	23,000	2,000
							$23,000		

*The calculation of $907 ($2,268 × 40%) is adjusted to $268 so that the carrying amount will equal the residual value.

The journal entry to record depreciation expense in 2017 would include a debit to Depreciation Expense for $7,500 and a credit to Accumulated Depreciation—Vehicles for $7,500.

Units-of-Production Depreciation in a Partial Year. This method is easy to apply when assets are purchased during the year. The actual units of production already show how much the asset was used during the year. Therefore, the depreciation calculations do not need to be adjusted for partial periods as is done in the straight-line and diminishing-balance methods.

ACCOUNTING IN ACTION
BUSINESS INSIGHT

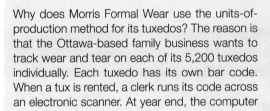

Why does Morris Formal Wear use the units-of-production method for its tuxedos? The reason is that the Ottawa-based family business wants to track wear and tear on each of its 5,200 tuxedos individually. Each tuxedo has its own bar code. When a tux is rented, a clerk runs its code across an electronic scanner. At year end, the computer adds up the total rentals for each of the tuxedos, then divides this number by expected total use to calculate the rate. For instance, on a two-button black tux, Morris expects a life of 30 rentals. In one year, the tux was rented 13 times. The depreciation rate for that period was 43% (13 ÷ 30) of the depreciable cost.

©istockphoto.com/DNY59

Q Is the units-of-production method the best depreciation method for Morris Formal Wear to use for its tuxedos or would you recommend another method?

Depreciation and Income Tax

The Canada Revenue Agency (CRA) prescribes the amount of depreciation that companies can deduct from gross revenues in order to determine taxable income. These prescribed amounts (determined using prescribed rates) are generally different from accounting depreciation methods. The CRA refers to these amounts as **capital cost allowance (CCA)**. Accounting for and determining income taxes will be covered in more advanced courses. For now, be aware that you may see a company deduct depreciation on its income statement, which is required by generally accepted accounting principles, and this amount will generally be different from the amount deducted for income tax purposes.

Helpful hint Depreciation for accounting purposes is usually different from depreciation for income tax purposes.

Action Plan

- Under straight-line depreciation, annual depreciation expense is equal to the depreciable amount (cost less residual value) divided by the estimated useful life.
- Under double diminishing-balance depreciation, annual depreciation expense is equal to double the straight-line rate of depreciation multiplied by the asset's carrying amount at the beginning of the year. Residual values are not used in this method.
- Under the straight-line and diminishing-balance methods, the annual depreciation expense must be pro-rated if the asset is purchased during the year.
- Under units-of-production depreciation, the depreciable amount per unit is equal to the total depreciable amount divided by the total estimated units of production. The annual depreciation expense is equal to the depreciable amount per unit times the actual usage in each year.

BEFORE YOU GO ON...DO IT **Methods of Depreciation**

On October 1, 2017, Iron Mountain Ski Company purchases a new snow grooming machine for $52,000. The machine is estimated to have a five-year useful life and a $4,000 residual value. It is also estimated to have a total useful life of 6,000 hours. It is used 1,000 hours in the year ended December 31, 2017, and 1,300 hours in the year ended December 31, 2018. How much depreciation expense should Iron Mountain Ski record in each of 2017 and 2018 under each depreciation method: (a) straight-line, (b) double diminishing-balance, and (c) units-of-production?

Solution

	2017	2018
Straight-line	$2,400	$ 9,600
Double diminishing-balance	5,200	18,720
Units-of-production	8,000	10,400

(a) Straight-line: ($52,000 − $4,000) ÷ 5 years = $9,600 per year; 2017: $9,600 × $^3/_{12}$ = $2,400
(b) Double diminishing-balance: 200% ÷ 5 years = 40% double diminishing-balance rate; 2017: $52,000 × 40% × $^3/_{12}$ = $5,200
2018: ($52,000 − $5,200) × 40% = $18,720
(c) Units-of-production: ($52,000 − $4,000) ÷ 6,000 hours = $8.00 per hour
2017: 1,000 × $8.00 = $8,000
2018: 1,300 × $8.00 = $10,400

Related exercise material: BE9–5, BE9–6, BE9–7, BE9–8, BE9–9, E9–2, E9–3, E9–4, E9–5, and E9–12.

LEARNING OBJECTIVE **Explain the factors that cause changes in periodic depreciation and calculate revised depreciation for property, plant, and equipment.**

REVISING PERIODIC DEPRECIATION

During the useful life of a long-lived asset, the annual depreciation expense needs to be revised if there are changes to the three factors that affect the calculation of depreciation: the asset's cost, useful life, or residual value. Thus, depreciation needs to be revised if there are

1. capital expenditures during the asset's useful life,
2. impairments in the value of an asset,
3. changes in the appropriate depreciation method, or in the asset's estimated useful life or residual value,
4. changes in the asset's fair value when using the revaluation model, and/or.

In the following sections, we discuss each of these items and then show how to revise depreciation calculations.

Capital Expenditures During Useful Life

Earlier in the chapter, we learned that companies can have both operating and capital expenditures when a long-lived asset is purchased. Similarly, during the useful life of a long-lived asset, a company may incur costs for ordinary repairs, or for additions or improvements.

Ordinary repairs are costs to *maintain* the asset's operating efficiency and expected productive life. Doing motor tune-ups and oil changes, repainting a building, or replacing worn-out gears on equipment are examples of ordinary repairs. These costs are frequently fairly small amounts that occur regularly. They may also be larger, infrequent amounts, but if they simply restore an asset to its prior condition, they are considered an ordinary repair. Such repairs are debited to Repairs Expense as they occur. Ordinary repairs are operating expenditures.

Additions and improvements are costs that are incurred to *increase* the asset's operating efficiency, productive capacity, or expected useful life. These costs are usually large and happen less often. Additions and improvements that add to the future cash flows associated with that asset are not expensed as they occur—they are capitalized. As capital expenditures, they are generally debited to the appropriate property, plant, or equipment account. The capital expenditure will be depreciated over the remaining life of the original structure or the useful life of the addition. Additions and improvements can also increase the useful life of the original structure. The depreciation calculations need to be revised when a company makes an addition or improvement.

Impairments

As noted earlier in the chapter, under the cost model, the carrying amount of property, plant, and equipment is cost less any accumulated depreciation since its acquisition. And, as already discussed, the carrying amount of property, plant, and equipment is rarely the same as its fair value. Remember that the fair value is normally not relevant since property, plant, and equipment are not purchased for resale, but rather for use in operations over the long term.

While it is accepted that long-lived assets such as property, plant, and equipment may be undervalued on the balance sheet, it is not appropriate if property, plant, and equipment are overvalued. Property, plant, and equipment are considered impaired if the asset's carrying amount exceeds its **recoverable amount**. The recoverable amount is the greater of the asset's fair value less costs to sell or its value in use, which is determined by discounting future estimated cash flows. When an asset is impaired, an **impairment loss** is recorded that is the amount by which the asset's carrying amount exceeds its recoverable amount. The rules for determining if an asset is impaired are somewhat different under ASPE and IFRS. While the details of these differences are left to an intermediate accounting course, it should be noted that under ASPE impairments are recorded less often.

Companies are required to determine on a regular basis if there is any indication of impairment. Some factors that would indicate an impairment of an asset include:

- Obsolescence or physical damage of the asset.
- Equipment used in the manufacture of a product where there is dramatically reduced demand or the market has become highly competitive.
- Bankruptcy of a supplier of replacement parts for equipment.

To illustrate an impairment loss on a long-lived asset, assume that on December 31, Piniwa Company reviews its equipment for possible impairment. The equipment has a cost of $800,000 and accumulated depreciation of $200,000. The equipment's recoverable amount is currently $500,000. The amount of the impairment loss is determined by comparing the asset's carrying amount with its recoverable amount as follows:

Carrying amount ($800,000 − $200,000)	$600,000
Recoverable amount	500,000
Impairment loss	$100,000

The journal entry to record the impairment is:

Dec. 31	Impairment Loss	100,000	
	Accumulated Depreciation—Equipment		100,000
	To record impairment loss on equipment.		

A	=	L	+	OE
−100,000				−100,000

Cash flows: no effect

Assuming that the asset will continue to be used in operations, the impairment loss is reported on the income statement. Often the loss is combined with depreciation expense on the income statement. The Accumulated Depreciation account, not the asset account, is credited for the impairment loss. The Accumulated Depreciation account will increase and the asset's carrying amount will decrease. Recording the loss this way keeps a record of the asset's original cost. Future depreciation calculations will need to be revised because of the reduction in the asset's carrying amount.

IFRS allows the reversal of a previously recorded impairment loss. Under IFRS, at each year end, the company must determine whether or not an impairment loss still exists by measuring the asset's recoverable amount. If this recoverable amount exceeds the current carrying amount, then a reversal is recorded. The **reversal of an asset is limited to the amount required to increase the asset's carrying amount to what it would have been if the impairment loss had not been recorded**. In other words, we cannot simply write the asset up to its recoverable amount—reversals are limited to the impairment loss originally recorded. When an impairment loss is reversed, we simply credit the impairment loss account and debit the accumulated depreciation account. If the asset is depreciable, additional revisions will be made to depreciation calculations. ASPE does not allow an impairment loss to be reversed.

Cost Model Versus Revaluation Model

As mentioned at the start of this chapter, under IFRS, companies can choose to account for their property, plant, and equipment under either the cost model or the revaluation model. We have used the cost model in this chapter because it is used by almost all companies. Only about 3% of companies reporting under IFRS use the revaluation model. The revaluation model is allowed under IFRS mainly because it is particularly useful in countries that experience high rates of inflation or for companies in certain industries, such as investment or real estate companies, where fair values are more relevant than cost. It is not allowed under ASPE.

Under the **revaluation model**, the carrying amount of property, plant, and equipment is its fair value less any accumulated depreciation less any subsequent impairment losses. This model can be applied only to assets whose fair value can be reliably measured. The accounting in the revaluation model will be studied further in more advanced courses. For now, be aware that if this model is used for property, plant, and equipment assets, depreciation will have to be revised regularly.

ACCOUNTING IN ACTION
ETHICS INSIGHT

Yue Wang/iStockphoto

Finney Container Company has been seeing sales go down for its main product, non-biodegradable plastic cartons. Although some expenses have also declined in line with the reduced revenues, there has been a decrease in profit because some expenses, such as depreciation, have not declined. The company uses the straight-line depreciation method.

The president, Philip Shapiro, recalling his college accounting classes, instructs his controller to lengthen the estimated asset lives used for depreciation calculations in order to reduce annual depreciation expense and increase profit. The president's compensation includes an annual bonus based on the amount of net profit reported in the income statement.

A processing line of automated plastic-extruding equipment that was purchased for $2.9 million in January 2015 was originally estimated to have a useful life between five and nine years. Therefore, the company used the middle of that estimate, or seven years, as the useful life and a residual value of $100,000 to calculate the annual straight-line depreciation for the first two years. However, the president now wants the equipment's estimated useful life to be changed to nine years (total), and to continue using the straight-line method.

The controller is hesitant to make the change, believing it is unethical to increase profit in this way. The president says, "Hey, the useful life is only an estimate. Besides, I've heard that our competition uses a nine-year estimated life on its production equipment. You want the company results to be competitive, don't you? So maybe we were wrong the first time and now we are getting it right. Or you can tell the auditors that we think maybe the equipment will last longer now that we are not using it as much."

 Is the president's requested change unethical? If so, why?

Changes in Depreciation Method, Estimated Useful Life, or Residual Value

As previously explained, the depreciation method used should be consistent with the pattern in which the asset's future economic benefits are expected to be consumed by the company. The appropriateness of the depreciation method should be reviewed at least annually in case there has been a change in the expected pattern.

Management must also review its estimates of the useful life and residual value of the company's depreciable assets at least at each year end. If wear and tear or obsolescence indicates that the estimates are too low or too high, estimates should be changed. If the depreciation method, estimated useful life, or residual values are changed, this will cause a revision to the depreciation calculations.

Revised Depreciation Calculations

All of the above-discussed factors will result in a revision to the depreciation calculation. In each case, the revision is made for current and future years only. The revision is not made retroactively for past periods. The rationale for this treatment is that the original calculation made in the past was based on the best information available at that time. The revision is based on new information that should affect only current and future periods. In addition, if past periods were often restated, users would feel less confident about financial statements.

Revised depreciation is calculated at the time of the change in estimate. To calculate the new annual depreciation expense, we must first calculate the asset's carrying amount at the time of the change. This is equal to the asset's original cost minus the accumulated depreciation to date, plus any capital expenditures, minus any impairment in value.

To illustrate how to revise depreciation, assume that JJ & Company decides on December 31, 2020—before recording its depreciation for 2020—to extend the original estimated useful life of its truck by one more year (to December 31, 2022) because of its good condition. As a result of using the truck for one additional year, the estimated residual value is expected to decline from its original estimate of $2,000 to $700. Assume that the company has been using straight-line depreciation and determines this is still the appropriate method. Recall that the truck was purchased on January 1, 2017, for $25,000 and originally had an estimated useful life of five years, with annual depreciation expense of $4,600.

The carrying amount at December 31, 2020—before recording depreciation for 2020—is $11,200 [$25,000 − (3 × $4,600)]. This is also the amount shown in Illustration 9-5 as the carrying amount at December 31, 2019. The remaining useful life of three years is calculated by taking the original useful life of five years, subtracting the three years where depreciation has already been recorded, and adding the additional estimated years of useful life—in this case, one year. The new annual depreciation is $3,500, calculated as in Illustration 9-14.

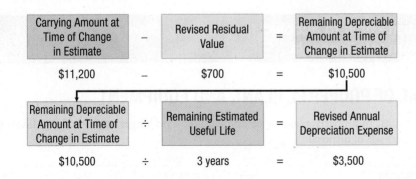

▶ **ILLUSTRATION** ⬤9-14
Formula for revised straight-line depreciation

As a result of the revision to the truck's estimated useful life and residual value, JJ & Company will record depreciation expense of $3,500 on December 31 of 2020, 2021, and 2022. The company will not go back and change the depreciation for 2017, 2018, and 2019. Accumulated depreciation will now equal $24,300 [($4,600 × 3) + ($3,500 × 3)] at the end of the six-year useful life instead of the $23,000 that was originally calculated.

If the units-of-production depreciation method is used, the calculation is the same as we just saw except that the remaining useful life is expressed as units rather than years. If the diminishing-balance method is used, the revised rate would be applied to the carrying amount at the time of the change in estimate. The rate must be revised because the useful life has changed.

BEFORE YOU GO ON...DO IT 3 | **Revised Depreciation**

Action Plan

- Understand the difference between an operating expenditure (benefits only the current period) and a capital expenditure (benefits future periods).
- To revise annual depreciation, calculate the carrying amount (cost less accumulated depreciation) at the revision date. Note that the cost of any capital expenditure will increase the carrying amount of the asset to be depreciated.
- Subtract any revised residual value from the carrying amount at the time of the change in estimate (plus the capital expenditure in this case) to determine the remaining depreciable amount.
- Allocate the revised depreciable amount over the remaining (not total) useful life.

On August 1, 2002, just after its year end, Fine Furniture Company purchased a building for $500,000. The company used straight-line depreciation to allocate the cost of this building, estimating a residual value of $50,000 and a useful life of 30 years. After 15 years of use, on August 1, 2017, the company was forced to replace the entire roof at a cost of $25,000 cash. The residual value was expected to remain at $50,000 but the total useful life was now expected to increase to 40 years. Prepare journal entries to record (a) depreciation for the year ended July 31, 2017; (b) the cost of the addition on August 1, 2017; and (c) depreciation for the year ended July 31, 2018.

Solution

(a)

July 31, 2017	Depreciation Expense [($500,000 – $50,000) ÷ 30]	15,000	
	Accumulated Depreciation—Building		15,000
	To record annual depreciation expense.		

(b)

Aug. 1, 2017	Building	25,000	
	Cash		25,000
	To record replacement of roof.		

(c)

Cost:	$ 500,000
Less: Accumulated depreciation $15,000 per year × 15 years	225,000
Carrying amount before replacement of roof, August 1, 2017	275,000
Add: Capital expenditure (roof)	25,000
Carrying amount after replacement of roof, August 1, 2017	300,000
Less: Residual value	50,000
Remaining depreciable amount	250,000
Divide by: Remaining useful life (40 – 15)	÷ 25 years
Revised annual depreciation	$ 10,000

July 31, 2018	Depreciation Expense	10,000	
	Accumulated Depreciation—Building		10,000
	To record revised annual depreciation expense.		

Related exercise material: BE9–10, BE9–11, E9–6, E9–7, and E9–8.

LEARNING OBJECTIVE 4 | **Demonstrate how to account for property, plant, and equipment disposals.**

DISPOSAL OF PROPERTY, PLANT, AND EQUIPMENT

▶ILLUSTRATION **9-15**
Methods of property, plant, and equipment disposal

Companies dispose of property, plant, or equipment that is no longer useful to them. Illustration 9-15 shows three methods of disposal.

Retirement
Equipment is scrapped or discarded.

Sale
Equipment is sold to another party.

Exchange
Existing equipment is traded for new equipment.

Steps in Recording Disposals of Property, Plant, and Equipment

Whatever the disposal method, a company must perform the following four steps to record the retirement, sale, or exchange of the property, plant, or equipment.

Step 1: Update Depreciation. Depreciation must be recorded over the entire period of time an asset is available for use. Therefore, if the disposal occurs in the middle of an accounting period, depreciation must be updated for the fraction of the year since the last time adjusting entries were recorded up to the date of disposal.

Step 2: Calculate the Carrying Amount. Calculate the carrying amount at the date of disposal after updating the accumulated depreciation for any partial year depreciation calculated in Step 1 above.

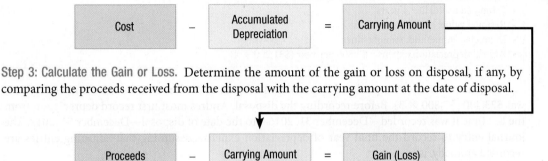

Step 3: Calculate the Gain or Loss. Determine the amount of the gain or loss on disposal, if any, by comparing the proceeds received from the disposal with the carrying amount at the date of disposal.

Gains and losses are similar to revenues and expenses except that gains and losses arise from activities that are peripheral to (outside of) a company's normal operating activities. For instance, Burger King's normal operating activities include earning revenue and incurring expenses related to the sale of hamburgers, french fries, salads, etc. If Burger King decided to dispose of a refrigerator, and the amount received is in excess of the carrying amount of the refrigerator, the excess would be recorded as a gain on the income statement.

If the proceeds of the sale are more than the carrying amount of the property, plant, or equipment, there is a gain on disposal. If the proceeds of the sale are less than the carrying amount of the asset sold, there is a loss on disposal.

Step 4: Record the Disposal. The journal entry to record the disposal always involves removing the asset's cost and the accumulated depreciation from the accounts. These are the same amounts used to calculate the carrying amount in Step 2 above. The journal entry may also include recording the proceeds and the gain or loss on disposal. Gains on disposal are recorded as credits because, like revenue, gains increase owner's equity; losses on disposal are recorded as debits because, like expenses, losses decrease owner's equity.

Gains and losses are reported in the operating section of a multiple-step income statement. Why? Recall that depreciation expense is an estimate. A loss results when the annual depreciation expense has not been high enough so that the carrying amount at the date of disposal is equal to the proceeds. Gains are caused because annual depreciation expense has been too high, so the carrying amount at the date of disposal is less than the proceeds. Thus gains and losses are adjustments to depreciation expense and should be recorded in the same section of the income statement.

Retirement of Property, Plant, and Equipment

Instead of being sold or exchanged, some assets are simply retired at the end of their useful lives. For example, some productive assets used in manufacturing may have highly specialized uses and

Alternative terminology
Derecognition is a term used under IFRS to describe the removal of a long-lived asset from the accounts after it is disposed of or no longer provides any future benefit.

Helpful hint "Proceeds" generally refers to cash or other assets received.

consequently have no market when the company no longer needs the asset. In this case, the asset is retired.

When an asset is retired, there are often no proceeds on disposal. The Accumulated Depreciation account is decreased (debited) for the full amount of depreciation recorded over the life of the asset. The asset account is reduced (credited) for the asset's original cost. Even if the carrying amount equals zero, a journal entry is still required to remove the asset and its related depreciation account from the books, as shown in the following example.

To illustrate the retirement of a piece of property, plant, and equipment, refer to the information below for Andres Enterprises:

- Date of retirement: December 31, 2017
- Equipment cost: $31,200
- Equipment acquisition date: January 2, 2014
- Estimated useful life: 4 years
- Residual value: none
- Depreciation method: straight-line
- Annual depreciation expense: $7,800 per year ($31,200 ÷ 4)

The balance in the Accumulated Depreciation account at Andres' year end, December 31, 2016, was $23,400 ($7,800 × 3). Before recording the disposal, Andres must first record depreciation from the last time it was recorded—December 31, 2016—to the date of disposal—December 31, 2017. The journal entry to record the final year of depreciation expense, assuming that adjusting entries are recorded annually, is:

A = L + OE			
−7,800 −7,800	2017 Dec. 31	Depreciation Expense Accumulated Depreciation—Equipment To record depreciation expense from last time it was recorded to date of disposal.	7,800 7,800
Cash flows: no effect			

After this journal entry is posted, the Equipment and Accumulated Depreciation accounts appear as follows:

Equipment		Accumulated Depreciation—Equipment	
Jan. 2, 2014 31,200		Dec. 31, 2014 7,800	
		Dec. 31, 2015 7,800	
		Dec. 31, 2016 7,800	
		Balance 23,400	
		Dec. 31, 2017 7,800	
		Balance 31,200	

The equipment is now fully depreciated with a carrying amount of zero (cost of $31,200 − accumulated depreciation of $31,200). As the equipment is being retired, there are zero proceeds, and since the carrying amount is equal to the proceeds, there is no gain or loss on disposal. All that is required is an entry to remove the cost and accumulated depreciation of the equipment, as follows:

A = L + OE			
+31,200 −31,200	2017 Dec. 31	Accumulated Depreciation—Equipment Equipment To record retirement of fully depreciated equipment.	31,200 31,200
Cash flows: no effect			

After this entry is posted, the balance in the Equipment and Accumulated Depreciation—Equipment accounts will be zero.

What happens if a company is still using a fully depreciated asset? In this case, the asset and its accumulated depreciation continue to be reported on the balance sheet, without further depreciation, until the asset is retired. Reporting the asset and related depreciation on the balance sheet informs the reader of the financial statements that the asset is still being used by the company. Once an asset is fully depreciated, even if it is still being used, no additional depreciation should be taken. Accumulated depreciation on a piece of property, plant, and equipment can never be more than the asset's cost.

If a piece of property, plant, and equipment is retired before it is fully depreciated and no proceeds are received, a loss on disposal occurs. Assume that Andres Enterprises retires its equipment on January 2, 2017 instead of December 31, 2017. The loss on disposal is calculated by subtracting the asset's carrying amount from the proceeds that are received. In this case, there are no proceeds and the carrying amount is $7,800 (cost of $31,200 − accumulated depreciation of $23,400), resulting in a loss of $7,800:

Proceeds	−	Carrying amount	=	Gain (Loss)
$0	−	$7,800	=	$(7,800)
		($31,200 − $23,400)		

The entry to record the retirement of equipment in 2017 is as follows:

Jan. 2	Accumulated Depreciation—Equipment	23,400	
	Loss on Disposal	7,800	
	Equipment		31,200
	To record retirement of equipment at a loss.		

A	=	L	+	OE
+23,400				−7,800
−31,200				

Cash flows: no effect

You should also note that there will never be a gain when an asset is retired with no proceeds. The proceeds would be zero and therefore cannot be greater than the carrying amount of the retired asset.

Sale of Property, Plant, and Equipment

In a disposal by sale, there are proceeds that must be recorded. Both gains and losses on disposal are common when an asset is sold. Only by coincidence will the asset's carrying amount and fair value (the proceeds) be the same when the asset is sold. We will illustrate the sale of furniture at both a gain and a loss in the following sections.

Gain on Disposal. To illustrate a gain, assume that on April 1, 2017, Andres Enterprises sells office furniture for $15,000 cash. The office furniture had originally been purchased on January 2, 2013, at a cost of $60,200. At that time, it was estimated that the furniture would have a residual value of $5,000 and a useful life of five years.

The first step is to update any unrecorded depreciation. Annual depreciation using the straight-line method is $11,040 [($60,200 − $5,000) ÷ 5]. The entry to record the depreciation expense and update accumulated depreciation for the first three months of 2017 is as follows:

2017 Apr. 1	Depreciation Expense ($11,040 × $^3/_{12}$)	2,760	
	Accumulated Depreciation—Furniture		2,760
	To record depreciation expense for the first three months of 2017.		

A	=	L	+	OE
−2,760				−2,760

Cash flows: no effect

After this journal entry is posted, the Furniture and Accumulated Depreciation accounts appear as follows:

Furniture	
Jan. 2, 2013 60,200	

Accumulated Depreciation—Furniture	
Dec. 31, 2013   11,040
Dec. 31, 2014   11,040
Dec. 31, 2015   11,040
Dec. 31, 2016   11,040
Apr. 1, 2017   2,760
Balance   46,920

The second step is to calculate the carrying amount on April 1, 2017. Note that the balance in Accumulated Depreciation is now $46,920.

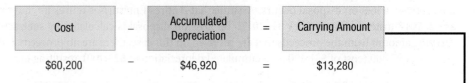

Cost	−	Accumulated Depreciation	=	Carrying Amount
$60,200	−	$46,920	=	$13,280

The third step is to calculate the gain or loss on disposal. A $1,720 gain on disposal is determined as follows:

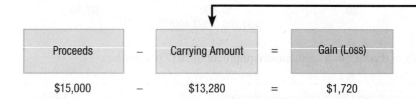

Proceeds	−	Carrying Amount	=	Gain (Loss)
$15,000	−	$13,280	=	$1,720

The fourth step is the entry to record the sale of the office furniture as follows:

```
 A      =  L   +   OE
+15,000          +1,720
+46,920
−60,200

↑Cash flows: +15,000
```

Apr. 1	Cash	15,000	
	Accumulated Depreciation—Furniture	46,920	
	Gain on Disposal		1,720
	Furniture		60,200
	To record the sale of office furniture at a gain.		

Notice that the carrying amount of $13,280 does not appear in the journal entry. Instead, the asset's cost ($60,200) and the total accumulated depreciation ($46,920) are used. **Remember: the carrying amount is simply a calculated amount to determine the gain or loss.** It is not an account and cannot be debited or credited.

Loss on Disposal. Assume that, instead of selling the furniture for $15,000, Andres sells it for $9,000. In this case, a loss of $4,280 is calculated as follows:

Proceeds	−	Carrying Amount	=	Gain (Loss)
$9,000	−	$13,280	=	$(4,280)

The entry to record the sale of the office furniture is as follows:

```
 A      =  L   +   OE
+9,000           −4,280
+46,920
−60,200

↑Cash flows: +9,000
```

Apr. 1	Cash	9,000	
	Accumulated Depreciation—Furniture	46,920	
	Loss on Disposal	4,280	
	Furniture		60,200
	To record the sale of office furniture at a loss.		

Exchanges of Property, Plant, and Equipment

An exchange of assets is recorded as the purchase of a new asset and the sale of an old asset. Typically a **trade-in allowance** on the old asset is given toward the purchase price of the new asset. An additional cash payment is usually also required for the difference between the trade-in allowance and the stated purchase price (list price) of the new asset. The trade-in allowance amount is often just a price concession and does not reflect the fair value of the asset that is given up. Consequently, as fair value is what matters, trade-in allowances are only used to determine the remaining cash that must be paid and are not recorded in the accounting records.

Instead of using the stated purchase price, **the new asset is recorded at the fair value of the asset given up plus any cash paid (or less any cash received) unless the fair value of the asset given up cannot be determined reliably, in which case the fair value of the asset *received* should be used**. The fair value of the asset given up is used to calculate the gain or loss on the asset being given up. A loss results if the carrying amount of the asset being given up is more than its fair value. A gain results if the carrying amount is less than its fair value.

Thus, the procedure to account for exchanges of assets is as follows:

Step 1: Update any unrecorded depreciation expense on the asset being given up to the date of the exchange.
Step 2: Calculate the carrying amount of the asset being given up (cost – accumulated depreciation).
Step 3: Calculate any gain or loss on disposal (fair value – carrying amount = gain [loss]).
Step 4: Record the exchange as follows:
- Remove the cost and the accumulated depreciation of the asset that is given up.
- Record any gain or loss on disposal.
- Record the new asset at the fair value of the old asset plus any cash paid (or less any cash received).
- Record the cash paid or received.

To illustrate an exchange of long-lived assets, assume that Chilko Company exchanged an old vehicle for a new vehicle on October 1, 2017. The details for the exchange are:

Original cost of the old vehicle: $61,000
Date of acquisition of old vehicle: January 1, 2012
Depreciation method: straight-line method
Estimated useful life: 6 years
Estimated residual value: $1,000
Fair value of the old vehicle (asset given up) on October 1, 2017: $3,000

The list price of the new vehicle was $51,000. Chilko received an $8,000 trade-in allowance from the vehicle dealership for the old vehicle and paid $43,000 cash ($51,000 – $8,000) for the new vehicle. Chilko's year end is December 31.

The first step is to update the depreciation on the old vehicle for the nine months ended October 1, 2017. Annual depreciation expense is $10,000 [($61,000 – $1,000) ÷ 6], so depreciation for nine months is $7,500 ($10,000 × $9/12$).

Oct. 1	Depreciation Expense	7,500	
	Accumulated Depreciation—Vehicles		7,500
	To record depreciation expense for the first nine months of 2017.		

A	=	L	+	OE
−7,500				−7,500

Cash flows: no effect

After this journal entry is posted, the Vehicles and Accumulated Depreciation accounts appear as follows:

Vehicles	
Jan. 1, 2012 61,000	

Accumulated Depreciation—Vehicles	
	Dec. 31, 2012 10,000
	Dec. 31, 2013 10,000
	Dec. 31, 2014 10,000
	Dec. 31, 2015 10,000
	Dec. 31, 2016 10,000
	Oct. 1, 2017 7,500
	Balance 57,500

The next step is to calculate the carrying amount of the old vehicle on October 1, 2017. Note that the balance in Accumulated Depreciation of $57,500 is equal to five years (January 1, 2012, to December 31, 2016) at $10,000/year plus $7,500 for 2017.

On October 1, 2017, the carrying amount is $3,500 (cost of $61,000 – accumulated depreciation of $57,500). The loss on disposal on the old vehicle is determined by comparing the carrying amount with the fair value:

Fair Value of Old Vehicle	–	Carrying Amount (Old Vehicle)	=	Gain (Loss)
$3,000	–	$3,500 ($61,000 – $57,500)	=	($500)

The cost of the new vehicle is determined by summing the fair value of the assets given up, that is:

Fair value of the old vehicle	$ 3,000
Cash paid	43,000
Cost of new vehicle	$46,000

The entry to record the exchange of vehicles is as follows:

A = L + OE
+46,000   −500
+57,500
−61,000
−43,000

Oct. 1	Vehicles (cost of new vehicle)	46,000	
	Accumulated Depreciation—Vehicles (on the old vehicle)	57,500	
	Loss on Disposal	500	
	Vehicles (cost of old vehicle)		61,000
	Cash		43,000
	To record exchange of vehicles, plus cash.		

Note that the exchange of vehicles is not netted. That is, it is shown as a separate increase and decrease to the general ledger account Vehicles. Also note that the list price of $51,000 and the trade-in allowance of $8,000 are ignored in determining the recorded cost of the new vehicle.

In the example above, the company recorded a loss on the exchange because the exchange was assumed to have **commercial substance**. An exchange has commercial substance if future cash flows change as a result of the exchange. That is, a company's operations will be altered in some fashion and future cash flows will change significantly.

In some situations, the exchange lacks commercial substance or else the fair value of the asset acquired or the asset given up cannot be determined. In such cases, the new long-lived asset is recorded at the carrying amount of the old asset that was given up, plus any cash paid (or less any cash received).

BEFORE YOU GO ON...DO IT   **Plant Asset Disposal**

Overland Trucking has a truck that was purchased on January 2, 2014, for $80,000. The truck had been depreciated on a straight-line basis with an estimated residual value of $5,000 and an estimated useful life of five years. Overland has a December 31 year end. Assume each of the following four independent situations:

1. On January 2, 2019, Overland retires the truck.
2. On May 1, 2018, Overland sells the truck for $9,500 cash.
3. On October 1, 2018, Overland sells the truck for $9,500 cash.
4. On November 1, 2018, Overland exchanges the old truck, plus $60,000 cash, for a new truck. The old truck has a fair value of $9,500. The new truck has a list price of $70,000, but the dealer gives Overland a $10,000 trade-in allowance on the old truck.

Prepare the journal entry to record each of these situations.

(continued)

BEFORE YOU GO ON...DO IT **Plant Asset Disposal** *(continued)*

Solution

$$\frac{\$80,000 - \$5,000}{5 \text{ years}} = \$15,000 \text{ annual depreciation expense}$$

$$\$15,000 \div 12 = \$1,250 \text{ per month}$$

1. Retirement of truck:

Jan. 2, 2019	Accumulated Depreciation—Vehicles ($1,250 × 60 months)	75,000	
	Loss on Disposal [$0 – ($80,000 – $75,000)]	5,000	
	Vehicles		80,000
	To record retirement of truck.		

2. Sale of truck for $9,500 on May 1, 2018:

May 1, 2018	Depreciation Expense ($1,250 × 4 months)	5,000	
	Accumulated Depreciation—Vehicles		5,000
	To record depreciation for four months.		
	Cash	9,500	
	Accumulated Depreciation—Vehicles ($1,250 × 52 months)	65,000	
	Loss on Disposal [$9,500 – ($80,000 – $65,000)]	5,500	
	Vehicles		80,000
	To record sale of truck at a loss.		

3. Sale of truck for $9,500 on Oct. 1, 2018:

Oct. 1, 2018	Depreciation Expense ($1,250 × 9 months)	11,250	
	Accumulated Depreciation—Vehicles		11,250
	To record depreciation for nine months.		
	Cash	9,500	
	Accumulated Depreciation—Vehicles ($1,250 × 57 months)	71,250	
	Gain on Disposal [$9,500 – ($80,000 – $71,250)]		750
	Vehicles		80,000
	To record sale of truck at a gain.		

4. Exchange of truck on Nov. 1, 2018:

Nov. 1, 2018	Depreciation Expense ($1,250 × 10 months)	12,500	
	Accumulated Depreciation—Vehicles		12,500
	To record depreciation for 10 months.		
	Vehicles (cost of new) ($9,500 + $60,000)	69,500	
	Accumulated Depreciation—Vehicles ($1,250 × 58 months)	72,500	
	Gain on Disposal [$9,500 – ($80,000 – $72,500)]		2,000
	Vehicles (cost of old)		80,000
	Cash ($70,000 – $10,000)		60,000
	To record exchange of trucks, plus cash.		

Related exercise material: BE9–12, BE9–13, BE9–14, E9–9, and E9–10.

Action Plan
- Update any unrecorded depreciation for dispositions during the fiscal year.
- Compare the proceeds with the asset's carrying amount to determine if there has been a gain or loss.
- Record any proceeds received and any gain or loss. Remove both the asset and any related accumulated depreciation from the accounts.
- Determine the cash paid in an exchange situation as the difference between the list price and the trade-in allowance.
- Record the cost of the new asset in an exchange situation as the fair value of the asset given up, plus the cash paid.

LEARNING OBJECTIVE 5 **Record natural resource transactions and calculate depletion.**

Natural Resources

Natural resources consist of standing timber and underground deposits of oil, gas, and minerals. Canada is rich in natural resources, ranging from the towering rainforests in coastal British Columbia to one of the world's largest nickel deposits in Voisey's Bay, Labrador. These long-lived assets have two characteristics that make them different from other long-lived assets: (1) they are physically extracted in operations such as mining, cutting, or pumping; and (2) only an act of nature can replace them.

Natural resources are tangible assets, similar to property, plant, and equipment. A key distinction between natural resources and property, plant, and equipment is that natural resources physically lose substance, or deplete, as they are used. For example, there is less of a tract of timberland (a natural resource) as the timber is cut and sold. When we use equipment, its physical substance remains the same regardless of the product it produces.

COST

The cost of a natural resource is determined in the same way as the cost of property, plant, and equipment and includes all expenditures necessary in acquiring the resource and preparing it for its intended use. These costs are often referred to as acquisition, exploration, and development costs. The cost of a natural resource also includes the estimated future removal and site restoration cleanup costs, which are often large. Restoration costs are usually required in order to return the resource as closely as possible to its natural state at the end of its useful life.

Detailed discussion on determining the cost of a natural resource will be left for more advanced accounting courses. In this section, we will look at how the acquisition cost of a natural resource is allocated over its useful life.

DEPLETION

Helpful hint Depreciation for natural resources is frequently called *depletion* because the assets physically deplete as the resource is extracted.

The units-of-production method (learned earlier in the chapter) is generally used to calculate the depreciation of natural resources. Under the units-of-production method, the total cost of the natural resource less its residual value is divided by the number of units estimated to be in the resource. The result is a depletion amount per unit of product. The depletion amount per unit is then multiplied by the number of units extracted, to determine the annual depletion expense.

To illustrate, assume that Fox Lake Company invests $5.5 million in a mine that is estimated to have 10 million tonnes (t) of uranium and a $200,000 residual value. In the first year, 800,000 tonnes of uranium are extracted. Illustration 9-16 shows the formulas and calculations.

▶ **ILLUSTRATION** 9-16
Formula for units-of-production method for natural resources

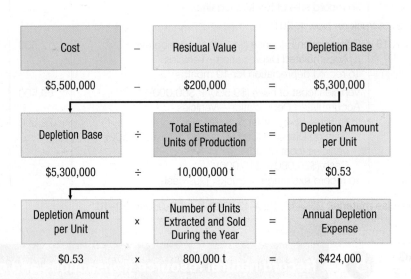

The calculated annual depletion expense is initially debited to an inventory account, a current asset. Note that this is not the same as depreciation for property, plant, and equipment, which is recorded as an expense. Depletion of natural resources is accounted for in this way because the resource extracted is available for sale—similar to merchandise that has been purchased or manufactured for sale, as we learned in Chapter 5.

The entry to record depletion of the uranium mine for Fox Lake Company's first year of operation, ended December 31, 2017, is as follows:

Dec. 31	Inventory ($0.53 × 800,000 t)	424,000	
	Accumulated Depletion—Resource		424,000
	To record depletion expense on uranium mine.		

A = L + OE
+424,000
−424,000

Cash flows: no effect

All costs of extracting the natural resource—both current production costs such as labour and depletion of the natural resource—are recorded as inventory. When the resource is sold, the inventory costs, which include depletion, are transferred to cost of goods sold and matched with the period's revenue. In other words, the depletion is charged to the income statement only in the period in which the related goods are sold. Depletion related to goods not yet sold remains in inventory and is reported as a current asset.

For example, assume that Fox Lake Company does not sell all of the 800,000 tonnes of uranium extracted in 2017. It sells 700,000 tonnes and stores 100,000 tonnes for later sale. In this situation, Fox Lake Company would include $371,000 (700,000 × $0.53) in cost of goods sold in 2017. The remaining depletion of $53,000 ($424,000 – $371,000) is for the 100,000 tonnes kept for later sale and will be included in inventory in the current assets section of the company's balance sheet.

Like depreciation for property, plant, and equipment, the depletion of a natural resource needs to be revised if there are capital expenditures during the useful life. Also, the depletion amount per unit of a natural resource needs to be revised whenever the estimated total units of the resource have changed as a result of new information. Natural resources such as oil and gas deposits and some metals have provided the greatest challenges. Estimates of the total units (also called reserves) of these natural resources are mostly knowledgeable guesses and may be revised whenever more information becomes available.

Natural resources must also be reviewed and tested for impairment annually or more frequently whenever circumstances make this appropriate. As with other long-lived assets, if there is impairment, the natural resource must be written down to its fair value, an impairment loss must be recorded, and current and future depreciation needs to be revised accordingly.

DISPOSAL

At disposal, just as with property, plant, and equipment, any unrecorded depletion of natural resources must be updated for the portion of the year up to the date of the disposal. Then proceeds are recorded, the cost and the accumulated depletion of the natural resource are removed, and a gain or loss, if any, is recorded.

Action Plan
- Use units-of-production depreciation for natural resources.
- Calculate the depletion amount per unit by dividing the total cost minus the estimated residual value by the total estimated units.
- Multiply the depletion amount per unit by the number of units cut to determine the total depletion.
- Allocate the depletion related to the units that have been cut but not yet sold to inventory.
- Allocate the depletion related to the units that have been cut and sold to expense.

| BEFORE YOU GO ON...DO IT | **Calculating Depletion for Natural Assets** |

High Timber Company invests $14 million in a tract of timber land. It is estimated to have 10 million cunits (1 cunit = 100 cubic feet) of timber and a $500,000 residual value. In the first year, 40,000 cunits of timber are cut, and 30,000 of these cunits are sold. Calculate depletion for High Timber's first year of operations and allocate it between inventory and cost of goods sold.

Solution

1. Depletion amount per unit: ($14,000,000 – 500,000) ÷ 10,000,000 cunits = $1.35 per cunit
2. Total depletion for the year: $1.35 per cunit × 40,000 cunits cut = $54,000
3. Depletion allocated to inventory: $1.35 per cunit × 10,000 cunits on hand = $13,500
4. Depletion allocated to expense: $1.35 per cunit × 30,000 cunits sold = $40,500

Related exercise material: BE9–15 and E9–11.

LEARNING OBJECTIVE **6** Identify the basic accounting issues for intangible assets and goodwill.

Intangible Assets and Goodwill

Similar to property, plant, and equipment, and natural resources, intangible assets provide economic benefits in future periods. They are used to produce products or provide services over these periods and are not intended for sale to customers. However, unlike property, plant, and equipment, and natural resources, which are **tangible assets** because they have a physical substance, **intangible assets** involve rights, privileges, and competitive advantages that have no physical substance. In other words, they are not physical things. Many companies' most valuable assets are intangible. Some widely known intangibles are Apple's trademark logo, Dr. Frederick G. Banting and Dr. Charles H. Best's patent for insulin, the franchises of Tim Hortons, the trade name of President's Choice, and the trade name of BMW.

An intangible asset must be identifiable, which means it must meet one of the two following criteria:

1. It can be separated from the company and sold, whether or not the company intends to do so, or
2. It is based on contractual or legal rights, regardless of whether or not it can be separated from the company.

Goodwill is a unique type of intangible asset. Because it cannot be separated from a company and sold, there are differences in the accounting for goodwill versus other intangible assets. We will discuss goodwill later in this section.

ACCOUNTING FOR INTANGIBLE ASSETS

Like tangible assets (property, plant, and equipment, and natural resources), intangible assets are recorded at cost. Cost includes all the costs of acquisition and other costs that are needed to make the intangible asset ready for its intended use—including legal fees and similar charges.

As with tangible assets, companies have a choice of following the cost model or the revaluation model when accounting for intangible assets subsequent to acquisition. The majority of companies use the cost model for all long-lived assets. So we will leave further study of the revaluation model, as it applies to intangible assets, for a later accounting course.

Under the cost model, if an intangible asset has a finite (limited) life, its cost must be systematically allocated over its useful life. We called this "depreciation" when discussing tangible assets. With intangible assets, we use the term **amortization**.

For an intangible asset with a finite life, its **amortizable amount** (cost less residual value) should be **allocated over the shorter of the (1) estimated useful life and (2) legal life**. Intangible assets, by their nature, rarely have any residual value, so the amortizable amount is normally equal to the cost. In addition, the useful life of an intangible asset is usually shorter than its legal life, so useful life is most often used as the amortization period.

When a company estimates the useful life of an intangible asset, it must consider factors such as how long the company expects to use the asset, obsolescence, demand, and other factors that can make the intangible asset ineffective at helping to earn revenue. For example, a patent on a computer chip may have a legal life of 20 years, but with technology changing as rapidly as it does, the chip's useful life may be only four or five years maximum.

Amortization begins as soon as the asset is ready to be used as intended by management. Similar to depreciation, the company must use the amortization method that best matches the pattern with which the asset's future economic benefits are expected to be consumed. If that pattern cannot be determined reliably, the straight-line method should be used.

Just as land is considered to have an indefinite life, there are also intangible assets with an indefinite life. An intangible asset is considered to have an indefinite (unlimited) life when, based on an analysis of all of the relevant factors, there is no foreseeable limit to the period over which the intangible asset is expected to generate net cash inflows for the company. If an intangible has an indefinite life, it is not amortized.

As with tangible assets, companies must determine if there are indicators of impairment on intangible assets' definite lives. If there are indicators, an impairment test is performed. Under IFRS, intangible assets with indefinite lives must be tested for impairment at least once a year even if no indications of impairment are evident. Under ASPE, this annual test is not required unless indicators are present.

Similar to tangible assets, the amortization is revised if there are changes in cost or useful life, or an impairment loss.

At disposal, just as with tangible assets, the carrying amount of the intangible asset is removed, and a gain or loss, if any, is recorded.

INTANGIBLE ASSETS WITH FINITE LIVES

Examples of intangible assets with finite lives include patents and copyrights. We also include research and development costs in this section because these costs often lead to the creation of patents and copyrights.

Patents

A **patent** is an exclusive right issued by the Canadian Intellectual Property Office of Industry Canada that allows the patent holder to manufacture, sell, or otherwise control an invention for a period of 20 years from the date of the application. A patent cannot be renewed. But the legal life of a patent may be extended if the patent holder obtains new patents for improvements or other changes in the basic design.

The initial cost of a patent is the price paid to acquire it. After it has been acquired, legal costs are often incurred. Legal costs to successfully defend a patent in an infringement suit are considered necessary to prove the patent's validity. They are added to the Patent account and amortized over the patent's remaining life.

The cost of a patent should be amortized over its 20-year legal life or its useful life, whichever is shorter. As mentioned earlier in this chapter, the useful life should be carefully assessed by considering whether the patent is likely to become ineffective at contributing to revenue before the end of its legal life.

Copyrights

A **copyright** is granted by the Canadian Intellectual Property Office, giving the owner an exclusive right to reproduce and sell an artistic or published work. Copyrights extend for the life of the creator plus 50 years. Generally, a copyright's useful life is significantly shorter than its legal life.

The cost of a copyright consists of the cost of acquiring and defending it. The cost may only be the fee paid to register the copyright, or it may amount to a great deal more if a copyright infringement suit is involved.

ACCOUNTING IN ACTION
ALL ABOUT YOU INSIGHT

If you copy a song from a CD that has a "digital lock" on it to prevent unauthorized copying to your smart phone, you could be liable for a fine ranging from $100 to $5,000 for breaking the digital lock and copying the CD. This is one of the provisions in Canada's Copyright Modernization Act, passed in 2012. The last time the copyright laws were changed was in 1997, before the first MP3 player came on the market. Since that time, the Internet and other new technologies have changed the way we produce and access copyright material. Supporters of the law argue that companies and individuals in the entertainment and creative fields need to have their songs, videos, TV shows, software, electronic books, and other works protected in order to foster creativity and innovation. But the amendments are also intended to give more flexibility to consumers such as officially legalizing the recording of television programs to watch at their convenience.

Sources: Bea Vongdouangchanh, "Parliament Passes New Copyright Law; Geist Says Feds Caved to U.S. on Digital Locks," *The Hill Times*, July 2, 2012; CBC News, "Copyright Bill Finally Clears Commons," CBC.ca, June 19, 2012; Mary Teresa Bitti, "Chambers: Copyright Lawyers Prepare for New Rules," *Financial Post*, March 26, 2012.

Getty Images/Moxie Productions

 Q Why is it important that the copyrights of artists, writers, musicians, and the entertainment industry be protected?

Research and Development Costs

Research and development (R&D) costs are not intangible assets by themselves. But they may lead to patents and copyrights, new processes, and new products. Many companies spend large sums of money on research and development in an ongoing effort to develop new products or processes.

Research and development costs present two accounting problems: (1) it is sometimes difficult to determine the costs related to specific projects, and (2) it is also hard to know the extent and timing of future benefits. As a result, accounting distinguishes between research costs and development costs.

Research is original, planned investigation that is done to gain *new knowledge and understanding*. It is not known at this stage if a future benefit will exist as a result of the research. Therefore, **all research costs should be expensed when they are incurred**.

Development is the *use of research findings and knowledge* for a plan or design before the start of commercial production. Development costs with probable future benefits should be capitalized. Specific criteria must be met before development costs can be recognized as an asset. If the conditions are not met, the development costs must be expensed. Illustration 9-17 shows the distinction between research and development. After development is completed, the capitalized development costs are amortized over the useful life of the project developed.

▶ **ILLUSTRATION** (9-17)
Distinction between research and development

Research	Development

Research

Examples
- Laboratory research aimed at the discovery of new knowledge
- Searching for ways to use new research findings or other knowledge
- Forming concepts and designs of possible product or process alternatives

Development

Examples
- Testing in search or evaluation of product or process alternatives
- Design, construction, and testing of pre-production prototypes and models
- Design of tools, jigs, moulds, and dies involving new technology or materials

INTANGIBLE ASSETS WITH INDEFINITE LIVES

An intangible asset is considered to have an indefinite life when there is no foreseeable limit to the length of time over which the asset is expected to generate cash. Examples of intangible assets with indefinite lives include trademarks and trade names, franchises, and licences. Intangible assets do not always fit perfectly in a specific category. Sometimes trademarks, trade names, franchises, or licences do have finite lives. In such cases, they would be amortized over the shorter of their legal or useful lives. It is more usual, however, for these intangible assets, along with goodwill, to have indefinite lives.

Trademarks, Trade Names, and Brands

A **trademark** or **trade name** is a word, phrase, jingle, or symbol that identifies a particular enterprise or product. Trade names like President's Choice, Starbucks, adidas, the Toronto Maple Leafs, and TSN create immediate brand recognition and generally help the sale of a product or service. Each year, Interbrand ranks the world's best brands. In 2014, it ranked Apple as the most successful brand in the world, followed by Google, Coca-Cola, and IBM. In Canada, the most valuable brands in retail included Shoppers Drug Mart and lululemon.

The creator can get an exclusive legal right to the trademark or trade name by registering it with the Canadian Intellectual Property Office. This registration gives continuous protection. It may be renewed every 15 years, as long as the trademark or trade name is in use. In most cases, companies continuously renew their trademarks or trade names. In such cases, as long as the trademark or trade name continues to be marketable, it will have an indefinite useful life.

If the trademark or trade name is purchased, the cost is the purchase price. If the trademark or trade name is developed internally rather than purchased, it cannot be recognized as an intangible asset on the balance sheet. The reason is that expenditures on internally developed trademarks or brands cannot be distinguished from the cost of developing the business as a whole. The cost cannot be separately measured.

Franchises and Licences

When you purchase a Civic from a Honda dealer, fill up your gas tank at the corner Mohawk station, or buy coffee from Tim Hortons, you are dealing with franchises. A **franchise** is a contractual arrangement under which the franchisor grants the franchisee the right to sell certain products, to provide specific services, or to use certain trademarks or trade names, usually inside a specific geographic area.

Another type of franchise is granted by a government body that allows a company to use public property in performing its services. Examples are the use of city streets for a bus line or taxi service; the use of public land for telephone, power, and cable lines; and the use of airwaves for radio or TV broadcasting. Such operating rights are called **licences**.

When costs can be identified with the acquisition of the franchise or licence, an intangible asset should be recognized. These rights have indefinite lives and are not amortized. Annual payments, which are often in proportion to the franchise's total sales, are sometimes required under a franchise agreement. These payments are called **royalties** and are recorded as operating expenses in the period in which they are incurred.

GOODWILL

Unlike other assets, which can be sold individually in the marketplace, goodwill cannot be sold individually because it is part of the business as a whole. It cannot be separated from the company, nor is it based on legal rights. **Goodwill** represents the value of favourable attributes related to a business such as exceptional management, a desirable location, good customer relations, skilled employees, high-quality products, fair pricing policies, and harmonious relations with labour unions.

If goodwill can be identified only with the business as a whole, how can it be determined? An accountant could try to put a dollar value on the attributes (exceptional management, a desirable location, and so on), but the results would be very subjective. Subjective valuations would not contribute to the reliability of financial statements. For this reason, internally generated goodwill is not recognized as an asset.

Goodwill is recorded only when there is a purchase of an entire business. The cost of goodwill is measured by comparing the amount paid to purchase the entire business with the fair value of its net assets (assets less liabilities). If the amount paid is greater than the net identifiable assets, then the purchaser has paid for something that cannot be separated and sold—goodwill. In this situation, because a transaction has occurred, the cost of the purchased goodwill can be measured and therefore recorded as an asset.

Because goodwill has an indefinite life, just as the company has an indefinite life, it is not amortized. Since goodwill is measured using the company's fair value—a value that can easily change—IFRS requires goodwill to be tested annually for impairment even if there is no indication of impairment. Under ASPE, impairment tests of goodwill are only conducted if there is an indication that impairment exists.

BEFORE YOU GO ON...DO IT **6** **Accounting for Intangible Assets**

Dummies 'R' Us Company purchased a copyright to a new book series for $15,000 cash on August 1, 2016. The books are expected to have a saleable life of three years. One year later, the company spends an additional $6,000 cash to successfully defend this copyright in court. The company's year end is July 31. Record (a) the purchase of the copyright on August 1, 2016; (b) the year-end amortization at July 31, 2017; (c) the legal costs incurred on August 1, 2017; and (d) the year-end amortization at July 31, 2018.

(continued)

Action Plan

- Amortize intangible assets with finite lives over the shorter of their useful life and legal life (the legal life of a copyright is the life of the author plus 50 years).
- Treat costs to successfully defend an intangible asset as a capital expenditure because they benefit future periods.
- Revise amortization for additions to the cost of the asset, using the carrying amount at the time of the addition and the remaining useful life.

BEFORE YOU GO ON...DO IT 6   **Accounting for Intangible Assets** *(continued)*

Solution

(a)

Aug. 1, 2016	Copyrights	15,000	
	Cash		15,000
	To record purchase of copyright.		

(b)

July 31, 2017	Amortization Expense ($15,000 ÷ 3)	5,000	
	Accumulated Amortization—Copyrights		5,000
	To record amortization expense.		

(c)

Aug. 1, 2017	Copyrights	6,000	
	Cash		6,000
	To record costs incurred to defend copyright.		

(d)

July 31, 2018	Amortization Expense	8,000*	
	Accumulated Amortization—Copyrights		8,000
	To record revised amortization expense.		

*$15,000 − $5,000 + $6,000 = $16,000 carrying amount; $16,000 carrying amount ÷ 2 years remaining = $8,000

Related exercise material: BE9–16, E9–12, E9–13, and E9–14.

LEARNING OBJECTIVE 7   **Illustrate the reporting and analysis of long-lived assets.**

Statement Presentation and Analysis

PRESENTATION

Long-lived assets are normally reported in the balance sheet under the headings "property, plant, and equipment," "intangible assets," and "goodwill". Natural resource assets are generally reported under "property, plant and equipment." Some companies combine property, plant, and equipment and intangible assets under the heading "capital assets." Goodwill must be disclosed separately.

The cost and the accumulated depreciation and/or amortization for each major class of assets are disclosed in either the balance sheet or notes. In addition, the depreciation and amortization methods that are used must be described. The amount of depreciation and amortization expense for the period should also be disclosed. As previously explained, gains or losses on disposals of long-lived assets are included in operating expenses on the income statement.

 Under IFRS, companies also have to disclose if they are using the cost or the revaluation model for each class of assets, and include a reconciliation of the carrying amount at the beginning and end of the period for each class of long-lived assets in the notes to the financial statements. This means they must show all of the following for each class of long-lived assets: (1) additions, (2) disposals, (3) depreciation or amortization, (4) impairment losses, and (5) reversals of impairment losses. ASPE does not require disclosure of all of these details.

Illustration 9-18 contains an excerpt from Enerflex's 2014 balance sheet (which it calls the statement of financial position). Enerflex is a Calgary-based supplier of products and services to the oil and gas production industry.

▶ ILLUSTRATION **9-18**
Presentation of
long-lived assets

ENERFLEX LTD. Statement of Financial Position (partial) December 31, 2014 (in thousands)	
Assets	
Property, plant, and equipment (note 11)	$152,898
Rental equipment (note 11)	290,577
Intangible assets (note 13)	42,104
Goodwill (note 14)	707,913

Enerflex provides additional details on the long-lived assets in the notes to its financial statements. For example, in note 11, Enerflex discloses the required information about all of its property, plant, and equipment, which include land, buildings, equipment, assets under construction, assets held for sale, and rental equipment.

Another note, the summary of significant accounting policies, discloses that Enerflex uses straight-line depreciation and provides information on the estimated useful lives of the company's long-lived assets. This note also states that major renewals and improvements in rental equipment and property, plant, and equipment are capitalized. It explains that significant components of property, plant, and equipment that require replacement at regular intervals are accounted for separately. The notes also include information on Enerflex's policies on testing its long-lived assets for impairment. Property, plant, and equipment, rental equipment, and intangible assets are assessed for impairment whenever changes in events or changes in circumstances indicate that the asset's carrying amount may not be recovered. Goodwill is tested for impairment at least annually.

ANALYSIS

Information in the financial statements about long-lived assets allows decision makers to analyze a company's use of its total assets. We will use two ratios to analyze total assets: asset turnover and return on assets.

Asset Turnover

The **asset turnover** ratio indicates how efficiently a company uses its assets; that is, how many dollars of sales are generated by each dollar that is invested in assets. It is calculated by dividing net sales by average total assets. If a company is using its assets efficiently, each dollar of assets will create a high amount of sales. When we compare two companies in the same industry, the one with the higher asset turnover is operating more efficiently. The asset turnover ratio for fiscal 2014 for Corus Entertainment Inc. (dollars in thousands) is calculated in Illustration 9-19. (Note that Corus reports "Revenues" and not "Net Sales" but the two account names can be used interchangeably for the purposes of the ratio calculation.)

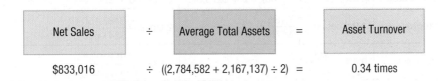

▶ ILLUSTRATION **9-19**
Asset turnover

The asset turnover ratio shows that each dollar invested in assets produced $0.34 in sales for Corus. This ratio varies greatly among different industries—from those that have a large investment in assets (e.g., utility companies) to those that have much less invested in assets (e.g., service companies). Asset turnover ratios, therefore, should only be compared for companies that are in the same industry. According to Reuters.com, the average for Corus's industry is 0.53. This means that generally the diversified entertainment industry as a whole has an asset turnover of 0.53. When compared with the industry, Corus is producing slightly less in sales per dollar invested in assets than the industry as a whole.

Return on Assets

The **return on assets** ratio measures overall profitability. This ratio is calculated by dividing profit by average total assets. The return on assets ratio indicates the amount of profit that is generated by each dollar invested in assets. A high return on assets indicates a profitable company. Illustration 9-20 shows the return on assets for Corus (dollars in thousands).

 **ILLUSTRATION** **9-20**
Return on assets

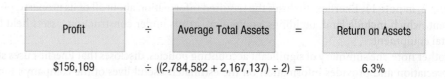

Profit	÷	Average Total Assets	=	Return on Assets
$156,169	÷	((2,784,582 + 2,167,137) ÷ 2) =		6.3%

Corus's return on assets was 6.3% for 2014. As with other ratios, the return on assets should be compared with previous years, with other companies in the same industry, and with industry averages, to determine how well the company has performed.

BEFORE YOU GO ON...DO IT **7** | **Asset Turnover and Return on Assets**

The following information is available for Toni's Sporting Goods for three recent years:

	2017	2016	2015
Total assets	$299,650	$259,700	$223,540
Net sales	521,180	487,150	441,280
Profit	26,390	18,210	13,540

Calculate the asset turnover and return on assets ratios for Toni's Sporting Goods for 2017 and 2016 and comment on any trends.

Action Plan

- Calculate average total assets using the total assets at the beginning and end of the year.
- Divide net sales by the average total assets for that year to calculate asset turnover.
- Divide profit by the average total assets for that year to calculate return on assets.
- Recall if it is better for asset turnover and return on assets to increase or decrease.

Solution

	2017	2016
Average total assets	($299,650 + $259,700) ÷ 2 = $279,675	($259,700 + $223,540) ÷ 2 = $241,620
Asset turnover	$1.9 \text{ times} = \dfrac{\$521,180}{\$279,675}$	$2 \text{ times} = \dfrac{\$487,150}{\$241,620}$
Return on assets	$9.4\% = \dfrac{\$26,390}{\$279,675}$	$7.5\% = \dfrac{\$18,210}{\$241,620}$

In general, it is better to have a higher asset turnover and return on assets. Toni's Sporting Goods' lower asset turnover may indicate it is not using its assets as efficiently in 2017 as compared with 2016. However, the increase in the return on assets indicates improved profitability. Given the decrease in turnover, this is a positive result.

Related exercise material: BE9–17, BE9–18, BE9–19, E9–15, and E9–16.

Comparing IFRS and ASPE

Key Differences	International Financial Reporting Standards (IFRS)	Accounting Standards for Private Enterprises (ASPE)
Valuing property, plant, and equipment	Choice of cost or revaluation model.	Must use cost model.
Terminology	The term "depreciation" is used for allocating the cost of property, plant, and equipment.	The term "amortization" may be used for allocating the cost of property, plant, and equipment. The term "depreciation" is also accepted.
Impairment of property, plant, and equipment, and finite-life intangible assets	Must look for indicators of impairment annually. If they exist, then must test for impairment. Allow for recoveries of previously recorded impairments.	No requirement to look for indicators of impairment annually. Perform tests only if it is apparent they exist. Impairments recorded less often, but cannot later reverse an impairment loss.
Test for impairment of indefinite-life intangible assets	Must perform impairment tests annually. Allows for recoveries of previously recorded impairments.	Same approach as for property, plant, and equipment, and intangible assets with finite lives.
Test for impairment of goodwill	Must be conducted every year.	Conducted only if there is an indication of impairment.
Disclosure	Must provide a reconciliation of the opening and closing carrying amount of each class of assets.	Reconciliation not required.

Demonstration Problem 1

DuPage Company purchases a factory machine at a cost of $17,500 on June 1, 2017. The machine is expected to have a residual value of $1,500 at the end of its four-year useful life on May 31, 2021. DuPage has a December 31 year end.

During its useful life, the machine is expected to be used for 10,000 hours. Actual annual use is as follows: 1,300 hours in 2017; 2,800 hours in 2018; 3,300 hours in 2019; 1,900 hours in 2020; and 700 hours in 2021.

Instructions
Prepare depreciation schedules for the following methods: (a) straight-line, (b) units-of-production, and (c) diminishing-balance using double the straight-line rate.

SOLUTION TO DEMONSTRATION PROBLEM 1

(a) Straight-line method

Year	Amount	×	Rate	=	Expense	End of Year Depreciation	Amount
							$17,500
2017	$16,000[a]		25%[b] × 7/12		$2,333	$ 2,333	15,167
2018	16,000		25%		4,000	6,333	11,167
2019	16,000		25%		4,000	10,333	7,167
2020	16,000		25%		4,000	14,333	3,167
2021	16,000		25% × 5/12		1,667	16,000	1,500

[a] $17,500 − $1,500 = $16,000
[b] 100% ÷ 4 years = 25%

ACTION PLAN

- Deduct the residual value in the straight-line and units-of-production methods, but not in the diminishing-balance method.
- In the diminishing-balance method, the depreciation rate is applied to the carrying amount (cost – accumulated depreciation). The residual value is not used in the calculations except to make sure the carrying amount is not reduced below the residual value.
- When the asset is purchased during the year, the first year's depreciation for the straight-line and diminishing-balance methods must be adjusted for the part of the year that the asset is owned. No adjustment is required for the units-of-production method. In the straight-line method, the final year must also be adjusted.
- Depreciation should never reduce the asset's carrying amount below its estimated residual value.

(b) Units-of-production method

| | | | | | End of Year | |
Year	Units of Production	× Depreciable Amount/Unit =	Depreciation Expense	Accumulated Depreciation	Carrying Amount
					$17,500
2017	1,300	$1.60[a]	$2,080	$ 2,080	15,420
2018	2,800	1.60	4,480	6,560	10,940
2019	3,300	1.60	5,280	11,840	5,660
2020	1,900	1.60	3,040	14,880	2,620
2021	700	1.60	1,120	16,000	1,500

[a] $17,500 – $1,500 = $16,000 depreciable amount ÷ 10,000 total units = $1.60/unit

(c) Diminishing-balance method

| | | | | End of Year | |
Year	Carrying Amount Beginning of Year	× Depreciable Rate (25% × 2) =	Depreciation Expense	Accumulated Depreciation	Carrying Amount
					$17,500
2017	$17,500	50% × 7/12	$5,104	$ 5,104	12,396
2018	12,396	50%	6,198	11,302	6,198
2019	6,198	50%	3,099	14,401	3,099
2020	3,099	50%	1,549	15,950	1,550
2021	1,550	50%	50[a]	16,000	1,500

[a] Adjusted to $50 so that the carrying amount at the end of the year is not less than the residual value.

Demonstration Problem 2

On January 2, 2017, Skyline Limousine Co. purchased a specialty limo for $78,000. The vehicle is being amortized by the straight-line method using a four-year service life and a $4,000 residual value. The company's fiscal year ends on December 31.

Instructions

Prepare the journal entry or entries to record the disposal of the limo, assuming that it is:
(a) retired for no proceeds on January 2, 2020.
(b) sold for $15,000 on July 1, 2020.
(c) traded in on a new limousine on January 2, 2020, for a trade-in allowance of $25,000 and cash of $52,000. The fair value of the old vehicle on January 2, 2020, was $20,000.

ACTION PLAN

- Calculate the annual depreciation expense and accumulated depreciation at the end of the previous year.
- Update the depreciation to the date of the disposal for any partial period.
- Determine the asset's carrying amount at the time of disposal.

SOLUTION TO DEMONSTRATION PROBLEM 2

$78,000 – $4,000 ÷ 4 years = $18,500 annual depreciation expense

Accumulated Depreciation at December 31, 2019: $18,500 × 3 years = $55,500

(a)

Jan. 2, 2020	Accumulated Depreciation—Vehicles	55,500	
	Loss on Disposal [$0 – ($78,000 – $55,500)]	22,500	
	Vehicles		78,000
	To record retirement of limo.		

(b)

July 1, 2020	Depreciation Expense ($18,500 × $^6/_{12}$)	9,250	
	Accumulated Depreciation—Vehicles		9,250
	To record depreciation for six months.		
	Cash	15,000	
	Accumulated Depreciation—Vehicles		
	($55,500 + $9,250)	64,750	
	Gain on Disposal [$15,000 − ($78,000 − $64,750)]		1,750
	Vehicles		78,000
	To record sale of limo.		

(c)

Jan. 2, 2020	Vehicles (cost of new) ($20,000 + $52,000)	72,000	
	Accumulated Depreciation—Vehicles	55,500	
	Loss on Disposal [$20,000 − ($78,000 − $55,500)]	2,500	
	Vehicles (cost of old)		78,000
	Cash		52,000
	To record exchange of limousines, plus cash.		

- Calculate any gain or loss by comparing proceeds with the carrying amount.
- Remove the asset's carrying amount by debiting accumulated depreciation (for the total depreciation to the date of disposal) and crediting the asset account for the cost of the asset. Record proceeds and any gain or loss.
- Ignore trade-in allowances.
- Record the new asset in an exchange situation at the fair value of the asset given up, plus the cash paid.

▶ Summary of Learning Objectives

1. **Calculate the cost of property, plant, and equipment.** The cost of property, plant, and equipment includes all costs that are necessary to acquire the asset and make it ready for its intended use. All costs that benefit future periods (that is, capital expenditures) are included in the cost of the asset. When applicable, cost also includes asset retirement costs. When multiple assets are purchased in one transaction, or when an asset has significant components, the cost is allocated to each individual asset or component using their relative fair values.

2. **Apply depreciation methods to property, plant, and equipment.** After acquisition, assets are accounted for using the cost model or the revaluation model. Depreciation is recorded and assets are carried at cost less accumulated depreciation. Depreciation is the allocation of the cost of a long-lived asset to expense over its useful life (its service life) in a rational and systematic way. Depreciation is not a process of valuation and it does not result in an accumulation of cash. There are three commonly used depreciation methods:

Method	Effect on Annual Depreciation	Calculation
Straight-line	Constant amount	(Cost − residual value) ÷ estimated useful life (in years)
Diminishing-balance	Diminishing amount	Carrying amount at beginning of year × diminishing-balance rate
Units-of-production	Varying amount	(Cost − residual value) ÷ total estimated units of production × actual activity during the year

Each method results in the same amount of depreciation over the asset's useful life. Depreciation expense for income tax purposes is called capital cost allowance (CCA).

3. **Explain the factors that cause changes in periodic depreciation and calculate revised depreciation for property, plant, and equipment.** A revision to depreciation will be required if there are (a) capital expenditures during the asset's useful life; (b) impairments in the asset's fair value; (c) changes in the asset's fair value when using the revaluation model; and/or (d) changes in the appropriate depreciation method, estimated useful life, or residual value. An impairment loss must be recorded if the recoverable amount is less than the carrying amount. Revisions of periodic depreciation are made in present and future periods, not retroactively. The new annual depreciation is determined by using the depreciable amount (carrying amount less the revised residual value), and the remaining useful life, at the time of the revision.

4. **Demonstrate how to account for property, plant, and equipment disposals.** The accounting for the disposal of a piece of property, plant, or equipment through retirement or sale is as follows:

  (a) Update any unrecorded depreciation for partial periods since depreciation was last recorded.
  (b) Calculate the carrying amount (cost − accumulated depreciation).
  (c) Calculate any gain (proceeds > carrying amount) or loss (proceeds < carrying amount) on disposal.
  (d) Remove the asset and accumulated depreciation accounts at the date of disposal. Record the proceeds received and the gain or loss, if any.

An exchange of assets is recorded as the purchase of a new asset and the sale of an old asset. The new asset is recorded at the fair value of the asset given up plus any cash paid (or less any cash received). The fair value of the asset given up is compared with its carrying amount to calculate the gain or loss. If the fair value of the new asset or the asset given up cannot be determined, the new long-lived asset is recorded at the carrying amount of the old asset that was given up, plus any cash paid (or less any cash received).

5. ***Record natural resource transactions and calculate depletion.*** The units-of-production method of depreciation is generally used for natural resources. The depreciable amount per unit is calculated by dividing the total depreciable amount by the number of units estimated to be in the resource. The depreciable amount per unit is multiplied by the number of units that have been extracted to determine the annual depreciation. The depreciation and any other costs to extract the resource are recorded as inventory until the resource is sold. At that time, the costs are transferred to cost of resource sold on the income statement. Revisions to depreciation will be required for capital expenditures during the asset's useful life, for impairments, and for changes in the total estimated units of the resource.

6. ***Identify the basic accounting issues for intangible assets and goodwill.*** The accounting for tangible and intangible assets is much the same. Intangible assets are reported at cost, which includes all expenditures necessary to prepare the asset for its intended use. An intangible asset with a finite life is amortized over the shorter of its useful life and legal life, usually on a straight-line basis. The extent of the

annual impairment tests depends on whether IFRS or ASPE is followed and whether the intangible asset had a finite or indefinite life. Intangible assets with indefinite lives and goodwill are not amortized and are tested at least annually for impairment. Impairment losses on goodwill are never reversed under both IFRS and ASPE.

7. ***Illustrate the reporting and analysis of long-lived assets.*** It is common for property, plant, and equipment, and natural resources to be combined in financial statements under the heading "property, plant, and equipment." Intangible assets with finite and indefinite lives are sometimes combined under the heading "intangible assets" or are listed separately. Goodwill must be presented separately. Either on the balance sheet or in the notes, the cost of the major classes of long-lived assets is presented. Accumulated depreciation (if the asset is depreciable) and carrying amount must be disclosed either in the balance sheet or in the notes. The depreciation and amortization methods and rates, as well as the annual depreciation expense, must also be indicated. The company's impairment policy and any impairment losses should be described and reported. Under IFRS, companies must include a reconciliation of the carrying amount at the beginning and end of the period for each class of long-lived assets and state whether the cost or revaluation model is used.

The asset turnover ratio (net sales ÷ average total assets) is one measure that is used by companies to show how efficiently they are using their assets to generate sales revenue. A second ratio, return on assets (profit ÷ average total assets), calculates how profitable the company is in terms of using its assets to generate profit.

▶ Glossary

Additions and improvements Costs that are incurred to increase the operating efficiency, productive capacity, or expected useful life of property, plant, or equipment. (p. 483)

Amortizable amount The cost minus the residual value of a finite-life intangible asset that is amortized over its useful life. (p. 496)

Amortization The systematic allocation of the amortizable amount of a finite-life intangible asset over its useful life. (p. 496)

Asset retirement costs The cost to dismantle, remove, or restore an asset when it is retired. (p. 470)

Asset turnover A measure of how efficiently a company uses its total assets to generate sales. It is calculated by dividing net sales by average total assets. (p. 501)

Basket purchase The acquisition of a group of assets for a single price. Individual asset costs are determined by allocating relative fair values. (p. 472)

Capitalized Capital expenditures recorded as property, plant and equipment or other long-lived asset rather than being recorded as an expense. (p. 470)

Capital cost allowance (CCA) The depreciation of long-lived assets that is allowed by the Income Tax Act for income tax purposes.

It is calculated on a class (group) basis and mainly uses the diminishing-balance method with maximum rates specified for each class of assets. (p. 481)

Capital expenditures Expenditures related to long-lived assets that benefit the company over several accounting periods. (p. 470)

Commercial substance An exchange of long-lived assets that results in a change in future cash flows of each party to the transaction. (p. 492)

Copyright An exclusive right granted by the federal government allowing the owner to reproduce and sell an artistic or published work. (p. 497)

Cost model A model of accounting for a long-lived asset that carries the asset at its cost less accumulated depreciation or amortization and any impairment losses. (p. 468)

Depreciable amount The cost of a depreciable asset (property, plant, and equipment, or natural resources) less its residual value. (p. 475)

Diminishing-balance method A depreciation method that applies a constant rate to the asset's diminishing carrying amount. This method produces a decreasing annual depreciation expense over the useful life of the asset. (p. 476)

Double diminishing-balance method A diminishing-balance method of depreciation that uses a rate equal to two times the straight-line rate. (p. 477)

Franchise A contractual arrangement under which the franchisor grants the franchisee the right to sell certain products, offer specific services, or use certain trademarks or trade names, usually inside a specific geographical area. (p. 499)

Goodwill The amount paid to purchase another company that is more than the fair value of the company's net identifiable assets. (p. 499)

Impairment loss The amount by which an asset's carrying amount exceeds its recoverable amount. (p. 483)

Intangible assets Rights, privileges, and competitive advantages that result from owning long-lived assets that have no physical substance. (p. 496)

Land improvements Structural additions to land that have limited useful lives, such as paving, fencing, and lighting. (p. 471)

Licences Operating rights to use public property, granted by a government agency to a company. (p. 499)

Natural resources Long-lived tangible assets, such as standing timber and underground deposits of oil, gas, and minerals, that are physically extracted and are only replaceable by an act of nature. (p. 493)

Operating expenditures Expenditures that benefit only the current period. They are immediately charged against revenues as expenses. (p. 470)

Ordinary repairs Expenditures to maintain the operating efficiency and productive life of the unit. (p. 483)

Patent An exclusive right issued by the federal government that enables the recipient to manufacture, sell, or otherwise control an invention for a period of 20 years from the date of the application. (p. 497)

Property, plant, and equipment Identifiable, long-lived tangible assets, such as land, land improvements, buildings, and equipment, that the company owns and uses for the production and sale of goods or services. (p. 470)

Recoverable amount The higher of the asset's fair value, less costs to sell, and its value in use. (p. 483)

Research and development (R&D) costs Expenditures that may lead to patents, copyrights, new processes, and new products. (p. 498)

Residual value The estimated amount that a company would currently obtain from disposing of the asset if the asset were already as old as it will be, and in the condition it is expected to be in, at the end of its useful life. (p. 475)

Return on assets An overall measure of profitability that indicates the amount of profit that is earned from each dollar invested in assets. It is calculated by dividing profit by average total assets. (p. 502)

Revaluation model A model of accounting for a long-lived asset in which it is carried at its fair value less accumulated depreciation or amortization and any impairment losses. (p. 484)

Royalties Recurring payments that may be required under a franchise agreement and are paid by the franchisee to the franchisor for services provided (e.g., advertising, purchasing), and are often proportionate to sales. (p. 499)

Straight-line method A depreciation method in which an asset's depreciable amount is divided by its estimated useful life. This method produces the same periodic depreciation for each year of the asset's useful life. (p. 475)

Tangible assets Long-lived resources that have physical substance, are used in the operations of the business, and are not intended for sale to customers. Tangible assets include property, plant, and equipment, and natural resources. (p. 496)

Trade-in allowance A price reduction offered by the seller when a used asset is exchanged for a new asset as part of the deal. (p. 490)

Trademark (trade name) A word, phrase, jingle, or symbol that distinguishes or identifies a particular enterprise or product. (p. 498)

Units-of-production method A depreciation method in which useful life is expressed in terms of the total estimated units of production or use expected from the asset. Depreciation expense is calculated by multiplying the depreciable amount per unit (cost less residual value divided by total estimated activity) by the actual activity that occurs during the year. (p. 478)

Useful life The period of time over which an asset is expected to be available for use, or the number of units of production (such as machine hours) or units of output that are expected to be obtained from an asset. (p. 474)

▶ Self-Study Questions

Answers are at the end of the chapter.

(LO 1) K 1. Additions to property, plant, and equipment are:
   (a) operating expenditures.
   (b) debited to the Repairs Expense account.
   (c) debited to the Inventory account.
   (d) capital expenditures.

(LO 1) AP 2. Bulyea Company purchased equipment and incurred the following costs:

Cash price	$36,000
Freight—FOB shipping point	1,000
Insurance during transit	200
Annual insurance policy	500
Installation and testing	400
Total cost	$38,100

What amount should be recorded as the cost of the equipment?
   (a) $36,000   (c) $37,600
   (b) $36,200   (d) $38,100

(LO 1) AP 3. Asura Company purchased land, a building, and equipment for a package price of $190,000. The land's fair value at the time of acquisition was $75,000. The building's fair value was $80,000. The equipment's fair value was $50,000. What costs should be debited to the Land account?
   (a) $74,146   (c) $46,341
   (b) $69,512   (d) $75,000

(LO 2) AP 4. Cuso Company purchased equipment on January 2, 2016, at a cost of $40,000. The equipment has an estimated residual value of $10,000 and an estimated useful life of five years. If the straight-line method of depreciation is used, what is depreciation expense on December 31, 2017?

(a) $6,000   (c) $18,000

(b) $12,000   (d) $24,000

(LO 2) AP 5. Kant Enterprises purchases a truck for $33,000 on July 1, 2017. The truck has an estimated residual value of $3,000, and an estimated useful life of five years, or a total distance of 300,000 km. If 50,000 km are driven in 2017, what amount of depreciation expense would Kant record at December 31, 2017, assuming it uses the units-of-production method?

(a) $2,500   (c) $5,000

(b) $3,000   (d) $5,333

(LO 2) AP 6. Refer to the data for Kant Enterprises in question 5. If Kant uses the double diminishing-balance method of depreciation, what amount of depreciation expense would it record at December 31, 2017?

(a) $6,000   (c) $12,000

(b) $6,600   (d) $13,200

(LO 3) K 7. When depreciation is revised:

(a) previous depreciation should be corrected.

(b) current and future years' depreciation should be revised.

(c) only future years' depreciation should be revised.

(d) None of the above.

(LO 4) AP 8. Oviatt Company sold equipment for $10,000. At that time, the equipment had a cost of $45,000 and accumulated depreciation of $30,000. Oviatt should record a:

(a) $5,000 loss on disposal.

(b) $5,000 gain on disposal.

(c) $15,000 loss on disposal.

(d) $15,000 gain on disposal.

(LO 4) AP 9. St. Laurent Company exchanged an old machine with a carrying amount of $10,000 and a fair value of $6,000 for a new machine. The new machine had a list price of $53,000. St. Laurent paid $42,000 cash and was offered $11,000 as a trade-in allowance in the exchange. At what amount should the new machine be recorded on St. Laurent's books?

(a) $42,000   (c) $52,000

(b) $48,000   (d) $53,000

(LO 5) AP 10. Titus Proudfoot Company expects to extract 20 million tonnes of coal from a mine that cost $12 million. If no residual value is expected and 2 million tonnes are mined in the first year, the entry to record depletion will include a:

(a) debit to Accumulated Depletion for $2,000,000.

(b) credit to Depletion Expense of $1,200,000.

(c) debit to Inventory of $1,200,000.

(d) credit to Accumulated Depletion of $2,000,000.

(LO 6) K 11. Which of the following statements about intangible assets is *false*:

(a) If an intangible asset has a finite life, it should be amortized.

(b) The amortization period should never be less than 20 years.

(c) Goodwill is recorded only when a business is purchased.

(d) Research costs should always be expensed.

(LO 7) AP 12. Cross Continental Rail Services reported net sales of $2,550 million, profit of $178 million, and average total assets of $3,132 million in 2017. What are the company's return on assets and asset turnover?

(a) 0.81% and 5.7 times

(b) 5.7% and 1.2 times

(c) 7.0% and 5.7 times

(d) 5.7% and 0.81 times

▶ Questions

(LO 1) K 1. What are the three characteristics of property, plant, and equipment?

(LO 1) K 2. What are some examples of land improvements?

(LO 1) C 3. Blue Hosta Company recently purchased a new vehicle. The company also had to pay for the company's logo to be painted on the vehicle, for a safety inspection, and for an annual insurance policy on the vehicle. Explain how each of these costs should be recorded and why.

(LO 1) C 4. In a recent newspaper article, the president of Altas Company asserted that something has to be done about depreciation. The president said, "Depreciation does not come close to accumulating the cash needed to replace the asset at the end of its useful life." What is your response to the president?

(LO 1) C 5. Jacques asks why the total cost in a basket purchase has to be allocated to the individual assets. For example, if we purchase land and a building for $250,000, why can we not just debit an account called Land and Building for $250,000? Answer his question.

(LO 2) C 6. Victor is studying for the next accounting examination. He asks your help on two questions: (a) What is residual value? (b) Is residual value used in determining periodic depreciation under each depreciation method? Answer Victor's questions.

(LO 2) K 7. Explain the factors that are used to calculate depreciation.

(LO 2) C 8. Contrast the effects of the three depreciation methods on annual depreciation expense.

(LO 2, 3) K 9. What factors should be considered when choosing a depreciation method?

(LO 3) C 10. Explain the difference between operating expenditures and capital expenditures during an asset's useful life and describe the accounting treatment of each.

(LO 3) C 11. Under what circumstances will depreciation need to be revised? Should these circumstances also result in the revision of previously recorded depreciation?

(LO 3) K 12. What factors contribute to an impairment loss?

(LO 3) C 13. In the fourth year of an asset's five-year useful life, the company decides that the asset will have an eight-year service life. How should the revision of depreciation be recorded? Why?

(LO 4) C 14. If equipment is sold in the middle of a fiscal year, why does depreciation expense have to be recorded for the partial period? Doesn't the subsequent journal entry to record the sale remove the accumulated depreciation from the books anyway?

(LO 4) C 15. Ewing Company owns a machine that is fully depreciated but is still being used. How should Ewing account for this asset and report it in the financial statements?

(LO 4) K 16. How is a gain or loss on the sale of an item of property, plant, or equipment calculated? Is the calculation the same for an exchange of a piece of property, plant, or equipment?

(LO 4) C 17. How is the carrying amount of an item of property, plant, or equipment calculated? Why does this amount NOT appear in the journal entry to record the disposition of an item of property, plant, or equipment?

(LO 5) K 18. What are natural resources, and what are their distinguishing characteristics?

(LO 5) C 19. Why is the units-of-production method used frequently to calculate depletion for natural resources?

(LO 6) C 20. Zeus Company's manager believes that all intangible assets should be amortized over their legal lives. Do you agree or disagree? Explain.

(LO 6) C 21. What are the similarities and differences between accounting for intangible and tangible assets?

(LO 6) C 22. What is goodwill? Why can it not be sold to raise cash if a company is planning to expand?

(LO 7) K 23. How should long-lived assets be reported on the balance sheet and income statement? What information should be disclosed in the notes to the financial statements?

(LO 7) C 24. Balpreet believes that when comparing the ratios for one company over a two-year period, it is more important for a company to have an improved asset turnover than it is to have an improved return on assets. Do you agree or disagree? Why?

▶ Brief Exercises

BE9–1 The following costs were incurred by Shumway Company in purchasing land: cash price, $85,000; legal fees, $1,500; removal of old building, $5,000; clearing and grading, $3,500; installation of a parking lot, $5,000. (a) What is the cost of the land? (b) What is the cost of the land improvements?

Determine cost of land and land improvements. (LO 1) AP

BE9–2 Surkis Company incurs the following costs in purchasing equipment: invoice price, $40,375; shipping, $625; installation and testing, $1,000; one-year insurance policy, $1,750. What is the cost of the equipment?

Determine cost of equipment. (LO 1) AP

BE9–3 In the space provided, indicate whether each of the following items is an operating expenditure (O) or a capital expenditure (C):

Identify operating and capital expenditures. (LO 1) K

(a) _____ Repaired building roof, $1,500
(b) _____ Replaced building roof, $27,500
(c) _____ Purchased building, $480,000
(d) _____ Paid insurance on equipment in transit, $550
(e) _____ Purchased supplies, $350
(f) _____ Purchased truck, $55,000
(g) _____ Purchased oil and gas for truck, $125
(h) _____ Rebuilt engine on truck, $5,000
(i) _____ Added new wing to building, $250,000
(j) _____ Painted interior of building, $1,500

BE9–4 Rainbow Company purchased land, a building, and equipment on January 2, 2017, for $850,000. The company paid $170,000 cash and signed a mortgage note payable for the remainder. Management's best estimate of the value of the land was $352,000; of the building, $396,000; and of the equipment, $132,000. Record the purchase.

Record basket purchase. (LO 1) AP

BE9–5 Surkis Company acquires equipment at a cost of $42,000 on January 3, 2017. Management estimates the equipment will have a residual value of $6,000 at the end of its four-year useful life. Assume the company uses the straight-line method of depreciation. Calculate the depreciation expense for each year of the equipment's life. Surkis has a December 31 fiscal year end.

Calculate straight-line depreciation. (LO 2) AP

Calculate diminishing-balance depreciation. (LO 2) AP

BE9–6   Refer to the data given for Surkis Company in BE9–5. Assume instead that the company uses the diminishing-balance method and that the diminishing-balance depreciation rate is double the straight-line rate. Calculate the depreciation expense for each year of the equipment's life.

Calculate units-of-production depreciation. (LO 2) AP

BE9–7   Speedy Taxi Service uses the units-of-production method in calculating depreciation on its taxicabs. Each cab is expected to be driven 550,000 km. Taxi 10 cost $38,950 and is expected to have a residual value of $4,300. Taxi 10 is driven 90,000 km in 2016, and 135,000 km in 2017. Calculate (a) the depreciable amount per kilometre (use three decimals), and (b) the depreciation expense for 2016 and 2017.

Calculate partial-year straight-line depreciation. (LO 2) AP

BE9–8   Pandora Pants Company acquires a delivery truck on April 6, 2017, at a cost of $38,000. The truck is expected to have a residual value of $6,000 at the end of its four-year life. Pandora uses the nearest month method to pro-rate depreciation expense. Calculate annual depreciation expense for the first and second years using straight-line depreciation, assuming Pandora has a calendar year end.

Calculate partial-year diminishing-balance depreciation. (LO 2) AP

BE9–9   Refer to the data given for Pandora Pants Company given in BE9–8. Assume now that the company has a policy of recording a half-year's depreciation in the year of acquisition and a half-year's depreciation in the year of disposal. Using the double diminishing-balance method, calculate the depreciation expense for each year of the equipment's life.

Determine carrying amount and record impairment loss. (LO 3) AP

BE9–10   Cherry Technology purchased equipment on January 4, 2015, for $250,000. The equipment had an estimated useful life of six years and a residual value of $10,000. The company has a December 31 year end and uses straight-line depreciation. On December 31, 2017, the company tests for impairment and determines that the equipment's recoverable amount is $100,000. (a) Calculate the equipment's carrying amount at December 31, 2017 (after recording the annual depreciation). (b) Record the impairment loss.

Calculate revised depreciation. (LO 3) AP

BE9–11   On January 2, 2017, Ares Enterprises reports balances in the Equipment account of $32,000 and Accumulated Depreciation—Equipment account of $9,000. The equipment had an original residual value of $2,000 and a 10-year useful life. Ares uses straight-line depreciation for equipment. On this date, the company decides that the equipment has a remaining useful life of only four years with the same residual value. Calculate the revised annual depreciation.

Record disposal by retirement. (LO 4) AP

BE9–12   On January 3, 2017, Ruiz Company retires equipment, which cost $25,700. No residual value is received. Prepare journal entries to record the transaction if accumulated depreciation is also $25,700 on this equipment. Ruiz has a December 31 fiscal year end.

Record disposal by sale. (LO 4) AP

BE9–13   Wilbur Company sells equipment on March 31, 2017, for $35,000 cash. The equipment was purchased on January 5, 2014, at a cost of $86,400, and had an estimated useful life of five years and a residual value of $2,200. Wilbur Company uses straight-line depreciation for equipment. Adjusting journal entries are made annually at the company's year end, December 31. Prepare the journal entries to (a) update depreciation to March 31, 2017, (b) record the sale of the equipment, and (c) record the sale of the equipment if Wilbur Company received $29,000 cash for it.

Record disposal by exchange of equipment. (LO 4) AP

BE9–14   Demeter Company exchanges an industrial oven for an industrial freezer. The carrying amount of the industrial oven is $31,000 (cost $61,000 less accumulated depreciation $30,000). The oven's fair value is $24,000 and cash of $5,000 is paid by Demeter in the exchange. Prepare the entry to record the exchange.

Record depletion for natural resources. (LO 5) AP

BE9–15   Cuono Mining Co. purchased a mine for $6.5 million that is estimated to have 25 million tonnes of ore and a residual value of $500,000. In the first year, 5 million tonnes of ore are extracted and 3 million tonnes are sold. Record annual depletion for the first year, ended August 31, 2017.

Record acquisition, legal expenditure, and amortization for patent. (LO 6) AP

BE9–16   Mabasa Company purchases a patent for $150,000 cash on January 2, 2017. Its legal life is 20 years and its estimated useful life is 8 years.

(a) Record the purchase of the patent on January 2, 2017.
(b) Record amortization expense for the year ended December 31, 2017.

Identify and classify long-lived assets. (LO 7) K

BE9–17   Indicate whether each of the following items is property, plant, and equipment (write "PPE"), a natural resource ("NR"), or an intangible asset ("I"). If the item does not fit any of these categories, write "NA" (not applicable) in the space provided.

(a) _____ Building
(b) _____ Cost of goods sold
(c) _____ Franchise
(d) _____ Diamond mine
(e) _____ Inventory
(f) _____ Land

(g) _____ Mining equipment
(h) _____ Note receivable, due in three years
(i) _____ Parking lot
(j) _____ Patent
(k) _____ Research costs
(l) _____ Trademark

BE9–18 Information related to property, plant, and equipment; natural resources; and intangibles on December 31, 2017 for H. Dent Company is as follows: land $400,000, building $1,100,000, accumulated depreciation—building $600,000, goodwill $410,000, nickel mine $500,000, and accumulated depletion—nickel mine $108,000. Prepare a partial balance sheet for H. Dent Company.

Prepare partial balance sheet. (LO 7) AP

BE9–19 **Agrium Inc.,** a global agricultural nutrients producer headquartered in Calgary, reports the following in its 2014 financial statements (in millions of US$):

Calculate ratios. (LO 7) AP

	2014	2013
Sales	$16,042	$15,727
Net earnings	720	1,063
Total assets	17,108	15,977

Note: "Sales" can be used in place of "Net sales" and "Net earnings" can be used in place of "Profit" in your ratio calculations.

Calculate Agrium's return on assets and asset turnover for 2014.

▶ Exercises

E9–1 The following expenditures related to property, plant, and equipment were made by Pascal Company:

Classify expenditures. (LO 1) AP

1. Paid $400,000 for a new plant site.
2. Paid $5,000 in legal fees on the purchase of the plant site.
3. Paid $7,500 for grading the plant site.
4. Paid $4,800 to demolish an old building on the plant site; residual materials were sold for $900.
5. Paid $54,000 for a new delivery truck.
6. Paid $200 freight to have the new delivery truck delivered.
7. Paid the $95 motor vehicle licence fee on the new truck.
8. Paid $17,500 for paving the parking lots and driveways on the plant site.

Instructions

(a) Explain what types of costs should be included in determining the cost of property, plant, and equipment.
(b) List the numbers of the preceding transactions, and beside each number write the account title that the expenditure should be debited to.

E9–2 Hohenberger Farms purchased real estate for $1,280,000, which included $5,000 in legal fees. It paid $255,000 cash and incurred a mortgage payable for the balance. The real estate included land that was appraised at $476,000, a building appraised at $748,000, and fences and other land improvements appraised at $136,000. The building has an estimated useful life of 60 years and a $50,000 residual value. Land improvements have an estimated 15-year useful life and no residual value.

Record basket purchase and calculate depreciation. (LO 1, 2) AP

Instructions

(a) Calculate the cost that should be allocated to each asset purchased.
(b) Record the purchase of the real estate.
(c) Calculate the annual depreciation expense for the building and land improvements assuming Hohenberger Farms uses straight-line depreciation.

E9–3 Jeffrey Parker has prepared the following list of statements about depreciation.

Understand depreciation concepts. (LO 1, 2) C

1. Depreciation is a process of asset valuation, not cost allocation.
2. Depreciation provides for the proper matching of expenses with revenues.
3. The carrying amount of a plant asset should approximate its fair value.
4. Depreciation applies to three types of assets: land, buildings, and equipment.
5. Depreciation does not apply to a building because its usefulness and revenue-producing ability generally remain intact over time.
6. The revenue-producing ability of a depreciable asset will decline due to wear and tear and to obsolescence.
7. Recognizing depreciation on an asset results in an accumulation of cash for replacement of the asset.
8. The balance in Accumulated Depreciation represents the total cost that has been charged to expense.
9. Depreciation expense and accumulated depreciation are reported on the income statement.
10. Four factors affect the calculation of depreciation: cost, useful life, residual value, and fair value.

Instructions

Identify each statement as true or false. If false, indicate how to correct the statement.

Calculate depreciation using three methods; recommend method. (LO 2) AP

E9-4 On June 9, 2016, Blue Ribbon Company purchased manufacturing equipment at a cost of $345,000. Blue Ribbon estimated that the equipment will produce 600,000 units over its five-year useful life, and have a residual value of $15,000. The company has a December 31 fiscal year end and has a policy of recording a half-year's depreciation in the year of acquisition.

Instructions

(a) Calculate depreciation under the straight-line method for 2016 and 2017.

(b) Calculate the depreciation expense under the double diminishing-balance method for 2016 and 2017.

(c) Calculate the depreciation expense under the units-of-production method, assuming the actual number of units produced was 71,000 in 2016 and 118,600 in 2017.

(d) In this situation, what factors should the company consider in determining which depreciation method it should use?

Prepare depreciation schedules and answer questions. (LO 2) AP

E9-5 On April 22, 2016, Sandstone Enterprises purchased equipment for $129,200. The company expects to use the equipment for 12,000 working hours during its four-year life and that it will have a residual value of $14,000. Sandstone has a December 31 year end and pro-rates depreciation to the nearest month. The actual machine usage was: 1,900 hours in 2016; 2,800 hours in 2017; 3,700 hours in 2018; 2,700 hours in 2019; and 1,100 hours in 2020.

Instructions

(a) Prepare a depreciation schedule for the life of the asset under each of the following methods:
    1. straight-line,
    2. double diminishing-balance, and
    3. units-of-production.

(b) Which method results in the lowest profit over the life of the asset?

(c) Which method results in the least cash used for depreciation over the life of the asset?

Record depreciation and impairment. (LO 3) AP

E9-6 Bisor Company has a December 31 year end and uses straight-line depreciation for all property, plant, and equipment. On July 1, 2015, the company purchased equipment for $500,000. The equipment had an expected useful life of 10 years and no residual value. The company uses the nearest month method for partial year depreciation.

On December 31, 2016, after recording annual depreciation, Bisor reviewed its equipment for possible impairment. Bisor determined that the equipment has a recoverable amount of $325,000. It is not known if the recoverable amount will increase or decrease in the future.

Instructions

(a) Prepare journal entries to record the purchase of the asset on July 1, 2015, and to record depreciation expense on December 31, 2015, and December 31, 2016.

(b) Determine if there is an impairment loss at December 31, 2016, and if there is, prepare a journal entry to record it.

(c) Calculate depreciation expense for 2017 and the carrying amount of the equipment at December 31, 2017.

Calculate revised depreciation. (LO 3) AP

E9-7 Lindy Weink, the new controller of Lafrenière Company, has reviewed the expected useful lives and residual values of selected depreciable assets at December 31, 2017. (Depreciation for 2017 has not been recorded yet.) Her findings are as follows:

Type of Asset	Date Acquired	Cost	Total Useful Life in Years		Residual Value	
			Current	Proposed	Current	Proposed
Building	Jan. 1, 2002	$800,000	20	30	$40,000	$60,500
Equipment	Jan. 1, 2015	125,000	5	4	5,000	4,000

After discussion, management agrees to accept Lindy's proposed changes. All assets are depreciated by the straight-line method. Lafrenière Company has a December 31 year end.

Instructions

(a) For each asset, calculate the annual depreciation expense using the original estimated useful life and residual value.

(b) Calculate the carrying amount of each asset as at January 1, 2017.

(c) For each asset, calculate the revised annual depreciation expense and the carrying amount at December 31, 2017.

Record asset addition and revised depreciation. (LO 3) AP

E9-8 On October 1, 2015, Chignecto Manufacturing Company purchased a piece of high-tech equipment for $90,000 cash. Chignecto estimated the equipment would have a six-year useful life and a residual value of $9,000. The company uses straight-line depreciation and has a September 30 fiscal year end.

On October 1, 2017, Chignecto paid $15,000 cash to upgrade the equipment. It is expected that the upgrade will significantly reduce the operating costs of the equipment. Chignecto also reviewed the equipment's expected useful life and estimated that, due to changing technology, the equipment's total expected useful life will be four years and its residual value will be $5,000.

Instructions

(a) Calculate the annual depreciation expense for the first two years of the equipment's life.
(b) Calculate the carrying amount of the equipment at September 30, 2017.
(c) Record the expenditure to upgrade the equipment on October 1, 2017.
(d) Record the annual depreciation of the equipment on September 30, 2018.

E9–9 The following are some transactions of Surendal Company for 2017. Surendal Company uses straight-line depreciation and has a December 31 year end.

Record disposal of property, plant, and equipment. (LO 4) AP

Apr. 1   Retired a piece of equipment that was purchased on January 1, 2008, for $45,000. The equipment had an expected useful life of 10 years with no residual value.

July 30   Sold equipment for $1,100 cash. The equipment was purchased on January 3, 2015, for $12,600 and was depreciated over an expected useful life of three years with no residual value.

Nov. 1   Traded in an old vehicle for a new vehicle, receiving a $10,000 trade-in allowance and paying $36,000 cash. The old vehicle had been purchased on November 1, 2011, at a cost of $35,000. The estimated useful life was eight years and the estimated residual value was $5,000. The fair value of the old vehicle was $7,000 on November 1, 2017.

Instructions

(a) For each of these disposals, prepare a journal entry to record depreciation from January 1, 2017, to the date of disposal, if required.
(b) Record the disposals.

E9–10 Plessis Company owns equipment that cost $65,000 when purchased on January 2, 2017. It has been depreciated using the straight-line method based on estimated residual value of $5,000 and an estimated useful life of five years.

Calculate gain or loss on disposal. (LO 4) AP

Instructions

Prepare Plessis Company's journal entries to record the sale of the equipment in these four independent situations.

(a) Sold for $31,000 on January 2, 2020
(b) Sold for $31,000 on May 1, 2020
(c) Sold for $11,000 on January 2, 2020
(d) Sold for $11,000 on October 1, 2020

E9–11 On July 1, 2017, Phillips Exploration invests $1.3 million in a mine that is estimated to have 800,000 tonnes of ore. The company estimates that the property will be sold for $100,000 when production at the mine has ended. During the last six months of 2017, 100,000 tonnes of ore are mined and sold. Phillips has a December 31 fiscal year end.

Record depletion for natural resources; show financial statement presentation. (LO 5) AP

Instructions

(a) Explain why the units-of-production method is often used for depleting natural resources.
(b) Record the 2017 depletion.
(c) Show how the mine and any related accounts are reported on the December 31, 2017, income statement and balance sheet.

E9–12 An accounting student encountered the following situations at Chin Company:

Apply accounting concepts. (LO 1, 2, 6) AP

1. During the year, Chin Company purchased land and paid legal fees on the purchase. The land had an old building, which was demolished. The land was then cleared and graded. Construction of a new building will start next year. All of these costs were included in the cost of land. The student decided that this was incorrect, and prepared a journal entry to put the cost of removing the building and clearing and grading the land in land improvements and the legal fees in legal fee expense.

2. The student decided that Chin's amortization policy on its intangible assets is wrong. The company is currently amortizing its patents but not its trademarks. The student fixed that for the current year end by adding trademarks to her adjusting entry for amortization. She told a fellow student that she felt she had improved the consistency of the company's accounting policies by making these changes.

3. One of the buildings that Chin uses has a zero carrying amount but a substantial fair value. The student felt that leaving the carrying amount at zero did not benefit the financial information's users—especially the bank—and wrote the building up to its fair value. After all, she reasoned, you write down assets if fair values are lower. She feels that writing them up if their fair value is higher is yet another example of the improved consistency that her employment has brought to the company's accounting practices.

Instructions

Explain whether or not the student's accounting treatment in each of the above situations follows generally accepted accounting principles. If it does not, explain why and what the appropriate accounting treatment should be.

Record acquisition, amortization, and impairment of intangible assets. (LO 6) AP

E9-13 Karsch Enterprises has a December 31 fiscal year end and uses straight-line amortization to the nearest month for its finite-life intangible assets. The company has provided you with the following information related to its intangible assets and goodwill during 2016 and 2017:

2016

Jan. 9	Purchased a patent with an estimated useful life of five years and a legal life of 20 years for $45,000 cash.
May 15	Purchased another company and recorded goodwill of $450,000 as part of the purchase.
Dec. 31	Recorded adjusting entries as required for amortization.
Dec. 31	Tested assets for impairment and determined the patent and the goodwill's recoverable amounts were $40,000 and $400,000, respectively.

2017

Jan. 2	Incurred legal fees of $30,000 to successfully defend the patent.
Mar. 31	Incurred research costs of $175,000.
Apr. 1	Purchased a copyright for $66,000 cash. The company expects the copyright will benefit the company for 10 years.
July 1	Purchased a trademark with an indefinite expected life for $275,000 cash.
Dec. 31	Recorded adjusting entries as required for amortization.

Instructions

(a) Record the transactions and adjusting entries as required.

(b) Show the balance sheet presentation of the intangible assets and goodwill at December 31, 2017.

Determine balance sheet and income statement presentation for intangible assets. (LO 6) AP

E9-14 Whiteway Company has a December 31 fiscal year end. Selected information follows for Whiteway Company for two independent situations as at December 31, 2017:

1. Whiteway purchased a patent from Hopkins Inc. for $400,000 on January 1, 2014. The patent expires on January 1, 2022. Whiteway has been amortizing it over its legal life. During 2017, Whiteway determined that the patent's economic benefits would not last longer than six years from the date of acquisition.

2. Whiteway has a trademark that had been purchased in 2010 for $250,000. During 2016, the company spent $50,000 on a lawsuit that successfully defended the trademark. On December 31, 2017, it was assessed for impairment and the recoverable amount was determined to be $275,000.

Instructions

(a) For each of these assets, determine the amount that will be reported on Whiteway's December 31, 2016 and 2017, balance sheets.

(b) For each of these assets, determine what, if anything, will be recorded on Whiteway's 2017 income statement. Be specific about the account name and the amount.

Classify long-lived assets; prepare partial balance sheet. (LO 7) AP

E9-15 **The North West Company Inc.,** a leading retailer to underserved rural and urban areas in hard-to-reach markets, reported the following selected information as at January 31, 2015 (in thousands):

Accumulated amortization—buildings	$209,584
Accumulated amortization—leasehold improvements	30,296
Accumulated amortization—fixtures and equipment	186,617
Accumulated amortization—computer equipment	62,074
Accumulated amortization—software	17,032
Accumulated amortization—other intangibles	5,750
Buildings	377,061
Cost-U-Less banner (trademark)	8,902
Computer equipment	73,151
Fixtures and equipment	265,706
Goodwill	33,653
Interest expenses	6,673
Land	16,041
Leasehold improvements	51,845
Other intangible assets	7,989
Other non-current assets	12,555
Software	28,376

Instructions

(a) Identify in which financial statement (balance sheet or income statement) and which section (e.g., property, plant, and equipment) each of the above items should be reported.

(b) Prepare the non-current assets section of the balance sheet as at January 31, 2015.

E9–16 **Suncor Energy Inc.** reported the following information for the fiscal years ended December 31, 2014, and December 31, 2013 (in millions):

Calculate asset turnover and return on assets. (LO 7) AN

	Dec. 31, 2014	Dec. 31, 2013
Net revenues	$39,862	$39,593
Net earnings	2,699	3,911
Total assets, end of year	79,671	78,315
Total assets, beginning of year	78,315	76,401

Instructions

(a) Calculate Suncor's asset turnover and return on assets for the two years.
(b) Comment on what the ratios reveal about Suncor Energy Inc.'s effectiveness in using its assets to generate revenues and produce profit.

▶ Problems: Set A

P9–1A   In 2017, Kadlec Company had the following transactions related to the purchase of a property. All transactions were for cash unless otherwise stated.

Record property transactions. (LO 1) AP

Jan.	12	Purchased real estate for a future plant site for $420,000, paying $95,000 cash and signing a note payable for the balance. On the site, there was an old building. The fair values of the land and building were $400,000 and $40,000, respectively. The old building will be demolished and a new one built.
	16	Paid $8,500 for legal fees on the real estate purchase.
	31	Paid $25,000 to demolish the old building to make room for the new plant.
Feb.	13	Received $10,000 for residual materials from the demolished building.
	28	Graded and filled the land in preparation for the construction for $9,000.
Mar.	14	Paid $38,000 in architect fees for the building plans.
	31	Paid the local municipality $15,000 for building permits.
Apr.	22	Paid excavation costs for the new building of $17,000.
Sept.	26	The construction of the building was completed. The full cost was $750,000. Paid $150,000 cash and signed a mortgage payable for the balance.
Sept.	30	Purchased a one-year insurance policy for the building, $4,500.
Oct.	20	Paved the parking lots, driveways, and sidewalks for $45,000.
Nov.	15	Installed a fence for $12,000.

Instructions

(a) Record the above transactions.
(b) Determine the cost of the land, land improvements, and building that will appear on Kadlec's December 31, 2017, balance sheet.

TAKING IT FURTHER   When should Kadlec start to record depreciation and on which assets?

P9–2A   In its first year of business, ChalkBoard purchased land, a building, and equipment on March 5, 2016, for $650,000 in total. The land was valued at $275,000, the building at $343,750, and the equipment at $68,750. Additional information on the depreciable assets follows:

Allocate cost and calculate partial period depreciation. (LO 1, 2) AP

Asset	Residual Value	Useful Life in Years	Depreciation Method
Building	$25,000	60	Straight-line
Equipment	5,000	8	Double diminishing-balance

Instructions

(a) Allocate the purchase cost of the land, building, and equipment to each of the assets.
(b) ChalkBoard has a December 31 fiscal year end and is trying to decide how to calculate depreciation for assets purchased during the year. Calculate depreciation expense for the building and equipment for 2016 and 2017 assuming:
1. depreciation is calculated to the nearest month.
2. a half-year's depreciation is recorded in the year of acquisition.
(c) Which policy should ChalkBoard follow in the year of acquisition: recording depreciation to the nearest month or recording a half year of depreciation?

TAKING IT FURTHER   In the year the asset is purchased, should ChalkBoard record depreciation for the exact number of days the asset is owned? Why or why not?

Determine cost; calculate and compare depreciation under different methods.
(LO 1, 2) AP

P9-3A   Payne Company purchased equipment on account on September 3, 2015, at an invoice price of $210,000. On September 4, 2015, it paid $4,400 for delivery of the equipment. A one-year, $1,975 insurance policy on the equipment was purchased on September 6, 2015. On September 20, 2015, Payne paid $5,600 for installation and testing of the equipment. The equipment was ready for use on October 1, 2015.

Payne estimates that the equipment's useful life will be four years, with a residual value of $15,000. It also estimates that, in terms of activity, the equipment's useful life will be 82,000 units. Payne has a September 30 fiscal year end. Assume that actual usage is as follows:

# of Units	Year Ended September 30
16,750	2016
27,600	2017
22,200	2018
16,350	2019

Instructions

(a) Determine the cost of the equipment.
(b) Prepare depreciation schedules for the life of the asset under the following depreciation methods:
   1. straight-line
   2. double diminishing-balance
   3. units-of-production
(c) Which method would result in the highest profit for the year ended September 30, 2017? Over the life of the asset?

TAKING IT FURTHER   Assume instead that, when Payne purchased the equipment, it had a legal obligation to ensure that the equipment was recycled at the end of its useful life. Assume the cost of doing this is significant. Would this have had an impact on the answers to parts (a) and (b) above? Explain.

Account for operating and capital expenditures and asset impairments.
(LO 1, 3) AP

P9-4A   Arnison Company has a December 31 fiscal year end and follows ASPE. The following selected transactions are related to its property, plant, and equipment in 2017:

Jan. 12   All of the company's light bulbs were converted to energy-efficient bulbs for $2,200. Arnison expects that this will save money on its utility bills in the future.
Feb. 6   Paid $5,400 to paint equipment that had started to rust.
Apr. 24   An air conditioning system was installed in the factory for $75,000.
May 17   Safety training was given to factory employees on using the equipment at a cost of $3,100.
July 19   Windows broken in a labour dispute (not covered by insurance) were replaced for $5,900.
Aug. 21   Paid $26,000 to convert the company's delivery vehicles from gasoline to propane. Arnison expects this will substantially reduce the vehicles' future operating costs and consequently improve efficiency, but it will not extend the vehicles' useful lives.
Sept. 20   The exhaust system in a delivery vehicle was repaired for $2,700.
Oct. 25   New parts were added to equipment for $20,000. Arnison expects this will increase the equipment's useful life by four years.
Dec. 31   After recording annual depreciation, Arnison reviewed its property, plant, and equipment for possible impairment. Arnison determined the following:
   1. Land that originally cost $200,000 had previously been written down to $175,000 in 2014 as a result of a decline in the recoverable amount. The current recoverable amount of the land is $220,000.
   2. The recoverable amount of equipment that originally cost $150,000 and has accumulated depreciation of $62,500 is $50,000.

Instructions

(a) For each of these transactions, indicate if the transaction increased (+) or decreased (−) Land, Building, Equipment, Accumulated Depreciation, total property, plant, and equipment (PP&E), and profit, and by how much. If the item is not changed, write "NE" to indicate there is no effect. Use the following format, in which the first one has been done for you as an example.

Transaction	Land	Building	Equipment	Accumulated Depreciation	Total PP&E	Profit
Jan. 12	NE	NE	NE	NE	NE	−$2,200

(b) Prepare journal entries to record the above transactions. All transactions are paid in cash.

TAKING IT FURTHER   Assume that Arnison also purchases equipment with an expected useful life of 12 years. Assume also that the equipment's engine will need to be replaced every four years. Which useful life should Arnison use when calculating depreciation on the equipment? Explain.

P9-5A Slope Style Snowboarding Company, a public company, purchased equipment on January 10, 2013, for $750,000. At that time, management estimated that the equipment would have a useful life of 10 years and a residual value of $50,000. Slope Style uses the straight-line method of depreciation and has a December 31 year end.

Slope Style tested the equipment for impairment on December 31, 2017, after recording the annual depreciation expense. It was determined that the equipment's recoverable amount was $320,000, and that the total estimated useful life would be eight years instead of 10, with a residual value of $10,000 instead of $50,000.

Record impairment and calculate revised depreciation. (LO 3) AP

Instructions

(a) Calculate the annual depreciation expense for the years 2013 to 2017 and the carrying amount at December 31, 2017.
(b) Record the impairment loss, if any, on December 31, 2017.
(c) What will appear on Slope Style's 2017 income statement and balance sheet with regard to this equipment?
(d) Assuming no further impairments or recoveries, calculate the annual depreciation expense for the years 2018 to 2020.

TAKING IT FURTHER Suggest some possible reasons why companies are allowed to record recoveries of previously recorded impairments under IFRS but not under ASPE.

P9-6A NW Tool Supply Company purchased land and a building on April 1, 2015, for $385,000. The company paid $115,000 in cash and signed a 5% note payable for the balance. At that time, it was estimated that the land was worth $150,000 and the building, $235,000. The building was estimated to have a 25-year useful life with a $35,000 residual value. The company has a December 31 year end, prepares adjusting entries annually, and uses the straight-line method for buildings; depreciation is calculated to the nearest month. The following are related transactions and adjustments during the next three years.

Record acquisition, depreciation, impairment, and disposal of land and building. (LO 1, 2, 3, 4) AP

2015

Dec. 31	Recorded annual depreciation.
31	Paid the interest owing on the note payable.

2016

Feb. 17	Paid $225 to have the furnace cleaned and serviced.
Dec. 31	Recorded annual depreciation.
31	Paid the interest owing on the note payable.
31	The land and building were tested for impairment. The land had a recoverable amount of $120,000 and the building, $240,000.

2017

Jan. 31	Sold the land and building for $320,000 cash: $110,000 for the land and $210,000 for the building.
Feb. 1	Paid the note payable and interest owing.

Instructions

(a) Record the above transactions and adjustments, including the acquisition on April 1, 2015. (Round depreciation calculation to the nearest dollar.)
(b) What factors may have been responsible for the impairment?
(c) Assume instead that the company sold the land and building on October 31, 2017, for $400,000 cash: $160,000 for the land and $240,000 for the building. Prepare the journal entries to record the sale. (*Hint*: Any impairment loss for land is credited directly to the Land account.)

TAKING IT FURTHER How might management determine the recoverable amount of the land and building at each year end? Would the company need to test the assets for impairment every year?

P9-7A On December 27, 2014, Wolcott Windows purchased a piece of equipment for $107,500. The estimated useful life of the equipment is either three years or 60,000 units, with a residual value of $10,500. The company has a December 31 fiscal year end and normally uses straight-line depreciation. Management is considering the merits of using the units-of-production or diminishing-balance method of depreciation instead of the straight-line method. The actual numbers of units produced by the equipment were 10,000 in 2015, 20,000 in 2016, and 29,000 in 2017. The equipment was sold on January 5, 2018, for $15,000.

Calculate and compare depreciation and gain or loss on disposal under three methods of depreciation. (LO 2, 4) AP

Instructions

(a) Calculate the depreciation for the equipment for 2015 to 2017 under (1) the straight-line method; (2) the diminishing-balance method, using a 40% rate; and (3) units-of-production. (*Hint*: Round the depreciable cost per unit to three decimal places.)
(b) Calculate the gain or loss on the sale of the equipment under each of the three methods.
(c) Calculate the total depreciation expense plus the loss on sale (or minus the gain on sale) under each of the three depreciation methods. Comment on your results.

TAKING IT FURTHER The owner of Wolcott Windows believes that having a gain or loss on sale indicates the company had made a mistake in calculating depreciation. Do you agree or disagree? Explain.

Record acquisition, depreciation, and disposal of equipment. (LO 2, 4) AP

P9–8A   Express Co. purchased equipment on March 1, 2015, for $95,000 on account. The equipment had an estimated useful life of five years, with a residual value of $5,000. The equipment is disposed of on February 1, 2018. Express Co. uses the diminishing-balance method of depreciation with a 20% rate and calculates depreciation for partial periods to the nearest month. The company has an August 31 year end.

Instructions

(a) Record the acquisition of the equipment on March 1, 2015.

(b) Record depreciation at August 31, 2015, 2016, and 2017.

(c) Record the disposal on February 1, 2018, under the following assumptions:

1. It was scrapped with no residual value.
2. It was sold for $55,000.
3. It was sold for $45,000.
4. It was traded for new equipment with a list price of $97,000. Express was given a trade-in allowance of $52,000 on the old equipment and paid the balance in cash. Express determined the old equipment's fair value to be $47,000 at the date of the exchange.

TAKING IT FURTHER   What are the arguments in favour of recording gains and losses on disposals of property, plant, and equipment as part of profit from operations? What are the arguments in favour of recording them as non-operating items?

Record property, plant, and equipment transactions; prepare partial financial statements. (LO 2, 4, 7) AP

P9–9A   At January 1, 2017, Hamsmith Corporation, a public company, reported the following property, plant, and equipment accounts:

Accumulated depreciation—buildings	$31,100,000
Accumulated depreciation—equipment	27,000,000
Buildings	48,700,000
Equipment	75,000,000
Land	10,000,000

Hamsmith uses straight-line depreciation for buildings and equipment and its fiscal year end is December 31. The buildings are estimated to have a 50-year useful life and no residual value; the equipment is estimated to have a 10-year useful life and no residual value. Interest on the notes is payable or collectible annually on the anniversary date of the issue.

During 2017, the following selected transactions occurred:

Apr. 1   Purchased land for $2.2 million. Paid $550,000 cash and issued a three-year, 6% note for the balance.

May 1   Sold equipment for $150,000 cash. The equipment cost $1.4 million when originally purchased on January 1, 2009.

June 1   Sold land for $1.8 million. Received $450,000 cash and accepted a three-year, 5% note for the balance. The land cost $700,000.

July 1   Purchased equipment for $1.1 million cash.

Dec. 31   Retired equipment that cost $500,000 when purchased on December 31, 2010.

Instructions

(a) Record the above transactions.

(b) Record any adjusting entries required at December 31, 2017.

(c) Prepare the property, plant, and equipment section of Hamsmith's balance sheet at December 31, 2017.

TAKING IT FURTHER   The owner of Hamsmith is considering using the revaluation model to account for property, plant, and equipment. What are some reasons to use the revaluation model?

Correct errors in recording intangible asset transactions. (LO 6) AP

P9–10A   Due to rapid turnover in the accounting department, several transactions involving intangible assets were improperly recorded by Riley Co. in the year ended December 31, 2017:

1. Riley developed a new manufacturing process early in the year, incurring research and development costs of $160,000. Of this amount, 45% was considered to be development costs that could be capitalized. Riley recorded the entire $160,000 in the Patents account and amortized it using a 15-year estimated useful life.

2. On July 1, 2017, Riley purchased a small company and, as a result of the purchase, recorded goodwill of $400,000. Riley recorded a half-year's amortization on the goodwill in 2017 based on a 40-year useful life and credited the Goodwill account.

3. Several years ago, Riley paid $70,000 for a licence to be the exclusive Canadian distributor of a Danish beer. In 2014, Riley determined there was an impairment of $40,000 in the value of the licence and recorded the loss. In 2017, because of a change in consumer tastes, the value of the licence increased to $80,000. Riley recorded the $50,000 increase in the licence's value by crediting Impairment Loss and debiting the Licence account. Management felt the company should consistently record increases and decreases in value.

Instructions

Assuming that Riley reports under IFRS, prepare the journal entries that are needed to correct the errors made during 2017.

TAKING IT FURTHER   The majority of the intangible assets reported on a balance sheet have been purchased as opposed to being internally generated. Why? What happens to the cost of an internally generated intangible asset if it is not recorded as an asset?

P9–11A   The intangible assets reported by Ip Company at December 31, 2016, follow:

Patent #1	$80,000	
Less: Accumulated amortization	16,000	$ 64,000
Copyright #1	48,000	
Less: Accumulated amortization	28,800	19,200
Goodwill		220,000
Total		$303,200

Patent #1 was acquired in January 2015 and has an estimated useful life of 10 years. Copyright #1 was acquired in January 2011 and also has an estimated useful life of 10 years. The following cash transactions may have affected intangible assets and goodwill during the year 2017:

Jan.   2   Paid $23,200 of legal costs to successfully defend Patent #1 against infringement by another company.
June 30   Developed a new product, incurring $180,000 in research costs and $60,000 in development costs, which were paid in cash. The development costs were directly related to Patent #2, which was granted for the product on July 1. Its estimated useful life is equal to its legal life of 20 years.
Sept. 1   Paid $12,000 to an Olympic athlete to appear in commercials advertising the company's products. The commercials will air in September.
Oct.   1   Acquired a second copyright for $18,000 cash. Copyright #2 has an estimated useful life of six years.

Instructions

(a) Record the above transactions.
(b) Prepare any adjusting journal entries required at December 31, 2017, the company's year end, and update the account balances.
(c) Show how the intangible assets and goodwill will be reported on the balance sheet at December 31, 2017.

TAKING IT FURTHER   Since intangible assets do not have physical substance, why are they considered to be assets?

P9–12A   Rivers Mining Company has a December 31 fiscal year end. The following information relates to its Golden Grove mine:

1. Rivers purchased the Golden Grove mine on March 31, 2016, for $2.6 million cash. On the same day, modernization of the mine was completed at a cash cost of $260,000. It is estimated that this mine will yield 560,000 tonnes of ore. The mine's estimated residual value is $200,000. Rivers expects it will extract all the ore, and then close and sell the mine site in four years.
2. During 2016, Rivers extracted and sold 120,000 tonnes of ore from the mine.
3. At the beginning of 2017, Rivers reassessed its estimate of the remaining ore in the mine. Rivers estimates that there are still 550,000 tonnes of ore in the mine at January 1, 2017. The estimated residual value remains at $200,000.
4. During 2017, Rivers extracted and sold 100,000 tonnes of ore from the mine.

Instructions

(a) Prepare the 2016 and 2017 journal entries for the above, including any year-end adjustments.
(b) Show how the Golden Grove mine will be reported on Rivers's December 31, 2017, income statement and balance sheet.

TAKING IT FURTHER   If the total estimated amount of units that will be produced (extracted) changes during the life of the natural resource, is it still appropriate to use the units-of-production method? Explain.

P9–13A   Andruski Company and Brar Company both manufacture school science equipment. The following financial information is for three years ended December 31 (in thousands):

Record intangible asset transactions; prepare partial balance sheet. (LO 6, 7) AP

Record natural resource transactions; prepare partial financial statements. (LO 3, 5, 7) AP

Calculate ratios and comment. (LO 7) AN

Andruski Company	2017	2016	2015
Net sales	$ 552.0	$ 515.9	$ 469.0
Profit	21.4	20.6	18.7
Total assets	702.5	662.8	602.5

Brar Company	2017	2016	2015
Net sales	$1,762.9	$1,588.2	$1,484.3
Profit	96.5	85.4	79.8
Total assets	1,523.5	1,410.7	1,318.4

Instructions

(a) Calculate the asset turnover and return on assets ratios for both companies for 2016 and 2017. Round your answers to two decimal points.

(b) Comment on how effective each of the companies is at using its assets to generate sales and produce profit.

TAKING IT FURTHER   After reading the notes to the financial statements, you have determined that Andruski Company uses diminishing-balance depreciation and Brar uses straight-line. Does this affect your ability to compare these two companies?

▶ Problems: Set B

Record property transactions.
(LO 1) AP

P9-1B   In 2017, Weisman Company had the following transactions related to the purchase of a property. All transactions are for cash unless otherwise stated.

Feb. 7   Purchased real estate for $575,000, paying $115,000 cash and signing a note payable for the balance. The site had an old building on it and the fair value of the land and building were $555,000 and $30,000, respectively. Weisman intends to demolish the old building and construct a new apartment building on the site.

9   Paid legal fees of $7,500 on the real estate purchase on February 7.

15   Paid $19,000 to demolish the old building and make the land ready for the construction of the apartment building.

17   Received $8,500 from the sale of material from the demolished building.

25   Graded and filled the land in preparation for the building construction at a cost of $10,500.

Mar. 2   Architect's fees on the apartment building were $28,000.

15   Excavation costs were $18,000. Construction began on March 20.

Aug. 31   The apartment building was completed. The full cost of construction was $850,000. Paid $170,000 cash and signed a note payable for the balance.

Sept. 3   Paid $40,000 for sidewalks and a parking lot for the building.

10   Purchased a one-year insurance policy on the finished building for $3,750.

Oct. 31   Paid $37,750 for landscaping.

Instructions

(a) Record the above transactions.

(b) Determine the cost of the land, land improvements, and building that will appear on Weisman's December 31, 2017, balance sheet.

TAKING IT FURTHER   When should Weisman begin recording depreciation on this property and on which assets?

Allocate cost and calculate partial period depreciation.
(LO 1, 2) AP

P9-2B   In its first year of business, Solinger Company purchased land, a building, and equipment on November 5, 2016, for $700,000 in total. The land was valued at $262,500, the building at $337,500, and the equipment at $150,000. Additional information on the depreciable assets follows:

Asset	Residual Value	Useful Life in Years	Depreciation Method
Building	$15,000	60	Straight-line
Equipment	15,000	8	Double diminishing-balance

Instructions

(a) Allocate the purchase cost of the land, building, and equipment to each of the assets.

(b) Solinger has a December 31 fiscal year end and is trying to decide how to calculate depreciation for assets purchased during the year. Calculate depreciation expense for the building and equipment for 2016 and 2017 assuming:

1. depreciation is calculated to the nearest month.

2. a half-year's depreciation is recorded in the year of acquisition.

(c) Which policy should Solinger follow in the year of acquisition: recording depreciation to the nearest month or recording a half year of depreciation?

TAKING IT FURTHER   Suppose that Solinger decided to use the units-of-production depreciation method instead of diminishing-balance for its equipment. How would this affect your answer to part (c) above?

P9–3B   Glans Company purchased equipment on account on April 6, 2015, at an invoice price of $442,000. On April 7, 2015, it paid $4,000 for delivery of the equipment. A one-year, $3,000 insurance policy on the equipment was purchased on April 9, 2015. On April 22, 2015, Glans paid $6,000 for installation and testing of the equipment. The equipment was ready for use on May 1, 2015.

Determine cost; calculate and compare depreciation under different methods.
(LO 1, 2) AP

    Glans estimates that the equipment's useful life will be four years, with a residual value of $20,000. It also estimates that, in terms of activity, the equipment's useful life will be 150,000 units. Glans has an April 30 fiscal year end. Assume that actual usage is as follows:

# of Units	Year Ended April 30
22,600	2016
45,600	2017
49,700	2018
32,200	2019

Instructions

(a) Determine the cost of the equipment.
(b) Prepare depreciation schedules for the life of the asset under the following depreciation methods:
   1. straight-line
   2. double diminishing-balance
   3. units-of-production
(c) Which method would result in the highest profit for the year ended April 30, 2017? Over the life of the asset?

TAKING IT FURTHER   Assume instead that, at the time Glans purchased the equipment, it had a legal obligation to ensure that the equipment was recycled at the end of its useful life. Assume the cost of doing this is significant. Would this have had an impact on the answers to parts (a) and (b) above? Explain.

P9–4B   Sugden Company has a December 31 fiscal year end and follows IFRS. The following selected transactions are related to its property, plant, and equipment in 2017:

Account for operating and capital expenditures and asset impairments. (LO 1, 3) AP

Jan. 22   Performed an annual safety inspection on the equipment for $4,600.
Apr. 10   Installed a conveyor belt system in the factory for $95,000, which is expected to increase efficiency and allow the company to produce more products each year.
May 6   Painted the interior of the entire building at a cost of $30,500.
July 20   Repaired a machine for $10,000. An employee had used incorrect material in the machine, which resulted in a complete mechanical breakdown.
Aug. 7   Overhauled equipment that originally cost $100,000 for $35,000. This increased the equipment's expected useful life by three years.
15   Trained several new employees to operate the company's equipment at a cost of $1,900.
Oct. 25   Paid $16,700 for the purchase of new equipment and $1,500 to a consultant for testing and installing the equipment.
Nov. 6   Added an elevator and ramps to a building owned by the company to make it wheelchair-accessible for $120,000.
Dec. 31   After recording annual depreciation, Sugden reviewed its property, plant, and equipment for possible impairment. Sugden determined the following:
   1. The recoverable amount of equipment that originally cost $250,000 and has accumulated depreciation of $75,000 is $90,000.
   2. Land that originally cost $575,000 had previously been written down to $500,000 as a result of an impairment in 2014. Circumstances have changed, and the land's recoverable amount is now $600,000.

Instructions

(a) For each of these transactions, indicate if the transaction increased (+) or decreased (−) Land, Building, Equipment, Accumulated Depreciation, total property, plant, and equipment (PP&E), and profit, and by how much. If the item is not changed, write "NE" to indicate there is no effect. Use the following format, in which the first one has been done for you as an example.

Transaction	Land	Building	Equipment	Accumulated Depreciation	Total PP&E	Profit
Jan. 22	NE	NE	NE	NE	NE	−$4,600

(b) Prepare journal entries to record the above transactions. All transactions are on account.

TAKING IT FURTHER   Assume that Sugden also purchased equipment with an expected useful life of 15 years and that the equipment's engine will need to be replaced every five years. Which useful life should Sugden use when calculating depreciation on the equipment? Explain.

Record impairment and calculate revised depreciation. (LO 3) AP

P9–5B   Short Track Speed Skating, a public company, purchased equipment on January 10, 2013, for $600,000. At that time, management estimated that the equipment would have a useful life of 10 years and a residual value of $25,000. Short Track uses the straight line method of depreciation and has a December 31 year end.

     Short Track tested the equipment for impairment on December 31, 2017, after recording the annual depreciation expense. It was determined that the equipment's recoverable amount was $260,000, and that the total estimated useful life would be seven years instead of 10, with a residual value of $10,000 instead of $25,000.

Instructions

(a) Calculate the annual depreciation expense for the years 2013 to 2017 and the carrying amount at December 31, 2017.
(b) Record the impairment loss, if any, on December 31, 2017.
(c) What will appear on Short Track's 2017 income statement and balance sheet with regard to this equipment?
(d) Assuming no further impairments or recoveries, calculate the annual depreciation expense for the years 2018 and 2019.

TAKING IT FURTHER   Why is it important to recognize impairment losses?

Record acquisition, depreciation, impairment, and disposal of land and buildings. (LO 1, 2, 3, 4) AP

P9–6B   SE Parts Supply Company purchased an industrial robot on July 1, 2015, for $395,000. It paid $100,000 in cash and signed a 5% note payable for the balance. The industrial robot was estimated to have a 20-year useful life with a $15,000 residual value. The company has a December 31 year end and prepares adjusting entries annually. It uses the double diminishing-balance method of depreciation to the nearest month for equipment. The following are related transactions and adjustments during the next three years.

2015

Dec. 31	Recorded annual depreciation.
31	Paid the interest owing on the note payable.

2016

May 21	Paid $2,000 to update robot's software system. The updates are required annually.
Dec. 31	Recorded annual depreciation.
31	Paid the interest owing on the note payable.
31	The equipment was tested for impairment. It had a recoverable amount of $275,000.

2017

Mar. 31	Sold the industrial robot for $240,000 cash.
Apr. 1	Paid the note payable and interest owing.

Instructions

(a) Record the above transactions and adjustments, including the acquisition on July 1, 2015.
(b) What factors may have been responsible for the impairment?
(c) Assume instead that the company sold the robot on September 30, 2017, for $260,000 cash. Prepare the journal entries to record the sale.

TAKING IT FURTHER   How might management determine the recoverable amount of the robot at each year end? Does the company need to test the asset for impairment every year?

Calculate and compare depreciation and gain or loss on disposal under three methods of depreciation. (LO 2, 4) AP

P9–7B   On January 3, 2016, Ajax Argyle purchased a piece of equipment for $125,000. The equipment's estimated useful life is either three years or 12,000 units, with a residual value of $18,000. The company has a December 31 fiscal year end and normally uses straight-line depreciation. Management is considering the merits of using the units-of-production or diminishing-balance method of depreciation instead of the straight-line method. The actual numbers of units produced by the equipment were 6,000 in 2016, 2,000 in 2017, and 3,800 in 2018. The equipment was sold on January 5, 2019, for $21,000.

Instructions

(a) Calculate the depreciation for the equipment for 2016 to 2018 under (1) the straight-line method; (2) the diminishing-balance method, using a 45% rate; and (3) units-of-production. (*Hint:* Round the depreciable cost per unit to three decimal places.)
(b) Calculate the gain or loss on the sale of the equipment under each of the three methods.
(c) Calculate the total depreciation expense plus the loss on sale (or minus the gain on sale) under each of the three depreciation methods. Comment on your results.

TAKING IT FURTHER   The owner of Ajax Argyle believes that having a gain or loss on sale indicates the company had made a mistake in calculating depreciation. Do you agree or disagree? Explain.

P9-8B Walker Co. purchased furniture on February 4, 2015, for $70,000 on account. At that time, it was expected to have a useful life of five years and a $1,000 residual value. The furniture was disposed of on January 26, 2018, when the company moved to new premises. Walker Co. uses the diminishing-balance method of depreciation with a 20% rate and calculates depreciation for partial periods to the nearest month. The company has a September 30 year end.

Record acquisition, depreciation, and disposal of furniture. (LO 2, 4) AP

Instructions

(a) Record the acquisition of the furniture on February 4, 2015.
(b) Record depreciation for each of 2015, 2016, and 2017.
(c) Record the disposal on January 26, 2018, under the following assumptions:
  1. It was scrapped and has no residual value.
  2. It was sold for $30,000.
  3. It was sold for $40,000.
  4. It was traded for new furniture with a catalogue price of $100,000. Walker Co. was given a trade-in allowance of $45,000 on the old furniture and paid the balance in cash. Walker Co. determined that the old furniture's fair value was $30,000 at the date of the exchange.

TAKING IT FURTHER What are the arguments in favour of recording gains and losses on disposals of property, plant, and equipment as part of profit from operations? What are the arguments in favour of recording them as non-operating items?

P9-9B At January 1, 2017, Jaina Company, a public company, reported the following property, plant, and equipment accounts:

Record property, plant, and equipment transactions; prepare partial financial statements. (LO 2, 4, 7) AP

Accumulated depreciation—buildings	$12,100,000
Accumulated depreciation—equipment	15,000,000
Building	28,500,000
Equipment	48,000,000
Land	4,000,000

Jaina uses straight-line depreciation for buildings and equipment, and its fiscal year end is December 31. The buildings are estimated to have a 50-year life and no residual value; the equipment is estimated to have a 10-year useful life and no residual value. Interest on all notes is payable or collectible at maturity on the anniversary date of the issue.

During 2017, the following selected transactions occurred:

Apr. 1 Purchased land for $1.9 million. Paid $475,000 cash and issued a 10-year, 6% note for the balance.
May 1 Sold equipment that cost $750,000 when purchased on January 1, 2010. The equipment was sold for $350,000 cash.
June 1 Sold land purchased on June 1, 1996, for $1.2 million. Received $380,000 cash and accepted a 6% note for the balance. The land cost $300,000.
July 1 Purchased equipment for $1 million on account, terms n/60.
Dec. 31 Retired equipment that cost $470,000 when purchased on December 31, 2010.

Instructions

(a) Record the above transactions.
(b) Record any adjusting entries required at December 31, 2017, and update account balances.
(c) Prepare the property, plant, and equipment section of Jaina's balance sheet at December 31, 2017.

TAKING IT FURTHER Why do most companies use the cost model instead of the revaluation model to account for property, plant, and equipment?

P9-10B Due to rapid employee turnover in the accounting department, the following transactions involving intangible assets were recorded in a questionable way by Hahn Company in the year ended August 31, 2017:

Correct errors in recording intangible asset transactions. (LO 6) AP

1. Hahn developed an electronic monitoring device for running shoes. It incurred research costs of $70,000 and development costs of $45,000. It recorded all of these costs in the Patent account.
2. The company registered the patent for the monitoring device developed in transaction 1. Legal fees and registration costs totalled $21,000. These costs were recorded in the Professional Fees Expense account.
3. The company recorded $5,750 of annual amortization on the patent over its legal life of 20 years [($70,000 + $45,000 = $115,000) ÷ 20 years]. The patent's expected economic life is five years. Assume that for amortization purposes, all costs occurred at the beginning of the year.

Instructions

Assuming Hahn reports under ASPE, prepare the journal entries that are needed to correct the errors made during 2017.

TAKING IT FURTHER The majority of the intangible assets reported on a balance sheet have been purchased as opposed to being internally generated. Why? What happens to the cost of an internally generated intangible asset if it is not recorded as an asset?

Record intangible asset transactions; prepare partial balance sheet. (LO 6, 7) AP

P9–11B   The intangible assets section of Ghani Corporation's balance sheet at December 31, 2016, is as follows:

Copyright #1	$36,000	
Less: Accumulated amortization	24,000	$ 12,000
Trademark		52,000
Goodwill		150,000
Total		$214,000

The copyright was acquired in January 2015 and has an estimated useful life of three years. The trademark was acquired in January 2010 and is expected to have an indefinite useful life. The following cash transactions may have affected intangible assets during 2017:

Jan.   2   Paid $7,000 in legal costs to successfully defend the trademark against infringement by another company.

July   1   Developed a new product, incurring $275,000 in research costs and $50,000 in development costs. A patent was granted for the product on July 1, and its useful life is equal to its legal life.

Aug. 1   Paid $45,000 to a popular hockey player to appear in commercials advertising the company's products. The commercials will air in September and October.

Oct.   1   Acquired a second copyright for $168,000. The new copyright has an estimated useful life of six years.

Dec. 31   Recorded annual amortization.

Instructions

(a) Prepare journal entries to record the transactions.

(b) Show how the intangible assets and goodwill will be presented on the balance sheet at December 31, 2017.

TAKING IT FURTHER   Since intangible assets do not have physical substance, why are they considered to be assets?

Record equipment, note payable, and natural resource transactions; prepare partial financial statements. (LO 2, 5, 7) AP

P9–12B   Cypress Timber Company has a December 31 fiscal year end. The following information is related to its Westerlund tract of timber land:

1. Cypress purchased a 50,000-hectare tract of timber land at Westerlund on June 7, 2016, for $50 million, paying $10 million cash and signing a 7% note payable for the balance. Annual interest on the mortgage is due each December 31. The note payable is due December 31, 2018. It is estimated that this tract will yield 1 million tonnes of timber. The timber tract's estimated residual value is $2 million. Cypress expects it will cut all the trees and then sell the Westerlund site in seven years.

2. On June 26, 2016, Cypress purchased and installed equipment at the Westerlund timber site for $196,000 cash. The equipment will be depreciated on a straight-line basis over an estimated useful life of seven years with no residual value. Cypress has a policy of recording depreciation for partial periods to the nearest month. The equipment will be scrapped after the Westerlund site is harvested.

3. In 2016, Cypress cut and sold 110,000 tonnes of timber.

4. In 2017, Cypress cut and sold 240,000 tonnes of timber.

Instructions

(a) Prepare the 2016 and 2017 journal entries for the above, including any year-end adjustments.

(b) Show how property, plant, and equipment, natural resources, and related accounts will be reported on Cypress's December 31, 2017, income statement and balance sheet.

TAKING IT FURTHER   If the total estimated amount of units that will be produced (extracted) changes during the life of the natural resource, is it still appropriate to use the units-of-production method? Explain.

Calculate ratios and comment. (LO 7) AN

P9–13B   Mock Orange Company and Cotoneaster Company both manufacture pruning shears. The following financial information is for three years ended December 31 (in thousands):

Mock Orange Company	2017	2016	2015
Net sales	$9,428.0	$8,894.3	$8,235.5
Profit	627.7	597.8	553.5
Total assets	5,829.1	5,771.4	5,343.9

Cotoneaster Company	2017	2016	2015
Net sales	$3,839.8	$3,656.9	$3,417.7
Profit	143.4	137.9	128.9
Total assets	2,754.5	2,504.1	2,340.3

Instructions

(a) Calculate the asset turnover and return on assets ratios for both companies for 2016 and 2017. Round your answers to two decimal points.

(b) Comment on how effective each of the companies is at using its assets to generate sales and produce profit.

TAKING IT FURTHER   After reading the notes to the financial statements, you have determined that Mock Orange Company uses straight-line depreciation and Cotoneaster uses diminishing-balance. Does this affect your ability to compare these two companies?

CHAPTER 9: BROADENING YOUR PERSPECTIVE

▶ Financial Reporting and Analysis

Financial Reporting Problem

BYP9-1   Refer to the financial statements and the Notes to Consolidated Statements for **Corus Entertainment Inc.**, which are reproduced in Appendix A.

Instructions

(a) For each type of property and equipment that Corus reports in note 6 to its consolidated statement of financial position, identify the following amounts at August 31, 2014: (1) cost, (2) accumulated depreciation, and (3) net carrying amount.

(b) For the broadcast licences (intangible asset) and goodwill that Corus reports in note 9 and in its consolidated statement of financial position, identify the following amounts at August 31, 2014: (1) cost, (2) impairments, and (3) net carrying amount.

(c) Refer to note 6 again and identify the amount of disposals and retirements for the fiscal year ended August 31, 2014.

(d) What total amount did Corus report for depreciation and amortization expense?

(e) Note 3 includes additional details regarding property, plant, and equipment accounting policies. Read the note and answer the following questions:
1. Does Corus use the cost model or revaluation model for property, plant, and equipment?
2. What depreciation method does Corus use for these assets?
3. For each property, plant, and equipment asset, identify the estimated useful life ranges used by Corus for depreciation.
4. When does Corus derecognize assets and how does it calculate gains and losses?

Interpreting Financial Statements

BYP9-2   **WestJet Airlines Ltd.** is one of Canada's leading airlines, offering service to destinations in Canada, the United States, Mexico, and the Caribbean. The following is a partial extract from its December 31, 2014, notes to the financial statements:

Note. 1 (j) Statement of Significant Accounting Policies—Property and Equipment

Property and equipment is stated at cost and depreciated to its estimated residual value. Expected useful lives and depreciation methods are reviewed annually.

Asset class	Basis	Rate
Aircraft, net of estimated residual value	Straight-line	15–20 years
Engine, airframe and landing gear overhaul	Straight-line	5–15 years
Ground property and equipment	Straight-line	3–25 years
Spare engines and rotables, net of estimated residual value	Straight-line	15–20 years
Buildings	Straight-line	40 years
Leasehold improvements	Straight-line	5 years/Term of lease

Estimated residual values of the Corporation's aircraft range between $2,500 and $6,000 (in thousands of dollars) per aircraft. Spare engines have an estimated residual value equal to 10% of the original purchase price. Residual values, where applicable, are reviewed annually against prevailing market rates at the consolidated statement of financial position date.

   Major overhaul expenditures are capitalized and depreciated over the expected life between overhauls. All other costs relating to the maintenance of fleet assets are charged to the consolidated statement of earnings on consumption or as incurred.

Instructions

(a) WestJet uses straight-line depreciation for all of its depreciable property and equipment. For which of the assets shown above might WestJet consider using units-of-production instead of straight-line depreciation? Should WestJet use units-of-production for those assets?

(b) According to this note, major overhaul expenditures are treated differently than other fleet maintenance costs. Explain how WestJet records these items. Is this appropriate? Why or why not?

(c) WestJet depreciates the cost of leasehold improvements over the terms of the leases. Is this appropriate? Are these terms the same as the physical lives of these assets?

(d) Does WestJet use component depreciation for any of its property and equipment assets? Explain.

▶ Critical Thinking

Collaborative Learning Activity

Note to instructor: Additional instructions and material for this group activity can be found on the Instructor Resource Site and in *WileyPLUS*.

BYP9–3 In this learning activity, you will improve your understanding of depreciation by working in small groups to analyze and categorize, on a grid, information about the three methods of depreciation.

Communication Activity

BYP9–4 Long Trucking Corporation is a medium-sized trucking company with trucks that are driven across North America. The company owns large garages and equipment to repair and maintain the trucks. Ken Bond, the controller, knows that assets can be exchanged with or without money being paid or received. The company is considering exchanging a semi-truck with a carrying amount of $100,000 (original cost $165,000) for a garage in a rural area where the company can operate a branch of the repair operation. The garage has a fair value of $90,000 and the semi-truck has a fair value of $75,000. Long Trucking Corporation will also pay the seller an additional $15,000.

Instructions

Write an e-mail to Jason Long (the owner) that explains (1) the financial impact of the exchange on assets and profit and (2) how the transaction should be recorded in the accounting records. Suggest appropriate depreciation methods to use for the garage for future recording.

"All About You" Activity

BYP9–5 In the "All About You" feature, you learned about actions that were taken to strengthen Canada's copyright law and the radical changes in technology that drove the need to update the law. You have recently graduated from a music program and have composed two songs that you believe a recording artist may produce. You are wondering how you can best get copyright protection for your songs.

Instructions

Go to the Canadian Intellectual Property Office website at http://www.cipo.ic.gc.ca and search for its publication "A Guide to Copyright." The guide can be found by clicking on "Learn" in the "Copyright" box midway down the page. (Note that the links may change so a basic search of the site may be required.)

Answer the following questions:

(a) What is a copyright and to what does copyright apply?

(b) How can you obtain a copyright for your songs and what do you have to do to be protected?

(c) What are the benefits to you of getting copyright registration for your songs?

(d) How and where do you register a copyright?

(e) When you register a copyright, you are required to pay a fee for the registration. Should the registration fee for the copyright be recorded as an asset or an expense?

(f) Go to the glossary in "A Guide to Copyright." What is infringement of copyright? Provide a specific example of infringement.

(g) Go to frequently asked questions in "A Guide to Copyright." How long does copyright last?

 ▶ *Santé Smoothie Saga*

(**Note:** This is a continuation of the Santé Smoothie Saga from Chapters 1 through 8.)

BYP9–6 Natalie is thinking of buying a van that will be used only for business. She estimates that she can buy the van for $28,400. Natalie would spend an additional $3,000 to have the van painted. As well, she wants the back seat of the van removed so that she will have lots of room to transport her juicer inventory and smoothies and supplies. The cost of taking out the back seat and installing shelving units is estimated at $1,600. She expects the van to last about five years and to be driven for 200,000 km. The annual cost of vehicle insurance will be $1,440. Natalie estimates that, at the end of the five-year useful life, the van will sell for $5,000. Assume that she will buy the van on December 15, 2017, and it will be ready for use on January 2, 2018.

Natalie is concerned about the impact of the van's cost and related depreciation on Santé Smoothies' income statement and balance sheet.

Instructions

(a) Determine the cost of the van.

(b) Prepare depreciation schedules for the life of the van under the following depreciation methods:
1. straight-line.
2. diminishing-balance at double the straight-line rate.
3. It is estimated that the van will be driven as follows: 30,000 km in 2018, 37,500 km in 2019, 40,000 km in 2020, 47,500 km in 2021, 35,000 km in 2022, and 10,000 km in 2023.

Recall that Santé Smoothies has a May 31 year end.

(c) Which method of depreciation would result in the highest profit for the year ended May 31, 2019? Over the life of the asset?

(d) Which method would result in the highest carrying amount for the van for the year ended May 31, 2019? Over the life of the asset?

(e) Which method of depreciation would you recommend that Natalie use? Why?

ANSWERS TO CHAPTER QUESTIONS

ANSWERS TO ACCOUNTING IN ACTION INSIGHT QUESTIONS

Business Insight, p. 481

Q: Is the units-of-production method the best depreciation method for Morris Formal Wear to use for its tuxedos or would you recommend another method?

A: Since Morris Formal Wear wants to track wear and tear on each of its tuxedos, the units-of-production depreciation method is the best choice. Rental tuxedos are the type of long-lived asset that will physically wear out with use much faster than they would become obsolete due to changing tuxedo styles. By keeping track of how many times each tuxedo has been used, instead of just how old they are, the business can make better decisions about when to replace the tuxedos.

Ethics Insight, p. 484

Q: Is the president's requested change unethical? If so, why?

A: The president's requested change is unethical because he wants to revise the depreciation calculation solely to increase company profits and therefore his bonus. A change in estimate for an asset's useful life should only be made when management decides that wear and tear or obsolescence require a change. Otherwise, changing the asset's useful life just to boost the president's bonus is unfair to readers of financial statements, competitors, and even employees, who may suffer if the company's reputation were damaged because the marketplace found out. The move would also not be fair to the company's auditors, who have a professional obligation to ensure that such changes in estimates are not made for unethical reasons.

All About You Insight, p. 497

Q: Why is it important that the copyrights of artists, writers, musicians, and the entertainment industry be protected?

A: Just as it is important that you as an individual be compensated in your career, it is important that individuals in artistic, music, entertainment, and literary careers be compensated fairly for their creativity. Without fair compensation, Canada's creativity and innovation will be discouraged. Without copyright protection, it may be difficult to ensure that appropriate individuals are fairly compensated and companies may not be willing to invest in creative ventures if the work is not protected.

ANSWERS TO SELF-STUDY QUESTIONS

1. d   2. c   3. b   4. a   5. c   6. b   7. b   8. a   9. b   10. c   11. b   12. d

10 CURRENT LIABILITIES AND PAYROLL

CHAPTER PREVIEW Whether it is a huge company such as one of Canada's chartered banks, a medium-sized company like Nanotech Security Corp., or a small business such as your local convenience store, every company has liabilities. **Liabilities are present obligations resulting from past transactions that will involve future settlement**. Liabilities are classified as current and non-current. As explained in Chapter 4, current liabilities are obligations that are expected to be settled within one year from the balance sheet date or in the company's normal operating cycle. Obligations that are expected to be paid after one year or longer are classified as non-current liabilities. Financial statement users want to know whether a company's obligations are current or non-current. A company that has more current liabilities than current assets often lacks liquidity, or the ability to pay short-term obligations as they become due. This may signal financial difficulties. Therefore, users want to know the types of liabilities a company has and when they will be due.

In this chapter, we explain current liabilities; non-current liabilities will be discussed in Chapter 15. Payroll creates current liabilities and affects almost every company. It is also explained in this chapter.

FEATURE STORY ▶ BUTTERFLIES BRING ABOUT BETTER BANKNOTES

SURREY, B.C.—How does a Canadian company commercialize the same technology that makes a butterfly glow? Nanotech Security Corp., inspired by nature, has developed a way to imprint hologram-like images on objects as diverse as banknotes and designer purses to prevent counterfeiting.

Nanotech uses nanotechnology—a method of manipulating matter on a molecular scale—to chip holes no bigger than one-billionth of a metre (or one nanometre) on an item's surface. These tiny holes reflect light, mimicking the nanostructures of the blue morpho butterfly, whose wings are luminescent. Nanotech's patented process, first developed by the company founders while at Simon Fraser University, is unlike other anti-counterfeiting processes, which inject dyes or pigments onto the surface and can be more easily copied. Nanotech's machines that make the holes are proprietary and expensive—well beyond the reach of typical counterfeiters.

Nanotech is now signing contracts with foreign countries to produce anti-counterfeit images on bank notes. The company hopes to work with luxury goods manufacturers, which can use the technology to etch their logos onto purse clasps, for example, producing a shimmering image that can't be reproduced.

These contracts require a certain accounting treatment, because Nanotech is often asking for money up front before the service is delivered. This revenue that Nanotech collects, but hasn't earned yet until it produces the anti-counterfeiting images on products, is called unearned revenue (also known as deferred revenue). Deferred revenue is considered a current liability because it is an obligation—to provide services under contract—that will be fulfilled within a year.

The biggest share of Nanotech's current liabilities was accounts payable and accrued liabilities, which amounted to $1.6 million as at September 30, 2014.

Sources: Ivor Tossell, "Famous Butterfly Inspires Anti-counterfeiting Nanotechnology," *Globe and Mail*, April 1, 2013; Jameson Berkow, "Nanotech's Big Break," *Financial Post*, February 13, 2012; Nanotech Security Corp. annual report 2014; Nanotech corporate website, http://nanosecurity.ca.

Ingo Arndt/Getty Images

CHAPTER OUTLINE | LEARNING OBJECTIVES

1 **Account for determinable or certain current liabilities.**

Determinable (Certain) Current Liabilities
- Accounts payable
- Unearned revenues
- Operating line of credit and bank overdraft
- Short-term notes payable
- Sales taxes
- Property taxes
- Current maturities of long-term debt

DO IT 1
Reporting current liabilities

2 **Account for uncertain liabilities.**

Uncertain Liabilities
- Provisions
- Contingencies

DO IT 2a
Warranty provisions

DO IT 2b
Reporting and disclosing a contingency

3 **Determine payroll costs and record payroll transactions.**

Payroll
- Employee payroll costs
- Employer payroll costs
- Recording the payroll

DO IT 3
Payroll

4 **Prepare the current liabilities section of the balance sheet.**

Financial Statement Presentation

DO IT 4
Current liabilities on the balance sheet

5 **Calculate mandatory payroll deductions (Appendix 10A).**

Payroll Deductions
- Mandatory payroll deductions
- Using payroll deduction tables

DO IT 5
Employer's payroll deductions

Determinable (Certain) Current Liabilities

In this section of the chapter, we will discuss liabilities where there is no uncertainty about their existence, amount, or timing. Liabilities with a known amount, payee, and due date are often referred to as **determinable liabilities**.

Examples of determinable current liabilities include accounts payable, bank indebtedness from operating lines of credit, notes payable, sales taxes payable, unearned revenue, and current maturities of long-term debt. This category also includes accrued liabilities such as property taxes, payroll, and interest payable.

The entries for accounts payable and determinable unearned revenues have been explained in previous chapters, but we will provide a brief review in this section. We will also discuss the accounting for other types of current liabilities in this section, including bank indebtedness from an operating line of credit, notes payable, sales taxes payable, property taxes payable, and current maturities of long-term debt. Payroll and employee benefits payable are also examples of determinable liabilities, but as the accounting for payroll is complex, we discuss it in a separate section of this chapter.

Alternative terminology Determinable liabilities are also referred to as *certain liabilities* or *known liabilities.*

ACCOUNTS PAYABLE

Whenever an entity buys goods from a supplier with the agreement to pay at a later date, an **account payable** (sometimes referred to as a "trade payable") is created. Most businesses require payment within 30 days; therefore, accounts payable are classified as current liabilities. For example, recall from previous chapters that when an entity buys supplies, the required journal entry is as follows:

A	=	L	+	OE
+500		+500		

Cash flows: no effect

Apr. 6	Supplies	500	
	Accounts Payable		500
	To record purchase of supplies.		

When this journal entry is posted, the current liability is now recorded until the payment is made.

Accounts payable, or trade accounts payable, are often the largest current liability on a company's balance sheet, as is the case with Nanotech Security Corp. In another example, as shown on Corus Entertainment's balance sheet excerpt in Illustration 10-1, its trade and other payables amounted to $170,411 thousand, which is almost 97% of its total current liabilities.

▶ ILLUSTRATION 10-1
Corus Entertainment Inc.'s current liabilities

CORUS ENTERTAINMENT INC.	
Consolidated Statement of Financial Position (partial)	
August 31, 2014 (in thousands)	
Accounts payable and accrued liabilities (*note 11*)	170,411
Provisions (*note 12*)	5,314
Total current liabilities	175,725

UNEARNED REVENUES

As noted in the feature story on Nanotech, unearned revenues are common for many businesses. This is especially true for entities in the publishing, entertainment, and travel industries. For example, when a magazine publisher, such as Rogers Communications, sells magazine subscriptions to *Sportsnet* or *LouLou*, it receives payment in advance when the customer order is placed. An airline, such as WestJet, often receives cash when it sells tickets for future flights. Season tickets for concerts, sporting events (as we saw in the feature story on Maple Leaf Sports and Entertainment in Chapter 3), and theatre programs are also paid for in advance. How do companies account for unearned revenues that are received before goods are delivered or services are performed?

1. When a company receives the payment in advance, it debits cash and credits a current liability account identifying the source of the unearned revenue.
2. When the company provides the goods or performs the service, the performance obligation is satisfied, and the company recognizes the revenue earned as it debits an unearned revenue account and credits a revenue account.

To illustrate, assume that the Saint John Seadogs hockey team sells 10,000 season tickets at $50 each for its five-game home schedule. The Seadogs make the following entry for the sale of season tickets.

Aug. 6	Cash	500,000	
	Unearned Revenue		500,000
	To record sale of 10,000 season tickets.		

$$A = L + OE$$
$$+500,000 \quad +500,000$$
↑Cash flows: +500,000

As each game is completed, the team records the recognition of revenue with the following entry.

Sept. 7	Unearned Revenue	100,000	
	Ticket Revenue		100,000
	To record hockey ticket revenue earned.		

$$A = L + OE$$
$$-100,000 \quad +100,000$$
Cash flows: no effect

The account Unearned Revenue is reported as a current liability. As the Saint John team recognizes revenue, it reclassifies the amount from Unearned Revenue to Ticket Revenue. For some companies, unearned revenue is material. For example, in the airline industry, tickets sold for future flights can represent almost 50% of total current liabilities.

Illustration 10-2 shows common types of unearned and earned revenue in selected types of businesses.

	Types of Revenue	
Type of Business	**Unearned Revenue**	**Revenue**
Airline	Unearned Ticket Revenue	Ticket Revenue
Magazine publisher	Unearned Subscription Revenue	Subscription Revenue
Hotel	Unearned Rent Revenue	Rent Revenue

▶ILLUSTRATION **10-2**
Common types of unearned and earned revenue

Helpful hint Unearned revenues are the opposite of prepaid accounts. For prepaid assets, the cash is paid out before the service or goods are received. For unearned revenues, the cash is received before the goods or services are provided.

OPERATING LINE OF CREDIT AND BANK OVERDRAFT

Operating Line of Credit

Current assets (such as accounts receivable) do not always turn into cash at the exact time that current liabilities (such as accounts payable) must be paid. Consequently, most companies have an **operating line of credit** at their bank to help them manage temporary cash shortfalls. This means that the company has been pre-authorized by the bank to borrow money when it is needed, up to a pre-set limit.

Security, called **collateral**, is usually required by the bank as protection in case the company is unable to repay the loan. Collateral normally includes some, or all, of the company's current assets (e.g., accounts receivable or inventories); investments; or property, plant, and equipment.

Money borrowed through a line of credit is normally borrowed on a short-term basis, and is repayable on demand by the bank. In reality, repayment is rarely demanded without notice. A line of credit makes it very easy for a company to borrow money. It does not have to make a call or visit its bank to actually arrange the transaction. The bank simply covers any cheques written in excess of the bank account balance, up to the approved credit limit.

Bank Overdraft

Some companies have a negative (credit), or overdrawn, cash balance at year end. This amount is usually called *bank indebtedness*, *bank overdraft*, or *bank advances*. No special entry or account is required to record the overdrawn amount. The Cash account has a credit balance because the dollar amount of cheques written exceeded the dollar amount of deposits. The credit balance in Cash is reported as a current liability with the appropriate note disclosure.

Interest is usually charged on the overdrawn amount at a floating rate, such as prime plus a specified percentage. The **prime rate** is the interest rate that banks charge their best customers. This rate is usually increased by a specified percentage according to the company's risk profile.

SHORT-TERM NOTES PAYABLE

The line of credit described above is similar to a **note payable**. Notes payable are obligations in the form of written promissory notes. Notes payable are often used instead of accounts payable because they give the lender formal proof of the obligation in case legal remedies are needed to collect the debt. Companies frequently issue notes payable to meet short-term financing needs. Notes payable usually require the borrower to pay interest.

Notes are issued for varying periods. **Notes payable due for payment within one year of the balance sheet date are classified as current liabilities.** Most notes payable are interest-bearing, with interest due monthly or at maturity.

To illustrate the accounting for notes payable, assume that Koh Co. borrows $100,000 from the local caisse populaire (credit union) on March 1 for four months, at an interest rate of 6%.

Koh makes the following journal entry when it signs the note and receives the $100,000:

> **Helpful hint** Notes payable are the opposite of notes receivable, and the accounting is similar.

A	=	L	+ OE
+100,00		+100,00	

↑Cash flows: +100,000

Helpful hint Interest is normally calculated using the number of days. In this textbook, we use months in order to simplify the calculations.

Mar. 1	Cash	100,000	
	Notes Payable		100,000
	To record issue of four-month, 6% note to		
	Caisse Populaire Dumoulin.		

Interest accrues over the life of the note; therefore, the company must periodically record the interest accrual. If Koh prepares financial statements annually and it has an April 30 year end, it will have to make an adjusting entry to recognize the interest expense and interest payable at April 30.

Recall from Chapter 3 that **interest is calculated by multiplying the principal amount by the annual interest rate by the fraction of the year in the accrual.** The formula for calculating interest for Koh is shown in Illustration 10-3.

Helpful hint Interest rates are always expressed as annual rates, not the rate for the duration of the note.

▶**ILLUSTRATION**  **10-3**
Formula for calculating interest

Face Value of Note		Annual Interest Rate		Time in Terms of One Year		Interest
$100,000	×	6%	×	$^2/_{12}$	=	$1,000

The adjusting entry to record the interest is:

A	=	L	+ OE
		+1,000	−1,000

Cash flows: no effect

Apr. 30	Interest Expense	1,000	
	Interest Payable		1,000
	To accrue interest to April 30.		

In the April 30 financial statements, the current liabilities section of the balance sheet will show notes payable of $100,000 and interest payable of $1,000. In addition, interest expense of $1,000 will be reported as other expenses in the income statement. **Interest payable is shown separately from the note payable.**

At maturity (July 1), Koh Co. must pay the face value of the note ($100,000) plus $2,000 interest ($100,000 × 6% × $^4/_{12}$). Two months ($1,000) of this interest has already been accrued. Interest must also be updated for $1,000 ($100,000 $\times$ 6% $\times$ 2/12) for the two additional months—May and June—since interest was last recorded.

July 1	Interest Expense		1,000	
	Interest Payable			1,000
	To accrue interest for May and June.			
1	Notes Payable		100,000	
	Interest Payable ($1,000 + $1,000)		2,000	
	Cash ($100,000 + $2,000)			102,000
	To record payment of Caisse Populaire			
	Dumoulin note and accrued interest.			

A	=	L	+	OE
		+1,000		−1,000

Cash flows: no effect

A	=	L	+	OE
−102,000		−100,000		
		−2,000		

▼ Cash flows: −102,000

The calculation of total interest expense over the life of the note is shown in Illustration 10-4.

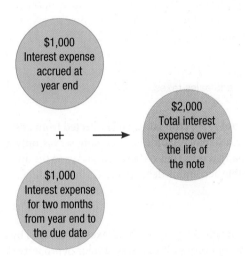

▶ ILLUSTRATION 10-4
Calculation of total interest expense over the life of the note

SALES TAXES

As a consumer, you are well aware that you pay sales taxes on most products and services. For businesses, sales taxes are collected from customers on behalf of the government. Taxes collected are therefore a liability. The business has an obligation to pay the amount collected to the appropriate government body.

Sales taxes are expressed as a percentage of the sales price. As discussed in earlier chapters and in Appendix B at the end of this textbook, sales taxes usually take the form of the federal Goods and Services Tax (GST) and Provincial Sales Tax (PST) or a combined Harmonized Sales Tax (HST). The following table summarizes the sales taxes by province or territory at the time of writing:

Province/Territory	GST	PST	HST
Newfoundland and Labrador			13%
Nova Scotia			15%
Prince Edward Island			14%
New Brunswick			13%
Quebec	5%	9.975%	
		(known as Quebec Sales Tax)	
Ontario			13%
Saskatchewan	5%	5%	
Manitoba	5%	8%	
Alberta	5%		
British Columbia	5%	7%	
Northwest Territories/Yukon/Nunavut	5%		

In Ontario, Newfoundland and Labrador, and New Brunswick, the PST and GST have been combined into one 13% HST. Prince Edward Island has a 14% HST and Nova Scotia a 15% HST. Quebec, Alberta, British Columbia, Manitoba, Saskatchewan, Yukon, Northwest Territories, and Nunavut do not have HST.

Whether GST, PST, or HST, the business collects the tax from the customer when the sale occurs. The business then pays (remits) the sales taxes collected to the designated federal and provincial collecting authorities. In the case of GST, HST, and the Quebec Sales Tax or QST, collections may be offset against sales taxes paid by the business on its purchases. In such cases, only the net amount owing or recoverable must be paid or refunded. Depending on the size of the business, the sales taxes must be sent to the government monthly, quarterly, or, for very small companies, annually.

The amount of the sale and the amount of the sales tax collected are usually rung up separately on the cash register. The cash register readings are then used to credit sales or services and the correct sales taxes payable accounts. For example, if the March 25 cash register reading for Comeau Company, in New Brunswick, shows sales of $10,000 and Harmonized Sales Tax of $1,300 ($10,000 × 13% HST rate), the entry is as follows:

A = L + OE
+11,300 +1,300 +10,000

⬆Cash flows: +11,300

Mar. 25	Cash	11,300	
	Sales		10,000
	HST Payable		1,300
	To record sales and sales taxes.		

Comeau Company does **not** report the sales taxes collected from customers as revenue; sales taxes collected from customers are a liability. Comeau Company serves only as a collection agent for the government. When the company remits (pays) these sales taxes to the appropriate government collecting authorities, the HST Payable account is debited and Cash is credited.

PROPERTY TAXES

Businesses that own property pay property taxes. These taxes are charged by municipal governments, and are calculated at a specified rate for every $100 of assessed value of property (land and buildings). Property taxes generally cover a full calendar year, although bills are not issued until the spring of each year.

To illustrate, assume that Tantramar Management owns land and a building in Regina. Tantramar's year end is December 31 and it makes adjusting entries annually. On March 1, it receives its property tax bill of $6,000 for the calendar year, which is due to be paid on May 31.

In March, when Tantramar receives the property tax bill for the calendar year, two months of that year have passed. The company records the property tax expense for the months of January and February and the liability owed at that point as follows:

A = L + OE
+1,000 −1,000

Cash flows: no effect

Mar. 1	Property Tax Expense ($6,000 × $^2/_{12}$)	1,000	
	Property Tax Payable		1,000
	To record property tax expense for January		
	and February and amount owing.		

On May 31, when Tantramar pays the property tax bill, the company records the payment of the liability recorded on March 1. It also records the expense incurred to date for the months of March, April, and May. As at May 31, five months have passed and should be recorded as property tax expense. The remaining seven months of the year are recorded as a prepayment, as shown in the following entry:

A = L + OE
+3,500 −1,000 −1,500
−6,000

⬇ Cash flows: −6,000

May. 31	Property Tax Payable	1,000	
	Property Tax Expense ($6,000 × $^3/_{12}$)	1,500	
	Prepaid Property Tax ($6,000 × $^7/_{12}$)	3,500	
	Cash		6,000
	To record payment of property tax expense		
	for March through May, and amount prepaid		
	for June through December.		

After the payment of the property tax, Tantramar has a zero balance in its liability account but still has a prepayment. Since Tantramar makes adjusting entries only annually, it would not adjust the prepaid property tax account until year end, December 31. At that time, it would make the following entry:

Dec. 31	Property Tax Expense	3,500	
	Prepaid Property Tax		3,500
	To record property tax expense for June through December.		

A	=	L	+	OE
−3,500				−3,500

Cash flows: no effect

There are other acceptable ways to record and adjust property taxes. Some companies would debit Property Tax Expense when the bill is recorded on March 1 and avoid a later adjusting entry. In addition, companies may prepare monthly or quarterly adjusting entries. Whatever way is used, at year end, the companies would have the same ending balances. In this case, the accounts Prepaid Property Tax and Property Tax Payable should each have a zero balance and Property Tax Expense should have a balance of $6,000.

CURRENT MATURITIES OF LONG-TERM DEBT

Companies often have a portion of long-term debt that will be due in the current year. That amount is considered a current liability. Assume that on January 1, 2017, Cudini Construction issues a $25,000, five-year note payable. Each January 1, starting on January 1, 2018, $5,000 of the note will be repaid. When financial statements are prepared on December 31, 2017, $5,000 should be reported on the balance sheet as a current liability and the remaining $20,000 of the note should be reported as a long-term liability. Companies often present this current liability as **current portion of long-term debt**. The Canadian winery Andrew Peller Ltd. reported almost $7.4 million of such debt (Illustration 10-5).

ANDREW PELLER LTD.
Balance Sheet (partial) March 31, 2014 (in thousands)
Current Portion of Long-Term Debt (note 11)   7,392

▶ILLUSTRATION 10-5
Andrew Peller Ltd.'s current portion of long-term debt

It is not necessary to prepare an adjusting entry to recognize the current maturity of long-term debt. The proper statement classification of each liability account is recognized when the balance sheet is prepared.

BEFORE YOU GO ON...DO IT	1	**Reporting Current Liabilities**

Prepare the journal entries to record the following transactions for DiMaria Enterprises. Round any calculations to the nearest dollar.

1. Accrue interest on January 31 (the company's year end) for a $10,000, 30-month, 8% note payable issued on December 1. Interest is payable the first of each month, beginning January 1.
2. The cash register total for sales on April 2 is $250,000. The HST tax rate is 13%. Record the sales and sales taxes.
3. A property tax bill of $12,000 for the calendar year is received on May 1 and is due on June 30. Record the entry on May 1, assuming the company has a January 31 year end.

(continued)

Action Plan

- The formula for interest is as follows: principal (face) value × annual interest rate × time.
- Record sales separately from sales taxes. To calculate sales taxes, multiply the sales total by the sales tax rate.
- Record the property tax expense and the property tax payable for amounts incurred (owed) to date.

BEFORE YOU GO ON...DO IT ❶   **Reporting Current Liabilities** *(continued)*

Solution

Jan. 31	Interest Expense ($10,000 × 8% × $^1/_{12}$)	67	
	Interest Payable		67
	To accrue interest on note payable.		
Apr. 2	Cash	282,500	
	Sales		250,000
	HST Payable ($250,000 × 13%)		32,500
	To record sales and sales taxes.		
May 1	Property Tax Expense ($12,000 × $^3/_{12}$)	3,000	
	Property Tax Payable		3,000
	To record property tax for February, March, and April.		

Related exercise material: BE10–1, BE10–2, BE10–3, BE10–4, BE10–5, BE10–6, BE10–7, E10–1, E10–2, E10–3, E10–4, E10–5, E10–6, E10–7, E10–8, and E10–9.

LEARNING OBJECTIVE ❷   **Account for uncertain liabilities.**

Uncertain Liabilities

In the previous section, we discussed current liabilities where there was a high degree of certainty. It was known who required payment, the amount to be paid, and when the payment was due. However, this may not always be the case. In this section, we will discuss liabilities that have a lower degree of certainty but are still likely to occur. We will then discuss situations where there is an even greater degree of uncertainty, as sometimes the determination of a liability may depend on a future event.

PROVISIONS

Alternative terminology Provisions are also known as *estimated liabilities.*

A **provision** is a liability that exists but the amount and the timing of the settlement are uncertain. We know we owe someone, but we are not sure how much and when. We may not even know whom we owe. Common provisions include product warranties, customer loyalty programs, and gift cards. We discuss these three provisions in the following sections.

Product Warranties

Product warranties are promises made by the seller to repair or replace a product if it is defective or does not perform as intended. Warranties (also known as guarantees) are usually issued by manufacturers. For a specified period of time after the item was sold, a manufacturer may promise to repair the item, replace it, or refund the buyer's money under certain conditions. As a buyer, it is important to read all warranty contracts carefully because the promises they make can be quite different.

Warranties will lead to future costs for the manufacturer for the repair or replacement of defective units. When goods are sold, it is not known which units will become defective. The company does not know whom it will have to pay, or when. The company does know a liability exists even though the payee and timing are unknown.

There are two possible approaches to accounting for product warranties: the expense approach and the revenue approach. In this chapter, we will illustrate the expense approach. The revenue approach is explained in an intermediate accounting textbook.

Under the expense approach, the warranty liability is measured using the estimated future cost of honouring the product's warranty. At the time the product is sold, the costs are not known, but based on past experience with a particular product, most companies are able to estimate it. Using the estimated amount, the company records a warranty expense and a liability. This ensures the company recognizes the full cost of the sale in the period in which the sale occurs. Recall that this is known as matching expenses with revenues. As the actual costs are incurred in subsequent periods, the liability is reduced.

To illustrate the expense approach of accounting for warranty liabilities, assume that Hermann Company sells 10,000 stereos at an average price of $600 in the year ended December 31, 2017. The selling price includes a one-year warranty on parts. Based on past experience, it is expected that 500 units (5%) will be defective, and that warranty repair costs will average $100 per unit.

At December 31, it is necessary to accrue the estimated warranty costs for the 2017 sales. The calculation is as follows:

Number of units sold	10,000
Estimated rate of defective units	× 5%
Total estimated defective units	500
Average warranty repair cost	× $100
Estimated product warranty liability	$50,000

The adjusting entry is:

Dec. 31	Warranty Expense	50,000	
	Warranty Liability		50,000
	To accrue estimated warranty costs.		

A = L + OE
+50,000 −50,000
Cash flows: no effect

In 2017, warranty contracts were honoured on 300 units at a total cost of $30,000. These costs are recorded when they are incurred, but for our illustration they are being recorded in one summary journal entry for the year:

Dec. 31	Warranty Liability	30,000	
	Repair Parts Inventory (and/or Wages Payable)		30,000
	To record honouring of 300 warranty contracts on 2017 sales.		

A = L + OE
−30,000 −30,000
Cash flows: no effect

As demonstrated in the T accounts below, in 2017, a warranty expense of $50,000 is reported as an operating expense in the income statement. The remaining estimated warranty liability of $20,000 ($50,000 − $30,000) is classified as a current liability on the balance sheet.

Warranty Expense		Warranty Liability		
50,000		Actual 30,000	Estimate	50,000
(Income Statement)			Bal. Dec. 31, 2017	20,000
			(Balance Sheet)	

In 2018, all costs incurred to honour warranty contracts on 2017 sales should be debited to the Warranty Liability account, like what was shown above for the 2017 sales. The Warranty Liability account will be carried forward from year to year—increased by the current year's estimated expense and decreased by the actual warranty costs incurred. It is quite likely that the actual expenses will not exactly equal the estimated liability amount. Every year, as is done with accounts receivable and the allowance for doubtful accounts, the warranty liability is reviewed and adjusted if necessary.

Customer Loyalty Programs

To attract or keep customers, many companies offer **customer loyalty programs.** Loyalty programs are designed to increase sales and are important for many businesses. These programs provide customers with future savings on the merchandise or services the company sells. Customer loyalty programs take varying forms. Some programs, such as airline frequent flyer programs, may require customers to collect points. Other programs may involve a credit reward that provides a cash discount on future sales.

The most successful loyalty program in Canadian retail history is Canadian Tire "money" (CTM), first introduced in 1958. The "money" resembles real currency (although the bills are considerably smaller than Bank of Canada notes) and is issued with no expiry date. CTM is given out by the cashiers for purchases paid for by cash, debit card, or the Canadian Tire Options MasterCard credit card. Customers can use CTM to buy anything at a Canadian Tire store. In fact, some privately owned businesses in Canada also accept CTM as payment since the owners of many of these businesses shop at Canadian Tire. Recently the company broadened the loyalty program and implemented an e-money program. Customers can now earn e-Canadian Tire "money" when store purchases are made. e-money is collected by the customer by showing their Canadian Tire mobile app, program card, or key fob with their payment. Like the paper money, the e-money never expires and it can be transferred to other loyalty program members.

Customer loyalty programs result in a liability to the business in the form of unearned or deferred revenue. When customers purchase goods or services and are awarded a loyalty benefit, there is a promise to deliver further goods or services in the future, either for free or at a discount. This promise results in a performance obligation to the entity. To record this future performance obligation, a portion of the original sales price should be allocated to unearned revenue until the future performance obligation is satisfied. The allocation of the selling price should be based on the stand-alone value of the goods or services sold and the stand-alone value of the goods or services promised. The stand-alone value is the amount at which the entity would sell the goods or services to the customer individually. The portion of the sale allocated to the loyalty program is recorded as unearned revenue. When the loyalty points are redeemed and the promised goods or services are delivered to the customer, the performance obligation is satisfied and the unearned revenue is earned.

To illustrate, assume that Greenville Co-op has a rewards program whereby customers get 1 point for every $10 spent on groceries. Each point is redeemable for a $1 discount towards the future purchase of groceries. During the month of April, the Co-op sells goods worth $100,000 and consequently awards customers 10,000 points. Based on past history, Greenville Co-op estimates that 90% of the rewards will be redeemed. Therefore, it is expected that 9,000 points will be redeemed with a stand-alone value of $9,000. A portion of the $100,000 of sales is to be allocated to the rewards program based on the total stand-alone value of $109,000 ($100,000 + $9,000). The revenue allocation for the current sales and the unearned revenue will be as follows:

Amount related to the revenue earned   = $100,000 ($100,000 ÷ $109,000)   = $91,743
Amount related to the loyalty points   = $100,000 ($9,000 ÷ $109,000)   = $8,257

Greenville will record the following journal entry to record the sale of the goods and the liability relating to the future redemption of the rewards points for the month of April:

A	=	L	+	OE
+100,000		+8,257		+91,743

↑Cash flows: +100,000

April 30	Cash	100,000	
	Sales		91,743
	Unearned Revenue—Loyalty Program		8,257
	To record the sales and unearned revenue related to the loyalty program.		

The account Unearned Revenue—Loyalty Program is a current liability that is reported on the balance sheet. It represents the unearned revenue related to the customer loyalty program. As the loyalty points are redeemed, the unearned revenue becomes earned.

To illustrate this, customers of the Greenville Co-op redeemed 4,500 points during the month of May. That is, half of the rewards issued in April were redeemed in May. This means half of the unearned revenue was earned during the month of May and must be recorded. Therefore, Greenville Co-op makes the following entry at the end of May (ignoring the cost of sales):

A	=	L	+	OE
		−4,129		+4,129

Cash flows: no effect

May 31	Unearned Revenue—Loyalty Program	4,129	
	Revenue from Rewards Program		4,129
	To record the redemption of rewards during May.		

Gift Cards

Gift cards or gift certificates have become an increasingly popular source of revenue for many companies. They are unearned revenues in that the company receives cash in advance of providing the goods or the services. Thus, when gift cards are issued, the Unearned Revenue account (liability) is credited. As the gift card is redeemed (used), the company will then record the sales or service revenue and reduce or debit the Unearned Revenue account.

Alternative terminology Unearned revenue is sometimes called *deferred revenue.*

As with customer loyalty programs, the difficulty with gift cards is that it is unknown when and even if the card will be redeemed. If an entity is able to estimate the gift card balances that will not be redeemed and there is little possibility of a reversal, the amount not expected to be redeemed may be taken into revenue as the gift card revenue is earned. If the entity is not able to estimate how much will remain unredeemed, then it may only recognize the related revenue once the possibility of redemption is remote. As with warranties and customer loyalty programs, a company with a gift card program will need to use past experience to estimate the appropriate balance for the liability.

ACCOUNTING IN ACTION
ACROSS THE ORGANIZATION

Almost every retailer offers some kind of customer loyalty program, through club memberships, discount cards, or points programs. Shoppers Drug Mart was one of the first retailers to take this trend a step further by having its Optimum Points program benefit others as well as customers. Shoppers Optimum Points® Donation Program allows Optimum card holders to donate some or all of their points to one of many registered charitable organizations. The organizations can then use the points to purchase products and supplies they need for their day-to-day activities and ongoing fundraising events. A wide variety of charitable organizations, both national and provincial, have signed up to receive the points.

LuckyImages/Shutterstock

Q A company's marketing department is responsible for designing customer loyalty programs. Why would Shoppers' marketing department add the option of donating points to charity?

BEFORE YOU GO ON...DO IT **2a** **Warranty Provisions**

Hockey Gear Company sells hockey skates with a two-year warranty against defects. The company expects that of the units sold each year, 5% will be returned in the first year after they are sold and 2% will be returned in the second year. The average cost to repair or replace a defective unit under warranty is $50. The company reported the following sales and warranty cost information:

	Units Sold	Actual Warranty Costs Incurred
2016	10,000	$20,000
2017	15,000	45,000

Calculate the balance in the Warranty Expense and Warranty Liability accounts at the end of 2017.

Solution

2016: Total defective units = 5% + 2% = 7%
10,000 × 7% = 700 × $50 = $35,000

Warranty Expense		Warranty Liability			
35,000		Actual	20,000	Estimate	35,000
				Bal. Dec. 31, 2016	15,000

2017: 15,000 × 7% = 1,050 × $50 = $52,500

Warranty Expense		Warranty Liability			
52,500		Actual	20,000	Estimate	35,000
				Bal. Dec. 31, 2016	15,000
		Actual	45,000	Estimate	52,500
				Bal. Dec. 31, 2017	22,500

Related exercise material: BE10–8, BE10–9, BE10–10, BE10–11, E10–11, E10–12, and E10–13.

Action Plan
- Calculate the warranty expense by multiplying the number of units sold by the percentage that is expected to be returned and by the average warranty cost.
- Record warranty expenses in the period of the sale.
- The warranty liability is increased by the expense in each period and decreased by the actual costs of repairs and replacements.

CONTINGENCIES

The current liabilities discussed earlier in this chapter were either definitely determinable or estimable. While it might have been necessary to estimate the timing or amount, in both cases there was no uncertainty about their existence. With **contingencies**, there is much more uncertainty about the timing and amount and even the existence of a liability.

In general, a **contingent liability** is a possible obligation resulting from a past event. Whether an actual liability exists is dependent on a future event that will confirm the liability's existence or non-existence.

Lawsuits are good examples of contingencies. The existence of a loss and the related liability depend on the outcome of the lawsuit. The settlement of the lawsuit will confirm the existence of the liability, the amount payable, the payee, and/or the date payable. Under IFRS, the term contingent liability refers only to possible obligations that are not recognized in the financial statements. A contingency that is considered probable would be classified as a provision and recorded under IRFS. Under ASPE, a liability for a contingent loss is recorded if **both** of the following conditions are met:

1. The contingency is *likely* (the chance of occurrence is high).
2. The amount of the contingency can be *reasonably estimated*.

Therefore, if it is likely that the company will lose a lawsuit, and if the amount can be reliably estimated, then the company must record the loss and the liability.

When a contingent loss is likely, but it cannot be reasonably estimated, or if its likelihood of occurrence is not determinable, it is necessary only to disclose the contingency in the notes to the financial statements. In that case, a liability is not recorded.

If a contingency is unlikely—the chance of occurrence is small—it should still be disclosed if the event could have a substantial negative effect on the company's financial position. Otherwise, it does not need to be disclosed. A loan guarantee is an example of a contingency that should be disclosed even if the chance of having to pay is small. General risk contingencies that can affect anyone who is operating a business, such as the possibility of a war, strike, or recession, are not reported in the notes to the financial statements.

In the sample note disclosure from Bombardier Inc.'s financial statements in Illustration 10-6, the company is unable to reasonably estimate probable losses. Therefore, they are only disclosed in this note.

▶ **ILLUSTRATION 10-6**
Note disclosure on contingencies by Bombardier Inc.

BOMBARDIER INC.
December 31, 2014
Excerpt: Note 37

Litigation
In the normal course of operations, the Corporation is a defendant in certain legal proceedings currently pending before various courts in relation to product liability and contract disputes with customers and other third parties.

The Corporation intends to vigorously defend its position in these matters.

While the Corporation cannot predict the final outcome of all legal proceedings pending as at December 31, 2014, based on information currently available, management believes that the resolution of these legal proceedings will not have a material adverse effect on its financial position.

S-Bahn claim
On March 4, 2013, S-Bahn Berlin GMBH ("SB") filed a claim against Bombardier Transportation GmbH, a wholly owned subsidiary of the Corporation, in the Berlin District Court ("Landgericht Berlin"), concerning the trains of the 481 Series delivered to SB between 1996 and 2004.

This lawsuit alleges damages of an aggregate value of €348 million ($423 million) related to allegedly defective wheels and braking systems. The claim is for payment of €241 million ($293 million) and also for a declaratory judgment obliging the Corporation to compensate SB for further damages. SB currently alleges such further damages to be €107 million ($130 million).

It is the Corporation's position that this claim i) is filed in absence of any defect, ii) is not founded on any enforceable warranty, iii) is filed after the expiry of any statute of limitations and iv) is based on inapplicable standards. The lawsuit contains allegations against the Corporation which the Corporation rejects as unfounded and defamatory. The Corporation intends to vigorously defend its position and will undertake all actions necessary to protect its reputation.

ACCOUNTING IN ACTION
ACROSS THE ORGANIZATION

Contingent liabilities abound in the real world, and their amounts are often large and difficult to estimate. The cost of government-regulated environmental cleanup of contaminated sites, for example, can run in the millions of dollars. Calgary-based Agrium Inc., a global producer and marketer of fertilizer and other agricultural products and services, reported environmental remediation liabilities for certain facilities and sites of an estimated $169 million as at December 31, 2014. The company is expected to settle those liabilities by 2038. Possible liabilities due to lawsuits are also common. Air Canada, for example, had a provision of $27 million as at December 31, 2014, relating to outstanding legal claims that it and other air carriers had violated European Union rules regarding cargo fees. The provision was an estimate based on Air Canada's assessment of the potential outcome of the legal proceedings.

Sources: Agrium 2014 annual report; Air Canada 2014 annual report.

Q Environmental contingencies are generally considered to be harder to estimate than contingencies from lawsuits. What might be the reason for this difference?

BEFORE YOU GO ON...DO IT **Reporting and Disclosing a Contingency**

A list of possible contingencies follows. Identify whether each of the following should be recorded, disclosed, or not reported:

1. A factory risks being damaged by floods. The building is located on a flood plain but has never experienced any damage from flooding in the past.
2. The government may expropriate a company's assets so that a new highway can be built. So far, there have been no discussions about how much the government might pay the company.
3. A public company is being sued for $1 million for wrongful dismissal of a company executive.
4. A company has guaranteed other companies' loans but the guarantees are unlikely to result in any payments.
5. A private company following ASPE is being sued for negligence and damages by a customer who slipped and broke a leg in the company's store.

Solution

1. No disclosure required.
2. Disclosure required.
3. If it is probable that the company will lose and the amount can be reasonably estimated, then this would be recorded as a provision; otherwise, just disclose.
4. Disclosure required.
5. If it is likely that the company will lose and the amount can be reasonably estimated, then this is recorded as a contingent liability; otherwise, just disclose.

Related exercise material: BE10–12, BE10–13, E10–14, and E10–15.

Action Plan
- Under IFRS, contingent liabilities are disclosed, as once they are recorded, they become provisions.
- Recall that under ASPE, contingent liabilities are recorded if they are likely and can be reasonably estimated.
- If the amounts cannot be estimated, they are only disclosed. Contingencies are not disclosed if they are unlikely unless they could have a substantial negative impact on the entity.

LEARNING OBJECTIVE 3 Determine payroll costs and record payroll transactions.

Payroll

Payroll and related fringe benefits often make up a large percentage of current liabilities. Employee compensation is often the most significant expense that a company incurs. For example, Costco recently reported 103,000 total employees and labour and fringe benefits costs that amounted to approximately 70% of the company's total cost of operations. Similarly, Nanotech, our chapter feature story, reports payroll-related expenses that are over 60% of its general and administration expenses.

Payroll accounting involves more than just paying employee salaries and wages. In addition to paying salaries and wages, companies are required by law to have payroll records for each employee, to report and remit payroll deductions, and to abide by provincial and federal laws on employee compensation. There are up to 190 different pieces of legislation and regulations that employers have to consider when doing payroll. In this section, we will discuss some of the basic issues regarding payroll costs, journalizing payroll, and payroll records. In the appendix to this chapter, we explain calculating mandatory payroll deductions.

There are two types of payroll costs to a company: (1) employee costs and (2) employer costs. Employee costs involve the gross amount earned by employees. Employer costs involve amounts paid by the employer on behalf of the employee (employee benefits). We will explore employee and employer payroll costs in the following sections.

EMPLOYEE PAYROLL COSTS

Accounting for employee payroll costs involves calculating (1) gross pay, (2) payroll deductions, and (3) net pay.

Gross Pay

Gross pay, or earnings, is the total compensation earned by an employee. It consists of salaries or wages, plus any bonuses and commissions. The terms "salaries" and "wages" are often used interchangeably and the total amount of salaries or wages earned by the employee is called **gross pay**, or gross earnings.

In addition to the hourly pay rate, most companies are required by law to pay hourly workers for overtime work at the rate of at least one and one-half times the government-regulated minimum hourly wage. The number of hours that need to be worked before overtime becomes payable is based on a standard workweek. A 44-hour standard workweek is fairly common but this will vary by industry and occupation. Most employees in executive, managerial, and administrative positions do not earn overtime pay.

To illustrate gross pay, assume that Mark Jordan works for Academy Company as a shipping clerk. His authorized pay rate is $20 per hour. The calculation of Mark's gross pay for the 48 hours shown on his time card for the weekly pay period ending June 23, 2017, is as follows:

Type of Pay	Hours	×	Rate	=	Gross Pay
Regular	44	×	$20	=	$ 880
Overtime	4	×	30	=	120
Total	48				$1,000

This calculation assumes that Mark receives one and one-half times his regular hourly rate ($20 × 1.5) for any hours worked in excess of 44 hours per week (overtime). Overtime rates can be as much as twice the regular rates.

ACCOUNTING IN ACTION
ETHICS INSIGHT

Robert Eberle owns and manages Robert's Restaurant, with 9 full-time and 16 part-time employees. He pays all of the full-time employees by cheque, but pays all of the part-time employees in cash, taken from the register. Robert says his part-timers prefer cash, and he doesn't withhold or pay any taxes or deductions because they go unrecorded and unnoticed. His accountant urges him to pay his part-timers by cheque and take off all required deductions.

 Who are the stakeholders regarding Robert's handling of his payroll?

Payroll Deductions

As anyone who has received a paycheque knows, the actual cash received is almost always less than the gross pay for the hours worked. The difference is caused by **payroll deductions**. Payroll deductions are also frequently called "withholdings" because these are the amounts that the employer withholds or holds back from the employee. Payroll deductions may be mandatory or voluntary. Illustration 10-7 shows the types of payroll deductions that most employers usually make.

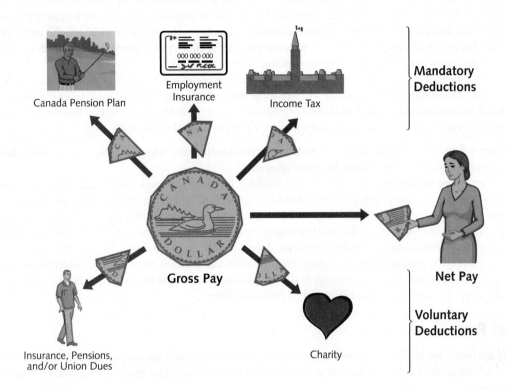

▶ **ILLUSTRATION 10-7**
Employee payroll deductions

Payroll deductions are not an expense to the employer. The employer only collects the amounts and forwards the collected amounts to the government at a later date. Required deductions include Canada Pension Plan, Employment Insurance, and income tax. Voluntary deductions may be union dues, extended benefits, or charitable donations.

The designated collection agency for the federal government is the Canada Revenue Agency (CRA), which collects money on behalf of the Receiver General for Canada, the cabinet minister responsible for accepting payments to the Government of Canada.

Mandatory Payroll Deductions. Mandatory deductions are required by law and include Canada Pension Plan contributions, Employment Insurance premiums, and personal income tax. We will discuss these three deductions in the following sections.

Canada Pension Plan. All employees between the ages of 18 and 70, except those employed in the province of Quebec, must contribute to the **Canada Pension Plan (CPP)**. Quebec has its own similar program, the Quebec Pension Plan (QPP). These mandatory plans give disability, retirement, and death benefits to qualifying Canadians.

Contribution rates are set by the federal government and are adjusted every January if there are increases in the cost of living. We will show how to calculate CPP contributions in Appendix 10A. For now, assume that Mark Jordan's CPP contribution for the weekly pay period ending June 23, 2017, is $46.17.

Employment Insurance. The Employment Insurance Act requires all Canadian workers who are not self-employed to pay **Employment Insurance (EI)** premiums. Employment insurance is designed to give income protection (in the form of payments representing a portion of one's earnings) for a limited period of time to employees who are temporarily laid off, who are on parental leave or compassionate leave, or who lose their jobs. Self-employed individuals may choose to pay EI to qualify for special benefits such as maternity or parental and compassionate care benefits. But this will not qualify them for Employment Insurance if they are not able to work.

Each year, the federal government determines the contribution rate and the maximum amount of premiums for the year. We will show how to calculate EI premiums in Appendix 10A. For now, assume that Mark Jordan's EI premium for the weekly pay period ending June 23, 2017, is $18.80.

Personal Income Tax. Under the Income Tax Act, employers are required to withhold income tax from employees for each pay period. The amount to be withheld is determined by three variables: (1) the employee's gross pay, (2) the number of credits claimed by the employee, and (3) the length of the pay period. The amount of provincial income taxes also depends on the province in which the employee works. There is no limit on the amount of gross pay that is subject to income tax withholdings. The higher the pay or earnings, the higher the amount of taxes withheld.

The calculation of personal income tax withholdings is complicated and is best done using payroll deduction tables supplied by the CRA. We will show this in Appendix 10A. For now, assume that Mark Jordan's federal income tax is $114.90 and provincial income tax is $58.15, for a total income tax owed of $173.05 on his gross pay of $1,000 for the weekly pay period ending June 23, 2017.

Voluntary Payroll Deductions. Unlike mandatory payroll deductions, which are required by law, voluntary payroll deductions are chosen by the employee.

Employees may choose to authorize withholdings for charitable, retirement, and other purposes. All voluntary deductions from gross pay should be authorized in writing by the employee. The authorization may be made individually or as part of a group plan. Deductions for charitable organizations, such as the United Way, or for financial arrangements, such as Canada Savings Bonds and the repayment of loans from company credit unions, are determined by each employee. In contrast, deductions for union dues, extended health insurance, life insurance, and pension plans are often determined on a group basis. In the calculation of net pay in the next section, we assume that Mark Jordan has voluntary deductions of $10 for the United Way and $5 for union dues.

Net Pay

The difference between an employee's gross pay, or total earnings, less any employee payroll deductions withheld from the earnings is known as **net pay**. This is the amount that the employer must pay to the employee.

Net pay is determined by subtracting payroll deductions from gross pay. For Mark Jordan, net pay for the weekly pay period ending June 23, 2017, is $746.98, as shown in Illustration 10-8.

▶ **ILLUSTRATION 10-8**
Employee payroll deductions

Gross pay		$1,000.00
Payroll deductions:		
CPP	$ 46.17	
EI	18.80	
Income tax (federal and provincial)	173.05	
United Way	10.00	
Union dues	5.00	253.02
Net pay		$ 746.98

Before we learn how to record employee payroll costs and deductions, we will turn our attention to *employer* payroll costs. After this discussion, we will record the total employee and employer payroll costs for Academy Company, where Mark Jordan works.

EMPLOYER PAYROLL COSTS

Employer payroll costs are amounts that the federal and provincial governments require employers to pay. The federal government requires CPP and EI contributions from employers. The provincial governments require employers to fund a workplace health, safety, and compensation plan. These contributions, plus such items as paid vacations and pensions, are referred to as **employee benefits**.

Employer payroll costs are not debited to the Salaries Expense account, but rather to a separate Employee Benefits Expense account.

Canada Pension Plan

Employers must also contribute to the CPP. **For each dollar withheld from the employee's gross pay, the employer must contribute an equal amount.** The CPP Payable account is credited for both the employees' and employer's CPP contributions.

Employment Insurance

Employers are required to contribute 1.4 times an employee's EI premiums. The EI Payable account is credited for both the employees' and employer's EI premiums.

Workplace Health, Safety, and Compensation

Each provincial workplace health, safety, and compensation plan gives benefits to workers who are injured or disabled on the job. The cost of this program is paid entirely by the employer; employees do not make contributions to these plans. Employers are assessed a rate—usually between 0.25% and 10% of their gross payroll—based on the risk of injury to employees in their industry and based on past experience.

Helpful hint CPP contributions and EI premiums are paid by both the employer and the employee. Workers' compensation premiums are paid entirely by the employer.

Additional Employee Benefits

In addition to the three employer payroll costs described above, employers have other employee benefit costs. Two of the most important are paid absences and post-employment benefits. We will describe these briefly here, but leave further details to an intermediate accounting course.

Paid Absences. Employees have the right to receive compensation for absences under certain conditions. The compensation may be for paid vacations, sick pay benefits, and paid statutory holidays. A liability should be estimated and accrued for future paid absences.

Post-Employment Benefits. Post-employment benefits are payments by employers to retired or terminated employees. These payments are for (1) pensions, and (2) supplemental health care, dental care, and life insurance. Employers must use the accrual basis in accounting for post-employment benefits. It is important to match the cost of these benefits with the periods where the employer benefits from the services of the employee.

RECORDING THE PAYROLL

Recording the payroll involves maintaining payroll records, recording payroll expenses and liabilities, paying the payroll, and filing and remitting payroll deductions.

Payroll Records

A separate record of an employee's gross pay, payroll deductions, and net pay for the calendar year is kept for each employee and updated after each pay period. It is called the **employee earnings record** and its cumulative payroll data are used by the employer to (1) determine when an employee has reached the maximum earnings subject to CPP and EI premiums, (2) file information returns with the CRA (as explained later in this section), and (3) give each employee a statement of gross pay and withholdings for the year.

An extract from Mark Jordan's employee earnings record for the month of June is shown in Illustration 10-9. This record includes the pay details shown in Illustration 10-8 for the weekly pay period ending June 23, 2017, highlighted in green.

ACADEMY COMPANY Employee Earnings Record Year Ending December 31, 2017												

Name Mark Jordan
Social Insurance Number 113-114-496
Date of Birth December 24, 1985
Date Employed September 1, 2010
Date Employment Ended
Job Title Shipping Clerk

Address 162 Bowood Avenue
Toronto
Ontario, M4N 1Y6
Telephone 416-486-0669
E-mail jordan@sympatico.ca
Claim Code 1

2017 Period Ending	Total Hours	Gross Pay				Deductions						Payment	
		Regular	Overtime	Total	Cumulative	CPP	EI	Income Tax	United Way	Union Dues	Total	Net Amount	Cheque #
June 9	46	880.00	60.00	940.00	19,940.00	43.20	17.67	154.15	10.00	5.00	230.02	709.98	974
June 16	47	880.00	90.00	970.00	20,910.00	44.68	18.24	163.15	10.00	5.00	241.07	728.93	1028
June 23	48	880.00	120.00	1,000.00	21,910.00	46.17	18.80	173.05	10.00	5.00	253.02	746.98	1077
June 30	46	880.00	60.00	940.00	22,850.00	43.20	17.67	154.15	10.00	5.00	230.02	709.98	1133

▶ **ILLUSTRATION** **10-9**
Employee earnings record

In addition to employee earnings records, many companies find it useful to prepare a **payroll register**. This record accumulates the gross pay, deductions, and net pay per employee for each pay period and becomes the documentation for preparing paycheques for each employee. Academy Company's payroll register for the weekly pay period ended June 23, 2017, is presented in Illustration 10-10. It shows the data for Mark Jordan in the wages section, highlighted in green. In this example, Academy Company's total payroll is $34,420, as shown in the gross pay column.

ACADEMY COMPANY Payroll Register Week Ending June 23, 2017												

Employee	Total Hours	Gross Pay			Deductions						Payment	
		Regular	Overtime	Gross	CPP	EI	Income Tax	United Way	Union Dues	Total	Net Amount	Cheque #
Aung, Ng	44	1,276.00		1,276.00	59.83	23.99	257.86	15.00		356.68	919.32	998
Canton, Maggie	44	1,298.00		1,298.00	60.92	24.40	264.72	20.00		370.04	927.96	999
Caron, William	44	1,166.00		1,166.00	54.89	21.92	223.60	11.00		311.41	854.59	1000
Deol, Rejean	44	880.00	60.00	940.00	43.20	17.67	154.15	10.00	5.00	230.02	709.98	1001
Jordan, Mark	48	880.00	120.00	1,000.00	46.17	18.80	173.05	10.00	5.00	253.02	746.98	1,077
Lee, Milroy	47	880.00	90.00	970.00	44.68	18.24	163.15	10.00	5.00	241.07	728.93	1078
Total		32,400.00	2,020.00	34,420.00	1,497.28	629.89	6,722.86	480.00	150.00	9,480.03	24,939.97	

▶ **ILLUSTRATION** **10-10**
Payroll register

Note that this record is a listing of each employee's payroll data for the June 23, 2017, pay period. In some companies, the payroll register is a special journal. Postings are made directly to ledger accounts. In other companies, the payroll register is a supplementary record that gives the data for a general journal entry and later posting to the ledger accounts. At Academy Company, the second procedure is used.

Recording Payroll Expenses and Liabilities

Helpful hint Total Payroll Expense = Gross Salaries and Wages + Employer's Portion of Payroll Costs

Employer payroll expenses are made up of two components: (1) employees' gross salaries and wages and (2) employer's payroll costs. Therefore, when recording, two journal entries are typically required.

1. Employee Payroll Costs.

The first journal entry records the employee gross wages and the related withholding taxes. In the following example, Academy Company records its total payroll for the week ended June 23 as follows:

June 23	Salaries Expense	34,420.00	
	CPP Payable		1,497.28
	EI Payable		629.89
	Income Tax Payable		6,722.86
	United Way Payable		480.00
	Union Dues Payable		150.00
	Salaries Payable		24,939.97
	To record payroll for week ending June 23.		

A = L + OE
+1,497.28 −34,420.00
+629.89
+6,722.86
+480.00
+150.00
+24,939.97

Cash flows: no effect

The above journal entry records the gross pay of $34,420 in Academy Company's Salaries Expense account. Sometimes companies will use separate accounts to record office worker expenses, salary expenses, and hourly wages. In this example, the net pay of $24,939.97 that is owed to employees is recorded in the Salaries Payable account. This is equal to the amount the employees will receive when the payroll is paid. Academy Company uses separate liability accounts for the amounts that it owes for its employee payroll deductions to the government for CPP, EI, and income tax, and amounts owed to third parties like United Way and for union dues.

2. Employer Payroll Costs.

Employer payroll costs are also usually recorded when the payroll is journalized. As discussed previously, employers must record their portion of CPP, EI, workers' compensation, and vacation pay. Therefore, as demonstrated below, Academy Company must record its share of CPP of $1,497.28 ($1,497.28 × 1) and its EI premium of $881.85 ($629.89 × 1.4).

Assume that Academy Company is also assessed for workers' compensation at a rate of 1%. It must also record this expense of $344.20 ($34,420 × 1%). Lastly, assuming that Academy Company employees accrue vacation days at an average rate of 4% of the gross payroll (equivalent to two weeks of vacation), Academy must record $1,376.80 ($34,420 × 4%) to recognize the accrued vacation benefits for one pay period.

Accordingly, the entry to record the employer payroll costs or employee benefits associated with the June 23 payroll is as follows:

June 23	Employee Benefits Expense	4,100.13	
	CPP Payable		1,497.28
	EI Payable		881.85
	Workers' Compensation Payable		344.20
	Vacation Pay Payable		1,376.80
	To record employer payroll costs on June 23 payroll.		

A = L + OE
+1,497.28 −4,100.13
+881.85
+344.20
+1,376.80

Cash flows: no effect

Employer payroll costs are debited to a separate expense account, normally called Employee Benefits Expense, so the employer can keep track of these costs. It may be combined with Salaries Expense on the income statement. The liability accounts are classified as current liabilities since they will be paid within the next year.

Recording Payment of the Payroll

Payment of the payroll by cheque or electronic funds transfer (EFT) is made from either the employer's regular bank account or a payroll bank account. Each paycheque or EFT is usually accompanied by a statement of earnings document. This shows the employee's gross pay, payroll deductions, and net pay for the period and for the year to date.

After the payroll has been paid, the cheque numbers are entered in the payroll register. The entry to record payment of the payroll for Academy Company follows:

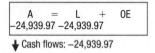

June 23	Salaries Payable		24,939.97	
	Cash			24,939.97
	To record payment of payroll.			

A = L + OE
−24,939.97 −24,939.97

↓ Cash flows: −24,939.97

Note that Academy Company is only recording payments to its employees, and not its payroll deductions, in this entry. Employee and employer deductions will be remitted to government authorities or other third parties when they are due.

Many companies use a separate bank account for payroll. Only the total amount of each period's payroll is transferred, or deposited, into that account before it is distributed. This helps the company determine if there are any unclaimed amounts.

When companies report and remit their payroll deductions, they combine withholdings of CPP, EI, and income tax. Generally, the withholdings must be reported and remitted monthly on a Statement of Account for Current Source Deductions (known by the CRA as the PD7A remittance form), and no later than the 15th day of the month following the month's pay period. Depending on the size of the payroll deductions, however, the employer's payment deadline could be different. For example, large employers must remit more often than once a month, and small employers with perfect payroll deduction remittance records can remit quarterly.

Workplace health, safety, and compensation costs are remitted quarterly to the provincial workers' compensation commission or board. Remittances can be made by mail or through deposits at any Canadian financial institution. When payroll deductions are remitted, payroll liability accounts are debited and Cash is credited.

The entry to record the remittance of payroll deductions by Academy Company in the following month is as follows:

A = L + OE
−12,203.36 −2,994.56
        −1,511.74
        −6,722.86
         −480.00
         −150.00
         −344.20

↓ Cash flows: −12,203.36

July 15	CPP Payable ($1,497.28 + $1,497.28)		2,994.56	
	EI Payable ($629.89 + $881.85)		1,511.74	
	Income Tax Payable		6,722.86	
	United Way Payable		480.00	
	Union Dues Payable		150.00	
	Workers' Compensation Payable		344.20	
	Cash			12,203.36
	To record payment of payroll deductions for June 23 payroll.			

Note that the vacation pay liability recorded on June 23 is not debited or "paid" until the employees actually take their vacation.

Other payroll information returns or forms must be filed by the employer with the government by the last day of February each year. In addition, as noted previously, employers must give employees a Statement of Remuneration Paid (called a T4 slip by the CRA) by the same date.

ACCOUNTING IN ACTION
ALL ABOUT YOU INSIGHT

Alex Hinds/Shutterstock

Employers are required by law each month to remit to the CRA mandatory payroll deductions as well as the employer's share of CPP and EI. Failure to do so can lead to interest and stiff penalties.

What happens if you are self-employed and providing consulting services to a company? If you are self-employed, you are required to pay CPP equal to both the employee's and employer's share, and you are also responsible for paying income tax. If you are self-employed, you can choose to pay EI to qualify for special benefits such as maternity or sickness benefits. But this will not qualify you for Employment Insurance if you are not able

to work. If you choose to pay EI, you will not be required to pay the employer's portion of the EI premium.

It may seem beneficial to some companies to hire consultants and avoid paying the employer's share of CPP and EI as well as other benefits. However, the CRA has strict guidelines as to whether an individual is considered an employee or a self-employed consultant. If a company inappropriately treats an individual as self-employed and fails to deduct CPP and EI, the company will be required to pay both the employer's and employee's share of CPP and EI as well as penalties and interest.

Sources: Service Canada website, "Frequently Asked Questions: Employment Insurance (EI) Special Benefits for Self-Employed People," available at www.servicecanada.gc.ca/eng/sc/ei/sew/faq.shtml; Canada Revenue Agency website, "Payroll," available at www.cra-arc.gc.ca/tx/bsnss/tpcs/pyrll/menu-eng.html; Canada Revenue Agency, "Employee or Self-Employed?", available at www.cra-arc.gc.ca/E/pub/tg/rc4110/README.html.

Q If you are providing services to a company, what are the advantages and disadvantages of being a self-employed consultant versus an employee of the company?

BEFORE YOU GO ON...DO IT **3**   **Payroll**

Prepare the journal entries to record the following transactions. Round any calculations to the nearest dollar.

1. A company's gross salaries amount to $10,000 for the week ended July 11. The following amounts are deducted from the employees' wages: CPP of $495, EI of $183, income tax of $3,965, and health insurance of $950. Assume employees are paid in cash on July 11.
2. The company accrues employer's payroll costs on the same day as it records payroll. Assume vacation days are accrued at an average rate of 4% of the gross payroll and that the health insurance is 100% funded by the employees.
3. Record the payment of the mandatory payroll deductions from the July 11 payroll on August 15.

Solution

July 11	Salaries Expense	10,000	
	CPP Payable		495
	EI Payable		183
	Income Tax Payable		3,965
	Health Insurance Payable		950
	Cash		4,407
	To record payment of wages for week ending July 11.		
July 11	Employee Benefits Expense	1,151	
	CPP Payable		495
	EI Payable ($183 × 1.4)		256
	Vacation Pay Payable ($10,000 × 4%)		400
	To record employer's payroll costs on July 11 payroll.		

(continued)

Action Plan
- Record both the employees' portion of the payroll and the benefits owed by the employer.
- Employee deductions are not an expense to the employer.
- The vacation pay liability is not "paid" until the employees actually take their vacation.

BEFORE YOU GO ON...DO IT 3   **Payroll** (continued)

Aug. 15	CPP Payable ($495 + $495)	990	
	EI Payable ($183 + $256)	439	
	Income Tax Payable	3,965	
	Health Insurance Payable	950	
	Cash		6,344
	To record payment of mandatory payroll deductions.		

Related exercise material: BE10–14, BE10–15, E10–16, and E10–17.

LEARNING OBJECTIVE 4   **Prepare the current liabilities section of the balance sheet.**

Financial Statement Presentation

Current liabilities are generally reported as the first category in the liabilities section of the balance sheet. Each of the main types of current liabilities is listed separately. In addition, the terms of operating lines of credit and notes payable and other information about the individual items are disclosed in the notes to the financial statements.

Similar to current assets, current liabilities are generally listed in order of liquidity (by maturity date). However, this is not always possible, because of the varying maturity dates that may exist for specific obligations such as notes payable. Many companies show bank loans, notes payable, and accounts payable first.

Illustration 10-11 shows how Air Canada presents its current liabilities in traditional order in its balance sheet.

▶ ILLUSTRATION **10-11**
Presentation of current liabilities

AIR CANADA Balance Sheet (partial) December 31, 2014 (in millions)	
Accounts payable and accrued liabilities	1,259
Advance ticket sales	1,794
Current portion of long-term debt and finance leases	484
Total current liabilities	3,537

Companies must carefully monitor the relationship of current liabilities to current assets. This relationship is critical in evaluating a company's short-term ability to pay debt. There is usually concern when a company has more current liabilities than current assets, because it may not be able to make its payments when they become due.

Air Canada had current assets of $3,478 million at December 31, 2014, which results in a current ratio of less than 1. You will recall from Chapter 4 that the current ratio is calculated by dividing current assets by current liabilities.

Air Canada's current ratio is 0.98:1 ($3,478 ÷ $3,537), which indicates that Air Canada does not have quite enough current assets to cover its current liabilities.

Recall also that the current ratio should never be interpreted without also looking at the receivables and inventory turnover ratios to ensure that all of the current assets are indeed liquid. It is also important to look at the acid-test ratio. If we wanted to do a more complete analysis of Air Canada's liquidity, we would need additional information.

BEFORE YOU GO ON...DO IT **4** **Current Liabilities on the Balance Sheet**

The following selected items were included in EastBoat Enterprises' adjusted trial balance at November 30, 2017:

Accounts payable	$ 52,775
Accounts receivable	30,250
Accrued liabilities	18,350
Bank indebtedness	10,400
Merchandise inventory	85,900
Notes payable	100,000
Prepaid expenses	12,000
Unearned revenue	6,500
Warranty liability	8,825

Additional information:

The $100,000 balance in notes payable consisted of: (1) a six-month, 5%, $25,000 note payable due on March 31, 2018; (2) a one-year, 5.5%, $15,000 note payable due on October 31, 2018; and (3) a three-year, 4.5%, $60,000 note payable due on September 30, 2020.

Prepare the current liabilities section of the balance sheet.

Solution

EASTBOAT ENTERPRISES
Balance Sheet (partial)
November 30, 2017

Current liabilities	
Bank indebtedness	$ 10,400
Accounts payable	52,775
Accrued liabilities	18,350
Unearned revenue	6,500
Warranty liability	8,825
Notes payable	40,000
Total current liabilities	136,850

Related exercise material: BE10–14, BE10–15, BE10–16, BE10–17, BE10–18, E10–18, and E10–19.

Action Plan
- Determine which items are liabilities.
- Recall that current liabilities are payable within one year of the balance sheet date.

Appendix 10A: PAYROLL DEDUCTIONS

LEARNING OBJECTIVE **5** **Calculate mandatory payroll deductions.**

MANDATORY PAYROLL DEDUCTIONS

As discussed in the chapter, payroll deductions may be mandatory or voluntary. Mandatory deductions are required by law and include Canada Pension Plan contributions, Employment Insurance premiums, and income tax. We discuss how to calculate these in the following sections.

Canada Pension Plan (CPP)

CPP contributions are based on a maximum ceiling or limit (called the maximum pensionable earnings) less a basic yearly exemption, and on the contribution rate set each year by the federal government. **Pensionable earnings** are gross earnings less the basic yearly exemption.

As at January 1, 2015, the following amounts were in effect:

Maximum pensionable earnings	$53,600
Basic yearly exemption	$3,500
CPP contribution rate	4.95%
Maximum annual employee CPP contribution	$2,479.95

Illustration 10A-1 shows the formulas and calculations used to determine Mark Jordan's CPP contribution on his gross pay of $1,000 for the weekly pay period ending June 23, 2017.

▶ILLUSTRATION
Formula for CPP
contributions

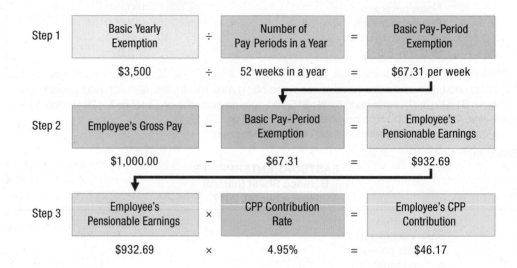

Note that the basic pay-period exemption of $67.31 is a per-week exemption and is used in this case because Academy Company pays its employees weekly. If a company pays its employees monthly, the basic pay-period exemption would be $291.67 ($3,500 ÷ 12).

An employer stops deducting CPP contributions if and when the employee's earnings are greater than the maximum pensionable earnings. In this way, the employee's CPP contributions will not be greater than the maximum annual CPP contribution. Self-employed individuals pay both the employee and employer share of CPP.

Employment Insurance (EI)

EI calculations are based on a maximum earnings ceiling (called the maximum annual insurable earnings) and the contribution rate set by the federal government each year. Different from CPP, there is no basic yearly exemption. For 2015, the following amounts were in effect:

Maximum insurable earnings	$49,500
EI contribution rate	1.88%
Maximum annual employee EI premium	$930.60

In most cases, **insurable earnings** are gross earnings.

The required EI premium is calculated by multiplying the employee's insurable earnings by the EI contribution rate. Illustration 10A-2 shows the formula and calculations to determine Mark Jordan's EI premium on his gross pay of $1,000 for the pay period ending June 23, 2017.

▶ILLUSTRATION
Formula for EI
premiums

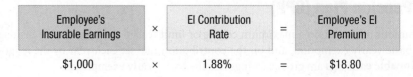

An employer stops deducting EI premiums if and when the employee's earnings are greater than the maximum insurable earnings. In this way, the employee's EI premiums will not be greater than the maximum annual EI premium. Self-employed individuals who have chosen to pay EI pay only the employee's share of EI.

Personal Income Tax

Income tax deductions are based on income tax rates set by the federal and provincial governments. The federal government uses a progressive tax scheme when calculating income taxes. Basically, this means that the higher the pay or earnings, the higher the income tax percentage, and thus the higher the amount of taxes withheld. For example, effective January 1, 2015, the federal tax rates were:

- 15% **on the first** $44,701 of taxable income, plus
- 22% **on the next** $44,700 of taxable income (on the portion of taxable income between $44,701 and $89,401), plus
- 26% **on the next** $49,185 of taxable income (on the portion of taxable income between $89,401 and $138,586), plus
- 29% of taxable income **over** $138,586.

Taxable income is determined by the employee's gross pay and the amount of personal tax credits claimed by the employee. **Personal tax credits** are amounts deducted from an individual's income taxes and they determine the amount of income taxes to be withheld. To indicate to the Canada Revenue Agency (CRA) which credits he or she wants to claim, the employee must complete a Personal Tax Credits Return (known as a TD1 form). In 2015, all individuals are entitled to a minimum personal credit (called the basic personal credit) of $11,327.

In addition, provincial income taxes must be calculated. Each province has its own specific tax rates and calculations.

As you can see, the calculation of personal income tax deductions is very complicated. Consequently, it is best done using one of the many payroll accounting software programs that are available or by using the payroll deduction tools provided by the CRA. These tools include payroll deduction tables and the Payroll Deductions Online Calculator. We will illustrate how to use the payroll deduction tables.

USING PAYROLL DEDUCTION TABLES

Payroll deduction tables are prepared by the CRA and can be easily downloaded from the CRA website (go to www.cra-arc.gc.ca and click on Businesses, then Payroll). There are separate payroll deduction tables for determining federal tax deductions, provincial tax deductions, Canada Pension Plan contributions, and Employment Insurance premiums.

These tables are updated at least once a year on January 1 to reflect the new rates for that year. Income tax tables are also reissued during the year if the federal or provincial governments make changes to income tax rates during the year. It is important to make sure you have the tables that are in effect during the payroll period for which you are calculating deductions.

There are separate sections of the federal and provincial income tax and CPP tables for weekly, biweekly, semi-monthly, and monthly pay periods. Thus, when determining these amounts, it is important to make sure you are using the table prepared for the company's pay period. The Academy Company would use the weekly tables.

Illustration 10A-3 shows excerpts from the CPP, EI, and federal and Ontario income tax tables effective January 1, 2015. You can use these tables to determine the appropriate deductions for Mark Jordan's gross pay of $1,000 during the pay period ended June 23, 2017.

In the CPP table, under the Pay column, find $1,000. The CPP deduction for the pay range $999.93 to $1,000.12 is $46.17. Earlier in the appendix, we showed how to calculate Mark Jordan's CPP and determined it was $46.17. The table has been created in such a way that within the ranges shown, the determination of the CPP will be exactly the same as the calculation carried out above (with a possible maximum rounding error of one cent).

▶**ILLUSTRATION 10A-3**
Excerpts from CPP, EI, and income tax deduction tables prepared by the Canada Revenue Agency, effective January 1, 2015

In the EI table, under the Insurable Earnings column, find $1,000. The EI deduction in the pay range $999.74 to $1,000.26 is $18.80. This is exactly the same amount we calculated earlier in the appendix.

Canada Pension Plan Contributions
Weekly (52 pay periods a year)

Pay From	To	CPP	Pay From	To	CPP	Pay From	To	CPP	Pay From	To	CPP
998.11	998.31	46.08	1012.66	1012.85	46.80	1027.20	1027.40	47.52	1570.84	1580.83	74.67
998.32	998.51	46.09	1012.86	1013.05	46.81	1027.41	1027.60	47.53	1580.84	1590.83	75.17
998.52	998.71	46.10	1013.06	1013.25	46.82	1027.61	1027.80	47.54	1590.84	1600.83	75.66
998.72	998.91	46.11	1013.26	1013.46	46.83	1027.81	1028.00	47.55	1600.84	1610.83	76.16
998.92	999.11	46.12	1013.47	1013.66	46.84	1028.01	1028.20	47.56	1610.84	1620.83	76.65
999.12	999.32	46.13	1013.67	1013.86	46.85	1028.21	1028.41	47.57	1620.84	1630.83	77.15
999.33	999.52	46.14	1013.87	1014.06	46.86	1028.42	1028.61	47.58	1630.84	1640.83	77.64
999.53	999.72	46.15	1014.07	1014.26	46.87	1028.62	1028.81	47.59	1640.84	1650.83	78.14
999.73	999.92	46.16	1014.27	1014.47	46.88	1028.82	1029.01	47.60	1650.84	1660.83	78.63
999.93	1000.12	46.17	1014.48	1014.67	46.89	1029.02	1029.21	47.61	1660.84	1670.83	79.13
1000.13	1000.33	46.18	1014.68	1014.87	46.90	1029.22	1029.42	47.62	1670.84	1680.83	79.62
1000.34	1000.53	46.19	1014.88	1015.07	46.91	1029.43	1029.62	47.63	1680.84	1690.83	80.12
1000.54	1000.73	46.20	1015.08	1015.27	46.92	1029.63	1029.82	47.64	1690.84	1700.83	80.61
1000.74	1000.93	46.21	1015.28	1015.48	46.93	1029.83	1030.02	47.65	1700.84	1710.83	81.11
1000.94	1001.13	46.22	1015.49	1015.68	46.94	1030.03	1030.22	47.66	1710.84	1720.83	81.60
1001.14	1001.34	46.23	1015.69	1015.88	46.95	1030.23	1030.43	47.67	1720.84	1730.83	82.10
1001.35	1001.54	46.24	1015.89	1016.08	46.96	1030.44	1030.63	47.68	1730.84	1740.83	82.59
1001.55	1001.74	46.25	1016.09	1016.28	46.97	1030.64	1030.83	47.69	1740.84	1750.83	83.09

Employment Insurance Premiums

Insurable Earnings From	To	EI premium	Insurable Earnings From	To	EI premium	Insurable Earnings From	To	EI premium	Insurable Earnings From	To	EI premium
919.42	919.94	17.29	957.72	958.24	18.01	996.02	996.54	18.73	1034.31	1034.84	19.45
919.95	920.47	17.30	958.25	958.77	18.02	996.55	997.07	18.74	1034.85	1035.37	19.46
920.48	921.01	17.31	958.78	959.30	18.03	997.08	997.60	18.75	1035.38	1035.90	19.47
921.02	921.54	17.32	959.31	959.84	18.04	997.61	998.13	18.76	1035.91	1036.43	19.48
921.55	922.07	17.33	959.85	960.37	18.05	998.14	998.67	18.77	1036.44	1036.96	19.49
922.08	922.60	17.34	960.38	960.90	18.06	998.68	999.20	18.78	1036.97	1037.49	19.50
922.61	923.13	17.35	960.91	961.43	18.07	999.21	999.73	18.79	1037.50	1038.03	19.51
923.14	923.67	17.36	961.44	961.96	18.08	999.74	1000.26	18.80	1038.04	1038.56	19.52
923.68	924.20	17.37	961.97	962.49	18.09	1000.27	1000.79	18.81	1038.57	1039.09	19.53
924.21	924.73	17.38	962.50	963.03	18.10	1000.80	1001.31	18.82	1039.10	1039.62	19.54
924.74	925.26	17.39	963.04	963.56	18.11	1001.32	1001.86	18.83	1039.63	1040.15	19.55
925.27	925.79	17.40	963.57	964.09	18.12	1001.87	1002.39	18.84	1040.16	1040.69	19.56
925.80	926.31	17.41	964.10	964.62	18.13	1002.40	1002.92	18.85	1040.70	1041.22	19.57
926.32	926.86	17.42	964.63	965.15	18.14	1002.93	1003.45	18.86	1041.23	1041.75	19.58
926.87	927.39	17.43	965.16	965.69	18.15	1003.46	1003.98	18.87	1041.76	1042.28	19.59
927.40	927.92	17.44	965.70	966.22	18.16	1003.99	1004.52	18.88	1042.29	1042.81	19.60
927.93	928.45	17.45	966.23	966.75	18.17	1004.53	1005.05	18.89	1042.82	1043.35	19.61
928.46	928.98	17.46	966.76	967.28	18.18	1005.06	1005.58	18.90	1043.36	1043.88	19.62
928.99	929.52	17.47	967.29	967.81	18.19	1005.59	1006.11	18.91	1043.89	1044.41	19.63
929.53	930.05	17.48	967.82	968.35	18.20	1006.12	1006.64	18.92	1044.42	1044.94	19.64
930.06	930.58	17.49	968.36	968.88	18.21	1006.65	1007.18	18.93	1044.95	1045.47	19.65
930.59	931.11	17.50	968.89	969.41	18.22	1007.19	1007.71	18.94	1045.48	1046.01	19.66
931.12	931.64	17.51	969.42	969.94	18.23	1007.72	1008.24	18.95	1046.02	1046.54	19.67
931.65	932.18	17.52	969.95	970.47	18.24	1008.25	1008.77	18.96	1046.55	1047.07	19.68
932.19	932.71	17.53	970.48	971.01	18.25	1008.78	1009.30	18.97	1047.08	1047.60	19.69
932.72	933.24	17.54	971.02	971.54	18.26	1009.31	1009.84	18.98	1047.61	1048.13	19.70
933.25	933.77	17.55	971.55	972.07	18.27	1009.85	1010.37	18.99	1048.14	1048.67	19.71
933.78	934.30	17.56	972.08	972.60	18.28	1010.38	1010.90	19.00	1048.68	1049.20	19.72
934.31	934.84	17.57	972.61	973.13	18.29	1010.91	1011.43	19.01	1049.21	1049.73	19.73
934.85	935.37	17.58	973.14	973.67	18.30	1011.44	1011.96	19.02	1049.74	1050.26	19.74
935.38	935.90	17.59	973.68	974.20	18.31	1011.97	1012.49	19.03	1050.27	1050.79	19.75
935.91	936.43	17.60	974.21	974.73	18.32	1012.50	1013.03	19.04	1050.80	1051.32	19.76
936.44	936.96	17.61	974.74	975.26	18.33	1013.04	1013.56	19.05	1051.32	1051.86	19.77
936.97	937.49	17.62	975.27	975.79	18.34	1013.57	1014.09	19.06	1051.87	1052.39	19.78
937.50	938.03	17.63	975.80	976.31	18.35	1014.10	1014.62	19.07	1052.40	1052.92	19.79
938.04	938.56	17.64	976.32	976.86	18.36	1014.63	1015.15	19.08	1052.93	1053.45	19.80
938.57	939.09	17.65	976.87	977.39	18.37	1015.16	1015.69	19.09	1053.46	1053.98	19.81
939.10	939.62	17.66	977.40	977.92	18.38	1015.70	1016.22	19.10	1053.99	1054.52	19.82
939.63	940.15	17.67	977.93	978.45	18.39	1016.23	1016.75	19.11	1054.53	1055.05	19.83

Federal tax deductions
Effective January 1, 2015
Weekly (52 pay periods a year)
Also look up the tax deductions in the provincial table

Pay From	Less than	CC 0	CC 1	CC 2	CC 3	CC 4
943 -	951	135.65	103.00	99.85	93.60	87.40
951 -	959	137.35	104.65	101.55	95.30	89.05
959 -	967	139.05	106.35	103.25	97.00	90.75
967 -	975	140.75	108.05	104.95	98.70	92.45
975 -	983	142.45	109.75	106.65	100.40	94.15
983 -	991	144.15	111.45	108.35	102.10	95.85
991 -	999	145.85	113.15	110.05	103.80	97.55
999 -	1007	147.55	114.90	111.75	105.50	99.25
1007 -	1015	149.25	116.60	113.45	107.20	100.95
1015 -	1023	150.95	118.30	115.15	108.90	102.65
1023 -	1035	153.10	120.40	117.30	111.05	104.80
1035 -	1047	155.70	123.05	119.90	113.65	107.40
1047 -	1059	158.35	125.65	122.55	116.30	110.05
1059 -	1071	161.00	128.30	125.20	118.95	112.70
1071 -	1083	163.60	130.95	127.85	121.60	115.35
1083 -	1095	166.25	133.60	130.45	124.25	118.00
1095 -	1107	168.90	136.25	133.10	126.85	120.60
1107 -	1119	171.55	138.85	135.75	129.50	123.25
1119 -	1131	174.20	141.50	138.40	132.15	125.90
1131 -	1143	176.80	144.15	141.05	134.80	128.55

Ontario provincial tax deductions
Effective January 1, 2015
Weekly (52 pay periods a year)
Also look up the tax deductions in the federal table

Pay From	Less than	CC 0	CC 1	CC 2	CC 3	CC 4
942 -	950	62.75	53.15	52.10	50.05	48.00
950 -	958	63.45	53.85	52.85	50.75	48.70
958 -	966	64.15	54.55	53.55	51.50	49.40
966 -	974	64.85	55.30	54.25	52.20	50.15
974 -	982	65.60	56.00	54.95	52.90	50.85
982 -	990	66.30	56.70	55.70	53.60	51.55
990 -	998	67.00	57.40	56.40	54.35	52.25
998 -	1006	67.70	58.15	57.10	55.05	52.95
1006 -	1014	68.40	58.85	57.80	55.75	53.70
1014 -	1022	69.15	59.55	58.55	56.45	54.40
1022 -	1030	69.85	60.25	59.25	57.15	55.10
1030 -	1038	70.55	61.00	59.95	57.90	55.85
1038 -	1046	71.30	61.70	60.70	58.65	56.55
1046 -	1054	72.05	62.45	61.40	59.35	57.30
1054 -	1062	72.75	63.20	62.15	60.10	58.05
1062 -	1074	73.70	64.10	63.05	61.00	58.95
1074 -	1086	74.80	65.20	64.15	62.10	60.05
1086 -	1098	75.90	66.30	65.25	63.20	61.15
1098 -	1110	76.95	67.40	66.35	64.30	62.25
1110 -	1122	78.05	68.50	67.45	65.40	63.35
1122 -	1134	79.15	69.60	68.55	66.50	64.45
1134 -	1146	80.25	70.70	69.65	67.60	65.55
1146 -	1158	81.35	71.80	70.75	68.70	66.65
1158 -	1170	82.45	72.90	71.85	69.80	67.75
1170 -	1182	83.55	74.00	72.95	70.90	68.80

Source: T4032 Payroll Deduction Tables, Effective July 1, 2015. Pages B-17, C-7, D-3, D-4, E-3, E4

In the federal tax deduction table, first find $1,000 in the Pay column. Now follow across the table to the Federal Claim Code 1 column. The federal tax deduction in the "from" $999 to "less than" $1,007 range, claim code 1, is $114.90. The same process is used in the Ontario provincial tax deduction table. In the "from" $998 to "less than" $1,006 range, provincial claim code 1, the provincial tax deduction is $58.15. The total of these amounts is $173.05 ($114.90 + $58.15).

Claim code 1 is used for individuals who qualify for only the basic personal credit on the TD1 form discussed earlier in the appendix. You will notice on the federal and provincial tax deduction tables that the higher the claim code, the lower the income tax deduction. These claim codes can be used for employees who have more personal tax credits. We have assumed that Mark Jordan qualifies for only the basic personal credit.

As mentioned earlier, employers may also use the payroll software packages or the CRA's Payroll Deductions Online Calculator to determine payroll deductions. All of these methods will provide correct deductions as long as the correct dates, gross pay, pay period, and claim codes are used.

BEFORE YOU GO ON...DO IT **5** **Employer's Payroll Deductions**

Highland Company pays salaries on a weekly basis. The payroll for the week ended May 26, 2015, includes three employees as follows:

Employee Name	Weekly Earnings	Claim Code
Hudson, James	$ 975	4
Randell, Findley	$ 975	2
Kim, Jaegeun	$1,015	1

Determine the appropriate mandatory payroll deductions and net pay for each employee. Calculate the CPP and EI deductions using the formula provided in Appendix 10A. Use the tables in Illustration 10A-3 to determine federal and provincial income taxes. *(continued)*

Action Plan
- The CPP basic pay-period deduction is the annual basic deduction divided by the number of pay periods in a year.
- CPP deductions are equal to an employee's pensionable earnings times the CPP contribution rate.

BEFORE YOU GO ON...DO IT **Employer's Payroll Deductions** *(continued)*

- EI premiums are equal to an employee's insurable earnings times the EI premium rate.
- The federal tax deduction is the amount in the correct Pay range and Claim Code column on the federal tax deduction table.
- The provincial tax deduction is the amount in the correct Pay range and Claim Code column on the provincial tax deduction table.

Solution

| | | | | Deductions | | | |
Employee	Gross Pay	CPP	EI	Federal Income Tax	Provincial Income Tax	Total	Net Pay
Hudson, James	$ 975.00	44.93[1]	18.33[3]	94.15	50.85	208.26	766.74
Randell, Findley	975.00	44.93	18.33	106.65	54.95	224.86	750.14
Kim, Jaegeun	1,015.00	46.91[2]	19.08[4]	118.30	59.55	243.84	771.16

Calculations:

Note: CPP basic pay-period exemption = $3,500 ÷ 52 = $67.31
[1] ($975.00 − $67.31) × 4.95% = $44.93
[2] ($1,015 − $67.31) × 4.95% = $46.91
[3] $975.00 × 1.88% = $18.33
[4] $1,015 × 1.88% = $19.08

Related exercise material: *BE10–19, *BE10–20, *E10–20, and *E10–21.

Comparing IFRS and ASPE

Key Differences	International Financial Reporting Standards (IFRS)	Accounting Standards for Private Enterprises (ASPE)
Conditions necessary to record a liability for a contingent loss.	Chance of occurrence is "probable" or "more likely than not."	Chance of occurrence is "likely."

Demonstration Problem

Benoit Company has the following selected transactions:

Feb. 1 Signed a $50,000, six-month, 7% note payable to the Central Canadian Bank, receiving $50,000 in cash. Interest is payable at maturity.

10 Cash register receipts totalled $37,565, plus 13% HST.

28 The payroll for the month is salaries of $50,000. CPP contributions and EI premiums withheld are $2,475 and $915, respectively. A total of $15,000 in income taxes is withheld. The salaries are paid on March 1.

The following adjustment data are noted at the end of the month:

1. Interest expense should be accrued on the note.
2. Employer payroll costs are recorded. In addition to mandatory costs, the company also pays $800 a month for a dental plan for all its employees.
3. Some sales were made under warranty. Of the units sold under warranty this month, 350 are expected to become defective. Repair costs are estimated to be $40 per defective unit.

Instructions
(a) Record the February transactions. Round your calculations to the nearest dollar.
(b) Record the adjusting entries at February 28.

SOLUTION TO DEMONSTRATION PROBLEM

(a)

Feb. 1	Cash		50,000	
	Notes Payable			50,000
	Issued six-month, 7% note.			
10	Cash ($37,565 + $4,883)		42,448	
	Sales			37,565
	HST Payable ($37,565 × 13%)			4,883
	To record sales and sales tax payable.			
28	Salaries Expense		50,000	
	Income Tax Payable			15,000
	CPP Payable			2,475
	EI Payable			915
	Salaries Payable			31,610
	To record February salaries.			

(b)

Feb. 28	Interest Expense ($50,000 × 7% × $^1/_{12}$)		292	
	Interest Payable			292
	To record accrued interest for February.			
28	Employee Benefits Expense		4,556	
	CPP Payable ($2,475 × 1)			2,475
	EI Payable ($915 × 1.4)			1,281
	Dental Plan Payable			800
	To record employee benefit costs for February.			
28	Warranty Expense (350 × $40)		14,000	
	Warranty Liability			14,000
	To record estimated product warranty liability.			

ACTION PLAN

- Remember that interest rates are annual rates and must be adjusted for periods of time less than one year.
- Remember that sales taxes collected must be sent to the government and are not part of sales revenue.
- Remember that employee deductions for CPP, EI, and income tax reduce the salaries payable.
- Employer contributions to CPP, EI, and the dental plan create an additional expense.
- Warranty costs are expensed in the period when the sales occur.

▶ Summary of Learning Objectives

1. **Account for determinable or certain current liabilities.** Liabilities are present obligations arising from past events, to make future payments of assets or services. Determinable liabilities have certainty about their existence, amount, and timing—in other words, they have a known amount, payee, and due date. Examples of determinable current liabilities include accounts payable, unearned revenues, operating lines of credit, notes payable, sales taxes, current maturities of long-term debt, and accrued liabilities such as property taxes, payroll, and interest.

2. **Account for uncertain liabilities.** Estimated liabilities exist, but their amount or timing is uncertain. As long as it is *likely* the company will have to settle the obligation, and the company can reasonably estimate the amount, the liability is recognized. Product warranties, customer loyalty programs, and gift cards result in liabilities that must be estimated. They are recorded as an expense (or as a decrease in revenue) and a liability in the period when the sales occur. These liabilities are reduced when repairs under warranty, redemptions, and returns occur. Gift cards are a type of unearned revenue because they result in a liability until the gift card is redeemed. Because some cards are never redeemed, it is necessary to estimate the liability and make adjustments.

A contingency is an existing condition or situation that is uncertain, where it cannot be known if a loss (and a related liability) will result until a future event happens or does not happen. Under ASPE, a liability for a contingent loss is recorded if it is likely that a loss will occur and the amount of the contingency can be reasonably estimated. Under IFRS, the threshold for recording the loss is lower. It is recorded if a loss is probable. Under ASPE, these liabilities are called contingent liabilities, and under IFRS, these liabilities are called provisions. If it is not possible to estimate the amount, these liabilities are only disclosed. They are not disclosed if they are unlikely unless they could have a substantial impact on the entity.

3. ***Determine payroll costs and record payroll transactions.*** Payroll costs consist of employee and employer payroll costs. In recording employee costs, Salaries Expense is debited for the gross pay, individual liability accounts are credited for payroll deductions, and Salaries Payable is credited for net pay. In recording employer payroll costs, Employee Benefits Expense is debited for the employer's share of Canada Pension Plan (CPP), Employment Insurance (EI), workers' compensation, vacation pay, and any other deductions or benefits

provided. Each benefit is credited to its specific current liability account.

4. ***Prepare the current liabilities section of the balance sheet.*** The nature and amount of each current liability and contingency should be reported in the balance sheet or in the notes accompanying the financial statements. Traditionally, current liabilities are reported first and in order of liquidity.

5. ***Calculate mandatory payroll deductions (Appendix 10A).*** Mandatory payroll deductions include CPP, EI, and income taxes. CPP is calculated by multiplying pensionable earnings (gross pay minus the pay-period exemption) by the CPP contribution rate. EI is calculated by multiplying insurable earnings by the EI contribution rate. Federal and provincial income taxes are calculated using a progressive tax scheme and are based on taxable earnings and personal tax credits. The calculations are very complex and it is best to use one of the Canada Revenue Agency income tax calculation tools such as payroll deduction tables.

Glossary

Accounts payable   Accounts payable that result from purchase transactions with suppliers. Also known as trade payables. (p. 530)

Canada Pension Plan (CPP)   A mandatory federal plan that gives disability, retirement, and death benefits to qualifying Canadians. (p. 543)

Collateral   Property pledged as security for a loan. (p. 531)

Contingency   An existing condition or situation that is uncertain, where it cannot be known if a loss (and a related liability) will result from the situation until one or more future events happen or do not happen. (p. 540)

Contingent liability   A liability whose existence will be confirmed only by the occurrence or non-occurrence of a future event. (p. 540)

Customer loyalty programs   Programs that result in future savings for members on the merchandise or services the company sells. (p. 537)

Determinable liability   A liability whose existence, amount, and timing are known with certainty. (p. 530)

Employee benefits   Payments made by an employer, in addition to wages and salaries, to give pension, insurance, medical, or other benefits to its employees. (p. 544)

Employee earnings record   A separate record of an employee's gross pay, payroll deductions, and net pay for the calendar year. (p. 545)

Employment Insurance (EI)   A federal mandatory insurance program designed to give income protection for a limited period of time to employees who are temporarily laid off, who are on parental leave, or who lose their jobs. (p. 543)

Gross pay   Total compensation earned by an employee. Also known as gross earnings. (p. 542)

Insurable earnings   Gross earnings used to calculate EI deductions. There is a maximum amount of insurable earnings set each year by the government. (p. 552)

Net pay   Gross pay less payroll deductions. (p. 544)

Notes payable   Obligations in the form of written promissory notes. (p. 532)

Operating line of credit   Pre-authorized approval to borrow money at a bank when it is needed, up to a pre-set limit. (p. 531)

Payroll deductions   Deductions from gross pay to determine the amount of a paycheque. (p. 543)

Payroll register   A record that accumulates the gross pay, deductions, and net pay per employee for each pay period and becomes the documentation for preparing a paycheque for each employee. (p. 546)

Pensionable earnings   Gross earnings less the basic yearly exemption. There is a maximum amount of pensionable earnings set each year by the government. (p. 551)

Personal tax credits   Amounts deducted from an individual's income taxes that determine the amount of income taxes to be withheld. (p. 553)

Prime rate   The interest rate banks charge their best customers. (p. 532)

Product warranties   Promises made by the seller to a buyer to repair or replace a product if it is defective or does not perform as intended. (p. 536)

Provisions   Liabilities of uncertain timing or amount. Also known as "estimated liabilities." (p. 536)

Note: All questions, exercises, and problems below with an asterisk (*) relate to material in Appendix 10A.

▶ Self-Study Questions

Answers are at the end of the chapter.

(LO 1) C 1. Which of the following statements is the best description of a liability?
(a) A liability is a commitment to pay an amount in the future.
(b) A liability arises when an expense is incurred.
(c) A liability is an amount that should have been paid in the past.
(d) A liability is a present obligation, arising from past events, to make future payments of assets or services.

(LO 1) C 2. The time period for classifying a liability as current is one year or the operating cycle, whichever is:
(a) longer.
(b) probable.
(c) shorter.
(d) possible.

(LO 1) AP 3. Gibraltar Company borrows $55,200 on July 31, 2017, from the East Coast Bank by signing a one-year, 5% note. Interest is payable at maturity. Assuming Gibraltar has a December 31 fiscal year end, how much interest expense will Gibraltar record in 2017?
(a) $0
(b) $1,150
(c) $1,380
(d) $2,760

(LO 1) AP 4. RS Company borrowed $70,000 on December 1 on a six-month, 6% note. At December 31:
(a) neither the note payable nor the interest payable is a current liability.
(b) the note payable is a current liability, but the interest payable is not.
(c) the interest payable is a current liability but the note payable is not.
(d) both the note payable and the interest payable are current liabilities.

(LO 1) AP 5. On March 1, Swift Current Company receives its property tax assessment of $13,200 for the 2017 calendar year. The property tax bill is due May 1. If Swift Current prepares quarterly financial statements, how much property tax expense should the company report for the quarter ended March 31, 2017?
(a) $3,300
(b) $4,400
(c) $1,100
(d) $13,200

(LO 2) AP 6. Big Al's Appliance Store offers a two-year warranty on all appliances sold. The company estimates that 5% of all appliances sold need to be serviced at an average cost of $100 each. At December 31, 2016, the

Warranty Liability account had a balance of $20,000. During 2017, the store spends $14,500 repairing 145 appliances. An additional 4,500 appliances are sold in 2017. On the 2017 income statement, warranty expense will be:
(a) $28,000.
(b) $22,500.
(c) $14,500.
(d) $20,000.

(LO 2) K 7. Friendly Department Store has a customer loyalty program in which customers receive points when they make a purchase. The points can be redeemed on future purchases. The value of the points issued should be recorded as:
(a) revenue when the points are issued.
(b) an expense when the points are issued.
(c) revenue when the points are redeemed.
(d) an expense when the points are redeemed.

(LO 2) K 8. Under IFRS, a contingent loss and the related liability should be recorded in the accounts when:
(a) it is probable the contingency will happen, but the amount cannot be reasonably estimated.
(b) it is probable the contingency will happen, and the amount can be reasonably estimated.
(c) it is highly unlikely the contingency will happen, but the amount can be reasonably estimated.
(d) it is unlikely that the users of the financial statements will read the notes.

(LO 3) AP 9. In a recent pay period, Blue Company employees have gross salaries of $17,250. Total deductions are: CPP $866, EI $316, and income taxes $4,312. What is Blue Company's total payroll expense for this pay period? Ignore vacation benefits and workers' compensation premiums.
(a) $17,250
(b) $18,558
(c) $11,765
(d) $18,432

(LO 4) K 10. On November 1, 2017, SSNL Company borrows $120,000 cash from the bank and issues a two-year, 4% note payable. SSNL must make payments of $5,000 plus interest at the end of each month. On December 31, 2017, what amount will be included in current and in non-current liabilities on the balance sheet?

	Current Liabilities	Non-current Liabilities
(a)	$60,000	$ 50,000
(b)	$60,000	$ 60,000
(c)	$10,000	$100,000
(d)	$50,000	$ 70,000

(LO 3, 5) *11. During the first week of May 2017, Emily Marquette
    AP   worked 35 hours at an hourly wage of $29.50 per
    hour for an employer in Ontario. Using the payroll
    deduction tables in Appendix 10A, what was the
    amount of federal tax withheld, assuming her only
    personal tax credit is the basic personal amount?

(a) $153.10
(b) $120.40
(c) $117.30
(d) $150.95

▶ Questions

(LO 1) K   1. What is a determinable liability? List some examples.

(LO 1) K   2. Why is a present commitment to purchase an asset
in the future not recorded as a liability?

(LO 1) AP 3. The Calgary Panthers sold 5,000 season football
tickets at $80 each for its six-game home schedule.
What entries should be made (a) when the tickets
were sold and (b) after each game?

(LO 1) K   4. How is interest calculated on a note payable? How is
the amount of interest payable at the fiscal year end
calculated?

(LO 1) K   5. What is the difference between an operating line of
credit and a bank overdraft?

(LO 1) C   6. Your roommate says, "Sales taxes are reported as an
expense in the income statement." Do you agree?
Explain.

(LO 1) C   7. Laurel Hyatt believes that if a company has a
long-term liability, the entire amount should be
classified as non-current liabilities. Is Laurel
correct? Explain.

(LO 2) C   8. The accountant for Amiable Appliances feels that warranty expense should not be recorded unless an appliance is returned for repair. "Otherwise, how do you
know if the appliance will be returned, and if so, how
much it will cost to fix?" he says. Do you agree? Explain.

(LO 2) C   9. Why does issuing a customer some form of future
savings, when the customer purchases goods or
services, result in a liability for the business?

(LO 2) C 10. A restaurant recently started a customer loyalty
program. For all bills in excess of $100, the customer
receives a 2-for-1 voucher for an appetizer for future
meals. How should the restaurant account for the
vouchers?

(LO 2) C 11. In what respects are gift cards similar to unearned
revenues and why are they classified as a liability?
How is a gift card different than an airline's unearned
passenger revenue for flights paid in advance?

(LO 1,2) K 12. What are the differences between determinable,
estimated, and contingent liabilities?

(LO 2) C 13. What is a contingency? How is it different from an
estimated liability?

(LO 2) C 14. If a company is using ASPE, under what circumstances
are a contingent loss and the related liability recorded
in the accounts? Under what circumstances are they
disclosed only in the notes to the financial statements?

(LO 2) C 15. If a company is using IFRS, under what circumstances
are a contingent loss and the related liability recorded
in the accounts? How is IFRS different from ASPE in
this respect?

(LO 2) C 16. When is it necessary to disclose a contingency even
if the chance of occurrence is small?

(LO 3) C 17. What is gross pay? How is it different than net pay?
Which amount (gross or net) should a company
record as salaries expense?

(LO 3) C 18. Explain the different types of employee and employer
payroll deductions, and give examples of each.

(LO 3) K 19. What are an employee earnings record and a payroll
register?

(LO 3) C 20. To whom, and how often, are payroll deductions
remitted?

(LO 4) K 21. In what order are current liabilities generally reported in the balance sheet? Why might this method not
always be possible?

(LO 4) K 22. What information about current liabilities
should be reported in the notes to the financial
statements?

(LO 4) K 23. How can a company determine if its current
liabilities are too high?

(LO 5) K *24. Explain how CPP and EI are calculated.

(LO 5) K *25. How is the amount deducted from an employee's
wages for income tax determined?

▶ Brief Exercises

Identify whether obligations
are current. (LO 1) AP

BE10-1   Jamison Jackets has the following obligations at December 31:
(a) a note payable for $100,000 due in two years
(b) salaries payable of $20,000
(c) a 10-year mortgage payable of $300,000, payable in 10 annual payments of $30,000 plus interest
(d) interest payable of $15,000 on the mortgage

(e) accounts payable of $60,000
(f) sales taxes payable of $6,500

For each obligation, indicate whether it should be classified as a current liability. (Assume an operating cycle of less than one year.)

BE10–2   The Brampton Bullet hockey team sold 2,000 tickets at $120 each for its six-game home schedule. Prepare the entry to record (a) the sale of the season's tickets and (b) the revenue recognized upon playing the first home game.

Journalize unearned revenue. (LO 1) AP

BE10–3   Satterfield publishes a monthly music magazine, *DiscOver*. Subscriptions to the magazine cost $18 per year. During November 2017, Satterfield sells 15,000 subscriptions beginning with the December issue. Satterfield prepares financial statements quarterly and recognizes subscription revenue earned at the end of the quarter. The company uses the accounts Unearned Revenue and Revenue. Prepare the entries to record (a) the receipt of the subscriptions and (b) the adjusting entry at December 31, 2017, to record revenue earned in December 2017.

Journalize unearned revenue. (LO 1) AP

BE10–4   Rabbitt Enterprises borrows $60,000 from LowLand Trust Co. on July 1, 2017 signing a 4%, one-year note payable. Interest is to be paid at maturity. Prepare journal entries for Rabbitt Enterprises to record: (a) the receipt of the proceeds of the note; (b) the journal entry to record the accrued interest at December 31, assuming adjusting entries are made only at year end; and (c) the payment of the note at maturity.

Record note payable. (LO 1) AP

BE10–5   Blue Robin Retail has one store in Ottawa and one in Regina. All sales in Ontario are subject to 13% HST; all sales in Saskatchewan are subject to 5% GST and 5% PST. On March 12, 2017, the Ottawa store reports cash sales of $7,200 and the Regina store reports cash sales of $8,400. (a) Calculate the sales taxes each store charged for these sales. (b) Prepare a journal entry for each store to record the sales on March 12, 2017.

Calculate sales taxes and record sales. (LO 1) AP

BE10–6   Backyard Shed Solutions sells its largest shed for $1,800 plus HST of 13%. On May 10, 2017, it sold 40 of these sheds. On May 17, 2017, the company sold 95 of these sheds. All sales are cash sales. For each day's sales, (a) calculate the HST and (b) prepare a journal entry to record the sales.

Calculate HST and record sales. (LO 1) AP

BE10–7   Dresner Company has a December 31 fiscal year end. It receives a $9,600 property tax bill for the 2017 calendar year on March 31, 2017. The bill is payable on June 30. Prepare entries for March 31, June 30, and December 31, assuming the company adjusts its accounts annually.

Record property tax. (LO 1) AP

BE10–8   In 2017, Song Company introduces a new product that includes a two-year warranty on parts. During 2017, 4,400 units are sold for $450 each. The cost of each unit was $175. The company estimates that 5% of the units will be defective and that the average warranty cost will be $85 per unit. The company has a December 31 fiscal year end and prepares adjusting entries on an annual basis. Prepare an adjusting entry at December 31, 2017, to accrue the estimated warranty cost.

Record warranty. (LO 2) AP

BE10–9   One-Stop Department Store has a loyalty program where customers are given One-Stop "Money" for cash or debit card purchases. The amount they receive is equal to 2% of the pre-tax sales total. Customers can use the One-Stop Money to pay for part or all of their next purchase at One-Stop Department Store. On July 3, 2017, Judy Wishloff purchases merchandise and uses $50 of One-Stop Department Store money. What entry or entries will One-Stop Department Store record for this transaction? Ignore taxes.

Record loyalty rewards issued and redeemed. (LO 2) AP

BE10–10   Metropolis Books sold 50,000 copies of a best-selling novel in July for $8 each. Included in each book was a $2 mail-in rebate for a future book purchase if the customer sends in proof of purchase with a completed rebate form. Metropolis estimates that 10% of the purchasers will claim the rebate. (a) Calculate the sales revenue and the unearned revenue related to the loyalty program that Metropolis earned in July on this book. (b) Prepare the journal entry to record the sale and the unearned revenue Metropolis Books should record.

Record estimated liability for a cash rebate program. (LO 2) AP

BE10–11   Rikard's Menswear sells $4,750 of gift cards for cash in December 2017. Rikard's has a December 31 fiscal year end and uses a perpetual inventory system. In January 2018, $2,425 of the gift cards are redeemed for merchandise with a cost of $1,070. Prepare journal entries for Rikard's for December 2017 and January 2018 assuming all gift card balances will be redeemed.

Record gift cards issued and redeemed. (LO 2) AP

BE10–12   For each of the following independent situations, indicate whether it should be (1) recorded, (2) disclosed, or (3) neither recorded nor disclosed. Explain your reasoning and indicate if the accounting treatment would be the same or different under IFRS and ASPE.
(a) A customer has sued a company for $1 million. Currently the company is unable to determine if it will win or lose the lawsuit.
(b) A customer has sued a company for $1 million. The company will likely lose the lawsuit.
(c) A competitor has sued a company for $2 million. The lawyers have advised that there is a 55% chance that the company will lose the lawsuit.

Account for contingencies. (LO 2) C

BE10–13   Athabasca Toil & Oil Company, a public company, is a defendant in a lawsuit for improper discharge of pollutants and waste into the Athabasca River. Athabasca's lawyers have advised that it is probable the company

Discuss contingency. (LO 2) AP

will lose this lawsuit and that it could settle out of court for $50,000. Should Athabasca record anything with regard to this lawsuit? Or should it disclose it in the notes to the financial statements? Explain.

Calculate gross and net pay, and employer costs.
(LO 3) AP

BE10–14   Becky Sherrick's regular hourly wage rate is $12.50, and she is paid time and a half for work over 40 hours per week. In the pay period ended March 16, Becky worked 46 hours. Becky's CPP deductions total $26.99, EI deductions total $11.21, and her income tax withholdings are $94.56. (a) Calculate Becky's gross and net pay for the pay period. (b) What are Becky's employer's costs for CPP, EI, and income tax?

Record payroll. (LO 3) AP

BE10–15   Bri Company's gross pay for the week ended August 22 totalled $70,000, from which $3,330 was deducted for CPP, $1,281 for EI, and $19,360 for income tax. Prepare the entry to record the employer payroll costs, assuming these will not be paid until September.

Identify current liabilities.
(LO 1, 2, 3, 4) K

BE10–16   Identify which of the following items should be classified as a current liability. For those that are not current liabilities, identify where they should be classified.
(a) A product warranty
(b) Cash received in advance for airline tickets
(c) HST collected on sales
(d) Bank indebtedness
(e) Interest owing on an overdue account payable
(f) Interest due on an overdue account receivable
(g) A lawsuit pending against a company. The company is not sure of the likely outcome.
(h) Amounts withheld from the employees' weekly pay
(i) Prepaid property tax
(j) A $75,000 mortgage payable, of which $5,000 is due in the next year

Calculate current and non-current portion of notes payable. (LO 1, 4) AP

BE10–17   Diamond Dealers has two notes payable outstanding on December 31, 2017, as follows:
(a) A five-year, 5.5%, $60,000 note payable issued on August 31, 2017. Diamond Dealers is required to pay $12,000 plus interest on August 31 each year starting in 2018.
(b) A four-year, 4.5%, $96,000 note payable issued on September 30, 2017. Diamond Dealers is required to pay $2,000 plus interest at the end of each month starting on October 31, 2017. All payments are up to date.

Calculate the amount of each note to be included in current and non-current liabilities on Diamond Dealers' December 31, 2017, balance sheet. Ignore interest.

Prepare current liabilities section and calculate ratios.
(LO 4) AP

BE10–18   **Suncor Energy Inc.** reported the following current assets and current liabilities (in millions) at December 31, 2014:

Accounts payable and accrued liabilities	$5,704
Accounts receivable	4,275
Cash and cash equivalents	5,495
Current portion of long-term debt	34
Current portion of provisions	752
Income taxes payable	1,058
Income taxes receivable	680
Inventories	3,466
Short-term debt	806

(a) Prepare the current liabilities section of the balance sheet.
(b) Calculate the current and acid-test ratios.

Calculate CPP and EI deductions. (LO 5) AP

*BE10–19   Cecilia Hernandez earned $60,100 in 2015 and was paid monthly. She worked for HillSide Tours for all of 2015. Using the formulas, what were her CPP and EI deductions in (a) January 2015 and (b) December 2015?

Calculate payroll deductions. (LO 5) AP

*BE10–20   In 2015, Viktor Petska was paid a gross salary of $1,075 on a weekly basis. For the week ended May 12, 2015: (a) calculate his CPP and EI deductions and (b) use the excerpts in Illustration 10A-3 to determine his income tax deductions assuming his TD1 claim code is 1.

▶ Exercises

Record various liabilities.
(LO 1, 3) AP

E10–1   Peter's Mini Putt was opened on March 1 by Peter Palazzi. The following selected transactions occurred during March:

Mar. 1   Purchased golf balls and other supplies for $350 from Stevenson Supplies payable in 30 days.
      5   Received a booking for a birthday party to be held the following week. The customer paid the mini golf fees of $200 in advance.

12   Provided the golf services for the birthday party.
15   Wages were paid to hourly workers. A total of $5,000 was paid out, with withholdings as follows: CPP $230, EI $94, and income tax $1,400.
30   Wrote a cheque to Stevenson Supplies for the $350 owing to settle the balance due.

Instructions

Journalize the transactions.

E10–2 Udala Uke's had the following transactions involving notes payable.

Record note payable and interest. (LO 1) AP

July 1, 2017	Borrows $50,000 from First National Bank by signing a nine-month, 8% note.
Nov. 1, 2017	Borrows $60,000 from Interprovincial Bank by signing a three-month, 6% note.
Dec. 31, 2017	Prepares adjusting entries.
Feb. 1, 2018	Pays principal and interest to Interprovincial Bank.
Apr. 1, 2018	Pays principal and interest to First National Bank.

Instructions

Prepare journal entries for each of the transactions.

E10–3 On June 1, Merando borrows $90,000 from First Bank on a six-month, $90,000, 6% note.

Record note payable and interest. (LO 1) AP

Instructions

(a) Prepare the entry on June 1.
(b) Prepare the adjusting entry on June 30.
(c) Prepare the entry at maturity (December 1), assuming monthly adjusting entries have been made through November 30.
(d) What was the total financing cost (interest expense)?

E10–4 On June 1, 2017, Novack Company purchases equipment on account from Moleski Manufacturers for $50,000. Novack is unable to pay its account on July 1, 2017, so Moleski agrees to accept a three-month, 7% note payable from Novack. Interest is payable the first of each month, starting August 1, 2017. Moleski has an August 31 fiscal year end and adjusts its accounts on an annual basis.

Record note payable, interest paid monthly. (LO 1) AP

Instructions

Record all transactions related to the note for Novack Company.

E10–5 On March 1, 2017, Tundra Trees purchased equipment from Edworthy Equipment Dealership in exchange for a seven-month, 8%, $30,000 note payable. Interest is due at maturity. Tundra Trees has a July 31 fiscal year end. Edworthy has a May 31 fiscal year end. Both companies adjust their accounts annually. Tundra honours the note at maturity.

Record note payable and note receivable; interest paid at maturity. (LO 1) AP

Instructions

(a) For Tundra Trees, record all transactions related to the note.
(b) For Edworthy Equipment, record all transactions related to the note. Assume the cost of the equipment to Edworthy was $18,000.

E10–6 In providing accounting services to small businesses, you encounter the following independent situations:

Record sales taxes. (LO 1) AP

1. Sainsbury rang up $13,200 of sales, plus HST of 13%, on its cash register on April 10.
2. Montgomery rang up $30,000 of sales, before sales taxes, on its cash register on April 21. The company charges 5% GST and no PST.
3. Winslow charges 5% GST and 7% PST on all sales. On April 27, the company collected $25,100 sales in cash plus sales taxes.

Instructions

Record the sales transactions and related taxes for each client.

E10–7 Scoggin rings up sales plus sales taxes on its cash register. On April 10, the register total for sales is $80,000.

Record sales taxes. (LO 1) AP

Instructions

Journalize the transactions assuming the sales were made in
(a) Quebec,
(b) Nova Scotia, and
(c) Alberta.

Account for unearned revenue. (LO 1) AP

E10–8 Charleswood Musical Theatre's season begins in November and ends in April, with a different play each month. In October 2017, Charleswood sold 100 season tickets for the 2017–18 season, for $210 each. Charleswood records all season ticket sales as unearned revenue and adjusts its accounts on a monthly basis. The company has a March 31 fiscal year end.

Instructions

(a) Prepare the entry for sale of the season tickets. Date the entry October 31.
(b) Prepare any required adjusting entries on:
    1. November 30, 2017
    2. March 31, 2018
    3. April 30, 2018
(c) Determine the balance (after any required adjustments) in Unearned Revenue on:
    1. November 30, 2017
    2. December 31, 2017
    3. March 31, 2018

Account for unearned revenue. (LO 1) AP

E10–9 Satterfield publishes a monthly sports magazine, *Hockey Hits*. Subscriptions to the magazine cost $18 per year. During November 2017, Satterfield sells 15,000 subscriptions beginning with the December issue. Satterfield prepares financial statements quarterly and recognizes revenue earned at the end of the quarter. The company uses the accounts Unearned Revenue and Revenue.

Instructions

(a) Prepare the entry in November for the receipt of the subscriptions.
(b) Prepare the adjusting entry at December 31, 2017, to record revenue earned in December 2017.
(c) Prepare the adjusting entry at March 31, 2018, to record revenue earned in the first quarter of 2018.

Record property tax; determine financial statement impact. (LO 1, 4) AP

E10–10 Seaboard Company receives its annual property tax bill of $24,000 for the 2017 calendar year on May 31, 2017, and it is payable on July 31, 2017. Seaboard has a December 31 fiscal year end.

Instructions

(a) Prepare the journal entries for Seaboard on May 31, July 31, and December 31, 2017, assuming that the company makes monthly adjusting entries. (Assume property tax expense in 2016 was $2,200 per month.)
(b) What is recorded on Seaboard's December 31, 2017, balance sheet and income statement for the year ended December 31, 2017, in regard to property taxes?

Record warranty costs. (LO 2) AP

E10–11 Castellitto Company began selling game consoles on November 1, 2017. The company offers a 75-day warranty for defective merchandise. Based on past experience with other similar products, Castellitto estimates that 2.5% of the units sold will become defective in the warranty period, and that the average cost of replacing or repairing a defective unit is $20. In November, Castellitto sold 30,000 units and 450 defective units were returned. In December, Castellitto sold 32,000 units and 630 defective units were returned. The actual cost of replacing the defective units was $21,600.

Instructions

(a) Prepare a journal entry to accrue for the estimated warranty costs for the November and December sales at December 31, 2017.
(b) Prepare one summary journal entry at December 31, 2017, to record the cost of replacing the defective game consoles returned during November and December.
(c) What amounts will be included in Castellitto's 2017 income statement and balance sheet at December 31, 2017, with regard to the warranty?

Calculate warranty costs for multiple years. (LO 2) AP

E10–12 Silver Cloud manufactures and sells computers for $2,000 each, with a two-year parts and labour warranty. Based on prior experience, the company expects, on average, to incur warranty costs equal to 5% of sales. The business reports the following sales and warranty cost information:

	Sales (units)	Actual Warranty Costs
2015	500	$30,000
2016	600	46,000
2017	525	53,500

Instructions

(a) Calculate the warranty expense for each year.
(b) Calculate the warranty liability at the end of each year.

E10–13 Steig's Sports Store has a customer loyalty program in which it issues points to customers for every cash purchase that can be applied to future purchases. For every dollar spent, a customer receives three points. Each point is worth one cent. There is no expiry date on the points. Steig's estimates that 35% of the points issued will eventually be redeemed. Steig's has a December 31 year end.

Calculate customer loyalty program liability. (LO 2) AP

The program was started in 2016. During 2016, 900,000 points were issued. Sales for 2016 were $300,000. In 2017, 1.2 million points were issued. Total sales for 2017 were $400,000.

Instructions

(a) What is the stand-alone value of the points issued in 2016? In 2017?
(b) Prepare the journal entries to record the sales for 2016 and 2017.
(c) When the points are redeemed, how is this accounted for? What is the impact of the point redemptions on profit and cash flow?

E10–14 A list of possible liabilities follows:

Identify type of liability. (LO 1, 2) C

1. An automobile company recalled a particular car model because of a possible problem with the brakes. The company will pay to replace the brakes.
2. A large retail store has a policy of refunding purchases to dissatisfied customers under a widely advertised "money-back, no questions asked" guarantee.
3. A manufacturer offers a three-year warranty at the time of sale.
4. To promote sales, a company offers prizes (such as a chance to win a trip) in return for a specific type of bottle cap.
5. A local community has filed suit against a chemical company for contamination of drinking water. The community is demanding compensation, and the amount is uncertain. The company is vigorously defending itself.

Instructions

(a) State whether you believe each of the above liabilities is determinable, estimable, or contingent, and explain why.
(b) If you identify the liability as contingent in part (a), state what factors should be considered in determining if it should be recorded, disclosed, or neither recorded nor disclosed in the financial statements.

E10–15 Sleep-a-Bye Baby Company, a public company, is the defendant in a lawsuit alleging that its portable baby cribs are unsafe. The company has offered to replace the cribs free of charge for any concerned parent. None-theless, it has been sued for damages and distress amounting to $1.5 million. The company plans to vigorously defend its product safety record in court.

Analyze contingency. (LO 2) AP

Instructions

(a) What should the company record or report in its financial statements for this situation? Explain why.
(b) What if Sleep-a-Bye Baby Company's lawyers advise that it is likely the company will have to pay damages of $100,000? Does this change what should be recorded or reported in the financial statements? Explain.
(c) How would your answers to parts (a) and (b) change if Sleep-a-Bye Baby Company were a private company that had chosen to follow ASPE?

E10–16 Hidden Dragon Restaurant's gross payroll for April is $46,600. The company deducted $2,162 for CPP, $853 for EI, and $9,011 for income taxes from the employees' cheques. Employees are paid monthly at the end of each month.

Record payroll. (LO 3) AP

Instructions

(a) Prepare a journal entry for Hidden Dragon on April 30 to record the payment of the April payroll to employees.
(b) Prepare a journal entry on April 30 to accrue Hidden Dragon's employer payroll costs. Assume that Hidden Dragon is assessed workers' compensation premiums at a rate of 1% per month and accrues for vacation pay at a rate of 4% per month.
(c) On May 15, Hidden Dragon pays the government the correct amounts for April's payroll. Prepare a journal entry to record this remittance.

Calculate gross pay; prepare payroll register, and record payroll. (LO 3) AP

E10–17 Ahmad Company has the following data for the weekly payroll ending May 31:

Employee	Hours Worked M	Tu	W	Th	F	S	Hourly Rate	CPP Deduction	Income Tax Withheld	Health Insurance
A. Kassam	9	8	9	8	10	3	$13	$29.17	$ 85.55	$10
H. Faas	8	8	8	8	8	5	14	29.59	87.10	15
G. Labute	9	10	9	10	8	0	15	33.05	102.55	15

Employees are paid 1.5 times the regular hourly rate for all hours worked over 40 hours per week. Ahmad Company must make payments to the workers' compensation plan equal to 2% of the gross payroll. In addition, Ahmad matches the employees' health insurance contributions and accrues vacation pay at a rate of 4%.

Instructions

(a) Prepare the payroll register for the weekly payroll. Calculate each employee's EI deduction at a rate of 1.88% of gross pay.

(b) Record the payroll and Ahmad Company's employee benefits.

Calculate current and non-current portion of notes payable, and interest payable. (LO 1, 4) AP

E10–18 Emerald Enterprises has three notes payable outstanding on December 31, 2016, as follows:

1. A six-year, 6%, $60,000 note payable issued on March 31, 2016. Emerald Enterprises is required to pay $10,000 plus interest on March 31 each year starting in 2017.
2. A seven-month, 4%, $30,000 note payable issued on July 1, 2016. Interest and principal are payable at maturity.
3. A 30-month, 5%, $120,000 note payable issued on September 1, 2016. Emerald Enterprises is required to pay $4,000 plus interest on the first day of each month starting on October 1, 2016. All payments are up to date.

Instructions

(a) Calculate the current portion of each note payable.

(b) Calculate the non-current portion of each note payable.

(c) Calculate any interest payable at December 31, 2016.

Prepare current liabilities section of balance sheet. (LO 4) AP

E10–19 Medlen Models has the following account balances at December 31, 2017:

Notes payable ($60,000 due after 12/31/18)	$100,000
Unearned service revenue	70,000
Mortgage Payable ($90,000 due in 2018)	250,000
Salaries payable	32,000
Accounts payable	63,000

In addition, Medlen is involved in a lawsuit. Legal counsel feels it is probable Medlen will pay damages of $25,000 in 2018. Medlen records contingent liabilities in the account Litigation Liability.

Instructions

Prepare the current liabilities section of Medlen's December 31, 2017, balance sheet.

Calculate gross pay and payroll deductions; record payroll. (LO 3, 5) AP

*E10–20 Kate Gough's regular hourly wage rate is $22.60, and she receives a wage of 1.5 times the regular hourly rate for work over 40 hours per week. For the weekly pay period ended June 15, 2017, Kate worked 44 hours. Kate lives in Ontario and has a claim code of 1 for tax deductions.

Instructions

(a) Calculate Kate's gross pay, payroll deductions, and net pay. Use Illustration 10A-3 to determine her income tax deductions.

(b) Record Kate's salary on June 15, assuming it was also paid on this date.

(c) Record the employer's related payroll costs on June 15, assuming they were not paid on this date.

Calculate gross pay and payroll deductions. (LO 5) AP

*E10–21 In 2017, Donald Green worked for the Green Red Company and earned a gross salary of $57,000 for the year ($4,750 per month). He was paid once a month at the end of each month.

Instructions

Calculate Donald's CPP and EI deductions for the following:

(a) September 2017

(b) October 2017

(c) November 2017

(d) December 2017

(e) In total for 2017

▶ Problems: Set A

P10–1A Motzer Company had the following selected transactions.

Prepare current liability entries and adjusting entries. (LO 1, 2) AP

Feb. 2   Purchases supplies from Supplies R Us on account for $2,500.
10   Cash register sales total $43,200, plus 5% GST and 8% PST.
15   Signs a $35,000, six-month, 6%-interest-bearing note payable to MidiBank and receives $35,000 in cash.
21   The payroll for the previous two weeks consists of salaries of $50,000. All salaries are subject to CPP of $2,308 and EI of $940 and income tax of $8,900. The salaries are paid on February 28. The employer's payroll expense is also recorded.
28   Accrues interest on the MidiBank note payable.
28   Accrues the required warranty provision because some of the sales were made under warranty. Of the units sold under warranty, 350 are expected to become defective. Repair costs are estimated to be $40 per unit.
28   Pays employees the salaries for the pay period ending February 21.
Mar. 1   Remits the sales taxes to the Province and GST to the Receiver General for the February 10 sales.
2   Makes the payment to Supplies R Us from the February purchase.
15   Remits the payroll taxes owing from the February 21 payroll to the Receiver General.

Instructions

Journalize the February and March transactions.

TAKING IT FURTHER   What are some additional employee benefits paid by employers? How are they accounted for?

P10–2A   On January 1, 2017, the ledger of Accardo Company contains the following liability accounts.

Prepare current liability entries, adjusting entries, and current liabilities section. (LO 1, 2, 4) AP

Accounts Payable	$52,000
HST Payable	7,700
Unearned Revenue	16,000

During January, the following selected transactions occurred.

Jan. 2   Borrowed $27,000 from Canada Bank on a three-month, 6%, $27,000 note.
5   Sold merchandise for cash totalling $20,500 plus 13% HST.
12   Performed services for customers who had made advance payments of $10,000. The payment included HST of $1,151. (Credit Service Revenue.)
14   Paid Receiver General for HST invoiced in December 2016 ($7,700).
20   Sold 900 units of a new product on credit at $50 per unit, plus 13% HST. This new product is subject to a one-year warranty.
25   Sold merchandise for cash totalling $12,500 plus 13% HST.

Instructions

(a) Journalize the January transactions.
(b) Journalize the adjusting entries at January 31 for (1) the outstanding notes payable, and (2) estimated warranty liability, assuming warranty costs are expected to equal 7% of sales of the new product sold January 20.
(c) Prepare the current liabilities section of the balance sheet at January 31, 2017. Assume no change in accounts payable.

TAKING IT FURTHER   Explain why warranty liabilities are recorded before a customer has any issues with the product.

P10–3A   Crab Apple Tree Farm has a December 31 fiscal year end. The company has six notes payable outstanding on December 31, 2017, as follows:

Calculate current and non-current portion of notes payable, and interest payable. (LO 1, 4) AP

1. A 10-month, 5%, $35,000 note payable issued on August 1, 2017. Interest is payable monthly on the first day of each month starting on September 1.
2. A four-month, 4%, $15,000 note payable issued on September 1, 2017. Interest and principal are payable at maturity.
3. A six-month, 4.5%, $26,000 note payable issued on November 1, 2017. Interest and principal are payable at maturity.
4. A five-year, 3.5%, $60,000 note payable issued on March 31, 2017. Crab Apple Tree Farm is required to pay $12,000 plus interest on March 31 each year starting in 2017.
5. A six-year, 5%, $100,000 note payable issued on October 1, 2017. Crab Apple Tree Farm is required to pay $2,000 plus interest on the first day of each month starting on November 1, 2017. All payments are up to date.
6. A four-year, 5%, $40,000 note payable issued on January 31, 2016. Crab Apple Tree Farm is required to pay $10,000 every January 31 starting in 2017. Interest is payable monthly on the last day of each month, starting on February 28, 2016.

Instructions

(a) Calculate the current portion of each note payable.

(b) Calculate the non-current portion of each note payable.

(c) Calculate any interest payable at December 31, 2017.

TAKING IT FURTHER   What are the costs and benefits to the maker and the payee of the note of using a note payable in place of an account payable?

Record note transactions; show financial statement presentation. (LO 1, 4) AP

P10–4A   The current liabilities section of the December 31, 2016, balance sheet of Learnstream Company included notes payable of $14,000 and interest payable of $490. The note payable was issued to Tanner Company on June 30, 2016. Interest of 7% is payable at maturity, March 31, 2017.

The following selected transactions occurred in the year ended December 31, 2017:

Jan. 12	Purchased merchandise on account from McCoy Company for $25,000, terms n/30. Learnstream uses a perpetual inventory system.
31	Issued a $25,000, three-month, 7% note to McCoy Company in payment of its account. Interest is payable monthly.
Feb. 28	Paid interest on the McCoy note (see January 31 transaction).
Mar. 31	Paid the Tanner note, plus interest.
31	Paid interest on the McCoy note (see January 31 transaction).
Apr. 30	Paid the McCoy note, plus one month's interest (see January 31 transaction).
Aug. 1	Purchased equipment from Drouin Equipment by paying $11,000 cash and signing a $30,000, 10-month, 6% note. Interest is payable at maturity.
Sept. 30	Borrowed $100,000 cash from the First Interprovincial Bank by signing a 10-year, 5% note payable. Interest is payable quarterly on December 31, March 31, June 30, and September 30. Of the principal, $10,000 must be paid each September 30.
Dec. 31	Paid interest on the First Interprovincial Bank note (see September 30 transaction).

Instructions

(a) Record the transactions and any adjustments required at December 31.

(b) Show the balance sheet presentation of notes payable and interest payable at December 31.

(c) Show the income statement presentation of interest expense for the year.

TAKING IT FURTHER   Why is it important to correctly classify notes payable as either current or non-current in the balance sheet?

Record current liability transactions; prepare current liabilities section. (LO 1, 2, 3, 4) AP

P10–5A   On January 1, 2017, Shumway Software Company's general ledger contained these liability accounts:

Accounts payable	$40,000
Unearned revenue—loyalty program	3,700
CPP payable	1,320
EI payable	680
HST payable	8,630
Income tax payable	3,340
Unearned revenue	15,300
Vacation pay payable	8,660

In January, the following selected transactions occurred:

Jan. 2	Issued a $46,000, four-month, 7% note. Interest is payable at maturity.
5	Sold merchandise for $8,600 cash, plus 13% HST. The cost of this sale was $4,100. Shumway Software uses a perpetual inventory system.
12	Provided services for customers who had paid $8,000 cash in advance. The payment included HST of $920.
14	Paid the Receiver General (federal government) for sales taxes collected in December 2016.
15	Paid the Receiver General for amounts owing from the December payroll for CPP, EI, and income tax.
17	Paid $14,800 to creditors on account.
20	Sold 1,900 units of a new product on account for $55 per unit, plus 13% HST. This new product has a one-year warranty. It is estimated that 9% of the units sold will be returned for repair at an average cost of $10 per unit. The cost of this sale was $25 per unit.
29	During the month, provided $2,300 of services for customers who redeemed their customer loyalty rewards. Assume that HST of $265 is included in the $2,300.
31	Issued 30,000 loyalty rewards points worth $1 each. Based on past experience, 20% of these points are expected to be redeemed. Cash sales related to the issuance of the loyalty points were $250,000.

31   Recorded and paid the monthly payroll. Gross salaries were $18,750. Amounts withheld included CPP of $764, EI of $343, and income tax of $3,481.

Instructions

(a) Record the transactions.
(b) Record adjusting entries for the following:
   1. Interest on the note payable
   2. The estimated warranty liability
   3. Employee benefits for CPP, EI, and vacation pay (accrued at a rate of 4%)
   4. Estimated property taxes of $8,820 for the 2017 calendar year
(c) Prepare the current liabilities section of the balance sheet at January 31.

TAKING IT FURTHER   Explain how and when the Vacation Pay Payable account balance is paid.

P10-6A   On January 1, 2015, Hopewell Company began a warranty program to stimulate sales. It is estimated that 5% of the units sold will be returned for repair at an estimated cost of $30 per unit. Sales and warranty figures for the three years ended December 31 are as follows: *Record warranty transactions. (LO 2) AP*

	2015	2016	2017
Sales (units)	1,500	1,700	1,800
Sales price per unit	$ 150	$ 120	$ 125
Units returned for repair under warranty	75	90	105
Actual warranty costs	$2,250	$2,400	$2,640

Instructions

(a) Calculate the warranty expense for each year and warranty liability at the end of each year.
(b) Record the warranty transactions for each year. Credit Repair Parts Inventory for the actual warranty costs.
(c) To date, what percentage of the units sold have been returned for repair under warranty? What has been the average actual warranty cost per unit for the three-year period?

TAKING IT FURTHER   Assume that at December 31, 2017, management reassesses its original estimates and decides that it is more likely that the company will have to service 7% of the units sold in 2017. Management also determines that the average actual cost per unit incurred to date (as calculated in part [c] above) is more reasonable than its original estimate. What should be the balance in the Warranty Liability account at December 31, 2017?

P10-7A   Save-Always Stores started a customer loyalty program at the beginning of 2016 in which customers making cash purchases of gasoline at Save-Always Gas Bars are issued rewards in the form of grocery coupons. For each litre of gasoline purchased, the customer gets a grocery coupon for 3.8 cents that can be redeemed in Save-Always Food Stores. The coupons have no expiry date. Save-Always Stores began selling gift cards in 2017 that do not have expiry dates.   *Record customer loyalty program and gift card transactions; determine impact on financial statements. (LO 2) AP*

   The following are selected transactions in 2016 and 2017:

1. In 2016, the Gas Bars sold 3.8 million litres of gasoline resulting in gas sales of $4,560,000. Grocery coupons were issued with these sales. The expected redemption rate for the grocery coupons is 80%.
2. In 2016, customers redeemed $46,000 of the grocery coupons in the Food Stores.
3. In 2017, the Gas Bars sold 4.65 million litres of gasoline resulting in gas sales of $6,045,000. Grocery coupons were issued with these sales. The expected redemption rate for the grocery coupons is 80%.
4. In 2017, customers redeemed $53,500 of the grocery coupons in the Food Stores.
5. In 2017, customers purchased $82,000 of gift cards, and $45,000 of the cards were redeemed by the end of the year.

Instructions

(a) Indicate if the following activities will increase, decrease, or have no effect on each of revenues, expenses, and profit:
   1. Issuing grocery coupons when sales are made
   2. Redeeming grocery coupons
   3. Issuing gift cards
   4. Redeeming gift cards
(b) Record the above transactions.
(c) What balances will be included in current liabilities at December 31, 2016 and 2017, regarding the customer loyalty program and gift cards?

TAKING IT FURTHER   What factors should management consider in determining if current liabilities are correctly valued at December 31, 2017?

Discuss reporting of contingencies and record provisions.

(LO 2, 4) AP

P10–8A   Mega Company, a public company, is preparing its financial statements for the year ended December 31, 2017. It is now January 31, 2018, and the following situations are being reviewed to determine the appropriate accounting treatment:

1. Mega Company is being sued for $4 million for a possible malfunction of one of its products. In July 2017, a customer suffered a serious injury while operating the product. The company is vigorously defending itself as it is clear the customer was intoxicated when using the product.
2. In a separate lawsuit, Mega is being sued for $3 million by an employee who was injured on the job in February 2017. It is likely that the company will lose this lawsuit, but a reasonable estimate cannot be made of the amount of the expected settlement.
3. On December 7, 2017, a potential customer injured himself when he slipped on the floor in the foyer of Mega Company's office building. Mega Company did not have appropriate floor mats in place and melting snow from the customer's boots made the floor very dangerous. Mega has negotiated a potential settlement of $200,000 with the individual's lawyer.

Instructions

For each of the above situations, recommend whether Mega Company should: (1) make an accrual in its December 31, 2017, financial statements; (2) disclose the situation in the notes to the financial statements; or (3) not report it. Provide a rationale for your recommendations.

TAKING IT FURTHER   What are the potential benefits and costs of making an accrual for a contingency as opposed to only disclosing it in the notes to the financial statements?

Prepare payroll register and record payroll. (LO 3) AP

P10–9A   Sure Value Hardware has four employees who are paid on an hourly basis, plus time and a half for hours worked in excess of 40 hours a week. Payroll data for the week ended March 14, 2017, follow:

Employee	Total Hours	Hourly Rate	CPP	EI	Income Tax	United Way
I. Dahl	37.5	$17.00	$27.80	11.83	$ 82.25	$ 7.50
F. Gualtieri	42.5	16.50	32.40	13.57	91.20	8.00
G. Ho	43.5	15.50	31.39	13.19	97.50	5.00
A. Israeli	45.0	15.00	31.94	13.40	107.75	10.00

Instructions

(a) Prepare a payroll register for the weekly payroll.
(b) Record the payroll on March 14 and the accrual of employee benefits expense. Assume the company accrues 4% for vacation pay.
(c) Record the payment of the payroll on March 14.
(d) Record the payment of remittances to the Receiver General on April 15.

TAKING IT FURTHER   Does the owner of a proprietorship need to deduct CPP, EI, and income taxes on his or her drawings?

Record payroll transactions and calculate balances in payroll liability accounts.

(LO 3) AP

P10–10A   On January 31, 2017, Cardston Company had the following payroll liability accounts in its ledger:

Canada Pension Plan payable	$ 7,887	Life insurance payable	$ 855
Disability insurance payable	1,280	Union dues payable	1,450
Employment Insurance payable	3,755	Vacation pay payable	20,520
Income tax payable	16,252	Workers' compensation payable	4,275

In February, the following transactions occurred:

Feb.	4	Sent a cheque to the union treasurer for union dues.
	7	Sent a cheque to the insurance company for the disability and life insurance.
	13	Issued a cheque to the Receiver General for the amounts due for CPP, EI, and income tax.
	20	Paid the amount due to the workers' compensation plan.
	28	Completed the monthly payroll register, which shows gross salaries $92,600; CPP withheld $4,281; EI withheld $1,695; income tax withheld $17,595; union dues withheld $1,574; and long-term disability insurance premiums $1,380.
	28	Prepared payroll cheques for the February net pay and distributed the cheques to the employees.
	28	Recorded an adjusting journal entry to record February employee benefits for CPP, EI, workers' compensation at 5% of gross pay, vacation pay at 4% of gross pay, and life insurance at 1% of gross pay.

Instructions

(a) Journalize the February transactions and adjustments.

(b) Calculate the balances in each of the payroll liability accounts at February 28, 2017.

TAKING IT FURTHER Why do employers need an employee earnings record for each employee as well as a payroll register?

P10–11A The following selected account balances are from LightHouse Distributors' adjusted trial balance at September 30, 2017:

Prepare current liabilities section; calculate and comment on ratios.

(LO 4) AP

Accounts payable	$ 90,000
Accounts receivable	182,000
Bank indebtedness	62,500
CPP payable	7,500
EI payable	3,750
HST payable	15,000
Income tax payable	35,000
Interest payable	10,000
Merchandise inventory	275,000
Mortgage payable	150,000
Notes payable	100,000
Prepaid expenses	12,500
Property taxes payable	10,000
Unearned revenue-loyalty program	5,000
Unearned revenue	30,000
Vacation pay payable	13,500
Warranty liability	22,500
Workers' compensation payable	1,250

Additional information:

1. On September 30, 2017, the unused operating line of credit is $75,000.
2. Redemption rewards, warranties, and gift cards are expected to be redeemed within one year. Unearned revenues relate to gift cards sold but not yet redeemed.
3. Of the mortgage, $10,000 is due each year.
4. Of the note payable, $1,000 is due at the end of each month.

Instructions

(a) Prepare the current liabilities section of the balance sheet.

(b) Calculate LightHouse's current ratio and acid-test ratio.

(c) Explain why the company did not report any cash as part of its current assets.

TAKING IT FURTHER The accountant for LightHouse argues that since property taxes are unavoidable, a company should record the full year's worth of property taxes as an expense when it is paid. Is the accountant correct? Explain.

P10–12A **Maple Leaf Foods Inc.** is a packaged meat producer. It reports biological assets on its balance sheet which consists of hogs and poultry livestock. These are considered current assets somewhat similar to inventory. The company reports the following current assets and current liabilities at December 31, 2014 (in thousands):

Prepare current liabilities section; calculate and comment on ratios.

(LO 4) AP

Cash	$496,328
Accounts payable and accruals	275,249
Accounts receivable	60,396
Biological assets	105,743
Current portion of long-term debt	472
Income taxes payable	26,614
Inventories	270,401
Notes receivable	110,209
Other current liabilities	24,383
Prepaid expenses and other assets	20,157
Provisions	60,443

Hint: Notes receivable are current assets that should be included in the acid-test ratio.

Instructions

(a) Prepare the current liabilities section of the balance sheet. The provisions are due within 12 months of the balance sheet date.

(b) Calculate the current and acid-test ratios.

(c) At December 31, 2013, Maple Leaf Foods Inc. had total current assets of $1,183,171 thousand, which included cash of $506,670 thousand, receivables of $111,034 thousand and notes receivable of $115,514. Current liabilities were $966,522 thousand. Did the current and acid-test ratios improve or weaken in 2014?

TAKING IT FURTHER What other factors should be considered in assessing Maple Leaf Foods' liquidity?

Calculate payroll deductions; prepare payroll register. (LO 5) AP

*P10-13A Western Electric Company pays its support staff weekly and its electricians on a semi-monthly basis. The following support staff payroll information is available for the week ended June 9, 2015:

Employee Name	Weekly Earnings	Claim Code
Chris Tanm	$ 945	2
Terry Ng	1,130	4
Olga Stavtech	1,130	1
Alana Mandell	1,067	1

The electricians' salaries are based on their experience in the field, as well as the number of years they have worked for the company. All three electricians have been with the company more than two years. The annual salaries of these employees are as follows:

Employee Name	Annual Salary for 2015
Sam Goodspeed	$43,440
Marino Giancarlo	64,770
Hillary Ridley	76,880

Instructions

(a) Prepare a payroll register for the June 9, 2015, weekly payroll for the support staff. Calculate the CPP and EI deductions using the formulas provided in Appendix 10A. Use the tables in Illustration 10A-3 to determine federal and provincial income taxes.

(b) Calculate the CPP and EI deductions for each of the electricians for their June 15, 2015, semi-monthly payroll.

(c) In which semi-monthly pay period will each of the electricians reach their maximum CPP and EI payments for 2015?

TAKING IT FURTHER Why are there separate payroll deduction tables for determining weekly, semi-monthly, and monthly income tax deductions?

▶ Problems: Set B

Prepare current liability entries and adjusting entries. (LO 1, 2) AP

P10-1B Vacation Villas had the following selected transactions.

Feb. 1 Signs a $30,000, eight-month, 5%-interest-bearing note payable to CountryBank and receives $30,000 in cash.

8 Sales on account of $14,500, plus 13% HST.

14 The payroll for the previous week consists of salaries of $15,000. All salaries are subject to CPP of $692 and EI of $282 and withholding taxes of $2,700. The salaries are paid on February 21. The employer's payroll expense is also recorded.

15 Purchase furniture worth $1,975 to be paid for in 30 days.

21 Pays employees the salaries for the pay period ending February 14.

28 Accrues interest on the CountryBank note payable.

28 Accrues the required warranty provision because some of the sales were made under warranty. Of the units sold under warranty, 20 are expected to become defective. Repair costs are estimated to be $25 per unit.

Instructions

Journalize the February transactions.

TAKING IT FURTHER The accountant at Vacation Villas believes a current liability is a debt that can be expected to be paid in one year. Is the accountant correct?

P10–2B On January 1, 2017, the ledger of Edmiston Software Company contains the following liability accounts:

Accounts Payable	$42,500
GST Payable	5,800
PST Payable	8,200
Unearned Revenue	15,000

During January, the following selected transactions occurred.

Jan.	1	Borrowed $30,000 in cash from Canada Bank on a four-month, 8%, $30,000 note.
	5	Sold merchandise for cash totalling $10,400, plus GST of 5% and PST 7%.
	12	Provided services for customers who had made advance payments of $9,000. The payment included GST of $402 and PST of $562.
	14	Paid the Province PST invoiced in December 2016 of $8,200 and paid the Receiver General GST invoiced in December 2016 of $5,800.
	20	Sold 900 units of a new product on credit at $52 per unit, plus GST of 5% and PST 7%. This new product is subject to a one-year warranty.
	25	Sold merchandise for cash totalling $18,720, plus GST of 5% and PST 7%.

Instructions

(a) Journalize the January transactions.

(b) Journalize the adjusting entries at January 31 for (1) the outstanding notes payable, and (2) estimated warranty liability, assuming warranty costs are expected to equal 5% of sales of the new product.

(c) Prepare the current liabilities section of the balance sheet at January 31, 2017. Assume no change in accounts payable.

TAKING IT FURTHER   James, an employee of the Edmiston Software Company, believes payroll taxes withheld are an expense to his employer. Is James correct? Explain.

P10–3B Juniper Bush Farm has a December 31 fiscal year end. The company has six notes payable outstanding on December 31, 2017, as follows:

1. A nine-month, 5%, $25,000 note payable issued on July 1, 2017. Interest is payable monthly on the first day of each month starting on August 1.
2. A six-month, 4%, $10,000 note payable issued on September 1, 2017. Interest and principal are payable at maturity.
3. A seven-month, 4.5%, $40,000 note payable issued on November 1, 2017. Interest and principal are payable at maturity.
4. A five-year, 3.75%, $80,000 note payable issued on May 31, 2017. Juniper Bush Farm is required to pay $16,000 plus interest on May 31 each year starting in 2018.
5. A three-year, 4.25%, $126,000 note payable issued on October 1, 2017. Juniper Bush Farm is required to pay $3,500 plus interest on the first day of each month starting on November 1, 2017. All payments are up to date.
6. A four-year, 5%, $50,000 note payable issued on March 31, 2016. Juniper Bush Farm is required to pay $12,500 every March 31 starting in 2017. Interest is payable monthly at the end of the month, starting on April 30, 2016.

Instructions

(a) Calculate the current portion of each note payable.

(b) Calculate the non-current portion of each note payable.

(c) Calculate any interest payable at December 31, 2017.

TAKING IT FURTHER   What are the costs and benefits to the maker and the payee of the note of using a note payable in place of an account payable?

P10–4B MileHi Mountain Bikes markets mountain-bike tours to clients vacationing in various locations in the mountains of British Columbia. The current liabilities section of the October 31, 2016, balance sheet included notes payable of $15,000 and interest payable of $375 related to a six-month, 6% note payable to Eifert Company on December 1, 2016.

During the year ended October 31, 2017, MileHi had the following transactions related to notes payable:

2016

Dec.	1	Paid the $15,000 Eifert note, plus interest.

2017

Apr.	1	Issued a $75,000, nine-month, 7% note to Mountain Real Estate for the purchase of additional mountain property on which to build bike trails. Interest is payable quarterly on July 1, October 1, and at maturity on January 1, 2018.
	30	Purchased Mongoose bikes to use as rentals for $8,000, terms n/30.

May 31   Issued Mongoose an $8,000, three-month, 8% note payable in settlement of its account (see April 30 transaction). Interest is payable at maturity.

July 1   Paid interest on the Mountain Real Estate note (see April 1 transaction).

Aug. 31   Paid the Mongoose note, plus interest (see May 31 transaction).

Oct. 1   Paid interest on the Mountain Real Estate note (see April 1 transaction).

1   Borrowed $90,000 cash from Western Bank by issuing a five-year, 6% note. Interest is payable monthly on the first of the month. Principal payments of $18,000 must be made on the anniversary of the note each year.

Instructions

(a) Record the transactions and any adjustments required at October 31, 2017.

(b) Show the balance sheet presentation of notes payable and interest payable at October 31, 2017.

(c) Show the income statement presentation of interest expense for the year.

TAKING IT FURTHER   Why is it important to correctly classify notes payable as either current or non-current in the balance sheet?

Record current liability transactions; prepare current liabilities section.
(LO 1, 2, 3, 4) AP

P10–5B   On January 1, 2017, Zaur Company's general ledger had these liability accounts:

Accounts payable	$63,700
Unearned revenue—loyalty program	2,150
CPP payable	2,152
EI payable	1,019
HST payable	11,390
Income tax payable	4,563
Unearned revenue	16,000
Vacation pay payable	9,120
Warranty liability	5,750

In January, the following selected transactions occurred:

Jan. 5   Sold merchandise for $15,800 cash, plus 13% HST. Zaur uses a periodic inventory system.

12   Provided services for customers who had previously made advance payments of $7,000. The payment included HST of $805.

14   Paid the Receiver General (federal government) for sales taxes collected in December 2016.

15   Paid the Receiver General for amounts owing from the December payroll for CPP, EI, and income tax.

16   Borrowed $18,000 from Second National Bank on a three-month, 6% note. Interest is payable monthly on the 15th day of the month.

17   Paid $35,000 to creditors on account.

20   Sold 500 units of a new product on account for $60 per unit, plus 13% HST. This new product has a two-year warranty. It is expected that 6% of the units sold will be returned for repair at an average cost of $10 per unit.

30   Customers redeemed $1,750 of loyalty rewards in exchange for services. Assume that HST of $201 is included in this amount.

31   Issued 50,000 loyalty points worth $1 each. Based on past experience, 10% of these points are expected to be redeemed. Sales related to the issuance of the loyalty points were $500,000.

31   Determined that the company had used $875 of parts inventory in January to honour warranty contracts.

31   Recorded and paid the monthly payroll. Gross salaries were $25,350. Amounts withheld include CPP of $1,183, EI of $464, and income tax of $4,563.

Instructions

(a) Record the transactions.

(b) Record adjusting entries for the following:
   1. Interest on the note payable for half a month
   2. The estimated warranty liability
   3. Employee benefits, which include CPP, EI, and vacation pay that is accrued at a rate of 4%

(c) Prepare the current liabilities section of the balance sheet at January 31.

TAKING IT FURTHER   Explain how and when the Vacation Pay Payable account balance is paid.

Record warranty transactions.
(LO 2) AP

P10–6B   On January 1, 2015, Logue Company began a warranty program to stimulate sales. It is estimated that 5% of the units sold will be returned for repair at an estimated cost of $25 per unit. Sales and warranty figures for the three years ended December 31 are as follows:

	2015	2016	2017
Sales (units)	1,200	1,320	1,420
Sales price per unit	$100	$105	$110
Units returned for repair under warranty	60	70	80
Actual warranty costs	$1,275	$1,600	$1,960

Instructions

(a) Calculate the warranty expense for each year and warranty liability at the end of each year.

(b) Record the warranty transactions for each year. Credit Repair Parts Inventory for the actual warranty costs.

(c) To date, what percentage of the units sold have been returned for repair under warranty? What has been the average actual warranty cost per unit for the three-year period?

TAKING IT FURTHER   Suppose at December 31, 2017, management reassesses its original estimates and decides that it is more likely that the company will have to service 7% of the units sold in 2017. Management also determines that the original estimate of the cost per unit is the appropriate cost to use for future repair work. What should be the balance in the Warranty Liability account at December 31, 2017?

P10–7B   Caribou County Service Station started a customer loyalty program at the beginning of 2016 in which customers making cash purchases of gasoline at the gas bar are issued rewards in the form of coupons. For each litre of gasoline purchased, the customer gets a coupon for 2.5 cents that can be redeemed in the service department toward such things as oil changes or repairs. The coupons have no expiry date. Caribou County Service Station began selling gift cards in 2017 that do not have expiry dates.

Record customer loyalty program and gift card transactions; determine impact on financial statements. (LO 2) AP

The following are selected transactions in 2016 and 2017:

1. In 2016, the gas bar sold 750,000 litres of gasoline resulting in gas sales of $1,050,000. Service department coupons were issued with these sales. The expected redemption rate for the grocery coupons is 70%.
2. In 2016, customers redeemed $5,950 of the coupons in the service department.
3. In 2017, the gas bar sold 810,000 litres of gasoline, resulting in gas sales of $1,255,000. Service department coupons were issued with these sales. The expected redemption rate for the grocery coupons is 70%.
4. In 2017, customers redeemed $9,500 of the coupons in the service department.
5. In 2017, customers purchased $3,950 of gift cards, and $1,500 of the cards were redeemed by the end of the year.

Instructions

(a) Indicate if the following items will increase, decrease, or have no effect on each of revenues, expenses, and profit:
   1. Issuing coupons when sales are made
   2. Redeeming coupons
   3. Issuing gift cards
   4. Redeeming gift cards

(b) Record the above transactions.

(c) What balances will be included in current liabilities at December 31, 2016 and 2017, regarding the customer loyalty program and gift cards?

TAKING IT FURTHER   What factors should management consider in determining if current liabilities are correctly valued at December 31, 2017?

P10–8B   Big Fork Company, a private company that follows ASPE, is preparing its financial statements for the year ended December 31, 2016. It is now February 15, 2017, and the following situations are being reviewed to determine the appropriate accounting treatment:

Discuss reporting of contingencies and record provisions. (LO 2, 4) AP

1. Big Fork is being sued for $3 million for a possible malfunction of one of its products. In March 2017, a customer suffered a serious injury while operating the product. The company is defending itself but it is clear that there was an error in the published operations manual for the product. It is likely that the company will lose this lawsuit, but it is unlikely it will have to pay the full $3 million. At this point, a reasonable estimate cannot be made of the amount of the expected settlement.
2. Big Fork is being sued for $1.5 million by an employee for wrongful dismissal and defamation of character. The employee was fired on August 2, 2017. The company is vigorously defending itself because the employee had a documented history of poor performance at work.
3. On December 16, 2017, a sales representative from one of the company's suppliers injured herself on a visit to Big Fork's offices. She tripped over equipment that had not been properly stored and will be unable to work for

several months as a result of her injuries. A $250,000 claim against Big Fork has been filed by the sales representative's insurance company.

Instructions

For each of the above situations, recommend whether Big Fork Company should (1) make an accrual in its December 31, 2017, financial statements; (2) disclose the situation in the notes to the financial statements; or (3) not report it. Provide a rationale for your recommendations.

TAKING IT FURTHER What are the potential benefits and costs of making an accrual for a contingency as opposed to only disclosing it in the notes to the financial statements?

Prepare payroll register and record payroll. (LO 3) AP

P10–9B Scoot Scooters has four employees who are paid on an hourly basis, plus time and a half for hours in excess of 40 hours a week. Payroll data for the week ended February 17, 2017, follow:

Employee	Total Hours	Hourly Rate	CPP	EI	Income Tax	United Way
P. Kilchyk	40	$15.25	$26.86	$11.16	$76.60	$5.00
B. Quon	42	15.00	28.60	11.80	83.70	7.25
C. Pospisil	40	16.25	28.84	11.90	84.10	5.50
B. Verwey	44	14.50	29.68	12.21	87.10	8.25

Instructions

(a) Prepare a payroll register for the weekly payroll.
(b) Record the payroll on February 15 and the accrual of employee benefits expense. Assume the company accrues 4% for vacation pay.
(c) Record the payment of the payroll on February 17.
(d) Record the payment of the remittances to the Receiver General on March 15.

TAKING IT FURTHER Does the owner of a proprietorship have to deduct CPP, EI, and income taxes from his or her own drawings?

Record payroll transactions and calculate balances in payroll liability accounts. (LO 3) AP

P10–10B On March 31, 2017, Babb Company had the following payroll liability accounts in its ledger:

Canada Pension Plan payable	$ 6,907	Life insurance payable	$ 756
Disability insurance payable	1,134	Union dues payable	1,285
Employment Insurance payable	3,320	Vacation pay payable	3,024
Income tax payable	14,364	Workers' compensation payable	3,780

In April, the following transactions occurred:

Apr.	4	Sent a cheque to the union treasurer for union dues.
	7	Sent a cheque to the insurance company for the disability and life insurance.
	13	Issued a cheque to the Receiver General for the amounts due for CPP, EI, and income tax.
	20	Paid the amount due to the workers' compensation plan.
	28	Completed the monthly payroll register, which shows gross salaries $83,160, CPP withheld $3,799, EI withheld $1,522, income tax withheld $15,800, union dues withheld $1,414, and long-term disability insurance premiums $1,247.
	28	Prepared payroll cheques for the April net pay and distributed the cheques to the employees.
	28	Recorded an adjusting journal entry to record April employee benefits for CPP, EI, workers' compensation at 5% of gross pay, vacation pay at 4% of gross pay, and life insurance at 1% of gross pay.

Instructions

(a) Journalize the April transactions and adjustments.
(b) Calculate the balances in each of the payroll liability accounts at April 30, 2017.

TAKING IT FURTHER Why do employers need an employee earnings record for each employee as well as a payroll register?

Prepare current liabilities section; calculate and comment on ratios. (LO 4) AP

P10–11B The following selected account balances are from Creative Carpentry's adjusted trial balance at March 31, 2017:

Accounts receivable	$184,000
Accounts payable	60,000
Bank overdraft	55,200
CPP payable	2,300
EI payable	1,750
HST payable	12,250
Income tax payable	25,000
Interest payable	8,000
Accumulated depreciation	115,000
Mortgage payable	200,000
Merchandise inventory	120,600
Notes payable	30,000
Prepaid expenses	500
Unearned revenue	9,385
Vacation pay payable	1,200
Warranty liability	12,500

Additional information:

1. On March 31, 2017, the unused operating line of credit is $25,000.
2. Redemption rewards, warranties, and gift cards are expected to be redeemed within one year. Unearned revenues relate to gift cards sold but not yet redeemed.
3. Of the mortgage, $50,000 is due each year.
4. Of the note payable, $5,000 is due at the end of each month.

Instructions

(a) Prepare the current liabilities section of the balance sheet.
(b) Calculate Creative's current ratio and acid-test ratio.
(c) Explain why the company did not report any cash as part of its current assets.

TAKING IT FURTHER   Explain to Peter, the owner of Creative Carpentry, why unearned gift card revenue is a current liability and how the liability will be settled.

P10–12B   BCE Inc., whose offerings include Bell Canada, reports the following current assets and current liabilities at December 31, 2014 (in millions of dollars):

Prepare current liabilities section; calculate and comment on ratios.
(LO 4) AP

Cash	$ 142
Cash equivalents	424
Current tax liabilities	269
Debt due within one year	3,743
Dividends payable	534
Interest payable	145
Inventory	333
Other current assets	198
Prepaid expenses	379
Trade and other receivables	3,069
Trade payables and other liabilities	4,398

Instructions

(a) Prepare the current liabilities section of the balance sheet.
(b) Calculate the current and the acid-test ratio.
(c) On December 31, 2013, BCE Inc. had current assets of $5,070 million. This included cash and cash equivalents of $335 million, and trade and other receivables of $3,043 million. Current liabilities were $7,890 million. Did the current and acid-test ratios improve or weaken in 2014?

TAKING IT FURTHER   What other factors should be considered in assessing BCE Inc.'s liquidity?

*P10–13B   Slovak Plumbing Company pays its support staff weekly and its plumbers on a semi-monthly basis. The following support staff payroll information is available for the week ended May 12, 2015:

Calculate payroll deductions and prepare payroll register.
(LO 5) AP

Employee Name	Weekly Earnings	Claim Code
Dan Quinn	$ 985	1
Karol Holub	1,037	3
Al Lowhorn	1,080	1
Irina Kostra	950	4

The plumbers' salaries are based on their experience in the field, as well as the number of years they have worked for the company. All three plumbers have been with the company more than two years. The annual salary of these employees is as follows:

Employee Name	Annual Salary for 2015
Branislav Dolina	$80,700
Henrietta Koleno	62,500
Aida Krneta	44,120

Instructions

(a) Prepare a payroll register for the May 12, 2015, weekly payroll for the support staff. Calculate the CPP and EI deductions using the formulas provided in Appendix 10A. Use the tables in Illustration 10A-3 to determine federal and provincial income taxes.

(b) Calculate the CPP and EI deductions for each of the plumbers for their May 15, 2015, semi-monthly payroll.

(c) In which semi-monthly pay period will each of the plumbers reach their maximum CPP and EI payments for 2015?

TAKING IT FURTHER   Why are there separate payroll deduction tables for determining income tax deductions for weekly, semi-monthly, and monthly pay periods?

▶ Cumulative Coverage—Chapters 3 to 10

The unadjusted trial balance of LeBrun Company at its year end, July 31, 2017, is as follows:

LEBRUN COMPANY Trial Balance July 31, 2017	Debit	Credit
Cash	$ 16,550	
Petty cash	200	
Accounts receivable	38,500	
Allowance for doubtful accounts		$ 2,000
Note receivable (due December 31, 2017)	10,000	
Merchandise inventory	45,900	
Prepaid expenses	16,000	
Land	50,000	
Building	155,000	
Accumulated depreciation—building		10,800
Equipment	25,000	
Accumulated depreciation—equipment		12,200
Patent	75,000	
Accumulated amortization—patent		15,000
Accounts payable		78,900
Warranty liability		6,000
Notes payable (due August 1, 2029)		124,200
S. LeBrun, capital		124,700
S. LeBrun, drawings	54,000	
Sales		750,000
Cost of goods sold	450,000	
Operating expenses	181,220	
Interest revenue		400
Interest expense	6,830	
Totals	$1,124,200	$1,124,200

Adjustment information:

1. The July 31 bank statement reported debit memos for service charges of $50 and a $650 NSF (not sufficient funds) cheque that had been received from a customer for the purchase of merchandise in July.
2. Estimated uncollectible accounts receivable at July 31 are $3,850.

3. The note receivable bears interest of 8% and was issued on December 31, 2016. Interest is payable the first of each month.
4. A physical count of inventory determined that $39,200 of inventory was actually on hand.
5. Prepaid expenses of $5,500 expired in the year (use the account Operating Expenses).
6. Depreciation is calculated on the long-lived assets using the following methods and useful lives:

> Building: straight-line, 25 years, $15,000 residual value
> Equipment: double diminishing-balance, five years, $2,500 residual value
> Patent: straight-line, five years, no residual value

7. The 6% note payable was issued on August 1, 2009. Interest is paid monthly at the beginning of each month for the previous month's interest. Of the note principal, $1,680 is currently due.
8. Estimated warranty costs for July are $1,975 (use Operating Expenses).

Instructions

(a) Prepare the adjusting journal entries required at July 31. (Round your calculations to the nearest dollar.)
(b) Prepare an adjusted trial balance at July 31.
(c) Prepare a multiple-step income statement and statement of owner's equity for the year and a balance sheet at July 31.

CHAPTER 10: BROADENING YOUR PERSPECTIVE

▶ Financial Reporting and Analysis

Financial Reporting Problem

BYP10–1 Refer to the financial statements of **Corus Entertainment** and the Notes to the Financial Statements in Appendix A.

Instructions

Answer the following questions about the company's current and contingent liabilities:

(a) What were Corus's total current liabilities at August 31, 2014? What was the increase (decrease) in total current liabilities from the previous year?

(b) Which specific current liabilities and in what order did Corus present on the August 31, 2014, statement of financial statement position?
(c) Calculate Corus's current ratio, acid-test ratio, and receivables turnover ratios for 2014 and 2013. Comment on Corus's overall liquidity.
(d) Does Corus report any contingencies? If so, where are they disclosed? Explain the nature, amount, and significance of Corus's contingencies, if any.

Interpreting Financial Statements

BYP10–2 **Loblaw Companies Limited** (which owns Shoppers Drug Mart) reported the following information about contingencies in the notes to its December 31, 2014, financial statements:

> **LOBLAW COMPANIES LIMITED**
> **Notes to the Consolidated Financial Statements**
> **December 31, 2014**
>
> **32. Contingent Liabilities (excerpt)**
> **Legal Proceedings** The Company is the subject of various legal proceedings and claims that arise in the ordinary course of business. The outcome of all of these proceedings and claims is uncertain. However, based on information currently available, these proceedings and claims, individually and in the aggregate, are not expected to have a material impact on the Company.
>
> Shoppers Drug Mart has been served with an Amended Statement of Claim in a proposed class action proceeding that has been filed under the Ontario Superior Court of Justice by two licensed Associates, claiming various declarations and damages resulting from Shoppers Drug Mart's alleged breaches of the Associate Agreement, in the amount of $500 million. The proposed class action comprises all of Shoppers Drug Mart's current and former licensed Associates residing in Canada, other than in Québec, who are parties to Shoppers Drug Mart's 2002 and 2010 forms of the Associate Agreement. On July 9, 2013, the Ontario Superior Court of Justice certified as a class proceeding portions of the action. While Shoppers Drug Mart continues to believe that the claim is without merit and will vigorously defend the claim, the outcome of this matter cannot be predicted with certainty.

Instructions

Why would Loblaw disclose information about these legal disputes, including the amount of the potential loss, in the notes to the financial statements instead of accruing an amount for these as liabilities in its accounting records?

 # Critical Thinking

Collaborative Learning Activity

Note to instructor: Additional instructions and material for this group activity can be found on the Instructor Resource Site and in *WileyPLUS.*

BYP10-3   In this group activity, your group must decide on the best accounting treatment for a contingency. Your instructor will provide the class with a scenario and each group will be required to decide if an accrual should be made and, if so, for how much. Groups will simultaneously report to the class and will be required to defend their decisions.

Communication Activity

BYP10-4   The Show Time movie theatre sells thousands of gift certificates every year. The certificates can be redeemed at any time because they have no expiry date. Some of them may never be redeemed (because they are lost or forgotten, for example). The owner of the theatre has raised some questions about the accounting for these gift certificates.

Instructions

Write an e-mail to answer the following questions from the owner:
(a) Why is a liability recorded when these certificates are sold? After all, they bring customers into the theatre, where they spend money on snacks and drinks. Why should something that helps generate additional revenue be treated as a liability?
(b) How should the gift certificates that are never redeemed be treated? At some point in the future, can the liability related to them be eliminated? If so, what type of journal entry would be made?

"All About You" Activity

BYP10-5   In the "All About You" feature, you learned who is responsible for remitting income tax, CPP, and EI to the Canada Revenue Agency (CRA) if you are an employee or self-employed. You also learned that the CRA has strict guidelines as to whether someone is self-employed or an employee.

Assume that as a new graduate you are accepting a position where you will be providing consulting services to a company. You have agreed to provide the services for $3,000 a month. The company's manager of human resources suggests that you may want to be considered self-employed rather than an employee of the company. Before you make your decision, you need to better understand the CRA's guidelines and the financial implications.

Instructions

(a) Go to the Canada Revenue Agency's website at www.cra-arc.gc.ca and search for document RC4110 "Employee or Self-Employed?"

What are the factors that should be considered when determining if a worker is an employee or self-employed?
(b) Assume you are an employee and you are paid monthly and that the following amounts are deducted from your gross earnings. (*Note:* The following deductions are based on the 2015 payroll tables for Ontario.)

CPP	$134.06
EI	54.90
Income tax	409.35

What is the amount of cash you will receive each month? What is the total amount of cash you will receive in a year?
(c) Based on the information in part (b), what is the total CPP you will pay in a year? What is the total EI you will pay in a year?
(d) Assume you are self-employed, and you have chosen to pay EI. What is the amount of cash you will receive each month from the company? What is the total CPP you will have to pay in a year? What is the total EI you will have to pay in a year?
(e) Assuming that you will pay the same amount of income tax as you would if you were an employee, calculate the amount of cash you will receive for the year if you are self-employed.
(f) Based on your answers to parts (c) and (e), do you want to be self-employed or an employee of the company? Explain.
(g) If you had the opportunity to provide consulting services to another company in your spare time, would your answer in part (f) be different? Explain.

 Santé Smoothie Saga

(*Note:* This is a continuation of the Santé Smoothie Saga from Chapters 1 through 9.)

BYP10-6   Natalie has had much success with her smoothies business over the past number of months. Some customers have shown an interest in purchasing gift certificates from Natalie. Natalie is considering a gift certificate that would include a recipe book and all of the supplies needed to create two cups of smoothies. Natalie wants to make sure that she has considered all of the risks and rewards of issuing gift certificates. She has come to you with the following questions:

1. From what I understand, if I sell a gift certificate, I need to be recording the money received as "unearned revenue." I am a little confused. How is the use of this account the same as the money that I received from customers that have paid me a deposit for premade smoothies?

2. What if I record the sale of gift certificates as revenue instead of unearned revenue? Technically, I have made a sale of a gift certificate and therefore should be recording amounts received as revenue for the sale of a gift certificate. What if a gift certificate is never used? Does this not justify a sale being recorded?

Instructions

Answer Natalie's questions.

ANSWERS TO CHAPTER QUESTIONS

ANSWERS TO ACCOUNTING IN ACTION INSIGHT QUESTIONS

Across the Organization Insight, p. 539

Q: A company's marketing department is responsible for designing customer loyalty programs. Why would Shoppers' marketing department add the option of donating points to charity?

A: Most customer loyalty programs were designed under the assumption that customers are motivated by cost savings. Shoppers realized that some customers have enough disposable income that cost saving is not a motivation. But many of these customers are motivated by the desire to help others. Thus the option to donate points has the potential to appeal to a wider base of customers and increase the program's success.

Across the Organization Insight, p. 541

Q: Environmental contingencies are generally considered to be harder to estimate than contingencies from lawsuits. What might be the reason for this difference?

A: The requirement to account for environmental contingencies is relatively new compared with the requirement to account for contingencies from lawsuits. Although it is difficult to predict whether the company will win or lose a lawsuit and what type of settlement may be involved, there is a vast history of case law that can be used to help a company form an opinion. Environmental regulations, in contrast, are still evolving and there is often no system (e.g., regulatory compliance audits or environmental site assessment data) that would help a company estimate the possible cost, or even the existence, of environmental contingencies for many years.

Ethics Insight, p. 542

Q: Who are the stakeholders regarding Robert's handling of his payroll?

A: The stakeholders include the part-time employees (who won't be covered by government programs such as EI and workers' compensation), the full-time employees (who are paying more taxes than the part-timers), the accountant (who is violating the professional code of conduct), the government (which is losing out on collecting income taxes, CPP premiums, and EI premiums, among other things), and the justice system (which would want to prosecute Robert for not making the legally required deductions).

All About You Insight, p. 549

Q: If you are providing services to a company, what are the advantages and disadvantages of being a self-employed consultant versus an employee of the company?

A: As a self-employed individual, your monthly cash received from the company would be higher as no CPP, EI, and income tax will be deducted. On the other hand, you will have to make quarterly instalment payments of CPP, EI (if you choose to pay it), and income taxes. If you are self-employed, you may be able to deduct certain expenses to reduce your income tax.

However, some individuals may not manage their cash properly and may be unable to make the remittances when required. In addition, you will have to pay twice as much for CPP and you will not qualify for EI benefits if you are unable to work. If you are self-employed, you would not qualify for other benefits offered to employees by the company, either.

ANSWERS TO SELF-STUDY QUESTIONS

1. d   2. a   3. b   4. d   5. a   6. b   7. c   8. b   *9. b   10. a   11. a

A | SPECIMEN FINANCIAL STATEMENTS

Corus Entertainment

In this appendix, we illustrate current financial reporting with a comprehensive set of corporate financial statements that are prepared in accordance with generally accepted accounting principles (IFRS). We are grateful for permission to use the actual financial statements of Corus Entertainment—one of Canada's foremost integrated media and entertainment companies.

Corus's financial statement package features consolidated statements of financial position, consolidated statements of income and comprehensive income, consolidated statements of changes in shareholders' equity, consolidated statements of cash flows, and notes to the financial statements. The financial statements are preceded by two reports: a statement of management's responsibility for financial reporting and the independent auditors' report.

We encourage students to use these financial statements in conjunction with relevant material in the textbook. As well, these statements can be used to solve the Financial Reporting Problem in the Broadening Your Perspective section of the end-of-chapter material.

Annual reports, including the financial statements, are reviewed in detail in *WileyPLUS* and on the companion website to this textbook.

MANAGEMENT'S RESPONSIBILITY FOR FINANCIAL REPORTING

The accompanying consolidated financial statements of Corus Entertainment Inc. ("Corus") and all the information in this Annual Report are the responsibility of management and have been approved by the Board of Directors (the "Board").

The consolidated financial statements have been prepared by management in accordance with International Financial Reporting Standards. When alternative accounting methods exist, management has chosen those it deems most appropriate in the circumstances. Financial statements are not precise since they include certain amounts based on estimates and judgments. Management has determined such amounts on a reasonable basis in order to ensure that the consolidated financial statements are presented fairly in all material respects. Management has prepared the financial information presented elsewhere in this Annual Report and has ensured that it is consistent with the consolidated financial statements.

Corus maintains systems of internal accounting and administrative controls of high quality, consistent with reasonable cost. Such systems are designed to provide reasonable assurance that the financial information is relevant, reliable and accurate, and that the Company's assets are appropriately accounted for and adequately safeguarded. During the past year, management has maintained the operating effectiveness of internal control over external financial reporting. As at August 31, 2014, the Company's Chief Executive Officer and Chief Financial Officer evaluated, or caused an evaluation of under their direct supervision, the design and operation of the Company's internal controls over financial reporting (as defined in National Instrument 52-109, Certification of Disclosure in Issuers' Annual and Interim Filings) and, based on that assessment, determined that the Company's internal controls over financial reporting were appropriately designed and operating effectively.

The Board is responsible for ensuring that management fulfills its responsibilities for financial reporting, and is ultimately responsible for reviewing and approving the consolidated financial statements. The Board carries out this responsibility through its Audit Committee (the "Committee").

The Committee is appointed by the Board, and all of its members are independent unrelated directors. The Committee meets periodically with management, as well as with the internal and external auditors, to discuss internal controls over the financial reporting process, auditing matters and financial reporting items, to satisfy itself that each party is properly discharging its responsibilities, and to review the Annual Report, the consolidated financial statements and the external auditors' report. The Committee reports its findings to the Board for consideration when approving the consolidated financial statements for issuance to the shareholders. The Committee also considers, for review by the Board and approval by the shareholders, the engagement or re-appointment of the external auditors.

The consolidated financial statements have been audited by Ernst & Young LLP, the external auditors on behalf of the shareholders. Ernst & Young LLP has full and free access to the Committee.

John M. Cassaday
*President and
Chief Executive Officer*

Thomas C. Peddie FCPA, FCA
*Executive Vice President
and Chief Financial Officer*

INDEPENDENT AUDITORS' REPORT

TO THE SHAREHOLDERS OF CORUS ENTERTAINMENT INC.

We have audited the accompanying consolidated financial statements of **Corus Entertainment Inc.**, which comprise the consolidated statements of financial position as at August 31, 2014 and 2013, and the consolidated statements of income and comprehensive income, changes in equity and cash flows for the years then ended, and a summary of significant accounting policies and other explanatory information.

MANAGEMENT'S RESPONSIBILITY FOR
THE CONSOLIDATED FINANCIAL STATEMENTS

Management is responsible for the preparation and fair presentation of these consolidated financial statements in accordance with International Financial Reporting Standards, and for such internal control as management determines is necessary to enable the preparation of consolidated financial statements that are free from material misstatement, whether due to fraud or error.

AUDITORS' RESPONSIBILITY

Our responsibility is to express an opinion on these consolidated financial statements based on our audits. We conducted our audits in accordance with Canadian generally accepted auditing standards. Those standards require that we comply with ethical requirements and plan and perform the audit to obtain reasonable assurance about whether the consolidated financial statements are free from material misstatement.

An audit involves performing procedures to obtain audit evidence about the amounts and disclosures in the consolidated financial statements. The procedures selected depend on the auditors' judgment, including the assessment of the risks of material misstatement of the consolidated financial statements, whether due to fraud or error. In making those risk assessments, the auditors consider internal control relevant to the entity's preparation and fair presentation of the consolidated financial statements in order to design audit procedures that are appropriate in the circumstances, but not for the purpose of expressing an opinion on the effectiveness of the entity's internal control. An audit also includes evaluating the appropriateness of accounting policies used and the reasonableness of accounting estimates made by management, as well as evaluating the overall presentation of the consolidated financial statements.

We believe that the audit evidence we have obtained in our audits is sufficient and appropriate to provide a basis for our audit opinion.

OPINION

In our opinion, the consolidated financial statements present fairly, in all material respects, the financial position of **Corus Entertainment Inc**. as at August 31, 2014 and 2013, and its financial performance and its cash flows for the years then ended in accordance with International Financial Reporting Standards.

Ernst & Young LLP

Toronto, Canada,
November 7, 2014

Chartered Professional Accountants
Licensed Public Accountants

CONSOLIDATED STATEMENTS OF FINANCIAL POSITION

(in thousands of Canadian dollars)	As at August 31, 2014	As at August 31, 2013	As at September 1, 2012
ASSETS			
Current			
Cash and cash equivalents	11,585	81,266	19,198
Accounts receivable (notes 4 and 23)	183,009	164,302	163,345
Promissory note receivable (note 26)	—	47,759	—
Income taxes recoverable	9,768	351	9,542
Prepaid expenses and other	13,032	16,392	12,619
Total current assets	217,394	310,070	204,704
Tax credits receivable	29,044	41,564	43,865
Investments and intangibles (note 5)	47,630	42,975	42,390
Investment in joint ventures (note 26)	—	125,931	121,704
Property, plant and equipment (note 6)	143,618	151,192	163,280
Program and film rights (note 7)	330,437	232,587	229,306
Film investments (note 8)	63,455	62,274	67,847
Broadcast licenses (note 9)	979,984	515,036	520,770
Goodwill (note 9)	934,859	646,045	646,045
Deferred tax assets (note 20)	38,161	39,463	28,327
	2,784,582	2,167,137	2,068,238
LIABILITIES AND SHAREHOLDERS' EQUITY			
Current			
Accounts payable and accrued liabilities (note 11)	170,411	164,443	177,367
Income taxes payable (note 20)	—	—	1,303
Provisions (note 12)	5,314	3,941	2,322
Total current liabilities	175,725	168,384	180,992
Long-term debt (note 13)	874,251	538,966	518,258
Other long-term liabilities (note 14)	171,793	93,241	87,588
Deferred tax liabilities (note 20)	252,687	145,713	145,310
Total liabilities	1,474,456	946,304	932,148
SHAREHOLDERS' EQUITY			
Share capital (note 15)	967,330	937,183	910,005
Contributed surplus	8,385	7,221	7,835
Retained earnings	313,361	256,517	198,445
Accumulated other comprehensive income (loss) (note 16)	3,767	1,653	(812)
Total equity attributable to shareholders	1,292,843	1,202,574	1,115,473
Equity attributable to non-controlling interest	17,283	18,259	20,617
Total shareholders' equity	1,310,126	1,220,833	1,136,090
	2,784,582	2,167,137	2,068,238

Commitments, contingencies and guarantees (notes 13 and 27)
See accompanying notes

CONSOLIDATED STATEMENTS OF INCOME AND COMPREHENSIVE INCOME

For the years ended August 31,

(in thousands of Canadian dollars, except per share amounts)	2014	2013
Revenues	833,016	751,536
Direct cost of sales, general and administrative expenses (note 17)	543,378	500,562
Depreciation and amortization (notes 5 and 6)	24,068	26,812
Interest expense (note 18)	48,320	44,795
Broadcast license and goodwill impairment (notes 9 and 10)	83,000	5,734
Debt refinancing (note 13)	—	25,033
Business acquisition, integration and restructuring costs (notes 12 and 26)	46,792	7,343
Gain on acquisition (note 26)	(127,884)	—
Gain on sale of associated company (note 26)	—	(55,394)
Other expense (income), net (note 19)	5,740	(3,560)
Income before income taxes	209,602	200,211
Income tax expense (note 20)	53,433	34,462
Net income for the period	**156,169**	165,749

Net income attributable to:		
Shareholders	150,408	159,895
Non-controlling interest	5,761	5,854
	156,169	165,749

Earnings per share attributable to shareholders:		
Basic	$ 1.77	$ 1.91
Diluted	$ 1.76	$ 1.90

Net income for the period	156,169	165,749

Other comprehensive income (loss), net of tax: (note 16)

Items that may be reclassified subsequently to net income:		
Unrealized foreign currency translation adjustment	1,720	2,333
Unrealized change in fair value of available-for-sale investments	446	132
Unrealized change in fair value of cash flow hedges	(52)	—
Actuarial (loss) gain on employee future benefits	(2,188)	616
	(74)	3,081
Comprehensive income for the period	**156,095**	168,830

Comprehensive income attributable to:		
Shareholders	150,334	162,976
Non-controlling interest	5,761	5,854
	156,095	168,830

See accompanying notes

CONSOLIDATED STATEMENTS OF CHANGES IN SHAREHOLDERS' EQUITY

(in thousands of Canadian dollars)	Share capital (note 15)	Contributed surplus	Retained earnings	Accumulated other comprehensive income (loss) (note 16)	Total equity attributable to shareholders	Non-controlling interest	Total shareholders' equity
At August 31, 2013	937,183	7,221	256,517	1,653	1,202,574	18,259	1,220,833
Comprehensive income (loss)	—	—	150,408	(74)	150,334	5,761	156,095
Actuarial loss transfer	—	—	(2,188)	2,188	—	—	—
Dividends declared	—	—	(91,376)	—	(91,376)	(6,737)	(98,113)
Issuance of shares under stock option plan	5,465	(862)	—	—	4,603	—	4,603
Issuance of shares under dividend reinvestment plan	24,682	—	—	—	24,682	—	24,682
Share-based compensation expense	—	2,026	—	—	2,026	—	2,026
At August 31, 2014	**967,330**	**8,385**	**313,361**	**3,767**	**1,292,843**	**17,283**	**1,310,126**
At August 31, 2012	910,005	7,835	198,445	(812)	1,115,473	20,617	1,136,090
Comprehensive income	—	—	159,895	3,081	162,976	5,854	168,830
Actuarial gain transfer	—	—	616	(616)	—	—	—
Dividends declared	—	—	(84,452)	—	(84,452)	(6,331)	(90,783)
Issuance of shares under stock option plan	1,155	(2,200)	—	—	(1,045)	—	(1,045)
Issuance of shares under dividend reinvestment plan	26,731	—	—	—	26,731	—	26,731
Shares repurchased	(708)	—	(756)	—	(1,464)	—	(1,464)
Share-based compensation expense	—	1,586	—	—	1,586	—	1,586
Acquisition of non-controlling interest (note 26)	—	—	(17,231)	—	(17,231)	(1,881)	(19,112)
At August 31, 2013	937,183	7,221	256,517	1,653	1,202,574	18,259	1,220,833

See accompanying notes

CONSOLIDATED STATEMENTS OF CASH FLOWS

For the years ended August 31,

(in thousands of Canadian dollars)	2014	2013
OPERATING ACTIVITIES		
Net income for the period	**156,169**	165,749
Add (deduct) non-cash items:		
Depreciation and amortization (*notes 5 and 6*)	**24,068**	26,812
Broadcast license and goodwill impairment (*notes 9 and 10*)	**83,000**	5,734
Amortization of program and film rights (*notes 7 and 17*)	**207,639**	168,883
Amortization of film investments (*notes 8 and 17*)	**19,808**	25,759
Deferred income taxes (*note 20*)	**5,638**	(11,332)
Increase in purchase price obligation (*note 26*)	**3,336**	—
Investment impairments (*notes 5, 8 and 19*)	**—**	7,121
Share-based compensation expense (*note 15*)	**2,026**	1,586
Imputed interest (*note 18*)	**14,698**	10,279
Tangible benefit obligation (*note 26*)	**31,916**	—
Debt refinancing (*note 13*)	**—**	25,033
Gain on sale of associated company (*note 26*)	**—**	(55,394)
Gain on acquisition (*note 26*)	**(127,884)**	—
Other	**2,402**	(14,393)
Net change in non-cash working capital balances related to operations (*note 24*)	**22,945**	6,768
Payment of program and film rights	**(225,935)**	(159,802)
Net additions to film investments	**(25,349)**	(46,074)
Cash provided by operating activities	**194,477**	156,729
INVESTING ACTIVITIES		
Additions to property, plant and equipment (*note 6*)	**(11,976)**	(13,029)
Business combinations (*note 26*)	**(497,393)**	—
Dividends from investment in joint ventures (*note 3*)	**—**	10,866
Net cash flows for investments and intangibles	**(11,493)**	(10,855)
Other	**(5,384)**	(652)
Cash used in investing activities	**(526,246)**	(13,670)
FINANCING ACTIVITIES		
Increase (decrease) in bank loans	**333,243**	(29,925)
Issuance of notes (*note 13*)	**—**	550,000
Redemption of notes (*note 13*)	**—**	(500,000)
Financing fees (*note 13*)	**(587)**	(26,732)
Issuance of shares under stock option plan	**4,603**	884
Shares repurchased (*note 15*)	**—**	(1,464)
Dividends paid	**(65,474)**	(56,696)
Dividends paid to non-controlling interest	**(6,737)**	(6,331)
Other	**(2,960)**	(10,727)
Cash provided by (used in) financing activities	**262,088**	(80,991)
Net change in cash and cash equivalents during the year	**(69,681)**	62,068
Cash and cash equivalents, beginning of the year	**81,266**	19,198
Cash and cash equivalents, end of the year	**11,585**	81,266

Supplemental cash flow disclosures (*note 24*)
See accompanying notes

NOTES TO CONSOLIDATED FINANCIAL STATEMENTS

(in thousands of Canadian dollars, except per share information)

1. CORPORATE INFORMATION

Corus Entertainment Inc. (the "Company" or "Corus") is a diversified Canadian communications and entertainment company. The Company is incorporated under the *Canada Business Corporations Act* and its Class B Non-Voting Shares are listed on the Toronto Stock Exchange (the "TSX") under the symbol CJR.B.

The Company's registered office is at 1500, 850 – 2nd Street SW, Calgary Alberta, T2P 0R8. The Company's executive office is at Corus Quay, 25 Dockside Drive, Toronto, Ontario, M5A 0B5.

These consolidated financial statements include the accounts of the Company and all its subsidiaries and joint ventures. The Company's principal business activities are: the operation of radio stations; the operation of specialty, pay and conventional television networks; and the Corus content business which consists of the production and distribution of films and television programs, merchandise licensing, publishing and the production and distribution of animation software.

2. BASIS OF PREPARATION AND STATEMENT OF COMPLIANCE

These consolidated financial statements have been prepared in accordance with International Financial Reporting Standards ("IFRS") as issued by the International Accounting Standards Board ("IASB"). These consolidated financial statements have been prepared using the accounting policies in note 3.

These consolidated financial statements have been authorized for use in accordance with a resolution from the Board of Directors on October 23, 2014.

3. SIGNIFICANT ACCOUNTING POLICIES

BASIS OF PRESENTATION

The consolidated financial statements have been prepared on a cost basis, except for derivative financial instruments and available-for-sale financial assets, which have been measured at fair value. The consolidated financial statements are presented in Canadian dollars, which is also the Company's functional currency and all values are rounded to the nearest thousand, except where otherwise noted. Each entity consolidated by the Company determines its own functional currency based on the primary economic environment in which the entity operates.

BASIS OF CONSOLIDATION

Subsidiaries

The consolidated financial statements comprise the financial statements of the Company and its subsidiaries, which are the entities over which the Company has control. Control exists when the entity is exposed, or has rights, to variable returns from its involvement with the entity and has the ability to affect those returns through its power over the entity. The non-controlling interest component of the Company's subsidiaries is included in equity.

Subsidiaries are fully consolidated from the date of acquisition, being the date on which the Company obtains control, and continue to be consolidated until the date when such control ceases. The determination of control is assessed either through share ownership and/or control of the subsidiaries board of directors, which may require significant judgment.

The financial statements of the Company's subsidiaries are prepared for the same reporting period as the Company, using consistent accounting policies. All intra-company balances, transactions, unrealized gains and losses resulting from intra-company transactions and dividends are eliminated in full.

Associates and joint arrangements

Associates are entities over which the Company has significant influence. Significant influence is the power to participate in the financial and operating policy decisions of the investee but is not control or joint control over those policies.

A joint venture is a type of joint arrangement in which the parties that have joint control of the arrangement have rights to the net assets of the joint venture. Joint control is the contractually agreed sharing of control of an arrangement, which exists only when decisions about the relevant activities require unanimous consent of the parties sharing control.

The considerations made in determining joint control or significant influence are similar to those necessary to determine control over subsidiaries. The Company accounts for investments in associates and joint ventures using the equity method.

Investments in associates and joint ventures accounted for using the equity method are originally recognized at cost. Under the equity method, the investment in the associate or joint venture is carried on the consolidated statements of financial position at cost plus post-acquisition changes in the Company's share of income and other comprehensive income ("OCI"), less distributions of the investee. Goodwill on the acquisition of the associates and joint ventures is included in the cost of the investments and is neither amortized nor assessed for impairment separately.

The financial statements of the Company's equity-accounted for investments are prepared for the same reporting period as the Company. Where necessary, adjustments are made to bring the accounting policies in line with those of the Company. All intra-company unrealized gains resulting from intra-company transactions and dividends are eliminated against the investment to the extent of the Company's interest in the associate. Unrealized losses are eliminated in the same way as unrealized gains, but only to the extent that there is no evidence of impairment.

After the application of the equity method, the Company determines at each reporting date whether there is any objective evidence that the investment in the associate or joint venture is impaired and consequently, whether it is necessary to recognize an additional impairment loss on the Company's investment in its associate or joint venture. If this is the case, the Company calculates the amount of impairment as the difference between the recoverable amount of the associate and its carrying value and recognizes the amount in the consolidated statements of income and comprehensive income.

BUSINESS COMBINATIONS

Business combinations are accounted for using the acquisition method of accounting, which requires the Company to identify and attribute values and estimated lives to the intangible assets acquired based on their estimated fair value. These determinations involve significant estimates and assumptions regarding cash flow projections, economic risk and weighted average cost of capital. The cost of an acquisition is measured as the aggregate of the consideration transferred, measured at acquisition-date fair value and the amount of any non-controlling interest in the acquiree.

For each business combination, the acquirer measures the non-controlling interest in the acquiree either at fair value or at the proportionate share of the acquiree's identifiable net assets. Acquisition costs incurred are expensed and included in business acquisition, integration and restructuring costs.

When the Company acquires a business, it assesses the financial assets and liabilities assumed for appropriate classification and designation in accordance with the contractual terms, economic circumstances and pertinent conditions as at the acquisition date. This includes the separation of embedded derivatives in host contracts by the acquiree.

If the business combination is achieved in stages, the acquisition date fair value of the acquirer's previously held equity interest in the acquiree is remeasured to fair value at the acquisition date through profit or loss.

Any contingent consideration to be transferred by the acquirer will be recognized at fair value at the acquisition date. Subsequent changes to the fair value of the contingent consideration which is deemed to be a financial asset or liability will be recognized in accordance with International Accounting Standard ("IAS") 39 - *Financial Instruments: Recognition and Measurement* either in profit or loss or as a change to OCI. If the contingent consideration is classified as equity, it should not be remeasured until it is finally settled within equity.

REVENUE RECOGNITION

Advertising revenues are recognized in the period in which the advertising is aired under broadcast contracts and collection is reasonably assured.

Subscriber fee revenues are recognized monthly based on estimated subscriber levels for the period-end, which are based on the preceding month's actual subscribers as submitted by the broadcast distribution undertakings.

The Company's revenues related to production and distribution revenues from the distribution and licensing of film rights; royalties from merchandise licensing, publishing and music contracts; sale of licenses, customer support, training and consulting related to the animation software business; revenues from customer support; and sale of books are recognized when the significant risks and rewards of ownership have transferred to the buyer; the amount of revenue can be measured reliably; it is probable that the economic benefits associated with the transaction will flow to the entity; the stage of completion of the transaction at the end of the reporting period can be measured reliably; the costs incurred for the transaction and the costs to complete the transaction can be measured reliably; and the Company does not retain either continuing managerial involvement or effective control.

Customer advances on contracts are recorded as unearned revenue until all of the foregoing revenue recognition conditions have been met.

Non-refundable advances, whether recoupable or non-recoupable, on royalties are recognized when the license period has commenced and collection is reasonably assured, unless there are future performance obligations associated with the royalty advance for which, in that case, revenue recognition is deferred and recognized when the performance obligations are discharged. Refundable advances are deferred and recognized as revenue as the performance obligations are discharged.

CASH AND CASH EQUIVALENTS

Cash and cash equivalents include cash and short-term deposits with maturities of less than three months at the date of purchase. Cash that is held in escrow, or otherwise restricted from use, is excluded from current assets and is reported separately from cash and cash equivalents.

PROPERTY, PLANT AND EQUIPMENT

Property, plant and equipment are stated at cost, net of accumulated depreciation and/or accumulated impairment losses, if any. Such cost includes the cost of replacing part of the property, plant and equipment, and borrowing costs for long-term construction projects if the recognition criteria are met. When significant parts of property, plant and equipment are required to be replaced at intervals, the Company recognizes such parts as individual assets with specific useful lives and depreciation, respectively. Repair and maintenance costs are recognized in the consolidated statements of income and comprehensive income as incurred.

Depreciation is recorded on a straight-line basis over the estimated useful lives of the assets as follows:

Land and assets not available for use	Not depreciated
Equipment	
Broadcasting	5 - 10 years
Computer	3 - 5 years
Leasehold improvements	Lease term
Buildings	
Structure	20 - 30 years
Components	10 - 20 years
Furniture and fixtures	7 years
Other	4 - 10 years

An item of property, plant and equipment and any significant part initially recognized are derecognized upon disposal or when no future economic benefits are expected from their use or disposal. Any gain or loss arising on derecognition of the asset (calculated as the difference between the net disposal proceeds and the carrying amount of the asset) is included in the consolidated statements of income and comprehensive income when the asset is derecognized.

The assets' residual values, useful lives and methods of depreciation are reviewed at least annually and the depreciation charge is adjusted prospectively, if appropriate.

BORROWING COSTS

Borrowing costs consist of interest and other costs that an entity incurs in connection with the borrowing of funds. Borrowing costs directly attributable to the acquisition, construction or production of an asset that necessarily takes a substantial period of time to get ready for its intended use or sale are capitalized as part of the cost of the asset. All other borrowing costs are expensed in the period they are incurred.

PROGRAM RIGHTS

Program rights represent contract rights acquired from third parties to broadcast television programs, feature films and radio programs. The assets and liabilities related to these rights are recorded when the Company controls the asset, the expected future economic benefits are probable and the cost is reliably measurable. The Company generally considers these criteria to be met and records the assets and liabilities when the license period has begun, the program material is accepted by the Company and the material is available for airing. Long-term liabilities related to these rights are recorded at the net present value of future cash flows, using an appropriate discount rate. These costs are amortized over the contracted exhibition period as the programs or feature films are aired. Program and film rights are carried at cost less accumulated amortization. At each reporting date, the Company assesses its program rights for indicators of impairment and, if any exist, the Company estimates the asset's or cash generating unit's ("CGUs") recoverable amount.

The amortization period and the amortization method for program rights are reviewed at least at the end of each reporting period. Changes in the expected useful life or the expected pattern of consumption of future economic benefits embodied in the assets are accounted for by changing the amortization period or method, as appropriate, and are treated as changes in accounting estimates. Amortization of program rights is included in direct cost of sales, general and administrative expenses and has been disclosed separately in the consolidated statements of cash flows.

FILM INVESTMENTS

Film investments represent the costs of projects in development, projects in process, the unamortized costs of proprietary films and television programs that have been produced by the Company or for which the Company has acquired distribution rights, and third-party-produced equity film investments. Such costs include development and production expenditures and attributed studio and other costs that are expected to benefit future periods. Costs are capitalized upon project greenlight for produced and acquired films and television programs.

The individual-film-forecast-computation method is used to determine amortization. Under this method, capitalized costs and the estimated total costs of participations and residuals, net of anticipated federal and provincial program contributions, production tax credits and coproducers' share of production costs, are charged to amortization expense on a series or program basis in the same ratio that current period actual revenues (numerator) bears to estimated remaining unrecognized future revenues as of the beginning of the current fiscal year (denominator). Future revenues are projected for periods generally not exceeding 10 years from the date of delivery or acquisition. For episodic television series, future revenues include estimates of revenues over a period generally not exceeding 10 years from the date of delivery of the first episode or, if still in production, five years from the date of delivery of the most recent episode, if later. Future revenues are based on historical sales performance for the genre of series or program, the number of episodes produced and the availability of rights in each territory. Estimates of future revenues can change significantly due to the level of market acceptance of film and television products. Accordingly, revenue estimates are reviewed periodically and amortization is adjusted prospectively. In addition, if revenue estimates change significantly with respect to a film or television program, the Company may be required to write down all or a portion of the unamortized costs of such film or television program, therefore impacting direct cost of sales, general and administrative expenses and profitability.

Projects in process represent the accumulated costs of television series or feature films currently in production.

Completed project and distribution rights are stated at the lower of unamortized cost and recoverable amount as determined on a series or program basis. Revenue and cost forecasts for each production are evaluated at each reporting date in connection with a comprehensive review of the Company's film investments, on a title-by-title basis. When an event or change in circumstances indicates that the recoverable amount of a film is less than its unamortized cost, the carrying value is compared to the recoverable amount and if the carrying value is higher, the carrying value is written down to the recoverable amount. The recoverable amount of the film is determined using management's estimates of future revenues under a discounted cash flow approach.

Third-party-produced equity film investments are carried at fair value. Cash received from an investment is recorded as a reduction of such investment on the consolidated statements of financial position and the Company records income on the consolidated statements of income and comprehensive income only when the investment is fully recouped.

Amortization of film investments is included in direct cost of sales, general and administrative expenses and has been disclosed separately in the consolidated statements of cash flows.

GOODWILL AND INTANGIBLE ASSETS

Intangible assets acquired separately are measured on initial recognition at cost. Intangible assets acquired in a business combination are measured at fair value as at the date of acquisition. Following initial recognition, intangible assets are carried at cost less accumulated amortization and accumulated impairment charges, if any. Internally generated intangible assets such as goodwill, brands and customer lists, excluding capitalized program and film development costs, are not capitalized and expenditures are reflected in the consolidated statements of income and comprehensive income in the year in which the expenditure is incurred.

Intangible assets are recognized separately from goodwill when they are separable or arise from contractual or other legal rights and their fair value can be measured reliably. The useful lives of intangible assets are assessed as either finite or indefinite.

Intangible assets with finite lives are amortized over their useful economic lives and assessed for impairment whenever there is an indication that the intangible assets may be impaired. The amortization period and the amortization method for intangible assets with finite useful lives are reviewed at least at the end of each reporting period. Changes in the expected useful life or the expected pattern of consumption of future economic benefits embodied in the assets are accounted for by changing the amortization period or method, as appropriate, and are treated as changes in accounting estimates. The amortization expense on intangible assets with finite lives is recognized in the consolidated statements of income and comprehensive income in the expense category, consistent with the function of the intangible assets.

Amortization is recorded on a straight-line basis over the estimated useful life of the asset as follows:

	Agreement term
Brand names, trade marks and digital rights	
Software, patents and customer lists	3 - 5 years

Intangible assets with indefinite useful lives are not amortized. Broadcast licenses are considered to have an indefinite life based on management's intent and ability to renew the licenses without significant cost and without material modification of the existing terms and conditions of the license. The assessment of indefinite life is reviewed annually to determine whether the indefinite life continues to be supportable. If not, the change in useful life from indefinite to finite is made on a prospective basis.

Goodwill is initially measured at cost, being the excess of the aggregate of the consideration transferred and the amount recognized for non-controlling interest over the net identifiable assets acquired and liabilities assumed. If this consideration is lower than the fair value of the net identifiable assets of the subsidiary acquired, the difference is recognized in profit or loss.

After initial recognition, goodwill is measured at cost less any accumulated impairment losses. For the purpose of impairment testing, goodwill acquired in a business combination is, from the acquisition date, allocated to a CGU or group of CGUs that are expected to benefit from the synergies of the combination, irrespective of whether other assets or liabilities of the acquiree are assigned to those units. The group of CGUs is not larger than the level at which management monitors goodwill or the Company's operating segments.

Where goodwill forms part of a CGU and part of the operation within that unit is disposed of, the goodwill associated with the operation disposed of is included in the carrying amount of the operation when determining the gain or loss on disposal of the operation. Goodwill disposed of in this circumstance is measured based on the relative fair value of the operation disposed of and the portion of the CGU retained.

Broadcast licenses and goodwill are tested for impairment annually or more frequently if events or circumstances indicate that they may be impaired. The Company completes its annual testing during the fourth quarter each year.

Broadcast licenses by themselves do not generate cash inflows and therefore, when assessing these assets for impairment, the Company looks to the CGU to which the asset belongs. The identification of CGUs involves judgment and is based on how senior management monitors operations; however, the lowest aggregations of assets that generate largely independent cash inflows represent CGUs for broadcast license impairment testing.

CGUs for broadcast license impairment testing

For the Television segment, the Company has determined that there are two CGUs: (1) specialty and pay television networks that are operated and managed directly by the Company; and (2) other, as these are the levels at which independent cash inflows have been identified.

For the Radio segment, the Company has determined that the CGU is a radio cluster whereby a cluster represents a geographic area, generally a city, where radio stations are combined for the purpose of managing performance. These clusters are managed as a single asset by a general manager and overhead costs are allocated amongst the cluster and have independent cash inflows at the cluster level.

Groups of CGUs for goodwill impairment testing

For purposes of impairment testing of goodwill, the Company has grouped the CGUs within the Television and Radio operating segments and is performing the test at the operating segment level. This is the lowest level at which management monitors goodwill for internal management purposes.

Gains or losses arising from derecognition of an intangible asset are measured as the difference between the net disposal proceeds and the carrying amount of the asset and are recognized in the consolidated statements of income and comprehensive income when the asset is derecognized.

INCOME TAXES

Tax expense comprises current and deferred income taxes. Tax expense is recognized in the consolidated statements of income, unless it relates to items recognized outside the consolidated statements of income. Tax expense relating to items recognized outside of the consolidated statements of income is recognized in correlation to the underlying transaction in either OCI or equity.

PROVISIONS

Provisions are recognized if the Company has a present legal or constructive obligation as a result of past events, if it is probable that an outflow of resources will be required to settle the obligation, and a reliable estimate can be made of the amount of the obligation.

The amount recognized as a provision is the best estimate of the consideration required to settle the present obligation as of the date of the consolidated statements of financial position, taking into account the risks and uncertainties surrounding the obligation. In some situations, external advice may be obtained to assist with the estimates.

Provisions are discounted and measured at the present value of the expenditure expected to be required to settle the obligation, using an after-tax discount rate that reflects the current market assessments of the time value of money and the risks specific to the obligation. The increase in the provision due to the passage of time is recognized as interest expense. Future information could change the estimates and thus impact the Company's financial position and results of operations.

FINANCIAL INSTRUMENTS

Financial assets within the scope of IAS 39 - *Financial Instruments: recognition and measurement* are classified as financial assets at fair value through profit or loss, loans and receivables or available-for-sale ("AFS"), as appropriate. The Company determines the classification of its financial assets at initial recognition.

Determination of fair value

Fair value is defined as the price at which an asset or liability could be exchanged in a current transaction between knowledgeable, willing parties, other than in a forced or liquidation sale. The fair value of instruments that are quoted in active markets is determined using the quoted prices where they represent those at which regularly and recently occurring transactions take place. The Company uses valuation techniques to establish the fair value of instruments where prices quoted in active markets are not available. Therefore, where possible, parameter inputs to the valuation techniques are based on observable data derived from prices of relevant instruments traded in an active market. These valuation techniques involve some level of management estimation and judgment, the degree of which will depend on the price transparency for the instrument or market and the instrument's complexity.

The Company categorizes its fair value measurements according to a three-level hierarchy. The hierarchy prioritizes the inputs used by the Company's valuation techniques. A level is assigned to each fair value measurement based on the lowest level input significant to the fair value measurement in its entirety. The three levels of the fair value hierarchy are defined as follows:

Level 1 – Unadjusted quoted prices at the measurement date for identical assets or liabilities in active markets.

Level 2 – Observable inputs other than quoted prices included in Level 1, such as quoted prices for similar assets and liabilities in active markets; quoted prices for identical or similar assets and liabilities in markets that are not active; or other inputs that are observable or can be corroborated by observable market data.

Level 3 – Significant unobservable inputs that are supported by little or no market activity.

The fair value hierarchy also requires an entity to maximize the use of observable inputs and minimize the use of unobservable inputs when measuring fair value.

The fair values of cash and cash equivalents are classified within Level 1 because they are based on quoted prices for identical assets in active markets.

The fair value of portfolio investments measured at fair value are classified within Level 2 because even though the security is listed, it is not actively traded. The Company determines the fair value for interest rate swaps as the net discounted future cash flows using the implied zero-coupon forward swap yield curve. The change in the difference between the discounted cash flow streams for the hedged item and the hedging item is deemed to be hedge ineffectiveness and is recorded in the consolidated statements of income. The fair value of the interest rate swap is based on forward yield curves, which are observable inputs provided by banks and available in other public data sources, and are classified within Level 2.

The fair value of the 4.25% Senior Unsecured Guaranteed Notes ("2020 Notes") are classified within Level 2 because they are traded, however, in what is not considered an active market.

Financial instruments classified at fair value through profit or loss and financial assets classified as AFS are recognized on the trade date, which is the date that the Company commits to purchase or sell the asset.

The Company has classified its financial instruments as follows:

Fair value through profit or loss	Loans and receivables	Available-for-sale	Other financial liabilities	Derivatives
• Cash and cash equivalents	• Accounts receivable • Loans and other receivables included in "Investments and intangibles" • Promissory note receivable	• Other portfolio investments included in "Investments and intangibles" • Third-party-produced equity film investments	• Accounts payable and accrued liabilities • Long-term debt • Other long-term financial liabilities included in "Other long-term liabilities"	• Derivatives that are part of a cash flow hedging relationship

Financial assets at fair value through profit or loss

Financial assets at fair value through profit or loss are carried at fair value. Changes in fair value are recognized in other income (expense) in the consolidated statements of income and comprehensive income.

Loans and receivables

Loans and receivables are initially recognized at fair value plus transaction costs. They are subsequently measured at amortized cost using the effective interest method less any impairment. Receivables are reduced by provisions for estimated bad debts which are determined by reference to past experience and expectations.

Financial assets classified as AFS

Financial assets that are not classified as at fair value through profit or loss or as loans and receivables are classified as AFS. A financial asset classified as AFS is initially recognized at its fair value plus transaction costs that are directly attributable to the acquisition of the financial asset. AFS financial instruments are subsequently measured at fair value, with unrealized gains and losses recognized in OCI and accumulated in accumulated other comprehensive income ("AOCI") until the investment is derecognized or determined to be impaired, at which time the cumulative gain or loss is reclassified to the consolidated statements of income and comprehensive income and removed from AOCI. AFS equity instruments not quoted in an active market where fair value is not reliably determinable are recorded at cost less impairment, if any, determined based on the present values of expected future cash flows.

Other financial liabilities

Financial liabilities within the scope of IAS 39 are classified as other financial liabilities. The Company determines the classification of its financial liabilities at initial recognition.

Other financial liabilities are measured at amortized cost using the effective interest rate method. Long-term debt instruments are initially measured at fair value, which is the consideration received, net of transaction costs incurred. Transaction costs related to the long-term debt instruments are included in the value of the instruments and amortized using the effective interest rate method.

Derecognition

A financial asset is derecognized when the rights to receive cash flows from the asset have expired, or when the Company transfers its rights to receive cash flows from the asset and the associated risks and rewards to a third party. The unrealized gains and losses recorded in AOCI are transferred to the consolidated statements of income and comprehensive income on disposal of an AFS asset.

A financial liability is derecognized when the obligation under the liability is discharged or cancelled or expires.

EARNINGS PER SHARE

Basic earnings per share are calculated using the weighted average number of common shares outstanding during the year. The computation of diluted earnings per share assumes the basic weighted average number of common shares outstanding during the year is increased to include the number of additional common shares that would have been outstanding if the dilutive potential common shares had been issued. The dilutive effect of stock options is determined using the treasury stock method.

CHANGES IN ACCOUNTING POLICIES

In December 2011, the IASB amended both IAS 32 - *Financial Instruments: Presentation* and IFRS 7 - *Financial Instruments: Disclosures* by moving the disclosure requirements in IAS 32 to IFRS 7 and enhancing the disclosures about offsetting financial assets and liabilities. The effective date of the amendments is for the Company's fiscal year commencing September 1, 2013. The Company has assessed the impact of these amendments and determined there is no impact on its consolidated financial statements.

4. ACCOUNTS RECEIVABLE

	2014	2013
Trade	168,969	152,911
Other	19,840	13,880
	188,809	166,791
Less allowance for doubtful accounts	5,800	2,489
	183,009	164,302

5. INVESTMENTS AND INTANGIBLES

	Intangibles	Investments in associates	Other	Total
Balance - September 1, 2012	13,452	20,438	8,500	42,390
Increase (decrease) in investment	10,690	(8,606)	7,887	9,971
Investment impairment	–	(3,399)	–	(3,399)
Equity loss in associates	–	(138)	–	(138)
Dividends from associates	–	(1,100)	–	(1,100)
Amortization of intangible assets	(4,416)	–	–	(4,416)
Fair value adjustment	–	(485)	152	(333)
Balance - August 31, 2013	19,726	6,710	16,539	42,975
Increase in investment	4,434	4,268	5,006	13,708
Investment impairment	–	(706)	–	(706)
Equity loss in associates	–	(1,685)	–	(1,685)
Amortization of intangible assets	(7,177)	–	–	(7,177)
Fair value adjustment	–	–	515	515
Balance - August 31, 2014	**16,983**	**8,587**	**22,060**	**47,630**

INTANGIBLES

Intangible assets are comprised of software, patents, customer lists, brand names, trade marks and digital rights. The Company expects the net book value of intangible assets with a finite life to be amortized by December 2020.

IMPAIRMENT OF LONG-LIVED ASSETS

At each reporting date, the Company assesses its long-lived assets, including property, plant and equipment, program and film rights, film investments, goodwill and intangible assets, for potential indicators of impairment, such as an adverse change in business climate that may indicate that these assets may be impaired. If any impairment indicator exists, the Company estimates the asset's recoverable amount. The recoverable amount is determined for an individual asset, unless the asset does not generate cash inflows that are largely independent of those from other assets, in which case the asset is assessed as part of the CGU to which it belongs. An asset's or CGU's recoverable amount is the higher of its fair value less costs to sell ("FVLCS") and its value in use ("VIU"). The determination of the recoverable amount in the impairment assessment requires estimates based on quoted market prices, prices of comparable businesses, present value or other valuation techniques, or a combination thereof, necessitating management to make subjective judgments and assumptions.

The Company records impairment losses on its long-lived assets when the Company believes that their carrying value may not be recoverable. For assets excluding goodwill, an assessment is made at each reporting date as to whether there is any indication that previously recognized impairment losses may no longer exist or may have decreased. If the reasons for impairment no longer apply, impairment losses may be reversed up to a maximum of the carrying amount of the respective asset if the impairment loss had not been recognized.

Goodwill

Goodwill is reviewed for impairment annually or more frequently if there are indications that impairment may have occurred.

Goodwill is allocated to a CGU or group of CGUs for the purposes of impairment testing based on the level at which management monitors it, which is not larger than an operating segment. The Company records an impairment loss if the recoverable amount of the CGU or group of CGUs is less than the carrying amount.

Refer to note 10 for further details on the Company's annual impairment testing for goodwill.

Broadcast licenses

Broadcast licenses are reviewed for impairment annually or more frequently if there are indications that impairment may have occurred.

Broadcast licenses are allocated to a CGU for the purposes of impairment testing. The Company records an impairment loss if the recoverable amount of the CGU is less than the carrying amount.

Refer to note 10 for further details on the Company's annual impairment testing for broadcast licenses.

Intangible assets and property, plant and equipment

The useful lives of the intangible assets with definite lives (which are amortized) and property, plant and equipment are confirmed at least annually and only tested for impairment if events or changes in circumstances indicate that an impairment may have occurred.

LEASES

The determination of whether an arrangement is, or contains, a lease is based on the substance of the arrangement at the inception date: whether fulfillment of the arrangement is dependent on the use of a specific asset or assets or the arrangement conveys a right to use the asset. Where the Company is the lessee, asset values recorded under finance leases are amortized on a straight-line basis over the period of expected use. Obligations recorded under finance leases are reduced by lease payments net of imputed interest. Operating lease commitments, for which lease payments are recognized as an expense in the consolidated statements of income and comprehensive income, are recognized on a straight-line basis over the lease term.

6. PROPERTY, PLANT AND EQUIPMENT

	Land	Broadcasting and computer equipment	Buildings and leasehold improvements	Furniture and fixtures	Other	Total
Cost						
Balance - September 1, 2012	5,539	155,009	104,666	20,210	3,732	289,156
Additions	–	11,505	2,161	810	–	14,476
Disposals and retirements	–	(25,642)	(726)	(2,233)	(1,269)	(29,870)
Balance - August 31, 2013	5,539	140,872	106,101	18,787	2,463	273,762
Additions	–	8,874	1,483	134	2,109	12,600
Acquisitions	–	783	–	37	80	900
Disposals and retirements	–	(4,414)	(154)	(383)	(92)	(5,043)
Balance - August 31, 2014	5,539	146,115	107,430	18,575	4,560	282,219
Accumulated depreciation						
Balance - September 1, 2012	–	97,826	17,906	8,825	1,319	125,876
Depreciation	–	16,545	5,791	2,541	118	24,995
Disposals and retirements	–	(25,286)	(587)	(2,227)	(201)	(28,301)
Balance - August 31, 2013	–	89,085	23,110	9,139	1,236	122,570
Depreciation	–	11,709	5,971	2,423	90	20,193
Impairments	–	–	1,240	–	–	1,240
Disposals and retirements	–	(4,886)	(123)	(369)	(24)	(5,402)
Balance - August 31, 2014	–	95,908	30,198	11,193	1,302	138,601
Net book value						
August 31, 2013	5,539	51,787	82,991	9,648	1,227	151,192
August 31, 2014	5,539	50,207	77,232	7,382	3,258	143,618

Included in property, plant and equipment are assets under finance lease with a cost of $28,297 at August 31, 2014 (2013 - $27,355) and accumulated depreciation of $19,080 (2013 - $16,764).

7. PROGRAM AND FILM RIGHTS

Balance - September 1, 2012	229,306
Additions	154,371
Transfers from film investments	17,793
Amortization	(168,883)
Balance - August 31, 2013	232,587
Additions	220,966
Transfers from film investments	6,984
Acquisitions (note 26)	77,539
Amortization	(207,639)
Balance - August 31, 2014	330,437

	2014	2013
Cost	967,159	710,824
Accumulated amortization	636,722	478,237
Net book value	330,437	232,587

The Company expects that 50% of the net book value of program and film rights will be amortized during the year ended August 31, 2015. The Company expects the net book value of program and film rights to be amortized by September 2019.

OTHER

Other is primarily comprised of investments in venture funds. These venture funds invest in early growth stage companies that are pursuing opportunities in technology, mobile media and consumer sectors.

INVESTMENTS IN ASSOCIATES

In assessing the level of control or influence that the Company has over an investment, management considers ownership percentages, board representation, as well as other relevant provisions in shareholder agreements. The Company exercises significant influence over the following investments which have been accounted for using the equity method and are included in investments in associates.

Fingerprint Digital Inc.

Fingerprint is a technology company providing a turnkey mobile solution to content creators and distributors seeking to link mobile offerings within one branded network. Its focus is educational gaming platforms for kids and their parents across any connected device.

Food Network Canada ("Food Network")

Food Network is a Canadian Category A specialty television network. This brand is the destination for Canadians for all things food-related and provides entertainment programming related to food and nutrition.

Food Network had been classified as an associated business based on management's judgment that the Company has, based on rights to board representation and other provisions in the shareholder agreement, significant influence despite owning only 19.9% of the voting rights. On April 30, 2013, the Company disposed of its interest in Food Network Canada, which had a carrying value of $11,388 on the disposition date (note 26).

KidsCo Limited

KidsCo Limited was an international children's television channel for preschoolers, children aged 6 to 10 and families. The channel was available in 18 languages and presented in over 100 territories on satellite, cable and IPTV platforms across Europe, Asia, Africa, Australia and the Middle East.

At August 31, 2013, the Company performed its annual impairment test for fiscal 2013 and determined that this investment was impaired based on expected future cash flows. As a result, an impairment charge was recorded in other expense (income), net of $3,399. On December 31, 2013, KidsCo ceased business and was wound up.

SoCast Inc. (formerly Supernova Interactive Inc.)

SoCast Inc. is a digital media company that develops and creates software service platforms, including its social relationship management platform for entertainment companies.

The following amounts represent the Company's share in the financial position and results of operations of the associates:

As at August 31,

	2014	2013
Assets	8,926	7,025
Liabilities	339	315
Net assets	8,587	6,710

For the year ended August 31,

	2014	2013
Revenues	320	13,620
Expenses	2,005	13,758
Net loss for the year	(1,685)	(138)

8. FILM INVESTMENTS

The following table sets out the continuity for film investments, which include the Company's internally produced proprietary film and television programs, acquired distribution rights and third-party-produced equity film investments:

	Total
Balance - September 1, 2012	67,847
Additions	63,670
Tax credit accrual	(21,969)
Transfer to program and film rights	(17,793)
Investment impairment	(3,722)
Amortization	(25,759)
Balance - August 31, 2013	62,274
Additions	47,774
Tax credit accrual	(19,801)
Transfer to program and film rights	(6,984)
Amortization	(19,808)
Balance - August 31, 2014	63,455

At August 31, 2014, the Company performed an impairment test on certain third-party-produced equity film investments and determined no impairments were present based on expected future cash flows. In 2013, an impairment charge was recorded in other expense of $3,722.

	2014	2013
Cost	953,238	925,885
Accumulated amortization	889,783	863,611
Net book value	63,455	62,274

The Company expects that 34% of the net book value of film investments will be amortized during the year ended August 31, 2015. The Company expects the net book value of film investments to be fully amortized by August 2023.

9. BROADCAST LICENSES AND GOODWILL

Broadcast licenses and goodwill are tested for impairment annually as at August 31, or more frequently if events or changes in circumstances indicate that they may be impaired. During the second and third quarters of fiscal 2014, the Company concluded that interim impairment tests were required for goodwill for the Radio segment and for broadcast licenses for certain Radio CGUs. As a result of these tests, the Company recorded goodwill and broadcast license impairment charges of $65.5 million and $17.5 million in fiscal 2014, respectively, as certain radio CGUs had actual results that fell short of previous estimates and the outlook for these markets was less robust.

At August 31, 2014, the Company performed its annual impairment test for fiscal 2014 and determined that there were no further impairments, other than those recorded in the second and third quarters of fiscal 2014, for the year then ended. The changes in the book value of goodwill were as follows:

	Total
Balance - August 31, 2012	646,045
Balance - August 31, 2013	646,045
Acquisitions (note 26)	354,363
Impairments (note 10)	(65,549)
Balance - August 31, 2014	934,859

The changes in the book value of broadcast licenses for the period ended August 31, 2014, were as follows:

	Total
Balance - August 31, 2012	520,770
Impairments	(5,734)
Balance - August 31, 2013	515,036
Acquisitions (note 26)	482,399
Impairments (note 10)	(17,451)
Balance - August 31, 2014	979,984

At August 31, 2013 the Company performed its annual impairment test for fiscal 2013. As certain CGUs had actual results that fell short of previous estimates and the outlook for these markets was less robust, impairment losses of $5,734 were recorded for certain Radio broadcast licenses.

Broadcast licenses and goodwill are located primarily in Canada.

10. IMPAIRMENT TESTING

At each reporting date, the Company is required to assess its intangible assets and goodwill for potential indicators of impairment such as an adverse change in business climate that may indicate that these assets may be impaired. If any such indication exists, the Company estimates the recoverable amount of the asset or CGU and compares it to the carrying value. In addition, irrespective of whether there is any indication of impairment, the Company is required to test intangible assets with an indefinite useful life and goodwill for impairment at least annually.

For long-lived assets other than goodwill, the Company is also required to assess, at each reporting date, whether there is any indication that previously recognized impairment losses may no longer exist or may have decreased.

The Company completes its annual testing during the fourth quarter of each fiscal year.

The test for impairment of either an intangible asset or goodwill is to compare the recoverable amount of the asset or CGU to the carrying value. The recoverable amount is the higher of an asset's or CGU's FVLCS and its VIU. The recoverable amount is determined for an individual asset unless the asset does not generate cash inflows that are largely independent of those from other assets or groups of assets (such as broadcast licenses and goodwill) and the asset's VIU cannot be determined to equal its FVLCS. If this is the case, the recoverable amount is determined for the CGU to which the asset belongs.

The Company has determined the VIU calculation is higher than FVLCS and therefore, the recoverable amount for all CGUs or groups of CGUs is based on VIU with the exception of two Radio CGUs.

In determining FVLCS, recent market transactions are taken into account, if available. If no such transactions can be identified, an appropriate valuation model is used. These calculations are corroborated by valuation multiples, quoted share prices for publicly traded subsidiaries or other available fair value indicators.

The VIU calculation uses cash flow projections generally for a five-year period and a terminal value. The terminal value is the value attributed to the CGU's operations beyond the projected period using a perpetuity growth rate. The assumptions in the VIU calculations are segment profit growth rates for periods within the cash flow projections and in perpetuity for the calculation of the terminal value), future levels of capital expenditures and discount rates.

Segment profit growth rates and future levels of capital expenditures are based on management's best estimates considering historical and expected operating plans, strategic plans, economic considerations and the general outlook for the industry and markets in which the CGU operates. The projections are prepared separately for each of the Company's CGUs to which the individual assets are allocated and are based on the most recent financial budgets approved by the Company's Board of Directors and management forecasts generally covering a period of five years with growth rate assumptions over this period. For longer periods, a terminal growth rate is determined and applied to project future cash flows after the fifth year.

• The discount rate applied to each asset, CGU or group of CGUs to determine VIU is a pre-tax rate that reflects an optimal debt-to-equity ratio and considers the risk-free rate, market equity risk premium, size premium and the risks specific to each asset or CGU's cash flow projections.

The recoverable amount for the Radio segment group of CGUs' overall goodwill impairment test was based on VIU. In the third quarter of fiscal 2014, the Company recognized an impairment charge of $65,549 based on the conclusions stated in the preceding paragraph. The recoverable amount and carrying value of the Radio segment group of CGUs after the impairment charge is approximately $378,689.

Sensitivity to changes in assumptions

An increase of 50 basis points in the pre-tax discount rate, a decrease of 50 basis points in the earnings growth rate each year, or a decrease of 50 basis points in the terminal growth rate, each used in isolation to perform the Radio goodwill impairment test, would have resulted in additional goodwill impairment in the Radio segment of between $1,600 and $8,000. However, no material additional broadcast license impairments would arise.

The Company has completed its annual impairment testing of goodwill and intangible assets for fiscal 2014. There were no additional impairment losses to be recorded as a result of the testing. The Company also assessed for any indicators of whether previous impairment losses had decreased. No previously recorded impairment losses on broadcast licenses were reversed.

The carrying amounts of goodwill and broadcast licenses allocated to each CGU and/or group of CGUs are set out in the following tables:

Goodwill	2014	2013
Television	760,760	412,764
Radio	174,099	233,281
	934,859	646,045

Broadcast licenses	2014	2013
Television		
Managed brands	825,000	351,101
Other	7,424	7,424
Radio[1]	147,560	156,511
	979,984	515,036

(1) Broadcast licenses for Radio consist of all Radio CGUs combined. There is no individual Radio CGU that comprises more than 10% of the total broadcast licenses balance.

11. ACCOUNTS PAYABLE AND ACCRUED LIABILITIES

Accounts payable and accrued liabilities are comprised of the following:

	2014	2013
Trade accounts payable and accrued liabilities	86,023	70,552
Program rights payable	63,061	74,456
Film investment accruals	3,111	2,620
Dividends payable	15,578	14,358
Financing lease accruals	2,638	2,457
	170,411	164,443

• In calculating the VIU, the Company uses an appropriate range of discount rates in order to establish a range of values for each CGU or group of CGUs.

The pre-tax discount and growth rates used by the Company for the purpose of its VIU calculations performed for each of the following groups of CGUs in the following periods were:

	2014	2013
Television		
Managed brands		
Pre-tax discount rate	11% - 13%	11% - 13%
Earnings growth rate	4.3% - 13.6%	0% - 4.6%
Terminal growth rate	2%	2%
Other		
Pre-tax discount rate	11% - 13%	11% - 13%
Earnings growth rate	4.3% - 13.6%	0% - 4.6%
Terminal growth rate	2%	2%
Radio		
Pre-tax discount rate	13% - 15%	12% - 14%
Earnings growth rate	2.0% - 8.1%	5.0% - 7.1%
Terminal growth rate	2%	2%

If the recoverable amount of an asset is less than its carrying amount, the carrying amount of the asset is reduced to the recoverable amount and the reduction is recorded as an impairment loss in the consolidated statements of income and comprehensive income.

If the recoverable amount of the CGU or group of CGUs is less than its carrying amount, an impairment loss is recognized. The impairment loss is allocated first to reduce the carrying amount of any goodwill allocated to the CGU or group of CGUs and then to the other assets of the CGU or group of CGUs pro rata on the basis of the carrying amount for each asset in the CGU or group of CGUs. The individual assets in the CGU cannot be written down below their fair value less costs to sell, if determinable.

Except for goodwill, a previously recognized impairment loss is reversed only if there has been a change in the assumptions used to determine the asset's recoverable amount since the last impairment loss was recognized. The reversal is limited so that the carrying amount of the asset does not exceed its recoverable amount, nor exceed the carrying amount that would have been determined, net of depreciation or amortization, had no impairment loss been recognized for the asset in prior years. Such reversal is recognized in the consolidated statements of income and comprehensive income.

In the second quarter of fiscal 2014, the Company determined that there was a broadcast license impairment in two Radio CGUs in Ontario. For one CGU, the Company used VIU to determine the recoverable amount, which resulted in an impairment charge of $6,000, while the FVLCS was used for the second CGU, which resulted in an impairment charge of $2,000 that reduced the carrying value (primarily broadcast licenses) of these CGUs to their recoverable amount. The recoverable amount for the Radio segment group of CGUs' overall goodwill impairment test was based on VIU.

In the third quarter of fiscal 2014, operating results in the Radio segment fell below previous estimates made in the second quarter, as the Radio segment continued to experience a soft advertising market and rating challenges in some markets. As well, the overall radio advertising market experienced a year-over-year decline in the quarter and on a year-to-date basis, causing the Company to lower its cash flow projections to reflect a weaker near term outlook. As a result, the Company determined there was a broadcast license impairment in three Radio CGUs in Ontario and one in British Columbia, as well as a goodwill impairment in the Radio segment group of CGUs overall.

In the third quarter of fiscal 2014, for three CGUs, the Company used VIU to determine the recoverable amount, while the FVLCS was used for one CGU, which resulted in impairment charges totalling $10,691 (predominantly comprised of broadcast license impairments) that reduced the carrying values of these CGUs to their recoverable amount at the end of the third quarter. The recoverable amount of these CGUs after the impairment charges is $49,171.

12. PROVISIONS

The Company recorded restructuring charges of $3,930 (2013 – $4,424) primarily related to severance and employee related costs as a result of the business acquisitions and the related integration. The Company anticipates that these provisions will be substantially paid by fiscal 2015.

The continuity of provisions is as follows:

	2014	2013
Restructuring		
Balance, beginning of period	4,441	2,452
Additions	3,930	4,424
Payments	(3,076)	(2,435)
Balance, end of period	**5,295**	**4,441**
Long term portion	(630)	(1,094)
Total current restructuring provision	**4,665**	**3,347**
Legal claims	649	594
Total current provisions balance, end of period	**5,314**	**3,941**

13. LONG-TERM DEBT

	2014	2013
Bank loans	333,677	–
Senior unsecured guaranteed notes	550,000	550,000
Unamortized financing fees	(9,426)	(11,034)
	874,251	538,966

Interest rates on the balance of the bank loans fluctuate with Canadian bankers' acceptances and/or LIBOR. As at August 31, 2014, the weighted average interest rate on the outstanding bank loans and Notes was 3.9% (2013 – 4.3%). Interest on the bank loans and Notes averaged 4.2% for fiscal 2014 (2013 – 5.8%).

The banks hold as collateral a first ranking charge on all assets and undertakings of Corus and certain of Corus' subsidiaries as designated under the credit agreement. Under the facility, the Company has undertaken to comply with financial covenants regarding a minimum interest coverage ratio and a maximum debt to cash flow ratio. Management has determined that the Company was in compliance with the covenants provided under the bank loans as at August 31, 2014.

On February 3, 2014, the Company's credit agreement with a syndicate of banks was amended and restated. The principal amendment effected was the establishment of a two year $150.0 million term facility, maturing February 3, 2016, incremental to the existing $500.0 million revolving facility maturing February 11, 2017. The $150.0 million term facility was fully drawn on inception and the proceeds were used to reduce the amount drawn on the revolving facility. Both the term and revolving facilities are subject to the same covenants and security. Interest rates on both the term and revolving facilities fluctuate with Canadian prime rate, Canadian bankers' acceptances and/or LIBOR plus an applicable margin.

Contemporaneously with the amendment and restatement of the credit agreement, the Company entered into Canadian dollar interest rate swap agreements to fix the interest rate on $150.0 million at 1.375%, plus an applicable margin, to February 3, 2016. The fair value of Level 2 financial instruments such as interest rate swap agreements is calculated by way of discounted cash flows, using market interest rates and applicable credit spreads. The Company has assessed that there is no ineffectiveness in the hedge of its interest rate exposure. The effectiveness of the hedging relationship is reviewed on a quarterly basis. As an effective hedge, unrealized gains or losses on the interest rate swap agreements are recognized in OCI.

In the second quarter of fiscal 2013, the Company issued $550.0 million principal amount of 4.25% Senior Unsecured Guaranteed Notes due February 11, 2020 ("2020 Notes") and redeemed the existing $500.0 million principal amount of 7.25% Senior Unsecured Guaranteed Notes due February 10, 2017 ("2017 Notes") effective March 16, 2013.

The issuance of the 2020 Notes and redemption of the 2017 Notes resulted in the Company recording debt refinancing costs of $25.0 million in the second quarter of fiscal 2013, which included the early redemption premium of $18.1 million and the non-cash write-off of unamortized financing fees of $6.9 million related to the 2017 Notes.

On February 27, 2013, the Company's $500.0 million credit facility, available on a revolving basis, with a syndicate of banks was amended. The principal amendment was to extend the maturity date to February 11, 2017.

14. OTHER LONG-TERM LIABILITIES

	2014	2013
Public benefits associated with acquisitions	27,604	1,414
Unearned revenue	6,611	8,751
Program rights payable	71,926	20,735
Long-term employee obligations	34,451	30,343
Deferred leasehold inducements	16,052	15,414
Derivative fair value	72	–
Merchandising and tradmark liabilities	11,021	13,486
Finance lease accrual	4,056	3,098
	171,793	93,241

15. SHARE CAPITAL

AUTHORIZED

The Company is authorized to issue, upon approval of holders of no less than two-thirds of the existing Class A shares, an unlimited number of Class A participating shares ("Class A Voting Shares"), as well as an unlimited number of Class B non-voting participating shares ("Class B Non-Voting Shares"), Class A Preferred Shares, and Class 1 and Class 2 Preferred Shares.

Class A Voting Shares are convertible at any time into an equivalent number of Class B Non-Voting Shares. The Class B Non-Voting Shares are convertible into an equivalent number of Class A Voting Shares in limited circumstances.

The Class A Preferred Shares are redeemable at any time at the demand of Corus and retractable at any time at the demand of a holder of a Class A Preferred Share for an amount equal to the consideration received by Corus at the time of issuance of such Class A Preferred Shares. Holders of Class A Preferred Shares are entitled to receive a non-cumulative dividend at such rate as Corus' Board of Directors may determine on the redemption amount of the Class A Preferred Shares. Each of the Class 1 Preferred Shares, the Class 2 Preferred Shares, the Class A Voting Shares and the Class B Non-Voting Shares rank junior to and are subject in all respects to the preferences, rights, conditions, restrictions, limitations and prohibitions attached to the Class A Preferred Shares in connection with the payment of dividends.

The Class 1 and Class 2 Preferred Shares are issuable in one or more series with attributes designated by the Board of Directors. The Class 1 Preferred Shares rank senior to the Class 2 Preferred Shares.

In the event of liquidation, dissolution or winding-up of Corus or other distribution of assets of Corus for the purpose of winding up its affairs, the holders of Class A Preferred Shares are entitled to a payment in priority to all other classes of shares of Corus to the extent of the redemption amount of the Class A Preferred Shares, but will not be entitled to any surplus in excess of that amount. The remaining property and assets will be available for distribution to the holders of the Class A Voting Shares and Class B Non-Voting Shares, which shall be paid or distributed equally, share for share, between the holders of the Class A Voting Shares and the Class B Non-Voting Shares, without preference or distinction.

EARNINGS PER SHARE

The following is a reconciliation of the numerator and denominator (in thousands) used for the computation of the basic and diluted earnings per share amounts:

	2014	2013
Net income attributable to shareholders (numerator)	**150,408**	**159,895**
Weighted average number of shares outstanding (denominator)		
Weighted average number of shares outstanding - basic	84,993	83,860
Effect of dilutive securities	334	330
Weighted average number of shares outstanding - diluted	**85,327**	**84,190**

The calculation of diluted earnings per share for fiscal 2014 excluded 12,618 (2013 – nil) weighted average Class B Non-Voting Shares issuable under the Company's Stock Option Plan because these options were not "in-the-money".

16. ACCUMULATED OTHER COMPREHENSIVE INCOME (LOSS)

	Unrealized Foreign currency translation adjustment	Unrealized change in fair value of available-for-sale investments	Unrealized change in fair value of cash flow hedges	Actuarial gains (losses) on defined benefit plans	Total
Balance – September 1, 2012	(1,065)	253	–	–	(812)
Items that may be subsequently reclassified to income:					
Amount	2,333	152	–	–	2,485
Income tax	–	(20)	–	–	(20)
	2,333	132	–	–	2,465
Items that will never be subsequently reclassified to net income:					
Amount	–	–	–	838	838
Income tax	–	–	–	(222)	(222)
	–	–	–	616	616
Transfer to retained earnings	–	–	–	(616)	(616)
Balance – August 31, 2013	**1,267**	**386**	–	–	**1,653**
Items that may be subsequently reclassified to income:					
Amount	1,720	515	(71)	–	2,164
Income tax	–	(69)	19	–	(50)
	1,720	446	(52)	–	2,114
Items that will never be subsequently reclassified to net income:					
Amount	–	–	–	(2,977)	(2,977)
Income tax	–	–	–	789	789
	–	–	–	(2,188)	(2,188)
Transfer to retained earnings	–	–	–	2,188	2,188
Balance – August 31, 2014	**2,987**	**832**	**(52)**	**–**	**3,767**

ISSUED AND OUTSTANDING

	Class A Voting Shares #	Class A Voting Shares $	Class B Non-Voting Shares #	Class B Non-Voting Shares $	Total $
Balance – September 1, 2012	3,434,292	26,595	79,924,384	883,410	910,005
Conversion of Class A Voting Shares to Class B Non-Voting Shares	(4,000)	(31)	4,000	31	–
Issuance of shares under stock option plan	–	–	50,200	1,155	1,155
Issuance of shares under dividend reinvestment plan	–	–	1,134,666	26,731	26,731
Shares repurchased	–	–	(64,104)	(708)	(708)
Balance – August 31, 2013	3,430,292	26,564	81,049,146	910,619	937,183
Conversion of Class A Voting Shares to Class B Non-Voting Shares	(2,000)	(15)	2,000	15	–
Issuance of shares under stock option plan	–	–	259,500	5,465	5,465
Issuance of shares under dividend reinvestment plan	–	–	1,024,947	24,682	24,682
Balance – August 31, 2014	**3,428,292**	**26,549**	**82,335,593**	**940,781**	**967,330**

No Class A Preferred Shares, Class 1 Preferred Shares or Class 2 Preferred Shares are outstanding at August 31, 2014.

DIVIDENDS

The holders of Class A Voting Shares and Class B Non-Voting Shares are entitled to receive such dividends as the Board of Directors determines to declare on a share-for-share basis, as and when any such dividends are declared or paid. The holders of Class B Non-Voting Shares are entitled to receive during each dividend period, in priority to the payment of dividends on the Class A Voting Shares, a dividend which is $0.005 per share per annum higher than that received on the Class A Voting Shares. This higher dividend rate is subject to proportionate adjustment in the event of future consolidations or subdivisions of shares and in the event of any issue of shares by way of stock dividend. After payment or setting aside for payment of the additional non-cumulative dividends on the Class B Non-Voting Shares, holders of Class A Voting Shares and Class B Non-Voting Shares participate equally, on a share-for-share basis, on all subsequent dividends declared.

2014 Date of record	Date paid	Class A Voting Shares Amount paid	Class B Non-Voting Shares Amount paid
September 16, 2013	September 30, 2013	$0.084583	$0.085000
October 15, 2013	October 31, 2013	$0.084583	$0.085000
November 15, 2013	November 29, 2013	$0.084583	$0.085000
December 13, 2013	December 30, 2013	$0.084583	$0.085000
January 15, 2014	January 31, 2014	$0.084583	$0.085000
February 14, 2014	February 28, 2014	$0.090417	$0.090833
March 14, 2014	March 31, 2014	$0.090417	$0.090833
April 15, 2014	April 30, 2014	$0.090417	$0.090833
May 15, 2014	May 30, 2014	$0.090417	$0.090833
June 16, 2014	June 30, 2014	$0.090417	$0.090833
July 15, 2014	July 31, 2014	$0.090417	$0.090833
August 15, 2014	August 29, 2014	$0.090417	$0.090833
		$1.055834	**$1.060831**

The total amount of dividends declared in fiscal 2014 was $91,376 (2013 - $84,452).

On October 23, 2014 the Company declared dividends of $0.090417 per Class A Voting Share and $0.090833 per Class B Non-Voting Share payable on each of November 28, 2014, December 30, 2014 and January 30, 2015 to the shareholders of record at the close of business on November 14, 2014, December 15, 2014 and January 15, 2015, respectively.

17. DIRECT COST OF SALES, GENERAL AND ADMINISTRATIVE EXPENSES

	2014	2013
Amortization of program and film rights	207,639	168,883
Amortization of film investments	19,808	25,759
Other cost of sales	27,615	35,276
Employee costs	149,459	155,687
Other general and administrative	138,857	114,957
	543,378	500,562

18. INTEREST EXPENSE

	2014	2013
Interest on long-term debt	32,121	32,814
Imputed interest on long-term liabilities	14,698	10,279
Other	1,501	1,702
	48,320	44,795

19. OTHER EXPENSE (INCOME), NET

	2014	2013
Interest income	(722)	(1,091)
Foreign exchange loss	649	876
Equity loss of investees	1,685	623
Third-party-produced film investment write down	—	3,722
Investment in associates (recovery) impairment	(256)	3,399
Income from joint ventures	—	(12,093)
Increase in purchase price obligation (note 26)	3,336	—
Other	1,048	1,004
	5,740	(3,560)

27. COMMITMENTS, CONTINGENCIES AND GUARANTEES

LEASES

The Company enters into operating leases for the use of facilities and equipment. During fiscal 2014, rental expenses in direct cost of sales, general and administrative expenses totalled approximately $21,422 (2013 - $21,239). Future minimum rental payments payable under non-cancellable operating leases at August 31, are as follows:

	2014	2013
Within one year	25,430	24,428
After one year but not more than five years	97,722	88,888
More than five years	290,617	279,157
	413,769	392,473

The Company has entered into finance leases for the use of computer equipment and software, telephones, furniture and broadcast equipment. The leases range between three and five years and bear interest rates varying from 2.1% to 7.0%. Future minimum lease payments under finance leases together with the present value of the net minimum lease payments are as follows:

	2014		2013	
	Minimum payments	Present value of payments	Minimum payments	Present value of payments
Within one year	2,921	2,638	2,556	2,147
After one year but not more than five years	4,362	4,056	3,247	3,098
Total minimum lease payments	7,283	6,694	5,803	5,245
Less amounts representing finance charges	589	—	558	—
Present value of minimum lease payments	6,694	6,694	5,245	5,245

PURCHASE COMMITMENTS

The Company has entered into various agreements for the right to broadcast or distribute certain film, television and radio programs in the future. These agreements, which range in term from one to five years, generally commit the Company to acquire specific films, television and radio programs or certain levels of future productions. The acquisition of these broadcast and distribution rights is contingent on the actual delivery of the productions. Management estimates that these agreements will result in future program and film expenditures of approximately $61,711 (2013 - $53,997). In addition, the Company has commitments of $97 (2013 - nil) for future television script production.

The Company has commitments related to trade marks and certain other intangible rights until February 2021, for a total of approximately $16,641 (2013 - $19,942). The Company has certain additional annual commitments, some of which are contingent on performance, to pay royalties for trade mark rights. In addition, the Company has licenses and other commitments over the next five years to use specific software, signal and satellite functions of approximately $29,549 (2013 - $40,352). Generally, it is not the Company's policy to issue guarantees to non-controlled affiliates or third parties, with limited exceptions.

LITIGATION

The Company, its subsidiaries and joint ventures are involved in litigation matters arising out of the ordinary course and conduct of its business. Although such matters cannot be predicted with certainty, management does not consider the Company's exposure to litigation to be material to these consolidated financial statements.

OTHER MATTERS

Many of the Company's agreements, specifically those related to acquisitions and dispositions of business assets, included indemnification provisions where the Company may be required to make payments to a vendor or purchaser for breach of fundamental representation and warranty terms in the agreements with respect to matters such as corporate status, title of assets, environmental issues, consents to transfer, employment matters, litigation, taxes payable and other potential material liabilities. The maximum potential amount of future payments that the Company could be required to make under these indemnification provisions is not reasonably quantifiable, as certain indemnifications are not subject to a monetary limitation. As at August 31, 2014, management believed there was only a remote possibility that the indemnification provisions would require any material cash payment.

The Company indemnifies its directors and officers against any and all claims or losses reasonably incurred in the performance of their service to the Company to the extent permitted by law. The Company has acquired and maintains liability insurance for directors and officers of the Company and its subsidiaries.

B SALES TAXES

All companies operating in Canada need to understand how sales taxes apply to their particular business in their province or territory. Sales taxes may take the form of the Goods and Services Tax (GST), Provincial Sales Tax (PST), or Harmonized Sales Tax (HST). GST is levied by the federal government. PST is levied by the provinces, with the exception of Alberta, the Northwest Territories, Nunavut, and Yukon, where no PST is charged. Ontario, Nova Scotia, New Brunswick, Newfoundland and Labrador, and Prince Edward Island have combined the GST and PST into one Harmonized Sales Tax or HST.

A business is considered an agent of the federal and provincial governments and is therefore required to collect sales taxes on behalf of these governing bodies. Sales taxes apply to most goods and services, but some exceptions do apply, which will be discussed in this appendix. We will discuss the collection, payment, recording, and remittance of each of these types of sales taxes in the following sections.

LEARNING OBJECTIVE ❶ ▶ Explain the different types of sales tax.

Types of Sales Taxes

GOODS AND SERVICES TAX

The GST is a federal sales tax on most goods and services provided in Canada. A business must register for the GST if it provides taxable goods or services in Canada and if it has revenues of more than $30,000 in any year. Businesses that have to register for the GST or decide to do so voluntarily are called registrants. Registrants can claim a credit—called an input tax credit (ITC)—for the amount of GST they pay or owe on purchases of goods or services against the GST they collect or are owed. GST returns are submitted quarterly for most registrants (monthly for large registrants) to the Canada Revenue Agency. The taxes are payable to the Receiver General for Canada, which is the collection agent for the federal government. We will discuss remittances of GST to the Canada Revenue Agency a little later in the appendix.

The GST applies at a rate of 5% on most transactions. Transactions subject to GST are called taxable supplies. There are two other categories of goods and services with respect to the GST:

1. zero-rated supplies, such as basic groceries and prescription drugs and
2. exempt supplies, such as educational services, health care services, and most financial services provided by financial institutions.

No GST applies to zero-rated or exempt supplies. However, businesses that supply zero-rated goods can claim input tax credits (ITCs) on the costs incurred to provide zero-rated goods. For example, assume that Jenna's Corner Grocery sells bananas to a customer. There is no requirement for Jenna to collect GST on the sale because bananas are a basic grocery item. However, the grocery store must pay for utilities to operate the store, and any GST paid on utility bills and other expenses can be claimed by Jenna against the sales of items such as bananas as an ITC.

HARMONIZED SALES TAX

The Harmonized Sales Tax or HST is a combined or harmonized tax. Provinces that adopt the HST combine their provincial sales tax rate with the federal GST rate and charge one combined rate on most goods and services. HST has the same regulations as GST; that is, HST is charged on taxable supplies, and no HST is charged on zero-rated and exempt supplies. In these provinces, the Receiver General for Canada is the collection agent for both the federal and provincial governments, reducing some of the administrative burden from the provinces. Similar to GST, HST returns are submitted quarterly for most registrants (monthly for large registrants). We will discuss remittances to the Canada Revenue Agency a little later in the appendix.

The provinces of Ontario, Nova Scotia, New Brunswick, Newfoundland and Labrador, and Prince Edward Island charge HST and they are referred to generally as participating provinces.

Illustration B-1 provides the GST/HST status of some typical goods and services.

▶ **ILLUSTRATION** **B-1**
Examples of GST/HST status

Taxable Supplies	Zero-Rated Supplies	Exempt Supplies
Building materials	Prescription drugs	Used house
Ready-to-eat pizza	Uncooked pizza	Dental services
Two doughnuts	Six or more doughnuts	Insurance policy

The reason ready-to-eat pizza and two doughnuts have GST/HST added to the purchase price is because they are considered convenience items, which are taxable, and not basic groceries, which are not taxable.

PROVINCIAL SALES TAX

Provincial sales taxes are charged on retail sales of certain goods and services. There are only four provinces that charge a separate Provincial Sales Tax: British Columbia, Saskatchewan, Manitoba, and Quebec. In Quebec, it is referred to as Quebec Sales Tax or QST. For businesses that have sales transactions in several provinces, the amount of PST they need to charge will depend on where the goods are being shipped. Consequently, a business could have several PST payable accounts while operating out of a province where only HST applies to sales. For example, Rogers Communications Inc. sells telecommunications services and products throughout Canada and is headquartered in Toronto, Ontario. When a sale is made to a customer in Saskatchewan, Rogers charges that customer both GST and Saskatchewan PST. Rogers is then responsible for submitting any PST collected on Saskatchewan sales to the Saskatchewan provincial government.

Provincial sales taxes are remitted periodically to the Minister of Finance in each province, which is the collection agent for provincial governments. PST rates vary by province and can change with each provincial budget. Certain goods are exempt and therefore can be purchased with no PST, such as children's clothing, textbooks, and residential rent. Examples of exempt services that are not taxable include personal services such as dental and medical services. Because rates and exemptions vary by province, it is important when starting a business to check with provincial officials for details on how to calculate the provincial tax that must be applied to sales.

To summarize, four provinces—British Columbia, Manitoba, Quebec, and Saskatchewan—apply both PST and GST to the selling price of a taxable good or service. The provincial tax rates used by these four provinces vary but the GST is consistent at the rate of 5%. Five provinces charge a combined HST: New Brunswick, Newfoundland and Labrador, Nova Scotia, Ontario, and Prince Edward Island. Four provinces and territories charge only the GST: Alberta, the Northwest Territories, Nunavut, and Yukon. GST/HST is charged on sales of most products and services and PST is also charged on most products and services but with notable exceptions.

The rates of sales tax in each province and territory are shown in Illustration B-2.

▶ILLUSTRATION **B-2**
Sales tax rates

Province/Territory	GST (HST) Rate[1]	PST Rate[3]
Alberta	5.0%	0.0%
British Columbia	5.0%	7.0%
Manitoba	5.0%	8.0%
New Brunswick	13.0%	N/A
Newfoundland and Labrador	15.0%[2]	N/A
Northwest Territories	5.0%	0.0%
Nova Scotia	15.0%	N/A
Nunavut	5.0%	0.0%
Ontario	13.0%	N/A
Prince Edward Island	14.0%	N/A
Quebec	5.0%	9.975%
Saskatchewan	5.0%	5.0%
Yukon	5.0%	0.0%

[1]These rates are in effect as of April 1, 2013, and are subject to change.
[2]Rate is effective January 1, 2016.
[3]These rates are current as of May 4, 2015, and are subject to change.

| LEARNING OBJECTIVE | | Record sales taxes collected by businesses on goods and services. |

Sales Taxes Collected on Receipts

Sales taxes are collected by businesses from consumers on taxable goods and services. It is important to understand that sales taxes are not a source of revenue for a company. They are collected by a company on behalf of the federal and provincial governments. Consequently, collected sales tax is a current liability to the company until remitted to the respective government at regular intervals.

SERVICES

Now let's look at how service companies record sales taxes on the services they provide.

Services with PST

Assume that $250.00 of cleaning services were provided by a company in Manitoba for cash on July 24. These services are subject to both PST (8%) and GST (5%), and would be recorded as follows:

July 24	Cash	282.50	
	Service Revenue		250.00
	PST Payable ($250 × 8%)		20.00
	GST Payable ($250 × 5%)		12.50
	To record cleaning service revenue.		

A	=	L	+	OE
+282.50		+20.00		+250.00
		+12.50		

↑Cash flows: +282.50

Note that the revenue recorded is $250.00, and not $282.50. The service revenue recognized is exclusive of the GST and PST amounts collected, which are recorded as current liabilities.

Services with HST

Assume now that these same services were provided by a company in New Brunswick, where HST is 13%. The entry would be as follows:

A	=	L	+	OE
+282.50		+32.50		+250.00

↑Cash flows: +282.50

July 24	Cash	282.50	
	Service Revenue		250.00
	HST Payable ($250.00 × 13%)		32.50
	To record cleaning service revenue.		

MERCHANDISE

Entries are needed to record the sales taxes owed when merchandise inventory (goods) is sold, or to reduce sales taxes payable when merchandise inventory is returned.

Sales with PST

Assume that Staples sells $1,000 of office furniture, on account, in the province of Manitoba, where PST is 8% and GST is 5%. Staples uses a perpetual inventory system and the cost of the furniture to Staples is $800. Staples will make the following two entries to record the sale and the cost of the sale on May 20:

A	=	L	+	OE
+1,130		+50		+1,000
		+80		

Cash flows: no effect

A	=	L	+	OE
−800				−800

Cash flows: no effect

May 20	Accounts Receivable	1,130	
	Sales		1,000
	GST Payable ($1,000 × 5%)		50
	PST Payable ($1,000 × 8%)		80
	To record sale of merchandise on account.		
20	Cost of Goods Sold	800	
	Merchandise Inventory		800
	To record cost of goods sold.		

The merchandise inventory does not include any sales taxes that may have been paid when the company purchased the merchandise. We will learn more about that in the next section of this appendix.

Under a periodic inventory system, the second entry would not be recorded.

Sales Returns and Allowances with PST

If the customer from the previous transaction returns $300 of the merchandise purchased from Staples on May 25 and the goods are returned to inventory, Staples entries to record the sales return would appear as follows (assuming an inventory cost of $240):

A	=	L	+	OE
−339		−15		−300
		−24		

Cash flows: no effect

A	=	L	+	OE
+240				+240

Cash flows: no effect

May 25	Sales Returns and Allowances	300	
	GST Payable ($300 × 5%)	15	
	PST Payable ($300 × 8%)	24	
	Accounts Receivable		339
	To record credit for returned merchandise.		
25	Merchandise Inventory	240	
	Cost of Goods Sold		240
	To record cost of merchandise returned.		

Note that the GST and PST payable accounts, rather than a receivable account, are debited, to indicate that this is a return of previously collected sales tax.

Under a periodic inventory system, the second entry would not be recorded.

Sales with HST

Assume now that Staples sells the same $1,000 of office furniture, on account, in the province of Ontario, where HST is 13%. Staples uses a perpetual inventory system and the cost of the furniture to Staples is $800. Staples will record the following two entries to record the sale and the cost of the sale on May 20:

May 20	Accounts Receivable	1,130	
	Sales		1,000
	HST Payable ($1,000 × 13%)		130
	To record sale of merchandise on account.		
20	Cost of Goods Sold	800	
	Merchandise Inventory		800
	To record cost of goods sold.		

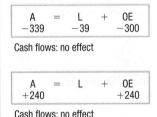

A = L + OE
+1,130   +130   +1,000
Cash flows: no effect

A = L + OE
−800   −800
Cash flows: no effect

Notice that no PST account is used because provinces that adopt HST are essentially replacing GST and PST with one tax only, HST.

Under a periodic inventory system, the second entry would not be recorded.

Sales Returns and Allowances with HST

Assume the same $300 of merchandise was returned to Staples on May 25. Staples entries to record the sales return would appear as follows:

May 25	Sales Returns and Allowances	300	
	HST Payable ($300 × 13%)	39	
	Accounts Receivable		339
	To record credit for returned merchandise.		
25	Merchandise Inventory ($300 ÷ $1,000 × $800)	240	
	Cost of Goods Sold		240
	To record cost of merchandise returned.		

A = L + OE
−339   −39   −300
Cash flows: no effect

A = L + OE
+240   +240
Cash flows: no effect

Under a periodic inventory system, the second entry would not be recorded.

LEARNING OBJECTIVE **3**   Record sales taxes paid on the purchase of goods and services.

Sales Taxes Paid on Payments

Businesses, similar to consumers, must pay the applicable PST and GST or HST charged by their suppliers on taxable goods and services.

PURCHASE OF MERCHANDISE FOR RESALE

When purchasing merchandise for resale, the treatment of the PST is different than that of the GST. In British Columbia, Manitoba, and Saskatchewan, PST is a single-stage tax collected from the final consumers of taxable goods and services. Consequently, wholesalers do not charge provincial sales tax to the retailer, which will in turn resell the merchandise, at a higher price, to the final consumer. By presenting a vendor licence number, retailers are able to buy merchandise for resale, exempt of the PST. In Quebec, however, QST is a provincial sales tax on most goods and services paid by both consumers and businesses alike.

Businesses in Canada must pay GST/HST on the purchase of merchandise but can then offset the GST/HST paid against any GST/HST collected. If a business is a registrant in Quebec, QST paid on most purchases can also be offset against any QST collected. Consequently, **when merchandise for resale is purchased, the GST/HST and QST paid by a business are not part of the inventory cost**. The GST/HST paid on purchases is debited to an account called GST or HST Recoverable and is called an input tax credit. The QST paid on purchases in Quebec is debited to an account called QST recoverable and is called an input tax refund (ITR).

Purchases with GST

The following is an entry to record the purchase of merchandise for resale in the province of Manitoba on May 4 at a price of $4,000, on account, using a perpetual inventory system:

A	=	L	+	OE
+4,000		+4,200		
+200				

Cash flows: no effect

May 4	Merchandise Inventory	4,000	
	GST Recoverable ($4,000 × 5%)	200	
	Accounts Payable		4,200
	To record merchandise purchased on account.		

As previously discussed, GST is not included in the Merchandise Inventory account, but is instead recorded as a receivable.

Under a periodic inventory system, the $4,000 debit would have been recorded to the Purchases account.

Purchase Returns and Allowances with GST

The entry to record a $300 return of merchandise on May 8 is as follows:

A	=	L	+	OE
−15		−315		
−300				

Cash flows: no effect

May 8	Accounts Payable	315	
	GST Recoverable ($300 × 5%)		15
	Merchandise Inventory		300
	To record the return of merchandise.		

Note that the GST Recoverable account is credited instead of the GST Payable account because this is a reduction of the previously recorded GST.

Under a periodic inventory system, the credit of $300 would have been recorded to the Purchase Returns and Allowances account.

To summarize, PST is not paid on purchases of merchandise for resale. GST paid on purchases is recoverable and recorded as a current asset in the GST Recoverable account. Purchase returns and allowances require an adjustment of GST only, since PST was not paid on the original purchase.

Purchases with HST

The following is an entry to record the purchase of merchandise for resale in the province of Prince Edward Island, where the HST rate is 14%, on May 4 at a price of $4,000, on account, using a perpetual inventory system:

A	=	L	+	OE
+4,000		+4,560		
+560				

Cash flows: no effect

May 4	Merchandise Inventory	4,000	
	HST Recoverable ($4,000 × 14%)	560	
	Accounts Payable		4,560
	To record merchandise purchased on account.		

The HST is not included in the Merchandise Inventory account but is instead recorded as a receivable.

Under a periodic inventory system, the $4,000 debit would have been recorded to the Purchases account.

Purchase Returns and Allowances with HST

The entry to record a $300 return of merchandise in the province of Prince Edward Island, where the HST rate is 14%, on May 8 is as follows:

May 8	Accounts Payable	342	
	HST Recoverable ($300 × 14%)		42
	Merchandise Inventory		300
	To record the return of merchandise.		

A	=	L	+	OE
−42		−342		
−300				

Cash flows: no effect

Note that the HST Recoverable account is credited instead of the HST Payable account because this is a reduction of the previously recorded HST.

Under a periodic inventory system, the credit of $300 would have been recorded to the Purchase Returns and Allowances account.

To summarize, HST paid on purchases is recoverable and recorded as a current asset in the HST Recoverable account.

OPERATING EXPENSES

The accounting treatment of sales taxes incurred on operating expenses depends on the type of sales taxes that the company is charged.

Operating Expenses with PST

Although PST is not charged on goods purchased for resale, it is charged to businesses that use taxable goods and services in their operations. For example, a business must pay GST and PST when it buys office supplies. As with all purchases made by a business that is a registrant, the GST is recoverable. (That is, it can be offset as an ITC against GST collected.) Because the PST is not recoverable, the PST forms part of the cost of the asset or expense that is being acquired.

The following is the entry for a cash purchase of office supplies on May 18 in the amount of $200 in the province of Saskatchewan, where PST is 5% and GST is 5%:

May 18	Supplies ($200 + $10* PST)	210	
	GST Recoverable ($200 × 5%)	10	
	Cash		220
	To record purchase of office supplies.		

*$200 × 5% = $10

A	=	L	+	OE
+210				
+10				
−220				

▼ Cash flows: −220

In this situation, the cost of the supplies includes both the supplies and the PST. Because GST is recoverable, it does not form part of the asset cost.

This same purchase would be recorded as follows if it occurred in the province of Quebec, where QST is 9.975% and GST is 5%:

May 18	Supplies	200.00	
	GST recoverable ($200.00 x 5%)	10.00	
	QST recoverable ($200.00 x 9.975%)	19.95	
	Cash		229.95
	To record purchase of office supplies		

A	=	L	+	OE
+200.00				
+10.00				
+19.95				
−229.95				

▼ Cash flows: −229.95

Operating Expenses with HST

When HST is applied, it is treated in the same manner as GST. HST is recoverable and does not form part of the cost of the item purchased. The purchase of office supplies would be recorded as follows if it had occurred in the province of Ontario, where HST is 13%:

A	=	L	+	OE
+200				
+26				
−226				

⬇ Cash flows: −226

May 18	Supplies	200	
	HST Recoverable ($200 × 13%)	26	
	Cash		226
	To record purchase of office supplies.		

Note that the type and amount of sales tax paid changes the amount recorded as the cost of office supplies in each province: $210.00 in Saskatchewan, $200.00 in Quebec, and $200.00 in Ontario.

PROPERTY, PLANT, AND EQUIPMENT

The PST and GST or HST apply to other purchases, such as the purchase of property, plant, and equipment, in the same manner as described in the Operating Expenses section above. All GST (or HST) paid is recoverable and is not part of the asset's cost. The PST, however, is part of the cost of the asset being purchased because it is not recoverable.

Property, Plant, and Equipment with PST

The following is the entry for the purchase of office furniture on May 20 from Staples, on account, for $1,000 plus applicable sales taxes in Manitoba, where PST is 8% and GST is 5%.

A	=	L	+	OE
+1,080		+1,130		
+50				

Cash flows: no effect

May 20	Furniture ($1,000 + $80* PST)	1,080	
	GST Recoverable ($1,000 × 5%)	50	
	Accounts Payable		1,130
	To record purchase of office furniture.		

*$1,000 × 8% = $80

Because the PST is not recoverable, the cost of the furniture is $1,080, inclusive of the PST. Compare this entry made by the buyer to record the purchase with the entry made by the seller (Staples) to record the sale, shown earlier in this appendix. Both companies record accounts payable and accounts receivable in the same amount, $1,130. However, the seller records both GST and PST payable while the buyer records only GST recoverable.

In Saskatchewan, where PST is 5% and GST is 5%, the same entry would be recorded as follows:

A	=	L	+	OE
+1,050		+1,100		
+50				

Cash flows: no effect

May 20	Furniture ($1,000 + $50* PST)	1,050	
	GST Recoverable ($1,000 × 5%)	50	
	Accounts Payable		1,100
	To record purchase of office furniture.		

*$1,000 × 5% = $50

Property, Plant, and Equipment with HST

In Ontario, where HST is 13%, the entry would be recorded as follows:

A	=	L	+	OE
+1,000		+1,130		
+130				

Cash flows: no effect

May 20	Furniture	1,000	
	HST Recoverable ($1,000 × 13%)	130	
	Accounts Payable		1,130
	To record purchase of office furniture.		

As we have noted before, the type and amount of sales taxes paid change the amount recorded as the cost of the office furniture in each province: $1,080 in Manitoba, $1,050 in Saskatchewan, and $1,000 in Ontario.

LEARNING OBJECTIVE 4 ▸ Record the remittance of sales taxes.

Remittance of Sales Taxes

As mentioned in the introduction, businesses act as agents of the federal and provincial governments in charging and later remitting taxes charged on sales and services. For example, Staples, the seller of office furniture shown earlier in the appendix, must remit GST or HST to the Receiver General for Canada and PST to the Minister of Finance, where applicable. Notice that, even if Staples has not received payment from a customer buying on account before the due date for the remittance, the tax must still be paid to the government authorities. As a registrant, however, Staples will also benefit from claiming ITCs and recording a reduction in amounts payable from applying GST/HST on sales.

GST (OR HST)

When remitting the amount owed to the federal government at the end of a reporting period for GST (or HST), the amount of GST/HST payable is reduced by any amount in the GST (or HST) Recoverable account.

To illustrate, Quasar Company operates retail clothing stores in British Columbia. Quasar collects GST and PST from its customers upon each sale and pays GST on all purchases. In British Columbia, GST is 5% and PST is 7%. At the end of the quarter, October 31, 2017, Quasar had total sales of $400,000 during the quarter and reported the following account balances related to GST:

GST Recoverable	$12,000
GST Payable	$20,000

Quasar will complete its GST return, prepare the required journal entry, and pay the amounts owing.

The difference between GST Recoverable and GST Payable is remitted to the Canada Revenue Agency. The journal entry to record the remittance is as follows:

Oct. 31	GST Payable	20,000	
	GST Recoverable		12,000
	Cash		8,000
	To record remittance of GST.		

A	=	L	+	OE
−12,000		−20,000		
−8,000				

↓ Cash flows: −8,000

If Quasar Company were located in a province that had HST, the journal entry would be the same but the accounts would be titled HST Payable and HST Recoverable. If Quasar Company collected both GST and HST (because sales are made to multiple provinces), the entry would also be the same but the accounts would be titled GST/HST Payable and GST/HST Recoverable.

GST/HST returns require the registrant to report at specified dates, depending on the business's volume of sales. The amount of the sales and other revenue as well as the amount of GST/HST charged on these sales, whether collected or not, is reported on the return. The amount of the ITCs claimed is also entered to reduce the amount owing to the Receiver General. If the amount of GST/HST recoverable exceeds the amount of GST/HST payable, the return should be filed as soon as possible in order to ask for a refund. The entry to record the cash receipt from a GST/HST refund will be similar to the entry shown above, except that there will be a debit to Cash, instead of a credit. Quasar would report for the period of August 1 to October 31, 2017, and it would report its total sales of $400,000 in addition to GST charged and GST ITCs.

The above discussion of the remittance of GST/HST explains why all registrants need two general ledger accounts—a payable account and a recoverable account. The GST (or HST) Payable account is used to keep track of all GST or HST charged on sales and revenues. The second account, GST (or HST) Recoverable, is used to keep track of the GST/HST ITCs that have been paid on all of the business's purchases. Both amounts must be reported on the return. Failure by a business to capture the proper amounts of ITCs has a significant impact on income and on cash flows.

PST

The remittance of PST to the Minister of Finance of the applicable province is similar to that of GST/HST except that, since no credit can be claimed, the amount paid at the end of each reporting period is the amount of the balance in the PST Payable account.

Total PST collected by Quasar Company during the quarter ending October 31, 2017, is $28,000. The entry to record a remittance of PST is as follows:

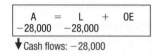

A = L + OE
−28,000 −28,000
↓ Cash flows: −28,000

Oct. 31	PST Payable	28,000	
	Cash		28,000
	To record remittance of PST.		

QST

The remittance of QST to the Minister of Revenue of Quebec is similar to that of GST/HST.

ROUNDING TAX AMOUNTS

Be careful when you record the amounts of taxes charged or claimed in the business accounts. Numbers must be rounded carefully. If the amount of the tax calculated on a credit sale is less than half a cent, the amount should be rounded down. If the amount of the tax as calculated comes to more than half a cent, the amount should be rounded up. For example, applying 13% HST on an amount of $49.20 would give you $6.396. The tax amount to be recorded must be rounded up to $6.40. On the other hand, if the sale is a cash sale, due to the abolition of the one-cent coin (the penny), the amount of the sale, including all taxes, must be rounded to the nearest five cents. Rounding might seem insignificant, but when a business has many transactions, the amounts can add up and the registrant is responsible to the government authorities for any shortfall created in error.

CONCLUSION

Sales tax law is intricate. It has added a lot of complexity to the accounting for most transactions flowing through today's businesses. Fortunately, computers that are programmed to automatically determine and record the correct sales tax rate for each good or service provided have simplified matters somewhat. Before recording sales tax transactions, however, it is important to understand all of the relevant sales tax regulations. Check the federal and provincial laws in your jurisdiction.

▶ Brief Exercises

Explain the different types of sales taxes. (LO 1) AP

BEB–1 List the various sales taxes in Canada and explain the main differences between the types. In what way are they alike to the consumer?

Record sales—perpetual inventory system—Quebec. (LO 2) AP

BEB–2 Record the sale on account, for $1,600, of merchandise costing $900 in the province of Quebec. Assume the company uses a perpetual inventory system. The QST is 9.975%. (Use QST payable for Quebec sales tax transactions.)

Record sales return—perpetual inventory system—Quebec. (LO 2) AP

BEB–3 Half of the shipment described in BEB–2 is returned because the incorrect sizes have been shipped. Record the return of merchandise on the seller's books.

Record sales and sales return—periodic inventory system—Quebec. (LO 2) AP

BEB–4 Record the sale in BEB–2 and the sales return in BEB–3 assuming the business uses a periodic inventory system.

BEB–5   Record the billing for $450 of services by D. R. Wong, dentist, in the province of British Columbia. Dental services are exempt from GST and PST.

Record exempt services—British Columbia. (LO 2) AP

BEB–6   Record the billing of accounting services of $700 for the preparation of personal income tax returns in the territory of Nunavut. GST is applicable on this service. Nunavut does not charge PST.

Record fees—Nunavut. (LO 2) AP

BEB–7   Record the purchase on account of $4,100 of merchandise for resale in the province of Manitoba, where the PST is 8%. The company uses a perpetual inventory system and the purchase is PST exempt.

Record inventory purchase—perpetual inventory system—Manitoba. (LO 3) AP

BEB–8   Record the return of $500 of the merchandise purchased in BEB–7.

Record purchase return—perpetual inventory system—Manitoba. (LO 3) AP

BEB–9   Record the purchase on account of $4,100 of merchandise for resale in the province of New Brunswick, where HST is 13%. The company uses a perpetual inventory system.

Record inventory purchase—perpetual inventory system—New Brunswick. (LO 3) AP

BEB–10   Record the return of $500 of the merchandise purchased in BEB–9.

Record purchase return—perpetual inventory system—New Brunswick. (LO 3) AP

BEB–11   Record the cash purchase of $600 of office supplies in the province of Saskatchewan, where PST is 5%.

Record purchase of supplies—Saskatchewan. (LO 3) AP

BEB–12   Record the cash purchase of $600 of office supplies in the province of Nova Scotia, where HST is 15%.

Record purchase of supplies—Nova Scotia. (LO 3) AP

BEB–13   Record the purchase on account of a $32,000 delivery truck in the province of Prince Edward Island, where HST is 14%.

Record purchase of vehicle—Prince Edward Island. (LO 3) AP

BEB–14   Record the purchase on account of a $32,000 delivery truck in the province of British Columbia, where the PST is 7%.

Record purchase of vehicle—British Columbia. (LO 3) AP

BEB–15   Record the purchase on account of $300 of office supplies and $5,000 of merchandise for resale in the province of Manitoba. The company uses a perpetual inventory system and the purchase of merchandise is PST exempt. The PST rate is 8%.

Record purchase of supplies and inventory—perpetual inventory system—Manitoba. (LO 3) AP

BEB–16   Record two payments: one cheque to the Receiver General for Canada for GST and one to the Minister of Finance of British Columbia for PST. The balances in the accounts are as follows: GST Payable $6,120, GST Recoverable $940, and PST Payable $8,570.

Record remittance of GST and PST—British Columbia. (LO 4) AP

BEB–17   Record the deposit of a cheque from the Receiver General for a refund of $690 following the filing of an HST return. The balances in the accounts are as follows: HST Payable $3,920 and HST Recoverable $4,610.

Record HST refund. (LO 4) AP

▶ Exercises

EB–1   Nebula Limited is a merchant operating in the province of Manitoba, where the PST rate is 8%. Nebula uses a perpetual inventory system. Transactions for the business are shown below:

Record purchase and sales transactions—perpetual inventory system—Manitoba. (LO 2, 3) AP

May 1   Paid May rent to the landlord for the rental of a warehouse. The lease calls for monthly payments of $7,300 plus 5% GST.
     3   Sold merchandise on account and shipped merchandise to Marvin Ltd. for $25,000, plus applicable sales taxes, terms n/30, FOB shipping point. This merchandise cost Nebula $18,600.
     5   Granted Marvin Ltd. a sales allowance of $800 for defective merchandise purchased on May 3. No merchandise was returned.
     7   Purchased on account from Macphee Ltd. merchandise for resale for $11,000, plus applicable tax.
    12   Made a cash purchase at Home Depot of a desk for the shipping clerk. The price of the desk was $600 before applicable taxes.
    31   Paid the quarterly remittance of GST to the Receiver General. The balances in the accounts were as follows: GST Payable $7,480 and GST Recoverable $1,917.

Instructions

Prepare the journal entries to record these transactions on the books of Nebula Limited.

Record purchase and sales transactions—perpetual inventory system—Alberta. (LO 2, 3) AP

EB-2 Refer to Nebula Limited in EB-1. Assume instead that the company operates in the province of Alberta, where PST is not applicable.

Instructions

Prepare the journal entries to record these transactions on the books of Nebula.

Record purchase and sales transactions—perpetual inventory system—Ontario. (LO 2, 3) AP

EB-3 Refer to Nebula Limited in EB-1. Assume instead that the company operates in the province of Ontario, where HST is 13%.

Instructions

Prepare the journal entries to record these transactions on the books of Nebula. Assume that the GST balances on May 31 are the balances in the HST accounts.

Record purchase and sales transactions—periodic inventory system—Manitoba. (LO 2, 3) AP

EB-4 Triton Company is a retailer operating in the province of Manitoba, where the PST rate is 8%. Triton uses a periodic inventory system. Transactions for the business are shown below:

Nov. 1   Paid November store rent to the landlord. The lease calls for monthly payments of $5,500 plus 5% GST.

4   Purchased merchandise for resale on account from Comet Industries. The merchandise cost $8,000 plus applicable tax.

6   Returned $500 of merchandise to Comet Industries.

7   Sold merchandise on account to Solar Star Company for $10,000 plus applicable sales taxes, terms, n/30, FOB shipping point. The merchandise was shipped to Solar Star. The cost of the merchandise to Triton was $6,000.

12   Purchased a new laptop computer at Staples for the marketing manager. The price of the laptop was $1,200 before applicable taxes.

30   Paid the quarterly remittance of GST to the Receiver General. The balances in the accounts were as follows: GST Payable $2,520 and GST Recoverable $985.

Instructions

Prepare the journal entries to record these transactions on the books of Triton Company.

Record purchase and sales transactions—periodic inventory system—Alberta. (LO 2, 3) AP

EB-5 Using the information for the transactions of Triton Company in EB-4, assume now that Triton operates in the province of Alberta, where PST is not applicable.

Instructions

Prepare the journal entries to record these transactions on the books of Triton.

Record purchase and sales transactions—periodic inventory system—Ontario. (LO 2, 3) AP

EB-6 Using the information for the transactions of Triton Company in EB-4, assume now that Triton operates in the province of Ontario, where HST is 13%.

Instructions

Prepare the journal entries to record these transactions on the books of Triton. Assume that the GST balances on May 31 provided in EB-4 are the balances in the HST accounts.

Record transactions for services, equipment, and supplies—British Columbia. (LO 2, 3, 4) AP

EB-7 Leon Cheng is a sole proprietor providing accounting services in the province of British Columbia, where PST is charged at the rate of 7% and GST is at the rate of 5%. Transactions for the business are shown below:

June 1   Paid cash to a local courier for the delivery of documents to several clients. The invoice was for $200 plus GST and PST.

5   Paid $800 cash plus GST and PST to have the office painted. Use the Repairs Expense account.

10   Purchased photocopy paper for $250 from a local stationery store, on account. The store added the appropriate sales taxes to the purchase price.

13   Billed a client for accounting services provided. The fee charged was $4,700 and the appropriate sales taxes were added to the fee billed.

15   Collected $896 on account. This included accounting services of $800, GST of $40, and PST of $56.

22   Paid $720 cash plus applicable taxes to Air Canada for an airline ticket to Ottawa to meet with a client. Airfare is subject to both PST and GST.

30   Received invoice from BC Tel for telephone service for the month of June. The invoice is for $150 plus GST and PST.

30   Paid the quarterly remittance of GST to the Receiver General. The balances in the accounts were as follows: GST Payable $1,890.50 and GST Recoverable $741.60.

30   Paid the quarterly remittance of PST to the Minister of Revenue for the province of British Columbia. The balance in the PST Payable account was $2,640.00.

Instructions

Prepare the journal entries to record these transactions on the books of Leon Cheng's accounting business.

EB–8 Ruby Gordon, L.L.B. is a sole proprietor providing legal services in the province of Newfoundland and Labrador, where the HST rate is 15%. Transactions for the business are shown below:

June 8 Purchased equipment for scanning and printing on account at a cost of $1,500. The appropriate taxes were added to this purchase price.

10 Purchased toner for the equipment for $100 cash from a local stationery store. The store added the appropriate taxes to the purchase price.

12 Billed Lee Ltd. for legal services provided. The fee charged was $1,250 plus appropriate taxes.

18 Paid cash of $220 plus applicable taxes to have a boardroom table repaired.

22 Collected the Lee Ltd. account billed on June 12.

30 Paid the quarterly remittance of HST to the Receiver General. The balances in the accounts were as follows: HST Payable $2,520.60 and HST Recoverable $820.45.

Record transactions for services, equipment, and supplies—Newfoundland and Labrador. (LO 2, 3, 4) AP

Instructions

Prepare the journal entries to record these transactions on the books of Ruby Gordon's legal practice.

EB–9 Refer to the data for Ruby Gordon, L.L.B. in EB–8. Assume instead that Ruby is operating her legal practice in Alberta and that on June 30 she paid a quarterly remittance of GST, as opposed to HST, to the Receiver General. Assume the balances were as follows: GST Payable $970.50 and GST Recoverable $315.55.

Record transactions for services, equipment, and supplies—Alberta. (LO 2, 3, 4) AP

Instructions

Prepare the journal entries to record these transactions on the books of Ruby Gordon's legal practice.

▶ Problems

PB–1 Mark's Music is a store that buys and sells musical instruments in Ontario, where the HST rate is 13%. Mark's Music uses a perpetual inventory system. Transactions for the business are shown below:

Record purchase and sales transactions—perpetual inventory system—Ontario. (LO 2, 3) AP

Nov. 2 Purchased three electric guitars from Fender Supply Limited, on account, at a cost of $900 each.

4 Made a cash sale of two keyboards for a total invoice price of $2,600 plus applicable taxes. The cost of each keyboard was $675.

5 Received a credit memorandum from Western Acoustic Inc. for the return of an acoustic guitar that was defective. The original invoice price before taxes was $700 and the guitar had been purchased on account. Mark's Music intends to return the defective guitar to the original supplier.

7 One of the keyboards from the cash sale of November 4 was returned to the store for a full cash refund because the customer was not satisfied with the instrument. The keyboard was returned to inventory.

8 Purchased supplies from a stationery store. The price of the supplies is $200 before all applicable taxes.

10 Sold one Omega trumpet to Regional Band, on account, for an invoice price of $5,100 before applicable taxes. The trumpet had cost Mark's Music $2,850.

13 Purchased two saxophones from Yamaha Canada Inc. on account. The invoice price was $1,900 for each saxophone, excluding applicable taxes.

14 Collected $4,150 on account. The payment included all applicable taxes.

16 Returned to Yamaha Canada Inc. one of the saxophones purchased on November 13, as it was the wrong model. Received a credit memorandum from Yamaha for the full purchase price.

20 Made a payment on account for the amount owing to Fender Supply Limited for the purchase of November 2.

Instructions

Prepare the journal entries to record the Mark's Music transactions.

PB–2 Transaction data for Mark's Music are available in PB–1. Assume instead that the company operates in the province of British Columbia, where the PST rate is 7% and the GST rate is 5%.

Record purchase and sales transactions—perpetual inventory system—British Columbia. (LO 2, 3) AP

Instructions

Prepare the journal entries to record these transactions on the books of Mark's Music.

PB–3 Transaction data for Mark's Music are available in PB–1. Assume that the company uses a periodic inventory system instead of a perpetual inventory system and operates in the province of Ontario, where the HST rate is 13%.

Record purchase and sales transactions—periodic inventory system—Ontario. (LO 2, 3) AP

Instructions

Prepare the journal entries to record the Mark's Music transactions.

Record purchase and sales transactions—periodic inventory system—British Columbia. (LO 2, 3) AP

PB–4 Transaction data for Mark's Music are available in PB–1. Assume that the company uses a periodic inventory system instead of a perpetual inventory system and operates in the province of British Columbia, where the PST rate is 7% and the GST rate is 5%.

Instructions

Prepare the journal entries to record these transactions on the books of Mark's Music.

Record service transactions— Alberta. (LO 2, 3, 4) AP

PB–5 Manny Lee, L.L.B., is a lawyer operating as a sole proprietor in the province of Alberta. Alberta does not charge provincial sales taxes and the GST rate is 5%. Transactions for the business are shown below:

May 1 Signed a two-year lease for the office space and immediately paid the first and last months' rent. The lease calls for monthly rent of $1,650 plus applicable taxes.

4 Purchased furniture, on account, from George's Furniture at a cost of $4,100. The appropriate sales taxes were added to this purchase price.

5 Returned one chair to George's due to a defect. The cost of the chair before taxes was $800.

6 Billed a client for the preparation of a contract. The client was very pleased with the document and immediately paid Manny's invoice for fees of $2,500 plus taxes.

10 Purchased paper for the photocopier for $300 cash from a local stationery store. The store added the appropriate sales taxes to the purchase price.

13 Billed Manson Ltd. for legal services rendered connected with the purchase of land. The fee charged is $1,100 plus applicable taxes.

18 Paid George's for the furniture purchase of May 4, net of returned items.

19 Paid $22 cash to a local grocery store for coffee beans for the office coffee machine. Coffee beans are zero-rated grocery products for GST and HST purposes. Use the Office Expense account.

21 In accordance with the lease agreement with the landlord, Manny must pay for water supplied by the municipality. The water invoice was received and the services amounted to $150. No GST is charged for municipal water.

25 Collected a full payment from Manson Ltd. for the May 13 bill.

27 Completed the preparation of a purchase and sale agreement for Pedneault Inc. and billed fees of $600.

Instructions

(a) Prepare the journal entries to record these transactions on the books of Manny Lee's law practice.

(b) Determine the balances in the GST Payable and GST Recoverable accounts. Determine if the company must make a payment to the Receiver General or if it will apply for a refund. Record the appropriate journal entry.

Record service transactions— Ontario. (LO 2, 3, 4) AP

PB–6 Refer to Manny Lee's law practice in PB–5. Assume instead that Mr. Lee operates in the province of Ontario, where the HST rate is 13%.

Instructions

(a) Prepare the journal entries to record these transactions on the books of Manny Lee's law practice.

(b) Determine the balances in the HST Payable and HST Recoverable accounts. Determine if the business must make a payment to the Receiver General or if it will apply for a refund. Record the appropriate journal entry.

SUBSIDIARY LEDGERS AND SPECIAL JOURNALS

In the textbook, we learned how to record accounting transactions in a general journal. Each journal entry was then individually posted to its respective general ledger account. However, such a practice is only useful in a company where the volume of transactions is low. Most companies use additional journals called special journals and ledgers called subsidiary ledgers to record transaction data.

We will look at subsidiary ledgers and special journals in the next sections. Both subsidiary ledgers and special journals can be used in either a manual accounting system or a computerized accounting system.

The illustrations provided in this appendix are taken from a manual accounting system. Computerized accounting systems vary in the way in which the accounting information is captured, processed, and reported. Nevertheless, the same basic information is maintained in a manual or computerized accounting system. If you can understand how a manual system works, you will be able to follow how a computerized system is capturing, recording, and reporting transactions for a business of any size or type.

| LEARNING OBJECTIVE **1** | Describe the purposes and advantages of maintaining subsidiary ledgers. |

Subsidiary Ledgers

Imagine a business that has several thousand customers who buy merchandise on account. If the business records the transactions with these customers in one general ledger account—Accounts Receivable—it would be virtually impossible to determine the balance owed by each customer at any point in time. Similarly, the amount owing to each creditor would be difficult to locate quickly if there were a single Accounts Payable account in the general ledger.

To track individual balances, companies use subsidiary ledgers (or "subledgers"). A subsidiary ledger is a group of accounts that share a common characteristic (for example, all accounts receivable). The subsidiary ledger maintains account details that the general ledger cannot capture. A subsidiary ledger is an addition to, and an expansion of, the general ledger.

Common subsidiary ledgers are:

1. The accounts receivable subledger, which collects transaction data for individual customers such as balances owing and the age of balances owing.
2. The accounts payable subledger, which collects transaction data for individual creditors such as invoice numbers and purchase dates.
3. The inventory ledger, which collects transaction data for each inventory item purchased and sold. The inventory ledger may also include information used by the purchasing department, such as the terms negotiated with suppliers. Computerized systems can be programmed to automatically produce purchase orders when the inventory is low to avoid shortages.
4. The payroll ledger, which details individual employee pay records.
5. The long-lived asset ledger, which keeps track of each item of property, plant, and equipment.

In each of these subsidiary ledgers, individual accounts are arranged in alphabetical, numerical, or alphanumerical order. The detailed data from each subsidiary ledger are summarized in the related general ledger account For example, the detailed data from the accounts receivable subsidiary ledger are summarized in the Accounts Receivable account. The general ledger account that summarizes subsidiary ledger data is called a control account.

Each general ledger control account balance must equal the total balance of the sum of the individual accounts in the related subsidiary ledger. This is an important internal control function.

EXAMPLE

An example of an accounts receivable control account and subsidiary ledger is shown in Illustration C-1 for Mercier Enterprises.

▶ILLUSTRATION **C-1**
Accounts receivable general ledger control account and subsidiary ledger

GENERAL LEDGER

Accounts Receivable — No. 112

Date	Explanation	Ref.	Debit	Credit	Balance
2017					
Jan. 31			12,000		12,000
31				8,000	4,000

ACCOUNTS RECEIVABLE SUBSIDIARY LEDGER

Aaron Co. — No. 112-172

Date	Explanation	Ref.	Debit	Credit	Balance
2017					
Jan. 11	Invoice 336		6,000		6,000
19	Payment			4,000	2,000

Branden Inc. — No. 112-173

Date	Explanation	Ref.	Debit	Credit	Balance
2017					
Jan. 12	Invoice 337		3,000		3,000
21	Payment			3,000	0

Caron Co. — No. 112-174

Date	Explanation	Ref.	Debit	Credit	Balance
2017					
Jan. 20	Invoice 339		3,000		3,000
29	Payment			1,000	2,000

The example is based on the following transactions:

Credit Sales			Collections on Account		
Jan. 11	Aaron Co.	$ 6,000	Jan. 19	Aaron Co.	$4,000
12	Branden Inc.	3,000	21	Branden Inc.	3,000
20	Caron Co.	3,000	29	Caron Co.	1,000
		$12,000			$8,000

During the month of January, Mercier makes three different sales to three different customers. When these sales are made, they are updated in each customer's subledger account. For example, we can see above that on January 11, Mercier makes a $6,000 sale to Aaron Co. on credit. A debit (increase) to Aaron's accounts receivable is recorded in Aaron's subledger account. On January 12, when a $3,000 sale is made to Branden Inc., again a debit is recorded in Branden Inc.'s subledger. Similarly, when customers make payments, such as when Caron Co. makes a $1,000 payment, a credit for $1,000 is made to the appropriate subledger account. The subledger maintains this level of customer detail.

At the end of the month, these data are updated in the general ledger in summary form. Therefore, we can see in the above general ledger that the Accounts Receivable account is debited with the total credit sales of $12,000 and credited $8,000, reflecting the total cash payments received. The result is that the total debits ($12,000) and credits ($8,000) in the Accounts Receivable control account in the general ledger match the detailed debits and credits in the subsidiary accounts. The balance of $4,000 in the control account agrees with the total of the balances in the individual Accounts Receivable accounts (Aaron $2,000 + Branden $0 + Caron $2,000) in the subsidiary ledger.

Rather than relying on customer or creditor names in a subsidiary ledger, a computer system expands the account number of the control account. For example, if the general ledger control account Accounts Receivable was numbered 112, the first customer account in the accounts receivable subsidiary ledger might be numbered 112-001, the second 112-002, and so on. Data entry in a computerized system is much faster if account numbers, rather than customer names, are used. Most systems allow inquiries about specific customer accounts in the subsidiary ledger (by account number) or about the control account.

As shown, postings are made monthly to the control account in the general ledger. Postings to the individual accounts in the subsidiary ledger are made daily. The rationale for posting daily is to ensure that account information is current. This enables Mercier Enterprises to monitor credit limits, send statements to customers, and answer inquiries from customers about their account balances. In a computerized accounting system, transactions are simultaneously recorded in journals and posted to both the general and subsidiary ledgers.

ADVANTAGES OF SUBSIDIARY LEDGERS

Subsidiary ledgers have several advantages:

1. They show transactions that affect one customer or one creditor in a single account. They provide up-to-date information on specific account balances.
2. They free the general ledger from excessive details. A trial balance of the general ledger does not contain vast numbers of individual customer account balances.
3. They strengthen internal controls by making the division of labour possible in posting. One employee can post to the general ledger while different employees post to the subsidiary ledgers.
4. They help locate errors in individual accounts. The potential for errors is minimized by reducing the number of accounts in one ledger and by using control accounts.

In a computerized accounting system, the internal control achieved by the double-checking by one employee of work performed by another employee, as described in item 3 above, doesn't happen as often. The accounting software is programmed to perform mathematical functions without error and to post entries to the subsidiary and general ledgers simultaneously. Consequently, computerized accounting systems do not make errors such as calculation errors and posting errors. Other errors, such as entry errors, can and do still occur. Internal control must be done using different means in computerized systems since account transactions are posted automatically.

LEARNING OBJECTIVE **2** ▶ Record transactions in special journals and post to subsidiary and general ledgers.

Special Journals

As mentioned earlier, due to the volume of transactions, most companies use special journals in addition to the general journal. If a company has large numbers of similar transactions, it is useful to create a special journal for those transactions. Examples of similar transactions that occur frequently are all sales of merchandise on account, or all cash receipts. The types of special journals a company will use depend largely on the types of transactions that occur frequently for that company.

While the form, type, and number of special journals used will vary among organizations, many merchandising companies use the journals shown in Illustration C-2 to record daily transactions. The letters that appear in parentheses following the journal name represent the posting reference used for each journal.

▶ILLUSTRATION **C-2**
Use of special journals and the general journal

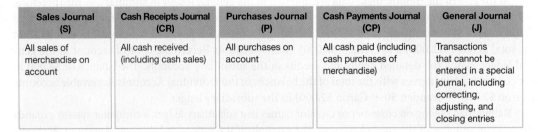

Sales Journal (S)	Cash Receipts Journal (CR)	Purchases Journal (P)	Cash Payments Journal (CP)	General Journal (J)
All sales of merchandise on account	All cash received (including cash sales)	All purchases on account	All cash paid (including cash purchases of merchandise)	Transactions that cannot be entered in a special journal, including correcting, adjusting, and closing entries

If a transaction cannot be recorded in a special journal, it is recorded in the general journal. For example, if you have four special journals, as listed in Illustration C-2, sales returns and allowances and purchase returns and allowances are recorded in the general journal. Similarly, correcting, adjusting, and closing entries are recorded in the general journal. Other types of special journals may sometimes be used in certain situations. For example, if sales returns and allowances are frequent, an additional special journal may be used to record these transactions. A payroll journal is another example of a special journal. It organizes and summarizes payroll details for companies with many employees.

For a merchandising company, the same special journals are used whether a company uses the periodic or perpetual system to account for its inventory. The only distinction is the number of, and title for, the columns each journal uses. We will use Karns Wholesale Supply to show the use of special journals in the following sections. Karns uses a perpetual inventory system. The variations between the periodic and perpetual inventory systems are highlighted in helpful hints for your information. In addition, special journals under a periodic inventory system are shown more fully at the end of this appendix.

SALES JOURNAL

The sales journal is used to record sales of merchandise on account. Cash sales of merchandise are entered in the cash receipts journal. Credit sales of assets other than merchandise are entered in the general journal.

Journalizing Credit Sales

Under the perpetual inventory system, each entry in the sales journal results in one entry at selling price and another entry at cost. The entry at selling price is a debit to Accounts Receivable (a control account supported by a subsidiary ledger) and a credit of an equal amount to Sales. The entry at cost is a debit to Cost of Goods Sold and a credit of an equal amount to Merchandise Inventory. Some companies also set up Merchandise Inventory as a control account supported by a subsidiary ledger.

A sales journal with two amount columns can show a sales transaction recognized at both selling price and cost on one line. The two-column sales journal of Karns Wholesale Supply is shown in Illustration C-3, using assumed credit sales transactions.

▶ILLUSTRATION **C-3**
Sales journal— perpetual inventory system

				KARNS WHOLESALE SUPPLY	
			Sales Journal		**S1**
Date	Account Debited	Invoice No.	Ref.	Accounts Receivable Dr Sales Cr.	Cost of Goods Sold Dr. Merchandise Inventory Cr.
2017					
May 3	Abbot Sisters	101		10,600	6,360
7	Babson Co.	102		11,350	7,370
14	Carson Bros.	103		7,800	5,070
19	Deli Co.	104		9,300	6,510
21	Abbot Sisters	105		15,400	10,780
24	Deli Co.	106		21,210	15,900
27	Babson Co.	107		14,570	10,200
				90,230	62,190

Helpful hint In a periodic inventory system, the sales journal would have only one column to record the sale at selling price (accounts receivable Dr., sales Cr.). The cost of goods sold is not recorded. It is calculated at the end of the period.

The reference (Ref.) column is not used in journalizing. It is used in posting the sales journal, as explained in the next section. Also, note that an explanation is not required for each entry in a special journal. Finally, note that each invoice is pre-numbered to ensure that all invoices are journalized.

If management wishes to record its sales by department, additional columns may be provided in the sales journal. For example, a department store may have columns for such things as home furnishings, sporting goods, and shoes. In addition, the federal government and practically all provinces require that sales taxes be charged on items sold. If sales taxes are collected, it is necessary to add more credit columns to the sales journal for GST Payable and PST Payable (or HST Payable).

Posting the Sales Journal

Postings from the sales journal are made daily to the individual accounts receivable accounts in the subsidiary ledger. Posting the total sales for the month to the general ledger is done monthly. Illustration C-4

> ▶ ILLUSTRATION **C-4**
> Posting the sales journal—perpetual inventory system

KARNS WHOLESALE SUPPLY
Sales Journal   S1

Date	Account Debited	Invoice No.	Ref.	Accts. Receivable Dr. Sales Cr.	Cost of Goods Sold Dr. Merchandise Inventory Cr.
2017					
May 3	Abbot Sisters	101	√	10,600	6,360
7	Babson Co.	102	√	11,350	7,370
14	Carson Bros.	103	√	7,800	5,070
19	Deli Co.	104	√	9,300	6,510
21	Abbot Sisters	105	√	15,400	10,780
24	Deli Co.	106	√	21,210	15,900
27	Babson Co.	107	√	14,570	10,200
				90,230	62,190
				(112)/(401)	(505)/(120)

> Individual amounts are posted daily to the subsidiary ledger.

> Totals are posted at the end of the accounting period to the general ledger.

ACCOUNTS RECEIVABLE SUBSIDIARY LEDGER

Abbot Sisters

Date	Ref.	Debit	Credit	Balance
2017				
May 3	S1	10,600		10,600
21	S1	15,400		26,000

Babson Co.

Date	Ref.	Debit	Credit	Balance
2017				
May 7	S1	11,350		11,350
27	S1	14,570		25,920

Carson Bros.

Date	Ref.	Debit	Credit	Balance
2017				
May 14	S1	7,800		7,800

Deli Co.

Date	Ref.	Debit	Credit	Balance
2017				
May 19	S1	9,300		9,300
24	S1	21,210		30,510

> The subsidiary ledger is separate from the general ledger.

GENERAL LEDGER

Accounts Receivable   No. 112

Date	Ref.	Debit	Credit	Balance
2017				
May 31	S1	90,230		90,230

Merchandise Inventory   No. 120

Date	Ref.	Debit	Credit	Balance
2017				
May 31	S1		62,190	62,190cr[1]

Sales   No. 401

Date	Ref.	Debit	Credit	Balance
2017				
May 31	S1		90,230	90,230

Cost of Goods Sold   No. 505

Date	Ref.	Debit	Credit	Balance
2017				
May 31	S1	62,190		62,190

> Accounts Receivable is a control account.

---

[1]The normal balance for Merchandise Inventory is a debit. But because of the sequence in which we have posted the special journals, with the sales journal first, the credits to Merchandise Inventory are posted before the debits. This posting sequence causes the temporary credit balance in Merchandise Inventory, which exists only until the other journals are posted.

shows both the daily postings to the accounts receivable subsidiary ledger and the monthly postings to the general ledger accounts. We have assumed that Karns Wholesale Supply does not maintain an inventory subsidiary ledger. However, if it did, the procedure is similar to that illustrated for the accounts receivable subsidiary ledger.

A check mark (✓) is inserted in the reference posting column of the sales journal to indicate that the daily posting to the customer's account has been made. A check mark is used when the subsidiary ledger accounts are not individually numbered. If the subsidiary ledger accounts are numbered, the account number would be used instead of the check mark. At the end of the month, the column totals of the sales journal are posted to the general ledger. Here, the column totals are posted as a debit of $90,230 to Accounts Receivable (account no. 112), a credit of $90,230 to Sales (account no. 401), a debit of $62,190 to Cost of Goods Sold (account no. 505), and a credit of $62,190 to Merchandise Inventory (account no. 120). Inserting the account numbers below the column totals indicates that the postings have been made. In both the general ledger and subsidiary ledger accounts, the reference S1 indicates that the posting came from page 1 of the sales journal.

Proving the Ledgers

The next step is to "prove" the ledgers. To do so, we must ensure two things:

1. The sum of the subsidiary ledger balances must equal the balance in the control account.
2. The total of the general ledger debit balances must equal the total of the general ledger credit balances.

The proof of the postings from the sales journal to the general and subsidiary ledgers follows:

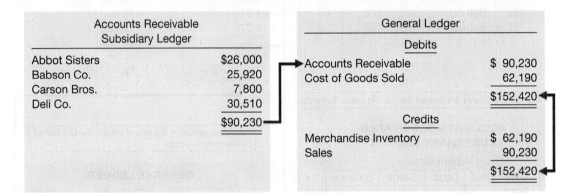

Accounts Receivable Subsidiary Ledger		General Ledger	
		Debits	
Abbot Sisters	$26,000	Accounts Receivable	$ 90,230
Babson Co.	25,920	Cost of Goods Sold	62,190
Carson Bros.	7,800		$152,420
Deli Co.	30,510		
	$90,230	**Credits**	
		Merchandise Inventory	$ 62,190
		Sales	90,230
			$152,420

Advantages of the Sales Journal

The use of a special journal to record sales on account has the following advantages:

1. The one-line–two-column entry for each sales transaction saves time. In the sales journal, it is not necessary to write out the four account titles for the two transactions.
2. Only totals, rather than individual entries, are posted to the general ledger. This saves posting time and reduces the possibility of errors in posting.
3. The sequential pre-numbering of sales invoices helps to ensure that all sales are recorded and that no sale is recorded more than once. This promotes good internal control.

There is a division of labour if the individual responsible for the sales journal is not given responsibility for other journals, such as cash receipts. This also promotes good internal control.

CASH RECEIPTS JOURNAL

All receipts of cash are recorded in the cash receipts journal. The most common types of cash receipts are cash sales of merchandise and collections of accounts receivable. Many other possibilities exist, such as a receipt of money from a bank loan. However, a one- or two-column cash receipts journal would not have enough space for all possible cash receipt transactions. A multiple-column cash receipts journal is therefore used.

Generally, a cash receipts journal includes the following columns: a debit column for cash, and credit columns for accounts receivable, sales, and other accounts. The other accounts column is used when the cash receipt does not involve a cash sale or a collection of accounts receivable. Under a perpetual inventory system, each sales entry is accompanied by another entry that debits Cost of Goods Sold and credits Merchandise Inventory. A separate column is added for this purpose

Additional credit columns may be used if they significantly reduce postings to a specific account. For example, cash receipts from cash sales normally include the collection of sales taxes, which are later remitted to the government. Most cash receipts journals have a separate credit column for sales tax collections.

Helpful hint In a periodic inventory system, the cash receipts journal would have one column fewer. The cost of goods sold Dr. and merchandise inventory Cr. would not be recorded.

Journalizing Cash Receipts Transactions

To illustrate the journalizing of cash receipts transactions, we will continue with the May transactions of Karns Wholesale Supply. Collections from customers are for the entries recorded in the sales journal in Illustration C-3. A five-column cash receipts journal is shown in Illustration C-5.

The entries in the cash receipts journal are based on the following cash receipts:

May	1	D. Karns makes an investment of $5,000 in the business.
	7	Cash receipts for merchandise sales total $1,900. The cost of goods sold is $1,240.
	10	A cheque for $10,600 is received from Abbot Sisters in full payment of invoice No. 101.
	12	Cash receipts for merchandise sales total $2,600. The cost of goods sold is $1,690.
	17	A cheque for $11,350 is received from Babson Co. in full payment of invoice No. 102.
	22	Cash is received by signing a 4% note for $6,000, payable September 22 to the National Bank.
	23	A cheque for $7,800 is received from Carson Bros. in full payment of invoice No. 103.
	28	A cheque for $9,300 is received from Deli Co. in full payment of invoice No. 104.

Further information about the columns in the cash receipts journal follows.

Debit columns:

1. Cash. The amount of cash actually received in each transaction is entered in this column. The column total indicates the total cash receipts for the month. The total of this column is posted to the Cash account in the general ledger.
2. Cost of goods sold. The cost of goods sold Dr./merchandise inventory Cr. column is used to record the cost of the merchandise sold. (The sales column records the selling price of the merchandise.) The cost of goods sold column is similar to the one found in the sales journal. The amount debited to Cost of Goods Sold is the same amount credited to Merchandise Inventory. One column total is posted to both accounts at the end of the month.

Credit columns:

3. Accounts receivable. The accounts receivable column is used to record cash collections on account. The amount entered here is the amount to be credited to the individual customer's account in the accounts receivable ledger.
4. Sales. The sales column is used to record all cash sales of merchandise. Cash sales of other assets (property, plant, and equipment, for example) are not reported in this column. The total of this column is posted to the account Sales.
5. Merchandise inventory. As noted above, the cost of goods sold Dr./merchandise inventory Cr. column is used to record the reduction in the merchandise available for future sale. The amount credited to Merchandise Inventory is the same amount debited to Cost of Goods Sold. One column total is posted to both accounts at the end of the month.
6. Other accounts. The other accounts column is used whenever the credit is not to Accounts Receivable, Sales, or Merchandise Inventory. For example, in the first entry, $5,000 is entered as a credit to D. Karns, Capital. This column is often referred to as the sundry accounts column.

In a multi-column journal, only one line is generally needed for each entry. In some cases, it is useful to add explanatory information, such as the details of the note payable, or to reference supporting documentation, such as invoice numbers if cash sales are invoiced. Note also that the account credited column is used to identify both general ledger and subsidiary ledger account titles. The former is shown in the May 1 entry for Karns' investment. The latter is shown in the May 10 entry for the collection from Abbot Sisters.

▶ILLUSTRATION **C-5**
Cash receipts journal—
perpetual inventory system

KARNS WHOLESALE SUPPLY
Cash Receipts Journal
CR1

Date	Account Credited	Ref.	Cash Dr.	Accounts Receivable Cr.	Sales Cr.	Cost of Goods Sold Dr. Mdse. Inv. Cr.	Other Accounts Cr.
2017							
May 1	D. Karns, Capital	301	5,000				5,000
7			1,900		1,900	1,240	
10	Abbot Sisters	√	10,600	10,600			
12			2,600		2,600	1,690	
17	Babson Co.	√	11,350	11,350			
22	Notes Payable	200	6,000				6,000
23	Carson Bros.	√	7,800	7,800			
28	Deli Co.	√	9,300	9,300			
			54,550	39,050	4,500	2,930	11,000
			(101)	(112)	(401)	(505)/(120)	(X)

Individual amounts are posted daily to the subsidiary ledger.

Totals are posted at the end of the accounting period to the general ledger.

ACCOUNTS RECEIVABLE SUBSIDIARY LEDGER

Abbot Sisters

Date	Ref.	Debit	Credit	Balance
2017				
May 3	S1	10,600		10,600
10	CR1		10,600	0
21	S1	15,400		15,400

Babson Co.

Date	Ref.	Debit	Credit	Balance
2017				
May 7	S1	11,350		11,350
17	CR1		11,350	0
27	S1	14,570		14,570

Carson Bros.

Date	Ref.	Debit	Credit	Balance
2017				
May 14	S1	7,800		7,800
23	CR1		7,800	0

Deli Co.

Date	Ref.	Debit	Credit	Balance
2017				
May 19	S1	9,300		9,300
24	S1	21,210		30,510
28	CR1		9,300	21,210

The subsidiary ledger is separate from the general ledger.

Accounts Receivable is a control account.

GENERAL LEDGER

Cash No. 101

Date	Ref.	Debit	Credit	Balance
2017				
May 31	CR1	54,550		54,550

Accounts Receivable No. 112

Date	Ref.	Debit	Credit	Balance
2017				
May 31	S1	90,230		90,230
31	CR1		39,050	51,180

Merchandise Inventory No. 120

Date	Ref.	Debit	Credit	Balance
2017				
May 31	S1		62,190	62,190cr.
31	CR1		2,930	65,120cr.

Notes Payable No. 200

Date	Ref.	Debit	Credit	Balance
2017				
May 22	CR1		6,000	6,000

D. Karns, Capital No. 301

Date	Ref.	Debit	Credit	Balance
2017				
May 1	CR1		5,000	5,000

Sales No. 401

Date	Ref.	Debit	Credit	Balance
2017				
May 31	S1		90,230	90,230
31	CR1		4,500	94,730

Cost of Goods Sold No. 505

Date	Ref.	Debit	Credit	Balance
2017				
May 31	S1	62,190		62,190
31	CR1	2,930		65,120

Debit and credit amounts for each line must be equal. Some accountants use the expression "the journal cross-adds" to describe this feature. When the journalizing has been completed, the amount columns are totalled. The totals are then compared to prove the equality of debits and credits in the cash receipts journal. Don't forget that the cost of goods sold Dr./merchandise inventory Cr. column total represents both a debit and a credit amount. Totalling the columns of a journal and proving the equality of the totals is called footing (adding down) and cross-footing (adding across) a journal.

The proof of the equality of Karns' cash receipts journal is as follows:

Debits		Credits	
Cash	$54,550	Accounts Receivable	$39,050
Cost of Goods Sold	2,930	Merchandise Inventory	2,930
	$57,480	Sales	4,500
		Other Accounts	11,000
			$57,480

Posting the Cash Receipts Journal

Posting a multi-column journal involves the following steps:

1. All column totals, except for the other accounts total, are posted once at the end of the month to the account title specified in the column heading, such as Cash, Accounts Receivable, Sales, Cost of Goods Sold, and Merchandise Inventory. Account numbers are entered below the column totals to show that the amounts have been posted to the general ledger.
2. The total of the other accounts column is not posted. Individual amounts that make up the other accounts total are posted separately to the general ledger accounts specified in the account credited column. See, for example, the credit posting to D. Karns, Capital. The symbol X is inserted below the total for the other accounts column to indicate that the amount has not been posted.
3. The individual amounts in a column (accounts receivable, in this case) are posted daily to the subsidiary ledger account name specified in the account credited column. See, for example, the credit posting of $10,600 to Abbot Sisters.

The abbreviation CR (not to be confused with "Cr." for credits) is used in both the subsidiary and general ledgers to identify postings from the cash receipts journal.

Proving the Ledgers

After the posting of the cash receipts journal is completed, it is necessary to prove the ledgers. As shown below, the sum of the subsidiary ledger account balances equals the control account balance. The general ledger totals of the accounts that have been affected by the entries are also in agreement.

Accounts Receivable Subsidiary Ledger		General Ledger	
Abbot Sisters	$15,400	**Debits**	
Babson Co.	14,570	Cash	$ 54,550
Deli Co.	21,210	Accounts Receivable	51,180
	$51,180	Cost of Goods Sold	65,120
			$170,850
		Credits	
		Merchandise Inventory	$ 65,120
		Notes Payable	6,000
		D. Karns, Capital	5,000
		Sales	94,730
			$170,850

PURCHASES JOURNAL

All purchases on account are recorded in the purchases journal. The most common types of purchases on account are inventory and supplies but there are a variety of other items purchased, or expenses incurred, on account. Each entry in this journal results in a credit to Accounts Payable and a debit to Inventory, Supplies, or other accounts as appropriate. Each business designs its purchases journal based on the types of transactions that occur frequently that involve a credit to Accounts Payable.

The purchases journal for Karns Wholesale Supply includes separate columns for purchases of inventory and for supplies because these are the most common types of transactions on account for Karns. All other purchases on account are recorded in the other accounts columns. Karns' purchases journal for May is shown in Illustration C-6, with assumed credit purchases.

▶ ILLUSTRATION **C-6**
Purchases journal—
perpetual inventory system

KARNS WHOLESALE SUPPLY
Purchases Journal   P1

Date	Account Credited	Terms	Ref.	Accounts Payable Cr.	Merchandise Inventory Dr.	Supplies Dr.	Other Accounts Account Debited	Ref.	Amount
2017									
May 6	Jasper Manufacturing Inc.	n/20	√	21,000	21,000				
10	Eaton and Howe Inc.	n/20	√	7,200			Equipment	151	7,200
14	Fabor and Son	n/20	√	6,900	5,000	1,900			
19	Jasper Manufacturing Inc.	n/20	√	17,500	17,500				
26	Fabor and Son	n/20	√	8,700	7,800	900			
28	Eaton and Howe Inc.	n/20	√	12,600	12,600				
				73,900	63,900	2,800			7,200
				(201)	(120)	(129)			(X)

Individual amounts are posted daily to the subsidiary ledger.

Totals are posted at the end of the accounting period to the general ledger.

Helpful hint When a periodic inventory system is used, the debit to the Merchandise Inventory account is replaced by a debit to the Purchases account.

ACCOUNTS PAYABLE SUBSIDIARY LEDGER

Eaton & Howe Inc.

Date	Ref.	Debit	Credit	Balance
2017				
May 10	P1		7,200	7,200
28	P1		12,600	19,800

Fabor and Son

Date	Ref.	Debit	Credit	Balance
2017				
May 14	P1		6,900	6,900
26	P1		8,700	15,600

Jasper Manufacturing Inc.

Date	Ref.	Debit	Credit	Balance
2017				
May 6	P1		21,000	21,000
19	P1		17,500	38,500

The subsidiary ledger is separate from the general ledger.

GENERAL LEDGER

Merchandise Inventory No. 120

Date	Ref.	Debit	Credit	Balance
2017				
May 31	S1		62,190	62,190Cr.
31	CR1		2,930	65,120Cr.
31	P1	63,900		1,220Cr.

Supplies No. 129

Date	Ref.	Debit	Credit	Balance
2017				
May 31	P1	2,800		2,800

Equipment No. 151

Date	Ref.	Debit	Credit	Balance
2017				
May 31	P1	7,200		7,200

Accounts Payable No. 201

Date	Ref.	Debit	Credit	Balance
2017				
May 31	P1		73,900	73,900

Accounts Payable is a control account.

Journalizing Credit Purchases

Entries in the purchases journal are made from purchase invoices. The journalizing procedure for the purchases journal is similar to that for the cash receipts journal. In contrast to the cash receipts journal, there is a column indicating the terms of the purchase to ensure that a purchase discount is not missed.

Posting the Purchases Journal

The procedures for posting the purchases journal are similar to those for the cash receipts journal. In this case, postings are made daily to the accounts payable subsidiary ledger accounts and monthly to the accounts in the general ledger. In both ledgers, P1 is used in the reference column to show that the postings are from page 1 of the purchases journal.

Proof of the equality of the postings from the purchases journal to both ledgers is shown by the following:

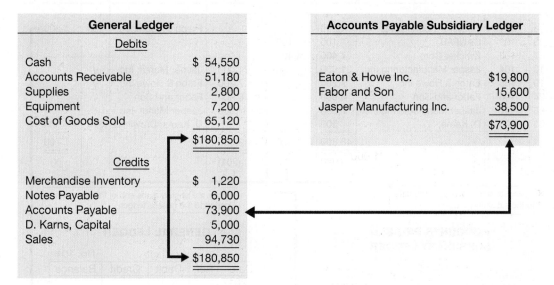

General Ledger	
Debits	
Cash	$ 54,550
Accounts Receivable	51,180
Supplies	2,800
Equipment	7,200
Cost of Goods Sold	65,120
	$180,850
Credits	
Merchandise Inventory	$ 1,220
Notes Payable	6,000
Accounts Payable	73,900
D. Karns, Capital	5,000
Sales	94,730
	$180,850

Accounts Payable Subsidiary Ledger	
Eaton & Howe Inc.	$19,800
Fabor and Son	15,600
Jasper Manufacturing Inc.	38,500
	$73,900

Note that not all the general ledger accounts listed above have been included in Illustration C-6. You will have to refer to Illustration C-5 to determine the balances for the accounts Cash; Accounts Receivable; Cost of Goods Sold; Notes Payable; D. Karns, Capital; and Sales.

CASH PAYMENTS JOURNAL

All payments of cash are entered in a cash payments journal. Entries are made from pre-numbered cheques. Because cash payments are made for various purposes, the cash payments journal has multiple columns. A four-column journal is shown in Illustration C-7.

Alternative terminology The cash payments journal is also called the cash disbursements journal.

Journalizing Cash Payments Transactions

The procedures for journalizing transactions in this journal are similar to those described earlier for the cash receipts journal. Each transaction is entered on one line, and for each line there must be equal debit and credit amounts. It is common practice in the cash payments journal to record the name of the company or individual receiving the cheque (the payee), so that later reference to the cheque is possible by name in addition to cheque number. The entries in the cash payments journal shown in Illustration C-7 are based on the following transactions for Karns Wholesale Supply:

> May 3   Cheque No. 101 for $1,200 issued for the annual premium on a fire insurance policy from Corporate General Insurance.
> 3   Cheque No. 102 for $100 issued to CANPAR in payment of freight charges on goods purchased.
> 7   Cheque No. 103 for $4,400 issued for the cash purchase of merchandise from Zwicker Corp.
> 10   Cheque No. 104 for $21,000 sent to Jasper Manufacturing Inc. in full payment of the May 6 invoice.
> 19   Cheque No. 105 for $7,200 mailed to Eaton & Howe Inc. in full payment of the May 10 invoice.
> 24   Cheque No. 106 for $6,900 sent to Fabor and Son in full payment of the May 14 invoice.
> 28   Cheque No. 107 for $7,500 sent to Jasper Manufacturing Inc. in partial payment of the May 19 invoice.
> 31   Cheque No. 108 for $500 issued to D. Karns as a cash withdrawal for personal use.

▶ ILLUSTRATION  C-7
Cash payments
journal—perpetual inventory system

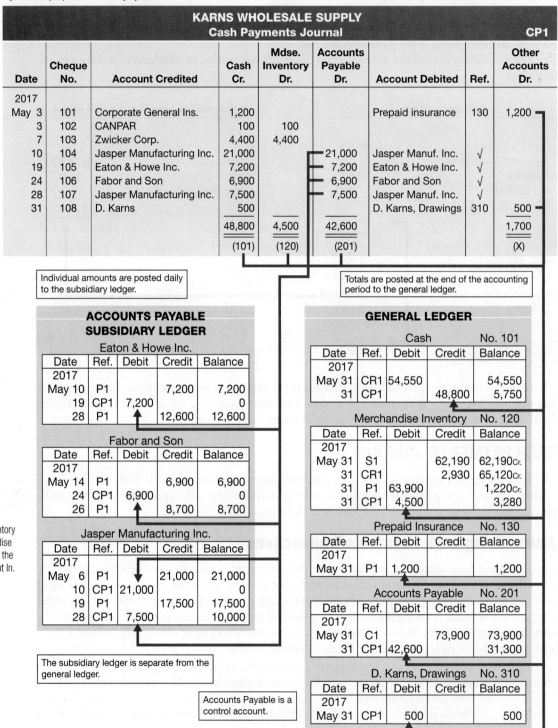

Helpful hint In a periodic inventory system, the debits to Merchandise Inventory would be recorded to the accounts Purchases and Freight In.

Note that, whenever an amount is entered in the other accounts column, a specific general ledger account must be identified in the account debited column. The entries for cheque numbers 101 and 108 show this situation. Similarly, a subsidiary account must be identified in the account debited column whenever an amount is entered in the accounts payable column (as, for example, the entry for cheque no. 104).

After the cash payments journal has been journalized, the columns are totalled. The totals are then balanced to prove the equality of debits and credits. Debits ($4,500 + $42,600 + $1,700 = $48,800) do equal credits ($48,800) in this case.

Posting the Cash Payments Journal

The procedures for posting the cash payments journal are similar to those for the cash receipts journal:

1. Cash and merchandise inventory are posted only as a total at the end of the month.
2. The amounts recorded in the accounts payable column are posted individually to the subsidiary ledger and in total to the general ledger control account.
3. Transactions in the other accounts column are posted individually to the appropriate account(s) noted in the account debited column. No totals are posted for the other accounts column.

The posting of the cash payments journal is shown in Illustration C-7. Note that the abbreviation CP is used as the posting reference. After postings are completed, the equality of the debit and credit balances in the general ledger should be determined. The control account balance should also agree with the subsidiary ledger total balance. The agreement of these balances is shown below. Note that not all the general ledger accounts have been included in Illustration C-7. You will also have to refer to Illustrations C-5 and C-6 to determine the balances for the Accounts Receivable, Supplies, Equipment, Cost of Goods Sold, Notes Payable, Capital, and Sales accounts.

Helpful hint If a company has a subsidiary ledger for merchandise inventory, amounts in the merchandise inventory column would be posted daily in the cash payments journal, as well as in the sales, cash receipts, and purchases journals.

General Ledger		Accounts Payable Subsidiary Ledger	
Debits			
Cash	$ 5,750	Eaton & Howe Inc.	$12,600
Accounts Receivable	51,180	Fabor and Son	8,700
Merchandise Inventory	3,280	Jasper Manufacturing Inc.	10,000
Supplies	2,800		$31,300
Prepaid Insurance	1,200		
Equipment	7,200		
D. Karns, Drawings	500		
Cost of Goods Sold	65,120		
	$137,030		
Credits			
Accounts Payable	$ 31,300		
Notes Payable	6,000		
D. Karns, Capital	5,000		
Sales	94,730		
	$137,030		

EFFECTS OF SPECIAL JOURNALS ON THE GENERAL JOURNAL

Special journals for sales, purchases, and cash greatly reduce the number of entries that are made in the general journal. Only transactions that cannot be entered in a special journal are recorded in the general journal. For example, the general journal may be used to record a transaction granting credit to a customer for a sales return or allowance. It may also be used to record the receipt of a credit from a supplier for purchase returns or allowances, the acceptance of a note receivable from a customer, and the purchase of equipment by issuing a note payable. Correcting, adjusting, and closing entries are also made in the general journal.

When control and subsidiary accounts are not used, the procedures for journalizing and posting transactions in the general journal are the same as those described in earlier chapters. When control and subsidiary accounts are used, two modifications of earlier procedures are required:

1. In journalizing, both the control and the subsidiary account must be identified.
2. In posting, there must be a dual posting: once to the control account and once to the subsidiary account.

To illustrate, assume that on May 31, Karns Wholesale Supply returns $500 of merchandise for credit to Fabor and Son. The entry in the general journal and the posting of the entry are shown in Illustration C-8. Note that, if cash had been received instead of the credit granted on this return, then the transaction would have been recorded in the cash receipts journal.

▶ ILLUSTRATION
General journal

Helpful hint In a periodic inventory system, the credit would be to the Purchase Returns and Allowances account rather than to Merchandise Inventory.

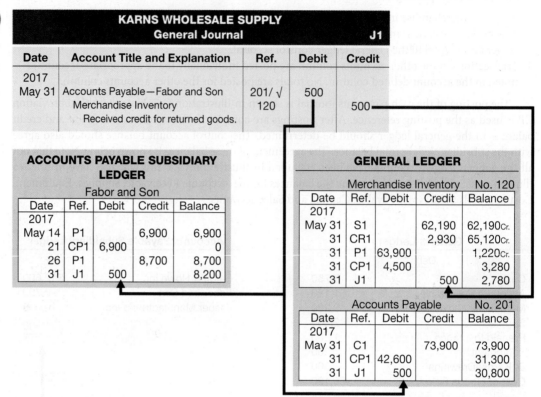

Notice that in the general journal, two accounts are indicated for the debit (the Accounts Payable control account and the Fabor and Son subsidiary account). Two postings (201/✓) are indicated in the reference column. One amount is posted to the control account in the general ledger (no. 201) and the other to the creditor's account in the subsidiary ledger (Fabor and Son).

SPECIAL JOURNALS IN A PERIODIC INVENTORY SYSTEM

Recording and posting transactions in special journals is essentially the same whether a perpetual or a periodic inventory system is used. But there are two differences. The first difference relates to the accounts Merchandise Inventory and Cost of Goods Sold in a perpetual inventory system. In this system, an additional column is required to record the cost of each sale in the sales and cash receipts journals, something that is not required in a periodic inventory system.

The second difference concerns the account titles used. In a perpetual inventory system, Merchandise Inventory and Cost of Goods Sold are used to record purchases and the cost of the merchandise sold. In a periodic inventory system, the accounts Purchases and Freight In accumulate the cost of the merchandise purchased until the end of the period. No cost of goods sold is recorded during the period. Cost of goods sold is calculated at the end of the period in a periodic inventory system.

Each of the special journals illustrated in this appendix is shown again here in Illustrations C-9 to C-12. Using the same transactions, we assume that Karns Wholesale Supply uses a periodic inventory system instead of a perpetual inventory system.

KARNS WHOLESALE SUPPLY
Sales Journal   S1

Date	Account Debited	Invoice No.	Ref.	Accts. Receivable Dr. Sales Cr.
2017				
May 3	Abbot Sisters	101	√	10,600
7	Babson Co.	102	√	11,350
14	Carson Bros.	103	√	7,800
19	Deli Co.	104	√	9,300
21	Abbot Sisters	105	√	15,400
24	Deli Co.	106	√	21,210
27	Babson Co.	107	√	14,570
				90,230

▶ ILLUSTRATION C-9
Sales journal—periodic inventory system

Helpful hint Compare this sales journal with the one presented in Illustration C-4.

KARNS WHOLESALE SUPPLY
Cash Receipts Journal   CR1

Date	Account Credited	Ref.	Cash Dr.	Accounts Receivable Cr.	Sales Cr.	Other Accounts Cr.
2017						
May 1	D. Karns, Capital	301	5,000			5,000
7			1,900		1,900	
10	Abbot Sisters	√	10,600	10,600		
12			2,600		2,600	
17	Babson Co.	√	11,350	11,350		
22	Notes Payable	200	6,000			6,000
23	Carson Bros.	√	7,800	7,800		
28	Deli Co.	√	9,300	9,300		
			54,550	39,050	4,500	11,000

▶ ILLUSTRATION C-10
Cash receipts journal—periodic inventory system

Helpful hint Compare this cash receipts journal with the one presented in Illustration C-5.

Helpful hint Compare this purchases journal with the one presented in Illustration C-6.

▶ ILLUSTRATION C-11
Purchases journal—periodic inventory system

KARNS WHOLESALE SUPPLY
Purchases Journal   P1

Date	Account Credited	Terms	Ref.	Accounts Payable Cr.	Purchases Dr.	Supplies Dr.	Other Accounts Account Debited	Ref.	Amount
2017									
May 6	Jasper Manufacturing Inc.	n/20	√	21,000	21,000				
10	Eaton and Howe Inc.	n/20	√	7,200			Equipment	151	7,200
14	Fabor and Son	n/20	√	6,900	5,000	1,900			
19	Jasper Manufacturing Inc.	n/20	√	17,500	17,500				
26	Fabor and Son	n/20	√	8,700	7,800	900			
28	Eaton and Howe Inc.	n/20	√	12,600	12,600				
				73,900	63,900	2,800			7,200

▶ILLUSTRATION C-12
Cash payments
journal—periodic
inventory system

Helpful hint Compare this cash
payments journal with the one
presented in Illustration C-7.

		KARNS WHOLESALE SUPPLY						
		Cash Payments Journal						CP1
Date	Cheque No.	Account Credited	Cash Cr.	Accounts Payable Dr.	Account Debited	Ref.		Other Accounts Dr.
2017								
May 3	101	Corporate General Ins.	1,200		Prepaid Insurance	130		1,200
3	102	CANPAR	100		Freight In	516		100
7	103	Zwicker Corp.	4,400		Purchases	510		4,400
10	104	Jasper Manufacturing Inc.	21,000	21,000	Jasper Manuf. Inc.	√		
19	105	Eaton & Howe Inc.	7,200	7,200	Eaton & Howe Inc.	√		
24	106	Fabor and Son	6,900	6,900	Fabor and Son	√		
28	107	Jasper Manufacturing Inc.	7,500	7,500	Jasper Manuf. Inc.	√		
31	108	D. Karns	500		D. Karns, Drawings	310		500
			48,800	42,600				6,200

▶ Brief Exercises

Calculate subsidiary ledger
and control account balances.
(LO 1) AP

BEC–1 Information related to Bryan Company is presented below for its first month of operations. Calculate (a) the balances that appear in the accounts receivable subsidiary ledger for each customer, and (b) the accounts receivable balance that appears in the general ledger at the end of January.

	Credit Sales			Cash Collections	
Jan. 7	Chiu Co.	$1,800	Jan. 17	Chiu Co.	$ 700
15	Elbaz Inc.	6,000	24	Elbaz Inc.	2,000
23	Lewis Co.	3,700	29	Lewis Co.	3,700

Identify general and
subsidiary ledger accounts.
(LO 1) K

BEC–2 Identify in which ledger (general or subsidiary) each of the following accounts is shown:
1. Rent Expense
2. Accounts Receivable—Chen
3. Bank Loan Payable
4. Service Revenue
5. Salaries Payable
6. Accounts Payable—Dhankar
7. Merchandise Inventory
8. Sales

Identify special journals.
(LO 2) K

BEC–3 Chisholm Co. uses special journals and a general journal. Identify the journal in which each of the following transactions is recorded:
1. Sold merchandise on account.
2. Granted a cash refund for a sales return.
3. Received a credit on account for a purchase return.
4. Sold merchandise for cash.
5. Purchased merchandise for cash.
6. Received a collection on account.
7. Recorded depreciation on vehicles.
8. Purchased equipment on account.
9. Purchased merchandise on credit.
10. Paid utility expense in cash.

Identify special journals—
perpetual inventory system.
(LO 2) K

BEC–4 Swirsky Company uses the cash receipts and cash payments journals illustrated in this appendix for a perpetual inventory system. In October, the following selected cash transactions occurred:
1. Made a refund to a customer for the return of damaged goods that had been purchased on credit.
2. Received payment from a customer.
3. Purchased merchandise for cash.

4. Paid a creditor.
5. Paid freight on merchandise purchased.
6. Paid cash for equipment.
7. Received a cash refund from a supplier for merchandise returned.
8. Withdrew cash for personal use of owner.
9. Made cash sales.

Indicate (a) the journal and (b) the columns in the journal that should be used in recording each transaction.

BEC–5 Identify the journal and the specific column title(s) in which each of the following transactions is recorded. Assume the company uses a periodic inventory system.
1. Cash sale
2. Credit sale
3. Sales return on account
4. Return of merchandise purchased for cash refund
5. Payment of freight on merchandise delivered to a customer
6. Cash purchase of merchandise
7. Credit purchase of supplies
8. Payment of freight on merchandise purchased from a supplier

Identify special journals—periodic inventory system. (LO 2) K

BEC–6 Willis Company has the following year-end account balances on April 30, 2017: Service Revenue $53,800; Rent Revenue $12,000; Salaries Expense $19,400; Depreciation Expense $8,000; Supplies Expense $3,500; B. Willis, Capital $97,000; and B. Willis, Drawings $18,000.
    Prepare the closing entries for Willis Company.

Use general journal for closing entries. (LO 2) AP

BEC–7 As part of the year-end procedures, depreciation for furniture was recorded in the amount of $6,800 for Leelantna Company. Prepare the adjusting entry dated November 30, 2017, using the appropriate journal.

Use general journal for adjusting entry. (LO 2) AP

BEC–8 Following the preparation of the bank reconciliation for Lolitta Services, a correcting journal entry was needed. A cheque issued for the correct amount of $960 for a payment on account was recorded in the amount of $690. Prepare the correcting entry dated February 28, 2017, using the appropriate journal.

Use general journal for correcting errors. (LO 2) AP

▶ Exercises

EC–1 Below are some transactions for Dartmouth Company:

1. Credit received for merchandise returned to a supplier
2. Payment of employee salaries
3. Sale of land for cash
4. Depreciation on equipment
5. Purchase of supplies on account
6. Purchase of merchandise on account
7. Purchase of land for cash
8. Payment on account
9. Return of merchandise sold for credit
10. Collection on account from customers
11. Revenues and expenses closed to income summary
12. Sale of merchandise on account
13. Sale of merchandise for cash

Identify special journals. (LO 2) K

Instructions

For each transaction, indicate whether it would normally be recorded in a cash receipts journal, cash payments journal, sales journal, purchases journal, or general journal.

EC–2 Wong Company, a sole proprietorship owned by V. Wong, uses special journals and a general journal. The company uses a perpetual inventory system and had the following transactions:

Sept. 2   Sold merchandise on account to T. Lu, $2,720, invoice #321, terms n/30. The cost of the merchandise sold was $1,960.
       3   Purchased supplies on account from Berko Co., $175.
      10   Purchased merchandise on account from Leonard Co., $800, FOB shipping point, terms n/30.

Record transactions in sales and purchases journals—perpetual inventory system. (LO 2) AP

11	Paid freight of $90 to A&F Shippers.
11	Returned unsatisfactory merchandise to Leonard Co., $200, for credit on account.
12	Purchased equipment on account from Wells Co., $7,700.
16	Sold merchandise for cash to L. Maille for $860. The cost of the merchandise sold was $490.
18	Purchased merchandise for cash from Leonard Co., $450, FOB destination.
20	Accepted returned merchandise from customer L. Maille, $860 (see Sept. 16 transaction). Gave full cash refund. Restored the merchandise to inventory.
24	Paid the correct amount owing for the merchandise purchased from Leonard earlier in the month.
25	Received payment from T. Lu for Sept. 2 sale.
26	Sold merchandise on account to M. Gafney, $890, invoice #322, terms n/30, FOB destination. The cost of the merchandise was $570. The appropriate party paid $75 to Freight Co. for shipping charges.
30	Paid September salaries, $2,360.
30	Withdrew cash for owner's personal use, $1,250.
30	Paid for supplies purchased on September 3.

Instructions

(a) Draw a sales journal and a purchases journal (see Illustrations C-3 and C-6). Use page 1 for each journal.
(b) Record the transaction(s) for September that should be recorded in the sales journal.
(c) Record the transaction(s) for September that should be recorded in the purchases journal.

Record transactions in cash receipts, cash payments, and general journals—perpetual inventory system. (LO 2) AP

EC–3   Refer to the information provided for Wong Company in EC–2.

Instructions

(a) Draw cash receipts and cash payments journals (see Illustrations C-5 and C-7) and a general journal. Use page 1 for each journal.
(b) Record the transaction(s) provided in EC–2 that should be recorded in the cash receipts journal.
(c) Record the transaction(s) provided in EC–2 that should be recorded in the cash payments journal.
(d) Record the transaction(s) provided in EC–2 that should be recorded in the general journal.

Record transactions in sales and purchases journals— periodic inventory system. (LO 2) AP

EC–4   Refer to the information provided for Wong Company in EC–2.

Instructions

(a) Draw a sales journal and a purchases journal (see Illustrations C-9 and C-11). Use page 1 for each journal.
(b) Record the transaction(s) for September that should be recorded in the sales journal.
(c) Record the transaction(s) for September that should be recorded in the purchases journal.

Record transactions in cash receipts, cash payments, and general journals—periodic inventory system. (LO 2) AP

EC–5   Refer to the information provided for Wong Company in EC–2.

Instructions

(a) Draw cash receipts and cash payments journals (see Illustrations C-10 and C-12) and a general journal. Use page 1 for each journal.
(b) Record the transaction(s) provided in EC–2 that should be recorded in the cash receipts journal.
(c) Record the transaction(s) provided in EC–2 that should be recorded in the cash payments journal.
(d) Record the transaction(s) provided in EC–2 that should be recorded in the general journal.

Record transactions in general journal and explain Posting. (LO 1, 2) AP

EC–6   Lee Ltd. has the following selected transactions during October:

Oct. 2   Purchased equipment on account costing $13,200 from Lifelong Inc.
      5   Received credit memorandum for $720 from Lyden Company for merchandise returned that had been damaged in shipment to Lee.
      7   Issued a credit memorandum for $600 to M. Presti for merchandise the customer returned. The returned merchandise has a cost of $375 and was restored to inventory.

Lee Ltd. uses a purchases journal, a sales journal, two cash journals (receipts and payments), and a general journal. Lee also uses a perpetual inventory system.

Instructions

(a) Record the appropriate transactions in the general journal. If a transaction should be recorded in one of the special journals, indicate the name of that journal.
(b) Assume now that Lee Ltd. uses a periodic inventory system. Record the appropriate transactions in the general journal.
(c) In a brief memo to the president of Lee Ltd., explain the postings to the control and subsidiary accounts.

Determine control account balances and explain posting. (LO 1, 2) AP

EC–7   Sven Co. uses both special journals and a general journal. On June 30, after all monthly postings had been completed, the Accounts Receivable control account in the general ledger had a debit balance of $137,800, and the Accounts Payable control account had a credit balance of $144,200.

The July transactions recorded in the special journals are summarized below. Sven Co. maintains a perpetual inventory system. No entries that affected accounts receivable and accounts payable were recorded in the general journal for July.

Sales journal: total sales, $98,670; cost of goods sold, $56,440
Purchases journal: total purchases, $39,700
Cash receipts journal: accounts receivable column total, $79,680
Cash payments journal: accounts payable column total, $42,300

Instructions

(a) What is the balance of the Accounts Receivable control account after the monthly postings on July 31?
(b) What is the balance of the Accounts Payable control account after the monthly postings on July 31?
(c) To what accounts are the column totals for total sales of $98,670 and cost of goods sold of $56,440 in the sales journal posted?
(d) To what account(s) is the accounts receivable column total of $79,680 in the cash receipts journal posted?

EC–8   On September 1, the balance of the Accounts Receivable control account in the general ledger of Mac Company was $10,960. The customers' subsidiary ledger contained account balances as follows: Jana, $2,440; London, $2,640; Cavanaugh, $2,060; and Zhang, $3,820. At the end of September, the various journals contained the following information:

Post journals to control and subsidiary accounts.
(LO 1, 2) AP

Sales journal: Sales to Zhang, $800; to Jana, $1,260; to Iman, $1,030; and to Cavanaugh, $1,100. The cost of each sale, respectively, was $480, $810, $620, and $660.
Cash receipts journal: Cash received from Cavanaugh, $1,310; from Zhang, $2,300; from Iman, $380; from London, $1,800; and from Jana, $1,240.
General journal: A $190 sales allowance is granted to Zhang on September 30.

Instructions

(a) Set up control and subsidiary accounts, and enter the beginning balances.
(b) Post the various journals to the control and subsidiary accounts. Post the items as individual items or as totals, whichever would be the appropriate procedure. Use page 1 for each journal.
(c) Prepare a list of customers and prove the agreement of the control account with the subsidiary ledger at September 30.

▶ Problems

PC–1   Selected accounts from the chart of accounts of Jinnah Ltd. are shown below:

Record transactions in special and general journals— perpetual inventory system.
(LO 2) AP

101	Cash	201	Accounts Payable
112	Accounts Receivable	401	Sales
120	Merchandise Inventory	412	Sales Returns and Allowances
126	Supplies	505	Cost of Goods Sold
157	Equipment	729	Salaries Expense

The company uses a perpetual inventory system. The cost of all merchandise sold is 60% of the sales price. During January, Jinnah completed the following transactions:

Jan. 3   Purchased merchandise on account from Sun Distributors, $7,800.
4   Purchased supplies on account from Moon Inc., $480.
4   Sold merchandise on account to R. Wong, $6,500, invoice no. 371.
5   Returned $1,450 of damaged goods to Sun Distributors.
6   Made cash sales for the week totalling $2,650.
8   Purchased merchandise on account from Irvine Co., $5,400.
9   Sold merchandise on account to Tops Corp., $2,600, invoice no. 372.
11   Purchased merchandise on account from Lewis Co., $4,300.
13   Paid Sun Distributors account in full.
13   Made cash sales for the week totalling $5,290.
15   Received payment from Tops Corp. for invoice no. 372.
15   Paid semi-monthly salaries of $11,300 to employees.
17   Received payment from R. Wong for invoice no. 371.
17   Sold merchandise on account to NFQ Co., $7,500, invoice no. 373.
19   Purchased equipment on account from Mark Corp., $6,600.

Jan. 20   Cash sales for the week totalled $1,400.
    20   Paid Irvine Co. account in full.
    23   Purchased merchandise on account from Sun Distributors, $4,800.
    24   Purchased merchandise on account from Levine Corp., $4,690.
    27   Made cash sales for the week totalling $4,370.
    30   Received payment from NFQ Co. for invoice no. 373.
    31   Paid semi-monthly salaries of $11,000 to employees.
    31   Sold merchandise on account to R. Wong, $7,380, invoice no. 374.

Jinnah Ltd. uses a sales journal, a purchases journal, a cash receipts journal, a cash payments journal, and a general journal.

Instructions

(a) Record the January transactions in the appropriate journals.
(b) Foot and cross-foot all special journals.
(c) Show how postings would be made by placing ledger account numbers and check marks as needed in the journals. (Actual posting to ledger accounts is not required.)

Record transactions in special and general journals—perpetual inventory system. (LO 2) AP

PC–2   Selected accounts from the chart of accounts of Zu Company are shown below:

101   Cash
112   Accounts Receivable
120   Merchandise Inventory
126   Supplies
140   Land
145   Buildings
201   Accounts Payable
401   Sales
505   Cost of Goods Sold
610   Advertising Expense

The company uses a perpetual inventory system. The cost of all merchandise sold was 65% of the sales price. During October, Zu Company completed the following transactions:

Oct. 2   Purchased merchandise on account from Madison Co., $5,800.
     4   Sold merchandise on account to Petro Corp., $8,600, invoice no. 204.
     5   Purchased supplies on account from Frey Co., $315.
     7   Made cash sales for the week that totalled $9,610.
     9   Paid the Madison Co. account in full.
    10   Purchased merchandise on account from Chen Corp., $4,900.
    12   Received payment from Petro Corp. for invoice no. 204.
    13   Issued a debit memorandum to Chen Corp. and returned $260 of damaged goods.
    14   Made cash sales for the week that totalled $8,810.
    16   Sold a parcel of land for $45,000 cash, the land's book value.
    17   Sold merchandise on account to Trudeau Co., $5,530, invoice no. 205.
    18   Purchased merchandise for cash, $2,215.
    21   Made cash sales for the week that totalled $8,640.
    23   Paid in full the Chen Corp. account for the goods kept.
    25   Purchased supplies on account from Frey Co., $260.
    25   Sold merchandise on account to Golden Corp., $5,520, invoice no. 206.
    25   Received payment from Trudeau Co. for invoice no. 205.
    26   Purchased for cash a small parcel of land and a building on the land to use as a storage facility. Of the total cost of $45,000, $26,000 was allocated to the land and $19,000 to the building.
    27   Purchased merchandise on account from Schmid Co., $9,000.
    28   Made cash sales for the week that totalled $9,320.
    30   Purchased merchandise on account from Madison Co., $16,200.
    30   Paid advertising bill for the month from The Gazette, $600.
    30   Sold merchandise on account to Trudeau Co., $5,200, invoice no. 207.

Zu Company uses a sales journal, purchases journal, cash receipts journal, cash payments journal, and general journal.

Instructions

(a) Record the October transactions in the appropriate journals.
(b) Foot and cross-foot all special journals.

(c) Show how postings would be made by placing ledger account numbers and check marks as needed in the journals. (Actual posting to ledger accounts is not required.)

PC–3 The post-closing trial balance for Perrault Music Co. follows:

Record transactions in special and general journals— perpetual inventory system. (LO 1, 2) AP

PERRAULT MUSIC CO.
Post-Closing Trial Balance
December 31, 2016

		Debit	Credit
101	Cash	$ 17,900	
112	Accounts receivable	38,000	
115	Notes receivable	45,000	
120	Merchandise inventory	22,600	
140	Land	25,000	
145	Building	75,000	
146	Accumulated depreciation—building		$ 38,800
157	Equipment	6,450	
158	Accumulated depreciation—equipment		1,950
200	Notes payable		–
201	Accounts payable		34,200
275	Mortgage payable		67,400
301	M. Perrault, capital		87,600
310	M. Perrault, drawings	–	
401	Sales	–	
410	Sales returns and allowances	–	
505	Cost of goods sold	–	
725	Salaries expense	–	
		$229,950	$229,950

The subsidiary ledgers contain the following information:

1. Accounts Receivable—S. Armstrong, $6,500; R. Goge, $30,000; B. Lu, $1,500
2. Accounts Payable—Denomme Corp., $4,000; Harms Distributors, $16,000; Watson & Co., $14,200

Perrault Music Co. uses a perpetual inventory system. The transactions for January 2017 are as follows:

Jan. 3 Sold merchandise to B. Rohl, $3,000. The cost of goods sold was $1,250.
      5 Purchased merchandise from Warren Parts, $2,900.
      7 Received a cheque from S. Armstrong, $4,000, in partial payment of its account.
     11 Paid Lindon Co. freight on merchandise purchased, $350.
     13 Received payment of account in full from B. Rohl.
     14 Issued a credit memo to R. Goge for $6,000 as a sales allowance for a previous sale on account.
     15 Sent Harms Distributors a cheque in full payment of account.
     17 Purchased merchandise from Voyer Co., $4,900.
     18 Paid salaries of $3,900.
     20 Gave Watson & Co. a 60-day note for $14,000 as a partial payment of account payable.
     23 Total cash sales amounted to $7,700. The cost of goods sold was $4,840.
     24 Sold merchandise on account to B. Lu, $7,800. The cost of goods sold was $3,300.
     27 Sent Warren Parts a cheque for $1,150 in partial payment of the account.
     29 Received payment on a note receivable of $35,000 from S. Lava.
     30 Returned merchandise costing $400 to Voyer Co. for credit.
     31 M. Perrault withdrew $1,300 cash for personal use.

Instructions

(a) Open general and subsidiary ledger accounts and record December 31, 2016, balances.
(b) Record the January transactions in a sales journal, a purchases journal, a cash receipts journal, a cash payments journal, and a general journal, as illustrated in this appendix.
(c) Post the appropriate amounts to the subsidiary and general ledger accounts.
(d) Prepare a trial balance at January 31, 2017.
(e) Determine whether the subsidiary ledgers agree with control accounts in the general ledger.

Record transactions in special and general journals, post, and prepare trial balance—perpetual inventory system. (LO 1, 2) AP

PC-4 The post-closing trial balance for Lee Co. follows. The subsidiary ledgers contain the following information:

	LEE CO. Post-Closing Trial Balance April 30, 2017		
		Debit	Credit
101	Cash	$ 36,700	
112	Accounts receivable	15,400	
115	Notes receivable—Cole Company	48,000	
120	Merchandise inventory	22,000	
157	Equipment	8,200	
158	Accumulated depreciation—equipment		$ 1,800
200	Notes payable		–
201	Accounts payable		43,400
301	C. Lee, capital		85,100
310	C. Lee, drawings	–	
401	Sales		–
410	Sales returns and allowances	–	
505	Cost of goods sold	–	
725	Salaries expense	–	
730	Rent expense	–	
		$130,300	$130,300

The subsidiary ledgers contain the following information:

1. Accounts Receivable—W. Karasch, $3,250; L. Cellars, $7,400; G. Parrish, $4,750
2. Accounts Payable—Summers Corp., $10,500; Cobalt Sports, $15,500; Buttercup Distributors, $17,400

Lee uses a perpetual inventory system. The transactions for May 2017 are as follows:

May	3	Sold merchandise on account to B. Simone, $2,400. The cost of the goods sold was $1,050.
	5	Purchased merchandise from WN Shaw, $2,600, on account.
	7	Received a cheque from G. Parrish, $2,800, in partial payment of account.
	11	Paid freight on merchandise purchased, $318.
	12	Paid rent of $1,500 for May.
	13	Received payment in full from B. Simone.
	14	Issued a credit memo to acknowledge $750 of merchandise returned by W. Karasch. The merchandise (original cost, $325) was restored to inventory.
	15	Sent Buttercup Distributors a cheque in full payment of account.
	17	Purchased merchandise from Lancio Co., $2,100, on account.
	18	Paid salaries of $4,700.
	20	Gave Cobalt Sports a two-month, 10% note for $15,500 in full payment of account payable.
	20	Returned merchandise costing $510 to Lancio for credit.
	23	Total cash sales amounted to $9,500. The cost of goods sold was $4,450.
	27	Sent WN Shaw a cheque for $1,000, in partial payment of account.
	29	Received payment on a note of $40,000 from Cole Company.
	30	Purchased equipment on account from Summers Corp., $4,000.
	31	C. Lee withdrew $1,000 cash for personal use.

Instructions

(a) Open general and subsidiary ledger accounts and record April 30, 2017, balances.
(b) Record the May transactions in a sales journal, a purchases journal, a cash receipts journal, a cash payments journal, and a general journal, as illustrated in this appendix.

(c) Post the appropriate amounts to the subsidiary and general ledger accounts.
(d) Prepare a trial balance at May 31, 2017.
(e) Determine whether the subsidiary ledgers agree with the control accounts in the general ledger.

PC–5   Selected accounts from the chart of accounts of Martin Ltd. are shown below:

101	Cash	401	Sales
112	Accounts Receivable	412	Sales Returns and Allowances
126	Supplies	510	Purchases
157	Equipment	512	Purchase Returns and Allowances
201	Accounts Payable	729	Salaries Expense

Record transactions in special and general journals—periodic inventory system. (LO 2) AP

During February, Martin completed the following transactions:

Feb.		
	3	Purchased merchandise on account from Zears Co., $4,200.
	4	Purchased supplies on account from Green Deer Inc., $290.
	4	Sold merchandise on account to Gilles Co., $5,220, invoice no. 371.
	5	Issued a debit memorandum to Zears Co. and returned $450 worth of goods.
	6	Made cash sales for the week totalling $1,950.
	8	Purchased merchandise on account from Fell Electronics, $7,200.
	9	Sold merchandise on account to Earlton Corp., $2,050, invoice no. 372.
	11	Purchased merchandise on account from Thomas Co., $9,100.
	13	Paid Zears Co. account in full.
	13	Made cash sales for the week totalling $3,850.
	15	Received payment from Earlton Corp. for invoice no. 372.
	15	Paid semi-monthly salaries of $14,100 to employees.
	17	Received payment from Gilles Co. for invoice no. 371.
	17	Sold merchandise on account to Lumber Co., $1,800, invoice no. 373.
	19	Purchased equipment on account from Brown Corp., $16,400.
	20	Cash sales for the week totalled $4,900.
	20	Paid Fell Electronics account in full.
	23	Purchased merchandise on account from Zears Co., $4,800.
	24	Purchased merchandise on account from Lewis Co., $5,130.
	27	Made cash sales for the week totalling $4,560.
	28	Received payment from Lumber Co. for invoice no. 373.
	28	Paid semi-monthly salaries of $14,900 to employees.
	28	Sold merchandise on account to Gilles Co., $9,810, invoice no. 374.

Martin Ltd. uses a sales journal, purchases journal, cash receipts journal, cash payments journal, and general journal. Martin uses a periodic inventory system.

Instructions

(a) Record the February transactions in the appropriate journal.
(b) Foot and cross-foot all special journals.
(c) Show how postings would be made by placing ledger account numbers and check marks as needed in the journals. (Actual posting to ledger accounts is not required.)

▶ Cumulative Coverage—Chapters 2 to 6 and Appendix C

Review the opening account balances in Winters Company's general and subsidiary ledgers on January 1, 2017. All accounts have normal debit and credit balances. Winters uses a perpetual inventory system. The cost of all merchandise sold was 40% of the sales price.

GENERAL LEDGER

Account No.	Account Title	January 1, 2017 Opening Balance
101	Cash	$ 35,050
112	Accounts receivable	14,000
115	Notes receivable	39,000
120	Merchandise inventory	20,000
125	Supplies	1,000
130	Prepaid insurance	2,000
140	Land	50,000
145	Building	100,000
146	Accumulated depreciation—building	25,000
157	Equipment	6,450
158	Accumulated depreciation—equipment	1,500
201	Accounts payable	36,000
275	Mortgage payable	125,000
301	A. Winters, capital	80,000

Accounts Receivable Subsidiary Ledger			Accounts Payable Subsidiary Ledger	
Customer	January 1, 2017 Opening Balance		Creditor	January 1, 2017 Opening Balance
R. Draves	$1,500		Liazuk Co.	$10,000
B. Jacovetti	7,500		Mikush Bros.	15,000
S. Tang	5,000		Nguyen & Son	11,000

Winters' January transactions follow:

Jan. 3 Sold merchandise on credit to B. Sota $3,100, invoice no. 510, and J. Ebel $1,800, invoice no. 511.
5 Purchased merchandise on account from Welz Wares for $3,000 and Laux Supplies for $2,700.
7 Received cheques for $5,000 from S. Tang and $2,000 from B. Jacovetti on accounts.
8 Paid freight on merchandise purchased, $180.
9 Sent cheques to Liazuk Co. for $10,000 and Nguyen & Son for $11,000 in full payment of accounts.
9 Issued credit memo for $400 to J. Ebel for merchandise returned. The merchandise was restored to inventory.
10 Summary cash sales totalled $16,500.
11 Sold merchandise on credit to R. Draves for $1,900, invoice no. 512, and to S. Tang for $900, invoice no. 513.
15 Withdrew $2,000 cash for Winters's personal use.
16 Purchased merchandise on account from Nguyen & Son for $15,000, from Liazuk Co. for $13,900, and from Welz Wares for $1,500.
17 Purchased supplies on account from Laux Supplies, $400.
18 Returned $500 of merchandise to Liazuk and received credit.
20 Summary cash sales totalled $17,500.
21 Issued $15,000 note to Mikush Bros. in payment of balance due. The note bears an interest rate of 10% and is due in three months.
21 Received payment in full from S. Tang.
22 Sold merchandise on credit to B. Soto for $1,700, invoice no. 514, and to R. Draves for $800, invoice no. 515.
23 Sent cheques to Nguyen & Son and Liazuk Co. in full payment of accounts.
25 Sold merchandise on credit to B. Jacovetti for $3,500, invoice no. 516, and to J. Ebel for $6,100, invoice no. 517.
27 Purchased merchandise on account from Nguyen & Son for $14,500, from Laux Supplies for $1,200, and from Welz Wares for $2,800.
28 Purchased supplies on account from Laux Supplies, $800.
31 Summary cash sales totalled $19,920.
31 Paid salaries of $6,900.
31 Received payment in full from B. Soto and J. Ebel on account.

In addition to the accounts identified in the trial balance, the chart of accounts shows the following: No. 200 Notes Payable, No. 230 Interest Payable, No. 300 Income Summary, No. 310 A. Winters, Drawings, No. 401 Sales, No. 410 Sales Returns and Allowances, No. 505 Cost of Goods Sold, No. 711 Depreciation Expense, No. 718 Interest Expense, No. 722 Insurance Expense, No. 725 Salaries Expense, and No. 728 Supplies Expense.

Instructions

(a) Record the January transactions in the appropriate journal—sales, purchases, cash receipts, cash payments, and general.

(b) Enter the opening balances in general and subsidiary ledger accounts. Post the journals to the general and subsidiary ledgers. New accounts should be added and numbered in an orderly fashion as needed.

(c) Prepare an unadjusted trial balance at January 31, 2017. Determine whether the subsidiary ledgers agree with the control accounts in the general ledger.

(d) Prepare and post adjusting journal entries. Prepare an adjusted trial balance, using the following information:
  1. Supplies at January 31 total $700.
  2. Insurance coverage expires on September 30, 2017.
  3. Annual depreciation on the building is $6,000 and on the equipment is $1,500.
  4. Interest of $45 has accrued on the note payable.
  5. A physical count of merchandise inventory has found $44,850 of goods on hand.

(e) Prepare a multiple-step income statement and a statement of owner's equity for January, and a classified balance sheet at the end of January.

(f) Prepare and post the closing entries.

(g) Prepare a post-closing trial balance.

Company Index

Subject Index